MW01688621

The Authors

John Daintith worked as a research chemist at the University of London and as a research assistant at Oxford University. He was science editor for the *Collins English Dictionary* and has compiled and edited a number of reference books, including the *Oxford Dictionary of Science.*

William Gould is an experienced reference-book compiler with a special interest in astronomy. He has contributed to a number of publications including the *World Book Encyclopedia* and the *Collins English Dictionary.*

Collins
dictionary *of*

Astronomy

William Collins' dream of knowledge for all began with the publication of his first book in 1819. A self-educated mill worker, he not only enriched millions of lives, but also founded a flourishing publishing house. Today, staying true to this spirit, Collins books are packed with inspiration, innovation, and practical expertise. They place you at the centre of a world of possibility and give you exactly what you need to explore it.

Collins. Do more.

Collins
dictionary *of*

Astronomy

John Daintith
William Gould

Collins

HarperCollins Publishers
Westerhill Road, Bishopbriggs
Glasgow G64 2QT

www.collins.co.uk

First published as *The Macmillan Dictionary of Astronomy* 1979
This edition first published 2006

Reprint 10 9 8 7 6 5 4 3 2 1 0

A catalogue record for this book is available from the British Library

ISBN-13 978-0-00-722092-2
ISBN-10 0-00-722092-8

Typeset by Market House Books Ltd, Aylesbury
Printed and bound in Great Britain by Clays Ltd, St Ives plc

Preface

For over 25 years we have been tracking the growth and developments in astronomy in this dictionary. For this new edition, the fifth in the book's life, we have completely reviewed and updated all the existing entries and have added around 200 entries to reflect recent advances in astronomy and related fields. An additional new feature is a listing of a selection of the most useful websites on astronomy, for the internet provides a very rich resource of information and images. The dictionary now contains over 3,500 entries and also includes an extensive set of appendices providing astronomical data. The book will provide a valuable resource both to those studying astronomy at school or university and to the many enthusiastic amateur astronomers.

The editors would like to express their thanks and appreciation to the many people who have been involved in the book. A list of the main contributors is given overleaf.

Contributors

Editor (previous editions):

Valerie Illingworth MPhil

Contributors:

Peter H. Cadogan PhD
John O. E. Clark BSc
Heather Couper BSc, FRAS
Carolin Crawford PhD, FRAS
Charles A. Cross MA, FRAS
Tony Dean PhD, FRAS
Peter Duffett-Smith PhD, FRAS
Andrew Fabian PhD, FRAS
Ian Furniss PhD, FRAS
Peter B. J. Gill FRAS
Nigel Henbest MSc, FRAS
David W. Hughes PhD, FRAS
Garry E. Hunt DSc, PhD, FIMA, FRAS, FMetS, MBCS
Philip L. Marsden PhD, FIP, FRAS
Rachael Padman PhD, FRAS
Alan Pickup FRAS
Phillipp Podsiadlowski PhD, FRAS
Ken Pounds PhD, FRS, CBE
Gareth Rees PhD, FRAS
Pam Spence MSc
Graham Woan PhD, FRAS
Allan J. Willis PhD, FRAS
John Zarnecki PhD, FRAS

Aa

A0620-00 a possible low-mass BLACK HOLE in the constellation Monoceros. See also X-RAY TRANSIENTS.

AAO *abbrev. for* Anglo–Australian Observatory.

AAT *abbrev. for* Anglo-Australian telescope.

Abell Catalog the standard catalog of rich CLUSTERS OF GALAXIES visible from the northern hemisphere. It was published by George Abell in 1958. A supplement for the southern hemisphere was published by Abell and others in 1988.

aberration 1 (**aberration of starlight**) the apparent displacement in the position of a star because of the finite speed of light and to the motion of the observer, which results primarily from the Earth's orbital motion around the Sun. It was discovered in 1729 by the English astronomer James Bradley. Light appears to approach the observer from a point that is displaced slightly in the direction of the Earth's motion. The angular displacement, α, is given by the relation $\tan \alpha = v/c$, where v is the Earth's orbital velocity and c is the speed of light. Using the Earth's mean orbital speed gives the *constant of aberration*, equal to 20.4955 arc seconds. Over the course of a year, the star appears to move in a small ellipse around its mean position; the ellipse becomes a circle for a star at the pole of the ECLIPTIC and a straight line for one on the ecliptic. The maximum displacement, i.e. the semimajor axis of the ellipse, is 20.5 arc seconds.

The aberration due to the Earth's orbital motion is sometimes termed *annual aberration* to distinguish it from the very much smaller *diurnal aberration* that results from the Earth's rotation on its axis. Compare ANNUAL PARALLAX.

2 a defect in the image formed by a lens or curved mirror, seen as a blurring and possible false coloration in the image. Aberrations occur for all light rays lying off the optical axis and also for those falling at oblique angles on the lens or mirror surface. The four principal aberrations are CHROMATIC ABERRATION (lenses only), SPHERICAL ABERRATION, COMA, and ASTIGMATISM. CURVATURE OF FIELD and DISTORTION are other aberrations. Chromatic aberration occurs when more than one wavelength is present in the incident light beam. For light of a single wavelength, only the latter five aberrations occur. These image defects may be reduced – but not completely eliminated – in an optical system by a suitable choice of optical materials, surface shape, and relative positions of optical elements and stops. See also ACHROMATIC LENS; CORRECTING PLATE.

3 a defect in the image produced by an electronic system using magnetic or electronic lenses.

ablation the loss of material from the surface of a moving body as a result of vaporization, friction, etc. For example, atmospheric atoms and molecules erode the surface of a meteoroid and damage the protective heat shield of a returning space shuttle.

absolute magnitude see MAGNITUDE.

absolute zero the zero value of the THERMODYNAMIC TEMPERATURE SCALE, i.e. 0 K (–273.15 °C). Absolute zero is the lowest temperature theoretically possible. At absolute zero molecular motion almost ceases.

absorption the conversion of all or part of the energy incident on a material medium into some other form of energy within the medium. For example, part of the energy of incident light or infrared radiation may be used in exciting the atoms or molecules of the absorbing substance.

absorption lines, bands see ABSORPTION SPECTRUM.

absorption nebula see DARK NEBULA.

absorption spectrum a SPECTRUM that is produced when ELECTROMAGNETIC RADIATION has been absorbed by matter. Typically, absorption spectra are produced when radiation from an incandescent source, i.e. radiation with a CONTINUOUS SPECTRUM, passes through cooler matter. Radiation is absorbed (i.e. its intensity is diminished) at selective wavelengths so that a pattern of very narrow dips or of wider troughs – i.e. *absorption lines* or *bands* – are superimposed on the continuous spectrum.

The wavelengths at which absorption occurs correspond to the energies required to cause transitions of the absorbing atoms or molecules from lower ENERGY LEVELS to higher levels. In the hydrogen atom, for example, absorption of a photon with the required energy results in a 'jump' of the electron from its normal orbit to one of higher energy (see HYDROGEN SPECTRUM).

The absorption lines (or bands) of a star are produced when elements (or compounds) in the outermost layers of the star absorb radiation from a continuous distribution of wavelengths generated at a lower level in the star. Basically the same elements occur in stars. Since each element has a characteristic pattern of absorption lines for any particular temperature (and pressure) range, there are several different types of stellar spectra depending on the surface temperature of the star. See SPECTRAL TYPES. See also EMISSION SPECTRUM.

abundance the relative proportion of each element, or of each isotope of an element, found in a celestial object or structure. See COSMIC ABUNDANCE.

Acamar see ERIDANUS.

acceleration 1 (**linear acceleration**) symbol: *a*. The rate of increase of velocity with time, measured in meters per second per second ($m\ s^{-2}$), etc.

2 (**angular acceleration**) symbol: α. The rate of increase of ANGULAR VELOCITY with time, usually measured in radians per second per second.

acceleration of gravity symbol: *g*. The acceleration to the center of a planet (or other massive body such as a natural satellite) of an object falling freely without air resistance, i.e. acceleration due to downward motion in a gravitational field. It is equal to GM/R^2, where G is the gravitational constant and M and R are the mass and radius of the planet. The acceleration is thus independent of the mass of the accelerated object, i.e. it is the same for all bodies (neglecting air resistance) falling at the same point on the surface of the planet, satellite, etc.

On Earth the value of the acceleration of gravity is about 9.81 meters per second per second. The value varies from place to place on the Earth's surface because of different distances to the Earth's center and greater acceleration toward the equator. In addition, it is affected by local deposits of light or heavy materials. See also MICROGRAVITY; WEIGHT; WEIGHTLESSNESS.

accretion (**aggregation**) the increase in mass of a body by the addition of smaller bodies that collide and stick to it. The relative velocity of any two colliding bodies must be low enough for them to coalesce on impact rather than fly apart. Once a large enough body forms, its gravitational attraction accelerates the accretion process. Accreting objects in the Universe are numerous and diverse. They include protoplanets, protostars, black holes, and X-ray binaries. The accretion process is thought to occur generally in the form of a disk. Accretion is now assumed to have had an important role in the formation of the planets from swarms of dust grains. In the outer Solar System the grains were like dirty snowflakes and thus accretion was accelerated. See SOLAR SYSTEM, ORIGIN.

accretion disk see BLACK HOLE; MASS TRANSFER; QUASAR.

ACE *abbrev. for* Advanced Composition Explorer.

Achernar (**α Eri**) a conspicuous bluish-white star that is the brightest in the constellation Eridanus. m_v: 0.5; M_v: –1.3; spectral type: B3 Vnp; distance: 22 pc.

Achilles (**(588) Achilles**) the first member of the TROJAN GROUP of ASTEROIDS to be discovered, by Maximilian Wolf, in 1906. It lies east of Jupiter and precedes the latter in its orbit of the Sun by 60°. See TABLE 3, BACKMATTER.

achondrite any of a class of STONY METEORITES that lack the characteristic CHONDRULES of the CHONDRITES. They are usually more coarsely crystallized than the chondritic stones and are more similar chemically and mineralogically to some terrestrial rocks. They contain very little iron and nickel. Achondrites resemble volcanic rocks and are thought to be products of large-scale melting on their parent bodies, i.e. they are differentiated or reprocessed matter. See also HED METEORITES; SNC METEORITES.

achromatic lens (**achromat**) a two-element lens – a doublet – that greatly reduces CHROMATIC ABERRATION in an optical system. The components, one converging and the other diverging in action, are of different types of glass (i.e. they have different REFRACTIVE INDICES); the combination focuses two selected colors, say red and blue, at a common image plane with a small spread in focal length for other colors. The difference in optical power (reciprocal of focal length) for the two colors in one element must cancel that in the other element. By a suitable choice of glasses and surface curvatures, the doublet can be aplanatic as well as achromatic, so that three major aberrations are minimized (see APLANATIC SYSTEM).

Residual color effects in an achromat can be further reduced by using a compound lens of three or more elements – an *apochromatic lens*; each element has an appropriate shape and dispersive power so that three or more colors can be focused in the same image plane.

Acidalia Planitia (formerly **Mare Acidalium**) The most prominent dark marking in the northern hemisphere of MARS; it is a low-lying area more than 2615 km in diameter located just below Mars' north pole and centered on the areographic coordinates 47° N latitude and 22° W longitude (see AREOGRAPHY). Much of the region seems to be volcanic in origin and is thought to be covered by black sand resulting from the erosion of dark basalts. There is a preponderance of rampart craters (see CRATERS) in the area, and ice lies just below the surface. In Mars' distant past, Acidalia Planitia may have been the receptacle for water discharged from adjacent major outflow channels such as Ares Valles. See also MARS, SURFACE FEATURES.

acoustic wave a pressure wave transmitted through a gas, liquid, or solid as a result of small displacements of the particles in the medium. The medium has elasticity and inertia; when set into motion it undergoes alternate compressions and rarefactions that travel through the medium with a speed characteristic of the medium.

acronical rising (**or setting**) the rising (or setting) of a star at or just after sunset.

Acrux see ALPHA CRUCIS.

actinometer an instrument for measuring the intensity of radiation.

active galactic nucleus (**AGN**) see ACTIVE GALAXY.

active galaxy a galaxy that is emitting unusually large amounts of energy from a very compact central source – hence the alternative name *active galactic nucleus* or AGN. (A separate category, STARBURST GALAXY, is employed for a galaxy where a high infrared luminosity arises from intense star formation.) The central powerhouse may be observed directly, as in SEYFERT GALAXIES, BL LAC OBJECTS, or QUASARS; in RADIO GALAXIES it is the radio-emitting lobes created by BEAMS emanating from the powerhouse that are observed. In general the host galaxies of powerful AGN are large, luminous elliptical galaxies, whereas the hosts of Seyferts are spiral. Although some radio-quiet QSO are found located in disklike hosts, most are found to lie in elliptical galaxies.

Observations of the motions of stars and gas in galaxies such as M87 (see VIRGO A) and NGC 4151 (see SEYFERT GALAXY), in addition to other arguments (see QUASAR; POWER-LAW SPECTRUM), strongly suggest that the energy output is derived from the gravitational potential of a supermassive BLACK HOLE: the energy arises from an accretion disk of matter spiraling into the black hole. This material could come from the interstellar medium of a spiral galaxy (especially when perturbed by gravitational effects in INTERACTING GALAXIES), from the tidal disruption of stars near the black hole, or from flows of intergalactic gas on to the central galaxy of a CLUSTER OF GALAXIES, as the gas cools. The X-ray CONTINUUM spectrum of many AGN features components of emission that are thought to be reflected off the accretion disk of the black hole, producing a *reflection spectrum.*

active optics the techniques by which corrections may be made to the shape of a large mirror or radio dish to adjust for minute-long or hour-long drifts from its designed shape. These variations in shape arise as a telescope is subjected to slowly changing forces, including the effects of gravity on different telescope orientations, temperature changes within and exterior to the structure, and wind; they result in an imperfect image and are particularly severe in large telescopes. With active optics, the shape of the reflector is adjusted to give a highly accurate surface and so maintain the quality of the image; in a segmented PRIMARY MIRROR, for example, the position, spacing, and tilt of individual segments can be controlled, while in a thin monolithic meniscus mirror, forces are applied at numerous positions on the mirror back to counteract naturally occurring changes in shape. Active optics are used on the latest generation of giant telescopes, including the 3.5-m NTT of the European Southern Observatory and the 10-m Keck Telescopes. An analogous system, in which the panels making up the receiving surface of a radio telescope can be individually controlled by actuators in order to change the overall shape of the dish, is in use on such instruments as the 100-m Green Bank Telescope. See also ADAPTIVE OPTICS.

active prominence see PROMINENCES.

active-region filament see PROMINENCES.

active regions regions of intense localized magnetic field on the Sun that extend from the PHOTOSPHERE, through the CHROMOSPHERE, to the CORONA. They may encompass a variety of phenomena, such as SUNSPOTS, FACULAEPLAGES, FILAMENTS (or PROMINENCES), and FLARES, and are characterized by enhanced emission of radiation at X-ray, extreme-ultraviolet, and radio wavelengths.

active Sun the term applied to the Sun around the maximum of the SUNSPOT CYCLE, when the profusion of ACTIVE REGIONS ensures a high level of SOLAR ACTIVITY. Compare QUIET SUN.

ADAF *Short for* advection-dominated accretion flow. See BLACK HOLE.

adaptive optics the techniques by which corrections may be made very rapidly (within hundredths of a second) to the shape of a mirror in order to adjust for distortions in a telescope image arising from turbulence in the Earth's atmosphere. The effects of SEEING on the image are thus greatly reduced or removed. Adaptive optics are being applied to new and modernized telescopes to increase the sensitivity and spatial RESOLUTION of the telescope, and should allow near-diffraction-limited imaging over the full aperture of large optical and infrared telescopes (see AIRY DISK). Techniques have been developed to monitor the atmospheric disturbance on the image of a bright reference star, or on an artificial reference star (or *beacon*), and to make rapid compensating adjustments to the shape of a small thin deformable mirror in the light path of the telescope. See also ACTIVE OPTICS.

Adhara (ε CMa) a very luminous remote blue-white giant that is the second brightest star in the constellation Canis Major. It is a visual binary star with an 8th-magnitude companion at a fixed separation of 8″. m_v: 1.5; M_v: –4.8; spectral type: B2 II; distance: 175 pc.

adiabatic process a process that takes place in a system with no heat transfer to or from the system. In general, a temperature change usually occurs in an adiabatic process.

Adonis ((2101) Adonis) a member of the APOLLO GROUP OF ASTEROIDS. Discovered in 1936 by Eugène Joseph Delporte, when it passed 0.015 AU from the Earth, it was not observed again until it was rediscovered in 1977 by Chartles T. Kowal. Its PERIHELION

DISTANCE is 0.51 AU and it has a diameter of about 1 km. See TABLE 3, BACKMATTER.

Adrastea a small irregularly shaped satellite of Jupiter, one of the planet's inner group of satellites, discovered in 1979. See JUPITER'S SATELLITES; TABLE 2, BACKMATTER.

ADS 1 *abbrev. for* Astrophysics Data System. 2 prefix used to designate an object as listed in the *New General Catalog of Double Stars*, 1932, a catalog of 17 180 double stars in the northern and equatorial skies, between DECLINATIONS +90° and –30°. The catalog was complied under the direction of the US astronomer Robert G. Aitken (the prefix is short for Aitken's Double Stars).

Advanced Composition Explorer (**ACE**) a NASA satellite, launched in 1997 to measure the isotope and element ABUNDANCES in the solar corona and COSMIC RAYS over a wide range of energies. It is in orbit around L_1, one of the Lagrangian points of the Sun–Earth system, 1.5 million km nearer to the Sun than Earth is.

Advanced X-ray Astrophysics Facility see AXAF.

advance of the perihelion the gradual movement of the PERIHELION of a planet's elliptical orbit in the same direction as that of the planet's orbital motion. This advance results from the slow rotation of the major axis of the planet's orbit due to gravitational disturbances by other planets and to the curvature of SPACETIME around the Sun. The small contribution from the curvature of spacetime was predicted by Einstein's general theory of RELATIVITY.

The value of this relativistic contribution toward the advance of the perihelion of Mercury is about 43 arc seconds per century. This agrees almost exactly with the discrepancy between the experimentally determined value for the advance and that predicted by classical Newtonian mechanics. It was therefore an important confirmation of general relativity. Recent measurements of the advance of the perihelia of Venus and Earth have also been very close to Einstein's predicted values for those planets.

aeon a period of one thousand million years: 10^9 years.

aerial see ANTENNA.

aeronomy the physics and chemistry of the upper atmosphere of the Earth, i.e. its temperature, density, motions, composition, chemical processes, reactions to solar and cosmic radiation, etc. The term has been extended to include the physics and chemistry of the atmospheres of the other planets.

aerospace the Earth's atmosphere and the space beyond.

Ae stars hot stars of SPECTRAL TYPE A that in addition to the normal absorption spectrum have bright emission lines of hydrogen. These lines are thought to arise in an expanding atmospheric shell of matter lost from the star. Like some BE STARS they are probably similar to T TAURI STARS except that they have larger masses.

afocal system an optical system in which both the object and the secondary image are infinitely distant. It is the usual adjustment in a simple refracting telescope and is produced when the objective and eyepiece lenses are separated by the sum of their focal lengths: the lenses are then *confocal*.

AG Catalog see AGK.

Agena see CENTAURUS.

age of the Earth the oldest rocks found in the Earth's crust have been assigned ages of 3.96 billion (10^9) years from radioisotope studies, but other properties of the rocks support the belief that the planet shares a common origin with the rest of the Solar System, about 4.57 billion years ago. The cycling of the crustal material by plate tectonics (see EARTH) and the eroding effects of ice, water, and wind mean that none of the earliest rocks survive intact and that evidence of an early meteoritic bombardment, so apparent on the Moon, Mercury, and Mars, is absent. See EARTH; SOLAR SYSTEM, ORIGIN.

age of the Universe the observed expansion and evolution of the Universe suggest that it has a finite age, considered as the time since the BIG BANG. The inverse HUBBLE CONSTANT, $1/H_0$, gives a measure of the age if the rate of expansion has always been constant. Since gravitation tends to diminish the expansion rate, H_0 can only give an upper limit. Using the value of H_0 of 75 km s^{-1} Mpc^{-1} gives an upper limit of 13 billion (10^9) years.

In the standard COSMOLOGY (solutions of

Einstein's field equations without a cosmological constant) with DECELERATION PARAMETER q_o, the age is given as one of the three alternatives:

$$H_o^{-1}q_o(2q_o - 1)^{-3/2}[\cos^{-1}(q_o^{-1} - 1) - q_o^{-1}(2q_o - 1)^{1/2}]$$

$$2/3H_o^{-1}$$

$$H_o^{-1}q_o(1 - 2q_o)^{-3/2}[q_o^{-1}(1 - 2q_o)^{1/2} - \cosh^{-1}(q_o^{-1} - 1)]$$

The choice depends on whether q_o exceeds, equals, or is less than ½ (and > 0), i.e. on whether the Universe is closed, flat, or open, respectively. Ages of 12 and 15×10^9 years thus correspond to values of q_o of ½ and 0.15, for H_o equal to 55 km s^{-1} Mpc^{-1}.

Lower limits to the age of the Universe, other than through measurements of H_o and q_o, can be found from RADIOMETRIC DATING of the Earth and Galaxy and from studies of GLOBULAR CLUSTERS. For example, the relative abundances of radioactive elements, such as uranium, and their decay products yield an estimate of the time since formation of that body of material e.g., the Earth. The results give an age for the Universe of $14–16 \times 10^9$ years. The age of a globular cluster may be estimated by comparison of the observed main-sequence TURNOFF POINT in the Hertzsprung–Russell diagram for the cluster with theoretical models. The oldest globular clusters in our Galaxy then work out to be $14–18 \times 10^9$ years old. Both of these ages should be less than the age of the Universe and in particular they must be less than H_o^{-1}. If the expansion of the Universe is now accelerating due to a cosmological constant, then the Universe will be slightly older than given by the above estimates.

aggregation see ACCRETION.

AGK (AG Catalog) *abbrev. for Astronomische Gesellschaft Katalog*. A general catalog of star positions originally proposed by the Prussian astronomer Friedrich Argelander in 1867. Argelander was the founder (in 1863) of the Astronomische Gesellschaft (Astronomical Society), which gave its name to the AGK. The first version, known as *AGK1*, covered the northern sky and by 1912 DECLINATION zones between +90° and –18° had been published. A revision, known as *AGK2*, was based on photographic measurements begun in the 1920s and was published 1951–58. A further set of photographic plates was produced in the 1950s to determine PROPER MOTIONS, which appeared in the *AGK3* version; this lists 183 145 stars and was distributed on magnetic tape from 1969, finally appearing in print in 1975. *AGK3R* (1977–78) gave more accurate positions of 20 194 northern-hemisphere reference stars, while an updated version, AGK3U (1992), using photographic plates supplied for the HST GUIDE STARS CATALOG in 1983, provided refinements to the positions of 170 464 stars.

AGN *abbrev. for* active galactic nucleus. See ACTIVE GALAXY.

Ahnighito meteorite the biggest (59 tonnes) of the three Cape York iron METEORITES, now on display in New York. It was brought back from the coast of west Greenland in 1897 by Robert Peary.

AIPS *abbrev. for* Astronomical Image-Processing System. A suite of computer programs produced by the NATIONAL RADIO ASTRONOMY OBSERVATORY (NRAO) covering over 300 astronomical data processing tasks. Designed primarily for radio astronomy, AIPS can accept APERTURE SYNTHESIS and VLBI data, process them to form images of the sky, and improve their quality using DECONVOLUTION methods. It can also display, analyze, and combine images. Data are usually transferred to and from AIPS using the FITS file format. The AIPS++ project is a more modern object-orientated package, written in C++, intended to supersede classic AIPS.

airglow (nightglow) the faint everpresent glow arising in the Earth's atmosphere that is light emitted (along with infrared radiation) during the recombination of ionized atoms and molecules following collisions with high-energy particles and radiation, mainly from the Sun. Airglow interferes with optical and infrared observations of faint celestial bodies.

air shower see COSMIC RAYS.

Airy disk the bright disklike image of a point source of light, such as a star, as seen in an optical system with a circular APERTURE. The disk is formed by DIFFRACTION effects in the instrument and is surrounded by faint diffraction rings that are only seen

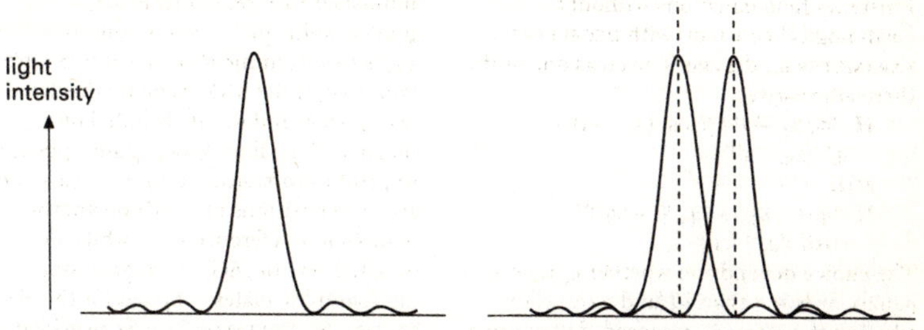

Airy disk: light distribution in Airy disk image of single point source (left) and two just resolvable point sources

under perfect conditions (see illustration). The disk diameter, first calculated by George Airy in 1834, is the factor limiting the angular RESOLUTION of the telescope.

Aitken see table at CRATERS.

AI Velorum stars see DWARF CEPHEIDS.

Alba Patera probably the largest central-vent volcanic structure on Mars. Located north of the THARSIS RIDGE, it is centered on the aerographic coordinates 40° N latitude, 109° W longitude (see AREOGRAPHY). It has a low dome containing a central caldera and enclosed by a ring of fractures 600 km in diameter. Associated lava flows cover an area more than 1500 km across. See MARS, VOLCANOES.

albedo the reflecting power of a nonluminous object, such as a planet or planetary surface feature. In general, it is the ratio of the total amount of light reflected in all directions to the amount of incident light: an albedo of 1.0 indicates a perfectly reflecting surface whereas a value of 0.0 indicates a totally black surface that absorbs all incident light.

Albedo can be expressed in several ways. The *Bond albedo* is the fraction of the total incident energy that a body reflects in all directions. It is calculated over all wavelengths and its value therefore depends on the spectrum of the incident radiation. This parameter determines the energy balance of a body such as a planet. The *geometrical albedo* is the ratio of the light reflected in the backscattering direction (zero phase angle or opposition) by an object, to that which would be reflected by a perfectly diffusing disk of the same size. The wavelength or range of wavelengths at which the geometrical albedo applies must be defined. Geometrical albedo is commonly used for Solar System objects. The *hemispherical albedo* is the reflecting power of a nonluminous body such as a planet, assuming the body is a sphere with a diffuse surface reflecting incoming parallel light rays in all directions. The *phase integral* is the ratio of the Bond albedo to the geometrical albedo averaged over the incident spectrum. See also TABLE 1, BACKMATTER.

Albert (**(719) Albert**) a small asteroid (2.6 km across) discovered by J. Palisa when it approached the Earth closely in 1911, but since lost.

Albireo (**β Cyg**) a beautiful double star, the second brightest star in the constellation Cygnus. The primary is an orange giant with a deep blue companion 35″ away. m_v: 3.1 (A), 5.1 (B); spectral type: K5 II (A), B8 V (B).

Alcaid (**Benatnasch; η UMa**) a blue-white star that is one of the seven brightest in the PLOUGH. m_v: 1.86; spectral type: B3 V; distance: 34 pc.

Alcor (**80 UMa**) a white star that lies in the 'handle' of the PLOUGH and forms an optical double with MIZAR. m_v: 4.0; spectral type: A5 V.

Alcyone (**η Tau**) a bluish-white giant star in the constellation Taurus that is the brightest star in the PLEIADES. m_v: 2.86; M_v: –1.5; spectral type: B7 IIIe.

Aldebaran (**α Tau**) a conspicuous red giant

that is the brightest star in the constellation Taurus and lies in the line of sight of but much nearer than the Hyades. It is a slow irregular variable. It has two companions: one of 11th magnitude at 122″ separation, the other of 13th magnitude at 30″. m_v: 0.85 (var.); M_v: –0.3; spectral type: K5 III; radius (by interferometer): 45 times solar radius; distance: 18 pc.

Alderamin see CEPHEUS.

Alfvén's theory a theory proposed by the Swedish physicist Hannes Alfvén in 1942 for the formation of the planets out of material captured by the Sun from an interstellar cloud of gas and dust. As atoms fall toward the Sun, they become ionized and subject to the control of the Sun's magnetic field. Ions are concentrated in the plane of the solar equator where the planets coalesce. The theory, in its original form, had difficulty in accounting for the inner planets, but was important in suggesting the role of MAGNETOHYDRODYNAMICS in the genesis of the Solar System. See SOLAR SYSTEM, ORIGIN.

Alfvén waves disturbances transmitted through a PLASMA in the presence of a magnetic field. The direction of propagation is parallel to the mean magnetic field, with the plasma particles vibrating at right angles to this direction. The speed of propagation, the *Alfvén speed*, depends on the magnetic field strength and the plasma density. The waves interact with the plasma particles, for example by exerting radiation pressure on the plasma. As the waves dissipate, the plasma particles are heated and accelerated. Alfvén waves are a type of magnetohydrodynamic (MHD) wave. They have been directly observed in the SOLAR WIND, particularly in the high-speed streams, and in planetary magnetospheres.

Algenib (γ Peg) a remote bluish-white subgiant that is one of the brighter stars of the constellation Pegasus and lies on the Great Square of Pegasus. It is a variable star with a very short period of about 4 hours, during which its visual magnitude ranges between 2.80 and 2.87. m_v: 2.83 (var.); M_v: –3.1; spectral type: B2 IV; distance: 153.5 pc. Algenib is also an old name for the star MIRFAK.

Algieba (γ Leo) an orange giant that is the second-brightest star in the constellation Leo. It is a multiple star, forming a visual binary (separation 4″.4, period 619 years) with a 3rd-magnitude yellow companion. m_v: 2.2 (A), 1.84 (AB); M_v: –0.5; spectral type: K0p III (A), G7 III (B); distance: 32 pc.

Algol (Demon Star; Winking Demon; β Per) a white star that is the second-brightest one in the constellation Perseus. It was the first ECLIPSING BINARY to be discovered, being the prototype of the ALGOL VARIABLES, although its variations in brightness were known to early astronomers. The theory of a darker companion periodically cutting off the light of the brighter star (Goodricke, 1782; Pickering, 1880) was confirmed spectroscopically in 1889. The brighter star (Algol A) is about three times the Sun's

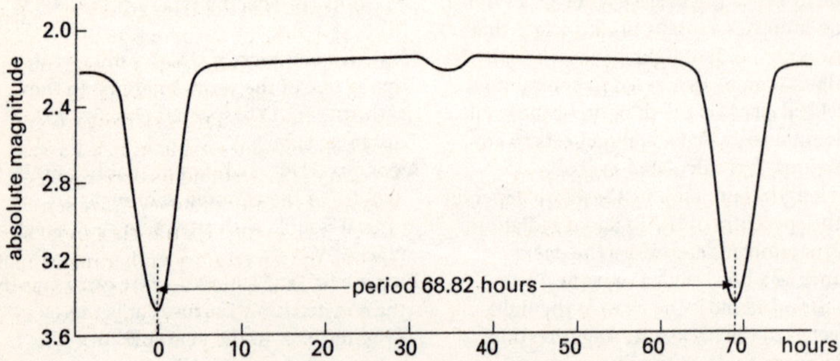

Algol: light curve of Algol

diameter; the fainter orange 3rd-magnitude companion (Algol B) is about 20% larger. The two stars revolve about one another in a period of 68.8 hours, and the eclipses cause the magnitude to drop from 2.2 to 3.5 (see illustration). There is also a third more distant star, Algol C, which orbits Algol A and B in 1.86 years.

Algol A is about 3.7 times as massive as the Sun, while Algol B has a mass of only 0.8 solar masses. According to STELLAR EVOLUTION theory, a more massive star evolves more rapidly; yet in the Algol system the more massive Algol A is still a main-sequence star while Algol B has evolved to become a subgiant. This is the *Algol paradox*, which is explained by slow and continuous MASS TRANSFER from Algol B to Algol A (see ALGOL VARIABLES). This mass transfer, along with APSIDAL MOTION, accounts for slight changes in the time of Algol's eclipses. The streams of gas passing from Algol B to Algol A make Algol an erratic radio and X-ray source. m_v: 2.1 (A), 3.5 (B); M_v: –0.2 (A), 1.2 (B); spectral type: B8 V (A), K0 IV (B); distance: 29 pc.

Algol paradox see ALGOL VARIABLES; ALGOL.

Algol variables (**Beta Persei stars**) a subclass of ECLIPSING BINARY stars, named after ALGOL, where the brighter and more massive star is still on the MAIN SEQUENCE while the less massive companion has evolved more and has become a SUBGIANT. This seemingly contradicts the theory of stellar evolution, which predicts that more massive stars evolve more rapidly, and is known as the *Algol paradox*. It is explained (Crawford 1955) as a result of extensive MASS TRANSFER: the now less-massive star originally contained most of the system's mass, and it evolved rapidly beyond the main sequence. As it expanded, this star lost up to 85% of its mass to the companion (see W SERPENTIS STAR) to end up as a faint low-mass subgiant, while the companion became a massive hot and brilliant star, still on the main sequence. Mass transfer continues at a very slow rate in Algol systems, causing variations in the orbital period and feeble radio and X-ray emission.

As a result of the mass transfer, the two stars have the unusual property of being roughly the same size (several times larger than the Sun) but having very different luminosities. They thus have a LIGHT CURVE characterized by deep primary minima when the dim subgiant eclipses the bright main-sequence star, alternating with scarcely detectable secondary minima when the subgiant is eclipsed.

Alhena see GEMINI.

alidade see ASTROLABE.

alignment effect see RADIO GALAXY.

Alioth (**ε UMa**) a white SPECTROSCOPIC BINARY, period 4.15 years, that is the brightest star in the constellation Ursa Major. It is a SPECTRUM VARIABLE star. m_v: 1.78; spectral type: A0p; distance: 19 pc. See also PLOUGH.

Alkaid see ALCAID.

Allegheny Observatory an observatory sited in Riverview Park, in the city of Pittsburgh, Pennsylvania, USA, and operated by the Physics and Astronomy Department of the University of Pittsburgh. Founded in 1859, the observatory was taken over by the university in 1867 and was fully established on its present site by 1912. The observatory has three telescopes housed in three separate domes. The Fitz-Clark Refractor, a 33.02-centimeter instrument, was the observatory's original telescope, purchased in 1861; it has a focal length of 4.62 meters and a focal ratio of f/14. The William Thaw Memorial Refractor (aperture 76.2 cm, focal length 14.3 m, focal ratio f/18.8) was built in 1912 and designed for photographic work. In 1985 its object lens was upgraded to focus red light, a region of the spectrum in which the Pittsburgh skies are still relatively clear. The James E. Keeler Memorial Reflector (aperture 73.7 cm, focal length 4.56 m, focal ratio f/6) is the observatory's main instrument. Built in 1905 as a Cassegrain telescope, it was originally used for spectroscopy. In 1992 its mirrors were replaced with ones made from a Russian version of CER-VIT and its optics were upgraded to an f/15 Ritchey–Chrétien system (see RITCHEY–CHRÉTIEN OPTICS). Among the observatory's other instruments is a nulti-channel astrometric photometer (MAP), designed by George A. Gatewood, the institution's director from 1977. The Allegheny Observatory is today a world leader in high-precision astrometry. Its measurements are being used most significantly in the search for extrasolar planetary systems.

Allende see METEORITE.

ALMA see ATACAMA LARGE MILLIMETER ARRAY.

Almach (γ And) an orange giant that is the third-brightest star in the constellation Andromeda. It is a triple star, forming a very fine visual binary with its apparently greenish companion (B), 10″ distant, with which it has a common proper motion; B is a spectroscopic binary, period 61 years. m_V: 2.28 (A), 5.1 (B), 2.16 (AB); spectral type: K3 II (A), A0p (B).

Almagest (Arabic: the Greatest) an astronomical work compiled by Ptolemy of Alexandria in about AD 140. It was translated from the original Greek into Arabic in the 9th century and became known in Europe when it was translated from Arabic into Latin in the late 12th century. Its 13 volumes cover the whole of astronomy as conceived in ancient times, with a detailed description of the PTOLEMAIC SYSTEM of the Solar System. It also included a star catalog giving positions and MAGNITUDES (from 1 to 6) of 1022 stars. This catalog was based mainly on the one produced in the 2nd century BC by Hipparchus of Nicaea.

almucantar a SMALL CIRCLE on the CELESTIAL SPHERE parallel to the horizon.

Alnath see ELNATH.

Alnilam see ORION.

Alnitak see ORION.

alpha (α) 1 the first letter of the Greek alphabet, used in STELLAR NOMENCLATURE usually to designate the brightest star in a constellation or sometimes to indicate a star's position in a group.
2 *symbol for* right ascension.

Alpha Capricornids see CAPRICORNIDS.

Alpha Centauri (Rigil Kentaurus; α Cen) a binary star that is the brightest star in the constellation Centaurus, one of the brightest in the sky, and the second nearest star to the Sun. The two components, A and B, form a yellow-orange VISUAL BINARY (separation 17″.7, period 80.1 years) and are similar in mass and size to the Sun. PROXIMA CENTAURI appears to be physically associated with α Cen; it is the nearest star to the Sun. m_v: –0.01 (A), 1.33 (B), –0.27 (AB); M_v: 4.4 (A), 5.7 (B), 4.1 (AB); spectral type: G2 V (A), K1 V (B); mass: 1.09 (A), 0.89 (B) times solar mass; distance: 1.33 pc.

Alpha Crucis (Acrux; α Cru) a conspicuous white star that is the brightest in the constellation Crux. It is a visual binary (separation 4″), both components being spectroscopic binaries. Alpha (α) and Gamma (γ) Crucis point towards the south celestial pole. m_v: 1.3 (A), 1.7 (B), 0.76 (AB); M_v: –4.2 (A), 3.2 (B); spectral type: B1 IV (A), B1 V (B); distance: 160 pc.

alpha particle (α particle) the nucleus of a helium atom, i.e. a positively charged particle consisting of two protons and two neutrons. It is thus a fully ionized helium atom. Alpha particles are very stable. They are often ejected in nuclear reactions, including *alpha decay* in which a parent nucleus disintegrates – or breaks up – into an alpha particle and a lighter daughter nucleus.

Alphard (α Hya) an orange giant that is the brightest star in the constellation Hydra and lies in a part of the sky where there are few other stars of comparable brightness. m_v: 2.05; spectral type: K4 III; distance: 35 pc.

Alpha Regio the first feature identified on Venus using Earth-based radar (it was discovered in 1963). It is a highland plateau about 1300 km across situated in the southern hemisphere of the planet (centered on the Venusian coordinates 25° S latitude, 4° E longitude). It exhibits multiple sets of intersecting ridges, troughs, and flat-floored fault valleys that together form a polygonal outline. Directly south of the complex ridged terrain is a large oval-shaped feature named *Eve.* A radar bright spot within Eve marks the location of the prime meridian of Venus.

Alphecca or **Alphekka (Gemma; α CrB)** a blue-white star that is the brightest one in the constellation Corona Borealis. It is an ECLIPSING BINARY (separation 42″, period 17.36 days). m_v: 2.23; spectral type: A0 V (A), G5 V (B); distance: 22 pc.

Alpheratz (Sirrah; α And) a bluish-white giant that is the brightest star in the constellation Andromeda. It is both a spectroscopic binary (period 96.7 days) and a SPECTRUM VARIABLE. It originally lay in the constellation Pegasus, as Delta (δ) Pegasi, and is still considered part of the Great Square of Pegasus. m_v: 2.07; spectral type: B9p III; distance: 31 pc.

Alphonsus see table at CRATERS.

Alps (Montes Alpes) see table at MOUNTAINS, LUNAR.

ALSEP *abbrev. for* Apollo Lunar Surface Experiments Package. Any of the experimental packages carried to the Moon by APOLLOS 11–17, set up by the astronauts, and left there to transmit information back to Earth. The content of each package differed, becoming more sophisticated as the program progressed. In the Apollo 17 ALSEP, a central station and thermal generator provided the main power; the experiments included an analysis of any residual atmosphere, detection and measurement of any lunar ejecta and meteorite impacts, measurement of any gravitational anomalies, lunar surface studies, and seismic measurements.

Altair (α Aql) a nearby conspicuous white star that is the brightest one in the constellation Aquila. m_v: 0.77; M_v: 2.3; spectral type: A7 Vn; distance: 5.0 pc.

altazimuth mounting (azimuthal mounting) a MOUNTING in which the telescope swings in azimuth about a vertical axis and in ALTITUDE about a horizontal axis (see illustration). It is easy to make and use and needs no counterpoise weights to balance the telescope. It provides a very firm support and is well adapted for terrestrial observations and for following rapidly moving objects such as artificial satellites. Its great disadvantage is the need to adjust both altitude and azimuth simultaneously and at different rates to follow the diurnal motion of a heavenly body. The application

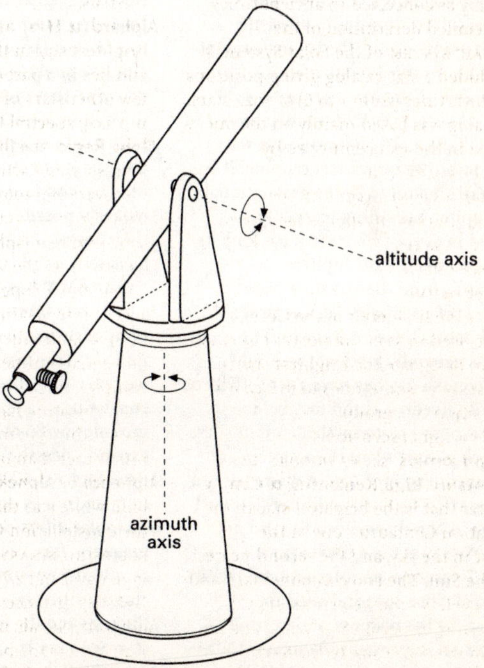

Altazimuth mounting

of very precise computer-controlled drive mechanisms to altazimuth mountings has led to their use in large optical and radio telescopes. The altazimuth design allows a smaller and less costly observatory DOME to be used on an optical telescope. Compare EQUATORIAL MOUNTING.

altitude the angular distance of a point or celestial object above or below the HORIZON, or of an object, such as an artificial satellite, above mean sea level. Altitude and azimuth are coordinates in the HORIZONTAL COORDINATE SYSTEM.

aluminizing a process whereby a very thin but perfectly uniform coating of aluminum is deposited by evaporation on a suitable base. It is used in astronomy to produce the reflective layer of a mirror. The aluminizing is done in an evacuated chamber. The aluminum layer is usually protected by a transparent coating of silica or magnesium fluoride. The surface is harder and more stable than silver and is also able to reflect shorter wavelengths than silver. The process was introduced into telescope manufacture in 1931 by the US instrument-maker John Strong. See SILVERING.

Amalthea one of the inner group of JUPITER'S SATELLITES that was discovered in 1892 by E.E. Barnard and until 1979 was thought to be the innermost satellite. It has been greatly distorted by the gravitational pull of Jupiter, becoming markedly elongated in shape (270 × 166 × 150 km); its long axis points toward Jupiter. Photographs from the VOYAGER PROBES show the surface is very red, due probably to sulfur contamination from IO. The ALBEDO is generally low, but the bright rather greenish patches have a reflectivity of up to 20% (albedo 0.2) and may be due to recently exposed material that contains less sulfur-rich glass. Its two main craters are bowl-shaped: *Pan* is 90 km in diameter and *Gaea* is 75 km. The Galileo orbiter flew past Amalthea in November 2002 but did not image it. See TABLE 2, BACKMATTER.

AMANDA Telescope an international facility operational since 1997 and sited in Antarctica for the purpose of detecting neutrinos. An improved version, AMANDA-II, came into service in 2000. AMANDA – the Antarctic Muon and Neutrino Detector Array – consists of an arrangement of 677 optical modules, each one as big as a glass basketball, strung on 19 electrical cables and buried deep in the pure clear ice beneath the South Pole. The AMANDA Telescope points downward to detect neutrinos passing right through the Earth from the skies above the northern hemisphere. Interference from other particles and from light radiation is filtered out by the body of the Earth and by the situation of the modules, located more than two kilometers below the surface of the ice.

A small number of the countless neutrinos that continually bombard and tear through our planet interact with subatomic particles in the polar ice and rock to produce negatively charged muons. Each muon speeding through the ice emits Cerenkov radiation, visible as a short-lived streak of faint blue light that illuminates phototubes within the modules. The phototubes convert the radiation to an electrical signal and transmit it to computers above ground. After an interaction, the muon continues to travel in almost exactly the same direction as the neutrino that produces it. Thus analysis of the muons' signals allows scientists to extrapolate information about their originating neutrinos, such as their paths, velocity, and frequency. Thus AMANDA makes it possible to track neutrinos back to their cosmic origins, such as gamma-ray bursts.

The AMANDA Telescope serves as a small-scale forerunner to a much larger array of neutrino detectors currently named *Ice Cube*. This device, covering a region of ice one cubic kilometer in volume and consisting of a planned 4800 optical modules on 80 cables, will include and expand upon the existing AMANDA detectors. Astronomers hope that it will be in operation by 2008.

ambipolar diffusion a process by which magnetic flux and angular momentum are removed from DENSE CORES in molecular clouds, ultimately leading to the collapse of the core and the formation of a low-mass star. See STAR FORMATION.

American Ephemeris and Nautical Almanac see ASTRONOMICAL ALMANAC.

Ames Research Center a NASA research establishment near San Francisco, California.

AM Herculis the archetypal magnetic white dwarf binary system, or polar, identified in 1976 from an UHURU X-ray source. Optically it is a faint variable binary star (mag. 12–15), exhibiting strong optical polarization and a photometric period of 185 minutes. X-ray emission is strongly modulated at the same period, due to rotation of the white dwarf. The characteristic high XUV-to-optical luminosity ratio has led to several other similar systems being found from X-ray and XUV surveys. See MAGNETIC CATACLYSMIC VARIABLES.

AM Herculis stars see MAGNETIC CATACLYSMIC VARIABLES.

Amor group a group of near-Earth ASTEROIDS that come within the PERIHELION DISTANCE of Mars but not within the orbit of the Earth. They have SEMIMAJOR AXES greater than 1 AU but perihelion distances between 1.017 and 1.3 AU. The group is named after the asteroid (1221) *Amor*, discovered in 1932 by Eugène Joseph Delporte. Compare APOLLO GROUP. See TABLE 3, BACKMATTER.

amplitude **1** symbol: Δm. The difference between the maximum and minimum MAGNITUDES of a VARIABLE STAR, i.e. the range in magnitude of the star. The amplitude of pulsating variables is related to the logarithm of the period.
2 the maximum instantaneous deviation of an oscillating quantity from its average value.

AMPTE *abbrev. for* active magnetospheric particle tracer explorer. Any of three satellites built by West Germany, the UK, and the USA that were launched from a Thor Delta rocket into different orbits on 9 Aug. 1984 for a series of interactive experiments to study the Earth's MAGNETOSPHERE. The German and UK satellites were put in highly eccentric orbits into the SOLAR WIND while the US craft was in a lower orbit. Lithium and later barium atoms released into the magnetosphere from the German satellite formed positive ions. These were used as tracers in a coordinated effort to study how solar energy, carried by the solar wind, is intercepted and stored in the magnetosphere as charged particles.

Am stars peculiar main-sequence stars (see PECULIAR STARS) of spectral types from A0 to F0 in which there is an over-abundance of heavier elements and rare earths and (less so) of iron, and an apparent under-abundance of calcium. They rotate slower than normal A stars and are almost all short-period SPECTROSCOPIC binaries. Current theory suggests that tidal effects slow the A star's rotation, leading to an unusually stable atmosphere where heavy elements can diffuse up from the interior. Compare AP STARS.

analemma the shape resembling a figure of eight obtained by plotting the position of the Sun relative to the intersection of a meridian and the celestial equator at a fixed (mean) time every day throughout the year. The analemma's vertical extent is a reflection of the changes in the Sun's declination arising from the inclination of the Earth's axis to the perpendicular to its orbit. The horizontal extent arises from the fact that the Earth's orbit is elliptical, which produces a difference between the length of the apparent solar day (the actual time between successive meridian transits of the Sun) and the mean solar day.

Ananke a small satellite of Jupiter, one of the planet's many outer satellites, discovered in 1951 by the US astronomer Seth Nicholson (1891–1963). See JUPITER'S SATELLITES; TABLE 2, BACKMATTER.

anastigmatic system an optical system that is able to produce an image essentially free of SPHERICAL ABERRATION, COMA, and ASTIGMATISM.

Andromeda a constellation in the northern hemisphere close to PEGASUS, the brightest stars being ALPHERATZ (α), the red giant Mirach (β), and the fine visual binary ALMACH (γ). It contains the MIRA STARS R and W Andromedae, the spiral ANDROMEDA GALAXY and its companion galaxies M32 (NGC 221) and M110 (NGC 205), and the bright planetary nebula NGC 7662. Other objects include the open cluster NGC 752 and the edge-on spiral galaxy NGC 891. The 4th-magnitude Upsilon (υ) Andromedae, a yellow dwarf star of spectral class F8 V located at a distance of 15.9 pc, is believed to have three giant planets in orbit around it. Abbrev.: And; genitive form: Andromedae; approx. position: RA 1h, dec +40°; area: 722 sq deg.

Andromeda galaxy (**M31; NGC 224**) the largest of the nearby galaxies, visible to the unaided eye as a faint oval patch of light in the constellation Andromeda. It is an intermediate (Sb) spiral (see HUBBLE CLASSIFICATION), orientated at an angle of about 15° from the edge-on position, and has a bright elliptical-shaped nucleus. Its distance is currently estimated as 725 kiloparsecs (2.36 million light years). With a total luminosity roughly double that of our own Galaxy and an overall diameter of approximately 60 kiloparsecs, M31 is the largest of the established members of the LOCAL GROUP. It has at least four elliptical satellites, including NGC 205 and NGC 221 (M32).

Andromedids see BIELIDS.

anemic galaxies disk galaxies that are intermediate in type between lenticular and normal spirals, possessing diffuse weak spiral arms; the BLACKEYE GALAXY is an example. See GALAXIES.

Anglo-Australian Observatory (**AAO**) an observatory at the Siding Spring Observatory site in New South Wales, Australia. The chief instruments are the 3.9-meter ANGLO-AUSTRALIAN TELESCOPE and the 1.2-meter UK SCHMIDT TELESCOPE.

Anglo-Australian Telescope (**AAT**) the 3.9-meter reflecting telescope of the ANGLO-AUSTRALIAN OBSERVATORY, sited at an altitude of 1150 meters. It was funded jointly by the governments of Australia and the UK, each country having a half share in observing time. It began regular operation in 1975 and is now equipped for both optical and infrared observations. It has RITCHEY–CHRÉTIEN OPTICS and a CER-VIT mirror and works at a FOCAL RATIO of f/3.3 at the prime focus, f/8 at the Cassegrain foci, f/15 for infrared work, and f/35 at the coudé focus. It has a limiting magnitude of 23–25 (depending on wavelength and technique used), the maximum field of view covering about one square degree of sky. The telescope has an EQUATORIAL MOUNTING, and is computer controlled so that the pointing and tracking are exceptionally accurate.

angstrom symbol: Å. A unit of length equal to 10^{-10} meters. It was formerly used to specify interatomic distances.

angular acceleration see ANGULAR VELOCITY.

angular diameter see APPARENT DIAMETER.

angular distance see APPARENT DISTANCE.

angular measure units of angle or length given in terms of degrees (°), arc minutes (′), and ARC SECONDS (″):

$60'' = 1'$

$60' = 1°$

$360° = 2\pi$ radians (a full circle).

angular momentum symbol: *L*. A property of any rotating or revolving system whose value depends on the distribution of mass and velocity about the axis of rotation or revolution. It is a vector directed along the axis and for a body orbiting about a point it is given by the vector product of the body's linear momentum and position vector *r*, i.e. it is the product $m(v \times r)$. It is also expressed as the product of the MOMENT OF INERTIA (I) and ANGULAR VELOCITY (ω) of the body.

In a closed system, such as the Solar System or an isolated star, there is always CONSERVATION OF MOMENTUM.

angular resolution see RESOLUTION.

angular separation see APPARENT DISTANCE.

angular velocity symbol: ω. The rate at which a body or particle moves about a fixed axis, i.e. the rate of change of angular displacement. It is expressed in radians per second. *Angular acceleration* is the rate of change of angular velocity.

anisotropy a dependence of physical properties upon direction; a lack of ISOTROPY. A lack of HOMOGENEITY implies anisotropy but the reverse is not necessarily true.

Ankaa see PHOENIX.

annihilation a reaction between an ELEMENTARY PARTICLE and its ANTIPARTICLE in which the two particles disappear and photons or other particles and antiparticles are created; energy and momentum are conserved. An electron and a positron, for example, interact and produce two gamma-ray photons. Hadrons, such as the proton and the antiproton, also undergo annihilation, as do QUARKS and antiquarks.

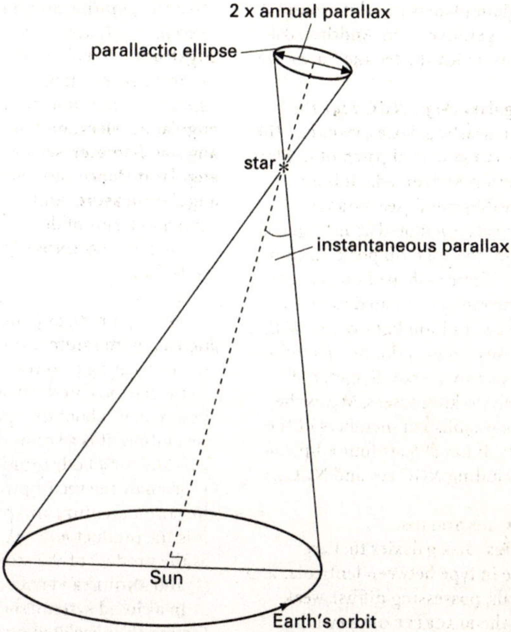

Annual parallax

annual aberration see ABERRATION.

annual equation (**annual inequality**) the periodic INEQUALITY in the Moon's motion that arises from variations in solar attraction due to the ECCENTRICITY of the Earth's orbit. Its period is the ANOMALISTIC YEAR and the maximum displacement in longitude is 11′8″.9. See also EVECTION; PARALLACTIC INEQUALITY; VARIATION.

annual inequality see ANNUAL EQUATION.

annual parallax (**heliocentric parallax**) the PARALLAX of a celestial body that results from the change in the position of an observational point during the Earth's annual revolution around the Sun: nearby stars are seen to be displaced in position relative to the more remote background stars. The instantaneous parallax of a given star is the angle formed by the radius of the Earth's orbit at the star; it varies through the year as the orbital radius varies. If the positions of a star are determined during one year they are found to describe an ellipse – a *parallactic ellipse* – on the celestial sphere. The annual parallax, π, of the star is equal to and can be measured from the semimajor axis of the ellipse.

Annual parallax is the maximum parallactic displacement of the star and occurs when the angle Earth-Sun-star is 90° (see illustration). It is thus expressed by the relation $\sin \pi = a/d$, where a is the semimajor axis of the Earth's orbit and d is the star's distance from Earth. Since π is extremely small (<1″), this reduces to $\pi = a/d$. If a is assumed to be unity (i.e. one ASTRONOMICAL UNIT) then a measurement of π in arc seconds will be equal to the reciprocal ($1/d$) of the distance in PARSECS.

The parallax of a star determined directly from a known baseline and using the principle of triangulation, i.e. from measurements of annual parallax, is termed *trigonometric parallax*. Due to its tiny value

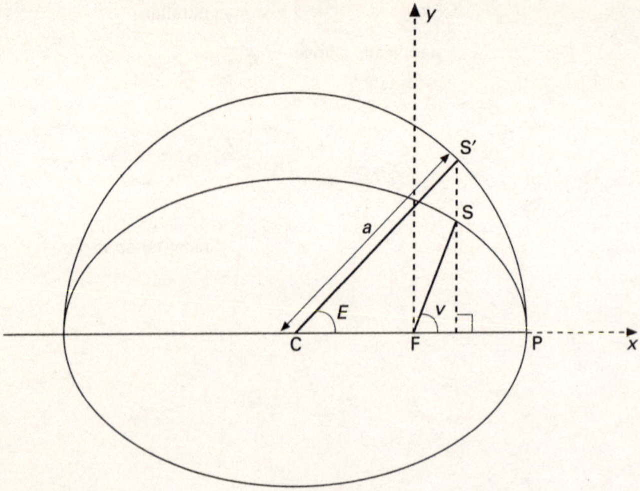

Anomaly

annual parallax from Earth can be measured only (photographically from Earth) with reasonable accuracy for stars within about 30 parsecs ($\pi > 0''.03$). Spacecraft such as HIPPARCOS can measure annual parallax with a very much greater accuracy, to 0″.002, allowing distances up to 500 parsecs to be determined. Microarcsecond measurements are planned for future spacecraft. Only about 3000 stars are known to have annual parallaxes exceeding 0″.04, the nearest star – Proxima Centauri – having the greatest value (0″.772).

annular eclipse see ECLIPSE.

anomalistic month the time interval of 27.554 55 days, on average, between two successive passages of the Moon through the PERIGEE of its orbit.

anomalistic year the time interval of 365.259 64 days between two successive passages of the Earth through the PERIHELION of its orbit. The anomalistic year is longer than the SIDEREAL and TROPICAL YEARS because of the ADVANCE OF THE PERIHELION caused (mainly) by planetary perturbations.

anomaly any of three related angles by means of which the position, at a particular time, of a body moving in an elliptical orbit can be calculated. For a body S moving around the focus, F, of an orbit (see illustration), the *true anomaly* is the angle v made by the body, the focus, and the point, P, of nearest approach. For a body orbiting the Sun, P is the perihelion. The angle is measured in the direction of motion of S. If an auxiliary circle is drawn centered on the midpoint, C, of the major axis of the elliptical orbit, then the *eccentric anomaly* is the angle E between CS′ and CP, where S′ lies on the circle and is vertically above S. The *mean anomaly* is the angle M between P, F, and a hypothetical body moving at a constant angular speed equal to the MEAN MOTION of S. It is thus the product of the mean motion and the time interval since S passed P.

The eccentric and mean anomalies are related by *Kepler's equation:*

$$E - e\sin E = M$$

where e is the ECCENTRICITY of the orbit. The coordinates (x, y) of the body S can be found from the equations

$$x = a(\cos E - e)$$
$$y = a\sin E\sqrt{(1 - e^2)}$$

where a is the semimajor axis of the orbit. See also EQUATION OF CENTER; ORBITAL ELEMENTS.

ANS *abbrev. for* Astronomical Netherlands Satellite.

ansae the parts of SATURN'S RINGS that are visible on each side of the planet as viewed from the Earth. They appear rather like handles on a double-handled cup (the Latin word *ansa* means 'handle').

antapex (solar antapex) see APEX.

Antarctic astronomy the high altitude, extreme cold, and low atmospheric water vapor content found on the Antarctic Plateau make it possibly the best site on Earth for astronomy at millimeter, submillimeter, and infrared wavelengths. The Center for Astronomical Research in Antarctica (CARA) coordinates year-round observations at the South Pole. These contribute to cosmic microwave background anisotropy studies and to investigations of young stars and molecular clouds.

Antares (α Sco) a huge remote but conspicuous red supergiant that is the brightest star in the constellation Scorpius. It is in an advanced stage of evolution. It is a visual binary (separation 3″, period 900 years), its 5th-magnitude B-type companion appearing green by contrast. The companion orbits inside the cool stellar wind and is a peculiar hot radio source. m_v: 0.96 (var.); M_v: –5.2; spectral type: M1.5 Iab; diameter: about 285 times solar diameter; distance: 160 pc.

antenna (aerial) a device used for the transmission or reception of radio waves. When connected to a transmitter, the oscillating electric currents induced in the antenna launch radio waves into space. When connected to a RECEIVER, incoming radio waves from a distant source generate oscillating electric currents in the antenna, which are detected by the receiver. A practical antenna neither radiates nor receives equally in all directions, which may be demonstrated by its *antenna pattern* – a plot of relative GAIN as a function of direction. The plot may be made in terms of the antenna's voltage response or power response, giving a *voltage pattern* or a *power pattern*. By the principle of reciprocity the antenna pattern for transmission is identical with that for reception.

A number of distinct *lobes* may often be identified in the antenna pattern. The lobe corresponding to the direction of best transmission or reception is the *main lobe* or *main beam*; all the others are called *side lobes* and are usually unwanted (see also BEAM). The ratio of the power received in the main beam to the total power received by all the lobes is called the *beam efficiency*. The angle between the two directions in the main beam at which the power response has fallen to half its maximum value is called the *beamwidth*; it is a measure of the antenna's DIRECTIVITY. If the angular separation of two cosmic radio sources is less than the beamwidth, the sources will not be resolved but will be observed as a single source. Some highly directional antennas have *pencil beams*, which are narrow main beams of circular cross section. Others have *fan beams* where the cross section of the main beam is greatly extended in one direction. See also ARRAY; DISH; RADIATION RESISTANCE.

Antennae (NGC 4038/9) a pair of INTERACTING GALAXIES that are in the process of merging. They lie at a distance of only 22 megaparsecs and are thus the best-studied example of this phenomenon. They were normal galaxies before their interaction, but during their point of closest approach about 200 million years ago tides have drawn out two long curved tails, hence their popular name. The galaxies are currently turning around toward their final MERGER.

antenna pattern (field pattern; polar diagram) see ANTENNA.

antenna temperature a measure of the strength of signal received by a RADIO TELESCOPE from a RADIO SOURCE. It is defined as the noise power received per unit BANDWIDTH, divided by the BOLTZMANN CONSTANT, *k*. Antenna temperature depends on the surface brightness of the sky weighted by the telescope's BEAM rather than physical temperature of the antenna. A radio source of flux density *S* with an angular diameter that is much smaller than the antenna's beam will give an antenna temperature of $SA_e/(2k)$, where A_e is the effective area (see ARRAY) of the antenna. If the beam is filled by a uniform source of BRIGHTNESS

TEMPERATURE T_B, the antenna temperature will also be T_B.

SYNCHROTRON EMISSION from COSMIC RAYS in the Galaxy produces a diffuse radio emission centered broadly on the galactic plane. Any practical observation of a radio source has to be made against this background emission, which at low frequencies limits the SENSITIVITY of the RADIO TELESCOPE. The antenna temperature of the diffuse emission is called the *background temperature*; the electrical NOISE it produces in radio receivers is often called *cosmic noise*.

anthropic principle a principle that was put forward in the 1960s by R. Dicke and maintains that the presence of life in the Universe places constraints on the ways in which the very early Universe evolved: the possible initial conditions are limited to those that give rise to an inhabited Universe, i.e. what we observe must be restricted by the conditions necessary for our presence as observers.

antimatter matter composed entirely of ANTIPARTICLES. Ordinary matter and antimatter would annihilate on contact. Although individual antiparticles are produced in cosmic-ray showers and in high-energy particle accelerators, the search for antimatter in the Universe has so far proved unsuccessful. It is thought therefore that the Universe is not now symmetric between matter and antimatter, although initially equal amounts were created. An excess of matter over antimatter may have resulted from processes occurring very early in the evolution of the Universe while it was out of equilibrium.

antiparticles a pair of ELEMENTARY PARTICLES, such as the electron plus positron or the proton plus antiproton, that have an identical rest mass but a charge, strangeness, and other fundamental properties of equal magnitude but opposite sign (positive rather than negative and vice versa). Thus, the electron has a negative charge and the positron an equal positive charge. A reaction of a particle with its antiparticle is called ANNIHILATION. See also PAIR PRODUCTION.

antitail a small spiky taillike structure on a comet that, unlike most COMET TAILS, seems to point toward the Sun. It is usually only seen when the observer is in the plane of the cometary orbit. The particles responsible for scattering the sunlight are much larger than those that produce the normal dust tail.

Antlia (**Air Pump, Pump**) a small inconspicuous constellation in the southern hemisphere near Centaurus, the brightest stars being of 4th magnitude. Abbrev.: Ant; genitive form: Antliae; approx. position: RA 10h, dec –35°; area: 239 sq deg.

Antoniadi scale see SEEING.

Apache Point Observatory an observatory near Sunspot, New Mexico, that opened in 1990 and is owned and operated by the Astrophysical Research Consortium (ARC), a consortium of US universities. The observatory is sited at an altitude of 2787.9 meters. The main instrument is a 3.5-meter telescope with a lightweight honeycomb PRIMARY MIRROR, for optical and infrared observations. The SLOAN DIGITAL SKY SURVEY's 2.5-meter telescope was commissioned there in 1997. There is also a 1-meter telescope operated by New Mexico State University.

apastron see PERIASTRON.

Apennines (**Montes Apenninus**) see table at MOUNTAINS, LUNAR.

aperture the diameter of the unobscured portion of the objective lens in a refracting telescope or of the primary mirror in a reflector. In a radio telescope it is the physical size of the antenna. As the aperture is increased, the telescope gathers more light, radio waves, etc., and thus will discern fainter objects: the radiation-gathering power depends on area, i.e. on the square of the aperture. A larger aperture also produces a smaller AIRY DISK and so has greater spatial RESOLUTION.

aperture ratio (**relative aperture**) the ratio d/f of the effective diameter (i.e. APERTURE), d, of a lens or mirror to its FOCAL LENGTH, f. The ratio f/d is the FOCAL RATIO.

aperture synthesis a technique originally of radio astronomy devised by Sir Martin Ryle in the late 1950s. It is used to obtain high RESOLUTION images by combining signals from a number of relatively small ANTENNAS spaced over an area equivalent to a large aperture. Although originally used only for *synthesized apertures* that were 'fully filled' by smaller antennas, the term is also applied to instruments for which no clearly definable equivalent large aperture exists. The antennas are connected in interferometric pairs (see RADIO TELESCOPE) and the AMPLITUDES and PHASES of the signals from a radio source are recorded on all antenna spacings necessary to cover the required area. The information is then processed in a computer where a FOURIER TRANSFORM is carried out to generate a radio map of the source.

In practice the rotation of the Earth is often used to move the antennas in space – a technique known as *Earth-rotation synthesis*. In such an arrangement, just 12 hours of observation generate all the baselines available from a particular configuration; the same baselines are repeated with the opposite sense during the next 12 hours. For a radio interferometer in which all the baselines are oriented east-west (e.g. the RYLE TELESCOPE and the WSRT), each baseline produces an elliptical track of synthesized aperture. The major axis of the ellipse is determined by the baseline length, whereas the minor axis depends on the sine of the DECLINATION of the source. Low declination sources cannot therefore be mapped with a uniformly high resolution by an east-west interferometer. The VLA largely overcomes this difficulty by arranging its dishes in a Y-shaped configuration.

The computer processing involved in map-making can become very sophisticated, and special software (such as AIPS) is usually used. The Fourier transform of the synthesized aperture defines the *synthesized beam* (or *dirty beam*) of the telescope, with which the final image will appear to be convolved (see CONVOLUTION). A synthesized aperture that is not fully filled will produce false features or *artifacts* in the map, and these must be suppressed using deconvolution algorithms such as Clean or MEM. An aperture consisting of only a few equally spaced strips will show bright, widely spaced concentric rings or *grating responses* (see ARRAY) around features in the map. Even a fully filled synthesized aperture may need to be *graded*, by gradually reducing the weight of contributions from the longer baselines. This reduces the *side-lobe response* of the telescope, which is the residual structure of the synthesized beam lying outside its central region. Other techniques such as *self-calibration* are used to remove artifacts generated by instrumental drifts and the effects of the atmosphere.

apex 1 (**solar apex**) the point on the celestial sphere toward which the Sun and the Solar System are moving relative to the stars in our vicinity. The apex lies in the constellation Hercules at a position RA 18h, dec +30°, close to the star Vega. The point diametrically opposite to the direction of this relative *solar motion* is the *antapex* (or *solar antapex*); it lies in the constellation Columba. The position of the apex can be determined from an analysis of the proper motions, radial velocities, and parallaxes of stars, based on the assumption that solar motion is equal and opposite to the group motion of stars. The velocity of this motion has been calculated as about 19.5 km s^{-1} with respect to the LOCAL STANDARD OF REST, when all available information on proper motion and radial velocity is used. The value is lower when only the stars in the Sun's immediate neighborhood are considered. Solar motion produces the SECULAR PARALLAX of stars.
2 the point on the celestial sphere toward which the Earth appears to be moving, at a given time, as a result of its orbital motion around the Sun.

aphelion the point in the orbit of a planet, comet, or artificial satellite in solar orbit that is farthest from the Sun. The Earth is at aphelion on or about July 3.

Aphrodite Terra a very extensive highland area on VENUS, situated mainly in the southern hemisphere but partly across the equator between about 70° and 210° Venusian longitude. It is a scorpion-shaped feature, 9700 × 3200 km in extent, with eastern and western mountains separated by a lower area. Several volcanoes are at its eastern limit, including the giant *Maat Mons*, which is 5 km high, *Ozza Mons*, and *Sapas Mons*. See also ISHTAR TERRA; BETA REGIO.

aplanatic Gregorian see GREGORIAN TELESCOPE.

aplanatic system an optical system that is able to produce an image essentially free from SPHERICAL ABERRATION and COMA.

APM *abbrev. for* automatic plate-measuring machine. A facility at the Royal Greenwich Observatory at Cambridge, used to digitize optical sky-survey photographic plates.

apocenter see PERICENTER.

apochromatic lens see ACHROMATIC LENS.

apodization any process suppressing the secondary maxima of a diffraction pattern, such as the faint rings around the AIRY DISK of an optical image; this allows finer detail to be resolved. It may be achieved, for example, by progressively reducing the transmission of the telescope from the center of the aperture to its periphery.

apogee 1 the point in the orbit of the Moon or an artificial Earth satellite that is farthest from the Earth and at which the body's velocity is at a minimum. Strictly the distance to the apogee is taken from the Earth's center. The distance to the Moon's apogee varies; on average it is about 405 500 km. When a spacecraft or satellite reaches apogee, its *apogee rocket* can be fired to boost it into a more circular orbit or to allow it to escape from Earth orbit. See also PERIGEE. 2 the highest point above the Earth's surface attained by a rocket, missile, etc.

Apollo the American space program for landing astronauts on the MOON and returning them safely to Earth. A manned lunar landing, to be achieved before 1970, was proposed to Congress in 1961 by President J.F. Kennedy following the first manned flight by what was then the USSR. Prior to Apollo 7, the missions were designed to test the Saturn 1B and Saturn V launch vehicles, the *command and service module* (*CSM*), and the *lunar module* (*LM*). After three astronauts were killed in a flash fire inside the *command module* (*CM*) during ground tests in Jan. 1967, the program was delayed for 18 months while the CM was redesigned. NASA commemorated the three astronauts by redesignating the mission that they would have flown in as Apollo 1. The subsequent Apollos 2–6 were crewless test flights.

The method selected for the flight program was *lunar orbit rendezvous*. The astronauts were to travel to and from the Moon in the command module, which contained the controls and instruments. Rocket engines and fuel supplies were housed in a separate *service module* (*SM*). On entering lunar orbit the command-module pilot would remain in the CM while the commander and lunar-module pilot made the landing in the LM. On completion of the mission on the Moon's surface, the descent stage was to remain on the Moon: the ascent stage of the LM was to carry the astronauts into lunar orbit and rendezvous with the command and service modules. The craft would then embark on its return journey, the LM being jettisoned. The SM was to be jettisoned just prior to reentering the Earth's atmosphere.

Details of the Apollo flights are given in the table. Apollo 7 was the first piloted test flight of the CSM. Apollo 8 was the first to be launched by Saturn V and to enter lunar orbit. The LM was tested in Earth orbit by Apollo 9, in lunar orbit by Apollo 10, and landed on the Moon for the first time by Apollo 11 on July 20 1969. Apollo 11's landing site, in Mare Tranquillitatis, was dubbed 'Tranquility Base'. Apollo 12 landed with higher accuracy than its predecessor, touching down in Oceanus Procellarum close to SURVEYOR 3, parts of which were returned to Earth. Both missions returned basalts from the MARIA. Apollo 13 was aborted safely after an explosion in the service module and its target was taken over by Apollo 14. This was to collect rocks from Cone crater (25 million years old) in the FRA MAURO FORMATION. Mobility was increased by the use of a Modular Equipment Transporter but the terrain was unexpectedly rugged. Complex non-mare basalt breccias were returned.

The last three Apollos visited sites with multiple objectives, collected deep (two meter) drill cores (in addition to wide cores, soils, pebbles, and larger rocks), and used a LUNAR ROVING VEHICLE. Apollo 15 returned samples of anorthosite and green glass from the Apennine MOUNTAINS and mare basalts from HADLEY RILLE. Apollo 16 landed in the vicinity of South Ray and North Ray craters (2 and 50 million years

Apollo Missions

Apollo Mission	*Astronauts (Commander) (LM pilot) (CM pilot)*	*Date of landing*	*Landing site coordinates (accomplishment)*	*EVA time (hr)*	*Dist-tance traversed (km)*	*Sample weight (kg)*
7	Schirra Eisele Cunningham	Oct. 1968	(first test of CSM in earth orbit)	–	–	–
8	Borman Lovell Anders	Dec. 1968	(first men in lunar orbit)	–	–	–
9	McDivitt Scott Schweickart	Mar. 1969	(test of LM in earth orbit)	–	–	–
10	Stafford Young Cernan	May 1969	(full dress rehearsal for lunar landing)	–	–	–
11	Armstrong* Aldrin* Collins	(20) July 1969	M. Tranquillitatis 0°67′N 23°49′E (first landing)	2.2	0.5	21.7
12	Conrad* Bean* Gordon	(19) Nov. 1969	Oc. Procellarum 3°12′S 23°23′W (Surveyor 3)	7.7	1.3	34.4
13	Lovell Swigert Haise	Apr. 1970	(Mission aborted: explosion in service module)	–	–	–
14	Shepard* Mitchell* Roosa	(31) Jan. 1971	Fra Mauro formation 3°40′S 17°28′E (Cone crater)	9.2	3.4	42.9
15	Scott* Irwin* Worden	(30) July 1971	Hadley Rille 26°06′N 3°39′E (first test of LRV)	18.3	27.9	76.8
16	Young* Duke* Mattingley	(21) Apr. 1972	Cayley-Descartes 8°59′S 15°31′E (lunar highlands)	20.1	27.0	94.7
17	Cernan* Schmitt* Evans	(11) Dec. 1972	Taurus-Littrow 20°10′N 30°46′E (first scientist)	22.0	30.0	110.5

*Astronauts marked with an asterisk landed on the moon.

old respectively) in the HIGHLANDS to sample the CAYLEY and DESCARTES FORMATIONS, but returned only anorthositic breccias rather than volcanic rocks. Apollo 17 included a scientist-astronaut for the first time. It landed in a dark and LIGHT MANTLED mare-filled valley between high massifs on the borders of Mare SERENITATIS. Several boulders were sampled and unusual orange glass was found near a 30-million-year-old DARK HALO crater, called Shorty.

Experiments performed on the Moon by Apollo included SOLAR-WIND, lunar-atmosphere, COSMIC-RAY and neutron detection, heat-flow and magnetic-field measurements, active and passive seismometry, and laser ranging. Apollos 15, 16, and 17 were equipped with experiments in the service module, including metric and panoramic photography, laser altimetry, radar sounding, magnetometry, and gamma-ray, ultraviolet, and alpha-particle spectrometry. Subsatellites were ejected from the SM for particle and field measurements. Spent boosters were crashed as seismic sources. After Apollo 17, the remaining hardware of the program was used in SKYLAB and the APOLLO-SOYUZ TEST PROJECT.

See also GEMINI PROJECT; LUNAR ORBITER PROBES; LUNA PROBES; MERCURY PROJECT; MOON ROCKS; RANGER; ZOND PROBES.

Apollo-Amor objects see APOLLO GROUP.

Apollo group a group of near-Earth ASTEROIDS, including (1566) ICARUS and (2201) OLJATO, that have PERIHELIA inside the orbit of the Earth (i.e. less than 1.017 AU). Like members of the AMOR GROUP, most are very small bodies and can be observed only when close to the Earth. The group takes its name from the 1.4-km-diameter asteroid (1862) *Apollo*, which was discovered when it approached within 0.07 AU of the Earth in 1932 by Karl Reinmuth but was lost because of uncertainties in its orbit; it was rediscovered in 1973. Radar observations of Apollo in 2005 by the ARECIBO RADIO TELESCOPE revealed that a satellite is in close orbit around it. The spectra of several of the Apollo group asteroids closely resemble those of CHONDRITE meteorites. Members of the Apollo and Amor groups are often classed collectively as *Apollo–Amor objects*, the perihelia of such bodies usually being taken as smaller than 1.3 AU. See TABLE 3, BACKMATTER.

Apollo-Soyuz test project (**ASTP**) the first international manned space flight, finally agreed to in 1972 and achieved by the USA and the USSR in 1975. An American APOLLO spacecraft – Apollo 18 – and a Soviet SOYUZ CRAFT – Soyuz 19 – were launched into Earth orbit on July 15, rendezvoused on July 17 at an altitude of 225 km, and successfully docked. The crews visited each other's craft and conducted joint experiments and surveys. The mission involved major design modifications in both spacecraft.

Apollo Telescope Mount (**ATM**) the complex telescope mount on NASA's orbiting space laboratory SKYLAB. The six principal instruments carried on the mount operated in the X-ray and/or ultraviolet spectral regions, not accessible to ground-based instruments. Two X-ray telescopes (0.3–6, 0.6–3.3 nm) and a white-light coronagraph (350–700 nm) were used in studying the solar CORONA. An XUV spectroheliograph (15–62 nm), a UV spectroheliometer (30–140 nm), and a UV spectrograph (97–394 nm) provided data on the Sun's CHROMOSPHERE. The observations were made between May 1973 and Feb. 1974.

apparent denoting a property of a star or other celestial body, such as altitude or brightness, as seen or measured by an observer. Corrections must be made to obtain the true value.

apparent diameter (**angular diameter**) the observed diameter of a celestial body, expressed in degrees, minutes, and/or seconds of arc. See also STELLAR DIAMETER.

apparent distance (**angular distance**; **angular separation**) the observed distance between two celestial bodies, expressed in degrees, minutes, and/or seconds of arc.

apparent magnitude see MAGNITUDE.

apparent noon the time at which the Sun's center is seen to cross the meridian. See APPARENT SOLAR TIME.

apparent place the position on a celestial sphere centered on the Earth, determined by removing from the directly observed position of a celestial body the effects depending on the observer's location on the Earth's surface – ATMOSPHERIC REFRACTION, diurnal ABERRATION, and diurnal PARALLAX. It is the position at which the object would be seen from the Earth's center, displaced by PLANETARY ABERRATION and referred to the TRUE EQUATOR AND EQUINOX.

apparent sidereal time see SIDEREAL TIME.

apparent solar time time measured by reference to the observed (apparent) motion of the Sun, i.e time as measured by a sundial. The *apparent solar day* is the interval between two successive APPARENT NOONS. The time on any day is given by the HOUR ANGLE of the Sun plus 12 hours. Because the Sun's motion is nonuniform (see MEAN SUN) apparent solar time does not have a constant rate of change and cannot be used for accurate timekeeping. The difference between apparent time and MEAN SOLAR TIME is the EQUATION OF TIME.

apparition the period of time during which a particular celestial object can be observed. The term is particularly applied to planets and periodic comets.

appulse 1 the apparent close approach of one celestial body to another. Often it refers to the close approach of a planet or asteroid to a star without the occurrence of an OCCULTATION.
2 a penumbral ECLIPSE of the Moon.

April Lyrids see LYRIDS.

apsidal motion rotation of the line of APSIDES (i.e. the major axis) of an elliptical orbit so that the orbit is not closed and there is a gradual shift in the position of periapsis. It can occur if the gravitational field of a third body can produce a significant effect on a two-body situation, as with the Earth, Moon, and Sun, or if one or both stars of a binary system is appreciably distorted from a spherical shape.

apsides (singular: **apsis**) the two points in an orbit that lie closest to – *periapsis* – and farthest from – *apapsis* – the center of gravitational attraction. The velocity of an orbiting body at the apsides is either maximal (at periapsis) or minimal (at apapsis). The *line of apsides* is the straight line connecting the two apsides and is the major axis of an elliptical orbit.

Ap stars peculiar main-sequence stars (see PECULIAR STARS) of spectral types from B5 to F5 in which the spectral lines of certain elements (mainly Mn, Si, Eu, Cr, and Sr) are selectively enhanced and are sometimes of varying intensity (see SPECTRUM VARIABLES). The enhancement and its variation is apparently associated with strong and often variable magnetic fields. Like the AM STARS, Ap stars are generally slow rotators, but they differ in being single stars rather than spectroscopic binaries. The relative enhancement may be due to diffusion in the stable atmosphere caused by slow rotation, modified by the effect of strong magnetism. The spectral peculiarities could also relate to stellar temperature, the *manganese stars* being hotter than the *silicon stars*, which in turn are hotter than the *europium-chromium-strontium stars*. See also MAGNETIC STARS.

Apus (Bird of Paradise) a small inconspicuous constellation in the southern hemisphere near Crux, the brightest stars being just above 4th magnitude. It contains the faint and slightly irregular globular cluster NGC 6101, visible as a misty patch through a small telescope. Abbrev.: Aps; genitive form: Apodis; approx. position: RA 16h, dec –75°; area: 206 sq deg.

Aquarids either of two active METEOR SHOWERS: the *Eta Aquarids*, radiant: RA 336°, dec 0°, maximize on May 6, having a peak duration of 10 days and a ZENITHAL HOURLY RATE (ZHR) of 45; the *Delta Aquarids*, double radiant: RA 340°, dec –17° and 0°, maximize on July 28 and Aug. 7, have a peak duration of about 20 days, and a ZHR of about 19 and 10. The Eta Aquarids have an orbit that is closely aligned to that of HALLEY'S COMET. They are observed near the descending node of the comet's orbit.

Aquarius (Water Bearer) an extensive zodiac constellation in the southern hemisphere near Pegasus, the brightest stars being of 3rd magnitude. It contains the planetary nebulae NGC 7293 (the HELIX NEBULA) and NGC 7009 (the *Saturn nebula*), and the globular clusters M2 (NGC 7089) and M72 (NGC 6981). Abbrev.: Aqr; genitive form: Aquarii; approx. position: RA 22h, dec –10°; area: 980 sq deg.

Aquila (Eagle) an equatorial constellation near Cygnus, lying in the Milky Way, the brightest stars being the 1st-magnitude

ALTAIR (α) and some of 2nd and 3rd magnitude. Eta (η) Aquilae is a bright CEPHEID VARIABLE, period 7.177 days. Abbrev.: Aql; genitive form: Aquilae; approx. position: RA 19.5h, dec +3°; area: 652 sq deg.

Ara (**Altar**) a small constellation in the southern hemisphere near Scorpius, lying in the Milky Way, the brightest stars being of 3rd magnitude. It contains the bright globular cluster NGC 6397, visible through powerful binoculars. This is possibly the nearest such cluster to the Solar System. Abbrev.: Ara; genitive form: Arae; approx. position: RA 17h, dec –55°; area: 237 sq deg.

ARC *abbrev. for* Astrophysical Research Consortium. See APACHE POINT OBSERVATORY.

archaeoastronomy the astronomy of early or nonliterate cultures, of interest to astronomers, archaeologists, and anthropologists. Many megalithic sites in the UK, Europe, and North and South America are thought to have been used for astronomical measurements and predictions.

arch filament see PROMINENCES.

arc minute (**arcmin**; **minute of arc**) see ARC SECOND.

arc second (**arcsec**; **second of arc**) symbol: ″. A unit of angular measure equal to 1/3600 of a degree. It is used, for example, to give the apparent diameter of objects, the angular separation of binary stars, and the proper motion and annual parallax of stars. An *arc minute*, symbol: ′, is 60 arc seconds, i.e. 1/60 of a degree. The full Moon is about 30′ in diameter.

Arcturus (**α Boo**) a conspicuous red giant that is the brightest star in the constellation Boötes and the second-brightest star in the northern sky (after the Sun). The three stars Alioth, Mizar, and Alcaid in the handle of the Plough point in its direction. Arcturus is a high-velocity star and shows spectral peculiarities. m_v: –0.04; M_v: –0.2; spectral type: K2 IIIp; radius (by interferometer): 28 times solar radius; distance: 10 pc.

areal velocity the velocity at which the RADIUS VECTOR sweeps out unit area. It is constant for motion in an elliptical orbit. See KEPLER'S LAWS.

Arecibo radio telescope a radio telescope, 305 meters in diameter and spherical in shape, sited in a natural hollow near the town and seaport of Arecibo, Puerto Rico. It is the world's largest single-dish telescope. It is operated by the National Astronomy and Ionosphere Center of Cornell University and has been in use since 1963. The original lining was replaced in the early 1970s by nearly 40 000 perforated aluminum panels in order to improve performance at shorter wavelengths, including the 21-cm line of hydrogen. It now observes at frequencies between 50 MHz and 10 GHz, using a small subreflector system (the 'mini-Gregorian') for work between 1–10 GHz. Although not steerable, the antenna can observe in any direction up to 20° from the zenith by moving the feed antennas along the north–south girder on which they are carried, 130 m above the dish. The Arecibo dish, with its huge collecting area, can also be used for RADAR ASTRONOMY and atmospheric science.

Arend–Roland comet (**1957 III**) a COMET discovered by S. Arend and G. Roland in the course of routine work on asteroids. It was unusual because it had a sunward spike: many of the solid particles ejected from the NUCLEUS near PERIHELION remained in the orbital plane of the comet; as the Earth passed through the orbital plane the sunlight reflected from the particles combined to give a luminous spike.

areography the geography of MARS. Surface coordinates are defined by *aerographic longitude* and *latitude*. Longitude is measured in degrees westward from a prime meridian chosen to pass through the dark-albedo feature Sinus Meridiani near the Martian equator. The exact position of the meridian is now fixed by a 0.5 km crater pit, Airy–0, within the crater Airy, 300 km south of the equator.

Argo (**Argo Navis**; **Ship**) a former very extensive unwieldy constellation in the southern hemisphere subdivided in the mid-18th century into the constellations CARINA, PUPPIS, VELA, and PYXIS. Its stars are still identified by a single set of Bayer letters (see STELLAR NOMENCLATURE), the brightest being CANOPUS or Alpha (α) Carinae.

argument of perihelion see ORBITAL ELEMENTS.

Argyre Planitia a 1000-km diameter basin in Mars' southern hemisphere, visible as a bright area to Earth-based observers and centered on the areographic coordinates 50° S latitude, 44° W longitude (see AREOGRAPHY). Like HELLAS PLANITIA it is probably an impact feature. See MARS, SURFACE FEATURES.

Ariane the three-stage LAUNCH VEHICLE built for the EUROPEAN SPACE AGENCY (ESA). The building program was officially approved in 1973, financed mainly by France. The original version, Ariane-1, first flew in Dec. 1979; its first successful operational flight took place in June 1983. Responsibility for production and marketing of Ariane was then transferred to the company *Arianespace*, which had been set up in 1980 to finance, build, sell, and launch Ariane; its first launch occurred in May 1984.

The launch site for Ariane is near the equator, at Kourou, French Guiana. The rocket is optimized for launching craft into geostationary orbit (that is, to an altitude of 36 000 km above the equator) for communications and meteorological purpose, into lower Earth orbits for scientific missions, and into Sun-synchronous Earth orbits for terrestrial observations. Ariane is an expendable probe, unlike NASA's reusable space shuttle.

Ariane-1 could carry a payload of up to 1.8 tonnes (1800 kg) into geostationary orbit. As the mass of satellites increased, Ariane-1 gave way, from 1984, to the more powerful Ariane-2 and Ariane-3. These in turn were superseded, from 1988, by the six versions of Ariane-4 – one 'bare', the others fitted with two or four solid-fuel booster rockets, depending on the payload mass. The most powerful Ariane-4, with four liquid-fuel boosters, can lift up to 4.46 tonnes into geostationary orbit.

Ariane-5 is radically different from the earlier Arianes. Shorter and squatter, it has two sections. The main unit is the 'lower composite', with engine and propellant flanked by two solid boosters, and is the same for all missions; the 'upper composite' is matched to the mission and its payload. It is designed to launch one, two, or three satellites weighing up to about 7 tonnes into geostationary orbit, 23 tonnes into low Earth orbit, or 10 tonnes into Sun-synchronous orbit. Its first launch in 1996 ended in disaster with total destruction after a flight of only 40 seconds. But by 2002 it had successfully launched several commercial craft, mostly communications satellites. The catastrophic launch failure of an upgraded version of Ariane-5 in December of that year, with the loss of two communications satellites, proved a major setback for ESA. Following the resumption of its launch program in April 2003, Ariane-5 continued to be used for commercial work and also for important European science missions – the lunar orbiter SMART-1 and the comet interceptor probe ROSETTA. In 2007 Ariane-5 will simultaneously carry both the Planck and Herschel Observatories into space.

Ariel a satellite of Uranus, discovered in 1851 by William Lasell. Extensively imaged by VOYAGER 2 in 1986, Ariel has many craters and broad branching smooth-floored valleys such as *Korrican Chasma* and *Kewpie Chasma*. Its surface carries the scars of numerous impacts dating back to a time when the Solar System was still being formed. See URANUS' SATELLITES; TABLE 2, BACKMATTER.

Ariel V the first and highly successful British X-RAY ASTRONOMY satellite launched into a 550-km equatorial orbit in Oct. 1974 from the San Marco platform off the Kenyan coast. Its six experiments (five UK, one US) were designed to detect, accurately locate, and measure spectral and temporal features of cosmic X-ray sources. Ariel V was spin-stabilized with the spin axis and period controlled by gas jets. Technically it was the first small scientific satellite to be operated in near real-time. Tracking, command, and data reception were carried out from NASA ground stations at Quito and on Ascension Island. The UK control station at the Rutherford Appleton Laboratory had data links to the experiment groups at the universities of Birmingham, Leicester, and London. The satellite and all experiments remained fully operational until mid-1977 when the control gas was exhausted.

Subsequent operation with magnetometer attitude control was extended up to reentry in Mar. 1980.

Ariel V's major scientific achievements were the production of a new atlas of X-RAY SOURCES (the 3A catalog), including a number of short-lived transients, the establishment of SEYFERT GALAXIES as powerful X-ray emitters, and the discovery of slow X-ray pulsators (now identified with magnetized NEUTRON STARS spinning with periods of minutes) and of abundant multimillion degree plasma in SUPERNOVA REMNANTS and in CLUSTERS OF GALAXIES.

Ariel VI a British satellite that was launched June 1979 and was the final small satellite in the Ariel series. Its three experiments were designed to measure the flux of heavy primary cosmic rays, i.e. those above iron in the periodic table, to produce a soft X-ray map of the sky (at energies 0.1–1.5 keV), and to determine the time variability and spectra of individual X-ray sources (many of which were discovered by ARIEL V) by means of a PROPORTIONAL COUNTER pointed for several hours toward each source. Each experiment operated successfully for most of the satellite's life (to early 1982) but the scientific returns were limited by a series of spacecraft problems, including interference, particularly over Eastern Europe, from powerful ground radars that caused random switching of both payload and spacecraft elements.

Aries (Ram) a zodiac constellation in the northern hemisphere near Taurus, the brightest stars being the 2nd-magnitude HAMAL (α) and 3rd-magnitude Sheratan (β). Mesarthim (γ) is a wide visual binary with components equal in magnitude (4.8) and both A stars. Abbrev.: Ari; genitive form: Arietis; approx. position: RA 2.5h, dec +21°; area: 441 sq deg. See also FIRST POINT OF ARIES.

Aries, first point of see FIRST POINT OF ARIES.

Aristarchus see table at CRATERS.

Arizona meteorite crater (Barringer Crater) the archetypal impact explosion crater in N Arizona, 1.2 km across and 180 m deep, formed about 25 000 years ago by a massive iron METEORITE, maybe 70 m in diameter. The rim is composed of folded and inverted rock layers that have been pushed out from a central point. The meteorite almost vaporized completely, only a few hundred tonnes being scattered over 80 km² around the crater in the form of tiny iron SPHERULES. It has been named after Daniel Barringer who studied it and first suggested its extraterrestrial origin.

armillary sphere a device, dating back to antiquity, composed of a set of graduated rings representing circles on the CELESTIAL SPHERE, such as the ecliptic, celestial equator, and colures. The whole globe often revolved about an axis – the polar axis – within horizon and meridian circles. Movable sighting adjustments enabled a star to be observed and its coordinates to be read off the relevant circles.

arm population young POPULATION I stars occurring in the spiral arms of the Galaxy.

Arneb see LEPUS.

Arp 220 two INTERACTING spiral galaxies in the process of merging to form an ULTRALUMINOUS IRAS GALAXY. The galaxy cores are separated by only 1200 light-years, and are surrounded by huge knots of recent star formation.

array 1 a system used in radio astronomy in which a number of discrete elements are connected to form a composite ANTENNA. An element may for example be a single DIPOLE or a DISH. The ratio of the aperture area occupied by all the elements to the area that would be occupied by a continuous aperture of the same overall length is called the *filling factor*; it is a measure of the fraction of the aperture that is actually there. The *effective area* for an array operating at a wavelength λ with a DIRECTIVITY D is given by

$$A_e = D\lambda^2/4\pi$$

It is usually less than the physical area, even when the filling factor is equal to unity, because of small irregularities in the aperture distribution. For a perfect array with a uniform aperture distribution the effective and physical areas are indeed equal.

An array may produce a *grating response* in one or more directions away from the main lobe (see ANTENNA) which, if the elements of the array were all nondirectional, would be as strong as the main lobe. However, the

ANTENNA PATTERNS of the elements together with geometrical effects usually reduce the power in the grating response to an acceptable level. See also APERTURE SYNTHESIS; BUTLER MATRIX; FEEDER.
2 (**detector array**) an electronic device, such as a CCD, consisting of thousands or millions of individual detectors fabricated on centimeter-sized wafers of silicon or some other material.

Arsia Mons a 14-km-high 400-km-wide volcano at the southern edge of the THARSIS RIDGE of Mars. It is located just south of the Martian equator at the aerographic coordinates 8.4° S latitude, 121.1° longitude (see AREOGRAPHY). It appears to be older than the other Tharsis volcanoes and has the largest summit caldera, 140 km across. See MARS, VOLCANOES.

artificial satellite see SATELLITE, ARTIFICIAL.

ASCA fourth in the series of small (500 kg) Japanese space science satellites devoted to X-ray astronomy. It was launched into a 560-km, 31° inclination orbit in Feb. 1993, carrying a payload of four identical GRAZING INCIDENCE X-ray telescopes (conical foil). Two telescopes had gas scintillation PROPORTIONAL COUNTERS in the focal plane and two had X-ray-sensitive CCDS (provided by NASA). The mission's main strength was X-ray spectroscopy. Both types of detector gave much improved energy resolutions over ASCA's working range of 0.5–10 keV, compared with the widely used imaging PROPORTIONAL COUNTER. Apart from a gradual deterioration in the energy resolution of the CCDs caused by in-orbit radiation damage, all instruments aboard ASCA continued to function up to the middle of 2000, by which time nearly 4000 separate observations had been carried out. Among many scientific advances were the detection of a population of partly obscured active galactic nuclei (see ACTIVE GALAXY), whose hard X-ray spectra suggested that they formed a major component of the X-RAY BACKGROUND RADIATION; the first evidence for strong gravity in the form of a broad iron fluorescence line; and the measurement of metal-rich spectra in the ejecta of several supernova remnants. The mission ended in July 2000 when a geomagnetic storm caused by an unusually large solar flare irrevocably altered the orbital attitude of the satellite and the orientation of its solar panels, taking the panels away from the Sun and effectively destroying ASCA's power supply. ASCA re-entered the Earth's atmosphere in 2001. See also ASTRO-E2; GINGA.

ascending node see NODES.

Ascraeus Mons a 19-km-high volcano on the THARSIS RIDGE of Mars, located at the areographic coordinates 11.9° N latitude, 104.5° W longitude (see AREOGRAPHY). It is 400 km wide at its base and has a summit caldera 50 km across. See MARS, VOLCANOES.

Asgard Basin see CALLISTO.

ashen light 1 the faint glow claimed to be occasionally observed on the unlit area of Venus in its crescent phase. Its cause is unknown but it might result from bombardment of atmospheric atoms and molecules by energetic particles and radiation, as with terrestrial AIRGLOW.
2 see EARTHSHINE.

aspect (**configuration**) the apparent position of any of the planets or the Moon relative to the Sun, as seen from Earth. Specific aspects include CONJUNCTION, OPPOSITION, and QUADRATURE, which differ in the ELONGATION of the object concerned.

aspheric surface any surface that does not form part of a sphere. A paraboloid reflector, used in both optical and radio telescopes, is aspheric. Although production costs are high, aspheric surfaces can greatly improve lens and mirror performance.

association a loose group of young stars of similar SPECTRAL TYPE. *OB associations* are groups of massive and highly luminous main-sequence stars of spectral types O and B. They occur in regions rich in gas and dust in the spiral arms of the Galaxy. They have dimensions ranging from a few parsecs to several hundred parsecs. Often an OPEN CLUSTER is found near the center of an association, e.g. the Zeta Persei association surrounds H AND CHI PERSEI. *R associations* are groups of bright young stars of slightly lower mass (3–10 solar masses) that illuminate REFLECTION NEBULAE. *T associations* are groups of T TAURI STARS, i.e. young stars of about the Sun's mass. Most contain less than 30 stars though some contain as many as 400. R and T associations are often found in the vicinity of young open clusters.

Associations are generally too sparsely populated to be gravitationally bound systems and there is strong evidence that they represent the aftereffects of comparatively recent multiple star births. In some cases the stars appear to be expanding from a common center: by extrapolating back their present velocities an estimate of the age of the system can be derived. For instance, the association II Persei shows an expansion age of slightly over one million years.

A stars stars of SPECTRAL TYPE A. They are blue-white or white and have a surface temperature (T_{eff}) of about 7500 to 9900 kelvin for main-sequence stars, and up to 12 000 K for supergiants. Balmer absorption lines of hydrogen dominate the spectrum, reaching maximum strength for A0 to A3 stars; lines of ionized and neutral metals slowly strengthen with the H and K lines of ionized calcium appearing in later subdivisions. A few A stars (AM and AP STARS) have anomalously high abundances of metals and rare earth elements. COLOR indices for A0 stars are zero. Vega, Sirius, Deneb, and Altair are A stars.

asterism a prominent grouping of stars forming a distinctive shape but not a complete or recognized constellation. The Plough is an asterism within the constellation Ursa Major. Other examples of asterisms are the Sickle in Leo, the FALSE CROSS and the SUMMER TRIANGLE.

asteroid belt (**main belt**) the zone near to the plane of the ECLIPTIC and between the orbits of Mars and Jupiter that contains the majority of ASTEROIDS, known as *main-belt asteroids*. The edges are well-defined at distances from the Sun of about 1.7 and 4.0 AU respectively and the orbits are strongly concentrated in the plane of the ecliptic. Even so, the individual asteroids in the main belt are widely spaced. The orbital INCLINATION becomes more scattered on moving through the belt. The average inclination is about 10° and the average eccentricity is 0.15. All the bodies are in DIRECT MOTION. Occasional collisions between asteroids occur at velocities of about 5 km s^{-1}. See also KIRKWOOD GAPS.

asteroid families see HIRAYAMA FAMILIES.

asteroids (**minor planets**; **planetoids**) small rocky Solar-System bodies without atmospheres that orbit the Sun but are too small to be considered planets. The distinction between an asteroid, a comet, and a KUIPER BELT object is rather blurred: the prevailing view is that most of these minor bodies are remnants of the protoplanetary nebula that failed to become incorporated into the planets during the accretion phase of the Solar System's formation. However, some astronomers have theorized that asteroids resulted from destructive collisions between a handful of Mars-sized bodies in the Solar System's remote past. These bodies would have been prevented from accreting into a planet by Jupiter's gravitational influence. Comets and Kuiper belt objects consist of a mixture of rock, dust, and ice, but asteroids, like meteoroids, are composed of rock and metal.

Most known asteroids (perhaps 95%) orbit in the asteroid belt, or main belt, between the orbits of Mars and Jupiter, at distances of 1.7 to 4.0 astronomical units from the Sun. These main-belt asteroids have periods between 3 and 6 years. The distribution of orbits within the belt is modified by KIRKWOOD GAPS, regions that have been swept clear of interplanetary bodies as a result of ORBITAL RESONANCE with Jupiter. Some asteroids have orbits that are very different from those in the main belt; these include the NEAR-EARTH ASTEROIDS (i.e. the AMOR, APOLLO, and ATEN GROUPS), and members of the TROJAN and HILDA GROUPS. These bodies are thought to be either fragments that have broken away from large main-belt asteroids or else comets that are no longer active. The objects (2060) CHIRON and Pholus, whose orbits lie out beyond Saturn, are sometimes considered to be asteroids but are technically classified as centaurs. There are also clusters or families of asteroids with very similar orbital characteristics (see HIRAYAMA FAMILIES). Like the planets, most asteroids follow direct orbits close to the plane of the ECLIPTIC, although the average orbit has a larger ECCENTRICITY (0.15) and a greater INCLINATION (9.7°) than those of most planets. A few objects, however, such as (944) HIDALGO, follow highly eccentric and inclined orbits more akin to those of some periodic COMETS. Their orbits taking them across the paths of the planets, and some make very close approaches.

Asteroids shine by reflected sunlight but only one, (4) VESTA, is bright enough to be seen with the naked eye. Astronomers believe that there may be several million asteroids in the Solar System, with about 60 000 new ones being discovered every year. Improved observational and photographic instruments and techniques account for this high discovery rate, but as of November 2005, only about 300 000 known asteroids had calculated orbits, and of these, only 120 000 had received permanent numbers. Many more, with less well-determined orbits, have been assigned temporary designations. Many numbered asteroids have also received names, usually bestowed on them by their discoverers, but today subject to strict guidelines issued by the Internal Astronomical Union's Small Bodies Names Committee.

Until the late 20th century, the diameters of even the largest asteroids could only be roughly estimated. Since 1970, however. studies of the POLARIZATION of reflected sunlight and of the brightness at visible and infrared wavelengths for a large number of asteroids has led to improved values for their ALBEDOS; the diameters have been recalculated from these values and from analysis of the occultation of stars by asteroids. Asteroids vary in size from the largest and first to be discovered – the 933-km-diameter (1) CERES – to objects smaller than 1 km. There probably exists a continuous distribution down to the size of METEOROIDS – boulder-size and smaller; but it has been suggested that bodies should be 50 m or more in diameter in order to qualify as asteroids. Most asteroids are thought to be irregular in shape, causing them to vary in brightness as they rotate every few hours. Smaller objects predominate. There are only about 30 asteroids with diameters greater than 200 km.

The total mass of the asteroids is estimated at 2.3×10^{21} kg (about 3% of the Moon's mass). Ceres accounts for more than one-third of this mass.

The composition of asteroids varies somewhat as a function of distance from the Sun. Studies of asteroid spectra and polarizations show that the surface rocks are diverse and are similar to those of METEORITES. It is now believed therefore that most meteorites are fragments of asteroids. The majority of asteroids resemble carbonaceous chondrite meteorites, whereas others appear to have a metallic or silicaceous surface; the latter are more common near the outer edge of the asteroid belt (see also C-TYPE ASTEROIDS; S-TYPE ASTEROIDS; M-TYPE ASTEROIDS). This is an important clue to the composition of the pre-solar nebula from which the proto-asteroids condensed.

Before the 1990s, our information about asteroids depended entirely on Earth-based observations. Then in 1991, NASA's GALILEO spacecraft, en route for Jupiter, encountered (951) GASPRA and took the first high-resolution photographs of an asteroid. Two years later, Galileo encountered (243) IDA and Ida's satellite Dactyl. Further asteroid encounters have followed, including the Near-Earth Asteroid Rendezvous (NEAR-Shoemaker) mission's visits to (253) Mathilde in 1997 and (433) Eros in 1999. NEAR-Shoemaker became the first human-made spacecraft to land on an asteroid when it touched down on Eros on Feb. 12, 2001, after orbiting it for a year.

See also TABLE 3, Appendix.

asthenosphere see EARTH.

astigmatism an ABERRATION of a lens or mirror system that occurs when light falls obliquely on the system and is focused not as a single point image but as two perpendicular and separated lines. In the reflecting system shown in the illustration rays from points A and B on the mirror converge to the vertical line image ab; rays from C and D converge to the horizontal line image cd. The pencil of reflected rays, elliptical in cross section, cannot produce a sharp image anywhere along its path; the plane of optimum focus occurs between ab and cd where the pencil has its smallest

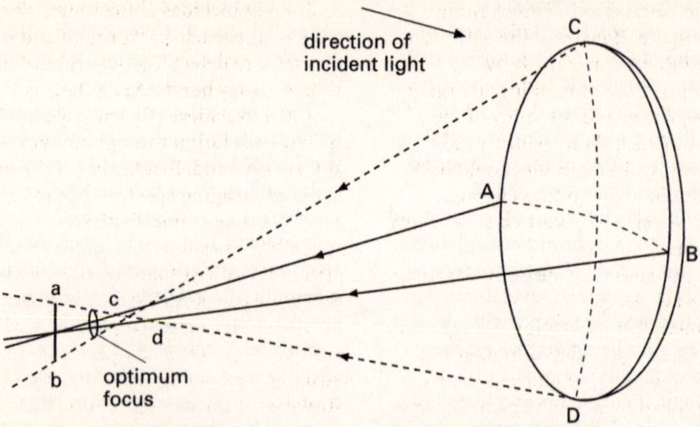

Astigmatism: astigmatism due to concave mirror

cross section. Astigmatism is not as severe an aberration as COMA.

ASTP *abbrev. for* Apollo-Soyuz test project.

Astraea the fifth ASTEROID to be discovered, in 1845 by K.L. Hencke. See TABLE 3, Appendix.

astration the continual cycling of material from the INTERSTELLAR MEDIUM into stars and back again, which steadily enriches the galaxies with elements heavier than hydrogen.

Astro an astrophysics mission launched by NASA in Dec. 1990 and operated for about 10 days from the bay of the space shuttle. The payload consisted of four instruments. The Wisconsin ultraviolet photopolarimeter experiment (WUPPE) provided polarization studies in the UV spectral region of 140–330 nm. The Hopkins ultraviolet telescope (HUT) made spectroscopic observations in the far-UV and extreme-UV wavebands. The ultraviolet imaging telescope (UIT), providing a 2″ resolution over a wide (40′) field of view, obtained many hundreds of UV images of a wide range of sources. The broad-band X-ray telescope (BBXRT) provided X-ray spectra of sources in the energy range 0.3–12 keV with an energy resolution of about 100 keV. The payload was returned to Earth after the mission. A second mission, Astro-2, was completed successfully in 1995.

ASTRO–B pre-launch name of the Japanese satellite TENMA.

astroblemes circular craterlike scars, usually ancient, left in the Earth's crust by meteorite impact. Criteria used for recognition are shatter cones, high-pressure silica polymorphs, shock microdeformations of quartz, impactite glasses, traces of nickel, and nickel-iron associations. All are of a geologically youthful age, none older than about 500 million years. The largest are Vredefort, South Africa (40 km diameter), Nordlinger Ries, Germany (25 km), Deep Bay, Saskatchewan, Canada (14 km), Lake Bosumtwi, Ghana (10 km), and Serpent Mound, Ohio (6.4 km).

The velocity of a large meteorite, i.e. one over thousands of tonnes, is dissipated very little by atmospheric braking effects and it hits the ground at its cosmic velocity of 11 to 74 km s^{-1} and explodes. Most of the kinetic energy goes to accelerate and excavate the material from the volume that eventually becomes the crater. Usually only an exceedingly small fraction (<0.01%) of the projectile survives. The resulting crater has a diameter between 20 and 60 times that of the impacting body, this factor depending on the incident velocity.

ASTRO–C pre-launch name of the Japanese satellite GINGA.

astrochemistry the study of the chemistry of

celestial bodies and of the intervening regions of space. It involves the detection and identification, principally by spectroscopy, of the inorganic and organic chemicals present and the study of the reactions by which these neutral and charged atoms and molecules could have been produced and of future chemical processes. See also MOLECULAR-LINE RADIO ASTRONOMY.

ASTRO–D pre-launch name of the Japanese satellite ASCA.

astrodynamics the application of CELESTIAL MECHANICS, the ballistics of high-speed solids through gases, propulsion theory, and other allied fields to the planning and production of the trajectories of spacecraft.

ASTRO–E2 sixth in the series of small Japanese-US science satellites, scheduled for launch in early 2005 as the eventual successor to ASCA. Its immediate predecessor, ASTRO–E, was an X-ray imaging and spectroscopy satellite that carried instruments originally intended for NASA's AXAF program and was supposed to complement NASA's Chandra and ESA's XMM-Newton spacecraft. Unfortunately, ASTRO–E was lost during launch in Feb. 2000. ASTRO–E2 was developed as its replacement by the Institute of Space and Astronautical Science of the Japan Aerospace Exploration Agency (ISAS/JAXA) and other Japanese institutions in collaboration with NASA, Goddard Space Flight Center (GSFC), and the Massachusetts Institute of Technology (MIT).

ASTRO–E2's mission is to cover the whole energy range 0.2–600 keV with the three elements of its instrumentation: (1) an X-ray Spectrometer (XRS) using a cryogenically cooled X-ray microcalorimeter and located behind a conical-foil mirror, the X-Ray Telescope (XRT); (2) four X-ray CCD cameras comprising the X-ray Imaging Spectrometer (XIS), situated in the focal plane of an X-ray telescope co-aligned with the center of the XRS field of view; and (3) the hard X-ray detector (HXD), a non-imaging instrument consisting of a collimated system of 'well' detectors. The HXD's sensitivity is unusually high, and its equipment includes anticounters that screen out particle background and may also serve to detect high-energy events such as gamma-ray bursts. ASTRO–E2 is expected to achieve particularly high X-ray spectral resolution throughout the 0.4–10 keV energy band. In addition, it is expected to obtain imaging spectroscopy of extended sources using its nondispersive spectrometers covering a larger area with a greater sensitivity than has been achieved in earlier missions. ASTRO–E2 is scheduled to be placed into a circular orbit with an altitude of 550 km and an inclination of 31°.

Astrographic Catalog see CARTE DU CIEL.

astrolabe an instrument, dating back to antiquity, used to measure the altitude of a celestial body and to solve problems of spherical astronomy. From the 15th century it was employed by mariners to determine latitude, until replaced by the sextant. There have been various types of astrolabes. One simple form consisted of a graduated disk that could be suspended by a ring to hang in a vertical plane. A movable sighting device – the *alidade* – pivoted at the center of the disk. Modern versions are still used to determine stellar positions and hence local time and latitude. See also PRISMATIC ASTROLABE.

astrometric binary see BINARY STAR.

astrometry (positional astronomy) the branch of astronomy concerned with the measurement of the positions of celestial bodies in the sky, with the factors, such as PRECESSION, NUTATION, and PROPER MOTION, that cause the positions to change with time, and with the concepts and observational methods involved in making the measurements. In *photographic astrometry* the positions of stars, planets, etc., are determined in relation to reference stars on photographic plates. In *meridian astrometry* the positions of celestial bodies are determined relative to the motions of the Earth. See also LONG-FOCUS PHOTOGRAPHIC ASTROMETRY; RADIO ASTROMETRY.

astronautics the science and technology of spaceflight.

Astronomer Royal an eminent British astronomer appointed by the UK sovereign to the post of Astronomer Royal of England. The appointment is made on the advice of the government-funded body responsible for astronomy research and facilities in the UK. Since 1994, this has been the PARTICLE PHYSICS AND ASTRONOMY RESEARCH COUNCIL (PPARC). The office of Astronomer Royal is an honorary position that, until the retirement of Sir Richard Woolley in 1971, was combined with the post of Director of the Royal Greenwich Observatory (RGO). The two titles were separated when Margaret Burbidge became Director of the RGO in 1971 and Sir Martin Ryle became Astronomer Royal in 1972. The first Astronomer Royal, John Flamsteed, was appointed by Charles II in 1675 following the foundation of the RGO in that year. The 15th Astronomer Royal, the cosmologist Sir Martin Rees, was appointed in 1995. A full list of Astronomers Royal appears in the table.

The office of *Astronomer Royal for Scotland* was created by Royal Warrant in 1834, with Thomas Henderson as its first incumbent. The title was originally held by the astronomer who served as both Director of the Royal Observatory, Edinburgh (ROE), and Regius Professor of Astronomy at the University of Edinburgh. Malcolm Longair was the ninth holder of the office, succeeding Vincent Reddish to the title in 1980. Longair held the post until 1991. The title then lapsed until 1995, by which time the decision had been taken to separate the Regius professorship and the directorship of the ROE. In the process, the office of Astronomer Royal for Scotland also became an independent post. The eminent solar and stellar specialist John Campbell Brown, professor of astrophysics at the University of Glasgow, was appointed Astronomer Royal for Scotland under the new regime in 1995.

Astronomers Royal

John Flamsteed	1675–1719
Edmund Halley	1720–42
James Bradley	1742–62
Nathaniel Bliss	1762–64
Nevil Maskelyne	1765–1811
John Pond	1811–35
Sir George Biddell Airy	1835–81
Sir William H.M. Christie	1881–1910
Sir Frank Watson Dyson	1910–33
Sir Harold Spencer Jones	1933–55
Sir Richard Woolley	1955–71
Sir Martin Ryle	1972–82
Sir F. Graham Smith	1982–90
Sir Arnold Wolfendale	1991–95
Sir Martin Rees	1995–

Astronomical Almanac the EPHEMERIS prepared jointly since 1981 by the United States Naval Observatory, Washington DC, and the Royal Greenwich Observatory in the UK. It replaced both the UK *Astronomical Ephemeris* and the *American Ephemeris and Nautical Almanac*, published separately in the UK since 1767 and in the USA since 1855.

astronomical data center see CENTRE DE DONNÉES ASTRONOMIQUES.

Astronomical Ephemeris see ASTRONOMICAL ALMANAC.

Astronomical Netherlands Satellite (ANS) a joint Netherlands/US satellite that was launched in Aug. 1974 and operated until 1976. It contained a 20-cm ultraviolet telescope providing broad-band (about 15 nm) photometric data on selected astronomical sources at wavelengths of 155 nm, 180 nm, 220 nm, 250 nm, and 350 nm. A catalog of such observations for about 3500 stars has been completed. In addition the satellite carried two X-ray telescopes that made the first observations of an X-RAY BURST SOURCE.

astronomical triangle a SPHERICAL TRIANGLE on the CELESTIAL SPHERE formed by the intersection of the great circles joining a celestial body, S, the observer's zenith, Z, and the north (or south) celestial pole, P (see illustration). The relationships between the angles and sides of a spherical triangle are used for transformation between EQUATORIAL and HORIZONTAL COORDINATE SYSTEMS: the angle at S (q) is the *parallactic angle*; that at P (t) is the HOUR ANGLE of S; that at Z (A) is the azimuth of S. The sides are equal to the ZENITH DISTANCE (ζ), the complement of the terrestrial latitude ($90°-\phi$), and the complement of the declination (90°–δ). The parallactic angle, for example, is given by the sine rule:

$$\sin q = (\cos \phi \sin t)/\sin \zeta = (\cos \phi \sin A)/\cos \delta$$

astronomical twilight see TWILIGHT.

astronomical unit (**AU** or **au**) a unit of length that is used for distances, especially within the Solar System. It is effectively the mean distance between Earth and Sun. It is defined formally in terms of Kepler's third law and the GAUSSIAN GRAVITATIONAL CONSTANT. One astronomical unit is equal to 149 597 870 kilometers or 499.005 light-seconds.

astronomy the observational and theoretical study of celestial bodies, of the intervening regions of space, and of the Universe as a whole. Astronomy is one of the oldest sciences and has developed in step with advances in instrumentation and other technology and with advances in physics, chemistry, and mathematics. The main branches are ASTROMETRY, CELESTIAL MECHANICS, and the major modern field of ASTROPHYSICS with its subsections of COSMOLOGY, RADIO ASTRONOMY, and X-RAY, GAMMA-RAY, INFRARED, and ULTRAVIOLET ASTRONOMY. STELLAR STATISTICS is another modern field.

astrophotography astronomical PHOTOGRAPHY.

astrophysics the study of the properties, constitution, and evolution of celestial bodies and the intervening regions of space. It is concerned in particular with the production and expenditure of energy in systems such as the stars and galaxies and in the Universe as a whole and with how this affects the evolution of such systems. Astrophysics developed in the 19th century with the application of spectroscopy to the study of light from celestial bodies. It is also now closely related to particle physics, plasma physics, thermodynamics, solid-

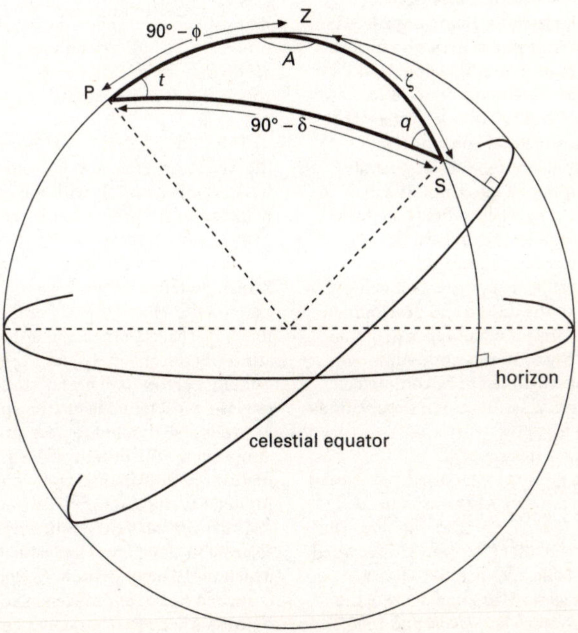

Astronomical triangle

state physics, and relativity. COSMOLOGY, RADIO ASTRONOMY, X-RAY, GAMMA-RAY, INFRARED, and ULTRAVIOLET ASTRONOMY are usually considered subsections of astrophysics.

Astrophysics Data System (ADS) a comprehensive computer database system, funded and maintained by NASA, that allows astronomers to locate, retrieve, and analyze astrophysical data stored at a large number of facilities by means of computer networks. The information, which covers all aspects of astronomy, astrophysics, and instrumentation, consists of bibliographical records, electronic versions of printed articles, and pointers and links to external resources. See also SIMBAD.

asymptotic giant branch see GIANT.

AT *abbrev. for* Australia Telescope.

Atacama Large Millimeter Array (ALMA) a large international project to construct a millimeter wavelength radio telescope in Llano de Chajnantor, near San Pedro de Atacama in northern Chile. The array comprises 64 separate dishes, each 12 meters in diameter, that can be arranged in a number of configurations with effective sizes of 150 m to 10 km, allowing ALMA to reach angular resolutions of up to 10 milliarcseconds. The altitude of the site (5000 m) ensures good atmospheric transparency at a number of wavebands between 10 mm and 0.350 mm. It will contribute to a number of fields of study including cosmology, extragalactic astronomy, star formation, molecular clouds and planetary science. Following completion of the design and development phase of the project in 2002, construction of the array began in Feb. 2003. Although ALMA is not scheduled to be completed until 2012, initial astronomical observations are planned for 2007.

ataxite see IRON METEORITE.

Aten group a group of near-Earth ASTEROIDS that have SEMIMAJOR AXES less than 1 AU and thus periods of less than one year. The group is named after (2062) *Aten*, discovered in 1976 (see Table 3, Appendix). Over a dozen Aten asteroids are now known, the largest being (2100) *Ra-Shalom* and 1986 To (asteroid number 3753).

Atlas **1** a small satellite of Saturn, discovered in 1980. It is the SHEPHERD SATELLITE for Saturn's A ring. See SATURN'S RINGS; TABLE 2, Appendix.
2 see PLEIADES.

atmosphere the gaseous envelope that surrounds a star, planet, or some other celestial body. The ability of a planet or planetary satellite to maintain an appreciable atmosphere depends on the ESCAPE VELOCITY at its surface and on its temperature. Small bodies, such as the Moon, have low escape velocities that may be exceeded comparatively easily by gas molecules traveling with the thermal speeds appropriate to their temperature and mass. The speed of a gas molecule increases with temperature and decreases with molecular weight; the lighter molecules, such as hydrogen, helium, methane, and ammonia, can therefore escape into space more readily than heavier ones such as nitrogen, oxygen, and carbon dioxide. Some bodies, such as Pluto, may be so cold that most potential atmospheric gases lie frozen on their surfaces. A body may gain an atmosphere by any of several processes, including a temporary acquisition by collision with an object containing frozen gases, such as a cometary nucleus.

The study of planetary atmospheres – their contents, meteorology, and evolution – has developed rapidly with the advent of planetary space probes in the 1960s. The planets EARTH, MARS, VENUS, JUPITER, SATURN, URANUS, and NEPTUNE, and Saturn's satellite TITAN, have been examined at close range by probes and much has been learned about their atmospheres. MERCURY and Neptune's satellite TRITON have been found to have only the most tenuous of atmospheres. PLUTO is also thought to have an atmosphere. The deep hydrogen, helium, methane, and ammonia atmospheres of Jupiter, Saturn, and the other GIANT PLANETS probably derive directly from the solar nebula and icy planetesimals from which the planets are now thought to have coalesced by accretion (see SOLAR SYSTEM, ORIGIN). The TERRESTRIAL PLANETS, however, were too small to capture the warm gases of the early nebula; the present atmospheres of Venus, Earth, and Mars are thought to have been released from volcanoes after being liberated from chemical combination in subsurface rocks by radioactive heating. The unusual abundance of free oxygen to be found in the Earth's atmosphere, accounting for about a fifth of its entire contents, is a direct result of the photosynthesizing action of living organisms.

Exploration of the Solar System has provided a unique opportunity to examine weather systems of planetary atmospheres. Venus: slowly rotating cloud over the planet with a huge GREENHOUSE EFFECT. Mars: a thin atmosphere where the weather systems are strongly influenced by the large topography of the surface. Jupiter and Saturn: large fluid atmospheres, rapidly rotating, with internal heating to assist in driving the weather phenomena. Each one of these examples is a natural laboratory for geophysical fluid dynamics that provides insight into general meteorological processes.

See also CHROMOSPHERE; CORONA; SOLAR WIND.

atmosphere, composition the percentage composition of clean dry air in the Earth's atmosphere is given in the table. The concentrations of CO_2, CO, SO_2, NO_2, and NO are greater in industrial areas. The amount of ozone increases in the ozone layer (see ATMOSPHERIC LAYERS) and depends on meteorological and geographical variations. The fraction of water vapor in normal air varies from 0.1–2.8% by volume and 0.06–1.7% by mass, with meteorological and geographical variations and a decrease with altitude.

The Earth's primitive atmosphere is thought to have formed as a result of outgassing from the Earth's interior, in proportions similar to those emitted by present-day volcanoes (mainly water vapor and CO_2 plus some SO_2 and N_2). The composition has since changed radically, initially as a result of geochemical cycling of the elements and the presence of plant and animal life, and recently by combustion processes and by industrial, technological, and agricultural activities. See also GREENHOUSE EFFECT.

atmospheric dispersion see DISPERSION.

atmospheric extinction see EXTINCTION.

atmospheric layers the gaseous layers into which the Earth's atmosphere is divided, mainly on the basis of the variation of temperature with altitude. The *troposphere* is the lowest layer, extending from sea level to

Composition of Earth's Lower Atmosphere

Gas		*Percentage composition of dry air*	
		By volume	*By mass*
nitrogen	N_2	78.084	75.523
oxygen	O_2	20.947	23.142
argon	Ar	0.932	1.290
carbon dioxide	CO_2	0.035	0.050
neon	Ne	0.0018	0.0013
helium	He	0.0005	0.0001
methane	CH_4	0.0002	0.0001
krypton	Kr	0.0001	0.0003
carbon monoxide	CO	0.0001	0.0001
sulfur dioxide	SO_2	0.0001	0.0002

With smaller traces of hydrogen (H_2), nitrous oxide (N_2O), ozone (O_3), xenon (Xe), nitrogen dioxide (NO_2), radon (Rn), and nitric oxide (NO).

the *tropopause* at an altitude of between 8 km at the poles and 18 km within the tropics. It contains three-quarters of the atmosphere by mass and is the layer of clouds and weather systems. It is a region, heated from the ground by infrared radiation and convection, in which the temperature falls with increasing height to reach a minimum of approximately –55 °C at the midlatitude and polar tropopause and maybe –80 °C at the equatorial tropopause.

The *stratosphere*, lying above the tropopause, is an atmospheric layer in which the temperature is at first steady with altitude before increasing to a maximum of 0°C at about 50 km, which marks the *stratopause*. This temperature variation inhibits vertical air movements and makes the stratosphere stable. The heating arises from the absorption of high-energy solar ultraviolet radiation by ozone (O_3) molecules. These molecules, themselves formed by the action of ultraviolet radiation on oxygen molecules, constitute the region known as the *ozone layer*. This contains about 90% of the atmosphere's ozone. Decreases in stratospheric ozone, observed especially in high latitudes in winter, are attributable mainly to increasing atmospheric levels of synthetic CFCs (chlorofluorocarbons). The Antarctic *ozone hole* in particular is allowing increased levels of potentially damaging solar ultraviolet radiation to reach the ground.

Above the stratopause is the *mesosphere*, in which the temperature falls with height to reach about –90 °C at the *mesopause* at an altitude of about 85 km. Within the mesosphere the heat contribution from ultraviolet absorption by ozone decreases as the ozone becomes less plentiful. The *thermosphere*, above the mesopause, has a temperature that rises with height as the Sun's far-ultraviolet radiation is absorbed by oxygen and nitrogen. This process gives rise to ionized atoms and molecules and leads to the formation of the IONOSPHERE layers above altitudes of about 60 km. This is also the domain of METEORS and AURORAE.

Although the temperature climbs to about 500 °C at 150 km and about 1300 °C at 500 km, these are the kinetic temperatures (i.e. measures of the average random motions) of the few atoms and molecules found at such heights: their combined heating ability is negligible. The atmospheric density decreases to about 0.25 of its sea-level value at the tropopause, 0.0009 at the stratopause, and 0.000 007 at the mesopause. The density at 500 km averages less than one million millionth of its sea level value but is prone to large variations resulting from solar heating and disturbances during periods of enhanced SOLAR ACTIVITY.

The *exosphere*, above 500 km, is the region in which atmospheric constituents lose collisional contact with each other because of their rarity and can leak away into space. It contains the VAN ALLEN RADIATION BELTS and the GEOCORONA and extends to the magnetopause, where it meets the interplanetary medium.

atmospheric pressure the force per unit area (i.e. pressure) exerted by a column of atmosphere extending vertically upwards to the limit of the atmosphere. It is usually expressed in millibars (mb) or newtons per square meter ($N\ m^{-2}$). The standard atmospheric pressure at the Earth's surface at sea level is 1013 mb or 101 325 $N\ m^{-2}$. On the surface of Venus and Mars the atmospheric pressure is about 90 000 mb and 7.5 mb, respectively.

atmospheric refraction REFRACTION of light passing obliquely through a body's atmosphere. Light entering the Earth's atmosphere is bent toward the Earth, with the result that stars and other celestial bodies appear to be displaced very slightly toward the ZENITH. The amount of displacement, i.e. the resulting increase in altitude, depends on the body's distance from the observer's zenith and is greatest (about 35 arc minutes) for objects on the horizon. See also ZENITH DISTANCE.

atmospheric windows wavebands of the ELECTROMAGNETIC SPECTRUM that can be transmitted through the Earth's atmosphere without significant absorption or reflection by atmospheric constituents. All spectral regions are at least partially absorbed but there are two nearly transparent ranges: the *radio window* and the *optical window* (see

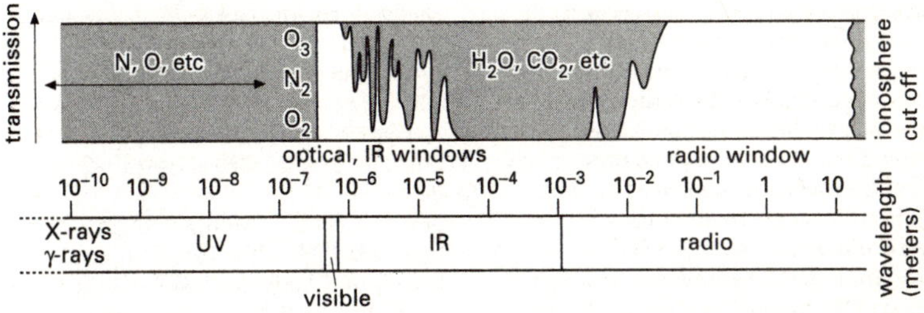

Atmospheric windows

illustration). The radio window extends from a wavelength of about a millimeter to about 30 meters (i.e. it includes frequencies from roughly 300 gigahertz to 10 megahertz); it thus allows high-energy radio waves from celestial RADIO SOURCES to be received by ground-based radio telescopes. Lower energies are reflected by the IONOSPHERE while above 100 GHz molecular absorption increases.

The optical window spans wavelengths of about 300 to 900 nanometers (nm) and thus includes some of the near-ultraviolet and near-infrared regions as well as the whole visible spectrum. In addition there are several narrow-band *infrared windows* at micrometer (μm) wavelengths. The photometric designations of these windows are J (1.25 μm), H (1.6 μm), K (2.2 μm), L (3.6 μm), M (5.0 μm), N (10.2 μm), and Q (21 μm). There are also small but useable windows at 350 and 460 μm. The atmospheric constituents responsible for the dominant absorptions are water vapor, carbon dioxide, nitrous oxide, and ozone. Observatories studying infrared sources are therefore best sited in very dry or mountainous regions where the effect of overlying water vapor is reduced and/or the atmosphere is thinner.

Beyond the low-wavelength end of the optical window no radiation can penetrate the atmosphere: ultraviolet radiation with wavelengths between about 230 and 300 nm is absorbed by atmospheric ozone; shorter wavelengths down to about 100 nm are blocked by oxygen and nitrogen molecules; the shortest wavelengths are absorbed by atoms of oxygen, nitrogen, etc., in the upper atmosphere. The spectral regions from space rendered inaccessible by atmospheric absorption must be studied by means of instruments carried in satellites, rockets, etc. Even then, high-energy ultraviolet and low-energy X-rays from distant stars can be absorbed by hydrogen and helium in the GEOCORONA.

ATNF *abbrev. for* Australia Telescope National Facility.

atom the smallest part of a chemical element that can retain its chemical identity, i.e. can take part in a chemical reaction without being destroyed. An atom can however be transformed into one or more other atoms by nuclear reactions. Nearly all the mass of an atom is concentrated in the small central nucleus, which is made up of protons and neutrons. Electrons occupy the remaining space in the atom and may be thought of as orbiting the nucleus. The number of protons in a particular nucleus, i.e. the atomic number of the atom, is equal to the number of electrons in a neutral (nonionized) atom. The arrangement and behaviour of these electrons determine the interactions of the atom with other atoms and thus govern chemical properties and most physical properties of matter. See also ENERGY LEVEL; ION; ISOTOPES.

atomic clock the most accurate type of clock to date, in which the periodic process used as the timing mechanism is an atomic or molecular event with which is associated a constant and very accurately known FREQUENCY. Various atoms and molecules have been employed in atomic clocks, the frequency involved in the timing mechanism being a microwave frequency; such frequencies can be produced and manipulated by sophisticated electronic techniques. The accuracy is at present better than one part in one thousand million million. See also ATOMIC TIME.

atomic number symbol: Z. The number of protons in the nucleus of an atom. This is equal to the number of electrons orbiting the nucleus in a neutral atom. The ISOTOPES of an element have the same atomic number but different MASS NUMBERS.

atomic time a time system that operates at a constant rate and that is measured by means of an ATOMIC CLOCK. The definition of the SECOND has been in terms of atomic time since 1967. See also INTERNATIONAL ATOMIC TIME.

Atria see TRIANGULUM AUSTRALE.

attenuation the reduction in magnitude of a quantity as a function of distance from source or of some other parameter. The attenuation of a beam of radiation, i.e. the reduction in intensity or flux density, results from absorption and/or scattering of the waves or particles as they pass through matter.

A-type asteroids a rare class of ASTEROID that have both a moderately high albedo and a reddish spectrum. An absorption feature around 1.05 μm in the near-infrared is thought to be caused by the presence of the mineral olivine.

AU or **au** *abbrev. for* astronomical unit.

audiofrequency any frequency at which a sound wave would be audible, i.e. a frequency in the range 15 hertz to 20 000 hertz.

Auger shower *another name for* air shower. See COSMIC RAYS.

augmentation the difference at a particular time between the topocentric and geocentric semidiameter of a celestial body. See also DIURNAL LIBRATION.

Auriga (**Charioteer**) a conspicuous constellation in the northern hemisphere near Orion, lying in the Milky Way, the brightest stars being CAPELLA (α) and the 2nd-magnitude ALGOL VARIABLE Menkalinan (β). Epsilon (ε) and Zeta (ζ) are eclipsing binaries (see EPSILON AURIGAE; ZETA AURIGAE). The area contains the bright open clusters M36 (NGC 1960), M37 (NGC 2099), and M38 (NGC 1912). Abbrev.: Aur; genitive form: Aurigae; approx. position: RA 5.5h, dec +40°; area: 657 sq deg.

aurora a display of diffuse changing colored light seen high in the Earth's atmosphere mainly in polar regions. Aurorae show varying colors from whitish green to deep red and often have spectacular formations of streamers or drapery. They occur principally at altitudes of approximately 100 km, forming around two irregular and changing *auroral ovals* that are centered on the Earth's magnetic poles; the ovals enlarge at times of high SOLAR ACTIVITY. Aurorae are caused by charged particles from the SOLAR WIND and solar FLARES that become trapped in the Earth's MAGNETOSPHERE. Formed into beams, they are focused by the magnetic fields into the upper atmosphere, spiraling along the Earth's magnetic field lines toward the poles. Their interactions with atmospheric atoms and molecules produce the auroral emissions.

Australian National Radio Astronomy Observatory see PARKES OBSERVATORY.

Australia Telescope (**Australia Telescope National Facility, ATNF, AT**) a radio telescope combining the principles of APERTURE SYNTHESIS and long baseline interferometry (LBI). Run by Australia's CSIRO, the AT produced its first image in April 1989. There are eight antennas in all, at three sites in New South Wales. Six 22-meter dishes at the Paul Wild Observatory, Narrabri, form the *Compact Array*. Five of these are movable along a 3-km railroad track, and the sixth lies a further 3 km to the west. The other two antennas are the 22-meter Mopra dish near Coonabarabran, close to the Siding Spring optical observatory, and the existing 64-meter dish at PARKES OBSERVATORY. When connected by radio links to the Compact Array they form the Australia Telescope *Long Baseline Array*. The AT can work up to 110 GHz with a BANDWIDTH of 1 GHz. It has a maximum BASELINE of 300 km.

autocorrelation function a mathematical

function that for a real function f(t) is given by

$$\int_{-\infty}^{\infty} f(u)f(u-t)du$$

It describes, for example, the time or distance over which a signal is coherent. The cross-correlation function describes how two different signals compare as they are displaced relative to one another; for two real functions f(t) and g(t), it is given by

$$\int_{-\infty}^{\infty} f(u)g(u-t)du$$

autoguider see GUIDE TELESCOPE.

automation the use of electronic equipment, especially computer systems, for the automatic control of instruments and processes and for automatically acquiring and processing information. The applications in astronomy include positioning and tracking of telescopes, direct control of instruments associated with telescopes, the storage of information and its reduction by sampling or simple analysis, and the processing of the information. See also COMPUTING; IMAGING; REMOTE OPERATION.

avalanche a process such as that in which a single ionization leads to a large number of ions. The electrons and ions produced ionize more atoms, so that the number of ions multiplies quickly. See GEIGER COUNTER.

AXAF the Advanced X-ray Astrophysics Facility, originally intended by NASA to follow the HUBBLE SPACE TELESCOPE as a long-lived X-ray observatory for the 1990s, with in-orbit servicing from the space shuttle. A direct successor to the EINSTEIN OBSERVATORY, AXAF was to carry an array of large (1.2-meter outer diameter) coaxial GRAZING INCIDENCE mirrors in a nested configuration, high-resolution cameras using both CCDs and MICROCHANNEL PLATES, and a cryogenically cooled X-ray spectrometer. Budgetary constraints led in 1992 to the restructuring of the AXAF into two smaller missions, AXAF-I (concerned with high-resolution X-ray imaging) and AXAF-S (dealing with X-ray spectroscopy). AXAF-I was scheduled for launch in 1998/99 into a highly eccentric orbit that would keep it out of the Earth's shadow for long periods, thereby maximizing its observation time. AXAF-S was to follow it into space in 1999, traveling in a near-Earth Sun-synchronous orbit to conduct high-resolution X-ray spectroscopy with no in-orbit servicing. In the event, NASA canceled AXAF-S, and its advanced X-ray spectroscopic instruments were transferred to the ill-fated Japanese Astro-E mission (see ASTRO-E2). Development of AXAF-I continued, however, and it was eventually successfully launched in July 1999 and renamed *Chandra* (see CHANDRA X-RAY OBSERVATORY).

axial period the period of time during which a body makes one complete ROTATION on its axis. For planets it is usually referred to the direction of a fixed star and is thus equivalent to the SIDEREAL DAY.

axion a hypothetical elementary particle of very low mass and zero charge. Axions have potentially important consequences in astrophysics and cosmology, such as having a possible effect on the cooling of stars and making up part or all of the DARK MATTER in the Universe. Some of these consequences enable limits to be calculated for the values of the properties of axions.

axis 1 an imaginary line that usually passes through the center of a body or system and about which the body has some form of symmetry. It is the imaginary line about which a rotating body turns or about which an object, such as the celestial sphere, appears to rotate.
2 a reference line on a graph.

azimuth see HORIZONTAL COORDINATE SYSTEM.

azimuthal mounting See ALTAZIMUTH MOUNTING.

Bb

Baade's star *another name for* Crab pulsar. See CRAB NEBULA.

baby universe a region of SPACE–TIME that is connected to another region of space–time by a WORMHOLE. It has been postulated that when a massive object in the Universe collapses to a black hole it could go through the SINGULARITY at the center of the black hole and create an expanding baby universe in another region of space–time. INFLATION could allow such a baby universe to become large very rapidly. It may be the case that the Universe we live in originated in this way. Although the idea of baby universes is highly speculative and requires a theory of QUANTUM GRAVITY before it can be formulated definitively, it has been investigated by a number of theorists. See also MULTIVERSE.

background radiation see COSMIC BACKGROUND RADIATION; MICROWAVE BACKGROUND RADIATION.

background temperature see ANTENNA TEMPERATURE.

Baikonur a space center or *cosmodrome* in Kazakhstan, NE of the Aral Sea, that is the location of the main launch site for spacecraft of the Russian Federation and (prior to 1992) the Soviet Union. First used for missile and rocket launches in the mid-1950s, the Baikonur Cosmodrome was the site from which the first artificial satellite, Sputnik 1, was launched, Oct. 4 1957, and from which Vostok 1 carried into orbit Yuri Gagarin, the first person ever to travel in space, Apr. 12 1961.

Baily see table at CRATERS.

Baily's beads a string of brilliant points of sunlight sometimes seen, very briefly, at the Moon's edge just before or just after totality in a solar ECLIPSE. They are the result of sunlight shining through the valleys on the Moon's limb as the Sun just disappears or emerges from behind the Moon. They were first described by Francis Baily after the eclipse of 1836. See also DIAMOND-RING EFFECT.

Baker–Nunn camera a wide-field astronomical camera, similar to the Schmidt camera (see SCHMIDT TELESCOPE), designed for satellite tracking. It uses a spherical primary mirror but replaces the Schmidt correcting plate with a three-element achromatic correcting lens.

Balmer series, lines see HYDROGEN SPECTRUM.

BAL quasar *short for* broad absorption line quasar. See QUASAR.

balun see FEEDER.

band 1 see WAVEBAND.
2 see BAND SPECTRUM.

band-pass filter see FILTER.

band spectrum a SPECTRUM consisting of one or more bands of emitted or absorbed radiation. The bands consist of numbers of closely spaced lines and result from transitions between ENERGY LEVELS in molecules, allowing different levels of vibration or rotation.

band-stop filter see FILTER.

bandwidth 1 the range of frequencies over which an instrument, such as a RADIO TELESCOPE, is sensitive. A wide bandwidth gives good SENSITIVITY to sources that emit over a wide range of frequencies (e.g. by SYNCHROTRON EMISSION), whereas a narrow bandwidth gives good sensitivity to spectral lines.

2 (**coherence bandwidth**) the range of frequencies over which electromagnetic or other emissions from a source maintain COHERENCE.

bar a unit of pressure equal to 10^5 pascals. The bar and the millibar (1/1000 bars, symbol: mbar or mb) are often used for planetary atmospheric pressures; the Earth's atmospheric pressure is about 1000 millibars.

barium stars a class of stars, usually G or K GIANTS, that show anomalous enhancements of barium, strontium, and other S-PROCESS elements in their spectra. Observations show that barium stars are exclusively found in BINARY STAR systems, with periods between a few months and a few years, in which the companion is a WHITE DWARF. Because the barium-rich star is usually not sufficiently evolved to have produced the chemical anomalies in its interior, it is now generally believed that it acquired material enriched in s-process elements by MASS TRANSFER from the companion, when the latter was an asymptotic GIANT (presumably an S STAR). See also CH STARS.

Barlow lens an achromatic diverging lens (see ACHROMATIC LENS) placed behind the eyepiece of a telescope, just inside the primary focal plane, in order to increase the effective focal length of the objective or primary mirror. This increases the magnification of the telescope so that a long-focus eyepiece may be used to give the higher powers needed to separate optical doubles, or for planetary observation under the best seeing conditions.

Barnard's loop or **ring** see ORION.

Barnard's star a red dwarf star in the constellation Ophiuchus that was discovered in 1916 by E.E. Barnard. The fourth-nearest star to the Sun, after the Alpha Centauri system, it has the largest known proper motion (10″.3 per year) and thus moves a distance equivalent to the Moon's diameter in 180 years. Observations of the star's position over many years show slight oscillating variations in right ascension and declination. It is thought that this wobbling motion is due to the presence of one or more planets orbiting the star. m_v: 9.53; M_v: 13.21; spectral type: M4 V; distance: 1.83 pc.

barred spiral galaxy see GALAXIES; HUBBLE CLASSIFICATION.

barrel distortion see DISTORTION.

Barringer crater see ARIZONA METEORITE CRATER.

Barwell meteorites a shower of about 44 kg of chondritic STONY METEORITES that fell in Dec. 1965 near Barwell in Leicestershire, England. This is one of only 22 observed falls in the British Isles in the last 370 years.

barycenter the CENTER OF MASS of a system of bodies, e.g. the Earth–Moon system or Solar System. The barycenter of the Solar System is offset from the Sun's center due to the presence of the planets, especially Jupiter, and moves as the relative positions of the planets change. *Barycentric coordinates* are a more rigorous coordinate system than heliocentric coordinates, specifying positions with respect to the Solar-System barycenter rather than the Sun's center.

barycentric coordinates see BARYCENTER.

barycentric dynamical time (**TDB**) see DYNAMICAL TIME.

baryon density parameter the ratio of the mean smooth density of baryons to the critical density of the Universe. It can be determined through studies of cosmic nucleosynthesis and observations of the helium and deuterium abundances in primordial material; the currently accepted value is around 0.06.

baryonic matter normal matter containing baryons, i.e. protons and neutrons. It is thought that a large proportion of DARK MATTER could be composed of nonbaryons, such as WIMPS.

baryons a class of ELEMENTARY PARTICLES, including the proton and neutron, that take part in strong interactions (see FUNDAMENTAL FORCES). Baryons are composed of a triplet of QUARKS. Antibaryons, i.e. the ANTIPARTICLES of baryons, consist of a triplet of antiquarks.

baseline the straight line between two observational points, as between the elements of an interferometer (see RADIO TELESCOPE). The longer the baseline between two radio telescopes, the finer the detail that can be resolved in a radio source. See also LBI; VLBI.

basin a huge CRATER. Lunar basins are multiringed structures that are several hundred kilometers in diameter and were all produced during the first 750 million years of lunar history by intense meteoritic impact. The youngest basins (ORIENTALE, IMBRIUM, CRISIUM, NECTARIS, and SERENITATIS) may have been excavated during a cataclysmic period around 3900 million years ago. The EJECTA BLANKETS of basins are extensive and provide the basis for HIGHLAND stratigraphy. Basins are so defined by their systems of concentric ring structures, most of which are now in the form of ridges and mountain arcs. Basins on the Moon's nearside were filled with lava at some time up to 3000 million years ago to produce MARIA: the resulting mare has the same name as the basin (e.g. Mare Imbrium). Several unfilled basins (*thassaloids*) exist on the farside, the largest of which was revealed as a vast depression by the APOLLO 15 laser altimeter. At least 28 basins are now known to exist. See also RILLE; MASCONS.

BATSE *abbrev. for* burst and transient source experiment. See COMPTON GAMMA RAY OBSERVATORY.

Bautz–Morgan classification a classification system for CLUSTERS OF GALAXIES that is based on the degree to which the cluster is dominated by its brightest galaxies. *Type I* clusters have a single central cD galaxy, *type II* have a normal giant elliptical galaxy at the center, and *type III* have no dominant cluster galaxy.

Bayer letters see STELLAR NOMENCLATURE.

BC *abbrev. for* bolometric correction. See MAGNITUDE.

BCD galaxy *short for* blue compact dwarf galaxy. See DWARF GALAXY.

BD see BONNER DURCHMUSTERUNG.

Beagle 2 see MARS EXPRESS.

beam 1 the region of sky to which a radio telescope is sensitive, equaling the region it would illuminate were its antennas to be used to transmit signals. In APERTURE SYNTHESIS the *primary beam* is the region to which the individual antennas are sensitive and defines the maximum size of the synthesized map. The *synthesized beam* is a theoretical beam pattern corresponding to the FOURIER TRANSFORM of the synthesized aperture and defines the resolution of the map. See also ANTENNA.
2 a well-defined elongated region of space down which energy is passing. In the beam model of double radio sources (see RADIO-SOURCE STRUCTURE), the central galaxy shoots out two beams in opposite directions in which the energy may be transported by RELATIVISTIC ELECTRONS, low-frequency waves, or some other mechanism. Hot spots are formed where the beams impinge on the surrounding INTERGALACTIC MEDIUM. See also JET.

beam efficiency see ANTENNA.

beamwidth see ANTENNA.

Becklin-Neugebauer object see BN OBJECT.

Becrux see BETA CRUCIS.

Beehive see PRAESEPE.

Bekenstein bound a result that relates the area of a surface and the maximum amount of information about the UNIVERSE on one side of the surface that can pass through to an observer on the other side. It states that the number of bits of information an observer can gain must be less than or equal to one quarter of the surface area in PLANCK UNITS. This result is related to the ENTROPY of black holes since entropy is related to both information theory and the area of the EVENT HORIZON of a black hole. The Bekenstein bound was derived and discussed by Jacob Bekenstein in papers he wrote in the mid 1970s but its importance was not appreciated until 20 years later.

Belinda a small satellite of Uranus, discovered in 1986. See URANUS' SATELLITES; Table 2, Appendix.

Bellatrix (γ Ori) a remote luminous blue-white giant that is the third brightest star in the constellation ORION. m_v: 1.64; M_v: –3.9; spectral type: B2 III; distance: 74 pc.

Bellerophon see 51 PEGASI.

Benatnasch see ALCAID.

Bennett's comet (1970 II) a long-period comet of inclination 90°, discovered by J.C. Bennett in Dec. 1969 from South Africa. Perihelion passage was on 20 Mar. 1971 and by mid-March 1971 the comet was a spectacular zero-magnitude object with a tail 11° long. The comet was observed by the Orbiting Geophysical Observatory and shown to be surrounded by a huge 9° by 6° hydrogen envelope.

bent double radio source see RADIO-SOURCE STRUCTURE.

BepiColombo a European Space Agency (ESA) mission to the planet MERCURY, run in collaboration with Japan and planned for launch in 2009. The mission will consist of two spacecraft, probably driven by solar electric propulsion: a Mercury orbiter and a magnetospheric satellite. Both craft will probably use the Moon's and Mercury's gravity to control their flight. The mission's basic objectives are to add to our understanding of the composition, structure, and history of Mercury and thereby extend our knowledge of the formation and history of the inner (terrestrial) planets of the Solar System in general. Consisting of two space vehicles incorporating many different modules, BepiColombo is set to map the whole of Mercury at several wavelengths. It will plot the planet's mineralogy and elemental composition and will be able to determine whether or not Mercury's interior is molten. BepiColombo is to be one of ESA's 'cornerstone' missions. Its use of two spacecraft makes it one of the most expensive ever mounted and, given Mercury's proximity to the Sun, one of the most technically challenging. The BepiColombo orbiter will have to endure extremes of temperature, from the furnacelike conditions of Mercury's sunlit side to the intense cold of its night side. The mission takes its name from a 20th-century Italian mathematician and spacecraft engineer Giuseppe ('Beppi') Colombo, who discovered that Mercury's axial rotation period equals two-thirds of that of its revolution around the Sun.

Bertele eyepiece see EYEPIECE.

Besselian year the length of the TROPICAL YEAR in 1900. Before 1976 it was defined as the period of one complete revolution in RIGHT ASCENSION of the MEAN SUN. The beginning of the Besselian year was used as a standard EPOCH until 1984.

Be stars IRREGULAR VARIABLES of spectral type B in which bright emission lines of hydrogen are superimposed on the normal absorption spectrum. They are now known to be identical to SHELL STARS. Some Be stars are young stars, rather more massive than AE STARS: together they are sometimes classed as *Herbig Ae-Be stars*, and are heavier versions of the T TAURI STARS. These Be stars are rotating very rapidly and are slowly losing mass to an expanding shell that surrounds the star and is drawn into a disk around the equator due to the rotation. Other Be stars are in close binary systems, with shells that consist of gas being accreted from an evolved companion star (see MASS TRANSFER).

beta (β) the second letter of the Greek alphabet, used in STELLAR NOMENCLATURE usually to designate the second-brightest star in a constellation or sometimes to indicate a star's position in a group.

Beta Canis Majoris stars see BETA CEPHEI STARS.

Beta Centauri (Hadar; Agena; β Cen) a luminous remote but still conspicuous blue-white giant that is the second-brightest star in the constellation Centaurus. It is a visual binary, separation 1″.2. m_v: 0.61 (var.); M_v: –4.4; spectral type: B1 II; distance: 100 pc.

Beta Cephei stars (Beta Canis Majoris stars) a small group of PULSATING VARIABLES, the prototypes being β Cep and β CMa. They are hot massive luminous stars of spectral types O9 to B3 with short periods of rotation (about 3–7 hours) and a very small variation in visual brightness (about 0.01–0.25 magnitudes), although the range is much greater at ultraviolet wavelengths. Some of the stars have two or even more periods of RADIAL-VELOCITY variation. The pulsation mechanism is still uncertain but could involve both radial and nonradial pulsations. Their position on the Hertzsprung–Russell diagram for PULSATING VARIABLES is just above the main sequence, beginning at type B3.

Beta Crucis (Mimosa; Becrux; β Cru) a remote luminous blue-white giant that is the second-brightest star in the constellation Crux. It is a variable star (period 0.25 days) and may also be a double star. m_v: 1.25 (var.); M_v: –4.7; spectral type: B0 III; distance: 150 pc.

beta decay a type of RADIOACTIVE DECAY in which an atomic nucleus spontaneously transforms into a daughter nucleus and either an electron plus antineutrino or a positron plus NEUTRINO. The daughter nucleus has the same MASS NUMBER as the parent nucleus but differs in ATOMIC NUMBER by one. The electrons or positrons ejected by beta decay have a spread of energies, extra energy being taken up by the antineutrinos or neutrinos, respectively.

Beta Lyrae, Beta Lyrae star see W SERPENTIS STAR.

beta particle an energetic electron or positron ejected by BETA DECAY.

Beta Persei stars see ALGOL VARIABLES.

Beta Pictoris (β Pic) a 4th-magnitude star in the constellation Pictor, about 19 parsecs from Earth. Following the IRAS survey in 1983, which showed the star to have an INFRARED EXCESS, optical detectors revealed a disk of dust and ices surrounding the star. Seen edge-on from the Earth, this disk may be a region in which planets could form. Analysis of the disk in the late 1990s and early 2000s revealed a warp or bulge in its outer regions that may have been caused when material was pulled from the disk by the gravitational effect of a passing star, a brown dwarf companion, or a planet several times the mass of Jupiter. Beta Pictoris is a young star a little larger than the Sun. M_v: 2.42; spectral type: A5 V

Beta Regio a highland area on VENUS, somewhat smaller than APHRODITE TERRA and ISHTAR TERRA. Located in the planet's northern hemisphere at Venusian coordinates 25.3° N latitude, 282.8° W longitude, it has a large rift valley and two large shield volcanoes, *Rhea Mons* and *Theia Mons*. Satellite tracking shows that there is a gravity anomaly over Beta Regio.

Betelgeuse (α Ori) a remote luminous red supergiant that is the second-brightest star in the constellation ORION. It is a semiregular variable with a period of about 5.8 years; the normal magnitude range is 0.3 to 0.9 but the magnitude has reached 0.15 and been as low as 1.3. It is a strong source of infrared radiation. IRAS found that the long-wavelength infrared is emitted from three concentric shells, the largest with a radius of 1.5 parsecs, ejected within the past 100 000 years. Images of the surface of Betelgeuse have been produced by various interferometry techniques, and indicate a nonuniform brightness. M_v: –5.7; spectral type: M2 Iab; diameter: about 500 times solar diameter; distance: 150 pc.

Bethe cycle, Bethe-Weizsäcker cycle *other names for* carbon cycle.

Bianca a small satellite of Uranus, discovered in 1986. See URANUS' SATELLITES; Table 2, Appendix.

Biela's comet (1852 III) a comet, discovered in 1826, having a period of 6.62 years and a perihelion distance of 0.86 AU. At the 1846 return it appeared to be distinctly elongated into a pear-shaped form and actually divided into two separate comets some 10 days later, these comets travelling in practically the same orbit, one preceding the other by 280 000 km. The brightness of the two parts fluctuated drastically. At the next return in 1852 their separation had increased eightfold, the two periods differing by about 15 days. Neither comet has been seen since. Other comets have been observed to break up and to have portions detatch from the main NUCLEUS; these include Brooks' comet (1889 V), Swift 1860 III, and 1882 III.

Bielids (Andromedids) a METEOR SHOWER with its RADIANT in Andromeda. It is named after BIELA'S COMET (1852 III), which passed within 30 000 km of the Earth's orbit in 1832 and broke up in the 1850s. The associated METEOROID STREAM is in the same orbit as the comet and produced a meteor storm on Earth on Nov. 27, 1872 and 1885, the latter having an observed rate of over 75 000 meteors per hour. Due to the rapid regression of the nodes of the orbit very little has been seen since.

Big Bang theory a COSMOLOGICAL MODEL in which all matter and radiation in the Universe originated in an explosion at a finite time in the past. This theory has been remarkably successful in explaining the expansion of the Universe, the MICROWAVE BACKGROUND RADIATION, and the cosmic abundance of HELIUM. An evolving Universe was first discussed in the 1920s by Aleksandr Friedmann, Georges Lemaître, and others. A *hot Big Bang*, in which the temperature of matter and radiation decreased with time, was suggested by George Gamow in the 1940s in an attempt to explain the observed abundances of the

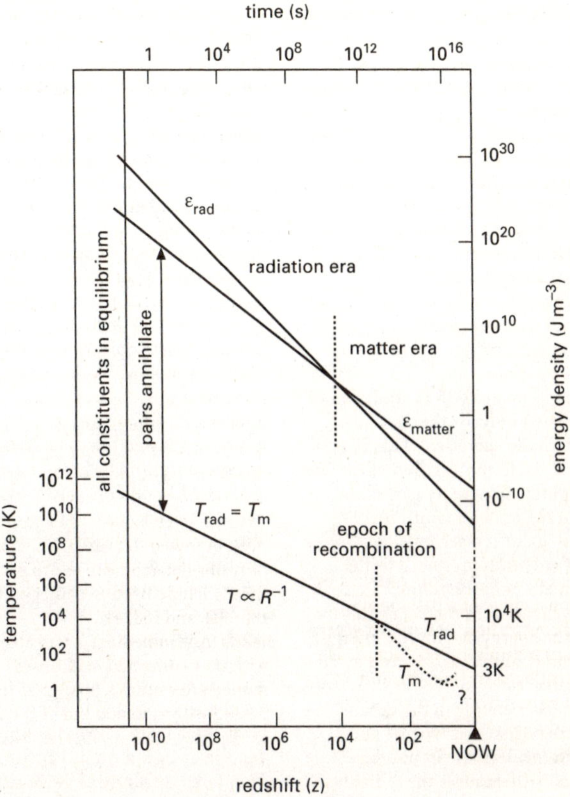

Big Bang theory

elements by cosmological NUCLEOSYNTHESIS. A neglected prediction of primeval-fireball radiation from the hot early phases following the Big Bang was verified by the discovery of the cosmic microwave background in 1965.

The Universe came into existence some 10 to 20 thousand million years ago (see AGE OF THE UNIVERSE) and has since been expanding and cooling from an initial state of extreme density and temperature. The uncertainty principle of quantum mechanics prevents our speculating on times shorter than 10^{-43} seconds after the Big Bang; this is known as the PLANCK TIME. Current theories of ELEMENTARY PARTICLES allow some calculation of the conditions from 10^{-35} seconds onward. At this time the Universe would have contained roughly equal amounts of matter and antimatter in the form of particles and their corresponding ANTIPARTICLES: ELECTRONS and positrons; NEUTRINOS and antineutrinos; QUARKS and antiquarks (quarks are the particles that make up PROTONS and NEUTRONS). The asymmetrical decay of hypothetical particles (called X-bosons) at this time into matter rather than antimatter may explain why the Universe is today apparently composed entirely of matter. The time from 10^{-35} to 10^{-24} seconds may have been the critical period of a sudden and enormous expansion of the Universe, according to the INFLATIONARY UNIVERSE theory.

The Universe cooled as it expanded with age, and the fall in temperature governed which particle reactions dominated at which era. During the *quark era* quarks and antiquarks had almost completely annihilated (see ANNIHILATION). The remaining small excess of quarks over antiquarks (by 1 in 10^9) then combined to form ordinary hadronic matter such as protons and neutrons during the *quark-hadron phase transition.* Conditions suitable for the interaction and self-annihilation of HADRONS existed only for the first millisecond, in the *hadron era.* This was followed by the self-annihilation of the less abundant lighter elementary particles – LEPTONS – in the *lepton era* until the Universe was about 100 seconds old. The PHOTONS of radiation produced by the matter-antimatter annihilation in these early epochs fueled the *primeval fireball* and dominated the energy density (i.e. energy per unit volume) of the early Universe. This was the *radiation era.*

Radiation loses energy in the expansion – by the COSMOLOGICAL REDSHIFT – and together with the decrease in photon number density this causes the radiation energy density, ε_{rad}, to vary with the COSMIC SCALE FACTOR, R, as R^{-4}. The matter density, ε_{matter}, decreases less slowly, as R^{-3}, and thus dominated the total energy density after about 10 000 years, when the temperature was about 10 000 K. This marked the beginning of the *matter era.* The matter was composed primarily of an ionized gas of electrons, protons, and helium nuclei. At about 3000 K electrons can recombine with protons to form neutral hydrogen. Prior to that epoch the scattering of photons on the electrons coupled matter and radiation so that they shared a common temperature. The possibility of recombination marked the beginning of the *decoupling era* some 300 000 years after the Big Bang, when the photons of radiation separated from the expanding matter and radiation could propagate freely in the Universe. Since recombination the radiation has cooled from about 3000 K down to the observed 3 K of the microwave background at a rate proportional to R. The matter, no longer coupled to the radiation, has interacted to form stars and galaxies (see GALAXIES, FORMATION AND EVOLUTION).

Deuterium and helium were synthesized in the dense hot phase at about 100 seconds after the Big Bang when the temperature was about 10^9 kelvin: primordial NEUTRONS combined with protons to form deuterium before the neutrons, with a half-life of 11 minutes, were able to decay. The deuterium nuclei then combined to give helium. Most of the helium in the Universe today was formed at this time. The lack of any stable nuclei with atomic numbers of 5 and 8 prevented formation of heavier elements, except lithium. (The heavier elements are generated by nuclear reactions in the stars – see NUCLEOSYNTHESIS.) Calculations yield estimates of approximately 25–30% by mass for the helium abundance if an expansion rate consistent with observations is used.

Big Bear Solar Observatory a solar observatory located on an artificial island in Big Bear Lake, southern California. The altitude is 2040 meters. It was formerly owned and operated by the California Institute of Technology, for which it was built in 1969, but it was handed over to the New Jersey Institute of Technology in 1997. The chief instrument is a 65-cm reflector. See also SOLAR TELESCOPE.

Big Crunch the time reversal of the Big Bang in which space–time collapses to a singularity. As the big crunch approaches galaxies would start to merge and the temperature associated with the background radiation would increase. The big crunch will occur at the end of time if there is enough mass in the Universe to make it closed. It is currently thought that this is not the case.

Big Dipper *US name for* the PLOUGH.

Big Ear Radio Telescope a large KRAUS-TYPE RADIO TELESCOPE at Ohio State University, dismantled in 1998. The telescope was famous for its early work in the search for extraterrestrial intelligence.

big splash *informal name for* giant impact hypothesis. See MOON.

BIMA array *abbrev. for* Berkeley-Illinois-Maryland Association array. See HAT CREEK OBSERVATORY.

binary galaxy *another name for* physical double galaxy. See DOUBLE GALAXY.

binary pulsar a PULSAR that is in orbit about another star, and is detected by its intrinsic emission of radiation (usually radio waves) rather than by radiation resulting from MASS TRANSFER (see X-RAY PULSATORS). The orbital motion is inferred from apparent changes in the pulse period as the pulsar orbits its companion; the companion star, which is not generally detected directly, can be a NEUTRON STAR, a WHITE DWARF, a low-mass STAR, or even a SUPERGIANT. Systematic surveys have discovered large numbers of binary pulsars, in particular binary MILLISECOND PULSARS, in GLOBULAR CLUSTERS, but they also occur in the galactic disk. The properties of the systems vary widely: the pulse period ranges from 0.0016 second (for PSR 1957+20) to about one second; the orbital periods range from several hours to several years.

PSR 1913+16 was the first binary pulsar to be discovered (in 1974), and is still sometimes called 'the binary pulsar'. It has a pulse period of 59 milliseconds. Its short period and highly eccentric ($e = 0.617$) orbit have led to accurate determinations of the system's parameters. The masses of the pulsar and the unseen companion are identical, and at 1.4 solar masses are equal to the CHANDRASEKHAR LIMIT for collapse to a neutron star. The orbital period is decreasing at a rate of 75 microseconds per year, implying that the stars are spiraling together. The only mechanism for losing orbital energy in this system is GRAVITATIONAL WAVES, and the analysis of PSR 1913+16 gives a rate of energy loss that is precisely in accord with the theory of general RELATIVITY. The pulsars PSR 2127+11C in the globular cluster M15 and PSR 1534+12 in the galactic disk are the two other examples of systems like PSR 1913+16 presently known. See also BLACK-WIDOW PULSARS; PLANET PULSAR.

binary star (binary) a pair of stars that are revolving about a common CENTER OF MASS under the influence of their mutual gravitational attraction. In most cases the stars may be considered to be moving in elliptical orbits described by KEPLER'S LAWS. Binary and MULTIPLE STARS are very common in the Galaxy: in a recent survey of 123 nearby sunlike stars over half (57%) were found to have one or more companions. Studies of the orbital motions in binaries are important because they provide the only direct means of obtaining stellar masses. Optical determination of orbits is only possible if the components are sufficiently far apart to be distinguished (see VISUAL BINARY). In an *astrometric binary* one component is too faint to be observed directly; the presence of this *unseen component* is inferred from perturbations in the motion of the visible component.

Orbital motion in SPECTROSCOPIC binaries is revealed by variations in radial velocity. Most spectroscopic binaries are *close binaries,* in which the components are too close together to be seen separately. Stars in a close binary are often distorted into nonspherical shapes by mutual TIDAL FORCES. If the two stars are physically separate, it is a *detached* binary system; in a *semidetached* system gas is drawn off one star on to the other; a *contact* binary consists of two stars sharing gas. In the latter two cases the gas flow from one star to the other (see EQUIPOTENTIAL SURFACES; MASS TRANSFER) profoundly alters the evolution of the stars (see W URSAE MAJORIS STARS; W SERPENTIS STAR; ALGOL VARIABLES). When one star is a compact WHITE DWARF or NEUTRON STAR, the infalling gas powers NOVAE outbursts and X-RAY BINARY systems.

The orbital planes of binaries are randomly oriented and only a minority of systems are ECLIPSING BINARIES, most of which are also spectroscopic binaries. See also CATACLYSMIC VARIABLE; COMMON ENVELOPE STAR; RS CANUM VENATICORUM STAR; SYMBIOTIC STAR.

binoculars a simple portable optical instrument that consists essentially of two short telescopes mounted side by side and held to both eyes; the optical system produces an erect image. Binoculars have a given combination of magnification × aperture (in mm), e.g. 8 × 40 or 10 × 50, and a wide field of view.

bipolar group see SUNSPOTS.

bipolar nebula a small emission or reflection nebula that appears hourglass-shaped and that represents outflow of gas in opposite directions from a central star that is often obscured by dust. Many have been detected as infrared or radio sources. A bipolar nebula can occur at two very different stages of a star's evolution. It can represent the early stages of a star's life, when it is the visible sign of the BIPOLAR OUTFLOW of T TAURI WIND from a young star. It can also result from the directional loss of matter from an evolved GIANT STAR as it begins to eject mass to become a PLANETARY NEBULA.

bipolar outflow a flow of gas from a very young star, forming two oppositely directed beams; it is apparently a common feature of STAR FORMATION. In the youngest stars the bipolar flow is detected by the radio emission from molecules such as CARBON MONOXIDE; when stars have dispersed most of the surrounding gas and dust, the outflow is visible optically as a BIPOLAR NEBULA or as 'jets' extending away from a T TAURI STAR for thousands of astronomical units. Both kinds of outflow can reach speeds of several hundred kilometers per second. The outflow from T Tauri stars can produce a line of HERBIG–HARO OBJECTS. These flows are too powerful to be driven by the pressure of the star's radiation. They are probably T TAURI WINDS that are channeled outward from the star's poles, a disk of dense gas around the equator preventing them from escaping isotropically. Such disks are indeed often detected in the centers of the different kinds of bipolar outflow at the correct orientation to account for the observed outflow of less-dense gas.

birefringent filter a type of narrow-band FILTER that uses a birefringent (double-refracting) medium between polarizers to produce selective absorption of polarized light. The earliest design is the *Lyot* (or *Lyot–Öhman) filter* devised independently by the French astronomer Bernard Lyot in 1933 and the Swedish astronomer Yngve Öhman in 1938. Its action depends on the extinction of polarized light occurring in birefringent crystalline laminae precisely orientated between Polaroid sheets: a stack of these elements, each of suitable thickness, transmits well-separated and very narrow wavebands of about 0.07 nanometer.

black body a body that absorbs all the radiation falling on it, i.e. a body that has no reflecting power. It is also a perfect emitter of radiation. The concept of a black body is a hypothetical ideal. The radiation from stars, and their EFFECTIVE and COLOR TEMPERATURES, can however be described by assuming that they are black bodies.

Black-body radiation is the thermal radiation (see THERMAL EMISSION) that would be emitted from a black body at a particular temperature. It has a continuous distribution of wavelengths. The graph of the energy, or intensity, of the radiation has a characteristic shape (see illustration) with a maximum value at a given wavelength, λ_{max}. At lower temperatures the black-body radiation is mainly in the infrared region of the spectrum. As the temperature increases the maximum of the curve moves to shorter wavelengths. Curves at different temperatures follow the relationship

$$\lambda_{max} T = 2.9 \times 10^3$$

where the wavelength is measured in micrometers. This is known as the *Wien displacement law*. The radiation from a hot black body is greater at every wavelength than the radiation from a cooler black body. The total radiation flux thus increases rapidly with increasing temperature, as described by STEFAN'S LAW.

Stefan's law gives the total energy emitted over all wavelengths per second per unit area of a black body. The energy emitted at a particular wavelength by a black body can be predicted from *Planck's radiation law*. This law was derived by Max Planck from his QUANTUM THEORY, propounded in 1900. If $E(\lambda,T)$ is the energy emitted per unit wavelength interval at wavelength λ, per second, per unit area, into unit solid angle, by a body at thermodynamic temperature T, then

$$E(\lambda,T) = (2\pi hc^2/\lambda^5)[e^{hc/\lambda kT} - 1]^{-1}$$

h is the Planck constant, k the Boltzmann constant, and c the speed of light. Stefan's law and the Wien displacement law can both be derived from Planck's law.

Planck's radiation law describes only the continuous spectrum emitted by a black body. The continuous radiation from a star, as opposed to a black body, does not usually follow Planck's law exactly, although over a broad region of the spectrum the law is a good approximation.

black drop an optical phenomenon seen near the beginning and end of TRANSITS of Venus and Mercury across the Sun's disk. It takes the form of an apparent elongation of the planet's silhouette against the solar surface, with a link being formed between the silhouette and the dark sky beyond the Sun's limb, as seen in photographs and telescopic projections. The effect makes the planet look rather like a teardrop. It appears to be caused by a combination of instability in the Earth's atmosphere (see SEEING) and the resolving power and sensitivity of the observing instrument being used. The black drop effect was a major factor in reducing the accuracy of early attempts to determine the SOLAR PARALLAX by observing transits from different parts of the Earth in the 18th and 19th centuries. During the transit of Venus in 2004, a large number of astronomers failed to notice the black drop effect at all, probably because of technical improvements that have been made in modern telescopes.

black dwarf see WHITE DWARF.

Blackeye galaxy (**M64; NGC 4826**) a nearby galaxy with smooth circular spiral arms and a prominent dark patch near its center due to obscuration by a dense DUST LANE, hence its name. It lies at a distance of 5.4 Mpc in the constellation of COMA BERENICES.

black hole an object so collapsed that its ESCAPE VELOCITY exceeds the speed of light. it becomes a black hole when its radius has shrunk to its SCHWARZSCHILD RADIUS and light can no longer escape. although gravity will make the object shrink beyond this limit, the 'surface' having this critical value of radius – the EVENT HORIZON – marks the boundary inside which all information is trapped. Calculations, however, indicate that space and time (see SPACETIME) become highly distorted inside the event horizon, and that the collapsing object's ultimate fate is to be compressed to an infinitely dense SINGULARITY at the center of the black hole. It has also been shown

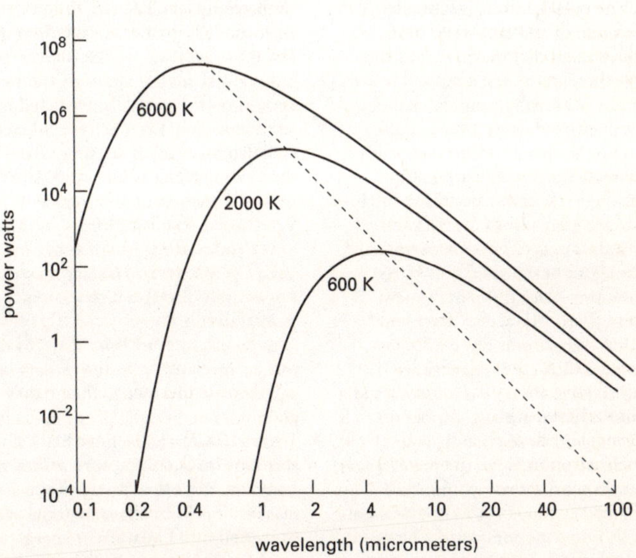

Black-body radiation curves for different temperatures

that the distortion of spacetime just outside the Schwarzschild radius causes the production of particles and radiation that gradually rob the black hole of energy and thus slowly diminish its mass. This *Hawking radiation* (Stephen Hawking, 1974) depends inversely on the black hole's mass, so the most massive black holes 'evaporate' most slowly. A black hole of the Sun's mass would last 10^{66} years.

Once matter (or antimatter) has disappeared into a black hole, only three of its original properties can be ascertained: the total mass, the net electric charge, and the total angular momentum. Because all black holes must have mass, there are four possible types of black hole: a *Schwarzschild black hole* (1916) has no charge and no angular momentum; a *Reissner–Nordstrom black hole* (1918) has charge but no angular momentum; a *Kerr black hole* (1963) has angular momentum but no charge; a *Kerr-Newman black hole* (1965) has charge and angular momentum. (The dates in brackets indicate when the named mathematician(s) solved the equations of general relativity for these particular cases.) In astrophysics the simple Schwarzschild solution is often used, but real black holes are almost certainly rotating and have very little electric charge, so that the Kerr solution should be the most applicable.

The most promising candidates for black holes are massive stars that explode as SUPERNOVAE, leaving a core in excess of 3 solar masses. This core must undergo complete GRAVITATIONAL COLLAPSE because it is above the stable limit for both WHITE DWARFS and NEUTRON STARS. Once formed, a black hole can be detected only by its gravity. Finding black holes only a few kilometers across (the size of the event horizon for a single-star black hole) is exceedingly difficult, but chances are increased if the black hole is a member of a close binary system. If the components of a binary system are close enough, mass transfer can occur between the primary star and its more compact companion (see EQUIPOTENTIAL SURFACES). Matter will not fall directly on to the companion, however, for it has too much angular momentum; instead it forms a rapidly spinning disk – an *accretion disk* – around the compact object. If the latter is a black hole considerable energy can be produced, predominantly at X-ray wavelengths, as matter in the accretion disk loses angular momentum and spirals in. When the accreting matter is unable to cool efficiently, most of the energy generated in the disk due to viscosity is not radiated away, but instead stored in the gas as internal energy and advected inward in an *advection-dominated accretion flow* onto the central object.

Candidates for black holes in a binary system fall into two classes, massive and low-mass black-hole binaries, depending on the mass of the companion star. The first massive black-hole candidate to be identified was the X-RAY BINARY CYGNUS X-1, comprising a 20 solar mass B0 supergiant accompanied by an invisible companion with a mass about 10 times that of the Sun. This massive nonluminous object is probably a black hole emitting X-rays from its accretion disk. Another promising massive black-hole candidate is the X-ray binary LMC X-3 in the Large Magellanic Cloud. While the probable mass of the compact objects in this system is of the order of 10 solar masses, rigorous lower limits are as low as 3 solar masses (possibly even lower), marginally consistent with the maximum theoretically predicted mass of a NEUTRON STAR. Even better evidence for a stellar-mass black hole comes from some of the low-mass black-hole candidates, in particular A0620-00 in Monoceros and V404 Cygni. Rigorous limits on the masses of the compact objects in A0620-00 and V404 Cygni are 3 and 6 solar masses, respectively. See also GAMMA-RAY TRANSIENTS.

Supermassive black holes of 10^6 to 10^9 solar masses probably lie in the centers of some galaxies and give rise to the QUASAR phenomenon and the phenomena of other ACTIVE GALAXIES. If a huge black hole is able to form and to capture sufficient gas and/or stars from its surroundings, the rest-mass energy of infalling material can be converted into radiation or energetic particles. There is now observational evidence to support this hypothesis. the dynamical motion of stars and ionized gas in the cores of nearby galaxies show that they are responding to a strong gravitational field, in excess of that expected from the number of stars accounting for the light at the galaxy center. These motions are thought to be due to the presence of the supermassive black hole (see SEYFERT GALAXY; VIRGO A). Other strong evidence for the presence of supermassive black holes is found from recent observations of an extremely broad iron fluorescence line in the X-rays from several SEYFERT GALAXIES; this line has a very particular shape, revealing its origin in an accretion disk very close to the central black hole.

At the other mass extreme are the more speculative *mini black holes*, weighing only 10^{11} kg and with radii of 10^{-10} meters. These could have formed in the highly turbulent conditions existing after the Big Bang. They create such intense localized gravitational fields that their Hawking radiation makes them explode within the lifetime of the Universe; their final burst of gamma rays and microwaves should be detectable but has not yet been found.

black-widow pulsars a class of binary MILLISECOND PULSARS in which the radiation from the pulsar is destroying ('evaporating') the companion star. The first system, discovered 1988, was PSR 1957+20. The pulsar has a spin period of 0.0016 seconds and the orbital period is 9.2 hours. The mass of the companion has already been reduced to about 0.02 solar masses, and the system is likely to become a single millisecond pulsar in about 20–30 million years. The system shows long radio eclipses lasting for some 10% of the orbital period. This implies that the material that causes the eclipses is outside the Roche lobe of the companion (see EQUIPOTENTIAL SURFACES) and therefore provides direct observational evidence for an 'irradiation-driven' evaporative wind. The pulsar PSR 1744–24A in the globular cluster Terzan 5 provides another example of this phenomenon.

blazars a very small percentage of the QUASAR population that appears to share some of the extreme characteristics of the BL LAC OBJECTS as a consequence of relativistic beaming (see SYNCHROTRON EMISSION). The luminosity of the emission lines stays constant while the CONTINUUM emission varies dramatically by factors as large as a hundred. The quasar is highly polarized and exhibits SUPERLUMINAL motion at radio wavelengths.

blazed grating a DIFFRACTION GRATING consisting of a series of nonsymmetrical grooves, thereby allowing a large proportion of the diffracted radiation to be concentrated into one order on one side of the zero order of the image.

Blazhko effect see RR LYRAE STARS.

blink comparator see COMPARATOR.

BL Lac objects extremely compact violently variable ACTIVE GALAXIES that resemble QUASARS but lack both emission and absorption lines in their spectra. More than two hundred are known, the first to be identified was BL Lacertae, which was mistakenly classified as a variable star in 1928 and later (1968) shown to be the optical counterpart of a peculiar radio source. BL Lac objects are most easily identified from X-ray and radio surveys (most of those known are strong radio sources) but, like quasars, the peak of their emission lies in the infrared.

Light and radio waves from these objects are strongly polarized, indicating intense magnetic fields, and there are rapid variations in both strength and direction. BL Lac objects are also violently variable in luminosity at all wavelengths, sometimes flaring up five magnitudes (a factor of 100) in only a few weeks. This indicates that the size of their energy-producing regions cannot be more than a few light-weeks across. During periods of faint luminosity, weak emission lines may sometimes be observed and a redshift measured but, in general, distance measurements to BL Lac objects have been hampered by their absence of spectral lines. Many BL Lac objects are embedded in a faint 'fuzz' identified as the surrounding galaxy. This contains weak absorption lines, from which it is possible to measure a REDSHIFT. Like other radio-loud active galaxies, BL Lac objects appear to lie in elliptical hosts. They are most populous in the low-redshift Universe, so that their space distribution appears to be very different from other active galaxies such as quasars. It has been proposed that they are mostly active galaxies with relativistic jets pointing along the line of sight. See also RADIO GALAXY.

bloomed lens see COATING OF LENSES.

BLR *abbrev. for* broad-line region. See QUASAR.

BLRG *abbrev. for* broad-line radio galaxy. See RADIO GALAXY.

blue compact dwarf (BCD) galaxy see DWARF GALAXY.

blueshift an overall shift of the spectral lines in a spectrum toward shorter wavelengths as a result of the DOPPLER EFFECT. It is observed in the spectra of celestial objects approaching the Earth. See REDSHIFT.

blue stragglers stars that are frequently found in OPEN and GLOBULAR CLUSTERS and that lie on the extension of the MAIN SEQUENCE beyond the TURNOFF POINT: they are 'blueward' of the turnoff in color-magnitude diagrams (see illustration at globular cluster). Because such stars have main-sequence lifetimes much shorter than the age of the cluster, they should already have evolved away from the main sequence. Their existence has been a long-standing puzzle. In one model, they are stars that have been rejuvenated by MASS TRANSFER from a binary companion. Alternatively, they may represent the result of the merger of two stars after a stellar collision. Recent observations have provided some support for both scenarios. Some blue stragglers are now known to be members of close binaries. In addition, observations with the HST have revealed large numbers of blue stragglers in the cores of several globular clusters, where collisions between stars are significant. See also TIDAL CAPTURE.

BN object *short for* Becklin-Neugebauer object. A pointlike infrared source in the ORION MOLECULAR CLOUD (OMC-1). It is thought to be a young B0 or B1 star, surrounded by a compact H II region and an expanding dust envelope characterized by a strong STELLAR WIND. The infrared luminosity of the dust is about a thousand times the Sun's luminosity at a temperature of about 600 K. The object is still above the MAIN SEQUENCE and evolving toward it, and may represent the earliest phase of stellar evolution that has so far been identified.

Bode's law (Titius–Bode law) a relationship between the distances of the planets from the Sun. Take the sequence 0, 3, 6, 12, 24,..., where each number (except the 3) is twice the previous one, add 4 to each, and divide by 10. The resulting sequence (0.4, 0.7, 1.0, 1.6, 2.8, 5.2,...) is in good agreement with the actual distances in ASTRONOMICAL UNITS (AU) of most planets, provided that the asteroids are included and considered as one entity at a mean distance of 2.8 AU. The law fails to predict the correct distances for Neptune and Pluto. Some astronomers think that the relationship may have some significance with respect to the formation of the Solar System; most consider the sequence purely fortuitous. Named after Johann Bode (1747–1826), who published it in 1772, it was formulated by Johann Titius (1729–96) of Wittenberg in 1766.

Bok globules small dark cool (10 K) clouds of gas and dust seen as near-circular objects against a background of stars or of an H II region; they are named after the American astronomer Bart J. Bok. They are believed to represent a late phase in the contraction of some DENSE CORES when the material has become sufficiently dense to be opaque at optical wavelengths. The main sites for STAR FORMATION are now known to be GIANT MOLECULAR CLOUDS, but Bok globules give rise to some of the Galaxy's lower-mass stars. Most globules have diameters between 0.2 and 0.6 parsecs, and absorb between one and five magnitudes of light. Their mass varies from 20 to 200 solar masses. IRAS and other infrared telescopes have located PROTOSTARS within some Bok globules; BIPOLAR OUTFLOWS from these produce HERBIG–HARO OBJECTS seen at the globule's edge.

bolide a brilliant METEOR that appears to explode, i.e. a detonating FIREBALL. The brighter ones are caused by ablating METEORITES that subsequently fall to Earth. About 5000 bolides occur in the Earth's atmosphere each year.

bolometer a radiation-sensing instrument that is used in astronomy to measure the total energy flux of radiation entering the Earth's atmosphere, and is especially useful in the infrared and microwave regions of the spectrum. It is essentially a small resistive element capable of absorbing electromagnetic radiation. The resulting temperature rise is a measure of the power absorbed. There is a large variety of bolometers, including semiconductor and supercooled devices; the semiconductor ones are normally of doped silicon or germanium. See also INFRARED DETECTORS.

bolometric correction (BC) see MAGNITUDE.

bolometric luminosity see LUMINOSITY.

bolometric magnitude see MAGNITUDE.

Bolshoi Altazimuth Telescope see ZELENCHUKSKAYA OBSERVATORY.

Boltzmann constant symbol: k. A constant given by the ratio of the molar gas constant to the Avogadro constant and equal to $1.380\,658 \times 10^{-23}$ joules per kelvin. It is the constant by which the mean kinetic energy of a gas particle can be related to its thermodynamic temperature.

Boltzmann equation an equation derived by the Austrian physicist Ludwig Boltzmann in the 1870s that shows how the distribution of molecules, atoms, or ions in their various ENERGY LEVELS depends on the temperature of the system; the system is in thermal equilibrium, with EXCITATION balanced by de-excitation. The equation gives the ratio of the number density (number per unit volume) of molecules, atoms, or ions, N_2, in one energy level to the number density, N_1, in another lower energy level as

$$N_2/N_1 = (g_2/g_1)e^{-E/kT}$$

g_1 and g_2 are the degeneracies of the two levels, i.e. the multiplicity of energy levels with the same energy, E is the energy required to excite the molecule, atom, or ion from the lower to the higher energy level, k is the Boltzmann constant, and T is the thermodynamic temperature. Thus as T increases a greater number of species will become excited.

The Boltzmann equation together with the SAHA IONIZATION EQUATION are widely used to interpret the absorption and emission spectra of stars and to determine stellar temperatures and densities.

Bond albedo see ALBEDO.

Bond–Lassell see HYPERION.

Bonner Durchmusterung (BD) the Bonn Survey, a general star catalog prepared under the direction of the Prussian astronomer Friedrich Argelander and published in Bonn 1859–62. The original catalog contained 324 189 stars – i.e. all those visible in the three-inch (76.2-centimeter) Bonn refractor – lying between DECLINATIONS of +90° and –2°. The limiting magnitude was about 9.5. Accompanying star charts were published in 1863. It was extended by Eduard Schönfeld in 1886 to a declination of –23° and then included 457 857 stars. The epoch for the whole catalog was 1855.0.

A cataloged star is identified by the prefix BD and a number giving its declination zone (each 1° wide), followed by its number (in order of right ascension) within that zone, as in BD +52 1638.

Cataloging was extended to the south polar regions through an analogous work, *The Córdoba Durchmusterung* (*CD*), compiled at the Córdoba Observatory, Argentina, and finally completed in 1930. This catalog contains about 614 000 stars, brighter than 10th magnitude, from declinations –23° to –90° for the epoch 1875.0. Computerized versions of the BD and CD are now available. See also CAPE PHOTOGRAPHIC DURCHMUSTERUNG.

Bonn Telescope see EFFELSBERG TELESCOPE.

Boötes (Herdsman) a large constellation in the northern hemisphere near Ursa Major. The brightest stars are ARCTURUS and the 2nd-magnitude yellow-blue visual binary Epsilon (ε) Boötis, one of several double stars. The area also contains one of the most distant RADIO GALAXIES, 3C–295. A giant planet 1.4 times as massive as Jupiter is thought to orbit the 4th-magnitude yellow subgiant Tau (τ) Boötis (spectral type: F6 IV; distance: 16 pc). Abbrev.: Boo; genitive form: Boötis; approx. position: RA 14.5h, dec +30°; area: 907 sq deg.

Boötes void see LARGE-SCALE STRUCTURE.

bosons a class of ELEMENTARY PARTICLES with integer values (positive, negative, or zero) of SPIN; the PHOTON is an example. More than one boson can exist with an identical set of quantum numbers (numbers assigned to the various quantities that describe a particle). See also FERMIONS; FUNDAMENTAL FORCES.

Boss General Catalog a whole-sky star catalog listing the positions and PROPER MOTIONS of 33 342 stars for the epoch 1950.0, down to a limiting magnitude of 7. It was prepared initially by the American astronomer Lewis Boss, with a preliminary publication in 1910, and was completed by his son Benjamin Boss in 1937.

bottom-up galaxy formation see DARK MATTER.

bound-free absorption a process of absorption that occurs when an electron bound to an atom or ion is given sufficient energy by an absorbed photon of radiation to free itself from the atom. If however the photon energy can only excite the electron to a higher energy level so that it remains bound to the atom, *bound-bound absorption* takes place. See also OPACITY.

bow shock see INTERPLANETARY MEDIUM; MAGNETOSPHERE.

BPM 37093 a relatively close white dwarf star located in the constellation Centaurus. It consists of a thin hydrogen atmosphere overlying a Moon-sized carbon core in which the atoms are believed to have been pushed so close together by gravitational pressure that they have stripped each other's electrons from around their positively charged nuclei and the mutual repulsion between the nuclei has forced them into a crystalline lattice structure. In February 2004 scientists at the Harvard-Smithsonian Center for Astrophysics announced that their recent investigations of the star had confirmed BPM 37093 to be a crystalline white dwarf, the first such object to be detected, The detection gave tangible proof to a theory advanced independently by Kirzhnitz (1960), Abrikosov (1960), and Salpeter (1961) that cool white dwarfs might crystallize. BPM 37093 is a pulsating star, and measurements of the pulsations indicate that the interior of the white dwarf is indeed solid crystalline carbon. Since BPM 37093 is effectively a vast cosmic diamond, it has been unofficially nicknamed 'Lucy', in recollection of the Beatles' song 'Lucy in the sky with diamonds'. m_v: 13; spectral type: DA V; diameter: about 4000 km; mass: 1.14 times solar mass; distance: 15.3 pc.

Bp stars the hottest types of AP STARS.

Brackett series see HYDROGEN SPECTRUM.

braking index a dimensionless number, *n*, characterizing the spin-down rate of a PULSAR, defined so that the rate of change of rotation frequency is proportional to frequency to the power *n*. A pulsar slowed by the loss of electromagnetic energy into the vacuum would have a braking index of three.

Brans–Dicke theory a relativistic theory of gravitation put forward in the 1960s by Carl Brans and Robert Dicke as a variant of Einstein's general theory of RELATIVITY. It is considered by many astronomers to be the most serious alternative to general relativity. It is a scalar-tensor theory, i.e. a theory in which the gravitational force on an object is due partly to the interaction with a scalar field and partly to a tensor interaction. Newton's gravitational constant is replaced by a slowly varying scalar field. The effect is to allow the strength of gravity to decrease with time. In the limit that this variation is zero, the various Brans–Dicke theories of gravitation that now exist reduce to Einstein's general relativity. Current observations limit the variation of Newton's gravitational constant to be less than one part in 10^{10} per year. This means that for local applications of a noncosmological nature Brans–Dicke theory is indistinguishable from general relativity.

bremsstrahlung (literally: 'braking radiation') Electromagnetic radiation arising from the rapid deceleration of electrons in the vicinity of an atom or ion. It has a continuous spectrum. See SYNCHROTRON EMISSION; THERMAL EMISSION.

bridge see RADIO-SOURCE STRUCTURE.

brightest stars the stars with the greatest apparent visual MAGNITUDE; there are about 9500 brighter than magnitude 6.5. Many are very much more luminous than the Sun and others appear bright because of their proximity. The most luminous stars lie in the supergiant and giant regions of the HERTZSPRUNG–RUSSELL DIAGRAM. See Table 6, Appendix.

bright nebula an EMISSION NEBULA or REFLECTION NEBULA as opposed to a DARK NEBULA. See also NEBULA.

brightness the intensity of light or other radiation emitted from – absolute or intrinsic brightness – or received from – apparent brightness – a celestial body, the latter decreasing as the distance from the body increases. Intrinsic brightness is directly related to the LUMINOSITY of a body in a given spectral region. Apparent brightness is considered in terms of apparent MAGNITUDE: a star one magnitude less than another is about 2.5 times brighter. If two stars belong to the MAIN SEQUENCE then the brighter star is the hotter of the two. See also RADIO BRIGHTNESS.

brightness temperature in radio astronomy, a source of surface brightness (i.e., FLUX DENSITY per unit solid angle) B has a brightness temperature of $T_B = B\lambda^2/(2k)$, where λ is the observing wavelength and k is the BOLTZMANN CONSTANT. If the source of that radiation is a BLACK BODY, and the observing wavelength sufficiently long, the brightness temperature will equal the temperature of the black body. In the case of an interstellar cloud, it may equal the physical temperature of the cloud if the radiation is by THERMAL EMISSION and the cloud is optically thick (see OPTICAL DEPTH). If the cloud is optically thin, the brightness temperature is reduced.

Sources that radiate by NONTHERMAL EMISSION can have very high brightness temperatures (>10^9 K). See also ANTENNA TEMPERATURE.

broad absorption line (BAL) quasar see QUASAR.

broad-line radio galaxy (BLRG) see RADIO GALAXY.

broad-line region (BLR) see QUASAR.

Brooks 2 see JUPITER'S COMET FAMILY.

brown dwarf a theoretical 'star' formed by the contraction of a lump of gas with a mass too small for nuclear reactions to begin in the core. This limit on STELLAR MASS is uncertain but is thought to be about 0.08 solar masses. An object below this limit will shine for only 100 million years as a result of gravitational contraction on the HAYASHI TRACK, and then cool off. Its interior consists of DEGENERATE MATTER. Some of the least luminous red DWARF STARS may actually be brown dwarfs. The first brown dwarf, named Gliese 229B, was unambiguously identified in 1995 with the Palomor 60-inch telescope. It orbits the red-dwarf star Gliese 229A. The presence of methane lines in its spectrum is believed to be a unique signature of a brown dwarf, which can be used to distinguish it from a very low-mass star. Since 1995 numerous other brown-dwarf candidates have been found.

BS prefix used to designate a star as listed in the *Bright Star Catalog*, the unofficial name for the *Yale Catalog of Bright Stars* (*YBS*). This catalog developed from the *Harvard Revised Photometry*, first published 1908 in *Harvard Annals*, Vol. 50, and also known as the *HR* Catalog. The BS Catalog took over the 9110 objects contained in the HR Catalog, preserving the HR numbering. Early editions of the BS Catalog listed 14 objects that were not stars. The latest (5th) edition (by D. Hoffleit and W.H. Warren Jr), published 1991, thus contains data on 9096 stars to a limiting magnitude of 6.5 for the epoch 2000.0. The BS Catalog is available in computerized form.

B stars stars of SPECTRAL TYPE B that are massive hot blue stars with a surface temperature (T_{eff}) of about 10 000 to 28 000 kelvin for main-sequence stars, and up to 30 000 kelvin for supergiants. Absorption lines of neutral helium (He I) dominate the spectrum, reaching maximum intensity for B2 stars. Balmer lines of hydrogen strengthen from B0 to B9; lines of ionized magnesium and silicon are also present. A few B stars – the BE STARS – also have emission lines from a circumstellar shell of gas. B0, B1, and B2 stars are found in OB ASSOCIATIONS in the spiral arms of galaxies. Spica, Rigel, Bellatrix, and Alpha Crucis are B stars.

B-type asteroids see C-TYPE ASTEROIDS.

bubble 1 *another name for* void. See LARGE-SCALE STRUCTURE.
2 see INTERSTELLAR BUBBLE.

bulge see GALAXIES; GALAXY.

burning conversion of one element to another by NUCLEAR FUSION, such as hydrogen to helium or helium to carbon.

burst a brief flux of intense radiation with a sudden onset and rapid decay, as is observed from JUPITER and from the Sun at radio wavelengths. Solar radio bursts are associated with FLARES. See also GAMMA-RAY BURSTS; X-RAY BURST SOURCES.

burst source (burster) see GAMMA-RAY BURSTS; X-RAY BURST SOURCES.

Butcher–Oemler effect see CLUSTERS OF GALAXIES.

Butler matrix an electronic phasing device by which the signals from 2^n separate elements of an ARRAY are combined with their correct relative PHASES to produce 2^n outputs, each of which corresponds to a main lobe (see ANTENNA) pointing in a different direction.

butterfly diagram see SUNSPOT CYCLE.

B-V see COLOR INDEX.

Bw stars blue stars that, unlike normal B STARS, have only weak helium lines.

Cc

Caelum (**Chisel**) a small inconspicuous constellation in the southern hemisphere near Orion, the brightest stars being of 4th magnitude. Abbrev.: Cae; genitive form: Caeli; approx. position: RA 4.5h, dec –40°; area: 125 sq deg.

Calar Alto mountain site in Spain of the GERMAN–SPANISH ASTRONOMICAL CENTER.

calendar any of various present-day, past, or proposed systems for the reckoning of time over extended periods: days are grouped into various periods that are suitable for regulating civil life, fixing religious observances, and meeting scientific needs. All calendars are based either on the motion of the Sun (solar calendar), or of the Moon (lunar calendar), or both (lunisolar calendar) so that the length of the year corresponds approximately to either the TROPICAL (SOLAR) YEAR or the LUNAR YEAR. Their complexity results primarily from the incommensurability of the natural periods of DAY, MONTH, and YEAR: the month is not a simple fraction of the year and the day is not a simple fraction of the month or the year. Present-day calendars include the GREGORIAN CALENDAR, which is in use throughout most of the world, and the Moslem, Jewish, and Chinese calendars.

calendar year the interval of time that is the basis of a CALENDAR. The GREGORIAN CALENDAR year contains an average of 365.2425 days.

Caliban see URANUS'S SATELLITES.

calibration a procedure carried out on a measuring instrument, such as a RADIO TELESCOPE, by means of which the magnitude of its response is determined as a function of the magnitude of the input signal. The calibration of a radio telescope provides an absolute scale of the output deflection against ANTENNA TEMPERATURE.

California nebula (**NGC 1499**) an emission nebula – an H II region – that lies in the constellation Perseus and is ionized by the star Xi (ξ) Persei.

Callisto the second largest of the four giant GALILEAN SATELLITES of Jupiter, with a radius of 2400 km and a density of 1.86 g cm^{-3}. It is the faintest of the Galileans, having an albedo of 0.2. It is the most heavily cratered object so far discovered in the Solar System, exhibiting a number of ray systems, i.e. craters from which bright streaks radiate. Some major systems of concentric ring mountains are prominent, particularly in the neighborhood of the huge *Valhalla Basin*, which is located slightly north of the equator. The basin is a bright circular region 600 km in diameter and is surrounded by concentric rings 50–200 km apart; the outermost ring is 3000 km across. This basin is comparable with ORIENTALE BASIN on the Moon, the Caloris Basin on MERCURY, and HELLAS PLANITIA on Mars. A second huge basin on Callisto, *Asgard Basin*, has a total diameter of 1600 km. Prior to the Galileo mission, Callisto was thought to have a thick crust of ice and rock extending to a depth of 200 to 300 km, beneath which there was believed to be a mantle of 1000 km of convecting water or soft ice. But preliminary analysis of the Galileo data has suggested that Callisto's internal structure is relatively undifferentiated, although the proportion of rock to ice may increase toward the center. Callisto, the outermost of the Galilean satellites, is beyond the major charged particle environment of Jupiter. It appears to be geologically inactive, its surface cratering being due to innumerable impacts during the early history of the Solar System. Scientists using the HUBBLE SPACE TELESCOPE have detected a tenuous oxygen atmosphere on Callisto, probably caused by the interaction between charged solar particles and water molecules in the satellite's icy crust. See also JUPITER's SATELLITES; Table 2, Appendix.

Caloris Basin see MERCURY.

Caltech Submillimeter Observatory (CSO) a 10.4-meter diameter dish situated near the summit of MAUNA KEA in Hawaii and run by the California Institute of Technology; it began operations in 1988. It is a CASSEGRAIN TELESCOPE, housed inside a dome with shutter doors, designed to operate at frequencies up to 900 GHz (a wavelength of about 330 micrometers). When connected to the JCMT with optical fibers, it can be used for submillimeter-wave interferometry. See also SUBMILLIMETER ASTRONOMY.

Calypso a small irregularly shaped satellite of Saturn, discovered in 1980. It is a COORBITAL SATELLITE with TELESTO and TETHYS. See Table 2, Appendix.

Camelopardalis (Giraffe) a large inconspicuous constellation in the northern hemisphere near Ursa Major, its brightest stars being of 4th magnitude. It contains the prototype of the Z Camelopardalis DWARF NOVAE stars. Abbrev.: Cam; genitive form: Camelopardalis; approx. position: RA 6h, dec +70°; area: 757 sq deg.

Canada–France–Hawaii Telescope (CFHT) a 3.6-meter telescope at the MAUNA KEA Observatory, Hawaii, that began regular operations in 1980 and is used for optical and infrared studies, mainly by Canadian and French observers and the University of Hawaii. It has a CER-VIT primary mirror with Cassegrain (f/8), coudé (f/20), and prime (f/3.8) foci, and an equatorial mounting.

canals linear markings on MARS that are now known to be illusory. They were first reported in 1877 by the Italian astronomer Giovanni Schiaparelli, who described them as 'canali' (channels). The mistranslation 'canals' gained popular currency, and the markings were later charted by many observers, most notably by the US astronomer Percival Lowell, who advocated that they were irrigation ditches dug by Martians to distribute their planet's scarce water resources. MARINER and VIKING spacecraft observations showed that the canals do not exist.

Cancer (Crab) an inconspicuous zodiac constellation in the northern hemisphere between Gemini and Leo, its brightest stars being of 3rd and 4th magnitude. There are many double and variable stars, including the multiple star Zeta (ζ) Cancri. The area also contains the open clusters PRAESEPE and the fainter M67 (NGC 2682) and the strong radio source NGC 2623. Abbrev.: Cnc; genitive form: Cancri; approx. position: RA 9h, dec +20°; area: 506 sq deg.

Canes Venatici (Hunting Dogs) an inconspicuous constellation in the northern hemisphere near Ursa Major, the brightest star being the 3rd-magnitude binary COR CAROLI. It contains the bright globular cluster M3 (NGC 5272) and the WHIRLPOOL GALAXY, M5l (NGC 4194–5). The star Y Canum Venaticorum is a variable star whose brightness ranges between magnitude 5.2 and 6.6 over 157 days. Abbrev.: CVn; genitive form: Canum Venaticorum; approx. position: RA 13h, dec +40°; area: 465 sq deg.

Canis Major (Great Dog) a conspicuous constellation in the southern hemisphere, lying partly in the Milky Way. The brightest stars are SIRIUS (α), the second brightest star in the sky (after the Sun) and one of the nearest stars to our Solar System; the 1st-magnitude giant ADHARA (ε); and the giant Mirzam (β) and supergiant Wezen (δ), both close to 2nd magnitude and very remote and luminous. The area contains the open cluster M41 (NGC 2287). Another cluster, NGC 2362, apparently centered on Tau (τ) Canis Majoris, makes an interesting telescopic sight. Abbrev.: CMa; genitive form: Canis Majoris; approx. position: RA 7h, dec −20°; area: 380 sq deg.

Canis Minor (Little Dog) a small constellation in the northern hemisphere near Orion, lying partly in the Milky Way. The brightest star is the visual binary PROCYON. Abbrev.: CMi; genitive form:

Canis Minoris; approx. position: RA 7.5h, dec +5°; area: 183 sq deg.

cannibalism 1 (**galactic cannibalism**) the swallowing of one galaxy by a larger galaxy. It occurs especially in the center of a CLUSTER OF GALAXIES, where successive acts of cannibalism in the early history of the cluster have probably contributed to the size of cD galaxies, the most massive galaxies known.
2 (**stellar cannibalism**) the process by which a GIANT STAR in a close binary system can swallow its companion.
See COMMON ENVELOPE STAR.

Canopus (**α Car**) a conspicuous and luminous white giant that is the brightest star in the constellation Carina and the third-brightest star in the sky after the Sun and Sirius. m_v: –0.72; M_v: –2.5; spectral type: A9 II; distance: 23 pc.

canyon see MARS, SURFACE FEATURES; VALLEY, LUNAR.

Cape Canaveral see KENNEDY SPACE CENTER.

Capella (**α Aur**) a conspicuous yellow giant that is the brightest star in the constellation Auriga. It is a visual binary (period 104 days), of which the components can only be resolved in the largest telescopes. The star has a high lithium content. m_v: 0.08; M_v: –0.4; spectral type: G6 III, G2 III; distance: 12.5 pc.

Cape Photographic Durchmusterung (**CPD**) a general star catalog of the southern sky compiled by J.C. Kapteyn from photographic plates produced by David Gill in Cape Town. It was published 1896–1900. It lists positions and MAGNITUDES of some 455 000 stars, brighter than 10th magnitude, from declinations –19° to –90°. A computerized version is now available.

Caph see CASSIOPEIA.

Capricornids a minor METEOR SHOWER, radiant: RA 315°, dec –15°, that maximizes on July 25. Another minor shower, the *Alpha Capricornids*, radiant: RA 309°, dec –10°, maximizes on Aug. 1.

Capricornus (**Sea Goat**) a zodiac constellation in the southern hemisphere near Sagittarius, the brightest stars being of 3rd magnitude. Alpha (α) Capricorni is a naked-eye double star (magnitudes 3.6, 4.2); both components are multiple stars. The area contains the globular cluster M30 (NGC 7099). Abbrev.: Cap; genitive form: Capricorni; approx. position: RA 21h, dec –20°; area: 414 sq deg.

captured rotation see SYNCHRONOUS ROTATION.

capture theory see ENCOUNTER THEORIES; MOON.

carbonaceous chondrite an uncommon class of METEORITES but very important because of their mineralogical and chemical composition, especially as regards the presence of hydrated minerals and organic (carbon) compounds. They are very easily crumbled and contain water-soluble compounds and must therefore be collected soon after they fall. Although all meteorites were formed very early in the Solar System's history, carbonaceous chondrites are possibly the most primitive form of matter in the Solar System. See also ASTEROIDS; CHONDRITE.

carbon cycle (**Bethe–Weizsächer cycle**) a chain of NUCLEAR FUSION reactions by which energy may be generated in stars. The overall effect of the cycle is the transformation of hydrogen nuclei into helium nuclei with emission of gamma-ray photons (γ), positrons (e^+), and neutrinos (ν). The major sequence of reactions is as follows:

$$^{12}C + {}^{1}H \rightarrow {}^{13}N + \gamma$$
$$^{13}N \rightarrow {}^{13}C + e^+ + \nu$$
$$^{1}H + {}^{13}C \rightarrow {}^{14}N + \gamma$$
$$^{1}H + {}^{14}N \rightarrow {}^{15}O + \gamma$$
$$^{15}O \rightarrow {}^{15}N + e^+ + \nu$$
$$^{1}H + {}^{15}N \rightarrow {}^{12}C + {}^{4}He$$

The carbon nucleus, ^{12}C, reappears at the end of the cycle and can be regarded as a catalyst for the reaction:

$$4\,{}^{1}H \rightarrow {}^{4}He + 2e^+ + 2\nu + 3\gamma$$

Because nitrogen (N) and oxygen (O) intermediates are involved, the cycle is often termed the *carbon-nitrogen-oxygen cycle* or *CNO cycle*.

The carbon cycle is very strongly temperature dependent and becomes the dominant energy-producing mechanism at core temperatures exceeding about 20 million K. It is therefore thought to be the major source of energy in hot massive stars of spectral types O, B, and A. The carbon cycle was proposed by Hans Bethe and independently by Carl von Weizsächer in

1938. See also PROTON-PROTON CHAIN REACTION.

carbon monoxide a molecule, CO, consisting of an atom of oxygen bound to a carbon atom. It is commonly found in GIANT MOLECULAR CLOUDS, where there is one CO molecule to about 10 000 hydrogen molecules. Collisions with hydrogen and other molecules easily excite the CO molecules and cause them to emit characteristic radio waves at wavelengths that are integer submultiples of 2.6 mm. Carbon monoxide is thus used in radio astronomy as the best tracer of molecular gas over wide areas: the molecular hydrogen in the cool clouds has no emission at radio wavelengths. The CO emission lines are analyzed to determine the density, velocity, and temperature of the molecules in the clouds.

carbon–nitrogen–oxygen cycle see CARBON CYCLE.

carbon stars (**C stars**) RED GIANT stars of low temperature that have an over-abundance of carbon relative to oxygen in their surface layers. In cool stars carbon and oxygen atoms combine to form stable carbon monoxide, and in carbon stars the excess carbon can then form other molecules. Their spectra therefore show strong bands of carbon compounds, including C_2, CN, and CH. All carbon stars undergo MASS LOSS, enriching the interstellar medium with considerable carbon, some nitrogen and oxygen, and also S-PROCESS elements. In the earlier Harvard classification (see SPECTRAL TYPES) carbon stars were divided into *R stars* and *N stars*: N stars are the 'classical' carbon stars, discovered spectroscopically by Angelo Secchi (1868). They are very cool and very luminous and many have been discovered in the Magellanic Clouds and other galaxies. They are observed to be losing mass rapidly and are much further evolved than the hotter less luminous R stars. The R stars are enriched in the isotopes ^{13}C and ^{14}N, but unlike most N stars, show no enhancement in s-process elements. See also R CORONAE BOREALIS STARS; S STARS.

cardinal points the four principal points on the HORIZON (see illustration). The *north*

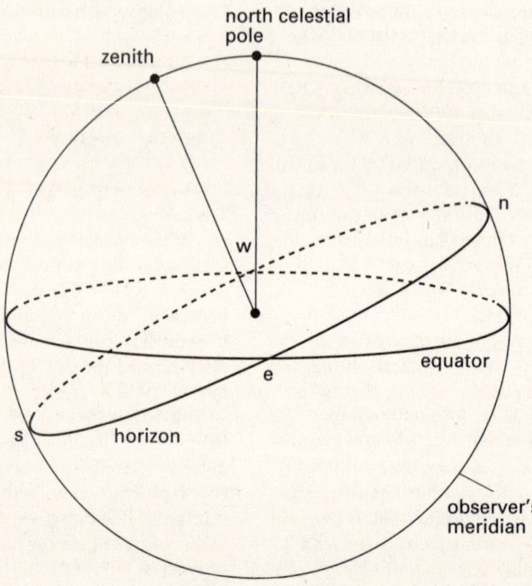

Cardinal points

point (n) lies at the intersection of the horizon with the celestial MERIDIAN nearest the north CELESTIAL POLE; the *south point* (s), diametrically opposite, is the equivalent intersection point closest to the south celestial pole. The *east point* (e) and *west point* (w) lie at the intersections of the horizon with the CELESTIAL EQUATOR, the east point being 90° and the west point 270° clockwise from the north point.

Carina (**Keel**) a constellation in the southern hemisphere near Crux. It was once part of the constellation ARGO. The brightest stars are the bright white giant CANOPUS (α) and some 1st- and 2nd-magnitude stars. The irregular variable star Eta (η) Carinae is associated with extensive nebulosity (see ETA CARINAE; ETA CARINAE NEBULA). The area also contains two open clusters: the 2nd-magnitude IC 2602, centered on Theta (θ) Carinae, and the brilliant NGC 3532, located just west of Eta Carinae; and the large globular cluster NGC 2808. Abbrev.: Car; genitive form: Carinae; approx. position: RA 9h, dec –60°; area: 494 sq deg.

Carina arm see GALAXY.

Carina system a dwarf elliptical galaxy that is a member of the LOCAL GROUP.

Carme a small satellite of Jupiter, discovered in 1938 by Seth Nicholson. See JUPITER'S SATELLITES; Table 2, Appendix.

Carpathians see table at MOUNTAINS, LUNAR.

Carrington rotation number a sequential number, introduced by R.C. Carrington, that identifies each solar rotation. Its starting date is 1853 November 9.489 (rotation 1). The number is based on the value of 27.2753 mean solar days that Carrington obtained for the mean synodic rotation period of the Sun from observations of sunspots. This value is equivalent to the Sun having a mean sidereal rotation period of 25.380 mean solar days.

Carte du Ciel a whole-sky photographic atlas proposed in Paris in 1887 and planned to include stars of magnitude 14 or brighter. This ambitious scheme involved 18 observatories in photographing areas of the sky only 2° square using specially designed 33-cm refracting telescopes. The survey has never been fully completed. Technical advances have since made it possible to photograph much greater areas with very much less work. The associated *Astrographic Catalog*, listing the positions of stars down to 12th magnitude, was essentially complete by 1958. The United States Naval Observatory (USNO) in co-operation with other institutions completed the process of converting the printed Astrographic Catalog into computerized format by the mid-1990s, updating the star positions to epoch 2000.0 in accordance with the HIPPARCOS Catalog. The resulting document, *AC 2000*, was released on CD-ROM in 1997. In 2001, following its collaboration with the University of Copenhagen Observatory in Denmark, on the Tycho-2 catalog, which uses AC 2000 data for many of its proper motions, the USNO issued a revised version of AC 2000, called *AC 2000.2*. This revision is also available on CD-ROM. AC 2000.2 is a whole-sky catalog listing more than 4.6 million stars.

Cartwheel galaxy a remnant of a large galaxy that has been distorted by a head-on collision with a small neighbor into a shape resembling a cartwheel. The 'hub' and 'spokes' of the wheel are formed by the old stars of the original galaxy and are surrounded by a 'rim' of young blue stars and ionized gas triggered by a rippling outward shock wave.

cascade see COSMIC RAYS.

Cassegrain configuration one of the configurations in which a large reflecting telescope can be used. A small secondary mirror with a convex hyperboloid shape intercepts the beam of radiation before it reaches the prime focus of the PRIMARY MIRROR (see illustration). The secondary reflects the beam back down the tube, through a central hole in the primary mirror, to a focal point just behind it. This is the *Cassegrain focus*. It is more accessible than the prime focus and is incorporated into many reflecting telescopes, notably the SCHMIDT TELESCOPE AND THE MAKSUTOV TELESCOPE.

Cassegrain focus see CASSEGRAIN CONFIGURATION.

Cassegrain telescope a compound REFLECTING TELESCOPE designed, according to some sources, by a French sculptor, Sieur

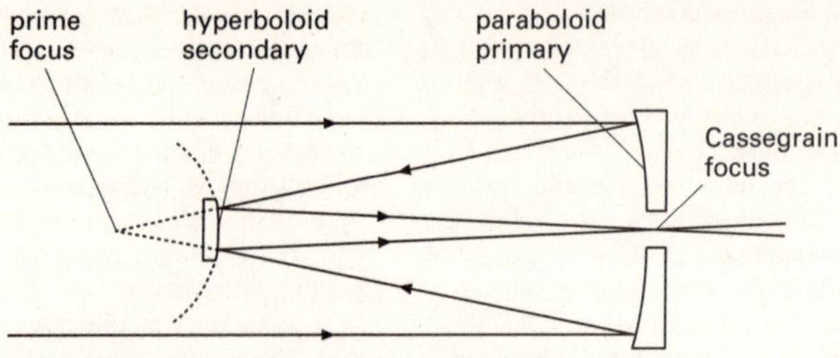

Cassegrain configuration

Guillaume Cassegrain, in 1672. Others attribute its invention to a 17th-century astronomer known to us only as N. Cassegrain. It is similar to the GREGORIAN TELESCOPE but has a secondary mirror with a convex hyperboloid shape mounted inside the focal plane of the primary mirror. The telescope has a small field, limited mainly by COMA, but is compact, portable, and easily mounted and thus very popular. Most large modern reflectors include this facility. See CASSEGRAIN CONFIGURATION; CATADIOPTRIC TELESCOPE; RITCHEY–CHRÉTIEN OPTICS; SCHMIDT TELESCOPE.

Cassini (**Cassini/Huygens**) a joint NASA/ESA mission to the Saturnian system, launched by a Titan IVB/Centaur rocket on Oct. 15 1997. It arrived at Saturn in 2004 and, after passing through a gap in the planet's complex ring system, entered orbit on June 30 of that year. The US *Cassini* probe carried 12 experiments, and on a 4-year tour orbiting Saturn was set to study the planet itself – atmosphere, rings, and magnetosphere – and some of its moons – TITAN and the icy satellites, such as Tethys, Iapetus, Dione, and Phoebe.

Cassini used the gravitational effects of both Venus and the Earth to catapult itself across interplanetary space and reduce its journey time to Saturn to a mere seven years. It completed a flyby of the asteroid (2685) Masursky in January 2000 and swung by Jupiter in December 2000, picking up even more momentum in the process. During its Jupiter flyby, it teamed up briefly with NASA's GALILEO probe in a joint investigation of the Jovian system. Cassini was scheduled to make 23 flybys of Saturn.

ESA's *Huygens* probe, carried aboard the Cassini spacecraft, was detached Dec. 24 2004 and landed on Titan Jan. 14 2005, after plunging into its dense atmosphere. During its parachute-controlled descent to the surface, which lasted about 2½ hours, and after touchdown, Huygens sent back a stream of data on the physics and chemistry of the satellite, including both pictures and sound. It transmitted from Titan's surface for about 70 minutes before its batteries ran out, and despite a computer malfunction aboard Cassini, which lost half the expected number of photographs, Huygens sent back via its mother ship about 350 pictures and a wealth of sensor readings. Ground-based radio telescopes also picked up some of Huygens' transmissions and rescued some science data that might have otherwise been lost. Preliminary analysis of the Huygens data appeared to confirm the view that Titan resembles the early Earth. Its atmosphere consists mostly of nitrogen, but concentrations of simple hydrocarbons such as methane exist near the surface. Evidence was found of liquid methane falling as 'rain' and penetrating just below the surfaces. At the Huygens landing site, the surface seemed to consist of a thin crust overlying a sandlike hydrocarbon soil; chunks of dirty water ice lay strewn nearby. High ridges were apparently cut by 'river channels' draining down to lower terrain or even to a 'lake' of liquid hydrocarbons.

Cassini Division see SATURN'S RINGS.

Cassini/Huygens see CASSINI.

Cassini Regio see IAPETUS.

Cassiopeia a conspicuous constellation in the northern hemisphere, lying partly in the Milky Way. The five brightest stars form a W-shape, which includes SCHEDAR (α), the blue-white visual binary *Cih* (γ), which is an irregular variable and an X-ray source, and the cream-colored *Caph* (β), all of 2nd magnitude. Eta, close to Schedar, is a 3rd-magnitude binary star. The area contains some fine open clusters (M52 [NGC 7654], M103 [NGC 581], NGC 457 and NGC 663) and globular clusters and the remnants of two recent supernovae – TYCHO'S STAR and the radio source CASSIOPEIA A. Abbrev.: Cas; genitive form: Cassiopeiae; approx. position: RA 1h, dec +60°; area: 598 sq deg.

Cassiopeia A an intense RADIO SOURCE 2.8 kiloparsecs distant in the constellation Cassiopeia. It has the largest FLUX DENSITY at low frequencies of all the discrete radio sources (apart from the Sun), the value being about 8200 JANSKY at 178 megahertz, and a SPECTRAL INDEX of –0.77. The flux drops by about 1% per year. It is a SUPERNOVA REMNANT – probably of a supernova explosion (unrecorded) of a massive (~50 $M_{\odot}$) star in the late 17th century – and has a ringlike structure about four arc minutes in diameter. The radio radiation is by SYNCHROTRON EMISSION and the radio shell is expanding at 2300 km s^{-1}. It is also an extended source of soft X-rays.

Castor (α Gem) a white star that is the second-brightest in the constellation Gemini. It is a visual triple star, the two brighter components having an orbital period of about 470 years; the third component, a flare star, is located some distance away. All three are spectroscopic binaries. m_v: 1.9 (A), 2.9 (B), 1.57 (AB); M_v: 0.5 (AB); spectral type: A1 V (A), A2 V (B); distance: 15 pc.

cat *abbrev. for* Cosmic Anisotropy Telescope.

cataclysmic variable (eruptive variable) a close BINARY-STAR system where one member is a WHITE DWARF, and MASS TRANSFER on to the latter causes sudden large and unpredictable changes in brightness. The main classes of cataclysmic variable are classical NOVAE, RECURRENT NOVAE, DWARF NOVAE, and SYMBIOTIC STARS. The outbursts of cataclysmic variables are also detected at ultraviolet and X-ray wavelengths; their X-ray output is however much less than that of X-RAY TRANSIENTS, which are similar systems where the compact star is a neutron star rather than a white dwarf.

It is generally believed that the progenitors of cataclysmic variables are wide binaries with periods of several months to several years. When the primary evolves and fills its Roche lobe as a giant, mass is lost from it (see EQUIPOTENTIAL SURFACES); this mass forms a COMMON ENVELOPE surrounding the core of the giant (a WHITE DWARF) and the companion. Due to frictional drag, the orbit of the immersed binary shrinks until the envelope is ejected forming a bright PLANETARY NEBULA and a short-period *precataclysmic binary*.

The distribution of orbital periods of cataclysmic variables displays a very pronounced gap between 2 and 3 hours, known as the *period gap*. It is widely believed that the gap is caused by the temporary cessation of mass transfer when the orbital period has decreased to three hours (possibly related to changes in the magnetic field of the mass-losing star when its interior becomes fully CONVECTIVE) so that the system has no longer the appearance of a cataclysmic variable.

catadioptric telescope a telescope that uses both refraction and reflection to form the image at the prime focus. By introducing a full-aperture CORRECTING PLATE in front of the primary mirror, the telescope designer can correct many ABERRATIONS over an exceptionally wide field of view, in a way that combines the best features of both REFRACTING and REFLECTING TELESCOPES. See SCHMIDT TELESCOPE; MAKSUTOV TELESCOPE.

catalog equinox the intersection of the HOUR CIRCLE of zero right ascension of a star catalog with the celestial equator. It is thus the origin of right ascension of the catalog. It is usually an approximation to the DYNAMICAL EQUINOX of some date, differing from it as a result of the limits of observational accuracy. There is also a difference, over a period of time, due to the motion of the dynamical equinox; this time-dependent difference is called *equinox motion.*

catena (plural: **catenae**) a chain of craters. The word is used in the approved name of such a surface feature on a planet or satellite.

catoptric system an optical system in which the principal optical elements are mirrors. Compare CATADIOPTRIC TELESCOPE; DIOPTRIC SYSTEM.

Cat's-eye nebula (NGC 6543) a complex PLANETARY NEBULA lying at a distance of about 1 kiloparsec in the constellation Draco. It represents the final stages in the life of an ordinary star. As it dies, the star blows off shells of glowing gas. The structure of this nebula appears to be so intricate, showing high-speed gas jets and unusual knots of gas as well as concentric gas shells, that some astronomers have theorized that the central star may be a binary.

Caucasus see table at MOUNTAINS, LUNAR.

cavus (plural: **cavi**) a steep-sided depression. The word is used in the approved name of such a surface feature on a planet or satellite.

Cayley formation see HIGHLAND LIGHT PLAINS.

CCD *abbrev. for* charge-coupled device. A light-sensitive electronic detector, invented 1970, now widely used in ground- and space-based astronomy for IMAGING, PHOTOMETRY, SPECTROSCOPY, ASTROMETRY, etc. CCDs are normally sensitive over a wide range of wavelengths from blue light to near-infrared; developments have extended the range further into the IR (see INFRARED DETECTORS), and into the ultraviolet and X-ray regions (to energies up to about 6 keV). A CCD is small (typically several square centimeters) compared with a photographic plate, and therefore covers a relatively small field of view. It also has a lower RESOLUTION than a fine-grained photographic emulsion. It does, however, have a much higher QUANTUM EFFICIENCY – i.e. is a much more efficient detector – than emulsion; exposure times are therefore relatively much shorter. CCDs are thus well suited to the imaging of faint objects. They also have a linear response over a wide range of illumination, and in a properly designed and operating CCD system, the response is very stable over long timescales.

Astronomical CCDs are fabricated as a two-dimensional array of tiny pixels (picture elements) on a thin wafer of semiconductor, usually silicon; there may be up to several thousand rows and columns of pixels. When light or other radiation is directed onto this array, each pixel responds to the PHOTONS falling on it by producing electrons. Electric charge thus accumulates in each pixel in proportion to the amount of incident radiation. After an exposure, these packets of charge are shifted out of the array and the accumulated charge in each pixel is measured, row by row. The values are digitized and stored in a computer, and may be used to form an image on a computer screen or may be further manipulated or analyzed. There is a direct relationship between the intensity of the recorded image and the original exposure, hence the linear response. NOISE is, however, introduced as the charges are moved out of the CCD, amplified, digitized, and stored in the computer, thus placing a lower limit on the signal that can be accurately recorded; this readout noise can be reduced by cooling the CCD.

CD *abbrev. for* Córdoba Durchmusterung. See BONNER DURCHMUSTERUNG.

CDA *abbrev. for* Centre de Données Astronomiques.

cD galaxy see CLUSTERS OF GALAXIES; GALAXIES.

CDM *abbrev. for* cold dark matter. See DARK MATTER.

CDS see CENTRE DE DONNÉES ASTRONOMIQUES.

celestial axis the line joining the north and south CELESTIAL POLES and passing through the center of the CELESTIAL SPHERE; the extension of the Earth's axis to the celestial sphere.

celestial equator the great circle in which the extension of the Earth's equatorial plane cuts the CELESTIAL SPHERE. The plane of the celestial (and hence terrestrial) equator is perpendicular to the celestial axis and is the reference plane for the equatorial coordinates RIGHT ASCENSION and DECLINATION. The orientation of the celestial equator is slowly changing as a result of the PRECESSION of the Earth's axis.

celestial latitude (**ecliptic latitude**) see ECLIPTIC COORDINATE SYSTEM.

celestial longitude (**ecliptic longitude**) see ECLIPTIC COORDINATE SYSTEM.

celestial mechanics the study of the motions and equilibria of celestial bodies subjected to mutual gravitational forces, usually by the application of Newton's law of GRAVITATION and the general laws of mechanics, based on NEWTON'S LAWS OF MOTION. Satellite and planetary motions, tides, precession of the Earth's axis, and lunar libration are all described by these laws within the limits of accuracy of measurements. Newtonian mechanics is much simpler to use than the more accurate general theory of RELATIVITY. Despite fundamental differences, the equations of relativistic mechanics, based on the concepts of relativity, reduce in a first approximation to those of Newtonian mechanics, observational and predicted Newtonian values normally being very close.

celestial meridian see MERIDIAN.

celestial poles the two points at which the extension of the Earth's axis of rotation cuts the CELESTIAL SPHERE. As a result of the PRECESSION of the Earth's axis the positions of the poles are not fixed but trace out a circle on the celestial sphere in a period of about 25 800 years. The *north celestial pole* revolves about a point in the constellation Draco and at present lies in Ursa Minor close to the star POLARIS. The *south celestial pole* lies in the constellation Octans. See also POLE STAR.

celestial sphere the sky considered as the

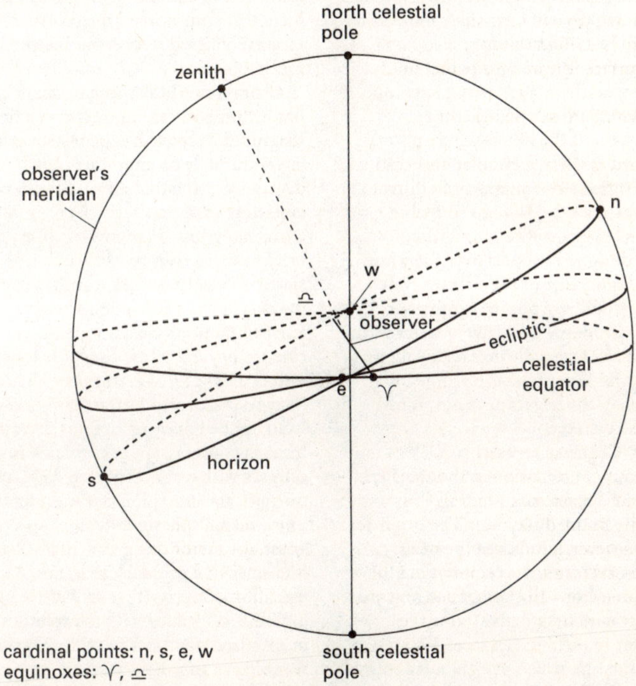

Celestial sphere

inside of an imaginary sphere of indeterminate but immense radius that surrounds the Earth. It provides a convenient surface on which to draw and study the directions and motions of celestial bodies and other points in the sky. The Earth's west-to-east rotation causes an apparent rotation of the celestial sphere about the same (extended) axis once every 24 hours but in an east-to-west direction.

The measurements that may be made with the celestial sphere, using the four main COORDINATE SYSTEMS of positional astronomy, concern not the distances but only the directions of celestial bodies. Angular relationships are established by the methods of spherical trigonometry (see SPHERICAL TRIANGLE). The principal reference circles on the celestial sphere are the CELESTIAL EQUATOR, the ECLIPTIC, and an observer's HORIZON, which are all great circles. The principal points are the poles of these circles and the points of intersection – the EQUINOXES and CARDINAL POINTS – of the circles (see illustration).

cell (**mirror cell**) the enclosure that holds the PRIMARY MIRROR in a reflecting telescope. It must hold the mirror so that the COLLIMATION of the optical elements is maintained as the direction of observation changes. It must also support the mirror so that it does not sag to an unacceptable degree under its own weight. Without carefully designed support over the whole rear face the mirror of the 5-meter Hale telescope would sag by 0.0625 mm, which is about 500 times the allowable quarter wave limit. The cell is usually provided with a closure or lid that protects the optical surface when the telescope is not in use.

centaur see CHIRON.

Centaurus (**Centaur**) an extensive conspicuous constellation in the southern hemisphere almost surrounding Crux and lying partly in the Milky Way. The brightest stars, of zero magnitude, are the nearby ALPHA (α) CENTAURI, the remote BETA (β) CENTAURI, and several stars of 2nd and 3rd magnitude. PROXIMA CENTAURI is the nearest star to the Sun. The area also contains the fine naked-eye globular cluster Omega (ω) Centauri (see OMEGA CENTAURI), the strong radio source CENTAURUS A, and the X-ray binary CENTAURUS X-3. Abbrev.: Cen; genitive form: Centauri; approx. position: RA 13h, dec –50°; area: 1060 sq deg.

Centaurus A an intense RADIO and X-RAY SOURCE in the southern constellation Centaurus and a source also of infrared radiation and gamma rays. It is identified with the galaxy NGC 5128 lying at a distance of only 5 megaparsecs from the Solar System, making it the nearest ACTIVE GALAXY. It is an elliptical galaxy, 100 kpc in diameter, cut across by broad belts of gas and dust. A complex elongated radio structure emerges from the center of the gas and dust belts, approximately along their axis of rotation and extending about 400 kpc in each direction. The radio structure consists broadly of two large lobes more or less symmetrically disposed about a central nucleus, from which a JET extends toward one of the lobes. The jet is broken up into a number of KNOTS. This huge radio galaxy, stretching over 9° of the sky, has a flux density at 86 megahertz of 8700 JANSKY, believed to be SYNCHROTRON EMISSION.

Centaurus A is also one of the brightest hard X-ray sources, its spectrum being measured to about 200 kiloelectronvolts. It is also variable on timescales down to a few days, suggesting that most of the X-ray emission arises in the nucleus. An Einstein Observatory image showed not only the bright nucleus but in addition a line of sources, i.e. an X-ray jet, significantly along the axis of the radio lobes. The X-ray emission follows closely the radio jet but extends beyond it into the radio lobe.

Centaurus X-3 an X-RAY BINARY, the first of its type, discovered by the UHURU satellite in 1971. The binary nature was determined from the observation of regular X-ray eclipses with a period of 2.09 days; in 1974 the optical companion star was identified as a 13th magnitude supergiant of spectral type O6.5, establishing Centaurus X-3 as a high-mass X-ray binary, or HMXB. Rapid pulsation of the X-ray source at a 4.8 second period is associated with the rotation of a magnetized NEUTRON STAR. It may thus be regarded as an X-RAY PULSAR.

Center for High Angular Resolution Astronomy (**CHARA**) an optical and infrared long baseline interferometry (LBI) facility operated at the MOUNT WILSON OBSERVATORY, California, by Georgia State University since 1984 with funding from the National Science Foundation and additional support from the W.M. Keck Foundation, the David and Lucille Packard Foundation, and private donations. The center also houses the Mount Wilson Institute, the non-profit corporation that controls the Mount Wilson Observatory by arrangement with the Carnegie Institution of Washington. In 1996 CHARA began construction of an interferometric array of six telescopes on Mount Wilson. The CHARA array became an active science instrument in 2002.

Each of the telescopes linked up in the array has an altazimuth mounting. Each instrument's primary mirror has an aperture of 1 meter. The instruments are deployed in a Y-shaped arrangement on the 1737-meter summit of Mount Wilson so as to form a two-dimensional layout that provides the resolving power of a single telescope with an aperture of up to 350 meters. Operating on dual wavelength regimes, the array has limiting resolutions of 200 μas at 500–800 nm and 1 mas at 2.0–2.4 μm. With these exceptionally high angular resolutions, astronomers should be able to make accurate measurements of the diameters of nearby stars, to detect any orbiting companions and measure the mass of such binary systems, and to contribute to the search for extrasolar planets.

center of gravity the point in a material body at which a single force, which is the resultant of all external forces on the body, may be considered to act. The center of gravity of a body in a uniform gravitational field coincides with the body's CENTER OF MASS. A body does not possess a center of gravity, however, if the external forces are not equivalent to a single resultant force or if the resultant does not always act on the same point of the system. This situation occurs in a nonuniform gravitational field. The Moon has strictly no center of gravity although the resultant force of the Earth's gravitational attraction always passes within a few meters of the center of mass.

center of inertia see CENTER OF MASS.

center of mass (**center of inertia**) the point in a material system at which the total mass of the system may be regarded as being concentrated and that moves as if all external forces on the system could be reduced to a single force acting at that point. When a body has a center of gravity, which it does in a uniform gravitational field, this point coincides with the center of mass.

Two bodies, moving under the influence of their mutual gravitation, will orbit around their center of mass, which lies on the line between them. The distances, r_1 and r_2, of the bodies from this point depend on their masses, m_1 and m_2, the more massive body lying closer. For circular orbits:

$$r_1/r_2 = m_2/m_1$$

central force a force on a moving body that is directed toward a fixed point or toward a point moving according to known laws. The gravitational attraction between the Sun and a planet is an example.

central meridian the imaginary N–S line bisecting the disk of a planet, satellite, etc., used as a reference.

central molecular zone see GALACTIC CENTER.

Centre de Données Astronomiques (**CDA**) the astronomical data center at the University of Strasbourg, France, established in 1972 as the *Centre de Données Stellaires* (*CDS*). It is concerned mainly with the collection and critical evaluation of data, the creation of new astronomical catalogs, and the distribution of data to astronomers worldwide. It manages the SIMBAD database, which is accessible over public transmission networks including the World Wide Web.

centrifugal force see CENTRIPETAL FORCE.

centripetal acceleration see CENTRIPETAL FORCE.

centripetal force a force, such as gravitation, that causes a body to deviate from motion in a straight line to motion along a curved path, the force being directed toward the center of curvature of the body's motion. The force reacting against this constraint, i.e. the force equal in magnitude but opposite in direction, is the *centrifugal force*. The centrifugal force results from the inertia of all solid bodies, i.e. their resistance to acceleration, and unlike gravitational or electrical forces, cannot be considered a real force. The centripetal force is equal to the product of the mass of the body and its *centripetal acceleration*. The latter is the acceleration toward the center, and for a body moving in a circle at a constant angular velocity ω it is given by $\omega^2 r$, where r is the radius.

Cepheid *short for* Cepheid variable.

Cepheid instability strip see PULSATING VARIABLES.

Cepheid variables a large and important group of very luminous yellow supergiants that are PULSATING VARIABLES with periods mainly in the range 1–50 days. Over 700 are known in our galaxy and several thousand in the Local Group. There are two categories: *classical Cepheids* (or *type I Cepheids*) are massive young population I objects found in spiral arms on the galactic plane; the less common *type II Cepheids* (also known as *W Virginis stars*) are much older and less massive population II objects found in the galactic center and halo, especially in GLOBULAR CLUSTERS, and are thus similar in distribution to RR LYRAE STARS. The classical Cepheids are about 1.5–2 magnitudes more luminous than type II Cepheids of the same period. The luminosity variations of both categories are continuous and extremely regular so that the periods can be measured very accurately. Characteristic periods are 5–10 days (classical) and 12–30 days (type II). The AMPLITUDES are typically 0.5–2 in magnitude in visual light; the fluctuation is more marked at blue than at red and infrared wavelengths. The two types are best distinguished by analysis of their spectra, the older type II Cepheids having a much lower abundance of METALS.

The prototype of the classical Cepheids is *Delta Cephei*, discovered 1784. The changes in brightness were found in the 1890s to be accompanied by and principally caused by changes in stellar temperature and also by changes in radius (see illustration overleaf). This was later explained in terms of pulsations in the outer layers of the stars that appear at a late evolutionary state (see PULSATING VARIABLES); according to theory, the pulsations die down as the star expands and its surface cools.

The relation between period of pulsation and average brightness of Cepheid variables was discovered during 1908–12 by Henrietta Leavitt. Leavitt was studying Cepheids in the Small Magellanic Cloud, which were thus all at about the same distance. She recognized that the relation between their period and their average apparent magnitude was equivalent to a relation between period and average absolute magnitude or luminosity (see DISTANCE MODULUS). An independent determination of the distance of a Cepheid of known period would lead to the graphical relation between period and luminosity. It was quickly realized by Shapley that this PERIOD-LUMINOSITY RELATION was an invaluable tool for measurements of distance out to the nearest galaxies and thus for studying the structure of our own galaxy and of the Universe (see DISTANCE DETERMINATION). The refurbished HUBBLE SPACE TELESCOPE can study classical Cepheids in galaxies as far away as the Virgo cluster (about 15 megaparsecs). Much work has been done to establish the graph of period versus absolute magnitude, mainly involving independent measurements of the distances or luminosities of Cepheids. Baade and Kukarkin were consequently able to demonstrate in the 1950s the existence of the two distinct categories of Cepheids, having separate but parallel period-luminosity relations.

Cepheus a constellation in the northern hemisphere near Cassiopeia, lying partly in the Milky Way, the brightest star, Alderamin (α), being of 2nd magnitude. As a result of PRECESSION, both Alderamin and the 3rd-magnitude Alrai (γ) have come close enough to the north celestial pole to serve as pole stars and will do so again. Cepheus contains several pulsating variable stars, including the prototype CEPHEID VARIABLE Delta (δ) Cephei, the red irregular variable Mu (μ) Cephei or GARNET STAR, and the prototype of the BETA CEPHEI STARS. Abbrev.: Cep.; genitive form: Cephei; approx. position: RA 22h, dec +70°; area: 588 sq deg.

Cerenkov counter an instrument for detecting and measuring the velocity of

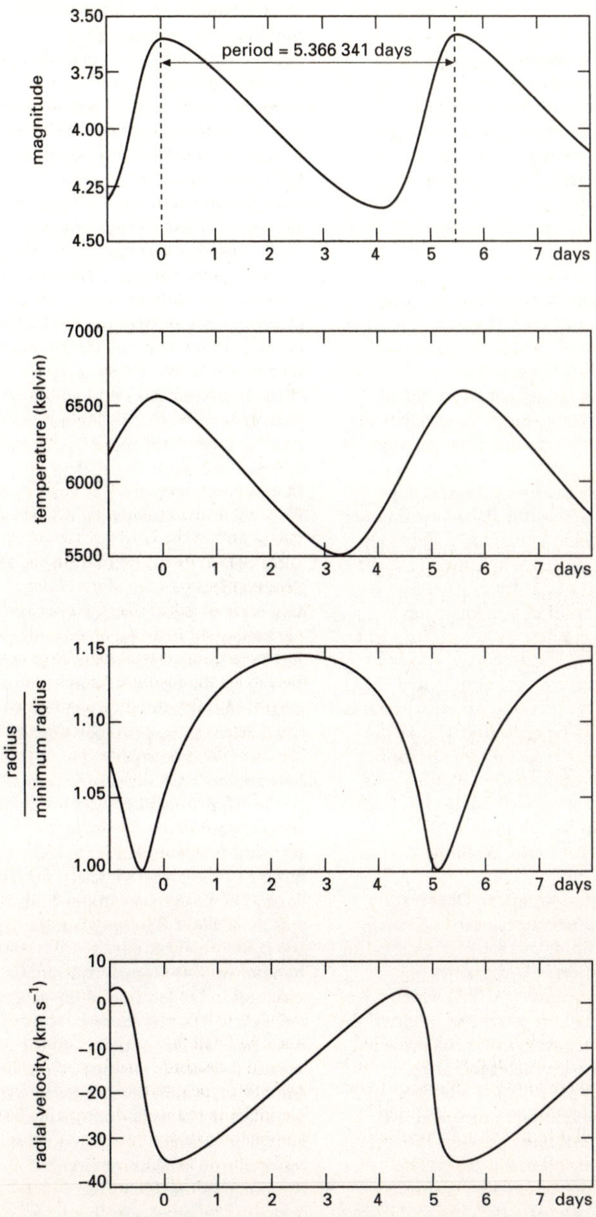

Cepheid variables: variation in brightness, temperature, radius, and radial velocity of expanding and contracting layers of Delta Cephei

very energetic particles such as cosmic rays or the cascades of electrons generated in the Earth's atmosphere by gamma rays. Faint blue light – *Cerenkov radiation* – is emitted by the particles as they pass through a transparent nonconducting (dielectric) material at a speed greater than the speed of light in that material. The radiation is emitted at a fixed angle, θ, to the direction of motion of the particle, such that

$$\cos \theta = c/nv$$

in which v is the particle velocity, n the refractive index of the transparent medium, and c the speed of light in a vacuum. This cone of light is focused on to a PHOTOMULTIPLIER so that an amplified electric pulse is registered. The velocity of the particle is determined from the angle of the cone.

Ceres (**(1) Ceres**) the first ASTEROID to be discovered, found by the Italian astronomer Giuseppe Piazzi in January 1801 following the predicted existence by BODE'S LAW of a planet at about 2.8 AU from the Sun. It is the largest asteroid known (diameter 933 km) and has a density of 2.7 g cm^{-3} and a mass of 9.5×10^{20} kg. It has a low ALBEDO of 0.10 and a spectrum similar to that of the CARBONACEOUS CHONDRITE meteorites. It is classified as a G-type asteroid. Unlike the rather smaller asteroid (4) VESTA, it cannot be seen by the unaided eye, attaining only 7th magnitude at opposition. NASA's Dawn mission, set for launch in 2006, is scheduled to visit Ceres. See Table 3, Appendix.

Cerro Tololo Inter-American Observatory (**CTIO**) a US observatory near La Serena, Chile, at an altitude of 2200 meters. It is run by the Association of Universities for Research in Astronomy (AURA), which operates through the NATIONAL OPTICAL ASTRONOMICAL OBSERVATORY. Its principal instruments are a 4-meter reflecting telescope, the Victor Blanco Telescope, which began operating in 1976, and two smaller reflectors, one 1.5 meters in aperture and the other 0.9 meter. The 4-meter telescope has a CER-VIT primary mirror, with Cassegrain (f/8), infrared (f/30), and prime (f/2.7) foci, on an equatorial mounting. The observatory also operates a Schmidt telescope at this site. Nearby Cerro Pachón is the location of the Gemini South telescope (see GEMINI TELESCOPES) and the SOAR TELESCOPE.

Cer-Vit *trademark* a glass-ceramic material that expands and contracts very little when its temperature changes and is thus used in telescope optics.

Cetus (**Whale**) an extensive but rather inconspicuous equatorial constellation near Orion, the brightest star being the 2nd-magnitude orange giant *Diphda* (β). It contains several MIRA STARS including the prototype MIRA Ceti (Omicron [o] Ceti), the FLARE STAR UV Ceti, the orange-red main-sequence star Tau (τ) Ceti, a close neighbor of the Sun (see TAU CETI), and the SEYFERT GALAXY M77 (NGC 1068). Abbrev.: Cet; genitive form: Ceti; approx. position: RA 1.5h, dec –10°; area: 1231 sq deg.

CfA survey see REDSHIFT SURVEY.

CFHT *abbrev. for* Canada–France–Hawaii Telescope.

CGRO *abbrev. for* Compton Gamma Ray Observatory.

chain craters see CRATER CHAIN.

Chamaeleon a small inconspicuous constellation in the southern hemisphere near Crux, the brightest stars being of 4th magnitude. Abbrev.: Cha; genitive form: Chamaeleontis; approx. position: RA 11h, dec –80°; area: 132 sq deg.

Champollion a US mission to comet Tempel 1 (1879 III) planned by NASA for launch in 2003. It would have arrived at the end of 2005 and released a lander to collect a sample of the comet's nucleus for return to Earth. The project was stopped for financial reasons while still in the planning stage. See ROSETTA; STARDUST.

Chandler wobble a small continuous variation in the location of the geographic poles on the Earth's surface. It leads to a *variation of latitude* of points on the Earth because latitude is measured from the equator midway between the poles. It does not affect the celestial coordinates of a body. The variation in polar location is resolved into two almost circular components, one (diameter: 6 meters; period: 12 months) resulting from seasonal changes in ice, snow, and atmospheric mass distribution; the second (diameter: 3–15 meters; period: 428 days) is believed to arise from movements of material within the Earth.

Chandra see AXAF.

Chandrasekhar limit (**Chandrasekhar mass**) the limiting mass for a nonrotating WHITE DWARF. It depends slightly on the star's composition, being 1.44 solar masses for a helium white dwarf, dropping to 1.40 solar masses for a carbon composition and 1.11 solar masses for an iron composition. The limit is raised substantially if the white dwarf has a rapidly rotating core. A star whose mass exceeds this limit will be forced to undergo further GRAVITATIONAL COLLAPSE to become a NEUTRON STAR or even a BLACK HOLE, because its material will be unable to support itself against the force of gravity.

Chandra X-Ray Observatory an orbiting X-RAY ASTRONOMY observatory launched by NASA in July 1999 as the third of its GREAT OBSERVATORIES. Chandra, which takes its name from the 20th-century Indian-born US astrophysicist Subrahmanyan Chandrasekhar, was originally developed as one of the craft making up NASA's Advanced X-Ray Astrophysics Facility (see AXAF); dubbed AXAF-I and renamed after its launch, Chandra was equipped for high-resolution X-ray imaging and was deployed by the space shuttle Columbia into a highly eccentric orbit (apogee 140 161 km, inclination 28.5°) that has allowed long periods of observation unimpeded by Earth shadowing. Chandra's optics consist of four nested pairs of GRAZING INCIDENCE paraboloid and hyperboloid mirrors, each having an outer diameter of 1.2 meters and a focal length of 10 meters. With its Advanced Charged Couple Imaging Spectrometer (ACIS) and its high-resolution camera using large field-of-view MICROCHANNEL plates to make X-ray images, Chandra's optical system achieves an angular resolution of 0.5 arcseconds over an operating range of 0.2–10 keV. Its high- and low-energy transmission gratings provide impressive spectral resolution throughout the range 0.09–10 keV.

Chandra has been called the most sophisticated X-ray observatory of its time, providing images of unprecedented detail at resolutions that are claimed to be about 50 times better than those achieved by ROSAT, the best X-ray astronomy satellite prior to 1999. In its first five years, Chandra has begun to penetrate the hottest, most energetic regions of the Universe. In particular, it has advanced our knowledge of BLACK HOLES, discovering among many other things how fast they spin, finding evidence of a star torn apart by a black hole, and emphatically confirming the reality of the EVENT HORIZON. It has revealed enormous tracts of hot gas, billions of parsecs distant and radiating at temperatures of tens of millions of degrees K. It has provided startling new images of supernova remnants such as the CRAB NEBULA, with its restless pulsar, showing intricate details never suspected before. It has made new studies of star-forming regions such as the ORION NEBULA and analyzed the effects of galaxy collisions and the merging of galaxy clusters. Most notably, it has gathered direct evidence of DARK ENERGY and the expansion of the Universe.

channels meandering valleys, some more than 1000 km long, that look like dried watercourses on the Martian surface. They are not related to the mythical Martian CANALS. See MARS, SURFACE FEATURES.

chaos broken terrain. The word is used in the approved name of such a surface feature on a planet or satellite.

chaos theory the theory of the unpredictable behavior that can arise in systems obeying deterministic scientific laws – laws that under ideal conditions completely determine the future states of a system from its preceding states. In practice, however, quantities cannot be measured with unlimited precision and the predictability suffers as a result of input errors. In a typical nonchaotic system, the errors accumulate with time but remain managable. In a chaotic system, there is a sensitivity to variations in the initial conditions. Input errors are multiplied at an escalating rate until all predictive power is lost and the system behaves in an apparently random manner.

There are many apparently simple physical systems in the Universe that obey deterministic laws but yet behave unpredictably.

charge a property of certain ELEMENTARY PARTICLES that causes them to attract or repel each other. Charged particles have associated electric and magnetic fields that allow them to interact with each other and with external electric and magnetic fields. Charge is conventionally 'negative' or 'positive': like charges repel, unlike charges attract. The ELECTRON possesses the natural unit of negative charge, equal to 1.6022×10^{-19} coulombs. The PROTON carries a positive charge of the same magnitude. If matter is charged, it is due to an excess or deficit of electrons with respect to protons.

charge-coupled device see CCD.

Charon the only confirmed satellite of PLUTO, discovered in 1978 by James W. Christy of the US Naval Observatory. The average distance between Charon and Pluto is less than 20 000 km. Charon is in SYNCHRONOUS ROTATION with Pluto (orbital period 6.39 days) and with a diameter of about 1190 km is more than half its size. It is, however, only one-tenth of Pluto's mass. See Table 2, Appendix.

chasma (plural: **chasmata**) A deep valley with steep sides. The word is used in the approved name of such a surface feature on a planet or satellite.

Chi Persei (**χ Per**) see H AND CHI PERSEI.

Chiron a large interplanetary object that has been classified both as an asteroid ((2060) Chiron) and as a comet (Kowal–Meech–Belton, or 95P/Chiron). It was discovered in 1977 by Charles T. Kowal but was subsequently identified on photographs taken as early as 1895. Studies of Chiron's light curve indicate that it rotates on its axis once every 5.9 hours. It has a 50.7-year orbit that lies almost entirely beyond that of Saturn; perihelion and aphelion distances are 8.46 and 18.94 AU respectively. The orbit is also highly elliptical, with an eccentricity of 0.383, and is inclined at an angle of 6.93° to the plane of the ECLIPTIC. Astronomers have found that this orbit is unstable over a time scale of a million years owing to perturbations by the giant planets. It is thought that Chiron has not occupied this orbit for more than a few million years and will in time either collide with a planet or be ejected from the Solar System. With a diameter estimated at 148 to 200 km, Chiron is much larger than most comets and comparable in size with an asteroid or icy satellite. But the case for assuming it to be a large comet was strengthened in 1988 when astronomers detected a gas and dust coma around it and confirmed in 1991 the presence of cyanogen radicals typical of comets but not normally found in asteroids. Chiron's anomalous status as a sort of half asteroid–half comet has led astronomers to give it a new classification, that of *centaur*. It may also be an object from the KUIPER BELT. Chiron's most recent passage through perihelion occurred in February 1996. See Table 3, Appendix.

chondrite a type of STONY METEORITE that contains CHONDRULES. They are the most abundant class of meteorite in the Solar System (about 86%). Chondrites are largely composed of iron- and magnesium-bearing silicate minerals with a wide range of compositions. Their chemical composition is similar to that of the Sun (but depleted in volatile gases like hydrogen and helium). Several types are recognized: CARBONACEOUS CHONDRITES have the highest proportions of volatile elements and are the most oxidized; *enstatite chondrites* contain the most refractory elements (withstanding high temperatures) and are reduced; 'ordinary' chondrites, the most common type, are intermediate in volatile element abundance and oxidation state. Ordinary chondrites plus some carbonaceous chondrites are thought to be primitive samples of early Solar-System material. See also ASTEROIDS. Compare ACHONDRITE.

chondrules near-spherical bodies composed chiefly of silicates, with sizes between 0.2 mm and 4 mm, found embedded in CHONDRITES. They are usually aggregates of olivine, $(Mg,Fe)_2SiO_4$, and pyroxene $(Mg,Fe)SiO_3$. They may also be single crystals, wholly glass, or crystal and glass, in a wide range of proportions. They appear to have been free fluid drops made spherical by surface tension and then solidified and crystallized. There is a possibility that these silicate drops were produced by lightning discharges in the dusty primitive solar nebula or that they are crystallized droplets of impact melt produced when two asteroids collided. Chondrulelike bodies have been found in lunar soils.

CHON particles dust particles that were discovered in the COMA of HALLEY'S COMET during the GIOTTO mission and were found to consist mainly of the light elements carbon, hydrogen, oxygen, and nitrogen and thus of a distinct compositional type. They are thought to be snowflakes that were being blown away from the cometary nucleus and would be short-lived.

christmas tree see FEEDER.

chromatic aberration an ABERRATION of a lens – but not a mirror – whereby the component wavelengths of light, i.e. ordinary white light, are brought to a focus at different distances from the lens (see illustration). It arises from the variation with wavelength of the REFRACTIVE INDEX of the lens material: red light is refracted (bent) less than blue light (see DISPERSION). False colors therefore arise in the image. Chromatic aberration can be reduced by using an ACHROMATIC LENS. Before the introduction of achromats, objective lenses of very long focal length were used in telescopes to reduce the aberration; this led to the production of very cumbersome instruments.

chromatic resolution see SPECTROGRAPH.

chromosphere the stratum of a star's atmosphere immediately above the PHOTOSPHERE and below the CORONA. The chromosphere is considerably less dense than the photosphere, and its gases are characterized by an emission rather than an absorption spectrum. The best-studied chromosphere is that of the Sun.

In the solar chromosphere the temperature rises over a few thousand kilometers from about 4000 K at the temperature minimum to around 50 000 K at the transition region (see SUN). The rise in temperature (which continues in the transition region and inner corona) was once thought to be the result of ascending shock waves, but this mechanism does not tally with detailed observations of the coronae of the Sun and other stars. It is now believed that magnetic heating is responsible (see CORONA).

The solar chromosphere is visible under natural circumstances only when the photosphere is totally eclipsed by the Moon (see ECLIPSE). It is then seen in profile at the Sun's limb. It may, however, be observed at times other than totality with the aid of a SPECTROHELIOGRAPH/SPECTROHELIOSCOPE or a telescope equipped with a suitable narrow-band INTERFERENCE FILTER. See also CHROMOSPHERIC NETWORK; FLASH SPECTRUM; SPICULES.

Chromospheres of other stars are studied by observing their strong ultraviolet emission lines or the narrow optical emission lines seen in the center of their photospheric broad absorption lines. In many stars of similar spectral type to the Sun, the chromospheric emission changes with a period of several years, indicating the presence of a cycle of activity akin to the solar cycle (see SUNSPOT CYCLE). Chromospheric brightness is related to speed of rotation, being greater for stars that rotate rapidly (either because they are

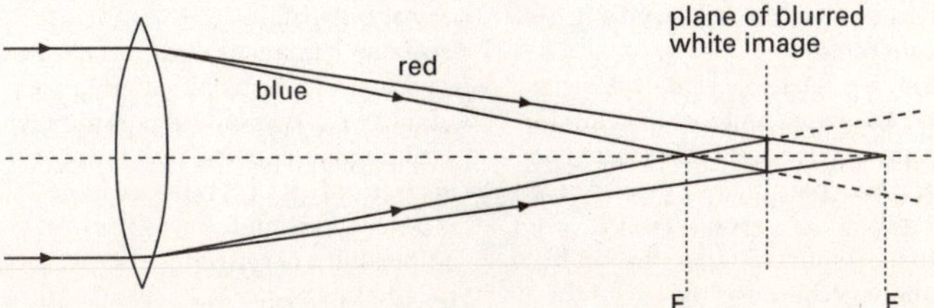

Chromatic aberration of convex lens

young or because of the effect of a companion – see RS CANUM VENATICORUM STAR).

chromospheric activity the collection of phenomena displayed by certain types of single and binary stars, including FLARE STARS, RS CANUM VENATICORUM STARS, and T TAURI STARS. The phenomena are similar to but usually much more extreme than SOLAR ACTIVITY, and are thought to require rapid rotation and a deep convective outer envelope. They include mass loss in stellar winds, starspots, rapid solarlike flares, and long-term cycles of activity analogous to the solar cycle (see SUNSPOT CYCLE).

chromospheric network a large-scale cellular pattern in the solar CHROMOSPHERE. It is most clearly defined at the center of the Sun's disk in the MONOCHROMATIC light of the K FRAUNHOFER LINE of singly ionized calcium (Ca II), when it appears as a mosaic of cells outlined (at least partly) by bright mottles. Its appearance is similar though less pronounced in the core of the hydrogen-alpha (Hα) line of neutral hydrogen, but in the WINGS the mottles appear dark instead of bright. Both bright and dark mottles have been tentatively identified with SPICULES, which are visible beyond the Sun's limb. They seem to differ only in their height above the PHOTOSPHERE, bright mottles being situated in the lower chromosphere, dark mottles at heights of up to about 10 000 km.

The chromospheric network coincides with the underlying SUPERGRANULATION, the horizontal flow within each supergranular cell concentrating magnetic flux at its boundary; at the boundary an enhanced vertical magnetic field is produced, which is responsible for the localized excess heating that manifests itself as the bright mottles.

Chryse Planitia a relatively smooth Martian plain, 1600 km across and 2.5 km below the average planetary surface. It is centered on the areographic coordinates 27° N latitude, 40° W longitude (see AREOGRAPHY). It appears to have suffered water erosion in the past and was chosen as the site of the VIKING 1 landing in 1976. See MARS, SURFACE FEATURES.

CH stars a class of stars, usually G or K giants or subgiants, that show very strong CH bands and enhancements in S-PROCESS elements. They are related to BARIUM STARS and are probably also found exclusively in binary systems.

Cih see CASSIOPEIA.

Circinus (Compasses) a small constellation in the southern hemisphere near Centaurus, lying in the Milky Way. The brightest star is of 3rd magnitude. CIRCINUS X-1 is an X-ray burst source. Abbrev.: Cir; genitive form: Circini; approx. position: RA 15h, dec –60°; area: 93 sq deg.

Circinus X-1 a luminous galactic X-ray source, showing recurrent flaring at a 16.6 day period. Spectral characteristics and variability on timescales down to milliseconds, similar to CYGNUS X-1, initially suggested Cir X-1 as a black hole candidate. Discovery by EXOSAT of X-RAY BURSTS have now shown that Cir X-1 is more likely to be a neutron star in an eccentric 16.6 day orbit with an early-type nondegenerate companion star. More recent observations with ASCA suggest the rapid X-ray variability may result from dense gas clouds passing across in front of the X-ray emission region.

circle of longitude any great circle that passes through the poles of the ECLIPTIC and is thus at right angles to the plane of the ecliptic. *Circles of latitude* lie parallel to the ecliptic plane.

circle of position an imaginary small circle on the Earth's surface on which an observer is located and that is centered on the SUBSTELLAR POINT of a particular star. Its radius is equal to the ZENITH DISTANCE of the star. The star will thus have the same zenith distance from every point on the circle of position.

circular polarization see POLARIZATION.

circulator a three- or four-port electronic device in which signals entering port number 1 appear only at port number 2, while signals entering port number 2 emerge only at port number 3, and so on. It is used, for example, in a RADIO TELESCOPE employing a negative-resistance preamplifier, such as a PARAMETRIC AMPLIFIER or a MASER AMPLIFIER; the circulator isolates the preamplifier from the

ANTENNA, which, if connected directly, might oscillate.

circumpolar stars stars that are permanently above the horizon from a given observational point on Earth, i.e. they never set. For stars to be circumpolar from a given geographical latitude ϕ, their declination (angular distance north or south of the celestial equator) must be greater than $90° - \phi$. For an observer at the north pole all stars in the northern hemisphere of the celestial sphere will be circumpolar whereas at the equator there are no circumpolar stars although almost all stars will be seen at some time during the year. For an observer at the south pole, all southern hemisphere stars will be circumpolar.

circumstellar cloud see INTERSTELLAR CLOUD.

cislunar of or in the region of space between the Earth and the Moon.

civil twilight see TWILIGHT.

civil year the length of the year as reckoned for ordinary purposes. Any civil year must contain an exact number of days, which in the GREGORIAN CALENDAR usually amounts to 365 but is equal to 366 in LEAP YEARS.

classical Cepheids see CEPHEID VARIABLES.

classical nova see NOVA.

classical T Tauri stars see T TAURI STARS.

Clavius see table at CRATERS.

Clementine a joint mission launched in 1994 by NASA and the US Strategic Defense Initiative Organization with the main aims of testing sensors and spacecraft components over a long period of exposure to the environment of space and carrying out scientific observations of the Moon and the near-Earth asteroid (1620) Geographos. The observations were intended to facilitate a thorough analysis of the surface relief and geology of both the Moon and Geographos by means of imaging at various wavelengths throughout the spectrum from infrared to ultraviolet, laser-ranging altimetry, and charged-particle measurement. The original purpose of these observations was to assess the surface mineralogy of the Moon between lunar latitudes 60° N and 60° S. The probe used for the Clementine mission was launched on Jan. 25 1994 from Vandenberg Air Force Base and achieved lunar orbit on Feb. 21. After completing its lunar investigations on May 7, the Clementine craft was about to maneuver into position to begin the journey to Greographos, when an onboard computer malfunction caused a thruster to fire and remain firing until it had exhausted all its fuel, sending the probe into an uncontrollable spin. Although Clementine remained in an Earth-centered orbit testing its equipment, the planned flyby of Geographos had to be abandoned. Despite being only partially successful, Clementine provided a wealth of photographic and other data. In 1996, analysis of its results led scientists to speculate that there might be reserves of water ice lying beneath the Moon's surface in deep craters whose interiors are in permanent shadow at the lunar poles. See also LUNAR PROSPECTOR.

CLFST see MULLARD RADIO ASTRONOMY OBSERVATORY.

clock star a bright star, usually situated near the celestial equator, whose position and proper motion are very accurately known so that it can be used for the exact determination of time, for the determination of the error of observatory clocks, and for correction of the positional observations of other stars.

close binary see BINARY STAR.

closed Universe see UNIVERSE.

closure phase the sum of PHASES around a loop of BASELINES in an INTERFEROMETER containing three or more elements. When applied to a radio interferometer, the sum is unaffected by phase drifts in the receivers or by variations in the ionosphere or troposphere above the telescopes and is therefore determined solely by the RADIO SOURCE under observation. The basic idea is used extensively in VLBI and in optical aperture-synthesis telescopes.

Cloverleaf a gravitationally lensed image of a very distant quasar (redshift 2.56) in the form of four images separated by about 1 arc second. The lensing galaxy has not yet been detected and may itself lie at comparatively high redshift. See GRAVITATIONAL LENS.

cluster a group of stars whose members are sufficiently close to each other to be physically associated. Clusters range from dense congregations of many thousands of stars to loose groups of only a few stars. Current theories of stellar evolution suggest that stars form in ASSOCIATIONS, whose densest groupings remain bound as clusters while the other stars disperse; this view is supported by the relatively well-defined HERTZSPRUNG–RUSSELL DIAGRAMS of clusters, which indicate that cluster members are of essentially the same composition and age (see also TURNOFF POINT). Because the stars in a cluster are all at approximately the same distance, the observed differences in appearance are believed to be due mainly to differences in mass. An estimate of distance is obtained from the technique of MAIN-SEQUENCE FITTING. See GLOBULAR CLUSTER; OPEN CLUSTER.

Cluster an ESA mission to study in three dimensions the shape and dynamic behavior of small-scale structures in the Earth's plasma environment. In effect, Cluster is examining 'space weather' – that is, the interaction between the particles of the solar wind and the Earth's magnetosphere. The mission consists of four identical 500-kg satellites, carrying the same 10 instruments. The satellites were carried into space in two pairs by Russian-made Soyuz rockets during the summer of 2000. The first pair, nicknamed Salsa and Samba, were launched July 16, followed by the second pair, Rumba and Tango, launched Aug. 9. The Cluster craft were scheduled to operate until 2005. The mission, which was designated Cluster II, was the replacement for an earlier failed mission. The original Cluster satellites were to have been sent into space together in June 1996, on an Ariane-5 rocket, but were destroyed when the rocket unexpectedly tilted and broke up soon after liftoff.

clusters of galaxies groups of galaxies that may contain up to a few thousand members. The majority of galaxies appear to occur in clusters or in smaller groups such as doubles or triples. Our own Galaxy is a member of a small irregular cluster – the LOCAL GROUP. The nearest large cluster is the VIRGO CLUSTER. The densest clusters, which typically contain a thousand or more members, are apparently roughly spherical and consist almost entirely of elliptical and S0 galaxies. Irregularly shaped clusters may be large, as with the Virgo cluster, or small, but tend to be less dense and to contain all types of galaxies. Adjacent clusters are loosely grouped into larger SUPERCLUSTERS.

Large clusters with an unusually high concentration of galaxies in the center are called *rich clusters*. Several thousand are listed in the ABELL CATALOG, examples being the COMA CLUSTER and PERSEUS CLUSTER. The comparison of the cluster mass derived from dynamical studies of its constituent galaxies, and that inferred by summing the contribution of luminous objects in the system shows that 90% of the mass of the cluster must be in the form of DARK MATTER. This is known as the *missing mass*. A rich cluster contains on average about a thousand galaxies, and has a total mass of 10^{15} solar masses within a radius of a megaparsec. X-ray observations show that clusters contain a large amount of hot (up to 10^8 K) gas; the mass of the gas is not, however, sufficient to explain the missing mass. In the irregularly shaped clusters the gas is associated with individual galaxies, but in the REGULAR CLUSTERS it forms a large pool between the galaxies, the INTRACLUSTER MEDIUM. This provides evidence that the regular clusters are more dynamically relaxed: their galaxies have interacted so often that their gases are stripped off and enrich the intracluster medium to about one-third solar METALLICITY.

The hot intracluster gas loses energy through the radiation of X-rays, and in the core of the cluster where the gas is most dense its COOLING TIME is substantially less than the presumed age of the cluster. Within this *cooling radius* the cooling gas flows inward to maintain the pressure required to support the weight of the outer hot atmosphere, thus forming a *cooling flow*. Cooling flows are detected from X-ray spectra and images of clusters and occur in 70–90% of all clusters. As the gas cools from X-ray temperatures it separates from the flow, and typically several hundreds of solar masses a year are deposited. Only a small percentage of the cooled matter goes into detectable star formation; the bulk of it is thought to form very low mass stars and large clouds of neutral hydrogen. Over the lifetime of the cluster, the cooling flow will contribute a significant mass to the centrally located *cD galaxy*, the most massive type of galaxy known.

Clusters evolve rapidly through the HIERARCHICAL merging of small clusters to form today's rich clusters. Merging of two equal subclusters leads to systems such as the COMA CLUSTER with two central dominant galaxies and no cooling flow. Cosmologically distant clusters of galaxies show a higher proportion of blue galaxies than do those at the present day, a feature known as the *Butcher–Oemler effect*, discovered by H. Butcher and A. Oemler in 1978. The galaxies are blue because of enhanced star formation, which is thought to be triggered either by RAM PRESSURE stripping by the INTRACLUSTER MEDIUM or by GALAXY HARASSMENT.

Measurements of the gas and galaxy content of clusters, coupled with limits on cosmic nucleosynthesis, suggest a low value of the cosmological density parameter, Ω. This is consistent with the lack of strong evolution in the X-ray luminosity of clusters.

C-M diagram *abbrev. for* color-magnitude diagram. See HERTZSPRUNG–RUSSELL DIAGRAM.

CME *abbrev. for* coronal mass ejection. See CORONAL TRANSIENTS.

CNES *abbrev. for* Centre nationale d'études spatiales. The French national space agency.

CNO cycle see CARBON CYCLE.

coalesced star see COMMON ENVELOPE STAR.

Coalsack (**Southern Coalsack**) a prominent DARK NEBULA about 170 parsecs away in the southern constellation Crux. It has an angular diameter of 6° and can be seen with the naked eye as a completely black shape silhouetted against the background of the Milky Way.

coaltitude see ZENITH DISTANCE.

COAST an optical interferometer at the MULLARD RADIO ASTRONOMY OBSERVATORY.

coating of lenses the deposition of one or more thin uniform transparent coatings on lens surfaces, usually by vacuum evaporation or other electronic techniques; these coatings reduce the amount of scattered light resulting from reflection at each refracting surface, say the interfaces between air and lens and between lens and air. A *bloomed lens* is coated with a single film of suitable refractive index and thickness: destructive INTERFERENCE can then occur between light reflected from the coating-air surface and light reflected from the lens-coating surface. *Multilayer coating* depends on thin-film interference. Using up to 30 layers of controlled thickness, extremely low levels of reflected light can be achieved. Multilayer coating can also be used to produce very high levels of reflection from a MIRROR.

COBE *abbrev. for* Cosmic Background Explorer. A NASA orbiting satellite launched Nov. 18 1989 and dedicated to the study of the cosmic MICROWAVE BACKGROUND RADIATION, and hence to cosmology. The mission ran for just over four years, being terminated by NASA on Dec. 23 1993.

COBE's scientific payload consisted of three instruments shielded from the adverse thermal and radiation effects of the Sun and Earth. Two cryogenically cooled instruments observed the sky at infrared wavelengths. DIRBE, the diffuse infrared background experiment, mapped the sky at 10 wavelengths over 1–300 μm in search of the cumulative uniform glow from earliest luminous objects. FIRAS, the far-infrared absolute spectrophotometer, measured the average temperature of the background with unprecedented precision: it showed the spectrum of the microwave background to be a perfect BLACK-BODY curve characteristic of a temperature of 2.735 ± 0.06 K. FIRAS was turned off after 10 months of flight when the helium coolant ran out.

The third detector, the DMR (differential microwave radiometer), consisted of six differential radiometers observing the sky at three radio wavelengths – 3.3, 5.7, and 9.5 mm. They made whole-sky surveys and were designed to detect any fluctuations in the brightness of the microwave background.

The microwave background is not completely uniform, showing a slight dipole anisotropy with an enhancement of one part in a thousand in the direction of the Galaxy's motion and an equal and opposite deficit in the opposite part of the sky. This results from the real motion of the Galaxy relative to the fixed background. It was announced in April 1992 that careful statistical analysis of the COBE measurements also revealed even weaker temperature fluctuations of one part in one hundred thousand on scales of ten degrees and larger. These are the imprints of quantum fluctuations in the early Universe. Further study of such fluctuations by such missions as the WILKINSON MICROWAVE ANISOTROPY PROBE have served to constrain cosmological models that determine how the early inhomogeneities collapsed to form the LARGE-SCALE STRUCTURE we see in today's Universe.

Cocoon nebula (**IC 5146**) an EMISSION NEBULA about 1 kiloparsec distant in the constellation Cygnus, surrounding a small cluster of faint stars. It is thought to be a region of active star formation.

coded-mask telescope a telescope system that enables high-quality sky images to be made using nonfocusing optics; it is a development of the simple pinhole camera. The technique is particularly applicable at gamma-ray wavelengths and greatly improves the accuracy with which cosmic γ-ray sources can be located within every point in the telescope's field of view, typically 10° square. The system consists of a crosswordlike mask of γ-ray opaque lead or tungsten elements positioned over, but separated from, a flat γ-ray detector. The detector is capable of measuring the point at which a γ-ray photon from a cosmic source makes contact, as well as its energy. A patterned shadow of the mask will be cast on the detector plane by photons not reaching the detector. The location of the γ-ray source can be determined uniquely from the position of the shadow and the known mask-detector separation.

coelostat a flat mirror that can be driven by a clock mechanism so as to rotate from east to west about an axis parallel to the Earth's rotational axis, thereby compensating for the west-to-east rotation of the Earth. The mirror may thus continuously reflect light from the same area of the sky into the field of view of an instrument that is fixed in position, usually by means of an additional optical system. See also HELIOSTAT; SIDEROSTAT; SOLAR TELESCOPE.

coherence the degree to which an oscillating quantity maintains a constant PHASE and AMPLITUDE relationship at points displaced in space or time. Hence the *coherence width* of a train of waves describes the distance along a wavefront over which the oscillations are appreciably correlated while the *coherence time* defines the time for which the character of the wavetrain remains more or less unchanged. A radio INTERFEROMETER measures coherence width. This is related to the shape of the radio source and can be used to generate an image of it. See also AUTOCORRELATION FUNCTION.

coherence bandwidth see BANDWIDTH.

coherence width see COHERENCE.

colatitude the complement of the celestial latitude (β) of a celestial body, i.e. the angle (90° – β). See ECLIPTIC COORDINATE SYSTEM.

cold camera a camera so designed that the film may be kept at a very low temperature to enhance its performance during long exposures. Cooling the PHOTOGRAPHIC EMULSION helps to overcome reciprocity failure.

cold dark matter (**CDM**) see DARK MATTER.

colles (singular: **collis**) low hills. The word is used in the approved name of such a surface feature on a planet or satellite.

collimation the alignment of the optical elements in a telescope. For a simple refractor the only adjustment required is to position the object lens at right angles to the optical axis by adjusting the screws on its supporting cell. In a simple Newtonian reflector the orientation of both the primary and diagonal mirrors must be adjusted, and the latter positioned correctly opposite the DRAW TUBE. Final small adjustments are then made to obtain bright star images as free as possible from COMA.

collimator a device used to produce a parallel or near parallel beam of light or other radiation in an instrument. One example, used in spectroscopes, is a converging lens or mirror at whose focal point is a narrow slit upon which light is focused from behind.

collision ejection hypothesis *another name for* giant impact hypothesis. See MOON.

color 1 the color of a star is measured and quoted in terms of its COLOR INDEX but basically depends on surface temperature: the star will radiate predominantly blue, white, yellow, orange, or red light in descending order of temperature (see SPECTRAL TYPES). Only the brightest stars have recognizable colors. Two stars of the same color may have very different LUMINOSITIES.
2 *short for* color index.

color coding see FALSE-COLOR IMAGERY.

color excess see COLOR INDEX.

color index the difference between the apparent MAGNITUDE of a star measured at one standard wavelength and the apparent magnitude at another (always longer) standard wavelength. Its value depends on the spectral distribution of the starlight, i.e. whether it is predominantly blue, red, etc., and it is therefore an indication of the color (i.e. temperature) of the star. It is independent of distance. Prior to the UBV system the *international color index* was mainly used; this is the difference between photographic and photovisual MAGNITUDES ($m_{pg} - m_{pv}$). In the now widely used UBV system (see MAGNITUDE) color index is usually expressed as the difference $B–V$, where B and V are the magnitudes measured with blue starlight (at a wavelength of 440 nanometers) and greenish-yellow starlight (550 nm), respectively. The color index $U–B$ is also used, where U is the apparent magnitude measured with ultraviolet radiation (365 nm) from a star.

Stars are classified into SPECTRAL TYPES, which are further subdivided into luminosity classes; each has a characteristic *intrinsic color index*, given as $(B–V)_0$ and $(U–B)_0$. These two indices are defined as zero for unreddened A0 main-sequence stars, such as Vega, and are therefore negative for hotter stars, i.e. those emitting more ultraviolet (O and B stars), and positive for cooler ones (A1 to M stars). Since color index is easily measured, it is usually used on graphs in preference to spectral type or temperature. Any excess of the measured value of color index of a star over the expected intrinsic value indicates that the starlight has become reddened by passage through interstellar dust (see EXTINCTION). The difference between the values is the *color excess*, E, of the star:

$$E = (B–V) - (B–V)_0$$

The value of E gives the amount of reddening.

There are also color indices relating to MAGNITUDES measured at red and infrared wavelengths. For example, in the indices $V–R$ and $V–I$, I and R are the magnitudes measured at 0.7 μm and 0.9 μm.

color-luminosity diagram see HERTZSPRUNG–RUSSELL DIAGRAM.

color-magnitude diagram (**C-M diagram**) see HERTZSPRUNG–RUSSELL DIAGRAM.

color temperature symbol: T_c. The surface temperature of a star expressed as the temperature of a BLACK BODY (i.e. a perfect radiator) whose energy distribution over a range of wavelengths corresponds to that of the star. It can thus be found by matching the energy distribution in the star's continuous spectrum to that of a black body (given by Planck's radiation law). With increasing temperature the star emits a higher proportion of blue and ultraviolet radiation and the position (wavelength) of maximum radiated energy on the energy distribution curve shifts accordingly; the basic shape of the curve remains unchanged (see illustration overleaf). Color temperature is related to COLOR INDEX ($B–V$) by an approximation of Planck's radiation law:

$$T_c = 7200/[(B–V) + 0.64] \text{ kelvin}$$

As a star's spectrum is not precisely that of a black body, the color temperature and EFFECTIVE TEMPERATURE are not equal: the difference is greatest for hot (O and B) stars. Although the color temperature is not as closely related to the star's surface temperature as is the effective temperature, it has the advantage of being found by measurements of the star's color index. The Sun's color temperature is 5700 K.

Columba (**Dove**) a constellation in the southern hemisphere near Canis Major, the two brightest stars being of 2nd and 3rd magnitude. Abbrev.: Col; genitive form: Columbae; approx. position: RA 6h, dec –35°; area: 270 sq deg.

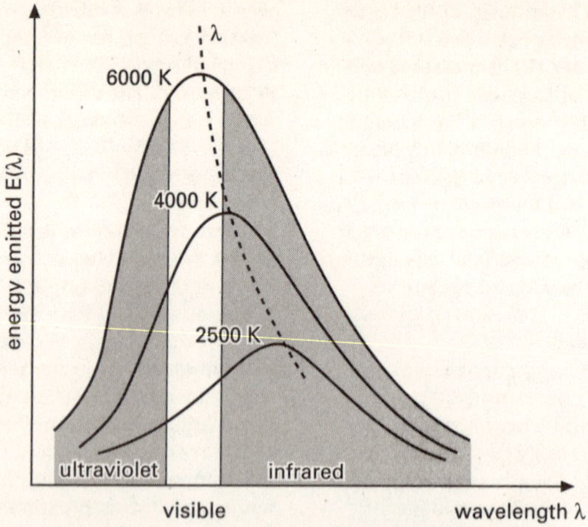

Planck radiation curves for various color temperatures

Columbus **1** a space program featuring a science module built by the European Space Agency (ESA) and incorporated into the International Space Station (ISS). The 4.5-meter pressurized cylindrical module is ESA's biggest single contribution to the ISS and is intended for use by Earth-based researchers working through the Columbus Control Center in Germany, with occasional assistance from the ISS crew. Permanently docked with the ISS, the Columbus module shares its basic structure and life-support systems with the Italian Space Agency's Multipurpose Logistics Modules. Its 75-cubic-meter interior is large enough to house a suite of scientific laboratories, allowing experiments to be carried out in microgravity across a range of scientific disciplines, including fluid physics, the biological sciences, and materials science. Four mounting points outside the pressurized hull of the Columbus module make provision for science packages that need to be exposed to the vacuum of space. Such packages may include investigations into the ability of bacteria to survive on the surface of an artificial meteorite or observations of volcanic activity on the Earth.
2 a telescope project involving two 8-meter telescopes on a single mount, planned by the University of Arizona and Ohio State University, with Italy as a partner. It was renamed the *Large Binocular Telescope* (*LBT*) in 1993 and was scheduled to begin operations in 2005. See STEWARD OBSERVATORY.

column density the number of atoms (of a particular element or ion) per unit area, often used to measure the amount of ABSORPTION caused by intervening matter along a line of sight.

colures the two great circles passing through the celestial poles and intersecting the ecliptic at either the EQUINOXES (*equinoctial colure*) or the SOLSTICES (*solstitial colure*).

coma **1** the most obvious part of a comet when it is close to the Sun. It consists of a diffuse luminous nebulous cloud of gas and dust that surrounds the comet's NUCLEUS and is formed by the sublimation of ices and ejection of dust particles from the nucleus. The brightest part of the coma is the central region nearest the surface of the nucleus, where the density of material being released is at its highest; the gas density in this region is typically 10^{13} molecules per cm^3. The visual boundary of the coma merges with the sky background.

A coma's size varies with the comet's distance from the Sun and with the amount of material being released from the nucleus but can grow to typically 10^4 to 10^5 km in diameter. The luminosity of the coma is mainly produced by FLUORESCENCE from a variety of carbon, nitrogen, hydrogen, and oxygen radicals and reflection of sunlight by dust particles. The shape seems roughly circular but fan-shaped comas have been reported. The material comprising the coma is extremely rarefied: even faint stars shine through.

See also HEAD.

2 an ABERRATION of a lens or mirror that occurs in a telescope when the light falls on the objective or primary mirror at an oblique angle. The light is not imaged as a point in the focal plane but as a fan-shaped area: each zone of the lens or mirror produces an off-axis image in the form of a circular patch of light, the diameter and position of the circle center varying steadily from zone to zone (see illustration). The dimensions of the resulting combination of zone images, i.e. the fan-shaped image, depends on the obliquity of the light falling on the lens or mirror. See also APLANATIC SYSTEM.

Coma Berenices (**Berenice's Hair**) an inconspicuous constellation in the northern hemisphere near Boötes, the brightest stars being of 4th magnitude. The north galactic pole lies in this constellation, which contains a huge cluster of faint galaxies, the very distant COMA CLUSTER. Part of a less remote collection of galaxies, the VIRGO CLUSTER, is also contained in this constellation. Other objects of interest include the globular cluster M53 (NGC 5024) and the so-called *Blackeye Galaxy* M64 (NGC 4826), a spiral galaxy whose center is completely obscured by an enormous dark nebula. NGC 4565 is a very faint spiral galaxy seen edge-on. Abbrev.: Com; genitive form: Comae Berenices; approx. position: RA 12.5h, dec +20°; area: 386 sq deg.

Coma cluster a very rich CLUSTER OF GALAXIES, near the north galactic pole, in the constellation Coma Berenices that contains at least 1000 bright elliptical and S0 galaxies. It is about 6 megaparsecs in diameter and is in the form of two equal subclumps, each with a central dominant galaxy associated with a radio source: an elliptical, NGC 4889, and an S0 galaxy, NGC 4874. The cluster is about 90 megaparsecs distant and is moving away from Earth at approximately 6700 km s^{-1}.

Comas Solá a COMET discovered in Nov. 1926 and subsequently found to have had its orbit severely disturbed when it approached within 0.19 AU of Jupiter in 1912. The major changes were in period (from 9.43 years to 8.53 years), PERIHELION DISTANCE (from 2.15 AU to 1.77 AU), and INCLINATION (from 18.1° to 13.7°).

combined magnitude the apparent

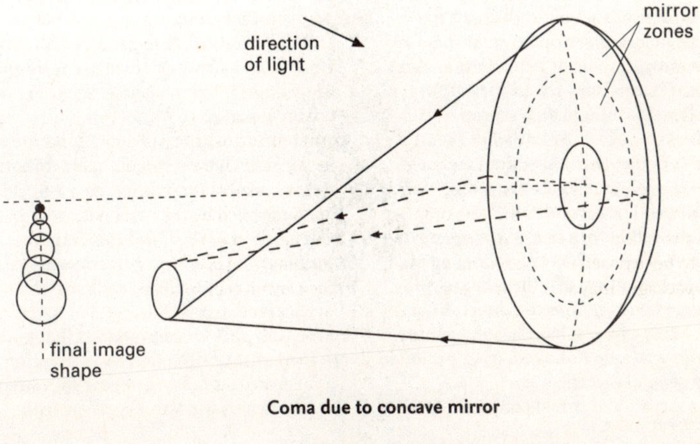

Coma due to concave mirror

brightness of two or more stars so close that they are observed as a single star. It is not equal to the sum of the individual magnitudes, m_1 and m_2, but is a logarithmic function:

$$m = m_1 - 2.5 \log\{1 + \text{antilog}[-0.4(m_2 - m_1)]\}$$

See MAGNITUDE.

comet a minor member of the Solar System that travels around the Sun in an orbit that generally is much more eccentric than the orbits of planets. Typical comets have three parts: the NUCLEUS, COMA, and COMET TAIL. The gas and dust tails of a comet appear only when the comet is near the Sun and always point away from the Sun. The nucleus is the permanent solid portion of a comet and is thought by the majority of astrophysicists to be a kilometer-sized *dirty snowball*; this model – the *Whipple model* – was first suggested by Fred L. Whipple in 1951. The Solar System contains only a few observable comets that have nuclei in the tens of kilometers size range. The numbers of actual (as opposed to observed) comets increase enormously as one goes to smaller and smaller sizes, but these are much less easy to see. The satellite missions to HALLEY'S COMET have revealed much about cometary composition and obtained the first image of a nucleus.

Cometary orbits fall into two classes. *Short-period comets* have periods of less than 200 years and orbits lying completely or almost completely inside the planetary system. They seem to have been captured into the inner Solar System by the gravitational attraction of the major planets. At any epoch about 50 of these are bright enough to be detected as they come to PERIHELION. They have a mean ECCENTRICITY of 0.56 and a mean INCLINATION of 11°. Nearly all of them (Halley's comet is an exception) are moving in direct orbits, i.e. in the same direction as the planets. The second class have near-parabolic orbits with periods in excess of 200 years. These orbits are orientated at random, indicating that these comets do not come from any specific direction in space. Many of them have been seen only once (for example Kohoutek has a period in excess of 70 000 years).

The majority of comets observed from Earth have perihelions near the Earth. This is simply due to observational selection. The brightness of a comet is proportional to $1/r^n\Delta^2$, where r is the distance between the comet and the Sun and Δ is the comet–Earth distance. The power n is on average 4.2 but can vary widely around this value. On average a comet passes perihelion about 1000 times before decaying away. Cometary decay produces METEOROID STREAMS.

Comets are named after their discoverers. In any year, say 1994, comets are designated 1994a, 1994b, etc., in order of discovery. Permanent designations 1994 I, 1994 II, etc., are given later, these being in order of date of perihelion passage.

There are two prevalent theories of cometary origin. In the first theory comets were produced as icy PLANETESIMALS in the Saturn–Neptune region, at the same time as the origin of the Solar System, and were then stored in the OORT CLOUD. In the second they are produced by gravitational accretion every time the Sun passes through an interstellar dust cloud. This latter theory predicts that the Solar System's cometary reservoir is periodically being topped up. The first theory predicts a cometary population that decreases with time.

cometary nebula a fan-shaped REFLECTION NEBULA whose illuminating star lies at the vertex of the fan. HUBBLE'S VARIABLE NEBULA is an example.

comet family a distinct group of comets, the members of which have APHELION distances that coincide approximately with points on the orbit of a giant planet, in particular Jupiter. Associations with Saturn, Uranus, and Neptune are now considered to be dynamically implausible. See JUPITER'S COMET FAMILY.

comet group a group of comets, occurring in the Solar System, which, apart from the time of perihelion passage, have very nearly the same orbital elements. 1668, 1843 I, 1880 I, 1882 II, 1887 I, and 1948 VII is a typical group. These groups have probably been formed by the tidal splitting of a larger comet.

comet tails tails of gas and dust that point in the antisolar direction away from the cometary NUCLEUS and appear only when a COMET is near the Sun, i.e. closer than about 2 AU (see illustration). Not all comets have tails. The luminosity is due to both molecular and atomic EMISSION and to reflection of sunlight. The gas and dust is forced away by RADIATION PRESSURE and by SOLAR-WIND interactions. There are two markedly different types of comet tails. The *ion tail* (or *plasma tail*) is usually straight and bluish, showing many diverse visible and rapidly changing structures. It consists exclusively of ionized molecules, moving at velocities between 10 and 100 km s^{-1}, the repulsive force being 20 to 100 times greater than gravity. The tail can be a million km wide and lengths of 10 million km are not uncommon. Sometimes large sections of the ion tail can break away (see DISCONNECTION EVENT). *Dust tails* are more strongly curved than ion tails. They contain solid particles, which simply reflect sunlight. Particles are ejected from the NUCLEUS along curved paths known as *syndynames*. The tail is an envelope over the reflection regions of particles of similar mass. The closer the dust tail is to the ion tail in curvature the smaller are the dust particles responsible for reflecting sunlight; they are usually 10–100 micrometers in diameter.

command module (**CM**) see APOLLO.

commensurable denoting orbital periods that are in rational proportion, i.e. in which one is a simple fraction (one-half, one-quarter, two-thirds, etc.) of the other. The condition is described as a *commensurability*. It is observed, for instance, between the orbital periods of planets (e.g. Neptune:Pluto is 2:3), and satellites (e.g. Io:Europa is 1:2). Commensurabilities arise from the effects of RESONANCE.

common envelope star a hypothetical type of GIANT STAR that consists of two stellar cores orbiting within a large common envelope of gas. Because the two cores are hidden within the envelope the star should superficially resemble a normal giant, and as a result no common envelope stars have yet been unambiguously identified. Their existence is strongly attested, however, by evidence for systems just before and just after this stage of evolution. Contact binaries of the W URSAE MAJORIS TYPE should become common envelope stars when one member expands as a red giant. Again, a close binary system where one member is a white dwarf must have had a common envelope at a previous evolutionary stage when the star now seen as a white dwarf went through its red giant phase: these systems are observed either as CATACLYSMIC VARIABLES or in the centers of some PLANETARY NEBULAE; the nebula's gas is probably the original common envelope, ejected as a result of the orbital motion of

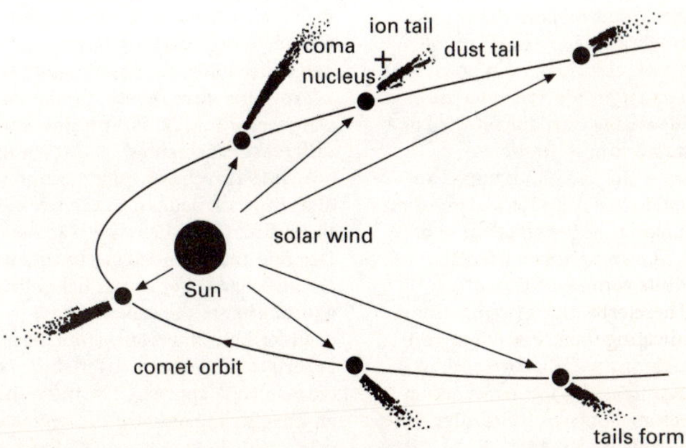

Comet tails

the two star cores within it. In some common envelope stars, the two cores may not eject the envelope gas but instead spiral together and eventually fuse into a single core. Angular momentum from the orbital motion would spin up the distended star; some rapidly spinning giant stars, like FK Comae and V Hydrae, may be examples of such *coalesced stars.*

common proper motion stars see VISUAL BINARY.

Compact Array see AUSTRALIA TELESCOPE.

compact galaxy a member of a class of PECULIAR GALAXIES, first catalogued by Fritz Zwicky in the 1960s. Their brightness is so concentrated that they are almost indistinguishable from stars on normal photographs and their constituent stars are unusually hot and blue. Detailed examination has shown that they are either ACTIVE GALAXIES, STARBURST galaxies, or EXTRAGALACTIC H II REGIONS, and the term compact galaxy is now rarely used.

compact groups of galaxies see GROUPS OF GALAXIES.

compact steep-spectrum radio sources see RADIO GALAXY.

comparator an instrument by means of which two photographs of the same area of the sky may be compared and any difference in the brightness or position of an object quickly detected without resorting to exact measurements. The movement of a comet, the proper motion of a star, or the presence of a variable star may thus be revealed. In the *blink comparator* the two photographs are viewed in rapid succession through an eyepiece: changes in position produce an apparent movement of an image while variable stars are detected as a pulsation in brightness. In the *stereocomparator* the two photographs are viewed simultaneously by binocular vision: objects that have changed in position or brightness (i.e. size) appear to stand out of the plane of the picture.

comparison spectrum the spectrum of one or more known substances under terrestrial conditions that is used in astronomy as a standard of comparison for investigating spectra of celestial objects; it provides, for example, a zero Doppler shift.

components stars, or possibly planets, that are constituent members of a BINARY STAR, TRIPLE STAR, or MULTIPLE-STAR system.

COMPTEL *abbrev. for* Compton Telescope. See COMPTON GAMMA RAY OBSERVATORY.

Compton Gamma Ray Observatory (**Compton Observatory**; **CGRO**) the second in NASA's series of GREAT OBSERVATORIES, launched by the space shuttle Atlantis into a low Earth orbit Apr. 1991. It took its name from the 20th-century US physicist Arthur Holly Compton. Providing nearly six orders of magnitude in spectral coverage, from 15 keV to 30 GeV, it studied a broad range of topics over its nine years of operational life. The 16-tonne observatory contained four gamma-ray telescopes on a stabilized platform.

BATSE, the burst and transient source experiment, measured gamma-ray brightness variations on time scales down to milliseconds; sources included GAMMA-RAY BURSTS, GAMMA-RAY TRANSIENTS, and solar FLARES. The instrument consisted of eight identical scintillator-crystal (NaI) detector modules that covered the entire sky, detecting photons in the energy band 0.03–1.9 MeV, plus a smaller spectroscopy detector optimized for broad energy coverage (0.015–110 MeV) and fine energy resolution.

OSSE, the oriented scintillation spectrometer experiment, observed gamma-ray sources in the 0.1–10 MeV range, with a limited capability above 10 MeV. The telescope consisted of four identical detector systems, each articulated to provide a 192° rotation. Normally, two detectors viewed the source, and two a nearby off-source region; the combination was reversed at regular intervals and the difference represented the net source flux.

COMPTEL, the imaging Compton Telescope, carried out a sensitive survey of the entire sky in the range 1–30 MeV. Discrete and extended sky images were reconstructed over a wide field of view with a resolution of the order of 1°.

EGRET, the energetic gamma-ray experiment telescope, covered the range 0.02–20 GeV (approx.). The instrument had an imaging capability at the degree level over a wide field of view. The basic imaging portion consisted of a SPARK CHAMBER arrangement within a plastic scintillator veto system; imaging was achieved by following the trajectories of the electron-positron pair through the spark chamber to a large NaI scintillation crystal where the photon energy was estimated.

The CGRO was one of the most efficient and successful space telescopes ever launched. It fulfilled its mission almost flawlessly, proving that gamma-ray bursts come from very distant regions of space and are the most powerful explosions in the Universe. In June 2000, NASA scientists deorbited the CGRO, which broke up during a controlled re-entry into the Earth's atmosphere. NASA plans to launch a successor to the CGRO, the Gamma-ray Large Area Space Telescope (GLAST), in 2006.

Compton scattering (**Compton effect**) an interaction between a PHOTON of electromagnetic radiation and a charged particle, such as an electron, in which some of the photon's energy is given to the particle. The photon is therefore reradiated at a lower frequency (i.e. with a lower energy) and the particle's energy is increased. In *inverse Compton emission* the reverse process takes place: photons of low frequency are scattered by moving charged particles and reradiated at a higher frequency.

Compton telescope a gamma-ray detector design based on the detection of a COMPTON SCATTERING interaction of a gamma ray in a first detector, usually a plastic scintillator, followed by the detection of the Compton scattered photon in a second detector. This method allows the simultaneous determination of photon direction and energy to be made. An imaging Compton telescope (COMPTEL) is part of the COMPTON GAMMA RAY OBSERVATORY.

concave curving inward. A concave mirror converges light. A biconcave or planoconcave lens, thinner in the middle than at the edges, has a diverging action.

concentration the diameter of the telescopic image of a point-source of light, such as a star. The image is increased from point size by unavoidable optical effects in the telescope, specifically diffraction (see AIRY DISK), and for ground-based telescopes it is further increased by distortion due to atmospheric conditions at the time of observation, i.e. by the SEEING.

Cone nebula see MONOCEROS.

configuration see ASPECT.

confocal lenses see AFOCAL SYSTEM.

confusion the running together of the traces from different radio sources in the output of a RADIO TELESCOPE. Confusion becomes important at the value of FLUX DENSITY when there is, on average, more than about one source in the BEAM at once. The radio telescope becomes *confusion limited* when this flux density is appreciably higher than its SENSITIVITY. Further increase in sensitivity will not then result in fainter sources being detected.

conic sections (**conics**) a family of curves that are the locus of a point that moves so that its distance from a fixed point (the focus) is a constant fraction of its distance from a fixed line (the directrix). The fraction, e, is the eccentricity of the conic. The value of the eccentricity determines the form of the conic. If e is less than 1 the conic is an ellipse. A circle is a special case of this with $e = 0$. If $e = 1$ the conic is a parabola and if e exceeds 1 the conic is a hyperbola.

These curves are known as conic sections because they can be obtained by taking sections of a right circular cone at different angles: a horizontal section gives a circle, an inclined one an ellipse, one parallel to the slope of the cone is a parabola, and one with an even greater inclination is a hyperbola (see illustration overleaf). Conics are important in astronomy since they represent the paths of bodies that move in a gravitational field. See also ORBIT.

conjunction the alignment of two bodies in the Solar System so that they have the same celestial longitude as seen from the Earth (see illustration at ELONGATION). The Sun and Moon are in conjunction at new Moon. An INFERIOR PLANET can be in conjunction twice in one revolution – at *inferior conjunction* when the planet lies between the Sun and the Earth and at *superior conjunction* when the planet lies on the opposite side of the Sun from the Earth. See also OPPOSITION.

conservation of mass-energy the principle that in any system of interacting bodies the total mass plus total energy is constant, where energy and mass are to be considered interconvertible according to the equation $E = mc^2$. The principle is a result of the theory of special RELATIVITY and is a generalization of the classical laws of *conservation of energy* and *conservation of mass*. These state that in a closed system energy (or matter) cannot appear or disappear spontaneously and cannot be lost or gained. Energy can only be transformed into different forms but the total energy must remain constant. According to relativity theory the transfer of energy by any process entails the transfer of mass, so that conservation of energy ensures conservation of mass.

conservation of momentum the principle that in any system of interacting bodies the total linear MOMENTUM in a fixed direction is constant provided that there is no external force acting on the system in that direction. The ANGULAR MOMENTUM of a system of bodies rotating and/or revolving about a fixed axis is also conserved provided that no external torque is applied.

constellation any of the 88 areas into which astronomers have divided the whole of the northern and southern hemispheres of the sky (or CELESTIAL SPHERE). Every star, galaxy, nebula, or other celestial body lies within, or sometimes overlaps, the boundaries of one of the constellations. These boundaries were established unambiguously by the International Astronomical Union in 1930 along arcs of RIGHT ASCENSION and DECLINATION for the epoch 1875, Jan. 1.

Originally the constellations had no fixed limits but were groups of stars considered by early civilizations to lie within the imagined outlines of mythological heroes, creatures, and other forms. In the *Almagest*, Ptolemy, in about AD 140, listed 48 constellations that were visible from the Mediterranean region. Their

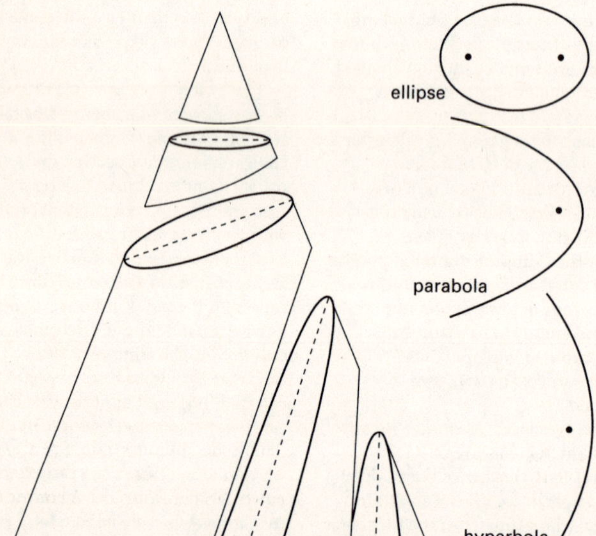

Conic sections

names were mostly derived from Greek and Roman mythology, which sought to explain their presence in the sky, but a few, such as Leo, the Lion, may be of much earlier origin. During the 16th, 17th, and 18th centuries many new groupings were identified and named (and several later discarded), especially in the previously uncharted regions of the southern hemisphere. These new groupings appeared principally in star atlases published by Bayer and Hevelius in the 17th century and Lacaille in the 18th. Since then further additions have proved unacceptable.

The constellations seen on any clear night depend on the latitude of the observer and change with the time of year and time of night. If, for a particular latitude, ϕ, the stars are CIRCUMPOLAR STARS (never set), they will be visible on every night of the year. Circumpolar stars are those with DECLINATIONS greater than $90 - \phi°$. Other stars never rise above the horizon at all: for observers in the northern hemisphere, these are the ones that have declinations beyond $\phi - 90°$; for observers in the southern hemisphere, they are the ones with declinations of $\phi + 90°$ (note that southern latitudes, like southern declinations, are taken to be negative for these calculations). The remaining stars can be seen only when they are above the horizon during the night, a star rising earlier, on average, by about two hours per month.

Each constellation bears a Latin name, as with Canis Major, the genitive form of which is used with the appropriate letter or number for the star name (see STELLAR NOMENCLATURE), as with Alpha Canis Majoris. For simplification the three-letter abbreviations for the constellations are more usually used, as with CMa. See Table 5, Appendix.

contact see ECLIPSE.

contact binary see BINARY STAR; EQUIPOTENTIAL SURFACES.

continuous spectrum a SPECTRUM consisting of a continuous region of emitted or absorbed radiation in which no discrete lines are resolvable. The emission from hot fairly dense matter will produce a continuous spectrum, as with the continuous emission of ultraviolet, visible, and infrared radiation from the Sun's PHOTOSPHERE. SYNCHROTRON EMISSION is another example of continuous emission.

continuum the CONTINUOUS SPECTRUM that would be measured for a body if no absorption or emission lines were present.

CONTOUR a NASA mission to be launched in July 2002 to study at least three comets: Encke (2003), Schwassmann–Wachmann-3 (2006), and d'Arrest (2008). The mission is designed so that it could be retargeted to intercept other unforseen comets.

contour map see RADIO-SOURCE STRUCTURE.

convection a process of heat transfer in which energy is transported from one region of a fluid to another by the flow of hot matter in bulk into cooler regions. See also CONVECTIVE ZONE; ENERGY TRANSPORT.

convective zone a zone in a star where CONVECTION is the main mode of ENERGY TRANSPORT. This occurs throughout a protostar on the HAYASHI TRACK, and beneath the surface of a MAIN-SEQUENCE STAR, where the temperature is sufficiently low to enable the nuclei of hydrogen and heavier elements to recombine with free electrons to form atoms and negative ions. The presence of these atoms and ions and their ability to absorb photons increases the OPACITY of the medium to the passage of radiation from below and results in a steeper temperature gradient, thereby triggering turbulent convection. Stars rather more massive than the Sun, fusing hydrogen by the CARBON CYCLE, have a convective zone at the core, which mixes the nuclear fusion region.

The surface convective zone of a sunlike or late-type star is almost certainly involved in the production of its magnetic field, and hence in the cycle of CHROMOSPHERIC ACTIVITY (or in the Sun's case SOLAR ACTIVITY) and in the heating of the CHROMOSPHERE and CORONA, but the details are still uncertain. See also GRANULATION; STELLAR STRUCTURE.

convex bulging outward. A convex mirror diverges light. A biconvex or planoconvex lens, fatter in the center than at the edges, has a converging action.

convolution a mathematical operation that is performed on two functions and expresses how the shape of one is 'smeared' by the other. Mathematically, the convolution of the functions f(x) and g(x) is given by

$$\int_{-\infty}^{\infty} f(u)g(x-u)du$$

It finds wide application in physics; it describes, for example, how the transfer function of an instrument affects the response to an input signal. See also AUTOCORRELATION FUNCTION; RADIO-SOURCE STRUCTURE.

cooling flow see CLUSTERS OF GALAXIES.

cooling time the time necessary for something to cool well below its present temperature. The *cooling function* is the rate of cooling of matter as a function of temperature, taking into account primary emission processes such as thermal BREMSSTRAHLUNG and line radiation.

coorbital satellites satellites that share the same orbit. For example, JANUS and EPIMETHEUS move in almost the same orbit around Saturn.

coordinated universal time (UTC) see UNIVERSAL TIME.

coordinate system a system, resembling that of latitude and longitude on the Earth, by which the direction of a celestial body or a point in the sky can be specified. The direction is defined and determined by two spherical coordinates, referred to a fundamental great circle lying on the CELESTIAL SPHERE and a point on the fundamental circle (see illustration). One coordinate (a) is the angular distance of the celestial body measured perpendicular to the fundamental circle along an auxiliary great circle passing through the body and the poles of the fundamental circle. The other coordinate (b) is the angular distance measured along the fundamental circle from a selected zero point to the intersection of the auxiliary circle.

There are four main coordinate systems: the EQUATORIAL, HORIZONTAL, ECLIPTIC, and GALACTIC COORDINATE SYSTEMS (see table). They are all centered on the Earth. Transformations can be made from one system to another by means of the relationships between the angles and sides of the relevant SPHERICAL TRIANGLES. The ASTRONOMICAL TRIANGLE, for example, relates equatorial and horizontal coordinates; the triangle formed by the celestial body and the poles of the equator and ecliptic relates equatorial and ecliptic coordinates. See also HELIOCENTRIC COORDINATE SYSTEM.

Copernican system a HELIOCENTRIC SYSTEM of the Solar System that was proposed by Nicolaus Copernicus and eventually published in 1543 in his book *De Revolutionibus*. It uses some of the basic ideas of the PTOLEMAIC SYSTEM, including circular orbits and epicycles, and was no more accurate in its predictions. Copernicus, however, maintained that the planets move around the Sun (in the relative positions accepted today), the Sun's position being offset from the center of the orbits. The apparent motions of celestial bodies such as the Sun were explained in terms of the rotation of the Earth about its axis and also the Earth's orbital motion.

The planetary motion can be represented by two uniform circular motions: one is an epicyclic motion of the planet about a point D on the circular orbit; the other, unlike that of the Ptolemaic system, is a uniform circular motion of D about the center, C, of the orbit. This requires that the rate of motion of D about C is exactly half that of the epicyclic rate of motion with respect to a fixed direction.

There was a strong and prolonged reaction – especially by the Church – to the Copernican system, which effectively displaced the Earth as the center of the Universe. There was also a sudden revival in astronomical observation in order to test the theory, notably by Tycho Brahe. Tycho's detailed observations, which showed the inadequacies of the Copernican system, were used in the formulation of KEPLER'S LAWS of planetary motion. The heliocentric cosmology became firmly established after Galileo had made telescopic observations of the phases of Venus.

Copernican System the youngest stratigraphic system of the Moon. It includes the freshest lunar CRATERS, formed during the last billion (10^9) years approximately, many of which have preserved RAYS. The period began with the

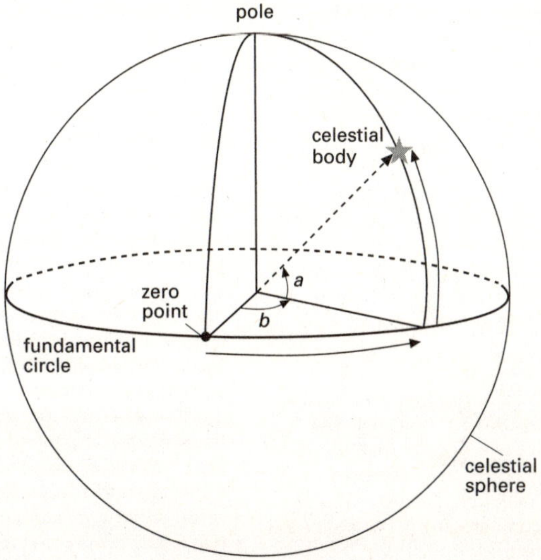

Coordinate system

The Four Main Coordinate Systems

Coordinate system	*Fundamental circle*	*Zero point*	*Coordinates*
equatorial	celestial equator	vernal equinox	right ascension declination
ecliptic	ecliptic	vernal equinox	celestial longitude celestial latitude
horizontal	horizon	north point	azimuth altitude
galactic	galactic equator	galactic center	galactic longitudes galactic latitude

formation of the crater COPERNICUS. The *Eratosthenian System* (for which Eratosthenes is the type crater) covers the earlier period extending from about 3.15 to 1 billion years ago. It includes slightly older more degraded craters with no visible rays, in addition to most of the youngest MARE deposits. See also IMBRIAN SYSTEM; NECTARIAN SYSTEM.

Copernicus 1 a young lunar crater to the south of Mare Imbrium that is 90 km in diameter and has an extensive system of RAYS and SECONDARY CRATERS. Possible ray material was collected by the crew of Apollo 12 and dated at 850 million years; this provides a calibration point for the COPERNICAN SYSTEM.
2 NASA's ORBITING ASTRONOMICAL SATELLITE OAO-3, launched in Aug. 1972 and operated until Dec. 1980. It carried a 0.9-meter telescope and a grating spectrometer used primarily for measurements of ultraviolet radiation, but also carried X-ray equipment. See ULTRAVIOLET ASTRONOMY; X-RAY SATELLITES.

Coprates canyon see VALLES MARINERIS.

Cor Caroli (**α CVn**) a bluish-white star that is the brightest one in the constellation Canes Venatici, Its name means 'Charles's Heart' and was given to it by Edmund Halley in honor of the English King Charles II. It is a visual binary (separation 20″), the brighter component (A or α^2 CVn) being the prototype of the SPECTRUM VARIABLE stars. It has a period of 5.469 days and its spectrum shows strong profuse lines of rare earths, iron-peak elements, and silicon. m_v: 2.9 (A), 5.5 (B); spectral type: B9.5 pv (A), F0 V (B).

Cordelia a small satellite of Uranus, discovered in 1986. Together with OPHELIA, it acts as a SHEPHERD SATELLITE to the outermost ring (the Epsilon ring) of Uranus. See URANUS' RINGS; URANUS' SATELLITES; Table 2, Appendix.

Córdoba Durchmusterung (**CD**) see BONNER DURCHMUSTERUNG.

core **1** the central region of a star, such as the Sun, in which energy is generated by thermonuclear reactions.
2 the central region of a differentiated planet or satellite, such as the EARTH or MOON.

core collapse supernova see SUPERNOVA.

Coriolis force a concept introduced to simplify calculations on the motion of bodies observed from a rotating frame of reference, such as the Earth. The effect of the Coriolis force is to deflect the object in a direction perpendicular to its course.

corona **1** the extremely tenuous outermost part of a star's atmosphere. The most easily observed corona is that of the Sun.

Optically, the solar corona has two main components: the K-CORONA (or inner corona) consists of rapidly moving free electrons, exhibits a CONTINUOUS SPECTRUM, and attains a temperature of around 2 000 000 K at a height of about 75 000 km; the F-CORONA (or outer corona) consists of relatively slow-moving particles of interplanetary dust, exhibits an ABSORPTION SPECTRUM, and extends for many million kilometers into the INTERPLANETARY MEDIUM. A third component, the E-CORONA, consists of relatively slow-moving ions and exhibits an EMISSION SPECTRUM superimposed on the CONTINUUM of the K-corona.

The *white-light corona* comprises the overlapping K-corona and F-corona. It is visible under natural circumstances only in profile beyond the Sun's limb on the rare occasions when the PHOTOSPHERE is totally eclipsed by the Moon. It may, however, be observed out to distances of several solar radii at times other than totality, with the aid of a balloon- or satellite-borne externally occulted CORONAGRAPH. Similarly, the E-corona may be observed at specific wavelengths with the aid of the Lyot coronagraph, used at certain high-altitude observatories.

The corona may also be observed against the Sun's disk at extreme-ultraviolet and X-ray wavelengths, using rocket- or satellite-borne instrumentation. X-ray observations reveal the structure of the corona at temperatures of several million kelvin. Strong X-ray emission is associated with ACTIVE REGIONS, and an absence of X-ray emission with CORONAL HOLES. There is little or no evidence for a uniform corona – its structure is determined by the strength and configuration of the localized magnetic fields. The X-ray telescopes on SKYLAB and the SOLAR MAXIMUM MISSION, in particular, provided much additional information on coronal structure (see CORONAL TRANSIENTS).

The overall shape of the solar corona changes with the phase of the SUNSPOT CYCLE. At sunspot minimum it is roughly symmetrical, with long equatorial *streamers*, and *plumes* orientated in the direction of the Sun's polar magnetic field. At sunspot maximum it is less symmetrical, although more evenly distributed about the Sun's disk as a whole. Its changing shape is due principally to the presence of individual streamers above active regions, the mean heliographic latitude of which progresses toward the equator as the sunspot cycle proceeds. Solar radio emission at meter wavelengths originates in the corona and may exhibit an intense burst or series of bursts at the time of a large FLARE.

It has been found that in general the coronae of normal stars are sources of X-rays: the X-ray telescope on the EINSTEIN

OBSERVATORY was able to detect all types of stars apart from red supergiants. The idea that coronae are heated by shock waves rising through the chromosphere from the photosphere (acoustic heating) is now considered untenable, because such heating would occur only in late-type stars like the Sun. Instead, the coronal output is thought to be linked to the star's rotation. In certain binary systems (RS CANUM VENATICORUM STARS and some FLARE STARS) the orbital motion forces the stars to spin rapidly, and they are unusually strong X-ray sources. Young stars, such as those in the Orion nebula or the Pleiades, rotate faster than older stars of the same spectral type; they too have powerful X-ray emitting coronae. The link is almost certainly that fast rotation considerably enhances the magnetic field, and this provides greater heat input to the corona; the details, however, are still obscure.
2 the DARK HALO of our Galaxy.
3 a surface feature on a planet or satellite, especially VENUS. The coronae on Venus are circular features that exceed 300 km in diameter and 0.5 km in elevation, and are surrounded by concentric rings of ridges. *Artemis Chasma* is the largest corona found so far, 2100 km across, with its outer ring of fractures forming a steep trough about 120 km wide and scarps up to 2.5 km high.

Corona Australids a minor METEOR SHOWER that is observable in the southern hemisphere, radiant: RA 245°, dec –48°, and that maximizes on March 16.

Corona Australis (Southern Crown) a small inconspicuous constellation in the southern hemisphere near Scorpius, lying partly in the Milky Way. The brightest stars are of 4th magnitude. It contains the just-visible globular cluster NGC 6541. Abbrev.: CrA; genitive form: Coronae Australis; approx. position: RA 19h, dec –40°; area: 128 sq deg.

Corona Borealis (Northern Crown) a small constellation in the northern hemisphere near Ursa Major in which there is a semicircle of stars, the brightest being the 2nd-magnitude ALPHECCA. It also contains the prototype of the variable R CORONAE Borealis stars and the RECURRENT NOVA T Coronae Borealis. Abbrev.: CrB; genitive form: Coronae Borealis; approx. position: RA 15.5h, dec +30°; area: 179 sq deg.

coronagraph an optical instrument designed in 1930 by the French astronomer Bernard Lyot for observing the solar CORONA at times other than a total solar eclipse. In the coronagraph, the bright image of the Sun is artificially eclipsed by means of a blackened occulting disk set at the prime focus of the objective lens of a refracting telescope. A lens is used because the scattering of light from its surface is much less than is the case with a mirror. It is important to reduce scattering to a minimum if the faint light of the corona is to be recorded on the photographic plate or other detector. To reduce atmospheric scattering, high-altitude sites are used; coronagraphs have also been operated from satellites, rockets, and balloon platforms. A narrow-band INTERFERENCE FILTER is usually placed in front of the detector so that the emission lines of the E-CORONA can be studied.

coronal gas collisionally ionized gas (mostly hydrogen) at a temperature of about 10^6 K. METALS typically have very high ionization states, as revealed by the ABSORPTION LINES of five-times-ionized oxygen (O^{+5}).

coronal holes regions of exceptionally low density and temperature compared with the surrounding solar or stellar CORONA. They overlie areas of the Sun's disk that are characterized by relatively weak divergent (and therefore primarily unipolar) magnetic fields, and are thought to be the primary source of the high-speed streams of energetic charged particles in the SOLAR WIND.

coronal lines bright emission lines observed in the spectrum of the Sun's E-CORONA.

coronal mass ejections (CMEs) see CORONAL TRANSIENTS.

coronal rain see PROMINENCES.

coronal transients (coronal mass ejections) huge eruptions of gas from the solar CORONA into the INTERPLANETARY MEDIUM, first observed from space in the early 1970s. They seem to occur at a rate of about one per day (around the time of sunspot maximum – see SUNSPOT CYCLE) and are in many cases associated with the sudden rapid ascent of a quiescent filament (see

DISPARATION BRUSQUE) or, to a lesser extent, with an energetic FLARE.

Typically, a coronal transient expels around 10^{12}–10^{13} kg of coronal material, often in the form of a 'bubble' with a clearly defined leading edge. This expands as it is accelerated outward to a final speed of 200–1000 km s^{-1} after about an hour. The passage of a transient through the corona 'straightens' the coronal magnetic field lines, making them more nearly radial, and thereby allows magnetic flux emerging from the photosphere to occupy a greater volume.

correcting plate (**correcting lens; corrector**) the aspherical element placed at the front of a CATADIOPTRIC TELESCOPE to correct the aberration of its spherical primary mirror. In this way a very wide field can be obtained, sensibly free from aberrations, even at FOCAL RATIOS well below one. See also MAKSUTOV TELESCOPE; SCHMIDT TELESCOPE.

correlation function a measure of the clustering on extragalactic scales obtained from REDSHIFT SURVEYS. It is the probability for a galaxy to have another neighbor within a given distance of separation, in excess of the probability expected from a uniform random distribution of galaxies, expressed as a function of that distance. Galaxy positions are highly correlated, with the probability decreasing approximately as the inverse square of the galaxy separation. The *correlation length* for clusters of galaxies is the radius within which the chance of finding another galaxy is double the chance expected from a uniform random distribution of galaxies. Galaxies cluster into groups and clusters on a length-scale of around 30 megaparsecs, whereas SUPERCLUSTERS have correlation lengths nearer 130 megaparsecs.

correlation length see CORRELATION FUNCTION.

correlation receiver a radio-astronomy RECEIVER in which either the NOISE POWER from a single ANTENNA is split and multiplied with itself or the noise power from the two arms of an interferometer (see RADIO TELESCOPE) are multiplied together. Signals that are uncorrelated (completely unrelated) give an output whose average value is zero when multiplied together. Correlated signals, however, produce components near zero frequency that give a steady deflection in the output of the multiplier. In addition to their use in radio interferometry, correlation receivers are also used to reduce the effect of INTERFERENCE and of changes in the GAIN and other parameters of the system. See also PHASE-SWITCHING INTERFEROMETER.

Corvus (**Crow**) a small fairly conspicuous constellation in the southern hemisphere near the star Spica, the four brightest stars being of 2nd and 3rd magnitude. It contains the associated radio sources NGC 4038 and 4039, a pair of galaxies in collision with each other. Abbrev.: Crv; genitive form: Corvi; approx. position: RA 12.5h, dec −20°; area: 184 sq deg.

COS-B a satellite of the European Space Agency that was launched in Aug. 1975 to investigate celestial objects emitting gamma rays and to measure time variations of such emission. It operated over the energy range 70 to 5000 MeV and performed so efficiently that the mission was twice extended, operations ceasing in 1982. See also GAMMA-RAY ASTRONOMY.

cosine rule see SPHERICAL TRIANGLE.

cosmic abundance the relative proportion of each ELEMENT found in the Universe. The standard cosmic abundance is based on that of the Solar System, determined from observations of the relative line strengths in the spectrum of solar radiation, from geological surveys of the Earth, and from analysis of meteorites (see table). The solar abundance in terms of numbers of atoms gives 90.8% hydrogen, 9.1% helium, and 0.1% other elements. Abundances deduced for most stars from their spectra usually agree quite well with the standard, although old stars tend to have rather less of the HEAVY ELEMENTS (see POPULATION I, POPULATION II) and there are a number of odd stars with abundances quite unlike the rest. The abundances deduced from the absorption and emission lines of the INTERSTELLAR MEDIUM do not agree so well, principally in that there is an apparent shortage of refractory elements such as iron. It is likely that these elements are present, however, but are bound up with the COSMIC DUST.

Cosmic Anisotropy Telescope (**CAT**) a three-element interferometer operating at frequencies between 13 and 17 GHz and on baselines of 1 to 5 m. Located at the MULLARD RADIO ASTRONOMY OBSERVATORY near Cambridge, England, CAT measured primordial temperature variations in the cosmic microwave background radiation. Its first set of results was published in 1996, followed by a second set in 1999. The telescope was turned off and partly dismantled in 2000.

Cosmic Background Explorer see COBE.

cosmic background radiation unresolved radiation from space. The cumulative effect of many unresolved – and individually weak – discrete sources provides the background at radio, X-ray, and possibly other wavelengths. One important form is the MICROWAVE BACKGROUND RADIATION, which peaks at about 1 mm wavelength (i.e. a frequency of 3×10^{10} hertz). This is considered to be due to the hot BIG BANG. See also COBE; GAMMA-RAY ASTRONOMY; INFRARED BACKGROUND RADIATION; RADIO SOURCE; X-RAY BACKGROUND RADIATION.

cosmic censorship, principle of see SINGULARITY.

cosmic dust small particles or grains of matter found in many regions of space. Their size ranges from about 10 μm to less than 0.01 μm. They are thought to be composed primarily of carbon and silicate material, which may in some cases have mantles of water and ammonia ice or of solid carbon dioxide. Within the Solar System they are associated with the ZODIACAL LIGHT. In the INTERSTELLAR MEDIUM they are found in MOLECULAR CLOUDS and DARK NEBULAE, causing INTERSTELLAR EXTINCTION. The grains are also found in circumstellar shells causing the INFRARED EXCESS seen in the spectrum of many stars.

cosmic jet see JET.

cosmic noise (**Jansky noise**) see ANTENNA TEMPERATURE.

cosmic power spectrum the spectrum of variations in power of the DARK MATTER. The quantum fluctuations in the very early Universe were stretched during the inflationary period to form the seeds from which present-day structure in the Universe has grown. One popular form of the cosmic power spectrum is a power-law known as the *Harrison–Wheeler spectrum.*

cosmic rays highly energetic particles that move through space at close to the speed of light and that continuously bombard the Earth's atmosphere from all directions. They were discovered by V.F. Hess during a balloon flight in 1912. The energies of the individual particles are immense, ranging from about 10^8 to over 10^{19} electronvolts (eV). The intensity (or particle flux) of cosmic rays is very low; it is greatest at low energies – several thousand particles per square meter per second – dropping with increasing energy but apparently leveling off at high energies. Cosmic rays are

Cosmic Abundance of Elements, using Solar System as Standard

Element	*Atomic number*	*Approx. composition by mass (%)*
hydrogen (H)	1	70.13
helium (He)	2	27.87
oxygen (O)	8	0.91
carbon (C)	6	0.41
neon (Ne)	10	0.14
nitrogen (N)	7	0.10
silicon (Si)	14	0.07
magnesium (Mg)	12	0.06
sulfur (S)	16	0.04

primarily nuclei of the most abundant elements (mass numbers up to 56) although all known nuclei are represented. PROTONS (hydrogen nuclei) form the highest proportion; heavy nuclei are very rare. Also present are a small number of ELECTRONS, POSITRONS, antiprotons, NEUTRINOS, and GAMMA-RAY photons. All these particles are known collectively as *primary cosmic rays.*

On entering the Earth's atmosphere the great majority collide violently with atomic nuclei in the atmosphere producing *secondary cosmic rays*; these consist mainly of ELEMENTARY PARTICLES. The large number of particles produced from one such collision form an *extensive air shower* (or simply an *air shower*), in which there is a very rapid, highly complex, but well-defined sequence of reactions. The initial products are principally charged and neutral PIONS. The neutral pions decay (disintegrate) almost immediately into gamma rays, which give rise to *cascades* of electrons and positrons by PAIR PRODUCTION and to more photons by BREMSSTRAHLUNG radiation from the decelerating electrons and positrons. The charged pions decay into MUONS, which subsequently decay into neutrinos and electrons. The original primary cosmic ray nucleus, and many of the secondary cosmic rays, undergo more collisions to create further generations of particles. Following the initial collision the number of particles in the shower increases to a maximum at some point high in the atmosphere, where the creation of new particles is balanced by absorption; the number then decreases. Very few primary cosmic rays reach the Earth's surface, the final products including electrons, muons, neutrinos, gamma rays, and some initial products of the primary collision. The maximum number of particles in an air shower depends on the energy of the primary cosmic ray: half a million particles can be produced at maximum development by a primary nucleus of 10^{15} eV. It is, however, a major problem to distinguish air showers produced by different primary nuclei of the same energy.

Lower-energy primary cosmic rays ($<10^{13}$ eV), i.e. those with the largest intensity, can be studied directly by sending particle detectors, such as scintillation counters, above the Earth's atmosphere in satellites, spaceprobes, rockets, and balloons. High-energy particles ($>10^{16}$ eV) have too low a flux for direct measurements and can be studied only through their extensive air showers using arrays of detectors at ground level; particles with energies exceeding 10^{20} eV have been detected with giant arrays of instruments covering areas greater than one km^2. Intermediate energies require sensitive detector arrays on mountaintops or large detectors in satellites.

Most of the lighter primary cosmic-ray nuclei are considered products of collisions of heavier nuclei that occur during their journey from source. These parent nuclei, with other heavy nuclei and most of the primary electrons, are created in some as yet unknown NUCLEOSYNTHESIS process of catastrophic origin. Medium and lower energy particles probably originate in SUPERNOVA explosions: both the Crab nebula and the supernova remnant of the Vela pulsar are thought to be sources. Shock waves associated with supernovae could provide the acceleration. The extraordinary acceleration processes that could produce the highest energies are not yet identified. There is no evidence as yet for a maximum energy for cosmic rays, although this has been predicted.

It is generally believed that almost all cosmic rays with energies less than about 10^{18} eV are generated by sources within the Galaxy. It is also thought that these particles are confined to the Galaxy for probably tens of millions of years by the complex and very weak GALACTIC MAGNETIC FIELD. Cosmic-ray particles, being charged, are affected by a magnetic field: they are deflected from their initial paths and become trapped in the galactic field, the lowest energies being most deflected. During their long confinement their directions of travel become almost uniformly scattered: these cosmic rays are nearly isotropic. As cosmic rays enter the Solar System they can be further scattered by magnetic irregularities in interplanetary space: the total intensity at the Earth's orbit is twice as great at sunspot minimum than at sunspot maximum.

Although lower-energy cosmic rays are confined very effectively, higher-energy particles tend to 'leak out' of the Galaxy; above a critical energy at which the effect of the magnetic field becomes negligible, they can all escape. Thus the cosmic-ray intensity should decrease with energy. The intensity, however, levels off at the highest energies, and the isotropy decreases; this has been taken as evidence of other sources of cosmic rays outside the Galaxy. Since high-energy particles travel in approximately straight lines (being almost unaffected by magnetic fields) their arrival direction should indicate their source direction: measurements made with the giant detector arrays point to sources well away from the galactic plane, i.e. to possible extragalactic sources. Gamma rays can arise in space from the interaction of primary cosmic rays with interstellar matter. It is hoped that measurements of the distribution of gamma rays in space, especially those of high energies ($>10^{18}$ eV), will reflect the distribution of cosmic rays and thus reveal the galactic or extragalactic nature of their sources.

cosmic scale factor symbol: R. A measure of the size of the Universe as a function of time. R is related to the REDSHIFT parameter, z, by

$$1 + z = R(t_0)/R(t_1)$$

where t_0 is the present time and t_1 is the time at emission of the radiation. The quantity $(1 + z)$ thus gives the factor by which the Universe has expanded in size between the time t_1 and the present, t_0. The *proper distance* between the origin and a point at a comoving coordinate r (i.e. in a system expanding with the Universe) is given by the product of $R(t)$ and $\sin^{-1}r$, r, or $\sinh^{-1}r$ depending on whether the UNIVERSE is closed, Euclidean, or open, respectively. R is also related to the HUBBLE CONSTANT H_0:

$$H_0 = R^{-1}(\mathrm{d}R/\mathrm{d}t)$$

cosmic strings linelike defects in SPACETIME that are infinitesimally thin but of very high mass. They can be either in an infinite linear form or a closed loop. Cosmic strings in the early Universe could act as gravitational condensates to promote galaxy formation. There is as yet no experimental support for their existence, but they could produce linelike anisotropies in the cosmic MICROWAVE BACKGROUND RADIATION.

cosmic year (**galactic year**) the period of revolution of the Sun about the center of the Galaxy, equal to about 220 million years.

cosmogony the study of the origin and evolution of cosmic objects and in particular the Solar System. See GALAXIES, FORMATION AND EVOLUTION; SOLAR SYSTEM, ORIGIN; STELLAR EVOLUTION. Compare COSMOLOGY.

cosmological constant a constant term that can be added to Einstein's field equations of GENERAL RELATIVITY THEORY. The cosmological constant was originally put forward by Albert EINSTEIN in 1917 to ensure that the application of general relativity theory to the Universe results in a static Universe rather than an expanding or contracting Universe. The discovery that the Universe is expanding removed the necessity for introducing the cosmological constant but cosmological models with a nonzero cosmological constant have been considered by theoreticians.

For many years it was thought that the value of the cosmological constant is exactly zero but, starting in the late 1990s, evidence began to accumulate that the cosmological constant has a small but nonzero value. This has the consequence that the expansion of the Universe is accelerating. There have been many attempts to show why the value of the cosmological constant is either zero or very small but there is no consensus as to why this should be the case.

cosmological models (**world models**) possible representations of the Universe in simple terms. Models are an essential link between observation and theory and act as the basis for prediction. Complications are added only when necessary (Occam's razor). A simple model for a two-dimensional Universe is the surface of an expanding balloon, on which HUBBLE'S LAW and the isotropy of the MICROWAVE BACKGROUND RADIATION may be demonstrated.

Most standard cosmological models of the Universe are mathematical and are based on the *Friedmann Universe*, derived by Aleksandr Friedmann in 1922 and independently by Georges Lemaître in 1927.

They assume the HOMOGENEITY and ISOTROPY of an expanding (or contracting) Universe in which the only force that need be considered is GRAVITATION. The BIG BANG THEORY is such a model. These models result from considerations of Einstein's field equations of general RELATIVITY. When the pressure is negligible the equations reduce to

$$(dR/dt)^2/R^2 + kc^2/R^2 = (8\pi/3)G\rho$$

for energy conservation – this is known as the *Friedmann equation* – and

$$\rho R^3 = \text{constant}$$

for mass conservation. R is the COSMIC SCALE FACTOR, ρ the MEAN DENSITY OF MATTER, G the gravitational constant, and c the speed of light; k is the curvature index of space of value +1 (closed UNIVERSE), –1 (open Universe), or 0 (flat or *Einstein–de Sitter Universe*). See illustration.

Other models involving the *cosmological constant*, Λ, have been proposed, such as the *de Sitter model*, in which no mass is present, the *Lemaître model*, which exhibits a coasting phase during which R is roughly constant, the STEADY-STATE THEORY, and those in which the gravitational constant, G, varies with time (see BRANS–DICKE THEORY). The cosmological constant is an arbitrary constant. Although it is possible for it to have any value that does not conflict with observation, it is highly probable that it is close to zero. Cosmological models involving Λ have recently come back into fashion. See also STATIC UNIVERSE.

cosmological principle a principle stating that there are no preferred places in the Universe. This is the basis for much of modern COSMOLOGY and is an extreme case of the Copernican view that the Earth is not the center of the Universe. Neglecting local irregularities, measurements of the limited regions of the Universe available to Earth-based observers are then valid samples of the whole Universe.

cosmological redshift the REDSHIFT resulting from the expansion of the Universe rather than from gravitational effects of intervening matter (see GRAVITATIONAL REDSHIFT) or from the motion of an intragalactic object away from the Solar System. See also COSMIC SCALE FACTOR.

cosmology the study of the origin, evolution, and large-scale structure of the UNIVERSE. COSMOLOGICAL MODELS describing the behavior of the COSMIC SCALE FACTOR with time are constructed from gravitational theory. These are then tested by comparison with, for example,

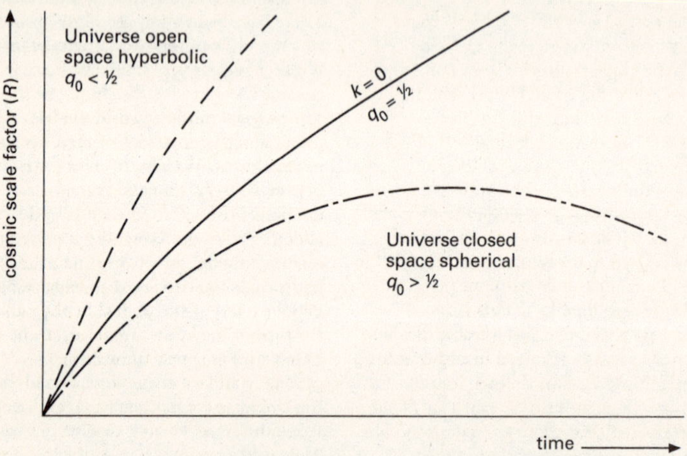

Cosmological models with different deceleration parameters, q_0

SOURCE COUNTS, the HUBBLE DIAGRAM, and the cosmic HELIUM abundance. The angular size of cosmic objects does not necessarily vary linearly with REDSHIFT and can be used as a further test – the *angular-size redshift test*. The nonlinearity arises because such objects were closer to us in the past and because radiation is bent by the gravitational attraction of intervening matter.

Cosmos a large series of Soviet satellites, the first of which was launched in March 1962. The many and varied applications of these satellites included astronomical, ionospheric, atmospheric, geomagnetic, geodetic, and biological studies. The satellites were also apparently used for navigation, reconnaissance, ocean surveillance, and military communications.

COSMOS a system of highly versatile automated plate-scanning equipment at the ROYAL OBSERVATORY, Edinburgh, used principally to extract data from the sky photographs of the UK SCHMIDT TELESCOPE and other Schmidts.

COSTAR see HUBBLE SPACE TELESCOPE.

coudé focus see COUDÉ TELESCOPE.

coudé telescope any telescope in which the light emerges along the POLAR AXIS so that its direction remains fixed while the object observed goes through its normal diurnal motion. This arrangement is essential when the light is to be subjected to analysis by bulky and delicate instruments, such as the SPECTROGRAPH, which can then be mounted in a fixed position at the *coudé focus*.

There are two main ways in which the fixed coudé focus can be secured. In one alternative, involving an equatorially mounted telescope, one or more extra mirrors can be placed so as to reflect or 'bend' the emerging light along the polar axis – the French word *coudé* means 'bent' or 'angled' (see illustration). This is the practice in large reflecting telescopes where the coudé focus is provided in addition to the prime and Cassegrain foci. It is also the basis for the amateurs' *Springfield mount*, in which the diagonal of a Newtonian telescope sends the light along the declination axis to an additional diagonal, which reflects it up the polar axis to the observer's eye.

In the other alternative, the whole telescope is mounted in a fixed position along the polar axis; a large moveable plane mirror is driven by a mechanism that allows it to reflect the observed object into the telescope for as long as observations may continue. This is the basis of many SOLAR TELESCOPES.

counterglow see GEGENSCHEIN.

covariance function a statistical measure of the association of astronomical objects in a sample. See CORRELATION FUNCTION.

CPD *abbrev. for* Cape Photographic Durchmusterung.

Crab nebula (Ml; NGC 1952) a turbulent expanding mass of gas and dust with luminous twisting filaments of ionized gas, lying about 2000 parsecs away and located in the sky near the star Zeta (ζ) Tauri in the constellation Taurus. It is a SUPERNOVA REMNANT, the result of a SUPERNOVA (probably of type II) that was almost certainly observed by Chinese and Japanese astronomers in 1054 and was sufficiently bright (magnitude about –5) to be visible in daylight for more than three weeks. At present it is about four parsecs in diameter. The Crab nebula emits SYNCHROTRON radiation of all wavelengths and is a particularly strong source of X-rays (Taurus X-1) and radio waves (TAURUS A). It was named the Crab nebula in 1848 by its first modern observer, the Irish astronomer William Parsons, 3rd Earl of Rosse (1800–67).

The star whose explosion produced the Crab nebula is now a young OPTICAL PULSAR (the *Crab pulsar* NP 0532), identified as such in 1967. Its pulsations are also observed at radio, infrared, X-ray, and gamma-ray wavelengths. These pulsations have a period of only 0.0331 seconds. The pulsar is the power house for the Crab nebula: energy is being lost by the pulsar in the form of highly energetic electrons, causing the pulsar to slow down very gradually; the electrons interact with the intense magnetic field extending into the nebula and radiate synchrotron emission. The energy loss of the pulsar equals the total energy radiated by the nebula (10^{30} to

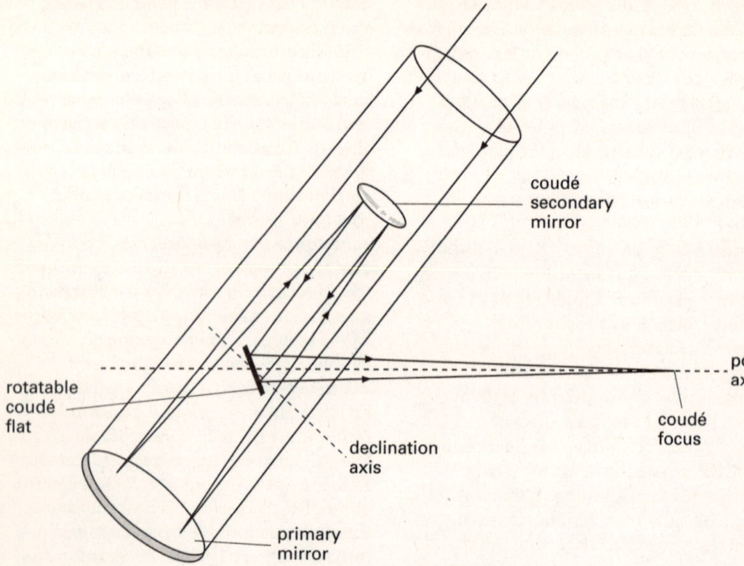

Light path in coudé telescope

10^{31} J s^{-1}). The ultraviolet component of this radiation ionizes the gas in the filaments, causing the atoms to fluoresce. The Crab nebula is the defining member of the class of filled SUPERNOVA REMNANTS, or plerions.

Crab pulsar see CRAB NEBULA.

Crater (Cup) a small inconspicuous constellation in the southern hemisphere near Leo, the brightest stars being of 3rd and 4th magnitude. Abbrev.: Crt; genitive form: Crateris; approx. position: RA 11.5h, dec –l5°; area: 282 sq deg.

crater chain (chain craters) any linear association of CRATERS. Some lunar crater chains are incipient sinuous RILLES, i.e. lava tubes (in MARIA) that have suffered only partial collapse. Others are not confined to the maria and consist of overlapping SECONDARY CRATERS. Chains of volcanic craters (as in fissure eruptions) have not been unequivocally recognized but see WRINKLE RIDGES.

crater cluster a group of SECONDARY CRATERS. Crater clusters were visited by the crews of Apollo 15 and 17.

crater counting see CRATERS.

craters circular depressions on the surface of the Moon and several other bodies in the Solar System. They have diameters ranging from less than 1 meter to more than 1000 km, although the larger structures are more usually termed BASINS. The largest lunar craters are considered to be the 200-km *walled plains*. Some of the more interesting lunar craters are listed in the table on p. 100. Craters appear all over the Moon's surface and are most prominent when near the terminator. Small craters are everywhere more numerous than larger ones and crater-size distribution curves provide the basis for the estimation of relative ages by *crater counting*. Most of the surface of MERCURY is heavily cratered and on Mars the craters predominate in the southern hemisphere (see MARS, SURFACE FEATURES). Many planetary satellites are now known to be cratered, some very heavily.

The vast majority of craters are now believed to have originated by meteoritic impact, although in some cases their present appearance results from later modification by erosion or volcanic processes. A few craters in the lunar maria, particularly those associated with sinuous RILLES, may be volcanic in origin. Some, such as those at the summits of the volcanoes of the Earth or Mars, are solely volcanic. Other small craters result from subsidence or surface collapse.

In profile, a typical crater has a floor slightly below the level of the surrounding surface and a raised rim that slopes gently outward but falls more steeply toward the crater floor. The inner slope of the rims of large craters may be *terraced*, while the terrain beyond the rim may be hummocky and broken with numerous very small craters. Some large craters also have mountainous *central peaks*.

The impact events that created most of the surviving craters on Solar System bodies are thought to have occurred between 3000 and 4000 million years ago as the bodies collided with numerous PLANETESIMALS. Possibly the planetesimals were themselves the debris from collisions between larger objects that accreted at the same time as the planets, about 4600 million years ago, between the orbits of Mars and Jupiter. Most of the present-day survivors of the planetesimals, the asteroids, orbit between Mars and Jupiter but the APOLLO and AMOR OBJECTS do stray within the orbits of the Earth or Mars and, together with cometary nuclei, still produce occasional impacts, although at a much reduced rate (see also NEAR-EARTH ASTEROID).

During a crater-forming impact, the kinetic energy of the impacting body, which may be several kilometers across and moving at many kilometers per second, goes toward vaporizing and compressing much of itself and the rock on which it impinges. It is the subsequent explosion of these gases that excavates the crater, throwing material (EJECTA) away from the crater center to form the rim and the crater's hummocky EJECTA BLANKET. Chunks within the ejecta give rise to secondary impact craters nearby. In a large crater the steep inner rim can then slump to form the observed terraces, while the central peaks may arise from a rebound of the rocks immediately below the site of the explosion. Craters may also initially have RAY systems, i.e. bright streaks radiating outward from the crater. In the equatorial and midlatitude regions of Mars, the ejecta deposits surrounding many impact craters consist of several overlapping lobes, so that they appear to be surrounded by 'moats' and rampart-like ridges. These so-called *rampart craters* have an ejecta morphology that is believed to result when an impacting object rapidly melts subsurface ice. The presence of liquid water mixed in with the ejecta material allows it to flow along the ground and produce the characteristic moat-and-rampart effect.

Later impacts may destroy an existing crater completely, form a new overlapping crater, or partly fill the crater with ejecta. Lava may well up through cracks in the floor of the largest impact features to produce lava plains, such as the lunar maria. There may be rim obliteration and erosion and the occurrence of isostatic uplift. As a result the depth-to-diameter ratio, which for lunar craters may be as high as 1:5, decreases. On the Earth, erosion by wind, water, ice, and tectonic forces has removed nearly all the evidence that our planet was subject to the same ancient bombardment as the Moon; only a few recent impact craters, such as the Barringer crater in Arizona, remain relatively intact. Over 120 space-impact sites have been identified on the Earth. They occur worldwide, and most are more than 50 million years old.

Crepe ring see SATURN'S RINGS.

Cressida a small satellite of Uranus, discovered in 1986. See URANUS' SATELLITES; Table 2, Appendix.

Crisium, Mare a lava-filled BASIN close to the Moon's eastern limb from which soil was returned by LUNA 24.

critical density see MEAN DENSITY OF MATTER.

Crommelin's comet an inconspicuous comet with a period of 27.7 years, first observed in 1818. Its apparition in March 1984 was observed internationally: the results were used to test techniques to be used in the observation of HALLEY'S COMET,

Lunar Craters

Lunar crater	*Characteristics**	*Coordinates*
Aitken	mare-filled, farside (L)	173°E 17°S
Alphonsus	dark halo crater, rilles (L)	3°W 13°S
Archimedes	flat-floored, Mare Imbrium (M)	4°W 29°N
Aristarchus	young, bright, TLP source (S)	47°W 24°N
Aristillus	young, close to Apollo 15 site (S)	2°E 34°N
Arzarchel	central peak, S of Alphonsus (M)	2°W 18°S
Autolycus	young, close to Apollo 15 site (S)	2°E 31°N
Baily	extremely large (L)	68°W 66°S
Clavius	very large (L)	14°W 58°S
Cleomedes	large, N of Crisium (L)	56°E 27°N
Copernicus	young, rayed, secondaries (M)	20°W 10°N
Cyrillus	overlaps with Theophilus (L)	24°E 3°S
Eratosthenes	type crater for Eratosthenian System (M)	12°W 14°N
Gassendi	N Mare Humorum, TLP source (L)	39°W 17°S
Giordano Bruno	extremely young, historical? (S)	119°E 46°N
Grimaldi	very dark floored, TLP source (L)	68°W 5°S
Jules Verne	farside crater (L)	148°E 35°S
Kepler	very young, rayed, Oc. Procellarum (S)	38°W 8°N
Langrenus	large, E Mare Fecunditatis (L)	62°E 9°S
Plato	very dark floored, N Mare Imbrium (L)	9°W 52°N
Proclus	partially rayed, W Mare Crisium (S)	47°E 16°N
Ptolemaeus	large, flat-floored (L)	2°W 9°S
Reiner	very deep, Oc. Procellarum (S)	55°W 7°N
Schickard	large, S Mare Humorum (L)	55°W 44°S
Schiller	elongated, secondary? (M)	39°W 52°S
Stevinus	young, bright, S Mare Fecunditatis (M)	54°E 33°S
Theophilus	young, unrayed, N Mare Nectaris (L)	27°E 2°S
Tsiolkovsky	mare-filled, farside (L)	130°E 21°S
Tycho	very young, prominent ray system (M)	11°W 43°S
Wargentin	flooded with Orientale ejecta (M)	60°W 49°S
Van de Graaff	double, farside, magnetic anomaly (L)	174°E 27°S

*diameter ranges: L, greater than 100 km; M, 50–100 km; S, smaller than 50 km

perihelion Feb. 1986, the observing conditions for the two comets being very similar.

cross-correlation function see AUTOCORRELATION FUNCTION.

crossing time 1 the time taken for an object to make a crossing of a larger system under the influence of gravitational dynamics, for example a star crossing a galaxy or a galaxy crossing a cluster of galaxies.
2 see TIME OF FLIGHT.

cross-talk the undesirable exchange of signals between closely spaced electrical elements. The ANTENNAS of a radio INTERFEROMETER can exhibit cross-talk when they are close together. It may also

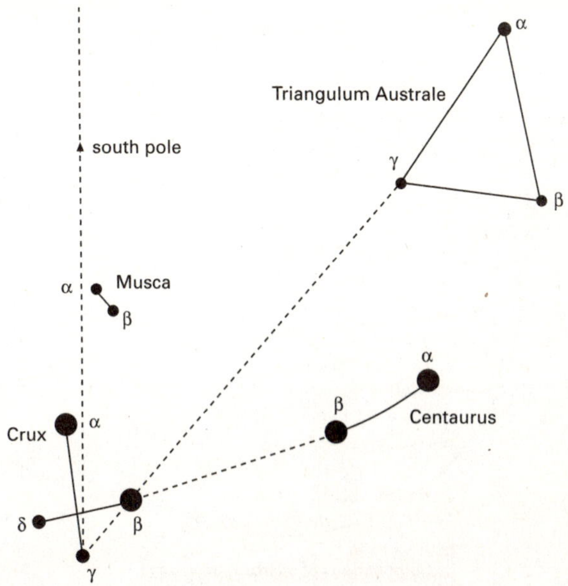

Crux and nearby bright constellations

occur if they are observing at low elevations, when one antenna may 'see' the back of another. Cross-coupling of noise produces an additional correlated output from the interferometer that must be accounted for. Some sorts of cross-talk can be removed by phase-switching the local oscillators supplied to different antennas at different frequencies (see PHASE-SWITCHING INTERFEROMETER).

CRRES *abbrev. for* Combined Release and Radiation Effects Satellite, a joint NASA/US Air Force satellite launched July 1990 into a highly elliptical Earth orbit to monitor the plasma in the MAGNETOSPHERE. Its instruments were designed to measure the energy, mass, and direction of flow of charged particles and check the effects of radiation on a package of electronic devices and components. The satellite performed several of its experiments well, but contact with it was lost Oct. 12 1991, presumably because of onboard battery failure.

crust the outermost solid layer of a terrestrial planet or a satellite, consisting of rock, ice, or a mixture of the two. See also EARTH.

Crux (**Crux Australis; Southern Cross**) the smallest but one of the most conspicuous of all the constellations in the sky, located in the southern hemisphere and lying in the Milky Way. The four brightest stars, ALPHA (α), BETA (β), Gamma (γ), and Delta (δ) Crucis form a cross (see illustration). The zero-magnitude Alpha and the 1st-magnitude red giant Gamma form the longer arm that points approximately to the south celestial pole. The 1st-magnitude Beta and 2nd-magnitude Delta form the transverse arm. The 3rd-magnitude Epsilon (ε), between Alpha and Delta, interferes with the figure's regularity. The area also contains the brilliant cluster the JEWEL BOX and the dark COALSACK nebula. Abbrev.: Cru; genitive form: Crucis; approx. position: RA 12.5h, dec –60°; area: 68 sq deg.

cryogenic cooling the cooling of instruments, etc., to very low temperatures,

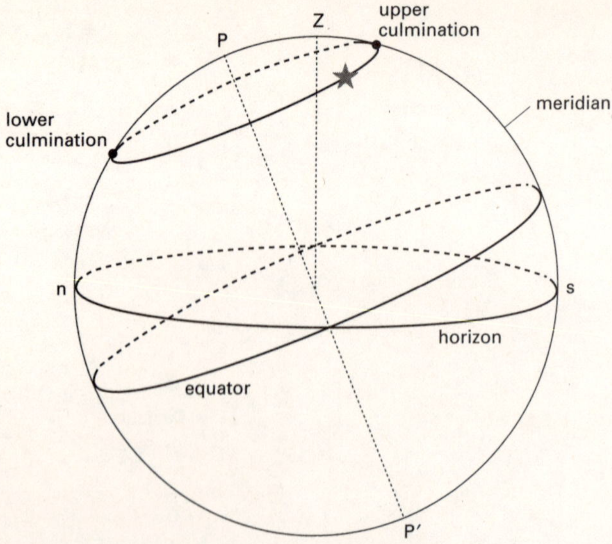

Culminations of a circumpolar star

usually using liquid helium or liquid nitrogen. See INFRARED DETECTORS; INFRARED TELESCOPE.

CSO *abbrev. for* Caltech Submillimeter Observatory.

C stars see CARBON STARS.

CTIO *abbrev. for* Cerro Tololo Inter-American Observatory.

C-type asteroids the most common class of ASTEROID in the outer main belt, having surfaces that are similar in composition to CARBONACEOUS CHONDRITE meteorites. Ultraviolet absorption features vary in relative strength according to the amount of water of hydration in the surface material. There are three subclasses: *B-type asteroids* have a higher ALBEDO than the average C; *F-types* have weak to nonexistent UV absorption features; *G-types* have a strong UV absorption feature.

Culgoora the site, near Narrabri, northern New South Wales. Australia, of the *Paul Wild Observatory* at which the AUSTRALIA TELESCOPE's Compact Array is located. It is also the site of Sydney University's Stellar Interferometer (SUSI), a radiospectrograph, and a 96-dish RADIO HELIOGRAPH, 3 km in diameter, used 1967–84 to make radio images of the Sun.

culmination (**meridian passage**) the passage of a celestial body across an observer's MERIDIAN. As a result of the Earth's rotation this occurs twice daily although both culminations can be observed only for CIRCUMPOLAR STARS. *Upper culmination* (or *transit*) is the crossing closer to the observer's ZENITH; for circumpolar stars and the Moon this is also called *culmination above pole*. *Lower culmination* (or *culmination below pole* for circumpolar stars and the Moon) is the crossing farther from the zenith (see illustration).

curvature see RADIUS OF CURVATURE.

curvature of field (**field curvature**) a minor ABERRATION of a lens or mirror whereby an object lying in a plane perpendicular to the optical axis produces an image lying not on a plane but on a curved surface. If there is any ASTIGMATISM present there will be two curved focal surfaces.

curvature of spacetime see SPACETIME.
cusp either of the tapering points of the crescent phase of the Moon, Venus, or Mercury.
cyclotron radiation electromagnetic radiation emitted by non-relativistic charged particles moving in a magnetic field. In a constant of *B* tesla, particles of mass *m* and charge *q* will perform helical motions around the field lines with a frequency $qB/(2\pi m)$, emitting cyclotron radiation at the same frequency. This type radiation is circularly polarized, and can be detected from the Sun, some planets and some X-ray pulsars including HERCULES X-1. At speeds approaching that of light the process is more complicated, and the particles emit SYNCHROTRON radiation over a range of frequencies.
Cygnids a minor METEOR SHOWER, radiant: RA 290°, dec +55° (near Kappa Cygnus), that maximizes on Aug. 20.
Cygnus (Swan) a large conspicuous constellation in the northern hemisphere, lying in the Milky Way. The five brightest stars – Alpha (α) (1st mag.), Gamma (γ), Epsilon (ε), and Delta (δ) (2nd mag.), and Beta (β) (3rd mag.) – form the *Northern Cross*: α, γ, β comprise the long arm and ε, γ, δ the transverse arm. Alpha is the extremely luminous supergiant DENEB and Beta the beautiful binary ALBIREO. There are several other noticeable binaries and some variables, including the MIRA STAR Chi (χ) Cygni, the brightest DWARF NOVA SS Cygni, and the highly luminous unstable P CYGNI. There is a large open cluster, M39 (NGC 7092), some complex emission and dark nebulosity, and the supernova remnant known as the CYGNUS LOOP, comprising several bright nebulae. The constellation also contains the star 61 CYGNI, the powerful radio source CYGNUS A, and the X-ray binaries CYGNUS X-1 and CYGNUS X-3. Cygnus X-1 and the object V404 Cygni are promising BLACK-HOLE candidates. Abbrev.: Cyg; genitive form: Cygni; approx position: RA 20.5h, dec +40°; area: 804 sq deg. See also NORTH AMERICA NEBULA.
Cygnus A an intense RADIO SOURCE in Cygnus that has a FLUX DENSITY at 178 megahertz of 8100 JANSKY. It is a typical double radio source (see illustration at RADIO-SOURCE STRUCTURE) and is identified with a 16-magnitude RADIO GALAXY; a narrow radio jet connects the central galaxy to the NW lobe. The galaxy has a REDSHIFT of 0.057, indicating a distance of about 230 megaparsecs, and a SPECTRAL INDEX of –0.8 below 1 GHz. It is the brightest low-redshift radio source, with a radio luminosity more typical of very distant radio galaxies (those above a redshift of one).

The galaxy is at the center of a cooling flow cluster (see CLUSTERS OF GALAXIES), and its optical spectrum is rich in forbidden emission lines. It also contains a polarized blue continuum that is due to scattered light from a hidden quasar nucleus.
Cygnus Loop an EMISSION NEBULA in the constellation Cygnus. The *Veil nebula* (NGC 6960, 6990, 6995) forms part of the Cygnus Loop. It is the SUPERNOVA REMNANT of a star that exploded probably some 50 000 years ago. The remnant now has an area of about 3 square degrees and is about 800 parsecs away. Its rate of expansion has gradually slowed to its present 100 km s^{-1} as the expanding shell collides with and sweeps up any surrounding interstellar matter. This creates a shock wave that compresses, heats, and ionizes the gas atoms, which then become visible as the emission nebula.
Cygnus X-1 an intense galactic X-ray source and the first to yield good observational evidence for the existence of a BLACK HOLE of stellar mass. Identification of Cygnus X-1 in 1971 with the luminous supergiant star HDE 226868 was followed by the discovery of a 5.6-day binary period. Analysis of the optical observations showed the mass of the 'unseen' companion star (the X-ray source) to lie in the range 6–15 solar masses, well above the limit allowed for a NEUTRON STAR (≤ 3 solar masses) or WHITE DWARF (≤ 1.4 solar masses). Support for the view that Cygnus X-1 involves gas accretion from the optical supergiant onto a black hole is provided by the rapid (millisecond) and irregular variability of the X-ray emission.
Cygnus X-3 a luminous X-RAY BINARY source with an unusually short (4.8 hour) binary period. The short period suggests that the

system consists of a NEUTRON STAR and a low-mass companion. Recent infrared spectra show strong helium emission lines as for a WOLF-RAYET companion star. The sinusoidal X-ray LIGHT CURVE is interpreted as being due to scattering of X-rays from the (unseen) central source by a hot dense wind driven off the companion star. Cygnus X-3 occasionally produces strong sometimes violent radio flares, first observed in 1972, between which it shows variable radio emission with a dominant component having a periodicity of 4.8 hours, similar to the X-ray period. Extremely high energy ($>10^{15}$ eV) gamma rays have also been detected, though not recently. These observations make Cygnus X-3 a unique source. It is postulated that the unusual properties may arise from very rapid rotation of the neutron star embedded in the dense wind of its companion star.

Dd

Dactyl see IDA.

Damocles ((5335) Damocles) an interplanetary object resembling an asteroid with an unusually elliptical orbit that carries it from 22 to 1.6 AU from the Sun. It was discovered in 1991 and is now believed to be the archetype of the Damocloids (see DAMOCLOID).

damped Lyman-alpha system see QUASAR.

dark ages the period between the recombination epoch and the formation of the first bright galaxies. Toward the end of this time the first generation of stars must have formed in PROTOGALAXIES, and created the first heavy elements. The absence of observable radiation renders this period 'dark'. Only when sufficient stars or quasars have formed to reionize the INTERGALACTIC medium (as revealed by the GUNN–PETERSON TEST) is this period observable.

dark cloud see DARK NEBULA.

dark energy the energy associated with the acceleration of the expansion of the Universe. About three-quarters of the energy of the Universe exists in the form of dark energy. The existence of dark energy can be taken into account using a nonzero value for the cosmological constant but the nature of this energy is not understood at the present time.

dark halo the large region around our Galaxy and other galaxies that is believed to contain distributed DARK MATTER. Its presence is revealed from the shape of ROTATION CURVES. See GALAXY.

dark halo crater a small lunar crater, originally believed to be volcanic (e.g. a cinder cone or fumarole) but now considered to be produced when an impacting meteorite excavates dark surface materials.

dark matter matter that probably comprises 75% (or more) of the mass of the Universe but is undetectable except by its gravitational effects. Dark matter was first suspected in CLUSTERS OF GALAXIES when the galaxies were found to move with too high a speed to be retained in the cluster by their gravitational influence on each other. The term *missing mass* was coined for the necessary invisible matter in the cluster, amounting to 10 to 100 times the amount of visible matter in the galaxies and in the INTERGALACTIC MEDIUM. In the 1970s investigations of the rotation of spiral galaxies indicated that these galaxies have a DARK HALO containing some 10 times as much matter as the visible galaxy. Simultaneously statistical analyses of the motions of galaxies on a larger scale than clusters suggested that the Universe in general has a ratio of perhaps 4:1 of dark matter to baryonic matter (except within galaxies, where ordinary matter dominates).

The nature of the dark matter is highly elusive, and there is no certainty even that the dark haloes of spiral galaxies consist of the same matter as the missing mass of clusters and the Universe at large. A proportion may consist of objects composed of normal matter, but according to standard BIG-BANG models the whole of the missing mass cannot consist of matter containing BARYONS (protons and neutrons) since that amount of baryonic matter would have produced a higher abundance of helium than is observed. The bulk of the dark matter does not therefore consist of dim stars or smaller chunks of solid matter, nor of BLACK HOLES that have formed from stars.

If the dark matter candidate was moving at velocities comparable to the speed of light as it decoupled from the early Universe, it would subsequently smear out all early fluctuations except on the very largest scales (see MICROWAVE BACKGROUND RADIATION). This candidate, known as *hot dark matter*, thus predicts that SUPERCLUSTERS of galaxies were the first structures to form, fragmenting later to form bound clusters and galaxies in a *top-down* scenario. This theory is no longer in favor because it has problems with the formation of galaxies at high REDSHIFTS, and is in contradiction with the anisotropies detected in the microwave background by the satellite COBE.

Alternatively, *cold dark matter* (*CDM*) particles are created and have low VELOCITY DISPERSIONS now and would have become trapped in baryonic gravitational potentials of galactic size when they decoupled. Clusters and superclusters would thus form later in the life of the Universe due to the mutual gravitational attraction of the galaxies. This *bottom-up* scenario is known as *hierarchical clustering*. Computer simulations of galaxy clustering, the observed galaxy CORRELATION FUNCTION, and recent X-ray observations of cluster evolution support the concept of cold dark matter. While consistent with the COBE observations, the CDM model needs further refinements to produce the observed LARGE-SCALE STRUCTURE of the Universe from the original spectrum of microwave-background fluctuations.

Candidates for cold dark matter are exotic elementary particles, including closed COSMIC STRINGS, WIMPS, AXIONS, and SUPERSYMMETRY particles, such as NEUTRALINOS, photinos, and gravitinos. Hot dark matter candidates include NEUTRINOS with nonzero but small mass.

See also GALAXIES, FORMATION AND EVOLUTION.

dark nebula (**dark cloud**; **absorption nebula**) a cloud of interstellar gas and dust that is sufficiently dense to obscure partially or completely the light from stars and other objects lying behind it and sufficiently large and suitably located to produce a noticeable effect. These NEBULAE can be observed as dark extrusions in front of bright (EMISSION OR REFLECTION) nebulae or as blank regions or regions with a greatly diminished number of stars in an otherwise bright area of sky. In external galaxies they are often observed against the bright spiral arms, where they appear as dark dust lanes. In our own Galaxy the dark clouds in Taurus are the nearest sites of STAR FORMATION to the Sun. Although the absorption is caused by COSMIC DUST, the dark nebulae are composed predominantly of molecular hydrogen. Small dark nebulae, called BOK GLOBULES, can sometimes be seen in large numbers superimposed on bright nebulae. Although having no optical features dark nebulae can be studied through their radio and infrared emissions. The COALSACK, HORSEHEAD NEBULA, and the GREAT RIFT are dark nebulae.

Darwin a 'cornerstone' mission of ESA's HORIZON 2000 program that aims to contribute to humanity's search for Earthlike planets around nearby stars on which life as we understand it may have evolved or could be supported. It takes the form of a space-based infrared interferometer that will be used to seek out such extrasolar planets and then discover by spectral analysis whether the planets have atmospheres containing carbon dioxide, ozone (showing evidence of photosynthesis), and water. Darwin will consist of seven spacecraft, six of them carrying a 1-meter-class telescope functioning in the near infrared (6–17 μm) and linked in to a nulling interferometer in the centrally placed seventh craft. All the telescopes will be focused on each selected nearby star in turn. If a planet is revolving about the star, any light it reflects will be swamped by light from the star. The separate images the telescopes pick up will be fed to the seventh craft where they will be combined to cancel out the star's light, leaving only that of the planet, if there is one. This ambitious project is planned for launch in or after 2015.

DA stars see WHITE DWARF.

database an organized collection of related

data that is stored in a computer system and is accessed by means of a set of programs known as a database management system. A database may provide data that is available to all users of a computer system and may be shared by a number of different applications. Examples include ESA's EXOSAT DATABASE and NASA's ASTROPHYSICS DATA SYSTEM.

data-relay satellite a satellite in geostationary orbit, used to pass data between other satellites or space platforms in low Earth orbits and stations on the ground. The *DRS* proposed by ESA will be compatible with NASA's TDRSS and Japan's *DTRS*.

Davida (**(511) Davida**) a large ellipsoidal C-type asteroid, discovered 1903 by Raymond Smith Dugan. It has a well-defined spin axis that is pointing in a fixed direction and is not precessing. The rotation period is about 5.13 hours. Davida orbits the Sun at a mean distance of 3.2 AU once every 5.64 years. Ground-based high-resolution pictures taken from the W.M. Keck Observatory reveal that the surface is very smooth and uniform. The mean diameter is about 326 km.

Davy Chain a prominent CRATER CHAIN on the Moon that was produced by secondary EJECTA.

Dawes limit see RESOLUTION.

Dawn a proposed NASA asteroid orbiter scheduled for launch in May 2006. Approved as a low-cost science mission for NASA's Discovery program in 2001, the Dawn spacecraft is set to visit two of the largest asteroids in the Solar System, (1) Ceres and (4) Vesta. The overall purpose of the mission is to investigate fully the physical makeup of these incipient planets and learn more about the origin of the Solar System and advance our understanding of the formation of the inner planets. The Dawn mission will build upon the highly successful ion-propulsion technology first used in NASA's DEEP SPACE 1. NASA scientists plan for the Dawn probe to visit Vesta first, arriving there in July 2010 and remaining in orbit for the following seven months or more. Dawn will be expected to rendezvous with Ceres in August 2014. In each case, the orbiter is expected to come as close as 100 km to the surface of the asteroid it will be circling.

day the period of the Earth's rotation on its axis, equal to 86 400 seconds (24 hours) unless otherwise specified.

day numbers quantities that depend on the position and motion of the Earth, and are used in reducing mean place of a celestial object to apparent place.

dec *short for* declination.

decametric radiation radio waves with wavelengths lying in the waveband 10–100 meters, i.e. in the frequency band 3–30 megahertz.

deceleration parameter symbol: q_0. The rate at which the expansion of the Universe changes with time as a result of self-gravitation. It is dimensionless and can be given in terms of the COSMIC SCALE FACTOR, *R*:

$$q_0 = -R(d^2R/dt^2)/(dR/dt)^2$$

Values of q_0 less than 0.5 are associated with an ever-expanding open Universe; values exceeding 0.5 imply that the Universe is closed and will collapse at a finite time in the future. If q_0 is equal to 0.5 then the Universe is infinite and space is Euclidean. See also MEAN DENSITY OF MATTER; UNIVERSE.

De Chéseaux's comet a magnificent comet of 1744 that reached magnitude –3 in late February. It is named for the Swiss astronomer who computed its orbit and described its impressive multiple fanlike tails.

decimetric radiation radio waves with wavelengths lying in the waveband 0.1–1 meter, i.e. in the frequency band 300–3000 megahertz.

declination (**dec**) symbol: δ. A coordinate used with RIGHT ASCENSION in the EQUATORIAL COORDINATE SYSTEM. The declination of a celestial body, etc., is its angular distance (from 0° to 90°) north (counted positive) or south (counted negative) of the celestial equator. It is measured along the hour circle passing through the body.

declination axis the axis at right angles to the POLAR AXIS about which a telescope on an EQUATORIAL MOUNTING is turned in order to make adjustments in declination.

The optical axis then follows a particular hour circle across the sky.

declination circle a SETTING CIRCLE on the declination axis that enables an equatorially mounted telescope to be set at the declination of the object to be observed. Its scales are graduated from 0°, when the telescope is aligned with the celestial equator, to ±90°, when it is aligned with the north or south poles.

deconvolution the recovery ('unsmearing') of data, such as an astronomical image, that has been convolved (see CONVOLUTION) with a response function, such as a telescope BEAM. The process is nearly always carried out on a computer using one or more *deconvolution algorithms* (see APERTURE SYNTHESIS). It can greatly improve the fidelity of images, particularly when the convolving function is well defined. The process is used extensively in aperture synthesis to remove artifacts generated by the synthesized beam and greatly improved the early performance of the HUBBLE SPACE TELESCOPE.

decoupling era see BIG BANG THEORY.

Deep Impact a NASA probe launched Jan. 12 2005 and set to rendezvous with Comet Tempel 1 in July of the same year. The spacecraft carried a copper-tipped projectile the size of a washing machine that was scheduled to crash into the comet, blasting a hole in its surface. Scientists intended that the impact should expose the comet's interior, revealing information on its chemical and physical makeup and providing data that would advance our understanding of what the Solar System was like when the planets began to form more than 4.6 billion years ago.

deep-sky object any object that is not a member of the Solar System. In general, the term is applied to nebulae, star clusters, galaxies, and clusters of galaxies, but not usually to stars.

Deep Space 1 an uncrewed NASA spacecraft, launched Oct. 1998 from Cape Canaveral, Florida, USA, on top of a Boeing Delta rocket. Its primary mission was to test advanced technologies that could lower the cost and risk involved in future scientific interplanetary exploration. Chief among these technologies was a new ion propulsion system utilizing atomic particles rather than conventional chemical fuel. An ion propulsion engine, first used for station-keeping by the PAS-5 telecommunications satellite in 1997, generates thrust by accelerating positively charged ions in a chamber of xenon through a series of gridded electrodes at one end of the chamber. Although such an engine produces only a tiny amount of thrust, the lack of atmospheric drag in outer space means that the thrust's effect builds up, allowing a probe to travel faster and farther. An ion propulsion engine is also very fuel-efficient, with a level of consumption about 10% of that of a conventional rocket engine. Thus, with an engine requiring less propellant than a normal spacecraft, Deep Space 1 was relatively light, its mass at liftoff, including fuel, being just 486.32 kg. By mid-August 2000, the ion propulsion engine had logged 200 days of operation. It continued functioning well until the probe was shut down in December 2001.

Deep Space 1 successfully tested 12 new technologies in all. Among the others were a Miniature Integrated Camera Spectrometer, low-power electronics, and a Small Deep Space Transponder. In the process the probe flew by two asteroids, (9969) Braille and 1992 KD. In September 1999 NASA decided to extend Deep Space 1's mission and sent it to encounter Comet Borelly. It successfully accomplished this activity in September 2001, returning valuable scientific data and excellent images. Deep Space 1 proved to be one of NASA's most successful low-budget missions, with total costs just short of $150 million.

Deep Space Network (**DSN**) a network of radio DISHES used by NASA for communications from and to spacecraft beyond the Moon, including the VOYAGER and PIONEER PROBES now in the outer Solar System. Some Earth-orbiting missions also utilize the DSN. Three standard radio dishes, 70 meters in diameter and equipped with highly sensitive receivers, are located at Goldstone in the Mojave Desert, California, at Tidinbilla near Canberra, Australia, and at Robledo near Madrid,

Spain. As the Earth rotates, there will always be one DSN station that can receive signals from a spacecraft.

deferent see PTOLEMAIC SYSTEM.

deflection of light see RELATIVITY, GENERAL THEORY.

dE galaxy *short for* dwarf elliptical galaxy. See DWARF GALAXY.

degeneracy pressure see DEGENERATE MATTER.

degenerate matter matter in a highly dense form that can exert a pressure as a result of quantum mechanical effects. Degenerate matter occurs in WHITE DWARFS and NEUTRON STARS. During the GRAVITATIONAL COLLAPSE of a dying star, the electrons are stripped from their atomic nuclei, and nuclei and electrons exist in a closely packed, highly dense mass. As the density increases, the number of electrons per unit volume increases to a point when the electrons can exert a considerable pressure, called *degeneracy pressure*. This pressure is a result of the laws of quantum mechanics. Unlike normal pressure, degeneracy pressure is essentially independent of temperature, depending primarily on density. At the immense densities typical of white dwarfs (10^7 kg m^{-3} or more) it becomes sufficiently large to counteract the gravitational force and thus prevents the star from collapsing further. The gross properties of a white dwarf are therefore described in terms of a gas of degenerate electrons.

Above a certain stellar mass (the CHANDRASEKHAR LIMIT) equilibrium cannot be attained by a balance of gravitational force and electron degeneracy pressure. The star must collapse further to become a neutron star. It is then the degeneracy pressure exerted by the tightly packed neutrons that balances the gravitational force. See also BLACK HOLE.

degenerate star a star composed primarily of degenerate matter, especially a WHITE DWARF or a NEUTRON STAR.

Deimos a satellite of Mars, lying farther from the planet than the slightly larger satellite PHOBOS. Like Phobos, it was discovered in 1877 by the US astronomer Asaph Hall. Deimos is an irregular body measuring 15 × 12 × 11 km, and orbits above Mars' equator at a distance of 23 460 km from the center of the planet in a period of 1.26 days. It orbits with its long axis radially aligned with the planet. Like Phobos, it may be a captured ASTEROID of a type similar to the CARBONACEOUS CHONDRITE meteorites. However, it appears to have none of the grooves and crater chains found on Phobos and many of its craters are less distinct, probably because of infilling by crater ejecta that may lie tens of meters thick on the surface. The larger craters, such as *Voltaire* and *Swift*, measure only about 1.3 km across. See Table 2, BACKMATTER.

Delphinus (**Dolphin**) a small constellation in the northern hemisphere near Cygnus, the brightest stars being of 3rd magnitude (α) and 4th magnitude (β, γ); all three are double stars. Abbrev.: Del; genitive form: Delphini; approx. position: RA 20.5h, dec +10°; area: 189 sq deg.

delta (**δ**) **1** the fourth letter of the Greek alphabet, used in STELLAR NOMENCLATURE usually to designate the fourth-brightest star in a constellation or sometimes to indicate a star's position in a group. **2** *symbol for* declination.

Delta Aquarids see AQUARIDS.

Delta Cephei see CEPHEID VARIABLES.

Delta Scuti stars a class of relatively young PULSATING VARIABLES, typified by Delta Scuti, that are about 1.5–3 solar masses and range in spectral type from about A3 to F6. They were originally grouped with the DWARF CEPHEIDS. They are numerous but tend to be inconspicuous because of the very small variation in brightness, usually about 0.01–0.4 magnitudes. Like dwarf Cepheids they have very short periods ranging from about 0.5–8 hours. A typical feature is a variation in the amplitude and shape of the light curve. Irregularities in the light-curve contour result from the superimposition of two or more harmonic modes in which the star is pulsating; nonradial pulsations may also be present.

delta T symbol: ΔT. From 1984, the increment to be added to UNIVERSAL TIME, UT1, to give terrestrial DYNAMICAL TIME, TDT. Prior to 1984 it was the increment to be applied to UT1 to give EPHEMERIS TIME. ΔT is not constant but at present is increasing in an irregular manner: between

1970 and 1990 it changed from +40 to +57 seconds, and is predicted to be +67 seconds by 2010.

Demon Star see ALGOL.

Deneb (α Cyg) a very luminous remote white supergiant that is the brightest star in the constellation Cygnus and lies at one end of the long arm of the Northern Cross, with ALBIREO (β Cyg) at the other (the name *Deneb* is Arabic for 'tail'). Deneb is one of the biggest and brightest stars known, with a mass at least 25 times that of the Sun. It has a luminosity of between 60 000 and 250 000 times the Sun's brightness, depending on the accuracy of our distance estimates for it. It has very low proper motion (0″.003 per year), and measurements of its very small parallax by Hipparcos suggest that it lies about 990 parsecs from the Sun, although other estimates place it 500 pc away. m_v: 1.25; M_v: –7.2 or –8.6; spectral type: A2 Ia.

Denebola (β Leo) a white star that is the third-brightest in the constellation Leo. It marks the 'tail' of Leo, the Lion. It is surrounded by a ring of dust that emits infrared radiation and may possibly indicate the early stages of a planetary system. m_v: 2.13; M_v: 1.5; spectral type: A3 V; distance: 13 pc.

dense core a small centrally condensed MOLECULAR CLOUD, typically of less than 500 solar masses. The central density is high enough to excite lines of ammonia and carbon monosulphide (CS), the latter observed with millimeter-wave telescopes. Many of these cores contain IRAS point sources that appear to be YSOs with luminosities indicating low-mass stars.

densitometer an instrument for measuring the density of exposure of a photographic emulsion. Densitometers have a light source and photocell to measure the transmission (or reflection) of the sample. They are used in obtaining quantitative measurements from photographic records of spectra, diffraction experiments, etc.

density 1 symbol: ρ. The mass per unit volume of a body or material. The mean density of a celestial body is its total mass divided by its total volume. A wide variation in densities is found in the Universe, ranging from about 10^{-20} kg m^{-3} for interstellar gas to over 10^{17} kg m^{-3} for neutron stars. The MEAN DENSITY OF MATTER in the Universe is of the order of 10^{-27} kg m^{-3}.
2 the number of electrons, ions, or other particles per unit volume.

density parameter symbol: ω. A key parameter in determining the fate of the Universe. It is defined as the ratio of the actual density of matter in the Universe to the critical density, where the critical density is the density of matter above which an expanding Universe will eventually recollapse. It is currently thought that the value of ω is about 0.3. Before 1980 it was one of the mysteries of cosmology as to why the value of ω is fairly close to 1. The theory of INFLATION provides an explanation of why this is the case.

density-wave theory a theory that attempts to explain how the structure of a spiral galaxy is sustained by the flow of material in and out of the regions of the spiral arms under the influence of gravity. It was proposed in 1964 by C.C. Lin and F.H. Shu and based on work by B. Lindblad. The spiral structure is not permanent: it is regarded as a wave pattern in which the spiral arms are regions of low gravitational potential where matter concentrates. The spiral arms therefore comprise the loci of wave crests of a density wave. The wave pattern is not tied to the matter but moves through it at an angular velocity that can differ appreciably from that of the matter; the relative motion is on average about 30 km s^{-1}. It is this motion that somehow maintains the overall appearance of the galaxy.

Stars move into the traveling gravitational troughs of the spiral arms and can remain there for a considerable time until their orbits take them out again. Interstellar gas also comes under the influence of the density wave. It has been suggested that when the gas encounters the moving wave it undergoes a sudden compression, which in turn could be a possible trigger for interstellar cloud collapse and star formation. Young stars should therefore be found preferentially in spiral arms, which is indeed the case.

Although the density-wave theory

explains the spiral shape of galaxies and the presence of young stars in spiral arms, it does not show how the density wave originated. In addition it predicts the dissipation of the spiral arms after only a few galactic rotations, i.e. after several hundred million years, which is much shorter than the lifetime of galaxies. The theory is widely believed to apply to galaxies suffering gravitational perturbations from a passing neighbor or from the central bar of a barred spiral galaxy: these galaxies have sharply defined arms. The patchier arms of many isolated galaxies may not be due to density waves but to SELF-PROPAGATING STAR FORMATION.

Descartes formation a range of lunar hills to the NW of Mare Nectaris that have an unusually high ALBEDO. They were once thought to consist of acid volcanics but are now considered to have been impact-generated.

descending node see NODES.

Desdemona a small satellite of Uranus, discovered in 1986. See URANUS' SATELLITES; TABLE 2, BACKMATTER.

de Sitter model see COSMOLOGICAL MODELS.

Despina a small satellite of Neptune, discovered in 1989. See Table 2, Appendix.

detached binary see BINARY STAR; EQUIPOTENTIAL SURFACES.

detector the component in an instrument that is sensitive to the radiation or particles under observation. It may, for example, be an array of CCDs or a photographic plate. See also IMAGING.

deuterium see HYDROGEN.

de Vaucouleurs' law a mathematical model that is a good fit to the observed radial brightness profile of elliptical galaxies. It was derived empirically from observations by G. de Vaucouleurs.

dew-cap an extension fitted to a telescope tube on a damp night to prevent the condensation of water vapor on the outer element of the telescope. It may simply be a nonconducting (e.g. card) tube or may contain a heating element.

diagonal mirror see NEWTONIAN TELESCOPE.

Diamond of Virgo see SPICA.

diamond-ring effect a bright flash of sunlight from a conspicuous BAILY'S BEAD sometimes very briefly observed, together with the solar CHROMOSPHERE, at the Moon's limb just before or after totality during a solar eclipse.

diaphragm see STOP.

dichotomy the moment of exact half-phase of the Moon, Mercury, or Venus.

dichroic extinction extinction by aligned grains of INTERSTELLAR DUST, which causes POLARIZATION of starlight. Light with its polarization vector lying along the projected long axis of the grain is absorbed more than light of the orthogonal polarization. This gives rise to a net excess of light polarized perpendicular to the direction of grain alignment. See also INTERSTELLAR EXTINCTION.

Dicke-switched receiver a radio-astronomy RECEIVER in which the input is continuously switched between the ANTENNA and a reference noise source of constant noise power. The switching, at a rate of between 10 and 1000 hertz, is carried out by a *Dicke switch*, which is typically a semiconductor-diode switch or a ferrite switch. The switching reduces the fluctuations in the output of the receiver that arise from GAIN changes in the amplification stages and seriously limit the performance of total-power RECEIVERS. The amplitude of the component at the switching frequency in the output of the first detector is proportional to the difference in powers between the noise source and the antenna; it is detected using a PHASE-SENSITIVE DETECTOR. The effect of a change in gain is much reduced provided that the change takes place much more slowly than in one switch cycle.

differential rotation rotation of different parts of a system at different speeds. It occurs in a system, such as a star, composed primarily of gas. A solid body, such as the Earth, rotates uniformly. The SUN and the giant planets, such as Jupiter, rotate differentially such that their equatorial regions move somewhat faster than areas closer to the poles. See also GALACTIC ROTATION.

differentiation the process by which layers of different density are formed from originally homogeneous molten rock. It is generally accepted that melting and differentiation occurred very early in the history of the Earth and resulted from the rapid increase in the young planet's temperature; the heat was generated by decay of radioactive elements in the planetary material, from the impact of infalling material, and from contraction of the planet. The widespread melting led to massive differentiation of the Earth into the iron-rich core and the lighter silicate (rocky) regions of the mantle and crust (see EARTH). Differentiation also occurred on other terrestrial planets and the Moon.

diffraction the bending of light or other electromagnetic radiation at the edges of obstacles, with the resulting formation of light and dark bands or rings (diffraction patterns) at the edges of the shadow. An example of a diffraction pattern is the AIRY DISK observed in telescope images of distant celestial objects. A small aperture or slit produces similar annular or banded patterns. Diffraction results from the wave nature of electromagnetic radiation. See also INTERFERENCE.

diffraction grating a device usually incorporated into a SPECTROGRAPH and employed in the production and study of SPECTRA. Its action depends on the DIFFRACTION of light or other radiation by a very large number of very close and exactly equidistant parallel linear grooves. The grooves are produced by ruling very fine closely spaced scratches on glass or polished metal, forming either a *transmission grating* in the first case or a *reflection grating* in the second. These *ruled gratings* are very costly, and *replica gratings* – accurate plastic casts of ruled gratings – are usually used instead. Reflection gratings can be plane or concave; the latter can act as a focusing element for incident radiation, which would otherwise be partly absorbed if a lens were employed .

The diffracted radiation, once focused, produces a series of sharp spectral lines for each resolvable wavelength present in the incident beam. For a plane wave of a single wavelength λ, incident on a transmission grating at angle i, the successive wave trains passing through the grooves will travel different pathlengths. If the path difference between two adjacent grooves is a whole number of wavelengths, the wave trains will be brought to a focus as a bright image of the radiation source at a particular angle of refraction, d (see illustration), where

$$\sin d = n\lambda/s - \sin i$$

s is the spacing between adjacent grooves and n is an integer. Bright images will in fact be produced for each of the angles d corresponding to $n = 1, 2, 3\ldots$ These numbers denote the *orders* of the image. If,

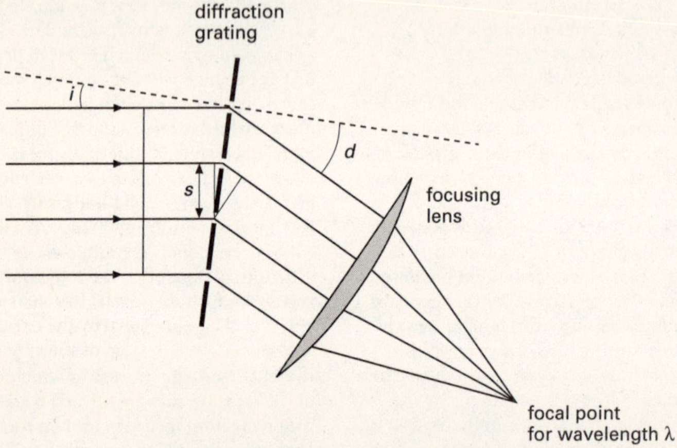

Diffraction by a plane transmission grating

for a particular order, *d* is made equal to *i*, then

$$\sin d = n\lambda/2s$$

If the incident beam is composed of various wavelengths, the image of any particular order, $n = 1, 2, 3\ldots$, will appear at different points because *d* varies with wavelength. Hence a grating produces several spectra on either side of the incident ray ($n = 0$). The angular dispersion of the spectral lines, i.e. $dd/d\lambda$, will be high when the grooves are very fine and closely spaced (i.e. *s* is small). For the spectral resolution – separation of images of very nearly equal wavelength – to be high, the total number of grooves must be large: several thousand grooves per centimeter are common for the visible and ultraviolet regions of the spectrum.

diffraction limit the finest detail that can be resolved by a telescope, limited by DIFFRACTION to a value proportional to λ/d, where λ is the wavelength of the radiation under observation and *d* is the telescope aperture. See also APERTURE; RESOLUTION.

diffraction pattern the pattern of alternating light and dark rings or bands produced when light is diffracted by a circular opening or object (rings) or a rectangular slit or an edge (bands). See also AIRY DISK; INTERFERENCE.

diffuse cloud a small atomic (H I) cloud that has too low a COLUMN DENSITY for it to be observed visually. Diffuse clouds constitute the bulk of the cold neutral medium in the three-phase description of the INTERSTELLAR MEDIUM. They are usually observed by means of absorption features, such as the sodium D lines, in the spectra of background stars.

diffuse interstellar bands a series of more than a dozen diffuse (wide) ABSORPTION features due to dust in INTERSTELLAR CLOUDS, of which the most intense include those at wavelengths of 443, 618, and 628 nm. There are at least three (but possibly more) families of bands. The carriers have not yet been identified, although they are almost certainly solids: evidence is mounting in favor of some sort of aromatic hydrocarbon.

dI galaxy *short for* dwarf irregular galaxy. See DWARF GALAXY.

Digitized Sky Survey either of two programs organized by the SPACE TELESCOPE SCIENCE INSTITUTE to make available in computerized form paper and plate photographs from major surveys of the whole sky undertaken between the 1970s and 1999. The sources of the computer files are plate images produced by the Oschin Schmidt Telescope at Mount Palomar, California, for the PALOMAR OBSERVATORY SKY SURVEY and the UK Schmidt at the Anglo-Australian Observatory for the ESO/SERC SOUTHERN SKY SURVEY and its extension northward to the celestial equator. Each digitized image file covers an area of sky 6.5° square. The images are being made available in compressed form on CD-ROM and on the World Wide Web.

Dione a satellite of Saturn, discovered in 1684 by Giovanni Domenico Cassini. It has a diameter of 1118 km and density of 1.4 g cm^{-3}, and is slightly larger than the satellite Tethys. An important characteristic of Dione is the nonuniformity of its brightness. The trailing hemisphere is dark, with an albedo of approximately 0.3, whereas the brightest features of the leading hemisphere have an albedo of approximately 0.6. Only Iapetus, of the Saturn system, displays a greater variation of brightness between the hemispheres. The surface shows evidence of a number of craters of 30–40 km, with a few large craters 165 km or more in diameter. There are some broad ridges in the southern part of the heavily cratered plains, with a long linear valley more than 500 km in length near the south pole. Dione's relatively high density compared with the neighboring satellites indicates a higher rock content of the interior. The most prominent feature is *Amata*, a crater 240 km in diameter associated with a system of bright wispy features that extend over the trailing hemisphere. The bright streaks on the surface first imaged by the two VOYAGER PROBES have been shown by the CASSINI probe to be a vast system of linear features scarring the satellite's surface. A minor satellite, *Helene*, has been discovered to share the orbit of Dione. See also TABLE 2, Appendix.

dioptric system an optical system, such as a

refracting telescope, in which all the optical elements are lenses.

Diphda see CETUS.

dipole a simple linear balanced ANTENNA that is fed from its center. It usually consists of two equal-length straight opposing elements, although these may sometimes be folded back on themselves and their far ends joined together in the middle to form a *folded dipole*. The elements may be of any length but the overall length of the dipole is usually a multiple of half a wavelength of the received (or transmitted) radio wave; the reactive component of the impedance seen at its feed point is then small.

A *half-wave dipole* has two elements of length one-quarter of a wavelength each and has a RADIATION RESISTANCE of about 70 ohms. A *full-wave dipole* is twice as long as a half-wave dipole and has a radiation resistance of several thousand ohms. The GAIN of a half-wave dipole over an isotropic radiator is about two decibels.

See also ARRAY; DISH; RADIO TELESCOPE.

directivity a measure of the ability of an ANTENNA to concentrate its radiation or response in a particular direction. It is defined as the ratio of the maximum radiation intensity in the forward direction to the average radiation intensity over all directions. If an antenna is operating at a wavelength λ and has an effective area A_e (see ARRAY), then the directivity, D, is given by

$$D = 4\pi A_e/\lambda^2$$

See also GAIN.

direct motion (prograde motion) **1** the apparent west to east motion of a planet or other object as seen from Earth against the background of stars. *Retrograde motion* is an apparent motion from east to west. When a superior planet near OPPOSITION is overtaken by the Earth, moving with higher relative velocity, its normal direct motion seems to become temporarily retrograde and it appears to undergo a loop or zigzag in the sky (see illustration); the turning points between these motions, when the planet appears motionless in the sky, are known as *stationary points*.

2 the anticlockwise orbital motion, as seen from the north pole of the ecliptic, of a planet or comet around the Sun or of a satellite around its primary. The body is then said to move in a *direct orbit* or *prograde orbit*. A clockwise orbital motion is *retrograde*. All the planets move in direct orbits.

3 The anticlockwise rotation of a planet, as seen from its north pole. Venus, Uranus, and Pluto have a clockwise *retrograde* rotation.

direct orbit see DIRECT MOTION.

dirty beam see APERTURE SYNTHESIS.

dirty-snowball theory see COMET; NUCLEUS.

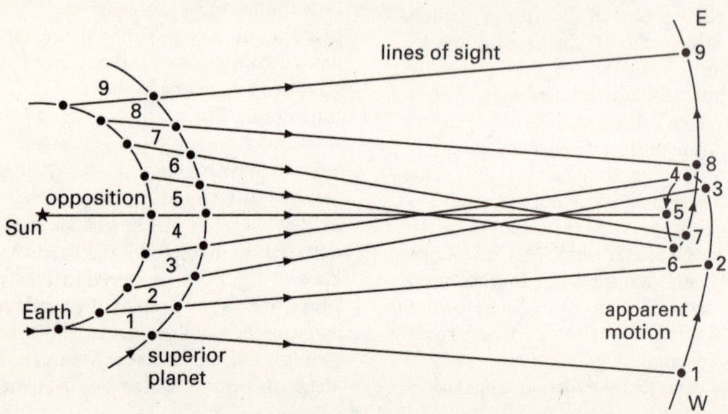

Direct and retrograde motion of superior planet

disconnection event the detachment of a cometary plasma tail from the coma of the COMET. The detached tail then 'flows' away from the comet, carried by a loop of interplanetary magnetic field lines that have become draped around the comet. The comet then quickly forms a new plasma tail.

dish a type of ANTENNA used in radio telescopes and consisting of a large spherical or parabolic metal reflector, usually circular in outline, by means of which radio waves are brought to a focus above the dish center. The waves are collected at the focus by a secondary antenna, called a FEED, or are reflected from a curved secondary to be brought to a focus elsewhere (see CASSEGRAIN CONFIGURATION). At low radio frequencies the feed may be a DIPOLE mounted in front of a small reflector; at high frequencies it is usually a horn antenna (see WAVEGUIDE). The signals picked up by the feed are transferred by means of the FEEDER to the RECEIVER for amplification and analysis. Both the angular RESOLUTION and the SENSITIVITY of the telescope to a point source increase with the area of the dish.

The dish is usually mounted so that it can be steered to point in different directions and can be made to track a moving object. Some dishes, however, can move in only one coordinate and rely on the Earth's rotation to provide coverage in the other coordinate. The 305-meter dish mounted in a natural hollow in the ground at the ARECIBO RADIO TELESCOPE, Puerto Rico, achieves partial beam steering by moving the feed.

disk 1 the two-dimensional projection of the surface of a star or planet.
2 see GALAXY; GALAXIES.

disk population stars see POPULATION I, POPULATION II.

disparation brusque (French) The sudden 'disappearance', over a few hours, of a quiescent solar FILAMENT as it is Doppler-shifted (see DOPPLER SHIFT) to a shorter wavelength in the line of sight, following disruption of the horizontal magnetic field supporting it and its subsequent rapid ascent and dissipation in the CORONA. The term is also sometimes used for the sudden disappearance of an active filament – although this may occur for a variety of reasons.

dispersion 1 the separation of a beam of light into its component colors, i.e. into its component wavelengths, so that a spectrum is formed. It arises because of the variation of the REFRACTIVE INDEX of the transmitting medium with wavelength. It occurs in a lens or prism, causing CHROMATIC ABERRATION. It also occurs to a small extent in the Earth's atmosphere, producing *atmospheric dispersion.* Normally the refractive index of a transparent substance increases as the wavelength decreases: blue light is refracted (bent) more than red light. See also SPECTROGRAPH.
2 the retardation of radio waves that occurs when they pass through ionized gas in the interstellar medium, the speed of propagation depending on frequency: the lower the frequency the greater the delay. This delay is not observable in a continuous radio signal but is detectable in a pulsed one, such as that from a pulsar. The amount of dispersion gives an indication of distance to a pulsar.

See also DISPERSION MEASURE.

dispersion measure (**DM**) the number of electrons per unit volume, n_e, integrated along the line of sight to a source:

$$\mathrm{DM} = \int n_e \mathrm{d}l$$

where dl is an element of the path. It is the factor that determines, for example, the time delay (i.e. DISPERSION) between the arrival of radio pulses from a PULSAR at two different frequencies. The value of n_e in the plane of our Galaxy is typically 0.03 cm^{-3}.

distance determination the distances of celestial objects can be determined directly by means of radar or laser ranging and from measurements of PARALLAX, and indirectly from photometric and spectroscopic methods. Radar and laser measurements can be made only for comparatively tiny distances, i.e. those within the Solar System: the Earth–Moon distance has been measured to a few cm by laser beaming; radar measurements of the distances of Venus, Mercury, and Mars have been used in determining planetary distances from the Sun by KEPLER'S LAWS. The distance from Earth to Sun is thus now known very accurately.

This Earth–Sun distance is used as the baseline in the determination of the ANNUAL PARALLAX of stars; using spacecraft measurements, stellar distances out to about 500 parsecs can be determined trigonometrically. At greater distances the error in measuring parallax becomes as large as the parallax itself. These distances have therefore to be found indirectly from measurements of LUMINOSITY, MAGNITUDE, and other stellar properties: distances are determined from relationships connecting these properties, including DISTANCE MODULUS, MOVING-CLUSTER PARALLAX, and the PERIOD-LUMINOSITY RELATION for CEPHEID VARIABLES.

A *distance scale* can be established whereby the distances found for one set of distance indicators, such as open clusters (using MAIN-SEQUENCE FITTING, for example), can be used to calibrate the next most distant indicators – Cepheid variables – occurring in such clusters. Cepheids, along with novae and the most luminous stars, are in turn used to measure the distances to galaxies in the LOCAL GROUP and in other nearby groups of galaxies. Out to this distance (a few megaparsecs), the distance scale is believed to be accurate to 10% or better. The HUBBLE SPACE TELESCOPE is able to measure Cepheid distances to about twenty nearby galaxies and in two of the nearer clusters, VIRGO and Fornax.

In the case of more distant galaxies, however, determination of distance currently differs by up to a factor of two. Traditional indicators of these larger distances include: the size of a galaxy's H II regions; the brightness of its GLOBULAR CLUSTERS; the maximum brightness of its Type Ia SUPERNOVAE; its total luminosity as inferred, for a luminous spiral, from its detailed appearance and as a standard brightness for cD galaxies (the brightest galaxies) in CLUSTERS OF GALAXIES. The stars or galaxies used in these techniques are known as *standard candles*, and their absolute luminosity is assumed not to vary with age. A further technique at present is the TULLY–FISHER METHOD, which relies on a relation between a spiral galaxy's absolute magnitude and the spread of its rotation velocities. An analogous technique applied to elliptical galaxies and the bulges of S0s is the FABER–JACKSON RELATION. Finally, the combination of the SUNYAEV–ZEL'DOVICH EFFECT and X-ray imaging of clusters of galaxies provides a distance measure independent of other measurements.

These methods provide distances out to at least 100 megaparsecs, where the motions of galaxies are dominated by the expansion of the Universe. A galaxy's recession velocity is determined from its REDSHIFT. The ratio of recession velocity to measured distance for the more distant galaxies gives a value for the HUBBLE CONSTANT; the Hubble constant is then used to derive distances to farther galaxies and quasars from their measured redshifts. The 20% uncertainty in the distance scale leads to a corresponding uncertainty in the value of the Hubble constant.

distance modulus the difference between the apparent magnitude, m, and the absolute magnitude, M, of a star and therefore a measure of distance (see MAGNITUDE):

$$m - M = 5\log(d/10) = 5\log d - 5$$

where d is the distance in parsecs. Distance modulus is used to determine the distances of stars and stellar clusters. It is corrected for INTERSTELLAR EXTINCTION by an additional term (see MAGNITUDE).

distance scale see DISTANCE DETERMINATION.

distortion (**field distortion**) an ABERRATION of a lens or mirror in which the image has a distorted shape as a result of nonuniform lateral magnification over the field of view. In *barrel distortion* the magnification decreases toward the edge of the field; in *pincushion distortion* there is greater magnification at the edge.

diurnal happening during a 24-hour day; daily.

diurnal circle see DIURNAL MOTION.

diurnal libration daily geometrical LIBRATION brought about by the change in the position of the observer with respect to the Earth–Moon line as the Earth rotates on its axis. This libration is most significant near the equator, where it amounts to 57′2″.6; this is equal to the Moon's mean equatorial horizontal parallax (see DIURNAL

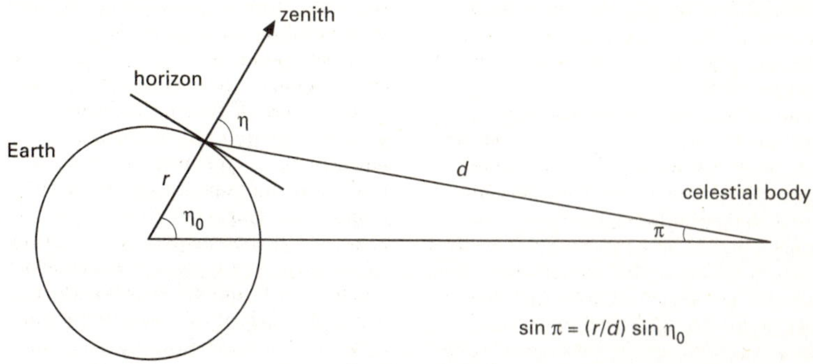

Diurnal parallax

PARALLAX). An observer closer to the poles will however experience an equivalent geometrical libration because of the displacement from the ECLIPTIC. See also AUGMENTATION; PHYSICAL LIBRATION.

diurnal motion the apparent daily motion of celestial bodies across the sky from east to west. It results from the Earth's rotation from west to east, the axis of the diurnal motion coinciding with the Earth's axis. The apparent path of a celestial body arising from diurnal motion is a circle parallel to the celestial equator and is termed a *diurnal circle*.

diurnal parallax (geocentric parallax) The PARALLAX of a celestial body that results from the change in position of an observational point during the Earth's daily rotation. It is the angle measured at a given celestial body between the direction to the Earth's center and that to an observer on the Earth's surface. It is thus equal to the difference between the topocentric and geocentric ZENITH DISTANCES, η and η_0, respectively (see illustration). It is appreciable only for members of the Solar System. As the observer's position changes during the day, the diurnal parallax of the body varies from a minimum, when the body is on the observer's meridian, to a maximum, when it is on the horizon. This maximum value is the object's *horizontal parallax*, π. It is given by:

$$\sin \pi = r/d$$

where r is the Earth's radius and d is the distance to the celestial object.

The Earth's nonspherical shape causes the length of the baseline to vary with latitude. If this variation is significant, as it is with nearby bodies like the Moon, then for the horizontal parallax to be a maximum it must be measured from the equator. This gives the *equatorial horizontal parallax:* the average value for the Moon – the *lunar parallax* – is 3422″.45; the mean value for the Sun – the SOLAR PARALLAX – is 8″.794.

D-layer (D-region) see IONOSPHERE.

D lines a close prominent doublet of lines in the yellow region of the visible spectrum of sodium. They occur at wavelengths of 589.6 nm and 589.0 nm and, being easily recognizable, are useful as standards in spectroscopy. The D lines are strong FRAUNHOFER LINES.

Dobsonian a telescope with a simple but highly stable ALTAZIMUTH MOUNTING that can be constructed and used by an amateur astronomer. It swings very smoothly between side bearings and is mounted on a simple sturdy rotating platform. The mounting, pioneered in the mid-20th century by John Dobson, a US telescope maker, is popular for large-aperture short-focus reflectors.

docking the locking together of two spacecraft in space following their rendezvous.

Dog Star see SIRIUS.

domain wall a two-dimensional defect in SPACETIME that, unlike COSMIC STRINGS, cannot survive the inflationary era. See INFLATIONARY UNIVERSE.

dome **1** the insulated roof of an observatory, which protects the telescope and associated equipment from bad weather and from the heating effect of the Sun. The telescope has access to the sky through a *shutter* in the dome, which is closed when the telescope is not in use. A delicate motorized mechanism ensures that, where necessary, the telescope is kept pointing through the opening at the same object throughout prolonged observations as the dome turns to compensate for the Earth's axial rotation. Where the telescope has an EQUATORIAL MOUNTING the dome is movable and hemispherical. Rotation of the dome on a circular track allows different areas of the sky to be brought into view. Built into the observatory's design and engineering is a complicated interaction between the dome's rotation and the movement of the telescope about its inclined axis. The dome must be much larger than the telescope so that it will be able to swing freely inside the structure.

For a telescope with an ALTAZIMUTH MOUNTING the rotation rates of dome and telescope are the same. The dome needs only to be slightly larger than the telescope, and can be square or oblong. The cost of the dome is thus greatly reduced.

2 a low hill with a gentle convex-upward profile, of probable volcanic origin, on a planetary or satellite surface. Lunar domes are confined to the MARIA and are generally less than 15 km in diameter.

Dominion Astrophysical Observatory an observatory near Victoria, British Columbia, Canada, at an altitude of 220 meters. The chief instruments are a 1.8-meter reflector, which went into use in 1918 and is now equipped with a new CER-VIT mirror, and a 1.2-meter reflector, in operation since 1962. They are used mainly for spectroscopy.

Dominion Radio Astrophysical Observatory (DRAO) a national facility, founded in 1959 and operated by the Herzberg Institute of Astrophysics, National Research Council of Canada; it is located near Penticton, British Columbia. Its main instruments are a 26-meter DISH and an APERTURE SYNTHESIS interferometer, working at 408 and 1420 MHz. The interferometer is composed of seven 9-meter paraboloid dishes on a 600-meter E–W track. Both telescopes are used to map continuum and hydrogen-line emission from the Galaxy. DRAO is one of the world's most radio-quiet sites.

Donati's comet (1858 VI) a spectacular COMET famous for its COMA with multiple *haloes*: parabolic envelopes with vertices toward the Sun and foci near the apparent NUCLEUS. These haloes were regular and sharp and are thought to have been produced by repetitive ejection of material from a single active area exposed successively to solar radiation as the solid cometary nucleus rotated every 4.6 hours.

Doppler broadening broadening of spectral lines due to the random motion of emitting or absorbing atoms. As a result of the DOPPLER EFFECT, atoms moving away from the observer show lines with a slight shift to longer wavelengths; atoms moving toward the observer show a slight shift to shorter wavelengths. The overall effect is that the line is broader than the natural width (determined by quantum mechanical uncertainty).

The motion of the atoms may be due to thermal motion, in which case the effect is larger for lighter atoms. Turbulence of stellar material, rapid rotation of a star, or an expanding stellar atmosphere can also produce Doppler broadening. See also LINE BROADENING.

Doppler effect a change in apparent frequency (and hence wavelength) of a wave motion as a result of relative motion of the source and observer. For ELECTROMAGNETIC RADIATION emitted from a moving source, the magnitude of this change is known as the *Doppler shift*. For a source moving away from the observer, the observed wavelength is longer than it would be if source and observer had no relative motion along the line joining them. This change to longer wavelengths (i.e. toward the red end of the visible spectrum for visible wavelengths) is called a REDSHIFT. Conversely, if the source is moving toward the observer, there is a change to shorter wavelengths, i.e. a BLUESHIFT.

When there is no relative motion between source and observer, the wavelength of a spectral line can be given by λ. If the relative velocity along the line of sight of source and observer is *v*, the change in wavelength (Δλ) of the spectral line is given by

$$\Delta\lambda/\lambda = v/c$$

where *c* is the speed of light. For values of *v* comparable with *c*, a relativistic expression is used:

$$\Delta\lambda/\lambda = [(c + v)/(c - v)]^{1/2} - 1$$

v is taken to be positive for a receding object and negative for an approaching one. Doppler shifts can be observed in all regions of the electromagnetic spectrum.

The Doppler effect was first suggested by the Austrian physicist C.J. Doppler in 1842. It has proved invaluable in astronomy for measuring the RADIAL VELOCITIES of celestial objects and is also used for determining the orbital motions (and in some cases the masses) of SPECTROSCOPIC binaries and the rotational motions of bodies. See also DOPPLER BROADENING.

Doppler shift see DOPPLER EFFECT.

Dorado (Swordfish; Goldfish) a small constellation in the southern hemisphere, the brightest star being of 3rd magnitude. It contains a large portion of the Large Magellanic Cloud in which lies the extremely luminous star S DORADUS and the complex Tarantula nebula, 30 DORADUS. Abbrev.: Dor; genitive form: Doradus; approx. position: RA 5.5h, dec –60°; area: 179 sq deg.

30 Doradus (Tarantula nebula; NGC 2070) a very extensive very luminous EMISSION NEBULA in the Large MAGELLANIC CLOUD (LMC) that is a grouping of H II REGIONS characterized by rapid complex motions. It is the brightest object (absolute magnitude –19) in the LMC and is visible to the naked eye. It is also the strongest radio source in the LMC. The most luminous object in the nebula, both at optical and ultraviolet wavelengths, lies near the center and is called R136. It is surrounded by dozens of fainter yet still very bright stars. R136 has at least three components, designated a, b, and c. R136a, the brightest component, is an intense UV source with a powerful STELLAR WIND. Observations with the Hubble Space Telescope have shown that R136a is an extremely dense cluster of at least 12 massive young O stars within a region only 0.25 parsecs across.

dorsum (plural: **dorsa**) a ridge. The word is used in the approved name of such a surface feature on a planet or satellite.

double cluster a pair of CLUSTERS that lie relatively close together. A well-known example is the pair H AND CHI PERSEI, in which the individual clusters appear to be of similar age.

Double Cluster in Perseus see H AND CHI PERSEI.

double galaxy two galaxies observed in close proximity. *Physical doubles* are spatially close pairs assumed to be in orbit about a common center of mass. They are known as a *dumbbell galaxy* when two elliptical galaxies of similar mass orbit each other in a common envelope. *Optical doubles* are widely separated pairs that appear close only because of a chance alignment along the line of sight. Although orbital motions cannot be directly observed, the relative radial velocities of galaxies in a gravitationally bound pair can be used to estimate their total mass, and hence their MASS-TO-LUMINOSITY RATIO.

double-lined spectroscopic binary see SPECTROSCOPIC BINARY.

double quasar the GRAVITATIONAL LENS, Q0957+561, where two images of a quasar, at a redshift of 1.41, are created by the gravitational effects of a galaxy at a redshift of 0.36. The two images are separated by 6″, and are observed in the radio, optical, and X-ray wavebands. It was the first bona fide gravitationally-lensed image to be discovered, by Walsh and collaborators in 1979. The spectra of the two images are almost identical, including common absorption lines from intervening matter along the line of sight. A 1.1-year TIME-OF-FLIGHT difference has been measured between the two images.

double radio source see RADIO-SOURCE STRUCTURE.

double star a pair of stars that appear close together in the sky. There are two types: *optical double stars* and *physical double stars*. Stars in an optical double, such as DENEB, appear close only because they happen to lie in very nearly the same direction from Earth; they are actually too far apart to be members of a dynamically linked system. Stars in a physical double are sufficiently close together for their motions to be affected by their mutual gravitational attraction. They are more usually known as VISUAL BINARIES.

Double Star Project an international mission studying the effects of solar radiation on the Earth's space environment – that is, its magnetosphere. The project, operated jointly by ESA and the China National Space Administration (CNSA), consists of two spacecraft, each designed, developed, launched, and operated by the Chinese Academy of Sciences (CAS) and the CNSA. The two small satellites, named Tan Ce 1 and Tan Ce 2, were launched in December 2003 and July 2004 respectively by a Long March 2C rocket from the Taiyuan spaceport, west of Beijing (*Tan Ce* is Mandarin Chinese for *Explorer*). Following on from ESA's successful CLUSTER (Cluster II) mission, the two Double Star Project spacecraft – one in a near-equatorial orbit, the other in a polar orbit – were designed to provide new measurements in key parts of the magnetosphere, especially the magnetotail, where storms of high-energy particles are generated. Their results were being coordinated with those of the Cluster mission.

DQ Herculis stars see MAGNETIC CATACLYSMIC VARIABLES.

Draco (Dragon) an extensive straggling constellation in the northern hemisphere near Ursa Major. The brightest stars are the 2nd-magnitude yellowish giant Eltanin (γ) and several of fainter 2nd and 3rd magnitude including THUBAN (α), which was the POLE STAR around 2700 BC and will assume that role again in 21 000 years' time because of PRECESSION. The area occupied by Draco contains several binaries, such as Epsilon (ε) and Eta (η) Draconis, and the bright planetary nebula NGC 6543 (see CAT'S-EYE NEBULA). Abbrev.: Dra; genitive form: Draconis; approx. position: RA 9.5 – 20.5h, dec 50° – 85°; area: 1083 sq deg.

draconic month (nodical month) the time interval of 27.2122 days, on average, between two successive passages of the Moon through the ascending NODE (or descending node) of its orbit.

Draconids see GIACOBINIDS.

Draco system a dwarf elliptical galaxy that is a member of the LOCAL GROUP.

DRAO *abbrev. for* Dominion Radio Astrophysical Observatory.

Draper classification *another name for* Harvard classification. See SPECTRAL TYPES.

draw tube a simple tube of 31.75, 25.4, or 50 mm bore into which fits the telescopic EYEPIECE in use. It is equipped with a mechanism, such as a rack and pinion, allowing fine adjustment of the eyepiece position in order to obtain a sharp focus.

drift chamber a position-sensitive detector of ionizing radiation. The point of formation of a cloud of electrons, caused by a particle ionizing a gas, is determined by timing the constant velocity drift of the cloud towards a fine wire anode, under the influence of an electric field. Drift chambers are used in high-energy gamma-ray telescopes for detecting photons by measuring the tracks of the electron-positron pair after a PAIR PRODUCTION absorption.

drift scan a profile of a RADIO SOURCE made with a radio telescope by aiming the ANTENNA at a point beside the source and allowing the rotation of the Earth to move the source through the antenna beam.

drive clock see EQUATORIAL MOUNTING.

DRS see DATA-RELAY SATELLITE.

DSN *abbrev. for* Deep Space Network.

D-type asteroids a class of ASTEROID whose members are rare in the main belt but become increasingly dominant in the regions beyond the 2:1 Jovian resonance at 3.2 AU (see KIRKWOOD GAPS). The observed surface coloring may be due to carbon-rich kerogenlike material.

Dubhe (α UMa) an orange-yellow giant that is one of the seven brightest stars in the PLOUGH and is one of the two POINTERS. It is a close visual binary (period 44 years) with a 4th-magnitude companion. m_v: 1.79; M_v: –0.8; spectral type: K0 IIIa; distance: 33 pc.

dumbbell galaxy see DOUBLE GALAXY.

Dumbbell nebula (M27; NGC 6853) a PLANETARY NEBULA in the constellation Vulpecula. It has an hourglass shape

(330 × 900 arc seconds) and a magnitude of 7.6.

Durchmusterung (German) an astronomical survey of the positional data of stars published in the form of a catalog. Such surveys are carried out either by sweeping successive narrow zones of the sky with a telescope and recording the position and magnitude of each star that transits the telescope's field down to a specified limiting magnitude or by analyzing wide-angle photographs taken with a Schmidt telescope or comparable instrument. See BONNER DURCHMUSTERUNG; CAPE PHOTOGRAPHIC DURCHMUSTERUNG.

dust see COSMIC DUST.

dust lane a belt of gas and dust that completely obscures the optical light from the center of an elliptical or S0 galaxy, forming a prominent dark band. Examples occur in CENTAURUS A and the BLACKEYE GALAXY. Dust lanes are seen in edge-on spiral systems caused by obscuring matter in the galactic disk, as in the SOMBRERO GALAXY.

dust tail see COMET TAILS.

dwarf *short for* dwarf star.

dwarf Cepheids (AI Velorum stars) a group of PULSATING VARIABLES that were classed as RR LYRAE STARS but have been shown to have a lower luminosity in addition to a shorter period of about 1 to 5 hours. The variation in apparent magnitude (i.e. AMPLITUDE) ranges from 0.3 up to 1.2 but can be higher. At the lower amplitudes they are difficult to differentiate from DELTA SCUTI STARS but are apparently older. Instabilities of period and light-curve shape are characteristic of these stars and many exhibit the Blazhko effect found in some RR LYRAE STARS. The pulsations are probably mixtures of oscillations of a fundamental mode and those at higher harmonic frequencies (see PULSATING VARIABLES).

dwarf elliptical (dE) see DWARF GALAXY.

dwarf galaxy a GALAXY that is unusually faint either because of its very small size, its very low surface brightness, or both. Since galaxies exist in a continuous range of sizes from the giant ellipticals downward, the dividing line between average and dwarf is somewhat arbitrary. Since no spiral or S0 galaxies have been observed with total magnitudes below –16, this is often used as a convenient demarcation line. They contain only a few million stars and are very difficult to observe against foreground stars because they are almost completely transparent. Dwarf galaxies may make up the bulk of the cosmic population and occur in all morphologies except as spiral galaxies.

The *dwarf irregulars* (*dI*) are the most numerous of these galaxies, and contain a significant fraction of their mass as neutral hydrogen gas in a dark halo (see also LSB GALAXIES). *Dwarf ellipticals* (*dE*) are dominated by metal-poor halo stars, and their lack of gas or dust suggests that any star formation occurred a long time ago in these systems. In contrast, the gas-rich *blue compact dwarf* (*BCD*) *galaxies* are undergoing active star formation with sizes and spectra resembling giant H II regions. See also EXTRAGALACTIC H II REGION.

dwarf irregular (dI) see DWARF GALAXY.

dwarf novae a small group of intrinsically faint stars that are characterized by sudden increases in brightness occurring at intervals of a few weeks or months, the maximum brightness lasting only a few days. The change in brightness (i.e. AMPLITUDE) is usually between 2–5 magnitudes. The first to be discovered, U Geminorum, is typical of the majority, which are therefore classified as *U Geminorum stars*. This subgroup displays a fairly smooth decline in brightness from the maximum, unlike the much smaller subgroup of *Z Camelopardalis stars* that can undergo *standstills*, i.e. periods of nearly constant intermediate brightness, before dropping to minimum brightness. Both the occurrence of the standstill and its duration – a few days to many months – are quite unpredictable. There are also periods of erratic light variations. *SU Ursae Majoris stars*, another subgroup, differ from U Gem stars by occasionally having particularly long outbursts – *superoutbursts* – that are brighter than normal outbursts.

Dwarf novae are a class of CATACLYSMIC VARIABLES, i.e. close BINARY STARS in which the primary is a WHITE DWARF. The secondary is a cooler main-sequence star, spectral type K or G. The components have similar masses (about 0.7 to 1.2 solar masses); the orbital periods are between about 3 to 15 hours. There are two popular models for dwarf novae. In the *mass-transfer instability model*, the secondary is undergoing irregular expansion and episodically fills its Roche lobe (see EQUIPOTENTIAL SURFACES. Hydrogen-rich gas then streams from the secondary and takes up a disk-shaped orbit around the primary, ultimately leading to an outburst. In the more popular *disk instability model*, the outbursts are caused by episodically recurring thermal instabilities in the accretion disk (see MASS TRANSFER), which is continually being fed by mass transfer from the Roche-lobe filling secondary. The outburst itself does not involve an explosion, and no significant amount of mass is ejected. The gas in the disk spirals down on to the white dwarf, where it may eventually cause a nova explosion.

dwarf planet any of the four TERRESTRIAL PLANETS.

dwarf star (**dwarf**) any star lying on the MAIN SEQUENCE of the HERTZSPRUNG–RUSSELL DIAGRAM. The term arises from the early dual classification of stars into giants (*g*) and dwarfs (*d*): the Sun was classified as *d*G2. This system has been superseded by that of luminosity classes (see SPECTRAL TYPES), and these 'dwarf' stars are of luminosity class V. The term *main-sequence star* is now more common, especially to prevent confusion with WHITE DWARFS; late-type main-sequence stars, however, are still referred to as RED DWARFS.

Dwingeloo Radio Observatory the administrative headquarters of the Netherlands Foundation for Research in Astronomy (NFRA) known as ASTRON (Stichting Astronomisch Onderzoek in Nederland) in Dutch. It is the site of a 25-meter radio telescope that came into operation in 1955 and can observe at 1.42, 1.66, and 5 GHz.

dynamical equinox (informal **vernal equinox**) The point of intersection of the ecliptic with the celestial equator at which the Sun's declination changes from south to north. It is thus the ascending NODE of the Earth's mean orbit on the Earth's equatorial plane. This point moves slowly with time. See also CATALOG EQUINOX; EQUINOXES.

dynamical friction see DYNAMICAL RELAXATION.

dynamical parallax an iterative method used to determine the distance and the mass of a VISUAL BINARY star, usually from measurements of the orbital period (P years) and apparent mean orbital size (l'') and an estimate of the mass of the two stars ($M_1 + M_2$ solar masses). The approximate semimajor axis (a AU) of the orbit is calculated from KEPLER'S THIRD LAW:

$$(M_1 + M_2)P^2 = a^3$$

The ratio of a/l gives an estimate of the distance of the binary. If the apparent magnitude is known, the absolute magnitude can be deduced from the DISTANCE MODULUS and a more accurate value of total mass is hence obtained using the MASS-LUMINOSITY RELATION. The process is repeated as necessary using the corrected mass estimates, an inaccurate estimate in mass leading to a much smaller error in distance.

dynamical relaxation a process occurring within a CLUSTER OF GALAXIES in which the collective gravitational potential acts on individual constituent galaxies. During the early stages of cluster formation the energy of a galaxy fluctuates very rapidly as the cluster undergoes *violent relaxation* to settle into a constant potential in VIRIAL EQUILIBRIUM. This process is modeled using N-BODY simulations that assume that gravitational interactions between individual galaxies are ignored in favor of modeling their response to the total mass. Once the cluster has collapsed, relaxation continues through TWO-BODY gravitational interactions. The galaxies lose orbital energy through the process and slow down due to this *dynamical friction*. This is particularly important for the most massive galaxies that gradually settle to the cluster center and may merge to form the massive dominant galaxy, often a cD galaxy. Most clusters are in a process of segregation of slow-moving massive galaxies at low cluster radii and lighter galaxies further out.

dynamical time the family of timescales that was introduced in 1984 to replace EPHEMERIS TIME, ET, as the independent variable of dynamical theories and ephemerides. Like ET these timescales are independent of the Earth's rotation.

Terrestrial dynamical time (*TDT*) is used as the timescale of ephemerides for observations from the Earth's surface. It is used for apparent geocentric ephemerides. For practical purposes

$$TDT = TAI + 32.184 \text{ seconds}$$

where TAI is the INTERNATIONAL ATOMIC TIME. This takes advantage of the direct (broadcast) availability of coordinated UNIVERSAL TIME, UTC, which is an integral number of seconds offset from TAI. Continuity with pre-1984 practices has been achieved by setting the difference between TDT and TAI to the 1984 estimate of the difference between ET and TAI. The increment to be applied to UNIVERSAL TIME, UT1, to give TDT is called DELTA T (ΔT). The unit of TDT is the day, 86 400 seconds, 24 hours, at mean sea level.

Barycentric dynamical time (*TDB*) is used for ephemerides and equations of motion that are referred to the BARYCENTER OF THE SOLAR SYSTEM. TDB differs from TDT only by periodic variations.

dynamics the study of the motion of material bodies under the influence of forces. Newton's laws of motion form the basis of classical dynamics. When speeds approach the speed of light the special theory of RELATIVITY must be taken into account.

Ee

Eagle nebula (**M16**; **NGC 6611**) a large EMISSION NEBULA – an H II region – that is located about 2.5 kiloparsecs away in the direction of the constellation Serpens Cauda (see SERPENS). It contains some hot young stars that are part of an open cluster.

early-type galaxies a general term now used for elliptical galaxies.

early-type stars hot stars of SPECTRAL TYPE O, B, and A. They were originally thought, wrongly, to be at an earlier stage of evolution than LATE-TYPE STARS.

early Universe the era in the evolution of the Universe soon after the BIG BANG when it was very hot and dense. As the Universe expanded it cooled, giving rise to a sequence of phase transitions associated with broken symmetries. The light elements such as helium were mostly formed in the early Universe. It has been suggested that in the early Universe *inflation*, i.e. very rapid expansion, occurred. The very early Universe, occurring immediately after the big bang, requires a fundamentally new physics involving the combination of quantum mechanics and general relativity theory before it will be understood.

Earth the third planet of the Solar System and the only one known to possess life. It is the largest of the inner planets (equatorial radius: 6378 km) and has one natural satellite, the MOON. A summary of the Earth's orbital and physical characteristics are given in Table 1, backmatter. The Earth has a substantial atmosphere, mainly of nitrogen and oxygen, and a MAGNETOSPHERE linked to a magnetic field. (See ATMOSPHERE, COMPOSITION; ATMOSPHERIC LAYERS; GEOMAGNETISM; VAN ALLEN RADIATION BELTS.) Two-thirds of the planet is covered by water, ocean depth ranging from 2500 to 6500 meters; the average land elevation is 860 meters. See also GEOID.

On average the Earth's surface transfers to the atmosphere an amount of energy equal to that it absorbs. The Earth's *mean surface temperature*, i.e. that needed to keep Earth and atmosphere in thermal equilibrium, is 13 °C. Temperatures in the atmosphere generally decrease from equator to poles and from low to high atmospheric altitudes. These temperature gradients, together with the Earth's rapid rotation, drive the circulation of the atmosphere. On average the Earth emits into space an amount of radiant energy equal to that absorbed by surface plus atmosphere. The Earth's *effective temperature*, i.e. that needed to keep Earth in thermal equilibrium with space, is –18 °C; this is the Earth's temperature as measured from space.

Studies of the refraction and reflection of seismic waves propagating through the Earth show that it consists of three main internal layers: the crust, mantle, and core. The *crust* has a thickness of about 30–40 km under the continents (but much thicker beneath mountains) and an average of 6 km under the oceans. It has a density of about 3 times that of water. It consists largely of sedimentary rocks, such as limestone and sandstone, resting on a base of igneous rocks, such as granite (under the continents) and basalt (under both the continents and oceans). The *mantle* extends to a depth of 2900 km, its density increasing with depth from 3.3 to 5.5 times that of water. Its composition is thought to include a high proportion of magnesium- and iron-rich silicate rocks. The *core* increases in density from 10 times that of water at its junction with the mantle to 13 times at the center. It is composed predominently of iron with several, possibly many, additional components. The *inner core* has a radius of about 1200 km and is solid. The *outer core* has a radius of 3485 km; it is liquid and is regarded as the seat of the Earth's magnetic field (see GEOMAGNETISM).

It is believed that the pressure at the Earth's center may reach 400 gigapascals (4 million atmospheres), while the internal temperature rises with increasing depth and may exceed 4000 °C at the center. The heat required to maintain these temperatures is derived from the natural radioactivity of the Earth's constituent rocks, but would have been greatly augmented soon after formation by gravitational compression and the impact of meteoritic material. This led to the widespread melting and DIFFERENTIATION that produced the present layered structure.

After 4.6 thousand million years the Earth's internal heat is still a source of mechanical power, producing earthquakes and volcanic eruptions, raising mountains, and moving continent-sized blocks about its surface. It is regarded as a convective heat engine. The crust and part of the upper mantle form a rigid zone, 50–70 km thick, known as the *lithosphere*. This lies above the weaker less rigid *asthenosphere*. According to the theory of *plate tectonics*, the lithosphere is broken up into fairly rigid *plates*; there are seven major plates and many smaller ones. Convection within the asthenosphere causes the plates, with their associated continental and/or oceanic crust, to move relative to each other: the phenomena of *continental drift* and *sea-floor spreading*. The relative motion amounts to a few cm per year. The plate boundaries are defined by a global map of earthquake epicenters. At *transform* boundaries between two plates the plates can slide past each other. At *constructive* boundaries two plates are moving apart. Where this occurs in mid-ocean, molten rock from the mantle is injected into the crust to form mid-oceanic ridges. At *destructive* boundaries two plates are moving toward each other. The oceanic part of one plate can plunge under another plate in a process called *subduction*, forming an island arc or mountain range.

See also AGE OF THE EARTH; SOLAR SYSTEM; SOLAR SYSTEM, ORIGIN.

Earth-grazers (**Earth-crossers**) NEAR-EARTH ASTEROIDS.

Earth-rotation synthesis (**supersynthesis**) see APERTURE SYNTHESIS.

earthshine (**ashen light**) sunlight reflected from Earth. Close to new Moon, earthshine reflected by the Moon back to the Earth enables the whole lunar disk to become visible – the old Moon in the new Moon's arms. An observer on the Moon sees the Earth illuminated by earthshine and at new Moon can measure the Earth's ALBEDO.

eastern elongation see ELONGATION.

east point see CARDINAL POINTS.

eccentric anomaly see ANOMALY.

eccentricity symbol: *e*. A measure of the extent to which an elliptical orbit departs from circularity. It is given by the ratio $c/2a$ where c is the distance between the focal points of the ellipse and $2a$ is the length of the major axis. For a circular orbit $e = 0$. The planets and most of their satellites have an eccentricity range of 0–0.25 (see table). Many comets and some of the asteroids and planetary satellites have very eccentric orbits. The eccentricity of an orbit varies over a long period due to changing gravitational effects: that of the Earth's orbit

Eccentricity

Planet	*Eccentricity*
Mercury	0.205 628
Venus	0.006 787
Earth	0.016 722
Mars	0.093 377
Jupiter	0.0483
Saturn	0.0560
Uranus	0.0461
Neptune	0.0097
Pluto	0.2482

varies between about 0.005 to 0.06 in a period of about 100 000 years. See also CONIC SECTIONS.

echelle grating a DIFFRACTION GRATING with very fine lines ruled much farther apart than in other gratings. Such a grating has very high resolution but only over a fairly narrow wavelength band. The resolving power at a given wavelength depends primarily on the total ruled width and the angles of incidence and refraction; a high resolution can be obtained with coarse ruling if the grooves are properly shaped (see BLAZED GRATING). The echelle grating of the *echelle spectrograph* is used at high-order diffraction to give larger angular dispersion. Since the high orders overlap, cross dispersion with, for example, a second grating must be used. The second grating is a standard grating with its direction of dispersion at right angles to that of the echelle; the spectral images of the different orders can then be separated and stacked above one another at the detector.

echelle spectrograph see ECHELLE GRATING.

eclipse the total or partial obscuration of light from a celestial body as it passes through the shadow of another body. A planetary satellite is eclipsed when it passes through the shadow of its primary or another satellite. An eclipse of the Sun is strictly an OCCULTATION.

An eclipse of the Sun – a *solar eclipse* – or the Moon – a *lunar eclipse* – occurs when the Sun, Moon, and Earth lie in or nearly in a straight line: see illustration (a). If the plane of the Moon's orbit lay exactly in the plane of the ECLIPTIC a solar eclipse would take place at each new Moon and a lunar eclipse at each full Moon. The two planes are however inclined at an angle of about 5°, intersecting at the NODES of the Moon's orbit. Eclipses are only observed when the Sun is at or near a node and the Moon is near the same node (solar eclipse) or the opposite one (lunar eclipse). The *ecliptic limits* are the maximum angular distances of the new or full Moon from its node for an eclipse to take place.

Although the Moon is 400 times smaller than the Sun, it is also about 400 times nearer the Earth. As a result, Sun and Moon have almost exactly the same angular size (about ½°), so that it is possible for the Moon to obscure the Sun. The Earth and Moon both cast shadows in sunlight, the shadow having a dark cone-shaped inner region – the UMBRA – and an outer lighter penumbral region. A solar eclipse occurs, between sunrise and sunset at new Moon, when the Moon passes directly in front of the Sun so that the Earth lies in the Moon's shadow: see illustration (b). When the Moon is sufficiently close to Earth so that its apparent diameter exceeds that of the Sun, then the umbra of the Moon's shadow can just reach the Earth's surface. It moves in a general west to east trend over a very narrow curved zone of the surface, known as the *path of totality*, which can be up to 250 km wide but averages about 160 km. An observer at a point where only the penumbra will move past sees a *partial eclipse*, in which only part of the Sun is obscured. An observer in the path of totality will experience a *total eclipse*, in which the Sun is completely obscured. If the Moon is far enough away to appear smaller than the Sun, a rim (or annulus) of light will be seen around the eclipsed Sun and an *annular eclipse* occurs. The period of annularity never exceeds 12.5 minutes and is normally much less.

In a total solar eclipse, *first contact* occurs when the Moon just appears to touch the Sun's western limb. As the Moon gradually covers the Sun, the landscape darkens and animals become disturbed. *Totality* begins at *second contact* when the Sun disappears from sight. The maximum duration of totality is 7m 31s but is usually much less. Totality ends at *third contact*, just as the crescent Sun emerges, and at *fourth contact* the whole disk of the Sun is once more seen. The time between first and last contact can approach four hours. During totality the CHROMOSPHERE, CORONA, and other phenomena can be observed and studied. There are between two and five solar eclipses each year. Total eclipses are, however, very rare at any particular place.

A lunar eclipse occurs, at full Moon, when the Moon passes into the shadow cone of the Earth. It can be seen from any place at which the Moon is visible above the horizon. A *total eclipse* occurs when the

Moon enters completely into the umbra of the Earth's shadow. If only part of the Moon enters the umbra the eclipse is *partial*. When the Moon only enters the penumbral region, a *penumbral eclipse* takes place in which a slight, usually quite unappreciable darkening of the Moon's surface occurs. The maximum duration of totality is 1h 47m. The Moon can usually be seen throughout totality, being illuminated by sunlight refracted by the Earth's atmosphere into the shadow area. Since the bluer wavelengths are removed by scattering, the Moon has a coppery-red color. There are up to either two or three lunar eclipses each year. Up to seven eclipses can occur in one year, either five solar and two lunar or four solar and three lunar.

See also SAROS.

eclipse year the period of time between two successive passages of the Sun through the same NODE of the Moon's orbit. It is equal to 346.620 days, being less than the

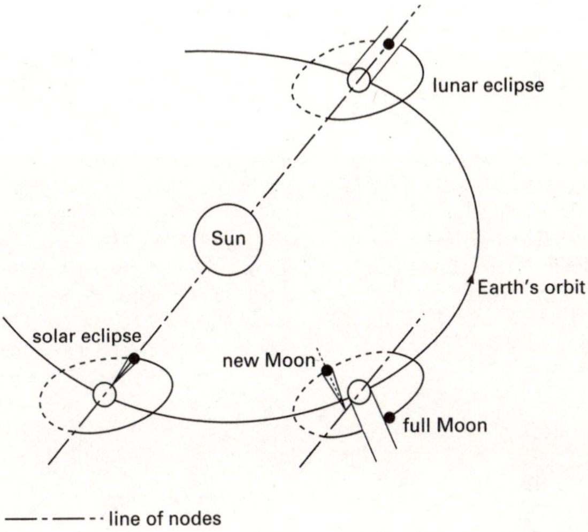

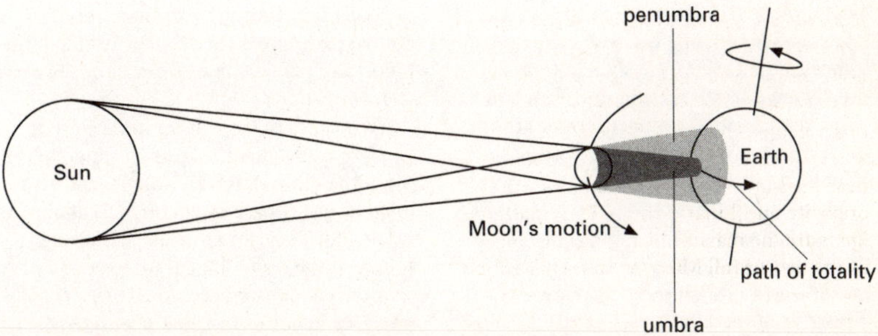

Eclipse: (a) solar and lunar eclipses; (b) lunar shadow in solar eclipse

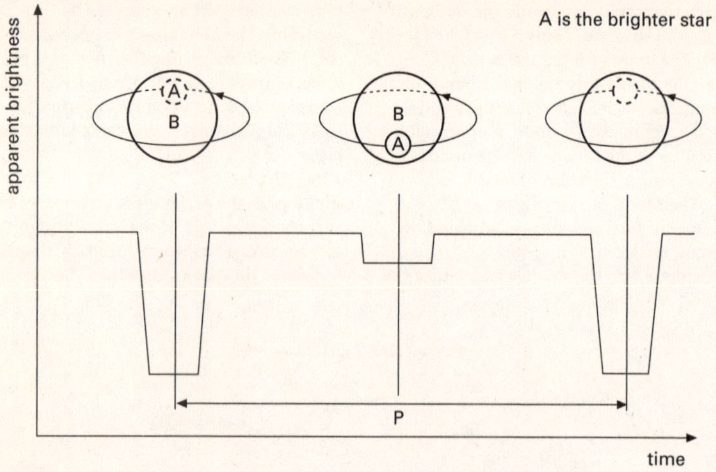

Schematic of orbits and light curve of eclipsing binary

SIDEREAL YEAR because of REGRESSION of the Moon's nodes. There are almost exactly 19 eclipse years in one SAROS.

eclipsing binary a BINARY STAR whose orbital plane is orientated such that each component is totally or partly eclipsed by the other during each orbital period. The effect observed is a periodic decrease in the light from the system (see illustration). The deeper minimum corresponds to the eclipse of the brighter star. The light curve gives the period of revolution, and from the depths and shapes of the minima it is possible to estimate the inclination of the orbital plane. The duration of the eclipses compared to the time between eclipses indicates the radii of the stars in terms of the distance between them. If the system is also a double-lined SPECTROSCOPIC BINARY the individual masses and radii of the stars can be calculated.

Eclipsing binaries tend to be composed of large stars with small orbits and therefore the majority are close binaries (see BINARY STAR). In these systems MASS TRANSFER affects the stars' evolution, leading to three main classes of eclipsing binaries. W URSAE MAJORIS STARS are in contact. In W SERPENTIS STARS one component is transferring mass rapidly to the other. In these two classes the stars are distorted into ellipsoids, an effect that shows in the light curve. ALGOL VARIABLES represent a later stage; mass transfer is almost complete and the stars are nearly spherical.

ecliptic the mean plane of the Earth's orbit around the Sun. Although the orbital plane is in fact defined by the motion of the center of mass of the Earth–Moon system around the sun, the ecliptic refers to the Earth alone, the resulting errors being negligible. The ecliptic may thus be taken as coincident with the Sun's apparent annual path across the sky. The orbits of the Moon and planets, apart from Pluto, lie very near the ecliptic.

The planes of the ecliptic and celestial equator are inclined at an angle equal to the tilt of the Earth's axis. This angle, known as the OBLIQUITY OF THE ECLIPTIC, is about 23°26′. The EQUINOXES lie on the celestial sphere at the two points of intersection of ecliptic and celestial equator. The *poles of the ecliptic* lie at 90° from all points on the ecliptic at the positions RA 18h, dec +66°.5 and RA 6h, dec –66°.5.

ecliptic coordinate system a COORDINATE

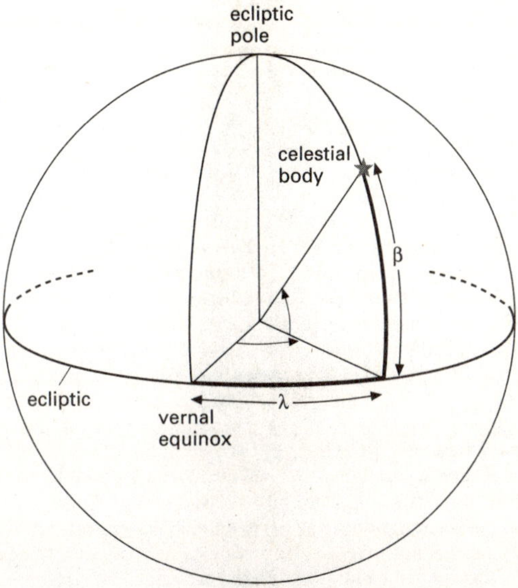

Ecliptic coordinate system

SYSTEM in which the fundamental reference circle is the ECLIPTIC and the zero point is the vernal (or dynamic) EQUINOX (γ). The coordinates are *celestial* (or *ecliptic*) *latitude* and *celestial* (or *ecliptic*) *longitude* (see illustration).

The celestial latitude (β) of a star, etc., is its angular distance (from 0° to 90°) north (counted positive) or south (counted negative) of the ecliptic; it is measured along the great circle through the body and the poles of the ecliptic. The celestial longitude (λ) of a body is its angular distance (from 0° to 360°) from the vernal equinox, measured eastward along the ecliptic to the intersection of the body's circle of longitude; it is measured in the same direction as the Sun's apparent annual motion. Although observations are taken from the Earth's surface the coordinates should strictly be geocentric and, tabulated as such, are universally applicable. A slight correction is therefore applied to convert surface (topocentric) observations to geocentric values.

The ecliptic system is older but less used than the EQUATORIAL and HORIZONTAL COORDINATE SYSTEMS. It is sometimes used to give the positions of the Sun, Moon, and planets. See also HELIOCENTRIC COORDINATE SYSTEM.

ecliptic limits see ECLIPSE.

E-corona the part of the solar CORONA that consists of relatively slow-moving ions and exhibits an EMISSION SPECTRUM superimposed on the CONTINUUM of the K-CORONA. The emission lines show that the E-corona is very highly ionized, some ions having lost up to 15 electrons. At visible wavelengths, only FORBIDDEN LINES are present, the most prominent of which are the 'red' line at 637.4 nm (caused by the presence of Fe X), the 'green' line at 530.3 nm (caused by Fe XIV), and the 'yellow' line at 569.4 nm (caused by Ca XV).

ecosphere the zone of space around the Sun or some other star in which a planet would experience external conditions that are not incompatible with the existence of life. Prevailing conditions, as of atmospheric content or pressure, might however prove too hostile.

Eddington limit an upper limit to the luminosity that can be radiated by a celestial object of a specified mass. Beyond this limit the forces on matter due to RADIATION PRESSURE in the emitting region would exceed the gravitational forces holding the object together.

effective area (of a radio telescope) see ARRAY.

effective focal length the property of a compound lens, such as an eyepiece, that is analogous to the FOCAL LENGTH of a single thin lens and can be used, for example, in the determination of magnifying power. For a two-lens system the effective focal length, f, is given by

$$1/f = 1/f_1 + 1/f_2 - d/f_1f_2$$

where f_1 and f_2 are the focal lengths of the components and d is their separation.

effective temperature symbol T_{eff}, T_e. The surface temperature of a star, expressed as the temperature of a BLACK BODY (i.e. a perfect radiator) having the same radius as the star and radiating the same total amount of energy (E) per unit area per second. A star is thus being considered a black body and its effective temperature is thus given by STEFAN'S LAW:

$$T_{\text{eff}}^4 = E/\sigma = L/4\pi R^2$$

σ is Stefan's constant and L and R are the star's luminosity and radius. Although accurate determinations of effective temperature are difficult, each SPECTRAL TYPE has a characteristic range of T_{eff}; the total range is from about 2500 to over 40 000 kelvin. The Sun's effective temperature is 5770 K. The effective temperature is the best measure of the actual temperature of the gas in a star's outer layers.

Radiation temperature, T_r, is equivalent to the effective temperature measured not over the whole spectral range but over a narrow portion of the spectrum, for example at visible wavelengths, which gives the *optical temperature*.

Effelsberg Telescope (**Bonn Telescope**) one of the world's largest fully steerable radio telescopes, built in 1972 in Bad Münstereifel-Effelsberg 40 km from Bonn, Germany, and operated by the Max Planck Institute for Radioastronomy (MPIR). The dish has a diameter of 100 meters and weighs 3200 tonnes. It was resurfaced in 1986 to an accuracy of 0.5 mm and can be used at frequencies up to 50 GHz. About 30% of the observing time on the telescope is assigned to VLBI observations.

EFR *abbrev. for* emerging flux region.

EGRET *abbrev. for* energetic gamma-ray experiment telescope. See COMPTON GAMMA RAY OBSERVATORY.

Einstein cross a gravitationally-lensed image of a distant quasar (redshift 1.7) by a foreground (redshift 0.039) spiral galaxy. The image of the quasar is split into four point sources forming a cross at the center of the galaxy. Gravitational microlensing has been observed as variations in the light between the four components. See GRAVITATIONAL LENS.

Einstein–de Sitter universe see COSMOLOGICAL MODELS.

Einstein Observatory nASA's second High-Energy Astrophysical Observatory, HEAO-2, launched in Nov. 1978 for X-ray observations and operated until loss of control gas in Apr. 1981. The (then) unique capabilities of its 60-cm GRAZING INCIDENCE telescope revolutionized X-ray astronomy, in the same way UHURU had done a decade before. High-resolution maps were obtained of many extended sources (clusters of galaxies, supernova remnants), the first high-resolution spectroscopy was achieved on a few bright sources, and the enhanced sensitivity led to the discovery of several thousand faint sources (down to ~10 nanojansky), mainly identified with normal galactic stars or active galaxies (quasars) at high redshifts. A catalog of Einstein Observatory sources is available as an extension to the EXOSAT DATABASE.

Einstein ring see GRAVITATIONAL LENS.

Einstein shift see GRAVITATIONAL REDSHIFT.

EISCAT *short for* European incoherent scatter radars. The sophisticated radar systems used in 1984–85 in N Scandinavia to study the Earth's IONOSPHERE.

ejecta material excavated during the formation of a CRATER or BASIN. See also EJECTA BLANKET; SECONDARY CRATERS.

ejecta blanket a deposit of EJECTA from a CRATER or BASIN, the thickness of which decreases with distance from the crater or

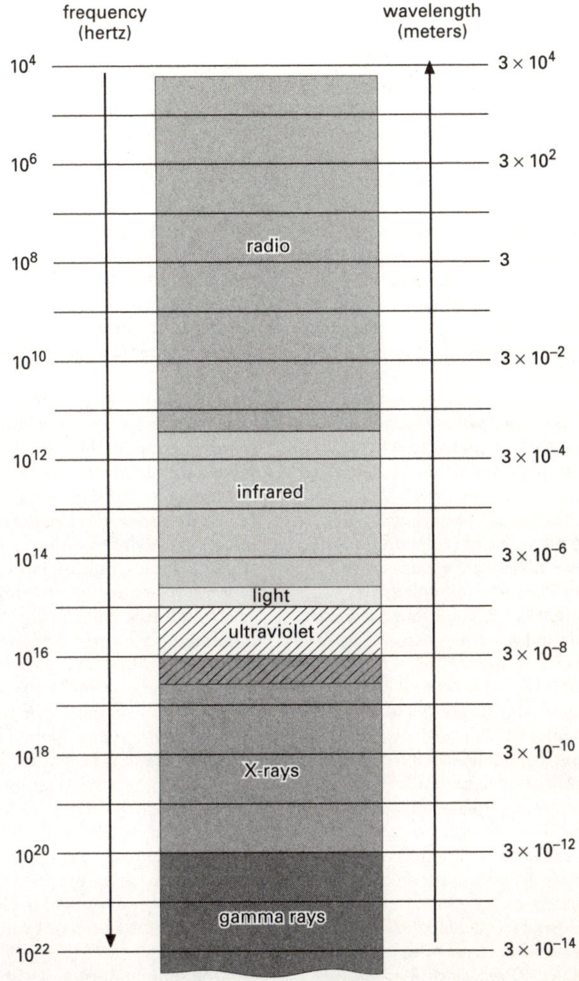

Electromagnetic spectrum

basin rim. The surface may exhibit transverse dunes, radial furrows, and SECONDARY CRATERS.

Elara a small satellite of Jupiter, discovered in 1905 by the US astronomer Charles Dillon Perrine. See JUPITER'S SATELLITES; Table 2, Appendix.

E-layer (E-region) see IONOSPHERE.

Electra see PLEIADES.

electromagnetic force see FUNDAMENTAL FORCES.

electromagnetic radiation a disturbance that can travel through a vacuum as well as through a material medium, light and radio waves being familiar forms. It consists of oscillating (time-varying) electric and magnetic fields with directions at right angles to each other and to the direction of propagation. The two fields are bound together, the time-varying electric and magnetic components regenerating each other in an endless cycle that moves from one point to the next through space. The radiation transfers energy and also momentum. It travels through a vacuum at the SPEED OF LIGHT, *c*, which is a fundamental constant equal to about 3×10^5 km s^{-1}. The speed is slightly reduced on entering a medium, such as air or glass.

Electromagnetic radiation is caused by the acceleration of charged particles, such as electrons. Its propagation through space can be fully described in terms of wave motion. Like other periodic waves, electromagnetic waves have a WAVELENGTH λ and a FREQUENCY ν, which are related by $\lambda\nu = c$. Reflection, refraction, interference, and polarization can be explained in terms of wave motion. When radiation interacts with matter, however, it exhibits particle-like behavior, as when it undergoes absorption or emission. It thus has a dual wave–particle nature. A particulate nature was originally proposed by Newton but in its present form the concept is part of QUANTUM THEORY. Light and other kinds of radiation interact with matter as quanta. A quantum of radiation of frequency ν transfers energy $h\nu$ and momentum $h\nu/c^2$, where h is the PLANCK CONSTANT. The quantum of electromagnetic radiation is the PHOTON. Light, etc., is thus absorbed by or emitted from atoms or molecules in the form of photons.

The range of frequencies (or wavelengths) of electromagnetic radiation is known as the *electromagnetic spectrum* (see illustration). The spectrum can be divided into various regions, which are not sharply delineated. These regions range from low-frequency low-energy RADIO WAVES through INFRARED RADIATION, LIGHT, ULTRAVIOLET RADIATION, X-RAYS, to high-frequency high-energy GAMMA RAYS. Most astronomical observations measure some form of electromagnetic radiation.

electromagnetic spectrum see ELECTROMAGNETIC RADIATION.

electron symbol: e. A stable ELEMENTARY PARTICLE (a lepton) that has a negative CHARGE of 1.6022×10^{-19} coulomb, a mass of 9.1094×10^{-28} gram, and SPIN ½. Although it has mass, the electron has no size: it is described as 'pointlike'. Electrons are constituents of all ATOMS, moving around the central nucleus. They can also exist independently. The ANTIPARTICLE of the electron is the *positron*, symbol e^+ or $\bar{e}$.

electron density symbol: n_e. The number of electrons per unit volume (e.g. per cubic meter) of the interstellar medium or some other medium.

electronic imaging see IMAGING.

electronographic camera a highly sensitive electronic device that can be used for recording astronomical images. It is an IMAGE TUBE in which the beam of electrons liberated from the photocathode is accelerated by an electric field and focused by a magnetic field on to a film coated with an *electronographic emulsion*. This is a very fine grain high-resolution 'nuclear' photographic emulsion in which electrons are recorded directly: every high-energy electron leaves a developable track so that an image can be produced by a process similar to that for a photograph. The resulting *electronograph* looks similar to a photograph with the important difference that the density at any point on the electronograph is proportional to the intensity at the corresponding point in the optical image through almost the whole intensity range. The device thus has a highly linear response. Photometric information can be obtained directly by measuring the density of the image. The device also has a high QUANTUM EFFICIENCY.

electron temperature a 'statistical' temperature required to account for the observed energy of electrons, assuming that the energy is kinetic energy. The electrons may be in a plasma, gas, or solid, however since they are not in equilibrium with their surroundings, they may have a much higher temperature.

electronvolt symbol: eV. A unit of energy equal to the energy acquired by an electron falling freely through a potential difference of one volt. It is equal to 1.6022×10^{-19} joule. High-energy ELECTROMAGNETIC RADIATION is usually referred to in terms of the energy of its photons: a photon energy of 100 eV is equivalent to a radiation frequency of 2.418 $\times 10^{16}$ hertz. The energies of ELEMENTARY PARTICLES are usually quoted in eV; their REST MASSES are generally referred to in terms of their energies in eV.

element any of a large number of substances, including HYDROGEN, HELIUM, carbon, nitrogen, oxygen, and iron, that consist entirely of ATOMS of the same ATOMIC NUMBER, i.e. with the same number of protons in their nuclei. The atoms are not all identical however: ISOTOPES of an element can occur with different numbers of neutrons in their nuclei. When arranged in order of increasing atomic number along a series of horizontal rows, elements with similar chemical and physical properties fall into groups. The similarities in properties arise from similarities in the electron arrangements within the atom. This table of elements is called the periodic table. Over 100 elements are now known, more than 90 of which occur naturally on Earth. The elements have stable isotopes and/or unstable (i.e. radioactive) isotopes.

The creation of the elements and the means by which they become distributed throughout the Universe are major areas of study in astronomy (see NUCLEOSYNTHESIS). The abundance of each element in the Universe, i.e. its COSMIC ABUNDANCE, depends on the method of its synthesis – by nuclear reactions in stars, by COSMIC-RAY collisions, etc. – and on its lifetime in its immediate surroundings and its long-term stability.

elementary particles the basic building blocks of matter. At present the only truly elementary particles containing no internal subcomponents are believed to be LEPTONS and QUARKS. There are six leptons: the ELECTRON, MUON, the massive tau lepton, and the three NEUTRINOS. There are also six so-called 'flavors' of quarks. At one time the constituents of atomic nuclei (NEUTRONS and PROTONS) were thought to be elementary but it is now known that they possess internal structure in the form of triplets of quarks. Particles with quark constituents are called *hadrons*. Those, like the proton, composed of three quarks are called *baryons*. Particles known as *mesons* are produced by a variety of high-energy reactions and decay into stable particles. Mesons, which include the PIONS, are composed of quark and antiquark pairs.

All the visible matter in the Universe can be described in terms of leptons and quarks and the forces acting between them. The simplest theoretical framework for this description is called the *standard model*. There are four known interactions between elementary particles: the strong interaction (in which only quarks and hadrons can take part), electromagnetism, the weak interaction, and gravitation (see FUNDAMENTAL FORCES).

elements, abundance see ABUNDANCE; COSMIC ABUNDANCE.

elements of an orbit see ORBITAL ELEMENTS.

ellipse a closed curve that is a type of CONIC SECTION with an eccentricity less than one. The longest line that can be drawn through the center of an ellipse is the major axis whereas the shortest line is the minor axis. The two axes are at right angles. There are two foci, which lie on the major axis and are symmetrically positioned on opposite sides of the center. The sum of the distances from the foci to a point moving round the ellipse is constant and equal to the length of the major axis. An orbiting body moves in an ellipse with the primary at one of the foci. See also KEPLER'S LAWS; ORBIT.

ellipsoid a surface or solid whose plane sections are circles or ellipses. An ellipse rotated about its major or minor axis is a particular type of ellipsoid, called a *prolate spheroid* (major axis) or an *oblate spheroid* (minor axis).

ellipsoidal reflector a reflector whose surface is part of an ellipsoid. An object situated at one focus will be imaged, after reflection, at the other focus.

elliptical galaxy see GALAXIES; HUBBLE CLASSIFICATION.

elliptical polarization see POLARIZATION.

ellipticity see OBLATENESS.

Elnath (**Alnath**; **β Tau**) a bluish-white giant that is the second-brightest star in the constellation Taurus. It was originally part of Auriga, as Gamma (γ) Aurigae. m_v: 1.65; M_v: –1.5; spectral type: B7 III; distance: 40 pc.

elongation the angular distance between the

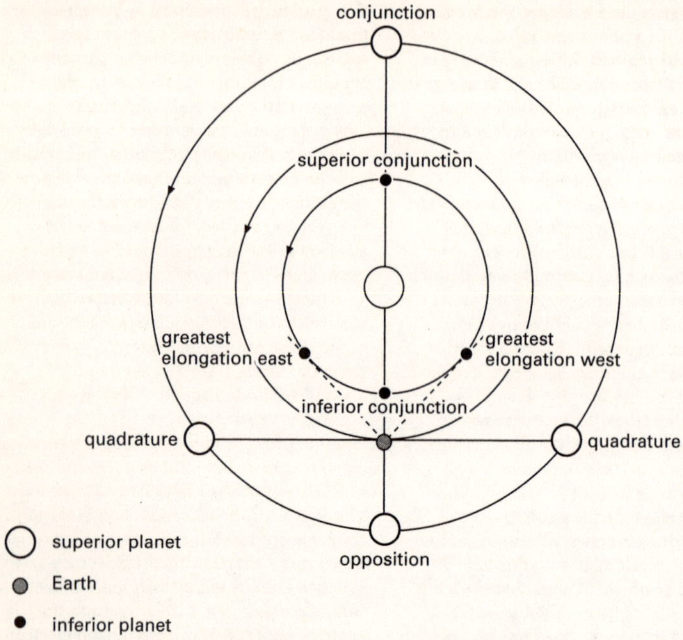

Elongations of superior and inferior planet

Sun and a planet, i.e. the angle Sun–Earth–planet, measured from 0° to 180° east or west of the Sun. It is also the angular distance between a planet and one of its satellites, i.e. the angle planet–Earth–satellite, measured from 0° east or west of the planet. An elongation of 0° is called CONJUNCTION, one of 180° is OPPOSITION, and one of 90° is QUADRATURE (see illustration). When an inferior planet follows the Sun in its daily motion, appearing east of the Sun in the evening, it is in *eastern elongation*. When it precedes the Sun, appearing west of the Sun in the morning, it is in *western elongation*. The inferior planets, which cannot come to quadrature, reach positions of *greatest elongation* (*GE*). The GE for both eastern and western elongation varies from 18° to 28° (Mercury) and from 45° to 47° (Venus).

Eltanin see DRACO.

Elysium Planitia Mars' second main center of volcanic activity, located on a bulge in the Martian crust about 3 km high and 5312 km in diameter, situated on the planet's equator. It is centered on the areograohic coordinates 2° N latitude, 205° W longitude (see AREOGRAPHY). Its principal volcano is *Elysium Mons* (25° N latitude, 213.1° W longitude), which is 250 km in base diameter and 15 km high. See MARS, VOLCANOES. In Feb, 2005, scientists examining images of Elysium Planitia taken by the European spacecraft MARS EXPRESS noted some that showed plated and rutted features over an extensive area measuring 800 by 900 km. The platelike fractures resemble ice floes seen in Earth's polar regions, leading the scientists to believe that a catastrophic event flooded the area about five million years ago forming a sea that then froze and became covered with dust and volcanic ash. They think it now survives as pack ice just below the Martian surface.

emerging flux regions (**EFRs**) new areas of intense localized magnetic field in the solar PHOTOSPHERE that are invariably the precursor of ACTIVE REGIONS. They are characterized by a small area of FACULAE in white light and by a small bipolar PLAGE connected by a few short arch filaments (see PROMINENCES) in the MONOCHROMATIC light of certain strong FRAUNHOFER LINES.

emersion the reappearence of a celestial body following its eclipse or occultation.

emission 1 the release of light or other radiation from an excited atom or molecule, or the radiation so emitted. See EMISSION SPECTRUM; NONTHERMAL EMISSION; THERMAL EMISSION.
2 the liberation of electrons from the surface of a solid or liquid. See PHOTOELECTRIC EFFECT.

emission lines see EMISSION SPECTRUM.

emission-line star a star, such as a BE STAR or OF STAR, whose spectrum exhibits nonstandard emission lines. See SPECTRAL TYPES.

emission measure see THERMAL EMISSION.

emission nebula a region of hot interstellar gas and dust that shines by its own light. Most of the gas atoms in the cloud are ionized – stripped of one or more electrons. The electrons liberated by the ionization process are free to move about the nebula. The light, and other radiation, emitted by the nebula results from subsequent interactions between ions and free electrons, and from the decay (de-excitation) of excited atoms.

There are three classes of emission nebula, all of extremely low gas density. In H II (ionized hydrogen) REGIONS, such as the ORION NEBULA, the gas is ionized by ultraviolet (UV) radiation from nearby hot young O and B stars; if there is sufficient gas close to one or more such stars a luminous nebula will form, surrounded by cooler neutral gas. The size is dependent on gas density and ultraviolet flux (see STRÖMGREN SPHERE), ranging up to several parsecs. The temperature is maintained at about 10 000 K by FORBIDDEN LINE radiation, mostly of oxygen and nitrogen. In PLANETARY NEBULAE, typified by the RING NEBULA, the gas is ionized by UV radiation from the remnant of a dying star lying within the nebula; the nebula comprises gas expelled from this star. In SUPERNOVA REMNANTS the ionization mechanisms are very complex: the atoms can be ionized by ultraviolet SYNCHROTRON radiation, as in the CRAB NEBULA, by interactions following the collision of an expanding remnant with surrounding interstellar gas atoms, as in the CYGNUS LOOP, or possibly by other processes.

Emission nebulae contain primarily free electrons and hydrogen ions, together with some helium ions and trace amounts of oxygen, carbon, nitrogen, and other elements. These components can interact in various ways. Firstly, an electron can be recaptured by an ion, usually a hydrogen ion. This recombination leads to the emission of radio, infrared, and optical CONTINUUM radiation, with line radiation then being emitted as the electron cascades down to lower ENERGY LEVELS. Secondly, an electron can collide with an ion, such as ionized oxygen, without being captured. Instead, energy is transferred from electron to ion, which becomes excited into an energy level just above the ground state. The excited ion returns to its normal energy state by emitting light at discrete wavelengths: at higher densities these transitions would be 'forbidden' (see FORBIDDEN LINES). Thirdly, free electrons can be decelerated when they pass near an ion, energy being radiated away as weak BREMSSTRAHLUNG – mainly radio waves.

The spectacular colors, predominantly red and green, of an emission nebula are due to recombination and excitation. The most intense visible radiation from hydrogen is the red hydrogen-alpha emission; red light is also emitted during a forbidden transition of singly ionized nitrogen. The strongest emission, however, results from a forbidden transition of doubly ionized oxygen (O^{++} or O III), the emission being green; the O III ions can only be produced by highly energetic UV photons. See also NEBULA.

emission spectrum a SPECTRUM formed by emission of ELECTROMAGNETIC RADIATION by matter. Energy has first to be supplied, either as heat (high temperature) or by some other mechanism such as absorption of electromagnetic radiation by the matter or by impact of electrons. The energy raises the atoms or molecules to higher ENERGY LEVELS. In a simple example, the electron in a hydrogen atom may 'jump' from its normal orbit to one farther from the nucleus (see HYDROGEN SPECTRUM). The emission spectrum of hydrogen, or any other emitting material, is formed by transitions from such excited states to lower energy states, the excess energy appearing in the form of photons with characteristic frequencies.

The emission spectrum therefore consists of a specific pattern of narrow peaks – *emission lines* – that occur at these frequencies. These lines may be superimposed on a CONTINUUM, but not necessarily so. Emission lines can occur in stellar spectra if, for example, the star is surrounded by a hot shell of diffuse gas. They also occur, for example, in the spectra of EMISSION NEBULAE, the interstellar medium (see MOLECULAR-LINE RADIO ASTRONOMY), and QUASARS. See also ABSORPTION SPECTRUM; EXCITATION.

emissivity symbol: ε. A measure of a body's ability to radiate ELECTROMAGNETIC RADIATION as compared to that of a perfect radiator – a BLACK BODY – at the same temperature.

Enceladus a satellite of Saturn, discovered in 1789 by William Herschel, that is one of the innermost moons of the planet, orbiting it at a distance of 238 100 km. It has been found to have a varied surface of ancient and youthful geological developments. Its diameter is only 500 km and its density 1.6 g cm^{-3}. Enceladus is the most highly reflective large object in the Solar System with an ALBEDO approaching 1.0. The surface shows evidence of highly cratered regions (5–35 km diameter), smooth plains, and ridged plains. The valleys and ridges indicate crustal movements that may have been associated with faulting and the extrusion of fluids. Tidal effects from the nearby and larger satellite DIONE may account for the production of the surface faulting and may have allowed the warmer fluid from the interior to resurface portions of the satellite. This situation also occurs on the Jovian satellite IO, so it is possible that Enceladus is still geologically active. During flybys in February and March 2005, the Cassini/Huygens spacecraft founded evidence of a significant atmosphere of ionized water vapor, due perhaps to volcanism, the eruption of geysers, or the escape of gases from the surface or the interior of Enceladus. The E ring of Saturn shows a pronounced peak of brightness in the orbit of Enceladus and may consist of particles that have escaped from the satellite. See also Table 2, Appendix.

Encke Division (**Encke Gap**) see SATURN'S RINGS.

Encke's comet the most observed comet, having been seen at 55 apparitions. The comet has a period of 3.30 years – one of the shortest – and is thought to be the parent body of the Taurid METEOROID STREAM. The period of Encke is decreasing by up to 2.7 hours per orbital revolution. This is caused by a jet effect from its rotating nucleus, which is not thermally symmetrical. The brightness of Encke has hardly decreased during the 165 years of observation. Since the orbit of Encke is extremely well known and a considerable bank of scientific data has been established, Encke is one of the prime targets for a spacecraft investigation of a comet.

encounter theories theories that propose that the planets formed from material ejected from the Sun or a companion star during an encounter with another object. Although the first such theory, by G.L.L. de Buffon in 1745, postulated that a comet collided with the Sun, most later theories have invoked an approach or collision involving another star, protostar, or a giant molecular cloud.

The *planetesimal theory* (1901–05) of T.C. Chamberlin and F.R. Moulton suggested that a passing star caused the Sun to eject filaments of material. These condensed into PLANETESIMALS from which the planets formed by ACCRETION.

Tidal theories (1916–18) of Harold Jeffreys and James Jeans suggested that a star grazed the Sun, drawing out into solar orbit a cigar-shaped filament of material that fragmented to form the planets: the larger planets – Jupiter and Saturn – condensed from the thicker central regions of the filament.

Variations on these ideas postulate that the encounter took place between a passing star and a binary companion star to the Sun. This overcomes one objection to most encounter theories: that material ejected from the Sun could not enter near-circular orbits at the observed planetary distances. However a remaining major problem with all these ideas is that most of the material drawn out from the Sun or its postulated companion would have stayed very close to the parent object. Also any material ejected at stellar temperatures would not condense but would expand violently and dissipate into space before it could form planets.

A modification of the Jeans–Jeffreys theory, the *capture theory* of M.M. Woolfson, attempts to overcome these problems. It proposes that the filament of matter was drawn off a relatively cool tenuous protostar moving past and tidally distorted by the condensed and more massive Sun. Condensations of protoplanets formed from the fragmented filament, of which six were captured by the Sun. A gradual rounding-off of the initial elliptical orbits and a major collision between the two innermost bodies led to the present distribution of solar-system bodies.

See also NEBULAR HYPOTHESIS; SOLAR SYSTEM, ORIGIN.

energy symbol: *E*. A measure of the capacity of a body or system for doing work, i.e. for changing the state of another body or system. The SI unit of energy is the joule; the erg (10^{-7} joule) is also used. There are various forms of energy including mechanical, electrical, nuclear, and radiant energy, all of which are interconvertible in the presence of matter. Mass is also regarded as a form of energy. In any closed system, the total energy, including mass, is always constant. See also CONSERVATION OF MASS-ENERGY; KINETIC ENERGY; POTENTIAL ENERGY.

energy level one of a number of discrete energies that, according to quantum mechanics, is associated with an atomic or molecular system. For instance, a hydrogen atom, which consists of a proton and an orbiting electron, has an energy due to electrostatic interaction between the electron and proton and to the motion of the electron. This energy can only have certain fixed values, which correspond to different orbits of the electron, and these constitute the *electronic energy levels* of the atom. The state of lowest energy is the *ground state* of the atom and higher states (in which the electron is farther from the nucleus) are known as *excited states*. Neither the hydrogen atom nor any other type of atom can take up energy continuously but can only 'jump' from one energy state to another: the energy is said to be *quantized*. This behavior is quite general, applying to energies of vibration and rotation in molecules and to energy difference due to interaction of magnetic moments of the electrons. See also EXCITATION; HYDROGEN SPECTRUM.

energy transport the flow of heat from a hot to a cooler region by means of radiation, convection, or conduction. In stars the heat flows from the hot interior to the surface, where it is radiated away into space. The most important means of energy transport in most stars is *radiative transport*, in which high-energy photons lose energy to the hot plasma through scattering, mainly by free electrons, and by absorption through photoionization of ions; this occurs in the *radiative zone* of the star. (The equation of radiative transport is given at *stellar structure*.) Convection is another mode of energy transport in which collections of hot fluid in the CONVECTIVE ZONE of a star rise toward the surface, release their energy, and sink again to pick up more energy. Convection is a highly efficient process but the conditions must be right for its onset. Conduction is negligible in most stars but becomes important in very dense degenerate stars, such as white dwarfs.

The mode of energy transport has important effects on a star's evolution: radiation (and conduction) do not affect the shells of different composition within an evolved star, but convection mixes them to a uniform composition.

English mounting *another name for* yoke mounting. See EQUATORIAL MOUNTING.

ENO *abbrev. for* European Northern

Observatory. See ROQUE DE LOS MUCHACHOS OBSERVATORY.

enstatite chondrite see CHONDRITE.

entrainment any process that involves the sweeping-up and transport of material by a fluid. The effect is thought to occur around JETS in RADIO GALAXIES. These jets are light, probably consisting of electrons and positrons, and generate surface instabilities as they sweep past the intergalactic medium. This leads to mixing, and the entrainment of heavier material, which affects the dynamics of the jet.

entropy a measure of the amount of disorder in a physical system. It never decreases in any physical interaction of a closed system.

entropy per baryon a cosmological parameter that measures the relative distribution of energy in disordered and ordered forms in the Universe. It is determined by the number of photons per baryon (proton or neutron) in the Universe today and has a value between 10^9 and 10^{10} according to present observations. BIG BANG theories must explain the value of this ratio.

Eos family a HIRAYAMA FAMILY of asteroids located at a distance of 3.0 AU from the Sun. The members are unusual and their color lies between that of C-TYPE and S-TYPE ASTEROIDS. Their reflection spectra are very similar to CHONDRITE meteorites. Observations of spin rates indicate that the family is old.

ephemeris (plural: **ephemerides**) **1** a work published regularly, usually annually, in which are tabulated the daily predicted positions of the Sun, Moon, planets, etc., for that period, together with information relating to certain stars, times of eclipses, etc. It is used in astronomical observation and navigation. See also ASTRONOMICAL ALMANAC.

2 a series of predicted geocentric positions of a celestial object at constant intervals of time.

ephemeris meridian the fictitious terrestrial meridian that rotates independently of Earth at the uniform rate defined by terrestrial DYNAMICAL TIME. It is

$$1.002\,738\,\Delta T$$

east of the Greenwich meridian (see DELTA T). *Ephemeris longitude* and *ephemeris hour angle* are measured relative to the ephemeris meridian.

ephemeris second see EPHEMERIS TIME.

ephemeris time (**ET**) a measure of time for which a constant rate was defined and that was used from 1958 to the end of 1983 as the independent variable in gravitational theories of the Solar System. It was superceded in 1984 by DYNAMICAL TIME. ET was reckoned from the instant, close to the beginning of 1900, when the Sun's mean geometric longitude was 279° 41′ 48″.04, at which instant the measure of ephemeris time was 1900 Jan. 0d 12h precisely. The primary unit of ET was the TROPICAL YEAR at this epoch of 1900 Jan. 0.5 ET, which contains a calculable number of seconds: the *ephemeris second* is the fraction 1/31 556 925.9747 of the tropical year 1900 Jan. 0.5 ET. The ephemeris second was adopted in 1957 as the fundamental invariable unit of time until replaced in 1967 by the second of ATOMIC TIME. This SI-adopted second was defined so that it was equal to the ephemeris second within the error of measurement. The ephemeris day contains 86 400 ephemeris seconds. ET could be found by adding a correction, DELTA T, to the UNIVERSAL TIME UT1.

epicycle see PTOLEMAIC SYSTEM.

Epimetheus a small irregularly shaped satellite of Saturn. It is a COORBITAL SATELLITE with JANUS; they orbit between the F ring and G ring. There are two named craters on Epimetheus, *Hilairea* and *Pollux*. See SATURN'S RINGS; Table 2, Appendix.

epoch an arbitrary fixed date or instant of time that is used as a reference datum, especially for stellar coordinates and ORBITAL ELEMENTS. For example, the coordinates right ascension and declination are continuously changing, primarily as a result of the PRECESSION OF THE EQUINOXES. Coordinates must therefore refer to a particular epoch, which can be the time of an observation, the beginning of the year in which a series of observations of an object was made, or the beginning of a half century. The *standard epoch* specifies the reference system to which coordinates are referred. Coordinates of star catalogs commonly referred to the MEAN EQUATOR

AND EQUINOX of the beginning of a BESSELIAN YEAR. Since 1984 the JULIAN YEAR has been used: the current standard epoch, designated J2000.0, is 2000 Jan. 1.5; it is exactly one Julian century removed from the standard epoch of 1900 Jan 0.5. Epochs for the beginning of a year now differ from the standard epoch by multiples of the Julian year. A standard epoch is usually retained for 50 years.

epsilon (ε) the fifth letter of the Greek alphabet, used in STELLAR NOMENCLATURE usually to designate the fifth-brightest star in a constellation.

Epsilon Aurigae an ECLIPSING BINARY star about 600 parsecs distant in the constellation Auriga, with a period of 9892 days, the eclipse lasting about 610 days. It consists of an extremely luminous F2 Ia supergiant about 15 times the mass of the Sun with a very large companion of about the same mass. Once thought to be a very distended cool supergiant, the large occulting object is now believed to be a ring or shell of gases surrounding the true companion, a main-sequence B star. The gases arise from rapid MASS TRANSFER from the F star (see W SERPENTIS STAR).

Epsilon Eridani (ε Eri) an orange-red main-sequence star located in the constellation Eridanus at a distance of 3.2 parsecs. It is a young star (about 500 million to a billion years old) and has between 75% and 85% of the Sun's mass and size but only 27% to 35% of its luminosity. In 1998, astronomers announced the detection of a cool dusty ring around the star, encircling it at a distance of between 35 and 75 AU. This is thought to be a belt of rocky and icy bodies equivalent to the Solar System's Edgworth–Kuiper Belt. In 2000, researchers announced the detection of a giant planet orbiting Epsilon Eridani at a mean distance of about 3.3 AU in an elliptical orbit (eccentricity: 0.6) with a period of 6.8 years. The planet is estimated to have a mass equal to about 1.2 times that of Jupiter. The existence of a second and smaller planet orbiting about 40 AU out from the star has been inferred from disturbances in the structure of the dust ring but remains unconfirmed. m_v: 3.73; spectral type: K2 V.

Epsilon Indi (ε Ind) an orange-red main-sequence dwarf star in the constellation Indus that is a near neighbor of the Sun, lying at a distance of almost 3.62 parsecs. It is about 1.3 billion years old and is smaller and much dimmer than the Sun, having a surface temperature of about 4300 K. In 2003, a team of astronomers announced the detection of a BROWN DWARF possibly with a methane atmosphere circling Epsilon Indi at a separation of 1500 AU. The brown dwarf, now known as Epsilon Indi ba, is thought to have the same diameter as Jupiter but nearly 50 times its mass. Epsilon Indi ba is itself orbited by a brown dwarf, named Epsilon Indi bb. The Epsilon Indi system has a very large proper motion (about 4.7 seconds of arc per year) and over the next few thousand years will move out of Indus into the neighboring constellation Tucana. m_v: 4.68; M_v: 6.89; spectral type: K5 Ve.

Epsilon ring see URANUS' RINGS.

equation of center the true ANOMALY minus the mean ANOMALY of a body moving in an elliptical orbit. It is the difference between the actual angular position of the body and the position it would have if its angular motion were uniform. It is a major INEQUALITY in the Moon's motion, being a direct result of the large ECCENTRICITY (0.0549) of the Moon's orbit and hence of its varying orbital velocity (see KEPLER'S LAWS).

equation of light see LIGHT-TIME.

equation of the equinoxes see SIDEREAL TIME.

equation of time the correction that must be applied to APPARENT SOLAR TIME to obtain MEAN SOLAR TIME, i.e. it is the difference in time as measured by a sundial and by a clock. The equation of time varies through the year; it has two maxima and two minima and is zero on four dates: April 15/16, June 14/15, Sept. 1/2, and Dec. 25/26. A positive value indicates that apparent time is ahead of mean time; the greatest positive value, which can be over 16 minutes, occurs in early Nov.; the greatest negative value, over 14 minutes, occurs in mid-Feb. The curve is the sum of two components, each reflecting a nonuniformity in the apparent motion of the Sun: one component arises from the ellipticity of the Earth's orbit, the

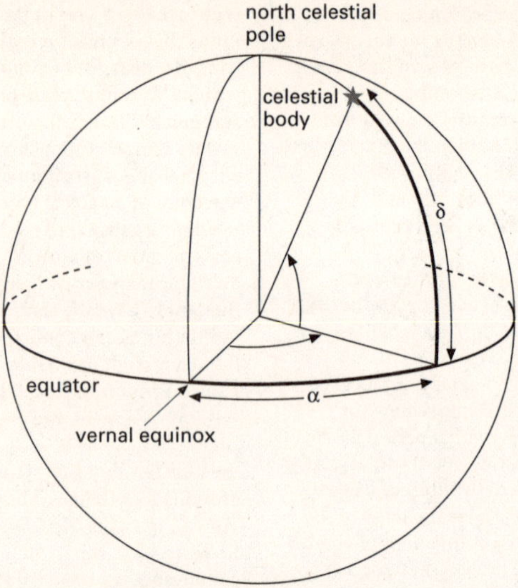

Equatorial coordinate system

other from the inclination of the ecliptic to the celestial equator (see MEAN SUN).

equator 1 the great circle on the surface of a planet or star that lies in a plane – the *equatorial plane* – passing through the center of the body and perpendicular to the axis of rotation.
2 *short for* celestial equator.

equatorial coordinate system the most widely used astronomical COORDINATE SYSTEM in which the fundamental reference circle is the celestial equator and the zero point is, strictly, a CATALOG EQUINOX, or less formally the vernal (or dynamical) EQUINOX. The coordinates are RIGHT ASCENSION (α) and DECLINATION (δ), which are measured along directions equivalent to those of terrestrial longitude and latitude, respectively (see illustration). SIDEREAL HOUR ANGLE is sometimes used instead of right ascension and NORTH OR SOUTH POLAR DISTANCE instead of declination. Because of the slow westerly drift of the dynamical equinox around the ecliptic the coordinates right ascension and declination are normally referred to the MEAN EQUATOR AND EQUINOX for a standard EPOCH, which in present use is 2000.0.

equatorial horizontal parallax see DIURNAL PARALLAX.

equatorial mounting a telescope MOUNTING in which one axis (the polar axis) is parallel to the Earth's axis of rotation, while the second axis (the declination axis) is at right angles to it. Its great advantage is that when the telescope is clamped in declination, and the polar axis is driven to turn once in 24 hours in the opposite direction to the Earth's rotation, any star will remain stationary in the FIELD OF VIEW. Until recently almost every large telescope was equatorially mounted, but the constantly changing stresses involved in swinging possibly hundreds of tonnes of asymmetrically shaped material about an inclined axis mean that the mounting must be extremely strong and hence extremely costly, so as a result many telescopes are now constructed with a computer-controlled ALTAZIMUTH MOUNTING.

There are several types of equatorial mountings, some being shown in the

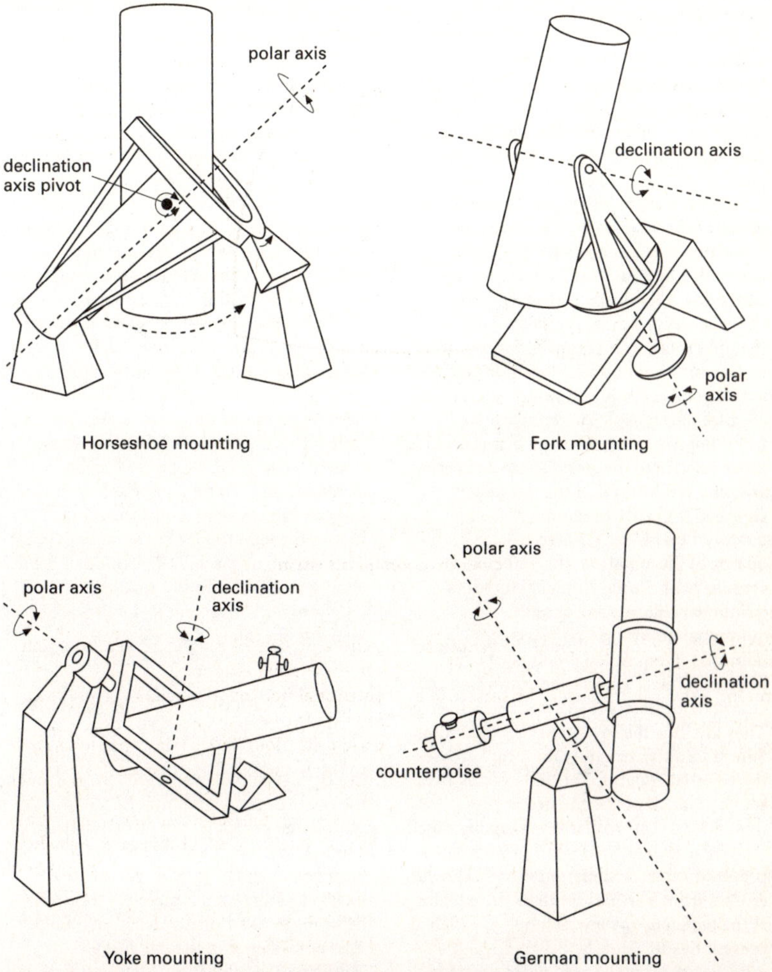

Equatorial mountings

illustration. In the *fork mounting* the telescope swings in declination about an axis carried on two prongs of a fork; the fork itself rotates about a shaft that is the polar axis. In the *yoke* (or *English*) *mounting* the polar axis is in the form of a long frame with a bearing at each end. The telescope swings in declination about an axis between the sides of the frame. This mounting is simple, very rigid, and needs no counterpoise weights; the polar region is, however, inaccessible. The *horseshoe mounting* is a modification of the fork and yoke mountings: the upper end of the polar axis frame is made into a horseshoe shape to accommodate the telescope tube; the polar region may then be observed. Many of the giant reflectors use this exceptionally stable mounting. In the *German mounting* the declination axis is carried as a tee on the top end of the polar axis. The telescope is carried on one end of the declination axis and there is a counterpoise on the other end.

The drive mechanism for the telescope is usually called a *drive clock*; in modern telescopes it is often an electric motor controlled by a variable frequency generator. A telescope is usually driven, about its polar axis, at the *sidereal rate* so that one rotation is completed in 23h 56m 4s, the duration of one sidereal day. Small corrections are required in drive rates because of atmospheric refraction and when following the Moon or planets, which move relative to the stars. These corrections are achieved by varying the frequency supplied to the drive motor.

equatorial plane see EQUATOR.

equator of illumination the plane of symmetry of a lunar or planetary PHASE.

equinoctial colure see COLURES.

equinoctial points see EQUINOXES.

equinoxes 1 (**equinoctial points**) the two points on the celestial sphere at which the ECLIPTIC intersects the CELESTIAL EQUATOR. They are thus the two points at which the Sun in its apparent annual motion crosses the celestial equator. The Sun crosses from south to north of the equator at the DYNAMICAL EQUINOX, still informally called the *vernal equinox*, symbol: ♈, which lies at present in the constellation Pisces. The Sun crosses from north to south of the equator at the *autumnal equinox*, symbol: ♎, which at present lies in Virgo. The dynamical or vernal equinox is the zero point for both the EQUATORIAL and ECLIPTIC COORDINATE SYSTEMS, although in star catalogs a CATALOG EQUINOX is now used. The equinoxes are not fixed in position but are moving westward around the ecliptic as a result of PRECESSION of the Earth's axis; the advance is about 50″ of arc per year. See also MEAN EQUATOR AND EQUINOX; TRUE EQUATOR AND EQUINOX.

2 the two instants at which the Sun crosses the equinoctial points, on about March 21 (dynamical equinox) and Sept. 23. On the days of the equinoxes the hours of daylight and of darkness are equal.

Compare SOLSTICES.

equinox motion see CATALOG EQUINOX.

equipotential surfaces imaginary surfaces surrounding a celestial body or system over which the gravitational field is constant. For a single star the surfaces are spherical and may be considered as the contours of the potential well of the star. In a close BINARY STAR the equipotential surfaces of the components interact to become hourglass-shaped (see illustration). The surfaces 'meet' at the inner LAGRANGIAN POINT, L_1, where the net gravitational force of each star on a small body vanishes; the contour line through this point defines the two *Roche lobes*. When both components are contained well within their Roche lobes they form a *detached binary system*. If one star has expanded so as to fill its Roche lobe it can only continue to expand by the escape of matter through the inner Lagrangian point. This stream of gas will then enter an orbit about or collide with the smaller component. The system is then a *semidetached binary*: DWARF NOVAE, W SERPENTIS STARS, and some ALGOL VARIABLES are examples. When both components fill their Roche lobes, as with W URSAE MAJORIS STARS, they form a *contact binary* sharing an outer layer of gas. Matter can then eventually spill into space through the outer Lagrangian point, L_2.

equivalence principle the principle that, on a local scale, the physical effects of a uniform acceleration of some FRAME OF REFERENCE imitates completely the behavior in a uniform gravitational field. This equivalence of the two frames of reference was introduced by Albert Einstein in his general theory of RELATIVITY. It is a generalization of the observed direct proportionality between gravitational and inertial MASS.

equivalent width a measure of the strength of a spectral line. The LINE PROFILE of an absorption line, for example, shows a dip below the CONTINUUM level, and the equivalent width is calculated as the area of the dip divided by the height of the continuum. It is the wavelength range of the spectral line if the amount of

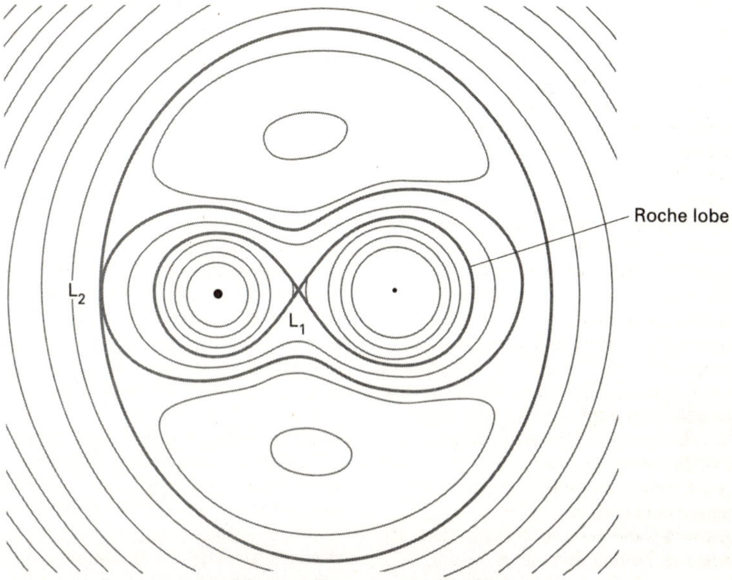

Equipotential surfaces of close binary star

absorption was redistributed into a rectangle having the intensity of the continuum.

Equuleus (**Little Horse**) a very small inconspicuous constellation in the northern hemisphere near Pegasus, the brightest star (γ) being a triple star of 4th magnitude. Delta (δ) and Beta (β) are double stars. Abbrev.: Equ; genitive form: Equulei; approx. position: RA 21h, dec +7°; area: 72 sq deg.

Eratosthenian System see COPERNICAN SYSTEM.

Erfle eyepiece see EYEPIECE.

Eridanus (**River**) a long straggling constellation in the southern hemisphere extending from Orion toward the southern polar region. Except for the zero-magnitude ACHERNAR (α), the brightest stars are of 2nd and 3rd magnitude. Zaurak (γ) is a red giant of apparent magnitude 2.95 and spectral type M1 IIIb, while Rana (δ) is somewhat hotter, an orange subgiant of apparent magnitude 3.54 and spectral type K0 IV. To the northwest of Zaurak lies Epsilon (ε) Eridani, a star close to the Sun that may be a planetary system in the making (see EPSILON ERIDANI). The 3rd-magnitude *Acamar* (θ) is a fine double star, possibly once much brighter than it is now. Abbrev.: Eri; genitive form: Eridani; approx. position: RA 1.5 to 5h, dec 0° to −58°; area: 1138 sq deg.

Eros (**(433) Eros**) an ASTEROID that was discovered in 1898 by the German astronomer Carl Gustav Witt and is a member of the AMOR GROUP. It passed within 23 million km of the Earth in 1975. It is the second largest of the near-Earth asteroids and the first to be discovered. It appears to be an S-type asteroid, a stony egg-shaped object measuring 13 × 13 × 33 km, and its varying light curve has been monitored since the early 20th century. Eros spins once every 5.27 hours and travels once around the Sun every 1.76 years in a slightly elliptical orbit that is inclined 10.8° to the ecliptic. In 2000, the NEAR-Shoemaker spacecraft, a NASA mission, entered orbit around Eros following a four-year journey from the Earth. On Feb. 15, 2001, it landed on the asteroid's surface, making Eros the first such body to be a landing site for a human-made spacecraft. Images sent back by NEAR-Shoemaker both before and after landing revealed that the surface of Eros shows fewer impact craters than expected and is covered with a regolith, which over hundreds of millions of years seems to have filled in many of the craters. The impacts appear to have left Eros in a shattered state, its pieces held together only by gravity. See Table 3, Appendix.

error box (**error circle**) the region of uncertainty in the position of a celestial source, defined on a statistical basis. The term is often used in sky surveys of X-ray, gamma-ray, and infrared sources.

ERS eSA's European Remote Sensing satellite. See REMOTE SENSING.

eruptive center an active volcanic area on a planet or satellite.

eruptive variable see CATACLYSMIC VARIABLE.

ESA *abbrev. for* European Space Agency.

escape velocity the minimum velocity required for an object to enter a parabolic trajectory around a massive body and hence escape from its vicinity. The object will keep moving away from the body although it travels at decreasingly lower speeds as the massive body's gravitational attraction continues to slow it down. If the object does not attain escape velocity it will enter an elliptical orbit around the body. If escape velocity is exceeded the object will follow a hyperbolic path. The escape velocity at a distance r from the center of a massive body, mass m, is given by $\sqrt{(2Gm/r)}$, where G is the gravitational constant. The escape velocity from the Earth's surface is about 11.2 km s^{-1}, from the Moon 2.4 km s^{-1}, and from the Sun 617.7 km s^{-1}. For a massive body to retain an atmosphere the average velocity of the gas molecules must be well below escape velocity.

ESO *abbrev. for* European Southern Observatory.

ESOC see EUROPEAN SPACE AGENCY.

ESO/SERC Southern Sky Survey see SOUTHERN SKY SURVEY.

ESRIN see EUROPEAN SPACE AGENCY.

ET *abbrev. for* ephemeris time.

eta (η) the seventh letter of the Greek alphabet, used in STELLAR NOMENCLATURE usually to designate the seventh-brightest star in a constellation or sometimes to indicate a star's position in a group.

Eta Aquarids see AQUARIDS.

Eta Carinae (**η Car**) one of the most luminous and unstable stars in the Galaxy, lying at a distance of 2000 parsecs in the constellation Carina. It displays a large variation in magnitude at very irregular periods. Halley cataloged it as a 4th-magnitude star in 1677. From 1835 to 1845 it outshone every star except Sirius, reaching a magnitude of –0.8 in 1843; it has since faded, the magnitude range having been between 5.9 and 7.9 since 1880. Eta Carinae is an example of a LUMINOUS BLUE VARIABLE. It is surrounded by a shell of cool dust that emits strongly at a wavelength of 20 μm. The decrease in light output observed after 1843 is assumed to have been caused by the ejection of the dust. The dust obscures the light output of the star (which may well have remained constant), converting the light to infrared radiation. Eta Carinae's total luminosity is about five million times that of the Sun, its temperature is 29 000 K, and its mass is about 120 solar masses. It is surrounded by a small cloud of ejected gas (the *Keyhole nebula*) that contains a high abundance of nitrogen, indicating that much NUCLEOSYNTHESIS has taken place.

Eta Carinae nebula (**NGC 3372**) a large complex of dust and glowing gas in the southern Milky Way. The nebulosity is an extended H II REGION in which there are clusters of young stars. Dark lanes of cool dust divide the nebula into islands of glowing gas. One of these dark and irregular dust lanes is known as the *Keyhole*, which is used to identify the bright emission *Keyhole nebula* in which the object ETA CARINAE is situated.

ether an extremely elastic medium of negligible density that was thought in the 19th century to permeate all space and thus provided a medium through which light and other electromagnetic waves from celestial bodies could travel. (At that time all waves were considered to require a medium for their propagation). The speed of travel of the electromagnetic waves, i.e. the speed of light, was assumed to be fixed with respect to the ether. The Earth, however, should move with respect to the ether and so, from considerations of relative motion, the speed of light should vary very slightly when measured in different directions.

Experiments were set up in the late 19th century to detect and measure the motion of the Earth relative to the ether. The most notable experiment was carried out in 1887 by A.A. Michelson and E.W. Morley (the *Michelson–Morley experiment*). No such motion was found, indicating both that the ether did not exist and that electromagnetic waves did not require any medium for their propagation. The concept of the ether was thus discarded. The result of these experiments was later explained by Einstein's special theory of RELATIVITY (1905) in which it was stated that the speed of light was independent of the velocity of the observer and was therefore invariant.

E-type asteroids a rare class of asteroid with a featureless spectrum between 0.3 and 1.1 micrometers. The surface composition may be similar to enstatite ACHONDRITE meteorites.

Eureca *short for* European retrievable carrier. A small reusable robotic space platform developed by the ESA. It was designed to be jettisoned from a space shuttle, propelling itself into the desired low Earth orbit, and to be retrieved on a subsequent shuttle flight some months later. It carried long-term computer-controlled scientific experiments. Small thruster motors controlled its position and solar panels provided power. It was first launched, as Eureca-1, in Aug. 1992, for collection by the shuttle in mid-1993. Its 1-tonne payload consisted mainly of experiments on the growth, under MICROGRAVITY, of large crystals of proteins, semiconductors, and zeolites. Eureca-1 was reckoned to be a great success, and ESA planned to launch five missions over the subsequent decade, but the plan came to nothing. A Eureca-2 mission was planned for 1995, but ESA ministerial meetings rejected further funding The Eureca craft was put into storage at the Bremen facilities of DASA, the aerospace subsidiary of the international automotive engineering firm DaimlerChrysler for possible use in commercial spaceflights.

Europa the smallest of the four GALILEAN SATELLITES of Jupiter and the only one inferior in size and mass to the Moon. It has a diameter of 3138 km and its density is 2.97 g cm^{-3}. Its albedo is 0.67. Studied by the two PIONEER spacecraft 10 and 11, by VOYAGER 2, and in particular depth by the GALILEO spacecraft, Europa has been found to be a smooth-surfaced world with no mountains and very few craters – none more than about 20 km in diameter. Its relatively young icy crust (at least 100 km thick) overlies what is thought to be a metallic core and is crisscrossed by a series of streaks and cracks. Most of the cracks appear to be filled with dark-colored material, some with a light-colored substance. The gravitational influence on Europa not only of Jupiter but also of the satellites Io and Ganymede serve to squeeze the satellite, resulting in tidal flexing, which is believed to heat Europa's interior. Tidal flexing may have melted some of the ice crust to form a substantial ocean of liquid water between it and the core. Water from this ocean may seep through cracks produced in the crust and may refreeze at the surface, thereby renewing it or forming icy ridges. It has been suggested that this ocean, if it exists, may provide a possible suitable environment for extraterrestrial microorganisms. The Hubble Space Telescope has revealed that Europa has a vanishingly thin oxygen atmosphere, due not to biological action but to the interaction between charged particles from the Sun and water molecules in the satellite's icy crust. The charged particles break up some of the water molecules, liberating hydrogen, which dissipates into space, and oxygen. See also JUPITER'S SATELLITES; Table 2, Appendix.

Europa Orbiter a NASA mission proposed for 2003 to investigate the surface ice of Europa and measure its thickness by radio sounding. The mission is planned to reach Europa in 2007.

European Northern Observatory see ROQUE DE LOS MUCHACHOS OBSERVATORY.

European Southern Observatory (ESO) a European intergovernmental organization (members: France, Germany, the Netherlands, Sweden, Belgium, Denmark, Italy, Switzerland, and – since 2002 – the United Kingdom), founded in 1962. Its headquarters are at Garching, near Munich, where all activities have been concentrated since 1980. Its observatory is at La Silla, near La Serena, Chile, at an altitude of 2400 meters; even in normal conditions the SEEING is exceptional due to the clear dry stable climate.

The chief instruments at La Silla are the 3.5-meter NEW TECHNOLOGY TELESCOPE (NTT), which began operating in 1989, and the older 3.6-meter telescope, sometimes referred to as the '360', which started operations in 1977. The 3.6-meter telescope works at focal ratios of f/3, f/8, and f/32 at the prime, Cassegrain, and coudé foci, and f/35 for infrared work. The limiting magnitude is 24 or more. The NTT has even better resolution than the 1 arcsec of the 3.6-meter and was a pioneer in the use of ACTIVE OPTICS. The 3.6-meter was upgraded in 1996 with an improved ADAPTIVE OPTICS system. There is also a 2.2-meter telescope, installed in 1983, which is identical to the one at Calar Alto, Spain; a 1-meter SCHMIDT TELESCOPE, operational since 1972 and involved in the SOUTHERN SKY SURVEY; and four telescopes of 1 to 1.5 meters. The 15-meter SWEDEN–ESO SUBMILLIMETER TELESCOPE became operational in 1989.

The ESO's VERY LARGE TELESCOPE (VLT), completed in 2001, is sited at Cerro Paranal, Chile. The VLT is the ESO's premier site for optical and infrared observations.

European Space Agency (**ESA**) an international organization for coordinating, promoting, and funding Europe's space program. Following ministerial meetings in Brussels in 1972 and 1973, ESA was formed from the merging of the European Space Research Organization (ESRO) and the European Launcher Development Organization (ELDO). It became operational at the end of May 1975. Originally consisting of 11 member countries, it now has a total of 15: Austria, Belgium, Denmark, Finland, France, Germany, Republic of Ireland, Italy, The Netherlands, Norway, Portugal, Spain, Sweden, Switzerland, and the UK. Greece was set to become a full member by the end of 2005. Canada is an associate member and participates in certain ESA projects, as does Hungary.

ESA has its headquarters in Paris. The European Space Research and Technology Centre (ESTEC) is at Noordwijk in the Netherlands and is concerned with management of science and applications programs. The European Space Operations Centre (ESOC) is at Darmstadt in Germany and is concerned with satellite and spaceprobe operations and data acquisition and processing; it controls a network of ground stations for data reception from satellites and interplanetary probes. ESRIN (European Space Research Institute) at Frascati, Italy, houses a major information-retrieval service and handles data from remote-sensing satellites. The European Astronaut Centre (EAC) at Cologne, Germany, selects and trains people for missions aboard the INTERNATIONAL SPACE STATION. ESA's launch base for its ARIANE launcher is at Kourou, French Guiana. It also operates sounding-rocket launch stations in Norway and Sweden, a meteorological program office at Toulon, in France, and satellite-tracking stations in Belgium, Germany, Italy, and Spain.

The programs carried out under the general budget and the science program budget are mandatory for all member countries. Other programs are optional, and members are free to decide on their level of scientific and financial involvement. Several of ESA's missions are carried out in collaboration with other space agencies, notably NASA, and ESA has made essential contributions to such long-term projects as the HUBBLE SPACE TELESCOPE. The ARIANE series of launch vehicles, SPACELAB, GIOTTO, SOHO, ISO, XMM-NEWTON, MARS EXPRESS, and the Huygens probe to Titan (see CASSINI-HUYGENS) are among ESA's most successful ventures into space. *Arianespace*, the world's first commercial space transportation company and a division of ESA, now conducts more than half of all commercial satellite launches. See also HORIZON 2000.

European VLBI Network see EVN.

EUV (**extreme ultraviolet**) *another name for* XUV. See XUV ASTRONOMY.

EUVE *abbrev. for* Extreme Ultraviolet Explorer.

eV *symbol for* electronvolt.

EVA *abbrev. for* extravehicular activity. Operations, including repair and maintenance, undertaken by an astronaut or cosmonaut outside a spacecraft. EVA was first achieved in 1965 by the Russians. See GEMINI PROJECT; VOSKHOD.

evection the periodic (31.807 day) INEQUALITY in the motion of the Moon that may amount to a displacement in longitude of up to 1°16′20″.4. It arises from changes in the ECCENTRICITY of the Moon's orbit (0.0432 to 0.0666) that are brought about by solar attraction. Evection was discovered by the Greek astronomer Hipparchus. See also ANNUAL EQUATION; EQUATION OF CENTER; PARALLACTIC INEQUALITY; VARIATION.

evening star an informal name for VENUS when it lies east of the Sun and is a brilliant object in the western sky after sunset. Such periods of visibility follow superior CONJUNCTION and precede inferior conjunction. The term is sometimes applied loosely to evening visibility of Mercury or other planets.

event horizon the boundary of a BLACK HOLE: for a nonrotating black hole it is a spherical 'surface' having a radius equal to the SCHWARZSCHILD RADIUS for a body of a given mass. The event horizon marks the critical limit where the ESCAPE VELOCITY of a collapsing body becomes equal to the speed of light and hence no information can reach an external observer. Calculations predict that a body shrinking within its event horizon – or indeed any body that falls inside the event horizon of another – inevitably contracts to a SINGULARITY at the precise center of the black hole.

Evershed effect a radial flow of material in the penumbra of a SUNSPOT, outward from the edge of the umbra, with a velocity of about 2 km s^{-1}. It forms part of a pattern of circulation determined by the configuration of the intense localized magnetic field. The gas ascends at or just beyond the outer edge of the penumbra, doubles back on itself in the CHROMOSPHERE, and then descends into the umbra (for the cycle to be repeated).

EVN *abbrev. for* European VLBI Network. An interferometric array of radio telescopes in Europe and beyond that regularly participate in VLBI observations at wavelengths between 1.3 and 90 cm; the network is administered by a consortium of institutes called the European Consortium for Very Long Baseline Interferometry. The founder-member telescopes are those at JODRELL BANK (UK), WESTERBORK (Netherlands), EFFELSBERG (Germany), ONSALA (Sweden), Medicina (Italy), and Noto (Italy). There are several associated members of the consortium.

evolved star a star, such as a GIANT or a WHITE DWARF, that has passed the main-sequence stage of its evolution. See STELLAR EVOLUTION.

excitation a process in which an electron bound to an atom is given sufficient energy to transfer from a lower to a higher ENERGY LEVEL but not to escape from the atom. The atom is then in an *excited state*. The atom may be excited in two ways. In collisional excitation a particle, such as a free electron, collides with the atom and transfers some of its energy to it. This energy corresponds exactly to the energy difference between two energy levels. The atom rapidly returns to a lower energy level, usually its ground state, possibly passing through several intermediate levels on the way. Photons are emitted during these transitions, so that an emission line spectrum results. The photon energies are equal to the energy differences between the levels involved.

In radiative excitation, a photon of radiation is absorbed by the atom. The photon energy must correspond exactly to the energy difference between two energy levels. This process produces an absorption line in a spectrum. The atom rapidly returns to its ground state, emitting photons in the process (as before). Since the photons can be emitted in any direction and can have different (lower) energies than the absorbed photon, the absorption line dominates the spectrum. See also BOLTZMANN EQUATION; IONIZATION.

excited state see ENERGY LEVEL; EXCITATION.

exclusion principle see PAULI EXCLUSION PRINCIPLE.

exit pupil (**Ramsden disk**; **Ramsden circle**) the image of the objective or primary mirror of a telescope formed on the eye side of the EYEPIECE. It is seen as a bright disk when the telescope is pointed at any extended bright surface. A convenient way to determine the magnification is to divide the telescope APERTURE by the diameter of the exit pupil.

exobiology the theories concerning 'living' systems that may exist on other planets or their satellites in the Solar System or on planetary systems of other stars, the methods of detecting them, and the study of their origin, development, distribution, etc. The probability of this *extraterrestrial life* occurring at some time on some planetary system of some star depends on the fraction of the possible 10^{20} stars in the Universe – 10^{11} in our Galaxy – that have planetary systems and on the fraction of these planetary systems that could support, on one or more members, these 'living' organisms.

The degree to which exobiology may differ from terrestrial biology is a matter of dispute. There are no universal laws of biology as there are assumed to be for physics; organisms could evolve on planets or satellites moderately different from Earth, in an unrecognizable form. There is no absolute definition of life but it is believed that any living material is built up from the common elements carbon, hydrogen, oxygen, and nitrogen and that the presence of water is probably necessary for sustaining life. In addition the environment should have an atmosphere to act as a shield from high-energy cosmic and stellar radiation, and to aid respiration where necessary, and the temperature should be reasonably uniform.

The course and rate of evolution of living organisms probably depends on the type of star in the planetary system, and its stability, as well as the planetary environment. The conditions may not be appropriate for the origin and evolution of living organisms in this present era. If they can form, however, many scientists believe that these organisms will inevitably become more developed. The number of life forms that might at this moment be 'intelligent' in a human sense and also able to communicate this intelligence is very uncertain: one group of scientists has suggested that at present there could be as many as one million advanced civilizations in our Galaxy; other estimates have been very much lower. Communications, however, are severely limited by distance: signals from a star 100 light-years (30.7 parsecs) away take 100 years to reach Earth.

There is to date no direct evidence for extraterrestrial life. Searches for microorganisms in the soils of the Moon and Mars have been unsuccessful. Searches for extraterrestrial intelligence (SETI) have also been made and are once more in progress.

EXOSAT the first European Space Agency mission in X-ray astronomy, a sophisticated 400-kg satellite launched in May 1983 carrying a payload of two GRAZING INCIDENCE telescopes, a large (1800 cm^2) array of PROPORTIONAL COUNTERS, and a (90 cm^2) gas scintillation PROPORTIONAL COUNTER. The unusual orbit of EXOSAT, initially 380 km perigee, 195 000 km apogee, gave it the unique capability of long (~80 hr) observations, uninterrupted by Earth occultation. With apogee over N Europe, direct contact with the ground station at Villafranca (Madrid) furthermore allowed EXOSAT to be operated directly by the astronomer, much like a ground-based telescope. Although problems occurred with two detectors early in the mission, rendering one telescope inoperable, the spacecraft systems, including on-board computer and 3-axis attitude control system, worked well until exhaustion of attitude control gas in Mar. 1986. Outstanding results were obtained on a wide range of SUPERNOVA REMNANTS, X-RAY BINARIES, X-RAY BURST SOURCES, ACTIVE GALAXIES, and CLUSTERS OF GALAXIES. The discovery of QUASI-PERIODIC OSCILLATIONS (QPOs) uncovered an important property of accreting binary systems not known before EXOSAT. See also EXOSAT DATABASE.

EXOSAT Database an X-RAY database containing a complete archive of reduced data and scientific data products from the EXOSAT mission. It was made available by ESA in 1990. The design of this database has since been adopted world-wide for subsequent archiving of X-ray astronomy (and related optical and radio) data.

exosphere see ATMOSPHERIC LAYERS.

expanding-cluster parallax see MOVING CLUSTER.

expanding Universe the observation that radiation from distant galaxies is redshifted leads to the conclusion that all galaxies (beyond the Local Group) are receding from us or, more precisely, that the distance between clusters of galaxies is continuously increasing. The Universe as a whole is therefore expanding. This expansion was discovered by Edwin Hubble in 1929 although it had already been suggested by theoretical cosmologists. It is the observational basis of the BIG BANG THEORY. The Universe may eventually contract if the DECELERATION PARAMETER exceeds 0.5. See HUBBLE CONSTANT; HUBBLE'S LAW; REDSHIFT.

Explorers a large group of US scientific satellites, the first of which – Explorer 1 – was America's first satellite and was launched on Jan. 31 1958; it weighed 14 kg. It was able to confirm the existence of one of the VAN ALLEN RADIATION BELTS. Explorers have been used in a wide range of scientific studies. Recent and proposed Explorers include IUE, COBE, EUVE, FUSE, and XTE. The *Small Explorer* (*SMEX*) class provides a more rapid access to space for small payloads (less than 200 kg); SWAS is an example.

extensive air shower see COSMIC RAYS.

extinction the reduction in the amount of light or other radiation received from a celestial body as a result of absorption and scattering of the radiation by intervening dust grains in space (INTERSTELLAR EXTINCTION) and in the Earth's atmosphere (atmospheric extinction). The extinction decreases with wavelength of the radiation and increases with the pathlength through the absorbing medium and with the density of the medium.

The starlight is also reddened since the extinction of blue light by dust is greater than that of red light. The reddening may be given in terms of the color excess, E,

$$E = (B–V) – (B–V)_0$$

where $(B–V)$ and $(B–V)_0$ are the observed and intrinsic COLOR INDICES of the star. Most stars are reddened by a few tenths of a magnitude although values of up to two magnitudes are not uncommon. Stars lying behind extremely dense matter might only be detectable at radio or infrared wavelengths. See also INFRARED SOURCES.

extragalactic H II region a cloud of hot ionized gas that is isolated in extragalactic space and is believed to consist of intergalactic gas that has begun to condense into stars and will probably become a DWARF IRREGULAR galaxy. Extragalactic H II regions were identified in 1970. They have no old stars, and a low METALLICITY indicates that some (like the COMPACT GALAXY IZw18) are less than 10^8 years old. These are the only 'galaxies' significantly different in age from our Galaxy.

extrasolar planet see PLANET.

extraterrestrial life see EXOBIOLOGY; SETI.

extravehicular activity see EVA.

extreme ultraviolet (**XUV**; **EUV**) the region of the electromagnetic spectrum bridging the gap between ultraviolet radiation and X-rays. See XUV ASTRONOMY.

Extreme Ultraviolet Explorer (**EUVE**) a NASA satellite launched June 1992 to carry out the first survey of the sky in the extreme ultraviolet (7–76 nm) region of the spectrum. Radiation at these wavelengths is totally screened out by the Earth's atmosphere, and so this mission was expected to be of groundbreaking significance. The 3.2-tonne satellite carried four photometric imaging systems and a three-channel EUV spectrometer. The imaging instruments were used to accomplish the sky survey. The spectrometers were used for the pointed spectroscopic programs, which collected data from over 350 unique astronomical targets. NASA authorized a Guest Observer Program of pointed spectroscopy that ended on Jan. 31, 2001, when the EUVE was shut down. The satellite fell out of orbit and broke up in the Earth's atmosphere at the end of Jan. 2002.

extrinsic variable see VARIABLE STAR.

eyelens see EYEPIECE.

eyepiece the magnifying system of lenses through which a telescopic image is viewed. It normally comprises a *field lens*, which receives the light rays, a stop, which defines the FIELD OF VIEW, and an *eyelens*, which

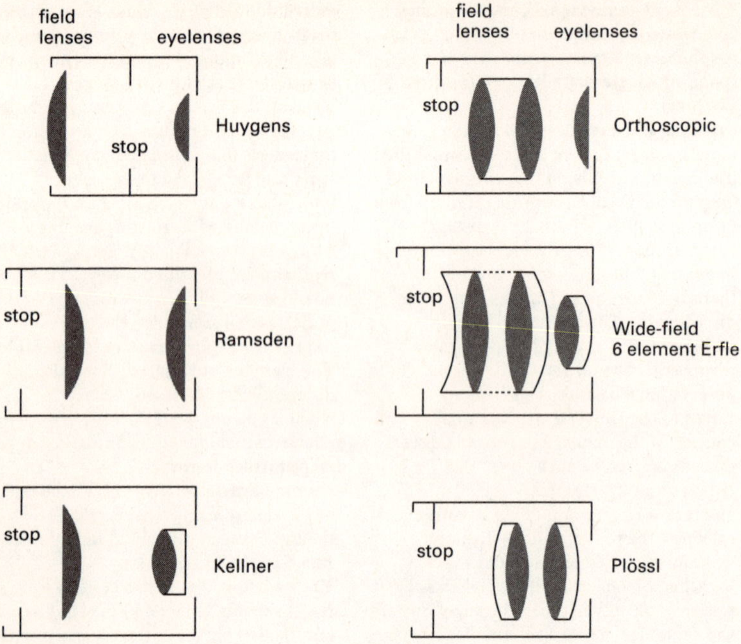

Types of eyepieces

directs the light into the eye. The magnification of a telescope is normally varied by using a short focal length eyepiece to give high powers, and one of long focal length for low powers.

Some eyepieces are shown in the illustration. The *Huygens eyepiece* consists of two planoconvex lenses with their flat faces toward the eye and a field stop between them. The field lens has two or three times the focal length of the eyelens and their separation is half the sum of their focal lengths. Although it has good EYE RELIEF and little CHROMATIC ABERRATION, the large SPHERICAL ABERRATION gives poor performance except with long-focus refractors. The *Ramsden eyepiece* has two identical planoconvex lenses mounted with their convex faces together and separated by 2/3 to 3/4 of their focal length. It has much less spherical aberration than the Huygens but suffers from troublesome chromatic defects. The *Kellner eyepiece* is a Ramsden with an achromatic eyelens. It is an excellent eyepiece, widely used in binoculars and field glasses. For best results the lenses must be coated to minimize ghost images formed by internal reflections. The *orthoscopic eyepiece*, in its commonest form, has a planoconvex eyelens and a cemented triplet field lens. Although it is expensive, this eyepiece gives excellent results and has a long eye relief, which suits the bespectacled user. The *Plössl eyepiece* has two identical achromatic doublets mounted close together with their biconvex elements facing each other. The field is wider (about 40°) and flatter than that given by orthoscopics, with sufficient eye relief for comfortable use, so that the Plössl is preferred by many observers. Several manufacturers have modified the design.

By the use of extra lens elements and

specially figured (aspheric) lenses, *wide-field eyepieces* may be obtained; these have fields subtending up to 90° at the eye; the *Erfle* has a field of 68° and the *Nagler* and *Bertele* up to 80°. Such eyepieces are useful for observation work requiring exceptionally wide fields, such as novae and comet searches, but they are very expensive and will not fit a standard DRAW TUBE. See also BARLOW LENS.

eye relief the distance between the human eyeball and the eyelens of an EYEPIECE at which the observer can see clearly the full FIELD OF VIEW. This is when the EXIT PUPIL corresponds with the pupil of the eye. Low-power eyepieces usually have good eye relief and high powers very little. An observer who must wear spectacles may find it difficult to use the higher powers.

Ff

Faber–Jackson relation a correlation between the luminosity of an elliptical galaxy and the VELOCITY DISPERSION of its stars. The gravitational potential of the galaxy is thus related to the kinetic energy of its constituents, so that the brightest most massive galaxies have the higher velocity dispersions. This relation, discovered by S.M. Faber and R.E. Jackson in 1976, is used in galactic DISTANCE DETERMINATION. See also TULLY–FISHER METHOD.

Fabry–Perot interferometer a type of INTERFEROMETER used in spectroscopy to study the fine structure within a spectrum. It has extremely high RESOLUTION. It consists essentially of two flat plates, separated and held parallel to each other very accurately. A beam of light, infrared, etc., is multiply reflected in the gap between the inner surfaces, so the plate material must have high reflectivity and low absorption in the wavelength region of interest. The gap is normally precisely controlled and adjustable.

The Fabry–Perot can be thought of as acting like a tunable filter. The gap (d) is related to the wavelength (λ) passed with maximum efficiency by the following equation:

$$2d \cos\theta = m\lambda,$$

where m is an integer known as the *order number* and θ is the angle of incidence of the beam on the plates (usually arranged to be zero so that $\cos\theta = 1$). When the beam is multiply reflected, the particular wavelengths that satisfy the above equation are partially transmitted. This transmitted radiation is focused by a lens or mirror system onto a detector or screen to produce an interference pattern consisting of narrow sharp bright rings on a dark background. The instrument is able to distinguish, or resolve, two very close wavelengths as two almost overlapping superimposed ring patterns, giving it its high resolving power. The wavelength producing the second ring pattern satisfies the equation for the same value of the gap (d) as the first wavelength, but with a different order number (m). The ring patterns can be separated by the use of a DIFFRACTION GRATING or dispersion by the prism of a SPECTROGRAPH, which acts as an *order sorter*. Instruments using two or three Fabry–Perots in series have even higher spectral resolutions.

faculae (singular: **facula**) **1** bright patches in the upper part of the solar PHOTOSPHERE that have a higher temperature than their surroundings and occur in areas where there is an enhancement of the relatively weak vertical magnetic field. With the exception of polar faculae, which consist of isolated granules and appear in high heliographic latitudes around the minimum of the SUNSPOT CYCLE, they are intimately related to SUNSPOTS, forming shortly before the spots – in the same vicinity – and persisting for several weeks after their disappearance. Faculae are best seen when near the Sun's limb, where LIMB DARKENING renders them more readily visible. They are approximately coincident, albeit at a lower level, with the PLAGES visible in monochromatic light.
2 bright patches observed on the surface of planetary satellites, especially GANYMEDE.

faint blue galaxies the faintest galaxies detectable, which show an enhancement in the number of blue, and hence star-forming, systems. The bulk of star formation occurred around redshifts 1 to 2, and the reason for the subsequent demise of this population of faint blue galaxies remains unclear.

fall see METEORITE.

falling star popular name for a meteor.

false-color imagery a process of color coding in the reproduction of an image in which colors unrelated to those of the original subject are used to indicate the distribution of certain quantities, such as the object's temperature, intensity of emitted radiation, etc. False-color images may be taken of such objects as the Sun, or over a region of the Earth, Sun, sky, etc. The colors are usually computer-generated. False color can also be used to indicate velocity since different DOPPLER SHIFTS from a single observational wavelength can be calculated and coded into different colors. In addition, images taken at different wavelengths, e.g. a radio and an optical wavelength, can each be allotted a color and can be superimposed to form a composite image. See also RADIO-SOURCE STRUCTURE.

False Cross a cross-shaped group of four 2nd-magnitude stars in the former constellation Argo. The group is now divided between Carina (Iota [ι] and Epsilon [ε]) and Vela (Kappa [κ] and Delta [δ]).

Fanaroff–Riley types I, II see FR I, FR II.

fan beam see ANTENNA.

Faraday rotation the rotation of the plane of polarization experienced by a beam of plane-polarized radiation when it passes through a region where there are free electrons and a magnetic field. The plane of polarization is rotated through an angle equal to λ^2RM, where λ denotes the radiation wavelength. RM is the *rotation measure* and is proportional to the integral along the line of sight of the product of the electron density, n_e, and the component of the magnetic flux density, B, parallel to the line of sight. Faraday rotation can occur in the interstellar medium, within radio sources themselves, or in the Earth's ionosphere. The interstellar magnetic field can be estimated by dividing the rotation measure by the DISPERSION MEASURE. The SYNCHROTRON EMISSION from a radio source may become depolarized by random Faraday rotation within the source.

far-infrared see INFRARED RADIATION.

Far Infrared and Submillimeter Space Telescope see FIRST.

farside see NEARSIDE.

far-ultraviolet see ULTRAVIOLET RADIATION.

Far Ultraviolet Spectroscopic Explorer (FUSE) a space observatory launched June 1999 as part of NASA's long-term Origins Program. It was developed for NASA by Johns Hopkins University, Baltimore, USA, in collaboration with the space agencies of Canada and France. It was placed into a circular orbit with an altitude of 775 kilometers. The science instrument carried aboard the FUSE spacecraft was the Integrated FUSE spectrograph (IFS), in which ultraviolet light was focused by four mirror segments and dispersed by four corresponding curved gratings allowing the achievement of very high spectral resolution over the operating range of approximately 90–120 nm. An electronic guide camera called the Fine Error Sensor (FES), functioning in the visible part of the spectrum down to the 14th magnitude, provided visual confirmation of where the IFS was being pointed. Computers controlled the targeting mechanism.

FUSE complemented other NASA observatories, revealing new information about the structure and chemical makeup of the Universe. It calculated the ratio of deuterium and the heavier elements to hydrogen in the Universe, and examined other aspects of the chemistry of interstellar and intergalactic space. Among its many discoveries, the satellite detected the immense 'cobweb' of helium that has pervaded space since soon after the Big Bang; it confirmed the haloes of hot gas surrounding the Milky Way Galaxy and the neighboring Magellanic Clouds; and it investigated SUPERNOVA REMNANTS and regions of star formation. In August 2001 it discovered what may be a cloud of millions of comets around the young star BETA PICTORIS. Much closer to home, it observed molecular hydrogen in the atmosphere of

Mars (a hitherto undetected phenomenon) and discovered molecular nitrogen outside the Solar System for the first time. Although FUSE was originally intended to run for about three years, it received a software upgrade in July 2003 and was still in operation at the beginning of 2005.

fast ejection see FLARES.

fast nova see NOVA.

fault a vertical or near vertical crustal displacement on the Earth, Moon, Mars, or some other solid body. Lunar faults are usually double but single-sided faults also occur. See also GRABEN; MARS, SURFACE FEATURES; RILLE; WRINKLE RIDGES.

Faye's comet a comet with a COMA that increased in size as it approached the Sun. Most comets, Encke being a typical example, have comas that decrease as they near the Sun. Between 1843 and 1955 Faye's brightness decreased from 4.2 to 11.1 magnitudes.

F-corona the outer part of the solar CORONA, responsible for the greater part of its intensity beyond a distance of about two solar radii. It consists of relatively slow-moving particles of interplanetary dust and exhibits an ABSORPTION SPECTRUM because the particles scatter light from the PHOTOSPHERE. The F-corona extends for many million kilometers into the INTERPLANETARY MEDIUM and merges, in the plane of the ecliptic, with the particles that give rise to the ZODIACAL LIGHT.

feed the electrical element at the focus of a radio DISH that collects the radio waves and feeds them to the receivers. The element may be a DIPOLE connected to a transmission line, or a horn (called a *feedhorn*) connected to a WAVEGUIDE. In both cases the physical size of the feed must be chosen to match the wavelength of the signal. A telescope capable of observing at a number of wavelengths may therefore possess a selection of feedhorns, any one of which may be moved to the focal point.

feeder a system of wires or WAVEGUIDES used to connect a distant radio ANTENNA with its transmitter or RECEIVER so that radio-frequency power is transferred with minimum loss (energy dissipation). The wires are arranged to form a *transmission line*, which carries the power in the form of electromagnetic waves. When a transmission line is terminated by a resistance equal to its characteristic impedance all the power traveling down the line is absorbed by the load and none is reflected. The line is then said to be *matched* to its load. Transmission lines are of two types: balanced, as with the open-wire feeder, and unbalanced, as with coaxial cable. It is important that a balanced load, such as a DIPOLE, is fed by a balanced feeder. Where an unbalanced feeder is required to drive a balanced load, a balanced-to-unbalanced transformer, or *balun*, must be used.

In an ARRAY many elements must be connected together to one receiver. One method of doing this is to join adjacent pairs of elements and then pairs of pairs and so on so that the total length of feeder from the receiver to any element is the same. Such an arrangement is sometimes called a *christmas tree*. See also BUTLER MATRIX.

feedhorn see FEED.

fermions a class of ELEMENTARY PARTICLES with half integer units of SPIN; examples are ELECTRONS, PROTONS, and NEUTRINOS. No two fermions can exist possessing an identical set of quantum numbers (numbers assigned to the various quantities that describe a particle). Compare BOSONS.

FFT *abbrev. for* Fast Fourier Transform. A particularly efficient implementation of the FOURIER TRANSFORM for computers. It is used extensively in APERTURE SYNTHESIS, digital signal processing and IMAGE PROCESSING.

FG Sagittae a rapidly evolving variable star in the constellation Sagitta that has recently cooled and expanded. It is now a pulsating yellow supergiant but in 1955 was a more compact hot blue supergiant. It is surrounded by a glowing expanding PLANETARY NEBULA, and it is thought that as the nebula gradually disperses the central star will again heat up and contract before eventually becoming a WHITE DWARF.

fibrils predominantly horizontal strands of gas in the solar lower CHROMOSPHERE – typically 11 000 km long and 725–2200 km wide – that are visible (in the MONOCHROMATIC light of certain strong

FRAUNHOFER LINES) as dark absorption features against the brighter disk. They form an ordered pattern in and around ACTIVE REGIONS, where they tend to be aligned in the direction of the localized magnetic field. The overall configuration of fibrils is stable over a period of several hours, though an individual fibril has a lifetime of only 10–20 minutes.

field 1 the region in which a physical agency exerts an influence, measured in terms of the force experienced by an object in that region. Thus a massive body has an associated gravitational field within which an object will feel an attractive force. There are several types of field, including gravitational, magnetic, electric, and nuclear fields, each of which has its own characteristics and exerts its influence, strong or weak, over a particular range. See also FUNDAMENTAL FORCES.
2 see FIELD OF VIEW.

field curvature see CURVATURE OF FIELD.

field distortion see DISTORTION.

field equation an equation describing the behavior of a FIELD, derived from the law governing how the associated physical agency varies in space and time. See also RELATIVITY, GENERAL THEORY.

field galaxy any galaxy that is not a member of a CLUSTER OF GALAXIES. Field galaxies are rare: the ratio of field galaxies to cluster galaxies is extremely uncertain, estimates ranging from 1:6 to essentially zero.

field lens see EYEPIECE.

field of view (**field**) the area made visible by the optical system of an instrument such as a telescope at a particular setting. It is expressed in the form of its angular diameter. The field of view of a telescope usually increases with decreasing magnification, and depends on the EYEPIECE in use. A *wide field* may be obtained with specially designed eyepieces or with telescopes such as the SCHMIDT. If the telescope optics produce a *flat field*, the image will be focused at the center as well as at the edge of the field of view.

field pattern *another name for* antenna pattern. See ANTENNA.

field stars stars that are not connected with an astronomical object being studied but which happen to appear in the same field of view when the object is observed through a telescope. Typical examples of field stars are those that appear in the foreground of a telescopic image of a distant galaxy.

figuring the process of grinding and polishing the surface of a lens or mirror base to the exact shape desired.

filamentary structure see LARGE-SCALE STRUCTURE.

filaments 1 clouds of gas in the solar upper CHROMOSPHERE/inner CORONA, with a higher density and at a lower temperature than their surroundings, that are visible (in the MONOCHROMATIC light of certain strong FRAUNHOFER LINES) as dark absorption features against the brighter disk. They were formerly sometimes called *dark flocculi*. When viewed beyond the limb they appear as bright projections and are termed prominences. See PROMINENCES.
2 see LARGE-SCALE STRUCTURE.

filar micrometer (**position micrometer**) a measuring device incorporated into the eyepiece of an instrument and used in astronomy to measure the angular separation and orientation of a visual binary star or to determine the position of an object relative to a nearby star whose coordinates are known. It consists essentially of two parallel wires that lie in the focal plane of the eyepiece and can be rotated about the optical axis of the telescope. A third wire lies perpendicular to the parallel wires. Two stars are aligned along this perpendicular wire. The position of one of the parallel wires can be controlled by turning a screw with a finely graduated micrometer head. The parallel wires are adjusted so as to coincide with the images of the two stars and the separation of the images can then be accurately measured.

filled supernova remnant (**plerion**) see SUPERNOVA REMNANT.

filling factor see ARRAY.

filter a device that transmits part of a received signal and rejects the rest. The signal may be in the form of a beam of light or other radiation or may be an electrical signal. Optical, ultraviolet, and infrared filters are dyed plastic or gelatin, glass or glasslike substances, or confined liquids, all of which absorb incident radiation except for a relatively narrow band of wavelengths. Such filters are used in astronomical PHOTOMETRY, especially in measurements of MAGNITUDES; transmitting bands typically 100 nanometers wide, they are termed broadband filters. Much narrower wavelength bands, of maybe 1 nm, can be obtained with INTERFERENCE and BIREFRINGENT FILTERS.

Electrical filters are devices whose ATTENUATION varies with frequency. Filters that allow low or high frequencies to pass without serious attenuation are called *low-pass* and *high-pass filters*, respectively. A filter that allows only a limited range of frequencies through is a *band-pass filter* while its converse is a *band-stop filter*. See also BANDWIDTH.

filtergram see SPECTROHELIOGRAM.

find see METEORITE.

finder a low-power telescope with a wide FIELD OF VIEW that has its optical axis aligned with that of the main telescope. It is used to locate an object to be observed and facilitate the training of the main telescope on that object. Because the field of view of the average amateur astronomer's telescope used at its lowest power is only about half a degree, some means of pointing it in the correct direction is needed. SETTING CIRCLES enable this to be done with a permanent EQUATORIAL MOUNTING but for a portable or a simple ALTAZIMUTH MOUNTING a finder is essential. It should have a field of view of at least four to eight degrees and be provided with illuminated cross wires or a graticule.

fireball a bright visual METEOR of MAGNITUDE greater than –10. About 50 000 to 100 000 occur in the Earth's atmosphere each year.

FIRST *abbrev. for* Far Infrared and Submillimeter Space Telescope. An orbiting telescope under design for ESA and at present scheduled for launch in 2007. It will be used primarily for interstellar spectroscopic studies. FIRST is at present considered to be a 4.5-meter radiatively cooled INFRARED (Cassegrain) telescope. It will feed two or three instruments working at wavelengths from about 100 μm to 1 mm and giving high spectral and angular RESOLUTION. A direct imaging FABRY–PEROT INTERFEROMETER (operating at 85–180 μm), a HETERODYNE DETECTOR (200–600 μm), and a multiband imaging bolometric system (70 μm up to maybe 1.2 mm) are under consideration; these will require active cooling. See also HORIZON 2000.

first point of Aries another name for the vernal EQUINOX, which over 2000 years ago, when Hipparchus first used the term, lay in the constellation Aries. Due to the westerly PRECESSION OF THE EQUINOXES the vernal equinox now lies in Pisces and will subsequently move into Aquarius. Likewise the *first point of Libra*, or the autumnal equinox, once lay in Libra but is now located in Virgo.

first point of Libra see FIRST POINT OF ARIES.

first quarter see PHASES, LUNAR.

fission see NUCLEAR FISSION.

FITS *abbrev. for* Flexible Image Transport System. A standard format for the transportation of astronomical images and other data between computers.

FitzGerald contraction see LORENTZ–FITZGERALD CONTRACTION.

Five-Kilometer Telescope see RYLE TELESCOPE.

fixed stars originally stars in general, which, until the early 18th century and the discovery of PROPER MOTION, were thought to have no relative motion and thus remained fixed in position in the sky. In comparison the planets were described as *wandering stars* (from the Greek *planetes*, a wanderer).

FK4, FK5, FK6 see FUNDAMENTAL CATALOG.

FK Comae stars a class of rapidly spinning giant stars, possibly examples of coalesced stars. See COMMON ENVELOPE STAR.

Flamsteed number see STELLAR NOMENCLATURE.

flares sudden short-lived brightenings of small areas of the Sun's upper CHROMOSPHERE/inner CORONA that are optically visible usually only in the MONOCHROMATIC light of certain strong FRAUNHOFER LINES. They represent an explosive release of energy – in the form of particles and radiation – that causes a temporary heating of the surrounding medium and may accelerate electrons, protons, and heavier ions to high velocities.

A typical flare attains its maximum

brilliance in a few minutes and then slowly fades over a period of up to an hour. Although attempts have been made to classify them according to their structure, the most objective system considers the maximum area covered by the flare and to a lesser extent its intensity. The overwhelming majority of flares are small, covering areas of less than several hundred million square kilometers, but those that are larger are sometimes associated with a number of interesting phenomena.

During the 'flash phase' of a large flare, when it suddenly increases in brightness and rapidly expands to its maximum extent, material may be ejected in the form of a SURGE, SPRAY, or (for a particularly energetic event) *fast ejection* – in which a compact portion of the flare is expelled without fragmentation, with a velocity of about 1000 km s^{-1}. Large flares may initiate a *Moreton wave*, which is a magnetohydrodynamic shock wave that spreads out from the center of disturbance, in a sector of about 90°, as it travels with a velocity of the order of 1000 km s^{-1} across the vertical magnetic fields of the inner corona. This causes a depression and subsequent relaxation of the underlying CHROMOSPHERIC NETWORK and may induce distant FILAMENTS, perhaps several hundred thousand kilometers from the flare, to undergo several damped vertical oscillations. Filaments in the vicinity of the flare may also be activated, before and/or during the flare, by changes in the configuration of the local magnetic field. This activation usually takes the form of increased internal motion or flow along the filament (small surges), sometimes accompanied by a gradual ascent of the filament itself. The aftermath of large flares may include coronal condensations of relatively dense material at temperatures of up to 4 000 000 K.

The effects of energetic flares are by no means confined to the Sun. Fade-out of short-wavelength radio signals is often experienced on the daylight hemisphere of the Earth and is caused by a temporary strengthening (by increased ionization) of the reflecting property of the D layer of the ionosphere (60–90 km altitude), which suppresses the passage of the signals to the higher layers from where they are normally reflected. This is accompanied by a sudden increase in the electrical conductivity of the E layer (90–120 km altitude) and by disturbances of the Earth's magnetic field. Ultraviolet radiation from the flare is responsible for these effects. X-rays may also be emitted and solar radio emission (from the inner corona) frequently exhibits an intense burst or series of bursts at centimeter or meter wavelengths. Occasionally, within about half an hour of the flare, energetic charged particles (energies up to 10^{10} eV) reach the Earth, and within about 26 hours, on average, less energetic charged particles may also arrive. These latter particles spiral around the Earth's magnetic field lines, causing GEOMAGNETIC STORMS and their luminous counterpart, AURORAL displays.

The nature of flares and the physical mechanism responsible for them are not completely understood. They invariably occur in ACTIVE REGIONS, close to the line of inversion (see SUNSPOTS), where the gradient of the horizontal component of the magnetic field is steepest and therefore stresses are greatest. It is thought that energy is released when the stressed field reconnects to a lower potential energy configuration, and that this produces the flare; but much remains to be done before a quantitative picture will emerge.

A phenomenon similar to solar flares, but far more energetic, is thought to be responsible for the rapid brightening of FLARE STARS.

flare stars (**UV Ceti stars**) intrinsically faint cool RED DWARF stars that undergo intense outbursts of energy from localized areas of the surface, causing transient but appreciable increases in the brightness of the star. The brightness can change by two magnitudes or more in several seconds, decreasing to its normal minimum in about 10 to 60 minutes; the output usually peaks in the near-ultraviolet. There are also radio and X-ray flares, not always coincident with optical flares. Flare stars are of SPECTRAL TYPE M or sometimes K with spectral emission lines of hydrogen and ionized calcium, i.e. they are ME STARS. They have unusually strong magnetic fields (typically

10^{-4} tesla), suggesting a similar mechanism to solar FLARES. Most flare stars are either young (found in ASSOCIATIONS) or are a component of a close BINARY STAR: the fast rotation due to youth or to tidal effects, respectively, is probably responsible for the strong magnetism. The nearby binary UV Ceti (M6e V) is a typical flare star.

flash spectrum the EMISSION SPECTRUM of the solar CHROMOSPHERE and E-CORONA. It is observable only for a few seconds during a total solar eclipse, at the beginning and end of totality. The majority of the spectral lines have the same wavelengths as the FRAUNHOFER LINES of the photospheric spectrum. Their presence in successive spectrograms taken during an eclipse provides information on the distribution of elements in the chromosphere.

flat field see FIELD OF VIEW.

flat-spectrum radio source see RADIO-SOURCE SPECTRUM.

flattening see OBLATENESS.

F-layer (F-region) see IONOSPHERE.

flexus (plural: **flexi**) a low curvilinear ridge with a scalloped pattern. The word is used in the approved name of such a surface feature on a planet or satellite.

flocculi a term that has been applied to several different solar phenomena. In the older literature PLAGES and FILAMENTS were often referred to as *bright* and *dark flocculi* respectively, while today the term is sometimes used to denote the bright mottles of the CHROMOSPHERIC NETWORK.

fluorescence the transformation of PHOTONS of relatively high energy (i.e. high frequencies, especially ultraviolet frequencies) to lower-energy photons through interactions with atoms. It is also the lower-energy radiation that is produced by the process.

flux **1** a measure of the energy, number of particles, etc., emitted from or passing through a surface per unit time. See also RADIANT FLUX.

2 a measure of the strength of a field of force, such as a magnetic field, through a specified area. See also MAGNETIC FLUX DENSITY.

flux collector see INFRARED TELESCOPE.

flux density **1** (**spectral flux density** or, strictly, **spectral power flux density**) symbol: *S*. A measure of the strength of the signal received from a discrete source of emission. The dimensions of flux density are energy per unit time per unit BANDWIDTH per unit area. The unit is the JANSKY.

2 see MAGNETIC FLUX DENSITY.

flyby a trajectory that takes a spaceprobe close to a planet or satellite but does not permit it to enter an orbit about the body or land on it.

f/number see FOCAL RATIO.

focal length symbol: *f*. The distance from the center of a reflecting surface or refracting medium to the *focal point* or *focus* (see illustration). With a converging system, such as a PARABOLOID surface, a concave mirror or thin convex lens, the focus, F, is the point to which a narrow beam of light, radio waves, etc., from a distant object, i.e. a parallel beam closely aligned to the axis, is brought to a sharply defined or focused image. In a convex mirror or thin concave lens it is the point from which a parallel beam, made divergent by the mirror or lens, appears to diverge. If the two surfaces of a lens do not have identical curvatures the lens will have two different focal lengths and focal points, depending on which surface the light falls.

The *focal plane* is the plane through the focus, at right angles to the optical axis, in which the image of a distant object will be formed. In some cases, as in the SCHMIDT TELESCOPE, the image is focused on a curved surface – the *focal surface* – rather than a plane. See also EFFECTIVE FOCAL LENGTH.

focal plane see FOCAL LENGTH.

focal-plane array an ARRAY of dipoles or horn antennas in the focal plane of a radio telescope. Each element in the array is fed to its own receiving system, so that the array can be used to map a region of sky with an efficiency much greater than that of a single element. These arrays may however be difficult to fabricate, especially at submillimeter wavelengths.

focal point (focus) see FOCAL LENGTH.

focal ratio the ratio *f/d* of the FOCAL LENGTH, *f*, of a reflecting surface or refracting medium to its effective diameter, *d*, i.e. to its aperture. The numerical value of the ratio (often called the *f/number*) is usually written

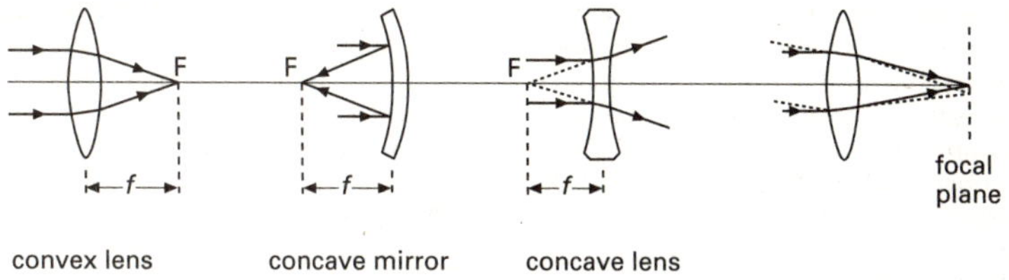

Focal length and focal plane

f/4 or f:4 for a ratio of 4, say. The reciprocal of the focal ratio (*d*/*f*) is the APERTURE RATIO. The LIMITING MAGNITUDE – i.e., the apparent brightness of the faintest detectable star – depends on the focal ratio of a telescope: for telescopes used under the same observing conditions, the larger the ratio the fainter the limit; if photographs are being taken, however, the larger the ratio the longer the necessary exposure time.

focal surface see FOCAL LENGTH.

focus (**focal point**) see FOCAL LENGTH.

folded dipole see DIPOLE.

following edge, following member see PRECEDING.

following spot (***f*-spot**) see SUNSPOTS.

Fomalhaut (**α PsA**) a white star that is the brightest in the constellation Piscis Austrinus. In 1983 the infrared satellite IRAS detected a shell of cool matter surrounding this star. The shell, which has a temperature of about 50 K, is thought to be solid material orbiting the star and forming a protoplanetary system. See also VEGA. m_v: 1.16; M_v: 2.0; spectral type: A3 V; distance: 6.7 pc.

forbidden lines lines that are not found in spectra under normal terrestrial conditions but are observed in certain astronomical spectra. In EMISSION NEBULAE, for example, atoms can be excited by impact of low-energy electrons. Under normal laboratory conditions such atoms would be de-excited by collisions with other atoms, etc., before they had time to radiate. Such collisions are very infrequent in nebulae and the *'forbidden' transitions* between the excited state and a state of lower energy can occur, producing the forbidden lines.

force symbol: F. According to NEWTON'S LAWS OF MOTION, any physical agency that alters or attempts to alter a body's state of rest or of uniform motion. The force required to accelerate a body of mass *m* is given by *ma*, where *a* is the acceleration imparted. There are many kinds of forces, including the gravitational force. The SI unit of force is the newton. See also FUNDAMENTAL FORCES; FIELD.

fork mounting see EQUATORIAL MOUNTING.

Fornax (**Furnace**) an inconspicuous constellation in the southern hemisphere fairly near Orion, the brightest stars being of 3rd and 4th magnitude. Abbrev.: For; genitive form: Fornacis; approx. position: RA 3h, dec –30°; area: 397 sq deg.

Fornax system a dwarf elliptical galaxy that is a member of the LOCAL GROUP.

fossa (plural: **fossae**) a long narrow shallow depression. The word is used in the approved name of such a surface feature on a planet or satellite.

Foucault's pendulum a simple pendulum that demonstrates the rotation of the Earth, first shown by J.B.L. Foucault in 1851. It consists of a massive metal ball that is suspended by a long wire and can swing freely with a minimum amount of friction. The pendulum swings steadily, tracing a straight line on the floor beneath it. The plane in which it swings, however, is observed to rotate during the day as a result of the Earth's rotation. The period of rotation of the plane depends on the latitude of the place: at the poles the plane would appear to move through a complete circle in one sidereal day (23h 56m 4s) while on the equator it would not rotate at all. The pendulum is in fact swinging in a plane that is fixed relative to the stars.

Fourier tachometer see HELIOSEISMOLOGY.

Fourier transform a mathematical operation by which a function expressed in terms of one variable, *x*, may be related to a function of a different variable, *s*, in a manner that finds wide application in physics. The Fourier transform, F(*s*), of the function f(*x*) is given by

$$F(s) = \int_{-\infty}^{\infty} f(x) \exp(-2\pi i x s)\, dx$$

and

$$f(x) = \int_{-\infty}^{\infty} F(s) \exp(2\pi i x s)\, ds$$

The variables *x* and *s* are often called *Fourier pairs*. Many such pairs are useful, for example, time and frequency: the Fourier transform of an electrical oscillation in time gives the spectrum, or the power contained in it at different frequencies.

Fourier transform spectrometer (FTS) a type of INTERFEROMETER that is used to study the constituent frequencies of a beam of radiation and can work in many wavelength regimes. A parallel beam of radiation is split into two coherent beams, which are then recombined so that they undergo INTERFERENCE. The distance traveled by one beam can be changed at a uniform rate. Any difference in distance traveled produces a PHASE DIFFERENCE between the two recombining beams. Different phase differences occur for the different frequencies present in the beams. If the recombined beams are focused onto a detector and the signal displayed as a function of time, the signal increases and decreases in a complex oscillatory fashion. The signal, digitized at regular intervals, is fed into a computer, where it can be processed by means of a FOURIER TRANSFORM to reveal the amplitudes of all the frequencies present in the spectrum of the input radiation, i.e. the POWER SPECTRUM of the source.

FR I, FR II *abbrev. for* Fanaroff–Riley types I, II. A simple but powerful classification, made in 1974, of RADIO GALAXIES that contain hot spots and diffuse emission. If the distance between the hot spots is less than half the total extent of the source, the radio galaxy is of *type I*, if greater than half, it is of *type II*. The distinction is thought to arise from the speed of the JET powering the radio lobes. A jet that is always faster than the sound speed in the intergalactic medium will produce an FR II source, whereas a subsonic jet will produce an FR I. The speed of the jet is affected by ENTRAINMENT. See also RADIO-SOURCE STRUCTURE.

Fred L. Whipple Observatory the observatory of the Smithsonian Institution, located at 2600 meters on Mount Hopkins, Arizona. Formerly the *Mount Hopkins Observatory*, it was renamed in 1982 to commemorate the 20th-century US astronomer Fred Lawrence Whipple, who had been a teacher at Harvard. The chief instrument is the 4.5-meter MULTIPLE MIRROR TELESCOPE, which was converted to a 6.5-meter single-mirror instrument and re-entered service for regular observation in early 2001. The other telescopes are a 1.5-meter reflector, and a 10-meter optical mosaic used for gamma-ray astronomy.

Freedom see INTERNATIONAL SPACE STATION.

Fra Mauro formation the EJECTA BLANKET associated with the IMBRIUM BASIN. It was the target for Apollo 14.

frame of reference a rigid framework, such as the Earth, the celestial sphere, or a set of coordinate axes, relative to which position, motion, etc., in a system may be measured.

Franklin-Adams charts a whole-sky photographic star atlas of 206 plates prepared by John Franklin-Adams and published in 1914 as the *Photographic Chart of the Sky*. It has a limiting magnitude of 16.

Fraunhofer lines absorption lines in the solar (photospheric) spectrum, first studied in detail by Joseph von Fraunhofer in 1814. He cataloged over 500 lines and labeled the more striking ones with letters. Over 25 000 lines have now been identified. The most prominent lines at visible wavelengths are due to the presence of singly ionized calcium, neutral hydrogen, sodium, and magnesium; many weaker lines are due to iron. The strength of a particular line depends not only on the quantity of the element present but also on the degree of IONIZATION and level of EXCITATION of its atoms. By isolating an individual strong line it is possible, by virtue of its residual intensity due to the reemission of radiation in the CHROMOSPHERE, to observe the chromosphere in the light of the element concerned. See SPECTROHELIOGRAM. See also D LINES; H AND K LINES; PHOTOSPHERE.

free-bound emission the radiation emitted when a free electron is captured by an ion. See RECOMBINATION LINE EMISSION.

free electron an ELECTRON that is not bound to an atom, molecule, or ion but is free to move under the influence of an electric or magnetic field.

free fall motion of a body under the influence of gravity alone, i.e. with no other forces acting. See also WEIGHTLESSNESS.

free-fall time the time it would take for a system to collapse in upon itself under force of gravity if it were not supported by either pressure or rotation.

free-free absorption a process of absorption that occurs when a free electron absorbs a photon of radiation and moves to a higher energy state: the difference between final and initial electron energy is equal to the photon energy. See also OPACITY.

free-free emission see THERMAL EMISSION.

frequency symbol: f, ν. The number of oscillations per unit time of a vibrating system. Frequency is measured in hertz. The frequency of a wave is the number of wave crests passing a point per unit time. For light and other ELECTROMAGNETIC RADIATION, it is related to wavelength λ by $\nu = c/\lambda$, where c is the speed of light.

Friedmann Universe, equation see COSMOLOGICAL MODELS.

fringe-stopping see PHASE ROTATOR.

f-spot *short for* following spot. See SUNSPOTS.

F stars stars of SPECTRAL TYPE F that are white with a surface temperature (T_{eff}) of about 6000 to 7400 kelvin. The hydrogen lines in the spectrum weaken rapidly and the lines of ionized calcium (Ca II, H and K) strengthen from F0 to F9; there are many lines of neutral and singly ionized metals and heavy atoms. Canopus, Polaris, and Procyon are F stars.

F-type asteroids see C-TYPE ASTEROIDS.

full Moon see PHASES, LUNAR.

full-wave dipole see DIPOLE.

fundamental catalog a catalog of FUNDAMENTAL STARS in which the precise mean positions and proper motions of the stars are listed for a given EPOCH; positions are determined as accurately as possible by recording transit times across the meridian at several observatories. The inclusion of data from many different observatories worldwide and from earlier catalogs helps to minimize errors. Other star catalogs can be compiled by reference to a fundamental catalog. A series of German fundamental catalogs commenced publication with the First Fundamental Catalog, prepared by G.F.J.A. Auwers for the Astronomische Gesellschaft in Berlin in 1879. It incorporated contemporary observations with the best of earlier data. The *Fourth Fundamental Catalog* (*Fundamentalkatalog* 4 or *FK4*) and its successors were prepared and published in Heidelberg by the Astronomisches Rechen-Institut. FK4, published 1963, contains data for 1535 classic reference stars to a limiting magnitude of 7 for the epoch 1950.0. Information from some 300 earlier catalogs contributed to FK4's dataset. The *Fifth Fundamental Catalog* (*FK5*) was published in 1988. It contains improved data on the same stars and is based on the standard epoch J2000.0 (see JULIAN YEAR); a supplement, FK5 Extension (FK5E), appeared in 1991, with data on an additional 3117 stars to magnitude 9.5. The *Sixth Fundamental Catalog* (*FK6*), which began publication in 1999, combines the results of the HIPPARCOS mission with the FK5 data. Parts I and III of FK6, which had appeared by the end of 2000, contain 878 fundamental stars and 3272 new stars respectively. The catalogs FK4 to FK6 are being made available in computerized form.

fundamental forces the four basic forces of nature: the GRAVITATIONAL FORCE, the *electromagnetic force* (both long established), and the two nuclear forces, the *strong force* and the *weak force*. These forces act between ELEMENTARY PARTICLES, i.e. the basic building blocks of matter. All the visible matter in the Universe and its behavior may be described in terms of these particles and the forces acting between them. The standard model of elementary particles uses *gauge theories* (based on the idea of symmetry) to describe the electromagnetic, strong, and weak forces: each is generated by the *interaction* between particles, which involves the exchange of an intermediate particle known as a *gauge boson*. These intermediates effectively 'carry' the force from one particle to another. Different gauge bosons are exchanged in the three types of interaction: the electromagnetic force is carried by photons, the strong force by gluons (see QUARK), and the weak force by neutral Z and charge W particles.

The gravitational force occurs between all particles, the electromagnetic force between charged particles, e.g. electrons and protons. The strong force arises between hadrons, e.g. protons and neutrons, and between the constituents of hadrons, i.e. QUARKS, and is the force binding together particles in the NUCLEI of atoms. The weak force occurs between both leptons and hadrons and is responsible for radioactivity. The four forces vary greatly in range: the gravitational and electromagnetic forces have an infinite range whereas the other two have an extremely short range. They also vary greatly in strength: the gravitational force is the weakest over very short distances ($\sim 10^{-39}$ times the strength of the strong force) but on a cosmic scale it dominates the others.

Attempts to construct a single theory unifying the four forces have been progressing. Steven Weinberg and Abdus Salam in the late 1960s found a mathematical description – the *electroweak theory* – that successfully unified the electromagnetic and weak forces so that they could be regarded as two aspects of the same phenomenon. There are various *grand unified theories* (*GUTs*) that aim to provide a mathematical framework in which the strong, electromagnetic, and weak forces emerge as parts of a single unified force. A symmetry is said to relate one force to another. Since the forces are very different in strength and character this symmetry is broken in the present-day Universe. GUTs predict that the symmetry holds only when the temperature is greater than about 10^{27} K, when particles would have extremely high energies, above 10^{24} electronvolts. Such extremes of temperature and energy occurred in the very young Universe immediately after the BIG BANG. GUTs are thus of great importance to cosmology.

The ultimate goal is to incorporate the gravitational force into the unification by formulating a satisfactory theory of QUANTUM GRAVITATION. This would produce a *theory of everything* (*TOE*); one candidate is STRING THEORY.

fundamental plane the tight correlation between properties of elliptical galaxies such as their total luminosity, SURFACE BRIGHTNESS and VELOCITY DISPERSION, and the relation between the luminosity and rotational velocity for spiral disks. Such relations are a natural consequence for self-gravitating systems with approximately constant mass-to-light ratio. See also FABER–JACKSON RELATION; TULLY–FISHER METHOD.

fundamental stars selected stars whose positions are determined with the greatest possible accuracy so that the positions of other stars can be compared with them. They are thus used as reference stars. A large number of observations of these stars, made at various times at several observatories throughout the world, contribute to the accuracy by minimizing errors. The positions of fundamental stars are recorded and published in a FUNDAMENTAL CATALOG.

FU Orionis a very young star, thought to be a T TAURI STAR, that is located in Orion in a cloud of gas and dust and is a strong source of infrared radiation. It flared up from about 16th to 10th magnitude in 1936 and has remained near that brightness. It has a high lithium content. It is the prototype of the *FU Orionis stars*, a group of very young stars all showing a persistent increase of several magnitudes, or thought to have recently done so.

FUSE *abbrev. for* Far Ultraviolet Spectroscopic Explorer.

fusion see NUCLEAR FUSION.

Gg

Gacrux *another name for* Gamma (γ) Crucis. See CRUX.

GAIA *abbrev. for* Global Astrometric Interferometer for Astrophysics, an ESA astrometric mission under consideration as part of ESA's HORIZON 2000 program. A successor to HIPPARCOS, GAIA will consist of a continuously scanning satellite providing a global astrometric system in which positions, proper motions, and trigonometric parallaxes will be worked out for about 50 million stars and other celestial objects to an accuracy of better than 10 μas. The satellite should achieve this unprecedented level of precision by its use of an interferometer using a modest baseline and a highly efficient detector incorporating a CCD and allowing parallel rather than sequential observations. The resulting catalog is intended to be complete to a limiting magnitude of 15, but millions of fainter objects down to magnitude 20 should be measurable with less accuracy. GAIA could be launched as early as 2009 or as late as 2014.

gain **1** a measure of the amplification of an electronic device. If the power input to the device is P_1 and the power output is P_2, the gain expressed in decibels is given by

$$G = 10 \log_{10}(P_2/P_1)$$

Gains measured in this way can be added when amplifying stages are connected in series.

2 a measure of the directional advantage of using one radio ANTENNA as compared with another. It is usual to express the gain, G, of a particular antenna over an isotropic radiator. For a lossless antenna it is given by

$$G = 4\pi A_e/\lambda^2$$

where A_e is the effective area (see ARRAY) and λ is the wavelength; the gain is equal to the DIRECTIVITY in this case. Sometimes the comparison is with a DIPOLE, which itself has a gain over an isotropic radiator of 1.5 (equivalent to 1.7 decibels, or dBi).

galactic bulge see GALAXIES; GALAXY.

galactic cannibalism see CANNIBALISM.

galactic center the innermost region of our GALAXY, or its exact center. INTERSTELLAR EXTINCTION obscures this region by up to 30 magnitudes at optical wavelengths and information on the very complex phenomena in the galactic center has been derived mainly from radio, infrared, and X-ray observations. The central region (with radius around 200 parsecs) is bright in radio and infrared continuum emission, particularly in lines of molecular CO and atomic C. This *central molecular zone* accounts for about 10% of the Galaxy's total molecular mass and has a high density and temperatures (30–200K). Star formation at rates of 0.5 solar masses a year is occurring at many places within this central molecular zone, probably triggered by external events, such as shocks. In particular the central parsec shows evidence for recent massive star formation, with many emission-line stars centered on the core of the central stellar cluster. The peak of this infrared emission and the stellar density coincide with the radio emission from an H II region in SAGITTARIUS A (West). This is generally considered to be the dynamic center of the galaxy. There is also extended X-ray line emission centered on the Galactic nucleus, with a size roughly half that of the central molecular zone,

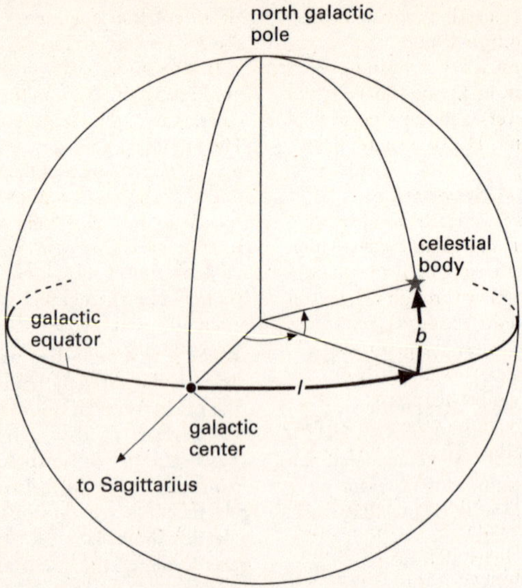

Galactic coordinate system

indicating that some of the gas not consumed by star formation is present as a hot plasma. The X-rays also reveal a point source at the position of Sgr A West.

The density of dust at the center is very low but probably increases beyond a radius of 1 parsec to give rise to a double-lobed structure, with a 100 μm luminosity of about $10^7 L_{\odot}$. This may be heated by ultraviolet radiation from a central object located at the position of Sgr A West. The source of this heating radiation is thought to be emission from a massive black hole.

Farther away from the center, radio observations indicate that there is a thin rapidly rotating disk of hydrogen extending out to a radius of about 750 parsecs and also gas moving rapidly away from the center. In particular there are two expanding arms of gas both roughly at a radius of 3 kiloparsecs. The arm on the sunward side of the center is approaching us with a speed of 50 km s^{-1} and the one on the other side is receding at 135 km s^{-1}.

galactic cluster 1 see OPEN CLUSTER. 2 see CLUSTERS OF GALAXIES.

galactic coordinate system A COORDINATE SYSTEM used to study the structure, surroundings, and contents of the GALAXY. The fundamental circle is the GALACTIC EQUATOR and the zero point lies in the direction of the galactic center (in the constellation Sagittarius) as seen from Earth (see illustration). The coordinates are *galactic latitude* and *longitude*.

The galactic latitude (*b*) of a celestial body is its angular distance (from 0° to 90°) north (counted positive) or south (counted negative) of the galactic equator; it is measured along the great circle passing through the body and the galactic poles. The galactic longitude (*l*) of a celestial body is its angular distance (from 0° to 360°) from the nominal galactic center measured eastward along the galactic equator to the intersection of the great circle passing through the body.

The position of zero galactic longitude, i.e. the nominal galactic center, was agreed (1959) by the International Astronomical Union (IAU); it lies at RA 17h 45.6m, dec –28°56′.3 (2000.0). More recent observations suggest the actual galactic center coincides with a radio and infrared souce, SAGITTARIUS A West, a few arc minutes from this nominal position; the nominal center is still used, however, as the zero point for galactic coordinates. The true center lies at $l = -3'.34$, $b = -2'.75$.

galactic disk see GALAXIES; GALAXY.

galactic equator a great circle on the CELESTIAL SPHERE. The *galactic plane,* which contains the galactic equator, is the plane that passes most nearly through the central plane of the spiral disk of our Galaxy. The galactic plane and celestial equator are inclined at an angle of about 63°. The nominal galactic center lies on the galactic equator in the direction of the constellation Sagittarius and is the zero point for the GALACTIC COORDINATE SYSTEM.

galactic fountain hot X-ray emitting gas from groups of SUPERNOVA REMNANTS that breaks free of the plane of our Galaxy and expands away until it cools and falls back onto the disk in a fountainlike behavior.

galactic halo see GALAXY. See also DARK HALO.

galactic latitude, longitude see GALACTIC COORDINATE SYSTEM.

galactic magnetic field a very weak and complex system of magnetic fields, known to exist in the interstellar regions of the Galaxy from observations of the FARADAY ROTATION of radiation from pulsars and other radio sources, of the ZEEMAN splitting of the 21-cm hydrogen line arising in interstellar clouds, and of INTERSTELLAR POLARIZATION. The magnetic flux density lies in the range 10^{-10} to 10^{-9} tesla, with 3–6 $\times 10^{-10}$ tesla being the best estimate. The direction of the field seems to be in the plane of the Galaxy, along the spiral arms. See also COSMIC RAYS.

galactic nucleus see ACTIVE GALAXY; GALAXIES; GALAXY.

galactic plane see GALACTIC EQUATOR; GALAXY.

galactic poles the two points on the celestial sphere that are 90° north and 90° south of every point on the GALACTIC EQUATOR. The *north galactic pole* lies in the constellation Coma Berenices at RA 12h 51.4m, dec +27°7′.7 (2000.0). The *south galactic pole,* diametrically opposite, lies in Sculptor.

galactic rotation the rotation of the GALAXY about its center, all its components sharing in this rotation to varying degrees. The predominant motion in the galactic disk is circular and parallel to the galactic plane. The orbital speed is determined by the mass within a star's orbit, not by the Galaxy's total mass, so the stars' rotation speeds do not follow KEPLER'S LAWS. The rotation speed increases from near zero to 150 km s^{-1} in the first kiloparsec of the Galaxy's radius, then increases more gradually to a peak near the Sun's orbit (at a radius of about 10 kpc). Farther away it may fall off gradually or remain roughly constant. The rotation velocity of the LOCAL STANDARD OF REST in the galactic plane was formerly taken to be 250 km s^{-1}, but the accepted value is now 220 km s^{-1} as a result of the Galaxy's massive DARK HALO. Objects in the galactic halo display much more random motions than those in the disk and the system as a whole has only a small residual rotation with respect to the galactic center. See also ROTATION CURVE.

galactic wind a substantial outflow of hot gas from a galaxy that has recently suffered a high burst of STAR FORMATION or a MERGER. The gas has a velocity of a few hundred kilometers per second and is usually hot enough to emit in X-rays. The occurrence of galactic winds has implications for the energetics, chemical enrichment, and evolution of galaxies and their environment.

galactic year see COSMIC YEAR.

Galatea a small satellite of Neptune, discovered in 1989. See Table 2, Appendix.

galaxies giant assemblies of stars, gas, and dust into which most of the visible matter in the Universe is concentrated. Each galaxy exists as a separate, though not always entirely independent, system held together and organized largely by the gravitational interactions between its various components. When capitalized, the term denotes specifically our own system, the Milky Way GALAXY. Owing to their cloudlike appearance when viewed by eye through simple telescopes, galaxies other than our own were once known as 'nebulae'. This term is now strictly applied only to clouds of interstellar gas and dust.

The majority of galaxies are composed of two structural components, the central spheroidal *bulge* and the flattened *disk*. The bulge is usually supported against gravitational collapse by the anisotropic VELOCITY DISPERSIONS of its stars, whereas a disk is maintained by rotation. Galaxies are divided into broad categories based on the relative importance of these two components.

Elliptical galaxies are those systems that have no disk component. They appear in photographs as fuzzy elliptical patches of light, diminishing smoothly in brightness from the center outward with no obvious internal structure. The shape of the outline varies from almost circular through to narrow ellipses about three times as long as they are wide. Traditionally the latter were regarded as oblate (flattened) systems but recent analyses show that prolate (elongated) systems are also possible. Most elliptical galaxies are probably triaxial ellipsoids with their three axes of different lengths. The shape of the outline is the basis of the HUBBLE CLASSIFICATION. Elliptical galaxies were long thought to be devoid of gas but X-ray and radio observations have shown them to have a significant and complex interstellar medium, with very hot (10^7 K) gas coexisting with clouds of neutral hydrogen. Some galaxies even show low-level emission-line activity. The stars within them are predominantly old (SPECTRAL TYPES K and M).

Galaxies with a second, disk-shaped component in addition to the bulge are known as *spiral galaxies*. They form flattened systems containing prominent *spiral arms* of interstellar matter and bright young stars that wind outward from a dense central bulge or *nucleus*. Although two-armed spirals are the most common, systems with one arm or even, very occasionally, three arms have also been observed. In *normal spirals* the arms emerge directly from the nucleus, usually from opposite sides; in *barred spirals* the arms emanate from each end of a bright central bar that extends across the nucleus. Both types exist in a wide range of forms. At one extreme there are galaxies with large dominant bulges and thin tightly wound spiral arms; at the other extreme there are galaxies with inconspicuous nuclei and prominent loosely wound spiral arms. The shape and structure of spirals and barred spirals is the basis of Hubble's classification.

Spiral galaxies are rich in gas and dust, most of which is distributed in clouds along the spiral arms. Stars in the nuclei of spirals appear to be predominantly well advanced in their evolution and the brightest individual stars observed there are RED GIANTS of POPULATION II. A fairly smooth axially symmetric distribution of old stars also extends beyond the nucleus. However, owing to the intrinsic faintness of most of its constituent stars, this system is much less conspicuous than the spiral arms embedded within it.

Although star formation is undoubtedly still taking place in the spiral arms, what triggers this process is still uncertain, as is the origin of the arms themselves. It has been proposed, in the DENSITY-WAVE THEORY, that the spiral structure is maintained over a long period by gravitational effects. Alternatively, it has been suggested that the spiral structure arises and persists as a result of SELF-PROPAGATING STAR FORMATION involving supernovae. All spiral galaxies are in differential rotation, stars in the outer parts completing their orbits on average more slowly than those nearer the center. As far as can be ascertained, the spiral arms always trail away from the direction of rotation.

Galaxies possessing a large bulge and small disk, intermediate between the spirals and ellipticals, are known as *So galaxies* or *lenticular galaxies*. The disk shows no evidence for spiral arms, although dark dust clouds are sometimes seen when the galaxy presents an edge-on aspect. The stars within So galaxies are predominantly old and little gas is apparent.

Irregular galaxies are those without discernable symmetry in shape or structure. They vary enormously in appearance but all are below average in size and contain large amounts of interstellar matter. In the early Hubble classification this term was applied to any galaxy that could not be fitted into the elliptical or spiral classes. Hubble's

Irr II galaxies are now reclassified as STARBURST, ACTIVE, and INTERACTING GALAXIES. The DWARF GALAXIES presently labelled as irregular correspond to Hubble's Irr I galaxies.

The colors of galaxies vary according to the age of the stars responsible for most of the light. In general, ellipticals and Sos are the most red and irregulars, because of their high content of very young stars, are the most blue. Differences in the dominant spectral type are also reflected in the mass to luminosity ratio, spirals and irregulars being, on average, brighter than ellipticals or Sos of similar mass.

The brightest and most massive galaxies are the *cD galaxies*, which resemble giant ellipticals; they have absolute magnitudes of about −22.5 and masses in excess of 10^{12} solar masses. cD galaxies are located exclusively at the gravitational center of clusters of galaxies. They possess an extra component in the form of a very faint but extensive (up to radii of 100 kiloparsecs) envelope of stars. They are the rarest galaxies, and usually contain the most powerful radio sources in the nearby Universe.

Ellipticals also display the greatest variation in mass, ranging down to extreme dwarfs (about 10^6 solar masses) that are no brighter than the most luminous GLOBULAR CLUSTERS. Spirals appear to exist only as large or giant systems, with masses typically of the order of 10^{10} or 10^{11} times that of the Sun. No irregulars are as bright as the giant spirals and some are extreme dwarfs.

Of the 1000 brightest galaxies, about 75% are spiral, 20% elliptical, and 5% irregular. However, when allowance is made for the many DWARF GALAXIES, the true proportions turn out to be nearer to 30:60:10. Few galaxies exist in total isolation. Double and multiple systems are common and many galaxies are also members of larger groups known as CLUSTERS OF GALAXIES. Clusters can in turn form loosely bound aggregates called SUPERCLUSTERS.

How and why galaxies have evolved to their present shapes is still uncertain although it appears that spirals contain much more ANGULAR MOMENTUM than ellipticals. Turbulence and vorticity in the early Universe may play a role. However, it is generally conceded now that the principal types of galaxy represent separate species rather than one species seen at different stages in its evolution. There is, in fact, no direct evidence that any other galaxy is significantly older than our own Galaxy (which is thought to be about 12 thousand million years old), and none younger apart from the minuscule EXTRAGALACTIC H II REGIONS. All galaxies appear to contain a mixture of stellar POPULATIONS.

See also GALAXIES, FORMATION AND EVOLUTION; RECESSION OF THE GALAXIES.

galaxies, classification galaxies may be classified according to a variety of criteria, including morphology (shape, concentration, and structure), spectroscopy (integrated spectrum, etc.) colorimetry (integrated color, etc.), photometry (luminosity, etc.), and unusual activity at various wavelengths (radio, infrared, X-ray, etc.). The HUBBLE CLASSIFICATION is based on morphology whereas MORGAN'S CLASSIFICATION is basically a quantitative spectroscopic classification.

galaxies, formation and evolution galaxies must have condensed out of the gases expanding from the BIG BANG, beginning at a time when the average density of the Universe was roughly the same as the current mean density of a galaxy. Details of the formation of galaxies are still highly uncertain, as is their subsequent evolution. Astronomers are not agreed, for example, on the extent to which the different types of GALAXY have been determined by conditions at formation or by later evolution. The current picture of galaxy formation assumes a COSMIC POWER SPECTRUM of fluctuations in the COLD DARK MATTER. Gravitational instability causes the overdense regions to collapse and the gas falls into these developing gravitational potential wells. This may lead to dissipation of gravitational energy heating the gas. That gas which can cool rapidly forms the visible stars of the galaxy; as time progresses more and more fluctuations become unstable and the potential wells of galaxies merge and cluster. This is known as *hierarchical* *clustering*. Although the details of the evolution of the cold dark matter can be calculated fairly precisely, the behavior of the gas is much more complicated, with energy and metals injected by SUPERNOVAE playing a major role in the visible appearance of the final galaxies.

Elliptical galaxies probably formed in the densest regions of the original fluctuations. Rapid star formation converted almost all the available gas to stars in less than a thousand million years. The most distant ellipticals should contain a proportion of younger bluer stars, and observations of distant RADIO GALAXIES display a bluer continuum that may be consistent with intense star formation. Spiral galaxies formed by the slower accumulation of fragments or collapse of larger clouds in less dense regions, and where turbulence caused the protogalaxy to rotate. Fairly rapid star birth during formation produced the old stars of the halo and central regions; the remaining gas settled into a disk, where stars continued to form much more slowly and interstellar gas remains to the present day.

The most dramatic examples of galaxy evolution are caused by external factors. For example, galaxies may collide and merge, or the hot INTRACLUSTER MEDIUM may strip gas from a rapidly moving galaxy.

Galaxy (**Milky Way System**) the giant star system to which the Sun belongs. The Galaxy has a spiral structure and, like other spiral galaxies, is highly flattened. It is estimated to contain of the order of 100 billion (10^{11}) stars, the bulk of which are organized into a relatively thin *disk* with an ellipsoidal *bulge*, or *nucleus*, at its center. This system is embedded in an approximately spherical *halo* of stars and GLOBULAR CLUSTERS (see illustration). The radius of the disk is approximately 20 kiloparsecs and its maximum thickness (at the center) is about 4 kpc. The halo is more sparsely populated than the disk and its full extent is uncertain, although its radius is known to be greater than that of the disk. There may also be a very much larger DARK HALO, or corona, of unseen matter stretching out to a radius of 100 kpc or more (see below). The characteristic *spiral arms*, which contain many of the brightest stars in the Galaxy, wind outward from the nuclear region, in or close to the central plane of the disk.

The Sun is situated only a few parsecs north of the central plane, near the inner edge of one of the spiral arms. Our distance from the center is nominally taken as 8.5 kpc (IAU, 1985).

The entire Galaxy is rotating about an axis through the center, the disk rotating fairly rapidly, the halo more slowly (see GALACTIC ROTATION). At the Sun's distance from the center, the systematic rotation of the disk stars is about 220 km s^{-1}, whereas the halo system is rotating with a speed of only about 50 km s^{-1}.

Many astronomers now believe that our Galaxy (and others) is enveloped in a huge dark halo. Its presence is inferred only from the ROTATION CURVE of the Galaxy and by its gravitational effect on the more distant globular clusters in the halo and on nearby dwarf galaxies. It contains ten times as much mass as the stars of the Galaxy. Most of the matter, like other dark matter, is likely to consist of some kind of elementary particle.

The objects in the halo are old stars or clusters of old stars, i.e. globular clusters, that belong to POPULATION II. They increase in density toward the center of the Galaxy but show little concentration toward the galactic plane. Stars in this system are believed to have condensed early in the life of the Galaxy, maybe 15 billion years ago, when the gas cloud from which it formed was still almost spherical. The bulk of the stars in the disk, and probably in the nucleus also, are stars of intermediate age (3–5 billion years) belonging to the disk POPULATION. The young POPULATION I stars are mainly confined to a layer about 500 pc thick along the center of the disk.

Most of the interstellar gas and dust detected in the Galaxy lies in or close to the galactic plane, and about half of it is concentrated into very dense MOLECULAR CLOUDS distributed along the spiral arms. The youngest stars in the Galaxy, notably the T TAURI STARS and the very bright, short-lived O and B STARS, are also largely confined to the spiral arms and it is almost

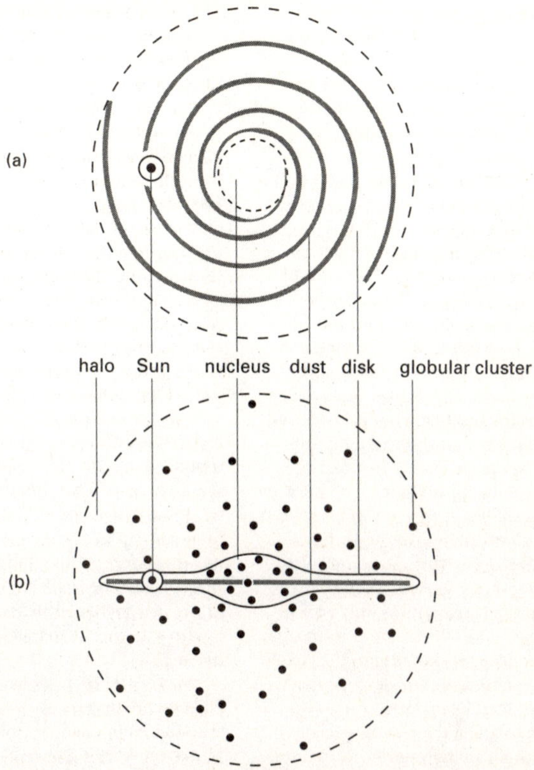

Schematic views of the Galaxy, (a) from above (b) from the side

certain that stars are still being formed from the molecular clouds there. Tracing of the spiral structure is complicated by our position in the disk. Three relatively nearby sections of arms have been traced optically – principally by mapping the distribution of O and B stars and associated EMISSION NEBULAE. These are the *Orion arm*, in which the Sun is located; the *Perseus arm*, located about 2 kpc farther out along the plane; and the *Sagittarius arm*, which lies about 2 kpc nearer the center. Another section, the *Carina arm*, may be a continuation of the Sagittarius arm, the concatenation being called the *Sagittarius-Carina arm*. INTERSTELLAR EXTINCTION makes optical tracing impossible beyond the first few kiloparsecs of the Sun in most directions. More distant spiral features have been traced by radio-astronomy techniques, mainly by mapping the distribution of neutral hydrogen in H I REGIONS and, more recently, the CARBON MONOXIDE in molecular clouds. The analysis is not simple, however, and it is even uncertain whether the Galaxy is a two-armed or four-armed spiral.

INTERSTELLAR EXTINCTION also obscures the central nucleus of the Galaxy at optical wavelengths. Information about this region has been derived mainly from radio, infrared, and X-ray observations. See GALACTIC CENTER.

The total mass of the Galaxy (ignoring

the dark halo) is estimated to be a little less than 2×10^{11} solar masses, of which about 10% exists in the form of interstellar matter. Where our Galaxy fits in the HUBBLE CLASSIFICATION is still open to argument. Some observations suggest a type Sb structure, others a type Sc. There is evidence of a central bar extending to a radius of at least 2.4 kpc, with a mass of around 10^{10} solar masses.

galaxy cluster see CLUSTERS OF GALAXIES.

Galaxy Evolution Explorer (GALEX) a NASA ultraviolet space telescope launched into a nearly circular orbit Apr. 2003 for the purpose of observing ultraviolet radiation from a range of galaxies, both near and remote, in order to advance our knowledge of the evolution and history of galaxies and of star formation. In a 29-month mission supervised by the California Institute of Technology (Caltech), GALEX carried out an extragalactic all-sky survey to produce the first comprehensive map of the Universe showing galaxies evolving. To accomplish this, the observatory looked back in time to an era when the Universe was only 20% of its present age. The UV radiation from such remote regions is redshifted into the visible and near infrared, and the telescope made provision for this. By making a fair comparison between the remote galaxies observed at such an early period with ones close to us in both space and time, GALEX helped provide a means of assessing what changes have occurred between then and now so that cosmologists can learn when and where the stars and elements found today had their origins. GALEX was also tasked with identifying celestial objects for further investigation by current and future missions and producing an all-embracing publicly available archive of data.

The GALEX satellite weighed 280 kg. Its telescope was equipped with f/6 Richey-Chrétien optics. Its 50-cm-diameter primary mirror and 22-cm-diameter secondary mirror were especially coated to screen out local background radiation, and its observations were made only while it was in the Earth's shadow. The mirrors focused incoming light onto two 65-mm microchannel plate detectors with a total ultraviolet sensitivity range of 135–280 nm. The GALEX telescope produced wide-field circular images of sky measuring 1.2° in diameter at a resolution of 5 arcseconds in the far and near ultraviolet light bands. Spectra with 10 to 20 angstrom resolution for all objects within the field of view were obtained by placing a crystalline prism in the light path.

galaxy harassment the morphological disruption of a galaxy similar to that experienced by INTERACTING GALAXIES, but the galaxy is responding to the gravitational potential of a whole cluster of galaxies rather than to another galaxy.

galaxy surveys see REDSHIFT SURVEY.

GALEX *abbrev. for* Galaxy Evolution Explorer.

Galilean satellites the satellites IO, EUROPA, GANYMEDE, and CALLISTO of Jupiter, discovered in 1610 by Galileo Galilei and, independently, by the German astronomer Simon Marius. They are bright enough to be seen with the aid of binoculars and have been studied in detail by PIONEER and VOYAGER spacecraft and the GALILEO spaceprobe. The Galilean satellites are Jupiter's largest satellites by far, comparable in size with the small planets. Ganymede, the largest satellite in the Solar System, is slighter bigger than Mercury in diameter, and all of them except Europa are larger than the Moon. Each is in SYNCHRONOUS ROTATION, keeping one face permanently turned toward Jupiter. Their maximum surface temperatures vary between the 120 K of Io to 155 K for Callisto, probably as a result of differences in ALBEDO; the albedo of Io is 0.61, of Europa 0.64, of Ganymede 0.42, and of Callisto as low as 0.20. They show a progressive decrease in bulk density from Io, the closest (3.57 times that of water) through Europa (2.97) and Ganymede (1.94) to Callisto, the farthest (1.86), indicating that the proportion of rocky material to ice is greater for the denser satellites. Ganymede and Callisto, unlike Io and Europa, are both heavily cratered bodies. The three Galilean satellites closest to Jupiter in order of distance – Io, Europa, and Ganymede – follow paths that are locked in to each other by ORBITAL RESONANCE. Thus for every single orbit completed by Ganymede, Europa completes two and Io four. One consequence of this orbital resonance takes the form of gravitational effects. Europa's gravitational influence on io has perturbed it into a more eccentric orbit around Jupiter, taking it both closer to and farther away from the giant planet and exposing it to the tidal stresses that produce the active volcanoes observed by the Voyager and Galileo spacecraft. Europa in its turn is acted upon by Ganymede and as a result its geology may have been subject to the effects of tidal friction and heating. It has been suggested that as Callisto's distance from Jupiter increases owing to the tidal exchange of angular momentum between it and the giant planet, it too will eventually reach a 2:1 resonance with Ganymede. See also JUPITER'S SATELLITES; Table 2, Appendix.

Galilean telescope the first type of astronomical telescope, developed in 1609 by Galileo from Hans Lippershey's 'magic tubes'. It is a refractor made up from a single long-focus object lens and a powerful diverging lens used as an eyepiece (see illustration). This optical system, which gives an upright image, survives in modern opera glasses. Galileo's best telescopes had a magnification of about 30 times; although very imperfect, they led to the great achievements of 17th-century astronomy. See also TELESCOPE.

Galileo a NASA mission to Jupiter and its moons, launched Oct. 18 1989 from the space shuttle Atlantis. With insufficient power to fly directly to Jupiter, Galileo first followed a circuitous 3-year flight path through the inner Solar System using the gravity of the celestial bodies it passed to catapult it on its way. Its trajectory involved the following events: Venus flyby (Feb. 1990), Earth flyby (Dec. 1990), flyby of asteroid (951) GASPRA in the inner asteroid belt (Oct. 1991), second Earth flyby (Dec. 1992). Its instruments sent back excellent images and data on Venus, the Moon, Earth, and Gaspra. The mission received a potentially disastrous blow when Galileo's communications system was crippled after its main transmission antenna failed to open properly in Apr. 1991. As a result, data could be relayed to Earth only using a slow weak backup link, greatly reducing the number of transmitted images. Despite this problem, the spacecraft was to prove a major success.

Following the second Earth flyby, Galileo had gained sufficient momentum to reach Jupiter (see GRAVITY ASSIST). On its flight there, it flew past the asteroid (243) IDA (Aug. 1993), where it discovered the first asteroidal moon, Dactyl, about 1.5 km in diameter, orbiting its primary at a distance of about 100 km. Galileo reached Jupiter in Dec. 1995, entering a 198-day, highly elliptical orbit around the gas giant. Among its first tasks was to relay data back to Earth from a probe it had released in 1995. The probe plunged into Jupiter just as Galileo entered orbit and sent back information on the physical and chemical nature of the upper reaches of the planet's deep atmosphere before being destroyed.

Galileo's mission to the Jovian system was at first set to run for 23 months. During this first period – its primary mission – the spacecraft made observations of Jupiter and flew by the Galilean satellites Ganymede, Callisto, and Europa. It also returned long-range images of the volcanically active Io. Its endurance in the hostile radiation-filled

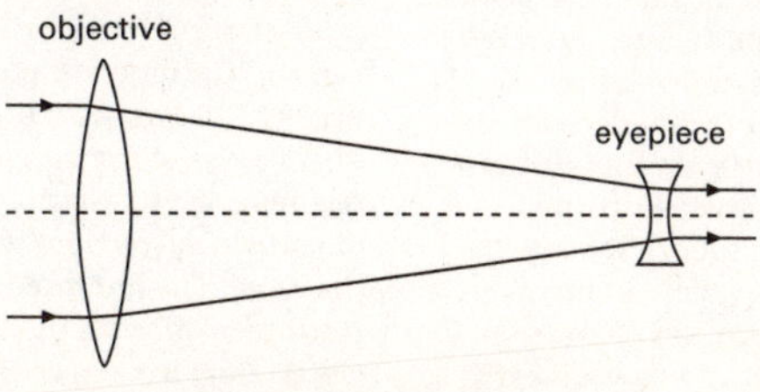

Ray path in Galilean telescope

environment around Jupiter and the excellence of the scientific data it sent back to Earth despite its communication problems persuaded NASA to prolong its stay after the end of its primary mission in Dec. 1997. It embarked on extended observations of Europa and Io. In 1999, it made its first close encounter with Io, returning during this and later visits valuable data on the satellite itself and on the Io torus, the doughnut-shaped cloud of highly energetic charged particles that surround the satellite's orbit. In late 2000, Galileo teamed up with the Saturn-bound Cassini–Huygens spacecraft to investigate the interaction between Jupiter's magnetosphere and the solar wind. The Galileo spacecraft remained operational in Jupiter's vicinity for nearly 8 years. In all, it made 35 circuits of Jupiter and completed 34 flybys of its major satellites. It returned a rich stream of information that transformed our understanding of the giant planet itself as well as its retinue of moons and its dusty rings. Altogether, it spent almost 14 years in space, traveling a total distance of 4 631 778 000 km. On Sept. 21 2003, Galileo was deliberately guided into Jupiter's atmosphere to be crushed out of existence.

Galileo Regio see GANYMEDE.

Galileo Telescope see ROQUE DE LOS MUCHACHOS OBSERVATORY.

Gallex see NEUTRINO ASTRONOMY.

gamma (γ) the third letter of the Greek alphabet, used in STELLAR NOMENCLATURE usually to designate the third-brightest star in a constellation or sometimes to indicate a star's position in a group.

gamma-ray astronomy the study of radiation from space at the extreme short-wavelength end of the electromagnetic spectrum (less than 0.01 nanometers) and with the largest photon energies (usually exceeding 100 000 electronvolts (eV), i.e. >100 keV). The immense range of gamma-ray energies (see GAMMA RAYS) has led to a variety of detection instruments and techniques, including SCINTILLATION COUNTERS, SPARK CHAMBERS, DRIFT CHAMBERS, CODED-MASK TELESCOPES, COMPTON TELESCOPES, and GAMMA-RAY SOLID-STATE DETECTORS.

Gamma rays from space cannot penetrate the Earth's atmosphere so that γ-ray observations only became possible when instruments could be carried above the atmosphere in satellites. The first cosmic γ-rays were detected with a scintillation counter on the OSO-3 satellite in 1968. More detailed observations confirmed their origin in a narrow band along the galactic plane, being particularly strong within 30° of the galactic center; these observations were provided by the NASA SAS-2 satellite launched in Nov. 1972 and suggested that the γ-rays come from interactions in interstellar gas. The spark-chamber detector on SAS-2, sensitive in the energy band 30–1000 MeV, also found discrete γ-ray sources coincident with two PULSARS, the Crab and Vela pulsars.

The European Space Agency's COS-B satellite, launched in Aug. 1975, also carried a large spark chamber and operated successfully for nearly seven years, providing improved exposure and angular resolution of medium-energy (70–5000 MeV) γ-rays. In addition to the Crab and Vela pulsars 22 other galactic sources, plus the bright QUASAR 3C273, were detected by COS-B. Identification of the remaining γ-ray emitters with known celestial objects has not, however, been possible. Detailed study of the COS-B positional ERROR BOXES has shown that none of these medium-energy γ-ray sources can have an X-ray luminosity more than a fraction of the γ-ray luminosity; this indicates that an understanding of their physical nature has to be found in the interpretation of γ-ray data and, furthermore, that they could represent a new class of cosmic object. At least two of the COS-B sources are coincident with MOLECULAR CLOUD regions (RHO OPHIUCHI and the ORION MOLECULAR CLOUD). The observed positional correlation between the γ-ray ISOPHOTES and the distribution of EXTINCTION from these regions suggests γ-ray production by means of particle interactions with the matter of the cloud. The improved sensitivity of instrumentation on the Compton Observatory has shown that a growing number of pulsars are powerful γ-ray emitters (see GAMMA-RAY PULSARS; GEMINGA).

Apart from the localized sources in our Galaxy, a clearly defined band (±15° latitude) of enhanced γ-ray continuum emission lying along the galactic equator has been observed; it has been interpreted as being mainly the result of interaction of COSMIC-RAY electrons (via BREMSSTRAHLUNG) and cosmic-ray nuclei (via neutral PION, π°, decay) with the interstellar gas. There is also evidence favouring local structure in the γ-ray emission coincident with the GOULD BELT as well as the Doliditz system. The Galaxy is also a rich source of low-energy (0.5–10 MeV) γ-ray emission, which encompasses a diffuse component as well as a number of discrete sources. The GALACTIC CENTER is a powerful emitter of electron-positron ANNIHILATION radiation. Detailed studies with germanium detectors of high spectral resolution have revealed that the line is narrow and shows some evidence for three-photon POSITRONIUM continuum below 511 keV.

The 1.809 MeV line of ^{26}Al has been detected from the general direction of the galactic plane. The emission intensity corresponds to approximately 3 $M_{\odot}$ of this long-lived (10^6 year) isotope within our Galaxy. The discovery of the 0.847 MeV γ-ray line from SN 1987A provided the first direct evidence of the explosive synthesis of elements. About 0.075 $M_{\odot}$ of the radioactive isotope ^{56}Ni were produced in this supernova explosion.

Although the quasar 3C273 was detected as a medium-energy γ-ray source, other types of ACTIVE GALAXIES have been discovered to be strong emitters of γ-rays. The γ-ray power output is found to dominate all emissions at other wavelengths. This high luminosity coupled with the timescale of the γ-ray variability (a few months) may be taken as evidence that the emissions are intimately related to the region containing the central power house.

A diffuse, and as far as can be measured isotropic, cosmic γ-ray flux has been observed to extend from 0.1 MeV to more than 1000 MeV. At the present time it is unclear if this COSMIC BACKGROUND flux is derived from particle interactions throughout the Universe, or whether it is derived from the contributions of a large number of active galaxies.

A growing number of galactic objects have been detected as very high energy (>10^{12} eV) γ-ray emitters. In two cases a NEUTRON STAR is almost certainly involved and the emission follows the period of pulsations at other wavelengths.

The measurement of γ-ray photons permits the study of the largest transfers of energy occurring in astrophysical processes. The extreme penetrating power of these high-energy photons offers a unique opportunity to probe deeply into the heart of violent galactic and extragalactic systems. The new generation of more sensitive γ-ray telescopes are revealing much new information on both the properties of astronomical objects and the high-energy processes that govern the dynamics of their evolution. See also COMPTON GAMMA RAY OBSERVATORY; GRANAT; HETE; INTEGRAL.

gamma-ray bursts intense flashes of hard X-rays or gamma rays, detected at energies up to one million electronvolts. They are of short duration (0.1–1000 seconds) and were discovered by US Air Force satellites in 1967 but not declassified until 1973. There are sharp temporal features in the burst time profile; this allows the measurement of differences in arrival times of wavefronts of the order of a few milliseconds over baselines separated by hundreds of light-seconds. For the strongest and most rapidly varying bursts, such measurements yield angular resolutions of the order of arc seconds. The most intense burst observed so far lies within the supernova remnant N49 in the Large MAGELLANIC CLOUD. The BATSE experiment on the COMPTON GAMMA RAY OBSERVATORY has detected hundreds of γ-ray bursts, averaging about one per day. Measurements have revealed that the distribution of the bursts is consistent with isotropy: they are uniformly distributed across the sky. Their origin still remains a mystery. γ-ray emission lines in their spectra may be related to ANNIHILATION radiation redshifted by the strong gravitational field of a NEUTRON STAR, and γ-ray absorption features to CYCLOTRON absorption in intense magnetic fields. The rapid temporal structure, including the periodic emission, is generally assumed to point to neutron star origins for γ-ray bursts, although sources at cosmological distances cannot be ruled out. The most probable energy source is thought to be either gravitational or nuclear in origin.

Gamma Ray Observatory (GRO) *original name of* Compton Gamma Ray Observatory.

gamma-ray pulsars the improved sensitivity of instrumentation on the COMPTON GAMMA RAY OBSERVATORY has shown that PULSARS can be powerful gamma-ray emitters. The gamma radiation is thought to originate in the star's outer magnetosphere, and in some cases it appears that a large fraction of the spin-down energy of the pulsar is emitted as pulsed gamma radiation. GEMINGA is now known to be a γ-ray pulsar, and, with a 180° phase separation of the two pulses, is thought to be an extreme case; nearly 100% of the available energy is emitted as γ-rays and the dipole magnetic field is inclined at a very large angle (>65°) to the spin axis.

gamma rays (γ-rays) very high energy ELECTROMAGNETIC RADIATION, i.e. radiation with the shortest wavelengths and the highest frequencies: γ-ray wavelengths are less than 10^{-11} meters. There is no sharp cutoff between the γ-ray region and the adjacent X-ray region of the electromagnetic spectrum.

Gamma rays, like X-rays, are usually described in terms of photon energy, $h\nu$, where ν is the frequency of the radiation and h is the Planck constant. The γ-ray region of the electromagnetic spectrum spans many decades of photon energy – from about 10^5 electronvolts (eV) to more than 10^{15} eV. The range is customarily subdivided into a number of energy bands that are related to changes in telescope technology:

low energy γ-rays, 10^5–10^7 eV;
medium energy γ-rays, 10^7–10^9 eV;
high energy γ-rays, 10^9–10^{11} eV;
very high energy γ-rays, 10^{11}–10^{14} eV;
ultra high energy γ-rays, $>10^{14}$ eV.

Low energy γ-ray photons ($h\nu \sim 10^6$ eV) are the most penetrating photons available to the astronomer. Traditionally γ-ray source spectra have been measured in units of photons per unit area per second per unit energy interval, i.e. treating the photons as individual events. At present the general move is to unify the measurement system by use of the JANSKY.

gamma-ray solid-state detectors semiconductor detectors designed to give high spectral resolution in the spectral domain in which the characteristic nuclear decay lines are emitted. Electron-hole pairs are created in a solid-state device along the path of the secondary electrons derived from γ-ray interactions, much as ion pairs are created in a gas-filled detector (see PROPORTIONAL COUNTER). Applying an electric field to the detector enables the electron-hole pairs to be collected and thus provides the basic electrical signal from the device. Semiconductor detectors may be rendered position-sensitive, and hence adapted to provide imaging systems, by appropriate geometric design of the electrode contacts.

A variety of semiconductors are suitable for such detector systems. Silicon, either in the form of silicon diodes or lithium-drifted silicon, provides high-quality detectors for operation at hard X-ray/γ-ray energies (<50 keV). High-purity germanium (HPGe), either in planar or coaxial form, currently provides the best-available spectral resolution for γ-rays (up to ~10 MeV); germanium devices, however, must be cooled to ~70 K for effective operation. Two semiconductors, mercuric iodide (HgI_2) and cadmium telluride (CdTe), currently show great promise for room-temperature operation, and hence in telescopes would not need cooling; difficult to produce with sufficient purity, they are best-employed as thin detector systems in hard X-ray/γ-ray telescopes that operate typically in the range 5–300 keV.

gamma-ray sources see GAMMA-RAY ASTRONOMY.

gamma-ray transients sources of transient gamma-ray outbursts, the vast majority of which lie within 10° of the galactic plane and have peak luminosities of 10^{29} to about 10^{28} joules per second. Both neutron star and black-hole systems exhibit such outbursts. The γ-ray emission features of black-hole candidates are particularly spectacular and may prove to be a collective signature of the presence of a black-hole system. They include hard ($E \geq 200$ keV) power-law emission tails, rapid stochastic flickering, broad electron-positron pair plasmalike spectral features; broadened and redshifted 511 keV line features; the presence of Compton backscattered spectral features near 170 keV.

Ganymede the brightest and largest of the four GALILEAN SATELLITES of Jupiter. With a diameter of 5262 km it is the largest satellite in the Solar System. It is in fact larger in diameter than the planet Mercury but is only half as massive. It has an albedo of 0.42 and a density of 1.94 g cm^{-3}. There are two main types of surface feature: ancient darkish heavily cratered terrain and the younger brighter regions, which have long parallel grooves or SULCI. The two types intermingle, giving a complex surface. The largest single feature on Ganymede is the vast dark area *Galileo Regio* with a diameter of 4000 km. The most ancient craters – ghost craters or palimpsests – are barely visible in the dark areas such as Galileo Regio. Some of the younger craters are surrounded by bright rays of exposed ice. The grooved terrain consists of parallel mountain ridges up to 1 km high, 10 to 15 km apart, which wander for thousands of kilometers across the surface forming intricate patterns. From data collected by the Galileo spacecraft, scientists have surmised that Ganymede's internal structure consists of three layers: a compact core consisting of molten iron or iron and sulfur, a surrounding mantle made up of rocky silicates, and an outer shell of ice. As in the case of Europa and Callisto, evidence has been discovered of a tenuous oxygen atmosphere, resulting from charged solar particles breaking down water molecules in the icy crust. See also JUPITER'S SATELLITES; Table 2, Appendix.

Gargantuan Basin see PROCELLARUM, OCEANUS.

Garnet star (**μ Cep**) a red supergiant in the constellation Cepheus. It is a SEMIREGULAR VARIABLE with a magnitude that ranges from 3.6 to 5.1 although it is usually about 4.5. It is also a triple star. Spectral type: M2 Ia.

gas hypersensitization (**hypering**) see HYPERSENSITIZATION.

Gaspra (**(951) Gaspra**) a typical S-TYPE ASTEROID discovered by the Ukrainian astronomer Grigoriy N. Neujmin in 1916. It became the first asteroid ever to be visited by a spacecraft from the Earth when it was imaged by the GALILEO probe in Oct. 1991 from a distance of about 16 000 km; the spacecraft was on its way to Jupiter. Gaspra was found to be conical in shape, being about 15 km across at its broadest. The shape was consistent with it being a fragment produced by the breakup of a much larger body some time in the past. The surface was, however, much smoother than anticipated and lacked the expected number of large craters.

gas scintillation proportional counter (**SPC**) see PROPORTIONAL COUNTER.

Gassendi see table at CRATERS.

gauge bosons, gauge theory see FUNDAMENTAL FORCES.

gauss symbol: G. The c.g.s. (electromagnetic) unit of MAGNETIC FLUX DENSITY. One gauss is equal to 10^{-4} tesla.

Gaussian gravitational constant symbol: k. A constant equal in value to

$$0.017\ 202\ 098\ 95$$

It defines the astronomical system of units of length (ASTRONOMICAL UNIT), mass (SOLAR MASS), and time (DAY) by means of Newton's form of KEPLER'S THIRD LAW:

$$n^2a^3 = k^2(1 + m)$$

n is the mean motion of a planet in radians per day, a is the semimajor axis of its orbit in astronomical units, and m is its mass in terms of solar mass. The dimensions of k^2 are those of Newton's GRAVITATIONAL CONSTANT.

GBT *abbrev. for* Green Bank Telescope. See GREEN BANK.

GC *abbrev. for* (Boss) General Catalog. See also NGC.

GCVS *abbrev. for General Catalog of Variable Stars*, a publication providing a comprehensive list of variable objects compiled under the direction of the Russian astronomer P.N. Kholopov. The fourth edition in its printed form (1985–90) listed 28 484 stars that had been confirmed as variables by 1982, giving their positions for the epoch 1950.0. The most salient sections of its five volumes are available in computerized form from the Sternberg Institute, Moscow. The first four volumes deal with variable stars within the Milky Way system, the fifth catalogs 10 979 variables in 35 extragalactic star systems, including the Magellanic Clouds and the Andromeda and Triangulum galaxies. There is also a catalog of 984 confirmed and suspected extragalactic supernovae. The *New Catalog of Suspected Variable Stars* (compiled by B.V. Kukarkin et al and published in its latest revision in 1982) gives the positions, magnitudes, variability types and alternative identifications of 14 811 stars whose variability was still not confirmed before 1980; a supplement to this publication lists 11 206 stars that were still unconfirmed as variables by 1997.

G-dwarf problem the observed lack of metal-poor stars in our Galaxy. There are expected to be some stars that formed early in the life of our Galaxy and, if of less than one solar mass (i.e. dwarf stars of SPECTRAL TYPE G), have not yet evolved away from the MAIN SEQUENCE. There should thus be a population of low-mass stars that display the very low metal abundances expected to be typical of the conditions at the time of the formation of the Galaxy. Subsequent generations of more massive POPULATION I stars have since enriched the environment. The lack of observed stars of the expected METALLICITY may be understood if the early initial mass function (see STELLAR MASS) was radically different, consisting of only massive stars, or by invoking a hypothetical POPULATION III whose very rapid evolution enriched the Galaxy as it formed.

GE *abbrev. for* greatest elongation. See ELONGATION.

gegenschein (counterglow) a very faint patch of light that can be seen on a clear moonless night on the ecliptic at a point 180° from the Sun's position at the time of observation. It is part of the ZODIACAL LIGHT.

Geminga an intense gamma-ray source in the constellation Gemini (hence the name), first discovered by the SAS-2 satellite. It is also an X-ray source, but more than 99% of its power output is observed in the γ-ray spectral range. Recent observations with the X-ray satellite ROSAT and the COMPTON GAMMA RAY OBSERVATORY have revealed that Geminga is a GAMMA-RAY PULSAR with a period of 237 milliseconds; this periodicity has been confirmed by the analysis of archive data from COS-B and SAS-2. Geminga is possibly the result of a nearby SUPERNOVA.

Gemini (Twins) a conspicuous zodiac constellation in the northern hemisphere near Orion, lying partly in the Milky Way. The brightest stars are the 1st-magnitude POLLUX (β) and the somewhat fainter multiple star CASTOR (α), the spectroscopic binary Alhena (γ), and several stars of 2nd and 3rd magnitude. There are many interesting objects including variable stars, such as the CEPHEID Zeta (ζ) Geminorum and the prototype of the U Geminorum DWARF NOVAE stars, binary stars, such as Eta (η) Geminorum, the open cluster M35 (NGC 2168) visible to the naked eye, and the planetary nebula NGC 2392 (known as the Clownface or Eskimo nebula). Abbrev.: Gem; genitive form: Geminorum; approx. position: RA 7h, dec +25°; area: 514 sq deg.

Geminids an important and active winter METEOR SHOWER that maximizes on Dec. 13, meteors being visible between Dec. 7 and Dec. 15. The shower has a radiant of RA 113°, dec +32°, and a ZENITHAL HOURLY RATE of about 80; the meteoroids hit the atmosphere with a velocity of about 36 km s^{-1}. The orbit of the METEOROID STREAM has a low semimajor axis (1.5 AU) and matches almost exactly the orbit of the Apollo asteroid PHAETHON. The shower has yielded a fairly constant rate during the last century. The meteoroids have a higher density than normal because the parent of the shower is an asteroid rather than a comet.

Gemini project a series of US space missions that extended the knowledge gained from the MERCURY PROJECT and preceded the APOLLO program. The project demonstrated that humans could function effectively over long periods of weightlessness, both inside and outside a spacecraft, and that two spacecraft could be made to rendezvous and dock while in orbit. Gemini 3 was the first manned flight, launched in Mar. 1965, with two astronauts on board. America's first spacewalk was made by Ed White in Gemini 4, launched in June 1965. Geminis 6 and 7 rendezvoused in Dec. 1965, and in Mar. 1966 Gemini 8 made the first successful docking with a crewless target. Gemini 7 remained in orbit for what was then a record 330.6 hours. Gemini 12, launched Nov. 1966, completed the project.

Gemini telescopes two 8.1-meter groundbased telescopes with identical capabilities for use in the infrared, visible, and near ultraviolet. One (completed in 1998) is sited in the northern hemisphere on MAUNA KEA in Hawaii and is known as the *Gillett Telescope* or Gemini North; the other (which saw first light in 2001) is in the southern hemisphere at Cerro Pachón in Chile and is known as Gemini South. The two telescopes together provide full sky coverage as well as similar performance in programs spanning both hemispheres. The telescopes are a joint venture between the USA, UK, Canada, Argentina, Chile, and Brazil. The US NATIONAL OPTICAL ASTRONOMY OBSERVATORY (NOAO) administers the work of the telescopes through the NOAO Gemini Science Center (NGSC), headquartered in Tucson, Arizona. Image quality at near-infrared wavelengths is better than 0.1 arcsecond over a 1-arcminute field of view. The use of ADAPTIVE OPTICS extends this near-diffraction-limited angular resolution to shorter wavelengths. A wide-field capability of 45′, for optical wavelengths, allows simultaneous spectroscopic sampling of multiple objects.

Gemma see ALPHECCA.

general precession see PRECESSION.

general relativity see RELATIVITY, GENERAL THEORY.

Genesis a NASA mission to obtain precise measurements of the abundances of the different elements and isotopes in the Sun and thereby gain more accurate information on its chemical makeup. The data gathered by Genesis would also advance scientists' understanding of the isotopic variations in meteorites, comets, lunar samples, and planetary atmospheres. The mission was set to collect samples of charged particles making up the solar wind and return them in a capsule to Earth. The aim was to provide a reservoir of solar material for scientific research and eliminate the need for future solar wind sample return missions. Part of NASA's Discovery program, Genesis was launched from Kennedy Space Center Aug. 8 2001 and took up a halo orbit around the Lagrangian point L_1, far beyond the Earth's magnetic influence, in Nov. 2001. For 16 months, between Dec. 3 2001 and Apr. 2 2004, it gathered its samples of the solar wind by exposing thin wafers of silicon, gold and other ultrapure substances to the particle stream. Some 10^{20} particles, about half a milligram in mass, embedded themselves in these collecting materials. Genesis then became the first spacecraft to make a return journey from L_1, flying by the Earth on May 2 2004 on its way to L_2. The capsule that it ejected reached Earth on Sept. 8 2004 and entered the atmosphere to be picked up in mid-air by a helicopter in order to minimize contamination. Unfortunately, the capsule's parachute failed to open, and the helicopter could not retrieve it before it fell to earth in the Utah desert, hitting the ground at more than 300 km/h. The capsule was smashed, but miraculously several of the wafer-thin collectors survived intact but soiled. NASA scientists remained confident that the collectors could be cleaned and that, despite its misfortunes, the Genesis mission would yield useful scientific results.

geocentric coordinate system a COORDINATE SYSTEM, such as the ECLIPTIC COORDINATE SYSTEM, in which the position of a celestial body is referred to the center of the Earth. Compare HELIOCENTRIC COORDINATE SYSTEM; TOPOCENTRIC COORDINATES.

geocentric gravitational constant the product of the GRAVITATIONAL CONSTANT and the Earth's mass, equal to

$$3.986\,005 \times 10^{14}\ \text{N m}^2\ \text{kg}^{-1}$$

geocentric parallax see DIURNAL PARALLAX.

geocentric system a model of the Solar System or of the Universe, such as the PTOLEMAIC SYSTEM, that has the Earth at its center.

geocentric zenith see ZENITH.

geocorona a tenuous cloud of hydrogen and some helium extending more than 50 000 km from the Earth's outermost ATMOSPHERIC LAYER to the MAGNETOSPHERE. It scatters Lyman-alpha radiation (see LYMAN SERIES) from the Sun, producing a glow that is visible on long-distance far-ultraviolet photographs of the Earth. It also interferes with far-ultraviolet astronomical observations from Earth orbit.

geodesy the study and measurement of the external shape of the Earth, and hence of its gravitational field and internal construction, using both the measurements of the precise form of the GEOID and observations of artificial Earth satellites.

geoid the form of the Earth obtained by taking the average sea level surface and extending it across the continents. It is an EQUIPOTENTIAL SURFACE defined by measurements of the variation of the Earth's gravitational attraction with latitude and longitude and the acceleration produced by the Earth's rotation. The geoid differs from a sphere in that the equatorial diameter (12 756.32 km) is greater than the diameter through the poles (12 713.51 km). The *flattening* of the Earth corresponds to the difference between these diameters as a fraction of the equatorial diameter and has a value of 1/298.257.

Studies of the PERTURBATIONS affecting the orbits of artificial Earth satellites have shown that the geoid departs from an oblate spheroid, or ellipsoid; this is a result of density anomalies within the Earth and supports the theory of dynamic convective processes in the mantle. There are more than ten elevations and depressions on the true geoid, scattered worldwide and typically of 40–60 meters. The greatest departures are a 105-meter depression to the south of India and a 75-meter elevation to the north of Australia.

geology the study of the history, structure, and composition of the EARTH's crust. The principle divisions of geology include *physical geology, historical geology,* and *economic geology.*

Physical geology includes mineralogy, which is the study of minerals; petrology, the study of the formation, composition, and structure of different types of rock; structural geology, concerned with how these rocks combine to form the crust; and geomorphology (or physiography), the study of the relation between geographical features and sub-surface geological structures.

Historical geology includes stratigraphy, which is concerned with the chronology of rock strata; paleogeography, the study of the distribution of geographical features (seas, deserts, mountains) during early periods of the Earth's history; and paleontology, dealing with the development of life as revealed by the fossil record on different geological strata.

Economic geology is concerned with the study of valuable mineral deposits, such as ores, coal, and oil.

geomagnetic storms sudden alterations in and subsequent recovery of the Earth's magnetic field due to the effects of solar FLARES. The variations are complex in the auroral zone and polar regions but at middle latitudes the horizontal component of the field shows four distinct phases.

The first is *storm sudden commencement* (*SSC*), when a sharp rise in field strength (over 2.5 to 5 minutes) is caused by compression of the MAGNETOSPHERE by a flare-generated shock wave. The second is the *initial phase* (*IP*), when the Earth is surrounded by the high-speed post-shock plasma and field, and is effectively isolated (for between about 30 minutes and several hours) from the interplanetary magnetic field. The surface field strength is higher than the pre-SSC value. In the *main phase* (*MP*) an increase in particle population, or in particle acceleration by reconnection of the geomagnetic and interplanetary fields, or in magnetospheric fluctuations produces a RING CURRENT at three to five Earth radii. This generates a magnetic field opposed to the Earth's and causes a decrease in the surface field strength of 50–400 nanoteslas, which lasts from a few hours to more than a day. During the fourth phase, *recovery phase* (*RP*), which is typically longer than the MP, the ring current decays by diffusion of the trapped particles and plasma instabilities. The surface field strength may return to, or just below, the pre-SSC value.

Geomagnetic storms are usually accompanied by ionospheric and auroral activity, and some may recur after 27 days owing to the persistence of a particular solar ACTIVE REGION or CORONAL HOLE.

geomagnetism the Earth's magnetic field (or its study), which at the Earth's surface approximates that of a bar magnet at the center of the Earth with its axis inclined by 11.4° to the Earth's rotation axis and somewhat off-centered: the north magnetic and geographical poles are much closer together than the south poles. Both sets of poles wander in position. The strength of the magnetic field varies from 0.6 gauss near the magnetic poles to 0.3 gauss near the equator, i.e. from 60–30 microtesla, but can depart by up to 20% from the average without any correlation with major surface features. The dipole field changes only slowly with time but there are larger local variations in strength and direction. Violent short-term fluctuations occur during GEOMAGNETIC STORMS. Studies of magnetized rocks show that the entire magnetic field has reversed in direction about twice every million years in the past 165 million years. Complete reversals (i.e. north pole switching from pointing toward geographic north to pointing south, or vice versa) can occur within a few thousand years. The source of the geomagnetic field is believed to lie in a complex dynamo action in the Earth's liquid iron-rich outer core. Convective motion in this rotating electrically conducting fluid, in the presence of a magnetic field, generates electric currents; these in turn induce a magnetic field. Hence the Earth's field has been maintained. The field existed since at least 2.5, probably 3.5, thousand million years ago. See also MAGNETOSPHERE; RING CURRENT.

geometrical albedo see ALBEDO.

geometrical libration (**optical libration**) see LIBRATION.

geophysics the physics of the Earth. It includes the study of the history, motion, and constitution of the planet; movements within it, such as those associated with continental drift, mountain-building, earthquakes, glaciers, tides, and atmospheric circulation; geomagnetism; and the interaction between the Earth and its interplanetary environment.

GEOS the first all-scientific satellite in geostationary orbit, built by the European Space Agency for the purpose of studying the Earth's MAGNETOSPHERE. GEOS–1, launched in April 1977, failed to reach its planned orbit; GEOS–2 was successfully launched in July 1978 and operated for two years with the reactivated GEOS–1 and some other satellites. Having become redundant it was boosted into a higher orbit in 1984.

geospace the region of space surrounding the Earth and containing the Earth's MAGNETOSPHERE and its various plasma regimes and complex magnetic and electric fields. Satellite missions to study the physics of geospace include EXPLORER I, the ORBITING GEOPHYSICAL OBSERVATORIES, the INTERNATIONAL SUN-EARTH EXPLORERS, the AMPTE missions, and the SOLAR/TERRESTRIAL ENERGY PROGRAM.

geostationary orbit see GEOSYNCHRONOUS ORBIT.

geosynchronous orbit an Earth orbit made by an artificial satellite (moving west to east) that has a period of 24 hours, equal to the Earth's period of rotation on its axis. If the orbit is inclined to the equatorial plane the satellite will appear from Earth to trace out a figure-of-eight, once per day, between latitudes corresponding to the angle of orbital inclination to the equator. If the 24-hour orbit lies in the equatorial plane, and is circular, the satellite will appear from Earth to be almost stationary; the orbit and orbiting body are then termed *geostationary*. A geostationary orbit has an altitude of 36 000 km.

A geosynchronous or geostationary orbit is very difficult to achieve, requiring a very high orbital velocity. Satellites in such orbits are used for communications and navigation and also for certain types of Earth observations. Most communications satellites are now geostationary, with groups of three or more, spaced around the orbit, giving global coverage.

German mounting see EQUATORIAL MOUNTING.

German-Spanish Astronomical Center an observatory on the mountain Calar Alto in

Almeria, Spain at an altitude of 2160 meters. A joint project of Germany and Spain, it is an outpost of the Max Planck Institute for Astronomy (MIPA), Heidelberg. The instruments include a 3.5-meter reflector with a Zerodur primary mirror, operational 1984, a 2.2-meter reflector, operational 1979 and with a twin at the EUROPEAN SOUTHERN OBSERVATORY at La Serena, a 1.5-meter reflector of Madrid University operational (independently) since 1979, a 1.2-meter reflector operational 1975, and a 0.8-meter Schmidt moved from Hamburg Observatory.

GHA *abbrev. for* Greenwich hour angle.

ghost crater a CRATER that has been almost totally buried by lava. Ghost craters survive in the shallow irregular MARIA on the Moon, where they can be made use of to calculate mare depths.

GHz *symbol for* gigahertz, i.e. 10^9 hertz.

Giacobinids (Draconids) a METEOR SHOWER, radiant RA 262°, dec 54° (in Draco), that maximizes on 8 Oct. The parent of the shower is comet GIACOBINI–ZINNER (period 6.6 years). The shower has been seen five times, in 1926, 1933, 1946, 1952, and 1985. In 1933 the Earth crossed the orbit about 80 days after the parent comet and the resulting METEOR STORM was the most spectacular this century. In 1946 the Earth crossed the orbit 15 days behind the comet, and the 4.2-meter radar at Jodrell Bank recorded a maximum of 10 000 meteors per hour; this observation was one of the first major successes of meteor radar astronomy.

Giacobini Zinner (1900 III) a short-period (6.6-year) comet with perihelion near 1 AU and aphelion near 6 AU, discovered in 1900 by M. Giacobini and rediscovered in 1913 by E. Zinner. It has been seen 14 times since discovery, every other apparition leading to a good view from Earth. Ground-based viewing in 1985 was excellent. The INTERNATIONAL-SUN-EARTH-EXPLORER satellite (ISEE–3) was reorbited so that it intercepted the comet on Sept. 11, 1985 when it was near perihelion. The interaction between the comet and the SOLAR WIND was investigated. See also GIACOBINIDS.

giant a large highly luminous star that lies above the MAIN SEQUENCE on the HERTZSPRUNG–RUSSELL DIAGRAM. Giants are grouped in luminosity classes II and III (see SPECTRAL TYPES) and generally have absolute MAGNITUDES brighter than 0. Despite their great size, they are not necessarily more massive than typical main-sequence stars; they have dense central cores, but their atmospheres are very tenuous – a feature that shows in their spectra.

Giants represent a late phase in STELLAR EVOLUTION, when the central hydrogen supplies have been exhausted and the star is 'burning' other nuclei in concentric shells near its core. As these nuclear processes change, the star's size, luminosity, and temperature gradually alter, and it moves about in the *giant region* and HORIZONTAL BRANCH region of the H–R diagram. Most stars cross the instability strip (see PULSATING VARIABLES) at least once, and are then CEPHEID or RR LYRAE variables. In its final stages, a giant becomes rather brighter and moves to the *asymptotic giant branch* just above the giants on the H–R diagram. Capella and Arcturus are typical examples of giant stars. See also GLOBULAR CLUSTER (ILLUSTRATION); RED GIANT; SUPERGIANT.

giant impact hypothesis see MOON.

Giant Meter-wave Radio Telescope see GMRT.

giant molecular clouds (GMCs) huge MOLECULAR CLOUDS that are the main sites for STAR FORMATION in our Galaxy and others. The average linear dimension of a GMC is about 40 parsecs, total mass about 5×10^5 solar masses, with gas temperatures of 15–30 K. GMCs are found to lie mostly in the Galactic plane. Warmer active clouds lie in the spiral arms; smaller cooler clouds are distributed almost randomly throughout the disk. It is estimated that there are between 4000 and 5000 GMCs in the Galaxy, implying a total mass of 2×10^9 solar masses. This represents a large proportion – possibly up to 50% – of the Galaxy's gas content, and is of importance in theories of galactic evolution and structure.

giant planets the planets Jupiter, Saturn, Uranus, and Neptune, which have diameters between 3.9 and 11.2 times that of the Earth and masses of between 14 and 318 Earth masses. They orbit the Sun at mean distances ranging from 5.21 AU for Jupiter to 30.06 AU for Neptune in periods from 11.86 to 164.79 years. All have low densities – from 0.7 to 1.8 times that of water – and are probably composed largely of hydrogen in its molecular or metallic state. Their visible surfaces are thought to be clouds of ammonia or methane. They all have PLANETARY RING systems and share at least 150 satellites between them (see Table 2, Appendix).

giant radio galaxy see RADIO GALAXY.

giant star see GIANT.

gibbous Moon see PHASES, LUNAR.

giga- symbol: G. A prefix to a unit, indicating a multiple of 10^9 of that unit. For example, one gigahertz is 10^9 hertz.

Gillett Telescope see GEMINI TELESCOPES.

Ginga a Japanese X-ray astronomy satellite that was launched into a 600 km, 31° inclination orbit in Feb. 1987, and operated near perfectly until reentry in Nov. 1991. It continued the X-ray studies begun with the satellites HAKUCHO and TENMA. The major payload was a 5000 cm^2 array of PROPORTIONAL COUNTER detectors capable of spectral and variability studies. The mission yielded the most detailed timing and broad-band spectral data available over the 2–20 keV band on a wide range of cosmic sources. Initially operated as a Japanese/UK collaboration, Ginga observations were subsequently opened up to world-wide use. Major advances included: the discovery of spectral features in ACTIVE GALACTIC NUCLEI, arising from reflection in previously unseen cold dense matter; measurement of temperature and chemical abundance differences in CLUSTERS OF GALAXIES, indicative of evolution and merging; resolution of DOPPLER shifted iron K-line emission from the galactic binary source SS433; the discovery of many new CATACLYSMIC VARIABLES and several galactic BLACK HOLE candidate systems. Complete archives (X-ray databases) of the Ginga data have now been established at ISAS and Leicester University, UK. See also ASCA.

Giotto an ESA spacecraft launched in July 1985 into Earth orbit from where it was fired into a trajectory that intercepted the path of HALLEY'S COMET on Mar. 13, 1986. Giotto was steered deep into the comet's coma to within 600 km of the cometary NUCLEUS. Data was gathered over a period of about 10 hours. Its 10 instruments recorded many images at various wavelengths, measured the composition of the coma and the mass, distribution, and composition of the dust tail, and analyzed the dynamics of the cometary plasma and its interaction with the solar wind. Though damaged by multiple impacts, Giotto continued its mission.

After a period of 'hibernation', the spacecraft was retargeted by an Earth flyby so that it would intersect the comet GRIGG–SKJELLERUP on July 12, 1992. It flew by at a distance of 200 km on the antisun side. Dust, gas, and plasma were investigated but the camera that had been so successful at Halley did not operate.

glitch see PULSAR; NEUTRON STAR.

Global Oscillations Network Group (GONG) a program for the continuous monitoring of solar oscillations (see HELIOSEISMOLOGY), coordinated by the US NATIONAL SOLAR OBSERVATORY. Six observatories spaced at approximately 60° intervals of longitude around the world form the observational network.

global positioning system (GPS) a satellite-based coordinate positioning tool and navigation system that can rapidly and accurately determine the latitude, longitude, and altitude of a point on or above the Earth's surface. It is based on a constellation of 24 satellites orbiting the Earth at a very high altitude and uses a form of triangulation based on the known positions and distances of three satellites relative to the surface of the Earth. First developed by the US Department of Defense to provide the military with a state-of-the-art positioning system, GPS receivers are now small enough and economical enough to be used by the general public. In meteorology and climatology, GPS receivers are increasingly used, for example, in RADIOSONDES, and have experimentally been used in the measurement of integrated (total column) precipitable water vapor.

globular cluster a spherically symmetrical

compact CLUSTER of stars, containing from several tens of thousands to maybe a million stars that are thought to share a common origin. An example is the GREAT CLUSTER IN HERCULES. A few globular clusters, such as OMEGA CENTAURI, appear to be slightly flattened. The concentration of stars increases greatly toward the center of the cluster, where the density may be as much as 1000 stars per cubic parsec. Globular clusters occur in our GALAXY and in other galaxies. About 150 are known in the Galaxy. Most appear to move in giant and highly eccentric elliptical orbits about the galactic center, and, unlike OPEN CLUSTERS, are not concentrated toward the galactic plane; instead they show a roughly spherical distribution in the galactic halo. About 20% are found in the galactic disk, moving in more circular orbits.

Globular clusters are POPULATION II systems (~80% halo population II): all the stars within them are relatively old (older than the Sun) and have a very low metal content; the METALLICITY varies from cluster to cluster, but in most clusters all stars have very similar chemical compositions. The galactic disk clusters are younger and more metal-rich than the halo objects. The stars that dominate the visual output of globular clusters are RED GIANTS, the bluer horizontal-branch GIANTS becoming dominant at shorter wavelengths. Although very few ordinary binary stars are observed in globular clusters, many contain strong X-ray sources typical of X-RAY BINARIES or CATACLYSMIC VARIABLES, i.e. systems containing a neutron star or a white dwarf, respectively.

The distribution and other characteristics of globular clusters suggest that they were formed early in the life of the Galaxy. The oldest formed possibly some 12 to 16 billion years ago, before the main body of the galactic disk had evolved. Because most of the member stars will have evolved away from the main sequence, the HERTZSPRUNG–RUSSELL DIAGRAM for stars

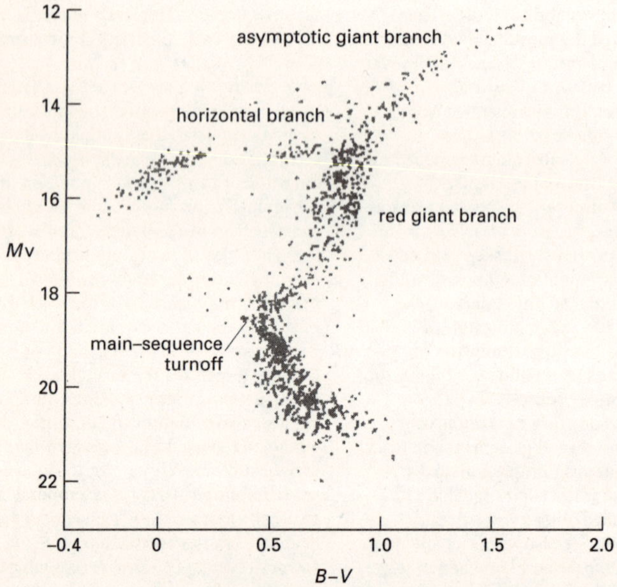

Color-magnitude diagram for typical globular cluster

of a globular cluster differs greatly from the conventional H–R diagram (see illustration). The luminosity at the TURNOFF POINT from the main sequence gives a measure of the age of a cluster, given the distance. Distances to globular clusters are usually calculated from the apparent magnitudes of the RR LYRAE STARS within them. Although the age of the oldest globular clusters is disputed, the difference between the ages of clusters can be measured more precisely. Evidence is mounting of a spread in ages of several billion years.

gluon see QUARK.

GMC *abbrev. for* giant molecular cloud.

GMRT *abbrev. for* Giant Meter-wave Radio Telescope. The world's largest radio telescope operating at meter and decimeter wavelengths, located 80 km north of Pune in India. It is an APERTURE SYNTHESIS array consisting of 30 fully steerable parabolic DISHES, each of 45-meter diameter, operating at six frequency bands in the range 38 to 1420 MHz. The dish surfaces are of a novel design called SMART, using a thin wire mesh stretched over rope trusses. Twelve of the dishes are in a central array one kilometer square, and the remaining eighteen are distributed along three 14-km tracks in a Y-shaped configuration (compare VLA). The telescope is designed to look for highly redshifted HYDROGEN-LINE emission from the early Universe, and to study MILLISECOND PULSARS with a view to measuring primordial GRAVITATIONAL WAVES.

GMST *abbrev. for* Greenwich mean sidereal time.

GMT *abbrev. for* Greenwich mean time.

gnomon a device used in ancient times to measure the altitude of the Sun and hence to determine the time of day and time of year. It consisted of a vertical shaft of known height (such as an upright rod or pillar) that cast a shadow of measurable length and direction on a graduated horizontal base. The ratio of height to shadow length gave the tangent of the altitude angle. The term is also applied to the metal projection on a sundial, used for the same purpose.

Goddard Space Flight Center a NASA establishment at Greenbelt, Maryland, that is a major center for basic astronomical research and the design, development, and management of near-Earth orbiting spacecraft. It is also concerned with suborbital flights. It is an astronomical data center.

Goldstone see DEEP SPACE NETWORK.

GONG *abbrev. for* Global Oscillations Network Group.

GOODS *abbrev. for* Great Observatories Origins Deep Survey. See GREAT OBSERVATORIES.

Gossamer Ring see JUPITER'S RINGS.

Gould Belt (**Local System**) a local formation of stars and clouds of gas and dust that appears to be a spur attached to the lower edge of the Orion arm of the GALAXY. It contains many of the apparently brightest stars in the sky, which follow the projection of the system across the sky in a 'belt' at 16° to the line of the Milky Way. The system is about 700 parsecs wide and 70 parsecs thick and includes the II Persei, Scorpio-Centaurus, and Orion OB-associations (see ASSOCIATION). The Sun lies approximately 12 parsecs north of the Belt's equatorial plane and about 100 parsecs from its center.

GPS see GLOBAL POSITIONING SYSTEM.

graben an elongated depression of land between two FAULTS. Lunar graben are usually 1–2 km wide and may be hundreds of kilometers in length.

gram a unit of mass equal to one thousandth of a KILOGRAM.

GRANAT a Russian satellite devoted to high-energy astronomy, launched in Dec. 1989 into a highly eccentric orbit (apogee: 30 Earth radii, perigee: 3000 km) with a period of 4.09 days and inclination 49°. The payload includes two types of instruments.

The narrow-field instruments – SIGMA, ART–P, and ART–S – are designed to observe point sources at a variety of energies. SIGMA is a CODED-MASK TELESCOPE imaging low-energy γ-ray sources in the energy range 30–2000 keV; it can also make spectral and temporal measurements. ART–P is an X-ray imaging telescope with a coded mask and four independent gas PROPORTIONAL COUNTERS; operating over thc energy range 3–100 keV, it is designed to provide X-ray images of localized sources. ART–S is a hard X-ray/γ-ray spectroscope constructed from four gas proportional counters; operating over the spectral range 3–150 keV, it performs spectral and time analysis of relatively bright localized sources.

The wide-field telescopes – Phebus and Konus – are designed to observe the entire sky and detect transient events, especially GAMMA-RAY BURSTS. Both have detector elements distributed around the spacecraft for all-sky coverage, and provide the location as well as a spectral and time analysis of the bursts. Phebus operates over the energy range 0.1–100 MeV, Konus over the range 0.02–20 MeV.

The payload also includes the Tournasol experiment, which has a narrow field of view but can also observe transient events because it is on a gimbal mount that can slew automatically to the direction of a burst localized by Konus. Mounted on the gimbal are two optical detectors and four proportional counters, designed for the optical detection of γ-ray bursts and the X-ray spectral analysis (2–20 keV) of any burst decay 'tails'.

grand unified theories (**GUTs**) see FUNDAMENTAL FORCES.

granulation a network of convective cells in the solar PHOTOSPHERE. It consists of bright irregularly shaped (often polygonal) *granules,* separated by dark narrow intergranular lanes. The individual granules are about 1000 km in diameter, have an upward velocity of about 0.5 km s^{-1}, and exhibit a horizontal flow of material – outward from the center – with a velocity of about 0.25 km s^{-1}; their average lifetime is about 8 minutes. They represent the changing tops of currents from the CONVECTIVE ZONE, bringing hot gases to the photosphere, where the gases cool and then return via the intergranular lanes.

Granulation is readily visible under favorable conditions, when it gives the photosphere a mottled appearance. It may be best seen near the center of the Sun's disk, where foreshortening is not significant. See also SUPERGRANULATION.

graticule a glass plate or cell bearing a grid, cross wires, or graduated scale that is set in the focal plane of the eyepiece of a telescope and is used for positioning or measuring.

grating *short for* diffraction grating.

grating response see ARRAY; APERTURE SYNTHESIS.

grating spectrograph a SPECTROGRAPH in which a DIFFRACTION GRATING is used to produce the spectra.

gravitation the ability of all material bodies to attract each other. This mutual attraction, or *gravitational force,* is the most familiar force of nature and was first expressed in mathematical form by Isaac Newton. *Newton's law of universal gravitation* was published in 1687 in *Principia.* It states that the force of attraction, F, between two bodies is proportional to the product of their masses, m_1 and m_2, and inversely proportional to the square of their distance apart, d:

$$F = Gm_1m_2/d^2$$

The constant of proportionality, G, is the GRAVITATIONAL CONSTANT. The force experienced by the mass m_1 is equal to but in the opposite direction to that felt by the mass m_2: the two masses are attracted toward each other. Newton showed that any body behaves, gravitationally, as if its mass were concentrated at its center. Thus gravitational force acts along a line joining the center of two bodies. In a system in equilibrium, such as the Solar System or a star like the Sun, gravitational force is balanced by an equal force acting in the opposite direction.

The region of space surrounding a massive body and in which the gravitational force is appreciable is the *gravitational field* of that body. The magnitude of the field at a particular point is the gravitational acceleration (in the direction of the massive body) that would be experienced by any object at that point; this is equivalent to the force that would be experienced by an object of unit mass at that point. A gravitational field depends on the distribution of matter that causes it. Its effect is on another distribution of matter. The *gravitational potential* at a point in a gravitational field is the work done in bringing unit mass to this point from a point infinitely distant from the cause of the field; it is thus the potential energy of a particle of unit mass arising from the mass of a material body.

Gravitation is the weakest force known. It is many orders of magnitude smaller than the other FUNDAMENTAL FORCES of nature – the strong, electromagnetic, and weak interactions. It is, however, the only means by which bodies can interact over immense distances.

Newton's theory of gravitation has proved adequate in most circumstances but was challenged by the more complex general theory of RELATIVITY put forward by Albert Einstein in 1915. According to general relativity, gravitational fields change the geometry of SPACETIME: both space and time are curved or warped around a massive body. Matter tells spacetime how to curve and spacetime tells matter how to move. See also KEPLER'S LAWS; QUANTUM GRAVITATION.

gravitational collapse contraction of a body arising from the mutual gravitational pull of all its constituents. Although there are several examples of such contraction processes in astronomy, 'gravitational collapse' usually refers to the sudden collapse of the core of a massive star at the end of nuclear burning, when its internal gas pressure can no longer support its weight. For a massive star this may initially result in a SUPERNOVA explosion, removing much of the star's mass. The eventual degree of gravitational collapse is determined by the mass that remains after a supernova, or after any other form of MASS LOSS. The three most likely end-products (in order of increasing mass) are WHITE DWARFS, NEUTRON STARS, and BLACK HOLES.

gravitational constant symbol: G. A universal constant that appears in Newton's law of GRAVITATION and is the force of attraction between two bodies of unit mass separated by unit distance. It is equal to 6.672×10^{-11} N m^2 kg^{-2}. Predictions that G is decreasing very slightly with time (by less than one part in 10^{10}) are not supported by experimental evidence.

gravitational field see GRAVITATION.

gravitational force see GRAVITATION.

gravitational instability the tendency for fluctuations in an inhomogeneous medium to grow because of self-gravitation. It is opposed by pressure forces. The critical length-scale beyond which such condensations collapse is known as a *Jeans length*, and the *Jeans mass* it encloses eventually forms a stable gravitationally bound system. The Jeans length is thus often taken as a characteristic length-scale for gravitational collapse; an INTERSTELLAR CLOUD larger than the Jeans length will fragment into clumps with this characteristic size. See also GALAXIES, FORMATION AND EVOLUTION.

gravitational lens a concept arising from the fact that a gravitational field bends light, and hence a concentration of mass can focus light rays in a manner similar to that of a lens. In the illustration overleaf, the observer at O sees two apparent images S′ of the background source S caused by *lensing* effects of the intervening galaxy. The theory of gravitational lensing was discussed by both Einstein and Lodge in 1919, and its applications to cosmology realized by Zwicky in 1937, but the first known gravitational lens (the DOUBLE QUASAR) was not discovered until 1979. Lensing by a smooth mass distribution such as a galaxy or a cluster of galaxies is known as *macrolensing*, and can occur in several forms.

The simplest form of gravitational lensing is where a pointlike background source, usually a QUASAR, is split into multiple images, the location and number of which are dependent on the relative geometry of the source and lens. The lens will distort and concentrate the original path of the light, so that an image will also appear brighter, or *magnified*. Different images forming a multiple system may have their luminosities magnified by different factors. Cases of double, triple and even quadruple lensing have been found (e.g. the CLOVERLEAF and the EINSTEIN CROSS). In most cases the lensing galaxy is not observed. Theoretical models of gravitational lensing predict that there should always be an odd number of images so both the double and quadruple systems are expected to have a central image that is too faint to be detected.

If the background object is a distant galaxy that is itself extended, the lensed images are smeared out into long luminous

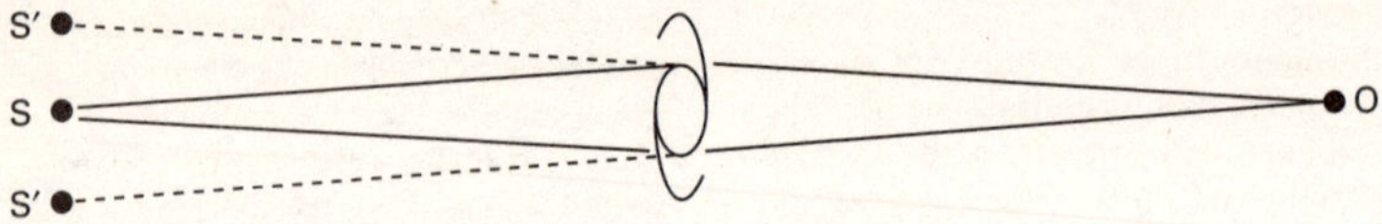

Gravitational lensing

arcs several arc seconds long. Such arcs are commonly observed in the core of rich clusters of galaxies, usually elongated tangentially to the cluster center and bluer in color than the cluster member galaxies. In several clusters many tens of smaller *arclets* are seen, which originate from *weak lensing* of background galaxies that are not so strongly magnified. The most extreme case of gravitational lensing is observed when an extended background source is exactly aligned with a symmetrical lens. The lensed image takes the form of an *Einstein ring*.

The alteration in the light path to the quasar will result in different TIMES OF FLIGHT for each image. If the quasar itself is variable, then a corresponding time delay for the brightening to be seen in each component of the image may be measured. The difference in the light travel time is related to the inverse of the HUBBLE CONSTANT, so it is theoretically possible to estimate H_0 from such time delays. In practice, precise modeling of the lens geometry is required before H_0 can be well constrained.

It is possible that individual stars in a lensing galaxy can cross the light path to the quasar and cause fluctuations in image brightness known as *microlensing*. This effect can also be seen when objects known as MACHOS in the galactic halo lens the light from an extragalactic star to cause a large amplification in its brightness, although such events are very rare.

gravitational mass see MASS.

gravitational potential see GRAVITATION.

gravitational radiation see GRAVITATIONAL WAVES.

gravitational redshift (Einstein shift) the REDSHIFT of spectral lines that occurs when radiation, including light, is emitted from a massive body. In order to 'climb out' of the body's gravitational field, the radiation must lose energy. The radiation frequency must therefore decrease and its wavelength λ, shift by Δλ toward a greater value. The redshift is given by

$$\Delta\lambda/\lambda = Gm/c^2r$$

G is the gravitational constant, *m* and *r* the mass and radius of the massive body, and *c* is the speed of light. Gravitational redshift was predicted by Einstein's general theory of RELATIVITY and although extremely small has been detected, for example, in the spectra of the Sun and several WHITE DWARFS. The redshift of the Earth's gravitational field has been determined very accurately using beams of radiation traveling upward through a tall building. Predicted and measured values agree very closely.

gravitational waves (gravitational radiation) extremely weak wavelike disturbances that were predicted by Einstein's general theory of RELATIVITY. They represent the radiation associated with the gravitational force, and are produced when massive bodies are accelerated or otherwise disturbed. They are ripples in the fabric of SPACETIME that travel at the speed of light, with a wide range of frequencies, and carry energy away from the source. They should affect all matter: gravitational waves hitting a suspended body, for example, should make it vibrate slightly. The interactions are very small, however.

No conclusive direct evidence of the existence of gravitational waves has been forthcoming from the various highly sensitive experiments designed to detect them. Laser interferometers could be sufficiently sensitive. They consist of two identical extremely long tubes, set at right angles and with mirrors at both ends. A laser beam is split and sent down the tubes. A relative change in the two lengths would indicate a passing gravitational wave, and would be seen in the interference patterns produced when the reflected beams are recombined.

Gravitational waves should be emitted during supernova explosions or energetic events in the cores of active galaxies. They should also be emitted by two massive stars in close orbit. Recent observations of the BINARY PULSAR PSR 1913+16 show that its orbital period is decreasing by 76 ± 2 microseconds per year. The observed value corresponds almost exactly with the decrease predicted to result from the emission of gravitational waves (75 μs per year) and is at present the best indirect evidence for their existence.

A quantum of gravitational radiation is known as a *graviton*, analogous to a PHOTON.

graviton see GRAVITATIONAL WAVES; QUANTUM GRAVITATION.

gravity 1 *another name for* gravitation. 2 the apparent force of gravitation on an object at or near the surface of a planet, satellite, etc.

gravity assist an astronautical technique whereby a spacecraft takes up a tiny fraction of the orbital energy of a planet that it is flying past, allowing it to change direction and speed. It has been used, for example, in the VOYAGER and ULYSSES missions.

Gravity Probe B a US mission to test two predictions of Einstein's general theory of relativity, launched Apr. 2004. The mission, developed jointly by NASA and Stanford University, aims to verify these predictions: it will seek to assess (1) how the presence of the Earth warps space and time and (2) how the Earth's rotation drags space and time around with it. The effects of the Earth on space and time are minute and have hitherto gone undetected and therefore unmeasured. The Gravity Probe B is designed to measure them for the first time. It will seek to do so using four gyroscopes housed within an artificial satellite orbiting directly over the Earth's poles at an altitude of 640 km. Free from external disturbances and cooled to near absolute zero to eliminate disruptions caused by their own molecular structures, the gyroscopes are near perfect spheres spinning in a vacuum and designed to provide direction measurements that are 30 million times as accurate as any gyroscope ever built before. If Einstein's predictions are correct, the gyroscopes should help to detect that very small amounts of space and time are missing from each orbit. In order to measure each orbit accurately, the gyroscopes are lined up with a guide star by means of a tracking telescope, and a magnetic-field measuring instrument records any changes with respect to the guide star. The mission was scheduled to run for a total of 18 months, including 16 months of data collection. It is set to end in late 2005.

grazing incidence X-rays reflect from surfaces for the same physical reason that light reflects, mainly due to coherent scattering in the surface material. However, since X-ray photon energies are large, the REFRACTIVE INDEX, n, is slightly less than unity and reflection occurs only up to a critical angle, θ, where $\cos \theta = n$. The angle θ is usually small and thus X-ray reflection is only high for rays that graze the surface; hence 'grazing incidence'. For example θ is about 1° for a gold surface and X-rays of wavelengths of about 0.3 nm (4 keV). θ is proportional to X-ray wavelength and also increases with the ATOMIC NUMBER of the reflecting surface.

The space station SKYLAB was the first space mission to carry a large grazing incidence X-ray telescope, in fact two, both of which produced many high-resolution X-ray images of the solar corona in 1973–74. With two coaxial reflectors (usually a paraboloid/hyperboloid pair), high-quality X-ray images are produced over a field of view of order of the grazing angle. The great potential of such optical systems for cosmic X-ray astronomy was first demonstrated with the flight of a 60-cm diameter grazing incidence telescope on the EINSTEIN OBSERVATORY in 1978–81. Subsequently, most X-ray astronomy satellites have employed or will employ this technique.

grazing occultation a lunar OCCULTATION in which the astronomical body is only momentarily occulted by mountain peaks along the Moon's limb.

Great Attractor a large concentration of mass that is detectable only by its powerful gravitational pull on our Galaxy and its LOCAL SUPERCLUSTER. Redshift surveys in the late 1980s revealed that the PECULIAR MOTION of the Local Group relative to the microwave background was not due solely to the gravitational effect of the VIRGO CLUSTER, but also to LARGE-SCALE STRUCTURE just beyond the Hydra–Centaurus supercluster in the southern sky.

Great Bear common name for URSA MAJOR.

great circle the circular intersection on the surface of a sphere of any plane passing through the center of the sphere. A sphere and its great circles are thus concentric and of equal radius. Compare SMALL CIRCLE.

Great Cluster in Hercules (M13; NGC 6205) the finest GLOBULAR CLUSTER to be seen from the northern hemisphere, discovered in Hercules by Edmund Halley in 1714. It has a dense broad center that is just visible to the naked eye; a 7.5-cm telescope will show some of the outer stars.

Great Dark Spot a prominent feature in Neptune's atmosphere, similar in many ways to Jupiter's GREAT RED SPOT. The Great Dark Spot measures roughly 12 000 km by 8000 km and, scaled down by the same factor that Neptune's diameter is smaller than Jupiter's, occupies a similar proportion of surface area to that occupied by the Great Red Spot. The Great Dark Spot is a high-pressure system around which winds flow in a counterclockwise direction. Wind speeds around the Great Dark Spot are near supersonic at about 700 m s^{-1}.

greatest elongation (GE) see ELONGATION.

Great Observatories NASA's four major orbiting observatories launched between 1990 and 2003. In chronological order of launch, they are: the HUBBLE SPACE TELESCOPE (HST), observing at ultraviolet and optical wavelengths; the COMPTON GAMMA RAY OBSERVATORY (CGRO); the CHANDRA X-RAY OBSERVATORY, which originally was to form part of the more ambitious Advanced X-Ray Astrophysics Facility (see AXAF); and the SPITZER SPACE TELESCOPE, formerly known as the Space Infrared Telescope Facility. Of the four satellites, only the Compton Gamma Ray Observatory had ended its mission by the start of 2005. In June 2004 NASA announced that the three Great Observatories still in orbit would collaborate with the European Space Agency's XMM-NEWTON satellite and some of the best groundbased observatories on a survey of deep sky objects called the Great Observatories Origins Deep Survey (*GOODS*). This survey will focus on two 150-square-arcminute portions of sky, one in the center of the Hubble Deep Field North, the other in the Chandra Deep Field South. GOODS will provide a multi-wavelength analysis of these regions to supply us with a rich legacy of data that will extend our knowledge about the remote and early universe.

Great Red Spot (GRS) an immense oval feature centered 22° south of Jupiter's equator. It is variable in size and color. At its largest it can be 40 000 by 14 000 km, but at the time of the VOYAGER flybys, it was only slightly larger than the Earth. Its color – possibly associated with the conversion of phosphene into red phosphorus – has varied from pale pink to bright red. Often visible from Earth through small telescopes, it has been persisted as a feature of Jupiter ever since astronomers made the first telescopic observations in the 17th century. Early explanations involved a solid island adrift in Jupiter's atmosphere or an atmospheric disturbance above a Jovian mountain or basin; the latter was disputed by evidence that it drifts in longitude. Infrared data from PIONEER, Voyager, and GALILEO spacecraft confirm that the spot is an anticyclonic high-pressure region that is much colder than its surroundings and at a higher elevation. In effect it is a vast high-pressure storm. Examination of cloud motions in and around the GRS reveal that the spot rotates counterclockwise with a period of about six days. The winds to the north of the spot are blowing to the west, the winds to the south move toward the east.

Great Rift a chainlike complex of large DARK NEBULAE that more or less obscures the light from a narrow but extensive band of the Milky Way between the constellations Cygnus and Sagittarius.

Great Square of Pegasus see PEGASUS.

Great Wall see LARGE-SCALE STRUCTURE.

Greek alphabet see STELLAR NOMENCLATURE; Table 5, Appendix.

Green Bank original location, in West Virginia, of the NATIONAL RADIO ASTRONOMY OBSERVATORY. In Nov. 1988, the 91-meter diameter meridian transit telescope at Green Bank collapsed after 26 years of use. Its replacement – the *Green Bank Telescope* (*GBT*) – is the world's largest fully steerable dish, with a height of nearly 145 meters and an aperture of 100 by 110 meters. The subreflector and prime-focus feed for the dish is supported on a long boom arm extending over the top edge of the structure and offset so that it does not block the view. The primary surface is composed of 2209 panels whose position can be determined and adjusted using laser distance-measuring equipment; the adjusted surface should have an accuracy of 220 μm and operate at up to 86 GHz.

green flash a shortlived phenomenon sometimes observed immediately before sunset whereby the last segment of the Sun's limb turns green just as it is about to sink below the horizon. The effect, resulting from refraction and absorption by the Earth's atmosphere, is sometimes followed by the appearance of a vertical green ray at the very instant of sunset. The same phenomenon may sometimes be observed at the moment of sunrise. The green flash is best seen in an area where the horizon is uninterrupted, typically at sea.

greenhouse effect a phenomenon in which a rise in temperature is caused because incoming radiation at certain wavelengths can pass through a barrier, be absorbed, and then re-emitted as radiation at longer wavelengths, which is absorbed by the barrier. In a glass greenhouse, solar radiation in the form of visible and (some) ultraviolet radiation is able to pass through the Earth's atmosphere and through the glass of the greenhouse. The radiation is absorbed by any surface it falls on, causing a rise in temperature. As a result these surfaces emit heat radiation (i.e. electromagnetic radiation in the infrared), which is absorbed by the glass, causing an overall increase in temperature inside the greenhouse. The analogous process occurs for a planet with the 'glass' being the planet's atmosphere. On Earth, for example, the atmosphere allows visible and ultraviolet through, but certain gases in the atmosphere absorb strongly in the infrared. These so-called *greenhouse gases* include water vapor (the main greenhouse gas), carbon dioxide, and methane. The greenhouse effect is not a bad thing – it is essential for keeping the Earth warm enough to support life. However, in recent times environmentalists have become concerned about the phenomenon of *global warming*, i.e. an increase of 0.3–0.6°C in the average temperature of air at the Earth's surface since the late 19th century. This could be a part of a natural cycle (essentially the end of the last 'Little Ice Age'), but there is evidence that this global warming could be the result of the greenhouse effect. The main suspect is carbon dioxide. The concentration of carbon dioxide in the atmosphere has risen by 25–30 % over the last 200 years as a result of human activity – deforestation and the burning of fossil fuels (coal, oil, and natural gas). Levels of methane in the atmosphere have also doubled in the last 100 years. There is a fear that an excess of greenhouse gases in the atmosphere will heat the planet too much and adversely affect weather patterns. A runaway greenhouse effect is responsible for the high surface temperature of Venus, where no water exists and life is impossible. A greenhouse effect also operates in the deep atmospheres of the giant planets and on Saturn's large satellite Titan.

Greenwich hour angle (**GHA**) the HOUR ANGLE of a celestial body or point on the Greenwich meridian. It is equal to the Greenwich sidereal time minus the right ascension (in hours) of the body or point.

Greenwich mean sidereal time (**GMST**) the GREENWICH HOUR ANGLE of the mean equinox of date (see MEAN EQUATOR AND EQUINOX). UNIVERSAL TIME is defined in terms of GMST by a mathematical formula.

Greenwich mean time (**GMT**) the MEAN SOLAR TIME on the longitude (0°) at

Greenwich, in the UK, reckoned from midnight. In 1928, on the recommendation of the IAU, GMT became known as UNIVERSAL TIME (UT) for scientific purposes; the version coordinated universal time, available since 1972 from broadcast signals, is now generally known as GMT.

Greenwich Observatory see ROYAL GREENWICH OBSERVATORY.

Greenwich sidereal date (GSD) a concept analogous to that of the JULIAN DATE. It is the number of SIDEREAL DAYS that have elapsed at Greenwich since the beginning of the sidereal day that was in progress on Julian date 0.0. The integral part of the date is the *Greenwich sidereal day number*; the fractional part is the GREENWICH SIDEREAL TIME.

Greenwich sidereal time (GST) the SIDEREAL TIME on the Greenwich meridian. See also LOCAL SIDEREAL TIME.

Gregorian calendar the calendar that is now in use throughout most of the world and that was instituted in 1582 by Pope Gregory XIII as the revised version of the JULIAN CALENDAR. The simple Julian four-year rule for leap years was modified so that when considering century years only one out of four, i.e. only those divisible by 400, were to be leap years: 1700, 1800, and 1900 were not leap years. There are therefore 365.2425 days per year averaged over 400 years. This greatly reduced the discrepancy between the year of 365.25 days used in the Julian calendar and the 365.2422 days of the TROPICAL YEAR, which had resulted in the accumulation of 14 days over the centuries.

The revision came into effect in Roman Catholic countries in 1582, the year being brought back into accord with the seasons by eliminating 10 days from October: Thursday Oct. 4 was followed by Friday Oct. 15. The vernal EQUINOX, which would have occurred on Mar. 11 and which had originally fallen on Mar. 25 in Julius Caesar's time was thus adjusted to Mar. 21. Gregory also stipulated that the New Year should begin on Jan. 1. Non-Catholic countries were slow to accept the advantages of the Gregorian reform. Britain and its colonies switched in 1752 when an additional day had accumulated between old and new calendars: Sept. 2, 1752 was followed by Sept. 14 and New Year's Day was changed from Mar. 25 to Jan. 1, beginning with the year 1752. The very slight discrepancy between the Gregorian year and the tropical year amounts to about three days in 10 000 years.

Gregorian telescope the first compound REFLECTING TELESCOPE to be devised, designed by the 17th-century Scottish mathematician James Gregory. It has a small concave secondary mirror that is mounted beyond the focal plane and reflects the light back through a central hole in the paraboloid primary mirror (see illustration). The design, published in 1663 in Gregory's book *Optica promota*, requires a secondary mirror of ellipsoid figure. It has a small field limited mainly by COMA. In the *aplanatic Gregorian*, which uses an ellipsoidal primary, coma and spherical aberration are both eliminated but the field is limited by astigmatism. Because of the imperfect grinding techniques available to him

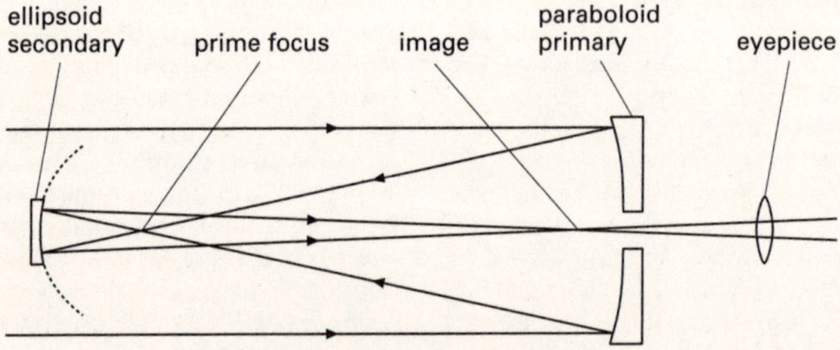

Ray path in Gregorian telescope

during the early 1660s, Gregory was unable to build the telescope he designed before Newton and Cassegarin produced their reflectors in the following decade. The more compact CASSEGRAIN CONFIGURATION, similar to the Gregorian design, is usually preferred.

Grigg–Skjellerup comet a comet that, after Encke, has the second shortest cometary period, 5.1 years. The retargeted spacecraft GIOTTO flew by the comet in July 1992 on the side away from the Sun at a distance of 200 km. Dust, gas, and plasma were investigated but no pictures could be taken.

Grimaldi see table at CRATERS.

ground state see ENERGY LEVEL.

groups of galaxies small isolated collections of from three to a hundred galaxies, examples being the LOCAL GROUP and STEPHAN'S QUINTET. Most are gravitationally bound systems but a few may be due to chance line-of-sight projections. If the groups are bound and stable their MASS-TO-LUMINOSITY RATIO must be high. The most extreme groups where several galaxies are in close proximity to each other are known as *compact groups of galaxies*. The members of such groups often show morphological features typical of INTERACTING GALAXIES.

Grus (Crane) a fairly conspicuous but isolated constellation in the southern hemisphere, the two brightest stars, Alpha (α) Gruis, or Alnair (a blue main sequence star) and Beta (β) Gruis, or Al Dhanab (a red giant), being of 1st and 2nd magnitude respectively. Abbrev.: Gru; genitive form: Gruis; approx. position: RA 22.5h, dec –50°; area: 366 sq deg.

GSD *abbrev. for* Greenwich sideral date.

GST *abbrev. for* Greenwich sidereal time.

G stars stars of SPECTRAL TYPE G that are yellow stars with a surface temperature (T_{eff}) of about 4900 to 6000 kelvin. The lines of ionized calcium (Ca II, H and K) dominate the spectrum and there are a large number of strong neutral metal lines (strengthening) and ionized metal lines (weakening) from G0 to G9. Molecular bands of CH and CN appear. The Sun, Alpha Centauri, and Capella are G stars.

G-type asteroids see C-TYPE ASTEROIDS.

guide star see GUIDE TELESCOPE.

Guide Star Catalog a catalog of celestial objects, mainly stars, compiled at the Space Telescope Science Institute during the early 1980s. It served as the database for the sensitive guidance system of the HUBBLE SPACE TELESCOPE. In its earliest published form, Version 1.2, it contained the positions of about 19 million objects, including some of the 16th magnitude. It was superseded by Version 2.2, which contained the positions for 435 million celestial objects down to the 19th magnitude. The Guide Star Catalog was compiled from the analysis of photographic plates and contains no proper motions. It is available on CD-ROM.

guide telescope a telescope carried upon the same mounting as one used for photography or with instruments, to ensure that the camera, etc., is accurately guided for the whole of an exposure, which may be of many hours duration. For this duty a high magnification and an illuminated graticule are required. The telescope drives must also be provided with slow motions in both axes so that corrections can be applied manually as the selected *guide star* begins to drift from the cross wires. Manual guidance may now be avoided by using automatic devices – *autoguiders* – that monitor the position of the guide star image electronically and adjust the drive to hold it steady.

Gum nebula an immense EMISSION NEBULA that dominates the Milky Way in the southern constellations Puppis and Vela. It is an expanding shell of ionized gas some 35° in diameter. It is thought to be one of the closest supernova remnants to the Solar System; the center is estimated to be about 400 parsecs distant but the outer edge closest to us may be as little as 100 parsecs away. It has been suggested that the Gum nebula is a fossil STRÖMGREN SPHERE produced by a supernova that exploded maybe up to a million years ago and gave off sufficient ultraviolet radiation to ionize interstellar gas out to an immense distance. Several very hot stars within the shell are now ionizing the gas, thus preventing it from returning to a neutral state. The nebula takes its name from the Australian astronomer Colin Gum (1924–1960), who first identified and photographed it in 1952.

The VELA PULSAR and its supernova remnant lie in the same direction as the Gum nebula.

Gunn–Peterson test a test for the presence of neutral hydrogen and singly-ionized helium in the diffuse INTERGALACTIC MEDIUM, first proposed by J.E. Gunn and B.A. Peterson in 1965. Such hydrogen and helium are expected to cause absorption of a quasar continuum shortward of its rest-frame Lyman emission lines; the fact that this continuum is detected (in between the Lyman-alpha forest) reveals that most of the IGM is already highly ionized, at least to a redshift of 4–5.

GUT *abbrev. for* grand unified theory. See FUNDAMENTAL FORCES.

gyrofrequency see SYNCHROTRON EMISSION.

Hh

H I *symbol for* spectrum of the neutral hydrogen atom, or the atom itself. See HYDROGEN; H I REGION.

H II *symbol for* spectrum of the singly ionized hydrogen ion, or the ion itself. See HYDROGEN; H II REGION.

HA *abbrev. for* hour angle.

Hadar see BETA CENTAURI.

Hadley Rille (**Rima Hadley**) a sinuous RILLE in Palus Putredinis, adjacent to the Apennine (third) ring of the IMBRIUM BASIN. It was sampled by the crew of APOLLO 15.

hadron see ELEMENTARY PARTICLES. See also BIG BANG THEORY.

Hakucho the first Japanese X-ray astronomy satellite, launched in Feb. 1979 and operating until re-entry in late 1984. Its payload included several small nonimaging detectors well matched to the study of variability in the brighter galactic X-ray sources. Extended observations of X-ray pulsars and of X-ray burst sources were the major scientific contributions. See also ASCA; GINGA; TENMA.

HALCA see VSOP.

Hale-Bopp (**1995 O1**) large bright comet discovered by Alan Hale and Thomas Bopp in July 1995. Reaching perihelion in 1997, its maximum brightness was about magnitude –1, with a core 40 km across.

Hale telescope see PALOMAR OBSERVATORY.

half-life the time taken for the number of atoms of a radioactive isotope to be reduced, by radioactive decay, to one half. The *mean life* is the average time before decay of a large number of similar elementary particles or atoms of a radioisotope. Mean life is equal to 1.44 times the half-life.

half-wave dipole see DIPOLE.

half-width half the width of a spectral line, measured at half the height. In some branches of spectroscopy it is customary to use the term to mean the full width at half height. See also EQUIVALENT WIDTH; LINE PROFILE.

Halley's comet a comet that was first positively recorded in 240 BC and has a period of 76 years on average, one return coinciding with the Battle of Hastings (1066) and leading to the comet's representation on the Bayeux Tapestry. The orbit is retrograde, the comet moving in the opposite direction to the planets. It is named after Edmund Halley, who showed that comets move around the Sun in accordance with Newton's theory of gravitation. He noticed that the orbits of the bright comets of 1531, 1607, and 1682 were very similar and concluded that they were actually one and the same comet. He calculated its orbit and predicted that this comet should return in 1758. Unfortunately Halley died 16 years before the comet returned.

Halley's comet was seen with the naked eye in October and November 1985 and in early spring 1986: PERIHELION was on Feb. 9, 1986 and it passed through its ascending and descending NODES on Nov. 27, 1985 and Apr. 11, 1986. Detailed observations were made using instruments on Earth and in five spacecraft: ESA's GIOTTO, the Soviet-led missions VEGA 1 and Vega 2, and the Japanese craft SAKIGAKE and Suisei. Pictures were obtained by Giotto of the dark potato-shaped NUCLEUS (16 × 8 km) and of structure and activity near the nucleus. The comet's development as it rounded the Sun was recorded and studies were made of cometary composition, of processes producing and occurring in the coma and tails, and the interaction between comet and SOLAR WIND. Halley's comet will return in 2061.

halo 1 see GALAXY.
2 see DARK HALO.
3 see DONATI'S COMET.

halo orbit a very stable orbit in which the periods of the planar and vertical components are equal. Spacecraft orbiting a Lagrangian point, such as L_1 or L_2 in the Sun–Earth system, follow such an orbit.

Halo Ring see JUPITER'S RINGS.

Hamal (α Ari) an orange giant that is the brightest star in the constellation Aries. m_v: 2.00; M_v: 0.1; spectral type: K2 IIIab; distance: 24 pc.

h and Chi Persei (Sword-Handle; Double Cluster in Perseus) a fine double cluster in the constellation Perseus. Both the constituent OPEN CLUSTERS, NGC 869 (h Persei) and NGC 884 (Chi [χ] Persei) are visible to the naked eye. They are relatively young clusters, about 10 million years old, and appear to be associated with the surrounding Zeta (ζ) Persei OB-association. See ASSOCIATION; OB CLUSTER.

H and K lines lines in the spectrum of singly ionized calcium, occurring at the visible/ultraviolet wavelengths of 393.4 nm (H) and 396.8 nm (K). They are very prominent FRAUNHOFER LINES.

Harrison–Wheeler spectrum see COSMIC POWER SPECTRUM.

Harvard classification (Henry-Draper system) see SPECTRAL TYPES.

harvest Moon the full Moon that occurs closest to the autumnal EQUINOX. At this time the RETARDATION is small (so that the Moon appears to rise at the same time on successive evenings) because of the low inclination of the plane of the Moon's orbit to the horizon.

Hat Creek Observatory a radio astronomy observatory in California operated by the University of California, Berkeley at an altitude of 1024 meters. The 26-meter dish, once used for millimeter-wave astronomy, blew down in Jan. 1993. The remaining major instrument at the site is the *Berkeley-Illinois-Maryland Association array* (*BIMA array*) – a millimeter-wave interferometer. The array consists of ten dishes, each of 6-meter diameter, on tracks that stretch 300 m E–W and 200 m N–S. It can observe at wavelengths between 1.3 and 2.6 mm.

Hawking radiation see BLACK HOLE.

Hawking's area theorem a result of general relativity theory proved by Stephen Hawking in papers published in 1971 and 1972, stating that in any process the area of a black hole can only increase. This increase in area is analogous to the increase in entropy in the second law of thermodynamics. The analogy led Jacob Bekenstein to postulate that a black hole has an entropy associated with its area.

Hayashi track a near-vertical downward-directed line on the HERTZSPRUNG–RUSSELL DIAGRAM that is believed to be followed by PROTOSTARS as they contract toward the MAIN SEQUENCE. C. Hayashi (1965) calculated these tracks as the evolutionary paths of stars that are convective throughout (see ENERGY TRANSPORT), as protostars are expected to be during at least their early contraction.

Haystack Observatory a facility in Massachusetts, NW of Boston, run by the Northeast Radio Observatory Corporation (NEROC) under agreement with the Massachusetts Institute of Technology. It has a 36.6-meter radio dish consisting of 96 stiff panel sections. The telescope is housed in a 45.7-meter diameter raydome, which reduces the effects of wind and rain; has a CASSEGRAIN FOCUS and an ALTAZIMUTH MOUNTING. It was originally used for radar astronomy, but is used mostly for spectral-line and VLBI work. It can observe in a selection of wavebands between 0.3 and 18 cm. At the shorter wavelengths the secondary mirror is deformed to take account of errors in the shape of the dish surface. The site contains a number of other radio and optical telescopes and radar antennas.

HD a prefix used to designate a star as listed in the HENRY DRAPER CATALOG.

HdC stars hydrogen-deficient CARBON STARS. They are supergiants that look much like R CORONAE BOREALIS STARS but are not variable.

H-D system *short for* Henry-Draper system. See SPECTRAL TYPES.

head the coma and nucleus of a COMET when seen together. In this context 'nucleus' means the diffuse starlike luminous condensation sometimes observed in the coma. The head generally contracts as PERIHELION is approached and expands again afterward. Remarkable changes in size, luminosity distribution, and the number of observed 'nuclei' can take place inside the head in a few hours.

head-tail galaxy see RADIO-SOURCE STRUCTURE.

HEAO *abbrev. for* High Energy Astrophysical Observatory. Any of three large (about 3000 kg) Earth satellites built by NASA for second-generation studies of X-RAY SOURCES, GAMMA-RAY SOURCES, and COSMIC RAYS.

HEAO-A, or HEAO-l after launch, was put into a 400-km, 22° inclination orbit in Aug. 1977 and carried a payload of large X-ray detectors with which to conduct a more sensitive sky survey than that of UHURU and ARIEL V. HEAO-l completed two-and-a-half surveys of the sky and several extended pointings at individual sources before reentry early in 1979. The eventual outcome was a catalog of 842 X-ray sources, brighter than about 1 microjansky, together with broad-band spectra of many active galaxies, clusters, and galactic sources.

HEAO-2, the EINSTEIN OBSERVATORY, operated from launch in Nov. 1978 until loss of control gas in Apr. 1981. The unique capabilities of its 60-cm GRAZING INCIDENCE telescope revolutionized X-ray astronomy in the same way that Uhuru had done a decade earlier.

HEAO-3 was launched in Sept. 1979. It carried a number of large cosmic-ray instruments to study the mass and charge distribution of primary cosmic rays, particularly the nuclei of the heavier elements, over a wide range of energies. The gamma-ray spectroscopy experiment was designed specifically to search for cosmic sources of narrow-line emission in the energy range 50 keV to 10 MeV. It consisted of a cluster of germanium solid-state detectors surrounded by an active cesium iodide scintillator shield. Apart from the study of gamma-ray line emission from solar FLARES, 511 keV ANNIHILATION radiation from the galactic center region, and 1.809 MeV line emission from radioactive ^{26}Al (see GAMMA-RAY ASTRONOMY), the spectrometer detected two strong gamma-ray line emissions from the extraordinary galactic object SS433. The various experiments on board HEAO-3 ceased operations during the years 1980-82.

heavy elements in astronomy, all elements heavier than hydrogen and helium. The COSMIC ABUNDANCE of the heavy elements is very much lower than that of hydrogen and helium.

Hector ((624) Hector) a member of the TROJAN GROUP of asteroids. It was discovered by Auguste Kopff in 1907. It is possibly a contact binary, or else an abnormally elongated single object, the ratio of its two principal axes being greater than two.

HED meteorites a group of stony (achondrite) METEORITES, named after the three types: *howardites, eucrites,* and *diogenites.* They are igneous rocks that are about 4.5 billion years old.

Heinrich Hertz Submillimeter Telescope a 10-meter radio telescope, commissioned in 1994 at the Mount Graham International Observatory in Arizona, that operates in the 0.3–1.0 mm waveband. It is run jointly by the University of Arizona and the Max-Planck Institut für Radioastronomie in Bonn, Germany.

Helene a small irregularly shaped satellite of Saturn, discovered in 1980. Helene is a COORBITAL SATELLITE with DIONE. See Table 2, Appendix.

heliacal rising the first appearance of a star or planet in the eastern sky just before dawn, following a period when it has been too close to the Sun to be visible. A *heliacal setting* is the last occasion on which a star or planet can be seen in the western sky just after sunset prior to its becoming too close to the Sun to be seen.

heliocentric coordinate system a COORDINATE SYSTEM referring usually to the plane of the ECLIPTIC but specifying position with respect to the center of the

Sun rather than that of Earth (see GEOCENTRIC COORDINATE SYSTEM). The coordinates – *heliocentric latitude* and *longitude* – are used to determine the relative positions of objects in the Solar System. See also BARYCENTER.

heliocentric gravitational constant the product of the GRAVITATIONAL CONSTANT and the SOLAR MASS, equal to

$$1.327\,124\,38 \times 10^{20}\ \mathrm{N\ m^2\ kg^{-1}}$$

It can be determined with greater precision than either quantity alone.

heliocentric parallax see ANNUAL PARALLAX.

heliocentric system a model of the Solar System or of the Universe that has the Sun at its center. Aristarchus of Samos proposed a heliocentric system in the third century BC in which the planets moved at uniform rates around the Sun in circular orbits. The theory was abandoned due to large discrepancies between prediction and observation, and the geocentric PTOLEMAIC SYSTEM was subsequently favored until the establishment of the heliocentric COPERNICAN SYSTEM.

heliographic latitude the angular distance from the Sun's equator, measured north or south along the meridian. The position of a point on the Sun's disk may be defined in terms of this and its HELIOGRAPHIC LONGITUDE.

heliographic longitude the angular distance from a standard meridian on the Sun (taken to be the meridian that passed through the ascending NODE of the Sun's equator on the ecliptic on 1854 Jan 1 at 12h 00m UT and calculated for the present day assuming a uniform SIDEREAL PERIOD of rotation of 25.38 days; see SUN), measured from east to west (0° to 360°) along the equator. The position of a point on the Sun's disk may be defined in terms of this and its HELIOGRAPHIC LATITUDE.

heliometer an obsolete refracting telescope with a split objective lens that was used to measure the angular distance between two stars and to measure position angles. The two sections of the objective were moved until the images of the stars produced in the two sections were made to coincide. The amount of movement gave a precise measure of the angular distance.

heliopause see HELIOSPHERE.

helioseismology the study of the Sun's interior by the observation of solar oscillations. First detected in 1960 by measuring the DOPPLER SHIFTS of FRAUNHOFER LINES at several points on the Sun's disk away from ACTIVE REGIONS, the oscillations are a rhythmic rise and fall of regions of the solar PHOTOSPHERE (and lower CHROMOSPHERE) several thousand kilometers in diameter. They have periods of about 5 minutes, persist at any one point for less than half an hour, and attain a maximum velocity of about 0.5 km s^{-1}. The oscillations are thought to be produced by the outward propagation of low-frequency sound waves, generated by turbulence in the CONVECTIVE ZONE, and by analyzing their global occurrence over an extended period of time it is possible to build up a picture of the Sun's interior.

Instruments used in the observation of solar oscillations include grating SPECTROGRAPHS, narrow-band INTERFERENCE FILTER (LYOT FILTER, magneto-optical filter, or FABRY–PEROT INTERFEROMETER) imagers, and Michelson interferometers – notably the *Fourier tachometer*, which has been in operation since 1985 and simultaneously monitors more than 60 000 points on the Sun's disk. A number of collaborative programs have been established, for example the GLOBAL OSCILLATIONS NETWORK GROUP (GONG). These are complemented by continuous monitoring by the helioseismology instrument on ESA's spacecraft, the SOLAR HELIOSPHERIC OBSERVATORY (SOHO).

heliosphere the vast region around the Sun that is permeated by the SOLAR WIND and the weak interplanetary magnetic field, and in which the solar-wind plasma plays a dominant role. It is bounded by the *heliopause*, which is estimated to be 100 AU or more from the Sun's center but has not yet been encountered by any spacecraft. The heliosphere may be very elongated owing to the presence of an *interstellar wind* of neutral hydrogen flowing from the direction of the galactic center.

heliostat a COELOSTAT mirror mounted on a synchronously controlled drive mechanism so that it may reflect sunlight in a fixed direction as the Sun moves across the sky.

Together with additional optical elements it is a basic component of most SOLAR TELESCOPES.

helium chemical symbol: He. A chemical ELEMENT with an ATOMIC NUMBER of two. In its most abundant form it consists of a nucleus of two protons and two neutrons, around which orbit two electrons. This nucleus, i.e. the positively charged helium ion, is exceptionally stable; it is called an alpha particle. A second far less abundant isotope, helium-3, has two protons and one neutron as its nucleus. Two radioactive (i.e. unstable) isotopes also exist.

Helium is the second most abundant element in the Universe (after HYDROGEN): about 25% by mass and 6% or more by numbers of atoms. All but about 1% of this approximate 25% cosmic abundance is now considered to have been synthesized in the first few minutes of the Universe (see BIG BANG THEORY). Helium is also synthesized, from hydrogen, by NUCLEAR FUSION reactions in the centers of main-sequence stars. It is by these reactions – the PROTON-PROTON CHAIN REACTION and the CARBON CYCLE – that the energy of the stars is generated. When the hydrogen supplies in the stellar cores are exhausted, the helium is itself consumed by further fusion processes to form carbon (see STELLAR EVOLUTION).

Helium is not easy to detect. It was first discovered in 1868 by Norman Lockyer: a yellow emission line of a then unknown element was observed in the spectrum of the Sun's chromosphere, recorded during a solar eclipse. High temperatures are required for helium to emit or absorb radiation. Absorption lines of neutral helium (He I) do not appear, for example, in the Sun's absorption spectrum, which originates in the photosphere, but they dominate the spectra of B STARS. Even greater temperatures are required to ionize helium, i.e. to remove one or both of its electrons. Singly ionized helium (He II) occurs, for instance, in O STARS and in EMISSION NEBULAE. Helium, although a minor component in the inner planets, is a major constituent in the atmospheres of Jupiter, Saturn, Uranus, and Neptune.

helium burning the NUCLEAR FUSION of three helium nuclei to form carbon. See TRIPLE ALPHA PROCESS.

helium flash the explosive onset of helium burning (by the TRIPLE ALPHA PROCESS) in the degenerate core of an evolved star (a GIANT) when the core temperature reaches about 10^8 kelvin. The sudden increase in energy production causes a rapid rise in temperature, in turn increasing the reaction rate, but this runaway process eventually removes the degeneracy and the reaction once again becomes sensitive to the gas pressure. The helium flash occurs in stars of about one to two solar masses.

helium shell flash a violent outburst of energy that occurs periodically in a highly evolved GIANT STAR. The star is producing energy in a shell of hydrogen and in an inner shell of helium surrounding the inert dense core of carbon and oxygen. Helium shell burning is unstable, producing energy mainly in short intense flashes. After a shell flash, which causes the star to expand then cool, the convective region in the outer part of the star goes deeper and may dredge up carbon to the surface.

helium star 1 one of a rare class of stars (excluding white dwarfs) whose outer layers contain more helium than hydrogen. These are evolved stars that have lost their hydrogen-rich envelope, possibly by the effect of a companion in a close binary system. Some helium stars are likely progenitors of type Ib/Ic SUPERNOVAE. See also WOLF–RAYET STARS.
2 *obsolete name for* B star.

Helix nebula (**NGC 7293**) a PLANETARY NEBULA lying in the southern hemisphere about 140 parsecs away in the direction of Aquarius. It has the largest apparent diameter (0°.2) of any planetary nebula but at magnitude 6.5 is too faint to be seen with the naked eye.

Hellas Planitia a vast, roughly circular impact basin in Mars' southern hemisphere, located in the planet's southern highland region at the areographic coordinates 40° S latitude, 290° W longitude (see AREOGRAPHY). It can be seen as a bright area from the Earth and is the largest impact feature on the planet. It is thought to be the result of an asteroidal impact about 3900 million years ago during the heavy bombardment phase of the formation of the Solar System. The crater excavated by the asteroid is about 9 km deep and 2100 km in diameter and is girdled by a ring of material forming an elevated rim that reaches a height of about 1.5 kilometers above the level of the surrounding area. See MARS, SURFACE FEATURES.

hemispherical albedo see ALBEDO.

Henry Draper Catalog (HD Catalog) a star catalog in nine volumes compiled by Annie J. Cannon and E.C. Pickering of the Harvard College Observatory and published 1918–24 as part of the *Harvard Annals*. It was the first catalog to assign stars to spectral classes as well as giving their positions and magnitudes. The catalog (a memorial to Henry Draper, a distinguished physician who, as an amateur astronomer, pioneered in the field of astronomical photography) was financed through a fund set up by Draper's wife after his death in 1882. It lists 225 300 stars for the epoch 1900.0, each allocated a SPECTRAL TYPE according to the Harvard classification. The *Henry Draper Extension (HDE)*, 1925–36, lists a further 133 700 stars. The entire catalog, of which the latest version appeared in 1985, is currently being reclassified on the MK system by a team from the University of Michigan led by Nancy Houk. Work on this publication, the *Michigan Catalog of Two-dimensional Spectral Types for the HD Stars*, began 1975.

Henry-Draper system (H-D system) *another name for* Harvard classification. See SPECTRAL TYPES.

Herbig Ae-Be stars (Herbig emission-line stars) see BE STARS.

Herbig–Haro objects (HH objects) small peculiar bright nebulae, containing concentrations of gas and dust, that have been lit up by the flux of radiation from, for example, T TAURI STARS or shocked into excitation in gas outflows from T Tauri stars or other protostellar objects. The latter may give rise to a string of HH objects, aligned along a BIPOLAR OUTFLOW.

Hercules an extensive but rather faint constellation in the northern hemisphere near Ursa Major. The brightest stars, Beta (β) and Zeta (ζ) Herculis, are of 2nd magnitude with many of 3rd and 4th magnitude. There are several binary stars, including Zeta and RASALGETHI (α) and the X-ray binary HERCULES X-1; globular clusters include the GREAT CLUSTER IN HERCULES (M13), visible to the naked eye, and the smaller and slightly fainter M92 (NGC 6341). Hercules A is a distant and very powerful radio galaxy. Abbrev.: Her; genitive form: Herculis; approx. position: RA 17h, dec +30°; area: 1225 sq deg.

Hercules X-1 an X-RAY BINARY star, the second to be established as such (after CENTAURUS X-3), based on UHURU satellite observations. It exhibits a complex behavior, with regular 1.24 second X-ray pulsations, eclipses (by the binary companion star) every 1.75 days, and longer-term modulation of the X-ray intensity over a 35-day cycle. Her X-1 was the first X-ray binary to be optically identified; the low-mass optical counterpart, HZ Her, varies through the binary period from SPECTRAL TYPE A/F to B due to X-ray heating. Its mass (about 1.5 times that of the Sun) and the 1.24-second pulsations strongly suggest the X-ray component to be a rotating NEUTRON STAR. It is thus often referred to as an X-ray pulsar, with the X-ray pulsations arising most probably from channeling of the accreting gas onto the magnetic poles of the neutron star. The discovery in 1976 of a hard X-ray 'emission line' at 55 keV, attributed to CYCLOTRON RADIATION from near the star's surface, provides support for this view and gave a direct measure of the intense polar magnetic field (about 10^8 tesla). More recent X-ray spectra have led to the re-interpretation of this feature as an absorption line, at 38 keV, arising from CYCLOTRON absorption of electrons in a magnetic field of 3×10^8 tesla.

Hermes 1 a spaceplane originally proposed by ESA as a crew-carrying space transport system to be launched by ARIANE-5. ESA approved the spaceplane project in 1987, aiming at a first launch in 1995. But the loss of the space shuttle Challenger in 1986 forced the craft's designers to add in extra safety features that increased its weight and drove up costs. After its budget was cut in 1992, ESA tried to revive it as a joint project

with Russia, but without success. Hermes was finally cancelled in 1993.
2 (**1937 UB** or **(69230) Hermes**) an ASTEROID discovered by Karl Reimuth in 1937 when it approached within 0.006 AU (780 000 km) of the Earth. A very small member of the APOLLO GROUP, it was lost for 66 years because of uncertain knowledge of its orbit. It was rediscovered in 2003 by US astronomer Brian A. Skiff and is now known to cross the Earth's orbit once every 777 days. By tracking its orbit back to the year of its discovery, astronomers have learned that it made very close approaches to Earth in 1942 (within 0.0044 AU), 1954, 1974, 1980, and 1986, but went unnoticed. Radar observations of Hermes made from the Arecibo observatory since its rediscovery indicate that it is in fact two rocky bodies in orbit around each other.

Herschel see MIMAS.

Herschel Space Observatory a spaceborne infrared and submillimeter imaging photometry and spectroscopy facility scheduled to be launched by the European Space Agency (ESA) in early 2007. It will enter space aboard the same launch vehicle, an Ariane-5 rocket, as the PLANCK mission. The observatory (known as Herschel for short) takes its name from the German-born English astronomer of the late 18th and early 19th century, Sir William Herschel. Originally designated the Far InfraRed and Submillimeter Telescope (FIRST), it is one of the cornerstones of ESA's science program. Its purpose is to observe the 'cool' universe, operating in the far infrared and submillimeter region of the spectrum over an approximate range of 57–670 μm. Functioning at these wavelengths, it will have the potential to look back into the Universe's remote past, discovering the earliest epoch proto-galaxies, revealing cosmologically evolving AGN/starburst symbiosis, and unraveling the mechanisms governing the formation of stars and planetary systems. Herschel will carry a 3.5-m-diameter passively cooled telescope. The science instruments – two cameras/medium resolution spectrometers and a very high resolution heterodyne spectrometer – will be housed in a superfluid helium cryostat. From its eventual observing position far out in space in orbit around L2, one of the Lagrangian points of the Sun–Earth system situated 1.5 million km from the Earth, Herschel will be able to benefit from a low and stable background and full access to the frequency range in which it is to work.

Herschel Telescope see WILLIAM HERSCHEL TELESCOPE.

Herstmonceux former site, in East Sussex, of the ROYAL GREENWICH OBSERVATORY.

Hertha family see NYSA FAMILY.

hertz symbol: Hz. The SI unit of frequency, defined as the frequency of a periodic phenomenon that has a period of one second. The frequency range of ELECTROMAGNETIC RADIATION is about 3000 Hz (very low frequency radio waves) to about 10^{22} Hz (high-frequency gamma rays).

Hertzsprung gap a region on the HERTZSPRUNG–RUSSELL DIAGRAM, to the right of the main sequence, in which few stars are found. This is because of a star's rapid evolution through this region, away from the main sequence. This occurs during the period when hydrogen is being burnt in a shell around the core of helium, before the onset of helium burning (see STELLAR EVOLUTION). The gap can be easily seen on H-R diagrams of open clusters.

Hertzsprung–Russell diagram (**H-R diagram**) a two-dimensional graph that demonstrates the correlation between SPECTRAL TYPE (and hence temperature) and LUMINOSITY of stars, discovered independently by the Danish astronomer E. Hertzsprung in 1911 and the American astronomer H.N. Russell in 1913. Instead of a uniform distribution, any large sample of stars is found to form well-defined groups or bands on the graph of spectral type plotted against absolute visual MAGNITUDE: about 90% lie along a diagonal band known as the MAIN SEQUENCE; the somewhat brighter GIANT STARS form another sequence as do the very brightest and relatively rare SUPERGIANTS; WHITE DWARFS and other groupings can also be distinguished.

There are several forms of H-R diagram. In most observational applications the absolute visual magnitude, M_V, is the vertical axis and the COLOR INDEX, $B–V$, the

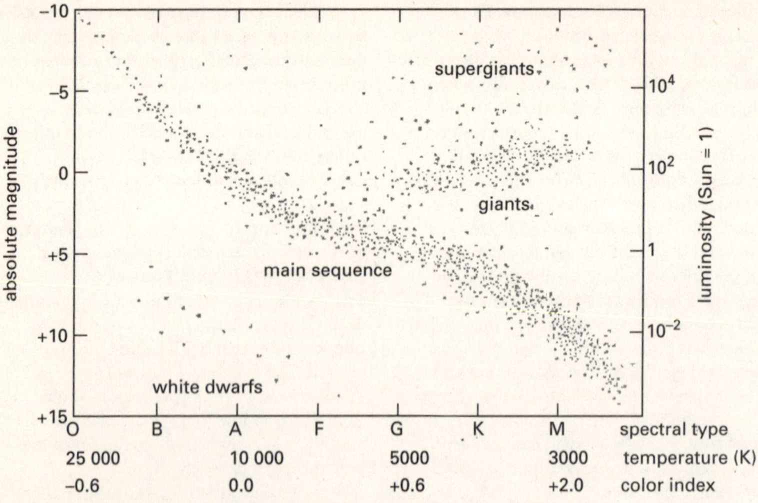

Hertzsprung–Russell diagram for bright stars

horizontal axis, color index being related to but more easily measured than spectral type. These are *color-magnitude H-R diagrams.* When studying a CLUSTER, whose stars are all at the same distance, apparent rather than absolute magnitude is used. Other studies use bolometric MAGNITUDE against EFFECTIVE TEMPERATURE – *theoretical H-R diagrams* – or luminosity against color index – *color-luminosity H-R diagrams.*

The H-R diagram is of great importance in studies of STELLAR EVOLUTION. Diagrams obtained on the basis of theoretical calculations can be tested against observationally determined diagrams. They can be drawn for the brightest stars (see illustration), for stars in a particular locality such as the solar neighborhood (mainly small cool main-sequence stars), for PULSATING VARIABLES, for GLOBULAR CLUSTERS, etc. The two broad stellar populations – POPULATIONS I and II – can be demonstrated by the H-R diagrams of a young OPEN CLUSTER (no giants), a somewhat older open cluster (a few giants), and a much older globular cluster (many giants and supergiants).

The H-R diagram can also be used for distance determination by both MAIN-SEQUENCE FITTING for stellar clusters and by spectroscopic PARALLAX for individual main-sequence stars, the star's spectral type fixing its position on the diagram and thus indicating its absolute magnitude and hence its DISTANCE MODULUS.

HET *abbrev. for* Hobby–Eberly Telescope.

HETE the High Energy Transient Experiment, an international mission scheduled by NASA for launch on a Pegasus rocket in 1994. The prime objective is to carry out the first multiwavelength study of GAMMA-RAY BURSTS with UV, X-ray, and γ-ray instruments mounted on a single spacecraft. Bursts can be localized with about 10 arcsec accuracy, in near real-time, on board the spacecraft, and these positions can be transmitted directly to a network of receivers at ground-based observatories, enabling rapid and sensitive follow-up studies in the radio, IR, and optical bands.

heterodyne detector a system that analyzes the frequency spectrum of a signal at very high spectral RESOLUTION. Originally developed in the radio-frequency region, systems are now being built to allow far-infrared and submillimeter studies of astronomical objects. Basically, the radiation collected by a telescope is converted to a signal of lower frequency that can then be handled electronically. This is achieved by *heterodyning*, or merging, the signal with one from a local oscillator (see RECEIVER). Once at the lower frequency the signal is much easier to process. It is analyzed in a spectrometer that further converts the signal from the time domain to the frequency domain and can in principle be analyzed at any resolution. The entire spectrum within the bandwidth is processed in parallel.

Hevelius formation the EJECTA BLANKET of the ORIENTALE BASIN. See also FRA MAURO FORMATION; HIGHLAND LIGHT PLAINS.

hexahedrite see IRON METEORITE.

HH object *short for* Herbig–Haro object.

Hidalgo ((944) Hidalgo) an ASTEROID that was discovered by Walter Baade in 1920 and has an eccentric 13.7 year orbit that carries it between 2.00 AU and 9.64 AU from the Sun, crossing the orbits of the main-belt asteroids and Jupiter and extending to that of Saturn. The eccentricity of its elliptical path is about 0.66 and its inclination to the ecliptic is 42.6°. It has a diameter estimated at between 20 and 30 km. Until the discovery of CHIRON in 1977, it had the farthest aphelion and longest period of any known asteroid. From the similarity of its orbit to those of the periodic COMETS, it has been suggested that Hidalgo represents the remains of a large comet nucleus. It has an albedo of 0.03 and a D-type spectrum. See Table 3, Appendix.

hierarchical clustering see DARK MATTER; GALAXIES, FORMATION AND EVOLUTION.

hierarchical Universe a COSMOLOGICAL MODEL, originally due to Charlier in 1908, in which inhomogeneities exist on increasingly larger scales: galaxies occur in CLUSTERS (as observed), which in turn are clustered into SUPERCLUSTERS (as observed), which may in turn aggregate as clusters of superclusters, and so on. As the level of clustering increases then the mean density of matter must decrease in the progressively larger volumes considered.

Higgs mechanism the mechanism by which the W BOSON and the Z BOSON and, more generally, all massive particles, acquire their mass. In the mid 1960s Peter HIGGS, and independently Robert Brout and François Englert, predicted the existence of a massive spin-zero particle is now known as the *Higgs boson*.

The Higgs boson is associated with a scalar field, now known as the *Higgs field*. In the WEINBERG–SALAM MODEL the W boson and the Z boson which mediate the weak interaction acquire their masses by the Higgs mechanism. Higgs bosons have not been found experimentally, although thorough searches up to 130 GeV have been conducted. It is thought that fermions in the STANDARD MODEL acquire their masses by the Higgs mechanism but it has not been possible to implement this suggestion.

High-Energy Astrophysical Observatory see HEAO; EINSTEIN OBSERVATORY.

highland light plains (Cayley formations) the widespread relatively level 'ponds' of light-colored materials that have accumulated in depressions in the lunar HIGHLANDS. Originally thought to be highland volcanics they are now believed to be rubble derived from impacts, possibly from the ORIENTALE BASIN.

highlands, lunar the topographically elevated and more rugged regions of the MOON. They have a higher ALBEDO – and thus appear brighter – than the MARIA and consist largely of anorthosite, a calcium-aluminum silicate rock. Lunar highland areas include most of the farside and southern part of the NEARSIDE of the Moon. CRATERS are larger and more abundant here than in the maria; this reflects the greater age of the highland crust, parts of which date back 4600 million years to the formation of the Moon. See also MOON ROCKS; MOUNTAINS, LUNAR.

high-pass filter see FILTER.

high-velocity clouds small MOLECULAR and DIFFUSE CLOUDS, often far from the galactic plane, that have radial velocities differing significantly – sometimes up to 100 km s^{-1} – from those predicted by a simple Galactic ROTATION CURVE. Some may be associated with tidal effects, such as the Magellanic Stream (see MAGELLANIC CLOUD), while others are more likely due to GALACTIC FOUNTAINS.

high-velocity stars very old (POPULATION II) stars in the galactic halo that are relatively near the Sun but do not share in the common circular motion around the galactic center of the Sun and other stars in the Sun's neighborhood (see LOCAL STANDARD OF REST). They are actually moving slower than the Sun in elliptical orbits that often carry them far out of the galactic plane. Their apparently high velocities (>65 km s^{-1}) relative to the Sun result from this difference in relative motions. High velocity provides an easy means of identifying individual old stars near the Sun, i.e. stars with a low abundance of heavy elements.

Hilda group a group of ASTEROIDS that have orbits with semimajor axes of around 4.0 AU and orbital periods that are very close to the 3:2 resonance with that of Jupiter. The group takes its name from (153) Hilda, the largest member in it, which was discovered by the Austrian astronomer Johann Palisa in 1875. In common with the TROJAN GROUP, Hildas are thought to have more elongated shapes than the more normal main-belt asteroids.

Hill sphere the spherical region around a planet (or satellite) within which that body dominates the motion of particles. Once the core of a planet exceeds a mass of about 10^{23} kg, it gravitationally attracts gas from the Hill sphere and is able to form an atmosphere in this way. Jupiter's Hill sphere, for example, had a volume about 1000 times greater than that of the Earth.

Himalia a satellite of Jupiter, discovered in 1904 by the US astronomer Charles Dillon Perrine (1867–1951). It is the largest of Jupiter's irregular satellites, with a diameter of 150 km. See JUPITER'S SATELLITES; Table 2, Appendix.

Hind's nebula (NGC 1554–5) a REFLECTION NEBULA in the constellation Taurus, illuminated by the young variable star T Tauri. The nebula has varied considerably in brightness since it was first observed in the 19th century.

Hipparcos (High-Precision Parallax Collecting Satellite) an astrometric satellite of the European Space Agency (ESA) launched in Aug. 1989 to gather modern data on the position, brightness and other properties of an input catalog of selected stars with an unprecedented level of accuracy. Although its name was an acronym, it was deliberately chosen to recall the ancient Greek astronomer Hippachus, who compiled an important star catalog in the 2nd century BC. A faulty booster motor failed to lift Hipparcos into its intended geostationary orbit, but, following a revision of its mission, it was operated successfully from its 10-hour orbit and completed its mission in 4 years (rather than the planned 2.5 years). Prolonged exposure to radiation eventually caused it to cease working in 1993.

The satellite's 29-cm Schmidt telescope plotted very exactly the position, magnitude, parallax, and proper motion of a large number of stars. The resulting *Hipparcos catalog* (published 1997) gave the positions of 118 218 stars with a precision (0.002 arcsec) not possible from the ground. It was complete to magnitude 7.5 but included many fainter stars down to magnitude 12.5. The mean epoch was 1991.25. The less accurate *Tycho catalog* was prepared using the Hipparcos satellite's less sensitive star tracker instrument and was published the same year. Tycho gave positional date and magnitudes for the 1 058 332 brightest stars, including many as faint as magnitude 11.5. Tycho 2, a collaborative venture between the United States Navy Observatory and the University of Copenhagen, Denmark, was released on CD-ROM in 2000. It extended the number of the brightest stars listed to 2 539 913, complete to magnitude 11, with their positions precessed to J2000.0.

Among its other achievements, Hipparcos helped to forecast the impacts on Jupiter of the fragments of Comet Shoemaker-Levy 9 and identified stars that in the far future will pass close to the Sun.

Hirayama families groupings of ASTEROIDS whose members orbit at approximately the same distance from the Sun and have very similar orbital characteristics (period, ECCENTRICITY, INCLINATION). More than 40 families are recognized, some containing more than 70 members. They are named after the Japanese astronomer Kiyotsugu Hirayama who discovered the first nine families in 1918. It is believed that each family represents debris resulting from a collision between larger asteroids in the past. In contrast, the AMOR GROUP and the APOLLO GROUP each comprise asteroids with a range of orbital characteristics. A large number of asteroids are members of Hirayama families.

H line see H AND K LINES.

HLIRG *abbrev. for* hyperluminous IRAS galaxy. See IRAS GALAXIES.

HMXB *abbrev. for* high-mass X-ray binary. See X-RAY BINARY.

Hoba meteorite the world's largest single meteorite mass, found in 1920 near Grootfontein, Namibia. It is an IRON METEORITE weighing 60 tonnes and measures 2.7 × 2.7 × 1 meters. It still lies at its original resting place and produced no crater, being only partly buried in the ground. A good percentage has rusted away.

Hobby–Eberly Telescope (HET) a telescope at the MCDONALD OBSERVATORY in Texas, used mainly for spectrographic surveys. It has an 11-meter segmented spherical mirror (f/1.3, with an effective aperture of 9.2 meters) on an altazimuth mounting, tipped at a permanent angle of 35° to the zenith. A movable secondary mirror reflects images onto it, and in this way it can survey 70% of the sky visible at the site. It was commissioned in 1997.

Hohmann transfer (Hohmann orbit) see TRANSFER ORBIT.

Holmberg radius the length of the semimajor axis of a galaxy down to a SURFACE BRIGHTNESS of 26.5 magnitudes per square arc second, expressed either in arc minutes, or if the distance to the galaxy is known, in kiloparsecs. It is a useful measurement of the visible size of the galaxy.

Homestake experiment see NEUTRINO ASTRONOMY.

homogeneity uniformity in space. A medium or process that is not homogeneous is called *inhomogeneous*. See COSMOLOGICAL PRINCIPLE; ISOTROPY.

honeycomb mirror see PRIMARY MIRROR.

Hooker telescope see MOUNT WILSON OBSERVATORY.

horizon 1 the horizontal plane perpendicular to a line through an observer's position and his or her ZENITH. The great circle in which an observer's horizon meets the celestial sphere is called the *astronomical horizon*, or simply the horizon; it separates the visible half of the celestial sphere from the invisible half for that observer or position. See also CARDINAL POINTS.

2 see EVENT HORIZON.

3 see HORIZON DISTANCE.

Horizon 2000 eSA's long-term space science research program covering the period from 1995 to the early 2000s. ESA originally introduced the program as early as 1984 and intended it to cover the years 1995–2007. There were four major 'cornerstone' missions. The first was ESA's contribution to the international SOLAR/TERRESTRIAL ENERGY PROGRAMME (STEP). The second was the X-ray spectroscopy mission XMM. The other two were the Far Infrared and Submillimeter Space Telescope (FIRST) and the ROSETTA cometary mission. There were also some less costly small and medium-sized projects. In 1992, ESA set up a survey committee to identify the main aims and challenges of future space missions and to design a new long-term program for the period up to 2016. This new program, Horizon 2000+, was approved in 1995. With the new project came a further four 'cornerstone' missions, including a Mercury orbiter (now under development as BEPICOLOMBO), an interferometry and astrometry mission (see GAIA), a project to observe gravity waves (now being developed as LISA), and a mission to join the search for extrasolar Earth-like planets (currently being considered under the name DARWIN). The new name for the program, Horizon 2000+, was shortlived, however, and ESA decided to refer to both the original plan and its extension as Horizon 2000.

The Horizon 2000 program provided a basis for a number of projects not originally included, such as GIOTTO, ULYSSES, and HIPPARCOS. It was also seen as the inspiration for the Huygens probe that formed ESA's contribution to the NASA CASSINI–HUYGENS mission to Saturn, landing on Titan in January 2004. The first two 'cornerstone' missions of Horizon 2000 have achieved implementation: SOHO and CLUSTER (ESA's contributions to STEP) and the XMM satellite (launched as XMM-NEWTON in 1999); the fourth, Rosetta, was launched in 2004. a year behind its original schedule and with a new target, Comet Churyumov-Gerasimenko. The remaining 'cornerstone' mission, FIRST, has been renamed HERSCHEL and is due for launch in 2007, alongside another ESA science mission, PLANCK. Horizon 2000 has been unanimously welcomed by the scientific community both within and outside Europe. Many non-European scientists collaborate on its missions. In 2004, ESA invited proposals for space projects to be considered covering the years 2016 to 2025.

horizon distance (**particle horizon**) the total distance that a light signal could have traveled since the beginning of the Universe, and hence the maximum distance that can be seen in a cosmological model.

horizon problem see INFLATION.

horizontal (or **horizon**) **coordinate system** a COORDINATE SYSTEM in which the fundamental reference circle is the observer's astronomical HORIZON and the zero point is the north point (see CARDINAL POINTS). The coordinates are *altitude* and *azimuth* (see illustration).

The altitude (h) of a celestial body is its angular distance north (counted positive) or south (counted negative) of the horizon; it is measured along the vertical circle through the body and ranges from 0°, when the object rises or sets, to 90°, when the object is directly overhead at the zenith. The ZENITH DISTANCE (ζ) is the complement of the altitude ($90° - h$) and is frequently used instead of altitude in the horizontal system. The azimuth (A) of a body is its angular distance measured eastward along the horizon from the north point (or sometimes the south point) to the intersection of the object's vertical circle.

The horizontal system is simple but is strictly a local system. At any given moment a celestial body will have a unique altitude and azimuth for a particular observation point, the coordinates changing with observer's position. The coordinates of a

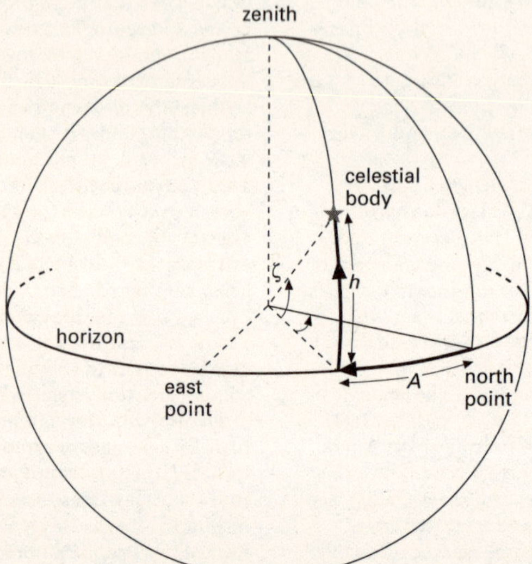

Horizontal coordinate system

star, etc., also change with time as the Earth rotates and the observer's zenith moves eastward among the stars.

horizontal branch a horizontal strip on the Hertzsprung–Russell diagram of a GLOBULAR CLUSTER, to the left of the red-giant branch. It consists of low-mass stars that have lost mass during the red-giant phase; they all have absolute magnitudes of about the same value. Where the instability strip associated with PULSATING VARIABLES crosses the horizontal branch, the stars are RR LYRAE STARS; in a conventional H-R diagram of nonvariable stars, this appears as a gap in the horizontal branch.

horizontal parallax see DIURNAL PARALLAX.

horn antenna see WAVEGUIDE.

Horologium (Clock) an inconspicuous constellation in the southern hemisphere near the star Achernar. Apart from Alpha (α), which is of magnitude 3.8, the brightest stars are of 4th magnitude. Abbrev.: Hor; genitive form: Horologii; approx. position: RA 3.5h, dec −50°; area: 249 sq deg.

Horsehead nebula (IC 434) a DARK NEBULA in Orion located near the star Zeta (ζ) Orionis. It is seen as a dark distinctively shaped region silhouetted against the bright background of an emission (H II) nebula.

horseshoe mounting see EQUATORIAL MOUNTING.

Horseshoe nebula see OMEGA NEBULA.

hot Big Bang see BIG BANG THEORY.

hot dark matter dark matter that consists of particles moving at speeds near to the speed of light. Since neutrinos have nonzero masses it is thought that they may contribute much of the hot dark matter in the Universe.

hot spot see RADIO-SOURCE STRUCTURE.

hour symbol: h. **1** a unit of time equal to 60 minutes, i.e. 1/24 of a DAY.
2 a unit of angle equal to 15° of arc, i.e. 1/24 of a circle. See RIGHT ASCENSION.

hour angle (HA) symbol: *t*. The angle measured westward along the CELESTIAL EQUATOR from an observer's meridian to the HOUR CIRCLE of a celestial body or point. It is usually expressed in hours, minutes, and seconds from 0h to 24h. It is thus measured in the same units but in the opposite direction to RIGHT ASCENSION. The angle measured eastward along the equator from the meridian is sometimes called the *meridian angle*. Due to the daily apparent rotation of the celestial sphere, a celestial body's hour angle increases daily from 0h at the meridian; after six hours the hour angle is 6h and 24 hours later the celestial body again crosses the meridian. See also SIDEREAL HOUR ANGLE.

hour circle any of a series of great circles on the CELESTIAL SPHERE along which DECLINATION is measured. The hour circle of a particular celestial body or point passes through the body or point and the north and south celestial poles. See also HOUR ANGLE.

HR prefix used to designate a star as listed in the *Harvard Revised Photometry*, 1908.

H-R diagram *short for* Hertzsprung–Russell diagram.

H I region a diffuse region of neutral, predominantly monatomic, hydrogen in interstellar space. A typical H I region is about 5 parsecs across, contains 50 solar masses of gas, and is at a temperature of 70 K. Between these clouds is more tenuous neutral hydrogen gas at a temperature of about 8000 K. Although the temperature is too low for optical emission, neutral hydrogen emits radio radiation at the spot frequency of 1.420 405 751 786 gigahertz, which corresponds to a wavelength of about 21 cm. This emission, termed the *hydrogen line* or *21 cm line emission*, is associated with a FORBIDDEN TRANSITION between two closely spaced ENERGY LEVELS of the ground state, related to the relative electron and proton spin orientation in the hydrogen atom. Predicted in 1944 by van der Hulst, it was first detected in 1951.

This radio emission has allowed the distribution and relative velocity of neutral hydrogen to be studied both in our own and in nearby spiral GALAXIES, using LINE RECEIVERS. Motions within the galaxy cause the observed frequency (1.4204 GHz) to be displaced by the DOPPLER EFFECT. The velocity is determined from the frequency shift. See also H II REGION; INTERSTELLAR MEDIUM.

H II region a region of predominantly ionized hydrogen in interstellar space, existing mainly in discrete clouds. The ionization is usually caused by

PHOTOIONIZATION by ultraviolet photons in regions of recent star formation, but cosmic rays, X-rays, or shock waves in the medium may sometimes be responsible. In comparison with the 21-cm radio emission of neutral hydrogen in H I REGIONS, the ionized hydrogen of H II regions emits radio waves by BREMSSTRAHLUNG (THERMAL EMISSION) and RECOMBINATION LINE EMISSION; the ionized hydrogen also emits recombination lines in the infrared, ultraviolet, and optical, the latter making an H II region appear as an EMISSION NEBULA. Younger H II regions are often roughly spherical with a sharply delineated boundary (see STRÖMGREN SPHERE). Their size is usually less than 200 parsecs, the largest being relatively constant in diameter from galaxy to galaxy. By studying the apparent diameters of the H II regions in a distant galaxy, the distance to the galaxy can be estimated. See also EXTRAGALACTIC H II REGION; INTERSTELLAR MEDIUM.

H–I rocket, H–II rocket see NASDA.

HST *abbrev. for* Hubble Space Telescope.

Hubble classification a classification scheme for galaxies introduced by Edwin Hubble in 1925. Although more complex and refined schemes have since been devised the simple but slightly revised Hubble scheme is still widely used. The scheme recognizes three main types of GALAXY: elliptical, spiral, and barred spiral. Each is divided into subtypes according to gross observable characteristics, the principle one being shape. These subtypes are arranged into a morphological sequence (see illustration).

Elliptical galaxies are denoted by the letter E followed by a number from 0 to 7 that indicates the apparent degree of flattening; this number is the nearest integer to $10(1 - b/a)$, where a and b are, respectively, the semimajor and semiminor axes of the observed profile. Thus E0 galaxies are almost circular in outline and E7, the most elliptical, have an $a{:}b$ ratio of about 3:1.

The spirals (type S) and barred spirals (type SB) are separated into subtypes a, b, and c along a sequence that follows a progressive decrease in central bulge luminosity compared to the disk and an increase in the openness and prominence of the spiral arms. An additional subtype, d, has been introduced. Galaxies with intermediate characteristics can be classified as Sab, SBab, Sbc, SBbc, etc. The S0 galaxies, placed at the junction of the elliptical and spiral sequences, resemble the spirals in general shape but lack spiral arms. This type was predicted by Hubble in 1925 but identified only later.

The less commonly observed irregular galaxies were not included in Hubble's original diagram, but are now placed to the right of the S and SB sequences. They were originally divided into two types. Irr I galaxies lack both symmetry and a nucleus and are mainly comprised of blue POPULATION I stars and H II REGIONS. Irr II galaxies were objects that could not otherwise be classified, possessing either a highly perturbed morphology or some prominent feature unusual for their class. The term irregular galaxy is now applied

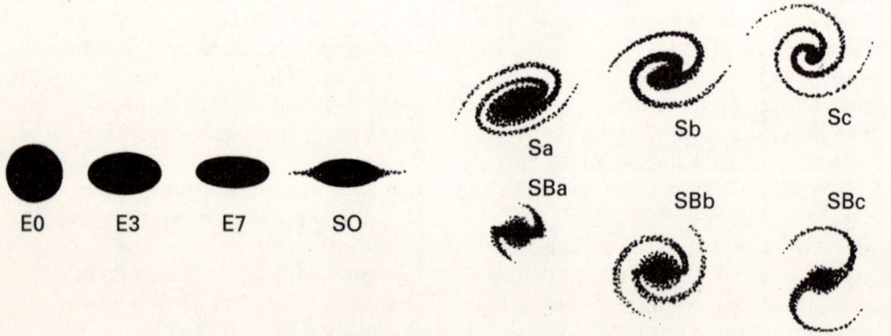

Hubble classification: Hubble's 'tuning fork' diagram

only to Hubble type Irr I, and Irr II systems are now usually reclassified as INTERACTING or STARBURST galaxies as appropriate.

Hubble constant symbol: H_0. The rate at which the expansion velocity of the Universe changes with distance; it is commonly measured in km s^{-1} megaparsec^{-1}. Current estimates place H_0 between 60 and 75 km s^{-1} Mpc^{-1}.

The value of H_0 is derived from the ratio of recession velocity to distance for galaxies beyond the LOCAL GROUP. The velocity can be measured accurately from the REDSHIFT in the galaxy's spectrum. It must be corrected for the Sun's motion (see GALACTIC ROTATION) and the VIRGOCENTRIC FLOW. The main source of dispute over the value of H_0 comes from the uncertainty of the distances to far-flung galaxies. Refinements in distance measurements have reduced the value since Hubble first determined it (as about 500 km s^{-1} Mpc^{-1}). Uncertainties in large extragalactic distances by a factor of two still leave H_0 in doubt by the same factor (see DISTANCE DETERMINATION).

The inverse of H_0 has the dimensions of time and is a measure of the age of an open Universe – the *Hubble time* (see AGE OF THE UNIVERSE). In an evolving Universe the Hubble 'constant' actually changes with time at a rate dependent upon the DECELERATION PARAMETER, q_0. It is independent of time only in a steady-state Universe where q_0 equals –1. In terms of the COSMIC SCALE FACTOR, R,

$$H_0 = R^{-1}(dR/dt)$$

See STEADY-STATE THEORY.

Hubble deep field an undistinguished – and therefore considered 'typical' – area of sky that was the subject of an extremely long observation taken with the HUBBLE SPACE TELESCOPE. The resulting image has enabled astonomers to study the ordinary galaxies at the edge of the Universe.

Hubble diagram a plot of the REDSHIFT of galaxies against their distance (see illustration) or of redshift against apparent magnitude. Apparent magnitude is a crude

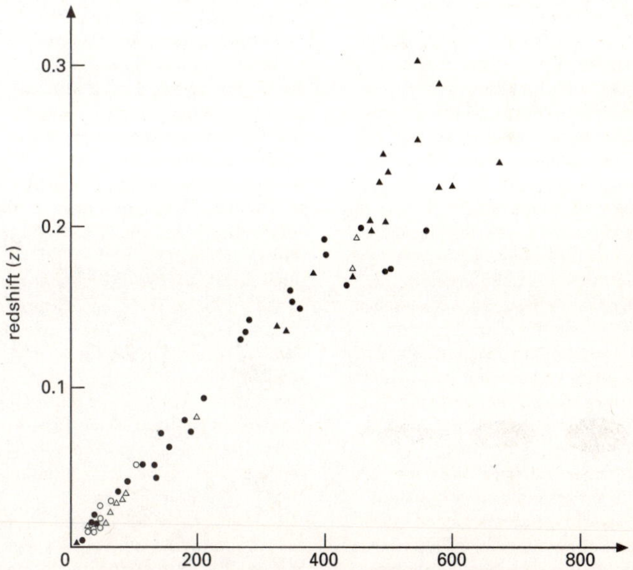

Hubble diagram compiled for several kinds of galaxies

measure of galactic distance, the value for the brightest or the third or tenth brightest member of a CLUSTER OF GALAXIES commonly being used. See HUBBLE CONSTANT; HUBBLE'S LAW.

Hubble flow see HUBBLE'S LAW.

Hubble radius the size of the observable Universe as derived from the ratio c/H_0, where H_0 is the HUBBLE CONSTANT and c the speed of light.

Hubble–Sandage variables the most massive and luminous stars ($M_v < -9$ and all spectral types) occurring in the nearby galaxies M31 and M33. Like other highly massive stars, they are VARIABLE STARS. The variations in brightness, discovered by E. Hubble and A. Sandage in 1953, were in most cases slow, small, and irregular although some displayed much greater variation. They are members of the class of LUMINOUS BLUE VARIABLES.

Hubble's law the law, first proposed by the American astronomer Edwin Hubble in 1929, stating that the recession velocity, v, of a distant extragalactic object (one outside the LOCAL GROUP) is directly proportional to its distance, D. The constant of proportionality is known as the HUBBLE CONSTANT, H_0, thus

$$v = H_0 D$$

The law is a direct consequence of a uniformly expanding isotropic Universe. The uniform outward STREAMING MOTION of all galaxies due to the cosmological expansion is called the *Hubble flow*. See also RECESSION OF THE GALAXIES.

Hubble Space Telescope (**HST**) the first of NASA's GREAT OBSERVATORIES, named after the US astronomer and cosmologist Edwin Hubble, and also the first mission in that agency's Origins Program. It was launched from the space shuttle Discovery in Apr. 1990 into a 600-km low-Earth orbit and in a projected 15-year mission was set to provide extensive imaging and spectroscopic observations over ultraviolet, optical, and near-infrared wavelengths. ESA's participation gave European observers at least 15% of the available observing time.

The science instruments carried into space aboard the HST included a 2.4-meter-diameter telescope and, in its focal plane, five highly sensitive scientific instruments functioning in the range 115–1000 nm. These were (1) the wide field/planetary camera (WF/PC), operating over 120–1000 nm; (2) ESA's faint object camera (FOC), operating over 120–650 nm; (3) a high-resolution spectrograph (115–320 nm); (4) a faint object spectrograph (115–700 nm); and (5) a high-speed photometer. In addition, one of the fine-guidance sensors made accurate astrometric measurements. The pointing accuracy was 0.007 arcsecond. Power was provided by solar arrays, and communication was made to Earth using relay satellites.

Free from the distortion and absorption effects of the Earth's atmosphere, the HST was expected to send back images that would have a resolution of 0.1 arcsecond or better. But initial observations revealed a flaw – SPHERICAL ABERRATION – in the primary mirror. This turned out to be the result of a manufacturing error. Most of the scientific programs originally envisaged, however, were carried out. There was important new spectroscopy and imaging of hot stars, late-type stellar chromospheres and coronae, the interstellar medium, galaxies and clusters, quasars and active galactic nuclei, and solar-system objects.

A servicing mission to the HST – the first of four – took place in 1993 using the space shuttle Endeavour, during which a corrective optics package, known as *COSTAR*, was emplaced and other repairs made. Pairs of mirrors in the COSTAR module focused light to five apertures serving three of the instruments – the two spectrographs and the FOC. COSTAR itself took the place of the high-speed photometer. The WF/PC was also replaced by the improved WF/PC-2. Sharply focused imaging began in 1994 and soon produced dazzling results. During the second servicing mission, by Discovery in 1997, a Near Infrared Camera and Multi-Object Spectrometer (NICMOS) and Space Telescope Imaging Spectrograph (STIS) replaced the previous high-resolution and faint-object spectrographs.

In October 1997 NASA announced that the HST mission would be extended another five years, taking its projected operational life up to 2010. In 1999, however, the cooling system for the NICMOS ceased to function and the instrument stopped working. More importantly, one of the HST's gyroscopes failed and the telescope could no longer be aimed. Astronauts crewing the space shuttle Discovery repaired the gyroscope, updated the onboard computers and carried out maintenance work. The telescope was upgraded again during a fourth service mission by the space shuttle Columbia in March 2002, with the installation of new solar arrays and a power control unit, a new cooling system for the NICMOS and a new scientific instrument, the Advanced Camera for Surveys (ACS). A fifth mission was cancelled because of safety concerns arising from the loss of Columbia in 2003. Any further missions were postponed indefinitely after NASA decided not to prolong HST's operations beyond 2010.

Despite its faults and problems, the HST proved one of NASA's outstanding successes. From 1994 it produced a long succession of sharply focused, beautiful photographs, showing in unprecedented detail a range of objects from nearby planets and asteroids to distant galaxies and gas clouds. Its famous Hubble Deep Field image of 1995, a 10-day exposure of a tiny patch of sky, revealed 1500 galaxies in various states of evolution and gave astronomers their best view back in time to the early dawn of the Universe. The HST discovered black holes at the centers of galaxies and made reliable distance measurements to galaxies using Cepheid variables as its yardsticks. In these ways, the HST helped researchers to peer into the Universe's deepest mysteries.

See also JAMES WEBB SPACE TELESCOPE.

Hubble's variable nebula (NGC 2261) a fan-shaped REFLECTION NEBULA in the constellation Monoceros that is illuminated by the variable star R Monocerotis. R Mon, an infrared source, is a very young stellar object surrounded by a disk of dust and ejecting a BIPOLAR OUTFLOW; this causes the brightness and outline of the nebula to vary. The nebula is a HERBIG–HARO OBJECT. It takes its name from the great US astronomer Edwin Hubble, who first noticed its variability.

Hubble time see HUBBLE CONSTANT.

Hungaria group a group of asteroids with a rather unusually high inclination of around 23° and semimajor axes close to 1.95 AU. It appears to be a HIRAYAMA FAMILY, which, in common with the *Phocaea group* (inclination 24°, semimajor axis 2.36 AU), consists of members that have been separated from the ASTEROID BELT by secular RESONANCES. Such orbital resonances occur when the precession of a minor body's orbit is some simple fraction of the rate at which a nearby major planet precesses. This kind of relationship makes certain orbital elements more popular than others. The group takes its name from (434) Hungaria, a small, E-type main-belt asteroid discovered by Maximilian Wolf in 1898.

Huygens eyepiece see EYEPIECE.

Huygens probe see CASSINI.

Hyades an OPEN CLUSTER of over 200 stars in the constellation Taurus. It is the nearest open cluster, about 46 parsecs away, and is scattered over an area of about 6°. Its brightest members form a V-shaped group that is visible to the naked eye, with ALDEBARAN in the foreground (but not a member). Its age is about 600 million years.

Hyakutake (1996 B2) a bright comet that passed within 15 million km of the Earth in 1996, reaching a brightness of zero magnitude.

hybrid ring a four-port device by which two input signals A and B are combined to give two output combinations $A + B$ and $A - B$, with a high degree of isolation between one input port and the other and between one output port and the other, and such that identical cables are matched (see MATCHING) at all four ports.

Hydra (Sea Serpent; Monster) the most extensive constellation in the sky, straggling between Leo in the northern hemisphere and Centaurus in the south. Its stars are rather faint apart from the solitary 2nd-magnitude ALPHARD. It contains several types of variable stars, the just-visible open cluster M48 (NGC 2548), the globular cluster M68 (NGC 4590), the bluish planetary nebula NGC 3242, and the spiral galaxy M83 (NGC 5236). Abbrev.: Hya; genitive form: Hydrae; approx. position: RA 8h to 15h, dec +7° to –35°; area: 1303 sq deg.

Hydra–Centaurus supercluster see SHAPLEY SUPERCLUSTER; SUPERCLUSTER.

hydrogen chemical symbol: H. The simplest chemical ELEMENT, with an ATOMIC NUMBER of one and the lowest density of all elements. In its most abundant form it consists of a PROTON orbited by a single electron. Two other forms, i.e. isotopes, exist: *deuterium* has a proton plus a neutron as its nucleus; *tritium*, which is radioactive (i.e. unstable), has a proton plus two neutrons.

Hydrogen is the most abundant element in the Universe: 91% by numbers of atoms, 70% by mass. All this hydrogen is primeval in origin, created in the earliest phase of the Universe (see BIG BANG THEORY). The amount of deuterium formed relative to the amount of hydrogen would have been very sensitive to the density of matter at the time of formation: deuterium readily combines with an additional neutron to form tritium, which rapidly decays into an isotope of helium. Thus if the Universe was very dense in its first few minutes, most of the deuterium would have been converted to helium. Deuterium is not easy to detect but recent measurements of the ratio of deuterium to hydrogen give an upper limit of about 2×10^{-5} for interstellar gas.

Hydrogen can exist in atomic, molecular, and ionized forms. Ionized hydrogen, H^+, more usually denoted H II, results when neutral atoms are stripped of their electrons. It occurs at high temperatures, as in the centers of stars and in H II REGIONS. NUCLEAR FUSION of hydrogen ions, i.e. protons, in the stellar core generates the energy of main-sequence stars by either the PROTON-PROTON CHAIN REACTION or the CARBON CYCLE. Ionized hydrogen can also be produced by PHOTOIONIZATION, as in EMISSION NEBULAE, and may then be detected by its RECOMBINATION LINE EMISSION.

In addition to the positive ion, the negative ion, H^-, can occur when an electron attaches itself loosely to a neutral atom. A continuous spectrum of radiation is emitted in the process. The negative ion is not very stable and breaks up easily with the second electron escaping with any amount of energy: this results in a continuous absorption spectrum. These two processes, producing continuous emission and absorption of both light and infrared radiation, take place concurrently, as happens in the Sun's PHOTOSPHERE. The H^{2-} ion has recently been discovered.

Neutral hydrogen, usually denoted H I, occurs throughout interstellar space as filaments and clouds (H I REGIONS) of varying density. It is detected by means of the 21-cm hydrogen line emission. At low temperatures and when the hydrogen density is sufficiently high, pairs of hydrogen atoms can combine to form molecular hydrogen, H_2, which exists in discrete MOLECULAR CLOUDS. The molecular ion H_3^+ forms in such clouds when a molecule, H_2, is ionized and then further reacts with H_2. The molecular ion is thought to have an important role in interstellar chemistry, allowing protons to be transferred to oxygen, carbon, and other heavy atoms, thereby leading to the formation of many different interstellar molecules. Molecular hydrogen is also a major constituent of the atmosphere of the GIANT PLANETS, with liquid hydrogen forming the bulk of the interiors of Jupiter and Saturn.

Hydrogen can be observed at a number of wavelengths including radio (21 cm), infrared, visible, and ultraviolet wavelengths (see HYDROGEN SPECTRUM).

hydrogen alpha line (Hα line) see HYDROGEN SPECTRUM.

hydrogen line (21 cm line) see H I REGION.

hydrogen region see H I REGION; H II REGION; INTERSTELLAR MEDIUM.

hydrogen spectrum emission and absorption spectra of hydrogen are relatively simple compared with spectra of heavier elements. Atomic hydrogen (H I) has a LINE SPECTRUM in which several series of lines can be distinguished. The Swiss physicist Johann Balmer showed, in 1885, that lines in the visible region of the hydrogen spectrum formed a series represented by the equation

$$1/\lambda = R_\infty(1/4 - 1/m^2)$$

λ is the wavelength of the line and m an integer greater than two. The constant R_∞ has a value of $1.097\,37 \times 10^7\ \mathrm{m}^{-1}$, and is called the *Rydberg constant.*

This series of spectral lines is called the *Balmer series*. Its existence was first explained by Niels Bohr in his theory of the atom (1913). Bohr postulated that only a discrete number of orbits is allowed to an electron in an atom and that when the electron jumps from one orbit to another, a photon of radiation is emitted or absorbed (see ENERGY LEVEL). The Balmer series is produced by transitions of the electron between the second permitted orbit, in order of distance from the nucleus, and higher orbits. When $m = 3$, the spectral line is produced by a transition from the second to the third orbit (or from the third to the second orbit). This line is referred to as Hα (the *hydrogen alpha line*) and has a wavelength of 656.4 nm, i.e. it falls in the red region of the visible spectrum. The next line, Hβ ($m = 4$), is at 486.1 nm in the blue. Hγ and Hδ occur at 434.2 nm and 410.2 nm, respectively. The lines in such a series get closer together at shorter wavelengths and the Balmer series converges to a limit at 364.6 nm in the ultraviolet region of the spectrum. Emission lines are produced by transitions from higher levels to the second orbit; absorption lines result from transitions from the second orbit to higher orbits.

In general, lines in the hydrogen spectrum can be represented by the equation $1/\lambda = R_{\infty}(1/n^2 - 1/m^2)$
where n and m are integers; n is called the *principal quantum number* and can have values from one to infinity. The Balmer series is formed for $n = 2$, i.e. the second orbit of the atom. Transitions from or to the first orbit, i.e. the ground state ($n = 1$), produce the LYMAN SERIES of spectral lines. This is in the far ultraviolet and extreme ultraviolet regions. *Lyman alpha*, denoted Ly α ($n = 1$, $m = 2$), occurs at 121.6 nm; the series Ly α, Ly β, Ly γ..., converges to a value of 91.2 nm, the *Lyman limit*. The *Paschen series* is produced by transitions to or from the third permitted orbit ($n = 3$) and occurs in the near infrared region of the spectrum. The *Brackett series* occurs at longer infrared wavelengths involving the fourth orbit ($n = 4$).

hydrostatic equilibrium a state of equilibrium in which the inwardly directed gravitational force in a star just balances the outwardly directed gas and radiation pressure. The star is thus held together but supported against collapse. The equation of hydrostatic equilibrium is given at STELLAR STRUCTURE.

hydroxyl radical the RADICAL OH, consisting of an oxygen and hydrogen atom bound together. It was the first interstellar molecule to be detected (1963) in the radio region of the spectrum and is also associated with certain red and infrared stars (see OH/IR STAR; MASER SOURCE). The spectral lines – OH lines – occur at 18, 6.3, 5.0, 3.7, and 2.2 cm.

Hydrus (Water Snake) a small constellation in the southern hemisphere lying between the Large and Small Magellanic Clouds. Its brightest star, Beta (β) Hydri, is of magnitude 2.8 and is the nearest conspicuous star to the south pole. Abbrev.: Hyi; genitive form: Hydri; approx. position: RA 2h, dec –70°; area: 243 sq deg.

Hygeia ((10) Hygeia) a large ASTEROID with a diameter of about 407 km and a quoted mass of $(9 \pm 5) \times 10^{19}$ kg. The Hubble Space Telescope has revealed that it has a spherical shape. Microwave measurements indicate that it has a surface soil layer that is very finely divided and at least 8 cm deep. This is similar to the depth of soil on VESTA and Pallas. The fourth largest asteroid, it was discovered in 1849 by the Italian astronomer Annibale de Gasparis. See Table 3, Appendix.

hyperbola a type of CONIC SECTION that has an eccentricity greater than one. See also ORBIT.

hyperboloid reflector a reflector whose surface is hyperboloid in shape, i.e. its curvature is that obtained by rotating a hyperbola about its axis. The secondary mirror in a CASSEGRAIN TELESCOPE is hyperboloid.

Hyperion a satellite of Saturn, discovered in 1848. Images taken by VOYAGER 2 in 1981 showed an elongated irregular body with a 'chaotic' spin orientation and rate; this tumbling is due to its irregular shape, its eccentric orbit, and the gravitational effects upon it of Saturn and TITAN. Hyperion has a low ALBEDO (0.03) compared with the other icy inner satellites of Saturn, although it is also probably composed largely of ice. The Voyager 2 pictures showed craters with diameters up to 120 km and one long ridge or scarp extending for 300 km; this is named *Bond–Lassell* in honor of the discoverers of Hyperion, William Cranch Bond, George Philips Bond, and William Lasell. The Cassini–Huygens probe flew by Hyperion in Sept. 2005 at a distance of 500 km. The images it returned reveal a heavily cratered world with a reddish tinge. In the Cassini images Hyperion shows evidence of possible multiple landslides in the past. A vast impact crater 200 km across is surrounded by rays. A mysterious dark material fills many of the craters, See Table 2, Appendix.

hyperluminous IRAS galaxies see IRAS GALAXIES.

hypernova a new type of SUPERNOVA, possibly related to cosmological GAMMA-RAY BURSTS. The prototype supernova, SN 1998bw, was an unusually energetic event, some 30 times more luminous than a normal core-collapse supernova. It was also detected as a gamma-ray burst, albeit a weak one. In the best model to date, the progenitor was a rapidly rotating, massive helium star that collapsed into a black hole forming a massive disk around it. Matter ejected along the spin axis in the form of a relativistic jet is believed to be responsible for the gamma-ray burst. Several more hypernovae have been identified since 1998.

hypersensitization the subjection of an unexposed PHOTOGRAPHIC EMULSION to one or more methods of treatment in order to improve its response to light or other radiation. This allows the emulsion to be used at the extremely low intensities of light and other electromagnetic radiation encountered in astronomy without an excessively long exposure time. Alternatively in a set period of telescope time the quantity or quality of information obtained can be increased by hypersensitization. Various techniques are used. One particularly suitable for light-sensitive emulsions is *gas hypersensitization* (or *hypering*). It involves heating the emulsion in either pure nitrogen gas or in nitrogen with a small admixture of hydrogen. The gas removes oxygen and water vapor from the emulsion; these impurities act as desensitizers. Heating speeds up this leaching process and can also increase the chemical sensitization, i.e. the possibility that grains in the emulsion if hit by light will be activated.

Hz *symbol for* hertz.

Ii

Iapetus a satellite of Saturn, discovered in 1671 by Giovanni Domenico Cassini. The diameter of Iapetus is 1440 km so that in size it is the twin of the satellite RHEA but its density, 1.21 g cm^{-3}, is much lower. It is a strange satellite with a dark leading hemisphere (albedo 0.04–0.05) compared with a bright trailing edge of albedo 0.6. The dark hemisphere carries the name *Cassini Regio*. It appears to be coated with some dark material. The demarcation between the dark and light regions is not abrupt and there is a transition region 200–300 km in width with a meandering boundary. The bright trailing edge is most heavily cratered; some of the craters have dark floors but it is not known if the dark material in them is the same as that covering Cassini Regio. The material on the leading edge is thought to be carbon-based, but it is unclear whether it was emitted from the interior of Iapetus or was debris from eruptions on other Saturnian satellites swept up by Iapetus from space.

Iapetus was photographed by Voyager 2 in 1981 and by Cassini–Huygens in 2004. The Cassini images revealed some new features not seen on the Voyager images, in particular a vast ancient impact basin over 400 km across, which has been heavily overprinted with more recent smaller craters, and a curious and extraordinary ridge that almost exactly coincides with Iapetus' equator. It appears as a 20-km-wide band, 1300 km long, that seems to girdle the whole satellite, extending above the surface of Iapetus to a height of up to 13 km. The equatorial ridge may be a mountain belt that has folded upward, or perhaps it was formed when material from inside Iapetus erupted onto the surface through a crack and accumulated locally.

See also TABLE 2, Appendix.

IAT *abbrev. for* International Atomic Time.

IAU *abbrev. for* International Astronomical Union.

IC *abbrev for* Index Catalog. See NGC.

Icarus (**(1566) Icarus**) An ASTEROID that was discovered in 1949 by Walter Baade and passed only 0.04 AU from the Earth in 1968. It belongs to the APOLLO GROUP of near-Earth asteroids and has one of the smallest PERIHELION DISTANCES (0.205 AU), well within the orbit of Mercury. See Table 3, Appendix.

icebergs see LSB GALAXIES; MALIN 1.

Ice Cube see AMANDA TELESCOPE.

ice dwarfs large distant interplanetary objects that exceed the size of a normal cometary nucleus and are much icier than an ordinary asteroid. The composition of asteroids varies somewhat as a function of distance from the Sun, so that the more distant HILDAS and TROJANS will certainly contain more icelike material than the main-belt asteroids. However, the vast majority of ice dwarfs are probably to be found in the KUIPER BELT and beyond. PLUTO, though traditionally considered a planet, is now regarded as among the largest icy dwarfs, along with other Kuiper belt objects and TRANS-NEPTUNIAN OBJECTS. CHIRON and PHOLUS may also be placed in this category.

ICM *abbrev. for* intracluster medium.

icy satellites see SATELLITE, NATURAL.

Ida-2 an asteroid that was discovered in

1880. It is an S-type asteroid, studied by the Galileo spacecraft in 1993, when it was found to have a satellite, named *Dactyl*. Ida is about 58 km × 23 km. Dactyl is about 1.5 km in diameter and orbits Ida at a distance of about 100 km.

Ikeya-Seki comet (**1965 VIII**) a COMET that was discovered by two amateur Japanese comet searchers. At one time it was actually thought that it would hit the Sun but it turned out to be a SUNGRAZING COMET with a perihelion distance of 0.0078 AU, missing the Sun's surface by 0.68 solar radii. The orbit is retrograde with an eccentricity of 0.99915.

image the representation of an object formed from the light or other electromagnetic radiation reflected or transmitted by the object and collected and brought to a focus by a telescope, camera, or similar instrument. Depending on the type of object being observed and telescope involved, images may be viewed directly by the observer, photographed, or recoded or analyzed by other instruments or electronic equipment. In an optical telescope, light is gathered by the PRIMARY MIRROR or OBJECTIVE, which bends the incoming rays until they meet at the focal point where the image is generated. In astronomy, the objects observed are so distant that images formed by all telescopes are upside down and real – that is, the light that produces them actually passes through them, making it possible for them to be projected onto a screen, for example. Such images are magnified by lenses in the EYEPIECE. In a refractor or Schmidt–Cassegrain, an angled device called a star diagonal, containing a prism or mirror, can be inserted in front of the eyepiece. Apart from making the telescope easier to use by making the eyepiece more accessible, this item of equipment turns the image up the right way but laterally inverts it, swapping it left to right as in a mirror. Radio telescopes work in a similar way to optical instruments, producing images from radio waves and converting them to a visible form by computer processing. See also IMAGING

image converter see IMAGE TUBE.

image intensifier see IMAGE TUBE.

image photon counting system see IPCS.

image processing see IMAGING.

image tube (**image intensifier**) an evacuated electronic device that is used to intensify a faint optical image. The beam of light (or near-ultraviolet radiation) falls on a PHOTOCATHODE so that electrons are liberated by the photoelectric effect. The electrons are accelerated by an electric field and may be detected and recorded by a variety of methods. They can be focused on a positively charged phosphor screen so that an optical image is produced, many times brighter than that of the original beam. This image can be directed onto a CCD detector. Alternatively, it can be made to fall on the photocathode of a second image tube and the intensification process repeated. Several image tubes can be linked in this way to form a *multistage image tube* but the coupling between phosphor screen and subsequent photocathode must be very efficient. The image on the final phosphor screen may then be photographed. The ELECTRONOGRAPHIC CAMERA and the IPCS (image photon counting system) use slightly different techniques.

In *image converters* a beam of infrared or ultraviolet radiation or X-rays is incident on the photosensitive surface. The liberated electrons can then produce a pictorial representation of a 'nonvisible' image.

imaging the representation, by means of TV pictures, photographs, graphs, etc., of an object or area by the sensing and recording of patterns of light or other radiation emitted by, reflected from, or transmitted through the object or area. Two broad classifications are *chemical imaging*, i.e. PHOTOGRAPHY, and *electronic imaging*. Both are important in astronomy, a variety of photographic emulsions and electronic devices being available for different frequency bands of the electromagnetic spectrum.

The majority of information gathered by ground-based and orbiting telescopes is in digital form so that it can be manipulated by computer. This information can be derived directly from electronic devices, such as CCDS, PHOTON-COUNTING DETECTORS, or PHOTOVOLTAIC DETECTORS, associated with the telescope. These devices respond to radiation by converting it to an electrical signal. They are more sensitive than photographic emulsions, responding to lower levels of intensity and/or producing an image in a shorter time. Photographic plates do, however, provide an image of a much greater area of the sky than existing electronic devices. Machines such as COSMOS have therefore been built to measure data on photographic plates rapidly and automatically and produce results in digital form.

An electronic detector can be moved across the focused image of an astronomical object or area of the sky, or the image can be moved across the detector. The electrical signal from the detector is sampled in such a way that an array of values corresponding to an array of portions of the complete image is obtained. Alternatively the image falls on a large number of closely packed detectors, all producing a signal. In each case the result is a set of numbers corresponding to some property of the individual image portions, e.g. the intensity at a particular wavelength. The individual portions into which the image is divided are called *pixels* (short for *picture elements*). The greater the number of pixels per image, the higher the resolution, i.e. the greater the detail seen.

This numerical version of the image will normally reside in a computer system, and can be manipulated in different ways in order to highlight different aspects of the original image; the manipulative techniques are known as *image processing*. The final form of the display can be a TV monitor, a visual display unit attached to a computer, a plotting device, or photographic film, and information derived from the image can also appear in graphs and tables, and be subjected to statistical and numerical analysis.

imaging proportional counter (**IPC**) see PROPORTIONAL COUNTER.

Imbrian System one of the stratigraphic systems of the Moon, defined by the deposits of the IMBRIUM BASIN and covering the period from about 3.85 to 3.15 billion (10^9) years ago. It includes the ORIENTALE BASIN, most visible MARE deposits, and many large CRATERS. See also COPERNICAN SYSTEM; NECTARIAN SYSTEM.

Imbrium Basin the second youngest lunar BASIN, of which much of the second and third rings survive as mountain arcs (see table at MOUNTAINS, LUNAR). The EJECTA BLANKET of the basin covers much of the NEARSIDE and provides the major reference horizon for lunar stratigraphy. The basin was formed 3850 million years ago and was flooded with basalt lavas during at least the following 600 million years. This produced *Mare Imbrium* (*Sea of Rains*), which was visited by Lunokhod 1, and also *Palus Putredinis*, which was sampled by Apollo 15. See also FRA MAURO FORMATION; IMBRIAN SYSTEM.

immersion entry of a celestial body into a state of invisibility during an ECLIPSE or OCCULTATION.

inclination **1** symbol: *i*. The angle between the orbital plane of a celestial body and a reference plane. For a planet or comet the reference plane is the plane of the ECLIPTIC, for a satellite it is the primary's equatorial plane, and for a double star it is the plane of the sky. Inclination is one of the ORBITAL ELEMENTS and varies between 0 and 180°, being less than 90° for a body with DIRECT MOTION.

2 (**axial inclination**) the angle between the rotational axis of a body and a line perpendicular to its orbital plane.

See also TABLES 1–3, Appendix.

Index Catalog (**IC**) see NGC.

Indus (**Indian**) a constellation in the southern hemisphere near Grus, the brightest stars being of 3rd magnitude. The star Epsilon (ε) Indi, one of the Sun's near neighbors, is located on the northwestern edge of the constellation (see EPSILON INDI). Abbrev.: Ind; genitive form: Indi; approx. position: RA 21h, dec –60°; area: 294 sq deg.

inequality an irregularity in the orbital motion of a celestial body. The inequalities of the Moon's motion are periodic terms whose sum gives the variation of either the spherical coordinates or the osculating elements of the lunar orbit. The principal inequalities of the Moon's motion are EVECTION and VARIATION.

inertia the property of a body by which it

resists change in its velocity. It is inertia that causes a body to continue in a state of rest or of uniform motion in a straight line (see NEWTON'S LAWS OF MOTION). The force required to give a specific acceleration to a body depends directly on its inertia. It is through the property of inertia that the concept of the MASS of a body (its *inertial mass*) arises.

inertial frame a FRAME OF REFERENCE in which an isolated particle placed at rest will remain at rest, and one in uniform motion will maintain a constant velocity. It is thus a frame of reference that is not subject to acceleration, as from a gravitational field, and in which Newton's first law of motion applies. According to Einstein's special theory of RELATIVITY, which is concerned only with inertial frames, all laws of physics are the same in every inertial frame.

inertial mass see INERTIA; MASS.

inferior conjunction see CONJUNCTION.

inferior planets the planets Mercury and Venus, which lie closer to the Sun than the Earth.

inflation a short period of very rapid expansion of the Universe postulated to occur very soon after the BIG BANG. The hypothesis of inflation in the EARLY UNIVERSE solves a number of cosmological problems. One of these is the *flatness problem*; i.e. the problem that the Universe appears to be almost exactly Euclidean. Another of these problems is the *horizon problem*; i.e. the problem of why the Universe looks the same on opposite horizons in spite of there not being enough time for light to traverse the Universe. The third problem is the *monopole problem*; i.e. the problem of why MAGNETIC MONOPOLES predicted by GRAND UNIFIED THEORIES are not plentiful.

If there was a period of rapid expansion when the size of the Universe was about the same as the PLANCK LENGTH then all these problems disappear. Space–time would become much flatter as a result of such an expansion. Before the inflation the Universe would have been sufficiently small for signals to go the very small distance from one side of it to the other.

In addition to solving these problems inflation provides a solution to the problem of STRUCTURE FORMATION in the Universe. It is postulated that quantum fluctuations in the early Universe were magnified by inflation, producing the irregularities necessary for the formation of structures. This theory made the prediction that there should be very slight variations in the temperature of the COSMIC MICROWAVE BACKGROUND (CMB) as a result of the irregularities in the early Universe. In the early 1990s COBE found precisely the expected variations. This finding was a major success for inflation theory. The theory also predicts that the irregularities in the early Universe produced GRAVITATIONAL RADIATION with distinct features. It is hoped that sufficiently sensitive detectors will detect this radiation within the first few decades of the twenty-first century.

Although the general idea of inflation theory is very successful it has proved very difficult to link it with any particular model of elementary particle theory. Theoretical frameworks for the early Universe invoke GUTS (see FUNDAMENTAL FORCES), where the fundamental forces are held in a symmetry not observed in the present Universe. It is hypothesized that the state of the Universe changed at an age of 10^{-35} seconds, when the electromagnetic and strong nuclear forces separated, or 'froze out' to different values. Mathematical solutions to this process of symmetry-breaking invoke the creation of defects in spacetime, such as MONOPOLES and DOMAIN WALLS, that are not observed in the present Universe. The phase transition caused by symmetry-breaking released energy that is calculated to have caused the Universe to expand or inflate catastrophically. Inflation theory was initially proposed by Alan GUTH in 1981 although his initial model was seriously flawed.

infrared astronomy the study of radiation from space with wavelengths beyond the red end of the visible spectrum, i.e. from about 0.8 micrometer (μm) to about 1000 μm; radiation above 300 μm is now described as submillimetric (see SUBMILLIMETER ASTRONOMY). Infrared observations are possible from the ground through several ATMOSPHERIC WINDOWS up to about 20 μm, but longer-wavelength observations require balloon-, rocket-, or satellite-platforms. The equipment used includes reflecting telescopes (see INFRARED TELESCOPE) and solid-state INFRARED DETECTORS, such as PHOTOVOLTAIC and PHOTOCONDUCTIVE devices and BOLOMETERS. The detectors need to be cooled to low temperatures, and in some cases the telescope optics are also cooled, to minimize the instrumental thermal emission and NOISE. The first satellite-borne infrared telescope, IRAS, was launched on Jan. 20 1983. IRAS has made an all-sky survey in the 10–100 μm waveband as well as investigating in more detail a wide range of astronomical sources. The European Space Agency launched the INFRARED SPACE OBSERVATORY (ISO) in 1995. ISO uses a cooled telescope to make observations in the 2–200 μm waveband.

Cosmic INFRARED SOURCES emit infrared radiation in a variety of ways. They may emit thermally as approximate BLACK-BODY radiators; such sources include the stars themselves, COSMIC DUST grains in the circumstellar shells around stars, and MOLECULAR CLOUDS, and have temperatures in the range 20–1000 K. In H II REGIONS electrons moving in the thermally heated and ionized gas emit infrared radiation by a process known as thermal bremsstrahlung (see THERMAL EMISSION). In PHOTODISSOCIATION REGIONS, where molecular clouds have interfaces with H II regions, highly ionized, ionized, and neutral species all occur, and collisional EXCITATION can produce FORBIDDEN LINES in the far-infrared and infrared spectra of these species. Infrared emission can also be produced by a nonthermal process in which high-energy electrons moving in a magnetic field emit SYNCHROTRON radiation.

infrared background radiation unresolved radiation from space in the infrared waveband 10–200 μm. The diffuse radiation is the sum of several components: ZODIACAL LIGHT, the infrared flux from stars, emission from COSMIC DUST in the Galaxy, INFRARED CIRRUS, and the infrared flux from external galaxies. Observations from the satellite IRAS show that zodiacal emission dominates the infrared background at 12–60 μm except near the galactic plane. The zodiacal emission is also present at 100 μm but diffuse galactic emission is prominent at this wavelength. See also COSMIC BACKGROUND RADIATION.

infrared cirrus extended sources of 60–100 μm infrared emission superimposed on the INFRARED BACKGROUND RADIATION. Such sources were first detected by the satellite IRAS. At high galactic latitudes some of these sources are associated with clouds of atomic hydrogen containing infrared-emitting dust at a temperature of about 30 K. Others are only poorly correlated with known interstellar gas clouds and may be due to cold material in the Solar System.

infrared detectors devices sensitive to INFRARED RADIATION in the region from 0.8 μm to about 400 μm. Present-day detectors are nearly all operated at cryogenic temperatures: 77 K using liquid nitrogen or 4 K or lower by using liquid helium. They are made from very pure semiconductor material, such as silicon or germanium, either as 1 mm cubes or smaller or as square arrays of tiny PIXELS (as with CCDS). For either form, electrical connections to the semiconductor allow monitoring of the electrical signal that is generated when the device is struck by infrared PHOTONS. Different conversion mechanisms from incident photon to electrical signal are involved, depending upon the detector (see BOLOMETER; PHOTOCONDUCTIVE DETECTOR; PHOTOVOLTAIC DETECTOR).

'Doping' the detector material with a particular impurity determines the wavelength region in which the detector will have its best response; impurities used include indium, gallium, copper, arsenic, antimony, beryllium, and boron. For example, a gallium-doped germanium detector (denoted, using chemical symbols, as Ge:Ga) has a useful wavelength region of 40–180 μm while an arsenic-doped silicon detector (denoted Si:As) has a useful range of 8–14 μm. A detector denoted InSb is made of indium antimonide, which is a compound rather than a crystalline mixture. Detectors of Ge:Ga can have their response limit extended to 205 μm by slightly squashing or stressing the material of the detector. Infrared detectors are susceptible to hits from COSMIC RAY particles, and work is progressing on detectors that are less vulnerable to this phenomenon.

infrared excess see INFRARED SOURCES.

infrared radiation ELECTROMAGNETIC RADIATION lying between the radio and the visible bands of the electromagnetic spectrum. The wavelengths range from about 0.8 micrometer (μm) to about 1000 μm. The definitions of the regions of the infrared are a little arbitrary, but are roughly as follows:

near-infrared: 0.8 to 8 μm
mid-infrared: 8.0 to 30 μm
far-infrared: 30 to 300 μm

The region around 8–13 μm has been described as far-infrared by some astronomers. Radiation above 300 μm is now called *submillimeter radiation*.

infrared sources a variety of objects emitting strongly in the infrared (see INFRARED RADIATION). Many stars exhibit an *infrared excess* in that they radiate more strongly in the 1–20 μm waveband than would be expected from their SPECTRAL TYPE. In most cases the excess arises from circumstellar shells containing COSMIC DUST grains that are heated by the visible and UV radiation from the central star. PROTOSTARS and their associated dust clouds are also strong infrared emitters. Many T TAURI STARS emit infrared radiation, in some cases by thermal bremsstrahlung and/or emission from heated dust. At longer wavelengths (60–200 μm) cool MOLECULAR CLOUDS containing dust are found to be infrared sources.

Infrared line emission occurs from a variety of different complex regions, particularly from H II REGIONS and associated molecular-cloud interfaces. Lines from atomic hydrogen are seen in the near-infrared (Brackett and Paschen lines), and in the mid- and far-infrared the lines occur from neutral and ionized states of neon, oxygen, nitrogen, sulfur, and iron. Highly ionized species of, for example, oxygen (O III) and nitrogen (N III) can be identified by the FORBIDDEN LINES in their infrared spectra. The molecule carbon monoxide has been detected in the far-infrared from some sources, the lines measured arising from the rotational spectrum of the molecule.

Infrared emission is also found in extragalactic sources (see IRAS) and is strongly correlated with galaxy type: elliptical and lenticular galaxies emit little or no infrared while most spiral galaxies are infrared emitters. Active galaxies, such as SEYFERT type II, BL LAC OBJECTS, and QUASARS, exhibit infrared emission from their nuclei. It is unclear at the present time whether this is thermal emission by dust in the nuclei or is due to nonthermal SYNCHROTRON EMISSION. Galaxies that are interacting or merging are also seen to be strong infrared CONTINUUM emitters. This may be due to the triggering of star formation in one or both galaxies.

Infrared Space Observatory (**ISO**) a satellite project funded by ESA. The spacecraft was launched in Nov. 1995, on an Ariane-4 rocket, and injected into a highly elliptical 24-hour orbit. Its telescope plus instruments were used to make photometric and spectroscopic studies of galactic, extragalactic, and Solar-System objects emitting in the infrared in the waveband 2–200 μm.

The payload consisted of a RITCHEY–CHRÉTIEN telescope with a 60-cm diameter primary mirror, and experiments mounted behind this at the CASSEGRAIN FOCUS. This equipment was all housed in a toroidal liquid-helium cryostat, which is insulated and Sun-shielded, the telescope looking out from one end of the enclosure. The tank of superfluid liquid helium, at a temperature below 2.17 K, provides the temperatures of 2–3 K that are necessary for the detectors to become sensitive. The telescope structure and mirrors were cooled to about 8 K by the gas boiling off from the helium.

Four cryogenically cooled instruments made up the scientific payload. ISOCAM is an infrared camera system that uses two infrared detector arrays (32 by 32 pixels) to view selected parts of the sky through the

ISO telescope. The first array operates over 2.5–5.5 μm and the second over 4–17 μm, bandpass filters being used to limit the spectral coverage. The total field of view can be as large as 3 arc minutes. ISOPHOT is a multiband imaging photometer-polarimeter operating over 2–200 μm. Its 23 infrared FILTERS can be used to limit the radiation reaching different detectors in the system. Some of these filters are common to those used on ISOCAM, and to those flown on the earlier satellite IRAS, thus providing overlap with both. The short-wavelength and long-wavelength spectrometers, SWS and LWS, are high-resolution spectrometers operating over 2–45 μm and 45–180 μm respectively. A variety of INFRARED DETECTORS can be used with both instruments, and FABRY–PEROT INTERFEROMETERS provide the highest resolutions.

Two ground stations were used to control and receive the data from ISO. One was provided by ESA and the second was provided by a Japanese/US collaboration.

infrared telescope (**flux collector**) a reflecting telescope used to detect and study infrared radiation from space; refractors cannot be employed because glass is opaque at these wavelengths. The mirror surface does not, however, need to be made to the same accuracy as one used for optical work because of the longer wavelengths of infrared radiation. Since neither the eye nor the photographic plate is sensitive to long-wavelength infrared radiation, special INFRARED DETECTORS are required, such as PHOTOVOLTAIC and PHOTOCONDUCTIVE DETECTORS and BOLOMETERS. The detectors, and in some cases the telescope optics, must be cooled to liquid-helium or liquid-nitrogen temperatures to reduce thermal emission from the instruments themselves and hence NOISE. As an alternative to active cooling by cryogenic liquids, space telescopes can be allowed to cool radiatively, i.e. passively, by being shielded from direct sunlight.

Infrared telescopes can detect sources partly or totally obscured at optical wavelengths by interstellar dust, and can identify those that are true infrared sources rather than highly reddened ordinary stars. Because water vapor in the Earth's atmosphere absorbs infrared radiation (see ATMOSPHERIC WINDOWS), the most advanced work is carried out with specially designed telescopes, such as the UK INFRARED TELESCOPE, at high-altitude observatories or with airborne or space observatories, such as KAO, IRAS, and ISO. Infrared telescopes can operate day and night.

Infrared Telescope Facility (**IRTF**) a 3.0-meter INFRARED TELESCOPE at the MAUNA KEA Observatory, Hawaii, that began operations in 1979 and is operated by the University of Hawaii's Institute of Astronomy on behalf of NASA, which funds the IRTF as a national facility. The telescope has a CER-VIT primary mirror and an equatorial mounting.

infrared windows see ATMOSPHERIC WINDOWS.

initial mass function (**IMF**) see STELLAR MASS.

injection (**insertion**) the process of boosting a spacecraft into a particular orbit or trajectory. It is also the time of such action or the entry itself.

inner Lagrangian point see EQUIPOTENTIAL SURFACES; LAGRANGIAN POINTS.

inner planets the terrestrial planets Mercury, Venus, Earth, and Mars, which lie closer to the Sun than the main ASTEROID BELT.

insolation the exposure of any surface or body to solar radiation. It is usually quoted as the radiant flux received from the Sun per unit area per unit time; it can therefore be considered as the heating effectiveness of solar radiation.

instability strip *short for* Cepheid instability strip. See PULSATING VARIABLES.

INT *abbrev. for* Isaac Newton Telescope.

INTEGRAL (**International Gamma-Ray Astrophysics Laboratory**) a European Space Agency (ESA) space observatory, launched Oct. 2002 aboard a Proton rocket from Baikonur in Kazakhstan and comprising four high-energy astronomical telescopes. The 4-tonne satellite, developed and operated by ESA in conjunction with Russia and the USA, was built to detect some of the most energetic radiation emanating from space, including that from gamma-ray bursts and neutron stars. Its achievements include spectral measurements of numerous gamma-ray sources and the mapping of the galactic plane in gamma radiation, the detection of some of the faintest and closest gamma-ray bursts ever found, the resolution of diffuse gamma-ray emissions from the center of the Milky Way Galaxy, the increase of our knowledge of active galactic nuclei, and the discovery of a new class of highly absorbed object. In a mission intended to last for two years, extendable to three, INTEGRAL followed a highly eccentric orbit (period 72 hours, inclination 51.6°) that carried it from 9000 km to 153 000 km above the Earth. Its four science instruments were (1) IBIS, a gamma-ray imager operating over the range 50–100 000 keV and imaging the sky at the arcminute level; (2) SPI, a gamma-ray spectrometer with a functional spectral range of 15–10 000 keV and a spectral resolution of about 500; (3) JEM-X, an X-ray monitor operating over the range 4–100 keV; and (4) OMC, an optical monitor with CCD and lens optics designed to detect the afterglow from a gamma-ray burst and identify the object associated with it.

integrated magnitude see TOTAL MAGNITUDE.

integration time the period for which a noisy signal is averaged in order to improve the signal to noise ratio in an electronic system. See SENSITIVITY.

intensity 1 (**radiant intensity**) the RADIANT FLUX emitted per unit solid angle by a point source in a given direction. It is measured in watts per steradian.
2 *obsolete name for* field strength of a magnetic or electric field.

interacting galaxies two, three, or (more rarely) four or more galaxies that show signs of mutual disturbance, such as perturbed morphologies or extruded filaments of stellar material, called *tidal tails*, which can sometimes link to form bridges between the galaxies. Examples include the ANTENNAE, ARP 220 and the MICE. Encounters of galaxies moving at low relative velocities are much more likely to produce MERGERS than fast encounters, where the interaction time is short and the galaxies pass through each other completely. The infrared satellite IRAS found that many interacting galaxies are powerful infrared sources: the interaction apparently stimulates star formation (see IRAS GALAXIES). There is also evidence that some radio-quiet QSO lie in interacting galaxies.

interference 1 unwanted signals picked up by a RADIO TELESCOPE or other electronic equipment; the signals usually arise from terrestrial sources but occasionally come from the Sun or Jupiter.
2 the interaction of two sets of waves to produce patterns of high and low intensity (*interference fringes*). For this to happen the two beams of light or other radiation must be coherent, i.e. they must be related with respect to PHASE and have the same, or nearly the same, WAVELENGTH. They must intersect at a fairly small angle and not differ too much in intensity. In addition, they must not be polarized in mutually perpendicular planes.

The interference pattern of fringes formed at a particular position is the sum of the intensities of the two interacting waves at that position. The fringes occur because of differences in pathlength between interacting waves, i.e. because of unequal distances from source to interaction point. If the difference is a whole number of wavelengths, then wave peaks (or troughs) of the two interacting waves coincide and the waves reinforce one another, producing a bright fringe when light waves are involved; this is termed *constructive interference*. If the path difference is an integral number of half wavelengths a peak coincides with a wave trough and a dark fringe results; this is *destructive interference*.

Both constructive and destructive interference of light can be produced by means of thin films of uniform thickness, as used in INTERFERENCE FILTERS. Waves of selected wavelengths are reflected from the front and back surfaces of the film and by a suitable choice of film composition and thickness the waves will either be reinforced or will cancel each other.

See also INTERFEROMETER.

interference filter an optical, ultraviolet, or infrared FILTER in which unwanted wavelengths are removed by destructive INTERFERENCE rather than by absorption. It produces a very narrow band of wavelengths, typically between 1 and 10 nanometers. One form, the *multilayer filter*, consists of a stack of transparently thin films with different refractive indices deposited on an optical glass substrate. The films allow only a selected waveband of 1 nm or less to be transmitted right through. The remaining wavelengths are reflected and caused to interfere destructively.

interference fringes see INTERFERENCE; RADIO TELESCOPE.

interferometer an instrument or system in which a beam of light or other radiation is split and subsequently recombined after the components of the split beam have traversed different pathlengths so that INTERFERENCE occurs and an interference pattern is produced. Interferometers use the effect of interference to measure some parameter – either the frequency components of the radiation undergoing interference, as with the FABRY–PEROT INTERFEROMETER or FOURIER TRANSFORM spectrometer, or spatial information about the radiation source, such as the apparent diameter of a star as with the MICHELSON STELLAR INTERFEROMETER or the laser interferometers being used to detect GRAVITATIONAL WAVES.

The *spatial interferometer* also uses interference to make measurements but takes a different form. Radio, infrared, or optical waves collected by a group of separate telescopes observing the same object and linked to a common receiver are combined in order to improve the spatial RESOLUTION of the system: the resolving power is equivalent to that of a single instrument with an aperture equal to the largest distance separating the component telescopes. The interference pattern from a particular pair of telescopes records information on the relative amplitude and phase of the two beams being collected by that pair. The interference patterns from different pairs can then be combined and processed by computer to produce a highly detailed image of the source of the beams.

The *radio interferometer* is one of the two basic forms of RADIO TELESCOPE. Very great separations (baselines) may now be used (see VLBI; LBI). Technical problems have slowed the successful development of this type of interferometer to operate at optical and infrared wavelengths. New technology, however, especially ADAPTIVE OPTICS, reduces the distorting effects of atmospheric turbulence, which is a serious problem for these *optical* and *infrared interferometers*. Since the end of the 1980s, optical interferometers, such as SUSI, have been used for the measurement of stellar diameters, the resolving of close binary stars, and wide-angle astrometry with milliarcsecond precision. Radio, IR, and optical interferometry carried out in space avoids the problems of atmospheric turbulence; see RADIOASTRON; VSOP.

intergalactic medium the matter contained in the space between the GALAXIES, about which very little is known. It exists in large amounts only in CLUSTERS OF GALAXIES where it is completely ionized and constitutes a significant proportion of the total observed mass of the cluster. Absorption lines in quasar spectra often indicate many clouds of intergalactic hydrogen along the line of sight but their total mass is very small.

intermediate-mass stars see STELLAR MASS.

intermediate polar system see MAGNETIC CATACLYSMIC VARIABLES.

International Astronomical Union (IAU) an international association of astronomers that is the controlling body of world astronomy. It was founded in Brussels in 1919. A general assembly is held every three years, the first one having occurred in 1922. In addition the IAU organizes periodic symposia for the discussion of current astronomical problems, establishes international standards and the official names for astronomical objects, produces several publications, and runs a telegram service for the rapid dispersal of information relating to transient phenomena such as novae and comets. One of the IAU's most important achievements was the establishment in 1929 of official constellation boundaries, making it possible to assign every star and the vast majority of other objects to one constellation and one only.

International Atomic Time (**TAI**) the most precisely determined timescale now available, set up by the Bureau Internationale de l'Heure in Paris, following analysis of ATOMIC TIME standards in many countries. It was adopted for all timing on Jan. 1 1972. The fundamental unit is the SI SECOND. It is a more precise scale than can be determined from astronomical observations. Coordinated UNIVERSAL TIME is based on TAI and is used for all civil timekeeping. See also DYNAMICAL TIME.

International Cometary Explorer (**ICE**) see INTERNATIONAL SUN-EARTH EXPLORER.

International Microgravity Laboratory a SPACELAB mission, launched in Jan. 1992 and dedicated to MICROGRAVITY research.

International Solar Polar Mission *former name of* Ulysses.

International Space Station (**ISS**) an internationally managed permanently crewed spacecraft providing an Earth-orbiting platform intended to function as an observatory, laboratory, manufacturing facility, assembly facility, and staging post. The ISS began as an ambitious program originated by the USA in 1984 under the name *Freedom*. The project went through several revisions of its design in order to reduce costs and meet Congressional budgetary limitations. Meanwhile Russia, with its considerable experience in building and running its SALYUT and MIR space stations, was contemplating the development of a successor to Mir, Mir-2. Following the break-up of the Soviet Union in 1991, however, the Russians too faced budgetary restrictions. In September 1993 the USA and the Russian Federation signed an agreement to merge the Freedom and Mir-2 projects, resulting in the birth of the ISS. Since then, the project has been widened to embrace contributions from 16 countries in all: the USA, Russia, Japan, and Canada; the ESA member countries Italy, Belgium, the Netherlands, Denmark, Norway, France, Spain, Germany, Sweden, Switzerland, and the UK; and Brazil.

Assembly of the ISS in space began Nov. 20 1998, when the first module, Zarya (Sunrise), was carried into orbit by a Russian Proton rocket from the Baikonur Cosmodrome in Kazakhstan. Zarya was the first of several elements originally intended by the Russians for incorporation into Mir-2. It served as the power and propulsion unit of the ISS. In Dec. 1998 the US space shuttle Endeavour lifted the US-made Unity module into orbit and linked it to Zarya. With the fifth ISS assembly mission, which took place in July 2000, the Russian-made Zvezda (Star) module was installed, providing living accommodation for the crew and housing the station's control room.

There followed two more missions to install supplies and equipment, including batteries and communications facilities as well as the US-made Z1 Truss, which among other things served as a framework for the attachment of early US solar arrays. Then on Oct. 31 2000, in the eighth mission to the ISS, the three-member Expedition 1, consisting of US Commander William Shepherd, Russian Commander Yuri Gidzenko and Russian Flight Engineer Sergey Krikalyev, blasted off from Baikonur aboard a Russian Soyuz launch vehicle. On Nov. 2 2000 these astronauts boarded the ISS to commence humanity's ongoing residence in Earth orbit. Their stay lasted four months, at the end of which they handed over to the newly arrived Expedition 2.

Assembly and maintenance of the space station continues, with each country in the ISS team making an important contribution. For example, the US-made Destiny Laboratory was delivered Feb. 2001 to provide a comfortable environment for year-round research in many fields. Canada's robotic arm, Canadarm2, was delivered Apr. 2001 and was used to install the US-made airlock, Quest. The tragic loss of the space shuttle Columbia in 2003 meant that for more than two years US participation in the ISS had to rely on Russia for transportation to and from the station. ESA's main contribution to the ISS is the COLUMBUS program, due for installation in 2006.

By the end of 2004, Expedition 10 had taken up residence aboard the ISS. Each crew had added greatly to the sum of human experience about living in space.

International Sun–Earth Explorer (**ISEE**) a joint project of NASA and ESA for studying the structure and interactions within the Earth's MAGNETOSPHERE and the solar phenomena producing such effects. The two satellites ISEE–1 and ISEE–2 were launched in tandem, in Oct. 1977, into a highly eccentric Earth orbit at a controllable distance apart. ISEE–3 was launched in Aug. 1978 into an orbit around the Sun–Earth Lagrangian point L_1, a point lying outside the magnetosphere, where it measured the SOLAR WIND, solar FLARES, and SUNSPOTS, unperturbed by the Earth's influence. It was thus a reference point for simultaneous observations made by ISEE–1 and ISEE–2. In 1982/83 the trajectory of ISEE–3 was altered so that it would intercept the comet GIACOBINI-ZINNER. The craft was renamed the *International Cometary Explorer* (*ICE*). It was the first spacecraft to rendezvous with two comets, flying through the plasma tail of Giacobini-Zinner in Sept. 1985, where it made particle, field and wave measurements, and passing between the Sun and Halley's comet in March 1986, at a distance from Halley's nucleus of 28 million km. By 1990, ICE had taken up a 355-day orbit around the Sun. In 1991, its mission was extended once more in order to study coronal mass ejections and cosmic rays. It was also occasionally linked up with ESA's Ulysses probe on certain science projects. NASA shut down the spacecraft in May 1997. It will return to the vicinity of the Earth in 2014. NASA has already agreed that, if the craft can be recovered successfully, it is to be donated to the Smithsonian Institute.

International Sunspot Number see RELATIVE SUNSPOT NUMBER.

International Ultraviolet Explorer (**IUE**) a satellite that is a joint project of NASA, ESA, and SERC (the UK's Scientific and Engineering Research Council) and was launched by NASA into an elliptical GEOSYNCHRONOUS ORBIT on Jan. 26 1978. Its 45-cm Ritchey-Chrétien telescope focuses ultraviolet radiation on either of two ECHELLE GRATING spectrographs providing about 0.01 nm spectral resolution; they operate in the wavelength range 115–190 nm and 180–320 nm. In addition lower resolution (about 0.6 nm) spectrographs are available for observations of faint sources. The satellite is controlled from ground stations in Maryland and Madrid by real-time data link, which permits operation in a manner similar to that of a ground-based observatory. In the 18 years of operation over 90 000 spectra were obtained on a wide variety of astronomical sources including planets, comets, interstellar dust and gas, stars of most spectral types, galaxies and galactic halos, Seyfert galaxies, and quasars (see ULTRAVIOLET ASTRONOMY). IUE became the longest-lived astronomical satellite ever, and finally ceased operating in 1996.

interplanetary dust the huge doughnut-shaped cloud of dust particles that orbit the Sun and have been produced mainly by the decay of the major comets such as Halley, Encke, Mellish, and Swift–Tuttle. The mass influx to this cloud is typically 200 kg per second. Dust particles in the cloud are continually colliding with each other, and the small debris from these collisions is then influenced by the POYNTING–ROBERTSON EFFECT and starts to spiral into the Sun. Particles with radii less than about 10^{-6} m can be blown out of the Solar System because the force exerted on them by RADIATION PRESSURE exceeds the gravitational attraction of the Sun. It is thought that in general this dust cloud is in equilibrium. See also ZODIACAL DUST CLOUD.

interplanetary magnetic field see INTERPLANETARY MEDIUM.

interplanetary medium the matter contained in the Solar System in the space between the planets. The term usually refers to the PLASMA and neutral gas (which comes from the local interstellar medium), but there is also INTERPLANETARY DUST. The Solar System is filled with a tenuous plasma – the SOLAR WIND – that streams outward from the Sun at supersonic speeds and in which is embedded the Sun's magnetic field wound into a spiral by the Sun's rotation (see PLASMA). This is called the *interplanetary magnetic field.* At the Earth the interplanetary medium has a density of about eight particles per cm^3 moving at a velocity of 300–400 km s^{-1}, and a magnetic flux density that averages about 5×10^{-9} tesla. The interplanetary magnetic field is crucial in coupling the solar wind plasma to the MAGNETOSPHERE of the Earth and other planets. The interplanetary medium moves at supersonic speed relative to the Earth, creating a shock front called the *bow shock,* rather like that set up by supersonic aircraft. Irregularities in the density of the solar wind cause interplanetary scintillations (see SCATTERING) on small RADIO SOURCES viewed through the medium.

interplanetary scintillation (IPS) see SCATTERING; INTERPLANETARY MEDIUM.

interpulse the weaker pulse of radio emission received after the main pulse and before the next main pulse in the signals from some PULSARS. The presence of an interpulse may indicate that we are seeing radiation from both magnetic poles of the pulsar.

interstellar bubble a large cavity in the distribution of gas in and near the plane of our Galaxy. The bubble is blown by the winds of multiple SUPERNOVAE from the most massive (and hence shortest-lived) stars in a stellar CLUSTER or ASSOCIATION. The bubble is usually filled with CORONAL GAS and is delineated by swept-up filaments and clouds of denser gas.

interstellar cloud a MOLECULAR CLOUD or H I REGION, as opposed to a cloud of the same composition more intimately connected with a star (*circumstellar cloud*).

interstellar dust COSMIC DUST occurring in the INTERSTELLAR MEDIUM.

interstellar extinction the reduction in brightness, i.e. the EXTINCTION, of light (and other radiation) from stars as a result of absorption and scattering of the radiation by INTERSTELLAR DUST. Although dust makes up only a small proportion of the interstellar medium, its effect on starlight is considerable. The amount of extinction, usually measured in MAGNITUDES, depends on the direction of observation. It is a maximum (about one magnitude per kiloparsec distance for visible wavelengths) toward the center of the Galaxy, where the density and extent of the dust is greatest. The extinction varies inversely with wavelength. Red light is thus less affected than blue light so that starlight appears reddened when observed through a dust cloud; this *interstellar reddening* can also be used to map the presence of dust in the Galaxy. Radio and infrared waves with their longer wavelengths can pass through the interstellar medium with ease compared with optical wavelengths. The presence of obscuring matter between the stars was first conclusively demonstrated by Robert Trumpler in 1930.

interstellar medium (ISM) the matter contained in the region between the stars of the GALAXY, constituting about 10% of the galactic mass. It is largely confined to a thin layer in the galactic plane and tends to be concentrated in the spiral arms. Several different constituents have been observed in the ISM, including clouds of ionized hydrogen – H II REGIONS – and smaller relatively cool (100 kelvin) clouds of neutral hydrogen – H I REGIONS – surrounded by more tenuous regions of hot gas (1000–10 000 K). The presence of some very much hotter regions has been inferred from a diffuse background of soft X-ray emission and by ultraviolet absorption lines. There are also very cool (10 K) dense clouds of molecular hydrogen – MOLECULAR CLOUDS – in which a number of other molecules and RADICALS have been observed.

There are several components of the ISM. In the *three phase model* of the ISM these are referred to as the *cold neutral medium* (H I gas at about 70 K and a density of 30 cm^{-3} filling 3–4% of the total volume), the *warm neutral medium* (H I, 6000 K, 0.3 cm^{-3}, 20% of the volume), and the *hot ionized medium* (H II, 10^6 K, 10^{-3} cm^{-3}, 70% of the volume). The three components are in approximate pressure equilibrium, and gas may cycle back and forth between the three phases.

In addition to the gas, COSMIC DUST is to be found throughout the medium. The dust comprises small solid grains that are between about 0.01 to 0.1 μm in size. The grains are thought to be composed of carbon, silicates, or iron material, with mantles of water and ammonia ice and possibly solid carbon dioxide, when they occur in dense molecular clouds. The total mass of interstellar dust is thought to be about 1% of the gas mass. The dust causes dimming and reddening of starlight (see INTERSTELLAR EXTINCTION) and also INTERSTELLAR POLARIZATION of starlight. The interstellar grains can undergo a complex life cycle, passing into and out of molecular clouds: the ISM is constantly churned up by shock waves from expanding SUPERNOVA REMNANTS, by STELLAR WINDS and BIPOLAR OUTFLOWS, and by other forces. While in a molecular cloud the grains may be incorporated in a newly forming star, and may later be ejected back into the ISM in a stellar wind or supernova explosion.

The medium is permeated by a flux of COSMIC RAYS that spiral along the field lines of the GALACTIC MAGNETIC FIELD of a few microgauss and cause the SYNCHROTRON EMISSION that is the *galactic radio background radiation*. RADIO MAPS show that this radiation is largely confined to the galactic plane but has several *spurs*, in particular the *north galactic spur*, radiating away from it. The north galactic spur is the most prominent segment of a huge fragmentary ring of gas detected at radio and X-ray wavelengths. This giant gas shell is probably a nearby old SUPERNOVA REMNANT.

interstellar molecules see MOLECULAR-LINE RADIO ASTRONOMY.

interstellar polarization the partial POLARIZATION of starlight caused by dust in the interstellar medium. Since only nonspherical particles with a nonrandom orientation can polarize light, the dust grains must be elongated and are thought to be partly aligned in a weak GALACTIC MAGNETIC FIELD.

Interstellar polarization may be due to reflection, absorption or emission. Reflection polarization is independent of grain alignment and is perpendicular to the line of sight from the reflecting dust to the light source; it is often used to determine the position of a hidden infrared source illuminating the dust. Emission and absorption polarization do depend on the grain alignment, which can be achieved with a very weak magnetic field. Since the grains tend to align perpendicular to the field, observations of dust polarization at infrared, submillimeter, and millimeter wavelengths can be used to probe the magnetic-field direction in increasingly dense regions of the dust clouds. Observations of absorption polarization require a bright (unpolarized) background source (usually a star), and hence are most commonly performed at IR wavelengths, and only at a few positions across the face of the cloud; emission polarization can be observed from the entire extent of the dust cloud.

interstellar reddening see INTERSTELLAR EXTINCTION.

interstellar scintillation see SCATTERING.

interstellar wind see HELIOSPHERE.

intracluster medium (ICM) the invisible medium that lies between the galaxies in a cluster. It is mostly comprised of hot (10^7–10^8 K) gas emitting strongly in X-rays. See CLUSTERS OF GALAXIES; X-RAY ASTRONOMY.

intrinsic color index see COLOR INDEX.

intrinsic variable see VARIABLE STAR.

invariable plane the unvarying reference plane through the CENTER OF MASS of the Solar System and perpendicular to the direction of the ANGULAR MOMENTUM vector of the Solar System. At present the ECLIPTIC is inclined by 1°.58 to the invariable plane.

inverse Compton emission see COMPTON SCATTERING.

Io the innermost of the four giant GALILEAN SATELLITES of Jupiter. It keeps one face permanently toward the planet (see SYNCHRONOUS ROTATION) as it orbits at a distance of 422 000 km, within Jupiter's MAGNETOSPHERE. Io is yellow-brown in color, has a high ALBEDO (0.61), and has a diameter of 3630 km. The orbital period of Io is one half that of EUROPA and one-fourth that of GANYMEDE; the three satellites are locked into an orbital resonance, the interaction of the satellites having caused their orbital distances to adjust until their periods were common multiples. Early photographs from the VOYAGER 1 probe March 1979 showed the surface of Io to lack impact craters. An explanation for this was found when intense volcanic action was observed on the satellite: at least nine active volcanoes were seen to eject material over a very wide area; seven were still active when Voyager 2 arrived four months later. Following the six passes of Io made by the Galileo spacecraft during its 33 orbits of Jupiter between 1996 and 2002, scientists now know there are at least 120 active volcanic regions. Few of Io's volcanoes resemble the crater-topped mountains seen on the Earth and Mars. Instead, most of Io's volcanic craters lie in relatively flat regions. Yet half the mountains on Io are located next to volcanic craters.

Io is the most active volcanic body known in the Solar System. The activity is thought to result from heating by tidal forces exerted by Jupiter. There are several types of activity: eruptive plumes, a few of which reach altitudes of hundreds of kilometers; huge calderas (volcanic collapse craters) with associated lava flows and/or surface markings; some possible lava lakes. The first volcano observed by Voyager 1 was an eruptive plume ascending to 280 km and visible above the satellite limb; material was deposited in concentric rings up to about 1400 km across. This volcano has been named *Pele*. The plume of *Loki* was active on both Voyager passes, rising to 100 km as measured by Voyager 1 and 200 km as measured by Voyager 2. Many of the plumes, such as that of *Prometheus*, were 50–120 km high and also apparently long-lived. Ionized matter – sulfur, oxygen, and hydrogen – escapes from the tenuous volcanic atmosphere of Io and forms a torus centered on Io and encompassing the whole of Io's orbit. The particles in the torus glow brightly in the ultraviolet. This matter interacts with Jupiter's magnetosphere: it controls the rate at which Jupiter radiates energy and probably affects aurorae on Jupiter, radio bursts from the planet, and other phenomena. See also GALILEAN SATELLITES; JUPITER; JUPITER'S SATELLITES; TABLE 2, Appendix.

ion an atom or molecule that has lost or gained one or more electrons, thus having a positive or negative charge.

ion engine a device consisting of a source for producing ions and an electromagnetic field for accelerating the ions in a particular direction. In practice, an ion engine can be used in a low-pressure environment to produce propulsion by reaction forces associated with the rapidly moving ions. It is also necessary to expel oppositely charged particles to the ions from the engine to ensure charge neutrality. Ion engines have been investigated as possible power sources for spacecraft.

ionization any of several processes by which normally neutral atoms or molecules are converted into IONS or by which one ion of an atom or molecule is changed to another ionic form, as by losing a second electron. Positive ions are commonly formed by impact of high-energy photons or particles with neutral atoms or molecules. The minimum energy required to remove an electron from an atom or molecule is the *ionization potential*, *I*, of that atom or molecule, and for ionization to occur the energy of the impacting photon or particle must exceed the ionization potential. It requires a higher energy (the *second ionization potential*) to remove a second more tightly bound electron, and an even greater energy to remove a third electron. For equilibrium to exist in a system, such as an EMISSION NEBULA, ionization processes must be balanced by recombination of positive ions and electrons.

Because of the high temperatures in stars, much of the matter present is in an ionized state; often more than one electron has been lost so that the atom or molecule is doubly or triply ionized, etc. In astronomy the neutral state of an element is conventionally denoted by I (H I, for example, denotes neutral hydrogen) whereas II denotes singly charged ions (H II is ionized hydrogen) and III indicates a doubly charged ion, and so on. See also PLASMA; SAHA IONIZATION EQUATION.

ionization front see STRÖMGREN SPHERE.

ionization potential see IONIZATION.

ionization zone see PULSATING VARIABLES.

ionosphere a region in the atmosphere of a planet, satellite, or comet that contains a high concentration of free electrons and ions produced by the ionizing action of solar X-ray and ultraviolet radiation on atmospheric constituents. The Earth's ionosphere extends from about 60 km to more than 1000 km in altitude. It disturbs the propagation of RADIO WAVES through it by reflecting or refracting them and attenuating them. The degree of ionization varies with time of day, season, latitude, and state of SOLAR ACTIVITY. The charged particles are found in four distinct layers: the *D-layer* lies below about 90 km, the *E-layer* lies between about 90 and 120 km, the F_1*-layer* (a daytime feature) is centered on about 150 km, and the F_2*-layer* is centered on about 300 km. Radio waves of sufficiently low frequency are reflected by the E- and F-layers. The D-layer, being lower in the atmosphere where collisions between molecules and ions are more frequent, is more an absorber than a reflector. The total DISPERSION MEASURE of the ionosphere is about 5×10^{17} m^{-2} by day and 5×10^{16} m^{-2} by night.

The ionosphere is important in radio communications, allowing long-distance propagation at frequencies up to about 30 megahertz by successive reflections between it and the ground. In RADIO ASTRONOMY, however, it makes ground-based observations almost impossible below 10 megahertz, causes PHASE and AMPLITUDE scintillations (see SCATTERING) on RADIO SOURCES viewed through it, and alters the observed POLARIZATION of radio waves by FARADAY ROTATION. Other bodies, including Mars, Venus, and the giant planets, the moons Titan and Triton, and comets Halley and Giacobini-Zinner, are now known to possess ionospheres.

ionospheric scintillation see SCATTERING.

ion tail see COMET TAILS.

iota (ι) the ninth letter of the Greek alphabet, used in STELLAR NOMENCLATURE usually to designate the ninth-brightest star in a constellation or sometimes to indicate a star's position in a group.

Io torus see IO; JUPITER.

IPC *abbrev. for* imaging proportional counter. See PROPORTIONAL COUNTER.

IPCS *abbrev. for* image photon counting system. A highly sensitive electronic system for detecting and accurately recording single photons of light or ultraviolet radiation; it was developed in 1973 by the British astronomer Alec Boksenberg. It enables very low intensities to be detected and recorded, or allows images to be recorded in a very short time. It is particularly useful for studying spectra. The light is first intensified by a high-gain multistage IMAGE TUBE and then recorded by a special TV camera. The TV signal is fed to and stored in a computer, where extraneous noise can be removed. A sharp and accurately recorded two-dimensional image is thus built up in the computer memory. This can be displayed on a screen, analyzed, or manipulated electronically.

IPS *abbrev. for* interplanetary scintillation. See SCATTERING.

IR *abbrev. for* infrared.

IRAF *abbrev. for* image reduction and analysis facility. A software package used in the reduction and display of astronomical images from optical and infrared telescopes. It is aimed specifically at the reduction of multislit spectrographic data obtained using CCD detector systems. IRAF was developed by NOAO.

IRAM *abbrev. for* Institute de Radio Astronomie Millimetrique. A French, German, and Spanish collaborative institute set up in 1979 for MILLIMETER ASTRONOMY. The main instruments are a 30-meter DISH on Pico Veleta in the Sierra Nevada (Southern Spain) operating between 70 and 345 GHz, and a five-element INTERFEROMETER built on the Plateau de Bure, south of Grenoble, France. The interferometer dishes are 15 meters in diameter and placed on a T-shaped track with arm lengths of 408 m and 232 m. It operates at frequencies between 80 and 115 GHz.

IRAS *abbrev. for* Infrared Astronomical Satellite. A satellite that has made an all-sky survey in the infrared wavelength range 10–100 μm using liquid helium-cooled optics and detectors. The project was developed and operated by the Netherlands Agency for Aerospace Programs (NIVR),

NASA, and the UK Science and Engineering Research Council (SERC). The satellite was launched into a 900 km orbit on Jan. 26 1983 and operated until Nov. 22 1983 when the helium supply was exhausted. By the end of the mission 95% of the sky had been surveyed with confirming scans, 3% surveyed only once, and the remaining 2% not surveyed at all.

IRAS consists of a spacecraft that pointed a liquid helium cryostat containing a 0.57-meter RITCHEY–CHRÉTIEN telescope cooled to less than 10 K. An array of cooled detectors was located in the focal plane at the Cassegrain focus of the telescope. The 62 PHOTOCONDUCTIVE DETECTORS responded to one of four wavebands centered on 100, 60, 25, or 12 μm. They were arranged so that every source crossing the field of view could be seen by at least two detectors in each of the wavebands. The low resolution SPECTROMETER (LRS) covered the range 8–23 μm with a spectral resolution, $\lambda/\Delta\lambda$, of about 20. The chopped photometric channel (CPC) mapped infrared sources on a 9 × 9 arcmin raster at 50 and 100 μm with a spatial resolution of about 1 arcmin.

The operation center for the satellite was at the SERC Rutherford-Appleton Laboratory, near Oxford, England where a preliminary analysis of the data was made. The final reduction of data was done in the USA and the Netherlands. The IRAS data has been issued in various catalogs, including the *IRAS Point Source Catalog* (*IPSC*) and the *IRAS Faint Source Survey* (*IFSS*) and corresponding catalog (*IFSC*). The *IRAS Sky Survey Atlas* (ISSA) for ecliptic latitude over 50° was released on CD–ROM in 1992 the remainder scheduled in 1994.

The results obtained so far relate to almost every aspect of astronomy. Some of the highlights are: the discovery of a dust shell around VEGA, which may be an early planetary system; the discovery of INFRARED CIRRUS in our Galaxy; the first detection from space using infrared of comets (IRAS discovered 5 new comets); the detailed mapping of the infrared emission from the galactic plane; observations on galaxies showing that most of the galaxies detected in the 60- and 100-μm wavebands are spirals; observations on low-luminosity PROTOSTARS in several MOLECULAR CLOUD complexes.

IRAS galaxies the class of galaxies revealed by the IRAS satellite to be ultraluminous at far-infrared wavelengths. Most galaxies detected by IRAS are isolated disk galaxies whose infrared emission can be accounted for by normal STAR FORMATION. IRAS galaxies have a bolometric LUMINOSITY as large as many QUASARS, and optical images show most of them to be strongly INTERACTING pairs of spiral galaxies with exceptionally luminous nuclei. Their spectra indicate the presence of intense star formation, sometimes with the addition of an active nucleus, and show that the galaxies are rich in molecular gas. Such galaxies may well be the dust-shrouded predecessors of quasars that have been triggered with the intense STARBURST activity by the MERGER of the two spiral galaxies. The most extreme examples, with a far-infrared luminosity in excess of 10^{12} solar luminosities, are known as *ultraluminous* and *hyperluminous IRAS galaxies.*

IRAS–Iraki–Alcock (1983 VII) a comet detected in 1983 by the infrared satellite IRAS and independently by G. Iraki and E. Alcock. It passed only 4.6×10^6 km (0.03 AU) from Earth and just before closest approach it brightened to 2nd magnitude and exceded 3° across. The huge HEAD was highly asymmetrical, with a fan of material spreading out sunwards from the off-centered starlike nucleus (which reached magnitude 12). No normal tail could be seen. Infrared and radar observations provided information on the composition and rotation of the nucleus.

iron 1 see NUCLEOSYNTHESIS.
2 *short for* iron meteorite.

iron meteorite (iron) one of the main classifications of METEORITES, containing nickel-iron alloys with small amounts of accessory minerals. The composition averages 90% iron, 10% nickel. The three main subdivisions are *octahedrites,* which have more than 6% nickel, the less common *hexahedrites,* with less than 6% nickel, and the nickel-rich *ataxites.* See also WIDMANSTÄTTEN FIGURES.

iron-peak elements see NUCLEOSYNTHESIS.

irregular cluster see REGULAR CLUSTER.

irregular galaxy see GALAXIES; HUBBLE CLASSIFICATION.

irregular variables stars, such as the majority of red giants, that are PULSATING VARIABLES showing slow luminosity changes either with no periodicity or with a very slight periodicity. The latter can be grouped into slow irregular variables of SPECTRAL TYPES F, G, K, M, C, and S that are usually giants, and slow irregular supergiants of spectral types M, C, and S.

IRTF *abbrev. for* Infrared Telescope Facility.

Isaac Newton Group see ROQUE DE LOS MUCHACHOS OBSERVATORY.

Isaac Newton Telescope (**INT**) a 2.5-meter reflecting telescope operated by the ROYAL GREENWICH OBSERVATORY at the ROQUE DE LOS MUCHACHOS OBSERVATORY on La Palma in the Canaries. It began operations in 1967 at the former RGO base in Herstmonceux, East Sussex, was dismantled in 1979, and, completely refurbished, resumed observations on La Palma in 1984. It is now part of the Isaac Newton Group. Its equatorial mounting was modified. Its new primary mirror has an extremely accurately figured paraboloidal surface made of ZERODUR. The focal ratio is 2.9. There is an f/15 Cassegrain focus and an f/50 coudé focus. The latest developments in telescope instrumentation have been incorporated, including CCD and IPCS detectors. Observing time is shared between the UK, Spain, and the Netherlands.

ISAS *abbrev. for* Institute of Space and Astronautical Science. The smaller of Japan's space agencies, responsible for implementing Japan's scientific space program. Its missions included two probes to HALLEY'S COMET in 1986 and the X-ray astronomy satellite GINGA. Originally part of the University of Tokyo, it became a separate institute in 1981 under the Ministry of Education. Its headquarters are near Tokyo. See also NASDA.

ISEE *abbrev. for* International Sun–Earth Explorer.

Ishtar Terra a large highland area in the northern hemisphere of VENUS. Centered on the Venusian coordinates 70.4° N latitude, 332.5° W longitude, it is a flattish plateau bounded on three sides by mountains, including MAXWELL MONTES, the highest range on Venus. The plains around Ishtar Terra feature many CORONAE. See also APHRODITE TERRA; BETA REGIO.

ISM *abbrev. for* interstellar medium.

ISO *abbrev. for* Infrared Space Observatory, an orbiting infrared astronomy observatory launched by the European Space Agency (ESA) on top of an Ariane-4 rocket from Kourou, French Guiana, Nov. 1995. The 2.5-tonne, 5.3-meter-long ISO was the most sensitive infrared satellite of its time, using four detectors cryogenically cooled by liquid helium to capture and study weak infrared radiation from such sources as cold gas and dust clouds and regions of star birth and star death, as well as quasars and remote galaxies. Lying in the focal plane of a telescope with a 60-centimeter mirror, the four detectors were (1) an infrared camera (ISOCAM) covering the range 2.5–17 μm; (2) a photopolarimeter (ISOPHOT) functioning between 2.5 and 240 μm; (3) a shortwave spectrometer covering the 2.4–45 μm band; and (4) a longwave spectrometer operating between 45 and 196.8 μm. These instruments revealed numerous hitherto unknown objects that were 'visible' only in infrared light. The satellite operated for about 30 months. Its mission ended in Apr. 1998 when its coolant finally ran out.

isophote a line on a diagram joining points of equal FLUX DENSITY or intensity.

isoplanatic angle the largest FIELD OF VIEW over which a distortion-free image can be formed looking through the Earth's atmosphere. At optical wavelengths it is a few arc seconds.

isotopes forms of an element in which the nuclei contain the same number of protons but different numbers of neutrons. For example, there are three isotopes of hydrogen: 'normal' hydrogen has a single proton, deuterium has one proton and one neutron, and tritium, which is a radioactive isotope, has one proton and two neutrons.

isotropy the property by which all directions

appear indistinguishable to an observer expanding with the Universe. Isotropy about every point in space implies HOMOGENEITY but the reverse is not necessarily true. See COSMOLOGICAL PRINCIPLE.

ISS 1 *abbrev. for* interstellar scintillation. See SCATTERING.
2 *abbrev. for* International Space Station.

Ithaca Chasma see TETHYS.

IUE *abbrev. for* International Ultraviolet Explorer.

Jj

Jacobus Kapteyn Telescope (JKT) see ROQUE DE LOS MUCHACHOS OBSERVATORY.

James Clerk Maxwell Telescope (JCMT) a 15-meter diameter radio telescope on MAUNA KEA, Hawaii, at an altitude of 4100 meters. It operates in the millimeter and submillimeter wavebands, between 2 mm and 350 µm. The primary reflector consists of 276 adjustable panels, which give a surface accuracy of better than 30 µm. It is equipped with LINE RECEIVERS and continuum RECEIVERS at the CASSEGRAIN and two NASMYTH foci; for maximum sensitivity the receivers are cryogenically cooled to 4 K (line) and as low as 0.1 K (continuum). The telescope has an ALTAZIMUTH MOUNTING and is housed in a carousel that rotates with the antenna. The JCMT became operational in Dec. 1986. It is operated by the Joint Astronomy Center in Hilo, Hawaii on behalf of its parent research councils in the United Kingdom, Canada, and the Netherlands.

James Webb Space Telescope (JWST) a next-generation space observatory optimized for infrared astronomy that NASA plans to launch in August 2011 as the successor to the HUBBLE SPACE TELESCOPE. It was named to commemorate a former NASA administrator, James E. Webb, who served from 1961 to 1968 during the time of the APOLLO missions. The observatory actually began its development as the *Next Generation Space Telescope* (NGST) following an initial proposal for such an instrument in 1996. The new name was adopted in 2002.

The chief goal of the JWST is to look across time and space 90% of the way back to the BIG BANG in order to explore the era when stars and galaxies started to form out of primeval gas and dust clouds. Radiation from this very remote region is redshifted so much that many spectral lines are moved into the infrared. Viewing the heavens in the infrared waveband also allows astronomers to penetrate dust and gas. For this reason, the JWST will have detectors that are highly sensitive to the infrared part of the spectrum, with some capability in the visible part. Its observing position will also be as stable and as isolated from unwanted background interference as possible, orbiting the Lagrangian point L2, well beyond the Moon's orbit at a location about 1.5 million kilometers from the Earth in the cold darkness of interplanetary space. The JWST's mission is scheduled to last between five and ten years.

The total mass of the JWST spacecraft is expected to be 6.2 tonnes, housing the telescope with its 6.5-meter 18-segment beryllium primary mirror (nearly three times the diameter of that of the Hubble Space Telescope but only about one-third as heavy, and foldable so that it can be carried conveniently within the spacecraft before being deployed). In the focal plane of the telescope, also known as the Optical Telescope Element (OTE), there will be an Integrated Science Instrument Module (ISIM), consisting of a cryogenic instrument module containing the infrared detectors linked into the telescope and to computers and software in the relatively warm part of the spacecraft. The science instruments within this module will be a Near-Infrared Camera (NIRCam), a Near-Infrared

Spectrometer (NIRSpec), a Mid-Infrared Instrument (MIRI), and the telescope's Fine Guidance System (FGS). To help maintain the operating temperature of the detectors at less than 50 K, they will be permanently in the shadow of a sun shield about the size of a tennis court (22 m × 10 m), which will be deployed between them and the Sun to screen out light, heat, and other solar radiation. The sun shield will turn as the spacecraft orbits. Like the primary mirror, the sun shield will be folded until the JWST is on station. The remaining part of the JWST spacecraft houses attitude and other control mechanisms and supplies electrical power and communications facilities to the science instruments and onboard computers.

jansky symbol: Jy. The unit of FLUX DENSITY adopted by the IAU in 1973 and used throughout the spectral range, especially for radio and far-infrared measurements; it is named after Karl Jansky, who discovered radio emission from the Milky Way in 1932. One jansky is equal to 10^{-26} watts per square meter per hertz. It is possible to calculate the equivalent flux density, S_ν, in janskys from a value of MAGNITUDE at the effective wavelength, λ_{eff}, appropriate to a particular optical or infrared filter (see table). For example, an R magnitude of 3.2 corresponds to a flux density at 0.7 μm of

$$2770 \times 10^{-0.4 \times 3.2}\ \mathrm{Jy}$$

i.e. 145 Jy. (The table gives the flux level for 0.0 magnitude.)

Jansky

Filter	λ_{eff} *(μm)*	S_ν *(jansky)*
U	0.365	1910
B	0.44	4260
V	0.55	3830
R	0.70	2770
I	0.90	2240
J	1.25	1720
K	2.20	645
L	3.40	310
M	5.0	183
N	10.2	41.5
Q	21	9.5

Jansky noise *another name for* cosmic noise. See ANTENNA TEMPERATURE.

Janus a small satellite of Saturn. The name Janus was originally given to a satellite of Saturn discovered in 1966 by the French astronomer Audouin Dollfus, but its existence was not confirmed. The name Janus has since been given to one of the two COORBITAL SATELLITES discovered in 1980 at approximately the orbital distance given by Dollfus. The other satellite is EPIMETHEUS. Four craters have been named on Janus: *Castor, Idas, Lynceus,* and *Phoibe.* See Table 2, Appendix.

JCMT *abbrev. for* James Clerk Maxwell Telescope.

JD *abbrev. for* Julian date.

Jeans instability an instability in a cloud of gas in space when fluctuations in the density of the gas cause clumping of the matter as a result of its mutual gravitational attraction. In 1902, Sir James Jeans worked out a criterion, now known as the *Jeans criterion,* which determines the conditions for this instability to occur in terms of the density and temperature of the gas. This calculation used Newtonian gravity in a static Universe. Extension of this calculation to the case of general relativity theory in an expanding Universe provides the starting point for understanding STRUCTURE FORMATION in the Universe.

Jeans length, Jeans mass see GRAVITATIONAL INSTABILITY.

jet a long thin linear feature of bright emission extending from a compact object, such as a galaxy. Jets are very common at radio wavelengths, but have also been seen in optical and X-ray emission. They are sometimes broken up into a number of bright KNOTS. In extragalactic sources a jet is usually associated with the presence of an ACTIVE GALACTIC NUCLEUS. An example is that found in the giant elliptical galaxy M87 (see VIRGO A). See also RADIO-SOURCE STRUCTURE.

Jet Propulsion Laboratory (JPL) an institution for space research and engineering at Pasadena, California, run by the California Institute of Technology under a contract from NASA. It is concerned primarily with the development and operation of crewless interplanetary spacecraft and control of planetary missions. These activities are facilitated by the use of the DEEP SPACE NETWORK, which is also run by JPL. The laboratory also manages more local science missions, such as NASA's Spitzer Space Telescope and the GALEX (Galaxy Evolution Explorer) satellite. JPL was founded in 1944 by a group of scientists that included Theodore von Kálmán, a Hungarian-born US engineer who worked on rockets and missiles at Caltech during World War II. JPL was responsible for Explorer 1, the first US artificial satellite launched in 1958, and has since controlled NASA's many interplanetary missions, including the Mariner and Pioneer series of probes, Voyagers 1 and 2, and Galileo.

Jewel Box (**NGC 4755**) a brilliant OPEN CLUSTER in the southern constellation Crux that contains over 100 stars of various colors, the brightest being the 6th-magnitude blue supergiant Kappa (κ) Crucis. It appears to be a young cluster of an estimated age of 10 million years, and is about 2400 parsecs away.

Jicamarca Radio Observatory (**JRO**) a large 49.92-MHz incoherent scatter radar antenna, located east of Lima, Peru. The antenna is a square-phased array of 18 432 dipoles covering an area of nearly 85 000 square meters.

JKT *abbrev. for* Jacobus Kapteyn Telescope. See ROQUE DE LOS MUCHACHOS OBSERVATORY.

Jodrell Bank the site near Holmes Chapel in Cheshire, about 30 kilometers south of the center of Manchester, UK, of the Jodrell Bank Observatory, part of the School of Physics and Astronomy of the University of Manchester. Originally founded in 1947 and later known for a time as Manchester University's Nuffield Radio Astronomy Laboratories, the observatory has played an active role in all branches of radio astronomy during the later 20th and early 21st centuries and has been at the forefront of pioneering research on such subjects as quasars and pulsars. Jodrell Bank's principal instrument is the *Lovell Telescope* (originally called the *Mark I*), a 76.2-meter (250-foot) fully steerable radio dish on an ALTAZIMUTH MOUNTING. This telescope has been in operation since 1957 and was formally named in 1987 for Sir Bernard Lovell, the observatory's first director (1951–81). It gained popular fame soon after it was completed by successfully tracking the world's first artificial satellite Sputnik I, It later went on to track many satellites and space probes in addition to carrying out its main radio astronomy programs. Modifications made to the telescope in 1970–71 included changes to the supporting structure and the fitting of a new reflecting membrane having an improved shape and longer focal length (22.9 m). In 2002 further refurbishments were completed, including the fitting of another new reflecting surface, this one of galvanized steel panels employing a recently developed holographic technique to ensure that the panels fit more accurately to the required parabolic shape. As a result of these upgrades, the Lovell will perform well at wavelengths of 6 cm and below. There is also a smaller elliptical-shaped reflector, the *Mark II*, 38 × 25.4 meters. This was completed in 1964 and can be used effectively at wavelengths down to 3 cm. Both instruments are part of the radio network MERLIN, whose component telescopes are controlled from Jodrell Bank.

Johnson Space Center (**JSC**) a NASA establishment in Houston, Texas, serving as the command and control center for every one of NASA's crewed space missions and other spaceflight activities involving humans, such as the space shuttle and the International Space Station. It organizes the training of astronauts and undertakes projects related to such fields as space medicine and aviation. Established in 1961 as the Manned Spacecraft Center, it was renamed in 1973 for President Lyndon B. Johnson, who had died that year.

joule symbol: J. The SI unit of energy, equal to the work done when the point of application of a force of one newton is moved one meter in the direction of the force.

Jovian planets a term derived from the Latin name for Jupiter and applied collectively to the giant planets Jupiter, Saturn, Uranus, and Neptune.

Jovian satellites see JUPITER'S SATELLITES.

JPL *abbrev. for* Jet Propulsion Laboratory.

JSC *abbrev. for* Johnson Space Center.

Julian calendar the calendar that was established in 46 BC in the Roman Empire by Julius Caesar, with Sosigenes of Alexandria as his chief advisor. It reached its final form in about 8 AD under Augustus and was in general use in the West up to 1582, when the GREGORIAN CALENDAR was instituted. Each year contained 12 months and there was an average of 365.25 days per year: three years of 365 days were followed by a leap year of 366 days. (Leap years were not correctly inserted until 8 AD.) Since the average length of the year was about 11 minutes 15 seconds longer than the 365.2422 days of the TROPICAL YEAR, a discrepancy arose between the calendar year and the seasons, with an extra day 'appearing' about every 128 years.

Julian century see JULIAN YEAR.

Julian date (JD) the number of days that have elapsed since noon GMT on Jan. 1 4713 BC – the *Julian day number* – plus the decimal fraction of the day that has elapsed since the preceding noon. The consecutive numbering of days makes the system independent of the length of month or year and the JD is thus used to calculate the frequency of occurrence or the periodicity of phenomena over long periods. The system was devised in 1582 by the French scholar Joseph Scaliger. A specific Julian date can be determined from astronomical tables of Julian day numbers: thus since March 1 1980, noon GMT, is tabulated as day number 244 4300 then March 17 1980, 6 p.m. GMT, is JD 244 4316.25 (see table). The *modified Julian date* (*MJD*) is found by subtracting 240 0000.5 from the Julian date.

Julian Date

Julian day at noon, UT, on March 1st

Year	*Julian day*	*Year*	*Julian day*
1800	2378556	1940	2429690
1820	2385861	1950	2433342
1840	2393166	1960	2436995
1860	2400471	1970	2440647
1880	2407776	1980	2444300
1900	2415080	1990	2447952
1920	2422385	2000	2451605

Julian year a period of 365.25 days (each containing 864 000 seconds, i.e. 24 hours). A *Julian century* is 100 Julian years. The Julian year has been used since 1984 for defining standard EPOCHS, replacing the BESSELIAN YEAR.

Juliet a small satellite of Uranus, discovered in 1986. See URANUS' SATELLITES; TABLE 2, Appendix.

June Lyrids a minor METEOR SHOWER, radiant: RA 278°, dec +35°, maximizing on June 16.

Juno (**(3) Juno**) the third ASTEROID to be discovered, found in 1804 by Karl Ludwig Harding. With a diameter of about 267 km it is the smallest of the first four asteroids to be found and numbered. It is a main belt asteroid, ranking as the seventh-largest of all the asteroids we know. It has a spectrum similar to that of the STONY-IRON METEORITES and is an S-type asteroid. Juno is unusually reflective, attaining a magnitude at opposition of 7.5. See Table 3, Appendix.

Juno mission an 8-day space mission in May 1991 that took the first UK astronaut, Helen Sharman, to the Soviet space station MIR. Conceived as a British commercially-funded science project, it was eventually paid for by the USSR, so that Sharman worked on Soviet experiments with just three experiments for British schools.

Jupiter the largest planet in the Solar System, orbiting the Sun at a mean distance of 5.2 AU once every 11.86 years. It has an equatorial diameter of 142 994 km (11 times that of the Earth) and a polar diameter of 133 708 km. This OBLATENESS results from a rotation period of less than 10 hours, shorter than that of any other planet. Jupiter has a mass more than twice that of all the other planets combined but its average density, only 1.3 times that of water, suggests that it contains a high proportion of the lightest elements, hydrogen and helium. Orbital and physical characteristics are given in Table 1, backmatter.

OPPOSITIONS recur at 13 month intervals; the planet then has, on average, an apparent diameter of 47 arc seconds and shines at about magnitude –2.5, brighter than every other night-time object apart from the Moon, Venus, and (rarely) Mars. Jupiter has 63 known satellites, including the four GALILEAN SATELLITES visible with a minimum of optical aid, and also a ring system (see JUPITER'S RINGS). Telescopes show the disk to be crossed by bands of light and dark clouds, called *zones* and *belts* respectively, running parallel to the equator. Irregular spots and streaks are seen, their motion across the disk indicating planetary rotation periods varying between about 9 hours 51 minutes in equatorial regions and 9 hours 56 minutes at high latitudes. Except for the GREAT RED SPOT and the white ovals, most of the markings are temporary, lasting for days or months.

Models for Jupiter's atmospheric and internal structure have been refined following the flybys of the spaceprobes PIONEER 10 and 11 in 1973 and 1974, the VOYAGER PROBES in 1979, and ULYSSES in 1992, and the detailed investigation of the Jovian system made by the Galileo spacecraft between 1996 and 2003; earlier spectroscopic work had, however, detected the presence of hydrogen, ammonia, and methane, and also water vapor, ethane, acetylene, phosphine, germanium tetrahydride, and carbon monoxide. It appears that the white or yellowish zones are areas of higher clouds supported by upward convection of warm gases; the reddish-brown belts have descending gas flows and lower clouds. With a rapidly rotating planet the weather systems are primarily zonal, and it is this that produces the banded colorful cloud systems superimposed with spots of a variety of different shades of colors; the spots are anticyclonically rotating systems. Huge convective storms are found in the equatorial region of Jupiter, and cyclonic storms, called *barges*, are seen in the northern latitudes. Eddies may give rise to the spots. At latitudes greater than about 45°, the belt/zone system gives way to a mottled surface appearance corresponding to ascending and descending convection cells (gas columns). The higher cloud zones appear to comprise ammonia crystals while the lower cloud belts may contain sulfur compounds, hydrogen and ammonium hydrosulfide, or complex organic compounds, possibly formed in photochemical reactions energized by ultraviolet radiation and by lightning discharges in the atmosphere. The highest cloud features, such as the Great Red Spot, may be colored red by traces of phosphorus brought up by convection from the lower atmosphere.

Jupiter radiates, as heat, about twice as much energy as it receives from the Sun, indicating that there is an internal reservoir of thermal energy left over from its creation 4.6 thousand million years ago. This internal energy source aids in driving Jupiter's weather system. In addition to the rapid rotation of Jupiter, the outflow of energy from the planet and a GREENHOUSE EFFECT ensure that there is little variation in temperature between the equator and poles, or between the day and night hemispheres. Atmospheric temperatures increase from –130°C at the cloud tops to about 30°C at the base of a lower cloud layer of water droplets and ice-crystals believed to lie about 70 km below the ammonia clouds. Over this same range the pressure rises from 0.5 to 4.5 (Earth) atmospheres. All Jupiter's weather occurs in this upper skin of its 1000-km deep gaseous atmosphere. At first sight the Jovian weather system appears quite different from that of the Earth. The analyses of the Voyager data have shown, however, that Jupiter (and also Saturn) and the Earth drive their meteorological systems in the same way, with energy being transported from the small-scale features into the main flow. The depth of the motions are unknown. However, they appear more stable than the specific cloud elements whose lifetimes vary from months to years to decades.

The atmosphere of Jupiter consists primarily of hydrogen and helium in the ratio 89.8 to 10.2 (by mass). The hydrogen becomes liquid at a depth of 1000 km; this marks the interface between atmosphere and planetary interior. At a depth of about 25 000 to 30 000 km, under an estimated two to three megabars of pressure, the hydrogen becomes metallic: the molecules dissociate into protons and a sea of unattached electrons. Temperatures may increase from 2000 K at 1000 km to some 20 000 K at the planet's center where there may be a rocky core 10 to 20 times more massive than the Earth. The bulk of Jupiter's interior is thus composed of liquid hydrogen, most of which is in metallic form.

A magnetic field, probably arising from a dynamo action within Jupiter's conductive metallic hydrogen, has a total strength about 19 000 times that of the Earth's magnetic field. Jupiter's field is tilted by 11° relative to its rotation axis and is reversed in polarity relative to that of the Earth. It supports a MAGNETOSPHERE, about 15 million km across, in which the eight inner satellites orbit. The magnetosphere contains radiation belts possibly 10 000 times more intense than the Earth's VAN ALLEN RADIATION BELTS.

Jupiter emits radio waves by three mechanisms: high-frequency thermal radio noise comes from the atmosphere along with infrared radiation; high-frequency nonthermal SYNCHROTRON EMISSION is generated by electrons in Jupiter's magnetic field; intense bursts of decametric radio waves are believed to arise from electrical discharges along Jovian magnetic field lines when IO, with its conductive ionosphere, moves across them. A small fraction of the sulfur and sulfur dioxide erupting from volcanoes on Io manages to escape Io's gravity and becomes part of Jupiter's magnetosphere. High temperatures ionize the material giving rise to the *Io torus*, a huge doughnut-shaped ring of plasma. The Io torus lies in the plane of Jupiter's magnetic equator, inclined by 11° to the plane of Io's orbit.

Jupiter-crosser a very rare class of ASTEROID whose orbit crosses that of Jupiter. The gravitational influence of Jupiter makes this type of orbit very short-lived. They include (944) HIDALGO and about 500 of the TROJANS.

Jupiter Icy Moons Orbiter a proposed NASA probe set to orbit Jupiter's large moons GANYMEDE, CALLISTO, and EUROPA. The earlier probe GALILEO found evidence suggesting that these satellites may harbor vast oceans beneath their icy surfaces. The Jupiter Icy Moons Orbiter is not planned for launch until 2015 or later. It may be the first nuclear-powered spacecraft.

Jupiter's comet family a COMET FAMILY whose distribution of aphelion distances (the comets' farthest points from the Sun) correlates with the mean distance of the planet Jupiter. Its members have aphelion distances of 4–8 AU. Jupiter is capable of substantially changing the orbits of comets that happen to pass close by. *Brooks 2* passed within two Jovian radii of Jupiter's surface in July 1886. Its period and aphelion distance were changed from 31 years and 14 AU to 7 years and 5.4 AU. The formation of the family is caused by such gravitational perturbations. Jupiter is also capable of throwing comets out of its family into long-period orbits (using a process similar to the one used to deflect spacecraft out of the Solar System). Over 90% of the Jovian family move in direct orbits. Comets with periods less than 10 years have a mean inclination to the ecliptic of 12°. After a comet has been captured by Jupiter it will take another 200 to 400 orbits (depending on perihelion distance) before it decays completely. No comet can remain in the Jupiter family for more than about 4000 years so the family is being replenished continually.

Jupiter's rings a system of planetary rings

Jupiter's Rings

Name	*Mean distance from planet center* (10^3 *km*)	*(planetary radii)*	*Radial width* *(km)*	*Thickness*	*Optical depth*
Halo	100–123	1.40–1.72	22 800	20 000	6×10^{-6}
Main	123–129	1.72–1.81	6400	< 30	10^{-6}
Gossamer	129–214	1.81–3	85 000	?	10^{-7}

composed of small rocky particles discovered around Jupiter in 1979 as the spacecraft Voyager 1 moved inside the orbit of the satellite Amalthea. There are three named rings: the vertically extended *Halo Ring*, the brighter *Main Ring*, and the tenuous *Gossamer Ring* (see table). Data from the GALILEO probe showed that the Gossamer ring is actually two rings, one embedded within the other, composed of debris from Almathea and Thebe. The satellite Metis is embedded in the Main Ring, while Adrastea orbits close to its gradual outer boundary.

Jupiter's satellites (Jovian satellites) a system of diverse satellites orbiting Jupiter at distances between 128 000 km and 24 million km and ranging in size from the planet-like GALILEAN SATELLITES to tiny worlds of rock and ice measuring barely 1 kilometer across. At the end of 2004, 63 Jovian satellites were known, most of which were discovered after 2000 through analysis of photographs taken either by spacecraft such as the VOYAGER PROBES or GALILEO mission or by high-quality groundbased instruments using large-format CCDs. Their physical and orbital properties are given in Table 2, backmatter.

The satellites can be divided into three main groups. The largest is an outer group of at least 48 small bodies moving in loosely bound retrograde orbits (see DIRECT MOTION) that are highly eccentric and are inclined to Jupiter's equatorial plane by an angle of about 150°–160°; most of them orbit the planet in periods of about 700 days and at mean distances of roughly 21 to 24 million km. Chief among them are Ananke, Carme, Pasiphae, and Sinope. The most remote one of this group so far known, designated S/2003 J2, in fact orbits Jupiter in more than 900 days at a mean distance of more than 28 million kmn. An intermediate group of five small satellites (Leda, Himalia, Lysithea, Elara, and S/2000 J11) move in approximately 250-day direct orbits at mean orbital distances between 11 and 12 million km; the orbits are generally less eccentric than those of the outer group and are inclined at an angle of about 28° to Jupiter's equatorial plane. Two other satellites follow direct orbits that do not fit neatly into either the outer or intermediate groups. These are Themisto, which orbits Jupiter in 130 days at a mean distance of about 7 million km and with an inclination of 43°, and S/2003 J20, which completes an orbit every 456 days at a mean distance of 17 million km and an inclination of 51°. The inner group is comprised of the four large GALILEAN SATELLITES – IO, EUROPA, GANYMEDE, and CALLISTO – together with AMALTHEA and the three satellites Thebe, Adrastea, and Metis; these all move in near-circular direct orbits that lie close to the plane of Jupiter's equator.

The members of the outer and intermediate groups are probably captured ASTEROIDS, although the capturing process that would place objects into one group rather than the other has not been defined. Possibly some of them were former members of the TROJAN GROUP of asteroids. All eight inner satellites are believed to have formed out of the dust particles that surrounded the disk of gas and dust from which Jupiter formed. These inner satellites all lie within Jupiter's MAGNETOSPHERE and are effective in sweeping up the charged particles found there, becoming intensely radioactive in the process.

Metis, Jupiter's innermost satellite, was unknown before Voyager 2 photographed it in 1979. So too were Thebe and Adrastea. The irregularly shaped Amalthea had been discovered in 1892, but few details of it were known before the visit of the Voyager probes. The Galilean satellites, however, have been studied throughout the telescopic era but came under much more intensive scrutiny from Pioneer 10 and 11, as well as the Voyager and Galileo missions.

Kk

Kamiokande see NEUTRINO ASTRONOMY.

KAO *abbrev. for* Kuiper Airborne Observatory.

kappa (κ) the tenth letter of the Greek alphabet, used in STELLAR NOMENCLATURE usually to designate the tenth-brightest star in a constellation or sometimes to indicate a star's position in a group.

Kapteyn's star a dim red SUBDWARF in the constellation Pictor that is a HIGH-VELOCITY STAR with a radial velocity of 242 km/s. It is one of the nearest stars to the Sun and is the nearest subdwarf. It has the second highest known proper motion, moving southeastward at a rate of 8.7 seconds of arc per year. Only BARNARD'S STAR exceeds this. Kapteyn's star was discovered in 1897 by the Dutch astronomer Jacobus Cornelius Kapteyn (1851–1922) through the analysis of photographic plates. m_v: 8.8; M_v: 10.8; spectral type: sdM0; distance: 3.91 pc.

Karl Schwarzschild Observatory an observatory founded 1960 at Tautenburg in Thuringia, Germany, at an altitude of 330 meters. The chief instrument is a reflector with a 2.0-meter spherical mirror that can be used with a 1.34-m correcting plate as a SCHMIDT TELESCOPE. A second correcting plate is ground so as to produce spectra of celestial bodies, i.e. it acts as an OBJECTIVE PRISM. The mirror can also be used at the Cassegrain and coudé foci.

Kaus Australis see SAGITTARIUS.

K-corona the inner part of the solar CORONA, responsible for the greater part of its intensity out to a distance of about two solar radii. It consists of rapidly moving free electrons, and exhibits a linearly polarized CONTINUOUS SPECTRUM owing to Thomson scattering, by the electrons, of light from the PHOTOSPHERE. The FRAUNHOFER LINES are not present in the spectrum: they have been sufficiently broadened by the large DOPPLER SHIFTS resulting from the rapid random motion of the electrons as to overlap and be indiscernible. The K-corona attains a temperature of around 2 000 000 kelvin at a height of about 75 000 km. It may exhibit considerable structure, with *streamers* (regions of higher than average density) overlying ACTIVE REGIONS and quiescent PROMINENCES, and CORONAL HOLES (regions of exceptionally low density) overlying areas characterized by relatively weak divergent (and therefore primarily unipolar) magnetic fields.

k-correction see REST FRAME.

Keck Telescopes two 10-meter diameter Ritchey–Chrétien telescopes housed at the W.M. Keck Observatory on MAUNA KEA in Hawaii. Built and operated by the California Association for Research in Astronomy (CARA), an organization whose Board of Directors includes representatives from the California Institute of Technology and the University of California, they are the world's largest reflecting telescopes, operating at optical and infrared wavelengths. The establishment of both the telescopes and the observatory was made possible by grants from the W.M. Keck Foundation. The first telescope, *Keck I*, was completed in 1992 and became operational in May 1993. *Keck II* was constructed 85 meters away, making it possible for the pair to be used as an optical INTERFEROMETER; it began working as a science instrument in October 1996.

Both telescopes have a segmented PRIMARY MIRROR (f/1.75) composed of 36 hexagonal segments, each 1.8 meters across and made of ZERODUR. In each case, the assembly is controlled with ACTIVE OPTICS. Interchangeable secondary mirrors allow optical or infrared observations at either a Cassegrain or two Nasmyth foci. The telescopes are also equipped with several spectrographs and spectrometers for operation in the visible (0.3–1 μm), near-infrared (1–5 μm), and mid-infrared (5–27 μm) wavebands.

In 1996, NASA joined CARA in running the W.M. Keck Observatory and made the observatory a cornerstone of its Origins program.

Keeler Gap (**Keeler Division**) see SATURN'S RINGS.

Kellner eyepiece see EYEPIECE.

kelvin symbol: K. The SI unit of temperature, equal to 1/273.16 of the THERMODYNAMIC TEMPERATURE of the triple point of water. A temperature in kelvin may be converted to one in degrees Celsius (°C) by the subtraction of 273.15.

Kelvin–Helmholtz contraction see KELVIN–HELMHOLTZ TIMESCALE.

Kelvin–Helmholtz instability a hydrodynamic instability where waves are set up at a surface boundary between two flows.

Kelvin–Helmholtz timescale the time taken for a mass of gas to collapse under its own gravitation. It is given by

$$\tau_{KH} = GM^2/RL$$

where G is the gravitational constant and M, R, and L are the mass, radius, and luminosity of the object. It is thought to describe the evolutionary timescale of a pre-main-sequence star. Such a collapse – known as the *Kelvin–Helmholtz contraction* – was proposed in the late 19th century as the source of the Sun's energy output. This theory was abandoned when the contraction timescale of only 10^7 years was shown to be too short. The energy source was subsequently shown to originate in nuclear-fusion reactions.

Kennedy Space Center (**KSC**) a NASA establishment at Cape Canaveral, Florida, from which many of the agency's satellites are launched. It is also the chief launch site for crewed spaceflights and is used for space shuttle payload integration and launching. Alan B. Shepard Jr., the United States' first astronaut, made his historic suborbital flight from this site in 1961, and it was also the starting point for Apollo 11's journey to the Moon in 1969. The site, on Merritt Island, comprises launchpads, runways, and space vehicle assembly areas.

Cape Canaveral began to be used as a missile-testing base by the US Air Force during the 1950s. In 1958, the newly created NASA came to Cape Canaveral and soon began building its Launch Operations Center, a spaceport and space-vehicle assembly facility, there. In 1963, following the assassination of President John F. Kennedy, the missile base and spaceport were integrated into the Kennedy Space Center. The surrounding area of Cape Canaveral was renamed Cape Kennedy in his memory. Changing the name of the whole cape proved unpopular with the local community, however, and it reverted to its previous name in 1973.

Kepler **1** see table at CRATERS.

2 a space telescope planned for launch by NASA in 2007 for the purpose of searching for Earth-sized extrasolar planets. The Kepler mission, to be managed by NASA's Jet Propulsion Laboratory, will seek to locate planets indirectly by watching for transits. The transit of a planet across the face of its parent star is only detectable if the planet is in direct line with the star and its orbit appears edge-on to the observer's line of sight. A transit should cause a minute decrease in the star's brightness, and Kepler will be designed to detect such dimming using a 1-meter telescope-photometer equipped with highly sensitive CCD technology. Using a relatively wide field of view, Kepler will measure the brightness of several thousand stars and check for brightness variations. Three transits, all with a consistent period, duration and change in brightness, provide strong confirmation of a planet's existence. From this information and the nature of the star concerned, Kepler's science team hopes to be able to measure the planet's orbit and work out whether it is in the habitable zone, the region of space around the star at the right distance for water to exist on the planet's surface. This will help determine whether or not the planet is like the Earth and can perhaps support life. Statistically it is estimated that the transit method is likely to detect only 0.5% of the number of planets there could possibly be in the Milky Way Galaxy.

Keplerian telescope the first major improvement of the GALILEAN TELESCOPE, developed by the German astronomer and mathematician Johannes Kepler, in which a positive (convex) lens was used as the eyepiece in place of the negative (concave) lens that Galileo used (see illustration). This gave a larger though inverted field of view and much higher magnifications.

Kepler's laws the three fundamental laws of planetary motion that were formulated by Johannes Kepler and were based on the detailed observations of the planets made by Tycho Brahe, with whom Kepler had worked. The laws state that

1 The orbit of each planet is an ellipse with the Sun at one focus of the ellipse.
2 Each planet revolves around the Sun so that the line connecting planet and Sun (the radius vector) sweeps out equal areas in equal times (see illustration). Thus a planet's velocity decreases as it moves farther from the Sun.
3 The squares of the sidereal periods of any two planets are proportional to the cubes of their mean distances from the Sun. If the period, P, is measured in years and the mean distance, a, in ASTRONOMICAL UNITS, then $P^2 \cong a^3$ for any planet.

The first two laws were published in 1609 in *Astronomia Nova* and the third law in 1619 in *Harmonices Mundi*. The third law, sometimes called the *harmonic law*, allowed the relative distances of the planets from the Sun to be calculated from measurements of the planetary orbital periods. Kepler's laws gave a correct description of planetary motion. The physical nature of the motion was not explained until Newton proposed his laws of motion and gravitation. From these laws can be obtained Newton's form of Kepler's third law:

$$P^2 = 4\pi^2 a^3/G(m_1 + m_2)$$

where G is the gravitational constant, m_1 and m_2 are the masses of the Sun and a planet, a is the semimajor axis of the planet, and P is its sidereal period; all quantities are in SI units. If P, a, and m are expressed in years, astronomical units, and solar masses, then

$$P^2 = a^3/(m_1 + m_2)$$

Kepler's star a SUPERNOVA that was observed in Oct. 1604 in the constellation Ophiuchus and could be seen with the naked eye for over a year. It was studied by astronomers in Europe, China, and Korea and its position was so accurately determined by Kepler and Fabricius that a small patch of nebulosity above the galactic plane could be identified as the remnant of the original 1604 supernova (Walter Baade, 1943). The light curve plotted from the original observations shows that the magnitude increased to a maximum of over −2.5, dropping to +4 in about 300 days, and that it was a type Ia supernova.

Kerr black hole, Kerr-Newman black hole see BLACK HOLE.

Keyhole nebula see ETA CARINAE NEBULA.

Kharkov radio telescope see UTR-2.

kilo- symbol: k. A prefix to a unit, indicating

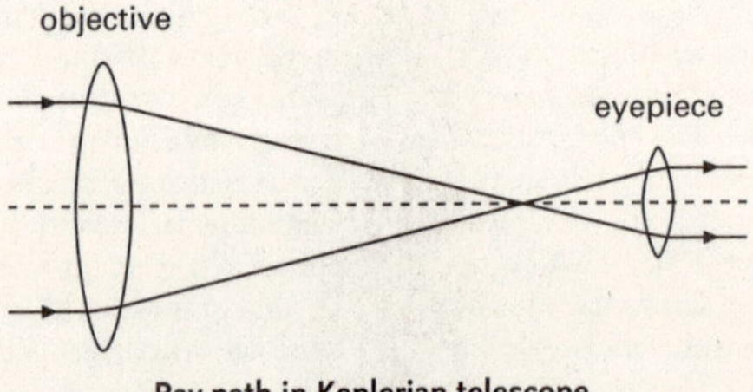

Ray path in Keplerian telescope

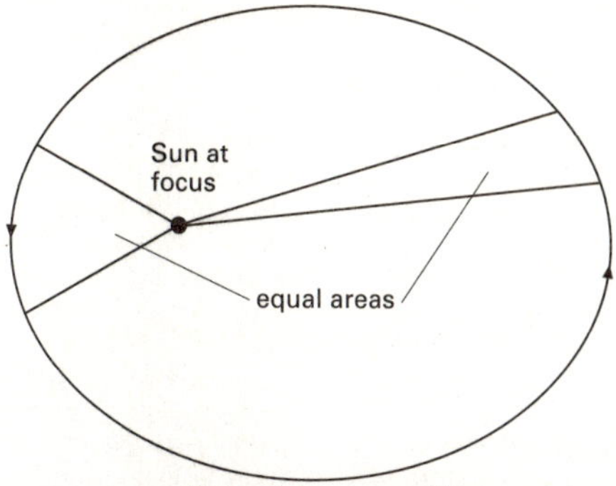

Kepler's second law

a multiple of 1000 or 10^3 of that unit. For example, one kiloparsec (symbol: kpc) equals 1000 parsecs.

kilogram symbol: kg. The SI unit of mass. It is defined as the mass of a prototype platinum-iridium cylinder kept at the International Bureau of Weights and Measures at Sèvres, France. See also SOLAR MASS.

kinetic energy energy possessed by a body by virtue of its motion, equal to the work that the body could do in coming to rest. In classical mechanics a body with mass m and velocity v has kinetic energy $\frac{1}{2}mv^2$. A body with moment of inertia I rotating with angular velocity ω has kinetic energy $\frac{1}{2}I\omega^2$.

King law a model due to I. King describing the radial brightness profile of a spheroidal system, such as an elliptical galaxy or a cluster of galaxies. While not such a good fit to many galaxies as the empirical DE VAUCOULEURS' LAW, it is closely derived from dynamical models of self-gravitating systems.

Kirkwood gaps gaps in the distribution of orbits within the main ASTEROID BELT, corresponding to the absence of orbits with periods that are simple fractions (1/4, 1/3, 2/5, 1/2, etc.) of the orbital period of Jupiter (see illustration overleaf). Asteroids with such orbital periods would be perturbed into orbits of high eccentricity by the regularly recurring gravitational pull of Jupiter. These asteroids would then cross the orbits of Mars and Earth, with a high chance of colliding with these planets. The US astronomer Daniel Kirkwood first explained these gaps in 1857.

Kitt Peak National Observatory (KPNO) an observatory near Tucson, Arizona, USA, at an altitude of 2100 meters. Founded in 1958, it is now one of the NATIONAL OPTICAL ASTRONOMY OBSERVATORY (NOAO). The site has a very large assembly of telescopes. The 4-meter *Mayall Telescope* began operating in 1973. It has a fused-quartz mirror, focal ratio (f/2.7), RITCHEY–CHRÉTIEN OPTICS, and Cassegrain (f/8) and infrared (f/16) foci. There are also a 2.1-meter reflector, operational since 1964, the 3.5-meter WIYN TELESCOPE (operated on behalf of the universities of Wisconsin, Indiana and Yale, and the NOAO), and a SCHMIDT TELESCOPE. Facilities of the NATIONAL SOLAR OBSERVATORY at Kitt Peak include the *McMath–Pierce Solar Telescope Facility*, with its 1.6-meter main telescope and its two 0.9-meter auxiliaries, and the *Vacuum Solar Telescope* (0.7 m, f/60) and the *Razdow Small Solar Patrol Telescope* (see SOLAR TELESCOPE). There is also the pioneering instrument for MILLIMETER ASTRONOMY, first used in 1967 and operated by the NATIONAL RADIO ASTRONOMY OBSERVATORY; since 1983 it has had a 12-m aperture and a more accurate reflecting surface.

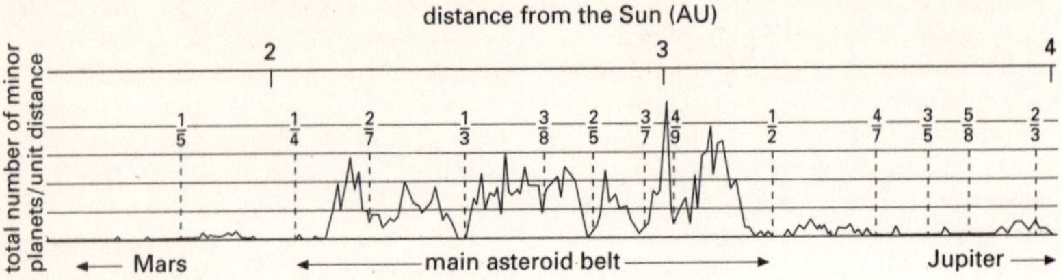

Kirkwood gaps, indicated by fractions

Kleinmann-Low nebula (**KL nebula**) a diffuse source of infrared radiation within the ORION MOLECULAR CLOUD (OMC-1). At far-infrared wavelengths (100 μm) it is the brightest member of the infrared cluster in the OMC-1 complex, with a luminosity about 10^5 times that of the Sun. The temperature of the dust within the nebula is found to be about 70 K.

K line see H AND K LINES.

knot a bright compact feature particularly in radio and X-ray JETS and in SUPERNOVA REMNANTS.

Kochab see URSA MINOR.

Kohoutek (**1973 XII**) a comet discovered in March 1973 by Lubos Kohoutek when he was looking for Biela's comet. At discovery comet Kohoutek was 4.6 AU away from the Sun and early predictions indicated that near perihelion, at its brightest, Kohoutek would reach a magnitude of about −12, comparable with the full Moon. This would make it visible in daylight. Comets however are among the most unpredictable astronomical objects and Kohoutek only just attained naked-eye visibility. It was extensively investigated from Skylab, astronaut Gibson being impressed by its overall orange color and its sunward spike.

Koronis family a HIRAYAMA FAMILY of asteroids located at 2.9 AU from the Sun. The members are S-TYPE ASTEROIDS with very similar color, spectra, and albedos. The precursor body was at least 90 km across. Many of the Koronis family 'remember' the original spin of the precursor, indicating that they have not collided enough since their formation to have had their spins randomized.

Kourou a coastal town in north central French Guiana, near which lies the launch site for ESA's ARIANE launcher. Originally owned by the European Launcher Development Organization (ELDO) and known as its Equatorial Space Range, the site passed to ESA upon its formation in the mid-1970s .

kpc *symbol for* kiloparsec, i.e. 10^3 parsecs.

KPNO *abbrev. for* Kitt Peak National Observatory.

Kraus-type radio telescope a RADIO TELESCOPE consisting of a long thin flat reflector that can be tilted about its long horizontal axis and that reflects radiation from the sky onto a large fixed curved reflector that forms part of a paraboloid. The radiation is collected at the focus of the paraboloid by the feed (see DISH). The telescope thus achieves a large collecting area that can be steered in one direction.

KREEP see MOON ROCKS.

Kreutz group a collection of SUNGRAZING COMETS that all have very similar orbital elements and were most probably formed by the breakup of a single large comet. The group was first recognized in 1888 by Heinrich Kreutz. Many members were detected by coronagraphs on spacecraft in the period 1979–89.

KSC *abbrev. for* Kennedy Space Center.

K stars stars of SPECTRAL TYPE K, orange in color and with a surface temperature (T_{eff}) of about 3500 to 4900 kelvin. The spectral lines of calcium (Ca II and Ca I) are strong and neutral metal lines are very prominent; molecular bands strengthen. Arcturus and Aldebaran are K stars.

Kuiper Airborne Observatory (**KAO**) an infrared and submillimeter observatory operated by NASA between 1975 and 1996, operationally based at the AMES Airforce base, California, and flown on a Lockheed C141 'Starlifter'. The plane normally flew at over 36 000 ft (nearly 11 000 meters), above most of the atmosphere's IR-absorbing water vapor. A 0.9-meter diameter NASMYTH Cassegrain telescope, mounted on an air bearing to reduce vibration, looked out of the aircraft through an uncovered aperture; a pressure bulkhead separating it from the operators. Observations, usually at wavelengths longer than 30 μm, were made with cryogenically cooled photometers, spectrometers, and interferometers. The observatory was named after the Dutch-born US astronomer Gerard P. Kuiper. See also SOFIA.

Kuiper belt a disk of some 10^7 to 10^9 COMETS that hugs the plane of the planetary system and lies between about 35 and 1000 AU from the Sun. CHIRON may have come from this disk.

Kvant see MIR.

Ll

labyrinthus (plural: **labyrinthi**) a system of intersecting narrow depressions. The word is used in the approved name of such a surface feature on a planet or satellite.

Lacerta (**Lizard**) a small inconspicuous constellation in the northern hemisphere near Cygnus, lying partly in the Milky Way, the brightest stars being of 4th magnitude. It contains the prototype of the quasarlike BL LAC OBJECTS. Abbrev.: Lac; genitive form: Lacertae; approx. position: RA 22.5h, dec +45°; area: 201 sq deg.

lacus a small relatively smooth dark isolated area. The word is used in the approved name of such a surface feature on the Moon and, now unofficially, on Mars. (Latin: lake)

Lagoon nebula (**M8; NGC 6523**) an EMISSION NEBULA in the form of an H II REGION that lies about 1 kiloparsec away in the direction of Sagittarius. It contains the open cluster NGC 6530. Its total apparent magnitude (5.8) makes it easily visible with binoculars.

Lagrangian points five locations in space where a small body can maintain a stable orbit despite the gravitational influence of two much more massive bodies, orbiting about a common center of mass. They are named after the French mathematician J.L. Lagrange who first suggested their existence in 1772. A Lagrangian point 60° ahead of Jupiter in its orbit around the Sun, and another 60° behind Jupiter, are the average locations of members of the TROJAN GROUP of asteroids; these points are denoted L_4 and L_5. The three other Lagrangian points in the Sun–Jupiter gravitational field do not permit stable asteroid orbits owing to the perturbing influence of the other planets. In any system these three points lie on the line joining the centers of mass of the two massive bodies and are denoted L_1 (the *inner Lagrangian point*) and L_2 and L_3 (the *outer Lagrangian points*); small bodies here would be in unstable equilibrium (see EQUIPOTENTIAL SURFACES).

lambda (λ) **1** the 11th letter of the Greek alphabet, used in STELLAR NOMENCLATURE usually to designate the 11th-brightest star in a constellation or sometimes to indicate a star's position in a group.
2 *symbol for* wavelength *or* longitude.

Langrenus see table at CRATERS.

La Palma Observatory see ROQUE DE LOS MUCHACHOS OBSERVATORY.

Laplace's nebular hypothesis see NEBULAR HYPOTHESIS.

Large Binocular Telescope (**LDT**) see STEWARD OBSERVATORY.

Large Magellanic Cloud (**LMC; Nubecula Major**) see MAGELLANIC CLOUDS.

large-scale structure the structure of matter on the largest scales (greater than 100 megaparsecs), revealed by the results from large-scale REDSHIFT SURVEYS of galaxies. This structure consists of very long *filaments* of matter surrounding huge *voids* or *bubbles* that are empty of matter. The largest SUPERCLUSTERS are elongated, and scattered CLUSTERS OF GALAXIES often link the ends of these superclusters into filaments. The filaments surround empty voids, the first of which was discovered in Boötes in 1981 and is about 100 Mpc across. Most of the matter in the Universe lies in the filaments, which occupy only 1% or 2% of the volume of space. The largest coherent structure so far detected in redshift surveys is the *Great Wall* at a distance of about 95 Mpc. This structure forms a thin sheet less than 10 Mpc thick but spans an area 80 by 225 Mpc.

Larissa a small satellite of Neptune, discovered in 1989. See Table 2, Appendix.

Las Campanas Observatory an observatory near La Serena, Chile, sited on Cerro Las Campanas, at an altitude of 2300 meters; the SEEING at this site is exceptional. The Observatory is owned by the Carnegie Institution of Washington. The principal instruments are the 2.5-meter Irenee du Pont Telescope, which went into operation in 1977, and the 1-meter *Swope Telescope*, which was named for Henrietta Swope and became operational in 1971. Two lightweight 6.5-meter telescopes – the *Magellan Telescopes* – came into operation at the start of the 21st century. Magellan I, also called the Walter Baade Telescope, saw first light in 2000; Magellan II, otherwise known as the Landon Clay Telescope, began working as a science instrument in 2002.

Las Campanas redshift survey see REDSHIFT SURVEY.

La Silla Observatory see EUROPEAN SOUTHERN OBSERVATORY.

last quarter (**third quarter**) see PHASES, LUNAR.

late-type galaxies a general term now used for spiral galaxies.

late-type stars relatively cool stars of SPECTRAL TYPES K, M, C (carbon), and S. They were originally thought, wrongly, to be at a much later stage of stellar evolution than EARLY-TYPE STARS.

latitude 1 *short for* celestial latitude. See ECLIPTIC COORDINATE SYSTEM.
2 *short for* galactic latitude. See GALACTIC COORDINATE SYSTEM.

launch vehicle any system by which the necessary energy is given to a satellite, spaceprobe, etc., in order to insert it into the desired orbit or trajectory. Expendable multistage launchers were used originally, and are still being used and developed: ESA's ARIANE and NASA's Titan and Delta families are examples. The reusable SPACE SHUTTLE was developed by NASA so that recovery of the vehicle is possible.

Rocket propulsion is a form of jet propulsion: all the propellant is carried in the vehicle at take-off and the hot combustion gases, resulting from the mixture of fuel with reactant, are ejected at high speed through a nozzle to produce the necessary force – termed *thrust* – to lift the vehicle off the ground. Modern launchers generally consist of two, three, or four stages; the final stage carries the spacecraft into the desired orbit, the satellite separating from the stage when orbital velocity is reached. There are design variations in the type of propellant used, which may be either solid or liquid, the means of carrying the propellant, and the process by which the tanks, etc., are discarded.

launch window an interval of time during which a planetary probe, etc., must be launched in order to attain a desired position at a desired time.

LBI *abbrev. for* long baseline interferometry. A technique of radio interferometry in which the antennas of an interferometer are connected by links such as microwave transponders rather than cables (see RADIO TELESCOPE). In this way the correlations can be done in real-time and the local oscillators at the antennas can maintain a constant PHASE relation. MERLIN is a long baseline interferometer. Compare VLBI.

LBT *abbrev. for* Large Binocular Telescope.

LBV *abbrev. for* luminous blue variable.

LDEF *abbrev. for* Long Duration Exposure Facility.

leading edge see PRECEDING.

leading spot *another name for* preceding (*p*-) spot. See SUNSPOTS.

leap month see LUNAR YEAR.

leap second see UNIVERSAL TIME.

leap year a year that contains one more day than the usual CALENDAR YEAR so that the average length of the year is brought closer to the TROPICAL YEAR of 365.2422 days or to the LUNAR YEAR. In the Julian calendar a leap year of 366 days occurred once every four years when the year was divisible by four. In the GREGORIAN CALENDAR this rule was modified so that century years are leap years only when they are divisible by 400. The additional day is now added at the end of February (Feb. 29).

Leda a small satellite of Jupiter, discovered in 1974 by Charles T. Cowall. See JUPITER'S SATELLITES; Table 2, Appendix.

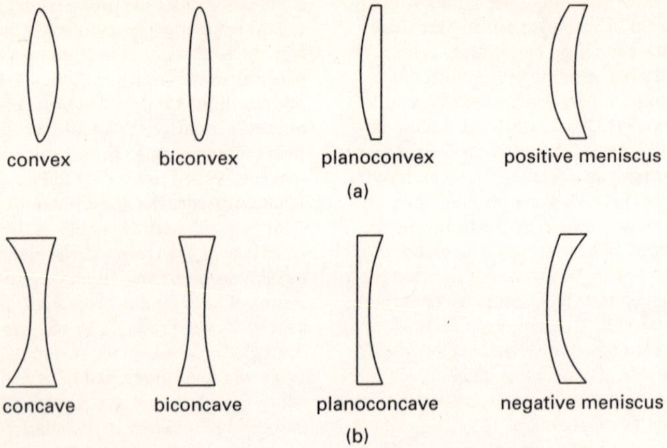

Lenses: (a) converging; (b) diverging

Lemaître model see COSMOLOGICAL MODELS.

lens a specially shaped piece of transparent material, such as glass, quartz, or plastic, bounded by two surfaces of a regular (usually spherical) but not necessarily identical curvature. A ray of light passing through a lens is bent as a result of REFRACTION. Spherical lenses may be either converging or diverging in their action on a light beam, depending on their shape (see illustration). See also ABERRATION; COATING OF LENSES; EYEPIECE; FOCAL LENGTH; OBJECTIVE.

lensing see GRAVITATIONAL LENS.

lenticular galaxy see GALAXIES.

Leo (**Lion**) a large conspicuous zodiac constellation in the northern hemisphere near Ursa Major. The brightest stars are the 1st-magnitude REGULUS (α) and Algieba (γ), three of 2nd magnitude including DENEBOLA (β), and several of 3rd magnitude. Regulus lies at the base of the *Sickle of Leo*, the other stars in the Sickle being (in order) Eta (η), Gamma (γ), Zeta (ζ), Mu (μ), and Epsilon (ε) Leonis. The area also contains the Mira star R Leonis, the dwarf nova X Leonis, and the spiral galaxies M65 (NGC 3623), M66 (NGC 3627), M95 (NGC 3351), and M96 (NGC 3368). Abbrev.: Leo; genitive form: Leonis; approx. position: RA 10.5h, dec +15°; area: 947 sq deg.

LEO *abbrev. for* low Earth orbit.

Leo Minor (**Little Lion**) a small inconspicuous constellation in the northern hemisphere near Leo, the brightest stars being of 4th magnitude. Abbrev.: LMi; genitive form: Leonis Minoris; approx. position: RA 10h, dec +35°; area: 232 sq deg.

Leonids (**November swarm**) a periodic METEOR SHOWER that tends to be insignificant most years (ZHR about 10) but at 33-year intervals produces a spectacular meteor storm. The shower, radiant: RA 152°, dec +22°, maximizes on the two days around Nov. 17 each year. The associated METEOROID STREAM is the dust debris from comet Tempel-Tuttle (1866 I) and storms occur when the Earth intersects the stream near the parent comet. This comet has an orbital period of 33 years. The last storm occurred in 1999. Spectacular storms occurred in 1799, 1833, 1866 and also in 1996; 1899 and 1933 were years of only mediocre displays.

Leo systems two dwarf elliptical galaxies that are members of the LOCAL GROUP.

leptons a class of pointlike ELEMENTARY PARTICLES that do not participate in strong interactions (see FUNDAMENTAL FORCES); it includes the ELECTRON, MUON, the massive tau lepton, the NEUTRINOS, and their associated ANTIPARTICLES. Leptons show no evidence of any internal structure. See also BIG BANG THEORY.

Lepus (Hare) a constellation in the southern hemisphere just south of Orion. The brightest star is the very luminous remote Arneb (α), which is of 2nd magnitude. R Leporis, an intensely red variable star with a period of 430 days during which it ranges in magnitude between 11.7 and about 5.5, is known as Hind's crimson star. The constellation also contains the globular cluster M79 (NGC 1904), a beautiful sight in a 200-millimeter telescope. Abbrev.: Lep; genitive form: Leporis; approx. position: RA 5.5h, dec −20°; area: 290 sq deg.

LEST *abbrev. for* large Earth-based solar telescope. See ROQUE DE LOS MUCHACHOS OBSERVATORY.

Lexell's comet a comet that was discovered by Messier in June 1770 but was named after the St. Petersburg mathematician who calculated its orbit. Prior to 1767 Lexell's comet had a period of 11.4 years; a close approach to Jupiter in 1770 changed this to 5.6 years and the next close approach to Jupiter in 1779 changed this period to a calculated 174 years. This last approach perturbed the comet so that it has a perihelion distance of 5.4 AU and it has never been seen again, always being too far away from Earth.

L* galaxy see LUMINOSITY FUNCTION.

LHA *abbrev. for* local hour angle.

Libra, first point of see FIRST POINT OF ARIES.

Libra (Balance) a fairly inconspicuous zodiac constellation in the southern hemisphere near Scorpius, the brightest star, Beta (β) Librae, being of 2nd magnitude and apparently green in color. Delta (δ) Librae is an ALGOL VARIABLE (magnitude 4.9 to 5.9) with a period of about 55 hours. Abbrev.: Lib; genitive form: Librae; approx. position: RA 15h, dec −15°; area: 538 sq deg.

libration the means by which 59% of the Moon's surface is made visible, over a 30-year period, to the terrestrial observer despite the lunar day being of the same length as the SIDEREAL MONTH (see SYNCHRONOUS ROTATION). PHYSICAL LIBRATION is a real irregularity in the Moon's rotation, arising from minor distortions in shape. *Geometrical librations,* including DIURNAL LIBRATIONS, are apparent oscillations due to the Moon being observed from slightly different directions at different times. A geometrical *libration in longitude* of 6°9′ (mean value) results from the inconstancy of the Moon's orbital velocity, which follows from the ECCENTRICITY of the Moon's orbit and KEPLER'S SECOND LAW. This libration reveals part of the eastern or western farside limbs at different times during one month. In addition the 5°9′ inclination of the Moon's orbital plane to the ecliptic, plus the 1°32′ tilt of the Moon's equator to its orbital plane, produces a monthly geometrical *libration in latitude* of 6°41′. This makes the Moon's north and south polar regions more readily observable during one month.

Lick Observatory an observatory on Mount Hamilton, California, at an altitude of 1280 meters. Endowed by James Lick, a 19th-century US financier and philanthropist, it was given to the University of California on the completion in 1888 of its (then) powerful 91-cm refracting telescope. The chief instrument today is the 3-meter *Shane Telescope,* with a Pyrex mirror having a comparatively large focal ratio of f/5. It was named for the US astronomer C. Donald Shane and became fully operational in 1959. There are also several smaller telescopes.

life in the Universe see EXOBIOLOGY; SETI.

light ELECTROMAGNETIC RADIATION to which the human eye is sensitive; light is thus also called *visible* or *optical radiation.* The wavelength range varies from person to person but usually lies within the limits of 380 to 750 nanometers (daytime). Light therefore forms a very narrow band of the electromagnetic spectrum between the infrared and ultraviolet bands. As the wavelength decreases, the color of the light changes through the spectral hues of red, orange, yellow, green, blue, indigo, and violet. These colors, which may be seen in a rainbow or produced by a prism, form the *visible spectrum.* In daylight, the eye is most sensitive to greenish-yellow light of wavelength about 550 nm; the dark-adapted eye has peak sensitivity around 510 nm, the range extending to about 620 nm. Optical astronomy covers wavelengths from about 300 to 900 nm, i.e. slightly wider than the human range. The Earth's atmosphere is transparent to light so that astronomy at optical wavelengths has not experienced the problems with detection and observation that have bedeviled studies at other wavelengths. Atmospheric turbulence does, however, adversely affect ground-based optical astronomy, as do clouds and precipitation. See ATMOSPHERIC WINDOWS. See also LIGHT POLLUTION.

light cone the representation of a light flash in SPACETIME. In three-dimensional space the wavefront of a light flash would be a sphere centered on the emitting point and growing in radius at the speed of light. In spacetime (with one spatial coordinate suppressed) the vertex of a cone represents the time and place at which a flash is emitted and the cone itself describes the history of the propagating flash. More generally a light cone defines the regions of the Universe accessible from a given point in space and moment in time, i.e. from a given position in spacetime. This position is called an *event* and is the vertex of the light cone.

light curve a graph of the brightness of a VARIABLE STAR or other variable object plotted against time, the brightness usually being expressed in terms of apparent or absolute MAGNITUDE. Different types of variable star can be distinguished by the shape of the curve; the period of the variable is one complete oscillation in brightness. The light curve of an eclipsing binary has two minima: a shallower one (the *secondary minimum*) and a deeper one (the *primary minimum*), which occurs when the brighter star is eclipsed. The minimum has a flat base if the eclipse is total or annular.

lightest superpartner (LSP) the lightest particle predicted to exist by SUPERSYMMETRY. The LSP must be a stable particle since there is no lighter supersymmetric particle it can decay to. The PHOTINO is a promising candidate to be the LSP. It is not possible to predict the mass of the LSP since the way in which supersymmetry is broken is not known. The LSP may contribute to the DARK MATTER in the Universe.

light-gathering power (light grasp) a measure of the ability of an optical telescope to collect light and thus discern fainter objects. It is proportional to the area of the telescope APERTURE, i.e. to the square of the diameter of the primary mirror or objective.

light mantle an avalanche of lunar HIGHLAND material, possibly triggered by the formation of SECONDARY CRATERS from TYCHO, that covers part of the TAURUS-LITTROW region and was sampled by the crew of Apollo 17.

light pollution one of the factors setting a limit on the faintness of stars that may be seen, photographed, or observed or recorded by telescope. Light pollution is an excessive amount of background light mostly arising from human activities and includes street and domestic lighting, lighting of public buildings, factories, and offices, and lighting of entertainment and sports facilities used at night. Not all light pollution is of human origin, however. On a moonless night there are still three natural sources, of roughly equal contribution; these are AIRGLOW and other atmospheric effects, the ZODIACAL LIGHT arising from the scattering of sunlight by Solar-System dust, and the background light of our Galaxy. See also SEEING.

light-time the time taken for light, radio waves, or other electromagnetic radiation to travel at the SPEED OF LIGHT (3×10^5 km s^{-1}) between two points. The light-time along the mean distance between Sun and Earth is 499 seconds. More precisely, the light-time for UNIT DISTANCE is a constant, τ_A, equal to 499.00478 seconds. Since the light-time between celestial bodies and Earth varies as the Earth revolves in its orbit, a correction – the *equation of light* – must be made to calculations involving measurements of time. Light-time produces a delay between transmission and reception of command signals and data between Earth and a spacecraft.

light-year (l.y.) a unit of distance equal to the distance traveled through space in one year by light, radio waves, or any other form of electromagnetic radiation. Since all electromagnetic radiation travels in a vacuum at the SPEED OF LIGHT, one light-year equals about 9.4605×10^{12} km. Distances expressed in light-years give the time that radiation would take to cross that distance. One light-year equals 0.3066 parsecs, 63 240 astronomical units, or a parallax of 3.259 arc seconds.

Analogous but smaller units of distance, such as the *light-month, light-week, light-day,* and *light-second* are also used, often to indicate the size of an object (such as the core of an ACTIVE GALAXY) whose output is varying: the timescale of the variations imposes an upper limit on the size, the conditions being unlikely to change more quickly than the time it takes for light to travel across the region.

limb the apparent edge of the Sun, Moon, or a planet, or any other celestial body with a detectable disk.

limb brightening the increase in intensity at X-ray and radio wavelengths from the center to the limb of the Sun's disk. It arises at radio wavelengths for the same reason as the LIMB DARKENING at visible wavelengths but has the opposite effect, because the radiation is emitted from the high-temperature upper CHROMOSPHERE/inner CORONA rather than from the PHOTOSPHERE. At X-ray wavelengths, where the material is less opaque, intensity is determined by path length rather than radiation temperature.

limb darkening the decrease in intensity at visible wavelengths from the center to the limb of the Sun's disk. Light from the central portion of the disk is radiated radially toward us, whereas light from closer to the limb has to pass obliquely through a greater thickness of the solar atmosphere. For a given limit of penetration we can therefore see deeper into the PHOTOSPHERE at the center of the disk than at the limb, where our line of sight passes through cooler gases. The limb consequently appears less bright.

Limb darkening has been detected in other stars, principally by the use of three-color PHOTOMETRY of the LIGHT CURVES of ECLIPSING BINARIES (the effect being more pronounced in blue light than in red) and by SPECKLE INTERFEROMETRY.

A similar effect is observed in planets with deep atmospheres, notably Jupiter and Saturn, and arises from the scattering of sunlight by atmospheric particles.

limiting magnitude the faintest apparent MAGNITUDE that may be observed through a telescope and/or recorded on a photographic plate or other device. It depends on the telescope aperture, on the sensitivity of the recording device, on atmospheric conditions, etc. Star catalogs usually list stars down to a specific limiting magnitude.

linea (plural: **lineae**) a dark or bright elongated marking, straight or curved, on the surface of a planet or satellite. The word is used in the approved name of such a feature.

linear momentum see MOMENTUM.

linear polarization see POLARIZATION.

line broadening the production of broadened spectral lines by various effects. The natural width of a spectral line is determined by quantum mechanical uncertainty. Other factors can, however, produce extra line width, including rapid ROTATION of a celestial body, DOPPLER broadening, PRESSURE BROADENING, and the ZEEMAN EFFECT. Considerations of the LINE PROFILE can give information about the physical conditions of celestial objects.

line of apsides see APSIDES.

line of cusps the plane passing through the CUSPS of a crescent Moon or planet. See also EQUATOR OF ILLUMINATION.

line of inversion see SUNSPOTS.

line of nodes see NODES.

line-of-sight velocity see RADIAL VELOCITY.

line profile the plot of radiation intensity against wavelength or frequency for a spectral line. See also LINE BROADENING.

line receiver a radio-astronomy RECEIVER that is either tuned to receive signals in only one narrow band of frequencies, the center frequency being adjustable, or that has a broad BANDWIDTH divided into many narrow channels of fixed frequency, the outputs of the channels being kept separate from one another. Line receivers are used in MOLECULAR-LINE RADIO ASTRONOMY where the radio emissions are of narrow bandwidth. They are also used to study the distribution and relative velocity of neutral hydrogen (H I) in our own and in nearby SPIRAL GALAXIES (see H I REGION).

LINER galaxies *abbrev. for* low-ionization nuclear emission-line region galaxies. A common class of otherwise normal galaxies which show low-ionization line emission around the nucleus, but not at the strength or scale observed in most ACTIVE GALAXIES.

line spectrum a SPECTRUM consisting of discrete lines (*spectral lines*) resulting from radiation emitted or absorbed at definite wavelengths. Line spectra are produced by atoms or ionized atoms when transitions occur between their ENERGY LEVELS as a result of emission or absorption of photons. The FRAUNHOFER LINES of the Sun are an example of an absorption line spectrum.

LISA *abbrev. for* Laser Interferometer Space Antenna. A 'cornerstone' mission of ESA's HORIZON 2000 program aimed at detecting and observing gravitational waves from massive black holes and binary stars in our Galaxy. The mission will seek to operate at frequencies between 0.1 and 0.0001 Hz, a range in which no useful groundbased measurements can be made. The LISA mission will consist of six identical spacecraft deployed in space in the configuration of an equilateral triangle having each side 5 million km long. Each spacecraft will carry a miniature laser emitting a continuous infrared beam at a wavelength of 1.064 μm. Each of the LISA craft will transmit the beam to its corresponding remote counterpart in the configuration via a 38-cm-aperture Cassegrain telescope and will in turn receive the much weaker return beam via the same telescope. Each telescope will focus the return beam it receives onto a sensitive photodetector where it will be superimposed with a small part of the original local light. The resulting interference signal from each arm of the triangle will be combined under computer control to screen out local phase noise. A polished platinum-gold cube (known as a test mass) inside a vacuum enclosure carried by each vehicle will serve as an optical reference (mirror) for the light beams. Any gravitational wave passing through the system should cause a fluctuation in the separation of the test masses and a concomitant fluctuation in the optical pathway between the test masses, and this should be detectable by the interferometry. Such a fluctuation will be extremely small but should be measurable. The mission is currently planned for launch in 2017.

lithium star a type of CARBON STAR with very strong lithium lines, suggesting that the lithium was freshly produced in the hydrogen-burning shell of the carbon star.

lithosphere see EARTH.

LMC *abbrev. for* Large Magellanic Cloud. See MAGELLANIC CLOUDS.

LMC X-3 a highly variable X-ray source in the Large Magellanic Cloud (LMC). Optical spectroscopy confirmed this to be an X-RAY BINARY system with an orbital period of 1.7 days and a high MASS FUNCTION. Along with A0620-00 and CYGNUS X-1, LMC X-3 is one of the best candidate sources for a galactic BLACK HOLE.

LMXB *abbrev. for* low-mass X-ray binary. See X-RAY BINARY.

lobate ridge a ramp-shaped feature occurring in the lunar MARIA. Lobate ridges are the surviving remnants of the margins of thick lava flows. Compare WRINKLE RIDGES.

lobate scarp see MERCURY.

lobe **1** see ANTENNA.
2 see RADIO-SOURCE STRUCTURE.

Local Group the CLUSTER OF GALAXIES of which our GALAXY is a member. It is a comparatively small cluster with around 40 known members and some other possible members, most of which are dwarf ellipticals or irregular galaxies (see table). The most massive members are the Galaxy and the ANDROMEDA GALAXY (M31). The other major members are the TRIANGULUM SPIRAL (M33) and the Large MAGELLANIC CLOUD. The group is irregular in shape with two notable subclusters: one around our Galaxy and the Magellanic Clouds, the other around M31 and M33.

local hour angle (**LHA**) the HOUR ANGLE of a celestial body as measured at a particular locality. It is the local apparent sidereal time minus the apparent right ascension (see LOCAL SIDEREAL TIME).

local oscillator see RECEIVER.

Local Group
(some nearer members)

Galaxy	*Position (2000)* *RA (h, m)*	*dec (°)*	*Type*	*Approx. distance (kpc)*	*Integrated magnitude*
Galaxy			Sb/Sc		
LMC	05 23.6	–69.7	Irr	50	0.1
SMC	00 52.7	–72.8	Irr	60	2.3
M31 (Andromeda)	00 42.7	+41.3	Sb	690	3.4
M33 (Triangulum)	01 33.9	+30.6	Sc	900	5.7
NGC 205	00 40.4	+41.7	E6	690	8.0
M32 (NGC 221)	00 42.7	+40.9	E2	690	8.2
NGC 185	00 39.0	+48.3	dE0	690	9.2
NGC 147	00 33.2	+48.5	dE4	690	9.3
IC 1613	01 04.8	+2.1	Irr	740	9.3
NGC 6822	19 44.9	–14.8	Irr	520	9
Fornax system	02 39.9	–34.5	dE3	140	8
Sculptor system	00 59.9	–33.7	dE3	80	10
Leo I system	10 08.4	+12.3	dE3	230	10
Leo II system	11 13.5	+22.2	dE0	230	11.5
Draco system	17 20.2	+57.9	dE3	80	11
UMi system	15 08.8	+67.2	dE6	70	12
Carina system	06 41.6	–59.0	dE	90	

local sidereal time (LST) the SIDEREAL TIME at a particular location. A celestial object crosses the local meridian when the LST is equal to the object's RIGHT ASCENSION. The *local mean sideral time* (*LMST*) is equal to the GREENWICH MEAN SIDERAL TIME plus four minutes for each degree of longitude that the location is east of Greenwich, four minutes being subtracted for each degree west. The *local apparent sideral time* (*LAST*) is obtained by adding the equation of the equinoxes (see SIDEREAL TIME) to the LMST.

local standard of rest (LSR) the frame of reference, centered on the Sun, in which the space velocities (see RADIAL VELOCITY) of all the stars average to zero. This LSR is called the *kinematic LSR*. The PECULIAR MOTIONS of these stars with respect to the LSR would also average to zero if the Sun were at rest. The Sun however is moving, relative to the LSR, at about 20 km s^{-1} toward the solar APEX. The stars reflect this solar motion in addition to their peculiar motions in their PROPER MOTIONS. A different LSR is sometimes useful. It is the reference frame, centered on the Sun, that moves in a circular orbit around the galactic center so that all neighboring stars (i.e. those in circular orbits) are essentially at rest. This is called the *dynamic LSR*. The rotation velocity of the dynamic LSR is about 250 km s^{-1} (*but see* GALACTIC ROTATION). These two definitions of the LSR do not exactly agree; the kinematic LSR lags behind the dynamic LSR.

Local Supercluster a huge flattened cloud of GALAXIES and CLUSTERS OF GALAXIES that is centered on or near the VIRGO CLUSTER and contains the LOCAL GROUP (including our Galaxy) as an outlying member. Its radius is believed to be about 30 megaparsecs. Although its reality was for long in doubt, the discovery of other SUPERCLUSTERS has convinced most astronomers that the Local Supercluster is a true physical system. The Local Group is moving toward Virgo at a velocity of 250–300 km s^{-1} in what is known as the *virgocentric flow*.

Local System see GOULD BELT.

local thermodynamic equilibrium (**LTE**) see THERMODYNAMIC EQUILIBRIUM.

log N–log S diagram see SOURCE COUNT.

Loki see IO.

Long Baseline Array see AUSTRALIA TELESCOPE.

long baseline interferometry see LBI.

Long Duration Exposure Facility (**LDEF**) a NASA satellite that was deployed from an orbiting space shuttle in Apr. 1984 and remained in orbit until retrieved by the shuttle in Jan. 1990, long after its scheduled retrieval after nine months. Its 57 experiments measured the effects of prolonged exposure of biological and electronic systems to the environment of space, or were studies requiring long exposures. For example, they recorded the quantity of artificial debris striking the satellite, the frequency of meteoroid impacts, levels of ultraviolet radiation, and concentrations of highly corrosive atomic oxygen; the whole spacecraft structure was examined in great detail, providing information that was to influence the design of future spacecraft. There were also major studies on cosmic rays.

long-focus photographic astrometry a branch of photographic ASTROMETRY in which (usually) refracting telescopes of long focal lengths of eight meters or more and focal ratios of f/15 to f/20 are used to produce sharp photographs of both the star under consideration plus three or more distant reference stars. Accuracies of about 0.01 arc seconds can be reached, distances being determined from ANNUAL PARALLAX. The technique is now also employed in the determination of orbital motion and masses of binary stars and of SECULAR PARALLAX.

longitude 1 *short for* celestial longitude. See ECLIPTIC COORDINATE SYSTEM.
2 *short for* galactic longitude. See GALACTIC COORDINATE SYSTEM.

longitude of perihelion see ORBITAL ELEMENTS.

longitude of the ascending node see ORBITAL ELEMENTS.

Long March (**Changzheng; Cz**) a family of liquid-fuelled rockets used as the main launch vehicles in China's space program. One of its members, the Long March 2F, carried the first Chinese astronaut into space in October 2003. The series of Long March rockets was the outcome of a gradual process that began with China's early attempts to build missiles in the mid-1950s, initially with help from the Soviet Union. Although hampered by political upheavals during the 1960s, Chinese rocket scientists had by 1970 completed the country's first intermediate-range and intercontinental ballistic missiles. One of these, the medium-range DF-3, became the basis of the Long March 1, which carried China's first artificial satellite, Mao 1, into orbit Apr 24 1970. The long-range ICBM DF-5 provided the template for the later Long March 2 (introduced 1975), 3 (1983), and 4 (1988).

Between 1970 and 2003, the Long March series carried out more than 70 launches. But a number of failures, some involving fatalities, attracted unfavorable criticism outside China. A human spaceflight project was abandoned, and in the 1980s China turned to developing less ambitious crewless spacecraft. Eventually, the Long March proved itself reliable enough for China to enter the international satellite-launching market. Using newly developed cryogenic engines and taking a modular approach to the design, the Chinese produced a family of Long March rockets. Between 1985 and 2000, Long March vehicles lifted 27 foreign satellites into space. The workhorse of the family, the Long March 4, is a three-stage rocket that can develop more than 272 000 kg of thrust and carry a payload of up to 5000 kg into low-Earth orbit, 3600 kg to medium orbit, and 2270 kg to geosynchronous orbit.

In April 1992, the Chinese government reinitiated its human spaceflight program using the Long March 2F, a two-stage rocket equipped with four liquid-fueled strap-on boosters. Between that year and 2003, this vehicle launched four crewless prototypes of a piloted spacecraft, the *Shenzhou* ('divine vessel'). The fifth, launched Oct 15 2003 from Jiuquan in the northern Gobi Desert of western China, one of the country's four isolated launch sites, carried Yang Liwei, China's first astronaut, on a 21-hour, 14-orbit spaceflight. The exploit made China only the third nation in the world to be capable of independently sending its citizens into space.

long-period variables a group of variable stars that are principally MIRA STARS but sometimes the red SEMIREGULAR STARS, type SRa, are included in the group. The longest periods (up to 5 years) are found in the OH/IR STARS, normally observable only at infrared wavelengths.

look-back time the time elapsed since a certain redshift.

loop prominence see PROMINENCES.

Lorentz–FitzGerald contraction the tiny contraction of a moving body in the direction of motion, put forward by H.A. Lorentz (1895) and independently by G.F. FitzGerald (1893) as an explanation for the result of the Michelson–Morley experiment (see ETHER). The contraction was later shown to be an effect of the special theory of RELATIVITY (1905).

Lorentz transformation a set of equations used in the special theory of RELATIVITY to transform the coordinates of an event (x, y, z, t) measured in one inertial frame of reference to the coordinates of the same event (x', y', z', t') measured in another frame moving relative to the first at constant velocity v:

$$x = (x' + vt')/\beta$$
$$y = y'$$
$$z = z'$$
$$t = (t' + x'v/c^2)/\beta$$

β is the factor $\sqrt{(1 - v^2/c^2)}$ and c is the speed of light. When v is very much less than c, these equations reduce to those used in classical mechanics.

Lovell Telescope see JODRELL BANK.

low Earth orbit (LEO) an orbit around the Earth of a satellite, etc., at an altitude of less than 5500 km.

Lowell Observatory a privately owned observatory at Flagstaff, Arizona, at an altitude of 2210 meters, set up by the US astronomer Percival Lowell in 1895. For many years it was the site of the huge *Clark Telescope*, a 24-inch (60.96-cm) refractor that was the largest of its generation. The US astronomer Clyde W. Tombaugh discovered the planet Pluto in 1930 while working at the Lowell Observatory. Currently the observatory's researchers work at Anderson Mesa, south of Flagstaff. But the Lowell Observatory is planned to be home to a 4-meter-class reflector, the *Discovery Channel Telescope*, which astronomers hope will be operational by about 2008.

lower culmination see CULMINATION.

low-mass stars see STELLAR MASS.

low-mass X-ray binary (LMXB) see X-RAY BINARY.

LSB galaxies *short for* low surface brightness galaxies. Galaxies with a very low central SURFACE BRIGHTNESS that may be very common and contain much of the mass in the Universe. They are difficult to detect against the brightness of the night sky and are thus missing from most galaxy catalogs. They are thought to be unevolved systems, with central regions resembling a DWARF GALAXY. Most of the mass is contained in a large gaseous disk that is observable only at radio wavelengths or with image-enhanced exposures. The galaxies are thus commonly referred to as *icebergs*. See MALIN 1.

LSR *abbrev. for* local standard of rest.

LST *abbrev. for* local sidereal time.

LTE *abbrev. for* local thermodynamic equilibrium. See THERMODYNAMIC EQUILIBRIUM.

Lucy an informal name for the white dwarf star BPM 37093.

luminosity symbol: L. The intrinsic or absolute brightness of a star or other celestial body, equal to the total energy radiated per second from the body, i.e. the total outflow of radiant flux. The luminosity of a body may be calculated over all wavelengths – the *bolometric luminosity* – or at particular wavebands. Bolometric luminosity is related to the body's surface area and EFFECTIVE TEMPERATURE, T_{eff}, by a form of Stefan's law:

$$L = 4\pi R^2 \sigma T_{eff}^4$$

where σ is Stefan's constant and R is the radius. Thus two stars with similar T_{eff} (i.e. of the same SPECTRAL TYPE) but greatly different luminosities must differ in size: they belong to different luminosity classes within that spectral type, as determined from their spectra. In the luminosity class of main-sequence stars, luminosity decreases as temperature decreases; the luminosity of GIANT stars however increases with decreasing temperature: RED GIANTS are much brighter than yellow giants; the luminosity of SUPERGIANTS drops and then rises with decreasing temperature. The luminosity of stars is in theory dependent on mass if their chemical composition is similar. It has been found that with the notable exception of highly evolved stars the MASS-LUMINOSITY RELATION is obeyed approximately.

The luminosity of a star or other body can be expressed as a multiple or fraction of the Sun's luminosity, $L_\odot$, which is equal to 3.83×10^{26} watts. The ratio $L/L_\odot$ is given by

$$2.5 \log_{10}(L/L_\odot) = M_\odot - M$$

where $M_\odot$ and M are the absolute bolometric MAGNITUDES of Sun and star; $M_\odot$ is equal to 4.76. There is a very great range in stellar luminosity from about a million times to less than one ten thousandth that of the Sun's luminosity.

luminosity classes see SPECTRAL TYPES.

luminosity distance the distance to an object enabling an intrinsic luminosity to be derived from an observed flux by the inverse square law. At large redshifts a relativistic correction must be included.

luminosity function the relative numbers of objects of different luminosities in a standard volume of space (usually a cubic parsec or cubic megaparsec). The luminosity may be in the optical band, the radio band, or at any other defined waveband. Observationally the luminosity function is determined as a histogram; theoreticians fit this with an algebraic expression.

In optical astronomy the luminosity function is given the symbol $\Phi(M)$ and is the number of stars per cubic parsec or the number of galaxies per cubic megaparsec with absolute magnitudes $M \pm ½$. The luminosity function for stars within 10 parsecs of the Sun shows a peak at an absolute magnitude of about +15: there is thus a predominance of intrinsically faint stars in the solar neighborhood. The luminosity function for any given magnitude interval is not the same everywhere in the Galaxy: for instance, the luminosity function of a GLOBULAR CLUSTER is different from that of an OPEN CLUSTER. Stars of all SPECTRAL TYPES contribute to the value $\Phi(M)$. The specific luminosity function $\Phi(M,S)$ considers one spectral type at a time, each showing a peak distribution at a different mean magnitude.

The luminosity function of galaxies (or quasars) is usually expressed as the number of galaxies in a given luminosity interval per cubic megaparsec and has a characteristic shape that is almost flat at faint magnitudes and falls off sharply at the bright end. The behavior of the bright and faint end of the luminosity function is divided by the 'typical' galaxy with an absolute magnitude of around −21.5, known as the L^* *galaxy*, at the 'knee' of the luminosity function.

The evolution of the quasar luminosity function is usually expressed as one of two forms of behavior: either the luminosity of all quasars is assumed to increase uniformly with REDSHIFT, or the number of quasars increases with redshift. In practice, present quasar luminosity functions fit a combination of the two models. See also LUMINOSITY–VOLUME TEST.

luminosity–volume test (**V/V_m test**) a method of testing for evolutionary effects in a sample of extragalactic sources of known REDSHIFT. All sources should be known over a particular region of the sky down to a certain FLUX DENSITY level. The volume, V, within the redshift of each object, together with the volume V_m within the maximum redshift out to which that object could have been and yet still remain in the sample, are computed from a cosmological model. If no evolution is present and the correct cosmological model is employed, then V ought to be uniformly distributed between 0 and V_m. The mean of V/V_m is then ½. If the mean differs significantly from ½ for all reasonable cosmological models, then evolution must be occurring; this is the case for QUASARS. See also LUMINOSITY FUNCTION.

luminous blue variables (**LBVs**) a class of very massive luminous blue stars known for sporadic mass ejections (eruptions); subclasses include P CYGNI STARS and HUBBLE–SANDAGE VARIABLES. They are generally found near the upper luminosity

Luna Probes

Spacecraft	*Launch date*	*Comments*
Lunik 1	1959, Jan. 2	Missed moon by 6000 km
Lunik 2	1959, Sept. 12	Struck moon in Palus Putredinis
Lunik 3	1959, Oct. 4	First farside photographs
Luna 4	1963, Apr. 2	Missed moon by 8500 km
Luna 5	1965, May 9	Struck moon
Luna 6	1965, June 8	Missed moon by 160 000 km
Luna 7	1965, Oct. 4	Struck moon
Luna 8	1965, Dec. 3	Struck moon
Luna 9	1966, Jan. 31	Soft landed in Oc. Procellarum
Luna 10	1966, Mar. 31	Performed experiments in lunar orbit
Luna 11	1966, Aug. 24	Performed experiments in lunar orbit
Luna 12	1966, Oct. 22	Returned photographs from lunar orbit
Luna 13	1966, Dec. 21	Soft landed in Oc. Procellarum
Luna 14	1968, Apr. 7	Performed experiments in lunar orbit
Luna 15	1969, July 13	Struck moon in Mare Crisium
Luna 16	1970, Sept. 12	Returned 101 g soil from Mare Fecunditatis
Luna 17	1970, Nov. 17	Landed Lunokhod 1 in Mare Imbrium
Luna 18	1971, Sept. 2	Struck moon
Luna 19	1971, Sept. 28	Performed experiments in lunar orbit
Luna 20	1972, Feb. 14	Returned 30 g soil, Crisium highlands
Luna 21	1973, Jan. 8	Landed Lunokhod 2 in Mare Serenitatis
Luna 22	1974, May 29	Performed experiments in lunar orbit
Luna 23	1974, Oct. 28	Soft-landed but drill failure
Luna 24	1976, Aug. 15	Returned 170 g soil from Mare Crisium

limit in the observed HERTZSPRUNG–RUSSELL DIAGRAM, and most are thought to have evolved from stars with initial masses exceeding 40 solar masses. The mass ejections are most likely due to instabilities in their stellar envelopes caused by RADIATION PRESSURE. LBVs show different types of variations occurring on a wide range of timescales. The largest variations are associated with sudden brightenings by more than 3 magnitudes lasting for several hundred to several thousand years. The smallest variations (<0.5 mag) last from several months to several years. Examples of LBVs are ETA CARINAE, AG Carinae, P CYGNI, and S DORADUS.

Luna probes (**Lunik probes**) a series of Soviet lunar probes (see table) that included the first craft to reach the vicinity of the Moon (1), the first to photograph the farside (3), the first crash lander (2), soft lander (9), orbiter (10), robotic sample-return mission (16), and robotic roving vehicle (17). See also LUNAR ORBITER PROBES; LUNOKHOD; RANGER; SURVEYOR; ZOND PROBES.

lunar calendar see LUNAR YEAR; CALENDAR.

lunar cycle see METONIC CYCLE.

lunar day the rotation period (27.322 Earth days) of the Moon, equal in length to the SIDEREAL MONTH. The Moon is thus in SYNCHRONOUS ROTATION with the Earth. See also LIBRATION.

lunar eclipse see ECLIPSE.

lunar module (**LM**) see APOLLO.

lunar month see SYNODIC MONTH.

Lunar Orbiter probes a series of five US space probes used for photographic reconnaissance of the Apollo landing sites (Lunar Orbiters 1, 2, and 3) and global mapping (4 and 5) of the Moon from equatorial and polar orbits respectively. The probes were launched between Aug. 1966 and Aug. 1967. Each spacecraft was equipped with medium- and high-resolution cameras, the films from which were scanned in strips for transmission back to Earth. Satellite tracking resulted in the discovery of MASCONS. The spacecraft were crashed onto the Moon on mission completion. See also LUNA PROBES; RANGER; SURVEYOR; ZOND PROBES.

lunar parallax see DIURNAL PARALLAX.

Lunar Prospector a lunar orbiter launched Jan. 6 1998 by NASA as part of its Discovery program. Its primary mission was to conduct a thorough investigation of the Moon from a low polar orbit. The investigation included mapping the composition of the Moon's surface and pinpointing lunar resources, making measurements of magnetic and gravity fields, and detecting radon outgassing events in the hope of partly accounting for the Moon's tenuous atmosphere. Following a 105-hour cruise to the Moon, the probe went into a nearly circular orbit taking it once around the satellite every 118 minutes at an altitude of 100 km. The Lunar Prospector carried five instruments, but it had no onboard cameras, unlike CLEMENTINE, an earlier Moon-mapping mission which had concentrated on equatorial and middle latitudes. Instead, it sought to collect its data using a gamma-ray spectrometer and a neutron spectrometer, a magnetometer and electron reflectometer, and an alpha particle spectrometer. In a part of the mission known as the Doppler Gravity Experiment, investigators used Doppler tracking of S-band radio signals to characterize the spacecraft's orbit and map the Moon's gravity field and topographical crustal structure. The Lunar Prospector's neutron spectrometer returned data that seemed to support the existence of water ice locked up in permanently shadowed polar craters, a situation suggested by analysis of Clementine's results. In December 1998, project scientists lowered the Lunar Prospector's orbit to 40 km and later to 30 km. On July 31 1999, the probe was guided into a polar crater and deliberately crashed in the hope of throwing up water in the impact plume, but none was observed.

lunar rocks see MOON ROCKS.

Lunar Roving Vehicle (**Lunar Rover**) the battery-driven car used to extend the sampling capabilities of APOLLOS 15, 16, and 17. Transported to the Moon in a compact form, the 213-kg Rover was equipped with a remote-controlled television camera and high-gain antenna for direct radio communication with Earth. It was left behind on the Moon after use. See also LUNOKHOD.

lunar year a year of 12 SYNODIC MONTHS, each of 29.5306 days, i.e. a year of 354.3672 days. A *lunar calendar* is based solely on the Moon's motion; it has a year of 354 days with a LEAP YEAR of 355 days and is composed of 12 months of 29 or 30 days. A *lunisolar calendar* is a lunar calendar that is brought into step with the solar or seasonal calendar by the intercalation (addition) of a 13th *leap month.*

lunation see SYNODIC MONTH.

Lunik probes see LUNA PROBES.

lunisolar calendar see LUNAR YEAR.

lunisolar precession see PRECESSION.

Lunokhod an eight-wheeled Soviet robotic lunar roving vehicle, soft-landed on the Moon by LUNAS 17 and 21. Lunokhod 1 was equipped with a laser reflector for lunar-ranging experiments; it was active in Mare Imbrium for 10 months during which time it completed a 10-km traverse, performing photographic tasks, magnetic field measurements, and chemical (X-ray) and cosmic-ray analyses. Lunokhod 2 traveled 37 km in four months in the vicinity of Le Monnier crater on the borders of Mare Serenitatis. See also LUNAR ROVING VEHICLE.

Lupus (**Wolf**) a constellation in the southern hemisphere near Centaurus, lying partly in the Milky Way, with several stars of 2nd magnitude. There are many naked-eye double stars and several globular and open star clusters. Abbrev.: Lup; genitive form: Lupi; approx. position: RA 15.3h, dec −45°; area: 334 sq deg.

l.y. *abbrev. for* light-year.

Lyman-alpha clouds see QUASAR.

Lyman-alpha forest see QUASAR.

Lyman-alpha line see LYMAN SERIES.

Lyman break galaxies see LYMAN LIMIT.

Lyman limit the observed cutoff in the light from a cosmologically distant object, observed shortward of rest-wavelength 912A, and caused by photoelectric absorption in intervening hydrogen. The system responsible for the absorption is known as a *Lyman limit system*. The observed sharp drop in the rest-wavelength spectrum at 912A permits the discovery of high-redshift *Lyman break galaxies*, where this region of the spectrum is redshifted into the optical waveband.

Lyman series a series of spectral lines of atomic hydrogen with wavelengths in the far ultraviolet and extreme ultraviolet regions of the spectrum (see HYDROGEN SPECTRUM). The *Lyman alpha* (Ly α) *line* occurs at 121.6 nm and the *Lyman limit* at 91.2 nm. Ly α emission and absorption lines occur, for example, in the spectra of QUASARS.

Lynds catalog a catalog of DARK NEBULAE compiled by Lynds in 1962 using the PALOMAR SKY SURVEY plates. Many of these clouds are now known to be the sites of low-mass STAR FORMATION. Clouds are designated by their Lynds number, an example being the L1641 complex (which includes the Orion molecular clouds).

Lynx a constellation in the northern hemisphere between Ursa Major and Gemini, the brightest stars being one (Alpha [α] Lyncis) of 3rd magnitude and several of 4th magnitude. The area contains many faint double stars. The faint globular cluster NGC 2419 is estimated to be more than 64 000 parsecs distant, further from us than the Magellanic Clouds and therefore beyond the confines of the Milky Way. As a result it has been nicknamed 'the Intergalactic Tramp'. Abbrev.: Lyn; genitive form: Lyncis; approx. position: RA 8h, dec +47°; area: 545 sq deg.

Lyot filter (**Lyot-Öhman filter**) see BIREFRINGENT FILTER.

Lyra (**Lyre**) a constellation in the northern hemisphere east of Cygnus, lying partly in the Milky Way, the brightest star being the blue zero-magnitude VEGA. It contains the prototype of the RR LYRAE STARS, the ECLIPSING BINARY Beta (β) Lyrae (see W SERPENTIS STAR), and the naked-eye pair Epsilon (ε) Lyrae, both of 4th magnitude and both double. It also contains the planetary RING NEBULA and a small globular cluster M56 (NGC 6779). Abbrev.: Lyr; genitive form: Lyrae; approx. position: RA 18.5h, dec +40°; area: 286 sq deg.

Lyrids (**April Lyrids**) a minor METEOR SHOWER, radiant: RA 272°, dec +32°, that maximizes on April 21. In the past it was much more active, the last great Lyrid shower occurring in 1803. Observations of Lyrids have been traced back 2500 years, Chinese observers describing a remarkable display in 15 BC. The associated METEOROID STREAM has the same orbit as comet Thatcher (1861 I). See also JUNE LYRIDS.

Lysithea a small satellite of Jupiter, discovered in 1938 by Seth Nicholson. See JUPITER'S SATELLITES; Table 2, Appendix.

Mm

$M_{\odot}$ *symbol for* solar mass.

M prefix used to designate a galaxy, star cluster, or nebula, as listed in the MESSIER CATALOG.

M87 see VIRGO A; VIRGO CLUSTER.

Maat Mons see APHRODITE TERRA.

McDonald Observatory an observatory of the University of Texas on Mount Locke, Texas, at an altitude of 2081 meters. It has a 2.7-meter and a 2.1-meter reflecting telescope, acquired in 1969 and 1939 respectively. When commissioned, the 2.1-meter *Otto Struve Telescope* was the second largest in the world; it has been modernized and equipped for infrared work. In 1996, the HOBBY–EBERLY TELESCOPE was installed.

MACHO *abbrev. for* massive astrophysical compact halo object. See GALAXY.

MACHO project a collaboration between universities in Australia and the USA to test the hypothesis that a major fraction of the dark matter in the halo of our Galaxy is made up of MACHOS, by searching for gravitational microlensing events toward the LMC and the GALACTIC BULGE. See GRAVITATIONAL LENS.

McMath–Pierce Solar Telescope see KITT PEAK NATIONAL OBSERVATORY; SOLAR TELESCOPE.

macrolensing see GRAVITATIONAL LENS.

macula (plural: **maculae**) a dark patch on the surface of a planet or satellite. The word is used in the approved name of such a feature.

Magellan NASA's planetary probe to VENUS that was launched from the space shuttle Atlantis May 4 1989 and reached the planet Aug. 10 1989. From three 8-month cycles of radar mapping (Sept. 1990–Sept. 1992), it produced a detailed radar map of almost 99% of the surface of Venus, revealing details as small as 100 meters across. It also provided a gravity map showing density variations in the surface features, and obtained an immense amount of data.

Magellan's mapping orbit carried it over the N pole and down the length of the planet almost to the S pole; it was close enough, during about 37 minutes of each orbit, for a 20–25-km swathe to be highlighted by the radar beam. In the remainder of the elliptical orbit Magellan transmitted data to Earth and fixed its position, before it resumed mapping over a new swathe of the slowly rotating planet. A topographical map was built up by radar altimetry, using signals from a small antenna pointing straight down. The larger antenna, pointing off to one side of the spacecraft, developed a detailed two-dimensional picture from the signals reflected off each object encountered; it also detected thermal emissions.

Impact craters, canyons, and other features were revealed on the planet's surface. Lava flows, fault zones, and volcanoes indicate volcanic activity and occur over about 85% of the surface of Venus, but no evidence was found for the type of plate tectonics found on Earth. There are relatively few impact craters, suggesting that Venus' surface is 'geologically' young. Craters are distributed randomly over the Venusian landscape, with roughly two-thirds showing no modification by volcanic activity. However, surface features include very long lava channels, vast lava plains, fields of small lava domes, shield volcanoes, and large 'pancake' domes that may have been formed from a type of lava produced by large-scale evolution of crustal rocks. Interpretation of these results in terms of past 'geological' activity is still under debate.

Gravity mapping of the surface commenced in Magellan's elliptical orbit. A successful aerobraking maneuver brought the craft into a low-altitude near-circular orbit in Aug. 1993, from which a detailed pole-to-pole gravity survey could be made. The Magellan mission ended Oct 11 1994 when the craft was sent plunging into Venus' dense atmosphere, sending back valuable data on its composition as it hurtled to its destruction.

Magellanic Clouds two comparatively small irregular GALAXIES that are close neighbors of our own Galaxy. Both are naked-eye objects but, being close to the south celestial pole, they are visible only from the southern hemisphere. They were first recorded in 1519 by Ferdinand Magellan. The *Large Magellanic Cloud* (*LMC*) has a diameter of about 10 000 parsecs; it lies in the constellation Dorado at a distance of about 50 000 parsecs. The *Small Magellanic Cloud* (*SMC*) has a diameter of about 6000 parsecs; it lies in the constellation Toucan and is about 60 000 parsecs away.

Both the LMC and SMC are rich in POPULATION I objects and contain a much greater proportion of gas than our own Galaxy. They are enveloped in a common cloud of cool neutral hydrogen, which extends into a narrow streamer. This *Magellanic Stream* stretches over 110° of the sky, extending toward the Galaxy. The Stream contains almost 10^9 solar masses of gas, probably ripped out of one or both Magellanic Clouds when they passed near the Galaxy about 200 million years ago and now strewn along the orbit of the Clouds. If the Galaxy has a massive DARK HALO, the Magellanic Clouds are gravitationally bound as satellites of the Galaxy and they have probably made several close approaches; otherwise, they have been involved in just one encounter, and the Magellanic Stream marks a hyperbolic ORBIT.

Magellanic Stream see MAGELLANIC CLOUDS.

Magellan Telescope see LAS CAMPANAS OBSERVATORY.

magnetars highly magnetized NEUTRON STARS, thought to be responsible for soft gamma repeaters (SGRs) and anomalous X-ray PULSARS (AXPs). A surface magnetic field of up to 10^{11} tesla (several hundred times that of a radio pulsar) rapidly slows the star's rotation, causing starquakes that deposit enough energy into the surrounding gases to generate bursts of soft gamma radiation. The field also heats the rotating surface sufficiently for it to emit X-rays, but the rotation is usually too slow for the neutron star to act as a radio pulsar. A large fraction of all neutron stars may be magnetars.

magnetic cataclysmic variables a class of CATACLYSMIC VARIABLES in which the large magnetic field of the WHITE DWARF (of order 10^3 tesla) affects the rotation of, and the accretion of material onto, the white dwarf. Two types can be distinguished: in *polar systems* (also known as *AM Herculis stars*) the white dwarf is in synchronism with the orbital period (i.e. the white dwarf's spin period is the same as the orbital period); in *intermediate polar systems* (also known as *DQ Herculis stars*) the spin period of the white dwarf is typically 10 times shorter than the orbital period. In both types, the accretion flow is channeled along the magnetic field lines directly onto the polar cap of the white dwarf. Accretion disks are generally absent in the case of polars, but may be present in the case of intermediate polars. See also MASS TRANSFER.

magnetic field the region surrounding a magnet, a conductor carrying an electric current, a stream of charged particles, etc., in which such a body or system exerts a detectable force. This force will be experienced by another magnetic substance or by a moving charged particle, such as an electron. The MAGNETIC FLUX DENSITY is a measure of the strength of the field, usually quoted in teslas or sometimes in gauss. See also GALACTIC MAGNETIC FIELD; GEOMAGNETISM; INTERPLANETARY MEDIUM; MAGNETIC STARS; SUNSPOT CYCLE.

magnetic flux density (**magnetic induction**) symbol: ***B***. A vector quantity that is a measure of the strength of a magnetic field in a particular direction at a particular point. It may be given in terms of the force, *F*, on a charge, *q*, moving in the magnetic field:

$$\boldsymbol{B} = F/(qv \sin\theta)$$

where *v* is the velocity of the charge, which is moving at an angle θ to the direction of the field. Magnetic flux density is usually measured in teslas. The *magnetic flux*, symbol: Φ, is the surface integral of ***B***, i.e.

$$\Phi = \int \boldsymbol{B}.\mathrm{d}A = \int \boldsymbol{B} \cos\alpha \, \mathrm{d}A$$

where α is the angle between ***B*** and a line perpendicular to the surface. The magnetic flux density is thus the magnetic flux passing perpendicularly through unit area. Magnetic flux is measured in webers.

magnetic induction see MAGNETIC FLUX DENSITY.

magnetic reconnection see MAGNETOSPHERE.

magnetic stars stars that have detectable and often very large magnetic fields, up to a few tesla. Magnetic stars are found in spectral classes B to F, but most are peculiar A stars (AP STARS). Many of these stars show either periodic or irregular variations of the field together with a reversal of the polarity; others show irregular field variations but constant polarity. Magnetic variability is usually accompanied by very small changes in brightness. Magnetic stars are studied by measurements of the Zeeman splitting (see ZEEMAN EFFECT) of spectral lines caused by a magnetic field; these give the average magnetic field over the entire disk. Periodic variations in the magnetic field could result from the magnetic axis of the star being tilted with respect to the rotational axis so that areas of different magnetic field strength are presented to the observer as the star rotates: this is the *oblique rotator theory*. Evidence for chromospheric activity and starspots on RED DWARF stars and RS CANUM VENATICORUM binaries indicates that they have weaker magnetic fields, similar to the Sun's. A few WHITE DWARFS have fields up to 10^5 tesla while some NEUTRON STARS detected as pulsars have fields of up to 10^9 tesla. See also MAGNETIC CATACLYSMIC VARIABLES; SPECTRUM VARIABLES.

magnetic storms see GEOMAGNETIC STORMS.

magnetobremsstrahlung see SYNCHROTRON EMISSION.

magnetograph an instrument used to map the distribution, strength, and polarity (direction) of magnetic fields over the Sun's disk. It is usually an automatic scanning system employing instruments to detect and measure the Zeeman splitting of a selected spectral line (see ZEEMAN EFFECT). The resulting diagram is called a *magnetogram*.

magnetohydrodynamics (MHD) the study of the behavior of electrically conducting fluids, i.e. a PLASMA or some other collection of charged particles, in a magnetic field. The collective motion of the particles gives rise to an electric field that interacts with the magnetic field and causes the plasma motion to alter. This coupling between hydrodynamic forces and magnetic forces means that the magnetic field is effectively 'frozen into' the plasma; the field lines flow with the plasma, and can be stretched, squeezed, or looped. One consequence is that the frozen-in field lines of two plasmas prevent them from mixing. MHD has contributed to the understanding of the SOLAR WIND and its interaction with planetary MAGNETOSPHERES, of solar FLARES and PROMINENCES, the SUNSPOT CYCLE, the formation and heating of the solar CORONA, star formation, and many other processes. See also ALFVÉN WAVES.

magnetometer any of a variety of instruments used to measure the strength and direction of a magnetic field.

magnetopause see MAGNETOSPHERE.

magnetosheath see MAGNETOSPHERE.

magnetosphere a region of space surrounding a planet within which charged particles are controlled by the magnetic field of the planet rather than by the Sun's magnetic field, which is carried by the solar wind (see INTERPLANETARY MEDIUM). The solar wind is the source of most of the charged particles, which form a tenuous gas known as a PLASMA. The region of a planet's magnetosphere is delimited by a boundary called the *magnetopause* and includes any radiation belts of the planet, such as the VAN ALLEN BELTS of the Earth. The Earth's

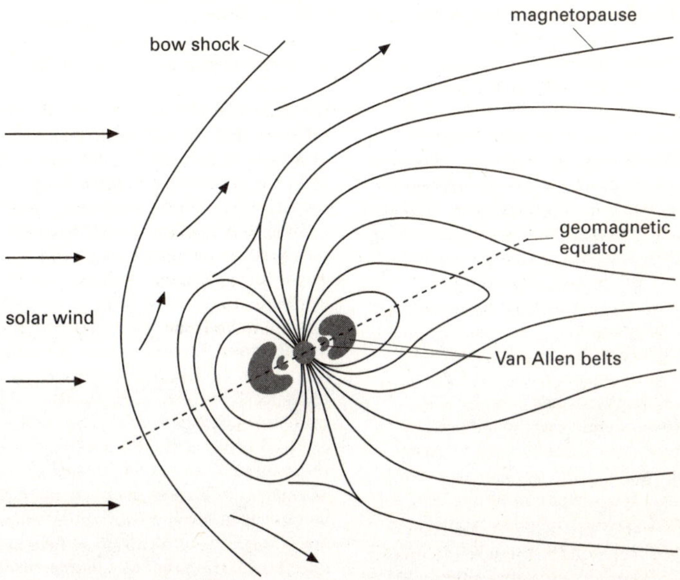

Earth's magnetosphere and magnetic field lines, shaped by the solar wind

magnetosphere extends to 60 000 km on the sunward side of the planet but is drawn out by the solar wind into an elongated extension called a *magnetotail* stretching many times this distance on the side away from the Sun (see illustration). *Magnetic reconnection* of the magnetic field lines of the Sun and Earth occurs across the sunward surface of the magnetopause (at points where two lines are in opposing directions); reconnection allows energy and particles to be transferred to the magnetosphere from the solar wind. Above the magnetopause is a layer of turbulent magnetic field, the *magnetosheath*, enclosed by a shock wave where the smooth flow of solar-wind particles past the planet is first interrupted. Mercury, Jupiter, Saturn, Uranus, and Neptune are also known to possess magnetospheres. See also GEOSPACE.

magnetotail see MAGNETOSPHERE.

magnifying power (**magnification**) the angle subtended by the image of an object seen through a telescope, divided by the angle subtended by the same object seen without telescopic aid. Where the object is too small or too distant to be resolved, the magnifying power may be calculated from the ratio of the focal lengths of the OBJECTIVE (or PRIMARY MIRROR) and EYEPIECE, or from the APERTURE divided by the diameter of the EXIT PUPIL.

magnitude a measure of the brightness of stars and other celestial objects. The brighter the object the lower its assigned magnitude. Expressions of magnitude are used primarily in the visible, near-infrared, and near-ultraviolet regions of the spectrum.

The *apparent magnitude*, symbol: *m*, is a measure of the brightness of a star, etc., as observed from Earth. Its value depends on the star's LUMINOSITY (i.e. its intrinsic brightness), its distance, and the amount of light absorption by interstellar matter between the star and Earth. In ancient times the visible stars were ranked in six classes of apparent magnitude: the brightest stars were of first magnitude and those just visible to the naked eye were of sixth magnitude. This system became inadequate as fainter stars were discovered with the telescope and instruments became available for measuring apparent brightness. In the 1850s it was proposed that the physiological response of the eye to a physical stimulus was proportional to the logarithm of that stimulus (Weber-Fechner law). A difference in apparent magnitude of two stars is thus proportional to the difference in the logarithms of their brightness, i.e. to the logarithm of the ratio of their brightness.

In order to make the magnitude scale precise the English astronomer N.R. Pogson proposed, in 1856, that a difference of five magnitudes should correspond exactly to a brightness ratio of 100 to 1. (W. Herschel had shown this to be approximately true.) Hence two stars that differ by one magnitude have a brightness ratio of $100^{1/5}$:1, i.e. a ratio – known as the *Pogson ratio* – of 2.512. A star two magnitudes less than another is $(2.512)^2$, i.e. 6.3 times, brighter, and so on. In general the apparent magnitudes m_1 and m_2 of two stars with apparent brightness I_1 and I_2 are related by:

$$m_1 - m_2 = 2.5 \log_{10}(I_2/I_1)$$

The Pogson scale, based on the Pogson ratio, is now the universally adopted scale of magnitude (see table). The zero of the scale was established by assigning magnitudes to a group of standard stars near the north celestial pole, known as the *North Polar Sequence*, or more recently by photoelectric measurements. The class of magnitude-one stars was found to contain too great a range of brightness and zero and negative magnitudes were consequently introduced: the higher the negative number, the greater the brightness. The scale also had to be extended in the positive direction as fainter objects were discovered. Values can be recorded in tenths, hundredths, even thousandths of a magnitude.

Originally apparent magnitude was measured by eye – *visual magnitude*, m_{vis} – usually in conjunction with an instrument by which brightnesses could be compared. It is now measured much more accurately by photometric techniques but previous to that photographic methods were used. *Photographic magnitudes*, m_{pg}, are determined from the optical density of images on ordinary film, i.e. film that has a maximum response to blue light. *Photovisual magnitudes*, m_{pv}, are measured using film that has been sensitized to light – yellowish green in color – to which the human eye is most sensitive. In the early *International Color System* these two magnitudes were measured with films having a maximum response to a wavelength of 425 nanometers (m_{pg}) and 570 nm (m_{pv}), the magnitudes being equal for A0 stars.

A suitable combination of PHOTOMETER and filter can select light or other radiation of a desired wavelength band and measure its intensity. These *photoelectric magnitudes* can be measured over either narrow or broad bands. The *UBV system* of stellar magnitudes is based on photoelectric PHOTOMETRY and has been widely adopted as the successor of the International System. The photoelectric magnitudes, denoted *U*, *B*, and *V* are measured at three broad bands: *U* (ultraviolet radiation) centered on a wavelength of 365 nm, *B* (blue) centered on 440 nm, and *V* (visual, i.e. yellowish green) centered on 550 nm. These magnitudes can also be written m_U, m_B, and m_V. The zero point of the UBV system is defined in terms of standard stars having a carefully studied and agreed magnitude. Another important photometric system, the UVBY SYSTEM, uses filters passing narrower wavelength bands than in the UVB system.

The UBV system has been extended by the use of magnitudes at red and infrared

Pogson Scale of Magnitudes

m_1–m_2	I_2/I_1	m_1–m_2	I_2/I_1
0.2	1.202	3.5	25.12
0.4	1.445	4.0	39.81
0.6	1.738	4.5	63.1
0.8	2.089	5.0	100
1.0	2.512	6.0	251
1.5	3.981	7.0	631
2.0	6.310	8.0	1585
2.5	10.0	9.0	3981
3.0	15.85	10.0	10000

wavelengths. The photometric designations are *R* (700 nm, i.e. 0.7 μm), *I* (0.9 μm), *J* (1.25 μm), *H* (1.6 μm), *K* (2.20 μm), *L* (3.40 μm), *M* (5.0 μm), *N* (10.2 μm), *Q* (21 μm). The designations *J*–*Q* relate to the infrared ATMOSPHERIC WINDOWS; two alternative values for *R* (640 nm) and *I* (800 nm) have recently gained acceptance.

Apparent magnitude is a measure of the radiation in a particular wavelength band, say of blue light, received from the celestial body. Apparent *bolometric magnitude*, m_{bol}, is a measure of the total radiation received from the body. The *bolometric correction* (*BC*) is the difference $m_V - m_{bol}$ between the apparent visual (*V*) and bolometric magnitudes; it is generally defined to be zero for stars with surface temperatures similar to the Sun. Other wavebands apart from *V* are sometimes used in calculating BC.

Apparent magnitude gives no indication of a body's LUMINOSITY: a very distant very luminous star may have a similar apparent magnitude as a closer but fainter star. Luminosity is defined in terms of *absolute magnitude*, M, which is the apparent magnitude of a body if it were at a standard distance of 10 parsecs. It can be shown that the two magnitudes of a body are related to distance *d* (in parsecs) or its ANNUAL PARALLAX, π (in arc seconds):

$$M = m + 5 - 5 \log d - A$$

$$M = m + 5 + 5 \log \pi - A$$

A is the INTERSTELLAR EXTINCTION. As with apparent magnitude there are values of absolute photoelectric magnitudes: M_U, M_B, M_V, etc.; of bolometric magnitude: M_{bol}; and of photographic magnitudes: M_{pg} and M_{pv}. Knowledge of a body's absolute bolometric magnitude enables its LUMINOSITY to be found. The flux density in JANSKY of a body can be determined from a value of absolute magnitude at one of the photometric designations J–Q.

magnitude at opposition a measure of the brightness of a planet or asteroid when at OPPOSITION; it corresponds, normally, to the maximum brightness attained by the object during the APPARITION, since it is then viewed at its fullest phase and is near its closest point to the Earth.

Maia see PLEIADES.

main-belt asteroid see ASTEROID BELT.

main lobe (**main beam**) see ANTENNA.

Main Ring see JUPITER'S RINGS.

main sequence the principal sequence of stars on the HERTZSPRUNG–RUSSELL DIAGRAM, running diagonally from upper left (high temperature, high luminosity) to lower right (low temperature, low luminosity) and containing about 90% of all known stars. A star spends most of its life on the main sequence. A newly formed star appears on the main sequence when it first achieves a stable state whereby its core temperature is sufficient for nuclear reactions to begin. It is then at age zero. The positions of the age-zero stars on the H-R diagram are specified by reference to the *zero-age main sequence* (*ZAMS*). As hydrogen is converted to helium, changes in chemical composition and stellar structure cause the star's position to shift slightly to the right from its zero-age position.

A star's position on the main sequence depends primarily on its mass, the more massive and thus more luminous stars occurring higher up the sequence. This gives a well-defined MASS-LUMINOSITY RELATIONSHIP for main-sequence stars. The star's lifetime there also depends on its mass, the more massive stars having much shorter lifetimes: the lifetime is approximately

$$10^{10}(M/M_{\odot})^{-3} \text{ years}$$

where *M* and $M_{\odot}$ are the stellar and solar mass. After the star has consumed most of the helium in its core (see STELLAR EVOLUTION) it evolves away from the main sequence: its radius and luminosity increase and it eventually becomes a GIANT.

main-sequence fitting a technique for measuring the distance modulus and hence distance for a star CLUSTER, especially an OPEN CLUSTER: the main-sequence portion of a graph of color index versus apparent magnitude for the cluster is superimposed on the main sequence of a HERTZSPRUNG–RUSSELL DIAGRAM, the color indices of the two curves being made to overlap. The difference between cluster magnitudes and the superimposed absolute magnitudes of the H-R diagram is approximately constant and equal to the distance modulus.

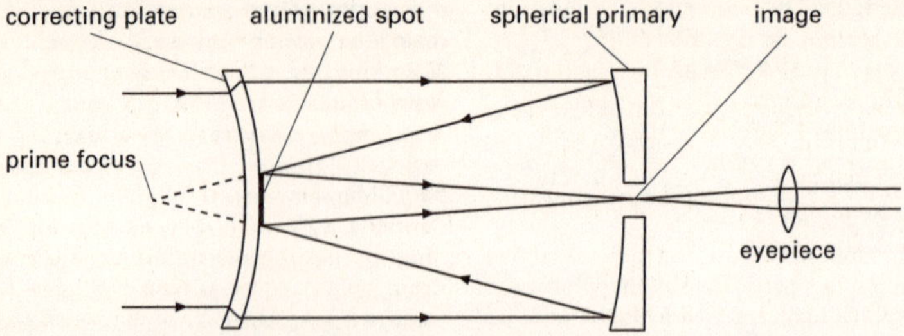

Maksutov telescope: ray path in Maksutov–Cassegrain telescope

main-sequence star a star lying on the MAIN SEQUENCE.

major axis see SEMIMAJOR AXIS.

major planets the planets Mercury, Venus, Earth, Mars, Jupiter, Saturn, Uranus, Neptune, and Pluto, which have diameters significantly larger than the 933 km diameter of Ceres, the largest ASTEROID (or minor planet). See Table 1, Appendix.

Maksutov telescope (**meniscus telescope**) a CATADIOPTRIC TELESCOPE named after its Soviet inventor, Dmitri Dmitriyevich Maksutov, who published its design in 1941. A Dutch telescope maker, Albert A. Bouwers of Amsterdam, arrived independently at the same design in the same year. It differs from the SCHMIDT TELESCOPE in that the CORRECTING PLATE is a deeply curved meniscus lens. Since the primary mirror is also spherical, all three optical surfaces are simple to make. Its commonest form (see illustration) is a Cassegrain adaptation in which the image is reflected by an aluminized spot on the meniscus lens back through a hole in the primary mirror. It performs well as a prime-focus camera. It can also be made in Newtonian and Gregorian configurations. Although the Maksutov telescope has exceptional performance and compactness, its thick correcting plate limits it to relatively small sizes both because of its weight and because of the very thick glass blanks needed to make larger diameters.

Malin 1 an extreme example of a LSB GALAXY at a distance of 330 Mpc. It has a very extended, extremely low surface brightness disk comprised of an enormous mass of neutral hydrogen, with a low-luminosity Seyfert nucleus at its core. It is interpreted as an unevolving disk galaxy with such a low mass density that the chemical composition and gas fraction change very slowly over the lifetime of the galaxy. It may be a prototype for damped LYMAN-ALPHA absorption systems seen in the spectra of quasars at high redshift.

Malmquist bias the bias inherent in any flux-limited sample due to the fact that only the very brightest systems will be detected at greater cosmological distances, and thus such sources will be over-represented in the sample. This can cause errors in DISTANCE DETERMINATION, such as the distance to the further STANDARD CANDLES being underestimated.

manganese stars see AP STARS.

mantle the zone within a planet or satellite, lying below the crust. See also EARTH.

mare (plural: **maria**) a large relatively smooth dark area on the surface of a planet or satellite. The word is used in the approved name of such a surface feature. (Latin: sea)

maria, lunar (**ring plains**) expanses of volcanic lavas of low ALBEDO (i.e. comparatively dark) that were erupted onto the lunar surface mainly between 3900 and 3000 million years ago. The maria are largely confined to the NEARSIDE of the Moon where the crust is thinnest. The youngest BASINS were flooded to produce the *circular maria* with their associated MASCONS. The *irregular maria* are shallower and fill the older less well-defined basins. The mare rocks are basalts. Chemical

Lunar Maria in Approximate Order of Size

Oceanus Procellarum	Ocean of Storms
Mare Imbrium	Sea of Rains
Mare Serenitatis	Sea of Serenity
Mare Fecunditatis	Sea of Fertility
Mare Tranquillitatis	Sea of Tranquillity
Mare Crisium	Sea of Crises
Mare Humorum	Sea of Moisture
Mare Nectaris	Sea of Nectar
Mare Frigoris	Sea of Cold
Mare Orientale	Eastern Sea
Mare Australe	Southern Sea
Mare Cognitum	Sea of Knowledge
Mare Nubium	Sea of Clouds
Mare Marginis	Border Sea
Mare Smythii	Smyth's Sea
Mare Spumans	Foaming Sea
Mare Undarum	Sea of Waves
Mare Humboldtianum	Humboldt's Sea
Mare Moscoviense	Sea of Moscow
Mare Ingenii	Sea of Ingenuity
Mare Anguis	Serpent's Sea
Mare Vaporum	Sea of Vapors
Sinus Medii	Central Bay
Sinus Aestuum	Bay of Heats
Sinus Roris	Bay of Dews
Sinus Amoris	Bay of Love
Sinus Iridum	Bay of Rainbows
Palus Putredinis	Marsh of Decay
Palus Somnii	Marsh of Sleep
Palus Epidemiarum	Marsh of Epidemics
Palus Nebularum	Marsh of Mists
Lacus Mortis	Lake of Death
Lacus Somniorum	Lake of Dreams
Lacus Veris	Lake of Spring
Lacus Autumni	Lake of Autumn

variations between the maria are revealed in REFLECTANCE SPECTRA and by color-difference photography. Age differences are apparent from their crater densities, which are invariably lower than in the older HIGHLANDS. Maria are mainly named after mental or meteorological states (see table); the terms LACUS, SINUS, and PALUS describe smaller lunar maria while OCEANUS describes a large feature. See also MOON ROCKS.

maria, Martian see MARS.

Mariner 2 a 202-kg US probe that made the first successful planetary flyby, 34 830 km from Venus, on Dec. 14 1962. Its flight confirmed the existence of the SOLAR WIND and measured Venus' temperature, but did not detect a Venusian magnetic field.

Mariner 4 a 261-kg US spacecraft that was the first successful probe to Mars. It passed the planet at a distance of 9844 km on July 14 1965, returning 22 photographs revealing an arid cratered surface.

Mariner 5 a 245-kg US spacecraft that passed Venus at a distance of 3990 km on Oct. 19 1967. It measured Venus' temperature and atmospheric profile, accurately determined its mass and diameter, but failed to detect any magnetic field.

Mariner 6, 7 two identical 413-kg US probes that passed Mars at distances of 3412 km and 3424 km on July 31 and Aug. 5, 1969, respectively. Mariner 6 photographed part of Mars' equatorial region while Mariner 7 examined the southern hemisphere and southern polar cap. A total of 201 photographs were returned, while other experiments measured surface temperatures, atmospheric pressure and composition, and Mars' diameter.

Mariner 9 a 1031-kg US probe that became the first artificial satellite of another planet when it entered a 12-hour orbit of Mars on Nov. 13 1971. This orbit, ranging in altitude from 1650 km to 17 100 km approximately, allowed Mariner's two television cameras to return 7329 photographs before contact was terminated on Oct. 27 1972. The entire Martian surface was mapped and close-up views were obtained of Mars' two small natural satellites, PHOBOS and DEIMOS. Other equipment included infrared and ultraviolet spectrometers, used for atmospheric studies, and an infrared radiometer to measure surface temperatures.

The photographic reconnaissance was jeopardized by a violent planet-wide dust storm that developed in late September 1971. With the exception of four hazy spots, later found to be the summits of the principal Martian volcanoes of the THARSIS RIDGE, all surface features were obscured by dust when Mariner 9 arrived. As the dust settled during the following weeks, photographs revealed for the first time the extent of Martian volcanism and the existence of canyons, such as the VALLES MARINERIS, and channels, which suggest that water once flowed on Mars. The changing appearance of the POLAR CAPS with the Martian seasons was also followed. See MARS; MARS, SURFACE FEATURES.

Mariner 10 a US spacecraft that executed the first dual-planet mission by making close approaches to Venus and, three times, to Mercury. Weighing 503 kg, it carried two television cameras that returned the first close-up views of Venus and Mercury. Other instruments included an infrared radiometer to measure Mercury's surface temperature; an ultraviolet spectrometer to detect atmospheric airglow and another to measure atmospheric absorption of solar ultraviolet radiation; and two magnetometers to monitor magnetic field variations throughout the flight.

During the Venus flyby at a distance of 5760 km on Feb. 5 1974, Mariner 10 returned 3500 photographs – those taken in ultraviolet radiation showing the planet's cloud cover and atmospheric circulation in unprecedented detail. Using the gravitational pull of Venus, the probe was placed on course for a Mercury flyby on Mar. 29 1974. After course corrections two more visits to Mercury took place on Sept. 21 1974 and Mar. 19 1975, each after two solar orbits by Mercury and one by Mariner 10. The three Mercury encounters, at minimum distances of 740 km, 48 000 km, and 330 km respectively, provided more than 10 000 photographs of Mercury and led to the discovery of the planet's magnetic field. See also MERCURY; VENUS.

Mariner probes a series of US planetary probes. Mariners 2 and 5 made close-up observations of Venus while MARINER 10 became the first two-planet probe, visiting Venus and Mercury. MARINERS 4, 6, 7, and 9 were successful Mars probes, the latter becoming the first man-made orbiter of another planet. Mariners 11 and 12 were renamed VOYAGERS 1 and 2. Mariners 1 (to Venus) and 8 (to Mars) suffered launch failure while Mariner 3 failed to achieve its intended trajectory to Mars.

Markab (α Peg) a white giant that is the second brightest star in the constellation Pegasus and, with Algenib, lies on the S side of the Great Square of Pegasus. m_v: 2.49; M_v: –0.1; spectral type: B9.5 III; distance: 33 pc.

Markarian galaxies a number of galaxies that were discovered by the Soviet astronomer B.E. Markarian in the 1970s to have a strong ultraviolet continuum. The ultraviolet sources are either concentrated in a bright nucleus or are distributed throughout a more diffuse object. The former group consists of SEYFERT GALAXIES and QUASARS; the latter group are galaxies where star formation has recently taken place.

Mars the fourth PLANET in the Solar System in outward succession from the Sun. It orbits the Sun every 686.98 days at a distance that varies between 1.38 and 1.67 AU. Its reddish 6795-km-diameter disk is most favorably placed for observation during oppositions that coincide with the time when it is near its PERIHELION (see MARS, OPPOSITIONS). Mars rotates in 24h 37m 22.67s. A single rotation is called a *sol*. The planet's axis is tilted by 25.19° to its orbital plane. The rotation rate and axial tilt help to make the Red Planet the most earthlike of all the other planets, even though it has only 28% of the Earth's surface area and less than 38% of its gravity. Mars has two small natural satellites: PHOBOS and DEIMOS. Orbital and physical characteristics are given in Table 1, backmatter.

Telescopes reveal an orange-red surface with indistinct darker markings, once thought to be seas and named *maria*. White polar caps expand and contract with the Martian seasons. When it became apparent that the maria also varied in intensity and shape with the seasons, it was suggested that they were areas of lichenlike vegetation that flourished when water became available from the poles during each Martian spring. CANALS, charted by some observers, were postulated as an artificial planet-wide water distribution network. Observations by MARINER spacecraft showed that the canals were a myth and revealed the maria as areas of darker bedrock on which the Martian winds deposit varying amounts of lighter-colored dust, so changing their appearance. North of the Martian equator, lowlands of volcanic origin predominate and impact craters are relatively few. In the southern hemisphere, heavily cratered highlands overlying a thick but weak crust form the chief terrain. HELLAS PLANITIA, a deep impact basin in the southern hemisphere, is the largest such feature so far known in the Solar System, while OLYMPUS MONS, in the northern hemisphere, is the Solar System's largest volcano. For details of Martian topography see MARS, POLAR CAPS; MARS, SURFACE FEATURES; MARS, VOLCANOES.

The Martian atmosphere has a surface pressure of about 7 millibars, or 0.007 times the average pressure at the Earth's surface, and extends to include an ionosphere at altitudes between 100 and 300 km. Daytime surface temperatures rarely climb above 0 °C (273 K) except during summer in the southern hemisphere, when they can rise to 20 °C (293 K). Most areas experience minimum temperatures as low as –140 °C (133 K) before sunrise each morning. NASA's MARS GLOBAL SURVEYOR, launched in 1996, confirmed that Mars' weather is driven by convection currents in the atmosphere that cause warm gases to rise from the summer hemisphere and descend upon the winter hemisphere.

Tests by the VIKING spacecraft, which landed in 1976, show an atmosphere comprising mainly carbon dioxide (95%), with nitrogen (2.7%), argon (1.6%), oxygen (0.15%), a variable trace of water vapor, and traces of carbon monoxide, krypton, and xenon. The water vapor sometimes freezes to form clouds of ice crystals, especially above high topographic features such as the volcanoes, or condenses as fog in low-lying areas, such as HELLAS PLANITIA and the VALLES MARINERIS. The rich variety of clouds systems – leewaves, cirrus, orographically produced clouds – are a major part of the planet's meteorology. More extensive surface obscurations occur during dust storms, which can engulf the entire planet. Such events happened in 1971 at the beginning of the Mariner 9 mission and in 1977 during the Viking mission. These global phenomena, which can occur both just before and just after perihelion when summer occurs in the southern hemisphere, will distribute material to altitudes of more than 40 km and last for several months. However, global storms do not seem to appear every Martian year.

Mars has no radiation belts and only a weak magnetic field, at most 0.2% as strong as the Earth's; this suggests that it lacks a molten nickel-iron core and may have no iron core at all. The surface rocks, however, appear to be rich in iron, resembling the minerals hematite and magnetite and lending the planet its red coloration. NASA's Mars Pathfinder mission of 1997 also discovered that Martian dust contains magnetic composite particles. See also VIKING PROBES.

Mars, oppositions OPPOSITIONS recur at an average interval of 2 years 50 days, although this varies by 30 days either way because of the ECCENTRICITY of Mars' orbit. Favorable oppositions for observation of surface features recur every 15–17 years when Mars is near PERIHELION and may approach within 56 million km of the Earth, attaining an apparent diameter of 25.7 arc seconds. Perihelion oppositions are, however, much less frequent than aphelion ones. The most favorable perihelion opposition of the 21st century occurred in August 2003, when Mars and Earth came within 55.8 million km of each other. This was estimated to be the closest proximity the two planets had achieved in 60 000 years. But even closer oppositions are due in 2287, 2650, 2729, 2808, and 2934, when the planetary distances will in each case be less than 55.7 million km. At APHELION oppositions Mars may be as much as 101 million km distant with an apparent diameter of 14 arc seconds.

Mars, polar caps two variable white areas at the Martian poles, visible to Earth-based observers but studied in detail by the MARINER and VIKING Orbiter spacecraft and more recently by the MARS GLOBAL

SURVEYOR and MARS ODYSSEY orbiters. Each cap grows under a haze of cloud during the winter in its hemisphere, reaching a latitude of 50° N or S at its greatest extent. During summer it retreats to leave a small irregular patch about 500 km across. This residual (permanent) cap probably consists almost entirely of water ice, while the variable cap appears to be a frost of frozen carbon dioxide, which is appears to be deposited out of the thin Martian atmosphere by dust storms in winter. At latitudes greater than 80°, the polar terrain exhibits a crater-free layered structure up to 6 km thick that possibly represents successive deposition of wind-borne dust. The covering of carbon dioxide is about 1 meter thick over the north pole but appears to be thicker over the south pole, where it is estimated to be up to 8 meters in depth. In summer the evaporation of carbon dioxide back into the atmosphere accompanies the retreat of the caps.

Mars, surface features impact CRATERS dominate Mars' mountainous southern hemisphere – and may be as old as 3500 million years – but are thinly scattered over the younger and mainly volcanic surface of most of the low-lying northern hemisphere. In addition there are white polar caps, volcanic features (see MARS, POLAR CAPS; MARS, VOLCANOES), and areas, particularly in equatorial regions, that show evidence of running water in the past. The existence of surface plates and ruts over an extensive area of the equatorial ELYSIUM PLANITIA has led some scientists to conclude that a frozen subterranean sea lies in this region.

Many of the Martian craters show the effects of erosion by dust, which is generally of a higher ALBEDO than uneroded surface rocks and forms bright deposits in low-lying terrain such as crater floors and the southern hemisphere impact basins of ARGYRE PLANITIA and HELLAS PLANITIA. In places the dust is swept into ridges or dunes by the wind. Bright or dark streaks occur in the lee of some craters where the prevailing wind has piled up the dust or has scoured the surface to reveal the underlying darker bedrock. Variations in dust deposition are responsible for albedo and outline changes of the darker markings, or maria, once attributed to life processes.

Southeast of the volcanoes of the THARSIS RIDGE lies the complex equatorial canyon system of VALLES MARINERIS, which measures 4500 km from east to west and 150 to 700 km from north to south. Individual canyons are up to 200 km wide and 7 km deep, dwarfing the maximum 28 km width and 2 km depth of Earth's Grand Canyon. They appear to result from faulting and collapse of the Martian surface – a process that may be continuing today. Other fault systems are found elsewhere, all of them apparently associated with areas of volcanic activity.

Smaller valleys, or channels, meander for up to 1000 km or more across equatorial areas of Mars. They appear to have been formed by running water derived, at least in part, from rain falling on the planet's surface. Some channels begin in areas of collapsed terrain as though the water they carried was originally frozen as a subsurface layer of permafrost that was subsequently thawed and released by volcanic heating. The enigma is that neither rain nor surface water can survive on Mars given present atmospheric constraints. Possibly the channels indicate that Mars has experienced spells of milder climatic conditions when the atmosphere was thicker than it is now, and the carbon dioxide could have trapped solar energy to warm the planet. Unfortunately, there is not enough carbon dioxide locked up in the polar caps today to support this view. In Mars' past, however, there may have been fluctuation in the Sun's output, variations in the planet's axial tilt, or periods of enhanced volcanic activity, during all of which polar and subsurface ice may have been released as liquid water. Further evidence for the existence of a permafrost layer comes from the shapes of the ejecta blankets surrounding some large craters.

Mars, volcanoes much of the northern hemisphere of Mars shows signs of volcanism with extensive lava plains sparsely pock-marked with impact craters: an indication of an age considerably less than the 3500 million years assigned to the heavily cratered southern hemisphere. This disparity may arise from the fact that the mean Martian surface lies at a lower level in the northern hemisphere than in the southern.

The two main areas of volcanic activity, both situated on bulges in the Martian crust, are the Tharsis region – with three huge volcanoes on the THARSIS RIDGE and the immense OLYMPUS MONS to the NW of the Ridge – and the ELYSIUM PLANITIA. The volcanoes are of the shield type, having long gently sloping flanks. Counts of the numbers of impact craters on the slopes suggest ages between 200 million and 800 million years for the Tharsis volcanoes, and about 1500 million years for those of Elysium Planitia. The extraordinary size of the volcanoes may be related to the absence of plate tectonics on Mars, so that the crust remains locked in relation to volcano-inducing 'hot spots' in the mantle below. See also MARS, SURFACE FEATURES.

Mars Climate Orbiter a NASA mission launched Dec. 1998 to produce information about the surface and climate of Mars. The mission was lost in Sept. 1999.

Mars Exploration Rovers two NASA robotic roving landers named *Spirit* and *Opportunity*, launched to Mars in summer 2003 from Cape Canaveral, Florida, by Delta 2 rockets. Spirit was launched on June 10, followed by Opportunity on July 7. The two landers made planetfall on Mars in Jan. 2004, using parachutes and giant airbags to cushion their landings. Spirit touched down in Gusev crater, just south of the Martian equator, on Jan. 3. Three weeks later, on Jan. 24, Opportunity landed in Meridiani Planum, an extensive plain just north of the equator but on the other side of the planet. Both rovers were equipped with a battery of cameras, spectrometers, microscopes and digging and sampling tools. Spirit's chief task was to explore Gusev, a large impact crater about 145 km wide, and investigate the possibility that it might have been a lake in Mars' remote past. Opportunity's landing site in Meridianum Planum was an area covered by an ancient layer of hematite, an oxide of iron that on Earth is usually found in watery environments with small amounts of the mineral goethite. Opportunity was to investigate this hematite layer in the hope of finding goethite and once again uncovering evidence that water once flowed on Mars. A software problem threatened to cut short Spirit's science-gathering program early on, but engineers found a way of working around the difficulty. Project scientists estimated that the rovers would function for no more than three months, but by the beginning of 2005 both were still transmitting back valuable scientific data, much of which seemed to confirm Mars' watery past.

Mars Express a mission organized by ESA and the Italian Space Agency to investigate the geology and subsurface structure of Mars and the composition and circulation of its atmosphere. Launched June 2 2003 from Baikonur Cosmodrome, Kazakhstan, on top of a Soyuz-Fregat rocket, the 12000-kg probe was the first all-European spacecraft to explore Mars. Built in record time and for a fraction of the cost of other comparable planetary missions, it consisted of an orbiter, the Mars Express craft itself, carrying seven instruments, including radar, for remote-sensing observations of the planet, and a lander, *Beagle 2*, which would be deployed by the orbiter and touch down on Mars to make on-site measurements of Martian rock and soil. After a six-month journey, Mars Express reached the vicinity of Mars and released Beagle 2 for descent to the planet's surface in Dec. 2003. Beagle 2 was scheduled to land on Mars on Dec. 25 and send a signal back to Earth to show that it was safely down, but the signal was never received and the lander was assumed lost. Meanwhile, Mars Express successfully entered orbit around Mars on the same day and began its scientific investigations. Still functioning in Feb. 2005, it had already sent back a wealth of scientific data. That month ESA scientists announced that Mars Express had detected a vast frozen sea beneath the surface of the planet in the region of the Martian equator.

Mars Global Surveyor (MGS) a NASA mission launched Nov 1996 to orbit Mars and send back scientific data on its surface features, atmosphere, and magnetic properties, all for the purposes of advancing scientific understanding of the Earth by comparing it with Mars and providing comprehensive information to aid future planetary missions. In the event, MGS proved one of NASA's most fruitful missions, and was a notable success at a time when other Martian missions failed. Following a polar orbit around the planet at an altitude of 450 km, MGS was able to cover the whole planet in a week. Its immediate mission, like that of the ill-fated MARS OBSERVER, was to map the planet and return data on its weather, geology and topography during the space of a Martian year (1.88 Earth years). It was still functioning and transmitting streams of images and other data at the start of 2005.

Mars Observer NASA's high-profile mission to Mars, the first visit since the Viking probes in 1976, that was launched in Sept. 1992 and reached the planet in Aug. 1993. Control was lost just before it was to be slowed by a rocket-firing maneuver to take it into Mars orbit, and communications could not be re-established. The Mars Observer was to have conducted a detailed survey of Mars – mapping the planet at high resolution and studying its climate, topography, and geology – over one Martian year or 687 Earth days. Failure of the mission affected future missions to Mars, especially Russia's Mars 94, which was to have used the Observer as a relay station. Other missions would have used the Observer data to select landing sites, etc. See MARS GLOBAL SURVEYOR.

Mars Odyssey a US probe, launched Apr. 7 2001, that was part of NASA's Mars Exploration Program, a long-term series of crewless investigations of Mars. It reached Mars in Oct. 2001 and commenced its primary mission to map the chemical makeup of the planet and scout out likely places where water or ice might be found by future probes searching for evidence of past life. Odyssey's primary mission ended on Aug. 24 2004 after well over 10 000 orbits, and it embarked upon an extended mission. During its first 34 months in orbit, Odyssey discovered ice just below the surface at the Martian poles and investigated the radiation environment in low Mars orbit, thereby aiding the assessment of radiation risk to future human spaceflight missions to the planet. In addition to its science activities, Odyssey served as a communications relay for the MARS EXPLORATION ROVERS Spirit and Opportunity. It would continue this role during its extended mission.

Mars 2001 Orbiter a NASA mission to Mars scheduled for launch in Mar. 2001 to map the mineralogy and morphology of the surface.

Mars Pathfinder a NASA mission launched Dec. 4 1996 to put a lander and a free-ranging instrument-packed roving vehicle directly onto the planet's surface. The probe landed on Mars on July 4 1997 in the region of the Ares Vallis, an extensive valley-like feature in the northern hemisphere. After landing, Mars Pathfinder released the rover, named *Sojourner*, which began investigations of the surrounding area. The Pathfinder mission lasted for nearly three months, sending back a wealth of science data about the planet's rocks and soil, its dust and dust storms, its winds and the effects of wind erosion, and possible evidence that water may have flowed on Mars during a warmer past. Pathfinder made its last complete data transmission on Sept. 27. After a month of unsuccessful attempts to communicate with it, mission controllers at the JET PROPULSION LABORATORY terminated further efforts to contact the probe on Nov. 4 1997.

The mission successfully demonstrated a low-cost method of delivering scientific instruments to Mars. It was possible to photograph local surface features, and the mission obtained 16 000 images from the lander and 550 from Sojourner.

Mars Polar Lander a NASA mission to Mars launched Jan. 1999 to land in the planet's southern polar region. The probe was lost as it entered the Martian atmosphere in Dec. 1999.

Mars probes 1 a series of ill-fated Soviet probes to Mars. Contact was lost with Mars 1, launched in Nov. 1962, after it had traveled 106 million km. Mars 2 and 3 entered orbit around Mars in Nov. and Dec. 1971 after detaching lander capsules: that from Mars 2 crashed and the other stopped transmitting within two minutes of touchdown. The orbiters made surface and atmospheric studies. Mars 4, an intended orbiter, passed the planet in Feb. 1974 after retrorocket failure. Mars 5 entered orbit two days later but ceased functioning after a few days of photographic reconnaissance. Mars 6 flew past Mars in Mar. 1974, ejecting a lander capsule that crashed on the surface. Mars 7 passed Mars three days before Mars 6 but its intended lander missed the planet completely.

2 space probes to Mars, such as the MARINER, VIKING, MARS GLOBAL SURVEYOR, MARS EXPRESS, and MARS ODYSSEY missions.

Mars Reconnaissance Orbiter a NASA Mars orbiter, part of the agency's Mars Exploration Program of crewless investigative probes, which was due for launch in August. 2005. It is set to provide the most thorough examination of Mars so far. Fitted with a high-resolution camera, it aims to send back close-up images of the Martian surface with unprecedented clarity. Chief among its tasks is the search for landing-sites close to sustainable sources of water, where future human missions will be able to establish themselves.

mascons *short for* mass concentrations. Positive gravitational anomalies associated with the young circular lunar MARIA, where relatively dense disk-shaped masses are now known to be located close to the surface: because the gravitational attraction is somewhat higher over these regions, mascons perturb the orbits of lunar satellites. They were produced either by the mare basalt itself as it flooded the basins or by the uplifting of higher-density mantle material during BASIN excavation. Mascons imply the existence of a rigid lunar crust for at least 3000 million years. The removal of crust during crater formation may also produce negative gravitational anomalies; these are observed in the younger large CRATERS and around the ORIENTALE BASIN, which is only partly lava-filled. Because the circular maria are topographic lows, mascons may be partially isostatically compensated, i.e. they may have sunk under their excess density until some sort of equilibrium depth was reached with relation to adjacent material.

maser amplifier a type of negative-resistance amplifier in which amplification is achieved by stimulating excited molecules to release photons in phase with the passing radiation. Amplifiers of this type have extremely low NOISE FIGURES, limited in practice by losses in the input and output circuits, and they therefore find application in RADIO TELESCOPES at microwave frequencies.

maser source a small celestial source of electromagnetic radiation, displaying narrow spectral lines and having an anomalously high BRIGHTNESS TEMPERATURE, in which the emission is thought to be by maser action: radiation at the maser frequency is amplified when excited molecules in the source emit PHOTONS in phase with the passing radiation (maser stands for microwave amplification by stimulated emission of radiation). Several different types have been identified including *OH (hydroxyl) masers* radiating at 1.665 gigahertz, *H_2O (water) masers* at 22.235, 321, 325, and 380 GHz, *SiO (silicon oxide) masers* at 43.424 and 86.243 GHz, and *CH_3OH (methanol) masers* at frequencies up to 338 GHz.

Maser sources have been detected, for example, in the atmospheres of old variable stars and in molecular clouds associated with newly formed or forming stars. The first maser source – an OH maser – was discovered in the Orion nebula in 1965. Hundreds of sources containing hydroxyl masers have since been found, some of which also have water masers. Masers are usually very VARIABLE RADIO SOURCES and produce highly polarized radio emission from regions that are typically about one parsec in diameter. Because of their small size, very precise position measurements are possible using VLBI. PROPER MOTION measurements over a period of several years have allowed a much more precise measurement of the distance to several GIANT MOLECULAR CLOUDS and to the GALACTIC CENTER, using the techniques of STATISTICAL PARALLAX and MOVING-CLUSTER PARALLAX. See also MIRA STARS; OH/IR STAR.

mass a measure of the quantity of matter in a body. The SI unit of mass is the kilogram. The astronomical unit of mass is the SOLAR MASS, i.e. 2×10^{30} kg. Mass is a property of matter that determines both the INERTIA of an object, i.e. its resistance to any change in its motion or state of rest, and the gravitational field that it can produce. The former is called *inertial mass*, defined by NEWTON'S LAWS OF MOTION, and the latter is *gravitational mass*. Inertial and gravitational mass have been found to be equivalent. This led to Einstein's principle of EQUIVALENCE between inertial and gravitational forces. See also RELATIVITY, SPECIAL THEORY; STELLAR MASS; WEIGHT.

mass function 1 the only information that can be determined about the masses m_1 and m_2 of the two components of a SPECTROSCOPIC BINARY when the spectral lines of only one component (of mass m_1) can be observed. It is equal to

$$(m_2^3 \sin^3 i)/(m_1 + m_2)^2$$

where m_1 and m_2 are measured in solar masses and i is the inclination of the orbit. 2 (**Salpeter mass function**) see STELLAR MASS.

mass loss the loss of mass by a star during its evolution by one or more processes. Mass is lost at a high rate in BIPOLAR OUTFLOWS during the formation of a star, and as a T TAURI WIND from some protostars. Mass is known to flow slowly into space from many stars, especially giants, in the form of a STELLAR WIND. Mass can also be ejected as the shell of a PLANETARY NEBULA or in a violent SUPERNOVA explosion. MASS TRANSFER can occur in close BINARY STARS, and mass can be lost from the binary in a NOVA explosion.

mass-luminosity relation (**M-L relation**) an approximate relation between the mass and LUMINOSITY of main-sequence stars, predicted by Eddington in 1924. Although having some basis in theory it is obtained empirically from a graph of absolute bolometric MAGNITUDE against the logarithm of mass (in SOLAR UNITS), i.e. $M/M_\odot$, for a large number of binary stars. Most points lie on an approximately straight line. Since a star's absolute bolometric magnitude is a function of the logarithm of its luminosity (in solar units), i.e. $L/L_\odot$, this line is represented by the M-L relation:

$$\log(L/L_\odot) = n \log(M/M_\odot)$$
$$L/L_\odot = (M/M_\odot)^n$$

n averages about 3 for bright massive stars, about 4 for Sun-type stars, and about 2.5 for dim red dwarfs of low mass. The relation holds for main-sequence stars, which all have a similar chemical composition and have similar internal structures and nuclear power sources. It is not obeyed by WHITE DWARFS (degenerate matter) or RED GIANTS (extended atmospheres).

mass number symbol: *A*. The number of protons and neutrons (i.e. nucleons) in the nucleus of a particular atom. It is the number closest to the mass of a nuclide in atomic mass units, i.e. in units equal to 1/12 of the mass of a carbon-12 atom. See also ATOMIC NUMBER.

mass-to-luminosity ratio the mass of a system divided by its luminosity, usually expressed in SOLAR UNITS such that the mass-to-luminosity ratio of the Sun is one. DARK MATTER is required to bind systems that have a high mass-to-luminosity ratio, such as groups and clusters of galaxies.

mass transfer a process occurring in close BINARY STARS when one of the stars has expanded to such an extent that mass can be transferred to its companion. This mass may strike the more compact companion directly or, more usually, may orbit the star and eventually form a ring of matter – an *accretion disk*. The mass transfer takes place through the inner Langrangian point, lying between the stars, and occurs when the larger star fills its Roche lobe (see EQUIPOTENTIAL SURFACES).

matching (**impedance matching**) arranging electrical impedances so that maximum power is transferred from one device to another. This occurs when the input impedance of one device equals the output impedance of the other to which it is connected. See also FEEDER.

Mathilde (**(253) Mathilde**) a C-TYPE MAIN-BELT ASTEROID, discovered in 1885 by the Austrian astronomer Johann Palisa. It was studied at close quarters in 1997 by the Near-Earth Asteroid Rendezvous (NEAR-Shoemaker) mission, which observed it to be 52 km across, with at least five craters more than 20 km across. It has an unusually long rotational period of 17.4 days.

matter–antimatter asymmetry the asymmetry between matter and antimatter in the Universe; i.e. the fact that all the matter in the Universe appears to be in the form of matter rather than an equal mixture of matter and antimatter, as might be expected from relativistic quantum mechanics. The problem of explaining this asymmetry is a major challenge for cosmology. SAKHAROV'S CONDITIONS provide a general explanation for how this asymmetry can arise. These conditions were implemented in the context of GRAND UNIFIED THEORIES in the late 1970s to provide an explanation of matter–antimatter asymmetry but it is not known whether this explanation is correct.

matter era see BIG BANG THEORY.

Mauna Kea a dormant volcano on the Big Island of Hawaii whose high-altitude summit (4200 meters, 13 800 ft) lies above almost half of the Earth's atmosphere. Conditions at the summit for astronomical observations, especially at infrared and submillimeter wavelengths, are extremely good. It is therefore the site of several major telescopes, administered overall as the *Mauna Kea Observatory* (MKO) by the University of Hawaii. The first telescope to be installed, 1968, was a 0.6-meter reflector of the University of Hawaii, followed two years later by a 2.2-meter instrument for the same institution. In 1979 three major telescopes for optical and infrared observations were inaugurated: the 3.8-meter UK INFRARED TELESCOPE (UKIRT), the 3.6-meter CANADA–FRANCE–HAWAII TELESCOPE (CFHT), used for optical and infrared studies, and the 3.0-meter INFRARED TELESCOPE FACILITY (IRTF), operated by NASA. There are also two major telescopes for submillimeter work: the 15-meter JAMES CLERK MAXWELL TELESCOPE (JCMT) and the 10.4-meter CALTECH SUBMILLIMETER OBSERVATORY (CSO), which began operations in 1986 and 1990 respectively. The US-Taiwanese 8 × 6-meter SUBMILLIMETER ARRAY began operations in 2002. Mauna Kea also has a 25-meter radio telescope, which is one of the ten antenna sites for the Very Long Baseline Array (VLBA).

Mauna Kea is the site of several new-generation telescopes. The two huge 10-meter KECK TELESCOPES, Keck I and Keck II, are part of the W.M. Keck Observatory. Additional projects include one of the two 8-meter GEMINI TELESCOPES and the 8.3-meter SUBARU TELESCOPE.

Maunder minimum see SUNSPOT CYCLE.

Max Planck Institute for Radio Astronomy (**MPIR; MPIfR**) see EFFELSBERG TELESCOPE.

Maxwell Gap (**Maxwell Division**) see SATURN'S RINGS.

Maxwell Montes the highest mountain range on VENUS, located on ISHTAR TERRA. It is centered on Venusian coordinates 65.2° N latitude, 356.7° W longitude. It rises to more than 11 km above the mean elevation of the surface, with complex folds and faults formed by extensive compression of the planet's crust. At high elevations, where the temperature and atmospheric pressure fall to a certain level, the rocks are coated with a metallic material similar to pyrite. Its western slopes are very steep, whereas its eastern slopes descend gradually into *Fortuna Tessera*.

Maxwell Observatory see JAMES CLERK MAXWELL TELESCOPE.

Mayall Telescope see KITT PEAK NATIONAL OBSERVATORY.

MCP detector see MICROCHANNEL PLATE DETECTOR.

mean anomaly see ANOMALY.

mean daily motion the angle through which a celestial body would move in one day if its orbital motion were uniform.

mean density of matter symbol: ρ_0. The factor that determines the dynamical behavior of the UNIVERSE, i.e. whether it is open or closed. The *density parameter*, Ω, is a dimensionless quantity given by

$$\Omega = 8\pi G\rho_0/(3H_0^2)$$

It is related to the DECELERATION PARAMETER, q_0, by

$$\Omega = 2q_0$$

If the Universe is a continuously expanding open system, Ω must be ≤1; if it exceeds unity the Universe is closed and must eventually collapse. The *critical density* for which Ω is unity is 5×10^{-27} kg m^{-3} for a HUBBLE CONSTANT H_0 equal to 55 km s^{-1} megaparsec^{-1}. Various estimates involving the mass to luminosity ratios of galaxies lead to values for Ω of about 0.01 due to galaxies. This is considerably less than the BARYON density parameter, the difference being due to the INTERGALACTIC MEDIUM. The missing-mass problem for CLUSTERS OF GALAXIES indicates the presence of DARK MATTER and suggests that the true value is about 0.3. A value of unity is not precluded by these observations; many theoretical cosmologists believe that $\Omega = 1$ precisely, because any deviation from unity in the early Universe would have been immensely amplified in the proposed inflationary phase (see INFLATIONARY UNIVERSE).

mean equator and equinox the reference system determined by ignoring small variations of short period in the motions of the celestial equator; it is affected only by PRECESSION. Positions in star catalogs are now usually referred to the mean catalog equator and equinox (see CATALOG EQUINOX) of a standard EPOCH. The coordinates of a celestial body on the (Sun-centered) celestial sphere, referred to the mean equator and equinox of a standard epoch, are its *mean place*. See also TRUE EQUATOR AND EQUINOX.

mean life see HALF-LIFE.

mean motion the constant angular speed that is required for a celestial body to complete one revolution of an (undisturbed) elliptical orbit of a specified semimajor axis.

mean parallax the PARALLAX obtained by statistical methods for a group of stars with different apparent magnitudes and proper motions.

mean place see MEAN EQUATOR AND EQUINOX.

mean sidereal time see SIDEREAL TIME.

mean solar time time measured with reference to the uniform motion of the MEAN SUN. The *mean solar day* is the interval of 24 hours between two successive passages of the mean Sun across the meridian. The mean solar second is 1/86 400 of the mean solar day. The difference between mean solar time and APPARENT SOLAR TIME on any particular day is the EQUATION OF TIME. Since the mean Sun is an abstract and hence unobservable point, mean solar time is defined in terms of SIDEREAL TIME. One mean solar day is equal to 24h 3m 56.555s of mean sidereal time.

Mean solar time was originally devised in order to provide a uniform measure of time based on the Earth's rate of rotation, which was assumed, incorrectly, to be constant. The Sun's mean daily motion does however conform closely to UNIVERSAL TIME.

mean Sun an abstract reference point that was introduced to define MEAN SOLAR TIME. It has a constant rate of motion and is used in timekeeping in preference to the real Sun whose observed motion is nonuniform. This nonuniformity results primarily from the Earth's elliptical orbit around the Sun, which causes the Earth's orbital speed, and hence the Sun's apparent speed, to vary (see KEPLER'S LAWS). Secondly the direction of the Sun's apparent motion is along the ecliptic and is thus inclined to the direction parallel to the celestial equator along which solar time is measured. An additional seasonal variation is therefore introduced when the Sun's motion is measured relative to the equator.

The mean Sun follows a circular orbit around the celestial equator so that it moves eastward at a constant speed and completes one circuit in the same time – one TROPICAL YEAR – as the apparent Sun takes to orbit the ecliptic, if the slight secular acceleration of the Sun is ignored. The mean Sun is defined by an expression for its right ascension, which fixes its position among the stars at every instant.

mega- symbol: M. A prefix to a unit, indicating a multiple of 10^6 (i.e. one million) of that unit. For example, one megaparsec (symbol: Mpc) is one million parsecs.

Megrez see PLOUGH.

meniscus lens a lens in which the two surfaces have different or sometimes equal curvatures but, unlike a concave or convex lens, curve in the same general direction. A *positive meniscus* is thicker at the center than at the edges; a *negative meniscus* is thinner at the center. See illustration at LENS.

meniscus mirror see PRIMARY MIRROR.

meniscus telescope see MAKSUTOV TELESCOPE.

Menkalinan see AURIGA.

mensa (plural: **mensae**) a flat-topped elevation with steep sides. The word is used in the approved name of such a surface feature on a planet or satellite.

Mensa (**Table Mountain**) a small

inconspicuous constellation in the southern hemisphere, close to the south pole, the brightest stars being of 5th magnitude. It contains part of the Large Magellanic Cloud. Abbrev.: Men; genitive form: Mensae; approx. position: RA 5.5h, dec –78°; area: 153 sq deg.

Merak (β UMa) one of the seven brightest stars in the PLOUGH and one of the two POINTERS. m_v: 2.37; M_v: 0.7; spectral type: A0mA1 IV-V; distance: 19 pc.

Mercury the innermost and, with a diameter of 4878 km, the second smallest planet in the Solar System, orbiting the Sun in 87.97 days at an average distance of 0.39 AU. It has no natural satellite. The distance from the Sun varies between 0.31 and 0.47 AU because of Mercury's high orbital ECCENTRICITY of 0.21. Maximum ELONGATION from the Sun varies between 28° and 18°, so that Mercury can be observed only when low in the twilight sky. Telescopes reveal a disk, between 4.5 and 12.9 arc seconds across, showing vague markings and PHASES varying from full at superior conjunction to new at inferior conjunction. TRANSITS across the Sun's disk recur at intervals of 7 or 13 years or in combinations of these figures. Orbital and physical characteristics are given in Table 1, backmatter.

Mercury's axial rotation period of 58.64 days, determined by radar in 1965, corresponds almost exactly to ⅔ of its orbital period, a fact discovered in 1965 by the Italian astronomer Giuseppi Colombo. The phenomenon is probably due to tidal coupling between the extra gravitational force of the Sun at PERIHELION and irregularities in Mercury's almost perfectly spherical form. This rotation period is close to half the planet's SYNODIC PERIOD; this explains why early observers, who saw the same face of the planet at favorable oppositions, concluded erroneously that it had a SYNCHRONOUS ROTATION period of 88 days.

MARINER 10, which made three close approaches to Mercury in 1974 and 1975, measured a maximum daytime temperature of 190 °C; this may reach 450 °C near perihelion. At night temperatures plunge to –180 °C beneath the most tenuous of atmospheres, consisting mainly of minute traces of helium, oxygen, and argon, plus some sodium and potassium. Mariner found that Mercury has a MAGNETOSPHERE supported by a magnetic field about 1% as strong as the Earth's; it is not clear whether this is generated within the planet's core or arises from permanent magnetization within the crust. Mercury's density, 5.4 times that of water, implies that it has a large nickel–iron core, perhaps 3600 km across.

Photography of half of Mercury's surface by Mariner 10 shows it to resemble the Moon in being heavily cratered with intervening areas of lava-flooded plains, called *maria*. The largest impact feature detected is the 1300 km diameter *Caloris Basin*, similar to the Moon's Mare IMBRIUM. Antipodal to Caloris is an area of chaotic terrain created, it is believed, by shock-waves from the same impact. Some recent craters possess radiating systems of light-colored surface streaks, similar to the lunar RAYS. The EJECTA BLANKETS surrounding many craters are half the size of those around lunar craters of similar diameter, probably because Mercury has twice the Moon's surface gravity. Of particular interest, and not seen on the Moon or Mars, are lines of cliffs, called *lobate scarps*, up to 3 km high and 500 km long. These may have resulted from wrinkling of the silicate-rich crust as Mercury's core cooled and contracted billions of years ago.

Mercury, perihelion see ADVANCE OF THE PERIHELION.

Mercury, transits see TRANSIT.

Mercury project the pioneering US space project to orbit a manned craft, to investigate human reactions to and ability to adapt to the weightlessness of space, and to recover both astronauts and spacecraft. Mercury MR3, launched May 5 1961 by a Redstone rocket, carried the first American, Alan Shepard, into the upper atmosphere in a suborbital hop. The first true orbital flight was made by John Glenn in Mercury MA6, launched Feb. 20 1962 by an Atlas rocket. The longest flight, 34.3 hours, was made by Gordon Cooper in the last capsule in the series, Mercury MA9, launched May 15 1963. See also APOLLO; GEMINI PROJECT.

merger the final gravitationally bound

product of closely INTERACTING GALAXIES or other interacting systems. Some IRAS GALAXIES are believed to be recent merger products.

meridian 1 an imaginary great circle passing through a point on the surface of a body, such as a planet or satellite, at right angles to the equator and passing through the north and south poles.

2 *short for* celestial meridian. The projection of the observer's terrestrial meridian on the CELESTIAL SPHERE. It is thus the great circle passing through the north and south CELESTIAL POLES and the observer's ZENITH and intersecting the observer's horizon at the north and south points (see CARDINAL POINTS).

meridian angle see HOUR ANGLE.

meridian circle see TRANSIT CIRCLE.

meridian passage the passage of a star across the meridian (see CULMINATION) or of an inferior planet across the Sun (see TRANSIT).

MERLIN *abbrev. for* Multi-Element Radio-Linked Interferometer Network (formerly known as MTRLI). A network of radio telescopes in England connected by microwave communication links to a control system at JODRELL BANK. In operation since 1980, it is used at wavelengths ranging from 1 meter to 1 centimeter approximately to build up high-resolution maps of RADIO SOURCES.

These telescopes in the network are as follows: Jodrell Bank's Lovell Telescope, Mark II telescope, or its 13-meter dish – the choice depends on wavelength, the 13 m being used at shorter wavelengths than the Mark II; the 25-meter dish at Defford, Worcestershire; three identical 25-meter dishes at Pickmere and Darnhall in Cheshire and Knockin in Shropshire; the 32-meter dish at MRAO, Cambridge, which can be used at frequencies of up to 90 GHz. The telescopes give BASELINES ranging from 11 to 217 km in length. MERLIN frequently observes simultaneously with the VLBA and the EVN to carry out global VLBI.

Merope see PLEIADES.

Mesarthim see ARIES.

mesons see ELEMENTARY PARTICLES.

mesosiderite see STONY-IRON METEORITE.

mesosphere, mesopause see ATMOSPHERIC LAYERS.

MESSENGER *abbrev. for* Mercury Surface, Space Environment, Geochemistry, and Ranging, a NASA mission to the planet Mercury, launched Aug. 3 2004 from Cape Canaveral by a Delta 2 Heavy rocket and forming part of the agency's Discovery Program. Although an acronym, the name recalls the planet's mythical association with Mercury the winged messenger of the gods. The MESSENGER spacecraft is NASA's first Mercury orbiter. Its chief goal is to investigate important scientific questions about Mercury's surface and interior composition and its environment. Among other things, the probe will seek to find out why Mercury's density is so high, what the composition and structure of its crust is, and whether there has been any volcanism. It will also look into the nature, dynamics and origin of Mercury's magnetic field (possibly driven by a liquid outer core) and its tenuous atmosphere. One focus of interest will be the mysterious polar deposits on Mercury, which some scientists believe could be water ice. The data for these questions will be gathered by an array of seven miniature instruments working in one of the most hostile environments in the Solar System, a mere 58 million km from the Sun.

To avoid overshooting its target and possibly falling into the Sun, the MESSENGER craft is following a 6½-year, 7.9-billion-km roundabout course to Mercury that should slow it down sufficiently to accomplish its task. The journey will involve 15 solar orbits, 6 trajectory-altering planetary flybys (including 1 of the Earth, 2 of Venus, and 3 of Mercury itself), and 6 crucial rocket firings. It will enter orbit around Mercury in March 2011 for a year of scientific data collection.

Messier Catalog a catalog of the brightest 'nebulae' prepared by the French astronomer Charles Messier and printed in final form in 1784. Messier compiled the list in order to avoid confusion of these cloudlike objects with comets, for which he was a keen searcher. 103 celestial objects, which appeared fuzzy and extended in telescopes of the time, were listed and given a number preceded by the letter M. This is the object's *Messier number*, an example being M42: the Orion nebula. It was later found that most of the objects were not true nebulae but galaxies and star clusters. Seven more objects were later added to Messier's list, bringing the total number of cataloged items to 110. See Table 8, Appendix; NGC.

Messier number see MESSIER CATALOG.

Me stars cool red stars whose spectra show emission lines of hydrogen in addition to the molecular bands of titanium oxide characteristic of M STARS. This occurs in both giant and dwarf (main-sequence) M stars, apparently for different reasons. The giant Me stars are mainly long-period variables, such as MIRA STARS, whose distended atmospheres are losing matter to space. The emission lines from dwarf Me stars seem to be related to the presence of strong magnetic fields; they are often FLARE STARS.

metal in astronomy, any element heavier than helium; the most abundant metals are oxygen, carbon, and nitrogen.

metallicity (**metal abundance**) symbol: Z. The fraction by mass of METALS in a star, cluster of stars, or in some other astronomical entity. Since metals are produced by NUCLEOSYNTHESIS in stars, the metallicity of an object or class of objects depends on when it was formed: objects of later origin in general have a higher metallicity. Metallicity is determined by photometry or high-resolution spectroscopy, and is usually expressed relative to solar metallicity (see COSMIC ABUNDANCE), and as the ratio of iron to hydrogen, Fe/H. See also POPULATION I, POPULATION II.

metal ratio the ratio of the abundance of a METAL to the abundance of hydrogen in a celestial body or system.

meteor the streak of light seen in the clear night sky when a small particle of interplanetary dust (a METEOROID) burns itself out in the Earth's upper atmosphere. On a clear moonless night at a time away from METEOR SHOWERS the dark-adapted eye can see about 10 per hour, the eye detecting meteors down to about fifth visual MAGNITUDE. The most probable magnitude seen is +2.5, 75% of the meteors observed having magnitudes in the range 3.75 to 0.75. The visual rate maximizes at about 04.00 local time when the observer is on the leading side of the Earth, 'plowing' into the cosmic dust cloud. The meteoroid enters the atmosphere at velocities between 11 and 74 km s^{-1} depending on whether the Earth just catches up the particle or they have a head-on collision. The ablating meteoroid not only leaves behind it a TRAIN of excited atoms that de-excite to produce the brief blaze of light – a *visual meteor* – but it also produces a column of ionized atoms and molecules (both atmospheric and meteoric) that can act as reflectors of radar pulses transmitted from ground-based telescopes – a *radio meteor*. The meteoroid dissipates its energy, distributes its disaggregated atoms and molecules, and produces the visual and radio meteor in the region between 70 km and 115 km above the Earth's surface. The mean altitude of maximum luminosity and electron density is 97 km.

A large percentage of the mass influx to the Earth's atmosphere (which totals some 220 000 tonnes per year) is made up of particles in the size range that produce visual and radio meteors, i.e. one millionth to one million grams. The meteoroid has a kinetic energy considerably in excess of the energy required to vaporize itself. Air molecules striking the meteoroid have a kinetic energy of about 400 electronvolts. As the binding energy of the atoms in the meteoroid is a few electronvolts, a hundred or so meteoroid atoms boil off for each adsorbed air molecule. The meteoroid starts to ablate at about 115 km. These ablated atoms then collide with the surrounding air molecules and by losing energy in these collisions produce EXCITATION and IONIZATION. After ten or so collisions the energy of the ablated atom has dropped below the excitation potential of the air molecules and ionization and excitation no longer occur. The ablated atom has moved about 50 cm from the meteoroid path during this process. The small meteoroid is completely evaporated after intercepting an air mass about 1% of its own mass. Owing to these processes the meteoroid TRAIN has a length of between 7 and 20 km and a width of about 100 cm. A 4th-magnitude meteor contains around 10^{18} electrons and 10^{18} positive ions. The atoms quickly de-excite and electrons and positive ions recombine and become attached to other atmospheric molecules. The time duration is related to the magnitude but is usually less than a second.

The meteor spectrum is a low-excitation one, ionization potentials lying in the range 1.9 to 13.9 volts (equivalent to temperatures roughly 1600 to 4800 K). The Ca II lines, H and K, are the main features of fast meteors whereas Na I, Mg I, and Fe I are dominant in slow ones.

meteorite interplanetary debris that falls to the Earth's surface. The first documented one was the stone that fell near Ensisheim, Alsace in 1492 but it was not until 1803 that meteorites were accepted by the scientific community as being extraterrestrial. One that is seen to hit the ground is known as a *fall*; one that is discovered accidentally some time after having fallen is termed a *find*. Roughly 6 falls and 10 finds are added to the list annually. About 3300 hit the Earth each year; the majority go unrecorded, falling in oceans, deserts, and other uninhabited regions.

Meteorites can be crudely divided into three types: STONY METEORITES, which subdivide into CHONDRITES and ACHONDRITES, IRON METEORITES, and STONY-IRON METEORITES. Iron meteorites have densities of about 7.8 g cm^{-3} and contain on average 91% iron, 8% nickel, and 0.6% cobalt. Stony meteorites have densities about 3.4 g cm^{-3} and on average contain 42% oxygen, 20.6% silicon, 15.8% magnesium, and 15.6% iron, no other element exceeding 2%. Stony-irons are intermediate in composition. The relative percentages of each type are shown in the table. The fall percentages give a reasonable approximation to the actual meteorite population of the Solar System. However the fragile CARBONACEOUS CHONDRITES mostly disintegrate on entry.

The largest iron meteorite that has been found is the 60-tonne HOBA METEORITE, the largest stony meteorite being 1 tonne, part of the Norton County, Kansas achondrite. The found meteorite might represent only a small percentage of the in-space mass of the body. Meteorite entry is accompanied by a brilliant BOLIDE, the meteorite usually being retarded to FREE-FALL velocity at a height of about 20 km. It hits the ground at about 300 km per hour. The surface of the meteorite can easily be heated up to several thousand kelvin during entry. This usually produces a black glassy fusion crust, which covers the meteorite. Most meteorites fragment on entry, scattering pieces over an elliptical area: the carbonaceous chondrite meteorite *Allende*, which fell in 1969 in Mexico, scattered 5 tonnes of material over an area 48 km long by 7 km wide.

Meteorites

Meteorite types		*Finds (%)*	*Falls (%)*
chondrites	stones	43.7	84.3
achondrites	stones	1.0	8.7
stony-irons		5.2	1.3
irons		50.1	5.7

Meteorites are named after the nearest topographical feature to the fall point. Recognizing meteorite finds relies mainly on analysing chemically for the presence of nickel, which is present in all iron meteorites. Etched and polished irons also show WIDMANSTÄTTEN FIGURES. Stony meteorites contain nickel-iron particles that can be extracted magnetically from a crushed sample.

Meteorites bring to our notice a type of rock existing in the Solar System but different from anything that occurs in the outer shell of the planet Earth. Studies of the chemical elements and compounds and the minerals present in meteorites allow their origin and history to be better understood; isotope ratios of given elements can give absolute ages. Most meteorites are believed to be fragments of ASTEROIDS. Two problems arise: firstly, meteorites seem to have had only a short exposure to cosmic rays; secondly, the dynamics by which a meteorite gets from the asteroid belt to the Earth's orbit is nontrivial, mainly relying on the orbital eccentricity being pumped up by gravitational perturbation when the semimajor axis approaches one of the KIRKWOOD GAP resonances. The carbonaceous chondrites are thought to originate as parts of cometary NUCLEI. The ages of meteorites have been obtained by radiometric-dating methods and have been estimated at up to 4.7×10^9 years. This indicates that meteorites were formed at about the same time as the Solar System.

meteorite craters circular impact structures produced by meteorite bombardment, usually known as ASTROBLEMES if they occur in the Earth's crust. See also CRATERS.

meteoroid the collective term applied to meteoritic material in the Solar System, usually replaced by the terms MICROMETEORITE for particles with mass less than 10^{-6} gram and METEORITE for bodies with mass greater than about 10^5 grams. The majority of the mass of the meteoroid cloud around the Sun is made up of particles with individual masses between 10^{-7} and 10^{-3} gram. Meteoroids are usually produced by the decay of short-period comets and the collisional fragmentation of asteroids. In the main they move around the Sun in low-inclination direct orbits. The space density of meteoroids maximizes near the orbit of Mars and then falls off as $1/r^{1.5}$, where r is the distance from the Sun. Individual meteoroids in the mass range 10^{-6} to 10^4 grams are fragile crumbly rocky dust particles with a composition similar to carbonaceous chondrite meteorites. See also METEOR.

meteoroid stream the annulus of METEOROIDS around the orbit of a decaying COMET. Dust particles are pushed away from the cometary NUCLEUS by gas pressure at the time when the nucleus is near PERIHELION. The particles then have slightly different orbital parameters to the comet. Stream-formation time depends on perihelion distance and meteoroid size, being anything from tens to hundreds of years. New streams only have meteoroids close to the parent comet and only produce METEOR SHOWERS periodically. Streams are about 100 times thicker at aphelion than at perihelion. They contain anywhere between 10^{14} grams and 10^{17} grams of dust and have volumes in the range 10^{21} to 10^{25} km^3.

meteor shower the increase in observed rate of appearance of METEORS – *shower meteors* – when the Earth passes through a METEOROID STREAM; a particular shower occurs at the same time each year. The increase in rate differs from stream to stream: it is a function of mass of the originating comet, age of stream, position of intersection point with respect to stream axis, and orbital elements (which can vary slowly with time). With many showers the rate varies from year to year because the meteoroids are not evenly distributed around the stream. The ratio between shower rate and sporadic-meteor rate is a function of the mass of the meteoroids being observed. This ratio can be as high as 10 for visual meteors, is about 1–2 for radio meteors, and is negligible for satellite-observed meteors. Shower meteors appear to emanate from a RADIANT, the shower being named after the constellation that contains the radiant. See Table 4, Appendix.

meteor storm (meteor swarm) a METEOR SHOWER with an enormous meteor rate that occurs when the Earth intersects a new METEOROID STREAM close to a large originating comet. The most famous was the Leonid storm of Nov. 12–13, 1833, when the rate exceeded 10 000 visual meteors an hour, single observers often seeing 20 a second.

meter symbol: m. The usual scientific unit of length and distance. It is defined (from Oct. 1983) as the length of the path traveled by light in vacuum during a time interval of 1/299 792 458 of a second. It is thus now defined in terms of the second and the fixed value of the SPEED OF LIGHT.

Metis a small irregularly shaped satellite of Jupiter, discovered in 1980 from photographs taken by Voyager 2 in 1979. It is Jupiter's closest known satellite, orbiting at a mean distance of 128 000 km. See JUPITER'S SATELLITES; Table 2, Appendix.

Metonic cycle (lunar cycle) a period of 19 years (tropical) after which the phases of the Moon recur on the same days of the year: the period contains 6939.60 days, which is very nearly equal to 235 SYNODIC MONTHS, i.e. 6939.69 days. Since it is also almost equal to 20 ECLIPSE YEARS, i.e. 6932.4 days, it is possible for a series of four or five eclipses to occur on the same dates at intervals of 19 years. The cycle was discovered by the Greek astronomer Meton in the fifth century BC and was used in determining how intercalary months could be inserted into a lunar calendar so that the calendar year and the tropical (seasonal) year were kept in step.

Meudon Observatory see PARIS OBSERVATORY.

MHD *abbrev. for* magnetohydrodynamics.

MHz *symbol for* megahertz, i.e. 10^6 hertz.

Mice (NGC 4676) two closely INTERACTING disk galaxies that have each thrown off major tidal features resembling mouse tails. They lie at a distance of 90 Mpc.

Michelson interferometer an early form of INTERFEROMETER in which a beam of light is split and subsequently recombined. Any difference in optical path traveled by the two beams leads to a phase difference between the recombining beams, and hence INTERFERENCE fringes are produced.

Michelson–Morley experiment see ETHER.

Michelson stellar interferometer any of a series of INTERFEROMETERS constructed by A.A. Michelson to measure the small angular dimensions of stellar objects, such as a star's apparent diameter or the angular separation of a double star. In the original version, a telescope objective was covered by a screen that was pierced with two parallel slits of adjustable separation. The components of a double star (or the two halves of a stellar disk) will each produce a set of interference fringes as a result of the double slit. By varying the slit separation, *d*, the bright fringes of one pattern can be made to coincide with the dark fringes of the other so that a continuous line of light is seen; the angular dimension is then proportional to *d*. Michelson was able to measure the diameters of several nearby stars down to about 0.01 arcsec, including that of the supergiant Betelgeuse. Much more sensitive measurements can now be made with modern optical INTERFEROMETERS.

micro- symbol: μ. A prefix to a unit, indicating a fraction of 10^{-6} (i.e. one millionth) of that unit. For example, one micrometer is 10^{-6} meter.

microchannel plate (MCP) detector a high-resolution (15–25 μm pixel) imaging device for recording X-ray, ultraviolet, or electron images. The incident photon (or electron) strikes the front surface of a thin glass plate consisting of a very large number of fine-bore tubes (usually aligned perpendicular to the plate surfaces). Secondary electrons are produced and are accelerated down the tubes by an applied voltage, striking the walls and creating further electrons. Charge multiplication factors of about 10^3 (or 10^6 in a 'cascaded pair' of MCPs) yield a signal that is easily read on a collector at the rear of the plate(s). Proximity focusing ensures retention of the initial photon (or electron) image and resolutions of 20–50 μm have been achieved. MCP detectors have been used successfully in a number of X-ray astronomy satellites, including the Einstein Observatory, EXOSAT, and ROSAT. MCPs are also the basis of the highest resolution X-ray camera in AXAF–I.

microdensitometer an optical instrument that measures and records small changes in the transmission density on a photographic plate, such as the faint features in a spectrum. The plate, mounted on a carriage, is moved through a light beam. A photomultiplier measures the amount of light transmitted by the plate and the output is fed to a chart recorder or computer.

microgravity the very low gravity encountered on spacecraft in Earth orbit, leading to a condition of near WEIGHTLESSNESS. The behavior of liquids and gases in microgravity differs markedly from that observed on Earth. Hydrostatic pressure is small, sedimentation is suppressed, and dynamic effects, such as thermal convection, disappear. Space missions dedicated to the study of materials and living matter in microgravity include EURECA, the International Microgravity Laboratory, and the US Microgravity Laboratory.

microlensing see EINSTEIN CROSS; GRAVITATIONAL LENS.

micrometeorite a COSMIC DUST particle of mass less than about 10^{-6} gram and diameter less than 0.1 mm. On impact with the Earth's atmosphere the heat absorbed by the particle from atmospheric friction is insufficient to raise it to boiling point. The ratio of heat radiated to heat absorbed is proportional to the inverse of the radius of a particle: those larger than 10^{-6} gram ablate and form METEORS; smaller ones do not. The micrometeorite will be decelerated to a normal free-fall velocity and then drift to the surface of the Earth. On the Moon, however, no deceleration occurs and they impact the surface with the normal geocentric velocity.

Microscopium (**Microscope**) a small inconspicuous constellation in the southern hemisphere near Sagittarius, the brightest star being of 4th magnitude. Abbrev.: Mic; genitive form: Microscopii; approx. position: RA 21h, dec −35°; area: 210 sq deg.

Microwave Anisotropy Probe see WILKINSON MICROWAVE ANISOTROPY PROBE.

microwave background radiation the remnant of the radiation content of the primordial fireball associated with the hot BIG BANG. It is the dominant radiation of deep intergalactic space. A microwave background was first considered by George Gamow in the 1940s, and its existence with a temperature close to 5 K was predicted in 1948 by Ralph Alpher and Robert Herman. The concept was generally neglected and the prediction forgotten until the radiation was discovered in 1965 by Arno Penzias and Robert Wilson.

The microwave radiation is highly isotropic, showing that it must be at cosmological distances when compared to the highly clumpy nearby Universe. The Earth's atmosphere complicates detailed observation of the microwave radiation at millimeter wavelengths where it is most intense (see illustration), and it is best studied by satellite-borne instruments such as were carried by NASA's Cosmic Background Explorer, COBE.

COBE has measured the spectrum of the microwave background to be a perfect BLACK-BODY curve characteristic of a temperature of 2.735 ± 0.06 K. The microwave background is not completely uniform, showing a slight *dipole anisotropy* with an enhancement of one part in a thousand in the direction of the Galaxy's motion and an equal and opposite deficit in the opposite part of the sky. This is due to

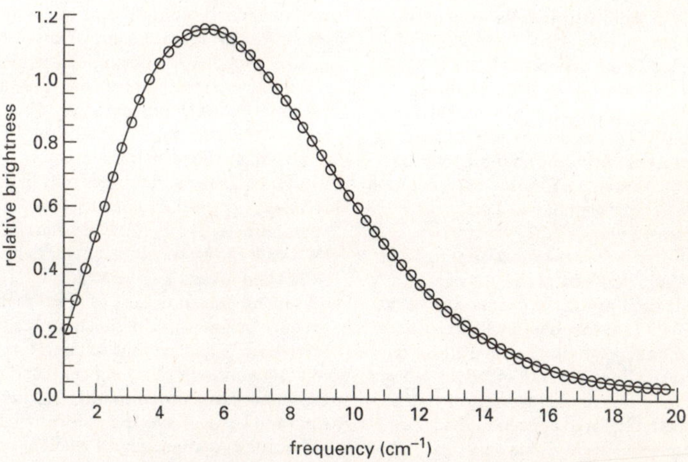

Spectrum of microwave background radiation determined by COBE (circles), compared with best-fit black-body spectrum (smooth curve)

aberration from the real motion of the Galaxy relative to the fixed background.

COBE has also revealed even weaker temperature fluctuations of one part in one hundred thousand on scales of ten degrees and larger. These are the imprints of quantum fluctuations in the early Universe. Further study of such fluctuations, in particular those due to acoustic oscillation of matter before recombination, will constrain cosmological models that determine how the early inhomogeneities collapse to form the LARGE-SCALE STRUCTURE we see in today's Universe. These can be directly related to the cosmic power spectrum.

The cosmological distance of the microwave background radiation implies that its photons were more energetic in the past. When the Universe was scarcely a few hundred thousand years old, they were energetic enough to photoionize hydrogen (see BIG BANG THEORY) and their mean free path was drastically reduced by scattering with the free electrons.

Microwave Observing Program see SETI.

microwaves very high frequency radio waves. Their frequencies are usually considered to lie in the range 1–300 gigahertz, so that their wavelength range is about 1–300 mm. *Microwave astronomy* is the branch of radio astronomy covering this wavelength range.

Midcourse Space Experiment (MSX) a spacecraft launched by the US Ballistic Missile Defense Organization in April 1996, carrying a combination of astronomical instruments (including an ultraviolet spectroscope and an infrared telescope) and military equipment. It had a planned lifetime of 4 years.

mid-infrared see INFRARED RADIATION.

Milky Way a dense band of faint stars that extends right round the CELESTIAL SPHERE, dividing it into roughly equal parts. Its central line marks the central plane of our GALAXY, inclined at about 63° to the celestial equator. Although the vast majority of the stars are too faint to be seen individually, they are collectively visible on a clear moonless night as a diffuse band of light. The Milky Way is seen because the Sun lies close to the central plane of the galactic disk. Because this region of the Galaxy is highly flattened, a much greater depth of stars is visible in directions along the plane (i.e. toward the Milky Way) than in other directions. The Milky Way has a distinctly patchy appearance; it also varies considerably in width and brightness and is noticeably brighter toward Sagittarius (the direction of the GALACTIC CENTER). Many of the apparent gaps are due to DARK NEBULAE, such as the Coalsack, along our line of sight, which prevent stars behind them from being seen.

Milky Way System see GALAXY.

milli- symbol: m. A prefix to a unit, indicating a fraction of 10^{-3} (i.e. 1/1000) of that unit. For example, one millisecond is 10^{-3} second.

millimeter astronomy a branch of radio astronomy covering the wavelength range from 1 to 10 millimeters approximately. When studies began in the late 1960s it was the highest frequency range, 30–300 gigahertz, in which radio astronomy could be carried out. SUBMILLIMETER ASTRONOMY has since become feasible. Both millimeter and submillimeter wavelengths are ideal for observations of giant MOLECULAR CLOUDS. A large variety of molecules form at the high densities in the clouds. The spectral lines emitted by the molecules are mainly in the millimeter and submillimeter range, and give information on chemical composition, relative abundances of isotopes, chemical reactions, and temperatures, densities, and velocities in the clouds (see also MOLECULAR-LINE RADIO ASTRONOMY).

Millimeter wave instrumentation – usually parabolic radio dishes plus line receivers – is similar to that used for submillimeter astronomy. One example is the JAMES CLERK MAXWELL TELESCOPE (JCMT) on Mauna Kea, Hawaii.

millisecond pulsars a class of PULSARS that produce pulses with a period of only a few milliseconds, and are thus NEUTRON STARS rotating hundreds of times per second. Unlike the fast 'normal' pulsars (e.g. the Crab and Vela pulsars), the millisecond pulsars' fast rotation is not a result of youth; they have almost certainly been 'spun up' by mass transfer in a close BINARY STAR at an earlier evolutionary stage. Rapid rotation of a neutron star is normally slowed precipitously because the star's strong magnetic field radiates away the rotational energy, as with the Crab pulsar (see CRAB NEBULA); the millisecond pulsars detected so far, however, have only a very gradual rate of slowing down, probably because their magnetic fields are comparatively weak (10^4–10^5 tesla).

PSR 1937+21 was the first millisecond pulsar to be found, 1982, and is currently the fastest known (period 1.56 ms, i.e. 642 rotations per second). The second to be found, PSR 1953+29 (6.1 ms), is a member of a BINARY PULSAR system; it orbits its unseen companion in 120 days. The old but rapidly spinning binary pulsar PSR 1913+16 also belongs in this class, although its period is rather longer (59 ms).

Recent surveys have discovered large numbers of millisecond pulsars in GLOBULAR CLUSTERS; more than half are close binary pulsars. It is generally believed that most of the single millisecond pulsars were initially members of binary systems, but lost their companion stars either because of a stellar collision (which is possible in globular clusters) or because the radiation emitted by the pulsars completely destroyed, or 'evaporated', the companion stars (see BLACK-WIDOW PULSARS). One millisecond pulsar (PSR 1257+12) appears to be orbited by two planet-mass objects (see PLANET PULSAR).

Mills cross antenna an interferometer (see RADIO TELESCOPE) using two long narrow ANTENNAS mounted in the form of a cross and producing a single pencil beam; it is named after B.Y. Mills, who constructed the first one near Sydney. One arm of the cross may be shortened to give a *T-antenna*, which has an antenna pattern very similar to that of the full cross but whose SENSITIVITY is less.

Mimas a satellite of Saturn, discovered in 1789 by William Herschel. It has a diameter of only 390 km and a density of 1.17 g cm^{-3}. The most striking feature is the crater *Herschel*, 130 km in diameter and nearly centered on the leading hemisphere. The walls rise on average to a height of 5 km above the floor. In the center of the crater is an enormous peak 20 × 30 km at its base and rising to 6 km. The diameter of the crater is a third of Mimas itself, and is probably close to the maximum size of impact crater that a body can sustain without being broken up. All other craters on the surface are small, being less than 50 km in diameter. There are valleys too on the surface, which is scored by grooves. The surface of the satellite is icy and there is every reason to suppose that the ice makes up much of the entire body, which now bears the scars of past bombardments. See also Table 2, Appendix.

Mimosa see BETA CRUCIS.

mini black hole see BLACK HOLE.

minor axis the least distance across an ellipse, crossing the major axis perpendicularly at the center of the ellipse. The length is usually given as 2*b*.

minor planet see ASTEROIDS; PLANETOIDS.

Mintaka see ORION.

minute of arc (**arc minute; arc min**) see ARC SECOND.

Mir (from the Russian for 'Peace' or 'World') The Soviet space station of modular design that superseded Salyut 7 (see SALYUT). The Soviet authorities announced the launch of Mir on Feb. 20 1986, and the first crew, cosmonauts Leonid Kizim and Vladimir Soloviev, arrived there Mar. 13 1986. The 20-tonne core unit was about 17.4 meters long by 4 meters wide and had large winglike solar panels. Permanently attached to this was a docking module with five ports, four in a cruciform arrangement and one aft. Large pressurized research modules, or transient spacecraft, could be docked to these ports. Each research module was dedicated to a different scientific or technical field; for example, the *Kvant* and *Kristall* modules were dedicated to astrophysical observations and experiments in Earth sciences, life sciences, and space-based materials-processing technologies. Kvant 1 and Kvant 2 were the first two modules to be added to the core unit in 1987 and 1989 respectively. Kristall followed in 1990. Then came *Spektr* (1995) and *Priroda* (1996).

Two cosmonauts routinely occupied Mir, although it could take six cosmonauts/ scientists. Very extended tours of duty by the cosmonauts and overlapping of successive crews ensured a virtually continuous presence on Mir. The cosmonaut Valeriy Polyakov set a space endurance record of 438 days aboard Mir between January 1994 and March 1995. Mir frequently hosted foreign crew members, and as time went on efforts were made to commercialize the station. In 1987, a Syrian spaceman briefly joined Mir's occupants. He was followed over the years by crew members from Bulgaria, Afghanistan, France, Austria, and Germany. In 1990, a Japanese journalist, Toyohiro Akiyama, joined the crew and broadcast live television reports from Mir. In 1991, Helen Sharman, the first UK citizen to travel in space, visited the station on the privately sponsored JUNO mission.

Mir continued to operate right through the collapse of the Soviet Union at the end of 1991. From 1995, when a module allowing the Space Shuttle to dock with the station was added, to 1998, seven US astronauts served with Russian crews aboard Mir. But by now Mir was aging. Accidents had dogged it throughout its career, many to do with the robotic Progress supply craft, which crashed into the station more than once. A few were due to human error. After a series of mishaps, Mir was finally abandoned in 1999. A commercial venture to reactivate it in 2000 came to nothing. Mir was destroyed in a controlled reentry into the Earth's atmosphere on Mar. 28 2001.

Miranda a satellite of Uranus, discovered in 1948 by G.P. Kuiper. A relatively small satellite with a diameter of 470 km, it orbits its primary once every 1.4 days at a mean distance of 129 000 km. Only half of Miranda's surface was available for study from VOYAGER 2 in 1986 (the northern hemisphere was in darkness) but a complex surface structure was revealed. Several distinct types of terrain exist: old cratered plains, younger brighter areas with cliffs and scarps, and regions of enclosed grooved areas about 200–300 km across. These features occupy distinct portions of the satellite, leading to the theory that Miranda was shattered by a collision and then subsequently reassembled into a single body. See URANUS' SATELLITES; Table 2, Appendix.

Mira or **Mira Ceti** (**the Wonderful; o Cet**) A RED GIANT in the constellation Cetus that is a long-period VARIABLE STAR with an average period of 331 days. It was known to early astronomers for its regular appearances and disappearances and was established in 1638 as a variable star. It is the prototype of the MIRA STARS. Its radius varies by 20 per cent during its cycle and at maximum size and brightness is over 330 times the Sun's radius. The surface temperature varies from about 2600 K at maximum luminosity down to about 1900 K. The visible light emitted varies considerably, usually by about 6 magnitudes, over the cycle (see illustration). The average maximum apparent magnitude, m_V, lies between 3 and 4 although it may reach 2nd magnitude. At minimum it is about 8th to 10th magnitude. Mira is also an INFRARED SOURCE, the emission arising from dust grains in the expanding envelope of gas.

Mira is both a visual binary with a faint peculiar companion that is also variable,

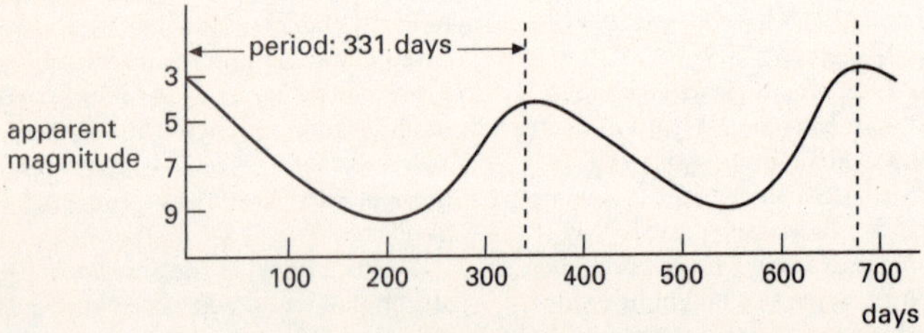

Light curve of Mira

and an optical double. M_V: –1.0 (var.); spectral type: M6e–M9e III; distance: 40 pc.

Mirach see ANDROMEDA.

Mira stars (Mira Ceti variables) long-period PULSATING VARIABLES, either red giants or red supergiants, that have periods ranging from about 80 to 1000 days and a range in brightness beginning at about 2.5 magnitudes and sometimes exceeding 10 magnitudes. They are numerous, MIRA Ceti being the prototype. The shape of the LIGHT CURVE is not constant, the maximum brightness varying quite considerably between periods (see MIRA). Because of the large amplitude they are easily recognizable, their high luminosity permitting detection at great distances.

Although their visual range is large, the range in bolometric and infrared MAGNITUDES is very much less, many of them being infrared sources. In terms of their spectra 90% can be classified as ME STARS, the rest being either CARBON STARS (Ce) or ZIRCONIUM (Se) stars, i.e. there are bright emission lines present in the spectra in addition to molecular bands. The pulsations of these huge stars are not very stable. There is evidence of shock waves developing within the tenuous atmosphere and traveling outward, thus heating the gas and causing the production of emission lines. The expanding envelopes often contain condensed dust grains, which produce detectable infrared emission, and simple molecules: Mira stars often show MASER emission from hydroxyl, water, and silicon monoxide molecules in the outer atmosphere. See also OH/IR STAR.

Mirfak (α Per) a remote creamy-yellow supergiant that is the brightest star in the constellation Perseus. m_v: 1.80; spectral type: F5 Ib; distance: 190 pc.

mirror an optical element designed to reflect light or other radiation, normally consisting of a glass or glasslike substrate on which is deposited a thin but uniform coating of highly reflective material. Aluminum is now usually used in telescope mirrors (see ALUMINIZING). A very high quality reflecting surface can also be made from a multilayered stack of very thin films. The films have alternately high and low REFRACTIVE INDICES and are of such a thickness and spacing that almost all the incident light is reflected.

Mirrors may be planar, i.e. flat. Alternatively the shapes may be concave (converging) or convex (diverging) and are generally spherical or paraboloid in form. The mirror base must be accurately ground and the surface polished to within one quarter of the wavelength used, i.e. to about 0.1 micrometer for optical wavelengths, if good quality images are to be produced. Paraboloid mirrors do not suffer from SPHERICAL ABERRATION but for wide fields have severe COMA. Spherical mirrors are free of coma and astigmatism if a suitable stop is used; they do, however, suffer from spherical aberration. See also GRAZING INCIDENCE; PRIMARY MIRROR.

mirror blank see PRIMARY MIRROR.

Mirzam see CANIS MAJOR.

missing mass the DARK MATTER in a CLUSTER OF GALAXIES. See CLUSTERS OF GALAXIES.

mixing layer a turbulent boundary layer formed where there is a velocity shear between two media at different temperatures. The turbulence draws long shreds from each side that mix and form a thick buffer layer at the mean temperature of the two media.

Mizar (ζ UMa) a white main-sequence dwarf that is one of the brighter stars of the PLOUGH. It forms an optical double with the 4th-magnitude ALCOR with a separation of 12′. But Mizar itself is also a double, a fact discovered by Riccioli in 1650. The two components of Mizar, A (the brighter) and B, are currently 14″ apart. It is thought that they complete one orbit about each other in 5000 years. Both components are spectroscopic binaries (see SPECTROSCOPIC BINARY). Mizar A was the first spectroscopic binary to be identified (E.C. Pickering, 1889) and has a period of 20.5 days; Mizar B has a period of 361 days. All the stars in the Mizar system are main-sequence dwarfs. The brighter components are of spectral type A2, while the fainter ones are of A5 or A7. m_v: 2.27; M_v: 0.07; spectral type: A2 V; distance: 23 pc.

MKO *abbrev. for* Mauna Kea Observatory. See MAUNA KEA.

MK system see SPECTRAL TYPES.

M-L relation see MASS-LUMINOSITY RELATION.

MMT 1 the 6.5-meter single-mirror telescope that was converted from the MULTIPLE MIRROR TELESCOPE on Mount Hopkins, Arizona. Its lightweight honeycomb PRIMARY MIRROR of borosilicate glass was cast in 1992. This replaced the six smaller mirrors of the original telescope. In 2001, the MMT was used in the first-ever discovery of a massive black hole in the galactic halo, thousands of parsecs above the plane of the Milky Way.
2 *abbrev. for* Multiple Mirror Telescope.

mock suns *another name for* SUN DOGS.

modified Julian date (MJD) see JULIAN DATE.

modulus of distance see DISTANCE MODULUS.

molecular clouds cool dense regions of interstellar matter within which atoms tend to be combined into molecules. The clouds are composed principally of molecular hydrogen (H_2), with between 300 and 2000 molecules/cm^3. There is also a small admixture of COSMIC DUST comprising about 1% of the mass, with gas temperatures between 10 and 20 K. Hydrogen molecules do not usually emit at radio and infrared wavelengths, and molecular clouds were discovered only in the mid-1970s in surveys of radio emission from CARBON MONOXIDE, CO, which is 10 000 times less common than hydrogen molecules in the clouds. The 2.6- and 1.33-mm CO lines are still the prime means of mapping and investigating the clouds. A wide variety of molecules, in addition to H_2 and CO, have been found in the clouds (see MOLECULAR-LINE RADIO ASTRONOMY); more than 80 types have been detected in the largest clouds, such as SAGITTARIUS B2.

Several DENSE CORE regions, with about 10^5 hydrogen molecules/cm^3 and mass about 10^2 to 10^3 solar masses, may be found within one molecular cloud. In GIANT MOLECULAR CLOUDS, these dense cores contain INFRARED SOURCES, H II REGIONS, MASER SOURCES, and the peak CO temperatures, which suggest that these regions are sites of massive STAR FORMATION. There are also smaller clouds, containing about 500 solar masses of molecular hydrogen, throughout which low-mass stars are forming and which may be relatively isolated, as in the Taurus–Auriga star-forming region.

molecular-line radio astronomy the study of celestial regions containing molecules by means of the radio emissions from the molecules themselves; unlike optical emissions, radio emissions are not obscured by material in the interstellar medium. A RADIO TELESCOPE using a LINE RECEIVER is best suited to the purpose. Many different molecules have now been detected in the Galaxy in MOLECULAR CLOUDS. The first interstellar molecules – CH, CH^+, and CN – were detected optically in the late 1930s. This list has been greatly extended by radio astronomy measurements (see table). Most of the molecules are organic, i.e. based on carbon, but some inorganic species, such as silicon oxide (SiO), have also been detected. Many molecules occur in different isotopic forms, e.g. with deuterium rather than hydrogen.

The radio emissions usually come from

Molecular-line Radio Astronomy
(Some observed interstellar molecules)

H_2	H^3+	NH_3	C_7
OH	H_2O	H_2CO	CH_3NH_2
CH	H_2S	H_2CS	CH_3CHO
CH^+	HCO	H_2C_2	CH_3C_2H
CN	HCO^+	HNCO	CH_2CHCN
CO	HCN	HNCS	HC_5N
CS	HNO	C_3N	
CS^+	HN_2^+		$HCOOCH_3$
C_2	HC_2	C_5	CH_3C_2CH
NO	SO_2	CH_4	
NS	OCS	CH_2NH	C_9
SO		CH_2CO	CH_3OCH_3
SiO		NH_2CN	CH_3CH_2OH
SiS		HCOOH	CH_3CH_2CN
		HC_3N	HC_7N
		HC_4	
			HC_9N
		CH_3OH	
		CH_3CN	$HC_{11}N$
		NH_2CHO	

transitions between different rotational states of the molecule and have wavelengths normally in the submillimeter and millimeter range, i.e. they lie in the gigahertz region of the radio spectrum. Some clouds of molecules appear to emit by maser action (see MASER SOURCE); for example, the OH line at 1.665 gigahertz in some radio sources is observed to be very narrow and highly polarized: characteristic features of a maser. Molecular-line radio astronomy is especially useful in determining cosmic isotope ratios.

Molonglo Radio Observatory an observatory at Hoskinstown, New South Wales, Australia, run by the University of Sydney. The main instrument is a MILLS CROSS ANTENNA, operational since 1966 although now modified for use as an APERTURE SYNTHESIS instrument (the *Molonglo Observatory Synthesis Telescope, MOST*) by abandoning the N–S arm and phasing the E–W arm. The arms are about 1.6 km long and consist of a series of 12-meter-wide cylindrical parabolic reflectors. MOST operates at 843 megahertz.

moment of inertia symbol: *I*. A property of any rotating body by which it resists any attempt to make it stop or change speed. If the body is rotating with angular velocity ω, the kinetic energy of the body is $\frac{1}{2}I\omega^2$ and its angular momentum is $I\omega$.

momentum 1 (**linear momentum**) symbol: p. A property of a body moving in a straight line. It is equal in magnitude to the product of the mass and velocity of the body. It is a vector quantity, mv, having the same direction as the velocity. See also CONSERVATION OF MOMENTUM; NEWTON'S LAWS OF MOTION.
2 see ANGULAR MOMENTUM.

Monoceros (**Unicorn**) an inconspicuous equatorial constellation near Orion, lying in the Milky Way, the brightest stars being of 3rd and 4th magnitude. It contains the triple star Beta (β) Monocerotis and the double Epsilon (ε) and several variables including R Monocerotis, a young stellar object that lights up HUBBLE'S VARIABLE NEBULA. There are many open clusters, including NGC 2244, surrounded by the ROSETTE NEBULA, and NGC 2264, which includes the multiple star S Mon and in whose surrounding nebulosity lies the dark *Cone nebula*. The object A0620-00 is a possible BLACK HOLE. Abbrev.: Mon; genitive form: Monocerotis; approx. position: RA 7h, dec 0°; area: 482 sq deg.

monochromatic of or producing a single wavelength or very narrow band of wavelengths.

monochromator an instrument in which one narrow band of wavelengths is isolated from a beam of light or other radiation. This is usually achieved by means of a narrow-band interference filter, or by a diffraction grating or prism, together with an exit slit through which the desired waveband may pass. Changes in the intensity of the monochromatic beam can then be investigated.

monolithic see PRIMARY MIRROR.

monopole a single unit of magnetic charge that is extremely massive and thought only to have been produced at the PLANCK TIME. Because there are none observed in the present Universe, few can have survived the inflationary era. See INFLATIONARY UNIVERSE.

mons (plural: **montes**) mountain. The word is used in the approved name of such a surface feature on a planet or satellite.

Month

Month	*Reference point*	*Length (days)*
tropical	equinox to equinox	27.321 58
sidereal	fixed star to fixed star	27.321 66
anomalistic	apse to apse	27.554 55
draconic	node to node	27.212 22
synodic	new moon to new moon	29.530 59

month the period of the Moon's revolution around the Earth with reference to some specified point in the sky (see table). The differences in the monthly periods result from the complicated motion of the moon.

Moon the only natural satellite of the Earth,

visible by virtue of reflected sunlight. It has a diameter of 3476 km, lies at a mean distance from the Earth of 384 400 km, and completes one orbit around the Earth in 27.322 days (see MONTH; SIDEREAL MONTH). Its mass in relation to that of the Earth is 1 : 81.3, i.e. 0.0123. It is in SYNCHRONOUS ROTATION, i.e. it keeps the same face – the NEARSIDE – toward the Earth, although more than 50% of the Moon's surface can be seen as a result of LIBRATION. The same face is not however always turned toward the Sun, the length of the solar day on the Moon being equal to the Moon's SYNODIC PERIOD, i.e. 29.530 59 days. During this period – the SYNODIC MONTH – the Moon exhibits a cycle of PHASES, reaching an apparent magnitude of –12.7 at full Moon. It can also undergo ECLIPSES and produce OCCULTATIONS.

The Moon's mean orbital velocity is 10 km s^{-1}. Its orbital motion is however subject to SECULAR ACCELERATION and periodic INEQUALITIES due to the gravitational attraction of the Sun, Earth, and other planets (see also ANNUAL EQUATION; EVECTION; PARALLACTIC INEQUALITY; VARIATION). In addition its PERIGEE and NODES move eastward and westward with periods of 8.85 years and 18.61 years, respectively: this results in different lengths for the sidereal, ANOMALISTIC, and DRACONIC MONTHS. Physical and orbital characteristics are given in the table.

Although Earth-based observations have revealed much lunar information, the Moon has now been carefully photographed, measured, and sampled by the APOLLO spacecraft and by RANGER, LUNAR ORBITER, SURVEYOR, LUNA, and ZOND spacecraft. It has an extremely tenuous atmosphere: a collisionless gas in which helium, neon, argon, and radon were detected by Apollo instruments. This near lack of atmosphere, together with the absence of an appreciable global magnetic field, exposes the REGOLITH to extremes of temperature (–180 °C to +110 °C) and to the SOLAR WIND, COSMIC RAYS, METEORITES, and MICROMETEORITES. Satellite magnetometer surveys and detailed analysis of lunar rocks have revealed that the Moon's magnetic field was originally considerably stronger and might have been generated internally by a fluid core rather than produced by some external means.

The Moon's interior structure is investigated from seismograms of MOONQUAKES and meteoritic and artificial impacts. The temperature of the central core may reach 1500 °C but a metallic iron composition is precluded by the Moon's moment of inertia. The Moon's CENTER OF MASS is displaced toward Earth by 2.5 km because of a thick farside crust.

The Moon was formed out of refractory (high melting point) materials about 4600 million years ago. Its outer layers were melted and differentiated to produce mafic cumulates (iron magnesium silicates) and a feldspathic crust (calcium aluminum silicates), below which radioactive elements were concentrated. The first 750 million years of lunar history constituted a period of intense bombardment, culminating in a cataclysm during which the BASINS and larger HIGHLAND craters were formed. The eruption of radioactive basalts (KREEP), or their excavation during formation of the Imbrium Basin, resulted in a concentration of natural radioactivity in the western hemisphere, as measured by gamma-ray spectrometers. A zone of melting then moved inward toward the Moon's center to generate a sequence of basaltic lavas that produced the MARIA. Since then the Moon has been relatively quiescent.

The origin of the Moon is still debatable. Similarities in composition indicate that the Earth and Moon are related and argue against *capture theories*, which propose formation elsewhere and subsequent capture by the Earth's gravitational field. Differences in composition, including the Moon's relative enrichment in refractory material and its depletion in iron and volatile material, including water, eliminate any direct formation from the Earth by fission. The *giant impact hypothesis* (or *big splash*) now seems more likely. This proposes that the glancing high-speed collision of a huge, possibly Mars-sized body with the primitive Earth smashed what crust the Earth had, melting rock to a great depth. A spray of molten rock from impactor and Earth (mantle rather than

Moon
(physical and orbital characteristics)

mass		7.35×10^{22} kg
diameter		3476 km
mean density		3.34 g cm^{-3}
surface gravity (Earth = 1)		0.1653
mean albedo		0.07
mean visual opposition magnitude		−12.7
interior structure:	crust	~60 km
	mantle	~1100 km
	core radius	~600 km
approximate age		4600 million years
mean horizontal parallax		3422″.46
moment of inertia		0.395 ± 0.005
mean distance		384 400 km
	maximum	405 500 km
	minimum	363 300 km
mean orbital velocity		10.1 km s^{-1}
escape velocity		2.38 km s^{-1}
mean eccentricity		0.0549
inclination of orbital plane to ecliptic		5°8′431″
inclination of equator to ecliptic		1°32′1″
sidereal month		27.321 66 days
anomalistic month		27.554 55 days
draconic month		27.212 22 days
synodic month		29.530 59 days

iron-rich core material) was ejected and condensed to form a ring of orbiting debris, and the Moon coalesced from this.

See also MOON ROCKS; MOON, SURFACE FEATURES.

Moon, surface features the surface of the Moon is characterized by light-colored HIGHLANDS interspersed with much lower ALBEDO (i.e. darker) and less rugged MARIA. The oldest and largest features on the Moon are the vast impact BASINS. These grade into large CRATERS, with which highland areas are saturated. There is no evidence for plate tectonics on the Moon but FAULTS, RILLES, WRINKLE and LOBATE RIDGES, DOMES, GHOST CRATERS, and volcanic plateaus are the expressions of past tectonic and igneous activity. Impact features include RAYS, DARK HALO CRATERS, SECONDARY CRATERS (including CRATER CLUSTERS and CRATER CHAINS), and textured EJECTA BLANKETS. See also MOUNTAINS, LUNAR.

moonquakes localized disturbances inside the Moon, detected by the APOLLO seismic network. Rare but strong moonquakes occur 50–300 km below the surface, although they are much less intense than earthquakes by a factor of about 1000. Weaker but more numerous moonquakes occur at depths of 800–1000 km and are triggered at PERIGEE by lunar TIDES. Seismic signals on the Moon are extended by scattering in the dry and porous lunar crust. Deep moonquakes provide information, through their arrival times, of the structure of the lunar interior: a 60 km crust on average, a mantle extending to a depth of 1100 km or more, and a central partly molten core roughly 500–600 km in radius.

Moon rocks (lunar rocks) samples of the Moon returned by APOLLO and LUNA spacecraft. Lunar soils, or fines, consist of glasses, aggregates, and meteorite debris in addition to recognizable fragments of larger rock types. Hand specimens include mare basalts (low titanium content from the western MARIA, high titanium content from the eastern maria, and aluminous basalts from Mare Fecunditatis), non-mare basalt (also known as *KREEP* because of its high content of potassium (symbol K), rare earth elements, and phosphorus (symbol P)), and anorthositic rocks from the HIGHLANDS. Rare lunar-rock types include granite, ultramafic green glass, pyroxenite, norite, troctolite, and dunite. Most highland rocks have been impact metamorphosed (to produce cataclastic, recrystallized, and impact melt textures), but cumulates are also observed and these date back to the formation of the first lunar crust.

Lunar rocks are depleted in volatile and siderophile elements. Strong correlations exist between elements that are geochemically similar to one another (e.g. iron and manganese) or that are both excluded by major minerals (e.g. potassium and lanthanum). The major lunar minerals are calcic plagioclase, clino- and ortho-pyroxene, olivine, and ilmenite. Minor phases include spinels, K-feldspar, troilite, metallic iron, quartz, tridymite, cristobalite, apatite, and whitlockite. Uniquely lunar minerals include armalcolite, tranquillityite, and pyroxferroite. No hydrated phases, highly oxidized minerals, diamonds, or mineralization have yet been found.

Moreton wave see FLARES.

Morgan–Keenan (MK) system see SPECTRAL TYPES.

Morgan's classification a classification scheme for galaxies, devised by W.W. Morgan, in which galaxies are grouped according to the composite spectra of their component stars and also by their form, i.e. spiral, barred spiral, elliptical, irregular, etc., by their degree of concentration, and by their orientation, which varies from face-on to edge-on.

morning star an informal name for VENUS when it lies west of the Sun and is a brilliant object in the eastern sky just before sunrise. Such periods of visibility follow inferior CONJUNCTION and precede superior conjunction. The term is sometimes applied loosely to morning visibility of Mercury or other planets.

mosaic mirror see PRIMARY MIRROR.

MOST *abbrev. for* Molonglo Observatory Synthesis Telescope. See MOLONGLO RADIO OBSERVATORY.

mountains, lunar raised regions on the Moon, most of which consist of crustal blocks uplifted to define the multiple ring structures of impact BASINS; these survive either as *ring mountains*, such as the Apennines, or as isolated peaks, such as La Hire (see table). In comparison the lunar HIGHLANDS are topographically higher than the MARIA but are characterized more by the elevated rims of craters and the rolling hills of basin EJECTA BLANKETS. Discrete mountains not associated with impact basins include the central peaks of CRATERS, such as Tsiolkovsky, and volcanic domes and plateaus. Despite their jagged appearance, few mountains have slopes that exceed 12°.

Mount Hopkins Observatory see FRED L. WHIPPLE OBSERVATORY.

mounting the structure that supports an astronomical telescope, designed so that the telescope may be pointed at almost every part of the heavens, preferably without forcing an observer into awkward positions. All telescope mountings must therefore be constructed so that the tube can turn about two axes at right angles. There are two main types: the EQUATORIAL MOUNTING, with one axis parallel to the Earth's axis, and the ALTAZIMUTH MOUNTING, with one axis vertical. Since high magnifications exaggerate any movement, the support must be rigid. In addition, because the Earth is turning through 0.25° per minute, means must be provided to move the telescope smoothly in the opposite direction; this counterbalances the diurnal motion of a star and keeps it in the field of view.

Mount Stromlo and Siding Spring Observatories optical observatories that are owned and run by the Australian

Lunar Mountains

Lunar mountains	*Location*
Alps	N Imbrium, part of second ring
Altai	SW Nectaris, part of third ring
Apennines	SE Imbrium, part of third ring
Apollonius	S Crisium, part of third ring
Aristarchus Plateau	Procellarum, volcanic province
Carpathians	S Imbrium, part of third ring
Caucasus	W Imbrium, part of third ring
Cordillera	Orientale Basin, third ring
Haemus	S Serenitatis, part of second ring
Harbinger	SW Imbrium, part of third ring
La Hire	Imbrium, isolated peak, part of first ring
Marius Hills	Procellarum, volcanic province
Piton	Imbrium, isolated peak
Pyrenees	W Nectaris, part of first ring
Riphaeus	W Cognitum
Rook	Orientale Basin, second ring
Rümker Hills	Sinus Roris, volcanic province
Spitzbergen	N Imbrium, part of first ring
Straight	N Imbrium, part of first ring
Taurus	E Serenitatis, part of second ring
Tenerife	N Imbrium, part of first ring

National University, Canberra, and located on Mount Stromlo near Canberra, altitude 770 meters, and on Siding Spring Mountain, altitude 1150 meters, in the Warrumbungle range, New South Wales. The main instrument on Mount Stromlo is a 1.9-meter reflector acquired in 1953. At Siding Spring, where the SEEING is much better, there is a 2.3-meter altazimuth reflector, operational since 1984, and some smaller reflectors. The ANGLO–AUSTRALIAN TELESCOPE and the UK SCHMIDT TELESCOPE are also located at Siding Spring.

Mount Wilson Observatory an observatory located on Mount Wilson near Pasadena, California, at an altitude of 1740 meters; the SEEING is often better than 1 arcsecond. It was founded in 1904 by George Ellery Hale. Until 1985 it was operated by the Carnegie Institution, and is now managed by the Mount Wilson Institute. The first major instrument was a 60-inch (1.5-meter) reflector, completed in 1908, which was followed by a 100-inch (2.5-meter) reflector. The 100-inch, named the *Hooker telescope* after its benefactor, began operation in 1917 as the world's largest telescope. Its great success led Hale to consider an even larger telescope, eventually sited at PALOMAR OBSERVATORY. The Hooker underwent renovation from 1985 to 1993. Mount Wilson is also the site of two SOLAR TELESCOPES and the CENTER FOR HIGH ANGULAR RESOLUTION ASTRONOMY, which operates the six optical telescopes of the CHARA interferometric array.

moving cluster an OPEN CLUSTER, such as the HYADES or the URSA MAJOR cluster, for which a distance can be derived from the individual radial velocities and proper motions of the member stars. The method is often termed *moving-cluster* (or *expanding-cluster*) *parallax*. The stars in a cluster share a common space motion and, if the system is sufficiently close to Earth, their paths will appear to diverge from or converge towards a point in space (point P in the illustration overleaf). The direction of P is parallel to the space motion of the cluster.

Considering each star in turn (illustration B overleaf):

$$v_r = v \cos \alpha$$
$$v_t = v \sin \alpha = 4.74\mu/p$$

where v, v_r, v_t are respectively the space, radial, and tangential velocities of the star in km/s, μ is the proper motion in arc seconds per year, and p is the PARALLAX in arc seconds. Determination of α, μ, and v_r for each star gives a value for the parallax of the system.

moving-cluster parallax see MOVING CLUSTER.

Mpc *symbol for* megaparsec, i.e. 10^6 parsecs.

MPIR (MPIfR) *abbrev. for* Max Planck Institute for Radio Astronomy. See EFFELSBERG TELESCOPE.

MRAO *abbrev. for* Mullard Radio Astronomy Observatory.

MS stars see S STARS.

M stars stars of SPECTRAL TYPE M, cool red stars with a surface temperature (T_{eff}) of about 2400 to 3480 kelvin. There is a greater abundance of oxygen to carbon in their surface layers (compare CARBON STARS), and the excess oxygen is available for the formation of molecular oxides. The spectra are characterized by broad absorption bands of titanium and vanadium oxides (TiO, VO). Lines of neutral metals are also present. Some show emission lines too, and are classed as ME STARS. Antares and Betelgeuse are M stars. See also S STARS.

MSX *abbrev. for* Midcourse Space Experiment.

M-type asteroids a class of ASTEROIDS that is fairly common in the main belt, having featureless spectra that are distinguished by high albedo. Their surfaces have a metallic composition (nickel and iron) plus a

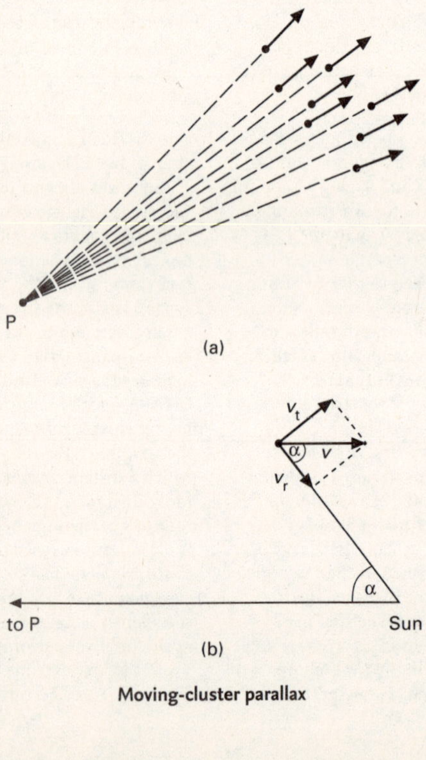

Moving-cluster parallax

varying amount of silicates. (16) Psyche, 250 km in diameter, is the largest of the M-Type asteroids.

mu (μ) **1** the 12th letter of the Greek alphabet, used in STELLAR NOMENCLATURE usually to designate the 12th-brightest star in a constellation or sometimes to indicate a star's position in a group.
2 *symbol for* proper motion.

Mullard Radio Astronomy Observatory (**MRAO**) the radio observatory of the Cavendish Laboratory, University of Cambridge, situated at Lord's Bridge, near Cambridge, UK. The main instruments at the site are antenna arrays: the RYLE TELESCOPE consists of eight 13-meter dishes and is used primarily for MICROWAVE BACKGROUND observations; the *Cambridge Low Frequency Synthesis Telescope* (*CLFST*), constructed in 1980 to survey the northern sky at 151 and 38 MHz, is carrying out the seventh and eighth Cambridge deep-sky radio surveys (7C, 8C); and the *Cambridge Optical Aperture Synthesis Telescope* (*COAST*) is an optical INTERFEROMETER working on radio APERTURE SYNTHESIS principles. The 3.6 Hectare Array, with which PULSARS were first discovered in 1967, took part in the Second Cambridge Pulsar Survey (completed 1998), a survey of the northern sky at the low frequency of 81.5 MHz, which detected 20 pulsars, all previously known. The COSMIC ANISOTROPY TELESCOPE (CAT) was built in 1993 to measure structure in the microwave background and was turned off and partially dismantled in 2000 after publishing two sets of results. MRAO is also the site of a major element of MERLIN.

multilayers see COATING OF LENSES; INTERFERENCE FILTER; MIRROR.

Multiple Mirror Telescope (**MMT**) a reflecting telescope of novel design, sited at the FRED L. WHIPPLE OBSERVATORY, on Mount Hopkins, near Tucson, Arizona at an altitude of 2600 meters. It was fully operational in 1980. The telescope, a joint project of the Smithsonian Institution and the University of Arizona, was in 1998 converted to a single-mirror instrument of diameter 6.5 meters (see MMT).

The original telescope was equivalent in light-gathering power to a single 4.5-meter mirror. It comprised six identical mirrors, 1.8 meters in diameter, arranged symmetrically about a central axis on an ALTAZIMUTH MOUNTING. A complex alignment and electronic guidance system brought all six images to a common focus, with one focus for optical work and another for infrared. The system was housed in a building that co-rotated on a rail with the telescope.

multiple star a group of two or more stars, such as Epsilon Lyrae, that are held together by their mutual gravitational attraction. Orbital motions within multiple systems are complex. For instance, systems containing two or more close binaries in orbit about each other appear to be quite common. See also BINARY STAR.

multiverse a speculative concept that the Universe we inhabit is not unique but is merely one of a very large number of Universes, which can have completely different physical laws and possibly even a different number of space–time dimensions. The multiverse concept emerged in the last few years of the 20th century due to the combination of the observation that 'fine tuning' of the basic physical laws is necessary for life to exist in the Universe and the realization that the collapse of stars to black holes and the emergence of 'baby Universes' sprouting into existence in inflation theory may allow other Universes to come into existence. There is no experimental or observational support for the multiverse concept.

muon symbol: μ. An ELEMENTARY PARTICLE (a lepton) with the same charge and SPIN as an ELECTRON but with a mass that is 207 times greater. It decays into electrons and neutrinos with a lifetime of two microseconds. COSMIC-RAY showers detected on Earth are comprised mainly of muons produced by PION decay. Muons do not interact strongly with matter and hence a large proportion of them reach the Earth's surface. The ANTIPARTICLE of the muon is the antimuon.

mural quadrant see QUADRANT.

Musca (**Fly**) a small constellation in the southern hemisphere near Crux, lying in the Milky Way, the brightest stars being of 2nd and 3rd magnitude. It contains the 7th-magnitude globular clusters NGC 4833 and NGC 4372. Abbrev.: Mus; genitive form: Muscae; approx. position: RA 13h, dec –70°; area: 138 sq deg.

MUSES–A (**Hiten**) a Japanese lunar probe launched in Jan. 1990 into an elongated 15-day Earth orbit. In Mar. 1990 it passed close to the Moon, and the small (30-cm) lunar probe swung into a lunar orbit using the Moon's gravity. The small lunar probe crashed onto the Moon in Apr. 1993.

MUSES–C (**Hayabusa**) a joint space mission by Japan and the USA to take samples from a small near-Earth asteroid (NEA) and return them to the Earth. It was launched on May 8 2003, more than a year behind schedule and with a change of target from the original (4660) Nereus to asteroid 1998SF36 (which was given the Japanese name Itokawa). After launch, MUSES-C was renamed Hayabusa (meaning 'Falcon'). The craft was scheduled to enter orbit around the asteroid in 2005 and was to investigate it using visible and infrared imaging. It was also set to fire three 'bullets' into the asteroid's surface and attempt to capture the particles of material ejected by the impacts. MUSES-C will return to Earth by 2007 and drop off the samples in a capsule attached to a parachute.

Nn

nadir the point on the CELESTIAL SPHERE that lies directly beneath an observer and is therefore unobservable. It is diametrically opposite the observer's ZENITH and with the zenith lies on the observer's MERIDIAN.

Nagler eyepiece see EYEPIECE.

Naiad a small satellite of Neptune, discovered in 1989. See Table 2, Appendix.

naked-eye object a star, etc., that can be seen without the aid of a telescope (under ideal viewing conditions).

naked singularity see SINGULARITY.

Nançay Radio Observatory a field station of the Paris Observatory located 200 km south of Paris and operated since 1953. It contains the *Decimetric Radio Telescope*, a transit instrument with a collecting area of 200 × 35 meters that can observe at 1.42, 1.66, and 3.2 GHz and has been used for VLBI since 1984, a 3.2 × 1.2 km T-shaped RADIO HELIOGRAPH used for fast solar imaging, and the *Decametric Array*, 100 × 10 meters in area, used at 15 to 100 MHz for planetary and solar observations.

nano- symbol: n. A prefix to a unit, indicating a fraction of 10^{-9} of that unit. For example, one nanometer (symbol: nm) is 10^{-9} meters.

Naos see PUPPIS.

narrow-band photometry see PHOTOMETRY.

NASA *abbrev. for* National Aeronautics and Space Administration. The US civilian government agency that is responsible for all nonmilitary aspects of the US space program. It was formed in Oct. 1958, largely in response to the Soviet Union's launch of Sputnik 1 in the previous year, and was given the task of researching and developing the equipment and activities involved in space exploration. NASA's headquarters are in Washington, DC, and it operates several field centers and other facilities. Chief among these are the JET PROPULSION LABORATORY, AMES RESEARCH CENTER, GODDARD SPACE FLIGHT CENTER, KENNEDY SPACE CENTER, JOHNSON SPACE CENTER, and the DEEP SPACE NETWORK. Other facilities include the Langley Research Center (Hampton, Virginia), the Marshall Space Flight Center (Huntsville, Alabama), and the John C. Stennis Space Center (near Starkville, Mississippi). NASA's current organizational structure is headed by an Administrator and Deputy Administrator, to whom the agency's other departments are responsible. These departments consist of four Mission Directorates: Aeronautics Research (concerned with the research and development of technologies for safe, reliable, and efficient aviation systems); Exploration Systems (concerned with developing the research and technology needed to enable sustainable and affordable human and robotic exploration of space); Space Operations (which directs all the agency's space launches, spaceflight operations and space communications); and Science (which is responsible for organizing and carrying out the scientific exploration of the Earth, the Solar System and beyond and reaping the rewards of Earth and space exploration for society). NASA's space activities currently fall into a series of long-term programs; for example, its Discovery program seeks to unlock the mysteries of the Solar System by means of low-cost exploration missions, while the Origins program focuses on observations of the earliest stars and galaxies, the search for planets around other stars, and the search for life elsewhere in the universe. NASA collaborates on projects with the EUROPEAN SPACE AGENCY (ESA) and with individual countries. One major focus of its international efforts is the INTERNATIONAL SPACE STATION. NASA funds and maintains the ASTROPHYSICS DATA SYSTEM and offers a satellite launcher service to other countries. See also SPACE SHUTTLE.

NASDA *abbrev. for* National Space Development Agency. The larger of Japan's two space agencies, established in 1969 and modeled on NASA. It is responsible for all space developments, especially for developing the technology to exploit space. Its launch site is on Tanegashima, a subtropical island (30°N), its launch vehicles including the *H–I* and its more powerful successor, the *H–II*. See also ISAS.

Nasmyth focus either of two fixed focal points on the altitude axis of a telescope with an ALTAZIMUTH MOUNTING. Light reflected from the secondary mirror of the telescope is diverted sideways by a third mirror mounted at 45° to the altitude axis. The light is brought to a focus at one of the two Nasmyth points on each side of the telescope, chosen by turning the third mirror. Bulky equipment can be mounted on observation platforms to use these foci. The arrangement was devised by James Nasmyth in the 1840s but came to prominence only in the late 20th century.

National Geographic Society-Palomar Observatory Sky Survey see PALOMAR OBSERVATORY SKY SURVEY.

National Optical Astronomy Observatory (NOAO) a US organization bringing under one administration the national facilities for optical astronomy at KITT PEAK NATIONAL OBSERVATORY, Arizona; CERRO TOLOLO INTER–AMERICAN OBSERVATORY, Chile; and SACRAMENTO PEAK OBSERVATORY, New Mexico. The NATIONAL SOLAR OBSERVATORY, formerly run by the NOAO, now has its own director. Founded in 1982, the NOAO was set up to consolidate all the groundbased optical astronomy observatories under the control of the US Association of Universities for Research in Astronomy (AURA), a consortium of US universities under contract to the National Science Foundation. The headquarters of the NOAO are in Tucson, Arizona. The NOAO also represents the US astronomical community in the International Gemini Project through its NOAO Gemini Science Center at Tucson (see GEMINI TELESCOPES).

National Radio Astronomy Observatory (NRAO) the US radio observatory administered from Charlottesville, Virginia, with various field stations. It is managed by a private consortium of universities in a cooperative agreement with the US government's National Science Foundation. Their principal instruments are the GREEN BANK Telescope, the VLA, the VLBA, and a millimeter-wavelength radio telescope at KITT PEAK, Arizona.

National Solar Observatory (NSO) the US solar observation facilities consisting of the solar telescopes of KITT PEAK NATIONAL OBSERVATORY, Arizona and SACRAMENTO PEAK OBSERVATORY, New Mexico. Formerly part of the US NATIONAL OPTICAL ASTRONOMY OBSERVATORY, it is currently headed by its own director and managed by the Association of Universities for Research in Astronomy (AURA).

National Space Development Agency see NASDA.

nautical twilight see TWILIGHT.

n-body problem any problem in celestial mechanics that involves the determination of the trajectories of *n* point masses whose only interaction is gravitational attraction. The bodies in the Solar System are an example if it is assumed that the masses of the planets, etc., are concentrated at their CENTERS OF MASS. A general solution exists for the TWO-BODY PROBLEM and in special cases a solution can be found for the THREE-BODY PROBLEM. The complete solution for a larger number is normally considered impossible.

NEAP *abbrev. for* Near-Earth Asteroid Prospector. A NASA mission to (4660) Nereus planned for launch between 2007 and 2010.

neap tide see TIDES.

NEAR *abbrev. for* Near-Earth Asteroid Rendezvous. A NASA mission launched in Feb. 1996. It was the first mission in NASA's

Discovery program, the series of projects dedicated to exploring the Solar System. In June 1997 NEAR encountered the asteroid (253) Mathilde before heading for its chief target, (433) Eros. The probe went into orbit around Eros in Feb. 2000, beginning a year-long intensive investigation of the tiny world, the first such examination ever undertaken. In March 2000, NASA decided to rename the probe *NEAR-Shoemaker*, to commemorate the comet expert Eugene Shoemaker, who had died in 1997. In a series of maneuvers, project scientists brought NEAR-Shoemaker ever closer to Eros and eventually made a surprise last-minute decision to land it. Thus NEAR–Shoemaker became the first human-built object to land on an asteroid. The landing took place Feb. 12 2001. The probe continued to function after landing and transmitted data back to the Earth, including stunning close-up images of the asteroid's surface, for another 16 days.

near-Earth asteroid (**NEA**) any asteroid that has a chance of hitting our planet, specifically any member of the APOLLO, AMOR, and ATEN GROUPS. Although the annual probability of the Earth being struck by a large asteroid or comet is extremely small, the consequences of such a collision are so catastrophic that it was thought prudent in the USA to assess the nature of the threat and to be prepared to deal with it.

nearest stars the stars nearest to the Sun are either comparable in luminosity to or fainter than the Sun. Most are less massive than the Sun and a large proportion belong to binary or triple star systems. See Table 7, Appendix.

near-infrared see INFRARED RADIATION.

NEAR-Shoemaker see NEAR.

nearside the hemisphere of the Moon that is permanently turned toward the Earth because of the tidal synchronization of the LUNAR DAY and the SIDEREAL MONTH. The lunar LIBRATIONS allow the terrestrial observer also to see 9% of the *farside*, the hemisphere that is permanently turned away from the Earth. The farside was first photographed by the Soviet LUNA 3 in 1959; it has no major MARIA.

near-ultraviolet see ULTRAVIOLET RADIATION.

nebula a cloud of interstellar gas and dust that can be observed either as a luminous patch of light – a bright nebula – or as a dark hole or band against a brighter background – a dark nebula. Interstellar clouds cannot usually be detected optically but various processes can cause them to become visible.

With EMISSION NEBULAE, ultraviolet radiation, generally coming from nearby or embedded hot stars, ionizes the interstellar gas atoms and light is emitted by the atoms as they interact with the free electrons in the nebula. Emission nebulae can be in the form of H II (ionized hydrogen) REGIONS, PLANETARY NEBULAE, or SUPERNOVA REMNANTS. With REFLECTION NEBULAE light from a nearby star or stellar group is scattered (irregularly reflected) by the dust grains in the cloud. Reflection and emission nebulae are bright nebulae. In contrast DARK NEBULAE are detected by what they obscure: the light from stars and other objects lying behind the cloud along our line of sight is significantly decreased or totally obscured by INTERSTELLAR EXTINCTION. Dark nebulae contain approximately the same mixture of gas and dust as bright nebulae but there are no nearby stars to illuminate them. If the COLUMN DENSITY is sufficiently high, the majority of the hydrogen is likely to be present in molecular form (see MOLECULAR CLOUDS).

The term 'nebula' was originally applied to any object that appeared fuzzy and extended in a telescope: over 100 were listed in the 18th-century MESSIER CATALOG. The majority of these objects were later identified as GALAXIES and star CLUSTERS.

nebular hypothesis a theory for the origin of the Solar System put forward by the French mathematician Pierre-Simon de Laplace in 1796 and similar to a suggestion of the philosopher Immanuel Kant in 1755. It was proposed that the Solar System formed from a great rotating cloud, or nebula, of material (gas and dust) collapsing under its own gravitational attraction. An interaction of forces caused the cloud to form a rotating flattened disk, called the *solar nebula*. To conserve ANGULAR MOMENTUM, the disk rotated more rapidly as the contraction progressed. Laplace suggested that rings of material became detached from the spinning disk when the velocity at its edge exceeded a critical value, and that the material in these rings later coalesced to form the planets. The central product of the contraction is the Sun, while the planetary satellites may have formed from further rings shed by the condensing planets.

The hypothesis, popular throughout the 19th century, went out of favor. The main problem was that it indicated that the Sun should still be spinning on the verge of rotational instability; it could not explain why the Sun has almost 99.9% of the mass of the Solar System but only about 2% of the total angular momentum. In addition, calculations showed that the rings would not condense to form planets. However, in a modified form, it is the basis of most modern ideas for the formation of the Sun and planets. See SOLAR SYSTEM, ORIGIN. Compare ENCOUNTER THEORIES.

Nectarian System one of the stratigraphic systems of the Moon, defined by the deposits of the NECTARIS BASIN and covering the period from 3.92 to 3.85 billion (10^9) years ago. It includes nearly four times as many large craters as the Imbrium Basin, and possibly some volcanic deposits. The *Pre-Nectarian System* is the oldest lunar stratigraphic system, covering the period from the Moon's origin and formation of the lunar crust to the Nectaris impact, i.e. 4.6 to 3.32 billion years ago. It includes crater and basin deposits from this period. See also COPERNICAN SYSTEM; IMBRIAN SYSTEM.

Nectaris Basin a large multiringed BASIN on the southeastern nearside of the Moon. It was formed about 3.9 billion years ago, and was later flooded with lava to produce *Mare Nectaris* (*Sea of Nectar*). See also NECTARIAN SYSTEM.

Neptune the eighth planet of the Solar System, orbiting the Sun every 164.79 years at an almost constant distance of 30.06 AU. It is the most distant GIANT PLANET. It has a diameter of 50 538 km, a mass of 17.2 Earth-masses, and a density of 1.76 times that of water. Neptune has 13 known satellites; TRITON and NEREID were detected from Earth and the rest were discovered as a result of the VOYAGER 2 flyby in Aug. 1989, during which NEPTUNE'S RINGS were also confirmed and photographed. Orbital and physical characteristics are given in Tables 1 and 2, backmatter.

Neptune was discovered in 1846 by Johann Gottfried Galle at the Berlin Observatory on the basis of predictions supplied by the Frenchman Urbain Leverrier, who had analyzed observed perturbations in the motion of Uranus. Similar predictions had been made by the English mathematician John Couch Adams.

The planet returns to OPPOSITION two days later each year, appearing as a magnitude 7.7 object visible in binoculars. When viewed by Earthbound telescopes, Neptune appears as a featureless greenish disk only 2.2 arc seconds across. As with URANUS, Neptune's color arises from the methane within its atmosphere, which is predominantly hydrogen and helium with a mixture of methane, water, and ammonia.

Voyager 2 was able to return excellent information and pictures from Neptune in 1989. The most conspicuous feature seen in Neptune's atmosphere is the GREAT DARK SPOT. There are also whitish cirruslike clouds of methane ice crystals. These clouds are at about 50–70 km above the main cloud deck. Neptune has belts and zones similar to JUPITER, but they are much fainter. The most prominent is a broad darkish band high in southern latitude. Embedded in this band is a smaller dark spot, about half the size of the Great Dark Spot.

Neptune's core is thought to be rocky, primarily iron and silicon; it rotates in about 16 hours. Neptune's atmosphere revolves more slowly. Some cloud features take as long as 18 hours to complete one revolution of the planet. This is contrary to the clouds of the other JOVIAN PLANETS, implying Neptune's atmospheric circulation is retrograde.

Neptune radiates more energy than it receives from the Sun, which implies it has an internal heat source. Temperatures in the upper atmosphere vary from around 60 K at the equator and poles to 50 K at mid-latitudes. The planet has a magnetic field, slightly weaker than the other GIANT PLANETS. It is inclined at 47° to its axis of

Neptune's Rings

Name	*Mean distance from planet center (10³ km)*	*(planetary radii)*	*Radial width (km)*	*Optical depth*
Galle	42–44	1.69	1700	10^{-4}
Le Verrier	53	2.15	15?	0.01–0.02
Plateau	53–59	2.15–2.4	5800	10^{-4}
Adams	63	2.53	<50	0.01–0.1

rotation and orientated opposite to that of the Earth's.

Neptune's rings four dark planetary rings around Neptune, discovered in 1976 during close observation of an occultation of a star by Neptune and confirmed during the VOYAGER 2 flyby in 1989 (see table). The *Adams* and *Le Verrier* rings are quite thin. The Adams ring has several brighter arcs of material, first observed from Earth. Two broad rings, *Galle* and *Plateau*, are diffuse sheets of fine particles. The Plateau has a brighter edge at a distance of about 57 500 km from the planet.

Neptune's satellites see NEPTUNE; Table 2, Appendix.

Nereid a small satellite of Neptune with a highly eccentric 360-day orbit that takes it between 1.3 and 9.6 million km from the planet. It was discovered in 1949 by G.P. Kuiper. Nereid is about 340 km in diameter, Voyager 2's best photographs of it were taken from a distance of nearly 5 million km and show that it has an albedo of about 0.14. See Table 2, Appendix.

network a group of computer systems situated at different locations and interconnected in such a way that they can exchange information by following agreed procedures. The information is transmitted as an encoded signal at high speed over communication lines. See also COMPUTING.

neutralinos the lightest supersymmetric particle. See DARK MATTER.

neutrino symbol: ν. An ELEMENTARY PARTICLE with zero CHARGE and SPIN ½. There are three types of neutrino, ν_e, ν_μ, and ν_τ, which are associated with the ELECTRON, MUON, and massive tau lepton respectively; the latter three particles together with the three neutrinos make up the family of LEPTONS. Neutrinos are thought to have either zero mass or a very small mass. The ANTIPARTICLE of the neutrino is the *antineutrino* ($\bar{\nu}$). Neutrinos have only a weak interaction with matter. See also NEUTRINO ASTRONOMY.

neutrino astronomy the study of NEUTRINOS produced in various processes, including energy-producing nuclear reactions in the centers of stars, reactions occurring during supernova explosions, and cosmic-ray collisions with matter. The detection of neutrinos from SUPERNOVA 1987A confirmed the basic ideas of stellar collapse. Neutrino interaction with other particles of matter is highly improbable, so the great majority escape from their source and travel unhindered through space and any intervening matter. They can thus provide direct information on the processes in which they were created, but their weak interaction with matter makes them difficult to detect.

Solar neutrinos are released by the PROTON–PROTON CHAIN, an energy-producing reaction in the Sun's core. The first experiment to detect solar neutrinos was set up by Raymond Davis in 1967 and is still in progress. It is conducted deep underground in the Homestake Gold Mine near Lead, South Dakota. A large quantity of dry-cleaning fluid is exposed for several months to the flux of solar neutrinos. A very small (but calculable) number of neutrinos react with the chlorine-37 atoms in the fluid to produce radioactive argon-37; the amount produced is a measure of the neutrino flux. The average flux detected is 30±14% of that predicted by the standard solar model.

The flux is measured in *solar neutrino units (SNU)*. One SNU equals one neutrino-induced event per 10^{36} target atoms in a detector. It is calculated from the expected conditions in the solar core and is very temperature dependent. The most widely accepted model predicts a neutrino flux of about 135 SNU. The expected neutrinos in the *Homestake* detector arise from one of the rarer pathways in the proton-proton chain reaction; they are emitted with high energy, mainly during the decay of boron-8. Another experiment designed to detect these high-energy neutrinos has been conducted since 1987 in the Kamioka mine in Japan. The *Kamiokande* detector measures the scattering of neutrinos by electrons in ultrapure water. It has measured 46±18% of the predicted flux.

Most solar neutrinos are produced in the initial step of the proton-proton chain, at energies too low to be detected by the Homestake and Kamiokande experiments; the production rate can, however, be more accurately predicted. Since the early 1990s, two international teams have been using large gallium detectors that are sensitive to the low-energy particles: neutrinos reacting with gallium–71 produce germanium–71 plus electrons. *SAGE* (Soviet–American gallium experiment) is located underground in the Caucasus in Russia. The European–Israeli–American *Gallex* experiment is in the underground Gran Sasso Laboratory near Rome. The Gallex average flux over two series of observations is 87±16 SNU. The first measurements at SAGE found only 20 SNU but a later run measured 85 SNU, and this has produced an overall figure of 58±14 SNU. The Gallex and SAGE measurements thus agree with each other, within the error limits, giving a combined average of about 60% of the predicted flux.

The discrepancy between the observed and predicted flux of solar neutrinos has not yet been explained. It could imply that the conditions in the Sun's interior and/or the nuclear reactions taking place there are not fully appreciated. Alternatively it could be that the characteristics of the neutrino itself are not fully appreciated and that its possible possession of rest mass could provide an explanation.

neutron symbol: n. An ELEMENTARY PARTICLE (a baryon) that is present in the NUCLEUS of all atoms except ordinary hydrogen, ^1H. It has zero CHARGE, SPIN ½, and a REST MASS of 1.6749×10^{-24} grams – slightly greater than that of the PROTON. The absence of charge enables the neutron to penetrate atoms easily since it has a negligible electromagnetic interaction with the constituents of the atom. Unlike free protons, free neutrons are unstable: they BETA DECAY into protons, electrons, plus antineutrinos with a mean life of 914 seconds. The small difference between the neutron and proton mass provides the energy for this decay. The neutron is stable, however, when bound in the nucleus of a nonradioactive atom. The ANTIPARTICLE of the neutron is the *antineutron.* See also ISOTOPES; NEUTRON STAR; NUCLEOSYNTHESIS; QUARK; R-PROCESS; S-PROCESS.

neutron star an extremely dense compact star that has undergone GRAVITATIONAL COLLAPSE to such a degree that most of its material has been compressed into NEUTRONS. Neutron stars were postulated in the 1930s by a number of astronomers including Landau and Zwicky. They are thought to form when the mass of the stellar core remaining after a SUPERNOVA explosion exceeds the CHANDRASEKHAR LIMIT, i.e. about 1.4 solar masses. Such a core is not stable as a WHITE DWARF star since even the pressure of DEGENERATE electrons cannot withstand the strong gravity. Collapse continues until the mean density reaches 10^{17} kg m^{-3} and the protons and electrons coalesce into neutrons, supporting the star against further contraction. Accretion of gas on to an existing white dwarf, raising its mass above the Chandrasekhar limit, may also lead to its collapse to become a neutron star.

With diameters of only 10–15 km, intense magnetic fields (10^8 tesla), and extremely rapid spin, young neutron stars are believed to be responsible for the PULSAR phenomenon. Their strong gravity is also thought to give rise to rapid heating of material observed in some X-RAY BINARY systems. Older pulsars, 'spun up' by accretion are detected as MILLISECOND PULSARS, the fastest rotating neutron stars.

GAMMA-RAY BURSTS probably have neutron star origins.

Models of the structure of neutron stars have been derived from sudden changes in pulsar spin rates – so-called *glitches*. A typical neutron star may have an atmosphere only a few centimeters thick, under which is a crystalline crust about one kilometer in depth. Beneath the crust the material is thought to act like a superfluid of neutrons (having zero viscosity) all the way through to a solid crystalline core.

New General Catalog see NGC.

New Horizons a Proposed NASA mission to explore the Pluto–Charon system and the objects of the Edgworth-Kuiper Belt. A launch date of Jan. 11 2006 would allow such a mission to benefit from a gravity assist from Jupiter in 2010 and arrive at the Pluto–Charon system by 2015. But much depends on whether the tight construction schedule can be kept.

new Moon see PHASES, LUNAR.

New Style (NS) the current method of measuring dates using the GREGORIAN CALENDAR as distinct from the former method – *Old Style* (OS) – that was based on the JULIAN CALENDAR. Britain and the American colonies switched calendars on Sept. 14 1752, the 11 days from Sept. 3 to Sept. 13 having been eliminated from that year.

New Technology Telescope (NTT) the 3.5-meter reflecting telescope of the EUROPEAN SOUTHERN OBSERVATORY in Chile, which began regular operations in 1990. Its major feature is an ACTIVE OPTICS system whereby small corrections can be made continuously to the shape of the PRIMARY MIRROR, which is a fast (f/2.2) lightweight meniscus mirror made of ZERODUR. In addition, it has an ALTAZIMUTH MOUNTING and is housed in an air-conditioned compact rotating building. As a result, it can produce very high resolution images of only 0.33 arcseconds.

newton symbol: N. The SI unit of force, equal to the force that gives a mass of one kilogram an acceleration of one meter per second per second.

Newtonian telescope the first REFLECTING TELESCOPE to be built, developed in about 1670 by Isaac Newton from the ideas of Zucchi and Gregory: Newton turned his attention to reflecting telescopes because he thought (wrongly) that there was no way in which the CHROMATIC ABERRATION of refracting telescopes could be corrected. The Newtonian has a paraboloid PRIMARY MIRROR and a flat *diagonal mirror* that reflects the light into an EYEPIECE mounted on the side of the tube (see illustration). A 45° prism can be used as an alternative to the diagonal mirror. The Newtonian is still

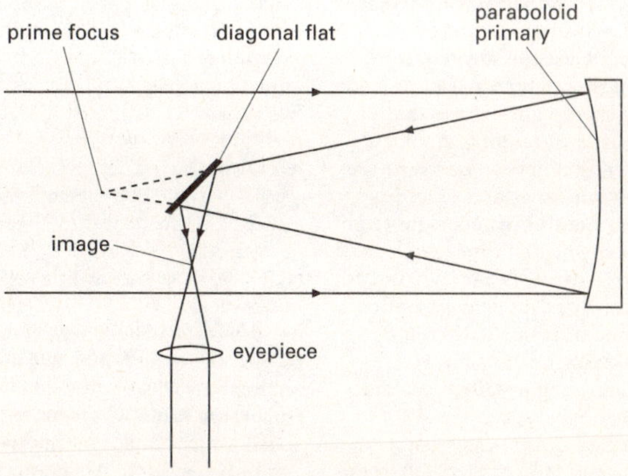

Ray path in Newtonian telescope

the form used by many amateurs, although it is somewhat inconvenient to use in larger form. Newton's original telescope had a mirror only 2.5 cm in diameter and made of SPECULUM METAL; it had a focal length of about 15 cm and magnified some 30 times.

Newton's law of gravitation see GRAVITATION.

Newton's laws of motion the three fundamental laws concerning the motion of bodies that were formulated by Isaac Newton and published together with the law of GRAVITATION in *Principia*, 1687. The laws are

1 Every body continues in a state of rest or of uniform motion in a straight line until that state is changed by the action of a force on the body.

2 The rate of change of linear MOMENTUM is proportional to the applied force, *F*, and occurs in the same direction as that of the force, i.e.

$$F = d(mv)/dt = m(dv/dt) = ma$$

where m is the mass, v the velocity, and a the resulting acceleration of the body.

3 Every action is opposed by a reaction of equal magnitude that acts in the opposite direction to the action.

The first law was conceived by Galileo, who first realized the falsity of the Greek notion that a force is required to maintain a body in motion. Newton's laws of motion and of gravitation are fundamental to CELESTIAL MECHANICS.

Next Generation Space Telescope (NGST) see JAMES WEBB SPACE TELESCOPE.

next-generation telescope any telescope, under development, under construction, or in operation, with design features that make use of the most recent technology. The next-generation optical telescopes are giant reflectors with apertures exceeding 6 meters. Their features include lightweight monolithic or segmented PRIMARY MIRRORS, ACTIVE OPTICS, ADAPTIVE OPTICS, computer control of the telescope, optics, and the attached instrumentation, and REMOTE OPERATION. Certain new technologies are being installed on older existing telescopes.

NGC short for *New General Catalogue of Nebulae and Clusters of Stars*, prepared by the Danish astronomer J.L.E. Dreyer at Armagh Observatory, Ireland, and published in 1888. It was based on an earlier *General Catalogue of Nebulae and Clusters of Stars* (GC),compiled in 1864 by Sir John Herschel from his own observations and previous catalogs by his father and aunt, Sir William and Caroline Herschel. Dreyer's work listed 7840 currently known nonstellar objects – nebulae, clusters, and galaxies (although the galaxies were not yet identified as such). Each object is numbered by RIGHT ASCENSION and its position and description given. The number is preceded by the letters NGC; this is the object's *NGC number*, an example being NGC 1976: the Orion nebula. Some of the brightest NGC objects also appear in the MESSIER CATALOG.

Dreyer listed 5386 further discoveries in two supplements to the original NGC. These were the first and second *Index Catalogs* (*IC*), published in 1895 and 1908. The three catalogs, now published as one volume, cover the whole sky.

The NGC underwent several revisions during its first hundred years. In 1988, on the centenary of Dreyer's original publication, Roger Sinnott published *NGC 2000.0*, a version of the NGC and IC containing the positions of 13 226 objects for the epoch 2000.0. In 2001 Wolfgang Steinicke produced a more thorough revision, adding a further 767 objects. The NGC/IC Project, accessible over the World Wide Web, seeks to eliminate observing errors and misidentifications inherent in Dreyer's original work to arrive at a clean version of the NGC and IC, with each object unambiguously numbered and identified and correctly attributed to its discoverer..

nightglow see AIRGLOW.

Nix Olympica earlier name for OLYMPUS MONS, assigned by telescopic observers to the bright-albedo feature they saw in its position.

NLR *abbrev. for* narrow-line region. See QUASAR.

nm *symbol for* nanometer, i.e. 10^{-9} meter.

NOAO *abbrev. for* National Optical Astronomy Observatory.

Nobeyama Radio Observatory a Japanese observatory run by the University of Tokyo and situated in the Nobeyama highland. It is concerned mainly with MILLIMETER

ASTRONOMY. Its 45-meter parabolic dish became operational in 1982 and was the first antenna of this size to be used efficiently at millimeter wavelengths. Other instruments include the Nobeyama Millimeter Array (NMA), an array of six movable antennas separated over a maximum baseline of 600 meters forming an APERTURE SYNTHESIS telescope of 600 meters or more; the Nobeyama Radioheliograph, an 84-antenna array aligned in a T-shaped configuration devoted to highly detailed solar observations; and a Very Long Baseline interferometer called VSOP, consisting of both satellites and groundbased instruments, that achieves angular resolutions equivalent to a single telescope with an aperture of 30 000 km. The Nobeyama Radio Observatory is one of the scientific institutions involved in the international ATACAMA LARGE MILLIMETER ARRAY.

Noctis Labyrinthus see THARSIS RIDGE.

nodes the two points at which the orbital plane of a celestial body intersects a reference plane, usually the plane of the ECLIPTIC or CELESTIAL EQUATOR. When the body, such as the Moon or a planet, crosses the reference plane from south to north it passes through the *ascending node;* crossing from north to south the body passes through its *descending node.* The line joining these two nodes is the *line of nodes.*

A celestial body might not cross the reference plane at the same points every time: the line of nodes then moves slowly forward or backward around the orbital plane, i.e. in the same or in the opposite direction to the body. This is termed *progression* or *regression of the nodes.* The Moon's nodes regress along its orbital plane, making one complete revolution in 18.61 years. This period is equal to the period of nutation.

nodical month see DRACONIC MONTH.

noise 1 fluctuations that occur in the output of any electronic or electrical device and, in a measuring instrument, ultimately limit its sensitivity. Noise can be caused by many different factors, for example by insufficient regulation of the voltage of a power supply, but the most important source is usually that produced by random agitation of electrons in a resistance, i.e. *thermal noise. White noise* is completely random and uncorrelated noise that is uniform in energy over equal intervals of frequency; up to a limiting frequency, thermal noise is white.

In electrical circuits a resistance at temperature T produces an exchangeable *noise power* in BANDWIDTH B of

$$P = kTB$$

where k is the Boltzmann constant. If this noise power is generated in the first stages of the measuring instrument, it is amplified along with the signal; the signal/noise ratio is therefore reduced by amplification, although the signal is made stronger. The contribution to the noise power of any part of an electric circuit can be specified by its *noise figure* or *noise factor, F,* which is defined by

$$F = (P_1 + P_0)/P_0$$

where P_1 is the extra noise power generated by the circuit and P_0 is the noise power present at the input terminals of the circuit due to the source resistance, i.e. the thermal noise. Thus if the circuit adds no extra noise, it has a noise figure of unity. F is usually expressed in decibels. Other forms of noise include *shot noise,* generated by the random arrival times of photons or electrons at a detector, and *pink noise.* See also SENSITIVITY.

2 fluctuations of a random nature in which the amplitude of the deflection from a given reference level cannot be predicted fom one moment to the next but whose statistical properties may be well-defined. Signals from RADIO SOURCES are of this kind, and in a RADIO TELESCOPE the problem is to detect these random signals in the presence of noise generated in the measuring instruments. These intrinsic fluctuations of the signal are called *self-noise,* and those from the equipment or any other source are *system noise.* See also RADIO-SOURCE SPECTRUM.

noise figure (noise factor) see NOISE.

noise power see NOISE.

noise temperature (system temperature) see SENSITIVITY.

nonrelativistic describing any phenomenon, object, etc., for which the effects of general or special RELATIVITY can be disregarded or do not apply.

nonthermal emission (nonthermal radiation) electromagnetic radiation, such as SYNCHROTRON EMISSION, that is produced, like THERMAL EMISSION, by the acceleration of electrons or other charged particles but is nonthermal in origin, i.e. its spectrum is not that of a perfect BLACK-BODY radiator.

noon the time of day at which the Sun crosses the local meridian and is at its highest point above the horizon. This time differs from 12.00 LOCAL time by up to about 15 minutes before or after midday, the amount – the EQUATION OF TIME – depending on the time of year.

Nordic Optical Telescope (NOT) see ROQUE DE LOS MUCHACHOS OBSERVATORY.

Norma (Rule; Level) a small inconspicuous constellation in the southern hemisphere near Centaurus, lying in the Milky Way, the brightest stars being of 4th magnitude. It contains the Mira stars R Nor and T Nor and several open clusters including the 5.6 magnitude NGC 6067. Abbrev.: Nor; genitive form: Normae; approx. position: RA 16h, dec –50°; area: 165 sq deg.

North America nebula (NGC 7000) an EMISSION NEBULA nearly 2° across lying in the constellation Cygnus. It is an H II REGION associated with the exceptionally luminous and remote A2 supergiant DENEB.

north celestial pole see CELESTIAL POLES.

Northern Cross see CYGNUS.

north galactic pole see GALACTIC POLES.

north galactic spur see INTERSTELLAR MEDIUM.

north point see CARDINAL POINTS.

north polar distance (NPD) the angular distance of a celestial object from the north CELESTIAL POLE, measured along the object's hour circle. It is the complement of the object's DECLINATION (90°–δ) and is sometimes used instead of this coordinate in the EQUATORIAL COORDINATE SYSTEM.

North Polar Sequence see MAGNITUDE.

North Star see POLARIS.

nova (classical nova) a close BINARY STAR system in which there is a sudden and unpredictable increase in brightness by maybe 10 magnitudes or more (see table). Novae are a class of CATACLYSMIC VARIABLE. In a typical spiral galaxy like our own, there are maybe 25 nova eruptions per year. The brightness increases to a maximum within days or sometimes weeks and then declines to a value probably close to its faint pre-nova magnitude, indicating that the eruption did not disrupt the bulk of the star. *Fast novae* usually increase in brightness by a factor of 10^5 in a few days, remaining at peak brightness for less than a week; they then decline steadily, initially quite rapidly, over several months. *Slow novae* reach maximum brightness more slowly and erratically, the increase being less than in fast novae, and then decline much more slowly. The total energy released, however, is about the same in both cases. Hydrogen-rich gas is ejected from the star resulting in the tremendous outflow of heat and light. The ejected matter forms a rapidly expanding shell of gas that can become visible as the nova fades. At later stages of the eruption the spectra of most novae show the bright forbidden lines characteristic of very low density EMISSION NEBULAE.

Like other cataclysmic variables, a classical nova is a close binary system in which one component is a WHITE DWARF. The other is a main-sequence star that is expanding to fill its Roche lobe (see EQUIPOTENTIAL SURFACES) and is hence losing mass to the white dwarf: some of its gases 'overflow' to form a disk surrounding the white dwarf. The rate of overflow is

Nova

Nova	*Type*	*Magnitude (m_v)* *before*	*max*
Nova Persei 1901 (GK Per 2)	fast	13.5	+0.2
Nova Aquilae 1918 (V603 Aql 3)	fast	10.6	–1.1
Nova Pictoris 1925 (RR Pic)	slow	12.7	+1.2
Nova Herculis 1934 (DQ Her)	slow	14.3	+1.4
Nova Cygni 1975 (V1500 Cyg)	fast	>20	+1.8

about 10^{-9} solar masses per year, about ten times higher than in a DWARF NOVA system, and as a result the disk is always as bright as a dwarf nova at maximum. Before a nova explosion the hot turbulent disk is the brightest part of the system, and its light makes a pre-nova appear as a bluish irregularly fluctuating 'star'. The hydrogen in the disk spirals down on to the surface of the white dwarf, and after a period of some 10 000 to 100 000 years enough has accumulated to react in a thermonuclear explosion – the nova outburst. The explosion leaves the system fundamentally unchanged, however, and the flow of gas resumes to reestablish the accretion disk around the white dwarf.

Novae are now named initially by constellation and year of observation; before 1925 they were numbered in order of observation. They are later given a variable star designation, as for example with DQ Herculis, i.e. Herculis 1934. See also RECURRENT NOVA; X-RAY TRANSIENTS.

November swarm see LEONIDS.

Nozomi a Japanese Mars probe launched July 4 1998. Designated Planet-B throughout its planning and design stages, the probe received the name Nozomi (the Japanese word for 'hope') immediately after launch. The craft was set to study the Martian atmosphere and ionosphere and examine the interaction between the ionosphere and the solar wind. But a trajectory alteration used up to much fuel, and the probe was unable to reach Mars orbit. Attempts to salvage the probe were finally abandoned in 2003.

NPD *abbrev. for* north polar distance.

NRAO *abbrev. for* National Radio Astronomy Observatory.

NSO *abbrev. for* National Solar Observatory.

N stars see CARBON STARS.

NTT *abbrev. for* New Technology Telescope.

Nubecula Major, Minor *alternative names for* Large and Small Magellanic Clouds, respectively. See MAGELLANIC CLOUDS.

nuclear fission a process in which an atomic nucleus splits into two smaller nuclei, usually with the emission of neutrons or gamma rays. Fission may be spontaneous or induced by neutron or photon bombardment. It occurs in heavy elements such as uranium, thorium, and plutonium. The process is accompanied by the release of large amounts of energy.

nuclear fusion a process in which two light nuclei join to yield a heavier nucleus. An example is the fusion of two hydrogen nuclei to give a deuterium nucleus plus a positron plus a neutrino; this reaction occurs in the Sun. Such processes take place at very high temperatures (millions of kelvin) and are consequently called *thermonuclear reactions*. With light elements, fusion releases immense amounts of energy: fusion is the energy-producing process in stars.

The lighter chemical elements evolve energy in fusion reactions whereas heavier elements (those with a MASS NUMBER above 56) require an input of energy to maintain the reaction. Thus although most elements up to iron can be formed by fusion reactions in stars (see NUCLEOSYNTHESIS), heavier elements must be synthesized by other nuclear reactions. See also CARBON CYCLE; PROTON-PROTON CHAIN REACTION.

nuclear reactions reactions involving changes in atomic nuclei. Nuclear reactions include NUCLEAR FUSION and fission and transformations of nuclei by bombardment with particles or photons. The energy released by nuclear reactions is equivalent to a decrease in mass according to Einstein's equation ($E = mc^2$) and appears in the form of kinetic energy of the particles or photons of electromagnetic radiation.

nuclear timescale the total nuclear-energy resources of a star divided by the rate of energy loss. For typical stars, the nuclear timescale is of the order of 10^{10} years, although the rate of energy loss may change during the star's lifetime if the reaction processes alter.

nucleon one of the constituents of the atomic nucleus, i.e. a proton or a neutron.

nucleosynthesis the creation of the ELEMENTS by nuclear reactions. To unravel the complex situation, the measured COSMIC ABUNDANCES of the elements are interpreted in terms of their nuclear properties and the set of environments (temperature, density, etc.) in which they can be synthesized. Nucleosynthesis began when the temperature of the primitive

Universe had dropped to about 10^9 kelvin. This occurred approximately 100 seconds after the Big Bang (see BIG BANG THEORY). Protons (hydrogen nuclei) fused with neutrons to form deuterium nuclei and deuterium nuclei could then fuse to form the two isotopes of helium. Most of the helium in the Universe was formed at this time, along with deuterium and lithium, but very little of the heavier elements. The nucleosynthesis ceased about 1000 seconds after the Big Bang when the Universe became too cool for nuclear reactions.

Helium and the heavier elements are synthesized in stars; this idea was first developed in 1956/57 by Fowler, Hoyle, and the Burbidges. Nucleosynthesis has occurred continuously in the Galaxy for many thousands of millions of years as a by-product of STELLAR EVOLUTION. While a star remains on the MAIN SEQUENCE, hydrogen in its central core will be converted to helium by the PROTON-PROTON CHAIN REACTION or the CARBON CYCLE; the core temperature is then about 10^7 K.

When the central hydrogen supplies are exhausted, the star will begin to evolve off the main sequence. Its core, now composed of helium, will contract until a temperature of 10^8 K is reached; carbon-12 can then be formed by the TRIPLE ALPHA PROCESS, i.e. by helium burning. In stars more than twice the Sun's mass a sequence of reactions, involving further nuclear fusion, produces oxygen, neon, and magnesium in the forms ^{16}O, ^{20}Ne, ^{24}Mg, and then, at temperatures increasing up to about 3.5×10^9 K, ^{28}Si to ^{56}Fe. Even higher temperatures will trigger reactions by which almost all elements up to a mass number (A) of 56 can be synthesized. The *iron-peak elements*, i.e. ^{56}Fe, ^{56}Ni, ^{56}Co, etc., represent the end of the nucleosynthesis sequence by nuclear fusion: further fusion would require rather than liberate energy because nuclei with this mass number have the maximum binding energy per nucleon.

The formation of nuclei with $A \geq 56$ requires nuclear reactions involving neutron capture: neutrons can be captured at comparatively low energies because of their lack of charge. If there is a supply of free neutrons in a star, produced as by-products of nuclear-fusion reactions, the S-PROCESS can slowly synthesize nuclei up to ^{209}Bi. An intense source of neutrons allows the R-PROCESS to generate nuclei up to ^{254}Cf, or higher, in a very short period. Such intense neutron fluxes arise in SUPERNOVAE.

The synthesized elements are precipitated into the INTERSTELLAR MEDIUM by various MASS-LOSS processes; these include stellar winds from giant stars, planetary nebulae, and nova explosions for elements up to silicon, and supernovae for the iron-peak elements and heavier nuclei.

nucleus 1 the dark kilometer-sized body that is the permanent portion of a COMET and is thought by most researchers to be the fount of all cometary activity. The density is about 0.2 g cm^{-3}. It contains about 75% by mass ice (mainly water ice, 85%, but with liberal amounts of CO_2, CO, H_2CO, CH_3OH, and NH_3) and 25% by mass dust thought to have a composition similar to carbonaceous chondritic meteorites (see CARBONACEOUS CHONDRITE). It is often described as a *dirty snowball*. A comet of mass 10^{18} grams would have a nucleus of diameter about 12 km. A positive identification of the nucleus of comets has recently been achieved using radar. The nucleus of comet HALLEY was imaged by the GIOTTO spacecraft in March 1986, and was found to be a huge potato-shaped object, 16 km long and 8 km wide. It was active only over 10% of its surface and was spinning every 54 hours, precessing every 7.4 days. A comet's nucleus of dirty ice is surrounded by a thin layer (a few cm) of insulating dust from which the ice has sublimated. This enables it to survive over 2000 perihelion passages. At each passage the nucleus loses on average a layer of material one meter thick. In Halley's comet this amounted to 3×10^{14} g. This material forms the COMA and COMET TAILS and also any associated METEOROID STREAM.
2 the small core of an ATOM, consisting of PROTONS and NEUTRONS bound together by strong nuclear forces. The nucleus has a positive charge equal to Ze, where e is the magnitude of the electron charge and Z the number of protons present – the atomic number. The total number of protons plus

neutrons is the mass number, A. A given element is characterized by its atomic number but may, within limits, have different numbers of neutrons in its nuclei, giving rise to different ISOTOPES of the element. The total mass of the protons and neutrons bound together in a nucleus is less than when the particles are unbound. This mass difference is equivalent to the energy required to bind the particles together. Nuclei are represented by their chemical symbols to which numbers are attached; usually the mass number is added as a left superscript to indicate a particular isotope, as in ^{4}He. The radii of nuclei are commonly measured in femtometers (1 fm = 10^{-15}m). The femtometer is sometimes referred to as a 'fermi'.

3 the central region of a galaxy.

nuclide a type of atom characterized by its atomic number and neutron number. The term 'isotope' is used for members of a series of atoms that have the same atomic number. 'Nuclide' is used for a particular species, e.g. the uranium–235 nuclide.

Nuffield Radio Astronomy Laboratories see JODRELL BANK.

number count the number of galaxies as a function of MAGNITUDE. See SOURCE COUNT.

Nunki see SAGITTARIUS.

nutation a slight periodic but irregular movement superimposed on the precessional circle (see PRECESSION) traced out by the celestial poles. It results from the varying distances and relative directions of the Moon and Sun, which continuously alter the strength and direction of their gravitational attraction on the Earth. The primary component is lunar nutation, which causes the celestial pole to wander by ±9 arc seconds from its mean position in a period of 18.6 years.

Changes in RIGHT ASCENSION and DECLINATION arising from precession are perceptibly modified by nutation.

Nysa family a HIRAYAMA FAMILY of asteroids containing a single large body ((44) Nysa) about 70 km in diameter and many small objects of 20 km or less. It is associated with the *Hertha family*; it is thought that (135) Hertha is the core of the parent body and that Nysa is a fragment of the outer mantle. The orbital elements are reasonably dispersed but family members can be easily recognized by their unique colors.

Oo

OAO *abbrev. for* Orbiting Astronomical Observatory.

OB association see ASSOCIATION.

OB cluster an OPEN CLUSTER that contains main-sequence O and B stars of high luminosity. These bright and very massive stars evolve more rapidly than less massive stars; their presence in a cluster suggests that it is comparatively young (10 million years or less) and that it may contain stars still in the process of formation. Examples are NGC 2264 and H AND CHI PERSEI. The young low-mass T TAURI STARS are often observed in these clusters. See also ASSOCIATION.

Oberon the outermost satellite of Uranus, discovered in 1787 by William Herschel. Photographed by VOYAGER 2, its surface shows some large craters with bright rays emanating from them and with dark patches on their floors, possibly due to eruptions of dirty water. Oberon also has large mountains up to 6 km high and steep curved slopes. See also URANUS' SATELLITES; Table 2, Appendix.

objective (**object lens; object glass**) the lens or lens system in a REFRACTING TELESCOPE that faces the observed object. The focal plane in which the image forms, in the absence of other components, is termed the *prime focus*. See also APERTURE.

objective grating see OBJECTIVE PRISM.

objective prism a narrow-angle prism placed in front of the primary mirror or objective lens of a telescope. The prism disperses the incident light very slightly so that each star image is spread out into a small SPECTRUM (see DISPERSION). A transmission DIFFRACTION GRATING (called an *objective grating*) is now often used for the same purpose. The spectra of a field of stars can thus be recorded in a single photographic or electronic image and the chief spectral features of the stars can be quickly assessed (see SPECTRAL TYPES).

oblateness (**ellipticity; flattening**) a parameter specifying the degree to which the form of a celestial object, such as a planet, differs from a true sphere, largely as a result of rotation. It is numerically equal to the difference between the equatorial and polar radii of the object divided by the equatorial radius. Saturn, with an oblateness of 0.108, is the most oblate planet in the Solar System.

oblique rotator theory see MAGNETIC STARS.

obliquity the angle between the equatorial and orbital planes of a celestial body.

obliquity of the ecliptic symbol: ε. The angle at which the ECLIPTIC is inclined to the CELESTIAL EQUATOR. This angle, equal to the tilt of the Earth's axis, is about 23°26′. PRECESSION and NUTATION cause this angle to change between the extremes of about 22.1° and 24.5°, altering (at present diminishing) by about 0″.47 per year. Its value on Jan. 1 2000 was 23°26′21″.

observatory a structure built primarily for astronomical observation, equipped nowadays with optical, radio, and/or infrared telescopes and, in the larger observatories, the associated equipment with which spectrographic, photometric, and other such measurements are made. The sites of modern optical and infrared observatories are selected very carefully so that there is maximum transmission of signals by the atmosphere (i.e. the sky is free from clouds and dust), minimal atmospheric turbulence (i.e. the SEEING is optimal), and minimum LIGHT POLLUTION (i.e. the night sky is dark). Most are sited in mountainous areas or on volcanic islands where the atmosphere is very thin and the absorption effects of water vapor are reduced. Radio observatories, less hampered by seeing conditions, clouds, and light pollution, must still be isolated from terrestrial radio and electrical interference.

Instruments can now be carried into space, away from the disturbing and absorbing effects of the Earth's atmosphere. The greatest hopes for future astronomical studies lie in space observatories and possible lunar observatories, permitting observations over the entire electromagnetic spectrum with a resolution that is limited only by the size of the telescope.

OB stars stars of spectral type O or B, i.e. O STARS or B STARS, all of which are ULTRAVIOLET STARS.

occultation complete or partial obscuration of an astronomical object by another of larger apparent diameter, especially the Moon or a planet. A solar eclipse is strictly an occultation. The precise timings of occultations provide information about planetary atmospheres, the dimensions of extended visible, radio, and X-ray objects, and the positions of objects, such as distant radio sources. See also ECLIPSE; GRAZING OCCULTATION.

oceanus a very large relatively smooth dark area on the surface of the Moon. The word is used in the approved name of such a feature. See also MARE. (Latin: ocean)

octahedrite see IRON METEORITE.

Octans (Octant) an inconspicuous constellation containing and surrounding the south celestial pole, the brightest stars being of 3rd magnitude. The faint (5th-magnitude) Sigma (σ) Octantis is the nearest naked-eye star to the south pole. Abbrev.: Oct; genitive form: Octantis; approx. position: RA 0 – 24h, dec –80°; area: 291 sq deg.

Odysseus see TETHYS.

Of stars young massive O stars that show selectively enhanced emission lines of ionized helium (He II) and nitrogen (N III) in addition to a well-developed absorption spectrum. The emission lines arise in an unstable atmosphere that is being lost from the star. Of stars are the hottest, most luminous, and probably the most massive stars in the Galaxy: the record holder is HD 93129A, near ETA CARINAE, with a temperature of 50 000 K, a luminosity of 3 million Suns, and a mass of probably 120 solar masses (see also SUPERMASSIVE STARS). Of stars are thought to be the evolutionary precursors of WOLF-RAYET STARS.

OG *abbrev. for* object glass (i.e. the objective of a refracting telescope), often used to indicate a refractor or its use.

OGO *abbrev. for* Orbiting Geophysical Observatory.

OH see HYDROXYL RADICAL.

OH/IR star a very large extremely cool giant or supergiant star that is losing mass very rapidly and is detected only by its infrared radiation and by its hydroxyl (OH) maser emission (see MASER SOURCE). The first OH/IR stars were found in a survey of OH maser sources in 1973; many more were detected by IRAS's infrared survey in 1983. These stars are usually very long period VARIABLES. MIRA STARS often show similar but weaker maser and infrared emission. The OH/IR stars, however, are losing mass a hundred times faster than the Mira stars. They are surrounded by a very dense shell of COSMIC DUST that shows absorption typical of silicates. The shells have temperatures ranging from 1000 K to only 100 K. Because the stars lose a solar mass of gas and dust in only 10 000 to 100 000 years, they must be changing very rapidly to their next evolutionary state, probably a PLANETARY NEBULA.

Olbers' paradox Why is the sky dark at night? Heinrich Olbers in 1826, and earlier J.P.L. Chesaux in 1744, pointed out that an infinite and uniform Universe, both unchanging and static, would produce a night sky of the same surface brightness as the Sun: every line of sight would eventually strike a star, a typical example of which is the Sun. This theoretical argument is obviously in disagreement with observation. The observable Universe is, however, neither uniform, unchanging, nor static and does not extend infinitely back into the past. The paradox is then resolved because the REDSHIFT of extragalactic radiation (i.e. the diminution in its energy) and in particular the youth of our Universe make the background radiation field at optical wavelengths very low indeed – less than about 10^{-21} times the surface brightness of the Sun.

Old Style (**OS**) see NEW STYLE.

Oljato (**(2201) Oljato**) An APOLLO asteroid that has a diameter of about 1.4 km and a high albedo of 0.42. Discovered in 1947 by the US astronomer Henry L. Giclas, Oljato has a chaotic orbit, its semimajor axis varying violently due to its many close approaches to Earth and Venus. It might possibly be a dormant or extinct cometary nucleus. It is also associated with several meteoroid streams.

Olympus Mons a lofty volcanic peak on Mars, located in the planet's northern hemisphere at 18.6° N latitude and 134.0° W longitude. It is the largest volcano on Mars and possibly the largest in the Solar System. With an estimated age of 200 million years, it may be younger than the volcanoes on the THARSIS RIDGE. It has a base more than 600 km across and rises to a 90 km diameter caldera at an elevation of 26 km above the surrounding plains. Around much of the base is an escarpment up to 6 km high. This giant feature is an important influence on Martian weather. For comparison, the largest volcano on Earth, Hawaii's Mauna Loa, rises only 9.3 km from its 120-km diameter base on the floor of the Pacific Ocean. See also MARS, VOLCANOES.

omega (ω) **1** the 24th and last letter of the Greek alphabet used in STELLAR NOMENCLATURE usually to designate the 24th-brightest star in a constellation or sometimes to indicate a star's position in a group. See also OMEGA CENTAURI..
2 *symbol for* angular velocity.
3 *symbol for* argument of perihelion (see ORBITAL ELEMENTS).
4 another name for density parameter. See MEAN DENSITY OF MATTER.

Omega Centauri (**ω Cen; NGC 5139**) a huge impressive GLOBULAR CLUSTER, magnitude 3.7, diameter 0°.6, in the constellation Centaurus. At about 5212 parsecs distant, it is one of the closest globulars to the Solar System. The million or so stars of which it is composed show a surprising range of metal content and possibly age. It is an X-ray source.

Omega nebula (**Swan nebula; Horseshoe nebula; M17; NGC 6618**) an EMISSION NEBULA with a conspicuous bar that lies at a distance of 2200 parsecs in the constellation of Sagittarius, very close to its northern boundary with Scutum. The nebula's apparent magnitude is 7. It is an H II region and a double radio source. The *M17SW molecular cloud* is a site of massive STAR FORMATION; the interface between the nebula and M17SW is an example of an edge-on PHOTODISSOCIATION REGION.

omicron (ο) the 15th letter of the Greek alphabet used in STELLAR NOMENCLATURE usually to designate the 15th-brightest star in a constellation or sometimes to indicate a star's position in a group.

Onsala Space Observatory a radio observatory of Chalmers University of Technology, Onsala, Sweden, located on the Onsala Peninsula south of Gothenburg. It has a 20-meter dish, enclosed in a golfball-like radome, for observations at millimeter wavelengths and a 26-meter radio telescope, in operation since 1965 at frequencies below 10 gigahertz.

Oort cloud (**Öpik–Oort cloud**) a cloud of COMETS that move in orbits round the Sun with perihelia in the range 5–50 AU and aphelia in a zone with heliocentric distances between 30 000 and 100 000 AU, i.e. in a zone far beyond Pluto's orbit. Since the nearest star to the Sun – Proxima Centauri – is 270 000 AU away these comets can be perturbed by passing stars; this changes their orbits and send them in closer toward our Sun (or out toward the perturbing star). These perturbed comets have periods of hundreds of thousands of years. The Oort cloud is so distant that it acts as a refrigerated cometary reservoir.

The existence of a distant long-lived cloud of comets was first suggested in 1932 by Ernst Öpik. The same idea was proposed in 1950 by J.H. Oort who thought that comets originated from the disintegration of a planet some time in the early history of the Solar System. After this the major planets, Jupiter in particular, drove the majority of the comets either into the inner Solar System, where they decayed, or into the outer regions. Of this latter group 98% would have been lost from the Solar System, only 2% remaining in the Oort cloud. The number of comets in the cloud is uncertain but it could be somewhere in the range 10^{11} to 10^{12} with a total mass in the region of 10^{28} grams. The orbits are oriented at random. A cometary cloud of radius 100 000 AU has a half life of at least 1.1×10^9 years. The existence of the cloud shows up very clearly when the number distribution of comets is considered as a function of the reciprocal of the semimajor axes of the orbits. See also KUIPER BELT.

Oort's constants see OORT'S FORMULAE.

Oort's formulae two mathematical expressions derived by Jan Oort that describe the effects of differential GALACTIC ROTATION on the radial velocities (v_r) and tangential velocities (v_t) of stars at an average distance r from the Sun. If each star is moving in a circular orbit about the galactic center, and if r is small in comparison with the Sun's distance from the center, then

$$v_r = Ar \sin 2l$$
$$v_t = Br + Ar \cos 2l$$

where l is the galactic longitude (see GALACTIC COORDINATE SYSTEM) and A and B are *Oort's constants*. Since v_t is not directly measurable the second equation is usually replaced by the expression for PROPER MOTION, μ:

$$\mu = 0.211(B + A \cos 2l)$$

The equations are valid for μ measured in arc seconds per year, velocities in km s^{-1}, and distances in parsecs. The most widely accepted values for Oort's constants are

A: 15 (km s^{-1})/kiloparsec
B: –10 (km s^{-1})/kpc

Most stars, including the Sun, do not move in precisely circular orbits but once a correction has been made for the Sun's velocity with respect to the average velocity of stars in the solar neighborhood (assumed to be circular), the measured variation of v_r and μ with l is sufficiently close to that predicted by the equations to support the theory that the general rotation pattern is circular and galactocentric.

Ooty Radio Telescope (**ORT**) a parabolic cylinder antenna, 350 meters long and 30 meters wide, built in Ooty, India by the National Center for Radio Astrophysics, Pune. The telescope is oriented N–S and built on the slope of a hill. It can rotate about its long axis and so track radio sources for about 9.5 hours every day. The pointing in the N–S direction is achieved by electrically phasing the 1056 DIPOLES along the focal line. The telescope operates at 326.5 MHz. The *Ooty Synthesis Radio Telescope* (*OSRT*) is an APERTURE SYNTHESIS telescope using the ORT and seven smaller parabolic cylinders up to 4 km away.

opacity a measure of the ability of a gaseous, solid, or liquid body to absorb radiation. It is the ratio of the total radiant energy received by the body to the total energy transmitted through it. For gaseous material of a particular chemical composition, opacity depends on both temperature and density. Various processes contribute to the opacity: energy absorption by electrons bound to an atom or ion, allowing them to jump to a higher level or to escape from the atom as free electrons (bound-bound or BOUND-FREE ABSORPTION); absorption by free electrons (FREE-FREE ABSORPTION); scattering of photone of radiation by free electrons or atoms (COMPTON SCATTERING); absorption of γ-ray photons by ambient 'gas' photons (PHOTON-PHOTON ABSORPTION). The negative HYDROGEN ion, H^-, is a particularly important source of opacity in a star like the Sun, and the solar opacity is seen to drop rapidly to zero at the Sun's limb.

open cluster (**galactic cluster**) a loose CLUSTER of stars that contains at most a few thousand stars and sometimes fewer than twenty. Examples visible to the naked eye are the HYADES and the PLEIADES. About 1200 open clusters are known. They are POPULATION I systems and occur in or close to the plane of the Galaxy. The brightest stars in an open cluster can be either red or blue giants, depending upon its age. Stars in the older clusters, such as M67 in Cancer, are similar in appearance to those in GLOBULAR CLUSTERS, although with some subtle differences due to the higher metal content of the material from which they were formed. Open clusters are more loosely bound systems than globular clusters and they tend to be gradually dispersed by the combined effects of the differential rotation of the Galaxy and perturbations due to close encounters with interstellar clouds. Calculations suggest that many will not survive more than one or two circuits of the Galaxy. Hence most open clusters are comparatively young systems. Some, such as NGC 2264, are less than 10 million years old and in these clusters star-formation is probably still taking place (see OB CLUSTER). See also HERTZSPRUNG–RUSSELL DIAGRAM; MOVING CLUSTER; TURNOFF POINT.

open Universe see DECELERATION PARAMETER; UNIVERSE.

Ophelia a small satellite of Uranus, discovered by Voyager 2 in 1986. Together with CORDELIA, it acts as a SHEPHERD SATELLITE to the outermost (Epsilon) ring. See URANUS' RINGS; URANUS' SATELLITES; Table 2, Appendix.

Ophiuchids a minor METEOR SHOWER, radiant: RA 260°, dec –20°, maximizing on June 20.

Ophiuchus (**Serpent Bearer**) a large equatorial constellation near Scorpius, lying partly in the Milky Way. The brightest star is the 2nd-magnitude white giant Rasalhague (α), which lies close to RASALGETHI (Alpha [α] Herculis). The area contains the supernova remnant of KEPLER'S STAR, the Rho (ρ) Ophiuchi cloud, in which there is active star formation (see RHO OPHIUCHI CLOUD), the loose open cluster IC 4665, and many globular clusters. Abbrev.: Oph; genitive form: Ophiuchi; approx. position: RA 17h, dec –7°; area: 948 sq deg.

Öpik–Oort cloud see OORT CLOUD.

Opportunity see MARS EXPLORATION ROVERS.

opposition the moment at which a body in the Solar System has a celestial longitude differing from that of the Sun by 180°, so that it lies opposite the Sun in the sky and crosses the meridian at about midnight (see ELONGATION). The term also applies to the alignment of the two bodies at this moment. Although the INFERIOR PLANETS cannot come to opposition, it is the most favorable time for observation of the other planets because they are then observable throughout the night and are near their closest point for that APPARITION. See also SYNODIC PERIOD.

optical astronomy the study of astronomical objects using radiation with wavelengths from about 300 to 900 nanometers. These wavelengths can pass through the Earth's atmosphere so that observations are possible from the ground. The human eye is sensitive to most of this waveband. See also LIGHT; REFLECTING TELESCOPE; REFRACTING TELESCOPE.

optical axis the imaginary line passing through the midpoint of a lens, mirror, or system of such elements and on which lies the focal point of parallel paraxial rays.

optical depth symbol: τ. A measure of the absorption of radiation of a particular wavelength as it passes through a gaseous medium. If the initial radiation flux Φ_o is reduced to Φ_x after a distance x through the medium then

$$\Phi_x/\Phi_o = \exp(-\tau)$$

where τ is the optical depth for the radiation wavelength. If τ equals zero the medium is transparent; if τ is much greater or much less than one the medium is *optically thick* or *optically thin* respectively. See also OPACITY.

optical double 1 see DOUBLE STAR. 2 see DOUBLE GALAXY.

optical interferometer see INTERFEROMETER.

optical libration *another name for* geometrical libration. See LIBRATION.

optical pathlength the distance, d, traveled by a light beam multiplied by the REFRACTIVE INDEX, n, of the medium through which the light has passed. If the light traverses more than one medium, then the optical pathlength is the sum

$$(n_1 d_1 + n_2 d_2 + \ldots)$$

for each medium.

optical pulsars PULSARS that flash at visible wavelengths. The two best known are the CRAB and the VELA PULSARS. The Crab pulsar appears as a 16th magnitude star but is pulsing with a period of 0.033 seconds; the optical flashes of the Vela pulsar, about 26th magnitude, were discovered by looking for faint pulses with exactly the period (0.089 seconds) of its radio emission.

Optical pulses have also been detected from X-RAY BINARY systems.

optical temperature see EFFECTIVE TEMPERATURE.

optical window see ATMOSPHERIC WINDOWS.

orbit the path followed by a celestial object or an artificial satellite or spaceprobe that is moving in a gravitational field. For a single object moving freely in the gravitational field of a massive body the orbit is a CONIC SECTION, in actuality either elliptical or hyperbolic. Closed (repeated) orbits are elliptical, most planetary orbits being almost circular. A hyperbolic orbit results in the object escaping from the vicinity of a massive body. See also KEPLER'S LAWS; ORBITAL ELEMENTS.

orbital elements the parameters that specify the position and motion of a celestial body in its orbit and that can be established by observation (see illustration). *Osculating elements* specify the instantaneous position and velocity of a body in a perturbed orbit (see OSCULATING ORBIT). *Mean elements* are those of some reference orbit that approximates the actual perturbed orbit. The shape and size of the orbit are specified by the ECCENTRICITY, *e*, and for an elliptical orbit by the SEMIMAJOR AXIS, *a*. The orientation of the orbit in space is specified firstly by the INCLINATION, *i*, of the orbital plane to the reference plane, usually that of the ecliptic, and secondly by the *longitude of the ascending node*, Ω; the latter is the angular distance from the dynamical or vernal EQUINOX, γ, to the ascending NODE, N. The orientation of the orbit in the orbital plane is usually specified by the angular distance, ω, between the periapsis, P (see APSIDES), and the ascending node. For an orbit round the Sun the periapsis is the PERIHELION and the angular distance ω is the *argument of perihelion*. It is measured along the direction of motion. The angular distance equal to the argument of perihelion plus the longitude of the ascending node is called the *longitude of perhelion*, which is also used as an orbital element.

The eccentric ANOMALY is used to determine the position of the body in its orbit. To calculate the position as a function of time an additional orbital element is used. This is the *time of periapsis* (or for a solar orbit *perihelion*) *passage*, t_o, by means of which Kepler's equation (see ANOMALY) can be solved. Analogous elements are used to describe the orbits of binary stars. To determine the orbit of a binary star system of unknown mass, the PERIOD must be established.

The Earth's orbital elements vary with time due to gravitational effects of the Moon and planets. The changes, approximately periodic, during the past several hundred thousand years have been calculated very accurately.

orbital resonance an effect in celestial

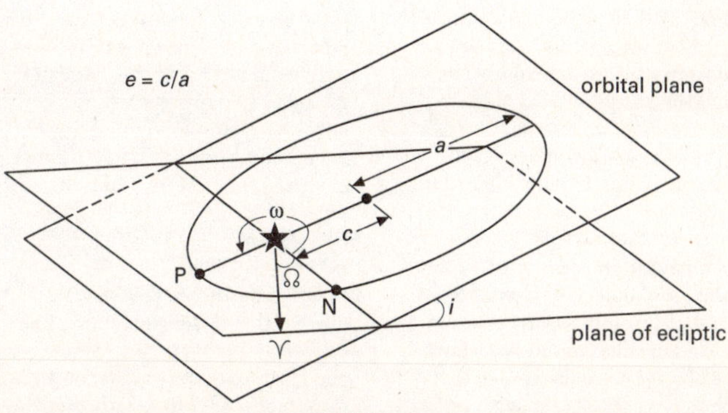

Orbital elements

mechanics that arises when two orbiting bodies have periods of revolution that are in a simple integer ratio allowing each body to have a regularly recurring gravitational influence on the other. Orbital resonance may stabilize the orbits and protect them from perturbation, as in the case of the TROJAN GROUP of asteroids, which are held in place by a 1:1 resonance with Jupiter. On the other hand, orbital resonance may destabilize one of the orbits, ejecting the body concerned, changing the eccentricity of its path, or sending it into a different orbit. This second effect of orbital resonance accounts for why there are virtually no asteroids in certain regions of the main asteroid belt (see KIRKWOOD GAPS). *Laplace resonance* is a form of orbital resonance that occurs when three or more orbiting objects have a simple integer ratio between their orbital periods. For example, the Jovian satellites IO, EUROPA, and GANYMEDE have periods of revolution in the ratio 4:2:1.

orbital velocity the velocity of a satellite or other orbiting body at any given point in its orbit. It is also the velocity required by a satellite to enter an orbit around a body. The orbital velocity, v, is given by the expression

$$v = \sqrt{[gR^2(2/r - 1/a)]}$$

where R is the radius of the orbited body, r is the distance from the CENTER OF MASS of the system (i.e. from the approximate center of the primary), a is the SEMIMAJOR AXIS of the orbit, and g is the standard acceleration of gravity. For a circular orbit, $r = a$ and the circular velocity is given by

$$v = \sqrt{(gR^2/r)}$$

To escape from an orbit a must tend to infinity and the escape velocity is then given by

$$v_e = \sqrt{(2gR^2/r)}$$

The orbital period for an elliptical orbit is given by

$$P = 2\pi a^{3/2}/\sqrt{gR^2}$$

orbit determination the derivation of the orbit of a celestial object, such as a comet, from several observations of its position by using the laws of celestial mechanics. At least three observations are needed to determine the ORBITAL ELEMENTS and many methods have been used.

Orbiting Astronomical Observatory (OAO) any of a series of four US satellites, two of which were successfully launched, that were primarily concerned with investigations in the ultraviolet (UV) region of the spectrum. OAO–2 was launched on Dec. 7 1968 and continued operating for over four years. In one group of experiments a UV survey of about one sixth of the sky was achieved by means of four telescopes plus UV-sensitive television camera tubes, which produced pictures in the wavelength range 115–320 nm. A catalogue of bright UV sources was compiled from the data. In the other experimental package measurements were made of the UV luminosity and spectra of a large number of preselected targets. OAO–3 was launched on Aug. 21 1972 and was named COPERNICUS after launch.

Orbiting Geophysical Observatory (OGO) any of a series of US geophysical satellites, first launched in Sept. 1964, for studying the Earth's atmosphere, ionosphere, magnetic field, radiation belts, etc., and how these are influenced by the SOLAR WIND and other phenomena. Moving mainly in highly elliptical orbits, the satellites could carry out many studies simultaneously for prolonged periods.

Orbiting Solar Observatory (OSO) any of a series of US satellites launched between 1962 (OSO–1) and 1975 (OSO–8) and designed to study the Sun and solar phenomena, especially solar flares, from Earth orbit. The quality and range of the observations improved as the series progressed, with high spectral and spatial resolution in ultraviolet and X-ray spectral regions in later craft. Instruments have included a CORONAGRAPH, SPECTROHELIOGRAPH, ultraviolet and X-ray SPECTROGRAPHS, PHOTOMETERS, gamma-ray detectors, and particle-flux sensors.

order sorter see FABRY–PEROT INTERFEROMETER.

Orientale Basin the youngest lunar BASIN, only partly filled by mare lava. The concentric ring structure of MOUNTAINS and the EJECTA BLANKET – the Hevelius formation – are exceptionally well preserved. Orientale is situated on the

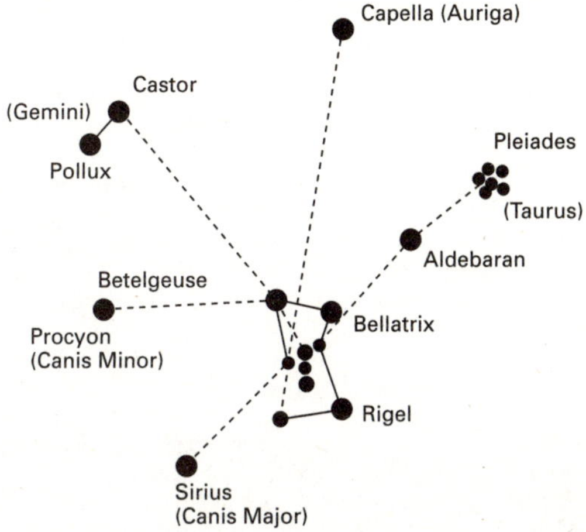

Orion and bright neighboring stars

western limb of the Moon and is visible from Earth only at times of favorable LIBRATION.

Orion a very conspicuous constellation on the celestial equator, close to the Milky Way, that is visible as a whole from most parts of the world and can be used to indicate the positions of many bright neighboring stars (see illustration). Five stars are of 1st magnitude or brighter; 15 are brighter than 4th magnitude. RIGEL (β), BETELGEUSE (α), BELLATRIX (γ), and 2nd-magnitude *Saiph* (κ) form the distinctive quadrilateral outline inside which are the three remote 1st- and 2nd-magnitude stars of *Orion's Belt*, Alnilam (ε), Alnitak (ζ), and Mintaka (δ). South of the Belt is *Orion's Sword*, in which lies the naked-eye gaseous ORION NEBULA. The area contains many double stars including Rigel, several variable stars, and the dark HORSEHEAD NEBULA. An immense oval ring of ionized hydrogen, *Barnard's loop*, surrounds most of Orion. Abbrev.: Ori; genitive form: Orionis; approx. position: RA 5.5h, dec 0°; area: 594 sq deg.

Orion arm see GALAXY.

Orion association (**I Orionis**) a large OB-association (see ASSOCIATION) that contains over 1000 stars and lies in the region of the Orion nebula. There are at least three clusters in the association: the Lambda (λ) Orionis cluster, the Belt group around Epsilon (ε) Orionis, and the TRAPEZIUM cluster.

Orionids an active METEOR SHOWER, radiant: RA 97°, dec +15°, that maximizes on Oct. 22 with a ZENITHAL HOURLY RATE of about 25. The activity has been observed to change by as much as a factor of four between one year and the next. The shower has been the center of controversy firstly because it was thought that the RADIANT was stationary during the three weeks of activity. This view has now been abandoned: all showers have radiants that move with respect to the stars as the Earth moves along its orbit. Secondly the shower is associated both with Halley's comet and the Eta AQUARIDS because of similarities in orbital elements.

Orion molecular cloud (**OMC-1**) a dense cloud of neutral molecular hydrogen lying slightly behind, but in contact with, the ORION NEBULA. It is part of a system of MOLECULAR CLOUDS in the Orion constellation, and is an example of a PHOTODISSOCIATION REGION seen face-on. It has a total mass of about 500 solar masses and has a temperature ranging up to 100 K. It is a very bright infrared source at a wavelength of 50 μm with a LUMINOSITY 10^5 times greater than the Sun's. It is likely that the TRAPEZIUM stars condensed from the same molecular cloud. Also associated with OMC-1 are the strong infrared sources, the BN OBJECT and KLEINMANN-LOW NEBULA, which together form the *BNKL complex.* Higher resolution measurements indicate that the center of the KL nebula consists of a cluster of small infrared sources that may be evolving toward the stage the Trapezium stars have already reached.

Orion nebula (**M42; NGC 1976**) one of the brightest EMISSION NEBULAE in the sky, about 400 parsecs distant. It is just visible to the naked eye as a diffuse luminous patch, 1° across, in the center of Orion's Sword; M43 (NGC 1982) is a small northern part of M42, a dust lane separating them. The Orion nebula is a complex region of ionized hydrogen (an H II REGION) that is associated with the ORION MOLECULAR CLOUD (OMC-1), part of a system of GIANT MOLECULAR CLOUDS in the Orion constellation. The Orion nebula is centered on a very dense stellar cluster – the TRAPEZIUM cluster – containing four hot young stars that excite and ionize the nebula, so producing both radio and optical radiation. Their total LUMINOSITY is about 3×10^5 times that of the Sun. The nebula is also a source of X-rays. The region is one of active STAR FORMATION, containing T TAURI STARS, MASER SOURCES, HERBIG–HARO OBJECTS, the BN OBJECT, and the KLEINMANN-LOW NEBULA. The interface between the nebula and the adjacent molecular cloud is an example of a PHOTODISSOCIATION REGION.

Orion's Belt see ORION.

Orion's Sword see ORION.

orrery an instrument or model that demonstrates the movements of some or all of the planets around the Sun, in their correct relative periods, by means of a set of small spheres mounted on wire rods and driven by an elaborate, usually clock-driven system of gears. The movements of satellites, such as the Moon, may be incorporated in the mechanism. The instrument takes its name from Charles Boyle, the 4th Earl of Orrery, who paid for such a device built in 1712; orreries were previously called *planetaria.*

ORT *abbrev. for* Ooty Radio Telescope.

orthoscopic eyepiece see EYEPIECE.

Oschin Telescope see PALOMAR OBSERVATORY.

oscillating Universe (**pulsating Universe**) a closed UNIVERSE in which collapse is followed by a reexpansion.

osculating orbit the truly elliptical orbit that a celestial object would follow if the perturbing forces of other bodies were to disappear so that it was subject only to the central gravitational field of a single massive body. In general elliptical motion is an approximation to the real motion of members of the Solar System. If all forces except the central gravitational force disappeared at time t, then the *osculating elements* would be the ORBITAL ELEMENTS of the ellipse followed by a body at a given instant after time t. For a real body in perturbed motion the instantaneous osculating elements are not constant but are functions of time. The osculating elements are often used to describe the perturbed motion of a body.

OSO *abbrev. for* Orbiting Solar Observatory.

OSSE *abbrev. for* oriented scintillation spectrometer experiment. See COMPTON GAMMA RAY OBSERVATORY.

O stars stars of SPECTRAL TYPE O that are very hot massive blue stars, emitting copious quantities of ultraviolet radiation, and with surface temperatures (T_{eff}) from about 28 000 to over 40 000 kelvin. Strong lines of singly ionized helium (He II) dominate the spectra. Lines of doubly and triply ionized elements are also present with lines of neutral helium (He I) and hydrogen strengthening in later subdivisions. No O0, O1, or O2 stars have been discovered and only a few O3 and O4 stars are known. Most O stars are found in the spiral arms of galaxies, often in OB ASSOCIATIONS, and are very fast rotators. They have short lifetimes of about three to six million years. See also OF STARS; ULTRAVIOLET STARS.

Otto Struve Telescope see MCDONALD OBSERVATORY.

outburst, cometary see SCHWASSMANN-WACHMANN 1.

outer planets the planets Jupiter, Saturn, Uranus, Neptune, and Pluto, which lie farther from the Sun than the main ASTEROID BELT. With the exception of Pluto, all are GIANT PLANETS.

OVV quasars *abbrev. for* optically violently variable quasars, a group of objects now classified as BLAZARS.

Owens Valley Radio Observatory (OVRO) the radio observatory of the California Institute of Technology, located in a semidesert region of California at an altitude of 1200 meters. It contains two 27-meter DISHES that were an early radio interferometer but are now used for solar observations, a 40-m dish used mostly for VLBI, and the *OVRO Millimeter Array*, an interferometer consisting of six 10.4-m dishes, laid out on a T-shaped track 200 m × 220 m.

Owl nebula (M97; NGC 3587) a relatively large, distinctively shaped PLANETARY NEBULA in the constellation Ursa Major, about 500 parsecs away.

Ozma project a pioneering project in the search for extraterrestrial intelligence. The 26-meter radio telescope at Green Bank, West Virginia, was used by Frank Drake in 1960 for about 150 hours in an unsuccessful attempt to detect signals – the 21-cm hydrogen line emission – from other civilizations. The targets were the two nearest and most sunlike stars Tau Ceti and Epsilon Eridani. See also EXOBIOLOGY; SETI.

ozone layer see ATMOSPHERIC LAYERS.

Pp

PA or **p.a.** *abbrev. for* position angle.

pair production the conversion of a high-energy (>1.022 MeV) gamma-ray PHOTON, usually in the field of an atomic nucleus, into an ELECTRON and positron, which are formed simultaneously. See also ANNIHILATION; PHOTON-PHOTON ABSORPTION.

Pallas ((2) **Pallas**) The second ASTEROID to be discovered, found in late March 1802 by the German astronomer H.W.M. Olbers. Measuring 570 × 525 × 500 km, it is the third largest asteroid and has a spectrum similar to that of the CARBONACEOUS CHONDRITE meteorites. Despite being a main-belt asteroid, Pallas follows an orbit that is inclined at 34.8° to the ECLIPTIC. Its mass has been measured at 2.2×10^{20} kg. It orbits the Sun once every 4.62 years at a mean distance of 2.77 AU. NASA's DAWN mission, set for launch in 2006, will, if successful, visit Pallas after (1) Ceres and (4) Vesta. See Table 3, Appendix.

pallasite see STONY-IRON METEORITE.

Palomar Observatory a world-famous observatory sited on Mount Palomar, about 65 kilometers northeast of San Diego, California, USA, at an altitude of 1713 meters. It is owned and operated by the Pasadena-based California Institute of Technology (Caltech). The site of the observatory was chosen by George Ellery Hale as suitable for a giant 200-inch (5.08-meter) telescope, following the success of the 100-inch Hooker telescope at MOUNT WILSON OBSERVATORY. The 200-inch reflector, now known as the *Hale telescope*, saw first light in Dec. 1947. Regular observing began in 1949. It was the world's largest telescope until the Soviet 6-meter instrument was built during the 1970s at ZELENCHUKSKAYA OBSERVATORY in the Caucasus. Now equipped with sophisticated electronic and computer systems, the Hale remains one of the world's most powerful telescopes.

The 200-inch mirror, ready for use in late 1947, almost 10 years after Hale's death, had been cast in 1934 after considerable design problems. It is of low-expansion Pyrex glass, with a reflecting surface of aluminum; it weighs 13.15 tonnes. The chosen FOCAL RATIO of f/3.3 meant that a much shorter tube could be used than with previous telescopes, which traditionally had an f/5 ratio. There is a Cassegrain focus, focal ratio f/16, and coudé foci of f/30.

In addition to the 200-inch, the Palomar Observatory has a 48-inch (1.24-meter) SCHMIDT TELESCOPE – the *Oschin Telescope*. This has a 1.83-meter primary mirror, focal ratio f/2.5, and a field of semiangle of 3°. It was used in the production of the PALOMAR SKY SURVEY. A new achromatic correcting plate was made in 1984. In addition there are an 18-inch (45.72-centimeter) Schmidt and a 60-inch (1.52-meter) reflector. Both the Oschin Telescope and the 60-inch have been modernized with the installation of CCD cameras.

Palomar Observatory Sky Survey (**POSS**) a photographic star atlas of the northern sky and part of the southern sky to a DECLINATION of –33°. It was prepared at the Mount Palomar Observatory, California, with the collaboration of the National Geographic Society, using the 48-inch Oschin Schmidt telescope. It was released

1954–58. It consisted of 935 pairs of photographic prints: one of each pair was made from an exposure on a blue-sensitive plate, the other was made from an exposure taken through a red filter. This survey, known as POSS-I, included stars to a limiting magnitude of 21 (20 in the southernmost plate). A second survey of the northern sky, known as POSS-II, was carried out in the 1980s with an upgraded version of the Palomar Oschin Schmidt, using much improved film. Objects four times as faint as those photographed by POSS-I were recorded. Identifications on POSS prints can be made using a set of labeled transparent overlays, prepared at Ohio State University by R. Dixon and published in 1981. The prints from both POSS-I and POSS-II are being converted to computerized digital format and are becoming accessible over the World Wide Web and as part of the DIGITIZED SKY SURVEY. See also SOUTHERN SKY SURVEY.

palus (plural: **paludes**) A mixed smooth and rough dark area on the surface of the Moon. The word is used in the approved name of such a feature. See also MARE. (Latin: marsh)

Pan a small satellite of Saturn, discovered in 1990 from photographs taken by Voyager 2 in 1981. It is the closest satellite to Saturn so far known, orbiting within the Encke Division of SATURN'S RINGS at a distance of 133 600 km from the center of the planet. It is a shepherd satellite, keeping the Encke Division open. See Table 2, Appendix.

Pandora a small irregularly shaped satellite of Saturn, discovered in 1980 from photographs taken by Voyager 1. It appears to be heavily cratered, the two largest craters being some 30 km in diameter. Together with PROMETHEUS, Pandora is a SHEPHERD SATELLITE for Saturn's F ring. See SATURN'S RINGS; Table 2, Appendix.

parabola a type of CONIC SECTION with an eccentricity equal to one. See also PARABOLOID.

parabolic velocity the velocity of an object following a *parabolic trajectory* around a massive body. Its velocity at a given distance from the massive body is equal to the ESCAPE VELOCITY at that distance.

paraboloid a curved surface formed by the rotation of a parabola about its axis. Cross sections along the central axis are circular. A beam of radiation striking such a surface parallel to its axis is reflected to a single point on the axis (the focus), no matter how wide the aperture (see illustration). A paraboloid mirror is thus free of SPHERICAL ABERRATION; it does however suffer from

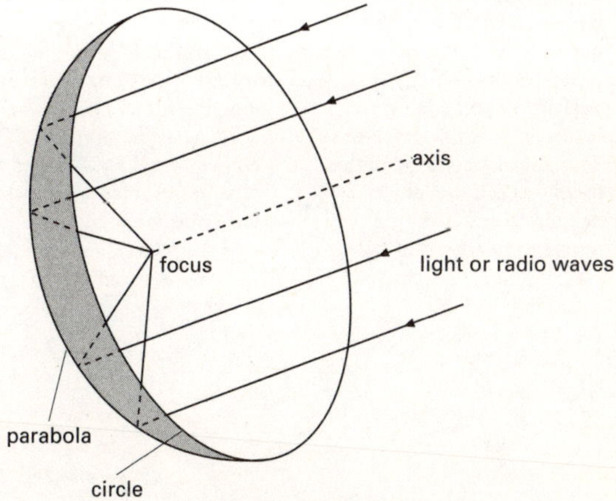

Paraboloid surface

COMA. Paraboloid surfaces are used in reflecting telescopes and radio telescopes. Over a small area a paraboloid differs only slightly from a sphere. A paraboloid mirror can therefore be made by deepening the center of a spherical mirror.

parallactic angle see ASTRONOMICAL TRIANGLE.

parallactic ellipse see ANNUAL PARALLAX.

parallactic inequality a minor periodic term in the Moon's motion that results from the gravitational attraction of the Sun and causes the Moon to be ahead at first quarter and to lag behind at last quarter (see PHASES, LUNAR). The inequality can be used to calculate SOLAR PARALLAX. See also EVECTION; VARIATION.

parallactic motion see PARALLAX.

parallax the angular displacement in the apparent position of a celestial body when observed from two widely separated points. It is thus the angle that the baseline connecting two viewpoints would subtend at the object (see illustration). It is very small in value and is usually expressed in arc seconds. If the baseline is of a fixed length then as the distance to the celestial object decreases, its parallax will increase accordingly. If the parallax can be measured then so can the distance.

The observer's position on Earth changes with the daily rotation of the Earth, the annual revolution of the Earth around the Sun, and the long-term motion of the Sun and Solar System relative to the background stars. Each motion produces a different measure of parallax: DIURNAL PARALLAX, ANNUAL PARALLAX, and SECULAR PARALLAX, respectively. The continual change in the apparent position of a celestial object, produced by the observer's changing position, is termed *parallactic motion* and must be distinguished from the star's own PECULIAR MOTION in space.

Methods used to determine the parallax and hence the distance of celestial bodies require an accurate knowledge of the baseline length. The baseline for diurnal parallax – the Earth's radius – can be used for distance measurements only within the Solar System. The baselines used in annual parallax – the semimajor axis of the Earth's orbit – and secular parallax are sufficiently great for stellar distances to be measured. Other methods based on the concept of parallax and used in distance determination include DYNAMICAL PARALLAX, MOVING-CLUSTER PARALLAX, and STATISTICAL PARALLAX.

Distances determined indirectly from stellar brightness are also sometimes called parallaxes: in *spectroscopic parallax* the absolute magnitude of a main-sequence star is deduced from the spectral type of the star using the HERTZSPRUNG–RUSSELL DIAGRAM and this together with the apparent magnitude gives the DISTANCE MODULUS and hence the distance. See also DISTANCE DETERMINATION.

parametric amplifier a type of negative-resistance amplifier that employs a nonlinear circuit element, such as a varactor diode, to act as a time-varying capacitance. These amplifiers have low NOISE FIGURES at high frequencies and are useful in RADIO TELESCOPES in the range 1–30 gigahertz.

paraxial lying close to the optical axis of a lens, mirror, or system of such elements.

parhelia *another name for* SUN DOGS.

Paris Observatory the French national astronomical research institute, located in Paris and founded in 1667. There are observing facilities at the *Meudon*

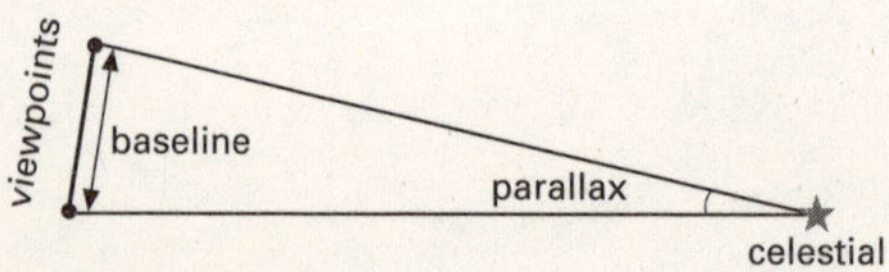

Parallax

Observatory, near Sèvres, which has two reflecting telescopes (1 meter and 0.6 meter) and forms the astrophysics section of the Paris Observatory, and at the NANÇAY RADIO OBSERVATORY.

Parkes Observatory (formerly **Australian National Radio Astronomy Observatory**) a radio astronomy observatory located near Parkes, New South Wales, Australia. It is operated by CSIRO's Division of Radio Astrophysics. The main instrument there is the *Parkes dish* – a fully steerable 64-meter telescope built in 1961 and now part of the AUSTRALIA TELESCOPE. It can observe at frequencies between 100 MHz and 45 GHz.

parking orbit an orbit in which a satellite or spacecraft can be placed before being injected into a final orbit or desired trajectory.

parsec *short for* parallax second. Symbol: pc. A unit of length normally used for distances beyond the Solar System. It is the distance at which the semimajor axis of the Earth's orbit subtends an angle of one arc second. It is thus the distance at which a star would have an ANNUAL PARALLAX of one arc second. A star with a parallax of p arc seconds is at a distance of d parsecs, given by $d = 1/p$ (accurate up to distances of about 30 pc). One parsec equals 30.857×10^{12} km, 206 265 astronomical units, and 3.2616 light-years.

partial eclipse see ECLIPSE.

particle see ELEMENTARY PARTICLES.

particle horizon see HORIZON DISTANCE.

Particle Physics and Astronomy Research Council (PPARC) an independent UK national organization funded by the government for the direction, co-ordination and financial support of British research into astronomy, particle physics, particle astrophysics and Solar System science. It was established by Royal Charter in 1994 and is one of seven UK research councils supporting advanced studies in various fields of learning. Its work is currently financed through an annual budget received from the Office of Science and Technology, a section of the Department of Trade and Industry. PPARC provides research grants and studentships to scientists in British universities, gives researchers access to world-class facilities and funds the UK membership of international organizations such as the European Particle Physics Laboratory, CERN, the EUROPEAN SPACE AGENCY (ESA) and the EUROPEAN SOUTHERN OBSERVATORY (ESO). It also makes financial contributions to the UK telescopes in La Palma, Hawaii, Australia and Chile, the UK Astronomy Technology Centre at the ROYAL OBSERVATORY, EDINBURGH (ROE), and the MERLIN/VLBI National Facility based at JODRELL BANK (see also MERLIN). PPARC is based in Swindon, UK, and has three scientific sites: the UK Astronomy Technology Centre at the ROE in Edinburgh, the ISAAC NEWTON GROUP of telescopes in La Palma, and the Joint Astronomy Centre in Hawaii. Among many other official tasks, PPARC advises the government on the appointment of the ASTRONOMER ROYAL and the Astronomer Royal for Scotland.

pascal symbol: Pa. The SI unit of pressure, equal to a pressure of one newton per square meter.

Paschen series see HYDROGEN SPECTRUM.

Pasiphae a small satellite of Jupiter, discovered in 1908 by the British astronomer Philibert Melotte. See JUPITER'S SATELLITES; Table 2, Appendix.

patera (plural: **paterae**) An irregular saucerlike volcanic structure with scalloped edges. The word is used in the approved name of such a surface feature on a planet or satellite.

pathlength see OPTICAL PATHLENGTH.

path of totality (**zone of totality**) see ECLIPSE.

Paul–Baker telescope a compact three-mirror telescope with a very wide field of view, designed by Maurice Paul in 1935 and modified by James Baker in about 1945 (see illustration overleaf). A paraboloidal primary mirror is used with a convex ellipsoidal secondary and concave spherical tertiary to produce a high-quality image on a flat focal plane; there is very low image spread.

Pauli exclusion principle the principle that no two particles can exist in exactly the same quantum state. It is obeyed by FERMIONS but not by BOSONS. The existence of WHITE DWARFS and NEUTRON STARS is a consequence of this.

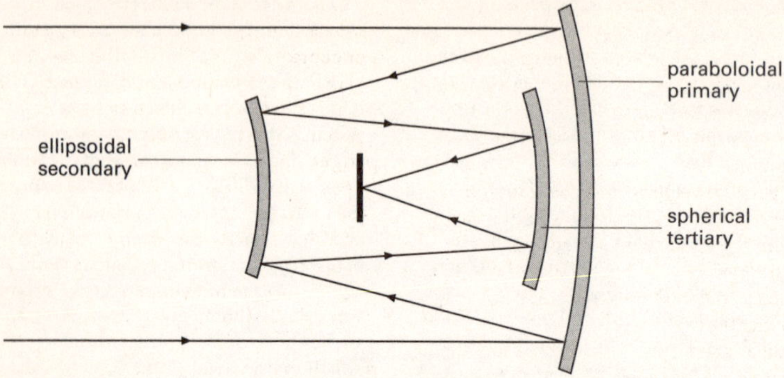

Paul–Baker telescope

Paul Wild Observatory see CULGOORA.

Pavo (Peacock) a constellation in the southern hemisphere near Grus, the brightest stars being the 1st-magnitude spectroscopic binary Alpha (α) Pavonis and several 3rd-magnitude stars. It contains several variables, including the bright Cepheid variable Kappa (κ) Pavonis, and the large bright globular cluster NGC 6752. Abbrev.: Pav; genitive form: Pavonis; approx. position: RA 19.5h, dec –65°; area: 378 sq deg.

Pavonis Mons a 19-km high volcano on the THARSIS RIDGE of Mars, located at 0.8° N latitude, 113.4 W longitude. It has a base diameter of 400 km, the diameter of the summit caldera being 45 km. See MARS, VOLCANOES.

payload 1 the total mass of a satellite, spacecraft, etc., that is carried into orbit by a launch vehicle. It is that part of the total launcher mass that is not necessary for the operation of the launcher. It is usually a small or very small fraction of the total launcher mass.

2 the mass of the experimental and operational equipment of a satellite, planetary probe, etc.

pc *symbol for* parsec.

P Cygni a massive LUMINOUS BLUE VARIABLE about 2000 parsecs away in the constellation Cygnus. It has undergone random outbursts: in both 1600 and 1653 it brightened considerably then faded, but since 1700 its brightness has very gradually increased. It is also an ultraviolet source that is gradually cooling, the UV brightness decreasing as the visual brightness increases. See also P CYGNI STARS.

P Cygni stars a small group of hot variable stars whose prototype is the BIe star P CYGNI. Their spectra show numerous strong emission lines, like those of BE STARS and WOLF-RAYET STARS, and sharp absorption lines that have a BLUESHIFT. The blueshifted absorption components originate in an expanding shell of low-density matter continuously ejected from the hot star. Many, like P Cygni, suffer random outbursts. The characteristic shape of the spectral lines – blueshifted absorption on an emission feature – has led to the term *P Cygni profile* being used for similarly shaped spectral lines in other types of astronomical bodies. In all cases it is due to an outflow of absorbing gases. See also LUMINOUS BLUE VARIABLES.

PDR *abbrev. for* photodissociation region.

peculiar galaxies galaxies that do not conveniently fit into the regular classification schemes of normal galaxies. These comparatively rare objects include ACTIVE GALAXIES, STARBURST GALAXIES, MARKARIAN GALAXIES, INTERACTING GALAXIES, single irregular or disturbed galaxies, DWARF GALAXIES, RING GALAXIES, and spiral galaxies with peculiar spiral arms or even with one or three arms.

peculiar motion 1 the motion of an

individual star relative to a group of neighboring stars.

2 that part of the PROPER MOTION of a star that results from its actual movement in space; it is the star's proper motion after elimination of the effects of the Sun's motion.

3 (**peculiar velocity**; **streaming motion**) a deviation of a galaxy or cluster of galaxies from the HUBBLE FLOW due to its real motion under local gravitational effects, such as the motion of the LOCAL GROUP due to the GREAT ATTRACTOR.

peculiar stars stars with spectral features that do not correspond exactly with the usual classification of SPECTRAL TYPES. In general they are designated by a 'p' after their spectral type, as with AP STARS, but specific features are given other suffixes, e.g. 'e' for emission or 'm' for metallic lines.

peculiar velocity see PECULIAR MOTION.

Pegasus an extensive conspicuous constellation in the northern hemisphere near Cygnus, with five 2nd-magnitude stars (ε, α, β, γ, and η Peg) and four of 3rd magnitude. The stars MARKAB (α), SCHEAT (β), and ALGENIB (γ) together with Alpha (α) Andromedae (ALPHERATZ) form the distinctive *Great Square of Pegasus.* The star 51 PEGASI, which is thought to have a planet orbiting it, is located within the Great Square. The constellation also contains the globular cluster M15 (NGC 7078), the dim spiral galaxy NGC 7331 and the group of faint galaxies known as STEPHAN'S QUINTET. Abbrev.: Peg; genitive form: Pegasi; approx. position: RA 23h, dec +20°; area: 1121 sq deg.

Pele see IO.

pencil beam see ANTENNA.

pencil-beam survey a form of REDSHIFT SURVEY where deep exposures of comparatively small fields are taken only at sparse intervals across the sky. This allows a compromise between sampling deep in the redshift direction with a wide sky coverage and an economical use of telescope time.

penumbra 1 see UMBRA.

2 see SUNSPOTS.

penumbral eclipse see ECLIPSE.

periapsis see APSIDES.

periastron the closest approach of the two components of a binary star. At greatest separation the components are at *apastron.*

pericenter the point in an orbit, e.g. of a planet or of a component of a binary star, that is nearest to the CENTER OF MASS of the system. The farthest point is the *apocenter.*

perigee the point in the orbit of the Moon or an artificial Earth satellite that is nearest the Earth and at which the body's velocity is maximal. Strictly, the distance to the perigee is taken from the Earth's center. The distance to the Moon's perigee varies; on average it is about 363 300 km. Compare APOGEE.

perihelion the point in the orbit of a planet, comet, or artificial satellite in solar orbit that is nearest the Sun. The Earth is at perihelion on or about Jan. 3. The time of year at which Earth reaches perihelion varies over a period of about 20 000 years, getting progressively later in the year. The perihelion distance *q*, and APHELION distance Q, of major planets and asteroids are given in Tables 1 and 3, backmatter. See also ADVANCE OF THE PERIHELION.

perihelion distance the distance from the Sun to the PERIHELION of a body in an elliptical orbit, or from the focus of a parabolic trajectory around the Sun to the vertex.

perihelion passage, time of see ORBITAL ELEMENTS.

period the time interval between two successive and similar phases of a regularly occurring event. The period of ROTATION or of REVOLUTION of a planet, etc., is the time to complete one rotation on its axis or one revolution around its primary. The period of a BINARY STAR is the time observed for the companion to orbit the primary. The period of a regular intrinsic VARIABLE STAR or an ECLIPSING BINARY is the time between two successive maxima or minima on the LIGHT CURVE.

period-density relation see PULSATING VARIABLES.

period gap see CATACLYSMIC VARIABLE.

periodic comet a comet that has been seen to orbit the Sun more than once. The names of such comets are prefixed by P/, as in P/Halley.

period-luminosity (P-L) relation a relation showing graphically how the period of the light variation of a CEPHEID VARIABLE depends on its mean luminosity: the longer the period the greater the luminosity and hence mean absolute magnitude of the star. The relation was discovered by Henrietta Leavitt in 1912 and much subsequent work was done in calibrating the graph. It was found, in the 1950s, that there are two types of Cepheid – classical Cepheids and the less luminous type II Cepheids – whose P-L relations are approximately parallel, as shown on the graph. The relation results from the dependence of both luminosity and period of light variation, i.e. of pulsation, on stellar radius (see PULSATING VARIABLES).

The relation is an invaluable means of determining the distances of Cepheids and hence of their surroundings. To calibrate the two curves, the mean absolute magnitude of a small number of Cepheids is determined from the measured value of their periods, and the distances must then be found from an independent measure. The distance to other Cepheids can then be calculated from their periods and mean apparent magnitudes (see DISTANCE MODULUS). Cepheids fluctuate more markedly at blue and near-UV wavelengths than at longer red and near-IR wavelengths. The mean brightness is thus more easily and accurately measured at longer wavelengths. Cepheids occur in many star clusters within our own Galaxy and because of their great luminosity can be observed in nearby galaxies. They can therefore be used for measuring an immense range of distances. See DISTANCE DETERMINATION.

Perseids a major METEOR SHOWER, radiant: RA 47°, dec +58°, maximizing on Aug. 12 with a ZENITHAL HOURLY RATE (ZHR) of about 80. Perseid meteors can be seen throughout the two weeks each side of maximum and are bright and flaring, with fine TRAINS. The geocentric velocity of the meteoroids is about 60 km s^{-1}. The METEOROID STREAM is closely associated with comet SWIFT–TUTTLE (1862 III), which returned to the inner Solar System in late 1992. Although the display is regarded as being constant in hourly rate there are exceptions, a ZHR of 250 being observed in 1921 and 1992 and a ZHR of less than 10 in 1911 and 1912. The shower has been regularly observed for over 100 years. The first record was in AD 36.

Perseus a fairly conspicuous constellation in the northern hemisphere near Cassiopeia, lying in the Milky Way. It has two bright stars – MIRFAK (α) and the prototype eclipsing binary ALGOL (β) – and several of about 3rd magnitude. It also contains the

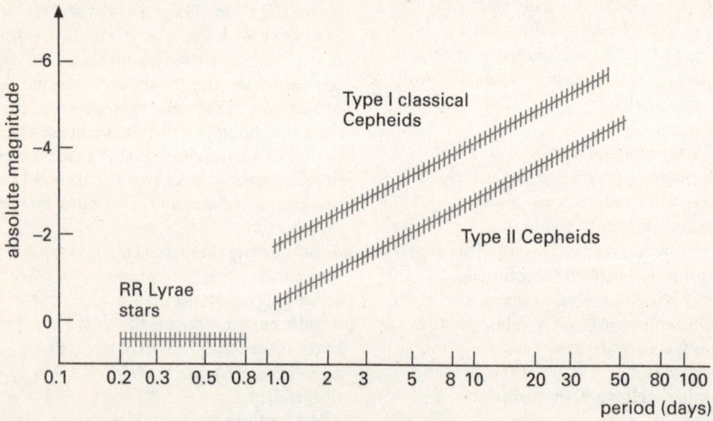

Period-luminosity relation

naked-eye double cluster H AND CHI PERSEI, several open clusters including the just-visible M34 (NGC 1039), the CALIFORNIA NEBULA, and the galaxy NGC 1275, which is a powerful radio source and lies in the PERSEUS CLUSTER. Abbrev.: Per; genitive form: Persei; approx. position: RA 3.5h, dec +45°; area: 615 sq deg.

Perseus A see PERSEUS CLUSTER.

Perseus arm see GALAXY.

Perseus cluster (Abell 426) A rich CLUSTER OF GALAXIES lying about 70 megaparsecs away in the direction of the constellation Perseus. It is the brightest cluster observed in the X-ray waveband. It also contains several strong radio sources, three of which have been identified with the galaxies IC 310, NGC 1265, and NGC 1275. The most intense radio source (3C84A or Perseus A) is associated with the dominant cD galaxy, NGC 1275. This lies at the center of the cluster's cooling flow, which has a mass deposition rate of around 200 solar masses a year (see CLUSTERS OF GALAXIES). NGC 1275 shows nuclear continuum activity (it was originally classified as a SEYFERT GALAXY) and is surrounded by a particularly extensive (up to 40 kiloparsecs in radius) nebula of line-emitting filaments. HST images show it is also surrounded by many GLOBULAR CLUSTERS. Study of the galaxy is complicated by the presence of an intervening disk galaxy, with its own emission-line spectrum, that is falling toward NGC 1275 along the line of sight at 3000 km s^{-1}.

perturbation a small disturbance that causes a system to deviate from a reference or equilibrium state. Periodic perturbations cancel out over the period involved and do not affect the system's stability. Secular perturbations have a progressive effect on the system that can cause it eventually to become unstable.

A single planet orbiting the Sun would follow an elliptical orbit according to Kepler's laws; in reality a planet is perturbed from its elliptical orbit by the gravitational effects of the other planets. Likewise the revolution of the Moon around the Earth is perturbed mainly by the Sun and to a much lesser extent by other bodies. The assumptions that the Sun is the only perturbing body and that the Earth orbits the Sun in a fixed elliptical orbit lead to a simplified theory of lunar motion. The orbits of comets and asteroids are strongly perturbed when the body passes close to a major planet, such as Jupiter. The influence of a perturbing body can be calculated from the orbital elements of an OSCULATING ORBIT, to which corrections are made.

Phaethon ((3200) Phaeton) A 6.9-km-diameter APOLLO asteroid discovered in 1983 on photographs taken by the infrared satellite IRAS. Its unusual orbit (eccentricity 0.89, inclination 22.17°) crosses the orbits of Mars, Earth, Venus, and Mercury and takes it to a perihelion of 0.14 AU from the Sun. This is the closest approach to the Sun of any known asteroid. Phaethon's 1.43-year orbit is almost identical to the Geminid METEOROID STREAM, and Phaethon is now generally assumed to be the parent of the GEMINIDS. Before Phaethon's discovery meteor showers were thought to be associated only with comets, and there has been considerable debate as to whether it is an extinct comet.

phase **1** the appearance of the illuminated surface of the Moon or a planet at a particular time during its orbit or of the Sun during an eclipse. Specifically it is the fraction of the object's apparent disk (taken to be circular) that is illuminated. Unlike the superior planets, Mercury and Venus can exhibit those phases in which half or less of the illuminated hemisphere is visible from Earth. See also PHASES, LUNAR. **2** the fraction of one complete cycle of a regularly recurring quantity that has elapsed with respect to a fixed datum point. The *phase difference*, ϕ, is the difference in phase between two electrical oscillations, wavetrains, etc., of the same frequency (i.e. coherent signals) and is usually expressed in terms of part of one complete cycle or wavelength. 'Phase difference' is often referred to simply as 'phase', as it is when considering the coherent signals in the two arms of a radio interferometer.

phase angle the angle between the lines connecting the Moon and Sun and the Moon and Earth or connecting a planet and the Sun and the planet and Earth (see illustration overleaf). At full or new Moon

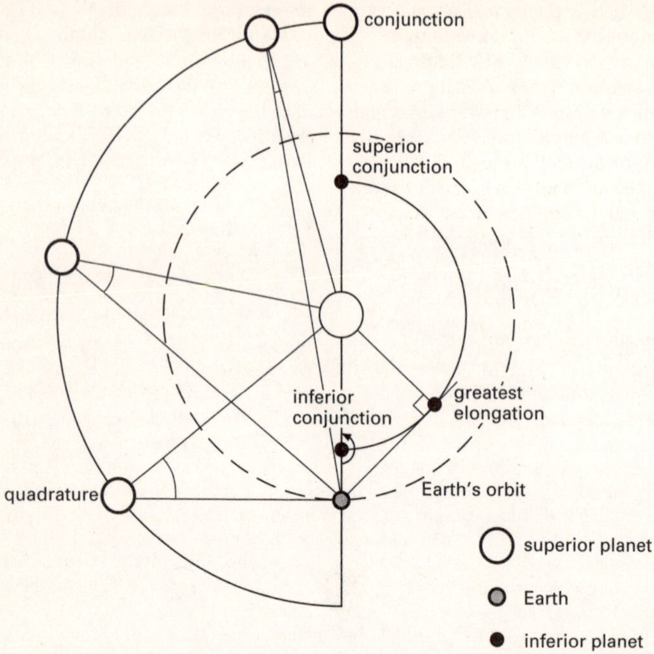

Phase angles for superior and inferior planet

the phase angle is 0° or 180°, respectively. At first and last quarters it is 90°. For the superior planets phase angle is greatest at quadrature. For the inferior planets it is greatest (180°) at inferior conjunction and equals 90° at greatest ELONGATION.

phased array an array of separate radio elements, such as DIPOLES or DISH antennas, connected together so as to behave as one large antenna. The BEAM of the array can be steered across the sky by adjusting the relative phases of signals from the elements. The adjustment does not involve mechanical movement and can be done very quickly, making the technique particularly useful for terrestrial radar. Radio interferometers such as the VLA are sometimes configured as sensitive phased arrays to detect weak transmissions from distant space probes.

phase defect the angular amount by which the illuminated area of the Moon differs from a circular disk at full Moon due to the inclination of the Moon's orbital plane to the ECLIPTIC.

phase difference see PHASE.

phase integral see ALBEDO.

phase rotator a device that adds extra delay to one arm of an interferometer (see RADIO TELESCOPE), especially one used for APERTURE SYNTHESIS, in order to keep the PHASE DIFFERENCE close to zero as a RADIO SOURCE moves across the sky. When the phase difference is made equal to zero, the process is called *fringe-stopping*.

phases, lunar the PHASES exhibited by the Moon (see illustration). A *new Moon* occurs when the Moon is at CONJUNCTION and the NEARSIDE is totally unilluminated by the Sun. As the moon moves eastward in its orbit around the Earth, the sunrise TERMINATOR crosses the nearside from east to west to produce a *crescent Moon*. The crescent waxes to *first quarter* when the Moon, at QUADRATURE, is half illuminated, through a *gibbous Moon*, and finally to *full Moon*, when the Moon is at OPPOSITION and the nearside is fully illuminated. The sunset TERMINATOR then follows to produce a waning gibbous Moon, *last quarter*, a waning crescent, and the next new Moon. New Moon, first quarter, full Moon, last quarter, and next new Moon occur on average about 7.4 days apart. See also ECLIPSE; SYNODIC MONTH.

phase-sensitive detector an electronic device capable of measuring the difference in phase between a periodic signal and a reference signal in the presence of NOISE. The signal plus noise is multiplied by a reference waveform whose shape and frequency are similar to those of the signal. Components near zero frequency are produced. When the output is smoothed by a low-pass FILTER a steady signal results, whose amplitude is related to the amplitude of the required signal and to the PHASE DIFFERENCE between the required signal and the reference waveform. The device is used, for example, in a PHASE-SWITCHING INTERFEROMETER to detect the component at the switching frequency in the output of the first DETECTOR.

phase-switching interferometer in its

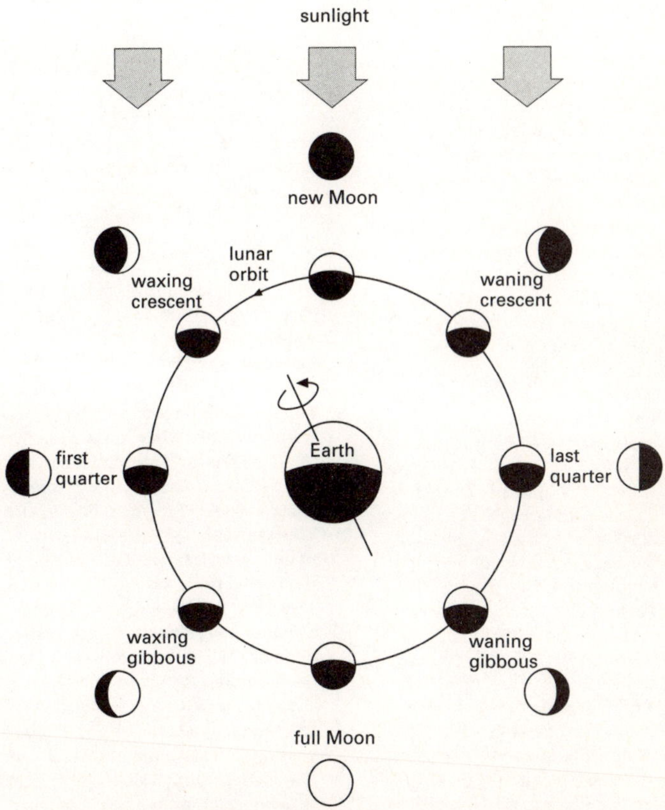

Lunar phases, outer circle showing phases as seen from Earth

simplest form, a correlating interferometer (see CORRELATION RECEIVER) in which the signals from two antennas, V_1 and V_2, are alternately added and subtracted before being applied to the input of a *square-law detector* to give outputs $(V_1 + V_2)^2$ and $(V_1 - V_2)^2$. The sign changing is carried out at a rate of between 10 and 1000 Hz by means of a *phase switch*, which adds an extra half wavelength to the path of the signal from the second antenna every alternate half cycle of the switching frequency. A PHASE-SENSITIVE DETECTOR, fed also by the switching signal, takes the difference between the two terms, equaling $4V_1V_2$. The time average of this is therefore proportional to the product of the two antenna signals, and is a measure of the correlated signal between the two antennas. Uncorrelated NOISE is reduced by the averaging process.

The strength of the correlated output depends on both the FLUX DENSITY of the radio source and the relative PHASE of the two signals at the antennas. As a RADIO SOURCE moves across the sky, interference fringes appear in the output of the phase-sensitive detector. The fringes are similar to those from an ordinary adding radio interferometer, except that their average is zero rather than being superimposed on a steady background deflection. Phase-switching makes the interferometer far less sensitive to INTERFERENCE and reduces the effects of changes in the gain and other parameters of the system.

Phase switches are sometimes used to modulate a weak, but relatively constant, signal before it is amplified and then to demodulate it afterwards. In this way any offsets introduced by the amplification process appear modulated at the output and can be removed with a FILTER.

Phecda (Phekda; γ UMa) one of the seven brightest stars in the PLOUGH. m_v: 2.44; M_v: 0.5; spectral type: A0 Van; distance: 24.5 pc.

Phobos the innermost and larger of the two satellites of Mars, both of which were discovered in 1877 by Asaph Hall. Observations from Mars-orbiting spacecraft show it to be an irregular potato-shaped body, measuring 27 × 22 × 19 km with a mass of 10^{16} kg and a density twice that of water. It orbits above the equator of Mars at a distance of 9380 km from the center of the planet every 7.65 hours, keeping its long axis pointing toward Mars. The low density, together with a low ALBEDO of 0.06, suggest that it resembles the water-rich CARBONACEOUS CHONDRITE meteorites, although it is difficult to see how such an object could have formed at the distance of Mars from the Sun. Possibly Phobos and DEIMOS, Mars' other small satellite, formed as more distant ASTEROIDS and were later captured by Mars in some way. The orbit of Phobos is decaying (contracting) because of tidal drag and the satellite may fall from orbit within another 100 million years.

Phobos has a REGOLITH-covered cratered surface with the two largest craters, *Stickney* and *Hall*, having diameters of 10 and 6 km. A network of pitted grooves, typically 100–200 meters wide and 20–30 meters deep, radiate around the satellite from Stickney and are thought to have arisen from severe internal fracturing and heating caused by the impact event that formed the crater. Chains of small craters parallel to the orbit of Phobos possibly represent the secondary impacts of clumps of material swept up from orbit around Mars after being ejected from the satellite during earlier primary impacts. See Table 2, Appendix.

Phobos mission either of two Soviet missions to land a probe on Mars' satellite Phobos. Phobos 1 was launched 1988, but contact was lost while it was still in transit. Phobos 2 was launched the following year, but signals from it ceased transmission about a week before the scheduled landing.

Phocaea group see HUNGARIA GROUP.

Phoebe a small satellite of Saturn, discovered in 1898 by William Henry Pickering. It is the largest of Saturn's outer satellites, roughly spherical in shape with a diameter of 220 km. It follows a retrograde orbit, circling the planet once every 548.2 days at a mean distance of nearly 13 million km. Voyager 2 photographed Phoebe after passing Saturn in 1981, revealing a surface that is dark, with an albedo of 0.06, Phoebe is red in color but not as red as Iapetus. Its rotation period is about 9.4 hours, so

Phoebe may not be in SYNCHRONOUS ROTATION with Saturn.

Phoebe was imaged again by the CASSINI probe in June 2004 just before the spacecraft entered orbit around Saturn. The images Cassini returned, taken from a distance of 2078 km, revealed a tiny world heavily scarred by impact craters. Many of the impacts had excavated material from within the satellite's crust, hurling enormous rocks out onto its surface. The images also revealed alternating light and dark material around some of the craters. Other sensors aboard Cassini found that Phoebe contains not only water ice but also carbon dioxide. The geological and chemical complexities of Phoebe lead scientists to believe that it is not a captured asteroid, as was first thought, but an icy planetesimal, similar in makeup to a Kuiper Belt object, that was captured about 4000 million years ago by the spinning gas disk that eventually became Saturn. See also Table 2, Appendix.

Phoenicids a minor southern hemisphere METEOR SHOWER, radiant: RA 15°, dec −55°, maximizing on Dec. 4.

Phoenix a constellation in the southern hemisphere near Grus, the brightest star, Ankaa (α) being of 2nd magnitude. Beta (β) Phoenicis is a binary, both components being of 4th magnitude. Abbrev.: Phe; genitive form: Phoenicis; approx. position: RA 1h, dec −50°; area: 469 sq deg.

Pholus a large interplanetary object, some 200 km in diameter, that moves in a highly elliptical orbit (9–32 AU) between the orbits of Saturn and Neptune. It was discovered in 1991. It may be similar to the object CHIRON.

photocathode an electrode in an electronic device, such as a photocell, photomultiplier, or image tube, that emits electrons when a beam of electromagnetic radiation strikes the surface. By a suitable choice of photocathode material, a reasonable response may be obtained from near-infrared wavelengths to low-energy X-ray wavelengths. The electrons result from the PHOTOELECTRIC EFFECT. As many as 30% of the incident photons can liberate electrons, although the percentage is usually lower when taken over a wide spectral region. The current of resulting electrons increases linearly with radiation intensity over a wide range of intensities.

photocell an electronic device that converts a light signal, or a signal in the infrared or ultraviolet, into an equivalent electrical signal. The earliest devices were *photoelectric cells*. These are evacuated and work by the PHOTOELECTRIC EFFECT. Electrons are emitted from a PHOTOCATHODE when a beam of radiation falls on the surface. The electrons are attracted to a positively charged anode so that a current flows in an external circuit. The word photocell is now commonly used to describe PHOTOCONDUCTIVE or PHOTOVOLTAIC devices.

photoconductive cell an electronic device that consists of a layer of semiconductor sandwiched between two electrical contacts. When light, infrared, or ultraviolet radiation falls on the sandwich its electrical conductivity increases markedly as a result of photoconductivity: the incident photons are absorbed in the material where they produce free electrical charge carriers that change the conductivity. A current therefore flows in the external circuit of the device. The current is proportional to the amount of radiation falling on the cell.

photoconductive detector a PHOTOCONDUCTIVE CELL used to detect photons in the infrared, usually made from either germanium or silicon doped with a variety of other metals, e.g. copper, arsenic, antimony. These detectors are used at wavelengths from about 10 to 200 μm, with liquid-helium cooling. In contrast to BOLOMETERS, the responsive elements of photoconductive detectors undergo no significant temperature change. See also INFRARED DETECTORS.

photodetector any electronic device designed to respond to, i.e. detect, photons of light or other radiation. Examples include the PHOTOMULTIPLIER and CCD.

photodiode a semiconductor device that produces an electric current when illuminated. Infrared-sensitive photodiodes are used, for example, in photometry.

photodissociation region (**PDR**) an interface between an H II REGION and a MOLECULAR CLOUD, where ULTRAVIOLET RADIATION escaping from the H II region dissociates molecules (including those of hydrogen and carbon monoxide), giving an increased abundance of the atomic forms of the constituents. The incident UV also leads to excitation and ionization of the dissociation products, and thus profoundly affects the chemistry in these regions. Well-known PDRs include those in the ORION NEBULA (face-on), and in the OMEGA NEBULA (edge-on).

photoelectric effect an effect whereby electrons are emitted by material exposed to electromagnetic radiation above a certain frequency. This frequency usually lies in the ultraviolet region of the spectrum for most solids, but can occur in the visible region. The number of ejected electrons depends on the intensity of the incident radiation. The electron velocity is proportional to the radiation frequency.

photoelectric magnitude see MAGNITUDE.

photoelectric photometry see PHOTOMETRY.

photographic emulsion a light-sensitive layer of silver halide crystals suspended in gelatin and coated on a flexible or rigid base, from which a permanent record of an optical or near-ultraviolet image, focused on the surface, may be produced. Both black-and-white and color films or plates are used in astronomy. Emulsions highly sensitive to infrared and ultraviolet radiation and to X-rays are also now available.

The sensitivity of a particular type of emulsion to light or other radiation is known as its *speed*. This is usually expressed numerically as its *ISO number*; very high speed color and black-and-white emulsions are commercially available and are suitable for astronomical work. The sensitivity of an emulsion can be increased by HYPERSENSITIZATION; this reduces the required exposure time or improves the image quality, sometimes both.

Photographic emulsions have high resolution, wide spectral response, and good dimensional stability and permanence, and they produce images with a reasonably high signal/noise ratio. The light from a star, well below the visual threshold, can be recorded during a long exposure: exposures of over an hour may be used. Emulsions are, however, inefficient detectors compared to electronic recording devices – they can record only a very small number of the incident photons of radiation. In addition, a linear relationship between intensity of incident radiation and resulting image density exists for only a narrow range of exposures ('exposure' here means intensity of illumination times exposure time); at shorter or longer exposures the relationship is nonlinear and the emulsion suffers from *reciprocity failure*. See also IMAGING; PHOTOGRAPHY.

photographic magnitude see MAGNITUDE.

photographic photometry see PHOTOMETRY.

photographic zenith tube (**PZT**) a specially designed telescope that is used for the accurate determination of time of transit of FUNDAMENTAL STARS, so ascertaining clock error arising from the Earth's irregular rotation and CHANDLER WOBBLE. It is also used to determine the ZENITH DISTANCE of those stars at transit. The telescope is fixed in a vertical position so that the observed stars are at or near the ZENITH of the observatory. The positions of the stars are recorded on a photographic plate.

photography the process of capturing light and other electromagnetic radiation reflected or transmitted from an object and chemically recording it as an image on emulsion-coated film or glass plates. Few professional astronomers employ traditional photographic methods any longer, using instead the modern techniques of electronic IMAGING. However, film photography remains an important aspect of amateur astronomy as a hobby, and plate photography retains much value in studying and recording wide areas of sky in the preparation of star catalogs.

The light or other radiation from a galaxy, nebula, star, Solar-System body or other celestial object visible at night is generally of very low intensity, requiring long exposure times of the film or plate (from minutes to many hours). In order to maintain a steady image and a constant field of view, the camera must be mounted in the focal plane of a telescope (or possibly in isolation) and the assembly has to be mechanically driven at a constant (usually sidereal) rate (see also GUIDE TELESCOPE). If the camera is not driven in this way, star images will be elongated into trails. Photography of the brighter Solar-System objects is fairly straightforward. For photographs of the well-illuminated Moon, for example, the best results can be achieved using a slow film with an ISO rating of 50 to 100. Wide-angle studies of the night sky, including constellation patterns and extended star fields, are somewhat more complicated: camera lenses of short FOCAL RATIO (less than f/5) should be used together with a high-speed photographic emulsion that is able to respond to the very low light levels and the long exposure times. Films of ISO 400, 800, and higher are now available from such manufacturers as Kodak and Fuji. Long exposures can be badly affected by stray light so that LIGHT POLLUTION must be minimal: the sites of both major observatories and small amateur instruments must be carefully selected to reduce pollution and to have the best possible SEEING. The use of filters, such as light-pollution reduction (LPR) filters or broadband filters, is of limited effect for night-sky photography. Such accessories may darken the background sky but usually alter the color balance of the image. However, filters are the most important aspect of solar photography. The safest ones to use are Mylar or metal-coated glass filters that cover the entire aperture of the telescope: eyepiece filters are not safe. For professional work, expensive filters that block all but a narrow wavelength of light may be necessary, especially hydrogen-alpha (Hα) filters, which allow the observer to see solar prominences.

Plates or films for long-exposure use must have fine-grained PHOTOGRAPHIC EMULSIONS with low reciprocity failure: they must be able to respond uniformly to a wide range of light intensity. When such emulsions are employed, the resulting photographic images are very uniform and have a very high resolution, especially when HYPERSENSITIZATION techniques are used to increase the speed. Some Kodak emulsions can be used for near-infrared work and can become very much faster when hypersensitized. A large area of the sky can be photographed at one time, much greater than that 'seen' at present using electronic IMAGING. This explains why photographic plates are used in SCHMIDT TELESCOPES for sky surveys. Information, in digital form, can be extracted rapidly and automatically from the plates using machines such as COSMOS.

photoionization the IONIZATION of an atom or molecule by photons of electromagnetic radiation. A photon can only remove an electron if the photon energy exceeds the first IONIZATION POTENTIAL of the atom or molecule. The excess energy is shared between the electron and the ion so that the electron can leave the atom with considerable velocity. If the radiation is of sufficiently high energy more strongly bound electrons will be removed, leaving the resulting ion in an excited state. See also RECOMBINATION LINE EMISSION.

photometer an instrument used in PHOTOMETRY, such as a CCD, PHOTOVOLTAIC DETECTOR, PHOTOMULTIPLIER, PHOTODIODE, or BOLOMETER. In these devices the incident radiation is converted into an electrical signal whose magnitude can be determined very precisely.

photometric binary a BINARY STAR that can be detected by virtue of periodic changes in its light curve. See ECLIPSING BINARY.

photometric redshift a way of estimating the REDSHIFT of a galaxy only from its COLORS when a spectrum is not available for direct redshift determination. The galaxy's MAGNITUDE in several broad-band filters is compared to that expected from theoretical spectra of different types of galaxy at a range of redshifts.

photometry the measurement of the brightness or intensity of a source of light or other electromagnetic radiation. In astronomy, photometric measurements are taken over particular ranges of frequency or wavelength (these ranges are called wavebands) and take account of how brightness varies with both waveband and time. Various properties of the source, including temperature, can then be inferred. At optical, infrared, and near-ultraviolet wavelengths, astronomers measure brightness or luminous intensity in terms of apparent MAGNITUDE. At other wavelengths measurements of FLUX DENSITY are made.

In some cases the eye can make comparisons, with a fair degree of accuracy (to 0.1 magnitude) between the known brightness of a reference star and the unknown brightness of the source under study. The greater accuracies now required in astronomy, however, are achieved with electronic instruments (photometers) or specially prepared photographic emulsions, leading to *photoelectric* or *photographic photometry*. A photometric system defines standard wavebands and sets of standard sources, measured with these wavebands, that are well-distributed around the sky. Different systems define different wavebands.

Photoelectric *broadband systems*, such as the UBV system (see MAGNITUDE), use a combination of a suitable FILTER and a device such as a CCD or PHOTOMULTIPLIER, to convert the radiation selected by the filter into an equivalent electrical signal, which is then amplified and measured. The U, B, and V magnitudes are determined over three relatively broad wavebands in the ultraviolet, blue, and yellow-green (visual) spectral regions. Magnitudes can also be measured for various infrared bands. In *narrow-band photometry*, narrower wavebands are used, as in the UVBY SYSTEM. Extremely narrow bands, now obtainable over the entire optical and infrared regions, can be studied by means of INTERFERENCE FILTERS: the distribution of, say, hydrogen in a source can be determined by isolating a particular spectral line of hydrogen.

Photoelectric photometry can be used to study an isolated star, region, etc., or with the latest detector arrays a narrow angle of sky containing several stars. In photographic photometry, measurements can be made of objects on a photographic image of a wide angle of sky; the photographs are taken at wavelengths varying from near-infrared to near-ultraviolet (depending on emulsion). Highly resolved features can be registered, often of much greater quality than can be obtained electronically. The image, for a given photographic exposure time, varies in density (and size) by an amount that, within relatively wide limits, depends on the original brightness. Densities can be measured accurately by means of microdensitometers, etc.

photomultiplier (**photomultiplier tube**; **phototube**) an electronic device used to convert a low-intensity light signal into an electrical signal and to amplify this signal very considerably. It contains a PHOTOCATHODE from which electrons are liberated by the incident light photons. The electrons are accelerated down an evacuated tube by a series of positively charged electrodes to which an increasingly high potential is applied. At each electrode a number of additional electrons are released by each impacting electron (by secondary emission). The electrons are all collected at the final electrode in the chain, which is held at a very high potential, and a large current pulse is produced.

photon symbol: γ. A quantum of ELECTROMAGNETIC RADIATION. The photon can be considered as an ELEMENTARY PARTICLE with zero REST MASS, CHARGE, and SPIN, traveling at the speed of light. A beam of electromagnetic radiation can thus be thought of as a beam of photons, with the intensity of the radiation proportional to the number of photons present. The energy of the photons, and hence of the radiation, is equal to the product, $h\nu$, of the PLANCK CONSTANT and the frequency of the radiation. Photons with sufficient energy can ionize atoms and disintegrate nuclei. Although photons have no rest mass they do have momentum and thus exert a pressure, usually referred to as RADIATION PRESSURE.

photon-counting detector a highly sensitive detecting system with a very high time resolution and very low readout noise. Many photon counters use an IMAGE TUBE or MICROCHANNEL PLATE as a first stage to intensify the incident beam of light or other radiation, and a CCD array as the final detector. The earliest version was Boksenberg's IPCS.

photon-photon absorption the absorption of gamma-ray photons on collision with ambient 'gas' photons to produce electron-positron pairs (see PAIR PRODUCTION). The

OPTICAL DEPTH for this process can be written as:

$$\tau_{\gamma\gamma} \cong R \int \sigma(E_T)\, N_T(E_T)\, dE_T$$

if the density of the target photons, N_T, is assumed constant throughout the source region of size R. $\sigma(E_T)$ is the cross-section for pair production with a target photon of energy E_T.

photosphere the 'visible' surface of the SUN and source of the ABSORPTION SPECTRUM that is characteristic of most stars. The photosphere of a star is considerably more dense than the atmospheric layers that lie above it, i.e. the CHROMOSPHERE and CORONA.

The solar photosphere is a stratum several hundred kilometers thick, from which almost all the energy emitted by the Sun is radiated into space. Within the photosphere the temperature falls from about 6000 K just above the CONVECTIVE ZONE to about 4000 K at the *temperature minimum*, where the photosphere merges with the chromosphere.

The intensity of the solar photosphere, which decreases at visible wavelengths from the center to the limb of the disk (see LIMB DARKENING), is due to the radiation emitted, principally by negative HYDROGEN ions (H^-), at depths of up to a few hundred kilometers. At higher levels, where the density of H^- ions is too low for appreciable OPACITY, the lower temperature gives rise to the absorption of radiation at discrete wavelengths. The FRAUNHOFER LINES of the resulting absorption spectrum have provided the key to determining the chemical composition of the photosphere, because a direct comparison can be made with the laboratory spectra of known elements under various conditions.

Regions of the solar photosphere (and lower chromosphere) several thousand kilometers in diameter rhythmically rise and fall with a period of about 5 minutes over a time span of less than half an hour, attaining a maximum velocity of about 0.5 km s^{-1}. These vertical oscillations are thought to be produced by the outward propagation of low-frequency sound waves, generated by turbulence in the convective zone. The internal vibrations of the Sun, the subject area of HELIOSEISMOLOGY, can reveal information on the solar interior.

See also FACULAE; GRANULATION; SUPERGRANULATION; SUNSPOTS.

phototube *short for* photomultiplier tube. See PHOTOMULTIPLIER.

photovisual magnitude see MAGNITUDE.

photovoltaic detector an electronic device designed to detect PHOTONS of electromagnetic radiation. It consists of a junction between two opposite-polarity semiconductors (a p-n junction). Photons absorbed at or near the junction cause the emission of charge carriers that are separated by the junction to produce an external voltage. The magnitude of the voltage is related to the number of incident photons. This type of instrument is used in astronomy to detect ultraviolet and infrared radiation; for example, an indium antimonide (InSb) detector is used in the near-infrared (see INFRARED DETECTORS). To achieve optimum performance in the infrared the detectors are cooled, for example by liquid nitrogen to operate at 77 K or with liquid helium to function at about 4 K. In contrast to BOLOMETERS, photovoltaic detectors exhibit no significant temperature change in their responsive elements.

physical double 1 see DOUBLE STAR. 2 see DOUBLE GALAXY.

physical libration slight variations in the Moon's rotation on its axis that are caused by minor irregularities in shape. They amount to less than two arc minutes but allow the Moon's principal moments of inertia, and hence the distribution of mass within the Moon, to be calculated. The mean orientation of the Moon with respect to its physical librations defines the Moon's PRIME MERIDIAN. See also LIBRATION.

pico- symbol: p. A prefix to a unit, indicating a fraction of 10^{-12} of that unit. For example, one picosecond is 10^{-12} seconds.

Pictor (**Painter**) a small inconspicuous constellation in the southern hemisphere alongside Canopus and north of the Large Magellanic Cloud, the brightest stars being the 3rd-magnitude Alpha (α) and the 4th-magnitude Beta (β) (see BETA PICTORIS). Abbrev.: Pic; genitive form: Pictoris; approx. position: RA 5.5h, dec $-50°$; area: 247 sq deg.

pincushion distortion see DISTORTION.

Pioneer probes a series of US Solar-System probes. Pioneers 1–3 were lunar probes intended for launch in 1958, Pioneer 2 suffered launch failure, and Pioneers 1 and 3 fell short of the Moon but did measure the extent of the VAN ALLEN RADIATION BELTS. Pioneer 4 began to orbit the Sun after overshooting the Moon and was followed into solar orbit in 1960 by Pioneer 5, which returned data about the SOLAR WIND and solar FLARES.

Pioneer 6, launched in 1965, was joined in solar orbit by Pioneer 7 in 1966, Pioneer 8 in 1967, and Pioneer 9 in 1968. Together they formed a network of 'solar weather stations' between 0.75 and 1.12 AU from the Sun. Monitoring SOLAR ACTIVITY and the solar wind, they provided early warnings of solar flares during the APOLLO program.

Pioneer 10, launched on Mar. 3 1972, made the first flyby of Jupiter at a distance of 130 300 km on Dec. 4 1973, after becoming the first probe to traverse the asteroid belt. It returned photographs of three of the GALILEAN SATELLITES of Jupiter (EUROPA, GANYMEDE, and CALLISTO), as well as of the Jovian atmosphere and the GREAT RED SPOT. Other experiments measured the strength and extent of Jupiter's radiation belts. Pioneer 11, launched on a similar mission on Apr. 5 1973, passed 42 940 km below Jupiter's south pole on Dec. 3 1974; it reached a top speed of 171 000 km per hour, faster than any previous man-made object. Nearly five years later it flew past Saturn, making its closest approach, 20 900 km above the clouds, on Sept. 1 1979. It twice crossed the plane of Saturn's rings. The probe, renamed *Pioneer Saturn*, returned 440 pictures and much new information on the planet, its satellites, and its rings. Pioneers 10 and 11 are heading out of the Solar System. Pioneer 10's mission was officially ended in 1997 but it continued to be tracked occasionally until its power source decayed below the point where its signal could be detected. The last attempt to contact Pioneer 10 was made on Feb. 7 2003. The last signals from Pioneer 11 were received on Sept. 30 1995. Since then the motion of the Earth has taken it out of alignment with Pioneer 11's radio antenna and no further communication is scheduled. Both Pioneers 10 and 11 carry messages from Earth that an alien civilization may decipher. Meanwhile, Pioneer 10 is heading out of the Solar System in the direction of the star Aldebaran in Taurus, while Pioneer 11 will pass near one of the stars in Aquila in about 4 million years.

Pioneer Venus probes two US probes, an orbiter and a multiprobe, launched in May and Aug. 1978, respectively, towards Venus. The orbiter, Pioneer Venus 1, entered a highly inclined elliptical orbit around Venus on Dec. 4 1978, approaching to within 150 km of the surface. It was designed to make observations over 243 days (Venus' rotational period) and do radar mapping of the surface, cloud studies at ultraviolet and infrared frequencies, and magnetometer studies.

The multiprobe, Pioneer Venus 2, released one large probe on Nov. 15 of 316 kg and three small probes on Nov. 19, each of 93 kg. These probes penetrated the Venusian atmosphere on Dec. 9 at different locations and continuously gathered and relayed data as they approached and hit the surface. One small probe survived the hard landing and continued transmitting for a further hour. Pioneer Venus 2 – the interplanetary 'bus' – entered the atmosphere on Dec. 9, shortly after its payload, as an upper-atmosphere probe.

The probe measurements revealed a surprisingly large amount of primordial argon, krypton, and neon in Venus' atmosphere, which relates to the early history of the planetary atmosphere. They also provided evidence of the layered structure of the clouds and confirmed the role of the GREENHOUSE EFFECT in maintaining the high surface temperature. Radar maps of the surface showed evidence of massive plateaus, volcanic areas, and large rift valleys greater than those seen on Earth. A major surprise was the evidence of lightning since it is not compatible with the meteorological observations. It is possible that volcanic activity at the time of the Pioneer mission may be related to this surprising observation.

pions symbol: π. A triplet of ELEMENTARY PARTICLES (mesons) that have SPIN zero and exist in three states: neutral, positively charged, and negatively charged. The magnitude of the charge is equal to that of the electron. The charged pions have a mass of 2.4886×10^{-25} grams, the neutral pion mass being slightly less at 2.4006×10^{-25} grams. Charged pions decay into MUONS and ELECTRONS with a mean life of 2.6×10^{-8} seconds; the neutral pion converts, usually directly, into gamma-ray photons with an average lifetime of 8.4×10^{-15} seconds. See also COSMIC RAYS.

Pisces (Fishes) a large but inconspicuous zodiac constellation mainly in the northern hemisphere near Pegasus. It contains the FIRST POINT OF ARIES, i.e. the vernal (or dynamical) EQUINOX. It has one 3rd-magnitude star and several of 4th magnitude. Objects of interest, visible only to an observer with a telescope, include the spiral galaxy M74 (NGC 628), the double star Zeta (ζ) Piscium, and *Van Maanen's star*, a white dwarf. Abbrev.: Psc; genitive form: Piscium; approx. position: RA 1h, dec +15°; area: 889 sq deg.

Pisces Australids a minor southern hemisphere METEOR SHOWER, radiant: RA 340°, dec −30°, maximizing on July 30.

Pisces–Perseus supercluster a very elongated local SUPERCLUSTER in the opposite part of the sky to the GREAT ATTRACTOR.

Piscis Austrinus (Southern Fish) a small constellation in the southern hemisphere near Grus, the brightest stars being of 4th magnitude apart from the 1st-magnitude FOMALHAUT. Abbrev.: PsA; genitive form: Piscis Austrini; approx. position: RA 22.5h, dec −30°; area: 245 sq deg.

Pistol Star one of the most luminous and most massive stars in our GALAXY. It has been estimated to have a luminosity of up to 10 million times the luminosity of the SUN and an original mass of around 200 times the mass of the Sun. It almost certainly has already shed a large fraction of its initial mass, forming the nebula that gave it its name in the process.

pixel *short for* picture element. The smallest element of a digital image, such as that produced by a CCD. See IMAGING.

plages (formerly sometimes termed **bright flocculi**) Bright patches in the solar CHROMOSPHERE, at a higher temperature than their surroundings, that occur in areas where there is an enhancement of the relatively weak vertical magnetic field. They are approximately coincident with photospheric FACULAE (though unlike the faculae they are visible, in the MONOCHROMATIC light of certain strong FRAUNHOFER LINES, anywhere on the Sun's disk) and may be considered as defining the extent of ACTIVE REGIONS.

Planck A space mission planned by the European Space Agency (ESA) for the purpose of surveying and mapping the anisotropies of the Cosmic Microwave Background (CMB) over the whole sky. The Planck spacecraft is scheduled to be launched by ESA in early 2007 and is to share its launch vehicle – an Ariane 5 rocket – with the HERSCHEL SPACE OBSERVATORY. After launch, the two craft will separate and be placed into different orbits around L2, one of the Lagrangian points of the Earth–Sun system. In this stable location 1.5 million kilometers from the Earth, almost wholly isolated from extraneous particle and radiation interference, the Planck observatory will be able to map the CMB anisotropies with improved sensitivity and angular resolution. It will also be able to help measure accurately the amplitude of the structures in the CMB. Planck will provide a major and up-to-date source of information on such issues as the accurate determination of the Hubble Constant and the testing of inflationary models of the early universe. The mission takes its name from Max Planck, the German theoretical physicist and creator of the quantum theory.

Planck constant symbol: h. A fundamental constant with the value $6.626\,076 \times 10^{-34}$ joule seconds. According to quantum theory, ELECTROMAGNETIC RADIATION has a dual nature. Although many phenomena, including reflection and refraction, can be explained in terms of the wavelike nature of radiation, radiation may also be considered to be composed of discrete packets of energy called PHOTONS, so that it acts as a stream of particles. The particle-like and wavelike properties are related by *Planck's* *law*, in which the Planck constant is the constant of proportionality:

$$E = h\nu = hc/\lambda$$

E is the energy of the photons and ν and λ the frequency and wavelength of the wave; c is the speed of light in a vacuum. The Planck constant appears in most equations of quantum theory and quantum mechanics, including Planck's radiation law for BLACK BODIES.

Planck's law see PLANCK CONSTANT.

Planck's radiation law see BLACK BODY.

Planck time a time equal to 5.4×10^{-44} second, and defined as $\sqrt{(hG/2\pi c^5)}$; h is the PLANCK CONSTANT, G the GRAVITATIONAL CONSTANT, and c the SPEED OF LIGHT. The uncertainty principle of quantum mechanics prevents any speculation on times shorter than the Planck time after the BIG BANG.

plane-polarized wave see POLARIZATION.

planet any of a class of rotating oblate spheroid bodies of substantial size that orbit the Sun or other stars and shine only by the light reflected from their primaries. In the Solar System there are nine known planets, varying in diameter from a little over 2000 km for Pluto to about 140 000 km for Jupiter and in mass from about 0.002 Earth masses for Pluto to 318 for Jupiter. All the planets follow elliptical paths of varying eccentricity and all but one have orbits that are more or less in the same plane. No planet shares its orbit with any other body of comparable size, although seven of them are attended by one or more satellites.

The planets of the Solar System and numerous ASTEROIDS (or minor planets), all probably share a common origin with the Sun about 4600 million years ago (see SOLAR SYSTEM, ORIGIN). But two very different classes of planet are found: four TERRESTRIAL PLANETS, rocky bodies with shallow atmospheres, which orbit close to the Sun, and four GIANT PLANETS, largely gaseous bodies, which circle it further out. PLUTO, by tradition regarded as the ninth planet, is too small to be a terrestrial planet. It also has the greatest eccentricity and inclination to the planetary plane of any of the planets. The discoveries in 2002 of QUAOAR, the largest KUIPER BELT OBJECT so far known, and in 2003 of SEDNA, a mysterious object apparently from the inner OORT CLOUD of comets, have prompted astronomers to reexamine their definition of the word 'planet' in respect of Pluto.

Planets of other stars (*extrasolar planets*) are too faint to be seen from Earth with present-day instruments, but very massive planets several times larger than Jupiter have been detected around the nearest stars by their perturbing effect on stellar motion. The slight wobble that would be produced in a star's motion can be determined by precise measurements of a star's position over many decades, or from characteristic changes in a star's radial velocity determined from its doppler shift (see also PLANET PULSAR). Future spaceborne observatories such as ESA's Darwin project may be able to detect directly light reflected from a planet orbiting a nearby star by masking out the star's light. Extrasolar planets with orbits edge-on to the Earth are particularly hard to detect, but the development of spacebased instruments sensitive enough to detect the minute drop in a star's light output as a large planet transits its disk are in the pipeline. Far-infrared observations can already reveal dust shells around stars and it may be possible to detect a PROTOPLANETARY system in this way (see BETA PICTORIS; VEGA). See also Table 1, Appendix.

planetarium an optical instrument by means of which an artificial night sky can be projected onto the interior of a fixed dome so that the positions of the Sun, Moon, planets, stars, etc., may be shown and their motions, real or apparent, demonstrated. The instruments were first built by the German firm of Carl Zeiss from 1913. The term also refers to the building housing such an instrument. Originally, *planetarium* was the name given to the device that later became known as an ORRERY.

planetary 1 of or involving a planet or the planets.
2 *short for* planetary nebula.

planetary aberration the apparent angular displacement of the observed position of a planet, etc., produced by motion of the observer (see ABERRATION) and by motion of the observed body (see LIGHT-TIME).

planetary alignment the rough alignment along a solar radius of the outer planets, Jupiter to Neptune, that takes place approximately every 179 years. The most recent planetary alignment took place at the beginning of the 1980s, making possible the two Voyager missions to Jupiter, Saturn, and beyond (see VOYAGER PROBES). The planetary alignment was thought to provide the only cost-effective way to visit the outer planets because using Jupiter's gravitational field to accelerate a probe, changing both its velocity and direction, saved fuel and took years off the journey time. But improved mathematical techniques for calculating accurate flightpaths, including gravity assists, mean that space scientists do not necessarily have to wait for planetary alignments to send probes to the outer Solar System. See also GRAVITY ASSIST.

Planetary Data System (PDS) a computer database system developed by NASA, allowing users to locate, retrieve, and analyze stored data on the planets and their satellites.

planetary nebula an expanding and usually symmetrical cloud of gas that has been ejected from a dying star. Most are believed to be the ejected envelopes of RED GIANT stars, shed as a result of instabilities late in their evolution. The gas cloud is ionized by the compact hot burnt-out stellar core that remains in the center of the cloud; the cloud is detected by virtue of the resulting light emission. Planetary nebulae are therefore a class of EMISSION NEBULAE. They are usually ring-shaped or sometimes hourglass-shaped. They are generally less than 50 000 years old, eventually fading and dispersing into the interstellar medium. The name refers to their resemblance to planetary disks rather than pointlike stars under low magnification. They have a large size range: the smallest objects have a starlike appearance on photographs – and are thus called *stellar planetaries* – but can be identified by the characteristic spectral emission lines. Planetary nebulae occur in isolation and usually lie close to the galactic plane, concentrated toward the galactic center.

A planetary nebula is believed to form as part of the normal evolution of single stars with masses of up to 8 solar masses; the immediately preceding stage is probably a rapid mass loss OH/IR STAR. Instabilities eject a succession of planetary nebula shells, reducing the mass of the star until the core (the *planetary nebula central star*) is only about 0.6 solar masses. This degenerate core becomes a WHITE DWARF. The recent discovery of planetary nebulae with close binary stars at the center suggests that some planetaries form as a result of interactions in a double star system. One star has expanded sufficiently to cocoon both in a COMMON ENVELOPE, with the two star cores orbiting inside; frictional drag transfers energy from the orbiting stars to the surrounding gas and thus expels the envelope as a planetary nebula.

Although planetary nebulae are less massive and more symmetrical than H II (ionized hydrogen) REGIONS, their optical spectra are similar. There are bright emission lines of oxygen, hydrogen, nitrogen, and other components, the characteristic green of the inner region being due to doubly ionized oxygen and the red of the outer periphery resulting from singly ionized nitrogen and from hydrogen alpha emission. About 1500 planetary nebulae are known in our Galaxy, the RING NEBULA in Lyra being a typical example. See also NEBULA.

planetary precession see PRECESSION.

planetary probe a crewless spacecraft designed and equipped to study conditions on or in the vicinity of the planets, their satellites, and other members of the Solar System, as well as in the interplanetary medium itself, and to transmit the information it gathers back to Earth. Probes have now made successful visits to all the planets of the Solar System except Pluto.

Planetary and interplanetary probes may use solar panels to derive power for communications and internal operation. However, spacecraft that travel farther from the Sun than the orbit of Mars receive comparatively little solar energy and must rely on other power systems, such as the radioisotope thermoelectric generators carried by Pioneers 10 and 11 and Voyagers 1 and 2. Most probes carry a main rocket propulsion system for course corrections as well as smaller thrusters for attitude adjustments. An alternative source of power for forward motion is ion propulsion, pioneered by NASA's DEEP SPACE 1 (1998–2001) and also to be used in the projected DAWN mission to the asteroids (1) Ceres and (4) Vesta (due for launch 2006).

planetary rings flat rings of material – consisting of numerous small bodies and particles of rock and ice – known to surround the four giant planets. SATURN'S RINGS were discovered in 1610 by Galileo but not recognized for what they were until Christiaan Huygens correctly described them in 1659. NASA's Pioneer and Voyager spacecraft confirmed that the rings were indeed made up of innumerable smaller bodies ranging in size from a fraction of a millimeter to 30 meters across. The two Voyager spacecraft confirmed the existence of JUPITER'S RINGS, URANUS' RINGS, and NEPTUNE'S RINGS, which are all much fainter than those of Saturn, All these ring systems probably came into being either because a satellite was shattered to fragments through collision with an asteroid or comet or because a satellite or captured interplanetary body came too close to the planet concerned and was torn apart by gravitational tidal forces. See also ROCHE LIMIT.

planetary system a system of PLANETS and other bodies, such as comets and meteoroids, that orbits a star. The Sun and its planetary system together comprise the SOLAR SYSTEM. Planetary systems may be common in the Galaxy, being formed along with stars from the gravitational contraction of interstellar clouds of gas and dust. See also PLANET PULSAR; PROTOPLANET.

planetary weather see ATMOSPHERE.

planetesimals bodies, ranging in size from less than a millimeter to many kilometers, that are thought to have formed the planets of the SOLAR SYSTEM by a process of ACCRETION.

planetesimal theory see ENCOUNTER THEORIES.

planetoids (minor planets) the minor members of the Solar System, especially ASTEROIDS, but also including COMETS, KUIPER BELT objects, and TRANS-NEPTUNIAN OBJECTS.

planetology the study of the planets of the Solar System – their history, internal and surface structures, and atmospheres – with particular regard as to how and why these differ from planet to planet.

planet pulsar the MILLISECOND PULSAR PSR 1257+12, which is orbited by at least two planetlike objects. The pulsar has a spin period of 6.2 milliseconds, and the two inferred PLANETS have masses of a few Earth masses and periods of 66 and 98 days, respectively. Because these orbits are close to a 3:1 RESONANCE, their mutual perturbations produce detectable variations in the pulse arrival times. Careful monitoring of the system has confirmed these predicted variations, unambiguously proving the planet hypothesis. In addition, it is likely that a third planet has now been identified in the system with an orbital period of 25 days and a mass similar to that of the Moon. It is presently not known how these 'planets' have formed. One of the more probable possibilities is that the system was a binary millisecond pulsar in which the companion star, a low-mass star or a white dwarf, was dynamically disrupted (see ROCHE LIMIT). The material of the disrupted star then formed a protoplanetary disk in which planets were able to form (see PROTOPLANET).

planets, origin see SOLAR SYSTEM, ORIGIN.

planet X unofficial designation given by Percival Lowell to the predicted hypothetical planet he believed existed beyond the orbit of Neptune. Pluto was eventually discovered by Clyde Tombaugh in 1930, but it was not the planet with a mass seven times that of Earth that Lowell had predicted. The trans-Neptunian region of the Solar System is now believed to consist of a host of icy, rocky planetoids, including KUIPER BELT OBJECTS and a shell of frozen comets called the OORT CLOUD.

planisphere a two-dimensional map projection centered on the northern or southern pole of the celestial sphere that shows the principal stars of the constellations, the Milky Way, etc., and is equipped with a movable overlay to indicate the stars visible at a particular time on any day of the year for a particular zone of terrestrial latitude.

planitia (plural: **planitiae**) A low plain on the surface of a planet or satellite. The word is used in the approved name of such a feature.

planum (plural: **plana**) A high plain or plateau. The word is used in the approved name of such a surface feature on a planet or satellite.

plasma a state of matter consisting of ions and electrons moving freely. A plasma is thus a fully ionized gas that can be formed at high temperatures (as in stars) or by PHOTOIONIZATION (as in interstellar gas). There is plasma in the INTERSTELLAR MEDIUM, in the INTERPLANETARY MEDIUM in the form of the solar wind, and within planetary MAGNETOSPHERES. The properties of plasmas differ from those of neutral gases primarily because of the effects of magnetic and electric fields on and arising from the moving charged particles. For example, in a plasma spread over a large area, plasma and magnetic field move together; the magnetic field is said to be 'frozen in' to the plasma. See also MAGNETOHYDRODYNAMICS.

plasmasphere a small toroidal region of PLASMA, primarily protons and electrons, that lies within the Earth's MAGNETOSPHERE above the ionosphere. The plasma is produced by the action of the Sun's ultraviolet radiation and X-rays on molecules, etc., in the upper atmosphere. The plasmasphere is bounded by the *plasmapause*, where the plasma density drops abruptly.

plasma tail see COMET TAILS.

plate tectonics see EARTH.

Plato see table at CRATERS.

Platonic year see PRECESSION.

Pleiades (**Seven Sisters**; **M45**) a young OPEN CLUSTER about 135 parsecs away in the constellation Taurus. It contains maybe 3000 stars of which at least six are visible to the naked eye: ALCYONE, Maia, Atlas, Electra, Merope, and Taygeta; PLEIONE could once have been brighter. The brightest stars are blue-white (B or Be) and highly luminous, the less bright ones being mainly A and F stars. Gas and dust surrounding the brighter stars reflect the starlight thus producing faint REFLECTION NEBULAE. Some of these nebulae have been separately cataloged. Thus NGC 1432 is the bright nebula surrounding Maia, while NGC 1435 refers to Tempel's nebula, the nebulosity within which Merope is embedded.

Pleione (**28 Tau**) one of the stars of the PLEIADES. It developed a surrounding envelope that was first observed in 1938, reached maximum intensity in 1945, and was just visible in 1954; another shell started to develop in 1972. It is thought to be unstable owing to its fast rotation rate. Spectral type: B8pe.

plerion see SUPERNOVA REMNANT.

Plössl eyepiece see EYEPIECE.

Plough (US **Big Dipper**) a group of stars in URSA MAJOR that contains the seven brightest stars in that constellation, nearly all with similar apparent magnitudes (m_v), and has a very distinctive shape (see illustration overleaf). The seven stars are ALIOTH, DUBHE, ALCAID, MIZAR, Merak (m_v: 2.36), Phecda (m_v: 2.43), and Megrez (m_v: 3.31), in order of brightness. Alcaid and Dubhe have different values and directions of PROPER MOTION than the other five so that the shape of the Plough is slowly but continuously changing.

P-L relation see PERIOD-LUMINOSITY RELATION.

Pluto the ninth and smallest planet of the Solar System, discovered in 1930 by Clyde Tombaugh at the Lowell Observatory in Arizona. Its 248.59 year orbit has a higher INCLINATION to the ecliptic (17.1°) and a greater ECCENTRICITY (0.25) than any other planet. Although it has the greatest mean planetary distance of about 39 AU from the Sun, it approaches within 30 AU at PERIHELION; between 1979 and 1999 Pluto was therefore closer to the Sun than Neptune. Orbital and physical characteristics are given in Table 1, backmatter.

OPPOSITIONS occur one or two days later each year, but Pluto's 14th-magnitude disk is too small to be measured using conventional Earth-based telescopes. Until 1978 the best estimate of its size was about 5900 km, a value based on negative observations of a predicted occultation of a star by Pluto during an APPULSE in 1965.

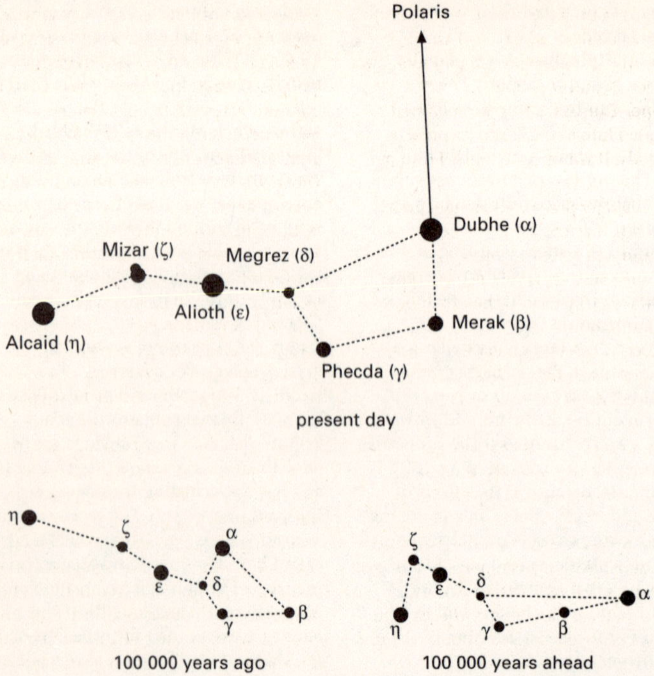

Plough

However, examination of photographs of Pluto in 1978 by James W. Christy of the US Naval Observatory revealed that it has a very close satellite, called CHARON, orbiting at a distance of about 20 000 km every 6.39 days – a period previously identified in the small light variation of the planet and ascribed to its axial rotation. The orbital parameters of Charon enable KEPLER'S THIRD LAW to be used to estimate Pluto's mass as about 0.20% that of the Earth. Apparently Pluto is a low-density body, about 2320 km across, while Charon is about 1186 km in diameter; it is thus the largest satellite in proportion to the size of its planet in the Solar System – a title previously credited to our own Moon. Because of their proximity, both Pluto and Charon are in SYNCHRONOUS ROTATION about their common center of mass. If the revised estimates of Pluto's size and density are correct, then it would appear to be smaller than our Moon. This possibility has helped to fuel debate among astronomers about whether Pluto is a fully-fledged planet or should be classed as a KUIPER BELT OBJECT.

At a temperature of 50 K, Pluto is too cold and small to have an appreciable atmosphere. Infrared spectroscopy has shown nitrogen and methane to be present but it is difficult to distinguish spectroscopically between gaseous and solid forms of methane at the temperature and pressure found on Pluto. Part of the surface, at least, could have a covering of methane ice; there is a suggestion that Pluto has bright POLAR CAPS.

In October 2005, NASA announced that the Hubble Space Telescope had photographed two new objects that may be satellites of Pluto. Observations suggest that the satellite candidates, provisionally named S/2005 P1 and S/2005 P2, orbit Pluto at distances of about 49 000 km and 65 000 km respectively. Their likely diameters may be between 45 and 160 km.

Pluto Kuiper Express a mission planned to investigate Pluto and Charon, at present under study. It is hoped to reach Pluto by 2010.

PMS star *short for* pre-main-sequence star. See STAR FORMATION.

Pogson ratio see MAGNITUDE.

Pointers the two stars in the PLOUGH that point toward POLARIS and the north pole; Dubhe and Merak.

point source a celestial object whose angular extent is too small to be measured.

polar (polar system) see MAGNETIC CATACLYSMIC VARIABLES.

polar axis 1 the axis in an EQUATORIAL MOUNTING that is parallel to the Earth's axis and hence points toward the celestial poles. 2 see POLES.

polar caps regions of ice that form around the northern and southern poles of a planet or planetary satellite. Earth's polar caps consist of water ice and snow whereas the caps of MARS are comprised of both water ice and frozen carbon dioxide. The southern polar cap of TRITON is pink and thought to be due to nitrogen snow and ice. Polar caps can show seasonal variation.

polar diagram *another name for* antenna pattern. See ANTENNA.

polar distance *short for* north polar distance or south polar distance.

polarimetry the measurement of the degree and direction of POLARIZATION of a beam of light or other radiation, using an instrument known as a *polarimeter*.

Polaris (North Star; α UMi) a remote creamy-yellow supergiant that is the brightest star in the constellation Ursa Minor. It lies very close to the north celestial pole (dec: 89°16′) and is the present POLE STAR. Its position is found by means of the POINTERS in the Plough. Polaris is a classical CEPHEID VARIABLE (period 3.97 days) but its pulsations have decreased rapidly since about the mid-1970s. It forms an optical double with a 9th-magnitude F3 V companion. m_v: 2.0; M_v: -2.9; spectral type: F8 Ib; distance: 97 pc.

polarization the degree to which the orientation of the electric or magnetic vector in ELECTROMAGNETIC RADIATION is predictable over time. In a partially polarized wave, the vector thus shows a less random orientation in the plane perpendicular to the direction of wave motion than occurs in an unpolarized (normal) wave. Waves in which the electric vectors are entirely vertical or horizontal with respect to the direction of motion are described as vertically or horizontally *plane* (or *linearly*) *polarized*. In general, both polarizations are present with a relative phase difference and the wave is then *elliptically polarized* in the right-handed or left-handed sense accordingly as the resultant vector rotates clockwise or counterclockwise when viewed along the direction of motion of the wave; in the case where the resultant vector rotates and its magnitude remains constant, the wave is *circularly polarized*.

Polarization is a measure of the way in which light or other ELECTROMAGNETIC RADIATION from a celestial body is affected by factors such as scattering due to cosmic dust or strong stellar or interstellar magnetic fields, or reflection from a surface. Radio emissions from celestial sources are usually *partially polarized*, i.e. the waves can be considered to be composed of a completely unpolarized component plus a small polarized component. SYNCHROTRON EMISSION, however, may be strongly polarized. The general situation is described by the four *Stokes parameters* (*I*, *Q*, *U*, and *V*), which are defined in such a manner that specifying their four values uniquely describes the state of polarization: *I* is a measure of the total power in the wave, *Q* and *U* define the degree of linear polarization, and *V* that of circular polarization. All four have dimensions of FLUX DENSITY. See also FARADAY ROTATION; INTERSTELLAR POLARIZATION.

polarization curve a curve showing the relationship between the angle of reflection of light from a surface and the degree of POLARIZATION of the reflected light. It depends on the surface characteristics (texture, composition). It is used to deduce the ALBEDO of the surfaces of ASTEROIDS so that their diameters may be calculated.

polar motion see CHANDLER WOBBLE.

polar orbit a satellite orbit that passes over the north and south poles of the Earth or of some other Solar-System body.

polar system see MAGNETIC CATACLYSMIC VARIABLES.

poles the two points on a sphere lying 90° above or below all points on a particular great circle. The *polar axis* is the imaginary straight line between the poles. See CELESTIAL POLES; GALACTIC POLES.

poles of the ecliptic see ECLIPTIC.

pole star the star closest to the north or south celestial pole at any particular time. As a result of PRECESSION the position of each pole traces out a circle in the sky in a period of about 25 800 years. There is thus a sequence of stars, including POLARIS, VEGA, and THUBAN, that have been and will become again the northern pole star (see illustration). The nearest naked-eye star to the south celestial pole is at present the 5th magnitude star Sigma Octantis. The altitude of the pole star is approximately equal to the local latitude.

Pollux (β Gem) an orange giant that is the brightest star in the constellation Gemini and is the nearest giant to the Earth. It has several optical companions, none of which are physically related to it. m_v: 1.14; M_v: 0.7; spectral type: K0 IIIb; distance: 12 pc.

poor cluster see CLUSTERS OF GALAXIES.

population I, population II the two classes into which stars and other celestial objects within a galaxy can be divided; the distinction is basically that of age, and the most obvious distinguishing characteristics are the objects' space distribution and chemical content (see METALLICITY). The classification was first made by W. Baade in 1944. He proposed that population I stars are the young metal-rich highly luminous stars found in spiral arms of galaxies – i.e. strongly concentrated in the galactic plane – and associated with interstellar gas and dust. In contrast population II stars are old red stars found throughout elliptical and lenticular galaxies and in spiral galaxies located in the galactic center, in the surrounding galactic halo, and in a disk coextending with the galactic plane but much thicker.

It is now known that in our Galaxy there is a continuum of populations existing between Baade's two classes (see table). The origin of population types is connected with the dynamic and chemical evolution of the Galaxy. Put very simply the earliest stars, formed from the original hydrogen-helium gas cloud, were *halo population II stars* followed, after further gas contraction produced a relatively thin extended disk, by *intermediate population II stars*; contraction of the remaining gas into an even thinner disk produced the *disk population*, which may be young population II stars or old population I stars. Successive generations of population I stars have subsequently formed from interstellar matter that has been slowly enriched with metals produced by MASS LOSS from stars and by SUPERNOVAE explosions. The youngest *extreme population stars* have 20 to 30 times the metallicity of the oldest halo objects.

population III a hypothetical population of supermassive stars that could have existed before the galaxies formed. They could have produced the large helium content of the Universe and the microwave background radiation, both usually attributed to the early stages of the BIG BANG. If population III stars did exist, cosmologists would need to severely modify current forms of the Big Bang theory.

pores see SUNSPOTS.

Porrima (γ Vir) a visual binary with cream components that lies in the constellation Virgo and has a highly eccentric orbit (period 171 years). The separation, about 5″ in the 1970s and 6″.6 at maximum, is decreasing and by 2010 the star will appear single except in the largest telescopes. Porrima is also an optical double. m_v: 3.5 (A and B), 2.75 (AB); spectral type: F0 V (A and B).

Portia a small satellite of Uranus, discovered in 1986 from photographs taken by Voyager 2. See URANUS' SATELLITES; Table 2, Appendix.

positional astronomy see ASTROMETRY.

position angle (PA; p.a.) 1 the direction in the sky of one celestial body with respect to another, measured from 0° to 360° in an easterly direction from north. It is used, for example, to give the position of the fainter

Characteristics of Populations I and II in the Galaxy

Population group	*Extreme population I*	*Older population I*	*Disk population*	*Intermediate population II*	*Halo population II*
typical objects	interstellar gas, dust H II regions T Tauri stars OB associations O, B stars supergiants young open clusters classical Cepheids	Sun strong-line stars A stars Me dwarfs giants older open clusters	weak-line stars planetary nebulae galactic bulge novae RR Lyrae stars ($P < 0.4$ day)	high-velocity stars long-period variables	globular clusters extreme metal-poor stars (subdwarfs) RR Lyrae stars ($P > 0.4$ day) type II Cepheids
distribution	spiral arms: extremely patchy	patchy	smooth	smooth	smooth
*z, Z, age	———	———	increasing	———	——→
concentration to Galactic center	none	little	considerable	strong	strong
Galactic orbits	circular	approx. circular	slightly eccentric	eccentric	very eccentric
brightness, metals/H ratio	←———	———	increasing	———	———

Adapted from A. Blaauw

*z, Z are mean distance from Galactic plane, mean of velocity components perpendicular to Galactic plane

component of a VISUAL BINARY with respect to the brighter component.
2 the angle at which the axis of a planet or star, or some other line on a celestial body, is inclined to the HOUR CIRCLE passing through the center of the body; it is measured eastwards from 0° to 360° from north.

position circle see CIRCLE OF POSITION.

position micrometer see FILAR MICROMETER.

positron the ANTIPARTICLE of an electron.

positronium a positron-electron system that lasts for a measurable time before combining to produce ANNIHILATION radiation. Positronium can be thought of as an atom analogous to that of hydrogen in which the electron and positron move in Bohr orbits about the center of mass, which is halfway between them. During formation, approximately 25% is formed in a singlet spin state and the other 75% is formed in a triplet state. The annihilation radiation emitted by the combining of a positron-electron pair in a singlet state consists of two γ-ray photons emitted simultaneously with energies of 511 keV each; the annihilation radiation from the triplet state consists of three γ-ray photons emitted simultaneously each with energy less than 511 keV.

POSS *abbrev. for* Palomar Observatory Sky Survey.

potential energy the energy possessed by a body or system by virtue of its position or configuration. It is equal to the work done by the system changing from its given state to some standard state. In a gravitational field, a mass *m* placed at a height *h* above a standard level (say the surface of the Earth) has potential energy *mgh*, where *g* is the acceleration of gravity.

power the rate at which ENERGY is expended by a source or work is done. It is measured in watts, i.e. in joules per second.

power-law spectrum a spectrum quantified in terms of a power law. A NONTHERMAL CONTINUUM spectrum is usually expressed by the dependence of the flux density *S* on the frequency ν raised to a certain power, $S \propto \nu^{-\alpha}$, where α is the SPECTRAL INDEX. The ubiquity of this power-law fit to the multiwavelength continuum spectrum of all ACTIVE GALACTIC NUCLEI is strong evidence for the emission to be powered by the same mechanism in all cases, such as an accreting BLACK HOLE. Only such an engine is capable of scaling its energy output through several orders of magnitude in luminosity without changing its fundamental spectrum.

power pattern see ANTENNA.

power spectrum a plot of the power contained in a signal versus the frequency, or of the power in a spatial distribution versus the wavenumber (reciprocal of wavelength). It may be obtained by taking a FOURIER TRANSFORM of the signal or distribution and squaring the amplitude of each component in the result.

Poynting–Robertson effect an effect whereby interplanetary particles slowly spiral toward the Sun. The particles interact with solar radiation (by absorbing and reradiating energy) so that they lose orbital momentum; this causes a decrease in orbital velocity so that they move into progressively smaller orbits around the Sun. For a particle moving in a circular orbit that is *d* astronomical units from the Sun, the time taken to fall into the Sun is given by

$$t = 7 \times 10^7 \rho r d^2 \text{ years}$$

where *r* and ρ are particle radius (in m) and density (in kg m^{-3}), respectively. The equation shows that the effect gets progressively more important as smaller particles are considered, and is particularly important in the 10^{-6} to 10^{-2} meter range.

RADIATION PRESSURE on the particles opposes the Poynting–Robertson effect and can overcome it for very small particles (radius less than 10^{-6} m). These particles are blown out of the Solar System by the action of the radiation pressure aided by the SOLAR WIND. Although these two processes remove dust from the Solar System, the dust level is constantly replenished by disintegrating comets, etc.

p-p chain see PROTON-PROTON CHAIN REACTION.

PPM Star Catalog a catalog prepared by S. Roeser, U. Bastian, et al, at the Astronomisches Rechen-Institut, Heidelberg, giving the positions, magnitudes, spectral types, and proper

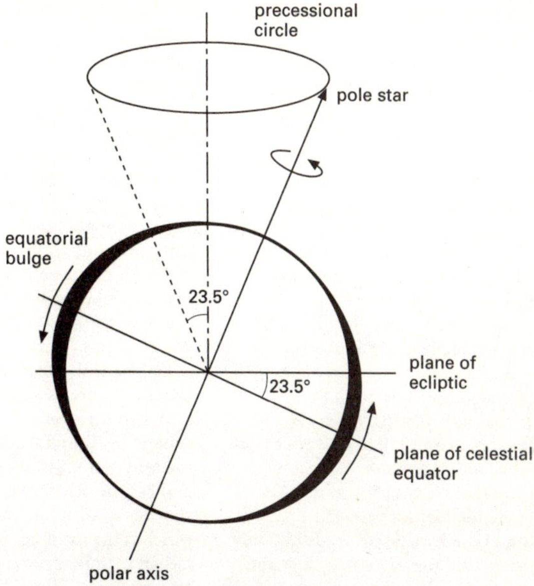

Precession of the Earth

motions of 378 910 stars down to a limiting magnitude of 12 for the epoch 2000.0. The *PPM* (Positions and Proper Motions) *Star Catalog* covers the whole sky in two volumes: one on the north (1991) and one on the south (1993). It is available in computerized form.

p-process a process of NUCLEOSYNTHESIS by which certain heavy proton-rich nuclei are thought to be produced.

Praesepe (**Beehive; M44; NGC 2632**) a large OPEN CLUSTER in the constellation Cancer with over 200 known stars. It can almost be resolved by the naked eye but is best viewed with a very low-power telescope or with binoculars.

preamplifier an amplifier used in a RADIO TELESCOPE to boost the signals from the ANTENNA before they are fed to the RECEIVER.

precataclysmic binary see CATACLYSMIC VARIABLE.

preceding 1 denoting the leading edge of a planet, etc., or the leading member of a pair of stars, as the Earth's rotation causes objects to drift across the sky from east to west.
2 denoting the leading edge of a surface feature on a planet, satellite, star, etc., or the leading member of a pair of features, the feature(s) moving as the body rotates.

In each case, the other edge or member is described as *following* or *trailing*.

preceding spot (***p*-spot**) see SUNSPOTS.

precession the slow periodic change in the direction of the axis of rotation of a spinning body due to the application of an external force (a torque). The extremities of the axis trace out circles in one complete precessional period if the rotational speed and applied torque are both constant. The Earth's axis precesses with a period of 25 800 years, the axial extremities, the celestial poles, tracing out circles about 23.5° in radius on the celestial sphere (see illustration). This radius is equal to the inclination of the Earth's equatorial plane to the plane of the ecliptic. The precession results primarily from the gravitational attraction of the Sun and Moon on the EQUATORIAL bulge of the nonspherical Earth. The Sun and Moon and also the planets pull on the bulge in an attempt to bring the equatorial plane into near coincidence with the plane of the ecliptic. The result of this gravitational action and the opposing rotation of the Earth is a precessional force that acts perpendicularly to both these actions.

The combined effect of the Sun and Moon leads to *luni-solar precession*, which together with the much smaller *planetary precession* gives the *general precession* of the Earth's axis and of the equinoxes. The *annual general precession* is given by

$$50.2564 + 0.0222T \text{ arcsecs}$$

where T is the time in Julian centuries from 1900.0. Thus one precessional circle is completed about every 25 800 years, this period being the *Platonic year*. The precession of the Earth's axis leads not only to the PRECESSION OF THE EQUINOXES and the consequential change in stellar coordinates but also to the changing position of the celestial poles and hence to the slow change in the two POLE STARS.

precession, constant of the ratio of the luni-solar PRECESSION to the cosine of the OBLIQUITY OF THE ECLIPTIC. It is about 54.94 arc seconds per year and varies very slightly with time.

precession of the equinoxes the slow continuous westward motion of the EQUINOXES around the ECLIPTIC that results from the PRECESSION of the Earth's axis. It was first described by Hipparchus in the second century BC. As the axis precesses, the celestial equator, which lies in the plane perpendicular to the axis, moves relative to the ecliptic. The two points at which the planes intersect – the equinoxes – thus move round the ecliptic in the precessional period of about 25 800 years, the annual rate being about 50.27 arc seconds. Coordinates such as RIGHT ASCENSION that refer to an equinox as their zero point thus change with time. Star catalogs therefore use a CATALOG EQUINOX as their origin.

precision catalog see STAR CATALOG.

pre-main-sequence (PMS) star see STAR FORMATION.

Pre-Nectarian System see NECTARIAN SYSTEM.

pressure the force per unit surface area at any point in a gas or liquid. The pressure of a gas is proportional to temperature and density: at constant temperature, as the density is increased the pressure increases accordingly. This law of classical physics does not apply to DEGENERATE MATTER.

pressure broadening broadening of spectral lines as a result of high density, and hence pressure, of the emitting or absorbing material: the greater the density and pressure, the greater the width of the spectral lines. The broadening is caused by collisions with other atoms while the atom is emitting or absorbing radiation. See also LINE BROADENING.

primary the celestial body that is nearest to the center of mass of a system of orbiting bodies. The other members, called *secondaries*, appear to orbit the primary, which is the most massive in the system. In fact all members move round the common center of mass. The Earth is the Moon's primary. See also VISUAL BINARY.

primary beam see BEAM.

primary cosmic rays see COSMIC RAYS.

primary mirror the optically worked mirror in a REFLECTING TELESCOPE that faces the observed object and collects its light. The front surface is coated, now usually with aluminum (see ALUMINIZING), to provide a high degree of reflectivity. Technical developments have led to 'superpolished' mirrors. Modern mirror-substrate materials are glass/ceramic compounds, such as Zerodur or Cer-Vit, or materials such as borosilicate glass, fused quartz, or Pyrex, all of which have very low coefficients of thermal expansion. The molten glass is first cast into an approximation of the designed concave shape, forming the *mirror blank*. After cooling, the surface must then be *figured*, i.e. accurately ground and polished. The designed shape of primary mirrors on most large telescopes is a PARABOLOID or HYPERBOLOID (see CASSEGRAIN TELESCOPE; RITCHEY–CHRÉTIAN OPTICS); spherical mirrors are used on, for example, SCHMIDT TELESCOPES. For high-quality images to be produced, the final surface must be polished to an accuracy of within one quarter of the wavelength used. The mirror is supported over its rear face, or from within its structure (see below), and can maintain an accurate profile up to considerable diameters without sagging. See also MOUNTING.

The new generation of ground-based reflectors have very large apertures and consequently high RESOLUTION. Technological problems and cost limit the diameter of a single one-piece (*monolithic*) primary mirror to 7–8 meters. Monolithic primaries are designed to be lightweight to prevent sagging. There are two types. *Honeycomb mirrors* have an interior honeycomb pattern of glass ribs formed, during casting, between the concave front surface and the flat back plate; this reduces the weight while retaining stiffness and strength. The 6.5-meter mirror of the MMT has such a structure. *Meniscus mirrors* are thin curved plates, concave on the front surface and usually convex on the back; because they are not very stiff, their shape has to be controlled and maintained by an ACTIVE OPTICS system. The 8-m mirrors of the VLT are so designed. The primary can alternatively be a *segmented mirror*, composed of many small mirrors that may fit together (as a *mosaic mirror*) or not, depending on their shapes. Each segment is individually supported and maneuvered by active optics so that the mirrors act together to form the image. Segmented mirrors can be larger than monolithic mirrors. The KECK TELESCOPES have 10-m mosaic mirrors. ADAPTIVE OPTICS further increase the resolution of all these designs.

The latest reflecting telescopes may have more than one primary mirror. The mirrors may be mounted together on a single structure, or on independent structures as in the VLT. The light collected may be routed by small mirrors or fiber optics to a central point, where it is combined and recorded. See also INTERFEROMETER.

prime focus the focal plane in which the image of the PRIMARY MIRROR or OBJECTIVE lens of a telescope forms, in the absence of other optical components.

prime meridian the arbitrary circle of zero longitude on the Earth or some other planet or mapped celestial body. The Earth's prime meridian is the *Greenwich meridian*.

primeval fireball The radiation-dominated phase of the Universe. See BIG BANG THEORY.

primeval galaxy see PROTOGALAXY.

primeval nebula the cloud of interstellar gas – mainly hydrogen and helium – and dust grains from which the Solar System developed. See NEBULAR HYPOTHESIS; SOLAR SYSTEM, ORIGIN.

prime vertical the VERTICAL CIRCLE that passes through an observer's zenith at right angles to the MERIDIAN and intersects the horizon at the east and west points (see CARDINAL POINTS).

prismatic astrolabe an astrometric instrument for determining the position of a celestial body by the accurate timing of its passage across a VERTICAL CIRCLE of the celestial sphere. It usually consists of an artificial horizon (such as a mercury surface) and a prism, which are placed in front of a telescope. The prism is fixed in position so that a fixed altitude, usually 45° or 60°, is used. Parallel rays of light falling on the artificial horizon and the prism are each reflected by the prism into the telescope (see illustration). As the celestial body moves toward the fixed altitude, the two images approach each other from top and bottom of the field of view. At the fixed altitude the two images lie close together on the same horizontal line through the center of the field. The time is then recorded, usually electronically.

probe (spaceprobe) see PLANETARY PROBE.

Procellarum, Oceanus (Ocean of Storms) a vast irregular MARE – possibly occupying an impact depression, the *Gargantuan Basin* – that covers a major part of the Moon's western NEARSIDE. It was the landing site for LUNAS 9 and 13, SURVEYORS 1 and 3, and APOLLO 12. It is one of the youngest areas on the Moon, parts of which may be less than 3000 million years old.

Procyon (α CMi) a conspicuous creamy-yellow star that is the brightest one in the constellation Canis Minor and is one of the NEAREST STARS to the Sun. It was found to be a visual binary in 1840 from observations of its variable proper motion. The companion (B) was discovered in 1896 to be

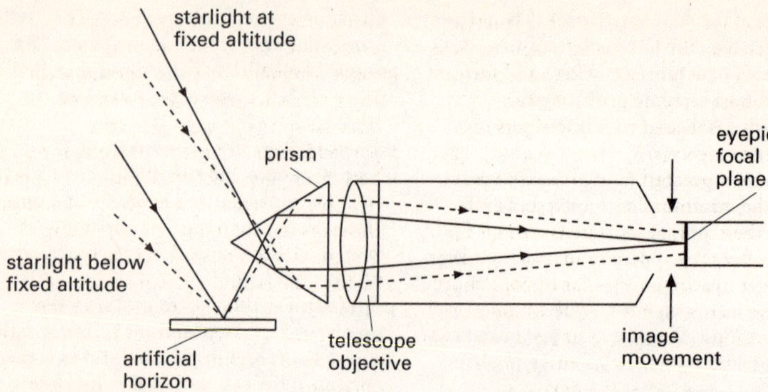

Optical path of prismatic astrolabe

a WHITE DWARF and is of magnitude 10.7. The period is 40.6 years, the separation 5″.2. m_v: 0.4; M_v: 2.6; spectral type: F5 IV-V (A), DZ (B); mass: 1.74 (A), 0.63 (B) times solar mass; radius: 1.7 (A), 0.01 (B) times solar radius; distance: 3.5 pc.

Prognoz a series of crewless Soviet observatories, first orbited in 1972. They have investigated the effect of solar activity on the interplanetary medium and the Earth's magnetosphere by measuring solar radiation (both electromagnetic and corpuscular) and magnetic fields in near-Earth space. They have also studied galactic ultraviolet radiation, X-rays, and gamma rays.

prograde motion DIRECT MOTION as opposed to retrograde motion.

Prometheus **1** a NASA program announced in 2003 for the purpose of developing technology and conducting advanced studies in the fields of radioisotope power systems and nuclear power and propulsion for the peaceful exploration of the Solar System. NASA's Office of Space Science is responsible for organizing the program, which is managed by the agency's JET PROPULSION LABORATORY. The program's goal is to develop the first reactor-powered spacecraft and demonstrate that it can be operated safely and reliably on long-duration missions in deep space.
2 a small satellite of Saturn, discovered in 1980 from Voyager photographs and officially named in 1985. It has an irregular, elongated shape, measuring 148 × 100 × 68 km. Its surface shows some ridges and valleys and a number of craters 20 km across. Its low density and high albedo suggest it is composed largely of ice. Together with PANDORA it is a SHEPHERD SATELLITE for Saturn's F ring. See SATURN'S RINGS; Table 2, Appendix.
3 An active volcanic plume on IO.

prominences clouds of gas in the Sun's upper CHROMOSPHERE/inner CORONA, with a higher density and at a lower temperature than their surroundings, that are visible (ordinarily only in the monochromatic light of certain strong FRAUNHOFER LINES) as bright projections beyond the limb. When viewed against the brighter disk they appear as dark absorption features and are termed *filaments.* They exhibit a great diversity of structure and are most conveniently classified according to their behavior, as either *quiescent* or *active.*

Quiescent prominences are particularly long-lived and are among the most stable of all solar features. They may persist for several months before breaking up or, less frequently, blowing up and have been known to reform at the same location with an almost identical configuration. Typically they are a couple of hundred thousand kilometers long, several tens of thousands of kilometers high, and several thousand kilometers thick. They occur in high

HELIOGRAPHIC LATITUDES, where they are supported by the horizontal magnetic field separating the polar field from the adjacent fields of opposite polarity that were formerly associated with the *f*-spots of ACTIVE REGIONS (see SUNSPOT CYCLE). They attain their greatest frequency a few years after the minimum of the sunspot cycle, when their average latitude is around ±50°. Thereafter they appear in increasingly high latitudes, reaching the polar regions shortly after sunspot maximum. Then, after a brief discontinuity, they reappear around latitude ±50° and remain there in small numbers until a few years after the next minimum, when they again progress poleward.

Active prominences are relatively short-lived and may alter their structure appreciably over a matter of minutes. There are many characteristic types, for example SURGES and SPRAYS, in which chromospheric material is ejected into the inner corona, and *loop prominences* and *coronal rain*, in which the reverse occurs. Loop prominences are impulsive events that often accompany FLARES, whereas coronal rain represents the return of flare-ejected material. In developing active regions *arch filaments* are usually present. These tend to connect regions of opposite polarity across the line of inversion and gradually ascend while material descends along both sides of the arch.

Intermediate between quiescent and active prominences are the so-called *active-region filaments*. These invariably lie along the line of inversion between the vertical magnetic fields of opposite polarity in well-developed active regions. Though long-lived, they may be distinguished from quiescent filaments by an almost continuous flow of material along their axis.

With the exception of surges and sprays, prominences may be regarded as an efficient (though limited) heat sink for the highly ionized corona, their material condensing out of it and then descending along the predominantly vertical magnetic field lines.

promontorium a brighter feature protruding into a darker area. The word is used in the approved name of such a surface feature on the moon. (Latin: promontory)

proper motion symbol: μ. The apparent angular motion per year of a star on the celestial sphere, i.e. in a direction perpendicular to the line of sight. It results both from the actual movement of the star in space – its PECULIAR MOTION – and from the star's motion relative to the Solar System. It was first detected in 1718 by Halley. The considerable distances of stars reduce their apparent motion to a very small amount, which for most stars is considered negligible. It is only after thousands of years that differences in the directions of proper motion cause groups of stars to change shape appreciably.

The proper motion of a star, usually a nearby star, can be determined if its cumulative effect over many decades produces a measurable change in the star's position. It is quoted in arc seconds per year, often in terms of two components: proper motion in right ascension (μ_α) and in declination (μ_δ). BARNARD'S STAR has the greatest proper motion (10″.3 per year). If the distance, d (in parsecs), of the star is known then the velocity along the direction of proper motion – the *tangential velocity*, v_t – can be found:

$$v_t = \mu d \text{ AU/year} = 4.74\mu d \text{ km s}^{-1}$$

proper time time measured by a clock that is sharing the observer's motion. Clocks moving with respect to the observer, or experiencing a different gravitational field, will measure time to flow at a different rate to that of proper time. See also RELATIVITY, SPECIAL THEORY.

proportional counter a gas-filled electronic device for the detection of X-rays, gamma rays, and other ionizing radiation and the counting of charged particles. A potential difference is maintained across a pair of electrodes. Radiation entering the tube ionizes the gas along its path and the resulting electrons are attracted toward the positively charged electrode. The size of the output pulse of the counter is proportional to the number of electron-ion pairs produced by the ionizing event and thus to the energy of the radiation. It is possible to differentiate between various forms of ionizing radiation. In astronomy proportional counters are used mainly for X-ray studies, where they provide sensitive detection and some spectral information.

Imaging proportional counters (*IPCs*) have now been developed, which record the position of each incident X-ray photon so that a two-dimensional image is built up. Linear resolutions of 200–500 μm are obtained in the 0.2–5 keV energy band. Such devices have been used successfully in a number of X-ray astronomy satellites, including the EINSTEIN OBSERVATORY, EXOSAT, and ROSAT. Another development is the *gas scintillation proportional counter* (*SPC*), which has an energy resolution about twice that of conventional counters, and has been successfully used on TENMA, EXOSAT, and ASCA.

Proteus the second-largest known satellite of Neptune, measuring 400 km across but irregular in shape, discovered in 1989 during the Voyager 2 flyby. It orbits close to its planet, completing one circuit in about 26 hours at a mean distance of nearly 93 000 km. Its path is almost parallel with Neptune's equator. Proteus has a low ALBEDO (about 0.06) and a large feature, the *Southern Hemisphere Depression*, which is 250 km in diameter and 10 km deep. There are also troughs, ridges, and several craters. See Table 2, Appendix.

protogalaxy an inhomogeneous gas cloud in the early stages of evolution into a galaxy. See GALAXIES, FORMATION AND EVOLUTION.

proton symbol: p. An ELEMENTARY PARTICLE (a hadron) that has a positive CHARGE, equal in magnitude to that of the ELECTRON. It forms the nucleus of the hydrogen atom and is present in differing numbers in all nuclei. The rest mass of the proton is 1.6726×10^{-24} gram, approximately 1836 times that of the electron. It has spin ½. It has a lifetime known to exceed 10^{31} years. The antiparticle of the proton is the *antiproton*. See also HYDROGEN; PROTON-PROTON CHAIN REACTION.

proton–proton chain reaction (p–p chain) a series of NUCLEAR FUSION reactions by which energy can be generated in the dense cores of stars. The overall effect of the chain reaction is the conversion of hydrogen nuclei to helium nuclei with the release of an immense amount of energy. The energy maintains the core temperature, some of it flowing to the stellar surface. The p-p chain is an efficient energy source even at core temperatures of only 15 million K; it is therefore believed to be the major source of energy in the Sun and in all main-sequence stars that are cooler (less massive) than the Sun. The CARBON CYCLE predominates in the hotter, somewhat more massive stars.

The sequence of steps of the p–p chain is shown in the illustration, with the principal sequence outlined heavily in black. The possible chains occur simultaneously but in what is thought to be 99.75% of the reactions, the sequence begins with two hydrogen nuclei (i.e. protons) combining to emit a positron and a neutrino and forming a nucleus of deuterium. The deuterium then combines with a proton to yield a nucleus of helium–3 and a photon. About 95% of the helium–3 nuclei will combine together to give helium–4, liberating two protons. Overall, each cycle thus converts four protons into one helium–4 nucleus with the release of energy. High collision speeds (plus a quantum-mechanical process known as tunneling) are required for the protons to fuse, since they have to overcome the mutual repulsion arising from their positive charge.

protoplanet an evolving planet in the process of ACCRETION, together with any of its satellites forming by accretion at the same time in the vicinity of the planet. The dust cocoon around some T TAURI stars has the attributes of a *protoplanetary system*. In the one typical case, HL Tauri, it forms a flattened disk, radius 160 AU, containing about one Earth mass of dust; allowing for dust condensed into planetesimals and the system's gas content, it could condense into several planets. Infrared observations from the satellite IRAS show dust around over 40 slightly older stars, including VEGA, indicating either a protoplanetary system or a swarm of comets. See also BETA PICTORIS.

protostar a stage in the evolution of a young star after it has fragmented from a gas cloud but before it has collapsed sufficiently for nuclear reactions to begin. This phase may take from 10^5 to 10^7 years, depending on the mass of the star. Simple theoretical models of protostars are probably

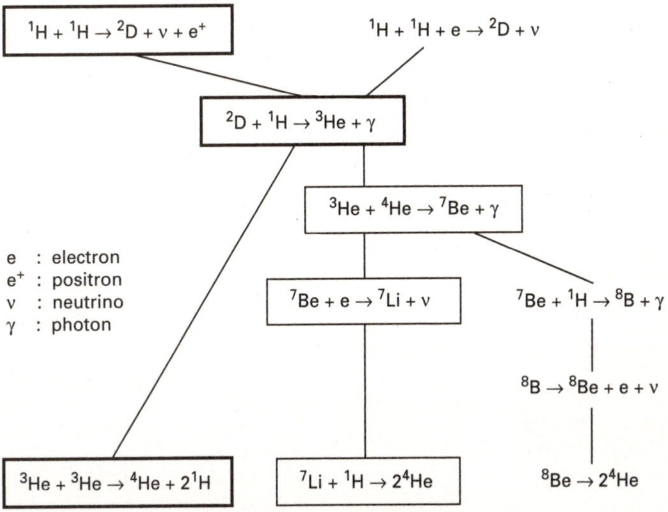

Proton–proton chain reaction

inaccurate, according to recent observations of star-formation regions. The satellite IRAS has probably detected many protostars in its infrared survey, but their identification requires clear criteria for distinguishing true protostars from young stars cocooned in dust. See also STAR FORMATION.

Proxima Centauri (**V645 Cen**) the nearest known star to the Sun. It is a FLARE STAR located in the constellation Centaurus and is a component of the ALPHA CENTAURI system, about 2°.2 from α Cen. Although very faint, it is an intense source of low-energy X-rays and high-energy ultraviolet – i.e. XUV wavelengths. m_v: 11.05 (var.); M_v: 15.5; spectral type: M5.5 Ve; mass: 0.1 times solar mass; distance: 1.29 pc. (4.2 l.y.).

proximity effect see QUASAR.

p-spot *short for* preceding spot. See SUNSPOTS.

PSR prefix used to designate a radio PULSAR, as in PSR 1913+16, the numbers indicating the pulsar's position (in right ascension and declination) on the sky.

PSR J0737–3039 a double radio pulsar system in the southern constellation Puppis and the first such system to be discovered. One component, a 23-millisecond pulsar now known as PSR J0737–3039 A, was discovered in 2003 by an international team of scientists using the 64-meter CSIRO radio telescope at the Parkes Observatory in New South Wales, Australia. At first it was assumed that this pulsar was orbiting a non-pulsing neutron star, but further observations made with the Parkes dish and the 76-meter Lovell radio telescope at the University of Manchester's Jodrell Bank Observatory in Cheshire, England, UK, revealed that the companion, now designated PSR J0737–3039 B, had a detectable slow pulse, rotating once every 2.8 seconds. The two pulsars are an estimated 800 000 kilometers apart and orbit around a common center of mass once every 2.4 hours. By chance the orbit appears edge-on, and each pulsar periodically eclipses the other, allowing researchers for the first time to analyze the physical conditions of a pulsar's magnetosphere or outer atmosphere. It is thought that the double-pulsar system evolved when, following the supernova explosion of the more massive PSR

J0737–3039 A and its transformation into a pulsar, a companion star was born and eventually developed into a giant. Material from the giant was accreted on the pulsar by mass transfer, making it spin faster. In time, the giant also exploded as a supernova and it too developed into a pulsar. Powerful gravitational forces are drawing the pulsars closer to each other, and scientists estimate that they will coalesce in 85 million years' time, possibly forming a black hole. Distance: 500–600 pc. See PULSAR.

Ptolemaeus see table at CRATERS.

Ptolemaic system a model that attempted to explain the observed motions of the Sun, Moon, and planets and predict their future positions. Originally proposed by Apollonius of Perga in the third century BC and developed by Hipparchus, it was completed by Claudius Ptolemaeus of Alexandria in the second century AD. Ptolemy assumed a GEOCENTRIC SYSTEM, possibly for ease of calculation, in which the Moon, Mercury, Venus, the Sun, Mars, Jupiter, and Saturn moved around the Earth in circular orbits of increasing radius. The position of the Earth, E, was somewhat offset from the center of the orbit, C (see illustration). The orbiting body moved at a uniform rate about a point A rather than about C. A, C, and E were colinear and AC = CE. This improved the accuracy of earlier theories in which Ptolemy had made the Moon or planet move in a small circle (an *epicycle*) the center of which moved around the circumference of a larger circle (the *deferent*), which was the body's orbit. By a suitable choice of the relative size of epicycle to deferent, the relative rates of motion in these circles, and the distance CE, Ptolemy was able to predict planetary positions to within about 1°. Comparison between prediction and observation were much simpler with a geocentric rather than a heliocentric system. It is not known however whether Ptolemy believed in an actual geocentric Solar System, as did his later followers. The Ptolemaic system, with minor modifications, was in use until the COPERNICAN SYSTEM was finally accepted.

P-type asteroid a fairly common main-belt asteroid type with an orbital distribution that peaks near the 3:2 orbital resonance with Jupiter, at a semimajor axis length of 4.0 AU. (An asteroid here will orbit three times for every two orbits of Jupiter.) These asteroids have featureless spectra and low albedos. Their surfaces are thought to be rich in organic material.

Puck a small roughly spherical satellite of Uranus, discovered in 1985 by Voyager 2. It has a low ALBEDO and three named craters: *Bogle*, *Lob*, and *Butz*. See URANUS' SATELLITES; Table 2, Appendix.

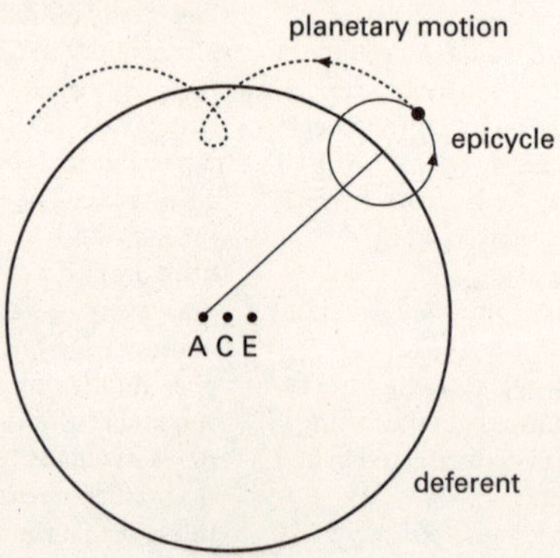

Ptolemaic system

Pulkovo Main Astronomical Observatory the chief astronomical observatory in Russia, built on the commanding heights of Pulkovo about 6 kilometers outside St Petersburg. It was founded in 1839 at the behest of Tsar Nicholas I, who appointed the German-born astronomer Friedrich Georg Wilhelm von Struve as its first director. It was completely destroyed in World War II, after which it was rebuilt. It reopened in 1954 with the surviving instruments repaired and modernized and some new instruments. In 1997, by presidential decree, it received the status of 'especially valuable object of the cultural heritage of the peoples of the Russian Federation'.

pulsar a very regularly 'pulsing' source of radiation, which almost certainly originates from a rotating NEUTRON STAR. Pulsars were originally discovered at radio wavelengths, and a few of these have been detected at optical and gamma-ray wavelengths; pulsars can be powerful gamma-ray emitters (see GAMMA-RAY PULSARS) and there is also a class of X-RAY PULSATORS or pulsars.

The first radio pulsar, PSR 1919+21, was detected by Antony Hewish and Jocelyn Bell during a pioneering study of interplanetary scintillation (see SCATTERING). More than 500 radio pulsars are now known. The periods range from 1.56 milliseconds to 4 seconds and can be measured to accuracies of, typically, one part in 10^{10}. The width of the pulse is usually a few per cent of the pulsar's period but can reach 50%. Pulsars with periods shorter than about 0.01 seconds constitute the distinct class of MILLISECOND PULSARS. Most pulsars are single, but BINARY PULSARS are now known, about half of which are millisecond pulsars.

The total number of pulsars in the Galaxy is estimated at about 100 000. Their rate of formation is now calculated as maybe 5 per century. Pulsars, together with a smaller number of black holes, are currently thought to originate in SUPERNOVA explosions. The estimated supernova production rate in the Galaxy is only 2–3 per century. The discrepancy is less than was thought a few years ago, but it may still be necessary to invoke the formation of some pulsars by another means (perhaps the accretion of gas on to a WHITE DWARF).

The received pulses occur when a beam of radio waves, emitted by a rotating neutron star, sweeps past the Earth in an identical manner to the flashes produced by a lighthouse lamp. This beam of radiation is comprised of SYNCHROTRON EMISSION; it arises from electrons moving in the neutron star's strong magnetic field (about 10^8 tesla), whose direction differs from that of the pulsar's rotation axis. There is still dispute over the emission site of the beam: it may be near the star, at the magnetic poles, so that radio waves are beamed down the magnetic axis; alternatively it may be farther out near the speed of light cylinder, where the magnetic field is rotating at almost the speed of light.

Despite their impressive regularity, the periods of all radio pulsars are very gradually increasing as the neutron star loses rotational energy. The central star of the CRAB NEBULA – the youngest known pulsar – is slowing at the rate of one part in a million per day. The slow-down rate of both this pulsar and the young VELA PULSAR are occasionally interrupted by *glitches* (or *spin-ups*): temporary changes in rotation rate. These are thought to be due to rearrangements of the crust or core of the neutron star. The Crab and Vela pulsars are both OPTICAL PULSARS. They are also among the brightest GAMMA-RAY SOURCES in the sky. Both optical and gamma-ray luminosity seem to decrease rapidly with a pulsar's age. The Crab pulsar is the fastest of the young pulsars (having a period of 33 milliseconds) but the millisecond pulsars represent a much faster and much older class of pulsar, probably 'spun-up' by mass transfer.

X-ray pulsars occur in close binary systems when gas from a companion is channeled on to the neutron star at its magnetic poles: the X-rays appear to pulse on and off as these hot gas patches are exposed by the star's rotation. The gas flow affects the neutron star's spin and as a result all X-ray pulsars are gradually speeding up. Although some have typical pulsar periods (up to a few seconds) there are many 'slow' X-ray pulsars (with periods of several minutes), whose rotation must somehow have been strongly 'braked'.

pulsating Universe see OSCILLATING UNIVERSE.

pulsating variables VARIABLE STARS that periodically brighten and fade as a result of large-scale and more or less rhythmical motions of their outer layers. Most stars evolve during their lifetime to a state where they naturally pulsate. The simplest motion is purely radial, a cycle of expansion and contraction in which the star remains spherical but changes volume. The idea that a periodic stellar expansion could lead to a variable light output was proposed by Shapley in 1914, with Eddington presenting the theory in 1918. The period of light variation is equal to the period of pulsation and is normally approximately constant. The spectrum of the star also changes periodically due to changes in surface temperature. The pulsation cycle is demonstrated by variations in RADIAL VELOCITY. All these variations are shown in the diagram at CEPHEID VARIABLES. The pulsation period, P, was shown by Eddington to be related to mean stellar density, ρ, by the *period-density relation* and hence to the star's radius, R, and mass, M:

$$P \propto 1/\sqrt{\rho} \propto \sqrt{(R^3/M)}$$

Combining this relation with STEFAN'S LAW and a MASS-LUMINOSITY RELATION shows that pulsation period should be related to luminosity (see PERIOD-LUMINOSITY RELATION). Types of pulsating variable include the CEPHEID VARIABLES, RR LYRAE STARS, DWARF CEPHEIDS, DELTA SCUTI STARS, long-period MIRA STARS, SEMIREGULAR VARIABLES (including RV TAURI STARS), IRREGULAR VARIABLES, and BETA CEPHEI STARS.

A star pulsates because there is a small imbalance between gravitational force and outward directed pressure so that it is not in hydrostatic equilibrium. When it pulsates it expands past its equilibrium size until the expansion is slowed and reversed by gravity. It then overshoots its

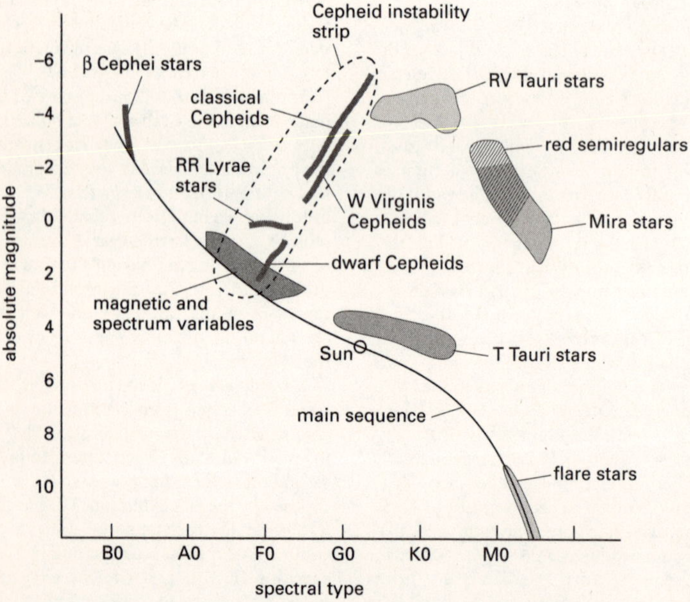

Hertzsprung–Russell diagram of pulsating and other variable stars

equilibrium size again until the contraction is slowed and reversed by the increased gas pressure within the star. The fact that the pulsations do not die away as energy is dissipated means that some process is continuously providing mechanical energy to drive the pulsations. The center of the star is not involved in the pulsation. For most pulsating variables the driving force is a valve mechanism in the form of a region of changing OPACITY near the stellar surface where the pulsation amplitude is greatest. This region is an *ionization zone* in which atoms, mainly helium, are partially ionized. Normally atoms become transparent, letting heat escape, as they are compressed. In an ionization zone the opacity increases with compression and the zone effectively acts as a heat engine, storing energy (in the form of the second ionization of helium); the energy is released during the expansion stage (as the helium recombines). As long as the zone lies at the required depth below the surface it can drive the pulsations. If the zones are too close to the surface, as in a very hot star, or if too deep, then pulsations cannot occur. The period of pulsation is complicated by the fact that the gas is thought to be able to undergo oscillations (as in an open musical pipe) either in a fundamental mode or as a harmonic of the fundamental.

The distribution of pulsating variables on the HERTZSPRUNG–RUSSELL DIAGRAM differs from that of normal stars. Most lie on a nearly vertical band – the *Cepheid instability strip* – that extends upward from the main sequence (and possibly below it) and merges into a broader instability region at top right (see illustration). Stars reach these instability regions by various evolutionary paths and may turn up there several times during their evolution. The existence of such instability regions indicates that with certain combinations of stellar luminosity and effective temperature a state of pulsation rather than of rest is favoured.

Puppis (**Poop**; **Stern**) a constellation in the southern hemisphere near Canis Major, lying partly in the Milky Way. It was once part of the constellation ARGO. The brightest star is the extremely remote and luminous 2nd-magnitude Naos (ζ). It also has several open clusters including M47 (NGC 2422), just visible, and M46 (NGC 2437), which contains the bright planetary nebula NGC 2438; the supernova remnant *Puppis A* is a strong radio and X-ray source. Abbrev.: Pup; genitive form: Puppis; approx. position: RA 7.5h, dec –30°; area: 673 sq deg.

Puppis A see PUPPIS.

Pyxis (**Mariner's Compass**) a small inconspicuous constellation in the southern hemisphere near Vela, lying partly in the Milky Way. It once formed part of the Mast of Argo, an obsolete division of ARGO. It has some 3rd- and 4th-magnitude stars and contains the peculiar RECURRENT NOVA T Pyxidis. Abbrev.: Pyx; genitive form: Pyxidis; approx. position: RA 9h, dec –30°; area: 221 sq deg.

PZT *abbrev. for* photographic zenith tube.

Qq

QPO *abbrev. for* quasi-periodic oscillation.

QSO *abbrev. for* quasi-stellar object. See QUASAR.

Q-type asteroids a rare class of asteroid that at present only contains (1862) APOLLO, (2063) Bacchus, and a few other NEAR-EARTH ASTEROIDS. The spectra are similar to ordinary CHONDRITE meteorites and have a strong absorption feature just below 0.7 μm.

quadrant an instrument dating back to antiquity and used for measuring altitudes and angular separations of stars. It remained the most important astronomical instrument until the telescope was invented. It consisted of a 90° graduated arc (a quarter circle) with a swiveling arm to which a sighting mechanism was attached. In the *mural quadrant* the graduated arc, often very large, was attached to a wall and was orientated along the observer's meridian. The mural quadrant was therefore the forerunner of the TRANSIT CIRCLE.

Quadrantids a major METEOR SHOWER, radiant: RA 232°, dec +50°, that maximizes on Jan. 3 when the SUN'S LONGITUDE is 282.8°. The ZENITHAL HOURLY RATE (ZHR) at maximum is about 90 and is constant from year to year. The METEOROID STREAM is narrow, the ZHR being greater than half maximum for only 17 hours: the stream's cross-sectional diameter is about 1.7 million km compared with 20 million and 13 million km for those of the PERSEIDS and GEMINIDS. The stream has its ascending NODE close to the orbit of Jupiter. Owing to gravitational and radiational perturbations the large 'visual' meteoroids are in a slightly different orbit to the smaller 'radio' meteoroids. The shower is thought to be associated with comet Machholz. It is named after the obsolete constellation Quadrans Murali found in early 19th-century star atlases. The radiant is actually in Boötes.

quadrature the position, or aspect, of a body in the Solar System when its ELONGATION from the Sun, as measured from the Earth, is 90°, i.e. when the angle Sun–Earth–body is a right angle.

quantum the minimum amount by which certain properties of a system, such as its energy or angular momentum, can change. The value of the property cannot therefore vary continuously but must change in steps: these steps are equal to or are integral multiples of the relevant quantum. This idea is the basis of QUANTUM THEORY and quantum mechanics. The PHOTON, for example, is a quantum of ELECTROMAGNETIC RADIATION.

quantum cosmology theories that encompass the meeting of gravity, quantum mechanics, and cosmology at a time – the PLANCK TIME – very shortly after the BIG BANG.

quantum efficiency a measure of the efficiency of conversion or utilization of light or other radiation. It is given by the proportion of incident PHOTONS, of a particular frequency, that are converted by a device into a useful form, such as a permanent record. Photographic emulsions, at best, record only a few photons out of every thousand falling on them. Electronic detectors have a much higher efficiency.

quantum gravitation any of various theories

of gravitation that are consistent with the theories of quantum mechanics and special relativity. It is postulated that the gravitational force between two particles is generated by the exchange of an intermediate particle. (This is similar to the explanation of the other FUNDAMENTAL FORCES.) In earlier theories the force was transmitted by the exchange of particles called *gravitons* of zero charge, zero rest mass, and spin 2; other particles have also been suggested.

quantum mechanics see QUANTUM THEORY.

quantum number one of a set of integers or half integers characterizing the energy states of an ELEMENTARY PARTICLE or system of particles. Physical properties, such as charge and spin, are described by quantum numbers.

quantum theory the theory put forward by the German physicist Max Planck in 1900. Classical physics regarded all changes in the physical properties of a system to be continuous. By departing from this viewpoint and allowing physical quantities such as energy, angular momentum, and action to change only by discrete amounts, quantum theory was born. It grew out of Planck's attempts to explain the form of the curves of intensity against wavelength for a BLACK-BODY radiator. By assuming that energy could only be emitted and absorbed in discrete amounts, called QUANTA, he was successful in describing the shape of the curves. Other early applications of quantum theory were Einstein's explanation of the PHOTOELECTRIC EFFECT and Bohr's theory of the atom (see HYDROGEN SPECTRUM; ENERGY LEVEL). The more precise mathematical theory that developed in the 1920s from quantum theory is called *quantum mechanics*. Relativistic quantum mechanics resulted from the extension of quantum mechanics to include the special theory of RELATIVITY.

Quaoar the largest known KUIPER BELT OBJECT, discovered in June 2002 by Chad Trujillo and Mike Brown of the California Institute of Technology using the 1.2-meter Oschin Telescope at PALOMAR OBSERVATORY. With an estimated diameter of about 1250 km, it is more than 30% larger than (1) CERES, the largest of the asteroids, and is larger in volume than all the known asteroids put together. It is half the diameter of PLUTO but has only 12½% of its volume. Quaoar, which takes its name from the creation mythology of the Tongva, a native American people who once inhabited the area around present-day Los Angeles, orbits the Sun in about 285 years at a mean distance of 42 AU. Its orbit is inclined at an angular of 8° to the ECLIPTIC and has an eccentricity of less than 0.04.

quark any of six pointlike ELEMENTARY PARTICLES (the up, down, strange, charm, bottom, and top quarks) that are thought to be the structural units from which other particles (excluding leptons) are formed. In the usual scheme, quarks all have spin ½, electric charges that are −⅓ or ⅔ of the proton charge, and other innate qualities. Corresponding to each quark is an *antiquark*, with opposite electric charge, etc. (see ANTIPARTICLES). The theory of quark interactions predicts that isolated quarks can never exist in the free state (under normal conditions of temperature and pressure); they occur only in particular pairs and triplets that form the class of particles called the hadrons. The proton, for example, is composed of one down and two up quarks, the neutron of one up and two down quarks. Quarks are held together through the exchange of massless particles called *gluons*; these are the carriers of the strong force, one of the four FUNDAMENTAL FORCES that particles experience.

At present there are tentative suggestions that states of condensed matter, such as the deep interiors of NEUTRON STARS, may consist of a soup of free quarks. See also BIG BANG THEORY.

quark–gluon plasma a state of matter thought to have existed in which isolated hadrons did not exist but in which quarks and gluons formed a 'hot soup'. It is thought that this state ended about 10^{-5} seconds after the big bang when there was a phase transition in which hadrons formed as the Universe cooled.

quark-hadron phase transition see BIG BANG THEORY.

quasar a compact extragalactic object that looks like a point of light but emits more energy than a hundred supergiant galaxies.

The name is a contraction of *quasi-stellar object* (*QSO*). Although they are bright optical sources, quasars emit most of their energy as infrared radiation. They are also strong X-ray sources. About 10% of quasars are also radio sources.

Quasars, of which several thousand are known, were discovered in 1963 as the optical counterparts to some powerful radio sources. The spectra of these objects were peculiar, with bright emission lines, apparently of an unknown element, superimposed on a continuum. Maarten Schmidt finally recognized the pattern of lines in one of these objects (3C 273) as the Balmer series of hydrogen redshifted to $z = 0.158$ (see REDSHIFT), showing that it was impossible for this to be a star within the Galaxy. Other quasars were then discovered to have far greater redshifts. The record is currently held by RD J030117+002025, whose redshift of 5.50 indicates that it is receding from us with more than 90% of the speed of light. Astronomers today interpret the quasar redshifts as Doppler shifts (see DOPPLER EFFECT) arising from the expansion of the Universe, making them among the most distant and hence the youngest extragalactic objects we observe.

To be visible at such great distances, quasars must be exceedingly luminous: many have absolute MAGNITUDES brighter than –27. There is however a great range in luminosity. In addition quasars themselves are often variable by a factor of two or greater, on timescales sometimes as short as a few hours. This indicates that their light-producing regions are sometimes less than a light-day across, which poses several problems in explaining their energy generation. The only process known to be efficient enough is accretion on to a supermassive BLACK HOLE (of the order of 10^9 solar masses) that is located at the nucleus of the quasar. This is in agreement with the nonthermal continuum emission observed at all wavelengths.

Matter is accreted on the central black hole via an *accretion disk*, which is heated by the dissipation of gravitational energy to produce a thermal component of emission in the quasar spectrum known as the *blue bump*. Gas clouds located around this system are also irradiated by the black hole to produce low-ionization emission lines (such as the Balmer series of hydrogen); the LINE BROADENING reveals speeds in excess of 10 000 km s^{-1}, indicative of the bulk motion of the clouds in orbit, accelerated by the central massive gravitational potential. This inner region of the quasar surrounding the black hole and its accretion disk is known as the *broad-line region* (*BLR*), and studies of the variability in the line emission show that it spans a region with radius typically of a few light-months. At larger radii of ten to a thousand light-years from the central ionization source, the gas clouds have more moderate speeds of a few hundred km s^{-1} and radiate strongly in FORBIDDEN LINES of ionized metals as well as hydrogen. There is probably a continuous transition between the BLR and this *narrow-line region* (*NLR*). Both the broad and narrow emission lines are superimposed on the nonthermal spectrum from the central black hole.

Deep exposures of quasars reveal that the nucleus is located in a large but otherwise normal 'host' elliptical galaxy. The radio quasars have also been shown to lie at the center of CLUSTERS OF GALAXIES for redshifts up to at least 0.7. Many quasars of both types are surrounded by emission-line nebulae extended over many tens of kiloparsecs in filaments and clouds. Some observations suggest that the host galaxy is distorted in shape and is partaking in an interaction that may supply fuel to the black hole. Alternatively, if a cooling flow is taking place in the galaxy CLUSTERS surrounding the radio quasars, these could be fueled by the mass deposition. Only one-tenth of a solar mass a year is required to power a luminous quasar.

There is a lack of quasars at very low redshift. The LUMINOSITY FUNCTION of quasars show that they were most numerous around a redshift of 2 (when the Universe was half its present age) and their numbers have declined catastrophically since. The reason is not yet established.

The lines of sight to distant quasars pass through many foreground systems, some of which leave their imprint on the quasar spectrum in the form of absorption lines of ionized metals such as carbon and magnesium. Many of these narrow absorption lines are thought to be due to extended DARK HALOS of ordinary galaxies. Some quasars show peculiar broadened line-of-sight absorption lines of LYMAN-ALPHA that have a high COLUMN DENSITY known as *damped Lyman-alpha systems.* The foreground systems are most likely either high-redshift LSB GALAXIES, or the progenitors of present-day disk galaxies.

Most of the very highest redshift quasars show a large number of very narrow single absorption lines that completely 'eat away' the quasar continuum emission just blueward of the quasar's Lyman-α emission line. This is the *Lyman-alpha forest* and is caused by Lyman-α absorption by a population of small clouds spread over a large range in redshift. The small width of individual lines precludes their association with the quasar, and they are thought to arise instead from intergalactic shreds of primordial matter. The tendency of the number density of these *Lyman-alpha clouds* to decrease along the line of sight toward an individual quasar, is known as the *proximity effect,* and is caused by the quasar radiation ionizing any clouds too close to it.

Absorption features intrinsic to the quasar are found only in *broad absorption line* (*BAL*) *quasars.* The width of the lines implies that massive outflows of absorbing gas are taking place at speeds of tens of thousands of kilometers per second away from the quasar.

See also RADIO GALAXY; ACTIVE GALAXY.

quasi-periodic oscillations (**QPOs**) short-lived, periodic flux changes, frequently observed in low-mass X-ray binaries. They were first detected in EXOSAT observations, with typical frequencies being 1–20 Hz, and coherence lasting for several tens of pulses; such pulses cause broad peaks in the X-ray POWER spectra of the sources. These QPOs are believed to arise in oscillations associated with the accretion of matter onto the compact star (white dwarf or neutron star) in these systems, and may prove to be a generic signature of such accretion. More recent observations, particularly with RXTE, have shown more rapid QPOs, at kHz frequencies, possibly associated with the neutron star spin frequency.

quasi-stellar object (**QSO**) see QUASAR.

quiescent prominence see PROMINENCES.

quiet Sun the term applied to the Sun around the minimum of the SUNSPOT CYCLE, when the absence of ACTIVE REGIONS allows relatively 'quiet' conditions to prevail. The Sun is not then free of all disturbance but there are few (if any) concentrations of intense magnetic flux to produce significant departures from a uniform distribution of radiative flux across the disk. Compare ACTIVE SUN.

Rr

RA *abbrev. for* right ascension.

radar astronomy the study of celestial bodies (as yet) within the Solar System by means of the faint reflections from them of powerful high-frequency radio transmissions aimed in their directions from the Earth. Some of the very large radio DISHES such as the 305-meter dish at ARECIBO, are equipped for radar work. The time interval between transmission of a signal and reception of the reflected signal is an accurate measure of intervening distance. The determination of planetary distances by this method led to a precise value for the ASTRONOMICAL UNIT. The transmitted frequency may be chosen to penetrate the atmosphere of a planet in order to establish a profile of the surface, which is otherwise hidden from view. In addition, rotation periods can be determined from the doppler shift produced in pulses bounced off different parts of an object. The rotation periods of Venus and Mercury were first determined by radar measurements.

radar meteor *another name for* radio meteor. See METEOR.

radial velocity (line-of-sight velocity) symbol: v_r. The velocity of a star along the line of sight of an observer. It is calculated directly from the doppler shift (see DOPPLER EFFECT) in the lines of the star's spectrum: if the star is receding there will be a REDSHIFT in its spectral lines and the radial velocity will be positive; an approaching star will produce a blueshift and the velocity will be negative. Most stars have values lying between +40 and –40 km s^{-1}. Radial velocity is usually given in terms of the Sun's position so that the Earth's orbital motion has no effect.

The velocity and direction of motion of the Sun relative to the LOCAL STANDARD OF REST can be determined from a statistical analysis of the observed radial velocities of nearby stars: stars in the region of the solar APEX have predominantly positive velocities while those around the antapex have predominantly negative ones.

A star's velocity in space relative to the Sun – its *space velocity* – is a vector quantity and can be split into two components: its radial velocity and its tangential velocity, v_t, along the direction of PROPER MOTION. Measurements of these components give both the magnitude, *V*, and direction, θ, of the star's space velocity (see illustration).

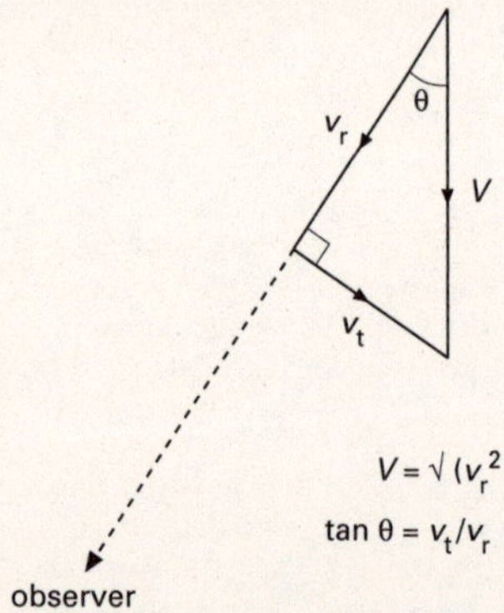

$$V = \sqrt{(v_r^2 + v_t^2)}$$

$$\tan \theta = v_t / v_r$$

Radial velocity: space velocity and its components

radial-velocity curve a curve showing how the radial velocity of a SPECTROSCOPIC BINARY changes during one revolution.

radian a unit of angle used in plane geometry that is the angle subtended at the center of a circle by an arc of the circle equal in length to the circle's radius. Thus 2π radians equals 360°, 1 radian equals 57°.296, and 1° equals 0.017 radians. Solid angles, used in spherical geometry, are measured in steradians.

radiant the point on the celestial sphere, usually given in the coordinates RIGHT ASCENSION and DECLINATION, from which a METEOR appears to originate. Shower meteors all seem to radiate from this point and the TRAINS of a series of shower meteors, extrapolated backwards, intercept at the radiant. Its position is found by calculating the intercept with the celestial sphere of the vector sum of the meteor's velocity vector and the Earth's velocity vector on collision. The radiant position changes slightly with time as the Earth moves through the METEOROID STREAM. Meteor showers are usually named after the constellation that contains the radiant.

radiant flux the total power emitted or received by a body in the form of radiation. It is measured in watts.

radiation see ELECTROMAGNETIC RADIATION; ENERGY TRANSPORT.

radiation belts one or more doughnut-shaped regions in the MAGNETOSPHERE of a planet in which energetic electrons and the ionized nuclei of atoms, chiefly protons from hydrogen atoms, are trapped by the planet's magnetic field. The particles within the belt, whose axis is the magnetic axis of the planet, spiral along magnetic field lines, traveling backward and forward between reflections which occur as they approach the magnetic poles. This motion produces SYNCHROTRON EMISSION from the particles. The particles are either captured from the SOLAR WIND or are formed by collisions between COSMIC RAYS and atoms or ions in the planet's outer atmosphere.

The Earth, Jupiter, Saturn, Uranus, and Neptune are all known to possess radiation belts. The magnetic field of Mercury appears to be too weak to sustain belts. The radiation belts of Jupiter are many times more intense than the VAN ALLEN RADIATION BELTS of the Earth and pose a threat to spacecraft systems in the vicinity of the planet.

radiation era see BIG BANG THEORY.

radiation pressure the very small pressure exerted on a surface by light or other electromagnetic radiation. The radiation is considered as a stream of PHOTONS, and the pressure is then due to the transfer of momentum from the photons to the surface. Although radiation pressure has a negligible effect on large particles or on dense matter, the effect is considerable with very small particles, which are driven away from the radiation source. Thus solar radiation pressure, aided by the SOLAR WIND, clears tiny particles of dust ($<1\ \mu m$) from the Solar System. See also POYNTING–ROBERTSON EFFECT.

radiation resistance a ficticious resistance in which the power radiated away from or collected by an ANTENNA is considered to be dissipated. For a perfect antenna made of superconducting material, the ohmic losses (power dissipation arising from resistance) in the elements themselves are zero; the resistive part of the impedance presented at the feed point is then equal to the radiation resistance. In any practical antenna the ohmic losses are kept as small as possible in comparison to the radiated power. Maximum power transfer between transmitter or RECEIVER and the antenna is effected when the FEEDER has a characteristic impedance equal to the radiation resistance.

radiation temperature see EFFECTIVE TEMPERATURE.

radiative transport, zone see ENERGY TRANSPORT.

radicals highly reactive groups of atoms that do not usually occur under terrestrial conditions but may be relatively abundant in some MOLECULAR CLOUDS, where collisions between reacting species happen only rarely. Radicals often have unpaired electrons in their outer shells. CN is an example.

radioactive decay the spontaneous transformation of one atomic nucleus into another with the emission of energy. The energy is released in the form of an energetic particle, usually an ALPHA PARTICLE, BETA PARTICLE (i.e. an electron), or positron, sometimes accompanied by a gamma-ray photon. The unstable isotopes of an element that can undergo such transformations are called radioactive isotopes, or *radioisotopes*. The emission of a particle from the nucleus of a radioisotope results in the production of an isotope of a different element, as in the beta decay of carbon–14 to nitrogen–14 or the alpha decay of radium–226 to radon–222. The isotope produced is itself often radioactive.

The average time taken for half a given number of nuclei of a particular radioisotope to decay is the HALF-LIFE of that radioisotope; values range from a fraction of a second to thousands of millions of years. See also RADIOMETRIC DATING.

radio astrometry a branch of ASTROMETRY in which the coordinates of celestial objects are measured with high precision using a RADIO TELESCOPE. It has become more accurate than its optical counterpart in recent years with the advent of interferometers having very long and accurately determined baselines. See VLBI.

RadioAstron an international collaborative mission to launch a 10-meter diameter RADIO TELESCOPE into an elliptical orbit (apogee 80 000 km, period 28 hours) around the Earth. The dish is made from 27 carbon-fiber petals with a surface accuracy of 0.5 mm. RadioAstron is designed to carry out VLBI observations in conjunction with ground-based telescopes, operating at wavelengths of 1.35, 6, 18 and 92 cm with an angular resolution of up to 30 milliarcseconds.

Initiated in the former Soviet Union, the project now has support from more than 20 countries and is planned for launch around 2007.

radio astronomy the study of celestial bodies and the media between them by means of the RADIO WAVES they emit. Extraterrestrial radio waves were first detected in 1932 by the American radio engineer Karl Jansky. The first RADIO TELESCOPE was built and operated by Grote Reber in the late 1930s but radio astronomy only developed after the war. It has benefitted greatly from advances in electronics and solid-state physics and is now a major branch of observational astronomy. It is particularly useful in the study of gaseous nebulae such as H I and H II REGIONS, PULSARS, SUPERNOVA REMNANTS, RADIO GALAXIES, QUASARS, and the MICROWAVE BACKGROUND. See also RADIO SOURCE.

radio background radiation see INTERSTELLAR MEDIUM; RADIO SOURCE.

radio brightness (**surface brightness**) the spectral FLUX DENSITY of a radio source per unit solid angle (see BRIGHTNESS TEMPERATURE). An image of the *radio brightness distribution* over the sky shows the shape of extended RADIO SOURCES in a form similar to an optical photograph. Maps made by APERTURE SYNTHESIS instruments, which naturally measure flux densities rather than brightnesses, are often calibrated in flux density units per synthesized beam area.

radio core see RADIO-SOURCE STRUCTURE.

radio frequency see RADIO WAVES.

radio galaxy an extragalactic radio source identified with an optical galaxy whose radio-power output lies in the range 10^{35} to 10^{38} watts. These sources often show symmetric tripolar structure (see RADIO-SOURCE STRUCTURE) and may be distinguished from normal galaxies, such as M31, whose radio emissions roughly follow the optical contours of the galaxy and whose radio powers are much lower, in the range 10^{30} to 10^{32} watts. Powerful radio sources are always located in elliptical galaxies, many of which are the central dominant member of a CLUSTER OF GALAXIES. Radio galaxies with diameters greater than one megaparsec are now known. An example of such a *giant radio galaxy* is 3C 236, which is a double radio source whose radio emission spans almost six megaparsecs of space, making it one of the biggest radio galaxies in the Universe.

Radio galaxies are a form of ACTIVE GALAXY. High-luminosity radio galaxies sometimes share some characteristics of QUASARS, such as broad optical emission lines and a bright optical nucleus in the galaxy and are termed *broad-line radio galaxies* (*BLRG*).

The similarities, in addition to their shared RADIO-SOURCE STRUCTURE, have led several astronomers to propose that the radio quasars and the very powerful FR II radio galaxies are the same type of object viewed at different inclinations to the line of sight. These *unification scenarios* suggest that when radio galaxies are observed along the radio source axis, the continuum emission from the central black hole is relativistically beamed into the line of sight, brightening the galaxy nucleus to appear as a quasar. When the system is viewed at a larger inclination, the continuum emission is no longer beamed into the line of sight and only the 'host' galaxy is seen. An optically thick torus around the nucleus may contribute to hiding it from sight. In this scenario, a BLRG is seen at some intermediate angle that is near the division of quasars and radio galaxies. Comparisons of orientation-independent properties of the systems, such as extended optical line emission, extended radio flux, the size and magnitude of the host galaxy, and cluster membership, broadly support the unification schemes. Similar schemes exist to unite the two types of SEYFERT GALAXY, and to identify BL LAC OBJECTS as the beamed apparition of the less powerful FR I radio galaxies.

High-redshift radio galaxies, such as those selected from the 3C catalog, are exceptionally luminous systems in both optical and radio emission. The galaxies possess optical emission-line nebulae and an optical-ultraviolet continuum (in the REST FRAME of the galaxy) that are extended over tens to hundreds of kiloparsecs. These structures are elongated and aligned with the direction of the radio-source axis, in an alignment effect, thought in part to be due to star formation induced in the surrounding medium by the passage of the radio jets. Other distant radio sources, known as *compact steep-spectrum radio sources*, show very STEEP radio spectra and subtend only a very small angular scale in the radio waveband. These are thought to be powerful radio galaxies in the early stages of their formation, when the radio jets are prevented by expanding from the active nucleus by a dense environment.

radio heliograph a RADIO TELESCOPE designed for making radio maps of the Sun. The radio heliograph at Nobeyama, Japan, is a particular example.

radio interferometer see APERTURE SYNTHESIS; PHASE-SWITCHING INTERFEROMETER; RADIO TELESCOPE.

radioisotope see RADIOACTIVE DECAY.

radioisotope thermoelectric generator (RTG) see THERMOELECTRIC GENERATOR.

radio lobe see RADIO-SOURCE STRUCTURE.

radio map see RADIO-SOURCE STRUCTURE.

radio meteor (radar meteor) see METEOR.

radiometer a device that measures the total energy or power received from a body in the form of radiation, especially infrared radiation. In radio astronomy, a radiometer measures the total received radio NOISE POWER.

radiometric dating the dating of rocks (and also fossils and archeological remains) by the accurate determination of the quantities of a long-lived radioactive isotope and its stable decay product in a sample. Assuming that the parent radioisotope was present at the time of formation of the rock, etc., then the number of daughter isotopes produced by RADIOACTIVE DECAY of the parent depends only on the HALF-LIFE of the parent and the age of the sample. Half-lives must therefore be known with great accuracy for precise dating and should range from about 10^5 to about 10^{10} years. In addition, there should be no loss or gain of parent or daughter isotope during the time the 'radioactive clock' is operating; if this condition is only partly satisfied, allowances must be made. The decay of radioisotopes can be used not only to date material but also to time very slow processes, such as the evolution of the Earth's atmosphere.

Pairs of isotopes used in radiometric dating include potassium–40 which decays to argon–40 with a half-life of 1.25×10^9 years, and rubidium–87 which decays to strontium–87 with a half-life of 4.88×10^{10} years.

radio receiver see RECEIVER.

radio source a celestial object whose radio emissions may be detected with a RADIO TELESCOPE. Within our Solar System these sources include Jupiter and the Sun, both of which emit powerful radio BURSTS. Galactic radio sources include PULSARS, SUPERNOVA REMNANTS, H I and H II REGIONS, MASER SOURCES, and the GALACTIC CENTER itself. SYNCHROTRON EMISSION from cosmic rays in the Galaxy gives rise to a diffuse background radiation, centered broadly on the galactic plane but having several spurs away from it (see INTERSTELLAR MEDIUM). This background radiation may limit the SENSITIVITY of a radio telescope, especially at frequencies below about 400 megahertz.

Extragalactic radio sources include spiral galaxies (whose H I and CARBON MONOXIDE emissions may be used to map the distribution of hydrogen within them), RADIO GALAXIES, and QUASARS. An extragalactic radio source is often classified according to the spatial distribution of the radio emission shown on a radio map of the source. See RADIO-SOURCE SPECTRUM; RADIO-SOURCE STRUCTURE.

radio-source catalog a numbered list of RADIO SOURCES detected in a survey at a given frequency down to a limiting FLUX DENSITY. A well-known example is the *third Cambridge catalog*, 3C. The catalog usually lists the source positions and flux densities together with any other information that may be available about angular sizes, etc. Early nomenclatures persist, such as 'Cassiopeia A' for the brightest source in Cassiopeia and 3C461 for the 461st source in the Cambridge 3C catalog, but most sources are classified by their position in the sky. Thus a source at RIGHT ASCENSION 23h21m07s and DECLINATION +58.5° is designated 2321+585. Positions are usually quoted at the standard EPOCHS of 1950.0 or 2000.0, and would need to be corrected for PRECESSION to find their actual position. Most of the sources in radio catalogs are RADIO GALAXIES or QUASARS.

From one or more catalogs SOURCE COUNTS can be compiled, in which the total number of sources per unit solid angle (steradian) above a given FLUX DENSITY is plotted as a function of the flux density. These counts are important in COSMOLOGY since different mathematical models of the Universe predict different source counts: they provide one method of comparing theory with the real world.

radio-source spectrum the variation of the FLUX DENSITY of a RADIO SOURCE with frequency. The emissions from most radio sources are NOISE signals displaying continuous spectra that rise or fall with increasing frequency more or less smoothly (see SPECTRAL INDEX). Sources of THERMAL and SYNCHROTRON EMISSION both give spectra of this type, sometimes showing a low-frequency cut-off due to self-absorption (see SYNCHROTRON EMISSION) or the RAZIN EFFECT. The spectra of the radiation from MASER SOURCES or from clouds of interstellar molecules, such as some H I REGIONS, have discrete lines of bright emission superimposed on a background continuum (see MOLECULAR-LINE RADIO ASTRONOMY). Extragalactic objects are often described as either *steep-spectrum* or *flat-spectrum radio sources* according to the size of the spectral index.

radio-source structure the spatial distribution of the radio emission from a RADIO SOURCE. It may be partly inferred from a *radio map* of the source, which is the CONVOLUTION of the true source distribution projected onto a plane and the ANTENNA PATTERN of the RADIO TELESCOPE, and which is often plotted in contours of constant BRIGHTNESS TEMPERATURE or FLUX DENSITY; such a map is called a *contour map*. Other features may be more easily seen in a *false-color map* or a *gray-scale map*, in which flux density or brightness are plotted in different colors or shades of gray. Where the angular size of the source is smaller than the antenna pattern, the radio map reveals no details of its structure; the source is then said to be *unresolved* and is described as a *point source*. In the converse case, the source is said to be *extended*.

Maps of extragalactic radio sources often show two distinct bright features called *lobes* to each side of the optical galaxy position, and usually separated from it by many hundreds of kiloparsecs. These may be joined back to any compact *core* emission associated with the galaxy nucleus by a faint *bridge* of diffuse emission, or in the case of quasars by a clearly collimated JET. The lobes are sometimes broken into distinct *hot spots* of bright emission with wide trailing extensions. These *double radio*

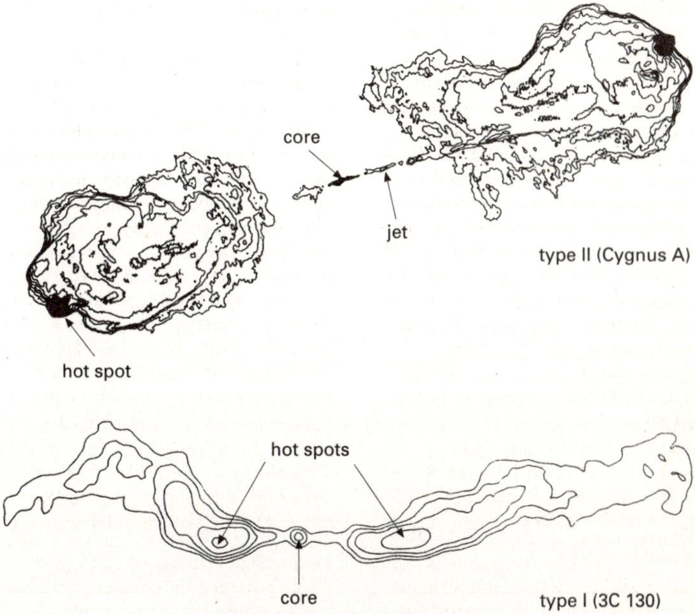

Double radio-source structures

sources are commonly separated into two *Fanaroff–Riley* (*FR*) *types*, according to both their morphology and power (see illustration). Type I systems are lower-luminosity radio galaxies with symmetric two-sided bridges extending into smooth lobes. Type II sources have powers above 5×10^{25} W Hz^{-1} at 178 MHz and are associated with quasars as well as radio galaxies. Type FR II have prominent lobes, with bright outer hotspots and usually display only a one-sided jet or bridge; CYGNUS A is a fine example.

If a radio galaxy is moving rapidly through a cluster, its extended lobes and connecting trails are swept back by the RAM PRESSURE of the intracluster medium and form a *bent double radio source.* If the bending is very great, the extended radio structures may combine into a single trail, forming a *head-tail source.*

radio telescope an instrument for recording and measuring the RADIO-FREQUENCY emissions from celestial RADIO SOURCES. All radio telescopes consist of an ANTENNA, or system of antennas, connected by FEEDERS to one or more RECEIVERS. The antennas may be in the form of DISHES, simple linear DIPOLES, or YAGI ANTENNAS. The receiver outputs may be displayed on suitable devices such as pen-recorders or, more usually, are passed directly to a computer for storage and analysis. Often the computer can then produce an image of the radio source similar to an optical photograph (see RADIO BRIGHTNESS).

The antenna system may consist of two separated units whose electrical signals are conveyed by feeders to a common receiver, forming an *interferometer.* The antenna units are often mounted on an east-west line and are arranged to point in the same direction. The Earth's rotation then causes a radio source to move through the antenna beam. Waves from the source interact when the identical signals are combined, alternately reinforcing each other (producing a signal) and canceling out (producing no signal) during the source's passage through the beam. The amplitude of the summed signal thus changes periodically, producing *interference fringes* at the output of the receiver. The fringes are sinusoidal variations whose maximum amplitude depends on the FLUX DENSITY of the source and whose period depends on both the radio wavelength and the spatial separation of the antenna units. Analysis of the changing interference fringes allows source position to be determined and source structure to be studied (see COHERENCE). An interferometer is generally used to improve the angular RESOLUTION of the telescope: the longer the distance, or baseline, between the antennas, the finer the detail that can be resolved. As resolution increases, however, large-scale structure is lost. See also APERTURE SYNTHESIS; ARRAY; LBI; VLBI.

radio waves traveling electromagnetic disturbances whose frequencies lie in the radio region of the electromagnetic spectrum, extending from about 20 kilohertz to over 300 gigahertz, the highest frequencies corresponding to millimeter and submillimeter wavelengths. RADIO ASTRONOMY may in principle be carried out at any radio frequency but in practice observations are confined to certain 'radio-astronomy bands' set aside for that purpose by international agreement to minimize INTERFERENCE from other services (see table). These bands lie within the radio window (see ATMOSPHERIC WINDOWS).

radio window see ATMOSPHERIC WINDOWS.

radius of curvature symbol: *r*, *R*. The radius of the sphere whose surface contains the surface of a spherical mirror, lens, or wavefront. The *curvature* of the mirror, etc.,

Radio Waves

(frequency allocations for radio astronomy – ITU 1990)

Frequency band (MHz)	*Bandwidth (%)*	*Frequency band (GHz)*	*Bandwidth (%)*
13.360–13.410	0.37	10.6–10.7	0.94
25.550–25.670	0.49	15.35–15.4	0.33
37.5–38.25(4)	1.98	22.21–22.50	1.30
73–74.6(1)	2.17	23.6–24.0	1.68
150.05–153(2)	1.95	31.3–31.8	1.58
322.0–328.6	2.03	42.5–43.5	2.33
406.1–410.0	0.96	86–92	6.74
608–614(3)	0.98	105–116	9.95
1400–1427	1.91	164–168	2.41
1660–1670	0.60	217–231	6.25
2655–2690(4)	1.31	265–275	3.70
2690–2700	0.37		
4800–4990(4)	3.88		
4990–5000	0.20		

1. Primary allocation in the Americas, protection recommended in Europe, Africa, Asia, and Australasia.
2. Primary allocation in Europe, Africa, North Asia, Australia, and India.
3. Primary allocation in the Americas, China, and India.
4. Secondary allocation.

is given by the reciprocal of the radius of curvature, i.e. by $1/r$. The radius of curvature of a mirror is twice its FOCAL LENGTH, f. That of a lens is given by

$$1/f = (n-1)(1/r_1 - 1/r_2)$$

where n is the refractive index; it is assumed that, in the direction of light travel, the radii, r_1 and r_2, for the convex and concave lens surfaces are positive and negative, respectively.

radius vector the line, of length r, joining a point on a curve to a reference point, such as the origin in spherical and cylindrical coordinate systems. In planetary motion the radius vector is the line between the position of a planet and the focus of its orbit, i.e. the Sun's position. See also KEPLER'S LAWS.

radome a protective covering over a radio ANTENNA that is transparent to radio waves at the frequency in use.

rampart crater see CRATER.

ram-pressure stripping the removal of gas from a rapidly moving system, such as a cluster galaxy, by the friction of its passage through a dense medium. This is observed to be happening to the galaxy M86 in the VIRGO CLUSTER as it moves through the intracluster medium.

Ramsden disk (**Ramsden circle**) see EXIT PUPIL.

Ramsden eyepiece see EYEPIECE.

Ranger an American space program, originally intended to hard-land instruments on the lunar surface but upgraded in 1963 into purely photographic missions. The first five Ranger craft were launched between August 1961 and October 1962. Ranger 6, launched Jan. 30 1964, reached its target but suffered camera malfunction. The last three – Rangers 7, 8, and 9 – were launched on July 28 1964, Feb. 17 1965, and Mar. 21 1965. They obtained the first close-ups of the Moon, revealing the existence of boulders and meter-sized CRATERS in the REGOLITH: over 4300, 7100, and 5800 photographs were transmitted by Rangers 7, 8, and 9 respectively, leading to a great advance in our knowledge of the Moon. See also LUNA PROBES; LUNAR ORBITER PROBES; SURVEYOR; ZOND PROBES.

Rasalgethi (**α Her**) a visual binary in the constellation Hercules. The primary (A) is a red supergiant that varies irregularly in magnitude from 2.7 to 4.0, the 5th-magnitude yellow giant companion (B) appearing green by contrast. B is a spectroscopic binary, period 51.6 days. Spectral type: M5 I (A), G5 III + F2 (B); distance: 193 pc.

Rasalhague see OPHIUCHUS.

Rasin effect see RAZIN EFFECT.

R association see ASSOCIATION.

RATAN 600 *abbrev. for* Radio Astronomical Telescope of the Academy of Sciences, a reflecting RING ANTENNA built (1976) at the Zelenchukskaya site of the SPECIAL ASTROPHYSICAL OBSERVATORY in the Caucasus. It consists of 895 metal panels, each 2 meters wide and 7.4 meters high, arranged in a circle 576 meters across. The panels can be tilted individually so that they form part of one large paraboloid surface and reflect radio waves horizontally to a smaller secondary mirror and antenna within the circle. Different sections of the ring can be used to image separate sources simultaneously. Observations can be made at wavelengths between 1 and 50 cm.

Rayleigh limit see RESOLUTION.

Rayleigh scattering see SCATTERING.

rays high ALBEDO (bright) streaks that surround the youngest Moon CRATERS and help to assign them to the Copernican System – the most recent era in lunar history. Rays consist of crater EJECTA that has not yet been darkened by radiation or by admixture with local materials. The most prominent systems are associated with TYCHO and Giordano Bruno. Similar bright features have been found around craters on other Solar-System bodies.

Razin effect (**Razin–Tsytovich effect**) the reduction of the SYNCHROTRON EMISSION from a relativistic electron due to the REFRACTIVE INDEX of the surrounding medium being less than one. The RADIO-SOURCE SPECTRUM will show a sharp cut-off below a frequency of about $20n_e/B$ MHz, where n_e is the electron density (in electrons per cubic meter) and B is the magnetic field strength (in tesla).

R Coronae Borealis stars (**R CrB stars**) a small group of VARIABLE STARS in which the brightness decreases – typically by about four MAGNITUDES – at irregular intervals and often quite rapidly, returning to its normal maximum often slowly and with considerable fluctuation. The frequency of occurrence of the decrease varies greatly between the stars. The prototype of the group is R Coronae Borealis, which drops from 6th magnitude usually down to 14th. R CrB stars are supergiant CARBON STARS that have an abnormally low proportion of hydrogen. The decrease in brightness apparently arises from the strong absorption of light by layers of carbon particles occasionally formed in the outer regions of the stellar atmosphere and gradually blown away by radiation pressure. This interpretation is supported by the observation that the infrared output remains nearly constant during the dramatic visual dimmings. Some R CrB stars, including the prototype, are also PULSATING VARIABLES. See also HDC STARS.

receiver an electronic device that, in radio astronomy, detects and measures the radio-frequency signals picked up by the ANTENNA of a radio telescope. A receiver that measures the total NOISE POWER from the antenna and from itself is called a *total-power receiver.* This is in distinction to other types that measure, for example, the correlated power in two antennas (see CORRELATION RECEIVER; DICKE-SWITCHED RECEIVER; PHASE-SWITCHING INTERFEROMETER).

Radio-astronomy receivers usually use the *superheterodyne* technique: the radio-frequency signals at frequency f_1 are combined in a *mixer* with signals from a *local oscillator* at frequency f_0 to produce a combination signal whose amplitude faithfully follows that of the radio-frequency signal but whose frequency is $f_1 - f_0$. This is the *intermediate frequency, IF,* which is amplified in the *IF amplifier* and presented to the first *detector.* The output of the nonlinear detector is a voltage that depends on the input power.

In a total-power receiver the output from the detector becomes the receiver output, having first been smoothed by a low-pass FILTER to reduce the fluctuations due to the system noise (see SENSITIVITY). In a switching receiver the first detector output is passed to a PHASE-SENSITIVE DETECTOR before smoothing in order to pick out the component at the switching frequency that is buried in the noise. See also LINE RECEIVER.

recession of the galaxies an important discovery made by Edwin Hubble in 1929 and based on the fact that the spectral lines of all galaxies beyond the LOCAL GROUP are systematically shifted toward longer wavelengths. These observed REDSHIFTS are interpreted as being due to the Doppler shift and imply that all distant galaxies are moving rapidly away from our own. The *recession velocities* of the galaxies can be determined from their redshifts and are found to be roughly proportional to their distances from us. Thus the Universe as a whole appears to be expanding, and it follows that the Universe was denser in the past. See BIG BANG THEORY; EXPANDING UNIVERSE; HUBBLE'S LAW.

reciprocal mass 1 (**of a planet**) the mass of the Sun divided by the mass of the planet, including its atmosphere and satellites. 2 (**of a satellite**) the mass of the satellite's planet divided by the mass of the satellite.

reciprocity failure see PHOTOGRAPHIC EMULSION.

recombination line emission electromagnetic radiation resulting from the *recombination* of a free electron (one not bound to a nucleus) and an ionized atom. The spectrum of the radiation consists of a continuum from the transition of free electrons to bound states and a number of distinct recombination lines, each one due to a transition between two ENERGY LEVELS in the atom. The emission lines occur at radio, infrared, and optical frequencies.

The energy levels are numbered in sequence starting at one for the ground state. Recombination lines are then classified according to the number of the energy level to which the electron moves and the number of energy levels that it passes. Recombination line emission occurs, for example, in EMISSION NEBULAE.

recombination time the period in the Universe's history, according to the BIG BANG THEORY, after which the temperature was low enough for atoms to form from free nuclei and electrons. This required a temperature of less than about 3000 K, which occurred when the Universe had expanded for about 300 000 years. At the time of recombination the radiation in the Universe began to propagate freely and ceased to interact with free electrons. This freely propagating radiation now resides in the MICROWAVE BACKGROUND. The name 'recombination' is a misnomer because neutral atoms are formed for the first time at the recombination era, never having existed previously.

recurrent nova a CATACLYSMIC VARIABLE that suffers a series of violent novalike outbursts at periodic intervals. The change in brightness is smaller and the decline in brightness more pronounced than with classical NOVAE. Like other cataclysmic variables, a recurrent nova is a close binary system in which one member is a WHITE DWARF; the other component is a RED GIANT, and gas is being transferred from the latter to the former. The red giant loses matter about a thousand times faster than the companion in a nova system, so that the transferred hydrogen builds up on the surface of the white dwarf at a much quicker rate. The accumulated hydrogen is hence sufficient to erupt in a thermonuclear explosion after only a few decades, and astronomers have been able to see multiple outbursts within the past century or so of systematic investigation of variable stars. Between outbursts, the system's light comprises both emission from hot gas circling the white dwarf and light from the cool red giant; as a result the spectrum shows what is apparently a star with two different temperatures (as with a SYMBIOTIC STAR). T Pyxidis (1890, 1902, 1920, 1944, 1965), RS Ophiuchi (1901, 1933, 1958, 1967, 1985), T Coronae Borealis (1866, 1946), U Scorpii (1863, 1906, 1936, 1979, 1987), and V394 Coronae Australis (1949, 1987) are recurrent novae.

reddening see EXTINCTION.

red dwarf any of a large group of MAIN-SEQUENCE STARS, mainly M and K STARS, that are much cooler, smaller, and less massive than the Sun (about 0.1–0.7 $M_\odot$). The convective motion within these stars, in combination with their rotation, generates a magnetic field, and the stars display a range of magnetically initiated phenomena similar to and sometimes more energetic than those occurring on the Sun. These include starspots, flares, and hot chromospheres and coronae. See also FLARE STARS; DWARF STAR.

red giant a GIANT STAR with a surface temperature between 2000–4000 kelvin and a diameter 10–1000 times greater than the Sun. Red giants are one of the final phases in the evolution of a normal star, reached when its central hydrogen has been used up. The star resorts to burning hydrogen in a shell around its dense inert helium core, which results in a rapid inflation of the outer layers of atmosphere. During subsequent evolution, interior structural and nuclear changes cause the star's temperature, size, and luminosity to alter (see GIANT); the star may change to a more compact hotter type of giant, then swell back to a red giant, more than once as it evolves. Because red giants are so distended, gravity has only a small effect on their surface layers and many lose considerable amounts of mass into space in the form of STELLAR WINDS. Condensing dust grains around the stars make them INFRARED SOURCES, while molecules here can emit maser radiation, making them MASER SOURCES.

Red giants are often VARIABLE STARS since their surface layers slowly expand and contract. Because these stars are so large, their pulsations usually take about a year to complete; red giants therefore belong to the class of MIRA STARS, or long-period pulsating variables. Low-mass red giants end up as PLANETARY NEBULAE, gently puffing off their distended atmospheres at low velocities (a few km s^{-1}) and leaving their dense cores exposed as WHITE DWARF stars, radiating away their heat into space. More massive red giants explode as Type II SUPERNOVAE. See also STELLAR EVOLUTION; SUPERGIANT.

Red Planet *another name for* Mars.

redshift a displacement of spectral lines toward longer wavelength values; for an optical line, the shift would be toward the red end of the visible spectrum. The *redshift parameter*, *z*, is given by the ratio $\Delta\lambda/\lambda$, where $\Delta\lambda$ is the observed increase in wavelength of the radiation and λ is the wavelength of the spectral line at the time of emission from a source, i.e. the wavelength in the 'normal' terrestrial spectrum.

The redshifts of astronomical objects within the Galaxy are interpreted as Doppler shifts (see DOPPLER EFFECT) caused by movement of the source away from the observer. The value of z is then v/c, where v is the relative RADIAL VELOCITY and c is the speed of light. The redshifts of extragalactic sources, including QUASARS, are also interpreted in terms of the Doppler effect, which for these objects results from the expansion of the Universe. The redshift parameter of a distant galaxy thus gives its velocity of recession; since recessional velocities can be very great, the relativistic expression for redshift must be used:

$$z = [(c + v)/(c - v)]^{1/2} - 1$$

From measurements of galactic redshifts it has been possible to calculate the distances of galaxies, using HUBBLE'S LAW (see DISTANCE DETERMINATION).

The redshifts described above represent a loss of energy by the photons of radiation in overcoming the effects of recession or expansion. There is another mechanism, however, by which redshifts can be produced, i.e. by which photons can lose energy – the presence of a strong gravitational field. This GRAVITATIONAL REDSHIFT was predicted by Einstein in his general theory of relativity. Although the redshifts of galaxies are often interpreted as being caused by the relativistic Doppler effect alone, both the expansion and the gravitational field of the Universe are involved. See also COSMOLOGICAL REDSHIFT.

redshift survey a three-dimensional mapping of galaxies in a large region of the sky, obtained by measuring the REDSHIFTS of all the galaxies down to a certain limiting magnitude. The redshifts allow distances to be determined using HUBBLE'S LAW; the sky positions are known. Many redshift surveys have been undertaken using different strategies varying from automatic measurement of optical photographic plates (see APM; COSMOS) and PENCIL-BEAM SURVEYS to galaxies selected by their infrared emission. Redshift surveys are important in tracing the LARGE-SCALE STRUCTURE of the Universe into its constituent superclusters, voids, and filaments. Major surveys include the Harvard–Smithsonian *CfA* (*Center for*

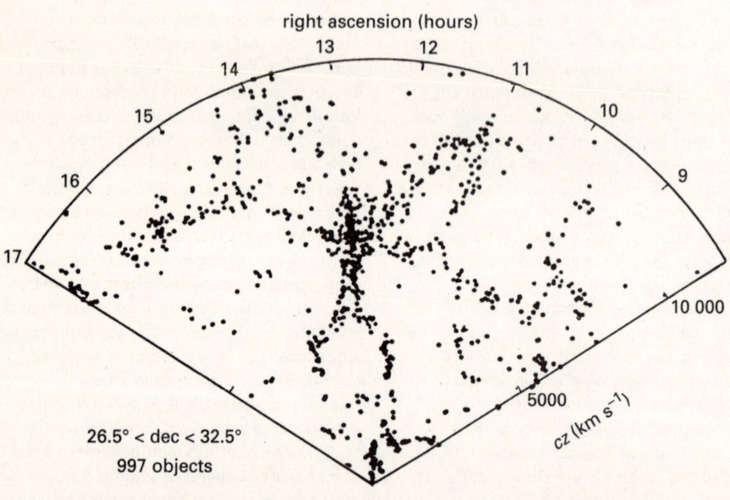

Redshift survey: slice of CfA survey for all galaxies down to magnitude 15.5 (courtesy of the Harvard–Smithsonian Center for Astrophysics)

Astrophysics) survey (see illustration), the *Las Campanas redshift survey*, the *2df survey*, and the SLOAN DIGITAL SKY SURVEY.

Red Spot see GREAT RED SPOT.

red variables the large group of variable stars, including MIRA STARS and IRREGULAR VARIABLES, that lie in the top right of the Hertzsprung–Russell diagram of PULSATING VARIABLES.

reflectance the ratio of the total radiant power reflected by a body to that incident on it.

reflectance spectra SPECTRA by means of which remote chemical analyses may be made, based on the REFLECTANCE efficiency of a planetary or satellite surface at various wavelengths, particularly near-infrared wavelengths.

reflecting telescope (reflector) a telescope that employs a mirror (the PRIMARY MIRROR) to bring light rays to a focus. The various configurations include the CASSEGRAIN, RITCHEY–CHRÉTIEN, NEWTONIAN, GREGORIAN, and COUDÉ TELESCOPES. There are also the MAKSUTOV and SCHMIDT TELESCOPES, which are CATADIOPTRIC TELESCOPES: these instruments differ in the shape of the primary, and in the additional optical system used to bring the image to a convenient point where it can be viewed through an EYEPIECE, photographed, or detected and recorded electronically, and subsequently analyzed. The ABERRATIONS in reflectors can be reduced to a very low level by suitable shaping of the primary mirror and with the possible use of a CORRECTING PLATE. In addition, a mirror, unlike a lens, suffers no CHROMATIC ABERRATION.

The first working reflector was a Newtonian. In the period following its introduction in about 1670, reflecting telescopes with mirrors made from SPECULUM METAL displaced the simple GALILEAN and KEPLERIAN REFRACTING TELESCOPES whose performance was limited by the chromatic aberration of their single-lens objectives. In the late 18th century, William Herschel developed a special ability in making speculum-metal mirrors of really accurate figure. In 1783 he built a reflector with an aperture of 46 cm and in 1789 one of 122 cm. He used these telescopes for a wide range of observations, making many important advances in stellar astronomy.

The end of the era was marked by the construction in 1842–45 of a 183-cm diameter speculum-metal mirror by William Parsons, 3rd Earl of Rosse, at his family seat of Birr Castle, at Parsonstown, Co. Offaly, Ireland. Known as Leviathan, this reflector was the largest such instrument built until the Mount Wilson 254-cm reflector – the Hooker Telescope – was brought into operation in 1917.

In the latter half of the 19th century, refracting telescopes with achromatic objectives overtook reflectors in performance and held their lead until the start of the 20th (see ACHROMATIC LENS). By then astronomers had come to realize that the reflectivity of silvered glass in mirror design made it far superior to speculum metal, which rapidly became obsolete. It was also realized that refractors had reached a real size limit at about 100 cm diameter: a lens can only be supported around its edge and larger lenses sag under their own weight to an unacceptable degree. A primary mirror can be supported over its whole rear face and thus escapes this limitation.

The modern era opened with the construction of the giant reflecting telescopes at Mount Wilson Observatory and then Palomar Observatory, both in California. The 5-meter Hale Telescope at Palomar, which saw first light in late 1947, remains one of the world's most powerful reflectors in use today. It was surpassed by the 6-meter Bolshoi Teleskop Azimutalnyi (Big Altazimuth Telescope) at the Zelenchukskaya Observatory in the Russian Caucasus mountains, which was the largest optical telescope in the world when it came into operation in the 1970s. The Big Altazimuth Telescope illustrates a trend among the most modern reflectors, whereby advantage has been taken of the developments in drive technology pioneered by radio astronomers to return from the EQUATORIAL to the simple ALTAZIMUTH MOUNTING. The 9.2-meter-effective-aperture HOBBY-EBERLY TELESCOPE at the McDonald Observatory on Mt

Fowlkes, Texas, a lightweight segmented primary mirror in an instrument set up at a fixed elevation angle of 55° to the horizon and able to rotate in azimuth to access 70% of the sky visible from its location, was built at about one-fifth of the cost of comparable instruments of similar diameter. Like the Hobby-Eberly, most of the world's largest telescopes have apertures greater than 8 meters. NEXT-GENERATION TELESCOPES, such as the 10-meter KECK TELESCOPES in Hawaii, with their new designs of PRIMARY MIRRORS, are also making use of other advanced technologies, including ADAPTIVE OPTICS to reduce the effects of atmospheric turbulence (see SEEING), ACTIVE OPTICS to reduce longer-term effects, and computer control. Telescope performance has also greatly improved as a result of new techniques for detection and analysis of the image, using complex electronic equipment and computer systems (see IMAGING). Further improvements in instrumentation is, however, unlikely to increase sensitivity very much. The observation of very faint objects is today being accomplished by the new generation of ground-based telescopes in combination with orbiting telescopes, such as the HUBBLE SPACE TELESCOPE and the planned JAMES WEBB SPACE TELESCOPE, operating in an environment undisturbed by the turbulence and absorption of the Earth's atmosphere.

See also INFRARED TELESCOPE.

reflection a phenomenon occurring when a beam of light or other wave motion strikes a surface separating two different media, such as air and glass or air and metal. Part of the wave has its direction changed, according to the laws of reflection, so that it does not enter the second medium. A rough surface will produce diffuse reflection. A smooth surface, as of polished metal, will reflect the radiation in a regular manner. The laws of reflection state firstly that the incident beam, the reflected beam, and the normal (the line perpendicular to the surface at the point of incidence) lie in the same plane, and secondly that the two beams are inclined at the same angle to but on either side of the normal.

reflection grating see DIFFRACTION GRATING.

reflection nebula a bright cloud of interstellar gas and dust that lies near and somewhat to one side of a star or stellar group, usually of SPECTRAL TYPE B2 or later. The starlight is scattered in all directions by the dust grains, the density of which is sufficient to produce a noticeable illumination of the cloud. The light scattered toward the observer is bluer than that of the illuminating star but the spectra of cloud and star are essentially the same – a continuous spectrum with absorption lines. (If there is sufficient dust in an EMISSION NEBULA, it will cause the stars' absorption spectra to be added to the normal emission spectrum of the nebula.) Reflection nebulosity is characteristic of young clusters and ASSOCIATIONS; the dust is dispersed in about 100 million years. Typical reflection nebulae occur around the brighter stars of the PLEIADES. See also NEBULA.

reflection spectrum see ACTIVE GALAXY.

reflector *short for* reflecting telescope.

refracting telescope (refractor) a telescope employing an OBJECTIVE lens to bring the light rays to a focus. The first telescopes were simple refractors with single-lens objectives: these were the GALILEAN and KEPLERIAN TELESCOPES, introduced in the early 17th century. They were supplanted by REFLECTING TELESCOPES in the last quarter of that century because no-one at that time could overcome their CHROMATIC ABERRATIONS, which introduced brilliant false color effects in the images. Although John Dollond discovered how to make an ACHROMATIC LENS in 1756, he could make only small diameters suitable for terrestrial telescopes; glass makers did not know how to make large uniform disks of crown and flint glass. This obstacle was overcome in the early 1800s by Joseph Fraunhofer, who made the 24-cm refractor at Dorpat and the 16-cm heliometer at Königsberg. His successor, Georg Merz, supplied the 32.4-cm equatorial refractor to the Royal Greenwich Observatory and manufactured the 38-cm refractor that was the first large telescope to be mounted in the USA, at Cambridge, Massachusetts, in 1847.

For years after this, American astronomers leaned strongly toward the refractor. By the 1880s Alvan Clark was making relatively large refractors: a 47-cm diameter instrument for the Dearborn Observatory, a 91-cm one for Lick Observatory, and a 102-cm one for Yerkes Observatory. Other very large refractors built in the late 19th century are the 61-cm at both Lowell Observatory, Arizona, and the Pic du Midi in France, the 75-cm at Pulkovo Observatory, St Petersburg, and the 83-cm at the Meudon Observatory in Paris. There are great technical problems in making large lenses free of imperfections and impurities, and of supporting these lenses (only around the edge) so that distortion of the image is minimal. The desire for ever larger APERTURES to reach ever farther and fainter objects in space has meant that the major telescopes built in the 20th and 21st centuries have been reflectors.

The surviving large refracting telescopes are mainly used in ASTROMETRY for the measurement of stellar positions, PROPER MOTIONS, and PARALLAX. Refractors are often preferred by visual observers because of their long focal length and closed tube; the latter avoids air currents in the tube, which often cause an unsteady image.

refraction a phenomenon occurring when a beam of light or other wave motion crosses a boundary between two different media, such as air and glass. On passing into the second medium, the direction of motion of the wave is 'bent' toward or away from the normal (the line perpendicular to the surface at the point of incidence). The incident and refracted rays and the normal all lie in the same plane. The direction of propagation is changed in accordance with *Snell's law*:

$$n_1 \sin i = n_2 \sin r$$

i and r are the angles made by the incident and refracted ray to the normal; n_1 and n_2 are the REFRACTIVE INDICES of the two media. The change in direction of motion results from a change of wave velocity as the wave passes from the first to the second medium.

refraction, angle of see ZENITH DISTANCE.

refraction, atmospheric see ATMOSPHERIC REFRACTION.

refractive index (**index of refraction**) symbol: n. The ratio of the SPEED OF LIGHT, c, in a vacuum to the speed of light in a given medium. This is the *absolute refractive index*; it is always greater than one. The relative refractive index is the ratio of the speeds of light in two given media. The refractive index of a medium depends on the wavelength of the refracted wave: with light waves, n increases as the wavelength decreases, i.e. blue light is refracted (bent) more than red light. See also REFRACTION.

refractor *short for* refracting telescope.

regio (plural: **regiones**) a large area distinguished by shading or color on the surface of a planet or satellite. The word is used in the approved name of such a feature.

regolith the layer of dust and broken rock, created by meteoritic bombardment, that covers much of the surfaces of the Moon and other planets and satellites in the Solar System.

regression of nodes see NODES.

regular cluster a rich CLUSTER OF GALAXIES exhibiting DYNAMICAL RELAXATION. These clusters have a smooth symmetric distribution with a high central concentration of galaxies to the core and very little subclustering. An *irregular cluster* is one that is dynamically less evolved, with significant substructure.

Regulus (**α Leo**) a bluish-white star that is the brightest one in the constellation Leo and lies at the base of the Sickle of Leo. It is a visual triple star, with the bright Regulus A being accompanied by an orange companion (B) orbiting A once every 130 000 years at a distance of more than 4000 AU. B itself has a 13th-magnitude red dwarf companion (C). The Regulus system has a common proper motion with a fourth star (D). m_v: 1.4 (A), 7.7 (B); M_v: −0.3; spectral type: B7 V (A), K1 V (B); distance: 21 pc.

relative aperture see APERTURE RATIO.

relative sunspot number symbol: R. A somewhat arbitrary index of the level of sunspot activity, derived from the formula $R = k(f + 10g)$, where g represents the number of sunspot groups, f the total number of their component spots, and k is a constant dependent on the estimated efficiency of, and also the equipment used by, a particular observer. Though a more objective assessment of the level of sunspot activity relies on the measurement of sunspot areas, relative sunspot numbers provide an almost continuous record back to the mid-18th century and yield graphs similar (at least so far as the yearly means are concerned) to those based on other indices.

The relative sunspot number was originally called the *Wolf number*, after Rudolf Wolf who introduced it at Zürich in 1848 and extended it back using old observations. It later became known as the *Zürich relative sunspot number* and then, when the Zürich tradition came to an end with the transfer of responsibility to the Sunspot Index Data Center in Brussels in Jan. 1981, the *International Sunspot Number* (symbol: *RI*). See also SUNSPOT CYCLE.

relativistic astrophysics high-energy ASTROPHYSICS, concerned with the extreme energies, velocities, densities, etc., associated with celestial objects such as WHITE DWARFS, NEUTRON STARS, BLACK HOLES, and ACTIVE GALAXIES, and with the very early Universe. It involves the theories of special and general RELATIVITY, QUANTUM MECHANICS, and the physics of ELEMENTARY PARTICLES.

relativistic beaming see SYNCHROTRON EMISSION.

relativistic electron an electron moving at close to the speed of light. The special theory of RELATIVITY must be used to describe associated phenomena.

relativity, general theory the theory put forward by Albert Einstein in 1915. It describes how the relationship between space and time, as developed in the special theory of relativity, is affected by the gravitational effects of matter. The basic conclusion is that gravitational fields change the geometry of SPACETIME, causing it to become curved. It is this curvature of spacetime that controls the natural motions of bodies. Thus matter tells spacetime how to curve and spacetime tells matter how to move. General relativity (GR) may therefore be considered as a theory of GRAVITATION, the differences between it and Newtonian gravitation appearing only when the gravitational fields become very strong, as with black holes, neutron stars, and white dwarfs, or when very accurate measurements can be made. GR also reduces to the special theory when gravitational effects are negligible.

The basic postulate from which GR was developed is the principle of EQUIVALENCE between gravitational and inertial forces: in two laboratories, one in a uniform gravitational field and the other suitably accelerated, the same laws of nature apply and thus the same phenomena, including optical ones, will be observed. Einstein was able to show that the natural motion of a body was in a 'straight line', i.e. along the shortest path between two points (a geodesic), in the geometry required to describe the physical world (compare NEWTON'S LAWS OF MOTION). Three-dimensional Euclidean geometry could not be used for this purpose. The requisite geometry had to be more flexible: this was the geometry of spacetime. The presence of gravitational fields leads to the curvature of spacetime. The curvature produced by a particular gravitational field can be calculated from Einstein's *field equations*, advanced as part of GR. It is then possible to calculate the geodesics followed by particles in this curved spacetime.

Experimental tests of GR require either very strong gravitational fields or very accurate measurements. These tests must verify the predictions of GR where they deviate from the predictions of Newtonian gravitation and also where they deviate from the predictions of other relativistic theories of gravitation (including the BRANS–DICKE THEORY) that have been developed since 1915. The main tests involve four predicted effects.

One effect is the bending of light or other electromagnetic radiation in a gravitational field. Measurements of the positions of stars when close to the Sun's limb (i.e. during total solar eclipses) and when some distance from the Sun have been shown to differ: the Sun's gravitational field changes the path of a photon of radiation from a straight line to a path bent toward the Sun. The angle by which the photon's path is deflected is called the *deflection of light*. The measured deflection for stars on the solar limb is near Einstein's predicted value, which is 1.75 arc secs.

Closer agreement (within 1%) has been found when the bending of radiation from radio sources such as quasars is determined (see also GRAVITATIONAL LENS). A related effect is the time delay in radio signals from spacecraft when they are close to the Sun. The measured delays from the Viking probes and other craft agree with Einstein's prediction within 0.1%.

The predicted GRAVITATIONAL REDSHIFT in the spectral lines of radiation emitted from a massive body has also been successfully demonstrated using both the Sun's and also the Earth's gravitational fields. A related prediction is that clocks run more slowly in a strong gravitational field than in a weaker one. An atomic clock flown at an altitude of 10 km has been shown to run faster than at sea level by a value within 0.02% of the predicted amount (47×10^{-9} seconds).

The effects of curved spacetime on the motions of orbiting bodies were shown convincingly when the ADVANCE OF THE PERIHELION of Mercury was found to be accounted for by GR. Recent measurements of the very much larger periastron shift of the BINARY PULSAR 1913+16 provided much stronger evidence, being in very close agreement with prediction.

The fourth test of GR concerns the predicted existence of GRAVITATIONAL WAVES. The emission of such waves causes a loss of energy from a system and in a binary system alters the orbital period. Recent measurements of the speed-up in the period of the binary pulsar 1913+16 are in almost precise agreement with the predicted value of GR. Many alternative theories of gravitation predict much higher values.

Other predictions of GR are the existence of SINGULARITIES in the structure of spacetime leading to black holes, and the constancy of the GRAVITATIONAL CONSTANT. There is no direct evidence as yet for (or against) these, although indirect evidence of black holes is accumulating.

It cannot be said that GR has been conclusively proved. The experimental evidence does, however, seem to be mounting in its favor.

relativity, special theory the theory proposed by Albert Einstein in 1905. It is concerned with the laws of physics as viewed by observers moving relative to one another at constant velocity (i.e. with observers in INERTIAL FRAMES), and with how relative motion affects measurements made by these observers. At low relative velocities, special relativity (SR) predicts the same results as the classical Newtonian laws of mechanics. As the relative velocity increases beyond that encountered in everyday experience, the predictions of the two theories diverge. It is those of SR that have been conclusively verified by experiment. SR must therefore be used to describe the behavior of bodies, such as electrons, when they are moving at velocities close to the SPEED OF LIGHT.

One of the basic principles of SR is that the speed of light is the same in any direction in free space, is the same for all observers, and is independent of the relative motion of the observer and the body emitting the light (or other electromagnetic radiation). This violates the classical concepts of relative motion but has been demonstrated experimentally.

Another basic principle is that all physical laws are the same for every inertial frame. Any law deduced in one inertial frame will be true in every other inertial frame. The values of the numerical constants appearing in these laws are also independent of the frame in which they are measured. The same does not, however, apply to certain variable quantities measured in different inertial frames.

Prior to SR it had been assumed that there was a universal 'absolute' time and 'absolute' space that were the same for all observers. Einstein showed that as a direct consequence of the invariance of the speed of light, time and space could not be considered as separate concepts, independent of each other and of the observer. Instead they must be regarded as a composite entity, called SPACETIME. Any event in an inertial frame must therefore be described in terms of four spacetime coordinates – three spatial and one time coordinate. The spacetime coordinates of the same event measured in two different frames will differ, but they can be interconverted by the LORENTZ TRANSFORMATION.

As the relative velocity (v) between inertial frames approaches the speed of light (c), very strange things are predicted. One is *time dilation*: two observers approaching at a relative velocity close to c will each see the clock of the other operating more slowly than their own. The time intervals will be dilated by a factor of $1/\beta$ where

$$\beta = \sqrt{(1 - v^2/c^2)}$$

Another prediction is the apparent contraction of a moving object that is observed, in the direction of motion of the object, by someone in a different inertial frame. The observed contraction, known as the *Lorentz contraction*, amounts to the factor β. The object also appears slightly rotated. No change in dimensions is observed in directions perpendicular to the direction of motion.

A further consequence of SR, when applied to the field of dynamics, is that the mass (m) of a body is not invariant but increases as the relative velocity between body and observer increases:

$$m = m_0/\beta$$

m_0 is the REST MASS of the body and is an invariant property of matter. It follows that no object with mass can reach the speed of light; only a particle with zero rest mass (such as the PHOTON) can travel at the speed of light. Einstein showed that the transfer of energy by any process entailed the transfer of mass, and concluded that the total energy E of any system of mass m is given by the equation $E = mc^2$.

relaxation time the time taken for the velocity of an object in a multiple-body system to become similar to the velocity of others in that system, and hence for the total system to become smooth and regular. See DYNAMICAL RELAXATION.

Relict a Soviet space mission launched in 1983 that made the first measurement of dipole anisotropy in the cosmic MICROWAVE BACKGROUND RADIATION.

remote operation the operation of a telescope and its associated instruments by off-site astronomers possibly thousands of kilometers away. Signals are passed over one or more communication links carrying voice, video, and digital information. Remote operation was a natural development from an earlier trend that involved transferring the operation of a telescope system from the actual physical position of the telescope to an on-site control room, which itself required the development of automated equipment and communication links (see AUTOMATION).

Remote operation by astronomers of a telescope-instrument-detector system in space was demonstrated in 1978 using the INTERNATIONAL ULTRAVIOLET EXPLORER satellite. It has since led on to such successful projects as the HUBBLE SPACE TELESCOPE. Remote operation of a ground-based telescope was first achieved in 1982 when the UK INFRARED TELESCOPE in Hawaii was remotely operated from the Royal Observatory, Edinburgh.

remote sensing the collection of information about the Earth or some other Solar-System body without direct contact of measuring instruments, especially from an orbiting satellite. High-resolution cameras, infrared detectors, and radar systems are used to survey the surface. The use of remote sensing from space to gather information about the Earth began soon after the start of the space age. NASA's first remote-sensing spacecraft was the Television and Infrared Observation Satellite (TIROS–1) launched April 1960. TIROS–1 proved that satellites could be used to study Earth's weather patterns. The TIROS series was followed by many other orbiting monitors of the Earth's environment and resources, including the *Landsat* series (beginning in 1972), the *Nimbus* series (the last of which, Nimbus 7, launched 1978, discovered the first evidence of 'holes' in the Earth's ozone layer caused by the destructive action of CFCs), and *TOPEX/Poseidon*, launched 1992, a US-French satellite that began to provide details about the links between the world's oceans and its climate. In 1999 NASA launched its Terra satellite, the flagship mission of its *Earth Observing System* (*EOS*), a series of low-inclination polar-orbiting satellites providing long-term global observations of the Earth's land surfaces, biosphere, oceans and atmosphere. Terra is one of more than 20 EOS missions scheduled to be launched between 1997 and 2010. Another is *Aura*, a satellite launched July 2004 to make detailed studies of the atmosphere. ESA's European Remote Sensing satellites, *ERS–I*, launched July 1991, and *ERS–2*, launched April 1995, have made continuous global observations of the oceans, polar caps, vegetation, etc., of the Earth. ERS–1 was taken out of service in 2000, but its successor was still operating in 2005. A third ESA satellite, Envisat, was launched into a Sun-synchronous orbit in March 2002. It is the largest Earth-observation spacecraft ever built and carries 10 sophisticated optical and radar instruments.

réseau a reference grid of fine lines that are photographically produced in the emulsion of a photographic plate and used in measurements of star positions.

residual the difference between an observed quantity, such as the position of a comet or the magnitude of a variable star, and its expected or calculated value.

resolution the ability of a telescope or other instrument to distinguish fine detail, or a numerical measure of that ability. A spectrometer has a *chromatic resolution*, and an imaging device has a *linear resolution* or a *spatial resolution*. Detectors can have an *energy resolution*.

The *spatial* or *angular resolution* of a telescope is the smallest angle between two point objects that produces distinct images. It depends on both the wavelength at which observations are made and on the diameter, or aperture, of the telescope. This minimum angle can be given by the *Rayleigh limit*:

$$2.52 \times 10^5 \, \lambda/d \text{ arc seconds}$$

where λ and d are the wavelength and aperture (in meters). For an optical system the Rayleigh limit is approximately

$$0.13/d \text{ arc seconds}$$

The *Dawes limit*, originally determined experimentally, gives the angular resolution as

$$0.12/d \text{ arc seconds}$$

When the angular separation of two stars is very small, it might be thought that the use of a large enough aperture or high enough magnification would always resolve the light into two distinct images. Because of diffraction effects however, the image of each star is not a point of light but a disk (see AIRY DISK). If the two disks substantially overlap then increased aperture or magnification merely gives a larger blur of light, and the telescope has not sufficient resolving power to separate the images. The stars will just be resolved, however, when their Airy disks touch. This gives the Dawes limit. Two stars are at a telescope's Rayleigh limit when the center of the Airy disk of one star falls on the first

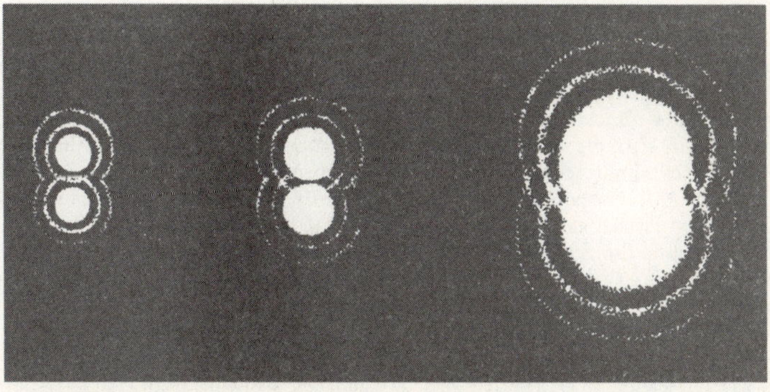

Resolution: images of an optical double of separation 0.8″ through apertures (left to right) of 30, 15, and 7.5

dark ring of the diffraction pattern of the other. The illustration shows the images of two stars of equal magnitude separated by 0.8 seconds of arc. Viewed under perfect SEEING conditions with a 7.5-cm aperture (right) they are not resolved; with 15-cm (center) they are just resolved and with 30-cm (left) they are clearly separated.

The discovery of Pluto's satellite Charon in 1978 shows that the Dawes (or Rayleigh) limit cannot be too strictly applied. Although well above the limiting angle for large telescopes, Charon had not been resolved; it was detected as an elongated photographic image. This is partly because of the difference in brightness and because Pluto is not a point source, but mainly because poor seeing prevented the larger-aperture telescopes from reaching the limiting angle. The distorting effects of the Earth's atmosphere are greatly reduced in telescopes with ACTIVE OR ADAPTIVE OPTICS, and are removed in orbiting telescopes. Very high spatial resolution is thus now feasible.

In radio astronomy, where the same formulae for spatial resolution apply but where very much greater wavelengths are studied, apertures maybe 30 times greater than those used in optical telescopes can only give poor resolution. The situation has been greatly improved by the use of APERTURE SYNTHESIS and very long baseline interferometry (VLBI).

resolving power the ability of a telescope, SPECTROGRAPH, DIFFRACTION GRATING, or some other system to distinguish fine detail. See RESOLUTION.

resonance a condition prevailing in a system when the frequency of some external stimulus coincides with a natural frequency of the system, and producing a selective or maximum response in the system. Resonance is responsible, for example, for COMMENSURABLE orbits, the KIRKWOOD GAPS in the asteroid belt, and divisions in SATURN'S RINGS.

resonance transition a change in the energy state of an atom, involving an electron jump from the ground state to a higher ENERGY LEVEL, leading to EXCITATION, or a return to the ground state from an excited state. This produces a *resonant* absorption or emission line in a spectrum. See also ULTRAVIOLET ASTRONOMY.

rest frame the FRAME OF REFERENCE for a distant or moving object that would appear to have zero velocity when observed from that object. Observed radiation has to be corrected for REDSHIFT to convert its emission to the intrinsic rest frame of the object, and this is known as a *k-correction.*

rest mass the mass of an elementary particle, etc., when at rest. According to the special theory of RELATIVITY, a body's mass increases as its speed increases. This is noticeable only at speeds close to the speed of light. Rest mass is often expressed in MeV (megaelectronvolts).

retardation the difference in the Moon's rising time between successive nights.

reticle a grid or pattern of two or more fine wires set in the focal plane of a telescope eyepiece and used in determining the position and/or size of a celestial object.

Reticulum (Net) a small constellation in the southern hemisphere near the Large Magellanic Cloud, the brightest stars being one of 3rd magnitude and some of 4th magnitude. Abbrev.: Ret; genitive form: Reticuli; approx. position: RA 4h, dec –60°; area: 114 sq deg.

retrograde motion see DIRECT MOTION.

retrorocket a small rocket motor attached to a spacecraft that, by ejecting gas in a forward direction, decelerates the craft. In this way the craft may change its orbit or, possibly with parachutes, achieve a soft landing.

reverbation mapping an observational method used to determine the relative distance of the BROAD-LINE REGION from its source of ionization, the central powerhouse of an ACTIVE GALAXY. Variations in the brightness of the nucleus are correlated with fluctuations in the intensity of the broad emission lines, and the inferred time delay reveals the separation of the nucleus and broad line gas.

revolution **1** orbital motion of a celestial body about a center of gravitational attraction, such as the Sun, another star, or a planet, as distinct from axial ROTATION. See also DIRECT MOTION.
2 one complete circuit of a celestial body

about a gravitational center. The Earth takes one year to make one revolution around the Sun.

RFT *abbrev. for* richest-field telescope.

RGO *abbrev. for* Royal Greenwich Observatory.

Rhea the second largest of the Saturn system of satellites, discovered in 1672 by Giovanni Domenico Cassini. It has a diameter of 1530 km and a density of 1.33 g cm^{-3}. The low density indicates that Rhea is composed of a rocky core making up about a third of the satellite's mass surrounded by water ice. The northern hemisphere is particularly heavily cratered and resembles the rolling cratered highlands of the Moon. The crater density on the surface is irregular and suggests a varied geological history. The craters vary in size up to 75 km, the most prominent of which is *Izanagi*. The leading edge of Rhea as it moves in its orbit is brighter than the trailing edge, which contains bright wispy markings. The Cassini/Huygens spacecraft flew by Rhea in November 2005 at a distance of 500 km and was scheduled to make a second, much more distant, flyby in August 2007. See also Table 2, Appendix.

rho (ρ) the 17th letter of the Greek alphabet, used in STELLAR NOMENCLATURE usually to designate the 17th-brightest star in a constellation or sometimes to indicate a star's position in a group.

Rho Ophiuchi Cloud a complex region of molecular and dark clouds and emission and reflection nebulae near the star ρ Oph in the constellation Ophiuchus. X-ray and infrared observations show that STAR FORMATION is occurring in the dark cloud.

rich cluster see CLUSTERS OF GALAXIES.

richest-field telescope (**RFT**) a telescope designed to show the largest possible number of stars at a single view when aimed at a dense field of faint stars, such as the Milky Way. This end is accomplished by combining a reasonably large aperture (100 to 150 mm) with a low power and the widest possible field of view. Although the true RFT is a special design, fitted with an expensive wide-field EYEPIECE, binoculars and most FINDER telescopes go a long way toward meeting these specifications. Apart from providing spectacular views of immense numbers of stars (which are not obtained with the high magnifications and narrow fields more usually employed), the RFT is an ideal instrument for scanning the heavens in the search for novae and comets.

rich-field adapter see TELECOMPRESSOR.

ridge (**scarp**) see LOBATE RIDGE; WRINKLE RIDGES.

Rigel (**β Ori**) a massive luminous and remote bluish-white supergiant that is very conspicuous and is the brightest star in the constellation ORION. It marks Orion's left foot. According to the Hipparcos catalog, its distance from the Sun is about 773 light-years (237 parsecs), though estimates have ranged between 900 and 1400 l.y. If the Hipparcos measurement is correct, Rigel is at least 40 000 times as luminous as the Sun. Rigel's diameter is thought to equal 70 solar diameters. It is a member of a large association that includes the stars of Orion's Belt and the Orion nebula. There is a 7th-magnitude companion at a separation of 9″.5, which is itself a binary. m_v: 0.18 (var.); M_v: –6.69(?); spectral type: B8 Iae.

right ascension (**RA**) symbol: α. A coordinate used with DECLINATION in the EQUATORIAL COORDINATE SYSTEM. The right ascension of a celestial body, etc., is its angular distance measured eastward along the celestial equator from the vernal (or dynamical) equinox, or more precisely from a CATALOG EQUINOX, to the intersection of the hour circle passing through the body. It is generally expressed in hours (h), minutes (m), and seconds (s) from 0 to 24h: one hour equals 15° of arc.

right-ascension circle the SETTING CIRCLE on the polar axis of an EQUATORIAL MOUNTING that measures the RIGHT ASCENSION at which the telescope is set.

Rigil Kentaurus see ALPHA CENTAURI.

rille (**rima**) either of two distinct types of elongated lunar depression (see table). *Sinuous rilles* are confined to the MARIA, where they follow local contours, are frequently discontinuous (or consist of rows of coalescing craters), and have V-shaped cross sections. They sometimes originate in volcanic caldera and are assumed to be channels, or collapsed tubes, carved out by molten basaltic lavas. Examples exist of sinuous rilles inside

Lunar Rilles and Valleys

Rille, valley	*Location; type*
Alpine Valley	NE Imbrium; radial fracture
Ariadaeus	W Mare Tranquillitatis; linear
Byrgius	W Mare Humorum; sinuous
Cauchy Fault	E Mare Tranquillitatis
Hadley	Palus Putredinus; sinuous
Hyginus	Mare Vaporum; forked rille
Lee Lincoln Scarp	Taurus Littrow area; fault
Posidonius	NE Mare Serenitatis; sinuous
Rheita Valley	S Nectaris; radial fracture
Schröter's Valley	Aristarchus Plateau; double sinuous
Schrödinger Canyon	S farside; radial fracture
Sirsalis	W Mare Humorum; sinuous
Straight Wall	Mare Nubium; linear fault

sinuous rilles but tributary systems are not observed.

Faulted *linear, arcuate,* and *forked rilles* have flat floors and do not recognize highland-mare boundaries. This second type of rille is frequently associated with impact basins and craters, where they may be concentric. See also CRATER CHAIN; FAULT; WRINKLE RIDGES.

rima (plural: **rimae**) a fissure. The word is used in the approved name of such a surface feature on a planet or satellite. It has been adopted as the official name for RILLE.

ring antenna a RADIO TELESCOPE consisting of many small elements arranged in a ring. For example, the RATAN 600 ring antenna is a *multiplate reflector* composed of reflecting panels that are adjusted to form part of a paraboloid surface with its axis directed at the source under observation. An advantage of the ring antenna over other shapes is that its side-lobe responses have no preferred direction and are small and widely distributed.

ring current an electric current flowing westward around the Earth; it arises from a net eastward flow of electrons and a net westward flow of protons trapped inside the VAN ALLEN RADIATION BELTS. The current produces a magnetic field that cancels part of the geomagnetic field at the Earth's surface. During GEOMAGNETIC STORMS, when the Van Allen belts are recharged with particles, the increased ring current results in a further decrease of the Earth's surface magnetic field strength.

ring galaxy a very rare type of galaxy that has the form of an elliptical ring either with a massive nucleus, often off-center, or with little or no luminous material visible in its interior. In many cases there is a small satellite galaxy devoid of interstellar gas. The ring configuration is thought to be unstable and it has been suggested that these systems may represent the after-effects of a collision between two galaxies.

ring mountains see BASIN; MOUNTAINS, LUNAR.

ring nebula a ring or arc of nebulosity centered on and ionized by ultraviolet radiation from a WOLF-RAYET STAR. The Ring nebula is, confusingly, not a ring nebula.

Ring nebula (**M57; NGC 6720**) a ring-shaped PLANETARY NEBULA, about 1′ across, in the constellation Lyra. The inner regions closest to the centrally placed ionizing star are green as a result of light emitted by doubly ionized oxygen; there is an approximately symmetrical transition to the reddish outer edge where the lower-energy transitions of hydrogen and nitrogen are responsible for the color. See EMISSION NEBULA.

ring plains see MARIA, LUNAR.

ring systems see JUPITER'S RINGS; NEPTUNE'S RINGS; PLANETARY RINGS; SATURN'S RINGS; URANUS' RINGS.

rising the daily appearance on an observer's horizon of a particular celestial body as a result of the Earth's rotation, the body disappearing below the horizon, or *setting,* at some time in the following 24 hours. A star rises, on average, 2 hours earlier per month. Stars always rise and set in the same position relative to other stars whereas the Sun, Moon, and planets rise and set at different points on successive days. This led to the early idea of FIXED STARS and wandering stars.

For an observer at the equator all stars in theory can be seen, rising and setting at right angles to the horizon. At the poles, only the stars in the observer's hemisphere can be seen, and these never rise nor set but move in circles parallel to the equator. At intermediate latitudes some stars (CIRCUMPOLAR STARS) never set and some, in a corresponding area in the sky around the opposite pole, never rise. The remaining stars rise and set at oblique angles to the horizon, the time spent above the horizon depending on the observer's latitude and the position of the star relative to the celestial pole. Stars on the celestial equator rise due east and set due west and for all observing positions except the poles remain 12 hours above the horizon.

Ritchey–Chrétien optics an optical system that is a variation on the CASSEGRAIN CONFIGURATION and was developed between 1910 and 1920 by George Willis Ritchey and Henri Chrétien. It corrects both SPHERICAL ABERRATION and COMA at the Cassegrain focus, and therefore gives a high-quality image over a relatively wide field of view. A primary mirror with a hyperbolic profile is used in conjunction with an appropriate departure from classical (hyperbolic) form at the secondary mirror.

R Monocerotis see HUBBLE'S VARIABLE NEBULA.

Roche limit the minimum distance from the center of a body at which a satellite can remain in equilibrium under the influence of its own gravitation and that of its primary. Assuming that the satellite is held together only by gravitational attraction, i.e. it has zero tensile strength, and that it has the same density as the primary, the Roche limit is about 2.45 times the radius of the primary. Inside the Roche limit a satellite would be torn apart by tidal forces. It is thought that the ring systems of the giant planets were formed when a satellite wandered inside the planet's Roche limit. The expression for the limit was discovered in 1849 by the French scientists Edouard Roche.

Roche lobe see EQUIPOTENTIAL SURFACES.

rocket see LAUNCH VEHICLE; SOUNDING ROCKET.

rockoon a device for exploring the upper atmosphere of the Earth. It consists of a large balloon to which is attached a small rocket. The rocket is fired at a considerable altitude, thus avoiding the air drag of the lower atmosphere. The balloons are usually *Skyhooks*: large nondilatable plastic balloons that can carry a heavy load to altitudes of over 30 km.

rocky dwarf any of the four rocky TERRESTRIAL PLANETS.

ROE *abbrev. for* Royal Observatory, Edinburgh.

Rood–Sastry classification a classification system for CLUSTERS OF GALAXIES based on the nature and spatial distribution of the ten brightest galaxies in the cluster.

Roque de los Muchachos Observatory an international observatory on La Palma in the Canary Islands, sited at an altitude of 2400 meters, where the observing conditions are superb. It was set up in 1979 by an international agreement involving the UK, Denmark, Spain (which owns the site), and Sweden; the Netherlands and the Republic of Ireland joined with the UK and share its telescopes. The observatory was ceremonially inaugurated in 1985.

The responsibility for running the Roque de los Muchachos Observatory lies with the Instituto de Astrofísica de Canarias (Institute of Astrophysics of the Canaries, IAC), which also operates the TEIDE OBSERVATORY on Tenerife. The two observatories together, along with associated technical facilities provided by the IAC on Tenerife and the planned Common Center for Astrophysics on La Palma, constitute the *European Northern Observatory*. About 60 institutions from 19 countries currently have telescopes and other instruments there.

The *Isaac Newton Group*, owned and funded by the UK PARTICLE PHYSICS AND ASTRONOMY RESEARCH COUNCIL (PPARC), is the largest collection of telescopes at the observatory. It includes the 4.2-meter WILLIAM HERSCHEL TELESCOPE, which began regular operations in 1987; the completely refurbished 2.5-meter ISAAC NEWTON TELESCOPE; and a 1-meter reflector, the *Jacobus Kapteyn Telescope*, specially designed for PHOTOMETRY and wide-field photography. The latter two began operations at their present location in 1984. So too did the Carlsberg Meridian Telescope, a telescope used for precision astrometry and operated jointly by institutions from Denmark, Spain, and the UK. Additional instruments include the 16-m Swedish solar tower, a high-resolution SOLAR TELESCOPE operational since 1983, and the 2.5-m *Nordic Optical Telescope* (*NOT*), with azimuthal mounting, that began regular operations in 1989.

The observatory has also been selected as the site for some new-generation telescopes, including the Italian *Galileo National Telescope* (*Telescopio Nazionale Galileo*, completed in 1997), with a 3.5-m meniscus PRIMARY MIRROR controlled by ACTIVE OPTICS, and the *Dutch Open Telescope*, an innovative solar telescope with a 45-centimeter primary mirror housed in a 15-meter-high open tower and used for high-resolution solar imaging simultaneously in multiple wavelengths, which was installed in 1996 and saw first light in 1997.

In return for necessary services, Spanish astronomers have 20% of available time on each telescope. International projects take up some of each telescope's time.

Rosalind a small satellite of Uranus, discovered in 1986 from Voyager 2 photographs. See URANUS' SATELLITES; Table 2, Appendix.

ROSAT *abbrev. for* Röntgenstrahlen Satellit. A major German X-RAY ASTRONOMY satellite, with UK and US collaboration, launched by a Delta II rocket into a 580 km, 53° inclination orbit in June 1990. The payload included a large (80-cm diameter) GRAZING INCIDENCE telescope to carry out the first deep all-sky survey in the 0.2–3 keV band. Use of such imaging optics over the first six months of the mission yielded an all-sky survey 100–1000 times deeper than those of UHURU, ARIEL V, and HEAO-1. The total number of cosmic X-ray sources detected, in this survey, some 60 000, was more than ten times the number previously recorded. A second ROSAT telescope, the Wide Field Camera (WFC), built by a consortium of UK university groups, uses grazing incidence optics at an unusually large angle and is optimized for the XUV band (0.2–0.02 keV). During the early ROSAT survey phase the WFC obtained the first all-sky survey in this energy band, detecting more than 1000 XUV sources, many being active stars or hot white dwarfs. Following the six-month survey phase, ROSAT embarked on a program of detailed observations of individual targets, chosen competitively from bids made by astronomers to the three ROSAT partners. The main spacecraft systems and three focal plane detectors (imaging PROPORTIONAL COUNTER and MICROCHANNEL PLATE arrays for the X-ray telescope plus XUV-sensitive MCP for the WFC) functioned until 1994. Thereafter observations continued with the microchannel plate array and the WFC. See also XUV ASTRONOMY.

ROSAT All-Sky Survey a survey by the X-ray ROSAT satellite. During its first year of operation it performed the first imaging survey of the whole sky in X-rays. The survey contains about 100 000 X-ray sources.

Rosetta an international ESA mission to rendezvous with a comet. It was approved in 1993 as a 'cornerstone' mission of ESA's HORIZON 2000 program, and the original plan was to bring back to Earth samples taken from a comet's nucleus. The spacecraft was to consist of a cruising module coupled with a landing module and Earth reentry module. The object of the mission was later changed to an 18-month analysis of cometary material. Rosetta was scheduled for launch in 2003 to rendezvous with Comet 46P/Wirtanen in 2011. But the timetable for launch slipped by a year and this fact necessitated the selection of a different target. Thus on Mar. 2 2004 the 3000-kg Rosetta craft was launched from Kourou, French Guiana, by an Ariane-5 rocket and set to encounter Comet 67P/Churyumov-Gerasimenko in 2014.

Rosetta's journey to the comet involves three gravity-assist flybys of the Earth and one of Mars. It will pass close to two asteroids, (2867) Steins and (21) Lutetia. Rosetta's task on reaching the comet will be to enter orbit around it and accompany it on its inward journey toward the Sun. The main Rosetta craft will deploy a lander called Philae, which will touch down on the comet's nucleus and carry out on-the-spot measurements of the chemical and physical makeup and properties of the nucleus and coma. It is hoped that these measurements will advance our understanding of the origin of comets, the relationship between cometary and interstellar material, and the implications of that relationship regarding the origins of the Solar System. The nominal end of the Rosetta mission will come when Churyumov-Gerasimenko passes through perihelion in late 2015.

Rosette nebula (**NGC 2237-38-39**) a large EMISSION NEBULA, about 1° in diameter, in the constellation Monoceros. It is an H II REGION heated and ionized by a centrally situated open cluster of hot young stars (NGC 2244).

Rossby number symbol: R_o. The ratio of the rotation period P to the turnover time τ_c of a convective cell in a star's interior or a planetary atmosphere; τ_c is the time required for hot gas to rise from the bottom to the top of a convective cell and then fall back as it cools. The Rossby number is a measure of the efficiency of a star's dynamo (which 'drives' its activity), smaller values of R_o indicating a greater influence of rotation upon convection, and therefore higher activity, irrespective of the surface temperature of the star.

rotating variable a star with a hotter or cooler region on its surface that periodically rotates into our line of sight and causes slight variations in the star's brightness. Many dwarf ME STARS show this effect (prototype BY Draconis), probably because their strong magnetic fields cause a large proportion of the star's surface to be covered by dark 'starspots'.

rotation **1** spinning motion of a celestial body or a group of gravitationally bound bodies, such as a galaxy, about an axis, as distinct from orbital REVOLUTION. Almost all celestial bodies show some degree of rotation. Young stars arrive on the MAIN SEQUENCE with a high rotation rate; this results from the conservation of ANGULAR MOMENTUM during their collapse from a cloud of interstellar gas. As a star ages, structural changes in its interior and interactions with its surroundings produce changes in its speed of rotation. The hottest (O and B) stars have very great rotation rates of about 200–250 km s^{-1}. Sunlike stars spin more slowly as they age, although some are able to retain their rapid rotation. The faster the rate of rotation the broader and shallower the star's spectral lines and the stronger the magnetic field (see CORONA). See also DIFFERENTIAL ROTATION; DIRECT MOTION; SYNCHRONOUS ROTATION.
2 one complete turn of a celestial body about its axis. The Earth takes one SIDEREAL DAY to make one rotation. Ideally the rotation period of other bodies is measured as the time interval between successive passages of a meridian line on the surface across the center of the disk, as seen from Earth. The solid surface may however be unobservable and indirect measurements, as by radar, are then employed. The rotation period of a gaseous body, such as the Sun or the planet Jupiter, varies with latitude, being greatest at the equator (see DIFFERENTIAL ROTATION).

rotation curve a plot of the rotational velocity, V, as a function of radius, R, in a spiral galaxy (see illustration overleaf). Rotation curves are an important tool in mapping the distribution of mass in a galaxy. The velocity increases rapidly with distance from the center of the galaxy, and then remains approximately constant, even in the outermost parts of the visible galaxy. This implies that the mass is not centrally concentrated, as might be expected, but is distributed into a DARK HALO extending up to five times the radius of the optical disk. The rotation velocities are measured from the Doppler shift in stellar absorption lines or the emission line spectra of H II regions in the plane of the galaxy. Neutral hydrogen extends farther than the luminous matter of a galactic disk and radio observations can trace out the rotation curve to radii of tens of kiloparsecs.

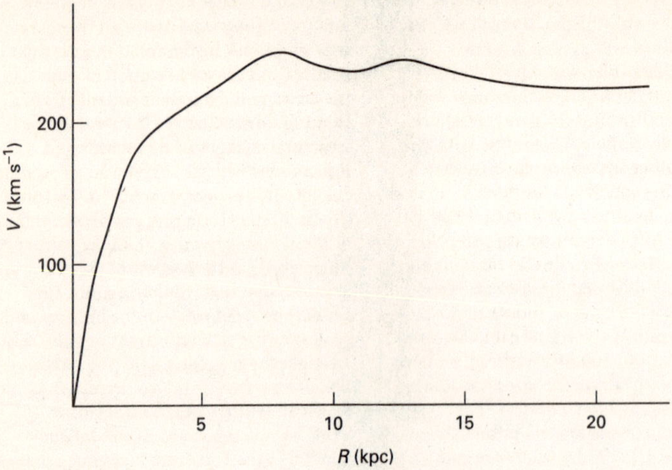

Typical rotation curve

rotation measure see FARADAY ROTATION.

Royal Greenwich Observatory (RGO) the former principal astronomical institute of the UK, sited originally at Greenwich, London, where some of its buildings still stand. It was founded (as the Royal Observatory) in 1675 by King Charles II so that astronomical measurements could be made and the data tabulated for the primary purpose of increasing the accuracy with which positions at sea could be determined. John Flamsteed was appointed the observatory's first director, with the title ASTRONOMER ROYAL, and took up his post in 1676. The Royal Observatory rapidly established itself as a center of accurate timekeeping and the place from which navigators could reckon their longitude. In 1767 it began publishing *The Nautical Almanac*, still an official source of astronomical and navigational information. In 1884, the meridian passing through the TRANSIT CIRCLE at the Royal Observatory was adopted internationally as the prime meridian, i.e. the meridian of zero longitude.

The increase in atmospheric and light pollution in the London area during the 19th and 20th centuries eventually necessitated the removal of the Royal Observatory to Herstmonceux Castle in East Sussex. The move was completed by 1954. The RGO was transferred from the Admiralty to the Science Research Council (later the Science and Engineering Research Council, SERC) in 1965. In addition to studying the positions and apparent motions of stars for the determination of longitude on Earth and in measuring time, the RGO's role widened to include ASTROPHYSICS. This led to the construction of the 2.5-meter ISAAC NEWTON TELESCOPE (INT) at Herstmonceux, completed 1967. But the increasing light pollution and poor SEEING that had driven the RGO from Greenwich again interfered with its activities in Sussex and resulted in the transfer of all observational work (and a modified INT) to La Palma in the Canary Islands. In 1988, the SERC relocated the RGO's UK-based administrative and research work to Cambridge, where it was accommodated by the *Cambridge Institute of Astronomy*, a department of the University of Cambridge set up in 1972 and devoted mainly to postgraduate teaching and research. The move to Cambridge was completed in 1990, and over the next eight years the RGO and the institute shared facilities and collaborated on some research programs.

In 1994, the SERC was replaced by the PARTICLE PHYSICS AND ASTRONOMY RESEARCH COUNCIL (PPARC) as the state-funded body responsible for the RGO and the UK's other astronomical research facilities. In 1998, having decided to rationalize its funding activities, the PPARC closed the RGO down after 323 years of operation. Most of the RGO's functions were taken over by the UNITED KINGDOM ASTRONOMY TECHNOLOGY CENTRE (UK ATC) in Edinburgh. The Nautical Almanac Office was transferred to Rutherford-Appleton Laboratories at Didcot, Oxfordshire. The original Royal Observatory site in Greenwich, now in the care of the UK's National Maritime Museum, is home to a museum and planetarium that attract large numbers of visitors each year. A public information service on astronomical matters is also centered there, and an amateur astronomy club, the Flamsteed Astronomy Society (founded 1999), holds regular meetings and observing sessions in the observatory's grounds. Refurbishment and expansion of the site began in 2004.

Royal Observatory, Edinburgh (**ROE**) an observatory situated on Blackford Hill in Edinburgh, Scotland, that was founded in 1818, gaining a Royal Charter in 1822. Originally sited on Calton Hill, Edinburgh, it was relocated to its present position in 1896. During nearly two centuries from its foundation, the ROE developed as an international center of research. In addition to astrophysical observations, it was concerned with the development of advanced technologies and their applications in astronomical and space research. From 1957 it established itself as a world leader in the analysis of photographic plates. In 1970 it introduced GALAXY, an automatic plate-measuring machine that was the forerunner of COSMOS. During the 1970s and 1980s it built up an immense Plate Library of thousands of photographs taken with the UK SCHMIDT TELESCOPE in Australia, an instrument it originally administered on behalf of its funding body, the Science and Engineering Research Council (SERC). The observatory also managed the 3.8-meter UK INFRARED TELESCOPE and the 15-meter JAMES CLERK MAXWELL TELESCOPE, both in Hawaii, for the same body. In 1994 responsibility for funding the ROE was transferred to the PARTICLE PHYSICS AND ASTRONOMY RESEARCH COUNCIL (PPARC). In 1998, under the PPARC's program to rationalize its funding activities (a program that saw the closure of the ROYAL GREENWICH OBSERVATORY), all the UK's overseas observatories and instruments became independent, including those administered by the ROE. The ROE itself became the site of the new UNITED KINGDOM ASTRONOMY TECHNOLOGY CENTRE (UK ATC). Its technology and research functions were shared between the UK ATC and the Institute of Astronomy, a department of the University of Edinburgh. See also ASTRONOMER ROYAL.

r-process a rapid process of NUCLEOSYNTHESIS that is thought to occur when there is a very high flux of neutrons, as in certain supernova explosions. All nuclei with a mass number greater than bismuth–209 (see S-PROCESS) and all neutron-rich isotopes heavier than iron have been produced by the r-process. The process involves the capture by a nucleus of two or more neutrons in quick succession. The nucleus will then undergo chains of beta decay, this beta-particle (electron) emission having been suppressed during the rapid capture process. The decay product will be a stable neutron-rich nucleus. Many heavy nuclei can be produced both by the r- and the s-process.

RR Lyrae stars a large group of PULSATING VARIABLES that are old giant stars (halo and disk POPULATION II stars) and are found principally in GLOBULAR CLUSTERS. They usually have periods of less than one day, light variations of 0.2–2 magnitudes, and median spectral types in the range A7 to F5. They were discovered in 1895 by Solon I. Bailey, the group being named after RR Lyrae, discovered in 1899. Available evidence indicates that all RR Lyrae stars have about the same mean absolute MAGNITUDE (about +0.6); they can therefore be used as distance

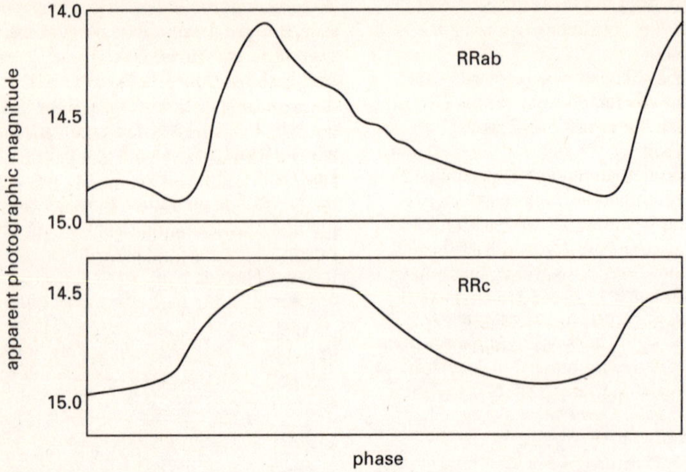

Typical light curves of RR Lyrae stars in subgroups RRab, RRc

indicators up to about 200 kiloparsecs (see DISTANCE MODULUS).

RR Lyrae stars are of a mixed nature. They were divided by Bailey into three groups – *RRa*, *RRb*, and *RRc* – depending on period and the asymmetry of their light curves (see illustration). Groups *a* and *b* are often combined today as *RRab* stars. Other groupings have been made according to period. Many RR Lyrae stars show a periodic variation in both period and shape of light curve – the *Blazhko effect*. In addition the periods of some RR Lyrae stars are slowly changing at a constant rate, as predicted by evolutionary theory, while others show abrupt changes in period. The pulsations of these stars are very complex and can be subdivided into one group (RRab) oscillating in fundamental mode (see PULSATING VARIABLES) and a second group (RRc) oscillating in first harmonic mode. See also HORIZONTAL BRANCH.

RS Canum Venaticorum star (**RS CVn star**) a short-period binary star system that contains a SUBGIANT of spectral type G or K exhibiting intense activity at radio, ultraviolet, and X-ray wavelengths; the other component is a normal F or G main-sequence star. The orbital period can range from 1 day to 2 weeks. The two stars are not undergoing MASS TRANSFER (they are a detached system), but TIDAL FORCES have locked the rotation of the subgiant so that it is forced to rotate once in each orbital period, much faster than a normal subgiant. This rapid rotation apparently causes strong magnetic fields, which then produce the observed activity.

The LIGHT CURVE of these stars shows a continuously changing brightness during the orbital period, believed to be due to dark *starspots* extensively blanketing one half of the subgiant's surface. Measurements of the ZEEMAN EFFECT in light from Lambda Andromedae show that the spotted hemisphere has a field strength of over 0.1 tesla, similar to that of sunspots. Some of these stars, including the prototype RS CVn, are also eclipsing binaries; the light curve shows regular dips of about a magnitude as the subgiant eclipses the main-sequence star. The subgiant's magnetic field also causes intense radio flares (compare FLARE STARS), strong ultraviolet emission lines from the CHROMOSPHERE, and powerful X-ray emission from a very hot CORONA.

As the subgiant swells to giant size, it

begins to transfer mass and become a W SERPENTIS STAR and then an ALGOL VARIABLE.

R stars see CARBON STARS.

RTG *abbrev. for* radioisotope thermoelectric generator. See THERMOELECTRIC GENERATOR.

runaway star a young star of spectral type O or early B with a very high space velocity, examples including AE Aurigae, 53 Arietis, and Mu Columbae. It has probably been flung out from a close BINARY STAR when its companion has exploded as a SUPERNOVA.

rupes a scarp. The word is used in the approved name of such a surface feature on a planet or satellite.

Russell–Vogt theorem see VOGT–RUSSELL THEOREM.

RV Tauri stars a small group of very luminous PULSATING VARIABLES, typified by RV Tauri, R Scuti, and R Sagittae, that are principally G and K stars with some F stars. They are yellow supergiants with extended atmospheres of gas that emit infrared radiation and have possibly been driven off by the pulsations. They have very characteristic light curves with alternating deep and shallow minima and periods ranging from 20 to 145 days. Because the luminosity fluctuations can be disturbed quite significantly in shape, period, etc., being most pronounced for longer-period stars, they are classified as SEMIREGULAR VARIABLES. RV Tauri stars can be distinguished from other similar yellow semiregular stars by the variation in their COLOR INDEX, which mimics the light curve but goes through its maximum a little before the luminosity minimum. A small group have double periodicity; DF Cygni has two separate luminosity oscillations, a rapid 50 day oscillation being superimposed on a much slower 780 day oscillation with a much greater amplitude.

Ryle Telescope (formerly **five-Kilometer Telescope**) an APERTURE SYNTHESIS radio telescope in Cambridge, UK, and part of the Mullard Radio Astronomy Observatory, University of Cambridge; it is named after Sir Martin Ryle. It consists of four fixed and four rail-mounted DISHES positioned along a 4.6 km E–W BASELINE, giving a total of 28 separate interferometer spacings. The dishes have a diameter of 13 meters and a surface accuracy of better than 1 mm. The telescope was refurbished in the late 1980s for microwave background work, and observes with a BANDWIDTH of 350 MHz at 15 and 5 GHz, giving fields of view of 5 and 15 arcminutes and resolutions of 0.7 and 2 arcseconds respectively.

Ss

SA *abbrev. for* spherical aberration.

Sachs–Wolfe effect the process by which density fluctuations in the early Universe have left an imprint on the COSMIC MICROWAVE BACKGROUND RADIATION. It is caused by the interaction of photons with a gravitational field with density fluctuations. This causes small variations in the temperature. It is thought that the 'ripples' found by the COBE satellite were due to the Sachs–Wolfe effect. The effect was predicted by Rainer Kurt Sachs and Arthur Michael Wolfe in 1967. See also STRUCTURE FORMATION.

Sacramento Peak Observatory a solar observatory sited on Sacramento Peak, New Mexico, at an altitude of 2800-meters. It is a facility of the US NATIONAL SOLAR OBSERVATORY. The main instrument is a 41-meter high vacuum tower telescope (see SOLAR TELESCOPE).

SAGE see NEUTRINO ASTRONOMY.

Sagitta (Arrow) a small constellation in the northern hemisphere near Cygnus, lying in the Milky Way, the brightest stars being Gamma (γ) and Delta (δ) of 3rd magnitude and some of 4th magnitude. It contains the globular cluster M71 (NGC 6838). Abbrev.: Sge; genitive form: Sagittae; approx. position: RA 19.7h, dec +18°; area: 80 sq deg.

Sagittarius (Archer) a large zodiac constellation in the southern hemisphere near Scorpius, lying partly in the Milky Way. The brightest stars are the 1.8-magnitude *Kaus Australis* (ε) and 2.0-magnitude *Nunki* (σ) with several others of 2nd and 3rd magnitude. The center of the Galaxy lies in the direction of Sagittarius. Although this region is obscured at optical wavelengths by considerable dark nebulosity, observations at other wavelengths have revealed very complex phenomena (see GALACTIC CENTER; SAGITTARIUS A). The constellation contains star clouds, many nebulae, including the OMEGA, LAGOON, and TRIFID NEBULAE, many globular clusters, including the bright ones M22 (NGC 6656) and M55 (NGC 6809), and some open clusters, including M25 (IC 4725). Abbrev.: Sgr; genitive form: Sagittarii; approx. position: RA 19h, dec –30°; area: 867 sq deg.

Sagittarius A the brightest member of a complex of radio sources at the GALACTIC CENTER. It has two components. *Sagittarius A East* is a source of NONTHERMAL EMISSION 8 parsecs across, and is probably a SUPERNOVA REMNANT. *Sagittarius A West* is a spiral-shaped source of THERMAL EMISSION from ionized gas and is about 2 parsecs across. It also contains an intense, very compact, and variable radio source, *Sagittarius A** (pronounced A star), that is probably smaller than 10 AU and lies very close to or at the Galaxy's exact center. This 'point' source resembles a scaled-down version of the central radio sources in ACTIVE GALAXIES, which are believed to be accretion disks of gases around a massive BLACK HOLE. X-ray and gamma-ray observations show similar resemblances to an active galaxy's core.

Infrared and radio observations show that Sgr A West contains gas and dust with velocities up to 250 km s^{-1}; there may be a ring of material in orbit about the compact central source, and also streams of gas falling toward the central source. The velocities indicate the gravitational influence of 6×10^6 solar masses within Sgr A West. Infrared observations of a source believed to be a cluster of stars at the Galaxy's core (almost coincident with the compact radio source) are consistent with only 3×10^6 solar masses of stars. The difference, 3×10^6 solar masses, may reside in a central black hole. Many of the properties of Sgr A West could, however, result from activity caused by star formation, as occurs in a STARBURST GALAXY, so that the case for a black hole is not accepted by all astronomers.

Sagittarius arm see GALAXY.

Sagittarius B an immense MOLECULAR CLOUD complex lying around the galactic center, maybe forming part or all of an expanding ring of clouds. The most massive cloud in the complex, and possibly in the Galaxy, is *Sagittarius B2*. A large number of the interstellar molecules detected so far were discovered in Sgr B2.

Sagittarius dwarf spheroidal galaxy the nearest galaxy to our own, the Sagittarius dwarf spheroidal galaxy was discovered in 1994, at a distance of only 24 kpc. Its detection is comparatively recent because it is faint, and its proximity means that its constituent stars are spread over a large part of the sky, heavily obscured by the many foreground stars of our own MILKY WAY. The galaxy is thought to be slowly being torn apart by the gravitational force of our own Galaxy.

Saha ionization equation an equation, put forward by the Indian physicist M.N. Saha in the 1920s, that gives the ratio of the number density (number per unit volume) of ions, N^+, to the number density of neutral atoms, N_o, in the ground state in a system of atoms, ions, and free electrons at a given temperature. The system is in equilibrium so that the rate of IONIZATION is equal to the rate of recombination of electrons and ions. The equation can be given in the form:

$$N^+/N_o = A(kT)^{3/2}\, e^{-I/kT} N_e$$

A is a constant, k is the Boltzmann constant, T the thermodynamic temperature, N_e the number of electrons per unit volume (the electron density), and I is the IONIZATION POTENTIAL of the atom. The equation also gives the ratio N^{2+}/N^+, N^{3+}/N^{2+}, etc., if I is replaced by the second (I_2) or the third (I_3) ionization potentials, etc.

The equation shows that the higher the temperature, the more highly ionized a particular atom will be. It can therefore be used to find the relative numbers of neutral, singly ionized, doubly ionized atoms, etc., in stars of known temperature and electron density. See also BOLTZMANN EQUATION.

Saiph see ORION.

Sakharov's conditions a set of three conditions in the EARLY UNIVERSE that can explain the asymmetry between matter and antimatter. These conditions are: (1) there is some process in which baryon number is not conserved; (2) CP violation occurs; (3) the early Universe is not in a state of thermal equilibrium. These conditions were put forward by Andrei SAKHAROV in 1967 and implemented in the context of grand unified theories (see FUNDAMENTAL FORCES) by a number of workers in the late 1970s.

Sakigake a Japanese spacecraft that was launched in Jan. 1985 and passed on the sunward side of HALLEY'S COMET on Mar. 11 1986 at a miss distance of 7 million km. The main aim was to investigate the PLASMA and magnetic field associated with the comet. A second Japanese spacecraft, *Suisei*, was launched in Aug. 1985 and passed Halley on the sunward side on Mar. 8 1986 at a miss distance of 151 000 km. This craft carried an ultraviolet imager and an instrument that measured the energy of the cometary plasma ions.

Salpeter mass function see STELLAR MASS.

Salpeter process see TRIPLE ALPHA PROCESS.

SALT *abbrev. for* Southern African Large Telescope.

Salyut a series of Soviet space stations launched into Earth orbit and visited and operated by crews of cosmonauts from the USSR and (usually) other Communist countries. The first station was launched in Apr. 1971. Others followed, Salyut-4 (1974–75), Salyut-6, and Salyut-7 being predominantly civilian in nature: in addition to medical, biological, and technological purposes, the stations served as platforms for terrestrial and astrophysical observations. Every Salyut was maneuverable in orbit, either by an engine on board the station or on a craft docked to it. When not carrying a crew, they were under automatic operation.

Salyut–6 was launched in Sept. 1977 and its program ended in July 1982. There were crews on board for a total of about two years: the last manned mission was completed in May 1981. There was a docking port at each end of the 15-meter long 19-tonne structure. Crews were transported to and from the station by SOYUZ CRAFT. Simultaneous use of the two docking ports allowed long-term and short-term visits to occur concurrently. Additional cargo and fuel were ferried to the station by unmanned Progress craft.

Salyut–7 was launched in Apr. 1982. Its exterior was similar to that of Salyut–6 but its interior had been modernized both in instrumentation and living conditions. There were several manned missions of long duration before Salyut–7 was abandoned in a high orbit in 1986 after the MIR space station was launched. Increased solar activity expanded the Earth's upper atmosphere, causing the orbit to decay, and the craft made an uncontrolled but safe landing in Feb. 1991 in Argentina.

S Andromedae a supernova that was observed, in 1885, in the Andromeda galaxy and at maximum was just visible to the naked eye.

SAO Star Catalog a general whole-sky catalog issued by the Smithsonian Astrophysical Observatory, Washington, in 1966. It lists positions and proper motions of 258 997 stars usually down to a limiting magnitude of 9 (epoch 1950.0), there being a uniform number of stars for each area of sky. An associated and highly accurate computer-plotted *Star Atlas* was published in 1968.

saros the period of 6585.32 days (about 18 years) that elapses before a particular sequence of solar and lunar ECLIPSES can recur in the same order and with approximately the same time intervals. Following such a period, the Earth, Sun, Moon, and NODES of the Moon's orbit return to about the same relative positions: the period is equal to 223 SYNODIC MONTHS and is almost equal to 19 ECLIPSE YEARS (6585.78 days). An eclipse repeated after one saros occurs 0.32 days later and hence 115°W of its predecessor. The saros was known in ancient times.

SAS *abbrev. for* Small Astronomical Satellite. Any of a series of US X-RAY and GAMMA-RAY ASTRONOMY satellites of the 1970s. SAS–1, later named UHURU, was launched in Dec. 1970. It was devoted entirely to X-ray astronomy and provided a wealth of data. SAS–2, launched in Nov. 1972, carried equipment, including a SPARK CHAMBER, for gamma-ray measurements while SAS–3, launched in May 1975, carried X-ray detectors.

satellite, artificial an object made by human beings that is boosted into a closed path (orbit) around the Earth, Moon, or some other celestial body. It is generally an unpiloted form of space vessel. Satellites carry a variety of detectors, cameras, and measuring instruments, depending on their function, plus equipment to support these: control systems to orientate them, power supplies such as solar panels, data storage facilities, and antennas for communications with Earth or with a data-relay satellite. The cost of the satellite and its equipment, plus the cost of launching it – e.g. from a space shuttle or on a Delta or Ariane rocket – and communicating with it, is now extremely high and countries are tending to collaborate on missions, sharing cost and expertise.

Although some malfunctioning satellites can be repaired by the crew of an orbiting shuttle, and in future may be repaired on the proposed SPACE STATIONS, repairs are at present usually impossible. Each material and component part must undergo extensive testing before launch, with a carefully considered degree of redundancy in electronic components and circuitry. The problems arising from the near vacuum environment of space, from the bombardment of cosmic rays, micrometeorites, etc., and from magnetic fields and radiation belts must also be considered.

Artificial satellites have a great range of functions. Some astronomical Earth satellites study the radiations from space that cannot penetrate the atmosphere:

X-RAY, GAMMA-RAY, ULTRAVIOLET, and INFRARED ASTRONOMY have been revolutionized by the recent launching of satellites specializing in these fields. Astronomical satellites can also make measurements at optical, radio, and infrared wavelengths that can penetrate, but may be severely affected by, the atmosphere. Other scientifically orientated satellites study the resources, atmosphere, and physical features of the Earth.

Satellites are also used for communications (usually in geostationary orbit and allowing global long-distance live television broadcasting and telephony), for weather forecasting, and as navigational aids. In addition, the military potential of satellites has been exploited.

satellite, natural (**moon**) a natural body that orbits a planet. The nine planets of the Solar System have a total of more than 150 known satellites between them. In addition, the numerous small bodies that comprise the PLANETARY RINGS of Saturn, Jupiter, Uranus, and Neptune may be regarded as natural satellites. A satellite may arise from one of two mechanisms, both of which probably applied in the Solar System: a body may grow by accretion from material (PLANETESIMALS) gravitationally attracted toward, and entering orbit around, a PROTOPLANET; secondly, bodies, such as ASTEROIDS, may be captured gravitationally by a planet. Another mechanism, involving formation from the debris of a major impact on the primary planet, may explain the MOON's origin. Most of the known satellites occur in the outer Solar System. Because of the low ambient temperature both now and during formation, many of these satellites are composed largely of water ice or of roughly equal mixtures of water ice and rock; these are the *icy satellites*. Three satellites – Titan, Triton, and Io – are now known to have atmospheres. For satellite properties, see Table 2, backmatter.

satellite galaxy a small galaxy that closely orbits a massive galaxy and will eventually lose orbital energy through DYNAMICAL FRICTION and fall into and merge with it. The MAGELLANIC CLOUDS are satellites of our Galaxy. See also CANNIBALISM.

Saturn the sixth planet of the Solar System and, with an equatorial diameter of 120 537 km, the second largest. It orbits at a distance of between 9.01 and 10.04 AU from the Sun once every 29.46 years; OPPOSITIONS recur two weeks later each year. It has a polar diameter of 107 519 km so that its OBLATENESS, 0.108, is the highest of any planet. Its mean density, 0.7 times that of water, is lower than that of any other planet. Before 1978 Saturn was thought to have 10 satellites, the three largest being Titan, Rhea, and Iapetus; the number is currently 47. Orbital and physical characteristics of planet and satellites are given in Tables 1 and 2, backmatter.

Saturn is the outermost of the five planets that were known to the astronomers of antiquity. The telescopic appearance of the planet is dominated by a prominent and beautiful system of rings (see SATURN'S RINGS) that lie in the plane of Saturn's equator, tilted by 27° with respect to its orbit. This tilting leads first one face of the rings, and then the other, to be inclined towards the Sun and the Earth by up to 27°. At approximately 15-year intervals, the rings become edge-on to the Earth and all but disappear. The bright rings, about 270 000 km across, can add appreciably to Saturn's average apparent magnitude of 0.7 at opposition, when the globe and rings are 19 and 44 arc seconds wide respectively.

Saturn's disk appears similar to that of Jupiter in being crossed by yellowish dark and light cloud bands running parallel to the equator; these are called *belts* and *zones* respectively. They are less prominent, however, than those of Jupiter and spots within them are much less common. The spots, typically white, that have been followed indicate that Saturn, like Jupiter, rotates more rapidly near the equator (in 10 hours 14 minutes or less) than at high latitudes (about 10 hours 40 minutes).

Saturn and its environment were studied by the PIONEER 11 probe in 1979, the VOYAGER PROBES in 1980 and 1981, and the Cassini/Huygens spacecraft from 2004. The Cassini craft was scheduled to make 74 orbits of the planet in the space of four years. These probes provided considerable information on the meteorology and atmosphere of Saturn, which resemble those of Jupiter. Like Jupiter, Saturn emits more radiation than it absorbs from the Sun and probably has an internal primordial energy reservoir. Escaping heat may drive the atmospheric convection processes that give rise to the observed cloud banks, probably of ammonia crystals at 100 K. The Saturnian weather systems, like those of Jupiter, are strongly zonal. At the equator the cloud top winds reach more than 500 m s^{-1}. There is evidence of a wide range of cloud systems of varied morphologies: the white spots are anticyclonically rotating systems and have features identical with Jupiter's GREAT RED SPOT; trains of vortex streets are seen in northern midlatitudes. Although there is a strong internal heat source, analyses of the Voyager data have shown that Saturn (and also Jupiter) and the Earth drive their meteorological systems in the same way, with energy being transported from the small-scale features into the main flow. Spectroscopic studies indicate hydrogen, methane, and ethane in the upper atmosphere; hydrogen probably forms the bulk of Saturn's mass.

Models for the internal structure of Saturn suggest an Earth-sized iron-rich rocky core with a 7500-km outer core of ammonia, methane, and water. This is enclosed by about 21 000 km of liquid metallic hydrogen above which lies liquid molecular hydrogen.

Saturn's magnetic field was detected by the Pioneer 11 probe. It has the same direction as Jupiter's field but is about 20 times weaker. Surprisingly, the magnetic axis corresponds almost exactly with Saturn's rotational axis. Pioneer also discovered RADIATION BELTS, mainly comprising energetic electrons and protons. Saturn emits intense radio waves that are thought to be generated as SYNCHROTRON EMISSION from the electrons spiralling in the magnetic field. Saturn's rings and its inner satellites sweep away these charged particles. The interactions with the rings give rise to electrostatic discharges and assist in the formation of the spoke patterns in ring B. The Cassini/Huygens probe found also that Saturn's radio emissions are generated along with aurorae on the planet.

Saturn nebula see AQUARIUS.

Saturn's rings a system of coplanar rings in Saturn's equatorial plane, with an overall diameter of possibly 960 000 km, measured to the outer edge of the outermost (E) ring and including the space occupied by Saturn itself. The ring system is tilted at nearly 27° to Saturn's orbital plane. It was seen indistinctly by Galileo in 1610 and was recognized for what it was by Christiaan Huygens in 1656. Huygens published a

Saturn's Rings

Name	*Mean distance from planet center* (10^3 *km*)	*(planetary radii)*	*Radial width (km)*	*Thickness*	*Optical depth*
D	67–75	1.11–1.24	7500	?	0.01?
C (Crepe)	75–92	1.24–1.52	17 500	?	0.08–0.15
Maxwell Gap	88	1.45	270		
B	92–118	1.52–1.95	25 500	0.1–1	1.21–1.76
Cassini Div.	118–122	1.95–2.02	4200	?	0.12
A	122–137	2.02–2.27	14 600	0.1–1	0.70
Encke Gap	134	2.21	325		
Keeler Gap	137	2.26	35		
F	140	2.32	30–500	?	0.01?
G	167–174	2.75–2.88	8000	100–1000	10^{-5}–10^{-4}
E	180–480?	3–8?	300 000?	1000?	10^{-7}–10^{-6}

description of the ring system three years later. But the true nature of the rings remained a matter of speculation until Pioneer 11 and Voyagers 1 and 2 visited Saturn in 1979–81.

The seven discernible main rings are now known to consist of thousands of narrow ringlets arranged concentrically and containing innumerable individual particles, chiefly of water ice. The particles are up to several centimeters or, in ring B, even a few meters in size, and each is a satellite of Saturn. The particulate nature of the rings is confirmed by the fact that the inner edge of each ring orbits Saturn faster than the outer edge. The rings are in general less than 1 km thick and almost disappear when edge-on to the Earth, as happens every 15 years or so, when the Earth crosses the rings' plane. Properties of the seven rings are given in the table.

The rings are designated by alphabetical letters reflecting the order of their discovery. The very faint and tenuous *D ring* is the closest to Saturn. There is no truly well-defined inner edge so that it would appear to extend right down to the cloud tops of Saturn. The C (or *Crepe*) *ring*, also known as the *Dusky ring*, fills the gap between the D ring and the inner edge of the brightest ring, ring B, at 25 000 km above the cloud tops. It is a complicated, 'grooved' region with a large number of discrete ringlets. There are at least two particularly noticeable gaps, the outer of which, the *Maxwell Gap*, is 270 km wide; these gaps contain narrow eccentric ringlets. *Ring B* is the brightest part of the entire ring system and is opaque when seen from the Earth. In the central portion of the ring *spokes* have been seen, measuring 10 000 km by 2000 km wide. The spokes move radially and they are thought to be created by the interaction of the local magnetic field with the particle distributions in the rings. There are also electrostatic (lightning) discharges in this region that may also be related to the spoke formation. The particles in ring B are reddish in color and may be as large as a few meters in diameter. These particles are quite different from those of the C and D regions.

The *Cassini Division* separates the B and A rings and is one of the most prominent features of the ring system. It is not empty of particles, but those to be found there are probably dust grains rather than specs of ice. The origin of the 4200-km gap may be related to the perturbation effect of the satellite Mimas, which is in a 2:1 orbital resonance with particles at the inner edge of the Cassini Division and the particles in the B ring area. A 285- to 400-km wide region near the inner edge of the Cassini Division, the *Huygens gap*, was discovered on Voyager photographs. The *A ring* is not as bright as its inner neighbor. It contains a large number of ringlets and minor gaps. These are quite separate from the principal division in the A ring, known as the *Encke Division*. This gap also contains several ringlets, and although only 325 km wide is visible from the Earth with moderate telescopes. The 35-km wide *Keeler Gap* lies in the outer A ring. The outer edge of ring A is a sharp boundary at a distance of 77 000 km above the cloud tops, which may be related to the presence of a tiny SHEPHERD SATELLITE, Atlas. The four rings have a thickness of 10–100 meters and are surrounded by a large rarefied cloud of neutral hydrogen extending to about 60 000 km above and below the ring plane.

Beyond the main rings are several diffuse ring systems. The braided *F ring* is not circular and its width varies over a range of 30–500 km. Two SHEPHERD SATELLITES, Prometheus and Pandora, are located on each side of the F ring, and in 2004 the Cassini/Huygens spacecraft discovered three other satellites in the F ring's vicinity, and two tenuous rings: R 2004/S2, close to Prometheus, and R 2004/S1, co-orbital with Atlas. Still farther out is the tenuous *G ring*, lying between the orbit of Mimas and that of the two COORBITAL SATELLITES Janus and Epimetheus. The distance between the F and G rings is about 30 000 km. Finally there is the *E ring*, which is very wide, possibly 300 000 km, and like the G ring is much thicker than the other rings; the brightest part of the E ring lies just inside Enceladus' orbit.

SAX (now **Beppo Sax**) an Italian satellite for observations of X-ray sources, launched in

April 1996 into an equatorial, near-Earth orbit. The combination of broad-band/narrow-field detectors, a wide-field camera, and a gamma ray burst monitor, provided a unique observing capability that gave rich dividends with the identification of the mysterious GAMMA RAY burst sources with powerful explosive events in distant galaxies.

scale factor see COSMIC SCALE FACTOR.

scattering 1 the random deflections suffered by light or other electromagnetic radiation passing through an irregular medium. If the source, medium, or observer are in relative motion, *scintillations* – random fluctuations of AMPLITUDE – may be seen as the source is observed through the medium: scattering in the Earth's atmosphere causes the stars to twinkle. Scintillations may only be seen if both the angular size of the source and the BANDWIDTH in which the waves are received are small enough. Otherwise, the effect of the scattering may simply be to broaden the apparent angular size of the source.

Scintillations of RADIO WAVES are observed to occur because of irregularities in the REFRACTIVE INDEX of the IONOSPHERE, the INTERPLANETARY MEDIUM, and the INTERSTELLAR MEDIUM giving *ionospheric scintillation, interplanetary scintillation* (*IPS*), and *interstellar scintillation* (*ISS*), respectively. IPS may be used in determining the angular sizes of RADIO SOURCES at meter wavelengths in the range 0.1 to 2 arc seconds, or for measuring parameters of the SOLAR WIND. ISS cause some of the random fluctuations in the intensity of pulses received from PULSARS.

Light may be deflected from its direction of travel by fine particles of solid, gaseous, or liquid matter. For very small particles (less than one wavelength in size) the effect results from DIFFRACTION, reflection playing a more important part with increasing size; this is known as *Rayleigh scattering* and is very dependent on wavelength. Very small particles scatter blue light more strongly than red light. This leads to the reddening of starlight by cosmic dust and to the reddening of the Sun when seen through a thick layer of atmospheric dust.

2 the deflection of individual particles (such as electrons or photons) from their direction of travel as a result of their interaction with other particles, nuclei, atoms, or molecules in the medium through which they are passing. There are various scattering processes including COMPTON SCATTERING.

Scheat (**β Peg**) a red giant that is one of the brightest stars in the constellation Pegasus and lies on the Great Square of Pegasus. It is a semiregular variable with a magnitude range of 2.3 to 2.7. Spectral type: M2 II-III; distance: 67 pc.

Schedar (**Shedir**; **α Cas**) an orange giant that is the brightest star in the constellation Cassiopeia. The magnitude is about 2.23 but it varies slightly. Spectral type: K0 IIIa; distance: 70 pc.

Schickard see table at CRATERS.

Schmidt–Cassegrain configuration see SCHMIDT TELESCOPE.

Schmidt telescope (**Schmidt camera**; **Schmidt**) a catadioptric wide-field telescopic camera first built in 1930 by the Estonian Bernhard Schmidt (see CATADIOPTRIC TELESCOPE). A short-focus reflecting telescope with a spherical mirror suffers from severe SPHERICAL ABERRATION. This is normally corrected by modifying the surface to a paraboloid. This method of correction is effective, however, only for a field of less than half a degree: outside this limit the star images are distorted by severe COMA. Schmidt overcame the spherical aberration of a spherical mirror, which does not suffer from coma, by placing a CORRECTING PLATE in the incoming light beam before it reached the short-focus spherical primary mirror. His correcting plate is a thin plate of complicated figure placed near the center of curvature of the mirror (see illustration). The corrected light comes to a focus on a curved focal surface but when a photographic plate is sprung to this curve very sharp star images are formed upon it over a field of maybe tens of degrees: the 1.2-meter UK SCHMIDT TELESCOPE covers 40 square degrees of sky. In addition relatively short photographic exposures are required, compared to a

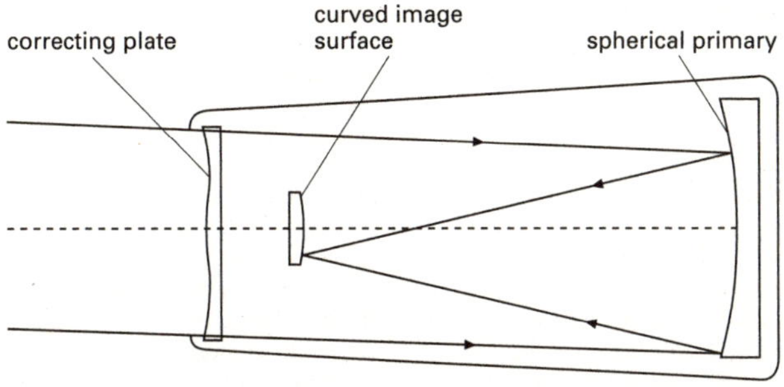

Ray path in Schmidt telescope

normal telescope, because of the small FOCAL RATIO of the Schmidt. The description '1.2 m/1.8 m/3.1 m Schmidt' indicates that the correcting plate has a diameter of 1.2 meters, and the spherical mirror a diameter of 1.8 m and a focal length of 3.1 m. This is normally abbreviated to '1.2-m Schmidt'.

The development of the Schmidt telescope has enabled whole-sky surveys, such as the PALOMAR OBSERVATORY SKY SURVEY and SOUTHERN SKY SURVEY, to include very faint (down to about 21st magnitude) stars. Information, in digital form, can now be extracted rapidly and automatically from the photographic plates using machines such as COSMOS.

The *Schmidt–Cassegrain configuration* offers a more accessible focal surface behind the primary mirror (which has a central hole) by means of an additional small convex mirror placed between correcting plate and primary (see CASSEGRAIN CONFIGURATION). This adaptation gives high-quality images over a reasonably wide field, and the focal surface can be flattened if at least one of the two mirrors is aspheric.

The *super Schmidt* is an extreme form of Schmidt developed by the American James Gilbert Baker in the late 1950s. By employing additional correcting plates he was able to retain the wide field while increasing the speed to focal ratios approaching 0.5. (Schmidt's original telescope was f/1.7). These extremely fast cameras were designed to record meteor and artificial satellite trails.

Schönberg–Chandrasekhar limit an upper limit on the mass of the core of a MAIN-SEQUENCE STAR: a star will leave the main sequence and become a RED GIANT when it has exhausted hydrogen supplies totalling some 12% of its original mass.

Schröter effect a discrepancy between the predicted phase of Venus and the one that is actually observed. In particular, the effect relates to the fact that the calculated date of dichotomy does not coincide with the date on which Venus is seen to have a completely straight terminator. Morning dichotomy is usually earlier than predicted, evening dichotomy later. The reason for the effect is unknown; it may be due to observational error or atmospheric distortions. The effect takes its name from the German astronomer Johann Hieronymus Schröter (1748–1816), who noted it in the 1790s.

Schwarzschild black hole a BLACK HOLE that possesses mass but has zero angular momentum and zero electric charge.

Schwarzschild radius the radius of the EVENT HORIZON of a BLACK HOLE: a critical radius that must be exceeded by a body if light from its surface is to reach an outside observer. For a body of mass M (but zero angular momentum and zero electric charge), the Schwarzschild radius, R_S, is given by

$$R_S = 2GM/c^2$$

where G is the gravitational constant and c the speed of light. If a body collapses so that its radius becomes less than this critical value, then the ESCAPE VELOCITY becomes equal to the speed of light and the object becomes a BLACK HOLE. The Schwarzschild radius is proportional to the mass of a body. For a star the size of the Sun, the Schwarzschild radius is some three km.

Schwassmann-Wachmann 1 a COMET that moves in a near-circular orbit between the orbits of Jupiter and Saturn and suffers from random *outbursts*: increases in brightness by up to seven magnitudes that last for a few weeks. A considerable number of comets suffer outbursts and many theories have been put forward to explain them. These include pressure release from gas pockets of methane and carbon dioxide, explosive chemical reactions involving free radicals (CH, OH, and NH), temperature-induced phase changes in amorphous ice, impact cratering by interplanetary boulders, and spin- and age-induced nuclear break-up. Impact and break-up are the most likely causes.

scintillation (**twinkling**) rapid irregular variations in the brightness of light received from celestial objects, noticeably stars, produced as the light passes through the Earth's atmosphere: irregularities in the atmosphere's refractive index occur in small mobile regions and can cause the direction of the light to change very slightly during its passage. In a telescope a star image will consequently wander rapidly about its mean position, producing an overall blurred enlarged image. With extended light sources, such as the planets, scintillation produces a hazy outline in a telescopic image. For stars near the horizon, where refraction effects including DISPERSION are much greater, changes in color can also be observed. See also SCATTERING; SPECKLE INTERFEROMETRY.

scintillation counter a radiation detector that is used in astronomy mainly for measurements of gamma rays. It consists of a layer of scintillator crystals that emit flashes of light when radiation passes through. Each scintillation is picked up by a PHOTOMULTIPLIER and an amplified pulse of current is produced. These pulses can be counted electronically and the activity of the gamma-ray source can be measured. It is also possible to determine the distribution of energy of the gamma rays. The energy of the electrons liberated from the photocathode of the photomultiplier depends on the frequency of the emitted light, which in turn depends on the energy of the incident beam. It is possible to exclude radiation of energies other than those under consideration by suitable electronic circuitry.

scopulus (plural: **scopuli**) a lobate or irregular scarp. The word is used in the approved name of such a surface feature on a planet or satellite.

Scorpius (**Scorpion**) a conspicuous zodiac constellation in the southern hemisphere, lying partly in the Milky Way. The brightest stars are ANTARES (α) and the blue subgiant *Shaula* (λ), both 1st magnitude, and several of 2nd and 3rd magnitude. The area contains many star clusters, including the bright naked-eye open clusters M6 (NGC 6405) and M7 (NGC 6475), the globular clusters M4 (NGC 6121) and M80 (NGC 6093), and the X-ray source SCORPIUS X-1. Abbrev.: Sco; genitive form: Scorpii; approx. position: RA 17h, dec –30°; area: 497 sq deg.

Scorpius X-1 the first cosmic X-ray source, discovered during a sounding rocket experiment from White Sands, New Mexico, in June 1962. By an order of magnitude Sco X-1 is the brightest of all non-transient cosmic X-ray sources. Optically identified in 1967 with the 13th magnitude variable star V818 Sco, it was confirmed as a low-mass X-ray binary system with an orbital period of 0.78 days. The distance of Sco X-1 remains uncertain, probably lying in the range 300–600 parsecs.

Sculptor an inconspicuous constellation in the southern hemisphere near Grus, the brightest stars being of 4th magnitude. R Sculptoris is an intense scarlet variable star. The south GALACTIC POLE lies in Sculptor and many faint galaxies can be observed. Abbrev.: Scl; genitive form: Sculptoris; approx. position: RA 0.5h, dec –30°; area: 475 sq deg.

Sculptor system a dwarf elliptical galaxy that is a member of the LOCAL GROUP.

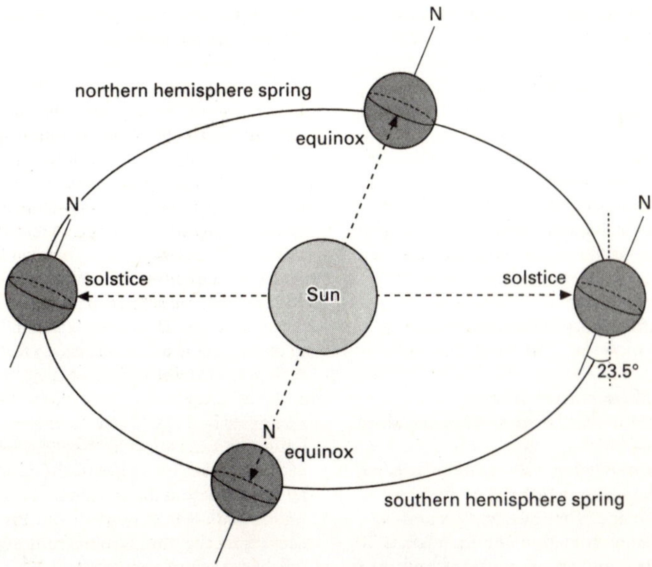

Annual change in seasons

Scutum (Shield) a small constellation in the southern hemisphere near Sagittarius, lying in the Milky Way, the brightest stars being of 3rd and 4th magnitude. It contains the bright RV TAURI STAR R Scuti, the prototype of the DELTA SCUTI STARS, and many star clusters, including the just-visible fan-shaped OPEN CLUSTER, the *Wild Duck* (M11 [NGC 6705]). Abbrev.: Sct; genitive form: Scuti; approx. position: RA 19h, dec –10°; area: 109 sq deg.

S Doradus an extremely luminous supergiant located in NGC 1910, a brilliant cluster of giant and supergiant stars lying in the Large Magellanic Cloud. S Dor is an IRREGULAR VARIABLE ranging in brightness between 9th and 11th magnitude. As with P CYGNI, the light variations are connected with sporadic ejections of material, resulting in a greatly enhanced mass outflow, and a slowly expanding cool shell of dust.

SDSS *abbrev. for* Sloan Digital Sky Survey.

sea interferometer an early form of radio interferometer (see RADIO TELESCOPE) that uses a single ANTENNA mounted on a clifftop overlooking the sea. Fringes are observed on a RADIO SOURCE at low elevation as a result of the INTERFERENCE between radio waves from the source itself and from its image reflected in the sea. Coastal radar antennas were used originally, left over from World War II.

seasons the four approximately equal divisions of the year, usually taken as lasting from EQUINOX to SOLSTICE – spring and autumn – or from solstice to equinox – summer and winter. The seasons, which are more noticeable away from the equator, result from the inclination (23°.45) of the Earth's axis to the perpendicular to the Earth's orbital plane so that the Sun spends half the year north and the remaining year south of the celestial equator (see illustration). The varying distance of the Earth from the Sun has a minor effect on the seasons. Mars, with an axial tilt of 24°, also has seasons.

Secchi classification see SPECTRAL TYPES.

second symbol: s. The scientific (SI) unit of

time, defined since 1967 in terms of ATOMIC TIME. The second is the duration of 9 192 631 770 periods of the radiation corresponding to the transition between two hyperfine energy levels of the ground state of the cesium–133 atom.

secondary 1 see PRIMARY.
2 *short for* secondary crater.

secondary cosmic rays see COSMIC RAYS.

secondary craters depressions produced by the impacts of low-velocity crater EJECTA. Secondary craters are usually elongated radially with respect to the primary CRATER and form loops, CRATER CHAINS, and CRATER CLUSTERS. They tend to lie outside the EJECTA BLANKET.

second of arc see ARC SECOND.

secular continuing or changing over a long period of time.

secular acceleration the apparent speeding up of the Moon in its orbit around the Earth, caused by TIDAL FRICTION and the gravitational attraction of other planets. It amounts to 10.3 arc seconds per century. It first became apparent from records of ancient ECLIPSES.

secular parallax the apparent and continuously increasing displacement of stars as a result of the Sun's motion through space. This form of PARALLAX can be used to determine the distance of nearby groups of stars. It is assumed that the stars are at approximately the same distance from the Sun and that their random individual proper motions tend to cancel out leaving only the parallactic motion. The baseline for this parallax measurement is the distance moved by the Sun relative to the LOCAL STANDARD OF REST and is hence increasing by the Sun's velocity of 19.5 km s^{-1}, i.e. 4.11 AU per year (see APEX). The secular parallax per annum, H (in arcsecs), is then given by:

$$\sin H = 4.11 \sin \alpha/d$$

where d is the mean distance to the group and α is the angle of the group to the solar apex (see illustration).

secular perturbation see PERTURBATION.

Sedna a body orbiting the Sun far out beyond the planet PLUTO at a mean distance of 90 AU. Its orbital period has been estimated at about 10 500 years. At the time of its discovery, made in November 2003 by a team led by Mike Brown from the California Institute of Technology, it was thought to be approaching perihelion, a point 76 AU from the Sun. A distinctive feature is its reddish color. Sedna takes its name from the Inuit goddess of the sea. It is believed to be an object made of ice and rock belonging to the inner OORT CLOUD. With an estimated diameter of about 1800 km, Sedna is thought to be about halfway in size between Pluto and the Kuiper Belt object QUAOAR. The temperature on Sedna is probably lower than 30 K.

seeing the quality of the observing conditions at the time of telescopic observation. The various degrees of good or bad seeing depend on the amount of turbulence in the Earth's atmosphere. Turbulence distorts the plane wavefront of

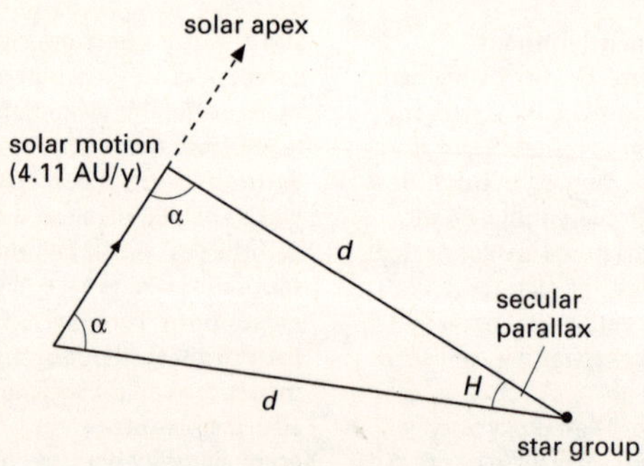

Secular parallax

a beam of radiation, which has traveled more or less undisturbed through space, and transforms it into a perturbed 'corrugated' wavefront. On the few occasions when atmospheric turbulence is very low, a small steady disk-shaped optical image of a point source (such as a star) results. Poor seeing mainly produces small erratic movements in the image position (see SCINTILLATION) so that the overall image is blurred, distorted and enlarged. In NEXT-GENERATION TELESCOPES, ADAPTIVE OPTICS is used to remove or greatly reduce the effects of atmospheric turbulence. Without such technology, it is the seeing that imposes the main limitation on the instrument's spatial RESOLUTION: the minimum diameter of the optical image, resulting from diffraction (see AIRY DISK), can be as low as 0.025 arc seconds but the spatial resolution may only be one or two arc seconds, or more, as a result of poor seeing.

In amateur astronomy the seeing can be evaluated using the *Antoniadi scale*, a system devised in the early 20th century by Eugène M. Antoniadi: the observer allocates a Roman numeral from I to V to conditions varying from perfect seeing, through good, moderate, poor, to appalling.

segmented mirror see PRIMARY MIRROR.

seismograph an instrument used in SEISMOLOGY to detect and record the passage of seismic waves, normally by making a continuous recording of the position of a suspended mass in relation to a frame fixed to the ground.

seismology the study of *seismic waves*, which propagate through the interior of the Earth, or other celestial bodies, such as the Moon, following earthquakes (or equivalent), explosions, or impact phenomena. There are two main types of wave: *S-waves* are shear waves that vibrate at right angles to their direction of motion; *P-waves* travel faster than S-waves and are compressional waves that oscillate along their direction of motion. The S- and P-waves travel deep into the body in question where they are refracted at the boundaries between layers of differing density. S-waves can travel only through a solid; P-waves can travel through solid, liquid, or gas. The waves are measured and analyzed to derive information about the events that generated them or about the internal structure of the body through which they travel. See also HELIOSEISMOLOGY.

SELENE *abbrev.* for Selenological and Engineering Explorer. A Japanese lunar orbiter originally planned for 2005 but expected to be launched in 2006. The name, although an acronym, recalls that of the Greek goddess of the Moon. The SELENE spacecraft, produced by ISAS for NASDA, is scheduled to consist of three separate units: (1) a main orbiter that will travel around the Moon carrying out observations and studying the origins, evolutionary development, and surface and subsurface structure of the Moon from orbit; (2) a relay satellite providing a communications link between the orbiter and the Earth; and (3) a VLBI satellite, which will be used along with instruments on the main orbiter in a Very Long Baseline Interferometry experiment to discover the exact position, precession and shape of the Moon. The mission is expected to last for one year.

selenography the study of the Moon's physical features. See MOON, SURFACE FEATURES.

selenology the scientific study of the MOON. See also MOONQUAKES; MOON ROCKS; STRATIGRAPHY.

self-absorption see SYNCHROTRON EMISSION.

self-noise see NOISE.

self-propagating star formation a process whereby spiral structure in galaxies is explained by waves of star formation triggered by the explosion of a previous generation of stars as SUPERNOVAE. Some of the new stars then explode in turn, and thus continue propagating the spiral pattern around the galaxy. P.E. Seiden and H. Gerola calculated in 1979 that the distribution of stars formed by supernova triggering would form spiral arms in a galaxy that was rotating. The theory gives a better fit than the rival DENSITY-WAVE THEORY to the patchy spiral arms found in many spiral galaxies.

semidetached binary see BINARY STAR; EQUIPOTENTIAL SURFACES.

semidiameter half the APPARENT DIAMETER of a celestial body.

semimajor axis symbol: *a*. The distance from the center of an ellipse to the edge, through the intervening focus. It is half the greatest distance across the ellipse, i.e. half the *major axis*. The semimajor axis of an elliptical orbit is one of the ORBITAL ELEMENTS.

semiregular variables (SR variables) a heterogeneous group of giant and supergiant PULSATING VARIABLES showing brightness variations that do not usually exceed one or two magnitudes, that have a noticeable periodicity ranging from several days to several years, but are also disturbed at times by various irregularities. The light curves have diverse shapes. Semiregular regulars have been divided into four subgroups: *SRa* and *SRb variables* are red giants of late spectral type (M, C, and S) either with relatively stable periods (SRa) or ill-defined periods (SRb) and are difficult to differentiate from long-period MIRA variables; *SRc variables* are red supergiants of late spectral type, such as Betelgeuse, Antares, and Mu Cephei; *SRd variables* are highly luminous yellow (F, G, and K) supergiants and giants.

sensitivity the minimum signal power that can be distinguished from the random fluctuations in the output of a measuring system caused by NOISE inherent in the system. In a RADIO TELESCOPE contributions to the *system noise* include noise generated in the first stage of the RECEIVER, thermal NOISE due to loss in the ANTENNA/FEEDER system, SYNCHROTRON EMISSION received by the antenna from the Galaxy (see RADIO SOURCE), and THERMAL EMISSION from the atmosphere and from the ground. If the system noise has a power P watts, then an equivalent *system temperature*, or *noise temperature*, can be ascribed to it given by

$$T = P/kB$$

where k is the Boltzmann constant and B the BANDWIDTH.

The *signal/noise ratio* of a radio telescope is the ratio of the power in the output that is due to the RADIO SOURCE under observation to that caused by the system noise. The sensitivity is usually defined as the FLUX DENSITY of a source that would produce the same signal power as the noise power, i.e. a signal/noise ratio of one. If the signal changes only slowly with time, the sensitivity may be improved by increasing the INTEGRATION TIME used in the measuring system. See also CONFUSION.

separation symbol: ρ. The angular distance between the two components of a VISUAL BINARY or optical DOUBLE STAR. Separation can be measured with a FILAR MICROMETER in the eyepiece of the telescope; its value is expressed in arc seconds (″).

Serenitatis Basin one of the youngest lunar BASINS, formed 4000 million years ago and filled with MARE lavas from at least 3800 million years ago to produce the circular *Mare Serenitatis* (*Sea of Serenity*). The Mare has striking color contrasts and numerous RILLES and WRINKLE RIDGES. It was visited by LUNOKHOD 2 and the margins sampled by the crew of APOLLO 17.

Serpens (Serpent) a constellation divided into two unequal parts, originally called *Serpens Caput* (Serpent's Head) and *Serpens Cauda* (Serpent's Tail), that lie on each side of the constellation Ophiuchus. The larger part (the Head) lies in the northern hemisphere near Corona Borealis; the smaller section (the Tail) lies in the southern hemisphere near Scorpius, partly in the Milky Way. The two sections use a single set of Bayer letters (see STELLAR NOMENCLATURE) to identify the stars. The brightest stars are Alpha (α) Serpentis, of 2nd magnitude, and several of 3rd magnitude. The globular cluster M5, in the larger part, contains over 100 RR Lyrae stars. The EAGLE NEBULA, M16, lies in the smaller section. Abbrev.: Ser; genitive form: Serpentis; approx. position: RA 15.5h, dec +10° (Head), RA 18.3h, dec −5° (Tail); area: 428 sq deg (Head), 208 sq deg (Tail).

service module (SM) see APOLLO.

SEST *abbrev. for* Sweden–ESO Submillimeter Telescope.

SETI *abbrev. for* search for extraterrestrial intelligence. Any of many searches in which neighboring stars, and sometimes more distant stars, have been studied primarily by means of radio telescopes for signals indicative of life (see EXOBIOLOGY). The SETI hypothesis is that the Universe holds many examples of intelligence of the human type – creatures with the power of abstract thought who can construct models of the external world and can use their skills to build things, including large radio telescopes and transmitters.

The pioneering program was Frank Drake's OZMA PROJECT of 1960. It was unsuccessful, as were subsequent projects using more sophisticated equipment and targeting more stars. Microwave frequencies (1–10 GHz, i.e. wavelengths of 3–30 cm) are thought to be the most favorable to study: natural sources of noise in our atmosphere and in the interstellar medium are at a minimum in this waveband and some common molecules have strong microwave emissions. These include neutral hydrogen at 1.42 GHz and the hydroxyl radical at 1.7 GHz. The longest full-time search was started in 1970 by Robert Dixon of Ohio State University and now covers the frequency range 1.4 to 1.7 GHz. Another long-term search began in 1983 under Paul Horowitz; assuming that artificial signals cover only a very narrow frequency band compared with natural radio emissions, highly sensitive receivers have been used to tune into particular frequencies, which are split into narrow bands (at present 0.05 Hz in width).

The latest and most ambitious SETI is NASA's 10-year *Microwave Observing Program*, which began in Oct. 1992. The targeted search, by the Ames Research Center, is examining at high sensitivity about 1000 nearby sunlike stars. The specially designed receiver is being used with radio telescopes at ARECIBO (305 meter dish), PARKES (64 m), and GREEN BANK (43 m); the equipment analyzes the frequency range 1–3 GHz, splitting it into two billion channels each 1 Hz wide, while software searches for different patterns of artificial signals. The other part of the program, the sky survey, which is undertaken by a team at the Jet Propulsion Laboratory, is systematically scanning the entire sky at lower sensitivities. The two receivers for this part of the project will be used with a 34-m telescope at Goldstone and a similar NASA telescope in the southern hemisphere; from 1996, the final systems covered the frequencies 1–10 GHz, and analyzed 32 million channels.

setting see RISING

setting circles the circular scales provided on the polar and declination axes of a nonportable EQUATORIAL MOUNTING. with their aid the telescope may be set to chosen values of RIGHT ASCENSION and DECLINATION, respectively, so as to bring an object of known position into the field of view.

seven sisters see PLEIADES.

Sextans (**Sextant**) an inconspicuous equatorial constellation near Leo, the brightest star being of 4th magnitude. Abbrev.: Sex; genitive form: Sextantis; approx. position: RA 10h, dec −2°; area: 314 sq deg.

Seyfert galaxy a galaxy with an exceptionally bright nucleus, first described by Carl Seyfert in 1943. Over 150 Seyfert galaxies have now been identified and the vast majority of these are otherwise normal nearby spiral galaxies. Seyferts have substantial NONTHERMAL EMISSION in their nuclei. The nuclei emit radiation at optical wavelengths (by definition) but most of their output is in the infrared; they are also strong X-ray and ultraviolet sources but are not often powerful at radio wavelengths. Their output can vary on a timescale of months. This indicates that the energy source in Seyfert galaxies must be a few light-months across and astronomers believe that Seyferts are a less powerful example (by a factor of 100) of the QUASAR phenomenon.

A region of hot ionized gas clouds surrounds the Seyfert nucleus, giving rise to an optical spectrum rich in emission lines. *Type 1 Seyferts* exhibit both broad Balmer line emission of hydrogen and narrow lines of ionized metals in a manner directly analogous to the broad and narrow line regions (BLR and NLR) of QUASARS. *Type 2 Seyferts* show only narrow lines of all species.

The distinction between the two types can be modeled as an effect of inclination. In type 1 Seyferts the nucleus of the galaxy can be viewed directly and thus the central BLR that surrounds the black hole is seen. In type 2 Seyferts, however, the view of the very central regions is obscured by a thick molecular torus that lies outside the BLR and so only the emission from the NLR is seen. Observations of faint reflected broad lines in some type 2s support this *unification* hypothesis.

Some 10% of giant spiral galaxies are Seyferts. As Seyfert activity is probably only a transitory period in the life of a galaxy, then it is possible that all giant spiral galaxies, including our own, spend 10% of their lives in a Seyfert phase.

So galaxy see GALAXIES.

shadow bands elongated patches or mottled patterns of light and shadow that have irregular form and movement and are briefly observed to cross rapidly over light surfaces on the Earth just before and after totality in a solar ECLIPSE. They probably result from irregular refraction, in the Earth's atmosphere, of light from the crescent Sun.

Shane telescope see LICK OBSERVATORY.

Shapley supercluster the richest SUPERCLUSTER known, containing more than 20 rich CLUSTERS OF GALAXIES within a 40 Mpc diameter. It was first noted by H. Shapley in 1930. It lies behind the Hydra–Centaurus supercluster, in the same direction as the GREAT ATTRACTOR, but three times farther away, at a distance of 180 Mpc.

Sharpless catalog a catalog of bright H II REGIONS visible on the PALOMAR SKY SURVEY plates, compiled by Sharpless in 1959. Sources are known by their Sharpless number; for example, S106 is a small BIPOLAR NEBULA in the direction of Cygnus.

Shaula see SCORPIUS.

Shedir see SCHEDAR.

shell burning see STELLAR EVOLUTION; GIANT.

shell galaxies elliptical or So galaxies that have been found, in deep exposures, to have faint sharp-edge shells of stars. The shells form alternate circular arcs on each side of the galaxy center and are identified with small-scale star formation triggered by a reverberating disturbance such as a galaxy MERGER.

shell star a hot main-sequence star, usually of spectral type B, whose complex spectrum shows sharp deep absorption lines with wings of bright emission lines superimposed on the normal absorption spectrum. It is now known that they are BE STARS, the differences in appearance between the two arising from the directions in which they are observed.

shell structure see STELLAR STRUCTURE.

shell supernova remnant see SUPERNOVA REMNANT.

Shenzhou a space capsule used in China's human spaceflight program. The name means 'divine vessel'. See LONG MARCH.

shepherd satellites (**shepherding satellites**) small satellites that gravitationally confine particles to a ring around a planet. In SATURN'S RING system, Atlas orbits close to the outer edge of ring A, while ring F is confined by Prometheus and Pandora. Voyager 2 discovered Cordelia and Ophelia among URANUS' RINGS.

Sheratan see ARIES.

shock wave (**shock front**) a discontinuity in the physical properties (pressure, temperature, density) of a gas, liquid, or solid that travels through the fluid or solid medium at supersonic speed without further change. Shock waves are generated, for example, by earthquakes, by explosions such as supernovae, or by impacts of supersonic bodies, as when the solar wind meets the Earth's magnetosphere. A shock wave can lose energy by heating the medium through which it travels.

Shoemaker-Levy 9 a comet discovered in 1993 in a 2-year orbit round Jupiter by Caroline and Eugene Shoemaker and David Levy. It had broken into about 20 fragments, which crashed successively into JUPITER over a period of 6 days in July 1994. Infrared fireballs and dark clouds were produced in Jupiter's atmosphere.

shooting star *colloquial name for* meteor.

short-period comet see COMET.

shot noise see NOISE.

shower meteor see METEOR SHOWER.

shuttle *short for* space shuttle.

Sickle of Leo see LEO.

side lobe see ANTENNA.

sidereal relating to or measured or determined with reference to the stars.

sidereal clock a clock regulated to measure the SIDEREAL TIME at an observatory. See also TRANSIT CIRCLE.

sidereal day the interval between two successive passages of a CATALOG EQUINOX across a given meridian. It is divided into 24 sidereal hours. The sidereal day is 3 minutes 56 seconds shorter than the mean solar day.

sidereal hour angle the angular distance measured westward along the celestial equator from a CATALOG EQUINOX to the intersection of the HOUR CIRCLE passing through a celestial body. It is equal to 360° minus the RIGHT ASCENSION (in degrees).

sidereal month the time taken by the Moon to complete one revolution around the Earth, measured with respect to a background star or stellar group considered fixed in position. The average time is 27.321 66 days.

sidereal noon see SIDEREAL TIME.

sidereal period the time taken by a planet or satellite to complete one revolution about its primary, measured by reference to the background of stars. The SIDEREAL MONTH and SIDEREAL YEAR are the sidereal periods of the Moon and Earth. See also SYNODIC PERIOD; Tables 1 and 2, Appendix.

sidereal rate see EQUATORIAL MOUNTING.

sidereal time time based on the rotation of the Earth with respect to the stars. It is measured in SIDEREAL DAYS and in sidereal hours, minutes, and seconds. The sidereal time at any instant is given by the SIDEREAL HOUR ANGLE of a CATALOG EQUINOX and ranges from 0 to 24 hours during one day. The day starts at *sidereal noon,* which is the instant at which the equinox crosses the local meridian. The hour angle at a particular location gives the LOCAL SIDEREAL TIME, the hour angle at Greenwich being the GREENWICH SIDEREAL TIME. A celestial object will be on the meridian of a particular place when the local sidereal time becomes equal to the object's RIGHT ASCENSION.

Apparent sidereal time is measured by the hour angle of the true equinox and thus suffers from periodic inequalities, the position of the true equinox being affected by the PRECESSION and NUTATION of the Earth's axis. *Mean sidereal time* relates to the motion of the mean equinox, which is only affected by long-term inequalities arising from PRECESSION. Apparent minus mean sidereal time equals the *equation of the equinoxes.* Sidereal time is directly related to UNIVERSAL TIME and MEAN SOLAR TIME and is used in their determination.

sidereal year the time taken by the Earth to complete one revolution around the Sun with reference to a background star or stellar group, which is regarded as fixed in position. It is thus the interval between two successive passages of the Sun, in its apparent annual motion around the celestial sphere, through a particular point relative to the stars. It is equal to 365.256 36 days and is about 20 minutes longer than the TROPICAL YEAR.

siderostat a flat mirror that is driven in such a way as to reflect light or infrared radiation from a celestial body to a fixed point, such as a spectrograph slit at the coudé focus of a telescope, over the duration of an observation. A siderostat is often installed outside the main dome of an observatory and can be used with a coudé spectrograph, say, at the same time as the main telescope is being used to study a different field of view. Siderostats often have computer-driven ALTAZIMUTH MOUNTINGS.

Siding Spring Observatory see MOUNT STROMLO AND SIDING SPRING OBSERVATORIES.

sigma (σ) the 18th letter of the Greek alphabet, used in STELLAR NOMENCLATURE usually to designate the 18th-brightest star in a constellation or sometimes to indicate a star's position in a group.

signal/noise ratio see SENSITIVITY.

signature a group of spectal lines usually in an emission spectrum that identifies a chemical – an atom or molecule, possibly ionized and/or in a rare isotopic form – in a star, stellar environment, galaxy, etc.

signs of the zodiac see ZODIAC.

silicon stars see AP STARS.

silvering a process whereby a reflective layer of silver is applied to a mirror base from a solution of silver salts containing reducing agents. Silvering was first used in the 1850s but has been supplanted by the ALUMINIZING process, which provides a reflective layer of greater durability and able to reflect lower wavelengths, i.e. into the ultraviolet.

SIMBAD a large computer database, developed in the early 1980s by staff at the

CENTRE DE DONNÉES ASTRONOMIQUES (CDA) in Strasbourg, France, allowing the user to access a large collection of astronomical data, including cross-identifications and measurements, together with bibliographic information on more than 2 750 000 celestial objects outside the Solar System, including stars, galaxies, nebulae, novae and supernovae. The name SIMBAD is an acronym for Sets of Identifications, Measurements, and Bibliography for Astronomical Data. The database went online for the first time in 1981 and since 1990 has been hosted by the Observatoire Astronomique de Strasbourg. In 1996 SIMBAD became accessible to astronomers over the World Wide Web as well as via public data transmission networks. It incorporates VizieR, a dedicated tool for retrieving astronomical data listed in published catalogs and tables, developed jointly by the CDA and the European Space Agency's European Space Research Institute. SIMBAD and its services are financed by sponsorship from major national and international agencies. NASA funds a mirror site of SIMBAD hosted by the Smithsonian Astrophysical Observatory.

sine formula see SPHERICAL TRIANGLE.

singularity a mathematical point at which space and time are infinitely distorted. Calculations predict that every BLACK HOLE must contain a singularity: matter falling into a black hole will ultimately be compressed to infinite densities at a single point, and in such conditions our laws of physics, including quantum mechanics, must break down. One black-hole theorem – the principle of *cosmic censorship* – states that singularities are always concealed by an event horizon so that they cannot communicate their existence to an observer in our Universe. However, if a *naked singularity* – a singularity without an event horizon – is found, then some of our physical concepts will need reexamination.

Sinope a small satellite of Jupiter, discovered in 1914 by Seth Nicholson. See JUPITER'S SATELLITES; Table 2, Appendix.

sinuous rille see RILLE.

sinus a semienclosed break along the borders of a lunar mare or in a scarp. The word is used in the approved name of such a feature on the Moon. (Latin: bay)

Sirius (**Dog Star; α CMa**) a white main-sequence star that is the brightest one in the constellation Canis Major and the brightest (after the Sun) and one of the nearest stars in the sky. It lies in a descending (southeasterly) line from Orion's Belt. Sirius is about 1.5 times as hot as the Sun, with a surface temperature of more than 9000 K, and is about 23 times as luminous. It is a visual binary (separation 4″.6, period 50 years), the companion, *Sirius B*, being the first WHITE DWARF to be discovered. Bessel suggested (1844) that Sirius had a dark companion to account for the star's wobbling movement. With improved telescope lenses Alvan G. Clark detected (1862) a tiny companion whose spectrum, first taken (1915) by W.S. Adams Jr., identified Sirius B as a white dwarf. The spectrum demonstrated the GRAVITATIONAL REDSHIFT predicted by the general theory of relativity. m_v: –1.46 (A), 8.3 (B); M_v: 1.4 (A), 11.2 (B); spectral type: A1 Vm (A), DA (B); mass: 2.31 (A), 0.98 (B) times solar mass; radius: 1.7 (A), 0.022 (B) times solar radius; distance: 2.65 pc.

Sirrah see ALPHERATZ.

SIRTF *abbrev. for* Space Infrared Telescope Facility.

SI units an internationally agreed system of coherent metric units, increasingly used for all scientific and technical purposes. It was developed from the MKS system of units and replaces the CGS and Imperial systems of units. There are seven base units that are arbitrarily defined and dimensionally independent (see Table 1). These include the kelvin and the second. The meter has been redefined but is still a base unit. The base units can be combined by multiplication and/or division to derive other units, such as the watt or the newton (see Table 2). A set of prefixes, including kilo- and micro-, can be used to form decimal multiples or submultiples of the units (see Table 3). Any physical quantity may then be expressed in terms of a number multiplied by the appropriate SI unit for that quantity.

SKA see SQUARE KILOMETER ARRAY.

Skyhook see ROCKOON.

Skylab a large crewed US space station

Table 1: Base and Dimensionless SI Units

Physical quantity	*Name of SI unit*	*Symbol for SI unit*
length	meter	m
mass	kilogram(me)	kg
time	second	s
electric current	ampere	A
thermodynamic temperature	kelvin	K
luminous intensity	candela	cd
amount of substance	mole	mol
*plane angle	radian	rad
*solid angle	steradian	sr

*dimensionless units

Table 2: Derived SI Units with Special Names

Physical quantity	*Name of SI unit*	*Symbol for SI unit*
frequency	hertz	Hz
energy	joule	J
force	newton	N
power	watt	Ω
pressure	pascal	Pa
electric charge	coulomb	C
electric potential difference	volt	V
electric resistance	ohm	Ω
electric conductance	siemens	S
electric capacitance	farad	F
magnetic flux	weber	Wb
inductance	henry	H
magnetic flux density	tesla	T
luminous flux	lumen	lm
illuminance (illumination)	lux	lx
absorbed dose	gray	Gy
activity	becquerel	Bq
dose equivalent	sievert	Sv

Table 3: Decimal Multiples and Submultiples used with SI Units

Submultiple	*Prefix*	*Symbol*	*Multiple*	*Prefix*	*Symbol*
10^{-1}	deci-	d	10^{1}	deca-	da
10^{-2}	centi-	c	10^{2}	hecto-	h
10^{-3}	milli-	m	10^{3}	kilo-	k
10^{-6}	micro-	μ	10^{6}	mega-	M
10^{-9}	nano-	n	10^{9}	giga-	G
10^{-12}	pico-	p	10^{12}	tera-	T
10^{-15}	femto-	f	10^{15}	peta-	P
10^{-18}	atto-	a	10^{18}	exa-	E
10^{-21}	zepto-	z	10^{21}	zetta-	Z
10^{-24}	yocto-	y	10^{24}	yotta-	Y

launched on May 14 1973 into a 435-km circular Earth orbit, inclined at about 50° to the equator. The station – Skylab 1 – provided an environment in which people could live and work under controlled but weightless conditions. During 1973 and 1974 three three-man crews were ferried to and from the station by APOLLO spacecraft consisting of a command and service module. The manned missions are known as Skylab 2, 3, and 4. With the Apollo craft docked, the overall length was 36 meters and the weight 82 000 kg; the orbital workshop was 14.7 meters long and 6.6 meters in diameter. Power was obtained from several panels of SOLAR CELLS.

Physiological and psychological reactions to weightlessness were carefully monitored and studied, and ability to perform experiments was tested. In over 513 man-days in space 73 experiments were conducted. The instruments of the APOLLO TELESCOPE MOUNT provided the majority of the observational data, other work including technological, biological, and materials-processing experiments. Over 180 000 solar photographs and 40 000 Earth-resources pictures were taken. The 740 hours spent on solar studies and 215 hours of astrophysical investigation, made above the Earth's distorting and absorbing atmosphere, led to great advances in astronomy.

NASA had assumed that Skylab would stay in orbit for 10 years, with the space shuttle being used to reboost it for further use or deboost it for controlled reentry and crash-landing in the Pacific. The orbit decayed, however, and despite rescue attempts by NASA the craft made an uncontrolled but safe landing in 1979 in the Indian Ocean, with fragments landing in Western Australia.

Sloan Digital Sky Survey (SDSS) a survey mapping one-quarter of the entire sky, using a dedicated telescope at the APACHE POINT OBSERVATORY. It will determine the position and magnitude of more than 100 million objects, and measure the distance to more than a million galaxies and quasars.

slow nova see NOVA.

slow pulsator see X-RAY PULSATORS.

small circle any circle on the surface of a sphere that is not a GREAT CIRCLE. It is the circular intersection on a sphere of any plane that does not pass through the center of the sphere.

Small Explorer (SMEX) see EXPLORERS.

Small Magellanic Cloud (SMC; Nubecula Minor) see MAGELLANIC CLOUDS.

SMART-1 a lunar probe launched on top of an Ariane-5 rocket by the European Space Agency (ESA) Sept. 2003 from Kourou, French Guiana. It was ESA's first Moon probe and the first craft to be sent into space as part of ESA's SMART program – SMART is short for Small Missions for Advanced Research in Technology. SMART-1 was placed in a transfer orbit from the Earth to the Moon before proceeding to an elliptical lunar orbit taking it over the Moon's poles. Driven by a very slow but inexpensive solar-powered electric ion propulsion drive, it took 14 months to reach lunar orbit. In addition to testing the ion drive, the 367-kg SMART-1 was due to attempt to set up a laser-beam communications link with the Earth. It also carried miniature instruments on board to conduct detailed mapping of the whole lunar surface, including the far side. Its tiny infrared detector was to be used in the search for water in deep craters at the lunar poles, while its spectrometer was to map the chemical makeup of the lunar surface and gather chemical data in order to learn more about the Moon's origins. SMART-1's mission was scheduled to last until late 2005 or 2006.

SMC *abbrev. for* Small Magellanic Cloud. See MAGELLANIC CLOUDS.

SMEX *abbrev. for* Small Explorer. See EXPLORERS.

Smithsonian Astrophysical Observatory (SAO) a research facility of the SMITHSONIAN INSTITUTION based in Cambridge, Massachusetts, USA. It was founded in 1890 and originally housed in a building attached to the Smithsonian Institution in Washington D.C. At first it concentrated mainly on solar research, especially into the solar constant. During the first half of the 20th century, it established several solar observing stations in the United States, South America, and Africa to conduct research on solar radiation. In 1955, under an agreement to cooperate on astrophysical research between the Smithsonian Institution and Harvard University, the SAO was transferred to Cambridge under the directorship of the astronomer Fred L. Whipple. The SAO's research activities widened to take in satellite tracking for the US space program, orbiting astronomical observatory experiments, the study of meteorites and comets, and involvement in theoretical astrophysics. In 1968, the SAO opened a major observatory on Mount Hopkins, Arizona. Here it collaborates with the University of Arizona in operating the MULTIPLE MIRROR TELESCOPE (MMT), dedicated in 1979 and converted to a 6.5-meter single-mirror telescope in 1998. The observatory in Arizona was renamed the FRED L. WHIPPLE OBSERVATORY in 1981. The SAO combines with the *Harvard College Observatory* (HCO) to form the *Harvard-Smithsonian Center for Astrophysics*, which was founded in 1973. The center coordinates the work of its constituent institutions under one director and carries out a broad program of research in astronomy, astrophysics, Earth and space sciences, and science education. Its current wide-ranging research activities cover atomic and molecular physics, high energy astrophysics, optical and infrared astronomy, planetary sciences, radio and geoastronomy, solar and stellar physics, and theoretical astrophysics. See also SAO STAR CATALOG.

SMTO *abbrev. for* Submillimeter Telescope Observatory. A joint facility of the University of Arizona's Steward Observatory and the Max-Planck-Institut für Radioastronomie (Bonn). The SMTO is located at an altitude of 3186 m on Mount Graham, northeast of Tucson, Arizona, and houses the Heinrich Hertz Submillimeter Telescope, a 10-m DISH with a surface accuracy of 12 micrometers.

SN 1987A see SUPERNOVA 1987A.

SNC meteorites a small group of stony (achondrite) METEORITES, named after its three main members *Shergotty*, *Nakhla*, and *Chassigny*. These igneous rocks seem to be only 1300 to 200 million years old. It is suggested that they have been ejected from Mars by some crater-producing event.

SNR *abbrev. for* supernova remnant.

SOAR Telescope southern Astrophysical Research Telescope, a 4.2-meter reflecting telescope located on the summit of Cerro Pachón, Chile, at an altitude of 2737 meters. It is one of the instruments of the CERRO TOLOLO INTER–AMERICAN OBSERVATORY and is administered jointly by the USA and Chile. Construction of the SOAR Telescope began in 1998. The instrument was dedicated Apr. 2004 and came into operation early 2005. Its aspherical primary mirror has a total diameter of 4.3 meters but is just 10 centimeters thick and weighs only 3.2 tonnes. It is equipped with ACTIVE OPTICS and its design gives it enhanced capabilities and performance in imaging and spectroscopy throughout the range of wavelengths from the near infrared to the blue/ultraviolet part of the spectrum. An Instrumental Support Box at each NASMYTH focus can carry a cluster of three instruments with a total weight of up to 3000 kg.

SOFIA stratospheric Observatory for Infrared Astronomy, a 2.5-meter telescope in a high-flying Boeing 747 aircraft. Scheduled to succeed the KUIPER AIRBORNE OBSERVATORY (KAO), which ceased operation in 1996, the telescope was installed in its aircraft in 2002 and was used to view the stars for the first time in Sept. 2004. The largest airborne observatory in the world, it is one of the missions included in NASA's long-term Origins Program. It is scheduled to enter regular service in 2005.

SOHO *abbrev. for* Solar Heliospheric Observatory.

solar activity the collective term for time-dependent phenomena on the Sun. SUNSPOTS, FACULAEPLAGES, FILAMENTS (or PROMINENCES), and FLARES all belong in this category, but the GRANULATION and CHROMOSPHERIC NETWORK do not since their gross configuration is stable. The level of solar activity at present varies over an average period of approximately 11 years – the so-called solar cycle (see SUNSPOT CYCLE).

solar antapex see APEX.

solar apex see APEX.

solar calendar any CALENDAR, such as the GREGORIAN CALENDAR, that is based solely on the motions of the Sun. See also LUNAR YEAR; TROPICAL YEAR.

solar cell a device by which incident solar radiation is converted directly into electrical energy. It is a semiconductor device that is identical in principle to the PHOTOVOLTAIC DETECTOR and has a p-n junction with a large surface area. Solar radiation falling on or near the junction produces an external voltage. A variety of different semiconductors, dopants, and fabrication techniques have been used to increase the conversion efficiency and the power delivered. The conversion efficiency can exceed 30%.

Solar cells form the main power supply in satellites, space stations, and short-range planetary probes. The cells are arranged on flat *solar panels* outside the craft to receive the maximum amount of radiation from the Sun. On probes traveling beyond Mars the radiation flux is insufficient to power the instruments: the solar constant at Jupiter's orbit is only about 4% of the value at the Earth's orbit. Power must then be obtained from other sources, such as THERMOELECTRIC GENERATORS.

solar constant the total energy radiated by the Sun that passes perpendicularly through unit area per unit time at a specified distance from the Sun. It is given by the ratio $L/4\pi r^2$, where L is the luminosity of the Sun and r the distance. The value measured at the mean Sun–Earth distance is about 1.367 kilowatts per square meter. Instruments on satellites such as the SOLAR MAXIMUM MISSION have shown that variations in the solar constant occur, the energy flux being reduced when SUNSPOTS are present, by an amount proportional to the area of the spots.

solar cycle see SUNSPOT CYCLE.

Solar Dynamics Observatory (SDO) a solar exploration mission planned for launch by NASA in 2007 and the first mission in the agency's Living with a Star (LWS) Program. Set to carry out studies of the Sun's atmosphere in several wavelengths at the same time, SDO will seek to investigate the various transient changes caused by variations in the Sun's magnetic field and thereby help advance our understanding of such phenomena as solar FLARES, coronal mass ejections, alterations in the SOLAR WIND, and other bursts of energy connected with SOLAR ACTIVITY. These phenomena produce a set of effects described as 'space weather', which have a profound influence on the Earth; they not only produce such events as the AURORA, but also cause immediate and long-term harm to electrical and communications equipment in groundbased systems, aircraft, and spacecraft. Unpredictable changes in solar radiation or energy output are potential hazards for astronauts working in the unprotected environment of space. SDO is also designed to study magnetic field variations in the Sun's interior, active regions and sunspots and how they develop, and the mechanisms that drive the 11-year solar cycle. Initially, its mission is set to last five years, with the possibility of an extension for a further five years.

solar eclipse see ECLIPSE.

Solar Heliospheric Observatory (SOHO) an ESA satellite, with some NASA instrumentation, launched in 1995 into a halo orbit around the L_1 LAGRANGIAN POINT – the point 1.5 million km from Earth at which the gravitational pull of Sun and Earth balance. SOHO is designed to study the Sun's internal structure (see HELIOSEISMOLOGY), and the physical processes that form and heat the solar CORONA and give rise to the SOLAR WIND, which permeates the HELIOSPHERE. SOHO is part of ESA's contribution to the SOLAR/TERRESTRIAL ENERGY PROGRAMME (STEP). Although its primary mission is to study the Sun, many of SOHO's solar images made using coronagraphs to block out the photosphere have revealed numerous hitherto unknown comets. By the start of 2005, SOHO had 'discovered' well over 900 comets.

solar luminosity see SOLAR UNITS.

solar mass symbol: $M_\odot$. The astronomical unit of mass. It is equal to the mass of the Sun, 1.9891×10^{30} kilograms. See also SOLAR UNITS.

Solar Maximum Mission (SMM) a NASA solar observatory that was launched into a 574-km, 96-minute Earth orbit in Feb. 1980 to study FLARES and other phenomena on the Sun during the then current maximum of SOLAR ACTIVITY. Instruments included gamma-ray, ultraviolet, and X-ray spectrometers, a coronagraph, and a radiometer. The SMM was the first multimission modular spacecraft. Later in 1980 a blown fuze and other control problems left it unable to point correctly. In Apr. 1984 Solar Max was maneuvered into the bay of a space shuttle, repaired, and successfully relaunched, and operated effectively until it reentered the Earth's atmosphere and burned up in Dec. 1989.

solar motion see APEX; GALACTIC ROTATION.

solar nebula see NEBULAR HYPOTHESIS.

solar neutrinos see NEUTRINO ASTRONOMY.

solar oscillations see HELIOSEISMOLOGY.

solar panel see SOLAR CELL.

solar parallax the angle subtended by the Earth's equatorial radius at the center of the Sun, at a distance of one astronomical unit. It is equal to 8.794 148 arc seconds, as defined by the IAU.

solar radius see SOLAR UNITS.

solar spectrum the Sun's spectrum extends from gamma-ray to radio wavelengths. It has an immense range in intensity, peaking at visible wavelengths. Although the central part of the curve varies little with SOLAR ACTIVITY, the long- and short-wavelength sections can be very considerably affected. The radiation intensity at visible and infrared wavelengths compares with that of a BLACK BODY at a temperature of about 6000 K; the maximum intensity occurs at wavelengths of about 460 nm. This is the continuous spectrum of the PHOTOSPHERE in which absorption lines – FRAUNHOFER LINES – appear. At the shortest and longest wavelengths, the solar spectrum corresponds to the radiation curve of a black body at about a million kelvin, which is representative of the temperatures of the CORONA and of solar FLARES. At ultraviolet and soft X-ray wavelengths the spectrum does not agree with either of these black-body curves. See also FLASH SPECTRUM.

Solar System a group of celestial bodies comprising the Sun and the large number of bodies that are bound gravitationally to the Sun and revolve in approximately elliptical orbits around it. The latter include the nine known planets, Mercury, Venus, Earth, Mars, Jupiter, Saturn, Uranus, Neptune, and Pluto (although Pluto may be an escaped satellite); more than 60 known natural satellites of the planets; the numerous asteroids mostly in orbits between the orbits of Mars and Jupiter; the comets, which exist in great numbers beyond the most distant planets; and countless meteoroids. The Sun contains 99.86% of all the mass of the system, while most of the remaining mass is concentrated in the planet Jupiter. In extent the Solar System may be considered as a sphere with a radius greater than 100 000 AU although the planets alone extend to a radius of less than 50 AU (see OORT CLOUD).

With the exception of the comets, all bodies of the Solar System orbit the Sun in the same direction as the Earth, along orbits that lie close to the plane of the Earth's orbit and the Sun's equator. Most objects in the Solar System spin in the same direction as their orbital motion. This motion reflects the common origin postulated for the Solar System by the contraction of a rotating cloud of interstellar gas and dust about 4600 million years ago (see SOLAR SYSTEM, ORIGIN).

The Sun and its entire retinue are moving in a nearly circular orbit around the center of the Galaxy, which lies about 8500 parsecs away in the constellation Sagittarius. They have a mean velocity of about 220 km s^{-1} (see GALACTIC ROTATION). In relation to the stars in its neighborhood, the Solar System is moving with a velocity of 19.4 km s^{-1} toward a point in the constellation Hercules – the solar APEX.

Solar System, origin there have been various theories on the origin of the Solar System, many of which have been discarded or modified as observational data has slowly accumulated. The Sun and planets are now believed to have formed together 4.56 billion years ago by the contraction of a cloud of interstellar gas, mainly hydrogen and helium, and dust grains – the *solar nebula*. The contraction may have been triggered by shock waves from a nearby supernova, but continued under the mutual gravitational attraction of the contents of the nebula (see STAR FORMATION).

Conservation of ANGULAR MOMENTUM dictated that as the cloud contracted its rotation rate increased, causing it to become disk-shaped around the developing Sun. Collisions between dust grains became frequent, leading to energy loss and a rapid concentration of particles in the plane of the disk, which lay close to the present plane of the ecliptic, and a gradual ACCRETION of grains into pebbles, boulders, and larger bodies began. Only when these PLANETESIMALS had reached a few kilometers across could their gravity accelerate the accretion process by attracting more solid material. Eventually the PROTOPLANETS of the present planets and satellite systems were built up, most of them rotating and revolving in the same sense as the parent nebula. Possibly any protoplanets that formed between the orbits of Mars and Jupiter suffered gravitational perturbations by Jupiter and were fragmented by collisions to leave the asteroids of today.

Although the Sun had yet to begin nuclear fusion processes, temperatures in the inner Solar System were high enough to maintain such volatile substances as water, methane, and ammonia in a gaseous state; the planetesimals that gave rise to the INNER PLANETS were therefore formed mainly from the nonvolatile component of the nebula, such as iron and silicates. Farther from the embryo Sun, beyond the ASTEROID BELT, lower temperatures allowed volatiles to become important constituents of the GIANT PLANETS, their satellite retinues, and their ring systems. The condensation of dirty snowflakes in these regions accelerated the accretion process. The origin of the volatile-rich comets is more obscure, but they may have formed concurrently as planetesimals in the Saturn to Neptune region and near the outer edge of the Solar System's disk. When the planetesimals had reached Moon size, the low temperatures also made it possible for them to greatly augment their masses by attracting and retaining large quantities of the light elements hydrogen and helium from the surrounding nebula. This produced the huge atmospheres of the giant planets.

As the Sun continued to collapse, the density and temperature in its central core rose (see STAR FORMATION). Once the core temperature reached some ten million kelvin, the Sun began to generate energy by the nuclear fusion of hydrogen. The onset of fusion processes in the Sun set up the SOLAR WIND, which drove uncollected gas and dust grains from the Solar System. Heating of the protoplanets by gravitational contraction and interior radioactivity caused partial melting that led to the present internal differentiated structure of the planets. Impacts by remaining planetesimals scarred the surfaces of the planets and their satellites, although the Earth's craters have been largely removed by erosion. Cratering events continue on a much reduced scale to the present day as errant asteroids or cometary nuclei collide with the planets or their satellites.

The suggestion that a contracting nebula formed the Solar System was the basis of the NEBULAR HYPOTHESIS, popular during the 19th century. However this was unable to explain why most of the Solar System's angular velocity resides in the revolution of the planets, rather than in the rotation of the Sun, and was replaced by various ENCOUNTER THEORIES early in the 20th century. The renaissance of a nebular theory came with the realization that MAGNETOHYDRODYNAMIC forces would transfer angular momentum from the early Sun to its surrounding nebula, and that the Sun would shed further angular momentum through the solar wind. In fact, the early Sun might have been twice its present mass and might have lost a large percentage of its angular momentum during its T Tauri phase when the solar T TAURI WIND was a gale. Calculations incorporating these ideas also suggest that the solar nebula contained at least three solar masses of material, most of which was expelled again into interstellar space.

solar telescope a reflecting (or refracting) telescope plus associated instruments used in studying the Sun. The Sun is the only star whose disk can be resolved and studied by a telescope. The diameter of the solar image is given by $0.00931f$, where f is the focal length of the telescope primary mirror

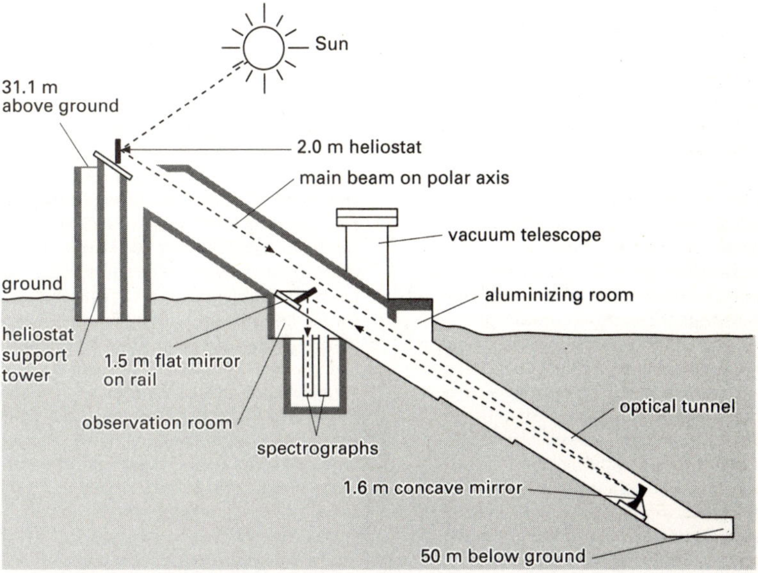

Optical path in McMath–Pierce Solar Telescope, Kitt Peak National Observatory

or objective. Long-focus telescopes must therefore be used in order for a large image to be formed. Such telescopes are usually fixed in position, with the sunlight being reflected on to the mirror or lens by a HELIOSTAT. This light is then directed in a fixed direction into a spectrograph or some other measuring instrument.

The intense heat of solar radiation requires the measuring instruments to be cooled. In some solar telescopes the entire building is cooled. In most cases the primary mirror and instruments are underground to facilitate this. The heat problem can be reduced by evacuating the air from the rooms housing the instruments and in some cases from the whole telescope housing.

Many large solar telescopes have been built as *tower telescopes* (or *solar towers*), in which the sunlight is directed down a vertical path inside a solid or girder construction and reflected into underground rooms containing the measuring instruments. In a *vacuum tower telescope*, the entire optical path is virtually air-free. The US NATIONAL SOLAR OBSERVATORY's vacuum tower telescope at Sacramento Peak, New Mexico, is 41 meters high with a further 67 meters underground; it has a 76-cm diameter mirror, FOCAL RATIO f/72. The 16-meter high Swedish solar tower on LA PALMA in the Canaries is patterned after the Sacramento Peak telescope, but has a more compact and optically simple system (50 cm, f/45 lens). Both telescopes give high-resolution images.

The *McMath–Pierce Solar Telescope* at the KITT PEAK NATIONAL OBSERVATORY, in Arizona, has a somewhat different design (see illustration). Sunlight is reflected from a 2.1-meter heliostat, which is 30 meters above the ground. It traverses 150 meters along the polar axis and is focused by a 1.6-meter concave mirror and a second flat mirror on to the various measuring instruments.

The best solar seeing is found above large lakes; in addition, a high altitude is required in order to reduce the disturbing effects of the Earth's atmosphere. The site of the BIG BEAR SOLAR OBSERVATORY, in California, has both these features.

Solar/Terrestrial Energy Programme (STEP) an international effort aimed at understanding the transfer of energy in the Solar System, and in particular on how energy reaches the Earth from the SOLAR WIND. It is a coordinated approach to understanding the physics of the Sun, plasma, and the heliosphere, combining results from satellite missions and ground-based observatories with theory and computer simulations. ESA's contribution has been twofold: the SOLAR HELIOSPHERIC OBSERVATORY (SOHO) and Cluster II (see CLUSTER).

solar time 1 *short for* mean solar time. 2 *short for* apparent solar time.

solar tower see SOLAR TELESCOPE.

solar units dimensionless units whereby the mass, luminosity, and other physical properties of a celestial body can be expressed in terms of the Sun's mass, luminosity, etc. For example, a star having 10 times the mass of the Sun is said to have a mass of 10 solar masses, or 10 $M_\odot$ (see SOLAR MASS). Likewise the luminosity of a source is frequently expressed as a multiple or fraction of the *solar luminosity*, $L_\odot$, which is equal to 3.826×10^{26} joules per second, and its radius in terms of the *solar radius*, $R_\odot$, equal to 1.392×10^6 km.

solar wind the flow of energetic charged particles – mainly PROTONS and ELECTRONS – from the solar CORONA into the INTERPLANETARY MEDIUM. The thermal energy of the ionized coronal gas is so great that the Sun's gravitational field cannot retain the gas in a confined static atmosphere. Instead, there is a continuous, near-radial, outflow of charged particles into interplanetary space. This highly tenuous PLASMA carries mass and angular momentum away from the Sun. The expansion is controlled by the Sun's magnetic field. The speed is low in the inner corona but rapidly becomes supersonic and reaches anywhere between 200 and 900 km s^{-1} at one astronomical unit, i.e. in the vicinity of the Earth's orbit. The density of the plasma decreases with increasing distance from the Sun, and at the Earth's orbit is only about eight particles per cm^3.

Two forms of the solar wind are readily recognizable: a slow-moving low-density flux (<400 km s^{-1}), and high-speed streams. The latter are thought to form the normal state and originate in areas of relatively weak divergent (and therefore primarily unipolar) magnetic field. The emission is greatly increased over CORONAL HOLES and the long-term stability of such regions may cause recurrent enhancement over several solar rotations. Similar long-lived jets are apparently emitted from the polar regions. Confinement by magnetic fields in the corona results in the slow-moving flow, and this is greatest around the maximum of the SUNSPOT CYCLE. In addition, transient mass ejections occur during FLARES and in some of the more frequent but less energetic active FILAMENTS/PROMINENCES (see CORONAL TRANSIENTS).

The Sun's magnetic field is transported by the expanding plasma and becomes the *interplanetary magnetic field*, the lines of which are wound into spirals by the Sun's rotation (see MAGNETOHYDRODYNAMICS). The region of expanding solar wind, or HELIOSPHERE, is bounded (at roughly 100–200 AU) by the heliopause.

solid-state detectors see GAMMA-RAY SOLID-STATE DETECTORS; INFRARED DETECTORS; CCD.

solstices 1 (**solstitial points**) the two points that lie on the ECLIPTIC midway between the vernal and autumnal EQUINOXES and at which the Sun, in its apparent annual motion, is at its greatest angular distance (23½°) north or south of the celestial equator.
2 the times at which the Sun reaches these points, on about June 21 and Dec. 22; the hours of daylight or of darkness are then at a maximum.

solstitial colure see COLURES.

solstitial points see SOLSTICES.

Sombrero galaxy (M104; NGC 4594) a spiral (Sa/Sb) galaxy in the constellation Virgo that has a relatively large bright nucleus and lies at a distance of 15 Mpc. The spiral structure is difficult to trace because the galaxy appears almost edge-on. A dark absorption band of interstellar dust in the galactic plane is clearly visible against the bright bulge component.

sonde a device, carried by rocket or balloon, for observations and measurements at high altitudes.

sounding rocket a rocket providing relatively inexpensive brief flights (typically 4–10 minutes) for studying the Earth's upper atmosphere and for making high-altitude astronomical observations. Information collected by instruments on board is radioed or sometimes parachuted back to Earth. First launched in 1946, sounding rockets are generally single-stage rockets. After completion of rocket motor firing they can coast upward before dropping back to Earth. The latest sounding rockets can reach an altitude of 1000 km.

source count (**number count**) a compilation of the number, *N*, of sources per unit solid angle that are brighter than a FLUX DENSITY level *S*. In Euclidean space the radius of the sphere out to which sources of a certain luminosity are observed varies as $S^{-1/2}$; the number of sources contained therein thus varies as $S^{-3/2}$. A plot of log *N* versus log *S* is a straight line of slope –1.5 and is independent of source luminosity. Deviations from this value may indicate source evolution, departures from a uniform space distribution, cosmological effects, or the effect of an intervening obscuring medium. Differential source counts (number per unit flux interval) are to be preferred when dealing with data since the errors on each point are then independent of other points. Radio source counts provided the first evidence for the BIG BANG THEORY as against STEADY-STATE THEORY. See also RADIO-SOURCE CATALOG.

south celestial pole see CELESTIAL POLES.

Southern African Large Telescope (**SALT**) a major telescope located at the main research and observing station of the *South African Astronomical Observatory* in Sutherland, in the Karoo region of the Northern Cape, South Africa. The telescope, which has a hexagonal mirror array measuring 11 meters in diameter, is the largest in the southern hemisphere, built at a cost of $30 million. Because of this high cost, SALT has had to be run as an international venture involving institutions from South Africa, Germany, New Zealand, Poland, the UK, and the USA. SALT is similar to the HOBBY-EBERLY TELESCOPE at the McDonald Observatory in Texas, USA, but employs redesigned optics to use a larger portion of the mirror array. Building of the telescope commenced in 2000 and it came into operation in 2005.

Southern Coalsack see COALSACK.

Southern Cross common name for CRUX.

Southern Sky Survey a photographic star atlas of the southern sky, comprising two sets of photographic plates covering overlapping areas of the sky and taken during the 1970s and 1980s. The celestial objects recorded were very much fainter and more distant than those on previous southern sky maps, and about four times as faint as objects on the PALOMAR OBSERVATORY SKY SURVEY of the northern and equatorial sky issued in the 1950s. The project was a joint effort involving the use of the 1.0-meter SCHMIDT TELESCOPE at the EUROPEAN SOUTHERN OBSERVATORY (ESO), Chile, and the 1.2-meter UK SCHMIDT telescope, funded by the UK Science and Engineering Research Council (SERC), at the ANGLO-AUSTRALIAN OBSERVATORY, Australia.

The UK Schmidt contribution was a set of sky-limited blue-sensitive plates; objects between a declination of –17° and –90° (the south celestial pole) were recorded, down to a magnitude of 22. The Southern Sky Survey was completed in 1984. The ESO Schmidt provided, 1987, a corresponding set of red-sensitive plates, covering the same area as the blue-sensitive plates. A further survey working northward toward the celestial equator was completed in 1998. Between 1985 and 1999, the UK Schmidt was used to take red plates for 'second epoch' survey of the southern sky. These plates, covering the same regions of sky as the red plates of the original Southern Sky Survey, are separated from them by a mean epoch difference of 15 years, thus allowing astronomers to check proper motions and other positional changes. Material from all the southern sky surveys was converted to digital format during the 1990s. Along with the material from the first and second Palomar Observatory Sky Surveys, the Southern Sky Survey data were incorporated into the First and Second Digitized Sky Surveys published by the SPACE TELESCOPE SCIENCE INSTITUTE.

south point see CARDINAL POINTS.

south polar distance the angular distance of a celestial body from the south celestial pole, measured along the object's hour circle.

Soyuz craft a series of Soviet crewed spacecraft, the first of which – Soyuz 1 – was launched Apr. 23 1967. The flight of Soyuz 1 ended tragically when its parachute became entangled during reentry and it crashed in Kazakhstan, killing its cosmonaut pilot Vladimir Komarov, the first person to die during a space mission. The program continued, however, and Soyuz 4 and 5 carried out the first docking of two spacecraft, and a transfer of crew, on Jan. 16 1969. In Oct. 1969 Soyuz achieved one of its most notable records, with three craft being launched in as many days, resulting in a total of seven cosmonauts being in space at the same time. In June 1971 three cosmonauts died aboard Soyuz 11 during a return trip from the space station Salyut 1. Further Soyuz launches were put on hold for three years.

In 1975, the Soyuz 19 spacecraft docked with the US Apollo 18 craft in the first international space effort, the APOLLO–SOYUZ TEST PROJECT. From then to the end of the 1990s, Soyuz craft ferried cosmonauts to and from the remaining SALYUT stations, and then from the MIR space station. From 1998, they shared the job of transporting personnel and materials to and from the INTERNATIONAL SPACE STATION with US space shuttles and carried on the task alone following the loss of Columbia in 2003 until shuttle flights resumed in 2005.

The Soyuz craft has undergone various design changes over the years, although it still carries some similarities to the VOSTOK and VOSHKOD craft of the early Soviet space era. The first notable changes came in 1980 with the introduction of the Soyuz T, which was equipped with more advanced electronics and navigation facilities and could carry three people instead of just two. In 1987 another upgrade, the Soyuz TM, was introduced for servicing Mir. It could act as a 'lifeboat' if Mir's computers failed and was equipped with life-support systems for the station's crew. The Soyuz TMA, now used for servicing the International Space Station, was introduced in 2002. It consists of three parts: the orbital module (the topmost and largest section, providing living accommodation and a working environment for the crew while in space), the reentry module (the central section, with room for three crew members and equipped with a climate control system, parachutes and retrorockets for the return to Earth), and the service module (the bottom section that carries the rocket fuel, oxygen tanks, thrusters, and communications and navigations equipment). Solar panels on the outside of the service module supply power to the whole craft while it is in space. Upgrades of the Soyuz, including the Soyuz-Fregat, are marketed by a Franco-Russian company, Starsem.

space the near-vacuum existing beyond the atmospheres of all bodies in the Universe. The extent of space, i.e. whether it is finite or infinite, is as yet unresolved. See INTERGALACTIC MEDIUM; INTERPLANETARY MEDIUM; INTERSTELLAR MEDIUM.

space density the spatial distribution of a type of astronomical object with redshift in the Universe. See LUMINOSITY FUNCTION; SOURCE COUNT.

Space Infrared Telescope Facility (SIRTF) original name of the SPITZER SPACE TELESCOPE.

Space Interferometry Mission (SIM) a spacebased astrometric observatory planned for launch by NASA in 2009. Placed in an Earth-trailing orbit around the Sun, SIM is designed to function as an optical Michelson interferometer operating over a wavelength range of 0.4–0.9 μm on a 10-meter baseline. The telescopic aperture is to be 0.3 meter. SIM is intended to measure the positions and distances of stars with unparalleled accuracy. With its silicon CCD detector it aims to achieve a precision of 1 microarcsecond (μas) in one measurement over a narrow field of view 1° in diameter. In this mode, SIM will search for planets orbiting nearby planets by detecting whether the stars 'wobble' relative to reference stars close to the same line of sight and by how much. For stars more widely separated, SIM aims to measure their absolute positions to an accuracy of 4 μas. These wide-angle measurements will be made relative to an astrometric grid of reference stars covering the whole sky. Construction of this grid is accomplished by repeatedly measuring the angle of separation between stars in overlapping grid boxes or 'tiles', each tile being 15° wide. The angle of 15° represents the area of sky accessible to SIM by retargeting the optical components without changing the attitude of the spacecraft. SIM aims to achieve a limiting magnitude of 20.

Spacelab a reusable space laboratory that was carried into Earth orbit as a payload aboard several of NASA's SPACE SHUTTLE missions between 1983 and 1998, and in which a team of scientists, known as *payload specialists*, were able to oversee or take part in short-term experiments devoted to science and technology. It remained in the cargo bay of the shuttle during an orbital flight. It was designed and constructed by ESA, and delivered to NASA in 1980. There were two basic sections in Spacelab: a long or short pressurized module in which the payload specialists could operate the experiments on board, and up to three unpressurized U-shaped 'pallets' or platforms on which instruments could be directly exposed to space. A pressurized tube connected the module to the shuttle's living quarters. Some Spacelab missions used only the pallets, together with a services module.

The first mission, Spacelab–1, was launched in Nov. 1983 and flew 72 experiments from ESA countries, the USA, Japan, and Canada, mainly devoted to human physiology and materials sciences. Spacelab–3, in Apr. 1985, had many microgravity experiments. Spacelab–2, in July 1985, was largely an astronomical mission; four telescopes were used on an ultraprecise pallet-mounted instrument-pointing system (IPS), which was also used in the ASTRO missions in Dec. 1990 and Nov. 1995. A joint German/ESA mission in Oct. 1985, Spacelab D1, flew microgravity and life-sciences experiments. There followed several dedicated series of missions: to the life sciences, starting with SLS–1 in June 1991; to microgravity, starting with IML–1 (the International Microgravity Laboratory) in Jan. 1992; and to atmospheric studies, with the Atmospheric Laboratory for Applications and Science (ATLAS–1) in Apr. 1992. The year 1992 also saw the Spacelab-J mission, a NASA collaboration with the Japanese space agency NASDA. This mission carried 34 US and Japanese experiments devoted to the life sciences and materials science. A joint US-Russian mission, Spacelab-Mir (Jun–Jul 1995) was carried aboard the space shuttle on a flight to the Mir space station, where life-sciences studies were carried out, including an evaluation of the Russian science research program, which sought to counter the effects of long stays in space. A final multinational Spacelab mission, designated Neurolab and devoted to a study of the nervous system in microgravity, was flown during April and May 1998.

spaceprobe see PLANETARY PROBE.

space shuttle a partially recoverable manned space transportation system developed and tested by NASA. The first orbital test flight, by the shuttle *Columbia*, took place on Apr. 12 1981, and the shuttle system, officially referred to by NASA as the space transportation system (STS), was operational by 1982. The shuttles *Challenger*, *Discovery*, and *Atlantis* were brought into service alongside Columbia in 1983, 1984, and 1985 respectively. Challenger was destroyed, and its seven-person crew killed, in an explosion on Jan. 28 1986, shortly after liftoff. Shuttle flights were then suspended until Sept. 1988. The shuttle *Endeavour* was built to replace Challenger, making its first flight in 1992. On Feb. 1 2003, Columbia broke up over Texas during its return from an orbital mission and was destroyed with the loss of all on board. Space shuttle flights were again suspended and did not resume until May 2005.

A shuttle consists of an *Orbiter* with the appearance of a delta-wing aircraft, a huge expendable external propellant tank, on which the Orbiter is mounted at launching, and two solid-fuel rocket boosters. The whole system weighs about 2000 tonnes at launch and has an overall length of about 56 meters. The Orbiter is 37 meters in length.

The shuttle is launched in a vertical position by the simultaneous firing of its two rocket boosters and three very powerful liquid hydrogen/liquid oxygen main engines. About two minutes into the flight the empty rocket boosters are detached, parachute into an ocean area, and are recovered for further use. Just before the craft reaches its orbit the propellant tank is discarded and burns up in the atmosphere. The Orbiter can then maneuver by means of two on-board engines. The altitude, eccentricity, and inclination of the orbit can be varied, within limits, as can the flight duration – between about 7 and 30 days. On mission completion the Orbiter uses its rocket motors to put it into a reentry path, enters the atmosphere in a shallow glide, and finally makes an unpowered landing like a conventional glider.

The Orbiter has a large cargo bay – 18.3 meters long and 4.6 meters in diameter – in which the payload is housed. SPACELAB first flew in the cargo bay in 1983. Satellites can be launched into orbit from the cargo bay and can also be brought back into the bay for servicing and redeployment or for return to Earth. Since the Challenger disaster, unpiloted boosters such as the Deltas have been used as the main launch vehicles for astronomy missions. But the space shuttle was employed for carrying the HUBBLE SPACE TELESCOPE into orbit in 1990 and later for service and repair missions to it. The shuttles are also used for medical, scientific, and technological experiments conducted by the astronauts. A total mass of 29.5 tonnes can be carried into a low-altitude orbit, with smaller loads for higher or less accessible orbits. Payloads to be placed in orbits above the shuttle ceiling, such as a geostationary orbit, require additional propulsion; the shuttle ceiling is about 1000 km in altitude. A payload of 11.5 tonnes can be returned to Earth.

In 1995 a shuttle made the first of several flights to and from the Russian space station MIR, in preparation for the construction and utilization of the INTERNATIONAL SPACE STATION (ISS). In 1998 shuttles and Russian SOYUZ CRAFT embarked upon the process of building the ISS, ferrying components into orbit and transferring personnel to and from the ISS modules as they were assembled. The suspension of shuttle flights after the loss of the Columbia temporarily halted the shuttles' contribution to this activity, but their collaboration in completing the ISS were scheduled to resume when they returned to service.

space station an orbiting space laboratory, with a lifetime of several years or more, on which people can live and work in controlled but weightless conditions. Crews are ferried to and from the station and remain on board either for short periods or on a continuous or near continuous rota basis. The first Soviet SALYUT space station was launched in 1971, and the one-off US SKYLAB station went into space in 1973. There followed six more Salyut stations before 1986, when the Soviet Union launched MIR, a modular space station that functioned almost continuously until it was abandoned in 1999. In its later years it was a focus of international cooperations, especially between Russia and the United States. It fell to Earth, burning up in the atmosphere, in 2001. The INTERNATIONAL SPACE STATION (ISS) is a venture involving contributions from 16 countries. Assembly of the ISS began in 1998, and the first long-stay crew took up residence there in Nov. 2000.

Space Telescope Science Institute (STScI) a research institute in Baltimore, Maryland, that defines the observing program of the HUBBLE SPACE TELESCOPE and collects the data on behalf of participating scientists. It is operated by a consortium of US universities (AURA) under contract to NASA.

spacetime the single physical entity into which the concepts of space and time can be unified such that an event may be specified mathematically by four coordinates, three giving the position in space and one the time. The path of a particle in spacetime is called its *world line.* The world line links events in the history of the particle.

The concept of spacetime was used by Einstein in both the special and the general theories of RELATIVITY. In special theory, where only INERTIAL FRAMES are considered, spacetime is flat. In the presence of gravitational fields, treated by general relativity, the geometry of spacetime changes: it becomes curved. The rules of geometry in curved space are not those of three-dimensional Euclidean geometry.

Matter tells spacetime how to curve: massive objects produce distortions and ripples in the local spacetime. The question of whether the spacetime of the real Universe is curved, and in what sense, has yet to be resolved. If the Universe contains sufficient matter, i.e. if the MEAN DENSITY of the Universe is high enough, then the spacetime of the Universe must be bent round on itself and closed.

space velocity see RADIAL VELOCITY.

spallation a particularly vigorous type of nuclear reaction in which several particles or nuclei result from a high-speed collision. Spallation occurs when COSMIC RAYS collide at high speed with atomic nuclei, the heavier nuclei breaking up to produce lighter nuclei.

spark chamber a device in which the tracks of charged particles are made visible and their location in space accurately recorded. It consists essentially of a stack of narrowly spaced thin plates or grids in a gaseous atmosphere, partially surrounded by one or more auxiliary particle detectors such as SCINTILLATION COUNTERS. Any particle detected in one of the auxiliary devices triggers the application of a high-voltage pulse to the stack of plates. The passage of the particle through the plates is then marked by a series of spark discharges along its path. The tracks are recorded by electronic or photographic means. Use of the auxiliary devices leads to a select triggering of the chamber for a particular type of energy or radiation. Spark chambers can be used to detect gamma rays following their conversion to an electron-positron pair.

spatial resolution see RESOLUTION.

Special Astrophysical Observatory the main observing facility, for optical and radio astronomy, of the Academy of Sciences of the former USSR. It is located in the Russian Caucasus between the Black Sea and Caspian Sea. The instruments include the 6-meter optical telescope at ZELENCHUKSKAYA OBSERVATORY and the RATAN 600 radio telescope.

special relativity see RELATIVITY, SPECIAL THEORY.

speckle interferometry a technique whereby the limit to the RESOLUTION of a telescope, imposed not by its design but by atmospheric turbulence (see SEEING), may be considerably improved: factors of 50 have been reported. A typical stellar image has, at best, a diameter given by that of the diffraction-limited AIRY DISK; atmospheric turbulence however causes small continuous erratic movements in image position on a long-exposure photograph, producing a final blurred image enlarged many times. In optical speckle interferometry and its more recent infrared counterpart, many short exposures (10–20 milliseconds) of the object are taken in rapid succession. These freeze the effects of turbulence so that the individual 'speckles' making up the overall image are distortion-free stellar images: those of supergiants are relatively large, those of binary stars are double. Substantial differences between the speckles of the many short exposures require the application of statistical analysis to the images. This leads to a range of information, including the separation and other properties of close binary stars, often hitherto unresolvable. In addition reconstructions have been achieved of the disks of supergiants, such as Betelgeuse; apparent diameters can thus be measured and large-scale surface details discerned. Very small areas of the Sun have also been studied.

spectral classes see SPECTRAL TYPES.

spectral flux density (spectral power flux density) see FLUX DENSITY.

spectral index the index, α, expressing how the FLUX DENSITY (S) of a radio source varies with frequency (ν). The spectrum is taken to be a power law so that either $S \propto \nu^{\alpha}$ or $S \propto \nu^{-\alpha}$. Because α is frequently stated without its sign, it is important to be clear which definition is being used in every case.

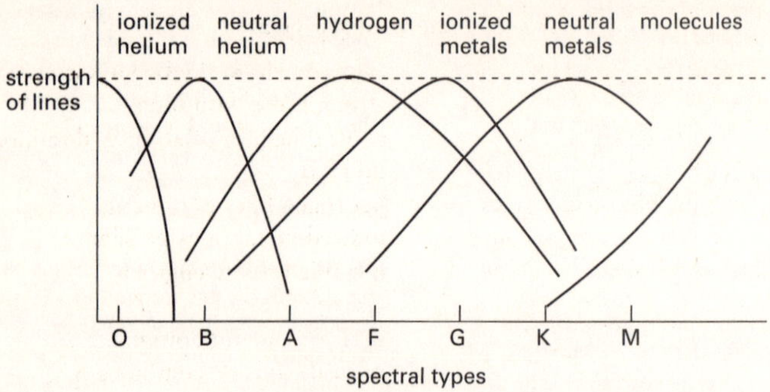

Spectral absorption features of spectral types

See also POWER-LAW SPECTRUM; RADIO-SOURCE SPECTRUM.

spectral lines see ABSORPTION SPECTRUM; EMISSION SPECTRUM; LINE SPECTRUM.

spectral types (**spectral classes**) the different groups into which stars may be classified according to the characteristics of their SPECTRA, principally the absorption lines and bands resulting from the presence of particular atoms and molecules in the star. Spectral lines of the various elements and compounds have widely different strengths in stars of different temperatures: this is the basis of the current classification. In the *Secchi classification* made in the 1860s by the Italian Angelo Secchi, stars were divided into four groups based on the visual observation of spectra. The subsequent development of photographic spectroscopy allowed a much more precise division. The *Harvard classification* was introduced by astronomers at Harvard Observatory in the 1890s and used in subsequent volumes of the HENRY DRAPER CATALOG. It was developed into its present form in the 1920s by E.C. Pickering, Annie J. Cannon, and others.

The original scheme was based on the strength of the hydrogen Balmer absorption lines in stellar spectra (see HYDROGEN SPECTRUM), the order being alphabetical from A to P: A stars had the strongest hydrogen lines. Some letters were later dropped and the ordering rearranged to correspond to a sequence of decreasing surface temperature. The majority of stars can be divided into seven spectral types – O, B, A, F, G, K, M – the order often remembered by the mnemonic 'Oh Be A Fine Girl (or Guy) Kiss Me'. The principal spectral features of these classes are shown on the graph (above) and listed in Table (facing) and also at separate entries: O STARS, B STARS, etc. Since temperature and COLOR are directly linked the Harvard classification is also a sequence of colors ranging from hot blue O stars to cool red M stars. Additional classes are the CARBON STARS (C stars) and the S STARS. The spectral types are further subdivided into 10 subclasses denoted by digits 0 to 9 placed after the spectral type letter, as with A5 – midway between A0 and F0. These subdivisions are based on a variety of complex empirical criteria, mainly the ratios of certain sets of lines in a spectrum, and may be further subdivided, as with O9.5. Other spectral characteristics, such as the presence of emission lines, are indicated by an additional small letter placed after the spectral type, as with M5e.

It was realized in the 1890s that stars of a particular spectral type could have widely differing LUMINOSITIES and several luminosity classifications were developed. The currently used *MK system* was first published in 1941 by W.W. Morgan and P.C. Keenan of Yerkes Observatory: stars of a

Spectral Features of Star Types

O	hottest blue stars	ionized helium (HeII) lines dominant strong UV continuum
B	hot blue stars	neutral helium (HeI) lines dominant no HeII
A	blue, blue-white stars	hydrogen lines dominant ionized metal lines present
F	white stars	metallic lines strengthen H lines weaken
G	yellow stars	ionized calcium dominant metallic lines strengthen
K	orange stars	neutral metal lines dominant molecular bands strengthen
M	coolest red stars	molecular bands dominant neutral metal lines strong

Nonstandard Spectral Features

e	emission lines present
n	diffuse lines
s	sharp lines
k	interstellar lines present
m	metallic lines present
p	peculiar spectrum
v	variable
wk	weak lines

Luminosity Classes

Ia	bright supergiants
Ib	supergiants
II	bright giants
III	giants
IV	subgiants
V	main sequence (dwarfs)
VI	subdwarfs
VII	white dwarfs

given spectral type are further classified into one of six *luminosity classes*, denoted by Roman numerals placed after the spectral type, as with G2 V, and indicating whether the star is a SUPERGIANT, GIANT, SUBGIANT, or MAIN-SEQUENCE STAR; SUBDWARFS and WHITE DWARFS are also sometimes considered as luminosity classes. All these classes occupy distinct positions on the HERTZSPRUNG–RUSSELL DIAGRAM. Stars of a similar temperature but different luminosities must differ in surface area and consequently in SURFACE GRAVITY and atmospheric density. These differences produce spectral effects that are used to differentiate between the luminosity classes. A major effect is the PRESSURE BROADENING of spectral lines, which increases as the atmospheric density and pressure increase (and radius decreases): spectral lines of a bright supergiant are much narrower than those of a main-sequence star of the same spectral type. The spectra of a set of standard stars are used in assigning spectral type and luminosity class to a star.

spectrograph an optical instrument used in separating and recording the spectral components of light or other radiation. Spectrographs are a major astronomical tool for analysing the emission and absorption spectra of stars and other celestial objects. They are used with reflecting (or refracting) telescopes, usually

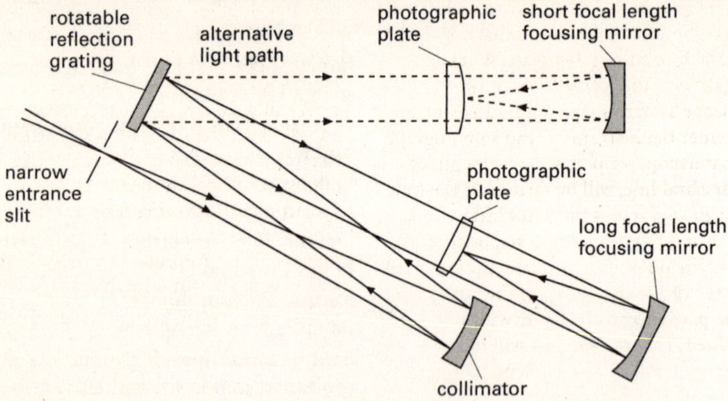

Optical path in spectrograph

mounted at the Cassegrain focus. If the telescope has a coudé or Nasmyth facility a spectrograph can be permanently positioned at these foci: such spectrographs are used for high-dispersion work. The *dispersion* of a spectrograph is the linear separation of spectral lines per unit wavelength difference, often quoted in millimeters per nanometer or per angstrom. The wavelength range over which the instrument will operate depends on the recording medium, and also on the optical elements of the device, but is generally in the region 300–1300 nanometers – i.e. light, near-infrared, and near-ultraviolet wavelengths.

The radiation is focused on and enters the instrument through a narrow rectangular slit. The diverging beam is made parallel by a collimator – a converging mirror or lens – and falls on or passes through a DIFFRACTION GRATING or prism. The beam is thus split into its component wavelengths. This spectrum is focused on a photographic plate or an electronic IMAGING device. Large quantities of digital information from highly sensitive electronic devices, such as CCD detectors, can be fed into a computer for rapid analysis and manipulation. The *chromatic resolution* or *resolving power* of a spectrograph is a measure of the detectable separation of wavelengths that are very nearly equal. It is given by the ratio $\lambda/\Delta\lambda$, if at a wavelength λ it is just possible to distinguish between two spectral lines of wavelength difference $\Delta\lambda$. In a large spectrograph, such as that in the illustration, there is often a choice of mirrors, of different focal lengths, for focusing the spectral image on the recording medium and also a choice of diffraction gratings.

spectroheliogram a photograph of the solar CHROMOSPHERE taken in the MONOCHROMATIC light of certain strong FRAUNHOFER LINES – usually the hydrogen-alpha (Hα) line of neutral hydrogen at 656.3 nm or the K line of singly ionized calcium at 393.4 nm – using a SPECTROHELIOGRAPH. When a photograph is taken using a telescope equipped with a suitable narrow-band INTERFERENCE FILTER, it is usually called a *filtergram*. By changing the wavelength slightly, different levels in the chromosphere can be photographed and information obtained on the vertical extent of any features present.

spectroheliograph a high-dispersion SPECTROGRAPH designed to be used, usually with a SOLAR TELESCOPE, for studying the Sun's spectrum and for obtaining photographs of the Sun at particular wavelengths, such as that of the HYDROGEN-ALPHA (Hα) line at 656.3 nm. In addition to an entrance slit, the instrument has a second narrow slit situated directly in front of the photographic plate so that only one spectral line falls on the plate. When the first slit is at the prime focus of the telescope a narrow strip of the Sun's image will enter the instrument and a photograph of that narrow strip, at the wavelength of the spectral line, will be formed. If the first slit is moved across the Sun's image, and the second slit is moved in step with it across the photographic plate, a photograph – a SPECTROHELIOGRAM – of the whole Sun, at the particular wavelength, will be obtained. This photograph will be composed of tiny line elements maybe 0.03 nm wide.

spectrohelioscope the optical counterpart of the SPECTROHELIOGRAPH, the principal difference being that both the entrance slit and secondary (viewing) slit are given a rapid oscillatory movement that enables the whole (or a part) of the Sun's disk to be seen by virtue of the observer's persistence of vision. Nowadays observation of the Sun in MONOCHROMATIC light is routinely undertaken using automatic photographic patrol telescopes utilizing a narrow-band INTERFERENCE FILTER, but the spectrohelioscope is still used at some observatories and by serious amateurs, particularly for measuring the velocities of material Doppler-shifted away from the center of the hydrogen-alpha (Hα) line.

spectrometer 1 an instrument, such as a SPECTROGRAPH, in which the spectrum of a source of radiation is produced, especially one in which the spectrum is recorded by electronic means so that wavelength, intensity, etc., can be measured. Spectrometers covering various wavelength ranges are used in ground-based and satellite and spaceprobe measurements. 2 an instrument for determining the distribution of energies in a beam of particles.

spectrophotometer an instrument designed to measure the intensity of a particular spectral line or a series of spectral lines in an absorption or emission spectrum.

spectroscopic binary a BINARY STAR in which the orbital motions of the components give rise to detectable variations in RADIAL VELOCITY, revealed by changes in DOPPLER SHIFT in their spectral lines (see illustration). Because a binary star is more likely to be detected spectroscopically if its orbital period is relatively short and the orbital velocities are relatively high, most spectroscopic binaries are close binaries (see BINARY STAR). Spectroscopic detection is not possible if the orbital plane lies at right angles to the line of sight.

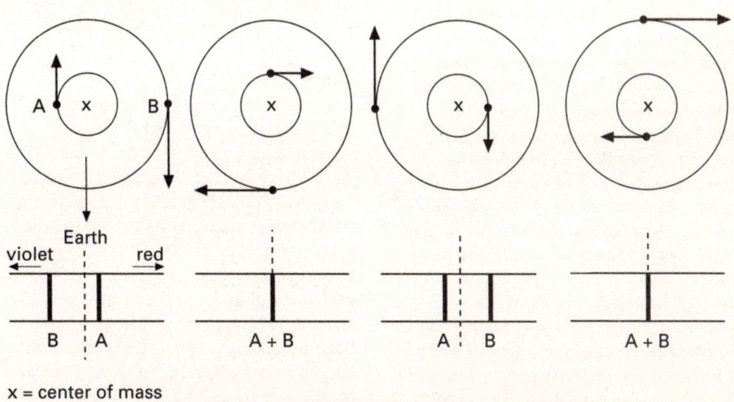

Doppler shifts of spectral lines at various orbital positions of spectroscopic binary

When the components are nearly equal in brightness both spectra are visible and the spectral lines appear double for most of each orbital period, coinciding only when the stars are moving at right angles to the line of sight. Such a system is called a *double-lined spectroscopic binary*. Comparison of the Doppler shifts in the component spectra gives the relative velocities and hence the relative masses of the two stars:

$$v_1/v_2 = M_2/M_1$$

The individual masses cannot be determined unless the inclination of the orbital plane to the line of sight is known (see ECLIPSING BINARY).

The presence of a comparatively faint component is revealed only by its gravitational effect on the motion of the brighter star. Invisible components of low mass are rarely detected because doppler shifts corresponding to orbital speeds of less than about 2 km s^{-1} are obscured by observational errors. See also MASS FUNCTION.

spectroscopic parallax see PARALLAX.

spectroscopy in general, the production and interpretation of spectra. The application of spectroscopy to the study of the light of celestial bodies began in the late 19th century. Astronomical spectroscopy is now used over the whole range of ELECTROMAGNETIC RADIATION from radio waves to gamma rays. It is the main source of information on the composition, temperature, and nature of celestial bodies.

The lines and bands in EMISSION and ABSORPTION SPECTRA are characteristic of the atoms, molecules, and ions producing them, and *spectral analysis* leads to the identification of these components in planetary atmospheres, comets, stars, nebulae, galaxies, and in the interstellar medium. Measurements of the intensities of spectral lines (*spectrophotometry*) can give quantitative information on the chemical composition.

In addition, spectroscopy yields information on the physical conditions and the processes occurring in celestial bodies. For instance, temperature may be measured by the vibrational excitation of molecules (if present) through analysis of the intensities of the individual lines in their band spectra. The degree of ionization can be used to measure higher temperatures. The width and shape of spectral lines indicates temperature, movement, pressure, and the presence of magnetic fields (see LINE BROADENING; ZEEMAN EFFECT). The processes occurring are often directly responsible for the production of the spectra, as in the recombination of ions and electrons in H II regions or synchrotron emission from electrons in magnetic fields. See also DOPPLER EFFECT; REDSHIFT.

spectrum a display or record of the distribution of intensity of ELECTROMAGNETIC RADIATION with wavelength or frequency. Thus, the spectrum of a celestial body is obtained by dispersing that radiation from it into its constituent wavelengths so that the wavelengths present and their intensities can be observed. A variety of techniques exist for obtaining spectra, depending on the part of the electromagnetic spectrum studied. The result may be a photographic record (as can be obtained in a SPECTROGRAPH) or a plot of intensity against wavelength or frequency (as can be produced by electronic and associated equipment).

The spectrum of a particular source of electromagnetic radiation depends on the processes producing emission of radiation (see EMISSION SPECTRUM) and/or on the way in which radiation is absorbed by intermediate material (see ABSORPTION SPECTRUM). Spectra are also classified by their appearance. A LINE SPECTRUM has discrete lines caused by emission or absorption of radiation at fixed wavelengths. A BAND SPECTRUM has distinctive bands of absorption or emission. A CONTINUOUS SPECTRUM occurs when continuous emission or absorption takes place over a wide range of wavelengths. See also SPECTROSCOPY.

spectrum variables (**α^2 CVn stars**) peculiar main-sequence AP STARS whose spectra have anomalously strong lines of metals and rare earths (Sr, Eu, Mn, Si, Cr) that vary in intensity by about 0.1 magnitudes over periods of about 1–25 days. These variations are related to changes in the stars' magnetic

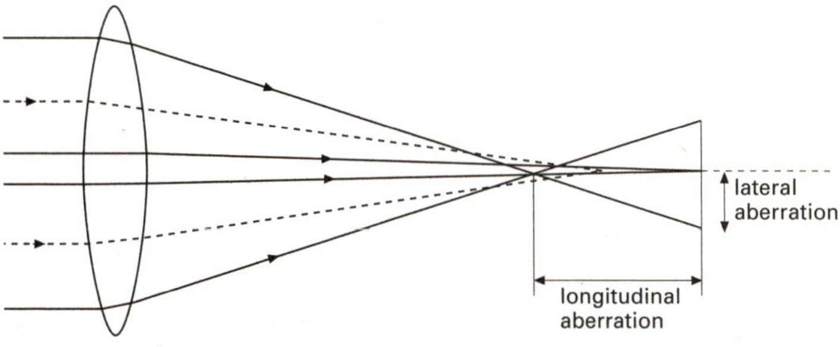

Spherical aberration in convex lens

fields. The brighter component of the binary star COR CAROLI (α^2 CVn) is typical.

Spectrum–X the first in a series of large astrophysics satellites developed in the former Soviet Union, planned for launch into an elliptical, 4-day period orbit on a Proton rocket. The 2.8-tonne scientific payload of Spectrum–X includes four main instruments: SODART, a large GRAZING INCIDENCE telescope equipped with imaging PROPORTIONAL COUNTERS, solid-state detectors, a polarimeter, and Bragg crystal spectrometers (a collaboration of Russian, Danish, US, and other nations); JET–X, a pair of higher-resolution telescopes feeding cooled CCDS (from the UK and Italy); MART, a high-energy X-ray telescope (an Italian/Russian collaboration); and EUVITA, an array of normal-incidence multilayer XUV telescopes (from Switzerland and Russia). Funding problems have delayed the launch of Spectrum-X, originally set for 1995, to 2001/2.

speculum metal an alloy of copper and tin used by Newton and his successors to make telescope mirrors because it could easily be cast, ground to shape, and took a good polish. It was made obsolete by the use of glass provided with a thin highly reflective silver coating.

speed of light symbol: *c*. The constant speed at which light and other ELECTROMAGNETIC RADIATION travels in a vacuum. It is equal to 299 792 458 m s^{-1} (value adopted by the IAU in 1976). Since space is not a perfect vacuum, radiation travels through space at a very slightly lower speed, which decreases somewhat when the radiation enters the Earth's atmosphere. The speed of light, *c*, is independent of the velocity of the observer: there can therefore be no relative motion between an observer and a light beam, i.e. the speed of light cannot be exceeded in a vacuum. This radical notion was basic to Einstein's special theory of RELATIVITY.

spherical aberration (SA) an ABERRATION of a spherical lens or mirror in which light rays converge not to a single point but to a series of points whose distances from the lens or mirror decrease as the light rays fall nearer the periphery of the optical element (see illustration). It is most obvious with elements of large diameter. It can be considerably reduced by using an APLANATIC SYSTEM, which also reduces COMA, or by using a CORRECTING PLATE. Paraboloid surfaces are free of spherical aberration, but not of coma. See also SCHMIDT TELESCOPE.

spherical angle see SPHERICAL TRIANGLE.

spherical triangle a triangle on the surface of a sphere formed by the intersections of three great circles (see illustration). The arcs BC, AC, and AB form the sides of the spherical triangle ABC. The lengths of these sides (*a*, *b*, and *c*), in angular measure, are equal to the angles BOC, COA, and AOB, respectively, where O is the center of the sphere. This assumes a radius of unity. The angles between the planes are the *spherical angles* A, B, and C of the triangle.

The relationships between the angles and sides of spherical triangles are

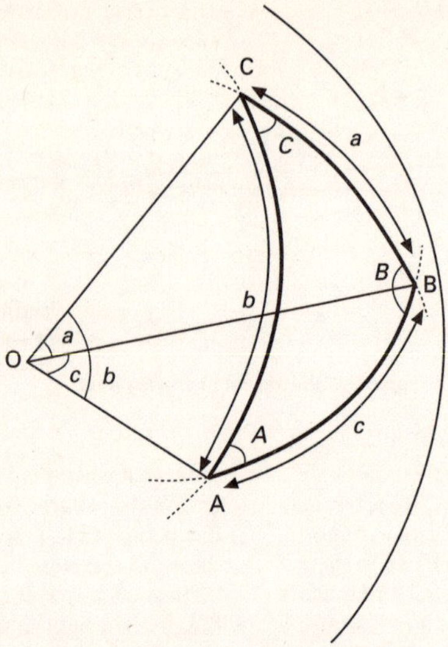

Spherical triangle

extensively used in ASTROMETRY. The three basic relationships are the *sine formula:*

$$\sin A/\sin a = \sin B/\sin b = \sin C/\sin c$$

the *cosine formula:*

$$\cos a = \cos b \cos c + \sin b \sin c \cos A$$
$$\cos b = \cos a \cos c + \sin a \sin c \cos B$$
$$\cos c = \cos a \cos b + \sin a \sin b \cos C$$

and the *extended cosine formula,* which can be derived from the other two.

For a *spherical right-angled triangle,* in which one angle, say C, is equal to 90° so that sin C = 1, cos C = 0, the formulae are much simplified. They are also simplified if the sides of the triangle are small so that, say, sin a tends to a and cos a to $1-a^2/2$. As a, b, and c approach zero the formulae reduce to those used in plane geometry. The formulae may be extended by replacing the sides and angles by the supplements of the corresponding angles and sides, respectively. Thus

$$\sin A = \sin a, \cos A = -\cos a$$

spheroid see ELLIPSOID.

spherules small round particles of rock and wüstite (iron oxide) formed by the solidification of molten meteoritic material that flows off a meteorite during its passage through the Earth's atmosphere. Magnetic spherules can easily be recognized in deep sea sediments. Sizes range typically from 10 µm to 200 µm.

Spica (α Vir) a conspicuous blue-white star that is the brightest one in the constellation Virgo. It is an ECLIPSING BINARY, period 4.014 days, the primary (A) being a BETA CEPHEI STAR near to core hydrogen exhaustion. Spica, Denebola, Arcturus, and Cor Caroli form the quadrilateral shape of the *Diamond of Virgo.* m_v: 0.98 (var.); M_v: –3.2; spectral type: B1 V; distance: 67 pc.

spicules predominantly vertical narrow (1000-km diameter) jets of gas, visible (in the monochromatic light of certain strong FRAUNHOFER LINES) beyond the Sun's limb. They ascend with velocities of up to 20–30 km s^{-1} from the lower CHROMOSPHERE for several thousand kilometers into the inner CORONA and then fall back and/or fade away. Their average lifetime is 5–10 minutes. They are closely associated with the CHROMOSPHERIC NETWORK, being located in regions of enhanced vertical magnetic field at the boundaries of supergranular cells (see SUPERGRANULATION), and have temperatures of the order of 10 000 to 20 000 K.

spider the diagonal support in a NEWTONIAN TELESCOPE.

spider diffraction the characteristic spikes of light in the form of a cross seen in the image formed by a Newtonian reflector. They result from diffraction effects caused by the diagonal supports – the spider – and are additional to the diffraction from the circular edge of an objective lens or a mirror, which converts a star image from a point to an AIRY DISK in refractors and reflectors.

spillover the part of the system noise (see SENSITIVITY) of a radio telescope using a DISH antenna that results from pick-up by the feed – the secondary antenna – from directions that do not intercept the reflecting surface of the dish.

spin 1 a fundamental intrinsic property of ELEMENTARY PARTICLES and atomic nuclei that describes the state of rotation of the particle or nucleus, i.e. its intrinsic angular momentum.
2 a quantum number that determines the values of this property and is either a whole or half integer. See also FERMIONS; BOSONS.

spiral arms see DENSITY-WAVE THEORY; GALAXIES; GALAXY; SELF-PROPAGATING STAR FORMATION.

spiral galaxy (**spiral**) see GALAXIES; HUBBLE CLASSIFICATION.

Spirit see MARS EXPLORATION ROVERS.

Spitzer Space Telescope an infrared astronomy space observatory launched Aug. 2003. It was the fourth and last of NASA's GREAT OBSERVATORIES and was also a significant scientific and technical element in the agency's long-term Origins Program. Lifted into space from Cape Canaveral, Florida, USA, by a Boeing Delta rocket, Spitzer was placed in an orbit around the Sun, following in the Earth's wake. Initially it was dubbed the *Space Infrared Telescope Facility* (*SIRTF*) but was renamed after launch to commemorate the US astrophysicist Lyman Spitzer, Jr, the first astronomer to propose placing a large telescope in space and one of the leading scientists involved in the development of the HUBBLE SPACE TELESCOPE. The 950-kg Spitzer spacecraft consists of a reflecting telescope with a beryllium mirror measuring 8.5 millimeters in diameter (focal ratio f/12), in the focal plane of which lie three cryogenically cooled science instruments incorporating technically advanced, large-format infrared detector arrays. Spitzer is designed to carry out imaging and photometry over the wavelength range of 3–180 micrometers (μm), spectroscopy over 5–40 μm, and spectrometry over 50–100 μm. The telescope and detectors are surrounded by liquid helium, which maintains them at their operating temperature of less than 5.5 K. NASA astronomers hope to operate the Spitzer Space Telescope for five years or more, using it to identify and investigate dusty disks around nearby stars that may be planet nurseries, to peer into clouds of dust and gas that may be the cradles of newborn stars, and to gaze beyond the Milky Way at very luminous infrared galaxies powered by gigantic black holes.

sporadic meteor a METEOR that is not associated with a specific METEOR SHOWER.

Spörer's law see SUNSPOT CYCLE.

sprays impulsive events on the Sun that are characterized by the ejection of chromospheric material into the inner CORONA with velocities exceeding the ESCAPE VELOCITY (618 km s^{-1}). They invariably occur during the 'flash phase' of FLARES and are less confined than SURGES, their material fragmenting as it flies out. See also PROMINENCES.

spring equinox *another name for* vernal equinox. See EQUINOXES.

Springfield mount see COUDÉ TELESCOPE.

spring tide see TIDES.

s-process a slow process of NUCLEOSYNTHESIS by which heavy stable nuclei are synthesized from the iron-peak elements (mass number 56) by successive captures of neutrons. The process occurs when there is a low density of neutrons in a star, the neutrons being by-products of nuclear-fusion reactions. If the nucleus produced by a neutron capture is stable it will eventually capture another neutron; if the nucleus is radioactive it will have sufficient time to emit a beta particle (i.e. an electron) to stabilize itself before further neutron capture. Thus the stable isotopes of an element are synthesized until a radioisotope is produced, at which point a new element forms by beta decay. Many years or decades may elapse between successive neutron captures. The most abundant nuclei produced by the s-process will be those with a low ability to capture neutrons. The s-process cannot synthesize nuclei beyond bismuth–209 because neutron capture by this nuclei results in rapid alpha decay. Compare R-PROCESS.

Sputnik any of a series of Soviet artificial satellites, the first of which – Sputnik 1 – was the first spacecraft to be placed in orbit. This 58-cm diameter sphere, weighing 84 kg, was launched on Oct. 4 1957; it burnt up in the Earth's atmosphere 92 days later. The orbit had a period of 96 minutes, an apogee and perigee (highest and lowest altitudes) of about 950 km and 230 km, and was inclined at 65° to the equator. Its radio signals were transmitted every 0.6 seconds. It contained few instruments, being intended as a test vehicle. The launching of Sputnik 1 had a profound effect in accelerating America's space program.

Sputnik 2, launched on Nov. 3 1957, was very much bigger. It carried about 500 kg in payload, including a live dog, Laika, which survived the launch, as well as 10 experiments. Sputnik 3, launched on May 15 1958, weighed about 1330 kg and remained in orbit for 691 days.

Square Kilometer Array (SKA) An international design project for a highly sensitive radio astronomical telescope operating between 0.15 and 20 GHz with an effective collecting area of one square kilometer. Countries involved include Australia, Canada, China, India, the Netherlands, the USA, and the UK.

SR variables see SEMIREGULAR VARIABLES.

SS433 a close BINARY STAR in Aquila that is ejecting a pair of oppositely directed jets at very extreme speed. It lies at a distance of 5 kiloparsecs in the old supernova remnant W50. The star system appears faint optically but is characterized by strong hydrogen emission lines, which led to its inclusion in the Stephenson–Sanduleak (SS) catalog of such stars (1977); its optical variability has led to an alternative variable-star designation, V1343 Aquilae. It is an X-ray source, discovered by Ariel V in 1976. It is also a radio source and a gamma-ray source. The discovery that it has weak hydrogen emission lines that move considerably in wavelength led to intense investigation and analysis in 1978–81; the following picture has emerged.

SS433 comprises a fairly normal star that is transferring mass at a high rate to a compact companion; as in other X-RAY BINARIES, the gas forms an accretion disk around the compact star. This hot accretion disk produces most of the system's light so that the nature of the normal star is not evident. It is probably a star of a few times the Sun's mass losing matter to a NEUTRON STAR or BLACK HOLE (see MASS TRANSFER). These two stars have an orbital period of 13 days, and the stars and the accretion disk form a partially ECLIPSING BINARY system.

Two jets of gas stream off the faces of the accretion disk, at a constant speed of 80 000 km s^{-1}. The disk precesses in a period of 164 days, so that the jets trace out a cone on each side with an opening angle of 40°. The component of velocity along the line of sight thus varies periodically, and the changing DOPPLER EFFECT causes the emission lines from the jets to move up and down the spectrum as the wavelength varies with the 164-day cycle. Radio observations show the precessing jets out to a distance of 0.05 parsecs; the Einstein Observatory recorded their X-ray emission in a broader band at distances up to 30 pc to each side, where they strike the surrounding supernova remnant W50. EXOSAT and GINGA observations showed that the innermost regions of each jet to be eclipsed by the normal star and to have a temperature of several million degrees.

SS433 may represent a transitory phase in the evolution of many X-ray binaries, and its apparent uniqueness may indicate that fast jets are only a short-lived phenomenon. The final outcome may be a THORNE–ŻYTKOW OBJECT. Two other instances of stars located within supernova remnants resemble SS433 superficially, and a similar phenomenon is apparently occurring on a more moderate scale in the jet-emitting SYMBIOTIC STAR R Aquarii.

SS Cygni the brightest DWARF NOVA.

Normally of 12th magnitude, it rises to maybe 8th magnitude every month or so: its period varies widely from the mean of 51 days; the maxima vary in shape, brightness, and duration. Like other dwarf novae it is a close binary system in which one component is a white dwarf; the other is a normal G5 star. The orbital period is 6.5 hours. SS Cygni is also an intense, soft X-ray source, i.e. an X-RAY BINARY.

S stars (**zirconium stars**) stars of SPECTRAL TYPE S, about half of which are IRREGULAR long-period variables. They are red giants similar to M STARS but distinguished spectroscopically by the presence of molecular bands of zirconium oxide (ZrO) rather than the oxides of titanium and vanadium. Pure S stars have very strong ZrO bands with either very weak or no TiO bands. *MS stars* are M-type stars showing ZrO bands. See also TECHNETIUM STARS.

standard candle see DISTANCE DETERMINATION.

standard epoch see EPOCH.

standard model the accepted but possibly incomplete theoretical framework for describing something such as the origin of the Universe, the processes in the interior of the Sun, or the interactions of elementary particles.

standard time the time in any of the 24 internationally agreed *time zones* into which the Earth's surface is divided; the primary division is centered on the Greenwich (0° longitude) meridian. All locations within a single zone keep the same time. Zone times differ by a whole number of hours, or in some cases of half hours, from GREENWICH MEAN TIME. Zones west of the Greenwich zone are behind GMT, those east of it are in front of GMT.

star a luminous gaseous body that generates energy by means of nuclear fusion reactions in its core. Below a certain mass (0.08 solar masses), the central pressures and temperatures in a body are insufficient to trigger fusion reactions; all stars must therefore exceed this mass limit. Stars of progressively higher mass are less and less common; the highest reliably determined values are about 60 to 120 solar masses, but there may be a very few more massive stars (see STELLAR MASS).

Although there is only a relatively narrow range in normal stellar masses, it is the mass of a star that determines its other properties – luminosity, temperature, size – and the way in which it evolves. These quantities are related to the mass by the equations of STELLAR STRUCTURE. Other stellar parameters show a far greater range than stellar mass: for example, the LUMINOSITY of a star is proportional to roughly the fourth power of its mass for a solar-type star, and the cube power of its mass for a massive star (see MASS-LUMINOSITY RELATION); stars therefore show a range in luminosity of some 10^{10}. A star's lifetime also depends on its mass: low-mass stars live considerably longer than high-mass ones.

All stars are composed predominantly of hydrogen and helium; this was first proposed in 1925 by Cecilia Payne-Gaposchkin and confirmed in 1929 by H.N. Russell. The proportions of the chemical elements in the SUN are not significantly different from those in most other stars. This general composition by mass is 70% hydrogen, 28% helium, with the remaining elements – known in astronomy as metals or heavy elements – making up just 2%; by numbers of atoms it is 90.8% hydrogen, 9.1% helium, 0.1% metals.

The characteristics of a star can be determined only when its distance is known. The method of DISTANCE DETERMINATION depends on the distance itself: the shortest distances are found directly by measuring a star's ANNUAL PARALLAX; greater distances require indirect methods. The nearest star, Proxima Centauri, is 1.3 parsecs away. The stars in our immediate locality are found in the main to be young stars occupying the outer parts of the disk of our Galaxy, rotating around the galactic center. Many still remain in open clusters, and over 50% of all the stars we observe are BINARY STARS or multiple stars.

See also MAGNITUDE; POPULATION I, POPULATION II; SPECTRAL TYPES; STAR FORMATION; STELLAR EVOLUTION; VARIABLE STAR.

star atlas a collection of maps of a particular region of the sky or of the whole sky, showing the relative positions of stars and other celestial objects down to a specified LIMITING MAGNITUDE. Many modern star atlases contain prints of photographic plates. The PALOMAR OBSERVATORY and SOUTHERN SKY SURVEYS and URANOMETRIA 2000.0 are examples. See also STAR CATALOG.

starburst galaxy a galaxy in which a massive burst of star formation is currently taking place: it is characterized by an infrared luminosity that is considerably larger than its optical luminosity, sometimes by a factor of 50 or more. The luminosity of starburst galaxies can compare to the bolometric luminosity of quasars, but is powered by a fundamentally different mechanism. The starburst occurs in a region over a kiloparsec in size, thus distinguishing these galaxies from ACTIVE GALAXIES, which have a tiny central powerhouse. A few nearby starburst galaxies (e.g. M82) have long been known from their disturbed optical appearance, but their widespread occurrence was only established when thousands were revealed by infrared satellite IRAS. They are basically spirals in which the star formation is proceeding at a rate that cannot be sustained for much of the lifetime of the galaxy. The trigger for the burst of star formation is unclear although in some cases the gravitational effect of a companion galaxy may be responsible (see INTERACTING GALAXIES). The new stars are still enveloped in the galaxy's dense MOLECULAR CLOUDS; their ultraviolet radiation is absorbed by dust in the clouds and reradiated as infrared. See also IRAS GALAXIES.

STARCAT *abbrev. for* Space Telescope Archive and Catalogue, a large computer database developed at the Space Telescope European Coordinating Facility and the headquarters of the European Southern Observatory, both in Garching, Germany. It allows users to access data from a large number of astronomical catalogs and databases.

star catalog a collection of data, compiled from observation, on stars in a specified area of the sky down to a specified LIMITING MAGNITUDE. For each entry it usually gives a position and apparent magnitude for identification, possibly with other information such as PROPER MOTION, RADIAL VELOCITY, SPECTRAL TYPE, etc. In a whole-sky catalog stars in both hemispheres will be included. Modern catalogs are divided into two general types: DURCHMUSTERUNGS, or *survey catalogs*, list a large number of stars whose positions are given with only moderate accuracy; *precision catalogs*, such as the FUNDAMENTAL CATALOG FK5 or the HIPPARCOS Catalog, give very precise positions for a relatively small number of stars. General catalogs include the BONNER DURCHMUSTERUNG and the AGK. There are also catalogs specifically for double stars, variable stars, nebulae, star clusters, galaxies, radio sources, X-ray sources, etc. Most new and revised catalogs are now made available in computerized form and may be accessed from many facilities over a computer network or over the Internet via the World Wide Web. See also CATALOG EQUINOX; STAR ATLAS.

star clouds areas of the sky where great numbers of stars are seen so close together that they appear as continuous irregular bright clouds. Star clouds are particularly noticeable in the direction of the galactic center in the constellation SAGITTARIUS.

star cluster see CLUSTER.

star density the number of stars per unit volume of space, usually per parsec cubed. It is often given in terms of the fraction of solar mass per volume. See also LUMINOSITY FUNCTION.

Stardust a NASA probe that was launched Feb. 7 1999 from Cape Canaveral, Florida, to rendezvous with Comet Wild 2 and collect particle samples from its coma for return to the Earth. The Stardust project formed part of NASA's Discovery program, dedicated to making low-cost investigations of the Solar System. It was managed for NASA by the JET PROPULSION LABORATORY, in Pasadena, California. Its target, Comet Wild 2, was discovered in 1978 by the astronomer Paul Wild. It travels around the Sun once every 6.39 years between the orbits of Mars and Jupiter. Stardust's journey to the comet took it across 3.2 billion kilometers of interplanetary space swept by cosmic rays, solar wind particles, and interstellar dust, and involved a gravity-assist flyby of the Earth in 2001 to speed it on its way. In 2000 and 2002, Stardust collected samples of interstellar dust. On Nov. 2 2002 the probe flew by asteroid (5535) Annefrank. Stardust encountered Comet Wild 2 on Jan. 2 2004, approaching to within 240 km of the comet. Protected by special shields from high-speed collisions with material blown off from the comet as it circles the Sun, the craft collected its samples of microscopic particles from the coma using a device that employs aerogel, a substance formed from silicon dioxide and air, as a particle trap. This device, which had also been used to capture the interstellar dust particles, was then folded down into the sealed sample-return capsule. The Stardust probe's on-board camera also captured detailed images of the comet and transmitted them back to Earth. Stardust returned to the vicinity of Earth on Jan. 15 2006, when it released the capsule, which entered Earth's atmosphere and made a parachute-assisted landing at the Utah Test and Training Range near Salt lake City. After this maneuver, the main Stardust craft entered permanent solar orbit.

star formation (stellar birth) stars are formed by the GRAVITATIONAL COLLAPSE of cool dense (10^9–10^{10} atoms per cubic meter) gas and dust clouds. Most are born in GIANT MOLECULAR CLOUDS; a few lower-mass stars condense from smaller molecular clouds and BOK GLOBULES. There are problems, however, in initiating the collapse of a gas cloud. It resists collapse because of firstly its internal motions and the heating effects of nearby stars, secondly the centrifugal support due to rotation, and thirdly the magnetic field pressure. In a massive dense cloud shielded by dust, it is believed that collapse can be triggered when the cloud is slowed on passing through the spiral density-wave pattern of our Galaxy (see DENSIRY-WAVE THEORY): it is noticeable that star formation preferentially occurs along spiral arms. Alternatively compression may be caused by a shock wave propagated by a nearby SUPERNOVA explosion – which may explain how stars are formed in galaxies without spiral arms or with only patchy spiral arms.

Once collapse starts, instabilities cause the cloud to divide into successively smaller fragments of about the Jeans mass (see GRAVITATIONAL INSTABILITY). At first, radiation can escape freely but eventually, when the cloud becomes dense enough, the OPACITY increases and the temperature rises, at which point fragmentation ceases. These final fragments are PROTOSTARS, which now collapse individually. This collapse is gentle at first but after some hundred thousand years (for a star of one solar mass) the density and temperature rise sharply at the center, forming a hot core that will be the future nucleus of the star. Theoretical models show that the protostar will contract along the HAYASHI TRACK in the HERTZSPRUNG–RUSSELL DIAGRAM. The slow contraction heats the core to a temperature of 10 million kelvin, which is sufficient to initiate NUCLEAR FUSION reactions in hydrogen. Once the nuclear energy source is established, the contraction is halted and the star joins the MAIN SEQUENCE.

Infrared and radio observations of star-formation regions are now filling out the theory. The infrared satellite IRAS found many small infrared sources within molecular clouds and Bok globules. Most are probably young stars still cocooned in dust, but a few may be true protostars. MOLECULAR-LINE radio astronomy has revealed the gas motions in regions of star formation. Predicted infall velocities are very low and are often masked by random motions in the gas. Despite this, infall has now possibly been detected in a few cases. In addition, surprisingly high velocity gas has been revealed near the young stars at the center, forming two oppositely directed beams – BIPOLAR OUTFLOWS – from the massive young stars. These outflows must affect star formation in the cloud, either disrupting protostars or promoting their formation by compressing the surrounding gas. Young stars are often surrounded by disks of dense gas and dust. The disks are apparently more common among single stars than in multiple-star systems, and may be the precursors of PLANETARY SYSTEMS. The gas in the disk may be spiraling inward and increasing the star's mass substantially, after hydrogen fusion begins. The effects of bipolar outflows and late accretion from a surrounding disk have yet to be incorporated into theoretical models; they may alter quite substantially the simple theory given above.

Although stars in small molecular clouds and Bok globules are often single, most stars form in dense clusters. Such clusters also contain compact gas clumps that emit powerful maser radiation from water molecules (see MASER SOURCE).

The young stars gradually dissipate the surrounding gas cloud by the effects of heating, RADIATION PRESSURE, and the gas outflows. The latter often break through first, indicating the presence of the star by an optical BIPOLAR NEBULA or a string of HERBIG–HARO OBJECTS. When massive O and B stars are present, they light up the residual gas as an H II REGION. The massive stars take the shortest time to form, 100 000 years or less, and are normal main-sequence stars by the time they become visible. Less-massive stars are seen while they are still contracting and have appreciable amounts of surrounding gas and dust: these *pre-main-sequence stars* appear as BE, AE, and T TAURI stars. A star like the Sun takes 50 million years to reach the main sequence.

star-formation efficiency (SFE) the fraction of gas in a given cloud or cloud complex that eventually ends up in the form of stars. The rest is presumed to be dispelled by STELLAR WINDS, BIPOLAR OUTFLOWS, and SUPERNOVA explosions before it can be incorporated into stars.

star-formation rate (SFR) the rate at which stars are formed in a given region, measured in units of solar masses per year. The SFR for the Galaxy is thought to be about 4 solar masses per year, but may be thousands of times higher in STARBURST galaxies.

star gauges systematic counts of stars in different regions of the sky. They were first made in the 1780s by William Herschel who counted the total number of stars visible in each of several adjoining areas within the region under study. By averaging the sample counts he obtained the star gauge for that region. Herschel compiled star gauges for several hundred regions representative of the northern hemisphere, his work being extended to the southern hemisphere by his son John. This provided the first precise information on the local distribution of stars in the Galaxy. By comparing gauges made to different limiting magnitudes (using larger and larger telescopes) they were able to show that the star system extends to great depths in directions toward the MILKY WAY. See also SOURCE COUNT.

starspots see RS CANUM VENATICORUM STAR; RED DWARF.

star trails curved images on a photographic plate that record the changing positions of stars when a telescope is not driven so as to keep up with their diurnal motion. Even if such a drive is being used, comet trails will still be recorded.

static Universe a Universe in which the COSMIC SCALE FACTOR is independent of time. Einstein proposed a static Universe in 1916 by including an ad hoc repulsion term – the *cosmological constant*, Λ – in his field equations of general RELATIVITY. This canceled out the natural tendency for a gravitating Universe either to expand or contract, depending on its energy content. See COSMOLOGICAL MODELS; EXPANDING UNIVERSE.

stationary orbit *short for* geostationary orbit. See GEOSYNCHRONOUS ORBIT.

stationary point see DIRECT MOTION.

statistical parallax the mean parallax of a group of stars that are all at about the same distance and whose space velocities are randomly orientated. It is derived from the RADIAL VELOCITIES and the tau components of the stars' PROPER MOTIONS: the tau component is measured perpendicular to the great circle joining a star to the solar APEX. It is thus perpendicular to and independent of the Sun's motion, i.e. it results entirely from the motion of the star. The average velocity in one direction will equal that in any other direction. The average radial velocity is thus a measure of average velocity. The average distance is then found from the ratio of average radial velocity to average tau component.

steady-state theory a cosmological theory obeying a perfect COSMOLOGICAL PRINCIPLE in which the Universe appears the same both at all points and all times: it thus had no beginning, will never end, and has a constant mean density of matter. Proposed by Hermann Bondi, Thomas Gold, and Fred Hoyle in 1948, the steady-state theory employs a flat space expanding at a constant rate. There is continuous creation of matter throughout the Universe – or perhaps in galactic centers – to compensate for the expansion. The creation rate is about 10^{-10} nucleons per meter cubed per year. The steady-state theory is not readily able to account for the MICROWAVE BACKGROUND RADIATION or the steep radio SOURCE COUNTS that indicate an evolving Universe. In its original form it has been abandoned, even by its originators.

steep-spectrum radio source see RADIO-SOURCE SPECTRUM.

Stefan's law (**Stefan-Boltzmann law**) the law relating the total energy, E, emitted over all wavelengths, per second, per unit area of a BLACK BODY, with the temperature, T, of the body:

$$E = \sigma T^4$$

σ is *Stefan's constant*, which has the value 5.6705×10^{-8} W m^{-2} K^{-4}. The law can be derived from Planck's radiation law (see BLACK BODY), but was first deduced by Josef Stefan in 1879 and then derived from thermodynamics by Ludwig Boltzmann in 1884. See also LUMINOSITY.

stellar association see ASSOCIATION.

stellar birth see STAR FORMATION.

stellar cannibalism see CANNIBALISM.

stellar diameter the diameters of stars range from several hundreds of millions of kilometers for SUPERGIANTS through about one million km for the Sun down to a few thousand km for WHITE DWARFS and about ten km for NEUTRON STARS. For convenience the diameter or radius is usually expressed in terms of the Sun's radius, $R_\odot$. For MAIN-SEQUENCE STARS, radii vary from 0.1 to over 10 $R_\odot$. The size of a star changes drastically toward the end of its life as it progresses through the RED GIANT stage to its final gravitational collapse. It can also change periodically (see PULSATING VARIABLES).

In most cases stars are too distant for their size to be determined directly. The diameter of a large star at a known distance can however be found geometrically if its APPARENT DIAMETER can be measured. Measuring techniques are based on the interference of light. The apparent diameters of bright supergiants and red giants were first measured in the 1920s (see MICHELSON STELLAR INTERFEROMETER). Very much smaller apparent diameters can now be measured with optical INTERFEROMETERS. A telescope cannot resolve the disk of a star; the disk of supergiants can however be imaged and measured using SPECKLE INTERFEROMETRY. OCCULTATIONS of stars by the Moon provide a further interference method: the star does not disappear instantaneously but fades over a few seconds; the unobstructed light produces a characteristic interference pattern of intensity against time from which angular size can be determined.

The sizes of many ECLIPSING BINARIES have been found from the shape of their LIGHT CURVES. In these measurements the sizes are obtained in terms of stellar radius relative to orbital radius. If the binary is also a SPECTROSCOPIC BINARY the absolute values of the radii can be found. For the majority of (smaller) stars diameters can be inferred only from STEFAN'S LAW, i.e. from known values of EFFECTIVE TEMPERATURE, T_{eff}, and luminosity, L:

$$L = 4\pi R^2 \sigma T_{\text{eff}}^4$$

where σ is Stefan's constant.

stellar evolution the progressive series of changes undergone by a star as it ages. Stars similar in mass to the Sun, having contracted from the PROTOSTAR phase (see STAR FORMATION) stay on the MAIN SEQUENCE for some 10^{10} years. During this period they give out energy by converting hydrogen to helium in their cores through the PROTON-PROTON CHAIN REACTION until the central hydrogen supplies are exhausted. Unsupported, the core collapses until sufficiently high temperatures are reached to burn hydrogen in a shell around the inert helium core. This *shell burning* causes the outer envelope of the star to expand and cool so that the star evolves off the main sequence to become a RED GIANT.

Further contraction of the core increases the temperature to 10^8 kelvin, at which stage the star can convert its helium core into carbon through the TRIPLE ALPHA PROCESS. The sudden onset of helium burning – the HELIUM FLASH – may disturb the equilibrium of a low-mass star. The triple alpha reaction gives out less energy than hydrogen fusion and soon the star finds itself once again without a nuclear energy source. Further contraction may result in helium-shell burning but it is doubtful if low-mass stars have sufficient gravitational energy to go further than this stage. The star becomes a red giant again, pulsating and varying in its brightness because of the vast extent of its atmosphere (see PULSATING VARIABLES). Eventually the atmosphere gently drifts away from the compact core of the star with velocities of only a few km s^{-1}, resulting in the formation of a PLANETARY NEBULA. The collapsed core forms a WHITE DWARF star, which continues to radiate its heat away into space for several millions of years.

Stars more than twice as massive as the Sun convert hydrogen to helium through the CARBON CYCLE, which makes their cores fully CONVECTIVE and therefore less dense than solar-mass stars. Their main-sequence lifetime decreases with increasing mass; it is only about 40 million years for a star of 8 solar masses and a few million years for the most massive stars. When they exhaust their hydrogen, the onset of helium burning occurs only gradually: this is because the core is nondegenerate, and so no instabilities arise. Having consumed its helium, a massive star has the potential energy to contract further so that carbon – formed by the triple alpha process – can burn to oxygen, neon, and magnesium (see NUCLEOSYNTHESIS). Should the star be sufficiently massive, it will build elements up to iron in its interior. But iron is at the limit of nuclear-fusion reactions and further contraction of a massive star's core can only result in catastrophic collapse, leading to a SUPERNOVA explosion. The core collapses to become a NEUTRON STAR or BLACK HOLE.

stellar mass the mass of a star is its most fundamental property, upon which its other properties depend strongly. It is usually given in terms of the Sun's mass, i.e. as some number of SOLAR MASSES, $M_{\odot}$; it ranges from about 0.08 to about 60 to 120 $M_{\odot}$. Stars of higher mass are much less common than those of low mass. *Low-mass stars* have an initial mass smaller than about 2.2–2.5 $M_{\odot}$, the exact value depending on chemical composition. *Intermediate-mass stars* have masses between about 2.2–8 $M_{\odot}$; they evolve from the main sequence without developing a degenerate core, unlike low-mass stars (see STELLAR EVOLUTION). More massive stars evolve to a state where their core temperatures are high enough to burn carbon under nondegenerate conditions.

The symbol ψ(M) is given to the number of stars with a particular mass *M* in a unit volume of space, and Salpeter (1955) showed that it is related to the star mass by the formula

$$\psi(M) \propto M^{-2.35}$$

Because of MASS LOSS and MASS TRANSFER, this *Salpeter mass function* holds strictly only for stars at the instant of birth, and it is therefore sometimes called the *initial mass function (IMF)*. The IMF is determined by fragmentation and other little-understood processes during STAR FORMATION.

The lower limit on a star's mass is the minimum amount of gas whose gravitational compression will raise the central temperature high enough for nuclear fusion to occur; less massive fragments from the initial cloud may contract directly to become a degenerate star known as a BROWN DWARF. It is still uncertain whether there is a theoretical upper limit to star masses, or whether the rarity of very massive stars means that a galaxy is unlikely to contain a star over about 120 $M_{\odot}$. Indirect methods indicate that ETA CARINAE and some other LUMINOUS BLUE VARIABLES may be as massive as 120 $M_{\odot}$.

Most stars lie on the main sequence of the HERTZSPRUNG–RUSSELL DIAGRAM. Their position on the main sequence, i.e. their SPECTRAL TYPE, depends on their mass, which varies from 0.1 $M_{\odot}$ (M stars) to over 20 $M_{\odot}$ (O stars). SUPERGIANTS are generally 10 to 20 $M_{\odot}$ but young O and B supergiants are much more massive.

The mass of a star can be determined directly if it has a significant gravitational effect on a neighboring star. Thus the combined mass and in some cases the individual masses of VISUAL and SPECTROSCOPIC BINARY stars have been found (see also DYNAMICAL PARALLAX). Mass can be estimated using the MASS-LUMINOSITY RELATION, or from a detailed study of the spectrum that indicates the star's surface gravity.

The evolutionary pattern and lifetime of a star depend on its mass. The least massive stars have the longest lifetimes of thousands of millions of years; the most massive exist only a few million years before exploding as SUPERNOVAE. At the end of its life, following mass loss in a PLANETARY NEBULA, etc., a star will become a WHITE DWARF if its mass is less than about 1.4 $M_{\odot}$; if the mass exceeds about 3 $M_{\odot}$ it is likely that the star will become a BLACK HOLE; a star with intermediate mass will end up a NEUTRON STAR.

stellar motion see PROPER MOTION; PECULIAR MOTION.

stellar nomenclature although most of the brighter stars have special names, as with Sirius or Aldebaran, the general and most convenient method of naming stars was introduced (1603) by Johann Bayer. In the system of *Bayer letters*, letters of the Greek alphabet – alpha (α), beta (β), gamma (γ), delta (δ), epsilon (ε), zeta (ζ), eta (η), etc. – are allotted to stars in each constellation, usually in order of brightness. The Greek letter is followed by the genitive of the Latin name of the constellation, as with Alpha Orionis or in abbreviated form α Ori. When the 24 Greek letters have been assigned, small Roman letters – a, b, c, etc. – and then capitals – A, B, C, etc. – are used. The letters R–Z were first used by Friedrich Wilhelm August Argelander (1862) to denote VARIABLE STARS in a particular constellation, and when those have been assigned the lettering RR–RZ, SS–SZ, etc., up to ZZ is employed. If that proves insufficient AA–AZ, BB–BZ, up to QZ (the 334th variable in the constellation) must be used (omitting Js), followed by V335, etc.

The fainter stars, usually invisible to the naked eye, are designated by their number in a star catalog. The numbers in John Flamsteed's *Historia Coelestis Britannica* (1725) are often adopted when a star has no Greek letter, as with 28 Tauri (PLEIONE in the Pleiades), the *Flamsteed number* generally being followed by the genitive of the constellation name. For stars unlisted in Flamsteed's catalog the number in some other catalog is used, the number being preceded by the abbreviation of the name – BD (BONNER DURCHMUSTERUNG), HD (HENRY DRAPER CATALOG), etc. Flamsteed numbered the stars in a constellation in order of RIGHT ASCENSION. Most modern catalogs ignore the constellation name and number purely by right ascension.

stellar planetaries see PLANETARY NEBULA.

stellar populations see POPULATION I, POPULATION II.

stellar statistics the use of statistical methods in the study of spatial and temporal distributions and motions of celestial objects within a galaxy, region of the Universe, etc., and of spatial and temporal distributions of certain features or of certain categories of these objects. The number of stars in a galaxy can be of the order of 10^{11} and the number of galaxies runs into countless millions. Only a very small number of stars, galaxies, radio sources, etc., can be examined in any detail and from this sample, analyzed statistically, a more general picture emerges. Much of the data that is used comes from STAR CATALOGS, SOURCE COUNTS, or detailed studies of selected areas. Almost all the information concerning the shape and structure of our Galaxy and the spatial distribution of other galaxies and of clusters of galaxies has been determined statistically.

stellar structure the interior constitution of a star, defining the run of temperature, pressure, density, chemical composition, energy flow, and energy production from the center to the surface. The structure of MAIN-SEQUENCE STARS, initially of uniform composition, is relatively simple: only very near the center are the temperature and pressure high enough for nuclear reactions to occur. In stars more than about twice the Sun's mass, convection currents in the core enlarge this zone and keep it mixed; less massive stars in contrast have a convective layer near the surface and an unmixed core.

Changes in structure as stars evolve can be calculated by following changes in chemical composition resulting from nuclear reactions, and recalculating the structure for the new composition. After the star has passed the SCHÖNBERG–CHANDRASEKHAR LIMIT, the structure changes to that of a GIANT, with an inert helium core surrounded by a hydrogen fusion shell and an extended envelope. Further core reactions in a very massive star will give it an onionlike *shell structure*, culminating in an iron core surrounded by successive shells of silicon, neon and oxygen, carbon, helium, and outermost, the hydrogen-rich envelope.

In principle, from an assumed composition, structure, and total mass, the other parameters of a stellar interior are derived by solving four differential equations:

(1) $dP/dr = -GM\rho/r^2$
(2) $dM/dr = 4\pi r^2\rho$
(3) $dL/dr = 4\pi r^2\rho\varepsilon$
(4) $dT/dr = 3\kappa L\rho/16\pi acr^2T^3$

Equation 1 is that of HYDROSTATIC EQUILIBRIUM, 2 is that of continuity of mass, 3 is that of energy generation, and 4 is that of radiative transport (see ENERGY TRANSPORT). Accurate solutions require a large computer since the pressure (P), opacity (κ), and energy generation rate (ε), also depend on the density (ρ), the temperature (T), and the chemical composition; in addition in some parts of the star energy may be transported by convection rather than by radiation. Of the other symbols, r is the radius, M the mass within that radius, G the gravitational constant, L the luminosity at radius r, a the radiation density constant, and c the speed of light.

stellar temperature see SURFACE TEMPERATURE.

stellar wind the steady stream of matter ejected from many types of stars, including the Sun (see SOLAR WIND). Although the mass loss is small in sunlike stars, it has been found to be very considerable in RED GIANTS and in hot luminous ULTRAVIOLET STARS, particularly in OF STARS and WOLF-RAYET STARS. This large mass loss could have a substantial effect on the final evolution of the stars into either white dwarfs or into more massive neutron stars (or black holes). In hot stars the stellar winds are thought to be produced by RADIATION PRESSURE of the intense ultraviolet radiation acting on the atoms in the stars' atmospheres. In red giants with hot coronae and low gravity the winds may simply be the expansion of the coronal gases into space. See also T TAURI WIND.

STEP *abbrev. for* Solar/Terrestrial Energy Programme.

Stephan's quintet a COMPACT GROUP of four galaxies, with a bright foreground galaxy in close proximity, first observed by M.E. Stephan in 1877. Three of the group members have a distorted morphology, indicating that they are INTERACTING GALAXIES.

STEREO *abbrev. for* Solar/Terrestrial Relations Observatory. A NASA mission for the agency's Office of Space Science Solar Terrestrial Probes Program that is set to provide revolutionary views of the Sun–Earth system and in particular solar eruptions and their effects on the Earth. The mission is due for launch in July. 2006 aboard a Delta 2 7925 rocket from Cape Canaveral. The STEREO mission is set to accomplish its task by imaging coronal mass ejections (see CORONAL TRANSIENTS) and background events simultaneously from two spaceborne observatories. The twin spacecraft are to be placed into solar orbit, one ahead of the Earth, the other behind it. The configuration should allow the observatories to obtain stereoscopic, or 3-D, images of the phenomena concerned.

stereocomparator see COMPARATOR.

Steward Observatory the observatory of the University of Arizona at Tucson, whose main instruments are at the KITT PEAK NATIONAL OBSERVATORY, including a 2.3-meter reflector. A number of telescopes are under construction or at the design stage at the Steward Observatory. Of these, one of the most important is the *Large Binocular Telescope* (*LBT*), due to become operational on Mount Graham, Arizona, in 2005. Equipped with twin 8.4-meter lightweight honeycomb mirrors sitting on the same mount and fitted with ADAPTIVE OPTICS, the LBT will arguably be the most advanced groundbased telescope in the world. Its configuration will provide an effective aperture of 22 meters, enabling it to be used in the search for Earth-sized extrasolar planets. The Steward Observatory Mirror Laboratory operates at the forefront of optical technology. It cast and polished the new 6.5-meter mirror that replaced the smaller mirrors of the MULTIPLE MIRROR TELESCOPE, operated jointly by the University and the SMITHSONIAN ASTROPHYSICAL OBSERVATORY. The Steward Observatory has also participated in several current and planned NASA space observatories, for example by making components for the HUBBLE SPACE TELESCOPE, the SPITZER SPACE TELESCOPE, and the JAMES WEBB SPACE TELESCOPE.

Stickney see PHOBOS.

Stokes parameters see POLARIZATION.

stone *short for* stony meteorite.

stony-iron meteorite any of a relatively small group of METEORITES containing on average 50% nickel-iron and 50% stony (mainly silicate) material. Stony irons can be subdivided into *pallasites*, which are composed of abundant grains of olivine (a magnesium silicate mineral) enclosed in metal, and *mesosiderites*, which are agglomerates of metal and silicates. See also S-TYPE ASTEROIDS.

stony meteorite (**stone**) a type of METEORITE that consists of silicate minerals generally with some nickel-iron. The two main subgroups are termed CHONDRITES and ACHONDRITES, depending on the presence or absence of CHONDRULES. The great majority (about 95%) of meteorites seen to fall to Earth are stony meteorites, and most of these are chondrites.

stop (**diaphragm**) a circular opening that sets the effective aperture (diameter) of a lens, mirror, EYEPIECE, etc., and also reduces stray light in an optical system.

stratigraphy the study of rock layers (strata). Younger geological units overlie, embay, or intrude older units. It is therefore possible to produce geological maps of the surface of a planet or satellite, and to form a stratigraphic classification to help to understand its history. Lunar stratigraphic systems include the COPERNICAN, IMBRIAN, and NECTARIAN SYSTEMS.

stratosphere, stratopause see ATMOSPHERIC LAYERS.

Stratospheric Observatory for Infrared Astronomy (**SOFIA**) a large-aperture telescope system to be installed in a Boeing 747SP aircraft, allowing infrared (especially far-IR) and submillimeter observations to be made from altitudes of over 41 000 feet, i.e. above most of the absorbing atmosphere (see ATMOSPHERIC WINDOWS). Under study by both NASA and the German Space Agency DASA, it will replace the KUIPER AIRBORNE OBSERVATORY. The planned telescope diameter is 2.5 meters and the spatial resolution 1–2 arc seconds. The expected lifetime is 20 years. SOFIA will provide a platform from which follow-up observations can be made on a short timescale for projects such as IRAS, ISO, and SIRTF. It is expected to be operational in 2009.

streaming motion the PECULIAR MOTION of a galaxy or cluster of galaxies.

strewn field see TEKTITES.

string theory a theory of ELEMENTARY PARTICLES based on the idea that the fundamental entities are not pointlike particles but finite lines, known as *strings*, or closed loops formed by strings (see also COSMIC STRINGS). Incorporating the concept of strings into SUPERSYMMETRY has led to *superstring theory*, in which all the FUNDAMENTAL FORCES are unified at the PLANCK TIME using a multidimensional framework called a *superstring*; this is still a highly speculative theory.

Strömgren sphere an approximately spherical region of ionized gas, mainly ionized hydrogen (H II), that surrounds a hot O or B star. If a hot star were embedded in very low-density gas of uniform distribution, the ultraviolet radiation from the star would almost completely ionize the gas out to a particular radius – the *Strömgren radius*. Equilibrium is established within this volume when the rate of ionization is balanced by the rate of recombination of ions with electrons. Outside this volume lies an *ionization front* – a thin transition zone between ionized gas and much cooler neutral gas. When the star 'turns on', the ionization front expands outward at about 10 km s^{-1} until the Strömgren radius is reached. If the gas cloud is relatively small and of low density, the entire cloud can be ionized. The Strömgren radius depends on the gas density and on the flux of ionizing radiation, i.e. of ultraviolet photons. The flux is dependent mainly on the star's temperature. See also EMISSION NEBULA.

strong force, interaction see FUNDAMENTAL FORCES.

structure formation the formation of large-scale structure such as galaxies, clusters of galaxies, etc. in the Universe. Most theories of structure formation are based on the JEANS INSTABILITY in the context of general relativity theory, with the large-scale structure emerging from the inhomogeneity of matter in the Universe. It is thought that quantum fluctuations in the EARLY UNIVERSE were responsible for the necessary inhomogeneities, with INFLATION expanding these fluctuations. Evidence that this theory is correct comes from the small variations in the cosmic microwave background radiation found by COBE. At present none of the detailed quantitative theories of structure formation can be regarded as definitive. One of the difficulties is that the nature of DARK MATTER is not known.

STScI see SPACE TELESCOPE SCIENCE INSTITUTE.

STSP see SOLAR/TERRESTRIAL ENERGY PROGRAMME.

S-type asteroids a common ASTEROID type found in the inner asteroid belt, having moderate albedos (0.1 to 0.2) and reddish spectra. Given their composition (metallic nickel-iron, combined with iron and magnesium silicates), they could be the parent bodies of the STONY-IRON METEORITES. (433) Eros is a prime example of an S-type asteroid.

Subaru Telescope an 8-meter Ritchey–Chrétien telescope of the Japan National Astronomy Observatory sited on MAUNA KEA, Hawaii. Its meniscus PRIMARY MIRROR (f/1.8) is controlled by ACTIVE OPTICS.

subdwarf a star that is smaller and about 1.5–2 magnitudes fainter than normal dwarf (main-sequence) stars of the same SPECTRAL TYPE. The subdwarfs are mainly old (halo population II) objects that lie just beneath the main sequence on the HERTZSPRUNG–RUSSELL DIAGRAM. Their anomalous position is due to their low metal content, which affects their apparent temperature and hence their spectral type. They are usually denoted by the prefix *sd*, as in sdK4, or given the luminosity class VI.

subgiant a GIANT STAR of smaller size and lower luminosity than normal giants of the same SPECTRAL TYPE, Alpha Crucis being an example. Subgiants form luminosity class IV, lying between the main-sequence stars and the giants on the HERTZSPRUNG–RUSSELL DIAGRAM.

subluminous stars types of stars, such as WHITE DWARFS, SUBDWARFS, and HIGH-VELOCITY STARS, that are fainter than main-sequence stars. Most are old (population II) stars.

sublunar point see SUBSTELLAR POINT.

submillimeter astronomy a branch of astronomy covering the wavelength range from 0.3 to 1 millimeter approximately. It is the highest frequency range, 300–1000 gigahertz, in which radio astronomy can be carried out, and is particularly important because of the large number of molecular emission lines to be found in the range (see MOLECULAR-LINE RADIO ASTRONOMY). These originate primarily from giant MOLECULAR CLOUDS.

Submillimeter astronomy usually involves a hybrid of radio and infrared techniques. A parabolic radio DISH plus a LINE RECEIVER is normally used. The receiver can be at the prime focus of the dish but is more usually at the Cassegrain focus behind the dish, to which radio waves are reflected by a small *subreflector* surface. The receiver is cooled to a very low temperature using liquid helium. To maintain SENSITIVITY the dish must be more accurately shaped and smooth than dishes for longer-wavelength studies, and must keep its shape under different orientations and weather conditions. Observations have to be made at high-altitude sites where there is very little atmospheric attenuation and absorption by water vapor. Submillimeter telescopes include JCMT, CSO, SMTO, and SEST. See also FIRST; MILLIMETER ASTRONOMY; SWAS.

Submillimeter Wave Astronomy Satellite see SWAS.

suborbital denoting instruments,

experiments, etc., on rockets, balloons, and aircraft rather than on Earth-orbiting spacecraft.

subsolar point see SUBSTELLAR POINT.

substellar point the point on the Earth's surface that lies directly beneath a star on the line connecting the center of Earth and star. The star would thus lie at the zenith of an observer at that point, the terrestrial latitude of which would equal the star's DECLINATION. The *sublunar point* and *subsolar point* are the equivalent points for the Moon and Sun, respectively.

Suisei see SAKIGAKE.

sulcus (plural: **sulci**) an area of subparallel furrows and ridges on the surface of a planet or satellite. The word is used in the approved name of such a feature.

summer triangle the large distinctive triangle formed by the three bright stars VEGA, ALTAIR, and DENEB. The stars are the first ones visible on northern summer evenings.

Sun the central body of the Solar System and nearest star to Earth, situated at an average distance of 149 600 000 km. A MAIN-SEQUENCE STAR of SPECTRAL TYPE G2 V, mass 1.9891×10^{30} kg, diameter 1 392 000 km, luminosity 3.83×10^{26} watts, and absolute visual magnitude +4.8, the Sun is a representative yellow dwarf. It is the only star whose surface and outer layers can be examined in detail.

The Sun is composed predominantly of hydrogen and helium (about 70% by mass hydrogen, 28% by mass helium), with about 2% of HEAVY ELEMENTS. It generates its energy by nuclear fusion processes, the most important of which is the PROTON-PROTON CHAIN REACTION, and is losing mass as a result, at a rate of about 4 000 000 tonnes per second. The generation of energy takes place in a central core, which has a temperature of around 15 000 000 K, is about 400 000 km in diameter and contains about 60% of the Sun's mass (in barely 2% of its volume). Outside the core is the *radiative zone*, an envelope of unevolved material through which energy from the core is transported by successive absorption and emission of radiation in collisions between the atomic particles (see ENERGY TRANSPORT). The individual particles proceed outward in a 'random walk', in which their direction of travel and energy change with each collision. It has been estimated that it may take as long as 20 million years for the energy generated in the core to reach the surface. The radiative zone extends to within about 200 000 km of the surface, where, the temperature having fallen to around 1 000 000 K, convection becomes the more important mode of energy transport (see CONVECTIVE ZONE).

The surface of the Sun, or PHOTOSPHERE, represents the boundary between the opaque convective zone and the transparent solar atmosphere. It is a stratum several hundred kilometers thick, from which almost all the energy emitted by the Sun is radiated into space. A permanent feature of the photosphere is the GRANULATION, which gives it a mottled appearance. More striking are the SUNSPOTS and their associated FACULAE, the numbers of which fluctuate over an average period of approximately 11 years – the so-called SUNSPOT CYCLE.

Observation of the transit of sunspots across the Sun's disk discloses a DIFFERENTIAL ROTATION, the SYNODIC PERIOD of which increases with HELIOGRAPHIC LATITUDE from 26.87 days at the equator to 29.65 days at ±40° (beyond which sunspots are seldom seen). The mean synodic period is taken to be 27.2753 days, which is equivalent to a SIDEREAL PERIOD of approximately 25.38 days (and corresponds to the actual period at around ±15° latitude). Spectroscopic measurements show that the rotation period continues to increase right up to the polar regions and that at any given latitude it decreases with height above the photosphere, except at the equator where the periods are approximately equal. The reason for this differential rotation is unknown, although it has been suggested that it may be caused by rapid rotation of the Sun's core. From the base to the top of the photosphere the temperature falls from about 6000 K to about 4000 K.

Immediately above the photosphere is the CHROMOSPHERE, a stratum a few thousand kilometers thick, in which the temperature rises from about 4000 K to around 50 000 K as the density decreases exponentially with height. Between this and the exceedingly rarified CORONA is the *transition region*, a stratum several hundred kilometers thick, in which the temperature rises further to around 500 000 K. The corona itself attains a temperature of around 2 000 000 K at a height of about 75 000 km. It extends for many million kilometers into the INTERPLANETARY MEDIUM, where the SOLAR WIND carries a stream of atomic particles to the depths of the Solar System.

The Sun is thought to possess a weak general magnetic field, although this has yet to be distinguished from the transient polar fields resulting from the dispersal of the intense localized fields of sunspots (see SUNSPOT CYCLE).

The age of the Sun is at least 4.6 billion (10^9) years and it may be regarded as a middle-aged star. After a similar period it is expected to expand to a RED GIANT and then to collapse to a WHITE DWARF (see STELLAR EVOLUTION).

See also ACTIVE SUN; NEUTRINO ASTRONOMY; QUIET SUN; SOLAR ACTIVITY.

sun dogs two bright, diffuse patches of light occasionally seen in the daytime sky, one each side of the Sun, and caused by refraction of the Sun's light by hexagonal ice crystals in the atmosphere. Each one is tinged red on the side near the Sun and blue on the other side. Sun dogs often appear on the fringe of a halo around the Sun, each one being separated from the Sun by an angular distance of 22°.

sungrazing comets comets whose PERIHELION points are very close to the Sun's surface. They actually pass through the solar corona. Comet 1882 II, for example, passed within 1.2 solar radii of the Sun's center. Sungrazing comets tend to be exceptionally bright. 1843 I, for example, was seen in broad daylight when it was only 4° from the Sun in the sky. Quite often, sungrazers are torn apart by tidal forces.

sunrise, sunset the times at which the apparent upper limb of the Sun is on the horizon. The true ZENITH DISTANCE (referred to the Earth's center) of the center of the disk is then 90°50′, the Sun's semidiameter being 16′ and horizontal ATMOSPHERIC REFRACTION being 34′. See also TWILIGHT.

sunrise, sunset terminator see TERMINATOR.

Sun's longitude a measure of the Earth's position around its orbit and more specifically the point in this orbit at which a METEOR SHOWER has its maximum intensity. It is the angle between the Earth–Sun line when the Sun is at the vernal EQUINOX and the Earth–Sun line at any other time, measured in the direction of the Earth's motion.

sunspot cycle the semiregular fluctuation of the number of SUNSPOTS over an average period of approximately 11 years – or 22 years if the respective magnetic polarities of the *p*- and *f*-spots are considered, because these reverse at sunspot minimum for the groups of the new cycle (see SUNSPOTS). The nature of the cycle is shown in the graph, where the index of sunspot activity is the RELATIVE SUNSPOT NUMBER. It can be seen that the rise to *sunspot maximum* usually occupies a shorter time than the fall to *minimum* and that the amount of activity may vary considerably between two consecutive cycles. There is some evidence for a modulation of the amplitude of the cycle over a period of around 80 years, but more data are required before the reality of this can be established.

The phase of the sunspot cycle also determines the mean HELIOGRAPHIC LATITUDE of all groups. At minimum the first groups of the new cycle appear at ±30–35°. Thereafter the latitude range moves progressively toward the equator, until by the next minimum the mean latitude is around ±7°. Then, while the equatorial groups are petering out, those of the next cycle begin to appear in their characteristic higher latitudes. This latitudinal progression is known as *Spörer's law*. At any one time there may be a considerable spread in latitude, but groups are seldom seen farther than 35° or closer than 5° from the equator. The *butterfly diagram* is a graphical representation of Spörer's law obtained by plotting the mean HELIOGRAPHIC LATITUDE of individual groups against time (see graph). Its appearance has been likened to successive pairs of butterfly wings, hence the name.

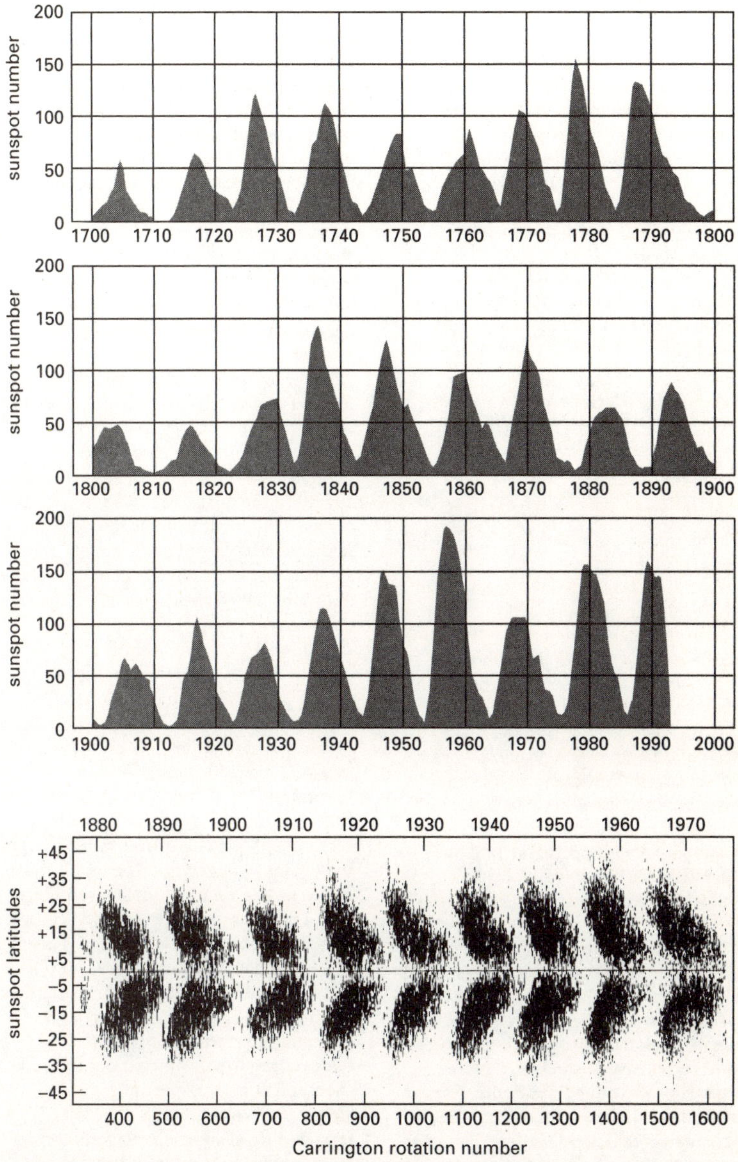

Sunspot cycle: (above) annual relative sunspot numbers 1700–1992 (courtesy of the National Geophysical Data Center, Boulder, Colorado, US); (below) butterfly diagram 1880–1976 (courtesy of the Royal Greenwich Observatory)

The underlying cause of the sunspot cycle is thought to be the interplay between a large-scale relatively weak poloidal magnetic field beneath the PHOTOSPHERE, DIFFERENTIAL ROTATION, and CONVECTION. The poloidal field, which is constrained to move with the ionized solar material, becomes increasingly distorted by differential rotation until an intense toroidal field is produced. The strength of this field is further enhanced by the perturbing effect of convection, which twists the field lines into ropelike configurations that may penetrate through the surface to form sunspots. This will occur first in intermediate latitudes, where the field's rate of shearing is greatest, and thereafter in increasingly low latitudes.

The inclination to the equator of the fields of opposite polarity associated with the *p*- and *f*-spots is such that they may drift apart in both longitude and latitude, as a result of differential rotation and the cyclonic rotation of individual supergranular cells (see SUPERGRANULATION). The latitudinal drift is responsible for an accumulation in the polar regions of magnetic flux of the same polarity as the *f*-spots in the respective hemispheres. Thus the intense (0.2–0.4 tesla) localized fields of sunspots are gradually dispersed to form weak ($1–2 \times 10^{-4}$ tesla) polar fields, which reverse polarity (not necessarily synchronously) around sunspot maximum. When this happens differential rotation no longer intensifies the subphotospheric toroidal field but rather weakens it and reestablishes a poloidal field of opposite direction to its predecessor.

The sunspot cycle may therefore be regarded (if this model is correct) as a relaxation process that is continually repeating itself. There is reason to believe, however, that at least some of the features of recent cycles may be transitory. In particular, a prolonged minimum, termed the *Maunder minimum*, from about 1645 to 1715, suggests that there is more than one circulatory mode available to the solar dynamo.

Sunspots are the most obvious but by no means the only manifestation of SOLAR ACTIVITY to undergo a cyclical change over a period of around 11 years. It is therefore proper to restrict the use of the term *sunspot cycle* to consideration of the fluctuation of the number of sunspots and to use the more general term *solar cycle* when considering the variation in the level of solar activity as a whole.

sunspot maximum, minimum see SUNSPOT CYCLE.

sunspots comparatively dark markings in the GRANULATION of the solar PHOTOSPHERE, ranging in size from *pores,* which are no larger than individual granules, to complex structures covering several thousand million square kilometers. All but the smallest spots consist of two distinct regions: a dark core or *umbra* and a lighter periphery or *penumbra.* The umbra usually appears featureless, while the penumbra – which can account for as much as 80% of the total area of a spot – may be resolved into delicate filaments, aligned radially in the case of regular spots. Most spots do not occur singly but tend to cluster in groups. The formation, development, and decay of large groups may occupy several weeks, or even months in exceptional cases, but the majority of groups are small, having lifetimes of not more than a couple of weeks.

Sunspots are the centers of intense localized magnetic fields, which are thought to suppress the currents bringing hot gases from the CONVECTIVE ZONE before they reach the photosphere. In the umbra, where the field is strongest (0.2–0.4 tesla), convection is almost completely inhibited; in the penumbra, where the field is more horizontal, a radial flow of material takes place (see EVERSHED EFFECT). The umbra is therefore much cooler than the penumbra, which is in turn cooler than the surrounding granulation, their temperatures being of the order of 4000, 5600, and 6000 K respectively. An alternative explanation for the lower temperature of sunspots suggests that far from inhibiting the flow of heat the magnetic field actually enhances it, converting at least three-quarters of the flux into magnetohydrodynamic waves (ALFVÉN

WAVES) that propagate rapidly along the field lines without dissipation.

Sunspot groups exhibit a great diversity of structure and are most conveniently classified according to the configuration of their magnetic field as unipolar, bipolar, or complex. *Bipolar groups* are by far the most common. In their simplest form they consist of two main spots of opposite magnetic polarity, termed (with respect to the direction of the Sun's rotation) the preceding (*p*-) and following (*f*-) spots, of which the *p*-spot usually lies slightly closer to the equator. The *line of inversion* separating the regions of opposite polarity (where the vertical component of the magnetic field is zero) is often the location of a relatively stable FILAMENT and the scene of violent FLARES, both of which occur above the sunspot group in the upper CHROMOSPHERE/inner CORONA.

The number of sunspots fluctuates over an average period of approximately 11 years – the so-called SUNSPOT CYCLE – during which time there is a corresponding variation in the mean heliographic latitude of all groups. Moreover the respective polarities of the *p*- and *f*-spots, which are consistent within a particular hemisphere but opposite on the other side of the equator, reverse at sunspot minimum for the groups of the new cycle.

Sunspots are the most obvious manifestation of SOLAR ACTIVITY. Together with their associated FACULAEPLAGES, filaments (or PROMINENCES), and flares, they constitute ACTIVE REGIONS, whose influence extends from the photosphere through the chromosphere to the corona.

Sunyaev–Zel'dovich effect (S–Z effect) the apparent change in temperature of the MICROWAVE BACKGROUND in the direction of very hot (10^8 K) plasma clouds, such as those around rich CLUSTERS OF GALAXIES. It is caused by inverse COMPTON SCATTERING of microwave background photons from highly energetic electrons in the plasma. When looked at with a radio telescope, the number of radio-frequency photons is depleted so the radiation appears cooler. The effect shows that the photons truly originated from behind the cluster (i.e. in the background) and can also be used to determine the distance to the cluster. The value of the HUBBLE CONSTANT can be measured by comparison of the X-ray luminosity of the galaxy to its microwave decrement.

supercluster a loosely bound aggregate of several CLUSTERS OF GALAXIES, about 100 megaparsecs in extent. As seen in the sky, different superclusters overlap; their members can be distinguished only after the distances of the constituent galaxies have been determined from a REDSHIFT SURVEY. Over a dozen superclusters have been identified, the nearest of which include the LOCAL SUPERCLUSTER, the PISCES–PERSEUS SUPERCLUSTER, the SHAPLEY SUPERCLUSTER, and Hydra–Centaurus. Superclusters contain between 2 and 15 rich clusters and have total masses of up to 10^{16} solar masses. Although the galaxies within each cluster are tightly bound, the clusters' gravitational effect on each other is not sufficient to overcome the expansion of the Universe. Each supercluster is thus growing in extent, although more slowly than the space between the superclusters. The larger superclusters appear to be elongated with no central concentration or axial symmetry, and form parts of filaments that surround empty voids (see LARGE-SCALE STRUCTURE).

supergalactic plane the dominant plane of the greatest concentration of nearby galaxy clusters in the sky, which passes through the VIRGO CLUSTER.

supergiant the largest and most luminous type of star, lying above both the MAIN SEQUENCE and the GIANT region in the HERTZSPRUNG–RUSSELL DIAGRAM. They are grouped in luminosity classes Ia and Ib (see SPECTRAL TYPES) and generally have absolute bolometric MAGNITUDES between –5 and –12. Only the most massive stars can become supergiants and consequently they are very rare. They are so bright, however, that they stand out in external galaxies. There is an upper limit to the absolute bolometric magnitude of cool red supergiants (–9.7), so the brightest supergiants can be used as approximate distance indicators. Examples of supergiant stars are Rigel and Betelgeuse in Orion,

Antares in Scorpius, and CEPHEID VARIABLE stars. See also LUMINOUS BLUE VARIABLES.

supergiant elliptical *another name for* cD galaxy. See CLUSTERS OF GALAXIES; GALAXIES.

supergranulation a network of large-scale (30 000 km diameter) convective cells in the solar PHOTOSPHERE. The individual cells have an upward velocity of about 0.1 km s^{-1} and exhibit a horizontal flow of material, outward from the center, with a velocity of about 0.4 km s^{-1}; their average lifetime is about one day (compare GRANULATION). The space between adjacent cells is the preferred birthplace of SUNSPOTS, whose intense localized magnetic fields are dispersed by differential rotation and a cyclonic rotation of the cells, to form a weak polar field in both hemispheres.

Supergranulation is not readily visible but may be detected in velocity-canceled SPECTROHELIOGRAMS. (These are obtained by the photographic cancellation of two spectroheliograms taken simultaneously in the wings, i.e. on either side of the core, of a strong FRAUNHOFER LINE.) It is seen as alternate bright–dark elements away from the center of the Sun's disk, corresponding to a predominantly horizontal flow of material in the line of sight that has been rendered visible by its doubled DOPPLER SHIFT. See also CHROMOSPHERIC NETWORK; SPICULES.

supergravity any of a number of theories seeking to unify the gravitational force with the three other FUNDAMENTAL FORCES of nature, the electromagnetic, strong, and weak forces. They involve SUPERSYMMETRY encompassing all four forces. Many theorists now believe that a unified theory to include gravity must be based on superstrings (see STRING THEORY).

superheterodyne receiver see RECEIVER.

superior conjunction see CONJUNCTION.

superior planets the planets Mars, Jupiter, Saturn, Uranus, Neptune, and Pluto, which orbit the Sun at distances greater than that of the Earth.

superlight source see SUPERLUMINAL SOURCE.

superluminal source (superlight source) a RADIO SOURCE in which components appear to be moving at velocities greater than the speed of light. Physical motion faster than light is impossible according to the special theory of RELATIVITY. It is possible, however, to explain such apparent superluminal velocities in terms of geometrical effects involving objects moving more slowly than light.

supermassive black hole see BLACK HOLE.

supermassive stars hypothetical very rare stars with masses of up to 1000 solar masses or more. The most massive of normal stars, such as ETA CARINAE and OF STARS, are about 100 solar masses, but it is not certain whether there is an actual upper limit to STELLAR MASS.

supernova a star that has exploded violently and is observed to brighten temporarily to an absolute MAGNITUDE brighter than about –15, over a hundred times more luminous than an ordinary NOVA. A supernova explosion blows off all or most of the star's material at high velocity, as a result of the final uncontrolled nuclear reactions in the small proportion of stars that reach an unstable state late in their evolution (see STELLAR EVOLUTION). The debris consists of an expanding gas shell (the SUPERNOVA REMNANT), and possibly a compact stellar object (a NEUTRON STAR or a BLACK HOLE), which is the original star's collapsed core. Supernovae are important in the NUCLEOSYNTHESIS of heavy elements.

Supernova searches, organized on a regular basis since 1936, have discovered more than 800 extragalactic supernovae. SUPERNOVA 1987A was a recent naked-eye supernova. In addition, past supernovae in our GALAXY have been recorded in Western Europe (TYCHO'S STAR of 1572 and KEPLER'S STAR of 1604) and in China and Korea (AD 185, 386?, 393, 1006, 1054, and 1181). The total supernova production rate in the Galaxy is currently estimated as two or three per century.

Theoretically, two different explosion mechanisms can be distinguished: thermonuclear explosions and core collapse supernovae. *Thermonuclear explosions* probably occur when a WHITE DWARF or the degenerate core of a moderately massive star is pushed over the CHANDRASEKHAR

LIMIT. The DEGENERATE MATTER containing mainly carbon and oxygen nuclei then ignites explosively, leading to a thermonuclear runaway and probably the complete disruption of the star. The ejecta will contain a large amount of radioactive nickel, produced in the nuclear runaway, whose decay to cobalt and then iron may explain the exponential decay observed in many supernova LIGHT CURVES. Supernovae of this type are probably a major source of iron in the Galaxy.

Core collapse supernovae occur when all the material in the core of a massive star has been completely burned to iron. Because an iron core is incapable of generating any more energy by NUCLEAR FUSION, it has to collapse (if its mass exceeds the Chandrasekhar mass) to become a neutron star; if the star is extremely massive it may collapse completely to a black hole. The link between the core's implosion and the explosion of the outer layers is still uncertain. One possibility is that, when the core reaches neutron-star densities, the newly formed neutron-star core suddenly presents a rigid surface to the infalling gas and the collapse stops, driving a shock wave into the overlying material that may blow off the star's outer layers. The high pressures and temperatures suddenly created in the layer just above the neutron star cause a spate of nuclear reactions; neutrons from these reactions build up very heavy nuclei by the R-PROCESS.

Observationally, supernovae have traditionally been divided into two main types, based on the absence (type I) or presence (type II) of hydrogen in their spectra. Recent observations have revealed a large diversity of supernova types and the need for further subclassification (e.g. type Ia, Ib, Ic; type II-P, II-L, IIb). This classification is further complicated by the fact that there is no simple one-to-one relationship between the theoretical explosion mechanisms and the two main observational types. Recently a more energetic type of supernova, called a *hypernova*, has been observed, possibly related to gamma-ray bursts.

Type Ia supernovae occur in both elliptical and spiral galaxies (but without notable preference for spiral arms); most of them have very similar light curves and absolute magnitudes (–19) at maximum. Contrary to earlier beliefs, type Ia supernovae are not perfect standard candles. However, observationally there appears to be a tight correlation between the shape of the supernova distances to fairly large redshifts ($z \sim 1$). In recent years, high-z supernova searches have found a large number of distant type Ia supernovae. These can be used to measure the expansion rate of the Universe when it was much younger. At face value, the results suggest that the expansion of the Universe if accelerating rather than decelerating – as it would in the standard cosmology. However, an alternative explanation might be that type Ia supernovae were systematically different at an earlier cosmological epoch than the present one. Their spectra reveal very broad absorption lines (for example, of silicon), but generally show no evidence for hydrogen in the ejected gas, which has a mass of roughly a solar mass and a velocity around 10 000 km s^{-1}; the total energy is about 10^{44} joules. The pre-supernova of a type Ia supernova is still uncertain, but a popular theory is that it is a white dwarf that accretes enough matter from a companion star or that merges with another lighter white dwarf to be pushed above the Chandrasekhar mass, leading to a thermonuclear explosion.

Type Ib/Ic supernovae, which unlike type Ia supernovae show no evidence for silicon in their spectra, probably make up the bulk of type I supernovae. They are less luminous than type Ia supernovae, indicating that they produce less radioactive material, and they are probably intrinsically related to type II supernovae. Their progenitors may be massive stars that have lost all of their hydrogen-rich envelopes in a stellar wind (see WOLF–RAYET STARS) or by MASS TRANSFER in a binary (see HELIUM STAR). Unlike type Ia supernovae, they probably experience core collapse and leave neutron-star or black-hole remnants.

Type II supernovae occur mainly in the spiral arms of spiral galaxies. They show more diversity in light curves and absolute magnitude than type I, although many of them reach a maximum of around –17. Their early spectra show a normal abundance of the elements and indicate that several solar masses are ejected at around 5000 km s^{-1}. The pre-supernova, in most cases (but not in the case of SUPERNOVA 1987A), is a red supergiant with a diameter of about 10 AU. The mass in its hydrogen-rich envelope may vary from a few tenths of a solar mass to several tens of solar masses. This large range in envelope masses is probably the main reason for the large diversity of type II light curves. The explosion mechanism in most cases is believed to be core collapse, but some type II supernovae may be caused by thermonuclear explosions.

supernova 1987A (**SN 1987A**) the first naked-eye supernova since 1604 (see KEPLER'S STAR). It occurred in the Large MAGELLANIC CLOUD (LMC) on Feb. 23 1987, and reached a visual magnitude of 2.9 by May 18 1987. It belonged to the class of type II SUPERNOVAE, but because its progenitor (Sanduleak –69°202) was a blue supergiant rather than a red supergiant, as is typical for type II supernovae, its peak luminosity was significantly lower and its spectral evolution much more rapid than expected. Initially it was suggested that the unusual color of the progenitor had to do with the lower METALLICITY of the LMC. However, it now appears more likely that this is a direct consequence of the binary nature of the progenitor system. In this model, the system initially consisted of two massive stars that merged some 30 000 years before the explosion to form a single, but unusual, star at the time of the explosion. This would also help explain the complex nebula surrounding the supernova, detected with the NTT and HST, consisting of three rings (interlocking in projection). The supernova is located at the center of the inner ring (which has a radius of 0.7 light-years). The outer rings are displaced above and below the plane of the inner ring at roughly twice the distance. This material was ejected by the supernova progenitor, presumably as a by-product of the merger event. The supernova blast wave is about to collide with the inner ring and will ultimately destroy it.

The detection of a burst of NEUTRINOS from the supernova has provided direct confirmation of the long-held belief that type II supernovae are triggered by the collapse of stellar cores. In addition, the detection of gamma-ray lines from the radioactive decay of cobalt (^{56}Co), the decay product of nickel (^{56}Ni), to iron (^{56}Fe) has provided evidence for explosive NUCLEOSYNTHESIS, i.e. the synthesis of iron-peak elements and other heavy nuclei during the supernova explosion.

supernova remnant (**SNR**) the expanding shell of gas from a supernova explosion, consisting of the supernova ejecta and 'swept-up' interstellar gas. Young (<1000 year old) supernova remnants are generally optically faint but are fairly strong radio and X-ray sources; the CRAB NEBULA is exceptionally bright because it is energized by a central PULSAR. Older supernova remnants appear as rings of bright filaments, again with associated radio and X-ray emission. Supernova remnants that have been observed at sufficiently high resolution can be loosely classified into two types. In *shell SNRs*, which constitute about 90% of all SNRs (including Tycho and Kepler), most of the observed radiation comes from a filamentary, often spherical shell; they seem to have no central power source and their luminosity is exclusively derived from the interaction of the supernova shell with the external medium. *Plerions* (or *filled* or *filled-center SNRs*) are now widely thought to be powered by a central pulsar – the Crab nebula is the archetypal example – and the observed radiation originates from the whole of the remnant. Compression by an expanding supernova remnant can trigger STAR FORMATION in interstellar clouds. See also EMISSION NEBULA.

super Schmidt see SCHMIDT TELESCOPE.

superstring theory see STRING THEORY.

supersymmetry (**SUSY**) an extension of the theories (GUTs) seeking to unify the four FUNDAMENTAL FORCES of nature. It unifies the particles called fermions (with half-integral spin) and the force particles, the bosons (with integral spin). In the simplest SUSY models, this leads to a new family of particles as every fermion has a supersymmetric boson partner and every boson has a supersymmetric fermion partner; for example, *photinos* and *gravitinos* are the hypothesized partners of the photon and graviton. Adding supersymmetric particles to the standard model of elementary particles remedies some of its discrepancies, but there is no experimental evidence for them. See also DARK MATTER.

surface brightness luminosity per unit area on the sky, usually expressed for optical data as magnitudes per square arc second. It is a useful distance-independent property to use in the comparison of low-redshift galaxies (where relativistic corrections are unimportant) because the angular area subtended and the luminosity both decrease with the inverse square of the distance.

surface gravity symbol: g. The ACCELERATION OF GRAVITY experienced by an object when it falls freely towards the surface of a planet or star.

surface temperature the temperature of the radiating layers of a star at which its continuous spectrum is produced. The star is assumed to be a perfect radiator, i.e. a BLACK BODY, and its temperature is usually expressed as its EFFECTIVE TEMPERATURE or its COLOR TEMPERATURE. Surface temperature is very much lower than the temperature at the center of a star.

surges impulsive events on the Sun that are characterized by the ejection of chromospheric material into the inner CORONA with velocities of 100–200 km s^{-1}. They occur in ACTIVE REGIONS, where they often accompany FLARES but more generally stem from small flarelike brightenings (termed *moustaches* or *Ellerman bombs*) at the outer edge of the penumbra of SUNSPOTS. The surge material, which is usually directed radially away from the spot, may reach a height of a couple of hundred thousand kilometers before fading or returning to the CHROMOSPHERE along either a curved trajectory or, more frequently, the trajectory of its ascent. Surges typically have a lifetime of 10–20 minutes and show a strong tendency to recur. See also PROMINENCES.

survey catalog see STAR CATALOG.

Surveyor a US unpiloted space program of the late 1960s that was designed to investigate the bearing strength, physical structure, and chemistry of the lunar REGOLITH by means of trenching devices and alpha-scattering analysis (see table). The spacecraft were soft-landed by retrorockets. Each was equipped with a television camera, powered by solar cells, for panoramic photography. The MARIA were shown to have a basaltic composition, whereas the HIGHLANDS were found to be richer in calcium and aluminum. See also LUNA PROBES; LUNAR ORBITER PROBES; RANGER; ZOND PROBES.

SUSI *abbrev. for* Sydney University Stellar

Surveyor Probes

Spacecraft	*Launch date*	*Comments**
Surveyor 1	1966, May 30	Soft-landed in Oc. Procellarum (11 150)
Surveyor 2	1966, Sept. 20	Struck moon in Oc. Procellarum
Surveyor 3	1967, Apr. 17	Tested soil in Oc. Procellarum (6315); later visited by Apollo 12
Surveyor 4	1967, July 14	Landed in Sinus Medii but radio contact lost
Surveyor 5	1967, Sept. 8	Analyzed soil in Mare Tranquillitatis (18 006)
Surveyor 6	1967, Nov. 7	Analyzed soil in Sinus Medii (30 000)
Surveyor 7	1968, Jan. 7	Analyzed/tested soil near Tycho (21 000)

*Figures in brackets indicate the number of photographs transmitted.

Interferometer. An optical INTERFEROMETER sited at Culgoora, New South Wales, Australia, in operation since 1991. It has 12 small mirrors located along a baseline 640 meters long. The effects of atmospheric turbulence are minimized firstly by using small apertures to gather a relatively clear fraction of the incoming light. In addition, rapid adjustments can be made to small mirrors within each telescope to counterbalance any remaining atmospheric distortion (see ADAPTIVE OPTICS).

SUSY *abbrev. for* supersymmetry.

SU Ursae Majoris stars (SU UMa stars) see DWARF NOVAE.

Swan nebula see OMEGA NEBULA.

SWAS *abbrev. for* Submillimeter Wave Astronomy Satellite. A SMALL EXPLORER payload consisting of a 1-meter class telescope feeding two HETERODYNE DETECTORS. Launched in 1997, SWAS conducted a survey of galactic MOLECULAR CLOUDS at high spectral RESOLUTION by studying submillimeter emission from H_2O, O_2, C, and ^{13}CO.

Sweden–ESO Submillimeter Telescope (SEST) a Cassegrain DISH antenna of 15-meter diameter for use at wavelengths as short as 0.8 mm. SEST is situated at an altitude of 2300 meters at the European Southern Observatory (ESO) site at La Silla, Chile, and has been in operation since 1989. The reflecting surface is made up of 176 panels positioned to a mean accuracy of 70 micrometers.

Swift Gamma-Ray Burst Explorer a NASA space observatory launched by a Boeing Delta 2 rocket from Cape Canaveral, Florida, Nov. 2004. Its three telescopes (one each operating in the gamma-ray, X-ray, and ultraviolet/visible wavelength ranges) will seek to discover the position, brightness, and physical nature of GAMMA-RAY BURSTS, the most powerful but also the most mysterious explosions in the Universe. What triggers them and what their relationship may be to black holes are also questions that Swift will help to address. Swift is designed for rapid pointing in order to home in on a detected gamma-ray burst as soon as possible after it has happened. Typically, the reaction time is expected to be within 20 and 70 seconds. The wide-field primary Burst Alert Telescope, which can scan about 16% of the sky at a time, will look for gamma-ray bursts and when it detects one the entire Swift craft will turn to target the explosion, bringing the other two telescope to bear on it, Gamma-ray bursts happen at least once a day, and one of Swift's goals is to acquire knowledge on at least 1000 of them over its three-year mission. Much can be learned from the afterglow of gamma-ray bursts, which cascades rapidly down through the wavelengths from gamma rays to radio waves. Thus Swift's three telescopes, with their multi-wavelength capabilities, represent a major advance in the study of these phenomena.

Swift–Tuttle (1737 II, 1862 III, 1992 t) a major comet that was independently discovered in 1862 by Lewis Swift and Horace Tuttle. It is the parent of the PERSEID meteoroid stream, which has a mass of well over 10^{14} kg. The comet has an orbital inclination of 113° and a period of around 128 years.

Sword-Handle see H AND CHI PERSEI.

Sycorax see URANUS'S SATELLITES.

symbiotic star a variable 'star' whose spectrum shows lines characteristic of gases at two very different temperatures, typically of an M star (3500 K) and a B star (20 000 K) superimposed. It is in fact a semidetached close BINARY STAR: a RED GIANT component produces the low-temperature spectrum whereas the higher-temperature spectrum comes from gas streams that are falling on to a companion star, usually a WHITE DWARF or a MAIN-SEQUENCE STAR, but sometimes possibly a NEUTRON STAR. The mass loss is due to the giant's STELLAR WIND, and so is much slower than the gravitational transfer in the otherwise-similar RECURRENT NOVAE. Symbiotic stars suffer smaller and more irregular outbursts than other CATACLYSMIC VARIABLES. An outburst in the R Aquarii system has produced a narrow jet some 1500 AU in length, visible to optical and radio telescopes. The gas in the jet is traveling at 2000 km s^{-1}, and is apparently a milder version of the ejection found in SS433. Some other well-studied symbiotic stars are Z Andromedae, BF Cygni, RW Hydrae, AG Pegasi, and AX Persei.

synchronous orbit an orbit made by an artificial satellite that has a period equal to the period of rotation of the orbited body. See also GEOSYNCHRONOUS ORBIT.

synchronous rotation 1 (**captured rotation**) the rotation of a natural satellite about its primary in which the period of rotation of the satellite is equal to its orbital period. The same hemisphere thus always faces the primary. The Moon is in synchronous rotation, although LIBRATION allows slightly more than one hemisphere to be seen from Earth. There are good dynamical reasons for satellites fairly close to their planet being locked in synchronous rotation. See TIDAL FORCE.

2 (**synchronism**) a situation in a close BINARY STAR in which the rotation period of a star is equal to the binary's orbital period (for circular orbits).

synchrotron emission (**synchrotron radiation; magnetobremsstrahlung**) ELECTROMAGNETIC RADIATION from very high energy ELECTRONS moving in a magnetic field. It is NONTHERMAL EMISSION and is also polarized (see POLARIZATION), usually strongly. It is the mechanism most often invoked to explain the radio emission from extragalactic RADIO SOURCES and the emission from SUPERNOVA REMNANTS and PULSARS.

When an electron moves in a magnetic field, it follows a circular path making $\nu = eB/2\pi m$ revolutions per second, where e and m are the electronic charge and mass and B is the magnetic flux density; ν is the *gyrofrequency*. The acceleration of the electron in its circular path causes it to radiate electromagnetic waves at frequency ν. This emission is called *cyclotron radiation*.

If the velocity of the electrons becomes comparable with the speed of light, the theory of RELATIVITY must be used to explain the observed phenomena. One effect is *relativistic beaming* in which the radiation is beamed forward in the direction of motion of the relativistic electron (see illustration (a)). The nature of

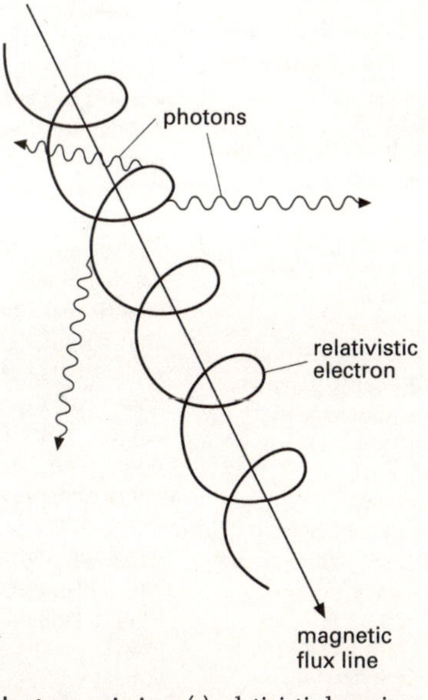

Synchrotron emission: (a) relativistic beaming

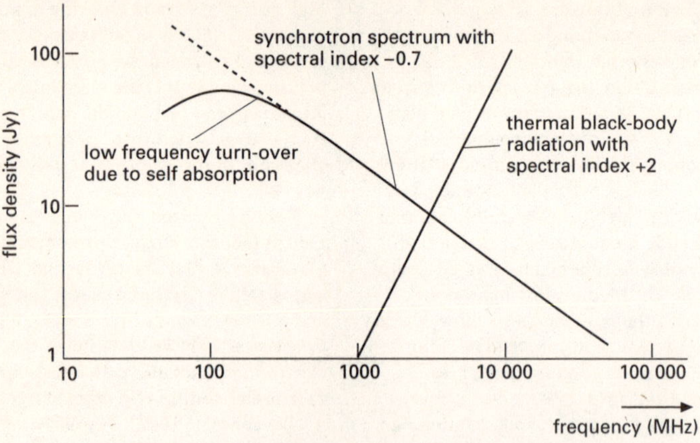

Synchrotron emission: (b) spectrum of synchrotron emission

the radiation changes from the simple cyclotron case and it becomes synchrotron emission. At low frequencies, the conditions in the source may cause the synchrotron emission to be reabsorbed before it can escape. The RADIO-SOURCE SPECTRUM then exhibits a turnover, as is often seen in extragalactic radio sources (see illustration (b)). This is called *synchrotron self-absorption.* See also RAZIN EFFECT.

syndynames see COMET TAILS.

synodic month (lunation; lunar month) the interval of 29.530 59 days, on average, between two successive new Moons.

synodic period the average time between successive CONJUNCTIONS of two planets as seen from the Earth, or between successive conjunctions of a satellite with the Sun as seen from the satellite's primary. Synodic period, P_s, and SIDEREAL PERIOD, P_1, of an inferior or superior planet are related, respectively, by the equations

$$1/P_s = 1/P_1 - 1/P_2$$
$$1/P_s = 1/P_2 - 1/P_1$$

P_2 is the sidereal period of the Earth, i.e. 365.256 days or 1 year. For a satellite the first equation applies, P_2 being the sidereal period of the primary.

synthesis telescope a system of radio telescopes that is used for APERTURE SYNTHESIS.

synthesized aperture, synthesized beam see APERTURE SYNTHESIS; BEAM.

Syrtis Major a dark triangular plateau near the Martian equator and prominent to Earth-based observers. It slopes downward to the east and is prone to strong winds that move and remove light-colored dust to expose the darker rocks below. See also MARS, SURFACE FEATURES.

Syrtis Major Planum a dark triangular plateau near the Martian equator and prominent to Earth-based observers. It is centered on the aerographic coordinates 10° N latitude, 290° W longitude (see AREOGRAPHY). The plateau is a low-relief volcanic shield, apparently composed of basaltic rock. It slopes downward to the east and is prone to strong winds that move and remove light-colored dust to expose the darker rocks beneath. See also MARS, SURFACE FEATURES.

system noise see SENSITIVITY.

system temperature (noise temperature) see SENSITIVITY.

syzygy the configuration arising when the Sun, Earth, and either the Moon or a planet lie approximately in line, i.e. when the Moon or planet is at OPPOSITION or CONJUNCTION.

S–Z effect see SUNYAEV–ZEL'DOVICH EFFECT.

Tt

TAI *abbrev. (French) for* International Atomic Time.

tail *short for* comet tail.

Tanegashima Space Center see NASDA.

tangential velocity (**transverse velocity**) see PROPER MOTION.

Tarantula nebula see 30 DORADUS.

T association see ASSOCIATION; T TAURI STARS.

tau (τ) the 19th letter of the Greek alphabet, used in STELLAR NOMENCLATURE usually to designate the 19th-brightest star in a constellation or sometimes to indicate a star's position in a group.

Tau Ceti (**τ Cet**) an orange-red main-sequence dwarf star in the constellation Cetus and one of the Sun's near neighbors. It is located in the sky just northeast of Diphda (β Ceti). Tau Ceti is comparable in size and mass with the Sun but is only about three-fifths as luminous. Dust has been detected around it but there is no hard evidence that Tau Ceti has a planetary or even a stellar companion. It appears, however, to be an optical double, with a 13th-magnitude red dwarf of spectral class M lying 90′ away from it. m_v: 3.5; M_v: 5.8; spectral type: G8 Vp; distance: 3.65 pc.

Taurids a minor METEOR SHOWER with a double radiant, RA 57°, dec +14° and +22°, that maximizes on Nov. 5. The METEOROID STREAM is associated with ENCKE'S COMET.

Taurus (**Bull**) a large zodiac constellation in the northern hemisphere near Orion, lying partly in the Milky Way. The brightest stars are the zero-magnitude ALDEBARAN, the 1st-magnitude ELNATH, which was once part of the constellation Auriga, and several of 2nd and 3rd magnitude. The area contains the prototypes of the RV TAURI and T TAURI STARS, the HYADES and PLEIADES, both beautiful open clusters, and the supernova remnant the CRAB NEBULA with its associated OPTICAL PULSAR. Abbrev.: Tau; genitive form: Tauri; approx. position: RA 4.5h, dec +15°; area: 314 sq deg.

Taurus A the RADIO SOURCE in the constellation Taurus that is identified with the CRAB NEBULA. It has a FLUX DENSITY at 178 megahertz of 1420 JANSKY, most of which comes from SYNCHROTRON EMISSION in the nebula, which is a SUPERNOVA REMNANT. A small fraction of the radio flux is pulsed, due to the PULSAR in the nebula rotating about 30 times per second. Unlike other supernova remnants, such as CASSIOPEIA A, the Crab nebula does not have a regular ringlike radio structure, probably because of its internal energy source – the pulsar.

Taurus-Littrow a HIGHLAND region on the Moon on the eastern borders of Mare SERENITATIS. It was the target for APOLLO 17.

Taurus X-1 the second X-ray source to be discovered (1963) and the first to be optically identified. It was found to coincide with the CRAB NEBULA supernova remnant.

TD-1 a satellite developed by the European Space Research Organization and launched in March 1972. It made a systematic ultraviolet survey of the whole sky, with one experiment on board recording spectrophotometric data at 3.5 nanometer resolution on thousands of stars in the wavelength range 135–274 nm. All hot O and B stars were recorded down to 9th magnitude in addition to observations of many of the brighter cooler stars of later spectral types. A catalog of more than 30 000 ultraviolet sources has been compiled from the data. A second UV instrument detected UV spectra, at about 0.2 nm resolution, of brighter preselected stars and a catalog of these data has also been prepared.

TDB *abbrev.* (*French*) *for* barycentric dynamical time. See DYNAMICAL TIME.

TDRSS *abbrev. for* tracking and data-relay satellite system. A network of four NASA satellites that transmits commands from a ground station to NASA spacecraft – including the HST – and returns their scientific data to the ground.

TDT *abbrev. for* terrestrial dynamical time. See DYNAMICAL TIME.

technetium stars a class of asymptotic GIANTS (usually S STARS or CARBON STARS) that show absorption lines of technetium in their spectra. Because technetium (^{99}Tc) is an unstable radioactive element decaying with a HALF-LIFE of 2.1×10^5 years, it must have been produced in the burning shell of the star in which it is observed. See also RADIOACTIVE DECAY.

tectonics large-scale movements of the crust of a planet or satellite, such as those that give rise to mountain building, faulting, and folding.

Teide Observatory an observatory at Izaña, altitude 2400 meters, on the island of Tenerife in the Canaries. Facilities are shared by the Instituto de Astrofísica de Canarias (Institute of Astrophysics of the Canaries) with several European countries. There are some major SOLAR TELESCOPES, including the German *Vacuum Tower Telescope*, which has a 70-cm aperture mirror, focal ratio f/76. The observatory also has eight telescopes for nocturnal use and three instruments or arrays for observing the COSMIC MICROWAVE BACKGROUND (see VSA). The observatory began operating in 1964. See also ROQUE DE LOS MUCHACHOS OBSERVATORY.

tektites small glassy rounded objects, about 0.1 to 3 cm in size, found only in certain parts of the world, often in vast *strewn fields*. They have shapes varying from spheroidal to pear-, lens-, and disk-shaped with surface-flow structures indicating that they were formed by rapid cooling of molten material. The chemical composition is that of silicic igneous rock with high SiO_2 content (70–80%) and moderate Al_2O_3 content (11–15%). They are named according to the place where they are found, e.g. *moldavites* (Moldavia), *australites* (Australia), etc. They were probably formed by the fusion of terrestrial material during the impact of giant METEORITES; terrestrial and lunar volcanic origins have also been proposed. They are between 0.75–65 million years old. Small tektitelike objects have been found in the lunar regolith.

telecompressor (**rich-field adapter**) a converging achromatic lens inserted inside the focus of a telescope in order to reduce the effective focal length and hence increase the telescope's field of view.

tele-extender an optical device located in an extension tube on a telescope and used with an eyepiece in order to increase the effective focal length of the telescope and hence increase the image scale.

telemetry the transmission of data to or from a satellite, space station, spaceprobe, etc., by means of radio waves.

telescope 1 an optical device for collecting light so as to form an image of a distant object. The light is collected and focused by an object lens in a REFRACTING TELESCOPE or by a primary mirror in a REFLECTING TELESCOPE. A telescope is usually described in terms of its APERTURE: LIGHT-GATHERING POWER, spatial RESOLUTION, and LIMITING MAGNITUDE all increase as the aperture increases.
2 any device by which radiation from a particular spectral region can be collected and focused on or brought to a suitable recording system for analysis. See CODED MASK TELESCOPE; GRAZING INCIDENCE; INFRARED TELESCOPE; RADIO TELESCOPE.

telescopic object a star or other celestial object that is less than 6th apparent MAGNITUDE and cannot be seen without a telescope.

Telescopium (**Telescope**) an inconspicuous constellation in the southern hemisphere near Scorpius, the brightest stars being of 3rd and 4th magnitude. Abbrev.: Tel; genitive form: Telescopii; approx. position: RA 19.5h, dec –50°; area: 252 sq deg.

Telesto a small irregularly shaped satellite of Saturn, discovered in 1981 from groundbased observations made in 1980. It is a COORBITAL SATELLITE with CALYPSO and TETHYS. See Table 2, Appendix.

television camera an electronic instrument that converts the optical image of a scene into an electrical signal, termed a *video signal*. This signal may then be transmitted by means of radio waves or by cable to a distant receiver. CCD cameras and VIDICONS are small highly sensitive TV cameras that are used in astronomy both in space probes and satellites and also in combination with ground-based telescopes.

telluric lines absorption lines seen in the spectrum of a celestial object but due to components, such as water vapor, oxygen, or carbon dioxide, in the Earth's atmosphere. Telluric lines can be distinguished because they are generally narrower than solar or stellar lines, etc. In addition, they vary in strength with the position of the source and are strongest when the source is on the horizon.

Tellus *Latin name for* the EARTH.

Tempel's comets two of the comets discovered by Ernst W. L. Tempel were named Tempel 1 (1879 III) and Tempel 2 (1957 II). The first disappeared after 1879 but reappeared in 1967. His most famous comet, 1866 I, named *Tempel-Tuttle*, has a period of 33.176 years and an orbit that is practically identical to that of the LEONID meteor stream. See CHAMPOLLION

temperature symbol: T. A property of a body or region that determines the direction of heat flow under thermal contact – always from a higher-temperature to a lower-temperature body or region. Numerical values of temperature are assigned by means of an internationally accepted scale of temperature, and for scientific purposes are now expressed in KELVIN (K) or degrees Celsius (°C): a temperature difference of 1 K is equal to a temperature difference of 1 °C, and a Celsius temperature t and a thermodynamic temperature T are related by the formula $t = T - 273.15$.

Astronomical temperatures are usually determined from spectroscopic measurements. Since astronomical bodies do not generally have a uniform temperature distribution and do not obey exactly the laws determining temperature, there are several different types of temperature; each characterizes a particular property of the body and has a slightly different value. They include EFFECTIVE, COLOR, BRIGHTNESS, ionization, and excitation temperature. The latter two are determined from the SAHA IONIZATION EQUATION and the BOLTZMANN EQUATION. See also THERMODYNAMIC TEMPERATURE SCALE.

temperature minimum see PHOTOSPHERE.

Tenma a Japanese X-RAY ASTRONOMY satellite launched in Feb. 1983. Like its predecessor, the satellite HAKUCHO, it was designed to study time variability and spectra of the brighter galactic and extragalactic X-ray sources. A feature of the satellite payload was a large area (~800 cm^2) gas scintillation PROPORTIONAL COUNTER (SPC). This SPC had an energy resolution a factor of two better than conventional proportional counters in the 1–50 keV band and provided impressive spectral data, particularly of the iron-line complex and absorption edges seen in many cosmic sources at 6–8 keV.

tera- symbol: T. A prefix to a unit, indicating a multiple of 10^{12} of that unit. For example, one terajoule is 10^{12} joules.

terminator the boundary between the dark and sunlit hemispheres of the Moon or a planet, the rotation of which gives rise to a *sunrise terminator* and a *sunset terminator*. The appearance of the terminator is affected by topographic irregularities, such as mountains, and by the presence of an atmosphere. See also PHASES, LUNAR.

terra (plural: **terrae**) an upland area on the surface of a planet or satellite, for example the lunar HIGHLANDS. The word is used in the approved name of such a feature.

terraced walls see CRATERS.

terrestrial of, relating to, or similar to the planet Earth.

terrestrial dynamical time (TDT) see DYNAMICAL TIME.

Terrestrial Planet Finder (TPF) a NASA space observatory planned for launch between 2014 and 2020. It will consist of two observatory spacecraft: one, a coronagraph, will be launched first, followed by a mid-infrared formation-flying interferometer. The observatory's mission is to survey nearby stars in a search for Earth-size planets orbiting the 'habitable zone' of their respective stars (the region where water might be able to exist and life night develop). The TPF will then follow up the brightest candidates it detects by subjecting them to spectroscopic analysis (e.g., to detect the chemical makeup of a possible atmosphere). In investigating atmospheric spectra, the craft may discover habitable conditions or even life itself. In addition, TPF is scheduled to conduct a program of high spatial-resolution astrophysics.

terrestrial planets the planets Mercury, Venus, Earth, and Mars. They are small rocky worlds with shallow atmospheres in comparison with the mainly gaseous GIANT PLANETS.

tesla symbol: T. The SI unit of MAGNETIC FLUX DENSITY, defined as one weber of magnetic flux per meter squared. One tesla is equal to 10^4 gauss.

tessera (plural: **tesserae**) a type of surface feature found on VENUS, consisting of a rugged elevated track extending for several thousand kilometers. The word is used in the approved name of such a feature.

Tethys the largest of the inner satellites of Saturn, having a diameter of 1050 km. It was discovered in 1684 by Giovanni Domenico Cassini. In size it is virtually the twin of the satellite Dione. Its low density of 1.2 g cm^{-3} indicates that it is probably made up mainly of water ice. Tethys has a feature currently unique in the Solar System: a huge canyon system, *Ithaca Chasma*, extending around the globe from near the north pole down to the equator and extending farther to the south pole; its average width is 100 km and its depth is 4–5 km. There is also an enormous crater, *Odysseus*, 400 km in diameter at 30° N latitude, 130° W longitude: its diameter is 40% that of the satellite and greater than the diameter of Mimas. The remainder of the surface is covered in craters of a range of sizes up to 20–50 km, indicating that Tethys has suffered intense bombardment in its history. Two much smaller satellites are held in the same orbit as Tethys. TELESTO travels about 60° ahead of it and CALYPSO follows it at the same angular distance. Telesto and Calypso are known as the *Tethys Trojans*. See also Table 2, Appendix.

Thalassa a small satellite of Neptune, discovered by Voyager 2 in 1989. See Table 2, Appendix.

Tharsis Ridge the principal area of volcanic activity on Mars, measuring 5000 km in diameter and elevated by up to 7 km from the average level of the planet's surface. It lies on the Martian equator and includes three of the largest Martian volcanoes: ASCRAEUS MONS, PAVONIS MONS, and ARSIA MONS. The highest Martian volcano, OLYMPUS MONS, lies several hundred km to the NW. On the E flank of the Tharsis Ridge is a vast maze of interconnecting canyons, *Noctis Labyrinthus*, which in turn lie at the W end of the VALLES MARINERIS. See also MARS, VOLCANOES.

thassaloid see BASIN.

Thebe a small irregularly shaped inner satellite of Jupiter, discovered by Voyager 2 in 1979. See JUPITER'S SATELLITES; Table 2, Appendix.

Themis family a HIRAYAMA FAMILY of asteroids located in the outer main belt at a distance of 3.2 AU from the Sun, most members having diameters less than 60 km. They all have low albedos, are of C-TYPE, and correspond to different metamorphic grades of CARBONACEOUS CHONDRITE material. These are thought to have been produced by different layers of the parent body suffering differing degrees of heating. The different types of material were then revealed when this body suffered collisional fragmentation. The Themis family is one of the most highly populated, with more than 500 members known. It takes its name from the asteroid Themis, discovered in 1853 by the Italian astronomer Annibale de Gasparis.

Themisto a small satellite of Jupiter, discovered in 1975 by Charles T. Cowall. See JUPITER'S SATELLITES; Table 2, Appendix.

Theophilus see table at CRATERS.

theory of everything (TOE) a unified theory of all the fundamental interactions, elementary particles, and cosmology. A theory of everything will involve a model that accounts for both quantum mechanics and gravity. It is hoped that SUPERSTRING

THEORY will be developed into such a theory.

thermal black-body radiation the electromagnetic emission from a perfect radiatior – a BLACK BODY – whose brightness follows Planck's radiation law.

thermal emission (**thermal radiation**; **thermal bremsstrahlung**) ELECTROMAGNETIC RADIATION resulting from interactions between electrons and atoms or molecules in a hot dense medium. The term usually refers to thermal emission from ionized gas (but see also THERMAL BLACK-BODY RADIATION). Free electrons in the ionized gas radiate when they are deflected in passing near PROTONS. The electrons are unbound to a nucleus before and after each encounter and the radiation is therefore also known as *free-free emission*. The radiation has a continuous spectrum, which at low frequencies has the SPECTRAL INDEX, α, of a thermal black-body radiator, i.e.

$$S \propto \nu^{-\alpha}; \alpha = -2$$

where S is the FLUX DENSITY and ν the frequency. At higher frequencies the spectrum flattens to a spectral index of α = 0. The *emission measure* of an ionized region of length l containing a density n_e of free electrons is given by

$$\mathrm{EM} = \int_0^l n_e^2 \, ds$$

where ds is an element of the path through the region. Compare NONTHERMAL EMISSION.

thermal field theory quantum field theory at nonzero temperatures. Thermal field theory is particularly useful in analyzing the sequence of phase transitions that is thought to have occurred in the EARLY UNIVERSE.

thermal noise see NOISE.

thermodynamic equilibrium a condition existing in a system when all the atoms and molecules have an equal share in the available heat energy. The temperature is then the same in all parts of the system by whatever method of measurement. A system that is not in thermodynamic equilibrium is unstable and the state of the system will change until equilibrium is reached. When strict equilibrium does not exist throughout a region, such as a stellar atmosphere, each small volume of gas may act as though in equilibrium even though a neighboring volume may have a slightly different temperature; this is a situation of *local thermodynamic equilibrium* (*LTE*).

thermodynamic temperature scale a temperature scale in which the temperature, T, is a function of the energy possessed by matter. Thermodynamic temperature is therefore a physical quantity that can be expressed in units, termed KELVIN. The zero of the scale is ABSOLUTE ZERO. The temperature of the ice point (0 °C) is 273.15 kelvin. Thermodynamic temperature can be converted to Celsius temperature by subtracting 273.15 from the thermodynamic temperature.

thermoelectric generator a device that converts heat directly into electric power. It consists basically of two dissimilar metals or semiconductors joined at two junctions: if the junctions are at different temperatures an electromotive force (e.m.f.) develops between the junctions. An e.m.f. can also be generated between two regions on one piece of metal when a temperature difference exists between the regions. In both cases the e.m.f. is proportional to the temperature difference and is also dependent on the materials used. The e.m.f. can be used to power an external electric circuit. Thermoelectric generators are used in long-range planetary probes when SOLAR CELLS are unable to produce sufficient power. The hot junction or region of the device is then often heated by means of the decay of a radioactive substance; this is the *radioisotope thermoelectric generator* (*RTG*).

thermonuclear explosion see SUPERNOVA.

thermonuclear reaction see NUCLEAR FUSION.

thermosphere see ATMOSPHERIC LAYERS.

theta (**θ**) the eighth letter of the Greek alphabet, used in STELLAR NOMENCLATURE usually to designate the eighth brightest star in a constellation or sometimes to indicate a star's position in a group.

third quarter *another name for* last quarter. See PHASES, LUNAR.

tholus (plural: **tholi**) a hill or dome on the surface of a planet or satellite. The word is used in the approved name of such a feature.

Thorne–Żytkow objects red supergiants

with neutron cores (first investigated by K. Thorne and A. Żytkow). Such objects are predicted to form either in the merger of a NEUTRON STAR with a massive companion in a massive X-RAY BINARY or in the collision of a neutron star with a low-mass star in a GLOBULAR CLUSTER. Although no Thorne–Żytkow has yet been identified, SS433 may be on the verge of becoming one. Thorne–Żytkow objects are expected to lose their envelopes in strong stellar winds and to ultimately become single (possibly spun-up) PULSARS.

three-body problem a specific case of the N-BODY PROBLEM in which the trajectories of three mutually interacting bodies are considered. There is no general solution for the problem although solutions exist for a few special instances. Thus the orbits can be determined if one of the bodies has negligible mass, as in the case of a planetary satellite, such as the Moon, subject to perturbations by the Sun or an asteroid whose motion is perturbed by Jupiter.

three kiloparsec arm see GALACTIC CENTER.

thrust see LAUNCH VEHICLE.

Thuban (α Dra) a white giant in the constellation Draco that was the POLE STAR about 2700 BC when it lay 10′ from the north celestial pole. Now of magnitude 3.6, its brightness has probably decreased in the past few hundred years. Because of PRECESSION, it will approach the pole again in about 21,000 years' time. Despite its designation as Alpha (α), it is in fact the fourth brightest star in the constellation. Spectral type: A0 III; distance: 95 pc.

tidal bulge see TIDES; TIDAL FORCE.

tidal capture a process by which a star can capture a passing, initially unbound star into a bound orbit. This is achieved by dissipating some of the orbital energy by raising TIDES in one or both stars. Since this process is effective only when the smaller star comes to within some three stellar radii of the larger star, tidal capture can only occur in very dense high-collision environments like GLOBULAR CLUSTERS. Low-mass X-RAY BINARIES and BLUE STRAGGLERS in globular clusters may be direct products of tidal captures.

tidal force a force arising in a system of one or more bodies as a result of differential gravitation: different parts of the system experience different accelerations. This can result in the production of TIDES and in general terms elongates a body in the direction of a nearby massive body, producing a *tidal bulge*. The force can alter a body's rotation rate until it is equal to the revolution period: this is true of most natural satellites of the planets, including the Moon, and is the case in some close binary stars, e.g. RS CANUM VENATICORUM STARS. Tidal forces can lead to *tidal heating* of the interior of a body, and in extreme cases can lead to the disruption of a body.

tidal friction energy dissipated by the raising of TIDES. As with tidal heights, the total energy dissipated on the Earth by tidal friction depends on the topography of coastlines and on the areal extent of adjacent continental shelves. Tidal friction is currently slowing down the Earth's rotation rate (i.e. the length of the day) by 16 seconds every million years and is causing the Moon to recede from the Earth by about 3.7 meters per century at present. See also SECULAR ACCELERATION.

tidal height see TIDES.

tidal lag see TIDES.

tidal tails see INTERACTING GALAXIES.

tidal theories see ENCOUNTER THEORIES.

tides distortions of a planet, star, etc., produced by the differential gravitational attraction of other astronomical bodies on parts of that planet, star, etc. The Sun and Moon combine to generate two *tidal bulges* in the Earth's oceans, one directed toward the Moon and the other diametrically opposite. If the Earth is assumed to be spherical and to be covered with water, then the gravitational pull of the Moon will have a different force at different points on the Earth's surface (see illustration (a i)). The gravitational acceleration at the Earth's center is equal to the centripetal acceleration of the Earth–Moon system. If this acceleration (which is a vector quantity) is subtracted from the surface accelerations, the differential (tidal) acceleration is found (illustration (a ii)), showing the two tidal bulges on the Earth–Moon line.

The daily rotation of the Earth and the slower eastward revolution of the Moon in its orbit produce (usually) two *high tides* and

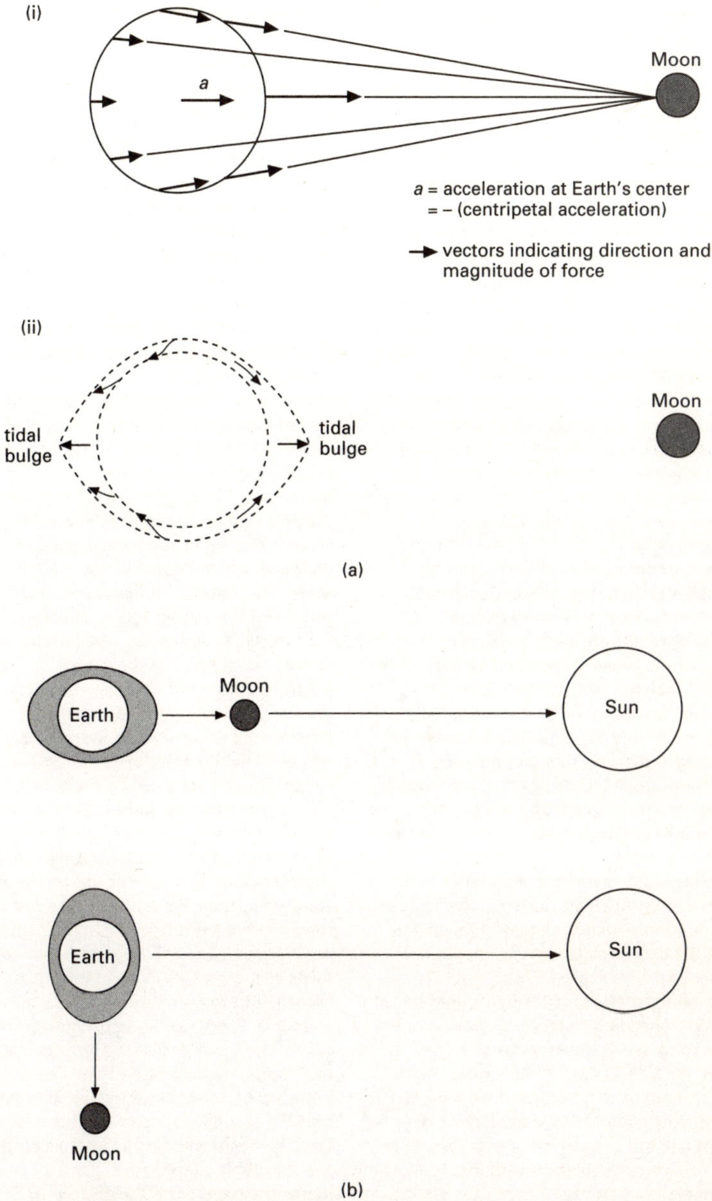

Tides: (a) (i) gravitational acceleration on Earth due to Moon, (ii) differential (tidal) acceleration found by subtracting *a* from other vectors on Fig. (i); (b) spring (top) and neap tides two *low tides* every 24 hours 50 minutes. The rotation and lunar revolution are also responsible for a *tidal lag* between the time when the Moon crosses the local MERIDIAN and the time of high tide.

The tidal pull of the Sun is less than half that of the Moon but reinforces it at full Moon and at new Moon to produce very high, or *spring tides*; these tides are exceptionally high when the Earth is close to PERIHELION and the Moon is close to PERIGEE (see illustration (b)). The lowest high tides, or *neap tides*, occur when the Moon is at QUADRATURE. The *tidal height* depends on the topography of the coastline and on the area of the adjacent continental shelf. Tides are also generated in the Earth's atmosphere and in the solid Earth.

Lunar tides are raised by the Earth as a consequence of the Moon's eccentric orbit. They trigger MOONQUAKES and TRANSIENT LUNAR PHENOMENA. See also TIDAL FRICTION.

time the continuous and nonreversible passage of existence, or some interval in this continuum. It is also a quantity measuring the duration of such an interval or of some process, etc. The unit of time in the SI system is the SECOND. The astronomical unit of time is often the interval of one day of 86 400 seconds. The time systems used in astronomy are INTERNATIONAL ATOMIC TIME, UNIVERSAL TIME, SIDEREAL TIME, and DYNAMICAL TIME (which has replaced EPHEMERIS TIME). See also SPACETIME.

time constant symbol: τ. A measure of the speed with which an electronic system can respond to a sudden change at its input.

time dilation see RELATIVITY, SPECIAL THEORY.

time of flight the time taken for light to travel a specified distance.

time zone see STANDARD TIME.

Titan the largest satellite of Saturn, discovered in 1655 by Christiaan Huygens. It orbits the planet at a mean distance of 1 221 900 km in a period of 15.95 days. It is in synchronous rotation with Saturn. With a diameter of 5150 km Titan is the second largest satellite in the Solar System, after Jupiter's Ganymede and, like Ganymede, it is somewhat larger but much less massive than the planet Mercury. The satellite appears reddish or orange in color but the two hemispheres are not identical. Titan has a thick, planetlike atmosphere made up almost entirely of nitrogen, with traces of argon, methane, ethane, acetylene, propane, diacetylene, methylacetylene, hydrogen cyanide, cyanoacetylene, cyanogen, carbon dioxide, and carbon monoxide. The surface pressure is 1.6 times that of the Earth and the surface temperature is 94 K, so that it is warmed by a small GREENHOUSE EFFECT. The coloration of the atmosphere is due to photochemical reactions and the production of fogs and aerosol particles, which probably extend nearly to the surface. Methane on Titan appears to play a similar role in the satellite's atmosphere to that of water on Earth, occurring in the three states of solid, liquid, and gas. The atoms and molecules of hydrogen that are produced by the photochemical reactions can easily escape from Titan and form a massive doughnut-shaped torus in the orbit of Titan. The material diffuses inward but is prevented from extending much beyond the orbit of Titan through the location of the boundary between the Saturn magnetosphere and the solar wind. The density of Titan is approximately 1.88 g cm^{-3}, nearly twice that of water. This suggests that the interior is composed roughly of half rock and half water ice. It has a surface that could be either liquid or solid in part, with oceans of methane. With no evidence of an intrinsic magnetic field, there would not seem to be an electrically conducting core. Voyager 1 in 1980 provided the first detailed images of Titan, including radar scans. The satellite became a major focus of the CASSINI mission to Saturn, launched in 1997. In January 2005 the European Space Agency's Huygens probe, part of the Cassini mission, touched down on Titan, giving scientists their first direct glimpses of its surface. Thus Titan became only the second planetary satellite to be the landing site of a human-made spacecraft. See also Table 2, Appendix.

Titania the largest satellite of Uranus, discovered in 1787 by William Herschel. Photographed by VOYAGER 2 in 1986, its icy surface shows many small craters, a few large impact basins, such as *Gertrude*, which is more than 200 km in diameter, and an extensive network of faults up to 5 km deep, such as the *Messina Chasma*, which runs up to 1500 km. See also URANUS' SATELLITES; Table 2, Appendix.

Titius–Bode law see BODE'S LAW.

TLP *abbrev. for* transient lunar phenomenon.

TOE see THEORY OF EVERYTHING.

tonne (**metric ton**) a unit of mass equal to 1000 kilograms and close to the long ton (1016 kg, 2240 lb).

top-down galaxy formation see DARK MATTER.

topocentric coordinates the coordinates of a celestial body measured from the surface of the Earth. For a star there is little or no detectable difference between topocentric coordinates and those referring to the Earth's center in a GEOCENTRIC COORDINATE SYSTEM. For a member of the Solar System the difference can be significant and a correction must be made.

topocentric zenith distance see ZENITH DISTANCE.

total eclipse see ECLIPSE.

totality see ECLIPSE.

total magnitude (**integrated magnitude**) a measure of the brightness of an extended object, such as a galaxy or nebula, obtained by summing the surface brightness over the entire image area or by measuring the amount of light received through a series of apertures of increasing diameter with a photoelectric photometer. The readings are found gradually to approach an upper limiting magnitude, which, corrected for night-sky brightness, gives the total magnitude.

total-power receiver see RECEIVER.

Toutatis (**(4179) Toutatis**) an APOLLO asteroid discovered in Jan. 1989 by the French astronomer Christian Pollas. It has a chaotic 4.01-year orbit that carries it between 0.9 and 4.1 AU from the Sun. In early Dec. 1992 Toutatis traveled within 3.5 million km of the Earth (10 times farther away than the Moon). In radar images the asteroid looked like a distorted peanut, the irregular ends being 4 and 2.5 km across. In 2004, it passed the Earth again at only four times the Moon's distance.

tower telescope (**solar tower**) see SOLAR TELESCOPE.

trailing edge see PRECEDING.

train **1** the faint glow sometimes left by a brighter METEOR along its path. It is much less conspicuous than the visible radiation that comes from the immediate vicinity of the ablating meteoroid. It is known as a *wake* if it glows for less than a second and a *persistent train* if the duration is longer. Sudden and brief enhancements of light during the meteor's passage are termed *flares* (or *bursts*).
2 the ionization and dust left along the meteoroid path.

trajectory the curved path followed by a moving spacecraft, rocket, etc., under the forces of gravity, lift, and/or drag.

Tranquillitatis, Mare (**Sea of Tranquillity**) an ancient irregular MARE on the eastern NEARSIDE of the Moon. It was the landing area for RANGER 8, SURVEYOR 5, and Apollo 11 (*Tranquillity Base* was the first manned landing point). The basaltic lavas in the mare are 3900 to 3600 million years old.

transfer orbit the trajectory followed by a spacecraft moving from one orbit to another, usually to the orbit of another body, such as another planet. The trajectory is generally part of an elongated ellipse – a *transfer ellipse* – that intersects the new orbit. The spacecraft would have to maneuver into an orbit around the planet by firing its rocket motors.

The transfer orbit requiring the minimum expenditure of energy is an ellipse that just touches the original (circular) orbit and the new coplanar orbit. This is called a *Hohmann transfer*, after the German engineer Walter Hohmann, who described it in 1925. Enough velocity is put in at the PERIGEE (or equivalent point) of the Hohmann transfer for the craft to reach the new orbit at APOGEE; at apogee an additional velocity input injects the craft into the desired orbit. Although requiring the lowest possible energy, Hohmann transfers between planets involve a long flight time. The flight time can be much reduced by using a somewhat greater velocity at perigee than that needed for a

Hohmann transfer. See also GRAVITY ASSIST.

transient lunar phenomena (**TLP**) short-lived changes in the appearance of lunar features, including reddish glows and obscurations of surface detail, that are triggered by lunar TIDES. They often occur within lunar CRATERS and around the perimeters of BASINS. A carbon spectrum was obtained from a TLP in the crater Alphonsus.

transit **1** the passage of an inferior planet across the Sun's disk. Normally when Venus or Mercury move between the Earth and Sun, at inferior CONJUNCTION, they pass above or below the Sun. A transit can occur only when the planet is at or near one of its NODES at inferior conjunction. Transits of Mercury take place either about May 7 (descending node) or Nov. 9 (ascending node) (see table). Transits occur at intervals of 7 or 13 years or in combinations of these figures, e.g. after 33 or 46 years. The much rarer transits of Venus take place either about June 7 (descending node) or Dec. 8 (ascending node). They currently occur in pairs with a separation of 8 years, the pairs themselves being separated by 105.5 or 121.5 years.
2 the passage of a planetary satellite or its shadow across the face of the planet.
3 (**upper culmination**) the passage of a celestial body, during its daily path, across an observer's meridian through the point closer to the observer's zenith. See also CULMINATION.

Transit Dates

Mercury		*Venus*	
November	*May*	*June*	*December*
1973	1970	1761 }	1874 }
1986	2003	1769 }	1882 }
1993	2016		
1999		2004 }	2117 }
2006		2012 }	2125 }

transit circle (**meridian circle**) an optical telescope mounted in such a way that it can swing only in a vertical north-south plane. It is used to measure the positions of celestial bodies with great accuracy as they cross the MERIDIAN of the telescope site (see CULMINATION). The ALTITUDE of a body as it crosses the meridian is now usually measured very precisely by electronic devices; earlier instruments used an accurately graded circular scale set in the vertical plane. The DECLINATION of the body can then be determined using the latitude of the observatory. Measurement of the precise LOCAL SIDEREAL TIME at the meridian passage determines the RIGHT ASCENSION of the body.

transition region see SUN. See also CHROMOSPHERE.

transit telescope any telescope that can swing in only one direction, up and down the north-south line in the sky, i.e. the observer's meridian. In optical astronomy a TRANSIT CIRCLE can be used to determine the positions of celestial bodies. In radio astronomy a transit telescope can be used to build up two-dimensional maps of radio sources: the Earth's daily rotation causes a radio source to move through the beam of the stationary telescope's ANTENNA, providing information in the east-west direction, the direction in which the telescope points being altered slightly each day.

transmission grating see DIFFRACTION GRATING.

transmission line see FEEDER.

transverse velocity *another name for* tangential velocity. See PROPER MOTION.

Trapezium a very young OPEN CLUSTER of stars, protostars, gas, and dust that lies in the ORION NEBULA and is part of the ORION ASSOCIATION. There are four prominent young main-sequence stars, which form the multiple star θ^1 Orionis and are of spectral class O6, B1, B1, and B3. These stars excite and ionize the nebula. They form a trapezium and are visible with a small telescope.

Triangulum (**Triangle**) a small constellation in the northern hemisphere near Perseus, the brightest stars being of 3rd magnitude. It contains the TRIANGULUM SPIRAL. Abbrev.: Tri; genitive form: Trianguli; approx. position: RA 2h, dec +30°; area: 132 sq deg.

Triangulum Australe (**Southern Triangle**) a

small constellation in the southern hemisphere near Crux, lying partly in the Milky Way. The brightest stars are the 1.9-magnitude orange giant Atria (α TrA) and 2nd-magnitude Beta (β) and Gamma (γ), which form a triangle. The area contains several Cepheid variables, such as R and S TrA and the bright open cluster NGC 6025. Abbrev.: TrA; genitive form: Trianguli Australis; approx. position: RA 16h, dec –65°; area: 110 sq deg.

Triangulum spiral (**M33; NGC 598**) a spiral (Sc) galaxy in the constellation Triangulum that is the third largest of the confirmed members of the LOCAL GROUP and is about 800 kiloparsecs distant. Although it is both smaller and more distant than the ANDROMEDA GALAXY it can appear larger because it is orientated face-on to us. The spiral arms are more open than those in our own Galaxy and the nucleus is relatively small and faint. It has a large number of young POPULATION I stars.

Trifid nebula (**M20; NGC 6514**) an EMISSION NEBULA about 2000 parsecs away in the direction of Sagittarius. There is dark matter associated with the nebula.

trigonometric parallax see ANNUAL PARALLAX.

triple alpha process (**Salpeter process**) a nuclear reaction occurring in an evolved star's interior when all the hydrogen has been used up and the core temperature has reached about 10^8 kelvin. Three helium nuclei (alpha particles) fuse together to form carbon by the reaction

$$3\,^4\text{He} > \,^{12}\text{C} + \gamma$$

This reaction gives out only 10% as much energy per unit mass as hydrogen burning.

triple star a MULTIPLE STAR with three components. See also BINARY STAR.

Triton the largest satellite of Neptune, discovered in 1846 by William Lassell. It has a retrograde orbit and is gradually spiraling in toward Neptune. In about 100 million years it will be inside Neptune's ROCHE LIMIT. Triton is very cold, with a surface temperature of only 37 K, and possesses a tenuous atmosphere mostly of nitrogen, but with some methane and traces of carbon monoxide. It has a pinkish south POLAR CAP, probably a layer of nitrogen snow and ice. Extensively photographed in 1989 by VOYAGER 2, Triton shows an extremely complex surface. Its largest crater is 27 km in diameter, it has no mountains, but it has long cracks up to 80 km wide. It also has a 'wrinkled' terrain resembling the skin of a cantaloupe melon, and nitrogen geysers reaching 8 km high. See also NEPTUNE'S SATELLITES; Table 2, Appendix.

Trojan group either of two groups of ASTEROIDS that lie in the vicinity of one of the two LAGRANGIAN POINTS in the orbit of Jupiter around the Sun: each group occupies one corner of an equilateral triangle with the Sun and Jupiter at the other corners. Beginning with the first Trojan to be discovered, (588) ACHILLES in 1906, most have been named after heroes from the two sides of the Trojan Wars. In fact, perturbations by other planets mean that each member of the group oscillates considerably in position (mainly in longitude along the orbit of Jupiter) from its stable Lagrangian point. It is likely that perturbations and collisions between them cause the total number of members of the group to change with time. Recent surveys suggest that more than 1000 Trojan group members may be bright enough to be seen from the Earth but fewer than 2% of these have yet received official asteroid designations. They are all exceptionally dark bodies.

tropical month the time of 27.321 58 days, on average, taken by the Moon to complete one revolution around the Earth, measured with respect to the vernal EQUINOX.

tropical year the interval between two successive passages of the Sun through the vernal EQUINOX, i.e. the time taken by the Sun, in its apparent annual motion, to complete one revolution around the celestial sphere relative to the vernal equinox. It is equal to 365.242 19 days. If the vernal equinox were a fixed point on the celestial sphere the tropical year would be equal to the SIDEREAL YEAR. PRECESSION however produces an annual retrograde motion of the equinoxes amounting to 50.28 seconds of arc relative to the fixed stars. The tropical year is thus about 20 minutes shorter than the sidereal year. Since the seasons recur after one tropical year, the average length of a CALENDAR YEAR should be as close as is practicable to the tropical year.

The tropical year of 1900 was the primary unit of EPHEMERIS TIME. Use of ephemeris time, and hence of the tropical year, was discontinued in 1984.

troposphere, tropopause see ATMOSPHERIC LAYERS.

true anomaly see ANOMALY.

true equator and equinox the coordinate system determined by instantaneous positions of CELESTIAL EQUATOR and ECLIPTIC. This reference system slowly changes as a result of the progressive effects of PRECESSION and the short-term variations of NUTATION. See also MEAN EQUATOR AND EQUINOX.

Trumpler's classification a method of classifying OPEN CLUSTERS according to their appearance, using the three criteria of stellar concentration toward the center, range in brightness of the member stars, and the total number of stars in the cluster. The method was devised by the Swiss-American astronomer Robert Trumpler who also found a correlation between this appearance classification and the cluster diameter.

Tsiolkovsky (**Tsiolkovskii**) See table at CRATERS.

T Tauri stars variable stars of spectral type G or later whose spectra are dominated by strong emission lines, usually attributed to CHROMOSPHERIC ACTIVITY and STELLAR WINDS in these stars. They are invariably embedded in dense patches of gas and dust that may require observations in the infrared: the dust absorbs the visible light of the star and reradiates it at longer wavelengths. The prototype is T Tauri. T Tauri stars are usually found together in groups (T associations) and are the youngest optically observable stages in the life of a star of about the Sun's mass; more massive counterparts are observed as AE and BE STARS. They are frequently associated with HERBIG–HARO OBJECTS.

There is much evidence that T Tauri stars are young objects, for instance they have a high abundance of lithium, an element destroyed fairly early in a star's life, and they are surrounded by gas and dust. They are thought to be young PROTOSTARS that have only recently contracted out of the interstellar medium (see STAR FORMATION). Lying above the main sequence in the HERTZSPRUNG–RUSSELL DIAGRAM, they are still contracting and losing mass (see T TAURI WIND). Their spectral lines reveal that some are extremely rapid rotators, throwing off material at speeds of up to 300 km s^{-1}. The irregular light variations are believed to arise partly from activity in the chromospheres of these young stars, and partly by the obscuring effect of the patchy dust in the cocoon as it moves in front of the star.

The original class of T Tauri stars, characterized by strong hydrogen emission lines, are often known as *classical T Tauri stars* (*CTTS*) to distinguish them from *naked* or *weak-line T Tauri stars* (*WTTS*); the latter have very weak hydrogen emission lines, often discovered in X-rays, and are much less active than the classical type. WTTS may represent a later phase of pre-main-sequence evolution than CTTS or a different evolutionary channel, as may be suggested by the apparently higher frequency of binaries among WTTS than among CTTS and main-sequence stars. See also FU ORIONIS; YY ORIONIS STARS.

T Tauri wind a continuous flow of material from the surface of a T TAURI star. Qualitatively this flux resembles the SOLAR WIND but the amount of material lost is far greater, approaching 10^{-7} solar masses per year in some cases. It is possible that this outflow acts as a braking mechanism for fast-spinning young stars. In some T Tauri stars this wind is collimated into a BIPOLAR OUTFLOW.

T-type asteroids a class of low-albedo asteroid.

Tucana (**Toucan**) a constellation in the southern hemisphere near Grus, the brightest stars being of 2nd and 3rd magnitude. The 3rd-magnitude double star Beta (β) has components that are also double. The area contains the Small MAGELLANIC CLOUD and the globular clusters 47 Tucanae (NGC 104), of 4th magnitude so easily visible, and NGC 362, just visible. Abbrev.: Tuc; genitive form: Tucanae; approx. position: RA 0h, dec −65°; area: 295 sq deg.

Tully–Fisher method the most accurate method for measuring the distances to distant spiral galaxies; it uses a relation between a galaxy's absolute magnitude and its rotation velocity that was discovered by R.B. Tully and J.R. Fisher in 1977. Radio observations at 21 cm wavelength give the rotation velocity; the Tully–Fisher relation then indicates the absolute magnitude, and a comparison with the apparent magnitude gives the distance. The Tully–Fisher relation must be calibrated by observations of nearby spirals, whose distances are known from CEPHEID VARIABLES, etc. (see DISTANCE DETERMINATION). See also FABER–JACKSON RELATION.

Tunguska event a gigantic explosion that occurred at about 7.17 a.m. on June 30, 1908 in the basin of the River Podkamennaya in Tunguska, Central Siberia. Devastation rained over an area 80 km in diameter and eye witnesses up to 500 km away saw in a cloudless sky the flight and explosion of a blindingly bright pale blue bolide. The sound of the explosion reverberated thousands of kilometers away, the explosion air wave recorded on microbarographs going twice round the world. The main explosion had an energy of 5×10^{16} joules and occurred at an altitude of 8.5 km. It was caused by the disintegration of an incoming object, most likely a Fragile Apollo asteroid or a small comet nucleus. When the object encountered the Earth it would have been coming from a point in the dawn sky comparatively close to the Sun and would thus have been most difficult to detect and observe.

turnoff point the point on the HERTZSPRUNG– RUSSELL DIAGRAM of a globular or open cluster at which stars are leaving the MAIN SEQUENCE and entering a more evolved phase (see illustration at GLOBULAR CLUSTER). Assuming that all the stars in a cluster contract out of a single gas cloud at approximately the same time, the locations of these stars on the H–R diagram depend on the time elapsed since the initial contraction. The length of time spent on the main sequence depends on stellar mass: stars of about solar mass will remain there for maybe 10^{10} years while more massive, and hence more rapidly evolving stars will turn off earlier. Since position on the main sequence also depends on mass, the lower the turnoff point, the older the cluster. The turnoff point of a cluster is the most accurate means of determining its age, and hence provides astronomers with a sample of stars of known age.

twenty-one cm line (**hydrogen line**) see H I REGION.

twilight the time preceding SUNRISE and following sunset when the sky is partly illuminated. *Civil twilight* is the interval when the true ZENITH DISTANCE (referred to the Earth's center) of the center of the Sun's disk is between 90°50′ and 96°, *nautical twilight* is the interval between 96° and 102°, and *astronomical twilight* is that between 102° and 108°. During nautical twilight, the sea horizon can be seen and the brightest stars are visible; during astronomical twilight, 6th-magnitude stars are just visible at the zenith in a clear sky.

twinkling see SCINTILLATION.

two-body problem a special case of the N-BODY PROBLEM in which a general solution can be found for the orbits of two bodies under the influence of their mutual gravitational attraction. The motion of a planet around the Sun is an example as long as the attractive forces of other planets are assumed to be negligible. A solution of the two-body problem is often acceptably realistic. Most theories of celestial motion thus use functions and principles, such as ORBITAL ELEMENTS and KEPLER'S LAWS, that have been derived by consideration of a two-body problem.

two-color diagram a plot of the COLOR INDICES *B–V* against *U–B*. Stars of different luminosity classes (see SPECTRAL TYPES) lie on slightly different curves.

Tycho a very recent lunar CRATER, possibly only about 100 million years old; it is 100 km in diameter. RAYS from the crater traverse much of the nearside of the Moon and are particularly striking at full Moon. The EJECTA BLANKET was sampled by SURVEYOR 7, the only Surveyor to land in the HIGHLANDS; some craters in the highland region of TAURUS-LITTROW may be SECONDARIES of Tycho.

Tycho catalogue see HIPPARCOS.

Tychonic system a model of the Solar

System proposed by Tycho Brahe in the 1580s and based on observations he made in order to test the COPERNICAN SYSTEM. He concluded that the Sun and Moon revolved around the Earth, which he maintained lay at the center of the Solar System, but suggested that the other planets orbited the Sun.

Tycho's star a type I SUPERNOVA that was observed in 1572 in the constellation Cassiopeia and was studied by astronomers in Europe, China, and Korea. Tycho Brahe's careful observations of its position have allowed modern astronomers to identify it with a known radio and X-ray source, which is the expanding supernova remnant. It was considerably brighter than Kepler's star of 1604, reaching a magnitude of –4 and remaining visible for about 18 months.

type I, type II Cepheids see CEPHEID VARIABLES.

type I, type II radio galaxies see FR I, FR II.

type I, type II Seyferts see SEYFERT GALAXY.

type I, type II supernovae see SUPERNOVA.

Uu

U–B see COLOR INDEX.

UBC–Lavall Telescope a rotating liquid-mercury mirror, 2.7 meters in diameter, on a fixed vertical mount. Operated by the University of British Columbia and Lavall University and located in Vancouver, it saw first light in 1992. It comprises a 2-mm-thick layer of mercury spread out by rotation over a paraboloidal support dish. It views a 21-arcmin field at the local zenith (centered on 49°.1).

UBV, UBVRI systems photometry systems for determining magnitudes at various broad wavebands, devised originally by H.L. Johnson and W.W. Morgan and extended to five wavebands by Johnson. See MAGNITUDE.

U Geminorum stars see DWARF NOVAE.

Uhuru ('Freedom' in Swahili) The first artificial Earth satellite for X-RAY ASTRONOMY (SAS–1), launched into a 500 km circular equatorial orbit in December 1970 from the San Marco platform off the coast of Kenya. Two sets of proportional gas counters, each 840 cm^2 in area and mounted on opposite sides of the slowly spinning spacecraft, scanned the sky for X-ray sources. Uhuru provided the first detailed X-ray sky map, leading to the *3U catalog* of 161 sources, published in 1974. Its most important discoveries were of X-RAY BINARIES (Cen X-3, Her X-1, etc.) and of extended regions of X-ray emission associated with CLUSTERS OF GALAXIES. Uhuru operated successfully until July 1971, when its transmitter failed. The 3U catalog is based on the data to that time. Subsequently the star sensors, used to determine the precise attitude of the spacecraft and hence the sky coordinates of each X-ray source, also degraded; surveying recommenced in Dec. 1971, however, after partial transmitter recovery. These later observations, with the aid of a magnetometer attitude solution, continued until Apr. 1973, when the Uhuru battery failed. All the Uhuru observations were finally put together to form the *4U catalog*, issued in 1978 and containing 339 X-ray sources.

UK Infrared Telescope (**UKIRT**) the British INFRARED TELESCOPE sited on MAUNA KEA, Hawaii, at the very high altitude of 4200 meters. The site is well above the main weather layers and the bulk of atmospheric water vapor, opaque to most infrared wavelengths; in addition there is excellent SEEING for work at visible wavelengths. The telescope is funded by the UK (by SERC), the Netherlands, and Canada, and is run by the Royal Observatory, Edinburgh. It became operational in 1979. The mirror is 3.8 meters (150 inches) in diameter, making the instrument the world's largest infrared telescope. It is unusually thin (29 cm) and weighs only 6.6 tonnes, allowing an extremely lightweight supporting structure to be used. The mirror surface has been ground sufficiently accurately that it can also be used at visible wavelengths for short exposures.

A full range of cryogenic (very low temperature) facilities is provided for cooling the detectors in order to reduce spurious signals generated by the warmth of the detectors. There are also means for removing spurious signals generated by the telescope itself. The instruments mounted at UKIRT's Cassegrain focus include infrared spectrometers and photometers; the latter work at various wavebands – optical, infrared (1–5 μm, 4–35 μm), and submillimeter (0.3–1 mm). Heavier instruments are mounted at the coudé focus.

UK Schmidt Telescope (**UKST**) the 1.2-meter SCHMIDT TELESCOPE at the ANGLO-AUSTRALIAN OBSERVATORY, Australia. Since 1988 it has been run by the Anglo–Australian Telescope Board, having been originally administered by the ROYAL OBSERVATORY, EDINBURGH (ROE). The UKST began regular observation in 1973, and was involved primarily in the production of photographic plates for the ESO/SERC SOUTHERN SKY SURVEY. It can reach limiting magnitudes in exposures of about an hour as a result of its low focal ratio of f/2.5. Each photograph covers a very wide area of the sky, amounting to 40 square degrees (in fact 6.6 × 6.6 degrees), and gives images of arc-second resolution over a wavelength range of 340–1000 nm. Its photographs are held in the plate library of the ROE. See also COSMOS.

ULIRG *abbrev. for* ultraluminous IRAS galaxy. See IRAS GALAXIES.

ultraluminous IRAS galaxies see IRAS GALAXIES.

ultraviolet astronomy astronomical observations in the waveband between the Lyman limit of atomic hydrogen at 91.2 nm and the Earth's atmospheric absorption cut-off at about 320 nm (see LYMAN SERIES; ATMOSPHERIC WINDOWS). The waveband between the Lyman limit and the X-ray band starting at about 12 nm is called the extreme ultraviolet (EUV or XUV – see XUV ASTRONOMY). Strong atomic and molecular absorption in the Earth's atmosphere requires UV observations to be carried out at balloon altitudes (about 30 km) for the 250–320 nm waveband and on rockets or satellites, at higher altitudes, for wavelengths below 250 nm. The UV band includes many of the resonant absorption and emission lines of most of the more abundant chemical elements, including hydrogen in both its atomic and molecular form. Such RESONANCE TRANSITIONS (to and from atomic ground states) are very important for the determination of the physical and chemical properties of astronomical sources, such as the interstellar gas, the outer atmospheres of stars, and the gaseous regions of active galaxies, in which the excitation is such that the electrons in atoms or molecules are mainly in the ground state.

Most ultraviolet astronomy has been carried out using satellite instrumentation either to survey the sky at low spatial and spectral resolution or to observe individual preselected sources at high resolution. The OAO–2 satellite, launched in 1968, carried a telescope that made a partial sky survey at 100–300 nm, while the TD-1 satellite carried an experiment that surveyed the whole sky between 135 and 274 nm, observing over 30 000 ULTRAVIOLET STARS. OAO–3, renamed *Copernicus* after launch in 1972, carried a reflecting telescope and high-resolution (about 0.02 nm) grating spectrometer that obtained spectra of many stars and interstellar regions in the wavelength range 90–300 nm over the following 8 years. Copernicus was restricted to observations of hot stars brighter than about 6th magnitude and concentrated on studies of the interstellar gas and the STELLAR WINDS of hot luminous stars. The ASTRONOMICAL NETHERLANDS SATELLITE (ANS), launched in 1974, provided UV photometric observations of many thousands of stars in the waveband 155–320 nm.

In Jan. 1978 the INTERNATIONAL ULTRAVIOLET EXPLORER (IUE) satellite was launched into a geosynchronous orbit over the mid-Atlantic. This satellite is operated like a ground-based observatory with astronomers carrying out observations at two stations in the USA and in Spain. IUE carries a 45-cm aperture ultraviolet telescope feeding two ECHELLE GRATING spectrographs, which cover the waveband 115–320 nm at about 0.01 nm resolution. IUE is much more sensitive than any previous UV satellite and has allowed observations of stars and active galaxies as faint as 17th magnitude. It has provided important data on a wide variety of astronomical fields: there have been studies of the Solar System, of stars and the interstellar medium in our own Galaxy and the Magellanic Clouds, and of external galaxies, Seyfert galaxies, and quasars.

It has been found that an extensive hot gaseous halo surrounds the Galaxy and the Magellanic Clouds, and that the Sun is located in a warm low-density 'hole' in the interstellar medium. Extensive MASS LOSS from hot stars, first studied in high-luminosity objects with Copernicus, has been discovered to exist also in low-luminosity hot stars such as O and B subdwarfs and the central stars of planetary nebulae; in many cases the mass loss rates are too high to be accounted for by current theory. Many stars have been found to show considerable variations in their mass loss. The outer chromospheres and coronae of the cool stars have been observed in the UV with IUE for the first time, allowing the densities and temperature distributions in these atmospheric regions to be mapped and shedding light on their energy balance. Because of the observatory nature of IUE it has been possible to respond quickly to the occurrence of transient events and the UV spectra of several novae and supernovae have been obtained. IUE observations of SN 1987A in the LMC showed that the star is surrounded by a nitrogen-rich circumstellar shell at a radius of 0.5 light-years, providing the first direct evidence for a supernova progenitor having gone through the red giant evolutionary phase prior to its explosion. IUE worked successfully for 18 years.

The NASA HUBBLE SPACE TELESCOPE (HST), launched 1990, is providing extensive new UV observations. It carries a 2.4-meter primary telescope and several cameras and spectrographs operating in the UV waveband 115–330 nm (as well as coverage at visible wavelengths) at greater sensitivity than IUE. The spherical aberration of the HST primary mirror initially limited its performance. Most of the scientific programs originally envisaged were carried out, however, with the satellite providing important new UV spectroscopy and imaging of hot stars, late-type stellar chromospheres and coronae, the interstellar medium, galaxies and clusters of galaxies, quasars and active galactic nuclei, and Solar System objects. The corrective optics package COSTAR, emplaced in Dec. 1993, brought the HST back to full capability.

ultraviolet radiation ELECTROMAGNETIC RADIATION lying in the wavelength range beyond the Earth's atmospheric absorption at about 320 nm to the hydrogen Lyman limit at 91.2 nm (see HYDROGEN SPECTRUM). The gap between the X-ray and UV wavebands is the XUV region. Long-wavelength ultraviolet radiation, i.e. with wavelengths up to 350 nm, near that of LIGHT, is often called *near-ultraviolet* with *far-ultraviolet* (*FUV*) being applied to short wavelengths, i.e. 91.2 nm up to about 200 nm.

ultraviolet stars hot stars that have considerable emission at ultraviolet and XUV wavelengths, i.e. between about 12–320 nm; these include early-type O and B STARS, WOLF-RAYET STARS, SUBDWARF O and B stars, hot WHITE DWARFS, and the central stars of most PLANETARY NEBULAE. For an O star with a surface temperature of about 30 000 K, over 80% of its radiation lies in the ultraviolet. In comparison the Sun, with a surface temperature of about 5800 K, emits most of its radiation in the visible region of the spectrum (380–750 nm). Space observations have allowed the UV energy distribution of such stars to be measured, providing a more precise determination of their total radiated power. In addition emission and absorption line spectra have given information on the structure and element abundances in the stellar atmospheres, and have shown for both luminous and subluminous hot stars the presence of strong STELLAR WINDS. In many cases such winds involve a rate of mass loss that will substantially affect the evolution of the star. Extensive regions of ionized interstellar gas – the H II REGIONS – surround many such hot luminous stars. See also ULTRAVIOLET ASTRONOMY.

Ulysses a joint ESA/NASA mission to study for the first time the properties of the INTERPLANETARY MEDIUM and SOLAR WIND away from the plane of the ecliptic and over the polar regions of the Sun. The ESA spacecraft was launched by NASA in Oct. 1990, toward Jupiter. It encountered Jupiter in Feb. 1992, approaching close over the north pole then swinging under the south pole, and the gravity of the massive planet accelerated the probe out of the ecliptic plane into a polar orbit of the Sun; the inclination of its orbit to the ecliptic is in fact 80°. (No rocket has sufficient thrust to launch a probe directly into such an orbit.) It passed under the Sun's south pole in May 1994 and over the north pole in May 1995, crossing the ecliptic in Feb. 1995. Its nine scientific instruments took measurements throughout the mission. They measured the solar wind from the Sun's polar regions at both solar maximum and minimum, they studied the interplanetary magnetic field and found that the magnetic flux emanating from the Sun is the same at all latitudes, and they discovered 'pools' of energetic particles surrounding the Sun. Ulysses also discovered the presence of interstellar dust in the Solar System, measured COSMIC RAYS flowing into the Solar System, made the first measurement of interstellar helium atoms in the Solar System, and analyzed solar X-rays, radio waves and plasma waves, and Jupiter's magnetosphere. Ulysses' mission continued throughout the 1990s and early 2000s and was extended several times; the latest extension, announced in 2004, continued Ulysses' operation up to 2008.

umbra 1 the dark inner region of a shadow cast by an object illuminated by a light of finite size rather than a pinpoint of light. The less dark outer region of the shadow is the *penumbra* (see illustration). The source of light is totally obscured to someone in the umbral region but only partly obscured in the penumbral region. See ECLIPSE. 2 see SUNSPOTS.

Umbriel a satellite of Uranus, discovered in 1851 by William Lassell. Photographed by VOYAGER 2 in 1986, it is very dark with an ALBEDO of only 0.18. It is heavily cratered, its most prominent feature being *Skyund*, a crater 100 km in diameter with a bright central peak. See also URANUS' SATELLITES; Table 2, Appendix.

unification schemes see RADIO GALAXY; SEYFERT GALAXY.

unit distance the astronomical unit of length, i.e. the length for which the GAUSSIAN GRAVITATIONAL CONSTANT takes its exact value when the units of measurement are the astronomical units of length, mass, and time. It is equal to the SPEED OF LIGHT, *c*, times the LIGHT-TIME for unit distance, τ_A, i.e. to $1.495\ 978\ 70 \times 10^{11}$ meters.

United Kingdom Astronomy Technology Centre (UK ATC) the United Kingdom's chief scientific establishment dedicated to astronomical technology. Its primary purpose is to provide a focus within the UK for the design, production, and promotion of cutting-edge advances in the development of astronomical and astrophysical instruments and techniques. Its scientists also carry out observational and theoretical research into fundamental issues in astronomy, such as the origins of planets and of galaxies. The UK ATC is funded and managed by the PARTICLE PHYSICS AND ASTRONOMY RESEARCH COUNCIL (PPARC). The UK ATC was formally established at the ROYAL OBSERVATORY, EDINBURGH (ROE) Apr. 1998, following PPARC's reorganization of its funding of UK astronomy. Part of that reorganization involved the closure of the ROYAL GREENWICH OBSERVATORY and the transfer of some of its functions, along with some of the functions of the ROE, to the

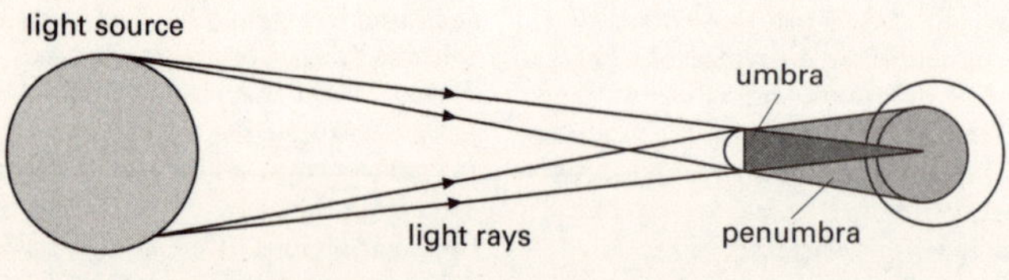

Umbral and penumbral regions of a shadow

UK ATC. The center collaborates with PPARC's overseas establishments – such as the ISAAC NEWTON GROUP of telescopes and the James Clerk Maxwell Telescope and the UK Infrared Telescope, both at MAUNA KEA in Hawaii – and international agencies such as NASA and ESA on a contractor-customer basis. It focuses its work around technologies for use in the optical, infrared and submillimeter wavebands and is involved in designing and making science instruments for such organizations as the GEMINI TELESCOPES, the EUROPEAN SOUTHERN OBSERVATORY, and the planned JAMES WEBB SPACE TELESCOPE project.

United States Naval Observatory (**USNO**) the national observatory in Washington D.C. concerned mainly with astrometric measurements for the purposes of timekeeping and navigation. The USNO is a department of the US Navy, and part of its mission is "to provide astronomical and timing data required by the Navy and other components of the Department of Defense for navigation, precise positioning, and command, control, and communications" and to make such information publicly available. The USNO was founded in 1830 as the Depot of Charts and Instruments. The original observatory was built in 1833, but the site has since been moved and expanded several times. In 1855, the UNSO began publishing astronomical and nautical almanacs, and in 1904 it broadcast the world's first time signal. Today its products include computer programs and Web-based astronomy- and time-related applications.

universal time (**UT**) the precise measure of time that forms the basis for all civil timekeeping. It conforms closely to the mean diurnal motion of the Sun.

UT is defined by a mathematical formula relating UT to SIDEREAL TIME. It is thus determined from observations of the diurnal motions of stars. It is not a uniform timescale, however, due to variations in the Earth's rotation. The timescale determined directly from stellar observations is dependent on the place of observation, and is designated UT0. The timescale independent of location is obtained by correcting UT0 for the variation in the observer's meridian that arises from the irregular varying motion of the Earth's geographical poles; it is designated UT1. This is the timescale used by astronomers. It is counted from 0 hours at midnight, and the unit is the mean solar day.

Coordinated universal time (*UTC*) is based on INTERNATIONAL ATOMIC TIME (TAI). Since Jan. 1 1972 the time given by broadcast time signals has been UTC. UTC differs from TAI by an integral number of seconds. UTC is kept within 0.90 seconds of UT1 by the insertion (or deletion) of exactly one second when necessary, usually at the end of December or June; these step adjustments are termed *leap seconds*. An approximation (DUT1) to the value of UT1 minus UTC is transmitted in code on broadcast time signals. TAI and UTC are recommended for the precise dating of observations. See also DYNAMICAL TIME.

Universe the sum total of potentially knowable objects. The study of the Universe on a grand scale is called COSMOLOGY. Barriers between potentially knowable and unknowable objects exist in even a simple expanding Euclidian Universe with flat space (i.e. in which the surface area of a sphere is $4\pi r^2$). More and more distant objects are seen to recede at faster and faster velocities. At a certain distance objects are receding at the speed of light and suffer an infinite REDSHIFT; they are then potentially unobservable.

Within the framework of general RELATIVITY the space of the Universe can be curved, and depending on the nature of the curvature the Universe may be *closed* or *open*. In a closed Universe gravitational distortion of light would cause space to be spherically curved: space would curve back on itself to form a finite volume with no boundary. The Universe would then be finite and the gravitational attraction among galaxies would be sufficient eventually to halt and reverse the expansion of the Universe so that it would begin to contract. In an open Universe space would still be curved but would not turn back on itself: the curvature would be hyperbolic rather than spherical. The Universe would then be infinite, with gravity too weak to halt the Universe's expansion. In a *flat Universe* space is not curved: it can be described by Euclidean geometry. The Universe would then be infinite and would expand forever, but less rapidly than an open Universe.

The dynamic behavior of the Universe, i.e. whether it is closed, open, or flat, depends on the value of the MEAN DENSITY OF MATTER, and hence on the DECELERATION PARAMETER q_0:

if $q_0 > ½$, Universe is closed
if $q_0 < ½$, Universe is open
if $q_0 = ½$, Universe is flat

The Universe exists close to the dividing line between the ever-expanding model and the eventually contracting model, but it is not yet certain which of these radically different prospects will occur. If the Universe is closed it will collapse in upon itself to form a final SINGULARITY known as the *big crunch.* Some theories speculate that there is an infinite cycle of OSCILLATING UNIVERSES where the end result of the collapse could be regarded instead as a *big bounce.* See also AGE OF THE UNIVERSE; BIG BANG THEORY; COSMOLOGICAL MODELS.

unresolved source a source of radiation whose angular size is too small for details of its structure to be revealed.

unsharp masking a process for amplifying fine detail in the image on a photographic plate. A positive contact copy is made through the glass on low-contrast film. The copy is blurred, containing only the large-scale features of the original image; this is the *unsharp mask.* When placed in contact with the back of the plate, it effectively cancels out the large-scale features, revealing the fine detail on the plate.

upper culmination see CULMINATION.

Uranometria 2000.0 a computer-plotted star atlas by W. Tirion et al, published 1987–88 in two volumes, displaying all stars and many other objects brighter than magnitude 9.5 in the northern and southern skies; the objects are precessed to the EPOCH 2000.0. There is also an associated catalog. The original *Uranometria* of Johann Bayer was published in 1603.

Uranus the seventh planet of the Solar System and the first to be discovered telescopically – by William Herschel in 1781. The third largest of the GIANT PLANETS, it has an equatorial diameter of about 51 119 km, a mass 14.5 times that of the Earth, and a density 1.3 times that of water. Uranus orbits the Sun every 84.01 years, varying in distance between 18.31 and 20.07 AU. At OPPOSITIONS, which recur four days later each year, it has a mean angular diameter of 3.7 arc seconds and a magnitude of 5.6, near the limit of naked eye visibility. Telescopically Uranus shows a featureless greenish disk making visual determination of its rotation period impossible. The period is about 16 hours and retrograde. Orbital and physical characteristics are given in Table 1, backmatter.

Uranus' equator is tilted by 98° with respect to its orbit, making it unique in having its rotation axis close to its orbital plane. This means that the north and south poles alternately point toward the Sun, giving highly exaggerated seasonal changes on the planet.

VOYAGER 2 flew by Uranus in 1986, and at this time its south pole was pointing almost directly at the Sun. Images of the planet show a remarkably featureless surface. Faint cloud markings determine that winds on Uranus blow at 40–160 m s^{-1} in the same direction as the planet rotates. These Uranian winds arrange the planet's cloud features into east-west bands.

The outer layers of Uranus are predominantly hydrogen and helium in gaseous state and with low density. The temperature in the upper atmosphere is around 60 K so methane and hydrogen condense to form clouds of ice crystals. The methane forms at higher altitudes, giving Uranus its blue-green color. Uranus' outer atmosphere rotates differentially between 16.2 and 16.9 hours at cloud-surface level, depending on latitude. Its internal rotation rate is about 17.23 hours. It is thought it has a rocky core, primarily iron and silicon, about the size of the Earth.

The equatorial region of Uranus receives little sunlight, but its effective temperature is almost the same as the sunlit pole. This implies that heat is efficiently transported between the poles and the equator.

Auroral activity noted before the Voyager probes gave indications that Uranus has a MAGNETOSPHERE. It is now known that Uranus has a magnetic field about the same

Uranus' rings

Name	*Mean distance from planet center (10³ km)*	*(planetary radii)*	*Radial width (km)*	*Thickness*	*Optical depth*
1986U2R	38	1.49	2500	0.1?	<0.001
6	42	1.60	1–3	0.1?	0.2–0.3
5	42	1.6	2–3	0.1?	0.5–0.6
4	43	1.63	2–3	0.1?	0.3
Alpha	45	1.71	7–12	0.1?	0.3–0.4
Beta	46	1.74	7–12	0.1?	0.2
Eta	47	1.80	0–2	0.1?	0.1–0.4
Gamma	48	1.82	1–4	0.1?	1.3–2.3
Delta	48	1.84	3–9	0.1?	0.3–0.4
1986U1R	50	1.91	1–2	0.1?	0.1
Epsilon	51	1.95	20–100	<0.15	0.5–2.1

as the Earth's. The magnetic axis is inclined by nearly 60° from its axis of rotation and, like the other JOVIAN PLANETS, is opposite in polarity to the Earth's.

Uranus has 27 known satellites and a ring system. See URANUS' RINGS; URANUS' SATELLITES.

Uranus' rings a system of planetary rings. The first six were discovered in 1977 when the planet occulted a star. Three further rings were found by Perth observatory, and Voyager 2 discovered two more rings in 1986. The 11 rings are narrow and dark, unlike Saturn's, which are broad and bright (see table). Most of them are less than 10 km wide and typical particles within them can be compared with large lumps of coal roughly 1 m in size. The Uranian rings have a low ALBEDO of about 0.01. The most prominent, the Epsilon ring, is gray in color and has segments that are nearly 100 km wide. All the rings are well within the ROCHE LIMIT. VOYAGER 2 found only two SHEPHERD SATELLITES – Cordelia and Ophelia, which together control the Epsilon ring –although the rings are confined to very narrow orbits.

Uranus' satellites prior to VOYAGER 2's flyby in 1986, five moderate-sized satellites were known to exist. The two largest, TITANIA and OBERON, are nearly the same size with diameters about 1550 km. ARIEL and UMBRIEL are also nearly the same size with diameters about 1160 km, whereas MIRANDA is only 472 km across. Voyager 2 discovered 10 very small satellites in 1986, most having diameters of less than 100 km. In 1997 two further moons were discovered by astronomers at Mount Palomar. These, given the provisional names Caliban (S/1997 U1) and Sycorax (S/1997 U2), were the first irregular satellites of Uranus to be identified. Subsequently, in 1999, a further satellite was identified by the Lunar and Planetary Lab at the University of Arizona from data collected by Voyager 2. This is a regular satellite, so far unnamed (S/1986 U10). Also in 1999, three more irregular satellites were discovered by astronomers using the Canada-France-Hawaii Telescope at Maunder Kea – Setebos (S/1999 U1), Stephano (S/1999 U2), and Prospero (S/1999 U3). Trinculo (S/2001 U1) was discovered in August 2001 by M. Holman and others, along with two other satellites as yet unnamed. With a further three satellites discovered in 2003, this gives Uranus a total of 27 satellites in all.

The average density of the Uranian satellites is about 1.5 g cm^{-3}, which is consistent with all 27 being composed of a mixture of rock and ice. Voyager data suggests the larger satellites are 50% water ice, 20% carbon- and nitrogen-based

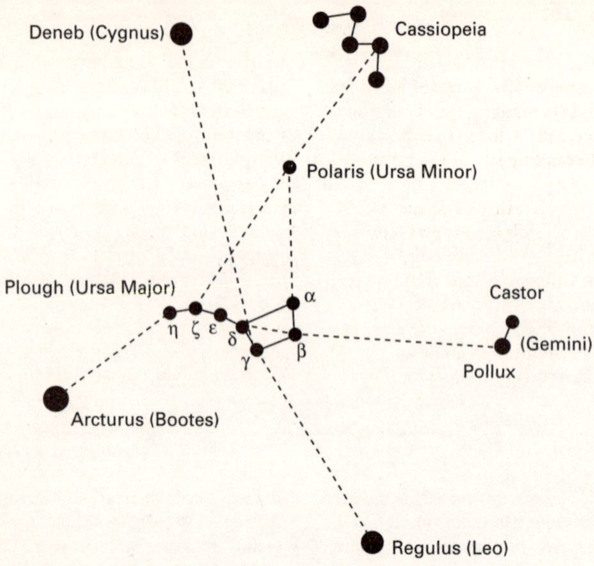

Ursa Major and bright neighboring stars

materials, and 30% rock. In addition, Uranus' satellites all have low ALBEDOS. Umbriel is one of the darkest moons in the Solar System with an albedo of 0.18. The most recent impact craters on Oberon and Titania appear to have exposed fresh undarkened ice, which implies the darkness is caused by a coating of dark sootlike material. See also Table 2, Appendix.

Ursa Major (**Great Bear**) an extensive very conspicuous constellation in the northern hemisphere that can be used to indicate the positions of brighter neighboring stars (see illustration). The seven brightest stars form the PLOUGH. Among these, the three brightest stars are ALIOTH, ALCAID, and DUBHE, all about magnitude 1.8. The area contains several double stars including the naked-eye double MIZAR and Alcor, the planetary OWL NEBULA, and the close spiral galaxies M81 (NGC 3031) and M82 (NGC 3034). M82 is a STARBURST GALAXY. Abbrev.: UMa; genitive form: Ursae Majoris; approx. position: RA 11.5h, dec +55°; area: 1280 sq deg.

Ursa Major cluster an OPEN CLUSTER containing over 100 stars that are scattered over an area of sky more than 1000 minutes of arc in diameter; its wide angular diameter is due to its proximity to Earth. It includes the stars Beta (β), Gamma (γ), Delta (δ), Epsilon (ε), and Zeta (ζ) Ursae Majoris in the PLOUGH, and also SIRIUS.

Ursa Minor (**Little Bear**) a constellation in the northern hemisphere that includes and surrounds the north celestial pole. The two brightest stars, both of 2nd magnitude, are POLARIS (α) (the present POLE STAR) and the orange subgiant Kochab (β), the star that marked the pole around 1000 BC, and will do so again about 23,000 years from now. Abbrev.: UMi; genitive form: Ursae Minoris; approx. position: RA 0 – 24h, dec +80°; area: 256 sq deg.

Ursa Minor system a dwarf elliptical galaxy that is a member of the LOCAL GROUP.

Ursids a minor METEOR SHOWER, radiant: RA 217°, dec +78°, maximizing on Dec. 22. The METEOROID STREAM is associated with comet Tuttle.

UT, UT0, UT1, UTC see UNIVERSAL TIME.

Utopia Planitia a smooth Martian plain located northwest of the ELYSIUM PLANITIA volcanoes and centered on the coordinates 50° N latitude, 242° W longitude. It was chosen as the landing site of the VIKING 2 Lander in 1976.

UTR-2 *abbrev. for* Ukrainian T-shape Radio telescope. The world's largest PHASED ARRAY operating at decametric wavelengths. Located near Grakovo village, about 80 km from Kharkov, northeast Ukraine, UTR-2 has a collecting area of 150 000 square meters and a resolution of about 40 arcminutes at its center frequency of 16.7 MHz.

UV *abbrev. for* ultraviolet.

uvby system a system of photometry, devised by B. Strömgren, in which photoelectric MAGNITUDES *u*, *v*, *b*, and *y* are measured at four wavelength bands: measurements of *u* (ultraviolet) are centered on 350 nm, *v* (violet) on 410 nm, *b* (blue) on 470 nm, and *y* (yellow) on 550 nm. The bandwidth (20–30 nm) is much narrower than for the UBV system. The uvby system can be used to measure METALLICITY, temperature, and Balmer discontinuity of A, B, and F stars.

UV Ceti stars see FLARE STARS.

***uv*-plane** unlike a conventional telescope, a radio INTERFEROMETER cannot produce an image of the sky directly. Instead it meathorsures the FOURIER TRANSFORM of the sky brightness distribution in a plane perpendicular to the direction of observation. A measurement on a particular BASELINE corresponds to a point on this plane with coordinates *u* and *v*, at a distance from the origin equal to the projected length of the baseline measured in wavelengths. The *uv*-plane is sometimes called the *aperture plane*, and a good coverage of points is essential for high-quality APERTURE SYNTHESIS mapping.

Vv

V404 Cygni the best candidate for a low-mass black hole known to date. See BLACK HOLE.

Vaca Muerta meteorite a rare stony-iron (mesosiderite) METEORITE, many kilograms of which were found in 1861 over an area of 12 × 2 km in the Atacama Desert in Chile. The dark meteorites were easy to spot against the pale sand of the desert. About 4 tonnes out of an estimated initial mass of 6 tonnes have now been recovered. The fall probably occurred about 3000 years ago.

vacuum fluctuation a fluctuation in the value of a quantity that is associated with the vacuum state having ZERO-POINT ENERGY. The existence of vacuum fluctuations is a specifically quantum-mechanical effect. It is thought that quantum fluctuations in the EARLY UNIVERSE were responsible for the large-scale structure in the Universe.

Vacuum Tower Telescope see TEIDE OBSERVATORY.

vacuum tower telescopes see SOLAR TELESCOPE.

Valhalla Basin see CALLISTO.

Valles Marineris a vast system of canyons on Mars photographed by MARINER 9. The canyons had long been recognized as a feature of the Martian surface, subject to changes in brightness, and known collectively as *Coprates canyon*. They were renamed Valles Marineris in commemoration of the Mariner project. The Valles Marineris are located near the Martian equator and centered on the coordinates 14° S latitude and 59° W longitude (see AREOGRAPHY). See MARS, SURFACE FEATURES.

valley, lunar (**canyon**) a radial fracture on the Moon associated with an impact basin or crater. See table at RILLE.

vallis (plural: **valles**) valley. The word is used in the approved name of such a surface feature on a planet or satellite.

Van Allen radiation belts two regions within the Earth's MAGNETOSPHERE in which charged particles become trapped and oscillate backward and forward between the magnetic poles as they spiral around magnetic field lines. The lower belt, which on average lies 5000 km above the equator, contains protons and electrons either captured from the SOLAR WIND or derived from collisions between upper atmosphere atoms and high-energy COSMIC RAYS. The upper belt lies between about 25 000 and 36 000 km or more above the equator but curving downward toward the magnetic poles; it contains fewer and less-energetic particles than the lower belt, mainly electrons from the solar wind. The belts were discovered by James Van Allen in the course of his analysis of observations by early EXPLORER satellites in 1958.

Van de Graaff see table at CRATERS.

Vanguard project part of the US program for the INTERNATIONAL GEOPHYSICAL YEAR, in which three small satellites were orbited. Vanguard 1, launched on Mar. 17 1958, was the first satellite powered by SOLAR CELLS: it continued transmitting for six years and long-term tracking of it later revealed the slight pear shape of the Earth. Two other Vanguards launched in 1959 completed the program, which provided information not only on the Earth's shape but on its surface and interior, its magnetic field and radiation belts, and its space environment.

Van Maanen's star see PISCES.

variable *short for* variable star.

variable radio source a RADIO SOURCE whose measured parameters change with time, especially the FLUX DENSITY. Many extragalactic radio sources have been observed at frequencies above 400 megahertz to vary over periods of weeks or months. The time-scale of the variations imposes an upper limit on the linear size of the varying region since the conditions are unlikely to change more quickly than the time it takes for light to travel across the region.

variable star a star whose physical properties, such as brightness, radial velocity, and spectral type, vary with time: about 30 000 have been cataloged so far. The variation in brightness is the easiest to detect, occurring in almost all variables. It can be seen on the LIGHT CURVE of the star and may be regular – with a period given by one complete cycle in brightness on the light curve – or may be irregular or semiregular. The periods range from minutes to years. The range between maximum and minimum brightness – the AMPLITUDE – is also very wide.

There are three major groups of variables: eclipsing, pulsating, and cataclysmic variables. The eclipsing or geometric variables are systems of two or more stars whose light varies as one star is periodically eclipsed by a companion star. These ECLIPSING BINARIES can be subdivided into ALGOL VARIABLES, W SERPENTIS STARS, and W URSAE MAJORIS STARS. PULSATING VARIABLES, such as the CEPHEID VARIABLES, periodically brighten and fade as their surface layers expand and contract. CATACLYSMIC VARIABLES are close BINARY STARS where one component is a white dwarf to which mass is being transferred from the other component. This group includes NOVAE, RECURRENT NOVAE, and DWARF NOVAE. Minor groups of variables include FLARE STARS, ROTATING VARIABLES, SPECTRUM VARIABLES, and R CORONAE BOREALIS STARS.

These many types also fall into three other main categories: with *extrinsic variables* the brightness variation results from some process external to the star, as with some eclipsing binaries; with *intrinsic variables* the variation results from some change in the star itself, as with the pulsating variables; in other cases, such as W Ursae Majoris stars, the variation can result from a combination of intrinsic and extrinsic agencies.

Different types of variable can be distinguished by period and also by light-curve shape: by amplitude of the variation, depth of the minima, size and shape of the maxima, characteristic irregularities, and by the continuous or steplike changes involved. Spectroscopic and photometric measurements can be used to differentiate between borderline cases and to investigate changes in temperature, radial velocity, and spectral type. See also STELLAR NOMENCLATURE.

variation the periodic INEQUALITY in the Moon's motion that results from the combined gravitational attraction of the Earth and Sun. Its period is half the SYNODIC MONTH, i.e. 14.77 days, and the maximum longitude displacement is 39′29″.9. See also ANNUAL EQUATION; EVECTION; PARALLACTIC INEQUALITY; SECULAR ACCELERATION.

vastitas (plural: **vastitates**) an extensive lowland plain. The word is used in the approved name of such a surface feature on a planet or satellite.

Vega (**α Lyr**) a conspicuous white star, apparently blue in color, that is the brightest star in the constellation Lyra. It was the POLE STAR about 12 000 years ago, at the end of the last Ice Age. Because of PRECESSION, it will be the pole star again around AD 14 000. Vega is the standard A0 V star (B–V = U–B = 0) in the UBV system. Observations of Vega by the satellite IRAS in 1983 revealed an INFRARED EXCESS beyond 10 μm. The excess is attributed to thermal radiation from particles more than 1mm in radius located about 85 AU from Vega and heated by the star to a temperature of 85 K. It appears that the large particles have arisen from the residual prenatal cloud of gas and dust and may perhaps represent an embryonic and developing planetary system. Because Vega is a bright A0 star with a short lifetime (3×10^8 years) a 'solar system' will not have sufficient time to form around it. (The age of our Solar System is 4.6×10^9 y.) m_v: 0.03; M_v: 0.6; spectral type: A0 Va; distance: 7.5 pc.

Vega mission either of two spacecraft missions, sponsored by the USSR, France, Germany, Austria, Bulgaria, Hungary, Poland, and Czechoslovakia. The main scientific goals were to study Venus by means of balloons and landers and to fly by HALLEY'S COMET. Vega 1 and Vega 2 were launched in 1984 (Dec. 15 and Dec. 21 respectively), flew past Venus on June 11 and June 15 1985, and used the gravitational assistance of that maneuver to fly by Halley on Mar. 6 and Mar. 9 1986 at miss distances of 8890 and 8030 km. The massive three-axis-stabilized TV systems on board unfortunately produced rather blurred images of the comet's nucleus. The dust mass spectrometers and dust detectors were, however, particularly successful. Results from the Vega mission enabled ESA to target the GIOTTO mission more accurately.

Veil nebula see CYGNUS LOOP.

Vela (Sails) a constellation in the southern hemisphere near Crux, lying partly in the Milky Way. It was once part of the large constellation ARGO. The four brightest stars, Gamma (γ), Delta (δ), Kappa (κ), and Lambda (λ) Velorum, are of 2nd magnitude and form a quadrilateral. The primary component of Gamma, a remote multiple star, is the only conspicuous WOLF-RAYET STAR. Delta and Kappa are two of the stars forming the FALSE CROSS. The 8th-magnitude planetary nebula NGC 3132 is a fine sight in a small telescope. The area also contains the VELA PULSAR. Abbrev.: Vel; genitive form: Velorum; approx. position: RA 9.5h, dec −50°; area: 500 sq deg.

Vela pulsar the second OPTICAL PULSAR to be discovered, the optical flashes being detected in 1977. With a brightness of only about 26 magnitudes – one of the faintest optical bodies to be detected – it is considerably fainter than the optical pulsar in the CRAB NEBULA, although at a distance of about 500 parsecs it is four times nearer. It was already known to emit pulses of radio emission in a period of 0.089 seconds and pulses of gamma rays twice every revolution. At gamma-ray wavelengths it is the brightest object in the sky. The optical pulses were found by sampling the light from a field only five arc seconds across, centered on the accurate radio position of the pulsar, and folding the data to the precise radio period.

Like other pulsars, the Vela pulsar is gradually slowing down in its rotation rate. Several brief and temporary increases in rotation rate – glitches – have however been observed since 1969 (see PULSAR). It is a young pulsar, some 10 000 years old, and (like the Crab pulsar) is one of the very few to be associated with a SUPERNOVA REMNANT. The remnant, Vela-X, has been observed at X-ray, XUV, optical, and radio wavelengths.

velocity dispersion a measure of the spread of velocities of members within a CLUSTER OF GALAXIES or of stars. If both radius, R, and velocity dispersion, V, of a cluster are measured, an estimate of mass, V^2R/G, is obtained.

velocity of light see SPEED OF LIGHT.

Venera probes (Venus probes) a series of Soviet probes to Venus, first launched in 1961. Veneras 1–3 were unsuccessful. Veneras 4–8 ejected capsules into Venus' atmosphere to measure the atmospheric temperature, pressure, and composition. The Venera 4 capsule transmitted for 94 minutes on Oct. 18 1967 during its parachute descent, while the capsules from Veneras 5 and 6 returned data for 53 and 51 minutes on May 16 and 17 1969 respectively; all were crushed by the atmospheric pressure before they reached the surface. The capsule from Venera 7 did survive to reach the surface on Dec. 15 1970, becoming the first human-made object to land on another planet. The Venera 7 capsule returned data for 23 minutes, indicating a temperature of 750 K and a pressure of 90 bar on the Venusian surface. Venera 8's capsule returned data from the surface for 50 minutes on July 22 1972.

A new generation of Venera probes traveled to Venus from 1975. Veneras 9 and 10 each consisted of a lander and an orbiter through which signals from the lander were relayed to Earth. On Oct. 22 1975, Venera 9's lander sent the first photograph from the surface of another planet, showing sharp angular rocks near the probe. Another panorama one day later from the Venera 10 lander revealed an apparently older more eroded landscape. The landers operated for 53 and 65 minutes respectively on the Venusian surface.

Veneras 11 and 12 reached Venus on Dec. 25 and Dec. 21 1978 respectively, and landers were sent to the surface. As they descended they transmitted information concerning the atmosphere to the two spacecraft, and continued relaying for about 100 minutes from the surface. No photographs were released. Veneras 13 and 14 reached Venus on Mar. 2 and Mar. 5 1982 and landers were sent to the surface. Colored panoramas were taken of the landing sites and soil analyses made, and this information, together with atmospheric data, was relayed back to the spacecraft.

Veneras 15 and 16 went into orbit around Venus on Oct. 11 and Oct. 16 1983. They studied the atmosphere and using radar mapped the mountains, craters, and other features on the N hemisphere of the planet's surface, to within about 20° of the equator and with a resolution of a few kilometers. See also VENUS.

Venus the second planet of the Solar System in outward succession from the Sun and the one that comes closest to the Earth. It orbits the Sun every 224.7 days at a distance varying between 0.72 and 0.73 AU. It has a size (12 104 km equatorial diameter), density, and, probably, internal constitution comparable with those of the Earth, but measurements by MARINER, PIONEER VENUS, VENERA, VEGA, MAGELLAN, and GALILEO spaceprobes have revealed extremely hostile surface and atmospheric conditions. Orbital and physical characteristics are given in Table 1, backmatter.

Venus is never far from the Sun in the sky, reaching its greatest ELONGATION of 45° to 47° about 72 days before and after inferior conjunctions, which recur at intervals of about 584 days. At greatest brilliancy the planet is near magnitude −4.4 and brighter than every other celestial object except the Sun and the Moon; this occurs at an elongation of 39° about 36 days before and after inferior conjunction, while Venus is an EVENING STAR or a MORNING STAR.

Telescopically the planet shows a brilliant yellowish-white cloud-covered disk. Because of its orbital position between Sun and Earth, Venus exhibits PHASES: gibbous and crescent phases occur between full at superior conjunction, when the planet's apparent diameter is 10 arc seconds, and new at inferior conjunction, when it has a diameter of about 61 arc seconds. TRANSITS of Venus across the Sun's disk at inferior conjunction are rare and currently come in pairs: the next will occur in 2012 – this will be the second of a pair, the first having taken place in 2004. After 2012, there will not be another until 2117.

The clouds never permit views of the surface of Venus; it was not until 1961 that radar established that Venus rotated in a retrograde direction 243.01 days relative to the stars, or 116.8 days in relation to the Sun (the Venusian day). Features in the clouds, seen indistinctly from the Earth but observed in detail by ultraviolet photography from Pioneer Venus and MARINER 10, indicate a four-day east to west rotation period for the upper atmosphere, corresponding to 350 km/hour winds. The atmosphere thus rotates in the same direction but about 60 times faster than the solid planet. The cloud patterns swirl from the equator toward the poles and appear to be driven by solar heating and convection near the subsolar point in the middle of the sunlit hemisphere.

Possibly because of the slow rotation of its nickel-iron core, Venus has little or no intrinsic magnetic field. A magnetic field is however induced in the planet's ionosphere by the SOLAR WIND. The resulting bow shock wave was found by one of the Pioneer Venus probes to be very strong and can therefore buffer the outer atmosphere of Venus from the solar wind.

The atmosphere extends to about 250 km above the surface. Pioneer Venus measurements showed there to be a layered structure to the Venusian clouds, which lie between altitudes of roughly 45–60 km within the troposphere of Venus (i.e. the region in which the atmospheric temperature decreases with altitude). There is haze above and below the clouds. Three cloud layers have been distinguished, having different concentrations and sizes of suspended particles; the particles are identified as liquid droplets of sulfuric acid with an admixture of water and solid and liquid particles of sulfur.

The temperature increases from about 300 K at the cloud tops to about 730 K at Venus' surface, which experiences a crushing atmospheric pressure 90 times that of the Earth. The surface temperature, higher than that of any other planet, is the result of a GREENHOUSE EFFECT involving the clouds and the large proportion of carbon dioxide in the atmosphere. Pioneer Venus showed that the atmosphere as a whole consists of about 98% carbon dioxide, 1–3% nitrogen, with a few parts per million (ppm) of helium, neon, krypton, and argon. Although the amounts of neon, krypton, and argon are small, they indicate very much greater amounts of primordial neon, krypton, and argon than those found in the Earth's atmosphere. This is currently raising problems concerning the established view of the origin of the Solar System. In the lower atmosphere, below the clouds, trace amounts of water vapor (0.1–0.4%) and free oxygen (60 ppm) were detected. The high surface temperature may have prevented any atmospheric water vapor from condensing into oceans, as occurred on Earth; it may also have prevented carbon dioxide from combining with the crustal material to form carbonaceous rocks. The upper atmospheric winds moderate to only 10 km/hour or so at the surface.

Photographs of the surface returned by the Venera 9 and 10 landers in 1975 showed a stony desert landscape, while tests for radioactive elements in the crust implied a composition similar to that of basalt or granite. Radar mapping of the surface of Venus was done by the Pioneer Venus, Venera 15 and 16, and Magellan spacecraft. Magellan mapped 98% of the surface, obtaining a resolution of 100 meters in places.

Huge rolling plains cover 65% of the surface, depressions cover 27%, and highland areas cover the remaining 8%, concentrated in two main areas – ISHTAR TERRA and APHRODITE TERRA. Ishtar Terra, the more northerly, is a flattish plateau bounded on three sides by mountains. MAXWELL MONTES, one of these mountainous regions, is the highest range on Venus, rising to more than 11 km above the mean elevation of the surface.

Almost everywhere, the surface of Venus displays evidence of volcanism. The larger shield volcanoes are generally located on top of the broad highland areas, while small volcanoes of only a few km across appear to exist over all the surface. Scores of small volcanic domes, all less than 15 km across, pepper the southern flank of the highland area *Tethus Regio*. The *Eistla* region has circular volcanic domes ('pancake' domes), some up to 65 km in diameter, with broad flat tops less than 1 km in height. These are formed from viscous lava.

Magellan observed more than 900 craters on Venus. The planet does not have impact craters less than a few km across because its thick atmosphere causes smaller objects to disintegrate totally before they reach the surface. Many craters are surrounded by huge radar-dark halos, the result of a shock wave that built up ahead of the object in Venus' atmosphere and pulverized the uppermost few meters of rock to produce a smooth blanket of material. The distribution of craters on Venus is statistically uniform and very few are altered by later volcanic activity.

Other features include wind streaks, TESSERAE, CORONAE, and deep chasms. Complex lava flows exist; the area of *Mylitta Fluctus* in *Lavinia Planitia* covers roughly 800 km by 400 km. Long narrow channels meander for great distances; for example *Hildr Fossa* extends for 6800 km but is only 1–2 km wide over its entire length with no lakes or tributaries. It may have been formed by extremely fluid lava flowing across a vast flat plain. It is clear that Venus has had an active geological history; no evidence has been found, however, for plate tectonics.

Venus, transits see TRANSIT.

Venus Express an ESA mission to Venus, launched in Nov. 2005 from Baikonur Cosmodrome by a Russian Soyuz/ST Fregat rocket. The mission is ESA's first to Earth's sister planet and was selected from a number of proposals for projects that would reuse the design first implemented for the Mars Express mission. Immediately after launch, the 1.27-tonne Venus Express spacecraft was placed into the transfer orbit needed for its 153-day journey to Venus. Once captured by the planet's gravity, it is scheduled to explore Venus from a polar orbit for a nominal 500 days (just over two Venusian rotations). Carrying some of the instruments left over from the Mars Express and Rosetta missions, Venus Express is to focus its investigations on the dense Venusian atmosphere and to find out what drives the planet's high-speed winds.

Venus probes see MAGELLAN; MARINER 2; MARINER 5; MARINER 10; PIONEER VENUS PROBES; VENERA PROBES; VENUS EXPRESS.

vernal equinox (spring equinox) see EQUINOXES.

vernier a short scale used to increase the accuracy of the graduated scale to which it is attached. If nine divisions of the vernier correspond to 10 divisions of the instrument scale, the latter can be read to a further decimal place.

vertical circle a great circle on the celestial sphere that passes through an observer's zenith and cuts the HORIZON at right angles.

Very Large Array see VLA.

Very Large Telescope (VLT) an optical telescope of the EUROPEAN SOUTHERN OBSERVATORY sited on Cerro Paranal in Chile, altitude 2600 meters. It consists of four 8.2-meter telescopes, each with a thin meniscus PRIMARY MIRROR mounted separately on a N–S baseline on an ALTAZIMUTH MOUNTING. The manufacture of the mirrors was completed between 1999 and 2001. The reflectors are usable in combination (equivalent to a 16-meter single telescope), individually, or as an INTERFEROMETER.

Very Long Baseline Array see VLBA.

very long baseline interferometry see VLBI.

Vesta ((4) Vesta) the fourth ASTEROID to be discovered, found in March 1807 by the German astronomer H.W.M. Olbers. It is the second largest asteroid, similar in volume to (2) Pallas but much more massive. Although it is only 60% as big as (1) Ceres, it has a much higher ALBEDO (0.423) than any other large asteroid and is the only one bright enough to be visible to the naked eye at favorable OPPOSITIONS, when it can reach magnitude 5.5. Its unusual spectrum suggests that it has a surface composed of basaltic minerals, similar to eucritic ACHONDRITE meteorites. It has a mass of about 3×10^{20} kg. Ejecta from a large impact crater in Vesta's southern hemisphere are believed to be the ultimate source of HED METEORITES. Vesta's path around the Sun is inclined 7.1° to the ecliptic, and it takes 3.63 years to complete one orbit. Its journey around the Sun carries it from a perihelion of 2.161 AU to an aphelion of 2.572 AU from the Sun. It is an oblate spheroid and its period of axial rotation is only 5.342 hours. NASA's DAWN mission, set for launch in 2006, is scheduled to visit Vesta. See Table 3, Appendix.

vidicon a sensitive semiconductor-based instrument derived from television technology and used in astronomy for detecting and measuring light, ultraviolet, and near-infrared radiation. The target area is photosensitive, responding to the radiation falling on it by producing an electronic signal that varies linearly with the intensity of the incident radiation. The vidicon has been superseded by CCD detectors.

vignetting uneven or reduced illumination over the image plane in a telescope, camera, etc., leading for example to an image that is dimmer at the edges.

Viking probes two identical American spacecraft, each comprising an Orbiter and a Lander, that were launched in 1975 on a mission to search for life on MARS. Each Orbiter weighed 2325 kg and carried two television cameras to photograph the surfaces of Mars and its satellites, and instruments to map atmospheric water vapor and surface temperature variations; 52 000 pictures were relayed to Earth. After detaching from its Orbiter, each Lander, weighing 1067 kg, made a successful landing using a combination of aerodynamic braking, parachute descent, and retro-assisted touchdown. The Viking 1 Lander set down on July 20 1976 in CHRYSE PLANITIA after a delay while Orbiter photographs were searched for a smooth landing area. Viking 2 landed on Sept. 3 1976 in UTOPIA PLANITIA, 7420 km northeast of the Viking 1 Lander.

Each Lander carried two television cameras, a meteorological station, a seismometer, and a set of soil-analysis experiments serviced by a sampling arm. Only the seismometer carried by Viking 1 failed to function; that on Viking 2 registered mainly wind vibrations and a few minor Martian 'earth' tremors. The television cameras returned views of a red rock-strewn surface under a pink dusty sky. Sand or dust dunes were evident at the Viking 1 site but no life forms were seen. The meteorology instruments reported temperatures varying between 190 K and 240 K with mainly light winds gusting to 50 km per hour.

X-ray analysis of soil samples showed a high proportion of silicon and iron, with smaller amounts of magnesium, aluminum, sulfur, cerium, calcium, and titanium. Gas chromatograph mass spectrometers carried by the Landers failed to detect any biological compounds in the Martian soil, but more ambiguous results were returned by three experiments designed to test for microorganisms in various soil samples.

A *labeled-release experiment* tested for radioactive gases that might have been expelled from organisms in a soil sample fed with a radioactive nutrient. In a *pyrolytic-release experiment* soil was placed with gases containing the radioactive isotope carbon–14. The idea was that Martian organisms might assimilate the isotope into their cell structure in a process similar to earthly photosynthesis. Later the soil was baked and a test made for the carbon isotope in gases driven off. Finally, a *gas exchange experiment* monitored the composition of gases above a soil sample, which might or might not have been fed with a nutrient. If Martian organisms were breathing the gases, a change in composition might be detected.

In practice, the pyrolytic release experiment produced negative results, while the gas exchange experiment gave a marginally positive response, which could be explained in terms of a chemical reaction involving the soil and nutrient. The positive response of the labeled-release experiment was marked but disappeared when the soil was sterilized by preheating.

Detailed analysis of the Viking Lander experiments led to the conclusion that there is no form of life on Mars.

violent relaxation see DYNAMICAL RELAXATION.

Virgo (Virgin) an extensive zodiac constellation straddling the equator between Boötes and Leo. The brightest stars are the 1st-magnitude SPICA (α) and some of 2nd and 3rd magnitude, including the binary PORRIMA (γ). The Mira-type variable R Virginis, which varies between magnitudes 6.2 and 12 over 145 days, makes an interesting telescope object. The area contains the CEPHEID VARIABLE W Virginis. The constellation is rich in faint galaxies, which are members of the VIRGO CLUSTER, and contains the first detected QUASAR 3C–273. Abbrev.: Vir; genitive form; Virginis; approx. position; RA 13.5h, dec –5°; area: 1294 sq deg.

Virgo A (3C274) an intense radio source in the VIRGO CLUSTER that is associated with the galaxy M87. It is 16 megaparsecs distant and has a flux density of 198 jansky at a wavelength of 20 cm. M87 is a giant elliptical galaxy that is unusual in possessing an optical JET extending from its central regions. Jet and nucleus are both sources of nonthermal radio and X-ray radiation due to SYNCHROTRON EMISSION from plasma as it is accelerated along the jet. M87 is the nearest ACTIVE GALAXY. HUBBLE SPACE TELESCOPE observations of a disk of hot gas in the core of M87 show it to be rotating rapidly, a signature of a supermassive black hole at the center of the galaxy, with a mass more than three billion times greater than that of our Sun.

The thermal X-ray emission in the Virgo cluster is strongly concentrated to the region around M87, and to bind this gas gravitationally the galaxy must have a total mass of more than 10^{13} solar masses. A direct determination of the MASS-TO-LUMINOSITY RATIO in this galaxy requires it to have a massive DARK HALO. The galaxy is surrounded by over a hundred thousand globular clusters.

virgocentric flow see LOCAL SUPERCLUSTER.

Virgo cluster a giant irregular CLUSTER OF GALAXIES lying near the north galactic pole in the constellation Virgo. It is the nearest large cluster: its distance is currently estimated as 15 megaparsecs. Some 2500 galaxies have been observed of which about 75% are spirals, the remainder being mainly ellipticals with a few irregulars. Its second-brightest member, the giant elliptical galaxy M87, is both a radio source (VIRGO A) and an X-ray source (Virgo X-1). The X-ray halo around M87 is taking part in a weak cooling flow of around 10 solar masses a year. A second large elliptical galaxy in Virgo, M86, is also an X-ray source, with the X-ray emission forming a plume directed away from the center of the galaxy. This is due to the hot gas being stripped from the galaxy by RAM PRESSURE as it falls into the cluster. The Virgo cluster is the center of the LOCAL SUPERCLUSTER, which exerts a significant gravitational pull on the LOCAL GROUP of galaxies, reducing the measured recession velocity of the Virgo cluster by some 250 km s^{-1} (to about 1000 km s^{-1}).

virial equilibrium, temperature see VIRIAL THEOREM.

virialization the way in which dissipative physics intervenes in the gravitational collapse of a body (e.g. a CLUSTER OF GALAXIES) to convert the kinetic energy of the collapse into random motions of the constituent members.

virial theorem the energy of a system in equilibrium is distributed between the KINETIC ENERGY E_K and the POTENTIAL ENERGY E_P such that, when averaged over time, $2E_K = -E_P$. Application of the virial theorem to a cluster of galaxies or stars allows an evaluation of its total mass from observations of its size and VELOCITY DISPERSION. The mean temperature at which the system would satisfy the virial theorem is the *virial temperature*, and the system is said to be in *virial equilibrium*.

visible radiation, spectrum see LIGHT.

Vision for Space Exploration NASA's main plan for its future and the future of US space exploration in the early 21st century. It emerged in a speech made by President George W. Bush on Jan. 14 2004, in which he 'set a new course for America's space program.' The Vision program outlined a 'building-block' strategy of human and robotic missions, commencing with the return of the SPACE SHUTTLE to regular service following the loss of Columbia in Feb. 2003 and the completion of the INTERNATIONAL SPACE STATION. The program calls for the return of humans to the Moon by 2020 and seeks to pave the way for human missions to explore Mars and beyond.

visual binary a BINARY STAR, such as SIRIUS or Gamma Centauri, whose components are sufficiently far apart to be seen separately, either with the naked eye or with a telescope. In most cases the components differ in brightness: the brighter star is designated the *primary* and the other is the *companion*. Observations over a period of time reveal the apparent orbit of the companion relative to the primary, from which the true orbit is derived by adjusting for the inclination of the orbital plane. If the distance is known the total mass of the binary can be obtained from Kepler's third law:

$$M_1 + M_2 = a^3/p^3P^2$$

a is the semimajor axis of the true orbit, p is the trigonometric parallax (both in arc seconds), and P is the orbital period in years; the total mass is obtained in terms of the solar mass. It is sometimes possible to measure the absolute orbit of each component against the background of more distant stars. Then, if a_1, a_2 are the semimajor axes of these orbits, the ratio of masses is given by

$$a_1/a_2 = M_2/M_1$$

and by applying both equations the individual masses can be obtained. If the distance is unknown, both it and the total mass can be found using the method of DYNAMICAL PARALLAX.

Visual binaries generally have long orbital periods and in some cases the period is too long for any orbital motion to be detected. Such pairs are called *common proper motion stars* because, unlike OPTICAL DOUBLE stars, they appear to stay together as they move across the sky.

visual magnitude see MAGNITUDE.

visual meteor see METEOR.

VLA *abbrev. for* Very Large Array. An APERTURE SYNTHESIS radio telescope near Socorro, New Mexico, and part of the NATIONAL RADIO ASTRONOMY OBSERVATORY. The VLA is the most effective instrument in the world for general-purpose radio-astronomical imaging. Its ANTENNAS are placed on a Y-shaped track that allows for high-resolution observations of sources over a wide range of DECLINATIONS. The three arms of the configuration are 21, 18.9, and 21 km long, and together hold 27 DISH antennas that can be positioned at 72 different observing locations. Each dish is 25 meters across, with a surface accuracy of 0.5 mm, and weighs 193 tonnes. The dishes can be arranged in one of four principal configurations, from 'A' (with a maximum BASELINE of 36.4 km) to 'D', which is the most compact and has a minimum baseline of 33 meters. Their scales vary by the ratios 1:3.2:10:32. The VLA generates 351 simultaneous baselines and can therefore synthesize maps relatively quickly. It has receivers for observing in six wavelength bands centered near 90, 20, 6, 3.6, 2, and 1.3 cm.

VLBA *abbrev. for* Very Long Baseline Array. A dedicated VLBI array run by the US NATIONAL RADIO ASTRONOMY OBSERVATORY. It consists of ten identical DISHES, each with a diameter of 25 meters, and a 20-station correlator (see CORRELATION RECEIVER); observations began in 1993. The dishes are at St Croix, VI, Hancock, NH, Liberty, IA, Fort Davis, TX, Los Alamos, NM, Pie Town, NM, KITT PEAK, AZ, OWENS VALLEY, CA, Brewster, WA, and MAUNA KEA, HI, giving a maximum BASELINE of 8600 km. The array is controlled remotely from a joint VLBA and VLA Array Operations Center in Socorro, New Mexico. It can observe in nine frequency bands between 327 MHz and 43 GHz, giving an angular RESOLUTION of up to 0.2 milliarcseconds. The dishes themselves are usable up to 86 GHz.

VLBI *abbrev. for* very long baseline interferometry. A method of using widely separated RADIO TELESCOPES as parts of an INTERFEROMETER without connecting them directly. The very long baselines achieved give the interferometer a high angular RESOLUTION and allow the study of fine structure in very distant RADIO SOURCES such as QUASARS.

Broad-bandwidth signals from each telescope are recorded on magnetic tape, together with timing information from high-precision clocks – usually based on hydrogen masers. The tapes are then transported to a central site where they are replayed to a *VLBI correlator* which processes them to produce an image (see APERTURE SYNTHESIS).

Telescopes at many observatories are routinely diverted from their normal programmes to make VLBI observations, and standard broad-bandwidth recording systems such as the 'Mark III' are used. Dedicated networks also exist (see VLBA) whose sole purpose is VLBI. Sometimes telescopes from around the world are combined to give *intercontinental VLBI* with baselines of more than 10 000 km. Baselines greater than the diameter of the Earth can be achieved by using a telescope mounted on an orbiting satellite, as is suggested for VSOP and RADIOASTRON.

VLBI can also be used to measure certain geodynamical phenomena, such as the movements of tectonic plates, polar wobble, and the rise and fall of Earth tides.

VLT *abbrev. for* Very Large Telescope.

VMO *abbrev. for* very massive object. A hypothetical POPULATION III star.

Vogt–Russell theorem a theorem proposed independently by H.N. Russell and H. Vogt in 1926 stating that, if the age, mass, and chemical composition of a star are specified, then its temperature and luminosity are (in almost all cases) uniquely determined. Hence for a star whose age, mass, and chemical composition are known, the equations of STELLAR STRUCTURE will have only one solution.

void see LARGE-SCALE STRUCTURE.

Volans (**Flying Fish**) a small inconspicuous constellation in the southern hemisphere near the Large Magellanic Cloud, the brightest stars being of 3rd magnitude. Abbrev.: Vol; genitive form: Volantis; approx. position: RA 8h, dec –70°; area: 141 sq deg.

volcanism any of various processes whereby molten material, produced by interior heating, rises along with associated gases through the crust of a planet or satellite and bursts out upon the surface in the form of volcanic eruptions, geysers, etc. Active volcanism, which produces new crustal material, occurs not only on Earth but also on the satellites IO and TRITON. Volcanism on the Moon produced the lava of the MARIA but largely ceased some three billion years ago. Evidence for past volcanism has also been found on Mars (see MARS, VOLCANOES), VENUS, and several outer-planet satellites, such as EUROPA, GANYMEDE, ENCELADUS, TETHYS, ARIEL, and TITANIA.

Voskhod two Soviet piloted spacecraft that followed the VOSTOK series. Voskhod 1 was launched Oct. 12 1964 and was the first multi-crewed spacecraft: three cosmonauts were on board. Voskhod 2 was launched on Mar. 18 1965, and during its flight one of the two-man crew, Alexsei Leonov, made the first spacewalk.

Vostok a series of six Soviet piloted spacecraft that were able to carry one person into orbit. Vostok 1 was launched on Apr. 12 1961. Its crew member, Yuri Gagarin, became the first man in space, the flight lasting 1.8 hours. In subsequent Vostok missions the flight duration was extended up to 119 hours so that the effects of prolonged weightlessness could be studied. The double launching of Vostoks 3 and 4 in Aug. 1962 and their close approach in orbit led to an appreciation of rendezvous techniques.

Voyager probes two 825-kg US probes launched in 1977 toward the planets of the outer Solar System and making use of the rare PLANETARY ALIGNMENT that occurred at the beginning of the 1980s. Voyager 1, launched on Sept. 5 1977, reached JUPITER in Mar. 1979, moving in a path that took it close to the satellites CALLISTO and GANYMEDE, then quite near EUROPA, and close to IO, before it made its closest approach (280 000 km) to Jupiter on Mar. 5; it then passed AMALTHEA. Using the slingshot action of Jupiter, Voyager 1 was set on a course for SATURN, which it reached in Nov. 1980. It approached within 125 000 km of that planet on Nov. 12, dipping below Saturn's rings just after passing close to the satellite TITAN. The spacecraft then headed out of the Solar System with no further planetary encounters.

Voyager 2, launched on Aug. 20, 1977, reached Jupiter in July 1979. It passed close to Callisto, Ganymede, and Europa, then passed Amalthea before its closest approach (714 000 km) to the planet on July 9. Since Voyager 1's encounter with Titan was successful, Voyager 2 was set on a path that took it past Saturn in Aug. 1981 and on toward Uranus and Neptune. It passed closer to several of Saturn's satellites (in particular IAPETUS, HYPERION, TETHYS, and ENCELADUS) than Voyager 1 had done, but farther from Titan. Moving above the plane of Saturn's rings it made its closest approach (101 300 km) to the planet on Aug. 25, 1981. Voyager 2 reached URANUS in Jan. 1986, making its closest approach (107 000 km) on Jan. 24 and discovering many hitherto unknown small satellites. It went on to NEPTUNE, making its closest approach (5000 km) on Aug. 25, 1989. Voyager 2 then also made its way out of the Solar System.

The two spacecraft carried a variety of instruments for scientific investigations, and three engineering subsystems for on-board control of spacecraft functions. Trajectory correction maneuvers could be enabled only from Earth. The science instruments for viewing the planets and their satellites and ring systems were mounted on a platform capable of being pointed very precisely. The instruments included a narrow-angle and a wide-angle TV camera for high-resolution imaging of satellite surfaces, etc., an infrared spectrometer, interferometer, and radiometer, an ultraviolet spectrometer, and instruments for studying plasmas, low-energy charged particles, and cosmic rays. In addition there were magnetometers mounted on an extendable boom and two planetary radio astronomy and plasma wave antennas. A 3.7-meter aperture high-gain radio dish pointed continuously toward

Earth, allowing two-way communications of commands and information. Power was provided by three radioisotope thermoelectric generators, and hot gas jets provided thrust for attitude stability and trajectory corrections. Not everything ran smoothly with the Voyager probes. During Voyager 2's Saturn encounter, its camera and science instruments platform became temporarily stuck. Another problem was that its radio antenna failed, and the team of Earth-based scientists were forced to use a less efficient backup system. Nevertheless, a. wealth of information was returned to Earth from the two Voyager craft, revealing many unexpected aspects concerning the satellites (especially the volcanic activity on Io), the fine details of Saturn's rings, and the existence of new satellites and planetary ring systems. (Details are given at individual entries in the Dictionary.)

After Voyager 2's encounter with the Neptune system, NASA redesignated the continuing Voyager journeys as the Voyager Interstellar Mission (VIM). Both Voyager craft are still making and transmitting observations on the outer HELIOSPHERE, monitored by the DEEP SPACE NETWORK. They are heading out of the Solar System in opposite directions. Voyager 1 is now the most distant human-made object in the Universe. At the start of 2005 it was more than 14 billion kilometers (93 AU) from the Sun, traveling away from it at a velocity of about 17.184 km/s (3.5 AU per year) and heading north at an angle of 35.55° to the plane of the ecliptic. Voyager 2 is heading out in a southerly direction at a velocity of 15.64 km/s (about 3.13 AU per year) and at an angle to the ecliptic of 47.46°. On their way out of the Solar System, both spacecraft are likely to have to negotiate a passage through the OORT CLOUD, which could take as long as 20 000 years. In about 40 000 years time, Voyager 1 will, if it survives, pass within 0.49 parsec of the red dwarf star AC+79 3888 in the constellation of Camelopardalis. By about the same time, Voyager 2 will pass within 0.52 parsec of another red dwarf, Ross 248 in Andromeda, and in 296 000 years it will pass Sirius at a distance of 1.32 parsecs. Both craft carry disks containing information about the Earth that an alien civilization might someday access.

VSA *abbrev. for* Very Small Array. A close-packed array of 14 small horn-reflector antennas, mounted on a tip-table and operating at frequencies between 26 and 36 GHz. The VSA is designed to make images of the COSMIC BACKGROUND RADIATION on angular scales of about one degree, and is located at the Teide Observatory in Tenerife. The project is a collaboration between MRAO, JODRELL BANK, and the Instituto de Astrofisica de Canarias (Tenerife).

VSOP *abbrev. for* VLBI Space Observatory Program. An 8-meter Earth-orbiting radio telescope, designed by the Japanese Institute of Space and Astronautical Science (ISAS) and launched into a highly elliptical orbit (apogee 21 000 km, perigee 560 km) in 1997. Renamed HALCA after its successful launch, the spacecraft performs VLBI observations, in collaboration with ground-based telescopes, on baselines up to three times longer than those achievable on Earth and at frequencies of 1.6, 5 and 22 GHz. HALCA is both an acronym for 'Highly Advanced Laboratory for Communications and Astronomy' and a Japanese pun for 'far away'.

Vulcan a hypothetical planet, thought during the 19th century to orbit the Sun within the orbit of Mercury. Searches for it during total solar eclipses and at suggested times of TRANSIT across the Sun were all unsuccessful. It is now known not to exist.

Vulpecula (**Fox**) a constellation in the northern hemisphere near Cygnus, lying in the Milky Way, the brightest stars being of 4th magnitude. It contains the DUMBBELL NEBULA. Abbrev.: Vul; genitive form: Vulpeculae; approx. position: RA 20h, dec +25°; area: 268 sq deg.

VV Cephei stars a class of massive interacting BINARY STARS, with orbital periods from somewhat less than a year to several decades, in which a massive supergiant (usually an M star) transfers mass to a blue companion (typically a B star). The mass donor appears to fill or almost fill its Roche lobe (see EQUIPOTENTIAL SURFACES). Because most VV Cephei stars have very eccentric orbits,

MASS TRANSFER often appears to be strongest near the phase of closest approach. VV Cephei systems are the more evolved counterparts of ZETA AURIGAE systems. Some well-studied examples include VV Cephei, AZ Cassiopeiae, and KQ Puppis.

V/V_m test see LUMINOSITY-VOLUME TEST.

Ww

walled plains see CRATERS.
wandering stars see FIXED STARS.
Washington Visual Double-Star Catalog a whole-sky catalog of binary and optical double stars prepared by Charles E. Worley and Geoffrey G. Douglass and issued by the US Naval Observatory, Washington D.C. The latest edition (1996) lists 78 100 objects, giving the position of each double and the magnitude of the brighter component. Multiple stars are split into pairs. The positions given in the catalog are those for 1900, as given in earlier catalogs, such as the 1961 Index Catalog of Visual Double stars (Jeffers and Van den Bos), but have been precessed to epoch 2000.0.
watt symbol: W. The SI unit of power, defined as the power resulting from the dissipation of one joule of energy in one second.
waveband (**band**) a region of the electromagnetic spectrum lying between frequency (or wavelength) limits that are defined according to some property of the radiation, or some requirement or functional aspect of a detecting device or system or transmission channel.
wavefront the imaginary surface of a wave of light or other radiation, connecting points of the same phase. The advancing wavefront is normally perpendicular to the direction of travel and may be plane, spherical, cylindrical, or more complex.
waveguide a metal tube, usually of rectangular cross section, down which traveling electromagnetic waves may be propagated. In a more general sense it is any system of material boundaries that fulfills the same purpose, such as layers of plasma in the IONOSPHERE. Waveguides are used at microwave frequencies where dielectric losses in radio cables become excessive; they are therefore used as FEEDERS in radio telescopes. The guided waves may be radiated away at the end of the waveguide by a *horn antenna*, which is a flared metal device having the dimensions of the waveguide at one end and opening out to a large aperture at the other end.
wavelength symbol: λ. The distance over which a periodic wave motion goes through one complete cycle of oscillation, i.e. the distance traveled during one period. Thus for a sinusoidal wave motion, such as ELECTROMAGNETIC RADIATION, it is the distance between two successive peaks or troughs. For electromagnetic radiation, wavelength is related to frequency, ν, by $\nu\lambda = c$, where c is the speed of light. Wavelength is measured in meters or in multiples or submultiples of meters; for example, the wavelength of light is usually given in nanometers while that of infrared radiation is usually quoted in micrometers.
waxing Moon the Moon as its illuminated face increases in size during one half of the synodic month. The illuminated face then decreases in size, as the *waning Moon*, for the remainder of the month. See PHASES, LUNAR.
WC stars see WOLF-RAYET STARS.
weak force see FUNDAMENTAL FORCES.
weak-line T Tauri stars see T TAURI STARS.
weber symbol: Wb. The SI unit of magnetic flux.
weight the force experienced by a body on the surface of a planet, natural satellite, etc., that results from the gravitational force

(directed towards the center of the planet, satellite, etc.) acting on the body. A body of mass *m* has a weight *mg*, where *g* is the acceleration of gravity.

weightlessness the condition associated with FREE FALL, i.e. the motion of an unpropelled body in a gravitational field. The acceleration of a person in a freely-falling object, such as a spacecraft, is equal to that of the freely-falling object. The person thus experiences no sensation of weight and floats freely. Many crew members on the US space shuttles and the USSR and US space stations have suffered a combination of symptoms, akin to those of motion sickness, as they adapt to conditions of weightlessness. It usually takes 1–3 days to overcome the problem (known as *space adaptation syndrome* or *space sickness*), duties being performed more slowly than scheduled. This can be serious on short-term missions. Other effects observed are a drop in activity of white blood cells, which fight disease, and a reduction in red blood cell count. The adaptation to conditions of normal Earth gravity following periods of weightlessness have been investigated by both the USSR and the USA after spaceflights of ever-increasing duration. No long-term effects have been observed to date. See also MICROGRAVITY.

West (**1976 VI**) a brilliant comet that passed within 30 million km of the Sun in Feb. 1976. The cometary nucleus broke into at least four fragments, accompanied by massive outbursts of gas and dust.

Westerbork Radio Observatory an observatory at Westerbork, near Groningen in the northern Netherlands. It has a highly sensitive APERTURE SYNTHESIS system (the Westerbork Synthesis Radio Telescope, or WSRT), which went into operation in 1970 and is run by the Netherlands Foundation for Radio Astronomy. Fourteen 25-meter radio dishes lie on a line running east-west and 2.8 km in length. (Originally there were 12 dishes on a 1.6-km baseline.) Four of the dishes are movable: two at one end of the line and a further two nearer the center of the line and the ten fixed dishes. It can observe at frequencies between 250 MHz and 8.65 GHz.

western elongation see ELONGATION.

west point see CARDINAL POINTS.

Wezen see CANIS MAJOR.

Whipple model see COMET.

Whipple Observatory see FRED L. WHIPPLE OBSERVATORY.

Whipple's comet a comet that started life with a near-circular orbit, eccentricity 0.167, period 10.3 years, and has been perturbed by Jupiter so that it now has an eccentricity of 0.26 and a period of 8.5 years. The comet seems to decrease in brightness by one magnitude at each return.

Whirlpool galaxy (**M51; NGC 5194**) a well-defined type Sc spiral galaxy (see HUBBLE CLASSIFICATION) that is face-on to us. It lies at a distance of 6 Mpc in the constellation Canes Venatici, the nearest bright star being Eta Ursae Majoris in the PLOUGH. A small companion galaxy, NGC 5195, appears to be connected to it by an extension of one of the spiral arms. Total magnitude: 8.1.

white dwarf an extremely dense compact star that has a mass below the CHANDRASEKHAR LIMIT (about 1.4 solar masses) and has undergone GRAVITATIONAL COLLAPSE. Having diameters only 1% that of the Sun these stars are consequently very faint, with absolute MAGNITUDES ranging from +10 to +15. The description 'white' is misleading because they display a range in color as they cool down, through white, yellow, and red, until finally ending up as cold black globes – called *black dwarfs*. However, the white ones are the brightest and were the first to be discovered.

White dwarfs are the final phase in the evolution of a low-mass star. Their progenitors are stars of up to 8 solar masses, which lose up to 90% of their matter in the form of PLANETARY NEBULAE. The core shrinks to become a white dwarf following the exhaustion of its nuclear fuel. Because most of the matter in the core of the collapsing star is in a DEGENERATE state – with the electrons stripped from their nuclei and packed tightly together – the star contracts until its gravity is balanced by the degeneracy pressure of the electrons, and the density rises to 10^7–10^{11} kg m^{-3}. Because of the peculiar behavior of degenerate material (which is subject to the quantum mechanical uncertainty principle), the most massive white dwarfs collapse to the smallest diameters and highest densities. Stars above the Chandrasekhar limit are too massive to be supported in this way and must collapse further to become NEUTRON STARS or BLACK HOLES. In practice, the addition of extra matter to a carbon-oxygen white dwarf at the Chandrasekhar limit may alternatively produce a runaway explosion as a type Ia SUPERNOVA.

The light from white dwarfs does not arise from internal nuclear reactions but in a thin gaseous atmosphere that slowly leaks away the star's heat into space. The spectral lines arising in this atmosphere are broadened by the extremely high surface gravity, and in extreme cases the light loses enough energy to suffer a measurable GRAVITATIONAL REDSHIFT. Over 75% of white dwarfs have hydrogen-rich atmospheres, and are designated DA (see below). Some white dwarfs show no hydrogen at all in their spectra, whereas others are enriched in helium, carbon, and calcium. A few have strong magnetic fields (10^5 tesla) and several have high rotational velocities. Some are pulsating variables (see ZZ CETI STARS). NOVAE, RECURRENT NOVAE, and DWARF NOVAE are close binary stars in which one component is a white dwarf (see CATACLYSMIC VARIABLE).

Spectroscopic classification of white dwarfs by SPECTRAL TYPE is inadequate because of the variety of surface composition. A classification scheme, introduced in 1983 by E. Sion and others, is based on the following spectral characteristics and temperature information:

- DA only lines of neutral hydrogen (H I)
- DB neutral helium (He I); no H or metals
- DC continuous spectrum
- DO ionized helium (He II) strong; no H or He
- DZ metal lines only; no H or He
- DQ carbon features

White dwarfs are further designated with a temperature index from 0–9, and with appropriate letters for magnetic fields/polarization (H,P), variability (V), and peculiar or unclassified spectra (X).

It has been estimated that there may be 10^{10} white dwarfs in our Galaxy, many having by now cooled to become black dwarfs. Best known of all white dwarfs is Sirius B, companion to SIRIUS (αCMa), which was discovered in 1862 by Alvan Clark after F.W. Bessel had predicted its existence (in 1844) from the unusual motion of Sirius. Sirius B has a radius of only 10^4 km, about twice that of the Earth, but a mass similar to that of the Sun.

white hole the reverse of a BLACK HOLE: a region where matter spontaneously appears. Early calculations on black holes indicated that the extreme distortion of space and time inside the EVENT HORIZON should connect our Universe with another through an Einstein–Rosen bridge (or *wormhole*). Matter falling into the black hole should then correspondingly appear in the other Universe as outpouring of material through a white hole. It now seems likely that such links, and hence white holes, do not exist.

white-light corona see CORONA.

white noise see NOISE.

wide field see FIELD OF VIEW; EYEPIECE.

Widmanstätten figures patterns of nickel-rich and nickel-poor bands crossing one another in two, three, or four directions that are revealed when polished surfaces of most IRON METEORITES are etched. They are lamellar intergrowths of kamacite, taenite, and plessite.

Wien displacement law see BLACK BODY.

Wild Duck see SCUTUM.

Wild's Trio a group of three irregular barred spiral galaxies that lies in the constellation Virgo. The galaxies appear to be connected by bridges of luminous material. Their differing radial velocities, derived from the REDSHIFTS in their spectra, suggest that the group is rapidly disintegrating.

Wilkinson Microwave Anisotropy Probe (WMAP) NASA probe investigating and mapping the fluctuations in the microwave background radiation that had been discovered by COBE. It was launched June 30 2001 into a halo orbit around the Sun–Earth Lagrangian point L_2, about 1.5 million km from the Earth. Originally known as MAP, it was later renamed in memory of the famous cosmologist David Todd Wilkinson, who died in Sept. 2002.

William Herschel Telescope a 4.2-meter

reflecting telescope with an ALTAZIMUTH MOUNTING sited at the ROQUE DE LOS MUCHACHOS OBSERVATORY in the Canaries and forming part of the Isaac Newton Group. It is largely a UK telescope with the Dutch and Spanish sharing observing time. It began regular operations in 1987. It has a glass-ceramic (Cer-Vit) primary mirror of great thermal stability and a focal ratio of f/2.4. The telescope can be used in a CASSEGRAIN CONFIGURATION (there is also an off-axis 'broken Cassegrain' focus). In addition, light from the secondary mirror can be diverted through the altitude bearings of the Y-shaped fork mounting to two NASMYTH foci, where heavy instruments can be mounted. Sophisticated electronic equipment detects and analyzes the light. In 2000, the William Herschel Infrared Camera (WHIRCAM) was replaced by the Isaac Newton Group Red Imaging Device (INGRID), a near-infrared camera for use mainly at the telescope's Cassegrain focus. INGRID is optimized for a wide field of view at relatively short wavelengths (0.8–2.5 µm). Its 1024 × 1024 near-infrared detector array provides imaging at a resolution of 0.25 arcseconds per pixel.

Willstrop telescope a compact three-mirror telescope with a very wide field of view, designed by Roderick Willstrop (see illustration). The focal plane lies at the center of the perforated primary mirror, which is approximately paraboloidal. The convex secondary and concave tertiary depart from sphericity. The system produces a high-quality image with very low image spread.

Wilson effect the apparent displacement of the umbra of a SUNSPOT relative to the penumbra as the spot is carried by the Sun's rotation from the east to the west limb of the disk. For a symmetrical sunspot, the side of the penumbra closest to the center of the disk is more foreshortened than that toward the limb. This was first interpreted as implying that the spot is a depression, but it is now known that the OPACITY of the umbra is less than that of the penumbra and that this also contributes to the effect.

WIMP *abbrev. for* weakly interacting massive particle. A hypothetical ELEMENTARY PARTICLE that is a candidate for DARK MATTER. It is a stable neutral particle, somewhat heavier than the neutron, that interacts only weakly with ordinary matter. Theory indicates that sufficient WIMPS could have formed in the early Universe to account for the high proportion of dark matter.

window see ATMOSPHERIC WINDOWS; LAUNCH WINDOW.

wing a broad feature occurring on one side of the position of a spectral line or band.

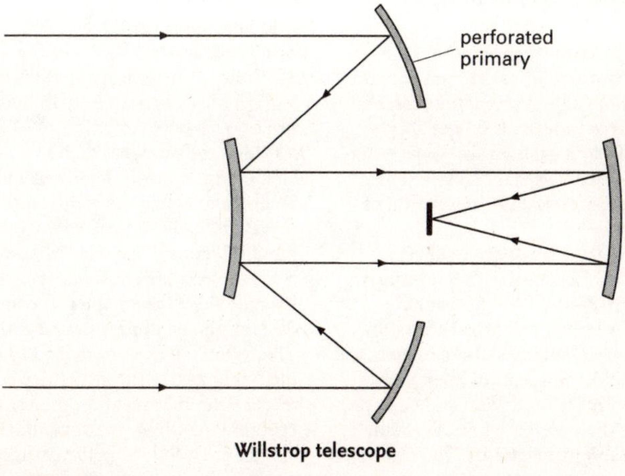

Willstrop telescope

The matter producing this feature is traveling at much greater speeds than that producing the main peak and thus has a greater Doppler shift. A redshifted wing (i.e. shifted to longer wavelengths) is produced by gas receding from us, a blueshifted (shorter-wavelength) wing by gas moving toward us.

WISE *abbrev. for* Wide-field Infrared Survey Explorer. A NASA satellite planned for a possible launch in 2008 that will scan the whole sky in the wavelength range from 3.5 to 23 microns in search of new sources of infrared radiation, including nearby cool stars and the most distant and very luminous galaxies. Using a cryogenically cooled space telescope, the survey is expected to be 1000 times as sensitive as IRAS and should add considerably to the catalog of known infrared sources by identifying millions of new objects. It is also hoped that WISE will supply the JAMES WEBB SPACE TELESCOPE with a full list of observational targets.

WIYN telescope a 3.5-meter telescope on Kitt Peak, Arizona, completed in 1994. It is a project of the University of Wisconsin, Indiana University, Yale University, and the NATIONAL OPTICAL ASTRONOMY OBSERVATORIES (NOAO). It has a lightweight borosilicate PRIMARY MIRROR, RITCHEY–CHRÉTIEN OPTICS, and an ALTAZIMUTH MOUNTING.

WN stars see WOLF RAYET STARS.

Wolf number see RELATIVE SUNSPOT NUMBER.

Wolf–Rayet galaxies a rare type of STARBURST GALAXY, whose spectra contain emission features that reveal the presence of hundreds to thousands of WOLF-RAYET STARS. Wolf-Rayet galaxies also show other indicators of massive stars, such as a blue continuum and emission-lines typical of H II REGIONS.

Wolf–Rayet stars a small group of very luminous very hot stars, with temperatures possibly as high as 90 000 K, that have anomalously strong and broad emission lines of ionized helium, carbon, oxygen, and nitrogen but few absorption lines. Since their discovery (by C.J.E. Wolf and G. Rayet, 1867), more than 300 have been found in our Galaxy and its neighbors. The majority either have lines of He, C, and O – *WC stars* – or He and N – *WN stars*; both types have anomalously low abundances of hydrogen. A further rare group, called *WO stars*, have recently been identified with very strong O emission lines. The emission lines are thought to arise in an expanding stellar atmosphere moving at very high speeds of up to 3000 km s^{-1} so that the star is continuously and rapidly losing mass. The average mass for Wolf–Rayets is 10 solar masses. About half are known to be binary stars, usually with O or B stars as companions, an example being Gamma Velorum (WC8 + O7).

These unusual properties provide clues that Wolf–Rayets are the centers of very massive OF STARS stripped of their outer envelopes with the products of interior nuclear burning being revealed. Because the Wolf–Rayets are the more evolved members of each binary, they must originally have been the more massive partner, a star of at least 20 solar masses. Half that mass has thus been lost in their stellar winds, whose high outflow rate would strip this mass off the star in only 100 000 years. This gas is in fact often visible as a ring nebula surrounding the Wolf–Rayet star. In a close binary the companion's gravity may assist the stripping, but for single stars the cause of the high mass loss is still uncertain, although RADIATION PRESSURE probably plays a major role.

world line see SPACETIME.

world models see COSMOLOGICAL MODELS.

wormhole a theoretical object bridging two regions of SPACETIME. See also WHITE HOLE.

WO stars see WOLF-RAYET STARS.

wrinkle ridges linear deformed and folded lunar features that are confined to the MARIA and may be elevated by several hundred meters; they may however continue into the HIGHLANDS as scarps. Wrinkle ridges are frequently compound, discontinuous, and associated with RILLES. They often reflect underlying topography, including BASIN ring structures beneath the maria. They may result from fissure eruptions, faulting, or the contraction of a surface crust following the draining away of subsurface lavas. SURVEYOR 6 landed close to a wrinkle ridge in Sinus Medii. See also LOBATE RIDGE.

W Serpentis star (**Beta Lyrae star**) a close BINARY STAR system where matter is being transferred very rapidly from one star to the other. This occurs when the more massive member of a close binary evolves to become a red giant (the previous stage may be an RS CANUM VENATICORUM STAR); the MASS TRANSFER can be so efficient that 85% of the red giant's mass is transferred to the other star. The system ends up as an ALGOL VARIABLE.

Observationally, W Ser stars are SPECTROSCOPIC binaries characterized by emission lines from an extended gas envelope that is hotter than either of the stars in the system; the emission is thousands of times brighter than the lines from a star's CHROMOSPHERE. This gas represents part of the giant star's mass that is lost to the system during the rapid transfer. The bulk of the gas forms an accretion disk around the giant's companion, and as this gas spirals inward the inner regions can heat up to 100 000 K and supply the radiation that ionizes the extensive tenuous gas producing the emission lines.

The outer cooler regions of the accretion disk can camouflage the accreting star and make it look larger and cooler than it actually is. This star will thus often have the appearance of a giant rather than that of the underlying main-sequence star. When mass transfer is most rapid, as in *Beta Lyrae*, the disk conceals this component entirely. Thus in Beta Lyrae we detect only the expanding giant star, a supergiant of spectral type B8.5 that is elongated towards its companion because it fills its Roche lobe (see EQUIPOTENTIAL SURFACES). The companion is hidden by a disk about twice as wide but only half as thick as the supergiant's diameter. The system is an ECLIPSING BINARY, with disk and star alternately eclipsing one another; the ellipsoidal shape of the supergiant causes the light curve to peak between eclipses, when the maximum extent of the star is seen. The B8.5 star is losing mass at a rate of about 10^{-5} solar masses per year, and this causes an increase in the orbital period (13 days) at a rate of 19 seconds per year.

WSRT *abbrev. for* Westerbork Synthesis Radio Telescope. See WESTERBORK RADIO OBSERVATORY.

W Ursae Majoris stars (**W UMa stars**) a class of contact ECLIPSING BINARIES that have very short periods amounting to only a few hours and components that are so close that they are grossly distorted by tidal forces into ellipsoidal shapes. Mass transfer occurs between the stars (see EQUIPOTENTIAL SURFACES). The components are approximately equal in brightness, as seen by the equal depths of the minima of the light curves. As with W SERPENTIS STARS the light curves show continuous variation resulting from the distorted stellar shapes and variable surface intensity. The two components are more similar in luminosity than in mass (the ratio of masses can be 12:1), so energy from the more massive star's core is being fed to the companion's photosphere. Resulting chromospheric activity is thought to be responsible for the unusually high X-ray output of these stars.

About 0.1% of all main-sequence stars should be born in close enough doubles to become contact systems: the lower mass F, G, and K stars are the W UMa class while the rare more massive analogs are called *SV Centauri stars*. In both cases as the more massive component swells to become a giant, its outer layers will surround both stars to create a COMMON ENVELOPE STAR; the final outcome will be a coalesced star.

W Virginis stars see CEPHEID VARIABLES.

Xx

XEUS the X-ray Evolving Universe Spectroscopy Mission, an advanced form of X-ray space observatory that the European Space Agency (ESA) plans to launch after 2010. The current probable launch date is Jan. 2014. The proposed mission is a long-lived observatory using cutting-edge X-ray spectroscopy technology to investigate the very hot young Universe, looking back to a time when stars and galaxies were developing through the gravitational collapse of gas and dust clouds. XEUS will also investigate the X-rays coming from material falling into black holes and associated with neutron stars and supernova remnants. Among its stated goals will be a better understanding of the largest collapsed objects in the Universe, clusters of galaxies, and how their properties can be used to probe DARK MATTER and DARK ENERGY, greater knowledge of the earliest massive black holes and their connection with the formation of galaxies, an investigation of the nature of gravity, space, and time around such massive black holes, and a clearer picture of matter under extreme conditions and the structure of highly collapsed stars. Proposed as a follow-on mission to ESA's successful XMM-NEWTON OBSERVATORY, XEUS is expected to be using cryogenically cooled X-ray detectors that will have 200 times the sensitivity of its predecessor. By using telescope barrels made of silicon instead of nickel, XEUS will be able to carry larger but lighter optics. Its X-ray detectors and spectrometers will deliver resolutions of unparalleled sensitivity. It will also be isolated from most extraneous background interference by being placed far out in interplanetary space, in a stable orbit around L2, one of the Lagrangian points of the Sun–Earth system.

XMM an X-ray mission, the second 'cornerstone' mission in the ESA HORIZON 2000 space science program launched into an elliptical orbit (apogee 115 000 km, perigee 7000 km, period 48 hr) by Ariane 5 in December 1999. Three identical nests of GRAZING INCIDENCE telescopes, each of 7.5 meters focal length, provide effective areas (1500 cm^2 at 6 keV and 4000 cm^2 at 1 keV) larger than on any previous or contemporary payload, making XMM particularly well-suited to the study of faint galactic and extragalactic sources. The telescopes feed a combination of X-ray-sensitive CCDs and reflection gratings, with spectroscopy and deep X-ray imaging being primary observational goals. XMM also carries a co-aligned optical telescope which will be used to provide simultaneous visible and UV fluxes of the observed X-ray sources and is intended to operate in orbit for up to 10 years.

XMM-Newton Observatory an important X-RAY ASTRONOMY satellite launched on top of an Ariane 5 rocket by the European Space Agency (ESA) in Dec. 1999 from Kourou, French Guiana. Named officially the High-Throughput X-ray Spectroscopy Mission, it became better known as XMM-Newton from the facts that it is an X-ray multi-mirror (XMM) space observatory and it commemorates the great English physicist Sir Isaac Newton, the 'father' of spectroscopy. Its mission was nominally to last two years but it was designed to function for a decade and was still operating smoothly at the end of 2004.

Launched less than six months after NASA's CHANDRA X-RAY OBSERVATORY, XMM-Newton rivals Chandra in technological sophistication. At the time of its launch, the 10-meter-long, 3.8-tonne XMM-Newton was the largest science satellite ever built by ESA. Like Chandra, it observes the hot, high-energy phenomena of the Universe with unprecedented sensitivity, revealing thousands of hitherto unknown X-ray sources. Its observing program is set to include monitoring of the hot regions surrounding black holes and the centers of galaxies, examining the X-ray output of SUPERNOVA REMNANTS, investigating the X-ray component of the cosmic background radiation, and analyzing the results of GAMMA-RAY BURSTS. It is also seeking to discover the true nature of the matter making up an ultradense NEUTRON STAR.

As its official name suggests, X-ray spectroscopy is a central element in XMM-Newton's mission program, and it carries scientific instruments designed to reveal the chemical makeup, temperature and velocity of the new X-ray sources it discovers. Its high-technology design consists of three huge coaligned X-ray telescope barrels made of nickel, each holding 58 wafer-thin cylindrical grazing-incidence mirrors nested inside each other, occupying an area the size of a tennis court. Each mirror has a coating of gold less than a millimeter thick to reflect X-rays that would normally pass right through. In the focal plane of each of the three X-ray telescopes lies a CCD camera providing imaging spectroscopy at a resolution of $E/\Delta E \cong 100$ at 6 keV over a 30 arc-minute-diameter field of view. Two of the telescopes also carry reflection-grating spectrometers delivering a resolution of between 100 and 600 in the energy range 0.35–2.5 keV. XMM-Newton also carries a small optical and ultraviolet telescope. Four small thrusters using hydrazine gas and four momentum wheels mounted on the spacecraft allow its attitude to be altered when aiming at a source. XMM-Newton's highly elliptical orbital path around the Earth (apogee 114 000 km, perigee 7000 km) takes it almost a third of the way to the Moon, and one orbit takes 48 hours to complete, so that astronomers can enjoy long, uninterrupted views of celestial objects and long exposure times unhindered by Earth shadowing.

X-ray astronomy the study of objects lying beyond the Solar System in the photon energy band 100 to 100 000 electronvolts (corresponding to wavelengths from 12 nanometers (nm) to 0.012 nm). X-ray observations are now an integral part of astronomy, relating particularly to galactic and extragalactic systems where violent or energetic phenomena give rise to copious high-energy particles or super-hot gas.

Opacity of the terrestrial atmosphere throughout the X-ray band requires that observations be made above about 150 km and hence X-ray astronomy could begin only after high-altitude rockets became available. The first detection of a cosmic X-ray source was made by Riccardo Giacconi and colleagues in July 1962, during an exploratory rocket launch equipped with an X-ray detector to search for lunar fluorescence. Confirmation of this source (SCORPIUS X-1) and the discovery of a second source (Taurus X-1) in 1963 began an active period of rocket and balloon observations that, by 1970, had yielded 25–30 sources spread throughout the Galaxy; there was also one likely extragalactic source, apparently associated with the powerful radio galaxy VIRGO A (M87). The first optical identification was of Taurus X-1, which was found to coincide with the CRAB NEBULA supernova remnant in a classical lunar occultation observation by Herbert Friedman and his colleagues in the USA.

The launch of the first X-ray astronomy satellite, UHURU, in Dec. 1970 accelerated the development of the subject, yielding many new sources including a large number at high galactic latitude. In particular, Uhuru discovered X-RAY BINARIES and showed these to be the most common form of galactic X-ray source. A second major discovery was of powerful X-ray emission from CLUSTERS OF GALAXIES, with evidence that this emission arose in an extended region comparable in size (about 0.5 megaparsecs) to the cluster.

The launch of other X-ray astronomy satellite experiments continued the rapid expansion of the subject. The ARIEL V sky survey extended the Uhuru catalog and led to the establishment of a second major class of extragalactic source: the X-ray SEYFERT GALAXIES. Observations by COPERNICUS and Ariel V, followed by SAS-3, found the slow X-RAY PULSATORS, periodically variable X-ray sources with periods of a few minutes, substantially longer than those of CENTAURUS X-3, HERCULES X-1, etc. Ariel V, followed by the satellite OSO-8, discovered an emission line near 7 keV in the spectra of several SUPERNOVA REMNANTS and many of the rich CLUSTERS OF GALAXIES, showing the X-rays to be of thermal origin, arising from hot gas at temperatures of 10^6 to 10^8 kelvin and containing an abundance of iron similar to that found in the Solar System. X-RAY TRANSIENTS and X-RAY BURST SOURCES were detected by several of the satellites. Optical identifications of a few of these have shown them to be most probably X-ray binaries in which the MASS TRANSFER or accretion rate is highly variable. Further major advances were made by the EINSTEIN OBSERVATORY, whose greater sensitivity revealed substantial X-ray emission from a wide range of normal stars. This emission comes from the stars' hot CORONAE.

More recent X-ray satellites, particularly EXOSAT, GINGA, ROSAT, and ASCA, have continued to extend the scope of X-ray observations to the point where it is now the major observational branch of high-energy astrophysics. Thus, for example, stellar activity, the form and evolution of young supernova remnants, the gravitational mass distribution and evolution of clusters of galaxies, the dynamics and energy processes in the centers of active galactic nuclei, as well as the study of accretion in the wide variety of compact-object binary-star systems, are most directly observed by their X-ray emission. This situation seems certain to continue with the diagnostic power of higher-resolution X-ray spectroscopy on future missions, such as AXAF, XMM, ASTRO-E, and SPECTRUM-X.

X-ray background radiation a diffuse sky background radiation that was one of the first discoveries in X-RAY ASTRONOMY. It is detected over 4 decades in frequency, and its origin varies across this band; most of the energy in the background is concentrated at 20–40keV. At very low energies the background is from hot gas in a 'Local Bubble'. In the 0.5–2keV energy band the ROSAT satellite has successfully identified the source as being mostly due to ACTIVE GALAXIES at moderate redshift. The 'hard' background above 3keV has a different spectrum and is thought to be due to the integrated emission from many heavily absorbed quasars at a range of redshifts.

X-ray binary the most common type of luminous galactic X-ray source, involving a close binary system in which gas flows (via the inner LAGRANGIAN POINT) or blows (by a strong STELLAR WIND) from a normal nondegenerate star on to a compact companion (see MASS TRANSFER; BINARY STAR). For the most luminous sources such as CENTAURUS X-3 and CYGNUS X-1, radiating X-rays at 10^{29}–10^{31} watts, this companion is probably a NEUTRON STAR or BLACK HOLE; in less luminous cases, such as SS Cygni and AM Herculis, it is more likely to be a WHITE DWARF. Gravitational energy powers these sources and both the luminosity (L) and temperature (T) are proportional to the mass-to-radius ratio (M/R) of the accreting star:

$$L \propto (M/R)Gm'$$

where G is the gravitational constant and m' is the rate of mass accretion, and

$$T \propto (M/R)G\varepsilon$$

where ε depends on the efficiency of the gas heating, being high for shocks and low for viscous heating.

Two main types of X-ray binary are distinguished: in *high-mass binaries* (*HMXBs*), such as Centaurus X-3 and Cygnus X-1, the nondegenerate star is a giant or supergiant of early spectral type (O, B, or A); in *low-mass binaries* (*LMXBs*) such as HERCULES X-1, the visible star is a middle or late main-sequence star of near solar mass. Several binaries contain a pulsating X-ray source, probably involving a rotating magnetized neutron star; these binaries, which include Centaurus X-3 and Hercules X-1, are among the best-determined of all binary systems.

The most luminous X-ray binaries, including Cygnus X-3, Scorpius X-1, and Circinus X-1, are also strong variable radio sources, sometimes also emitting radio flares.

X-ray burst sources (X-ray bursters) sources of intense flashes of cosmic X-rays, discovered in 1975. The bursts, seen primarily in the 1–30 keV energy band, are characterized by a rapid onset, often less than one second, followed by an exponential decay with a time constant of a few seconds to a minute. They are located in our Galaxy, mostly within 40° of the galactic center. Two types have been distinguished: *type I* repeat on timescales of hours or days; *type II* emit bursts every few minutes or less for a period of several days. It is widely believed that X-ray bursts arise in X-RAY BINARY systems and are due to thermonuclear flashes when material accreted on to the surface of a neutron star exceeds a critical temperature and pressure (type I) and to spasmodic mass accretion on to a neutron star (type II).

X-ray catalogs these have been published following successive (and increasingly sensitive) all-sky surveys. The first sky-survey mission was UHURU, which led finally to the *4U catalog* published in 1978. The ARIEL V survey yielded the *3A catalog* in 1981, followed by the more sensitive HEAO-1 catalog in 1984. ROSAT was the next spacecraft to carry out an all-sky X-ray survey, in 1990–91, yielding over 60 000 source detections (not yet published). ROSAT was also responsible for the first all-sky survey in the XUV waveband: the *Bright Source Catalog*, containing 384 XUV sources, was published in 1993, with a more extensive version of 479 XUV sources following in 1995.

X-ray nova see X-RAY TRANSIENTS.

X-ray pulsars see X-RAY PULSATORS.

X-ray pulsators regularly variable X-RAY BINARIES that have periods of a few seconds or in the case of the *slow pulsators* of a few minutes. This pulsation is widely interpreted as being associated with the rotation of a magnetized neutron star, so that these objects may be regarded as *X-ray pulsars*. The X-ray pulsations are believed to arise from channeling of the accreting gas onto the magnetic poles of the neutron star. The gas flow affects the neutron star's spin and as a result all X-ray pulsars (unlike other PULSARS) are gradually speeding up. Examples include CENTAURUS X-3, CYGNUS X-3, and HERCULES X-1.

X-rays high-energy ELECTROMAGNETIC RADIATION lying between gamma rays and ultraviolet radiation in the electromagnetic spectrum. The XUV region bridges the gap between the X-ray and ultraviolet bands. X-rays, unlike light and radio waves, are usually considered in terms of photon energy, $h\nu$, where ν is the frequency of the radiation and h is the Planck constant. X-ray energies range from about 100 electronvolts (eV) up to about 100 000 eV, corresponding to a wavelength range of about 12 nanometers (nm) to about 0.012 nm. Low-energy X-rays are sometimes called *soft X-rays* to distinguish them from high-energy or *hard X-rays*. In astronomy, thermal X-rays are produced from very high temperature gas ($\sim10^6$–10^8 K), with nonthermal X-rays arising from the interaction of high-energy electrons with a magnetic field (SYNCHROTRON EMISSION) or with low-energy photons (inverse Compton emission – see COMPTON SCATTERING). See also NONTHERMAL EMISSION; THERMAL EMISSION.

X-ray satellites artificial Earth satellites devoted to cosmic X-ray observations, the first of which was NASA's UHURU, launched in Dec. 1970. Up to this date, i.e. throughout the period 1962–70, X-RAY ASTRONOMY was carried out exclusively with sounding rockets and balloon experiments. Uhuru produced the first all-sky survey for cosmic X-ray sources and increased the catalog of known sources to 161 by 1974. The second X-ray astronomy satellite was the British satellite ARIEL V, which was launched in Oct. 1974 and occupied a similar 500-km circular equatorial orbit to Uhuru. It successfully extended the Uhuru sky map and made detailed spectral and temporal studies of individual sources.

Although X-ray experiments were also carried on other satellites principally devoted to the research fields (Copernicus, OSO-7, ANS, OSO-8), the next two dedicated X-ray astronomy satellites were SAS-3 and HEAO-1, launched respectively in 1975 and 1977. Both included modulation collimator experiments in their payloads and these provided the first accurate positions of many X-ray sources, leading to additional and more reliable optical identifications. In Nov. 1978 HEAo-2 (the EINSTEIN OBSERVATORY) was launched; its large GRAZING-INCIDENCE telescope produced major advances. After the Einstein Observatory ceased operation in Apr. 1981 only two small satellites, ARIEL VI and HAKUCHO, remained before the launch in 1983 of the Japanese TENMA and the European EXOSAT spacecraft. Subsequent X-ray satellites, of increasing sophistication, were the Japanese GINGA (launched 1987), German ROSAT (1990), and Japanese ASCA (1993), with still larger missions in preparation, including the Russian SPECTRUM–X (1995), NASA's XTE (1997) and AXAF (1998/99), and ESA's XMM (1999).

X-ray sources luminous sources of X-ray emission lying well beyond the Solar System. More than 120 000 are now known, the majority from the ROSAT all-sky survey and deep pointing observations. Optical counterparts include a wide range of astronomical objects, from high-redshift quasars to nearby stars, and even comets. The brightest sources lie in our Galaxy and are identified principally as X-RAY BINARIES (e.g. SCORPIUS X-1, CYGNUS X-1, CYGNUS X-3, CENTAURUS X-3, HERCULES X-1), many having an X-ray power 100 to 1000 times the power of the Sun. A smaller subset of bright galactic X-ray sources are identified with young supernova remnants, such as the CRAB NEBULA and the remnant of TYCHO'S STAR. Fainter but intrinsically much more powerful X-ray emission is detected from many extragalactic objects, especially rich CLUSTERS OF GALAXIES and ACTIVE GALAXIES – such as SEYFERT GALAXIES, QUASARS, and powerful RADIO GALAXIES, including Virgo A (M87) and Centaurus A.

X-ray telescope an instrument carried above the Earth's atmosphere by an X-RAY SATELLITE, etc., and by means of which X-rays from space can be detected and recorded. See also CCD; GRAZING INCIDENCE; MICROCHANNEL PLATE DETECTOR; PROPORTIONAL COUNTER.

X-ray Timing Explorer see XTE.

X-ray transients bright novalike cosmic X-ray sources that develop rapidly over a few days and remain visible for several weeks or months. ARIEL V observations, supported by simultaneous ground-based studies, led to the first optical identification of an X-ray transient source. This was A0620–00 (Nova Mon 1975), for a time in 1975 the brightest cosmic X-ray source ever seen, and found in the visible as a NOVA of about 11th magnitude. Both X-ray and optical stars then faded rapidly, to disappear by mid-1976. Subsequently, a star of 18th magnitude has been identified as the quiescent state of Nova Mon. Optical spectroscopy has shown the compact companion to be very probably a BLACK HOLE of at least 3 solar masses.

The sky distribution of X-ray transients shows them to be galactic, typically at distances of 1–10 kiloparsecs. Several have been found to have recurrent outbursts, usually on a timescale of several months or years. It is believed that X-ray transients represent close binary systems in which the MASS TRANSFER is highly variable. The qualitative difference from most optical novae (e.g. Nova Cygni 1975, which had no detectable X-ray emission) may be due to the compact star being a NEUTRON STAR or BLACK HOLE, rather than a WHITE DWARF as in the optical novae.

XTE *abbrev. for* X-ray Timing Explorer, a NASA satellite launched in December 1995 and designed to study variability and broad-band spectra of the brighter cosmic X-ray sources. The main payload consists of a large (6250 cm^2) array of PROPORTIONAL COUNTERS, sensitive over the 2–60 keV band. Other instruments extend coverage to 200 keV and provide an all-sky search for transient X-ray sources. All spacecraft systems remain operational up to the end of 2005 and the mission has yielded unique data on both short-term (e.g. kHz QPOs) and long-term variability of many X-ray binary sources and AGN.

XUV *short for* extreme ultraviolet.

XUV astronomy the study of objects beyond

the Solar System that emit radiation bridging the gap between X-rays and ultraviolet radiation (the *XUV region*), i.e. from about 12 nm to the hydrogen Lyman limit at 91.2 nm (see LYMAN SERIES). The high opacity of the interstellar gas at these wavelengths prevents observations beyond about 10 parsecs from 91.2 to about 50 nm, extending to about 200 parsecs at 12 nm. The first partial sky survey in the XUV was carried out in the APOLLO-SOYUZ mission in 1975, in which were found a number of intense sources, including HZ43 and Feige 24 (both hot WHITE DWARF stars) and PROXIMA CENTAURI.

The first deep all-sky survey in the XUV band was carried out by the UK Wide Field Camera (WFC) on the ROSAT satellite, launched in 1990. The WFC provided sky-survey observations into two photometric bands covering the range 6–30 nm, yielding over a thousand sources. A further XUV sky-survey was conducted by the NASA EUVE satellite, launched in 1992, providing observations in the waveband 7–76 nm. Most of the XUV sources found in these surveys are nearby hot WHITE DWARFS, late-type stellar chromospheres/coronae, and active stars. A few extragalactic sources have also been detected. Later EUVE observations provided the first resolved XUV spectra of a number of bright cosmic sources. See also X-RAY CATALOGS.

Yy

Yagi a directional ANTENNA comprising three or more parallel elements mounted on a straight beam and at right angles to it. The elements are a DIPOLE, to which the FEEDER is attached, behind which is a reflector and in front of which is one or more directors. Named after Hidetsugu Yagi, this type of aerial is commonly used for television reception although it is also used as an element in some radio telescopes.

year 1 the period of the Earth's revolution around the Sun or the period of the Sun's apparent motion around the celestial sphere, both periods being measured relative to a given point of reference. The choice of reference point determines the exact length of the year (see table). See also JULIAN YEAR.
2 *short for* calendar year.

Yerkes Observatory an astronomical station of the University of Chicago, located at Williams Bay, southeast Wisconsin, and operated by the university's Department of Astronomy and Astrophysics. It was endowed by Charles Tyson Yerkes, a Chicago businessman, at the suggestion of George Ellery Hale. It has five telescopes, including the world's largest refracting telescope, 40 inches (102 cm) in diameter, completed in 1897, the year the observatory opened.

yoke mounting (**English mounting**) see EQUATORIAL MOUNTING.

YSO *abbrev. for* young stellar object. Any object in an early stage of STAR FORMATION, ranging from a protostar through to a deeply embedded main-sequence star. The generality of the term reflects the difficulty in assigning a precise evolutionary state to these heavily obscured objects.

YY Orionis stars variable stars that appear to form a subclass of T TAURI STARS. However, their spectra reveal that matter is falling on to them rather than being ejected and so they could represent an earlier stage of evolution.

Year

Year	*Reference point*	*Length (days)*
tropical	equinox to equinox	365.242 19
sidereal	fixed star to fixed star	365.256 36
anomalistic	apse to apse	365.259 64
eclipse	Moon's node to Moon's node	346.620 07

Zz

z *symbol for* redshift.

ZAMS *abbrev. for* zero-age main sequence. See MAIN SEQUENCE.

Z Camelopardalis stars see DWARF NOVAE.

Zeeman effect an effect that occurs when atoms emit or absorb radiation in the presence of a magnetic field: the field modifies the energy configuration of the atom with the result that a spectral line is split into two, three, or more closely spaced components, each of which is polarized. (In some cases the components cannot be resolved and the effect appears as a broadening of the spectral line.) This Zeeman splitting can be used to study the magnetism of stars, including the Sun, since the spacing of the components is a measure of the magnetic field strength.

Zelenchukskaya Observatory the optical observatory of the SPECIAL ASTROPHYSICAL OBSERVATORY, sited on Mount Pastukhov, near Zelenchukskaya, in the Caucasus at an altitude of 2100 meters. The chief instrument is the 6-meter Bolshoi Teleskop Azimutalnyi (*Big Altazimuth Telescope*, BTA), which was the first large optical telescope to have an ALTAZIMUTH MOUNTING. Instruments can be placed at the prime focus (f/4) and the NASMYTH foci (f/30) of the primary mirror. The original Pyrex primary was replaced in 1984 by a glass-ceramic mirror, and a third one made of Sitall glass was installed in 1992. This reduces distortion of the image arising from temperature fluctuations. Stress-relieving systems have reduced changes in mirror shape arising from weight. The telescope was finally operational in 1977 after a long and difficult development period. Today it is mostly used for SPECKLE INTERFEROMETRY and SPECTROSCOPY. See also RATAN 600.

zenith the point on the CELESTIAL SPHERE that lies vertically above an observer and 90° from all points on that person's horizon. It lies on the observer's celestial meridian. The *geocentric zenith* lies at the point where the line connecting the Earth's center with the observer's position would meet the celestial sphere. Because the Earth is not spherical the two points rarely coincide. Compare NADIR.

zenithal hourly rate (ZHR) the probable number of METEORS observed per hour from a METEOR SHOWER that has its RADIANT in the observer's zenith. Shower rates vary as the zenith distance of the radiant changes. To obtain the normalized ZHR the observed rate must be multiplied by a factor, *F*, which varies for different values, *A*, of radiant altitude (see table).

Normalized Zenithal Hourly Rate

A	90°	52°	35°	27°	8.6°	2.6°
F	1	1.25	1.67	2	5	10

zenith attraction the corrections that must be subtracted from the observed velocity and direction of a meteoric body to give the true values. The gravitational attraction of the Earth on the body will increase the METEOROID's impact velocity, the effect being greatest for bodies with low initial values of geocentric velocity (i.e. meteoroids just catching up with the Earth). The path of the meteoroid will also change, the new RADIANT appearing to be closer to the observer's zenith than the original true radiant.

zenith distance (coaltitude) symbol: ζ. The angular distance of a celestial body from an observer's zenith measured along the vertical circle through the body. It is therefore the complement of the altitude (90° – *h*) of the body. The *topocentric zenith distance* is the zenith distance measured at the observation point; it differs from the true value due to ATMOSPHERIC REFRACTION, the difference being termed the *angle of refraction.* See also DIURNAL PARALLAX.

zenith stars stars that come to CULMINATION on the observer's zenith.

zenith tube a telescope mounted in a vertical plane so that stars at or near the zenith are observed. Atmospheric disturbance is minimal in this direction. See also PHOTOGRAPHIC ZENITH TUBE.

zero-age main-sequence (ZAMS) see MAIN SEQUENCE.

Zerodur *trademark* a glass-ceramic material that alters very little in size or shape when heated over normal temperature ranges. It is used in telescope mirrors.

zeta (ζ) the sixth letter in the Greek alphabet, used in STELLAR NOMENCLATURE usually to designate the sixth-brightest star in a constellation.

Zeta Aurigae (ζ Aur) an ECLIPSING BINARY in the constellation Auriga (period 972 days, magnitude range 5.0–5.7). The brighter component is a hot blue B8 main-sequence star and the secondary is a cool K4 supergiant 35 times the size of its companion. During the partial eclipse of the brighter star its light shines through the rarefied atmosphere of the supergiant and the spectral changes give information about the atmosphere's composition.

Zeta Aurigae stars are eclipsing binaries composed of a cool giant or supergiant and a hot companion, exhibiting atmospheric eclipses. The period often amounts to several years. See also VV CEPHEI STARS.

ZHR *abbrev. for* zenithal hourly rate.

zirconium stars see S STARS.

zodiac a band of sky passing around the CELESTIAL SPHERE and extending about 9° on each side of the ECLIPTIC. It thus includes the apparent annual path of the Sun as seen from Earth and also the orbits of the Moon and the principal planets apart from Pluto. In the 5th century BC, this band was divided by the ancient Babylonians into 12 parts, each 30° wide, known as the *signs of the zodiac.* The Greeks borrowed this scheme and redefined the boundaries of the signs so that the vernal equinox was included in the constellation Aries the Ram (their version of the Babylonian constellation of the Hired Man) – see FIRST POINT OF ARIES. Aries thus became the starting point of the zodiac, with each successive sign originally corresponding in name and position to each one of the 12 constellations lying along the path of the zodiac – the *zodiac constellations.* These signs and constellation names were given their final form by the Romans. Eventually, the names and signs were used simply to identify the 30° zones. PRECESSION OF THE EQUINOXES has since shifted the zodiac constellations eastward by over 30°, so that the constellations through which the Sun now passes include Ophiuchus, which is not considered a zodiac constellation.

zodiacal dust cloud the dust cloud that is mainly responsible for the ZODIACAL LIGHT. It is symmetrical about the ecliptic plane and is conical, having its maximum thickness at the Sun. The density then decreases as about $r^{-1.5}$ where r is the distance from the Sun. Most of the particles that can be seen have sizes in the range 10–100 micrometers. They are produced by decaying comets and are spiralling slowly in towards the solar surface.

zodiacal light a permanent phenomenon that can be seen as a faint glow, especially at tropical latitudes, on a clear moonless night in the west after sunset and in the east before sunrise. It is shaped like a slanting cone and extends from the horizon, tapering along the direction of the ECLIPTIC, and visible for maybe 20°. The zodiacal light has been shown, spectroscopically, to be sunlight scattered by minute dust particles in the interplanetary medium in the inner Solar System, mainly in the ZODIACAL DUST CLOUD. The zodiacal light can be detected right round the zodiac, there being a slight increase in size and brightness – the GEGENSCHEIN – directly opposite the Sun's position. See also INFRARED BACKGROUND RADIATION.

zodiac constellations see ZODIAC.

Zond probes a series of Soviet interplanetary and lunar probes. Zonds 1 and 2 passed Venus and Mars in 1964 and 1965 respectively but did not return data. Zond 3 photographed the farside of the Moon in 1965, obtaining the first high-quality pictures, while Zonds 5 and 6 (in 1968), 7 (1969), and 8 (1970) made circumlunar flights and were recovered on Earth. Zond 4, in 1968, may have been an unsuccessful attempt at a circumlunar flight.

zone a portion of a spherical surface lying between two parallel circles.

zone of avoidance a region of sky, which roughly coincides with the belt of the MILKY WAY, where no galaxies are seen at optical wavelengths. The apparent absence of galaxies is due to the presence of light-absorbing clouds of dust in the galactic plane.

zone of totality *another name for* path of totality. See ECLIPSE.

Zürich relative sunspot number see RELATIVE SUNSPOT NUMBER.

Zwicky catalog a multivolume catalog of galaxies and clusters of galaxies compiled from optical plates and published by Zwicky and collaborators during the 1960s. In the case of clusters, the criteria for inclusion in the catalog are less strict than those of the ABELL CATALOG, so there is a wider range of clusters, including larger lower-density systems with significant substructure.

ZZ Ceti stars a group of DA WHITE DWARFS that are PULSATING VARIABLES with multiperiod luminosity variations in the range 2–20 minutes and surface temperatures near 12 000 K; their prototype is ZZ Ceti. Two other groups of pulsating white dwarfs have been found with higher surface temperatures.

Appendix

Contents

Table 1A Planets, orbital characteristics

Planet	*Sidereal period*	*Perihelion (AU)*	*Aphelion (AU)*	*Inclination (deg)*
Mercury	87.97 d	0.31	0.47	7.0
Venus	224.70 d	0.72	0.73	3.4
Earth	365.26 d	0.98	1.02	0.0
Mars	686.98 d	1.38	1.67	1.9
Jupiter	11.86 y	4.95	5.46	1.3
Saturn	29.46 y	9.01	10.04	2.5
Uranus	84.01 y	18.31	20.07	0.8
Neptune	164.79 y	29.76	30.36	1.8
Pluto	247.92 y	29.73	49.33	17.1

Table 1B Planets, physical characteristics

Planet	*Equatorial diameter (km)*	*Oblateness*	*Mass‡ (Earth=1)*	*Density (water=1)*	*Albedo (geom.)*
Mercury	4878	0	0.06	5.4	0.11
Venus	12 104	0	0.82	5.2	0.65
Earth	12 756	0.003	1.00	5.5	0.37
Mars	6795	0.006	0.11	3.9	0.15
Jupiter	142 985	0.065	317.83	1.3	0.52
Saturn	120 537	0.098	95.16	0.7	0.47
Uranus	51 119	0.023	14.54	1.3	0.51
Neptune	50 538	0.017	17.15	1.7	0.41
Pluto	2320	0	0.002	2.0	0.3

‡ mass of Earth = 5.9742×10^{24} kg.

Table 1C Planets, axis and satellites

Planet	*Tilt (deg)*	*Period* (days hours minutes)*	*Satellites†*
Mercury	0.0	58d 15h 30.5m	0
Venus	177.3	243d 0h 14.4m r	0
Earth	23.45	23h 56.1m	1
Mars	25.19	1d 0h 37.4m	2
Jupiter	3.13	9h 55.5m	63 & R
Saturn	26.73	10h 39.4m	47 & R
Uranus	97.77	15h 36.0m r	27 & R
Neptune	28.32	18h 25.9m	13 & R
Pluto	122.53	6d 9h 16.8m r	1**

* r indicates retrograde axial rotation.

**Two other satellites reported for Pluto in 2005 but not confirmed.

The rotation periods for Jupiter and Saturn refer to equatorial regions; the periods exceed 9h 55m and 10h 38m at higher latitudes respectively.

† R indicates planetary rings (see individual entries for information).

Table 2 Planetary satellites

PLANET & satellite	*Year of discovery*	*Diameter (km)*	*Orbital radius (10^3 km)*	*Eccentricity*	*Orbital period (days)*	*Inclination (°)*
EARTH						
Moon	-	3476	384.4	0.055	27.32	18.3-28.6
MARS						
Phobos	1877	27 × 22 × 19	9.38	0.015	0.32	1.0
Deimos	1877	15 × 12 × 11	23.46	0.001	1.26	1.8
JUPITER						
Metis	1979	40	128	0	0.29	0
Adrastea	1979	25 × 20 × 15	129	0	0.30	0
Amalthea	1892	270 × 166 × 150	181	0.003	0.50	0.40
Thebe	1979	110 × 90	222	0.015	0.67	0.8
Io	1610	3643	422	0.004	1.77	0.04
Europa	1610	3122	671	0.010	3.55	0.47
Ganymede	1610	5262	1070	0.002	7.15	0.21
Callisto	1610	4823	1883	0.007	16.69	0.51
Thermisto	2000	9	7507	0.242	130.0	43.08
Leda	1974	16	11 094	0.148	238.72	26.07
Himalia	1904	186	11 480	0.158	250.57	27.63
Lysithea	1938	36	11 720	0.107	259.22	29.02
Elara	1905	76	11 737	0.207	259.65	24.77
Ananke	1951	30	21 200	0.169	631 R	147
Carme	1938	40	22 600	0.207	692 R	164
Pasiphae	1908	50	23 500	0.378	735 R	145
Sinope	1914	36	23 700	0.275	758 R	153
SATURN						
Pan	1991	20	134	low	0.58	low
Atlas	1980	37 × 34 × 27	138	0.002	0.60	0.3
Prometheus	1980	148 × 100 × 68	139	0.003	0.61	0.0
Pandora	1980	110 × 88 × 62	142	0.004	0.63	0.1
Epimetheus	1978	194 × 190 × 154	151	0.009	0.69	0.34
Janus	1978	276 × 220 × 160	151	0.007	0.69	0.14
Mimas	1789	421 × 395 × 385	186	0.020	0.94	1.5
Enceladus	1789	512 × 495 × 488	238	0.005	1.37	0.02
Tethys	1684	1050	295	0.000	1.89	1.86
Telesto	1980	34 × 28 × 26	295	0.0	1.89	2
Calypso	1980	34 × 22 × 22	295	0.0	1.89	2
Dione	1684	1120	377	0.002	2.74	0.02
Helene	1980	36 × 32 × 30	377	0.005	2.74	0.2

Table 2 Planetary satellites (cont.)

PLANET & satellite	*Year of discovery*	*Diameter (km)*	*Orbital radius (10^3 km)*	*Eccentricity*	*Orbital period (days)*	*Inclination (°)*
Mimas	1789	421 × 395 × 385	186	0.020	0.94	1.5
Enceladus	1789	512 × 495 × 488	238	0.005	1.37	0.02
Tethys	1684	1050	295	0.000	1.89	1.86
Telesto	1980	34 × 28 × 26	295	0.0	1.89	2
Calypso	1980	34 × 22 × 22	295	0.0	1.89	2
Dione	1684	1120	377	0.002	2.74	0.02
Helene	1980	36 × 32 × 30	377	0.005	2.74	0.2
Rhea	1672	1530	527	0.001	4.52	0.35
Titan	1655	5150	1222	0.029	15.95	0.33
Hyperion	1848	405 × 260 × 220	1481	0.104	21.28	0.43
Iapetus	1671	1440	3561	0.028	79.33	14.72
Kiving	2000	16	11 110	0.334	449.2	46.16
Ijiraq	2000	12	11 125	0.332	451.5	46.74
Phoebe	1898	230 × 220 × 210	12 952	0.163	550.48	
URANUS						
Cordelia	1986	40	50	< 0.001	0.34	0.1
Ophelia	1986	42	54	0.010	0.38	0.1
Bianca	1986	51	59	< 0.001	0.43	0.2
Cressida	1986	80	62	< 0.001	0.46	0.0
Desdemona	1986	64	63	< 0.001	0.47	0.2
Juliet	1986	93	64	0.001	0.49	0.1
Portia	1986	135	66	< 0.001	0.51	0.1
Rosalind	1986	72	70	< 0.001	0.56	0.3
Cupid	2003	10	75	< 0.001	0.62	-
Belinda	1986	80	75	< 0.001	0.62	0.0
Perdita	1986	20	76	< 0.001	0.64	-
Puck	1985	162	86	< 0.001	0.76	0.31
Mab	2003	10	98	< 0.001	0.92	-
Miranda	1948	471	129	0.001	1.41	4.34
Ariel	1851	1158	191	0.001	2.52	0.04
Umbriel	1851	1169	266	0.004	4.14	0.13
Titania	1787	1578	436	0.001	8.71	0.08
Oberon	1787	1522	583	0.001	13.46	0.07
Francisco	2001	22	4276	0.146	266.6	145.2
Caliban	1997	72	7231	0.159	579.7 R	139.2
Stephano	1999	32	8004	0.229	677.4 R	144.1
Trinculo	2001	18	8504	0.220	759.0 R	167.1
Sycorax	1997	150	12 179	0.509	1284.3 R	252.7
Margaret	2003	20	14 345	0.661	1694.8	56.6

Table 2 Planetary satellites (cont.)

PLANET & satellite	*Year of discovery*	*Diameter (km)*	*Orbital radius (10^3 km)*	*Eccentricity*	*Orbital period (days)*	*Inclination (°)*
Prospero	1999	50	16 256	0.445	1977.3 R	152.0
Setebos	1999	47	17 418	0.591	2243.8 R	158.2
Ferdinand	2003	21	20 901	0.368	2823.4	169.8
NEPTUNE						
Naiad	1989	96 × 60 × 52	48	< 0.001	0.29	4.74
Thalassa	1989	108 × 100 × 52	50	< 0.001	0.31	0.21
Despina	1989	180 × 148 × 128	53	< 0.001	0.33	0.07
Galatea	1989	204 × 184 × 144	62	< 0.001	0.43	0.05
Larissa	1989	216 × 204 × 168	74	0.001	0.55	0.20
Proteus	1989	436 × 416 × 402	118	< 0.001	1.12	0.04
Triton	1846	2707	355	0.000	5.88 R	157.35
Nereid	1949	340	5513	0.751	360.14	7.23
PLUTO						
Charon	1978	1186	20	< 0.001	6.39	98.8

Note: Only named planets are included. Neptune has four extra planets S2002 N1-N4 and Jupiter and Saturn have a large number of small satellites. The orbits of the outer satellites of Jupiter vary considerably with time.The distances refer to the center of the parent planet and the inclinations to the plane of the equator of the planet. R indicates retrograde motion.

Table 3 Asteroids

No.	*Name*	*Discovery year*	*Period (years)*	*Perihelion (AU)*	*Aphelion (AU)*	*Inc (°)*	*Diameter (km)*	*Rotation (hours)*
1	Ceres	1801	4.60	2.55	2.98	10.6	933	9.1
2	Pallas	1802	4.62	2.12	3.42	34.8	523	7.8
3	Juno	1804	4.36	1.98	3.35	13.0	267	7.2
4	Vesta	1807	3.63	2.15	2.57	7.1	501	5.3
5	Astraea	1845	4.13	2.08	3.07	5.4	125	16.8
6	Hebe	1847	3.78	1.93	2.92	14.8	192	7.3
7	Iris	1847	3.69	1.84	2.93	5.5	203	7.1
10	Hygiea	1849	5.55	2.76	3.51	3.8	429	18.4
15	Eunomia	1851	4.30	2.15	3.13	11.8	272	6.1
31	Euphrosyne	1854	5.58	2.43	3.86	26.3	248	5.5
433	Eros	1898	1.76	1.13	1.78	10.8	23	5.3
588	Achilles	1906	11.77	4.40	5.95	10.3	147	?
944	Hidalgo	1920	14.14	2.01	9.68	42.5	15	10.1
1221	Amor	1932	2.66	0.97	2.88	12.0	0.5	?
1566	Icarus	1949	1.12	0.21	1.95	18.0	0.9	2.3
1862	Apollo	1932	1.78	0.65	2.30	6.1	1.4	3.1
2060	Chiron	1977	50.38	8.46	18.82	6.9	300?	?
2062	Aten	1976	0.95	0.74	1.19	18.0	2.0	?
2101	Adonis	1936	2.57	0.51	3.24	2.0	1	?

Table 4 Meteor showers

Shower	*Normal limits*	*ZHR at max.*
Quadrantids	Jan. 1–6	90
Corona Australids	Mar. 14–18	5
April Lyrids	Apr. 19–24	12
η-Aquarids	May 1–8	45
June Lyrids	June 10–21	9
Ophiuchids	June 17–26	4
Capricornids	July 10–Aug. 15	6
δ-Aquarids	July 15–Aug. 15	19, 10
Pisces Australids	July 15–Aug. 20	5
α-Capricornids	July 15–Aug. 25	4
Perseids	July 25–Aug. 18	80
Cygnids	Aug. 19–22	3
Orionids	Oct. 16–26	25
Taurids	Oct. 20–Nov. 30	8
Cepheids	Nov. 7–11	8
Leonids	Nov. 15–19	10
Phoenicids	Dec. 4–5	6
Geminids	Dec. 7–15	80
Ursids	Dec. 17–24	9

Table 5 Constellations

Andromeda	And	Cygnus	Cyg	Pavo	Pav
Antlia	Ant	Delphinus	Del	Pegasus	Peg
Apus	Aps	Dorado	Dor	Perseus	Per
Aquarius	Aqr	Draco	Dra	Phoenix	Phe
Aquila	Aql	Equuleus	Equ	Pictor	Pic
Ara	Ara	Eridanus	Eri	Pisces	Psc
Aries	Ari	Fornax	For	Piscis Austrinus	PsA
Auriga	Aur	Gemini	Gem		
Boötes	Boo	Grus	Gru	Puppis	Pup
Caelum	Cae	Hercules	Her	Pyxis	Pyx
Camelopardalis	Cam	Horologium	Hor	Reticulum	Ret
Cancer	Cnc	Hydra	Hya	Sagitta	Sge
Canes Venatici	CVn	Hydrus	Hyi	Sagittarius	Sgr
Canis Major	CMa	Indus	Ind	Scorpius	Sco
Canis Minor	CMi	Lacerta	Lac	Sculptor	Scl
Capricornus	Cap	Leo	Leo	Scutum	Sct
Carina	Car	Leo Minor	LMi	Serpens	Ser
Cassiopeia	Cas	Lepus	Lep	Sextans	Sex
Centaurus	Cen	Libra	Lib	Taurus	Tau
Cepheus	Cep	Lupus	Lup	Telescopium	Tel
Cetus	Cet	Lynx	Lyn	Triangulum	Tri
Chamaeleon	Cha	Lyra	Lyr	Triangulum Australe	TrA
Circinus	Cir	Mensa	Men		
Columba	Col	Microscopium	Mic	Tucana	Tuc
Coma Berenices	Com	Monoceros	Mon	Ursa Major	UMa
Corona Australis	CrA	Musca	Mus	Ursa Minor	UMi
Corona Borealis	CrB	Norma	Nor	Vela	Vel
Corvus	Crv	Octans	Oct	Virgo	Vir
Crater	Crt	Ophiuchus	Oph	Volans	Vol
Crux	Cru	Orion	Ori	Vulpecula	Vul

Table 6 Brightest Stars

Star		*Position (2000.0) RA h m*	*dec ° ′*	*Apparent magnitude*	*Spectral type*	*Parallax ″*	*Distance (l.y.)*	*Absolute magnitude*
	Sun	—	—	−26.72	G2 V	—	—	4.8
α CMa	Sirius	06 45.1	−16 43	−1.46	A1 Vm	0.377	8.6	1.4
α Car	Canopus	06 24.0	−52 42	−0.72	A9 II	0.028	74	−2.5
α Cen	Rigil Kentaurus	14 39.6	−60 50	−0.27	G2 V	0.750	4.3	4.1
α Boo	Arcturus	14 15.7	+19 11	−0.04	K1.5 IIIp	0.097	34	0.2
α Lyr	Vega	18 36.9	+38 47	0.03	A0 V	0.133	25	0.6
α Aur	Capella	05 16.7	+46 00	0.08	G6 III+G2 III	0.080	41	0.4
β Ori	Rigel	05 14.5	−08 12	0.12	B8 Iae	0.013	1400[b]	−8.1
α CMi	Procyon	07 39.3	+05 14	0.38	F5 IV–V	0.285	11.4	2.6
α Eri	Achernar	01 37.7	−57 14	0.46	B3 Vnp	0.026	69	−1.3
α Ori	Betelgeuse	05 55.2	+07 24	0.50 (var.)	M2 Iab	0.005	500	−5.7
β Cen	Hadar	14 03.8	−60 22	0.61 (var.)	B1 II	0.009	320	−4.4
α Cru	Acrux	12 26.6	−63 06	0.76[a]	B0.5 IV+B1 Vn	0.008	510	−4.6[a]
α Aql	Altair	19 50.8	+08 52	0.77	A7 Vn	0.202	16	2.3
α Tau	Aldebaran	04 35.9	+16 31	0.85 (var.)	K5 III	0.054	60	−0.3
α Sco	Antares	16 29.4	−26 26	0.96 (var.)	M1.5 Iab	0.024	520[c]	−5.2
α Vir	Spica	13 25.2	−11 10	0.98 (var.)	B1 V	0.023	220	−3.2
β Gem	Pollux	07 45.3	+28 02	1.14	K0 III	0.094	40	0.7
α PsA	Fomalhaut	22 57.6	−29 37	1.16	A3 V	0.149	22	2.0
β Cru	Becrux	12 47.7	−59 41	1.25 (var.)	B0.5 III	-	460	−4.7
α Cyg	Deneb	20 41.4	+45 17	1.25	A2 Ia	0.000	1500	−7.2

Source: Robert F. Garrison, *Royal Astronomical Society of Canada Observers' Handbook* (1989). [a] Combined magnitude of double star. [b] Distance to Orion cluster. [c] Distance to Scorpius cluster.

Note: Parallaxes and absolute magnitudes of many stars are not well determined. For stars with a parallax smaller than 0″.05, absolute magnitudes and distances have been calculated from the spectral classification.

Table 7 Nearest Stars

Star	*Position (2000.0)* *RA* *h m*	*dec* *° ′*	*Parallax* *″*	*Distance* *(l.y.)*	*Apparent magnitude*	*Spectral type*	*Absolute magnitude*
Proxima (V645 Cen)	14 29.7	–62 41	0.772	4.2	11.05 (var.)	M5.5 Ve	15.5
α Cen A	14 39.6	–60 50	0.750	4.3	–0.01	G2 V	4.4
α Cen B					1.33	K1 V	5.7
Barnard's star	17 57.8	+04 34	0.545	6.0	9.54	M3.8 V	13.2
Wolf 359 (CN Leo)	10 56.5	+07 01	0.421	7.7	13.53 (var.)	M5.8 Ve	16.7
BD+36° 2147	11 03.3	+35 58	0.397	8.2	7.50	M2.1 Ve	10.5
UV Cet A	01 38.8	–17 57	0.387	8.4	12.52 (var.)	M5.6 Ve	15.5
UV Cet B					13.02 (var.)	M5.6 Ve	16.0
Sirius A	06 45.1	–16 43	0.377	8.6	–1.46	A1 Vm	1.4
Sirius B					8.3	DA	11.2
Ross 154	18 49.8	–23 50	0.345	9.4	10.45	M3.6 Ve	13.1
Ross 248	23 41.9	+44 10	0.314	10.4	12.29	M4.9 Ve	14.8
ε Eri	03 32.9	–09 28	0.303	10.8	3.73	K2 Ve	6.1
Ross 128	11 47.8	+00 48	0.298	10.9	11.10	M4.1 V	13.5
61 Cyg A (V1803 Cyg)	21 06.9	+38 45	0.294	11.1	5.22 (var.)	K3.5 Ve	7.6
61 Cyg B					6.03	K4.7 Ve	8.4
ε Ind	22 03.4	–56 47	0.291	11.2	4.68	K3 Ve	7.0
BD+43° 44 A	00 18.5	+44 01	0.290	11.2	8.08	M1.3 Ve	10.4
BD+43° 44 B					11.06	M3.8 Ve	13.4
L789-6	22 38.5	–15 19	0.290	11.2	12.18		14.5

Source: Alan Batten, *Royal Astronomical Society of Canada Observers' Handbook* (1989)
A, B refer to brightest, second brightest components of binary star
BD: Bonner Durchmusterung; CD: Córdoba Durchmusterung; L: Luyten

Table 8 Messier Numbers plus Equivalent NGC, IC Numbers

Messier no.	*NGC IC*	*Type**	*Const.*	*Messier no.*	*NGC IC*	*Type**	*Const.*
M1	1952	n	Tau	M36	1960	o.c.	Aur
2	7089	g.c.	Aqr	37	2099	o.c.	Aur
3	5272	g.c.	CVn	38	1912	o.c.	Aur
4	6121	g.c.	Sco	39	7092	o.c.	Cyg
5	5904	g.c.	Ser	40	—	d	UMa
6	6405	o.c.	Sco	41	2287	o.c	CMa
7	6475	o.c.	Sco	42	1976	n	Ori
8	6523	n	Sgr	43	1982	n	Ori
9	6333	g.c.	Oph	44	2632	o.c.	Cnc
10	6254	g.c.	Oph	45	—	o.c.	Tau
11	6705	o.c.	Sct	46	2437	o.c.	Pup
12	6218	g.c.	Oph	47	2422	o.c.	Pup
13	6205	g.c.	Her	48	2548	o.c.	Hya
14	6402	g.c.	Oph	49	4472	G E	Vir
15	7078	g.c.	Peg	50	2323	o.c.	Mon
16	6611	o.c.	Ser	51	5195	G Sc	CVn
17	6618	n	Sgr	52	7654	o.c.	Cas
18	6613	o.c.	Sgr	53	5024	g.c.	Com
19	6273	g.c.	Oph	54	6715	g.c.	Sgr
20	6514	n	Sgr	55	6809	g.c.	Sgr
21	6531	o.c.	Sgr	56	6779	g.c.	Lyr
22	6656	g.c.	Sgr	57	6720	p.n.	Lyr
23	6194	o.c.	Sgr	58	4579	G SBb	Vir
24	6603	o.c.	Sgr	59	4621	G E	Vir
25	IC4725	o.c.	Sgr	60	4649	G E	Vir
26	6694	o.c.	Sct	61	4303	G Sc	Vir
27	6853	p.n.	Vul	62	6266	g.c.	Oph
28	6626	g.c.	Sgr	63	5055	G Sb	CVn
29	6913	o.c.	Cyg	64	4826	G Sb	Com
30	7099	g.c.	Cap	65	3623	G Sa	Leo
31	224	G Sb	And	66	3627	G Sb	Leo
32	221	G E	And	67	2682	o.c.	Cnc
33	598	G Sc	Tri	68	4590	g.c.	Hya
34	1039	o.c.	Per	69	6637	g.c.	Sgr
35	2168	o.c.	Gem	70	6681	g.c.	Sgr

* n: nebula; p.n.: planetary nebula; o.c.: open cluster; g.c.: globular cluster; G: galaxy and classification (E: elliptical, S: spiral, Sb: barred spiral); d: double star.

Table 8 Messier Numbers (cont.)

Messier no.	*NGC IC*	*Type**	*Const.*	*Messier no.*	*NGC IC*	*Type**	*Const.*
M71	6838	g.c.	Sge	M91	4548	G S	Com
72	6981	g.c.	Aqr	92	6341	g.c.	Her
73	6994	s.g.	Aqr	93	2447	o.c.	Pup
74	628	G Sc	Psc	94	4736	G Sb	CVn
75	6864	g.c.	Sgr	95	3351	G Sb	Leo
76	651	p.n.	Per	96	3368	G Sa	Leo
77	1068	G Sb	Cet	97	3587	p.n.	UMa
78	2068	n	Ori	98	4192	G Sb	Com
79	1904	g.c.	Lep	99	4254	G Sc	Com
80	6093	g.c.	Sco	100	4321	G Sc	Com
81	3031	G Sb	UMa	101	5457	G Sc	UMa
82	3034	G Irr	UMa	102**			
83	5236	G Sc	Hya	103	581	o.c.	Cas
84	4374	G E	Vir	104	4594	G Sa	Vir
85	4382	G So	Com	105	3379	G E	Leo
86	4406	G E	Vir	106	4258	G Sb	CVn
87	4488	G E	Vir	107	6171	g.c.	Oph
88	4501	G S	Com	108	3556	G Sb	UMa
89	4552	G E	Vir	109	3992	G SBc	UMa
90	4569	G Sb	Vir	110	205	G E	And

* n: nebula; p.n.: planetary nebula; o.c.: open cluster; g.c.: globular cluster; G: galaxy and classification; s.g. stellar group.

**M102 was a duplication of M101.

Table 9 Astronomical and physical constants

astronomical unit, AU	$149.597\,870 \times 10^{-6}$ km
speed of light in vacuum, *c*	$2.997\,924\,58 \times 10^{5}$ km s^{-1}
light-time for 1 AU	499.004 78 s
gravitational constant, *G*	6.672×10^{-11} N m^{2} kg^{-2}
standard acceleration of free fall, *g*	9.806 65 m s^{-2}
mass of Earth	5.9742×10^{24} kg
Earth's equatorial radius	6378.140 km
Earth's polar radius	6356.775 km
mean density of Earth	5.517 g cm^{-3}
mean distance to Moon	384 403 km
lunar mass	7.35×10^{22} kg
lunar radius	1738 km
solar mass, $M_{\odot}$	1.9891×10^{30} kg
solar radius, $R_{\odot}$	696 000 km
solar luminosity, $L_{\odot}$	4×10^{26} W
solar parallax	8″.794 148
constant of sine parallax for Moon	3422″.451
constant of aberration (2000)	20″.495 52
obliquity of ecliptic (2000)	23°26′21″.4
general precession in longitude per Julian century (2000)	5029″.0966
constant of nutation (2000)	9″.2025
Gaussian gravitational constant, *k*	0.017 202 098 95 N$^{1/2}$ m kg^{-1}
Planck constant, *h*	$6.626\,076 \times 10^{-34}$ J s
Boltzmann constant, *k*	$1.380\,658 \times 10^{-23}$ J K^{-1}
Stefan's constant, σ	5.6705×10^{-8} W m^{-2} K^{-4}

Table 10 Famous people in the field of astronomy

Adams, John Couch	1819–92	English
Airy, Sir George Biddell	1801–92	English
Albategnius (or Al-Battani)	858–929 AD	Arabian
Aristarchus of Samos	c. 320–250 BC	Greek
Baade, Walter	1893–1960	German–American
Barnard, Edward Emerson	1857–1923	American
Bessel, Friedrich Wilhelm	1784–1846	German
Bradley, James	1693–1762	English
Brahe, Tycho	1546–1601	Danish
Cassini, Giovanni Domenico	1625–1712	Italian–French
Chandrasekhar, Subrahmanyan	1910–95	Indian–American
Clark, Alvan Graham	1832–97	American
Copernicus, Nicolas	1473–1543	Polish
Eddington, Sir Arthur Stanley	1882–1944	English
Einstein, Albert	1879–1955	German–American
Eratosthenes	c. 276–196 BC	Greek
Flamsteed, John	1646–1719	English
Fraunhofer, Joseph von	1787–1826	German
Galileo Galilei	1564–1642	Italian
Gamow, George	1904–68	Russian–American
Hale, George Ellery	1868–1938	American
Halley, Edmond	1656–1742	English
Hawking, Stephen	1942–	English
Herschel, Caroline	1750–1848	German–English
Herschel, Sir John	1792–1871	English
Herschel, Sir William	1738–1822	German–English
Hertzsprung, Ejnar	1873–1967	Danish
Hipparchus	c. 170–120 BC	Greek
Hoyle, Sir Fred	1915–2001	English
Hubble, Edwin Powell	1889–1953	American
Huggins, Sir William	1824–1910	English
Huygens, Christiaan	1629–95	Dutch
Jeans, Sir James	1877–1946	English
Kepler, Johann	1571–1630	German
Kuiper, Gerard Peter	1905–73	Dutch–American
Laplace, Pierre Simon, Marquis de	1749–1827	French
Leavitt, Henrietta	1868–1921	American
Lovell, Sir Bernard	1913–	English
Lowell, Percival	1855–1916	American
Morgan, William Wilson	1906–94	American
Newton, Sir Isaac	1642–1727	English
Pickering, Edward Charles	1846–1919	American
Ptolemy (Claudius Ptolemaeus)	c. 100–170 AD	Greek
Russell, Henry Norris	1877–1957	American
Ryle, Sir Martin	1918–84	English
Sandage, Allan	1926–	American
Schmidt, Bernhard	1879–1935	Estonian
Schmidt, Maarten	1929–	Dutch–American
Schwarzschild, Karl	1873–1916	German
Shapley, Harlow	1885–1972	American
Struve, Otto	1897–1963	Russian–American
Zwicky, Fritz	1898–1974	Swiss–American

Table 11 The Greek alphabet

Α	α	alpha	Ν	ν	nu
Β	β	beta	Ξ	ξ	xi
Γ	γ	gamma	Ο	ο	omikron
Δ	δ	delta	Π	π	pi
Ε	ε	epsilon	Ρ	ρ	rho
Ζ	ζ	zeta	Σ	σ	sigma
Η	η	eta	Τ	τ	tau
Θ	θ	theta	Υ	υ	upsilon
Ι	ι	iota	Φ	φ	phi
Κ	κ	kappa	Χ	χ	chi
Λ	λ	lambda	Ψ	ψ	psi
Μ	μ	mu	Ω	ω	omega

Internet links

There are many sites on the Internet giving information about astronomy and space science. A selection of useful sites is given below. In general, they are sites of universities or official organizations rather than web sites run by individuals.

Official organizations

American Astronomical Society	www.aas.org
European Space Agency	www.esa.int
International Astronomical Union	www.iau.org
National Aeronautics and Space Administration (NASA)	www.nasa.gov
Royal Astronomical Society	www.ras.org.uk
Royal Astronomical Society of Canada	www.rasc.ca
Royal Astronomical Society of New Zealand	www.rasnz.org.nz

Selected observatories

Anglo-Australian Observatory	www.aao.gov.au
Arecibo Observatory	www.naic.edu
Australia Telescope National Facility	www.atnf.csiro.au
European Southern Observatory	www.eso.org
Gemini Telescopes	www.gemini.edu
Hubble Space Telescope	http://hubble.nasa.gov
Jodrell Bank Observatory	www.jb.man.ac.uk
Mauna Kea Observatories	www.ifa.hawaii.edu/mko
Mount Stromlo and Siding Spring Observatories	www.mso.anu.edu.au
Mount Wilson Observatory	www.mtwilson.edu
National Optical Astronomy Observatory	www.noao.edu
National Radio Astronomy Observatory	www.nrao.edu
Palomar Observatory	www.astro.caltech.edu/palomar
Particle Physics and Astronomy Research Council	www.pparc.ac.uk
Roque de los Muchachos Observatory	www.iac.es/gabinete/orm/indice.html
Royal Greenwich Observatory	www.rog.nmm.ac.uk
Royal Observatory, Edinburgh	www.roe.ac.uk
Smithsonian Astrophysical Observatory	www.harvard.edu/saohome.html

United Kingdom Astronomy Technology Centre	www.roe.ac.uk/ukatc
Pulkovo Main Astronomical Observatory	www.gao.spb.ru
Spitzer Space Telescope	www.spitzer.caltech.edu
United States Naval Observatory	www.usno.navy.mil
Zelenchukskaya Observatory	www.sao.ru/Doc-en/index.html

Other useful sites

American Association of Variable Star Observers	www.aavso.org
Astronomical World Wide Web resources lites	www.ifa.hawaii.edu/~sheppard/satel-
BBC - Science and Nature - Space	www.bbc.co.uk/science/space
The Electronic Sky	www.glyphweb.com/esky
Mira Field Trips to the Stars	www.mira.org/ftso/text/txt001z.htm
JPL Solar System Dynamics	http://ssd.jpl.nasa.gov
Jupiter Satellite Page	www.ifa.hawaii.edu/~sheppard/satellites
The Kuiper belt page	www.ifa.hawaii.edu/~jewitt/kb.html
The Messier Catalog - online	http://seds.lpl.arizona.edu/messier
The NGC/IC Project	www.ngcic.org
The Nine Planets	www.ex.ac.uk/Mirrors/nineplanets
SIMBAD Astronomical Database	http://simbad.u-strasbg.fr/Simbad
SolStation	www.solstation.com
Space Now	www.spacenow.org.uk/index.cfm
United States Geological Survey Astrogeology Program	http://planetarynames.wr.usgs.gov
Views of the Solar System	www.solarviews.com